Paradigm PUBLISHING

# Microsoft® office 2007

BENCHMARK SERIES

## Nita Rutkosky
Pierce College at Puyallup
Puyallup, Washington

## Audrey Rutkosky Roggenkamp
Pierce College at Puyallup
Puyallup, Washington

| | |
|---|---|
| **Managing Editor** | Sonja Brown |
| **Production Editor** | Donna Mears |
| **Cover and Text Designer** | Leslie Anderson |
| **Copy Editor** | Susan Capecchi |
| **Desktop Production** | John Valo, Desktop Solutions |
| **Proofreader** | Laura Nelson |
| **Indexer** | Nancy Fulton |

**Acknowledgments:** The authors and editors wish to thank the following individuals for checking the accuracy of the instruction and exercises:

- Catherine Caldwell, Technical Writer, Memphis, Tennessee
- Theresa Jabs, Computer Applications Tester, Farmington, Minnesota
- Robertt Neilly, Professor, Computer Applications, Humber College, Toronto, Canada
- Pamela J. Silvers, Chairperson, Business Computer Technologies, Asheville-Buncombe Technical Community College, Asheville, North Carolina

Care has been taken to verify the accuracy of information presented in this book. However, the authors, editors, and publisher cannot accept responsibility for Web, e-mail, newsgroup, or chat room subject matter or content, or for consequences from application of the information in this book, and make no warranty, expressed or implied, with respect to its content.

**Photo Credits:** Introduction page 1 (clockwise from top), Lexmark International, Inc., courtesy of Dell Inc., all rights Hewlett-Packard Company, Logitech, Micron Technology, Inc.; Word Level 1 page 3, Asia Images Group/AsiaPix/Getty Images, page 4, © Corbis: Excel Level 1 pages 1, 3, 4, © Corbis: Access Level 1 page 1, © Corbis; PowerPoint pages 1, 2, and 4, © Corbis; photos in Student Resources CD, courtesy of Kelly Rutkosky and Michael Rutkosky.

**Trademarks:** Microsoft is a trademark or registered trademark of Microsoft Corporation in the United States and/or other countries. Some of the product names and company names included in this book have been used for identification purposes only and may be trademarks or registered trade names of their respective manufacturers and sellers. The authors, editors, and publisher disclaim any affiliation, association, or connection with, or sponsorship or endorsement by, such owners.

We have made every effort to trace the ownership of all copyrighted material and to secure permission from copyright holders. In the event of any question arising as to the use of any material, we will be pleased to make the necessary corrections in future printings. Thanks are due to the aforementioned authors, publishers, and agents for permission to use the materials indicated.

ISBN 978-0-76382-983-4 (Text)
ISBN 978-0-76382-999-5 (Text + CD)

© 2008 by Paradigm Publishing, Inc.
875 Montreal Way
St. Paul, MN 55102
E-mail: educate@emcp.com
Web site: www.emcp.com

Printed in the United States of America

16 15 14 13 12 11 10 09 08    3 4 5 6 7 8 9 10

*These activities appear at the end of every chapter.*

office

Benchmark Microsoft Office 2007 is designed for students who want to learn how to use the new version of Microsoft's popular suite to enhance their productivity for educational, workplace, and home use. Throughout this text, students are expected to develop and execute strategies for solving information processing and management problems using Word 2007; for solving numeric and mathematical problems using Excel 2007; for organizing, querying, and retrieving data using Access 2007; and for writing, creating, and producing presentations using PowerPoint 2007. After successfully completing a course using this textbook, students will be able to

- Analyze, synthesize, and evaluate school, work, or home information-processing tasks and use application software to meet those needs efficiently and effectively
- Access the Internet and use the browse, search, and hyperlink capabilities of Web browsers
- Create, design, and produce professional documents using word processing software
- Process, manipulate, and represent numeric data using spreadsheet software
- Plan, structure, and create databases for efficient data access and retrieval using database software
- Use presentation software to design and create informational and motivational slide shows that contain hyperlinks, tables, images, and animation
- Learn strategies for merging and integrating source data from different applications

In addition to mastering essential Word, Excel, Access, and PowerPoint skills, students will learn the basic features and functions of computer hardware, the Windows XP operating system, and Internet Explorer 7.0. Upon completing the text, they can expect to be proficient in using the major applications of the Office 2007 suite to organize, analyze, and present information.

# Achieving Proficiency in Office 2007

Since its inception several Office versions ago, the Benchmark Series has served as a standard of excellence in software instruction. Elements of the book function individually and collectively to create an inviting, comprehensive learning environment that produces successful computer users. On this and following pages, take a visual tour of the structure and features that comprise the highly popular Benchmark model.

MODULE OPENERS highlight key features of Word, Excel, Access, and PowerPoint 2007 within the context of organizing, analyzing, and presenting information.

# Level 1

## Microsoft® word

### Unit 1: Editing and Formatting Documents

➤ Preparing Documents
➤ Formatting Characters and Paragraphs
➤ Customizing Paragraphs
➤ Formatting Pages

**UNIT OPENERS** display the unit's four chapter titles. Each program module has two units, which conclude with a comprehensive unit performance assessment.

## Customizing Paragraphs

### CHAPTER 3

**CHAPTER OPENERS** present the Performance Objectives and highlight the practical relevance of the skills students will learn.

### PERFORMANCE OBJECTIVES

Upon successful completion of Chapter 3, you will be able to:

- Apply numbering and bulleting formatting to text
- Insert paragraph borders and shading
- Apply custom borders and shading
- Sort paragraph text
- Set, clear, and move tabs on the Ruler and at the Tabs dialog box
- Cut, copy, and paste text in a document
- Copy and paste text between documents

word Chapter 3

Tutorial 3.1
Using Formatting Features
Tutorial 3.2
Copying and Moving Text

CD icon identifies a folder of data files to be copied to student's storage medium.

SNAP icon alerts students to corresponding SNAP tutorial titles.

As you learned in Chapter 2, Word contains a variety of options for formatting text in paragraphs. In this chapter you will learn how to insert numbers and bullets in a document, how to apply borders and shading to paragraphs of text in a document, how to sort paragraphs of text, and how to manipulate tabs on the Ruler and at the Tabs dialog box. Editing some documents might include selecting and then deleting, moving, or copying text. You can perform this type of editing with buttons in the Clipboard group in the Home tab or with keyboard shortcuts.

*Note: Before beginning computer projects, copy to your storage medium the Word2007L1C3 subfolder from the Word2007L1 folder on the CD that accompanies this textbook and then make Word2007L1C3 the active folder.*

### Project 1  Format a Document on Computer Technology

You will open a document containing information on computer technology, type numbered text in the document, and apply numbering and bullet formatting to paragraphs in the document.

**New! PROJECT APPROACH** organizes instruction and practice into multipart projects that focus on related program features.

Project overview identifies tasks to accomplish and the key features to use in completing the work.

# PROJECT APPROACH: Builds Skill Mastery within Realistic Context

Each project exercise guides students step by step to the desired outcome. Screen captures illustrate what the screen should look like at key points.

Typically, a file remains open throughout a project. Students save their work incrementally.

Between project parts, the text presents instruction on the features and skills necessary to accomplish the next task.

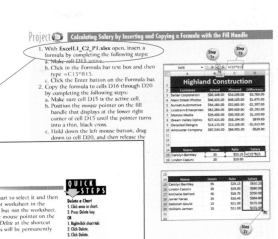

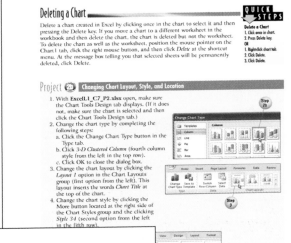

Text in magenta identifies material to type.

Quick Steps provide feature summaries for reference and review.

At or near the end of the project, students save and print their work. Locked, watermarked model answers in PDF format on the Student Resources CD allow students to check their results. This option rewards careful effort and builds software mastery.

# CHAPTER REVIEW ACTIVITIES: A Hierarchy of Learning Assessments

## CHAPTER summary

- Use the spelling feature to check spelling of slides in a presentation. Begin the spelling checker by clicking the Review tab and then clicking the Spelling button in the Proofing group.
- Refer to Table 2.1 for methods for selecting text in slides.
- Text in a placeholder is positioned inside of a placeholder. Click in a placeholder to select the placeholder and position the insertion point inside.
- Display the Find dialog box by clicking the Find button in the Editing group in the Home tab.
- Display the Replace dialog box by clicking the Replace button in the Editing group in the Home tab.
- With buttons in the Clipboard group or with optio[...] you can cut and paste or copy and paste text in sli[...]
- You can use the mouse to move text in the Slides/O[...] and then drag it to a new location or hold down th[...] copy text to a new location.
- Use the sizing handles that display around a selec[...] decrease the size of the placeholder. You can use t[...] placeholder to a new location in the slide.
- Use the New Slide button in the Home tab to inse[...]
- Delete a selected slide by clicking the Delete butto[...] Home tab or by pressing the Delete button.
- You can move or delete a selected slide in Normal [...] pane or in Slide Sorter view.
- Copy a selected slide by holding down the Ctrl key [...] the desired location.
- Use the Copy and Paste buttons in the Clipboard [...] copy a slide between presentations.
- Select adjacent slides in the Slides/Outline pane or [...] clicking the first slide, holding down the Shift key, [...] slide. Select nonadjacent slides by holding down th[...] each desired slide.
- Duplicate slides in a presentation by selecting the [...] Slides/Outline pane, clicking the New Slide button [...] the *Duplicate Selected Slides* option.
- You can copy slides from a presentation into the op[...] at the Reuse Slides task pane. Display this task pa[...] button arrow and then clicking *Reuse Slides* at the [...]
- Display a presentation in Print Preview by clicking [...] to *Print*, and then clicking *Print Preview*.

- In Print Preview, display the Header and Footer dialog box by clicking the Options button and then clicking *Header and Footer* at the drop-down list. Use options in the dialog box to insert the date and time, a header, a footer, slide numbers, or page numbers. The options will vary depending on which tab is selected—*Slide* or *Notes and Handouts*.
- Click the Help button in a dialog box and the PowerPoint Help window displays with information specific to the dialog box.
- Click the Microsoft Office Word Help button or press F1 to display the PowerPoint Help window.

**CHAPTER SUMMARY captures the purpose and execution of key features.**

## COMMANDS review

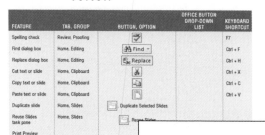

| FEATURE | TAB, GROUP | BUTTON, OPTION | OFFICE BUTTON DROP-DOWN LIST | KEYBOARD SHORTCUT |
|---|---|---|---|---|
| Spelling check | Review, Proofing | | | F7 |
| Find dialog box | Home, Editing | Find ▾ | | Ctrl + F |
| Replace dialog box | Home, Editing | Replace | | Ctrl + H |
| Cut text or slide | Home, Clipboard | | | Ctrl + X |
| Copy text or slide | Home, Clipboard | | | Ctrl + C |
| Paste text or slide | Home, Clipboard | | | Ctrl + V |
| Duplicate slide | Home, Slides | Duplicate Selected Slides | | |
| Reuse Slides task pane | Home, Slides | Reuse Slides | | |
| Print Preview | | | | |
| PowerPoint Help window | | | | |

**COMMANDS REVIEW summarizes visually the major features and alternative methods of access.**

## CONCEPTS check

### Test Your Knowledge

Completion: In the space provided at the right, indicate the correct term, symbol, or command.

1. The Spelling button is located in the Proofing group in this tab.

2. This is the keyboard shortcut to select all text in a placeholder.

3. The Find button is located in this group in the Home tab.

4. In the Slides/Outline pane with the Outline tab selected, hold down the left mouse button on this to select all text in the slide.

5. To copy text to a new location in the Slides/Outline pane with the Outline tab selected, hold down this key while dragging text.

6. The border of a selected placeholder displays these handles as well as a green rotation handle.

7. You can reorganize slides in a presentation in the Slides/Outline pane or in this view.

8. You can copy selected slides in a presentation using this option from the New Slide button drop-down list.

9. To select adjacent slides, click the first slide, hold down this key, and then click the last slide.

10. Click the New Slide button arrow and then click the *Reuse Slides* option at the drop-down list and this displays.

11. Display the presentation in Print Preview by clicking the Office button, pointing to this option, and then clicking *Print Preview*.

12. In Print Preview, display the Header and Footer dialog box by clicking this button in the Print Preview tab and then clicking *Header and Footer* at the drop-down list.

13. This is the keyboard shortcut to display the PowerPoint Help window.

**CONCEPTS CHECK questions assess knowledge recall.**

# SKILLS check

## Demonstrate Your Proficiency

Assessment

### 1 CREATE AN ELECTRONIC DESIGN PRESENTATION

1. Create the presentation shown in Figure 2.7 using a design theme of your choosing. (When typing bulleted text, press the Tab key to move the insertion point to the desired tab level.)
2. After creating the slides, complete a spelling check on the text in the slides.
3. Save the presentation into the PowerPoint2007C2 folder on your storage medium and name the presentation PP_C2_A1.
4. Run the presentation.
5. Preview the presentation, change the *Print What* option to *Handouts (4 Slides Per Page)*, change the orientation to landscape, and then print the presentation.
6. Make the following changes to the presentation:
   a. Change to Slide Sorter view and then move Slide 3 between Slides 1 and 2.
   b. Move Slide 4 between Slides 2 and 3.
   c. Search for the word *document* and replace it with the word *brochure*. (Make Slide 1 active and then capitalize the "b" in "brochure.")
   d. Add a transition and sound of your choosing to each slide.
7. Save the presentation.
8. Display the Reuse Slides task pane, browse to the PowerPoint2007C2 folder on your storage medium, and then double-click *LayoutTips.pptx*.
9. Insert the *Layout Punctuation Tips* slide below Slide 4.
10. Insert the *Layout Tips* slide below Slide 5.
11. Close the Reuse Slides task pane.
12. Find all occurrences of *Layout* and replace with *Design*. (Insert a check mark in the *Match case* check box.)
13. Move Slide 5 between Slides 1 and 2.
14. Move Slide 6 between Slides 2 and 3.
15. Save the presentation.
16. Print the presentation as a handout with six slides per page.
17. Close PP_C2_A1.pptx.

SKILLS CHECK exercises ask students to develop both standard and customized kinds of word processing, spreadsheet, database, or presentation documents without how-to directions.

# CASE study

## Apply Your Skills

Part 1

You are the office manager at the Company Connections agency. One of your responsibilities is to conduct workshops for preparing individuals for the job search process. A coworker has given you a presentation for the workshop but the presentation needs some editing and modifying. Open **JobAnalysis.pptx** and then save the presentation and name it **PP_C2_CS_P1**. Check each slide in the presentation and then make modifications to maintain consistency in the size and location of placeholders (consider using the Reset button to reset the formatting and size of the placeholders), maintain consistency in heading text, move text from an overcrowded slide to a new slide, complete a spelling check, apply a design theme, and make any other modifications to improve the presentation. Save **PP_C2_CS_P1.pptx**.

Part 2

After reviewing the presentation, you realize that you need to include slides on resumes. Open the **ResumePresentation.pptx** presentation and then copy Slides 2 and 3 into the **PP_C2_CS_P1.pptx** presentation. You want to add additional information on resume writing tips and decide to use the Internet to find information. Locate information on the Internet with tips on writing a resume and then create a slide (or two) with the information you find. Add a transition and sound to all slides in the presentation. Save the **PP_C2_CS_P1.pptx** presentation.

Part 3

You know that Microsoft Word offers a number of resume templates you can download from the Microsoft Office Online site. You decide to include information in the presentation on how to download resumes. Open Microsoft Word, click the Office button, and then click *New* at the drop-down list. At the New Document dialog box, click the Help button that displays in the upper right corner of the dialog box. Read the information on downloading templates and then experiment with downloading a template. With the **PP_C2_CS_P1.pptx** presentation open, add an additional slide to the end of the presentation that provides steps on how to download a resume in Microsoft Word. Print the presentation as a handout with six slides per page. Save, run, and then close the **PP_C2_CS_P1.pptx** presentation.

The chapter CASE STUDY requires analyzing a workplace scenario and then planning and executing multipart projects to meet the information needs.

Students search the Web and/or use the Help feature to locate additional information required to complete the Case Study.

# UNIT PERFORMANCE ASSESSMENT: Cross-Disciplinary, Comprehensive Evaluation

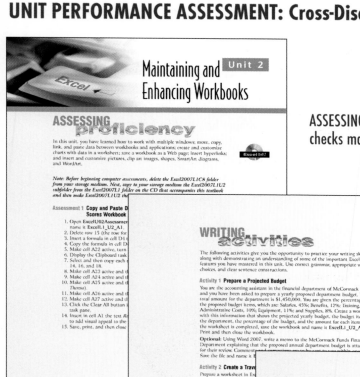

**ASSESSING PROFICIENCY** checks mastery of features.

**WRITING ACTIVITIES** involve applying program skills in a communication context.

**INTERNET RESEARCH** project reinforces research and information processing skills.

**JOB STUDY** at the end of Unit 2 presents a capstone assessment requiring critical thinking and problem solving.

An **INTEGRATED PROJECT** at the end of the text offers students the opportunity to experience the power of using the Office suite—importing and exporting data among the major applications to meet information processing needs most effectively.

# Student Courseware

**Student Resources CD** Each Benchmark Series textbook is packaged with a Student Resources CD containing the data files required for completing the projects and assessments. A CD icon and folder name displayed on the opening page of chapters reminds students to copy a folder of files from the CD to the desired storage medium before beginning the project exercises. Directions for copying folders are printed on the inside back cover. The Student Resources CD also contains the model answers in PDF format for the project exercises within chapters. Files are locked and watermarked, but students can compare their completed documents with the PDF files, either on screen or in hard copy (printed) format.

**Internet Resource Center** Additional learning tools and reference materials are available at the book-specific Web site at www.emcp.net/BenchmarkOffice07XP. Students can locate and use the same resources that are on the Student Resources CD along with study aids, Web links, and tips for working with computers effectively in academic and workplace settings.

**SNAP Training and Assessment** SNAP is a Web-based program that provides hands-on instruction, practice, and testing for learning Microsoft Office 2007 and Windows. SNAP course work simulates operations of Office 2007. The program is comprised of a Web-based learning management system, multimedia tutorials, performance skill items, a concept test bank, and online grade book and course planning tools. A CD-based set of tutorials teaching the basics of Office and Windows is also available for additional practice not requiring Internet access.

**Class Connections** Available for both WebCT and Blackboard e-learning platforms, Paradigm's Class Connection provides self-quizzes and study aids and facilitates communication among students and instructors via e-mail and e-discussion.

# Instructor Resources

**Curriculum Planner and Resources** Instructor support for the Benchmark Series has been expanded to include a *Curriculum Planner and Resources* binder with CD. This all-in-one print resource includes planning resources such as Lesson Blueprints, teaching hints, and sample course syllabi; presentation resources such as PowerPoint presentations and handouts; and assessment resources including an overview of assessment venues, live program and PDF model answers for intrachapter projects, and live program and annotated PDF model answers for end-of-chapter and end-of-unit assessments. Contents of the *Curriculum Planner and Resources* binder are also available on the Instructor's CD and on the password-protected Instructor's section of the Internet Resource Center for this title at www.emcp.com.

**Computerized Test Generator** Instructors can use ExamView test generating software and the provided bank of multiple-choice items to create customized Web-based or print tests.

# System Requirements

This text is designed for the student to complete projects and assessments on a computer running a standard installation of Microsoft Office 2007, Professional Edition, and the Microsoft Windows XP operating system with Service Pack 2 or later. To effectively run this suite and operating system, your computer should be outfitted with the following:

- 500 MHz processor or higher; 256 MB RAM or higher
- DVD drive
- 2 GB of available hard-disk space
- CD-ROM drive
- 800 by 600 minimum monitor resolution; 1024 by 768 recommended
  *Note: Screen captures in this book were created using 1024 by 768 resolution; screens with higher resolution may look different.*
- Computer mouse, or compatible pointing device

# About the Authors

**Nita Rutkosky** began teaching business education courses at Pierce College in Puyallup, Washington, in 1978. Since then she has taught a variety of software applications to students in postsecondary Information Technology certificate and degree programs. In addition to co-authoring texts in the *Benchmark Office 2007 Series*, she has co-authored *Signature Word 2007*, *Marquee Office 2007*, and *Using Computers in the Medical Office: Microsoft Word, Excel, and PowerPoint 2003*. Other textbooks she has written for Paradigm Publishing include books on previous versions of Microsoft Office along with WordPerfect, desktop publishing, keyboarding, and voice recognition.

**Audrey Rutkosky Roggenkamp** has been teaching courses in the Business Information Technology department at Pierce College in Puyallup including keyboarding, skill building, and Microsoft Office programs. In addition to titles in the *Benchmark Office 2007 Series*, she has co-authored *Using Computers in the Medical Office*, *Marquee Office 2007*, and *Signature Word 2007*.

# Getting Started in Office 2007

In this textbook, you will learn to operate several computer application programs that combine to make an application "suite." This suite of programs is called Microsoft Office 2007. The programs you will learn to operate are the software, which includes instructions telling the computer what to do. Some of the application programs in the suite include a word processing program named Word, a spreadsheet program named Excel, a database program named Access, and a presentation program named PowerPoint.

## Identifying Computer Hardware

The computer equipment you will use to operate the suite of programs is referred to as hardware. You will need access to a microcomputer system that should consist of the CPU, monitor, keyboard, printer, drives, and mouse. If you are not sure what equipment you will be operating, check with your instructor. The computer system shown in Figure G.1 consists of six components. Each component is discussed separately in the material that follows.

**Figure G.1** Microcomputer System

# CPU

CPU stands for Central Processing Unit and it is the intelligence of the computer. All the processing occurs in the CPU. Silicon chips, which contain miniaturized circuitry, are placed on boards that are plugged into slots within the CPU. Whenever an instruction is given to the computer, that instruction is processed through circuitry in the CPU.

## Monitor

The monitor is a piece of equipment that looks like a television screen. It displays the information of a program and the text being input at the keyboard. The quality of display for monitors varies depending on the type of monitor and the level of resolution. Monitors can also vary in size—generally from 14-inch size up to 21-inch size or larger.

## Keyboard

The keyboard is used to input information into the computer. Keyboards for microcomputers vary in the number and location of the keys. Microcomputers have the alphabetic and numeric keys in the same location as the keys on a typewriter. The symbol keys, however, may be placed in a variety of locations, depending on the manufacturer. In addition to letters, numbers, and symbols, most microcomputer keyboards contain function keys, arrow keys, and a numeric keypad. Figure G.2 shows an enhanced keyboard.

**Figure G.2** Keyboard

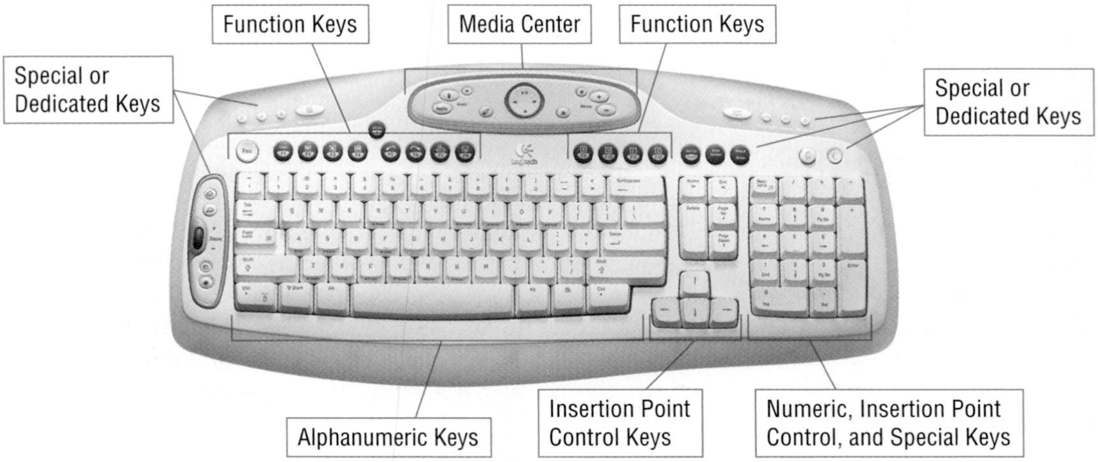

The 12 keys at the top of the keyboard, labeled with the letter F followed by a number, are called *function keys*. Use these keys to perform functions within each of the suite programs. To the right of the regular keys is a group of *special* or *dedicated keys*. These keys are labeled with specific functions that will be performed when you press the key. Below the special keys are arrow keys. Use these keys to move the insertion point in the document screen.

A keyboard generally includes three mode indicator lights. When you select certain modes, a light appears on the keyboard. For example, if you press the Caps Lock key, which disables the lowercase alphabet, a light appears next to Caps Lock. Similarly, pressing the Num Lock key will disable the special functions on the numeric keypad, which is located at the right side of the keyboard.

## Disk Drives

Depending on the computer system you are using, Microsoft Office 2007 is installed on a hard drive or as part of a network system. Whether you are using Office on a hard drive or network system, you will need to have available a DVD or CD drive and a USB drive or other storage medium. You will insert the CD (compact disc) that accompanies this textbook in the DVD or CD drive and then copy folders from the CD to your storage medium. You will also save documents you complete at the computer to folders on your storage medium.

## Printer

A document you create in Word is considered soft copy. If you want a hard copy of a document, you need to print it. To print documents you will need to access a printer, which will probably be either a laser printer or an ink-jet printer. A laser printer uses a laser beam combined with heat and pressure to print documents, while an ink-jet printer prints a document by spraying a fine mist of ink on the page.

## Mouse

Many functions in the suite of programs are designed to operate more efficiently with a mouse. A mouse is an input device that sits on a flat surface next to the computer. You can operate a mouse with the left or the right hand. Moving the mouse on the flat surface causes a corresponding mouse pointer to move on the screen. Figure G.1 shows an illustration of a mouse.

# Using the Mouse

The programs in the Microsoft Office suite can be operated using a keyboard or they can be operated with the keyboard and a mouse. The mouse may have two or three buttons on top, which are tapped to execute specific functions and commands. To use the mouse, rest it on a flat surface or a mouse pad. Put your hand over it with your palm resting on top of the mouse and your wrist resting on the table surface. As you move the mouse on the flat surface, a corresponding pointer moves on the screen.

When using the mouse, you should understand four terms—point, click, double-click, and drag. When operating the mouse, you may need to point to a specific command, button, or icon. Point means to position the mouse pointer on the desired item. With the mouse pointer positioned on the desired item, you may need to click a button on the mouse. Click means quickly tapping a button on the mouse once. To complete two steps at one time, such as choosing and then executing a function, double-click a mouse button. Double-click means to tap the left mouse button twice in quick succession. The term drag means to press and hold the left mouse button, move the mouse pointer to a specific location, and then release the button.

## Using the Mouse Pointer

The mouse pointer will change appearance depending on the function being performed or where the pointer is positioned. The mouse pointer may appear as one of the following images:

- The mouse pointer appears as an I-beam (called the I-beam pointer) in the document screen and can be used to move the insertion point or select text.

- The mouse pointer appears as an arrow pointing up and to the left (called the arrow pointer) when it is moved to the Title bar, Quick Access toolbar, ribbon, or an option in a dialog box. For example, to open a new document with the mouse, position the I-beam pointer on the Office button located in the upper left corner of the screen until the pointer turns into an arrow pointer and then click the left mouse button. At the drop-down list that displays, make a selection by positioning the arrow pointer on the desired option and then clicking the left mouse button.

- The mouse pointer becomes a double-headed arrow (either pointing left and right, pointing up and down, or pointing diagonally) when performing certain functions such as changing the size of an object.

- In certain situations, such as moving an object or image, the mouse pointer becomes a four-headed arrow. The four-headed arrow means that you can move the object left, right, up, or down.

- When a request is being processed or when a program is being loaded, the mouse pointer may appear with an hourglass beside it. The hourglass image means "please wait." When the process is completed, the hourglass image is removed.

- The mouse pointer displays as a hand with a pointing index finger in certain functions such as Help and indicates that more information is available about the item.

## Choosing Commands

Once a program is open, you can use several methods in the program to choose commands. A command is an instruction that tells the program to do something. You can choose a command using the mouse or the keyboard. When a program such as Word or PowerPoint is open, the ribbon contains buttons for completing tasks and contains tabs you click to display additional buttons. To choose a button on the Quick Access toolbar or in the ribbon, position the tip of the mouse arrow pointer on a button and then click the left mouse button.

The Office suite provides access keys you can press to use a command in a program. Press the Alt key on the keyboard to display KeyTips that identify the access key you need to press to execute a command. For example, press the Alt key in a Word document and KeyTips display as shown in Figure G.3. Continue pressing access keys until you execute the desired command. For example, if you want to begin spell checking a document, you would press the Alt key, press the R key on the keyboard to display the Review tab, and then press the letter S on the keyboard.

**Figure G.3** Word KeyTips

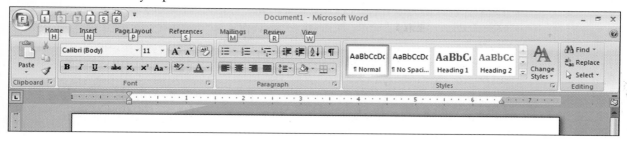

## Choosing Commands from Drop-Down Lists

To choose a command from a drop-down list with the mouse, position the mouse pointer on the desired option and then click the left mouse button. To make a selection from a drop-down list with the keyboard, type the underlined letter in the desired option.

Some options at a drop-down list may be gray-shaded (dimmed), indicating that the option is currently unavailable. If an option at a drop-down list displays preceded by a check mark, that indicates that the option is currently active. If an option at a drop-down list displays followed by an ellipsis (…), a dialog box will display when that option is chosen.

## Choosing Options from a Dialog Box

A dialog box contains options for applying formatting to a file or data within a file. Some dialog boxes display with tabs along the top providing additional options. For example, the Font dialog box shown in Figure G.4 contains two tabs—the Font tab and the Character Spacing tab. The tab that displays in the front is the

**Figure G.4** Word Font Dialog Box

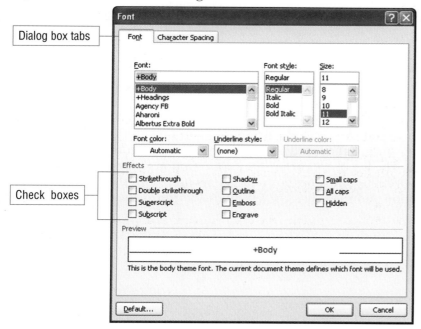

active tab. To make a tab active using the mouse, position the arrow pointer on the desired tab and then click the left mouse button. If you are using the keyboard, press Ctrl + Tab or press Alt + the underlined letter on the desired tab.

To choose options from a dialog box with the mouse, position the arrow pointer on the desired option and then click the left mouse button. If you are using the keyboard, press the Tab key to move the insertion point forward from option to option. Press Shift + Tab to move the insertion point backward from option to option. You can also hold down the Alt key and then press the underlined letter of the desired option. When an option is selected, it displays with a blue background or surrounded by a dashed box called a marquee. A dialog box contains one or more of the following elements: text boxes, list boxes, check boxes, option buttons, spin boxes, and command buttons.

## Text Boxes

Some options in a dialog box require you to enter text. For example, the boxes below the *Find what* and *Replace with* options at the Excel Find and Replace dialog box shown in Figure G.5 are text boxes. In a text box, you type text or edit existing text. Edit text in a text box in the same manner as normal text. Use the Left and Right Arrow keys on the keyboard to move the insertion point without deleting text and use the Delete key or Backspace key to delete text.

**Figure G.5** Excel Find and Replace Dialog Box

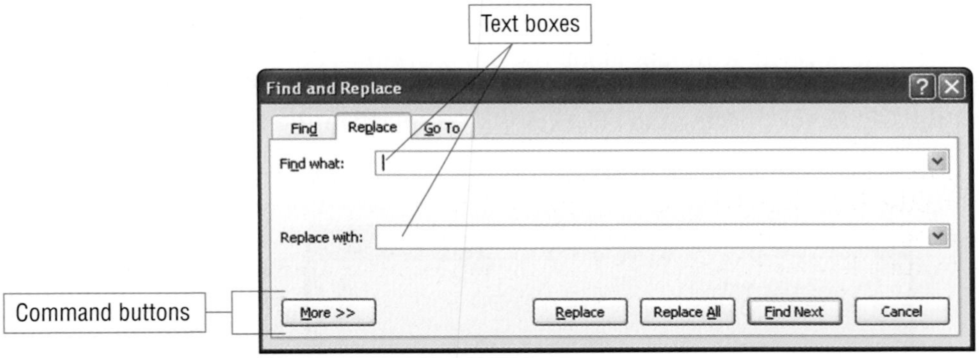

## List Boxes

Some dialog boxes such as the Word Open dialog box shown in Figure G.6 may contain a list box. The list of files below the *Look in* option is contained in a list box. To make a selection from a list box with the mouse, move the arrow pointer to the desired option and then click the left mouse button.

**Figure G.6** Word Open Dialog Box

Some list boxes may contain a scroll bar. This scroll bar will display at the right side of the list box (a vertical scroll bar) or at the bottom of the list box (a horizontal scroll bar). You can use a vertical scroll bar or a horizontal scroll bar to move through the list if the list is longer than the box. To move down through a list on a vertical scroll bar, position the arrow pointer on the down-pointing arrow and hold down the left mouse button. To scroll up through the list in a vertical scroll bar, position the arrow pointer on the up-pointing arrow and hold down the left mouse button. You can also move the arrow pointer above the scroll box and click the left mouse button to scroll up the list or move the arrow pointer below the scroll box and click the left mouse button to move down the list. To move through a list with a horizontal scroll bar, click the left-pointing arrow to scroll to the left of the list or click the right-pointing arrow to scroll to the right of the list.

To make a selection from a list using the keyboard, move the insertion point into the box by holding down the Alt key and pressing the underlined letter of the desired option. Press the Up and/or Down Arrow keys on the keyboard to move through the list.

In some dialog boxes where enough room is not available for a list box, lists of options are inserted in a drop-down list box. Options that contain a drop-down list box display with a down-pointing arrow. For example, the *Underline style* option at the Word Font dialog box shown in Figure G.4 contains a drop-down list. To display the list, click the down-pointing arrow to the right of the *Underline style* option box. If you are using the keyboard, press Alt + U.

## Check Boxes

Some dialog boxes contain options preceded by a box. A check mark may or may not appear in the box. The Word Font dialog box shown in Figure G.4 displays a variety of check boxes within the *Effects* section. If a check mark appears in the box, the option is active (turned on). If the check box does not contain a check mark, the option is inactive (turned off). Any number of check boxes can be active. For example, in the Word Font dialog box, you can insert a check mark in any or all of the boxes in the *Effects* section and these options will be active.

To make a check box active or inactive with the mouse, position the tip of the arrow pointer in the check box and then click the left mouse button. If you are using the keyboard, press Alt + the underlined letter of the desired option.

## *Option Buttons*

The Word Print dialog box shown in Figure G.7 contains options in the *Print range* section preceded by option buttons. Only one option button can be selected at any time. When an option button is selected, a green circle displays in the button. To select an option button with the mouse, position the tip of the arrow pointer inside the option button and then click the left mouse button. To make a selection with the keyboard, hold down the Alt key and then press the underlined letter of the desired option.

**Figure G.7** Word Print Dialog Box

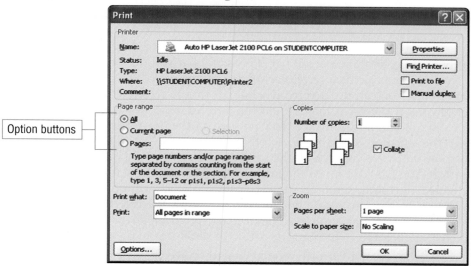

Option buttons

## *Spin Boxes*

Some options in a dialog box contain measurements or numbers you can increase or decrease. These options are generally located in a spin box. For example, the Word Paragraph dialog box shown in Figure G.8 contains spin boxes located after the *Left*, *Right*, *Before*, and *After* options. To increase a number in a spin box, position the tip of the arrow pointer on the up-pointing arrow to the right of the desired option and then click the left mouse button. To decrease the number, click the down-pointing arrow. If you are using the keyboard, press Alt + the underlined letter of the desired option and then press the Up Arrow key to increase the number or the Down Arrow key to decrease the number.

**Figure G.8** Word Paragraph Dialog Box

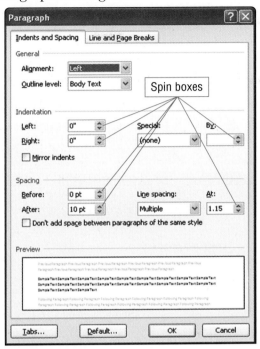

## Command Buttons

In the Excel Find and Replace dialog box shown in Figure G.5, the boxes along the bottom of the dialog box are called command buttons. Use a command button to execute or cancel a command. Some command buttons display with an ellipsis (...). A command button that displays with an ellipsis will open another dialog box. To choose a command button with the mouse, position the arrow pointer on the desired button and then click the left mouse button. To choose a command button with the keyboard, press the Tab key until the desired command button contains the marquee and then press the Enter key.

## Choosing Commands with Keyboard Shortcuts

Applications in the Office suite offer a variety of keyboard shortcuts you can use to executive specific commands. Keyboard shortcuts generally require two or more keys. For example, the keyboard shortcut to display the Open dialog box in an application is Ctrl + O. To use this keyboard shortcut, hold down the Ctrl key, type the letter O on the keyboard, and then release the Ctrl key. For a list of keyboard shortcuts, refer to the Help files.

## Choosing Commands with Shortcut Menus

The software programs in the suite include menus that contain commands related to the item with which you are working. A shortcut menu appears in the file in the location where you are working. To display a shortcut menu, click the right mouse button or press Shift + F10. For example, if the insertion point is positioned in a paragraph of text in a Word document, clicking the right mouse button or pressing Shift + F10 will cause the shortcut menu shown in Figure G.9 to display in the document screen.

**Figure G.9** Word Shortcut Menu

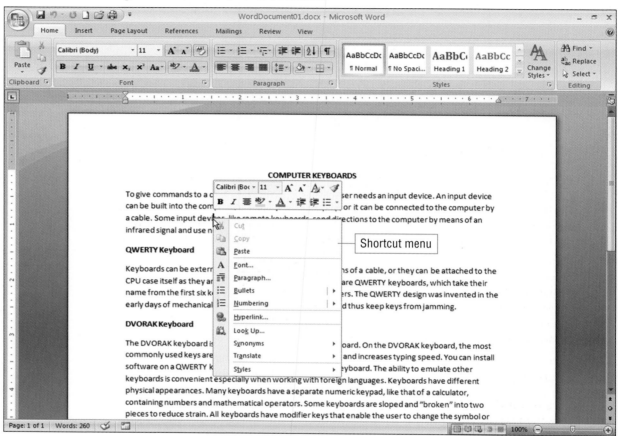

To select an option from a shortcut menu with the mouse, click the desired option. If you are using the keyboard, press the Up or Down Arrow key until the desired option is selected and then press the Enter key. To close a shortcut menu without choosing an option, click anywhere outside the shortcut menu or press the Esc key.

# Working with Multiple Programs

As you learn the various programs in the Microsoft Office suite, you will notice how executing commands in each is very similar. For example, the steps to save, close, and print are virtually the same whether you are working in Word, Excel, or PowerPoint. This consistency between programs greatly enhances a user's ability to transfer knowledge learned in one program to another within the suite. Another appeal of Microsoft Office is the ability to have more than one program open at the same time. For example, you can open Word, create a document, and then open Excel, create a spreadsheet, and copy the spreadsheet into Word.

When you open a program, the name of the program displays in the Taskbar. If you open a file within the program, the file name follows the program name on the button on the Taskbar. If you open another program, the program name displays on a button positioned to the right of the first program button. Figure G.10 shows the Taskbar with Word, Excel, and PowerPoint open. To move from one program to another, click the button on the Taskbar representing the desired program file.

**Figure G.10** Taskbar with Word, Excel, and PowerPoint Open

# Completing Computer Projects

Some computer projects in this textbook require that you open an existing file. Project files are saved on the Student CD that accompanies this textbook. The files you need for each chapter are saved in individual folders. Before beginning a chapter, copy the necessary folder from the CD to your storage medium. After completing projects in a chapter, delete the chapter folder before copying the next chapter folder. (Check with your instructor before deleting a folder.)

The Student CD also contains model answers in PDF format for the project exercises within (but not at the end of) each chapter so you can check your work. To access the PDF files, you will need to have Adobe Acrobat Reader installed on your computer's hard drive. A free download of Adobe Reader is available at Adobe Systems' Web site at www.adobe.com.

## Copying a Folder

As you begin working in a chapter, copy the chapter folder from the CD to your storage medium using the My Computer window by completing the following steps:
1. Insert the CD that accompanies this textbook in the CD drive.
2. Insert your storage medium in the appropriate drive.
3. At the Windows XP desktop, open the My Computer window by clicking the Start button and then clicking *My Computer* at the Start menu.
4. Double-click the CD drive in the contents pane (probably displays as *Office2007_Bench* or *Word2007, Excel 2007*, etc. followed by the drive letter).
5. Double-click the *StudentDataFiles* folder in the contents pane.
6. Double-click the desired folder name in the contents pane. (For example, if you are copying a folder for a Word Level 1 chapter, double-click the *Word2007L1* folder.)
7. Click once on the desired chapter subfolder name to select it.
8. Click the <u>Copy this folder</u> hyperlink in the *File and Folder Tasks* section of the task pane.
9. At the Copy Items dialog box, click the drive where your storage medium is located and then click the Copy button.
10. After the folder is copied to your storage medium, close the My Computer window by clicking the Close button (white X on red background) that displays in the upper right corner of the window.

## Deleting a Folder

Before copying a chapter folder onto your storage medium, you may need to delete any previous chapter folders. Do this in the My Computer window by completing the following steps:

1. Insert your storage medium in the appropriate drive.
2. At the Windows XP desktop, open the My Computer window by clicking the Start button and then clicking *My Computer* at the Start menu.
3. Double-click the drive where you storage medium is located in the contents pane.
4. Click the chapter folder in the list box.
5. Click the <u>Delete this folder</u> hyperlink in the *File and Folder Tasks* section of the task pane.
6. At the message asking if you want to remove the folder and all its contents, click the Yes button.
7. If a message displays asking if you want to delete a read-only file, click the Yes to All button.
8. Close the My Computer window by clicking the Close button (white X on red background) that displays in the upper right corner of the window.

## Viewing or Printing the Project Model Answers

If you want to access the PDF model answer files, first make sure that Adobe Acrobat Reader is installed on your hard drive. Double-click the folder, double-click the desired chapter subfolder name, and double-click the appropriate file name to open the file. You can view and/or print the file to compare it with your own completed exercise file.

# Customizing the Quick Access Toolbar

The four applications in the Office 2007 suite—Word, Excel, PowerPoint, and Access—each contain a Quick Access toolbar that displays at the top of the screen. By default, this toolbar contains three buttons: Save, Undo, and Redo. Before beginning chapters in this textbook, customize the Quick Access toolbar by adding three additional buttons: New, Open, and Quick Print. To add these three buttons to the Word Quick Access toolbar, complete the following steps:

1. Open Word.
2. Click the Customize Quick Access Toolbar button that displays at the right side of the toolbar.
3. At the drop-down list, click *New*. (This adds the New button to the toolbar.)
4. Click the Customize Quick Access Toolbar button and then click *Open* at the drop-down list. (This adds the Open button to the toolbar.)
5. Click the Customize Quick Access Toolbar button and then click *Quick Print* at the drop-down list. (This adds the Quick Print button to the toolbar.)

Complete the same steps for Excel, Access, and PowerPoint. You will only need to add the buttons once to the Quick Access toolbar. These buttons will remain on the toolbar even when you exit and then reopen the application.

# Using Windows XP

A computer requires an operating system to provide necessary instructions on a multitude of processes including loading programs, managing data, directing the flow of information to peripheral equipment, and displaying information. Windows XP Professional is an operating system that provides functions of this type (along with much more) in a graphical environment. Windows is referred to as a ***graphical user interface*** (GUI— pronounced *gooey*) that provides a visual display of information with features such as icons (pictures) and buttons. In this introduction, you will learn the basic features of Windows XP:

- Use desktop icons and the Taskbar to launch programs and open files or folders
- Organize and manage data, including copying, moving, creating, and deleting files and folders
- Customize the desktop by changing the theme, background, colors, and settings, and adding a screen saver
- Use the Help and Support Center features
- Customize monitor settings

Historically, Microsoft has produced two editions of Windows—one edition for individual users (on desktop and laptop computers) and another edition for servers (on computers that provide service over networks). Windows XP is an upgrade and a merging of these two Windows editions and is available in two versions. The Windows XP Home Edition is designed for home use and Windows XP Professional is designed for small office and workstation use. Whether you are using Windows XP Home Edition or Windows XP Professional, you will be able to complete the steps in the projects in this introduction.

Before using one of the software programs in the Microsoft Office suite, you will need to start the Windows XP operating system. To do this, turn on the computer. Depending on your computer equipment configuration, you may also need to turn on the monitor and printer. If you are using a computer that is part of a network system or if your computer is set up for multiple users, a screen will display showing the user accounts defined for your computer system. At this screen, click your user account name and, if necessary, type your password and then press the Enter key. The Windows XP operating system will start and, after a few moments, the desktop will display as shown in Figure W.1. (Your desktop may vary from what you see in Figure W.1.)

**Figure W.1**  Windows XP Desktop

icon

Taskbar

# Exploring the Desktop

When Windows XP is loaded, the main portion of the screen is called the ***desktop***. Think of the desktop in Windows as the top of a desk in an office. A business person places necessary tools—such as pencils, pens, paper, files, calculator—on the desktop to perform functions. Like the tools that are located on a desk, the desktop contains tools for operating the computer. These tools are logically grouped and placed in dialog boxes or panels that you can display using icons on the desktop. The desktop contains a variety of features for using your computer and software programs installed on the computer. The features available on the desktop are represented by icons and buttons.

## Using Icons

Icons are visual symbols that represent programs, files, or folders. Figure W.1 identifies the *Recycle Bin* icon located on the Windows XP desktop. The Windows XP desktop on your computer may contain additional icons. Programs that have been installed on your computer may be represented by an icon on the desktop. Also, icons may display on your desktop representing files or folders. Double-click an icon and the program, file, or folder it represents opens on the desktop.

## Using the Taskbar

The bar that displays at the bottom of the desktop (see Figure W.1) is called the Taskbar. The Taskbar, shown in Figure W.2, contains the Start button, a section that displays task buttons representing open programs, and the notification area.

**Figure W.2** Windows XP Taskbar

Start button          Task button area          Notification area

Click the Start button, located at the left side of the Taskbar, and the Start menu displays as shown in Figure W.3 (your Start menu may vary). You can also display the Start menu by pressing the Windows key on your keyboard or by pressing Ctrl + Esc. The left column of the Start menu contains **pinned programs**, which are programs that always appear in that particular location on the Start menu, and links to the most recently and frequently used programs. The right column contains links to folders, the Control Panel, online help, and the search feature.

**Figure W.3** Start Menu

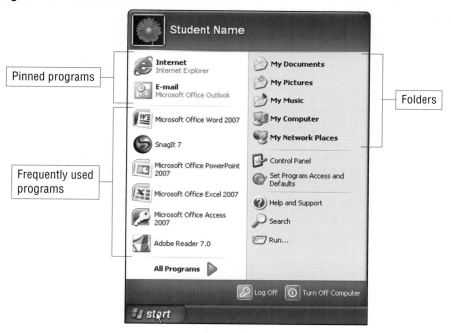

To choose an option from the Start menu, drag the arrow pointer to the desired option (referred to as **pointing**) and then click the left mouse button. Pointing to options at the Start menu that are followed by a right-pointing arrow will cause a side menu to display with additional options. When a program is open, a task button representing the program appears on the Taskbar. If multiple programs are open, each program will appear as a task button on the Taskbar (a few specialized tools may not).

# Project ① Opening Programs and Switching between Programs

1. Open Windows XP. (To do this, turn on the computer and, if necessary, turn on the monitor and/or printer. If you are using a computer that is part of a network system or if your computer is set up for multiple users, you may need to click your user account name and, if necessary, type your password and then press the Enter key. Check with your instructor to determine if you need to complete any additional steps.)
2. When the Windows XP desktop displays, open Microsoft Word by completing the following steps:
   a. Position the arrow pointer on the Start button on the Taskbar and then click the left mouse button.
   b. At the Start menu, point to *All Programs* (a side menu displays) and then point to *Microsoft Office* (another side menu displays).
   c. Drag the arrow pointer to *Microsoft Office Word 2007* in the side menu and then click the left mouse button.
   d. When the Microsoft Word program is open, notice that a task button representing Word displays on the Taskbar.

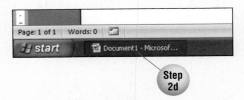

Step 2d

3. Open Microsoft Excel by completing the following steps:
   a. Position the arrow pointer on the Start button on the Taskbar and then click the left mouse button.
   b. At the Start menu, point to *All Programs* and then point to *Microsoft Office*.
   c. Drag the arrow pointer to *Microsoft Office Excel 2007* in the side menu and then click the left mouse button.
   d. When the Microsoft Excel program is open, notice that a task button representing Excel displays on the Taskbar to the right of the task button representing Word.
4. Switch to the Word program by clicking the task button on the Taskbar representing Word.

Step 4

Step 6

5. Switch to the Excel program by clicking the task button on the Taskbar representing Excel.
6. Exit Excel by clicking the Close button that displays in the upper right corner of the Excel window.
7. Exit Word by clicking the Close button that displays in the upper right corner of the Word window.

## Exploring the Notification Area

The notification area is located at the right side of the Taskbar and contains the system clock along with small icons representing specialized programs that run in the background. Position the arrow pointer over the current time in the notification area of the Taskbar and today's date displays in a small yellow box above the time. Double-click the current time displayed on the Taskbar and the Date and Time Properties dialog box displays as shown in Figure W.4.

**Figure W.4** Date and Time Properties Box

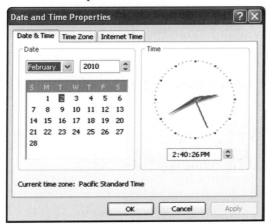

Change the date with options in the *Date* section of the dialog box. For example, to change the month, click the down-pointing arrow at the right side of the option box containing the current month and then click the desired month at the drop-down list. Change the year by clicking the up- or down-pointing arrow at the right side of the option box containing the current year until the desired year displays. To change the day, click the desired day in the monthly calendar that displays in the dialog box. To change the time, double-click either the hour, minute, or seconds and then type the appropriate time or use the up- and down-pointing arrows to adjust the time.

Some programs, when installed, will add an icon to the notification area of the Taskbar. Display the name of the icon by positioning the mouse pointer on the icon and, after approximately one second, the icon label displays in a small yellow box. Some icons may display information in the yellow box rather than the icon label. If more icons have been inserted in the notification area than can be viewed at one time, a left-pointing arrow button displays at the left side of the notification area. Click this left-pointing arrow button and the remaining icons display.

## Setting Taskbar Properties

By default, the Taskbar is locked in its current position and size. You can change this default setting, along with other default settings, with options at the Taskbar and Start Menu Properties dialog box, shown in Figure W.5. To display this dialog box, position the arrow pointer on any empty spot on the Taskbar and then click the right mouse button. At the shortcut menu that displays, click *Properties*.

**Figure W.5** Taskbar and Start Menu Properties Box

Each property is controlled by a check box. Property options containing a check mark are active. Click the option to remove the check mark and make the option inactive. If an option is inactive, clicking the option will insert a check mark in the check box and turn on the option (make it active).

## Project ② Changing Taskbar Properties

1. Make sure Windows XP is open and the desktop displays.
2. Hide the Taskbar and remove the display of the clock by completing the following steps:
   a. Position the arrow pointer on any empty area on the Taskbar and then click the right mouse button.
   b. At the shortcut menu that displays, click *Properties*.
   c. At the Taskbar and Start Menu Properties dialog box, click *Auto-hide the taskbar*. (This inserts a check mark in the check box.)
   d. Click *Show the clock*. (This removes the check mark from the check box.)
   e. Click the Apply button.
   f. Click OK to close the dialog box.

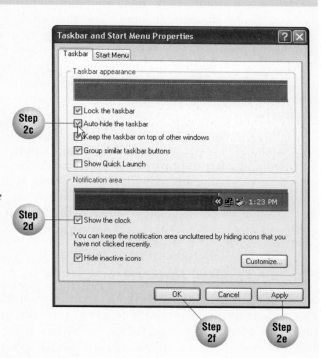

3. Display the Taskbar by positioning the mouse pointer at the bottom of the screen. When the Taskbar displays, notice that the time no longer displays at the right side of the Taskbar.
4. Return to the default settings for the Taskbar by completing the following steps:
    a. With the Taskbar displayed (if it does not display, position the mouse pointer at the bottom of the desktop), position the arrow pointer on any empty area on the Taskbar and then click the right mouse button.
    b. At the shortcut menu that displays, click *Properties*.
    c. At the Taskbar and Start Menu Properties dialog box, click *Auto-hide the taskbar*. (This removes the check mark from the check box.)
    d. Click *Show the clock*. (This inserts a check mark in the check box.)
    e. Click the Apply button.
    f. Click OK to close the dialog box.

# Turning Off the Computer

When you are finished working with your computer, you can choose to shut down the computer completely, shut down and then restart the computer, put the computer on standby, or tell the computer to hibernate. Do not turn off your computer until your screen goes blank. Important data is stored in memory while Windows XP is running and this data needs to be written to the hard drive before turning off the computer.

To shut down your computer, click the Start button on the Taskbar and then click *Turn Off Computer* at the Start menu. At the Turn off computer window, shown in Figure W.6, click the *Stand By* option and the computer switches to a low power state causing some devices such as the monitor and hard drives to turn off. With these devices off, the computer uses less power. Stand By is particularly useful for saving battery power for portable computers. Tell the computer to "hibernate" by holding down the Shift key while clicking the *Stand By* option. In hibernate mode, the computer saves everything in memory, turns off the monitor and hard drive, and then turns off the computer. Click the *Turn Off* option if you want to shut down Windows XP and turn off all power to the computer. Click the *Restart* option if you want to restart the computer and restore the desktop exactly as you left it. You can generally restore your desktop from either standby or hibernate by pressing once on the computer's power button. Usually, bringing a computer out of hibernation takes a little longer than bringing a computer out of standby.

**Figure W.6** Turn Off Computer Window

# Managing Files and Folders

As you begin working with programs in Windows XP, you will create files in which data (information) is saved. A file might contain a Word document, an Excel workbook, or a PowerPoint presentation. As you begin creating files, consider creating folders into which those files will be stored. You can complete file management tasks such as creating a folder and copying and moving files and folders at the My Computer window. To display the My Computer window shown in Figure W.7, click the Start button on the Taskbar and then click My Computer. The various components of the My Computer window are identified in Figure W.7.

**Figure W.7** My Computer Window

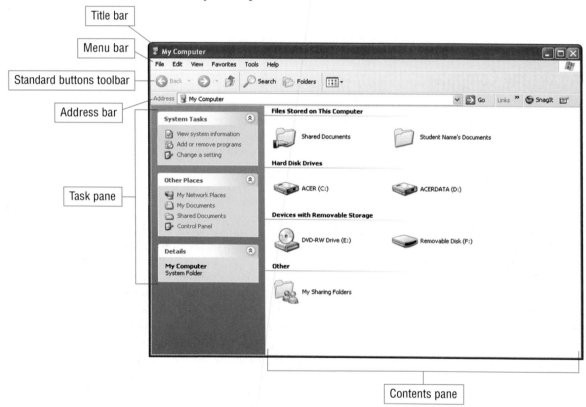

## Copying, Moving, and Deleting Files/Folders

File and folder management activities might include copying and moving files or folders from one folder or drive to another, or deleting files or folders. The My Computer window offers a variety of methods for copying, moving, and deleting files/folders. You can use options in the task pane, drop-down menu options, or shortcut menu options. This section will provide you with the steps for copying, moving, and deleting files/folders using options in the task pane.

To copy a file/folder to another folder or drive, first display the file in the contents pane by identifying the location of the file. If the file is located in the My Documents folder, click the My Documents hyperlink in the *Other Places* section of the task pane. If the file is located on the hard drive, double-click the desired drive in the contents pane; if the file is located on a USB drive, DVD, or CD, double-click the desired drive letter. Next, click the folder or file name in the contents pane that you want to copy. This changes the options in the task pane to include management options such as renaming, moving, copying, and deleting folders or files. Click the <u>Copy this folder</u> (or <u>Copy this file</u>) hyperlink in the task pane and the Copy Items dialog box displays as shown in Figure W.8. At the Copy Items dialog box, click the desired folder or drive and then click the Copy button.

**Figure W.8** Copy Items Dialog Box

To move adjacent files/folders, click the first file or folder, hold down the Shift key, and then click the last file or folder. This selects and highlights all files/folders from the first file/folder you clicked to the last file/folder you clicked. With the adjacent files/folders selected, click the <u>Move the selected items</u> hyperlink in the File and Folder Tasks section of the task pane and then specify the desired location at the Move Items dialog box. To select nonadjacent files/folders, click the first file/folder to select it, hold down the Ctrl key, and then click any other files/folders you want to move or copy.

You can easily remove (delete) a file or folder from the My Computer window. To delete a file or folder, click the file or folder in the contents pane, and then click the <u>Delete this folder</u> (or <u>Delete this file</u>) hyperlink in the task pane. At the dialog box asking you to confirm the deletion, click Yes. A deleted file or folder is sent to the Recycle Bin. You will learn more about the Recycle Bin in the next section.

In Project 3, you will insert the CD that accompanies this book into the DVD or CD drive. When the CD is inserted, the drive may automatically activate and a dialog box may display on the screen telling you that the disk or device contains more than one type of content and asking what you want Windows to do. If this dialog box displays, click Cancel to remove the dialog box.

# Project ③ Copying a File and Folder and Deleting a File

1. At the Windows XP desktop, insert the CD that accompanies this textbook into the appropriate drive. If a dialog box displays telling you that the disk or device contains more than one type of content and asking what you want Windows to do, click Cancel.
2. At the Windows XP desktop, open the My Computer window by clicking the Start button on the Taskbar and then clicking *My Computer* at the Start menu.
3. Copy a file from the CD that accompanies this textbook to the drive containing your storage medium by completing the following steps:
   a. Insert your storage medium in the appropriate drive.
   b. In the contents pane, double-click the drive containing the CD (probably displays as *Office2007_Bench* followed by a drive letter). (Make sure you double-click the mouse button because you want the contents of the CD to display in the contents pane.)
   c. Double-click the *StudentDataFiles* folder.
   d. Double-click the *WindowsXP* folder in the contents pane.
   e. Click **WordDocument01.docx** in the contents pane to select it.
   f. Click the Copy this file hyperlink located in the *File and Folder Tasks* section of the task pane.

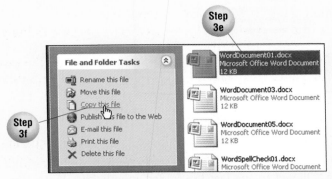

g. At the Copy Items dialog box, click in the list box the drive containing your storage medium.
h. Click the Copy button.

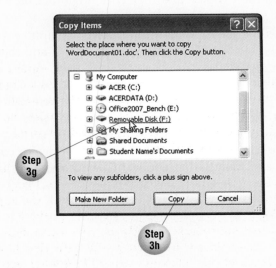

4. Delete **WordDocument01.docx** from your storage medium by completing the following steps:
   a. Click the <u>My Computer</u> hyperlink located in the *Other Places* section of the task pane.
   b. Double-click in the contents pane the drive containing your storage medium.
   c. Click ***WordDocument01.docx***.
   d. Click the <u>Delete this file</u> hyperlink in the *File and Folder Tasks* section of the task pane.

   e. At the message asking you to confirm the deletion, click Yes.
5. Copy the WindowsXP folder from the CD drive to the drive containing your storage medium by completing the following steps:
   a. Click the My Computer hyperlink in the *Other Places* section of the task pane.
   b. In the contents pane, double-click the drive containing the CD (probably displays as *Office2007_Bench* followed by a drive letter).
   c. Double-click the *StudentDataFiles* folder.
   d. Click the *WindowsXP* folder in the contents pane to select it.
   e. Click the <u>Copy this folder</u> hyperlink in the *File and Folder Tasks* section of the task pane.
   f. At the Copy Items dialog box, click the drive containing your storage medium.
   g. Click the Copy button.
6. Close the window by clicking the Close button (contains a white *X* on a red background) located in the upper right corner of the window. (You can also close the window by clicking File on the Menu bar and then clicking *Close* at the drop-down list.)


## *Selecting Files/Folders*

You can move, copy, or delete more than one file or folder at the same time. Before moving, copying, or deleting files/folders, select the desired files or folders. Selecting files/folders is easier when you change the display in the contents pane to List or Details. To change the display, open the My Computer window and then click the Views button on the Standard Buttons toolbar. At the drop-down list that displays, click the *List* option or the *Details* option.

To move adjacent files/folders, click the first file or folder, hold down the Shift key, and click the last file or folder. This selects and highlights all files/folders from the first file/folder you clicked to the last file/folder you clicked. With the adjacent files/folders selected, click the <u>Move the selected items</u> hyperlink in the *File and Folder Tasks* section of the task pane and then specify the desired location at the Move Items dialog box. To select nonadjacent files/folders, click the first file/folder to select it, hold down the Ctrl key, and then click any other files/folders you want to move or copy.

# Project ④    Copying and Deleting Files

1. At the Windows XP desktop, open the My Computer window by clicking the Start button and then clicking *My Computer* at the Start menu.
2. Copy files from the CD that accompanies this textbook to the drive containing your storage medium by completing the following steps:
   a. Make sure the CD that accompanies this textbook and your storage medium are inserted in the appropriate drives.
   b. Double-click the CD drive in the contents pane (probably displays as *Office2007_Bench* followed by the drive letter).
   c. Double-click the *StudentDataFiles* folder in the contents pane.
   d. Double-click the *WindowsXP* folder in the contents pane.
   e. Change the display to Details by clicking the Views button on the Standard Buttons toolbar and then clicking *Details* at the drop-down list.

   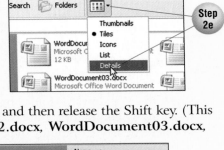

   f. Position the arrow pointer on **WordDocument01.docx** in the contents pane and then click the left mouse button.
   g. Hold down the Shift key, click ***WordDocument05.docx***, and then release the Shift key. (This selects **WordDocument01.docx**, **WordDocument02.docx**, **WordDocument03.docx**, **WordDocument04.docx**, and **WordDocument05.docx**.)

   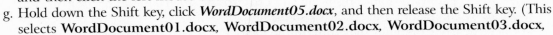

   h. Click the <u>Copy the selected items</u> hyperlink in the *File and Folder Tasks* section of the task pane.
   i. At the Copy Items dialog box, click the drive containing your storage medium and then click the Copy button.
3. Display the files and folder saved on your storage medium by completing the following steps:
   a. Click the <u>My Computer</u> hyperlink in the *Other Places* section of the task pane.
   b. Double-click the drive containing your storage medium.
4. Delete the files from your storage medium that you just copied by completing the following steps:
   a. Change the view by clicking the Views button on the Standard Buttons toolbar and then clicking *List* at the drop-down list.
   b. Click ***WordDocument01.docx*** in the contents pane.
   c. Hold down the Shift key, click ***WordDocument05.docx***, and then release the Shift key. (This selects **WordDocument01.docx**, **WordDocument02.docx**, **WordDocument03.docx**, **WordDocument04.docx**, and **WordDocument05.docx**.)
   d. Click the <u>Delete the selected items</u> hyperlink in the *File and Folder Tasks* section of the task pane.

   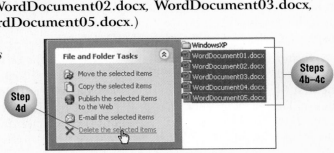

   e. At the message asking you to confirm the deletion, click Yes.
5. Close the window by clicking the Close button (white *X* on red background) that displays in the upper right corner of the window.

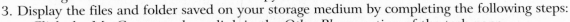

# Manipulating and Creating Folders

As you begin working with and creating a number of files, consider creating folders in which you can logically group the files. To create a folder, display the My Computer window and then display in the contents pane the drive where you want to create the folder. Click File on the Menu bar, point to *New*, and then click *Folder* at the side menu. This inserts a folder icon in the contents pane and names the folder *New Folder*. Type the desired name for the new folder and then press Enter.

## Project 5   Creating a New Folder

1. At the Windows XP desktop, open the My Computer window.
2. Create a new folder by completing the following steps:
   a. Double-click in the contents pane the drive that contains your storage medium.
   b. Double-click the *WindowsXP* folder in the contents pane. (This opens the folder.)
   c. Click File on the Menu bar, point to *New*, and then click *Folder*.
   d. Type **SpellCheckFiles** and then press Enter. (This changes the name from *New Folder* to *SpellCheckFiles*.)
3. Copy **WordSpellCheck01.docx**, **WordSpellCheck02.docx**, and **WordSpellCheck03.docx** into the SpellCheckFiles folder you just created by completing the following steps:
   a. Click the Views button on the Standard Buttons toolbar and then click *List* at the drop-down list.
   b. Click once on the file named ***WordSpellCheck01.docx*** located in the contents pane.
   c. Hold down the Shift key, click once on the file named ***WordSpellCheck03.docx***, and then release the Shift key. (This selects **WordSpellCheck01.docx, WordSpellCheck02.docx,** and **WordSpellCheck03.docx**.)
   d. Click the <u>Copy the selected items</u> hyperlink in the *File and Folder Tasks* section of the task pane.
   e. At the Copy Items dialog box, click in the list box the drive containing your storage medium.
   f. Click *WindowsXP* in the list box.
   g. Click *SpellCheckFiles* in the list box.
   h. Click the Copy button.
4. Display the files you just copied by double-clicking the *SpellCheckFiles* folder in the contents pane.

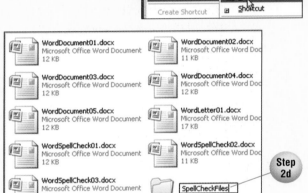

Step 2c

Step 2d

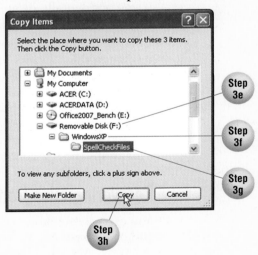

Step 3e

Step 3f

Step 3g

Step 3h

5. Delete the SpellCheckFiles folder and its contents by completing the following steps:

   a. Click the Up button on the Standard Buttons toolbar. (This displays the contents of the WindowsXP folder which is up one folder from the SpellCheckFiles folders.)

   b. Click the *SpellCheckFiles* folder in the contents pane to select it.

   c. Click the <u>Delete this folder</u> hyperlink in the *File and Folder Tasks* section of the task pane.

   d. At the message asking you to confirm the deletion, click Yes.

6. Close the window by clicking the Close button located in the upper right corner of the window.

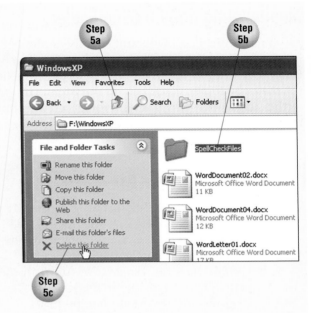

# Using the Recycle Bin

Deleting the wrong file can be a disaster but Windows XP helps protect your work with the Recycle Bin. The Recycle Bin acts just like an office wastepaper basket; you can "throw away" (delete) unwanted files, but you can "reach in" to the Recycle Bin and take out (restore) a file if you threw it away by accident.

## Deleting Files to the Recycle Bin

A file/folder or selected files/folders deleted from the hard drive are sent automatically to the Recycle Bin. Files/folders deleted from a disk are deleted permanently. (Recovery programs are available, however, that will help you recover deleted text. If you accidentally delete a file/folder from a disk, do not do anything more with the disk until you can run a recovery program.)

One method for deleting files is to display the My Computer window and then display in the contents pane the file(s) and/or folder(s) you want deleted. Click the file or folder or select multiple files or folders and then click the appropriate delete option in the task pane. At the message asking you to confirm the deletion, click Yes. Another method for deleting a file is to drag the file to the *Recycle Bin* icon on the desktop. Drag a file icon to the Recycle Bin until the *Recycle Bin* icon is selected (displays with a blue background) and then release the mouse button. This drops the file you are dragging into the Recycle Bin.

## Recovering Files from the Recycle Bin

You can easily restore a deleted file from the Recycle Bin. To restore a file, double-click the *Recycle Bin* icon on the desktop. This opens the Recycle Bin window shown in Figure W.9. (The contents of the Recycle Bin will vary.) To restore a file, click the file you want restored, and then click the <u>Restore this item</u> hyperlink in the *Recycle Bin Tasks* section of the task pane. This removes the file from the Recycle Bin and returns it to its original location. You can also restore a file by positioning the arrow pointer on the file, clicking the right mouse button, and then clicking *Restore* at the shortcut menu.

**Figure W.9** Recycle Bin Window

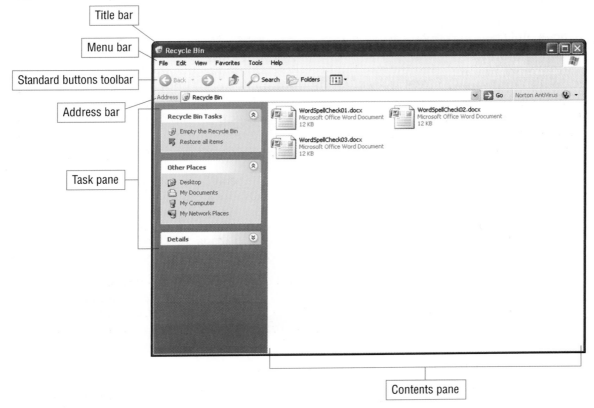

Contents pane

---

## Project ⑥  Deleting Files to and Recovering Files from the Recycle Bin

*Before beginning this project, check with your instructor to determine if you can copy files to the hard drive.*

1. At the Windows XP desktop, open the My Computer window.
2. Copy files from your storage medium to the My Documents folder on your hard drive by completing the following steps:
   a. Double-click in the contents pane the drive containing your storage medium.
   b. Double-click the *WindowsXP* folder in the contents pane.
   c. Click the Views button on the Standard Buttons toolbar and then click *List* at the drop-down list.
   d. Position the arrow pointer on **WordSpellCheck01.docx** and then click the left mouse button.
   e. Hold down the Shift key, click **WordSpellCheck03.docx**, and then release the Shift key.

f. Click the Copy the selected items hyperlink in the *File and Folder Tasks* section of the task pane.

g. At the Copy Items dialog box, click *My Documents* in the list box.

h. Click the Copy button.

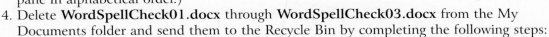

3. Click the <u>My Documents</u> hyperlink in the *Other Places* section of the task pane. (The files you copied, **WordSpellCheck01.docx** through **WordSpellCheck03.docx**, will display in the contents pane in alphabetical order.)

4. Delete **WordSpellCheck01.docx** through **WordSpellCheck03.docx** from the My Documents folder and send them to the Recycle Bin by completing the following steps:

a. Select **WordSpellCheck01.docx** through **WordSpellCheck03.docx** in the contents pane. (If these files are not visible, you will need to scroll down the list of files.)

b. Click the <u>Delete the selected items</u> hyperlink in the *File and Folder Tasks* section of the task pane.

c. At the message asking you to confirm the deletion to the Recycle Bin, click Yes.

5. Click the Close button to close the window.

6. At the desktop, display the contents of the Recycle Bin by double-clicking the *Recycle Bin* icon.

7. At the Recycle Bin window, restore **WordSpellCheck01.docx** through **WordSpellCheck03.docx** to the My Documents folder by completing the following steps:

a. Select **WordSpellCheck01.docx** through **WordSpellCheck03.docx** in the contents pane of the Recycle Bin window. (If these files are not visible, you will need to scroll down the list of files.)

b. With the files selected, click the <u>Restore the selected items</u> hyperlink in the *Recycle Bin Tasks* section of the task pane.

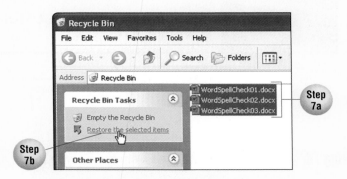

8. Close the Recycle Bin window by clicking the Close button located in the upper right corner of the window.

9. Display the My Computer window.

10. Click the <u>My Documents</u> hyperlink in the *Other Places* section of the task pane.

11. Delete the files you restored by completing the following steps:

a. Select **WordSpellCheck01.docx** through **WordSpellCheck03.docx** in the contents pane. (If these files are not visible, you will need to scroll down the list of files. These are the files you recovered from the Recycle Bin.)

b. Click the <u>Delete the selected items</u> hyperlink in the *File and Folder Tasks* section of the task pane.

c. At the message asking you to confirm the deletion, click Yes.

12. Close the window.

# Emptying the Recycle Bin

Just like a wastepaper basket, the Recycle Bin can get full. To empty the Recycle Bin, position the arrow pointer on the *Recycle Bin* icon on the desktop and then click the right mouse button. At the shortcut menu that displays, click *Empty Recycle Bin*. At the message asking you to confirm the deletion, click Yes. You can also empty the Recycle Bin by double-clicking the *Recycle Bin* icon. At the Recycle Bin window, click the Empty the Recycle Bin hyperlink in the *Recycle Bin Tasks* section of the task pane. At the message asking you to confirm the deletion, click Yes. (You can also empty the Recycle Bin by clicking File on the Menu bar and then clicking *Empty Recycle Bin* at the drop-down menu.)

Emptying the Recycle Bin deletes all files/folders. You can delete a specific file/folder from the Recycle Bin (rather than all files/folders). To do this, double-click the *Recycle Bin* icon on the desktop. At the Recycle Bin window, select the file/folder or files/folders you want to delete. Click File on the Menu bar and then click *Delete* at the drop-down menu. (You can also right-click a selected file/folder and then click *Delete* at the shortcut menu.) At the message asking you to confirm the deletion, click Yes.

## Project ⑦  Emptying the Recycle Bin

*Before beginning this project, check with your instructor to determine if you can delete files/folders from the Recycle Bin.*

1. At the Windows XP desktop, double-click the *Recycle Bin* icon.
2. At the Recycle Bin window, empty the contents of the Recycle Bin by completing the following steps:
   a. Click the Empty the Recycle Bin hyperlink in the *Recycle Bin Tasks* section of the task pane.

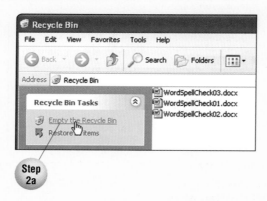

   b. At the message asking you to confirm the deletion, click Yes.
3. Close the Recycle Bin window by clicking the Close button located in the upper right corner of the window.

When you empty the Recycle Bin, the files cannot be recovered by the Recycle Bin or by Windows XP. If you have to recover a file, you will need to use a file recovery program such as Norton Utilities. These utilities are separate programs, but might be worth their cost if you ever need them.

# Creating a Shortcut

If you use a file or program on a consistent basis, consider creating a shortcut to the file or program. A shortcut is a specialized icon that represents very small files that point the operating system to the actual item, whether it is a file, a folder, or an application. If you create a shortcut to a Word document, the shortcut icon is not the actual document but a path to the document. Double-click the shortcut icon and Windows XP opens the document in Word.

One method for creating a shortcut is to display the My Computer window and then display the drive or folder where the file is located. Right-click the desired file, point to *Send To*, and then click *Desktop (create shortcut)*. You can easily delete a shortcut icon from the desktop by dragging the shortcut icon to the Recycle Bin icon. This deletes the shortcut icon but does not delete the file to which the shortcut pointed.

## Project 8  Creating a Shortcut

1. At the Windows XP desktop, display the My Computer window.
2. Double-click the drive containing your storage medium.
3. Double-click the *WindowsXP* folder in the contents pane.
4. Change the display of files to a list by clicking the Views button on the Standard Buttons toolbar and then clicking *List* at the drop-down list.
5. Create a shortcut to the file named **WordLetter01.docx** by right-clicking on **WordLetter01.docx**, pointing to *Send To*, and then clicking *Desktop (create shortcut)*.

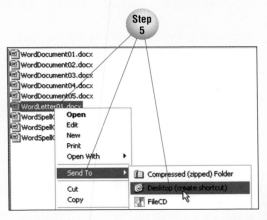

Step 5

6. Close the My Computer window by clicking the Close button located in the upper right corner of the window.
7. Open Word and the file named **WordLetter01.docx** by double-clicking the *WordLetter01.docx* shortcut icon on the desktop.
8. After viewing the file in Word, exit Word by clicking the Close button that displays in the upper right corner of the window.
9. Delete the *WordLetter01.docx* shortcut icon by completing the following steps:
   a. At the desktop, position the mouse pointer on the *WordLetter01.docx* shortcut icon.
   b. Hold down the left mouse button, drag the icon on top of the *Recycle Bin* icon, and then release the mouse button.

Step 7

# Customizing the Desktop

You can customize the Windows XP desktop to fit your particular needs and preferences. For example, you can choose a different theme, change the desktop background, add a screen saver, and apply a different appearance to windows, dialog boxes, and menus. To customize the desktop, position the arrow pointer on any empty location on the desktop and then click the right mouse button. At the shortcut menu that displays, click *Properties*. This displays the Display Properties dialog box with the Themes tab selected as shown in Figure W.10.

**Figure W.10** Display Properties Dialog Box

## Changing the Theme

A Windows XP theme specifies a variety of formatting such as fonts, sounds, icons, colors, mouse pointers, background, and screen saver. Windows XP contains two themes—Windows XP (the default) and Windows Classic (which appears like earlier versions of Windows). Other themes are available as downloads from the Microsoft Web site. Change the theme with the *Theme* option at the Display Properties dialog box with the Themes tab selected.

## Changing the Desktop

With options at the Display Properties dialog box with the Desktop tab selected, as shown in Figure W.11, you can choose a different desktop background and customize the desktop. Click any option in the *Background* list box and preview the results in the preview screen. With the *Position* option, you can specify that the background image is centered, tiled, or stretched on the desktop. Use the *Color* option to change the background color and click the Browse button to choose a background image from another location or Web site.

**Figure W.11** Display Properties Dialog Box with Desktop Tab Selected

## Adding a Screen Saver

If your computer sits idle for periods of time, consider adding a screen saver. A screen saver is a pattern that changes constantly, thus eliminating the problem of an image staying on the screen too long. To add a screen saver, display the Display Properties dialog box and then click the Screen Saver tab. This displays the dialog box as shown in Figure W.12.

**Figure W.12** Display Properties Dialog Box with Screen Saver Tab Selected

Click the down-pointing arrow at the right side of the *Screen saver* option box to display a list of installed screen savers. Click a screen saver and a preview displays in the monitor located toward the top of the dialog box. Click the Preview button and the dialog box is hidden and the screen saver displays on your monitor. Move the mouse or click a button on the mouse and the dialog box will reappear. Click the Power button in the *Monitor power* section and a dialog box displays with options for choosing a power scheme appropriate to the way you use your computer. The dialog box also includes options for specifying how long the computer can be left unused before the monitor and hard disk are turned off and the system goes to standby or hibernate mode.

## Changing Colors

Click the Appearance tab at the Display Properties dialog box and the dialog box displays as shown in Figure W.13. At this dialog box, you can change the desktop scheme. Schemes are predefined collections of colors used in windows, menus, title bars, and system fonts. Windows XP loads with the Windows XP style color scheme. Choose a different scheme with the Windows and buttons option and choose a specific color with the Color scheme option.

**Figure W.13** Display Properties Dialog Box with Appearance Tab Selected

## Changing Settings

Click the Settings tab at the Display Properties dialog box and the dialog box displays as shown in Figure W.14. At this dialog box, you can set color and screen resolution. The *Color quality* option determines how many colors your monitor displays. The more colors that are shown, the more realistic the images will appear. However, a lot of computer memory is required to show thousands of colors. Your exact choice is determined by the specific hardware you are using. The *Screen resolution* slide bar sets the screen's resolution. The higher the number, the more you can fit onto your screen. Again, your actual values depend on your particular hardware.

**Figure W.14** Display Properties Dialog Box with Settings Tab Selected

## Project 9   Customizing the Desktop

*Before beginning this project, check with your instructor to determine if you can customize the desktop.*

1. At the Windows XP desktop, display the Display Properties dialog box by positioning the arrow pointer on an empty location on the desktop, clicking the right mouse button, and then clicking *Properties* at the shortcut menu.

2. At the Display Properties dialog box, change the desktop background by completing the following steps:
   a. Click the Desktop tab.
   b. If a background is selected in the *Background* list box (other than the *(None)* option), make a note of this background name.
   c. Click *Blue Lace 16* in the *Background* list box. (If this option is not available, choose another background.)
   d. Make sure *Tile* is selected in the *Position* list box.
   e. Click OK to close the dialog box.

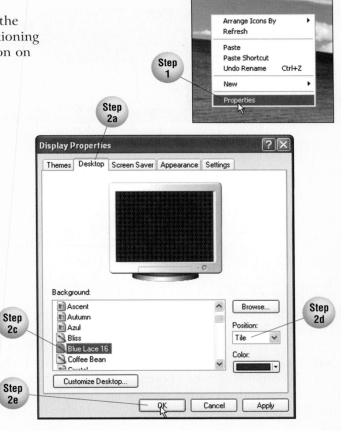

3. After viewing the desktop with the Blue Lace 16 background, remove the background image and change the background color by completing the following steps:
   a. Display the Display Properties dialog box.
   b. At the Display Properties dialog box, click the Desktop tab.
   c. Click *(None)* in the *Background* list box.
   d. Click the down-pointing arrow at the right side of the *Color* option and then click the dark red option at the color palette.
   e. Click OK to close the Display Properties dialog box.

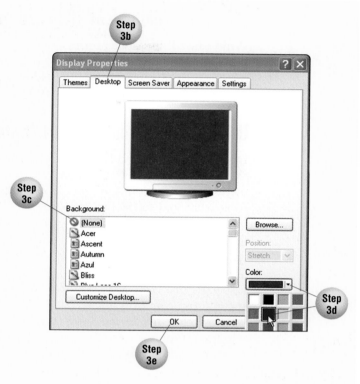

4. After viewing the desktop with the dark red background color, add a screen saver and change the wait time by completing the following steps:
   a. Display the Display Properties dialog box.
   b. At the Display Properties dialog box, click the Screen Saver tab. (If a screen saver is already selected in the *Screen saver* option box, make a note of this screen saver name.)
   c. Click the down-pointing arrow at the right side of the *Screen saver* option box.
   d. At the drop-down list that displays, click a screen saver that interests you. (A preview of the screen saver displays in the screen located toward the top of the dialog box.)
   e. Click a few other screen savers to see how they will display on the monitor.
   f. Click OK to close the Display Properties dialog box.

5. Return all settings back to the default by completing the following steps:
   a. Display the Display Properties dialog box.
   b. Click the Desktop tab.
   c. If a background and color were selected when you began this project, click that background name in the *Background* list box and change the color back to the original color.
   d. Click the Screen Saver tab.
   e. At the Display Properties dialog box with the Screen Saver tab selected, click the down-pointing arrow at the right side of the *Screen saver* option box, and then click *(None)*. (If a screen saver was selected before completing this project, return to that screen saver.)
   f. Click OK to close the Display Properties dialog box.

# Exploring Windows XP Help and Support

Windows XP includes an on-screen reference guide providing information, explanations, and interactive help on learning Windows features. The on-screen reference guide contains complex files with hypertext used to access additional information by clicking a word or phrase.

## Using the Help and Support Center Window

Display the Help and Support Center window shown in Figure W.15 by clicking the Start button on the Taskbar and then clicking *Help and Support* at the Start menu. The appearance of your Help and Support Center window may vary slightly from what you see in Figure W.15.

If you want to learn about a topic listed in the *Pick a Help topic* section of the window, click the desired topic and information about the topic displays in the window. Use the other options in the Help and Support Center window to get assistance or support from a remote computer or Windows XP newsgroups, pick a specific task, or learn about the additional help features. If you want help on a specific topic and do not see that topic listed in the *Pick a Help topic* section of the window, click inside the *Search* text box (generally located toward the top of the window), type the desired topic, and then press Enter or click the Start searching button (white arrow on a green background).

**Figure W.15** Help and Support Center Window

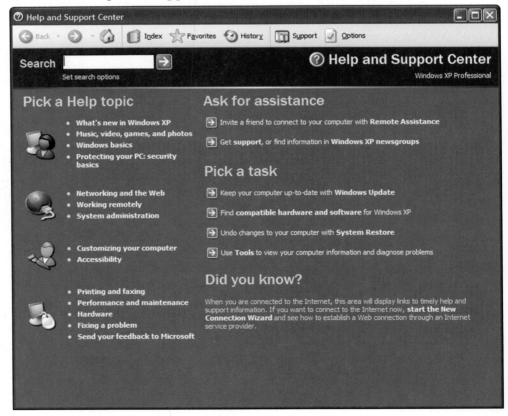

# Project ⑩  Using the Help and Support Center

1. At the Windows XP desktop, use the Help and Support feature to learn about new Windows XP features by completing the following steps:
   a. Click the Start button on the Taskbar and then click *Help and Support* at the Start menu.
   b. At the Help and Support Center window, click the <u>What's new in Windows XP</u> hyperlink located in the *Pick a Help topic* section of the window.

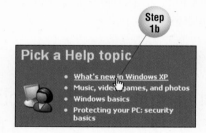

Step 1b

   c. Click the <u>What's new</u> hyperlink located in the *What's new in Windows XP* section of the window. (This displays a list of Help options at the right side of the window.)
   d. Click the <u>What's new in Windows XP</u> hyperlink located at the right side of the window below the subheading *Overviews, Articles, and Tutorials*.
   e. Read the information about Windows XP that displays at the right side of the window.
   f. Print the information by completing the following steps:
      1) Click the Print button located on the toolbar that displays above the information titled *What's new in Windows XP Professional*.

Step 1d

Step 1f1

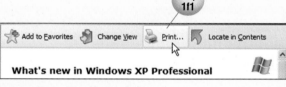

      2) At the Print dialog box, make sure the correct printer is selected and then click the Print button.
2. Return to the opening Help and Support Center window by clicking the Home button located on the Help and Support Center toolbar.
3. Use the *Search* text box to search for information on deleting files by completing the following steps:
   a. Click in the *Search* text box located toward the top of the Help and Support Center window.
   b. Type **deleting files** and then press Enter.
   c. Click the <u>Delete a file or folder</u> hyperlink that displays in the *Search Results* section of the window (below the *Pick a task* subheading).

Step 3b

Step 3c

d. Read the information about deleting a file or folder that displays at the right side of the window and then print the information by clicking the Print button on the toolbar and then clicking the Print button at the Print dialog box.

e. Click the <u>Delete or restore files in the Recycle Bin</u> hyperlink that displays in the *Search Results* section of the window.

f. Read the information that displays at the right side of the window about deleting and restoring files in the Recycle Bin and then print the information.

4. Close the Help and Support Center window by clicking the Close button located in the upper right corner of the window.

## Displaying an Index of Help and Support Topics

Display a list of help topics available by clicking the Index button on the Help and Support Center window toolbar. This displays an index of help topics at the left side of the window as shown in Figure W.16. Scroll through this list until the desired topic displays and then double-click the topic. Information about the selected topic displays at the right side of the window. If you are looking for a specific topic or keyword, click in the *Type in the keyword to find* text box, type the desired topic or keyword, and then press Enter.

**Figure W.16** Help and Support Center Window with Index Displayed

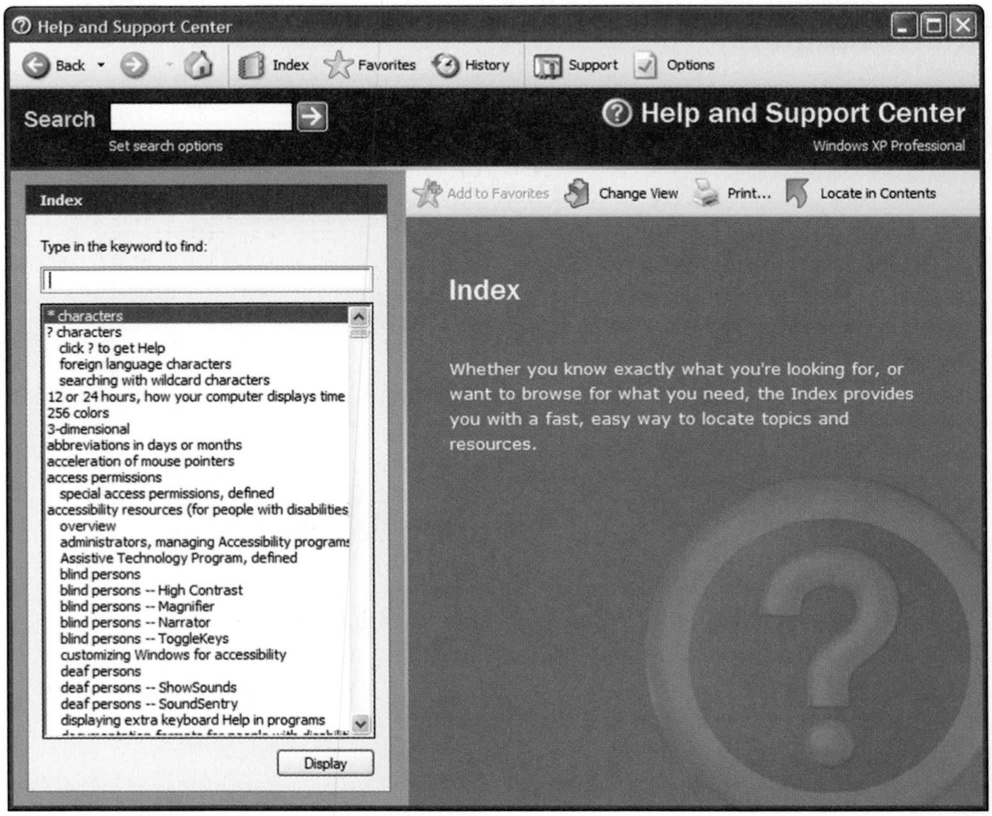

# Project 11  Using the Index to Search for Information

1. At the Windows XP desktop, use the Index to display information on accessing programs by completing the following steps:
   a. Click the Start button on the Taskbar and then click *Help and Support* at the Start menu.
   b. Click the Index button on the Help and Support Center window toolbar.
   c. Scroll down the list of Index topics until *accessing programs* is visible and then double-click the subheading *overview* that displays below *accessing programs*.

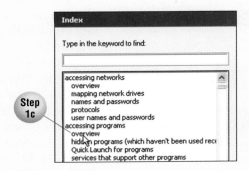

Step 1c

   d. Read the information that displays at the right side of the window and then print the information.
2. Find information on adding a shortcut to the desktop by completing the following steps:
   a. Select and delete the text *overview* that displays in the *Type in the keyword to find* text box and then type **shortcuts**.
   b. Double-click the subheading *for specific programs* that displays below the *shortcuts* heading.

Step 2a

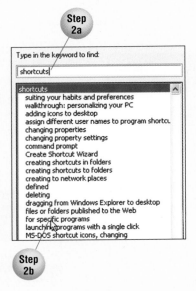

Step 2b

   c. Read the information that displays at the right side of the window and then print the information.
3. Close the Help and Support Center window by clicking the Close button located in the upper right corner of the window.

# Customizing Settings

Before beginning computer projects in this textbook, you may need to customize the monitor settings and turn on the display of file extensions. Projects in the chapters in this textbook assume that the monitor display is set to 1024 by 768 pixels and that the display of file extensions is turned on. To change the monitor display to 1024 by 768, complete the following steps:

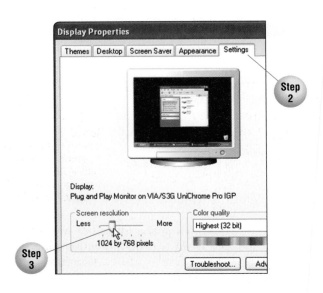

1. At the Windows XP desktop, right-click on any empty location on the desktop and then click *Properties* at the shortcut menu.
2. At the Display Properties dialog box, click the Settings tab.
3. Using the mouse, drag the slide bar button in the *Screen resolution* section to the left or right until *1024 by 768* displays below the slider bar.
4. Click the Apply button.
5. Click the OK button.

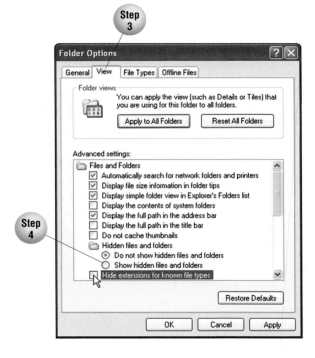

To turn on the display of file extensions, complete the following steps:

1. At the Windows XP desktop, click the Start button and then click *My Computer*.
2. At the My Computer window, click Tools on the Menu bar and then click *Folder Options* at the drop-down list.

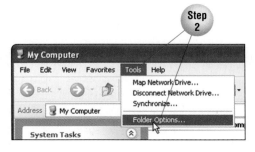

3. At the Folder Options dialog box, click the View tab.
4. Click the *Hide extentions for known file types* check box to remove the check mark.
5. Click the Apply button.
6. Click the OK button.

# Browsing the Internet Using Internet Explorer 7.0

Microsoft Internet Explorer 7.0 is a Web browser program with options and features for displaying sites as well as navigating and searching for information on the Internet. The *Internet* is a network of computers connected around the world. Users access the Internet for several purposes: to communicate using instant messaging and/or e-mail, to subscribe to newsgroups, to transfer files, to socialize with other users around the globe in "chat" rooms, and also to access virtually any kind of information imaginable.

**Tutorial IE1**
Browsing the Internet with Internet Explorer 7.0
**Tutorial IE2**
Gathering and Downloading Information and Files

Using the Internet, people can find a phenomenal amount of information for private or public use. To use the Internet, three things are generally required: an Internet Service Provider (ISP), a program to browse the Web (called a *Web browser*), and a *search engine*. In this section, you will learn how to:

- Navigate the Internet using URLs and hyperlinks
- Use search engines to locate information
- Download Web pages and images

## Browsing the Internet

You will use the Microsoft Internet Explorer Web browser to locate information on the Internet. Uniform Resource Locators, referred to as URLs, are the method used to identify locations on the Internet. The steps for browsing the Internet vary but generally include: opening Internet Explorer, typing the URL for the desired site, navigating the various pages of the site, navigating to other sites using links, and then closing Internet Explorer.

To launch Internet Explorer 7.0, double-click the *Internet Explorer* icon on the Windows desktop. Figure IE.1 identifies the elements of the Internet Explorer, version 7.0, window. The Web page that displays in your Internet Explorer window may vary from what you see in Figure IE.1.

**Figure IE.1** Internet Explorer Window

Title bar

Navigation bar

Address bar

Instant search box

Toolbar

Tabbed browsing— display multiple Web pages by inserting new tabs

Status bar

Change zoom level

If you know the URL for the desired Web site, click in the Address bar, type the URL, and then press Enter. The Web site's home page displays in a tab within the Internet Explorer window. URLs (Uniform Resource Locators) are the method used to identify locations on the Internet. The format of a URL is *http://server-name.path*. The first part of the URL, *http*, stands for HyperText Transfer Protocol, which is the protocol or language used to transfer data within the World Wide Web. The colon and slashes separate the protocol from the server name. The server name is the second component of the URL. For example, in the URL http://www.microsoft.com, the server name is *microsoft*. The last part of the URL specifies the domain to which the server belongs. For example, *.com* refers to "commercial" and establishes that the URL is a commercial company. Other examples of domains include *.edu* for "educational," *.gov* for "government," and *.mil* for "military."

## Project ① Browsing the Internet Using URLs

1. Make sure you are connected to the Internet through an Internet Service Provider and that the Windows desktop displays. (Check with your instructor to determine if you need to complete steps for accessing the Internet such as typing a user name and password to log on.)
2. Launch Microsoft Internet Explorer by double-clicking the *Internet Explorer* icon located on the Windows desktop.
3. At the Internet Explorer window, explore the Web site for Yosemite National Park by completing the following steps:
   a. Click in the Address bar, type www.nps.gov/yose, and then press Enter.

Step 3a

b. Scroll down the home page for Yosemite National Park by clicking the down-pointing arrow on the vertical scroll bar located at the right side of the Internet Explorer window.

Step 3b

c. Print the home page by clicking the Print button located on the Internet Explorer toolbar.

4. Explore the Web site for Glacier National Park by completing the following steps:

Step 3c

a. Click in the Address bar, type **www.nps.gov/glac**, and then press Enter.

Step 4a

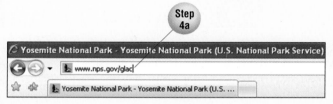

b. Print the home page by clicking the Print button located on the Internet Explorer toolbar.

5. Close Internet Explorer by clicking the Close button (contains an X) located in the upper right corner of the Internet Explorer window.

# Navigating Using Hyperlinks

Most Web pages contain "hyperlinks" that you click to connect to another page within the Web site or to another site on the Internet. Hyperlinks may display in a Web page as underlined text in a specific color or as images or icons. To use a hyperlink, position the mouse pointer on the desired hyperlink until the mouse pointer turns into a hand, and then click the left mouse button. Use hyperlinks to navigate within and between sites on the Internet. The navigation bar in the Internet Explorer window contains a Back button that, when clicked, takes you to the previous Web page viewed. If you click the Back button and then want to return to the previous page, click the Forward button. You can continue clicking the Back button to back your way out of several linked pages in reverse order since Internet Explorer maintains a history of the Web sites you visit.

## Project ② Navigating Using Hyperlinks

1. Make sure you are connected to the Internet and then double-click the *Internet Explorer* icon on the Windows desktop.
2. At the Internet Explorer window, display the White House Web page and navigate in the page by completing the following steps:
   a. Click in the Address bar, type **whitehouse.gov**, and then press Enter.
   b. At the White House home page, position the mouse pointer on a hyperlink that interests you until the pointer turns into a hand, and then click the left mouse button.
   c. At the linked Web page, click the Back button. (This returns you to the White House home page.)

Step 2c

d. At the White House home page, click the Forward button to return to the previous Web page viewed.

e. Print the Web page by clicking the Print button on the Internet Explorer toolbar.

3. Display the Web site for Amazon.com and navigate in the site by completing the following steps:

a. Click in the Address bar, type www.amazon.com, and then press Enter.

b. At the Amazon.com home page, click a hyperlink related to books.

c. When a book Web page displays, click the Print button on the Internet Explorer toolbar.

4. Close Internet Explorer by clicking the Close button (contains an X) located in the upper right corner of the Internet Explorer window.

## Searching for Specific Sites

If you do not know the URL for a specific site or you want to find information on the Internet but do not know what site to visit, complete a search with a search engine. A search engine is a software program created to search quickly and easily for desired information. A variety of search engines are available on the Internet, each offering the opportunity to search for specific information. One method for searching for information is to click in the *Instant Search* box (displays the text *Live Search*) located at the right end of the navigation bar, type a keyword or phrase related to your search, and then click the Search button or press Enter. Another method for completing a search is to visit the Web site for a search engine and use options at the site.

## Project ③  Searching for Information by Topic

1. Start Internet Explorer.

2. At the Internet Explorer window, search for sites on bluegrass music by completing the following steps:

a. Click in the *Instant Search* box (may display with *Live Search*) located at the right end of the of the navigation bar.

b. Type bluegrass music and then press Enter.

c. When a list of sites displays in the Live Search tab, click a site that interests you.

d. When the page displays, click the Print button.

3. Use the Yahoo! search engine to find sites on bluegrass music by completing the following steps:
   a. Click in the Address bar, type www.yahoo.com, and then press Enter.
   b. At the Yahoo! Web site, with the insertion point positioned in the *Search* text box, type bluegrass music and then press Enter. (Notice that the sites displayed vary from sites displayed in the earlier search.)

Step 3b

   c. Click hyperlinks until a Web site displays that interests you.
   d. Print the page.
4. Use the Google search engine to find sites on jazz music by completing the following steps:
   a. Click in the Address bar, type www.google.com, and then press Enter.
   b. At the Google Web site, with the insertion point positioned in the search text box, type jazz music and then press Enter.

   c. Click a site that interests you.

Step 4b

   d. Print the page.
5. Close Internet Explorer.

# Completing Advanced Searches for Specific Sites

The Internet contains an enormous amount of information. Depending on what you are searching for on the Internet and the search engine you use, some searches can result in several thousand "hits" (sites). Wading through a large number of sites can be very time-consuming and counterproductive. Narrowing a search to very specific criteria can greatly reduce the number of hits for a search. To narrow a search, use the advanced search options offered by the search engine.

Web Search

# Project ④  Narrowing a Search

1. Start Internet Explorer.
2. Search for sites on skydiving in Oregon by completing the following steps:
   a. Click in the Address bar and then type www.yahoo.com.
   b. At the Yahoo! Web site, click the Web Search button next to the Search text box and then click the <u>Advanced Search</u> hyperlink.

c. At the Advanced Web Search page, click in the search text box next to *all of these words*.
d. Type **skydiving Oregon tandem static line**. (This limits the search to Web pages containing all of the words typed in the search text box.)

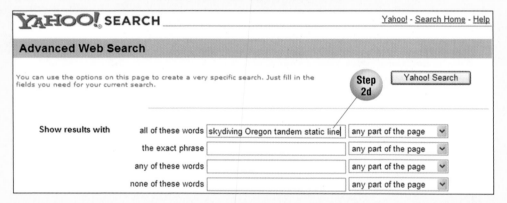

e. Choose any other options at the Advanced Web Search page that will narrow your search.
f. Click the Yahoo! Search button.
g. When the list of Web sites displays, click a hyperlink that interests you.
h. Print the page.
3. Close Internet Explorer.

## Downloading Images, Text, and Web Pages from the Internet

The image(s) and/or text that display when you open a Web page as well as the Web page itself can be saved as a separate file. This separate file can be viewed, printed, or inserted in another file. The information you want to save in a separate file is downloaded from the Internet by Internet Explorer and saved in a folder of your choosing with the name you specify. Copyright laws protect much of the information on the Internet. Before using information downloaded from the Internet, check the site for restrictions. If you do use information, make sure you properly cite the source.

# Project 5   Downloading Images and Web Pages

1. Start Internet Explorer.
2. Download a Web page and image from Banff National Park by completing the following steps:
   a. Search for sites on the Internet for Banff National Park.
   b. From the list of sites that displays, choose a site that contains information about Banff National Park and at least one image of the park.
   c. Save the Web page as a separate file by clicking the Page button on the Internet Explorer toolbar, and then clicking *Save As* at the drop-down list.
   d. At the Save Webpage dialog box, click the down-pointing arrow at the right side of the *Save in* option and then click the drive you are using as your storage medium at the drop-down list.
   e. Select the text in the *File name* text box, type **BanffWebPage**, and then press Enter.

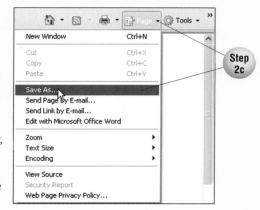

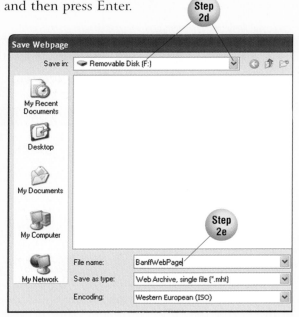

3. Save an image file by completing the following steps:
   a. Right-click an image that displays on the Web site. (The image that displays may vary from what you see below.)
   b. At the shortcut menu that displays, click *Save Picture As*.

c. At the Save Picture dialog box, change the *Save in* option to your storage medium.

d. Select the text in the *File name* text box, type **BanffImage**, and then press Enter.

4. Close Internet Explorer.

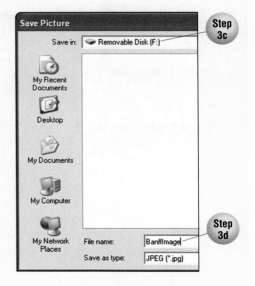

Step 3c

Step 3d

OPTIONAL

## Project  **Opening the Saved Web Page and Image in a Word Document**

1. Open Microsoft Word by clicking the Start button on the Taskbar, pointing to *All Programs*, pointing to *Microsoft Office*, and then clicking *Microsoft Office Word 2007*.

2. With Microsoft Word open, insert the image in a document by completing the following steps:

   a. Click the Insert tab and then click the Picture button in the Illustrations group.

   b. At the Insert Picture dialog box, change the *Look in* option to the location where you saved the Banff image and then double-click *BanffImage.jpg*.

   c. When the image displays in the Word document, print the document by clicking the Print button on the Quick Access toolbar.

   d. Close the document by clicking the Office button and then clicking *Close* at the drop-down menu. At the message asking if you want to save the changes, click No.

3. Open the **BanffWebPage.mht** file by completing the following steps:

   a. Click the Office button and then click *Open* at the drop-down menu.

   b. At the Open dialog box, change the *Look in* option to the location where you saved the Banff Web page and then double-click *BanffWebPage.mht*.

   c. Print the Web page by clicking the Print button on the Quick Access toolbar.

   d. Close the **BanffWebPage.mht** file by clicking the Office button and then *Close*.

4. Close Word by clicking the Close button (contains an X) that displays in the upper right corner of the screen.

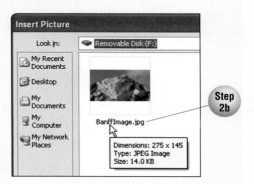

Step 2b

Step 3b

# Microsoft® WORD

## Making Word Work for You!

Communicating and managing information are needs that drive our entire economy. With Microsoft Word 2007, individuals and companies are in a better position than ever before to organize, analyze, and present information using word processing software.

## Organizing Information

You can create documents using Word 2007 and then organize the data in documents using a variety of tools such as columns and tables. Improve the readability of text in a document by organizing the text in columns. The shorter line length of column text helps increase the ease with which a person can read the text. Organizing text in tables can help readers interpret complex information much more quickly. For example, which is easier to understand: paragraphs of text identifying various stocks, their type, and their prices—or a table of the same information with columns for stock, stock type, and price? With Word's Table feature, you can create tables or convert existing data into a table.

To help organize personal or company documents, apply a theme to provide a uniform and consistent appearance and help "brand" documents. Apply a Word theme to customize the fonts, colors, and effects applied to data in a document.

Format text in columns to improve the readability of a document.

### COMPUTER INPUT DEVICES

Engineers have been especially creative in designing new ways to get information into computers. Some input methods are highly specialized and unusual, while common devices often undergo redesign to improve their capabilities or their ergonomics, the ways in which they affect people physically. Some common input devices include keyboards, mice, trackballs, and touch pads.

**Keyboard**

A keyboard can be an external device that is attached by means of a cable, or it can also have function keys, labeled F1, F2, F3, and so on. These keys allow the user to issue commands by pressing a single key.

**Mouse**

Graphical operating systems contain many elements that a user can choose by pointing at them. Such elements include buttons, tools, pull-down menus, and icons for file folders, programs, and document files. Often pointing to and clicking on one of these elements is more convenient than using the cursor or arrow keys on the keyboard. This pointing and clicking can be done by using a mouse. The mouse is

Organize text in tables to help readers interpret information more quickly.

### TRI-STATE PRODUCTS

**Computer Technology Department**
**Microsoft® Office 2007 Training**

| Application | # Enrolled | # Completed |
|---|---|---|
| Access 2007 | 20 | 15 |
| Excel 2007 | 62 | 56 |
| PowerPoint 2007 | 40 | 33 |
| Word 2007 | 80 | 72 |
| Total | 202 | 176 |

# Analyzing Information

Word's Spelling and Grammar features provide proofing tools that help you fine-tune your documents. The features mark words as you type so that you can immediately see if a word or sentence needs correction. With the view side-by-side feature, you can compare the contents of two documents to analyze similarities and differences. Use the Reveal Formatting feature to display formatting differences in documents.

In today's global workplace, it is common for two or more people to collaborate on a report or proposal, often with geographical distances between them. Word's ability to save files in different formats, such as PDF (Portable Document Format), allows a person to send files to other collaborators in a common file format. Each person can add comments to the document and return it to the sender for preparing a final version.

Right-click to choose correct spelling from suggestions list.

Green wavy underlines indicate potential grammatical errors.

Red wavy underlines indicate potential spelling errors.

When sending files to other collaborators, consider saving a document in a universal file format such as PDF.

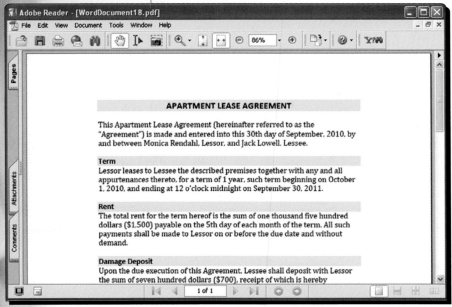

# Presenting Information

Word simplifies the task of creating, editing, and formatting text so that you can concentrate on the message rather than the process. Rich text enhancements give you the capability to create visually stimulating documents. Inserting pictures, drawings, and images is just a few mouse clicks away.

Word 2007 includes the SmartArt feature that you can use to create graphic designs and organizational charts. A SmartArt graphic is a visual presentation of information that helps the reader understand and interpret the data. If you need to illustrate visually hierarchical data, consider creating an organizational chart with the SmartArt feature.

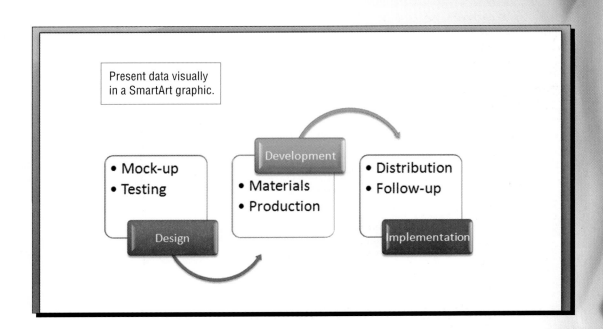

Present data visually in a SmartArt graphic.

When you are nearing the completion of your studies and getting ready to enter the workforce, consider using a resume template to help sell your capabilities to prospective employers. Microsoft provides a number of predesigned resume templates you can download from Microsoft Online. When designing your resume, be sure to note that you are Word 2007 proficient.

Display the New Document dialog box and then browse through the Microsoft Office Online templates. Consider using a cover page template to help you write a cover letter to send with your resume. After the interview, use another template to help you write a thank-you letter. With Word 2007, you can download templates for every imaginable need. Templates provide the formatting and standard text so that all you need to do in most cases is fill in the blanks.

Learning Word is an essential skill for today's employee. Microsoft Word 2007 is an easy-to-use program that will have you creating, editing, and formatting documents in no time—like a pro. You have our word.

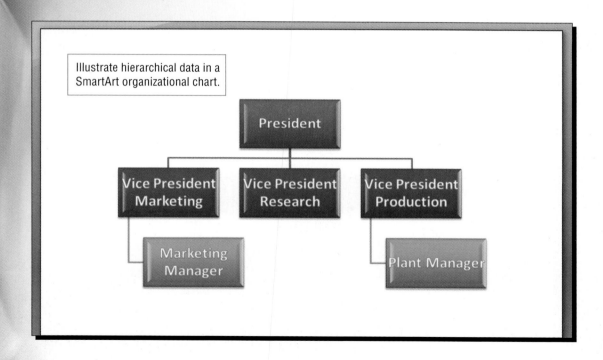

Illustrate hierarchical data in a SmartArt organizational chart.

Microsoft®

# word

## Unit 1: Editing and Formatting Documents

- ➤ Preparing Documents
- ➤ Formatting Characters and Paragraphs
- ➤ Customizing Paragraphs
- ➤ Formatting Pages

## Benchmark Microsoft® Word 2007 Level 1

### Microsoft Certified Application Specialist Skills—Unit 1

| Reference No. | Skill | Pages |
|---|---|---|
| **1** | **Creating and Customizing Documents** | |
| 1.1 | Create and format documents | |
| 1.1.2 | Apply styles from a Quick Styles set | 45-46 |
| 1.1.3 | Apply themes to documents | 47-48 |
| 1.1.4 | Modify themes | 47-48 |
| 1.1.5 | Format page backgrounds | 125-128 |
| 1.1.6 | Add a blank page or a cover page | 115-118, 116-118 |
| 1.2 | Lay out documents | |
| 1.2.1 | Change page format | 103-139, 109-118 |
| 1.2.2 | Insert and edit headers and footers (not using Quick Parts) | 120-125, 124, 125 |
| **2** | **Formatting Content** | |
| 2.1 | Format text and paragraphs | |
| 2.1.1 | Format with Format Painter | 57-58 |
| 2.1.3 | Change typestyles, fonts, and font effects | 36-44 |
| 2.1.4 | Customize paragraph formats | 48-56, 69-97 |
| 2.1.5 | Manipulate tabs | 82-85 |
| 2.2 | Manipulate text | |
| 2.2.1 | Cut, move, copy, and paste text | 88-93 |
| 2.2.2 | Use Find and Replace | 129-136 |
| 2.3 | Control pagination | |
| 2.3.1 | Insert and remove page breaks | 114-115 |
| **3** | **Working with Visual Content** | |
| 3.2 | Format illustrations | |
| 3.2.3 | Use Quick Styles | 45-46 |
| **5** | **Reviewing Documents** | |
| 5.1 | Navigate documents | 106-108 |
| 5.1.1 | Locate and move to locations in a document; use Find and Go To | 17-19 |
| 5.1.2 | Switch to a different window view | 104-109 |

*Note:* The Level 1 and Level 2 texts each address approximately half of the Microsoft Certified Application Specialist skills. Complete coverage of the skills is offered in the combined Level 1 and Level 2 text titled *Benchmark Series Microsoft® Word 2007: Levels 1 and 2,* which has been approved as certified courseware and which displays the Microsoft Certified Application Specialist logo on the cover.

# Preparing Documents

## PERFORMANCE OBJECTIVES

**Upon successful completion of Chapter 1, you will be able to:**

- Open Microsoft Word
- Create, save, name, print, open, and close a Word document
- Exit Word and Windows
- Edit a document
- Move the insertion point within a document
- Scroll within a document
- Select text in a document
- Use the Undo and Redo buttons
- Check spelling and grammar in a document
- Use the Help feature

Tutorial 1.1
Creating a Document

In this chapter, you will learn to create, save, name, print, open, close, and edit a Word document as well as complete a spelling and grammar check. You will also learn about the Help feature, which is an on-screen reference manual providing information on features and commands for each program in the Office suite. Before continuing, make sure you read the *Getting Started* section presented at the beginning of this book. This section contains information about computer hardware and software, using the mouse, executing commands, and exploring Help files.

*Note: Before beginning computer projects, copy to your storage medium the Word2007L1C1 subfolder from the Word2007L1 folder on the CD that accompanies this textbook. Steps on how to copy a folder are presented on the inside of the back cover of this textbook. Do this every time you start a chapter's projects.*

 **roject** **1** **Prepare a Word Document**

You will create a short document containing information on computers and then save, print, and close the document.

# Opening Microsoft Word

Microsoft Office 2007 contains a word processing program named Word that you can use to create, save, edit, and print documents. The steps to open Word may vary depending on your system setup. Generally, to open Word, you would click the Start button on the Taskbar at the Windows desktop, point to *All Programs*, point to *Microsoft Office*, and then click *Microsoft Office Word 2007*.

# Creating, Saving, Printing, and Closing a Document

When Microsoft Word is open, a blank document displays as shown in Figure 1.1. The features of the document screen are described in Table 1.1.

At a blank document, type information to create a document. A document is any information you choose—for instance, a letter, report, term paper, table, and so on. Some things to consider when typing text are:

- **Word Wrap:** As you type text to create a document, you do not need to press the Enter key at the end of each line because Word wraps text to the next line. A word is wrapped to the next line if it begins before the right margin and continues past the right margin. The only times you need to press Enter are to end a paragraph, create a blank line, or end a short line.

**Figure 1.1** Blank Document

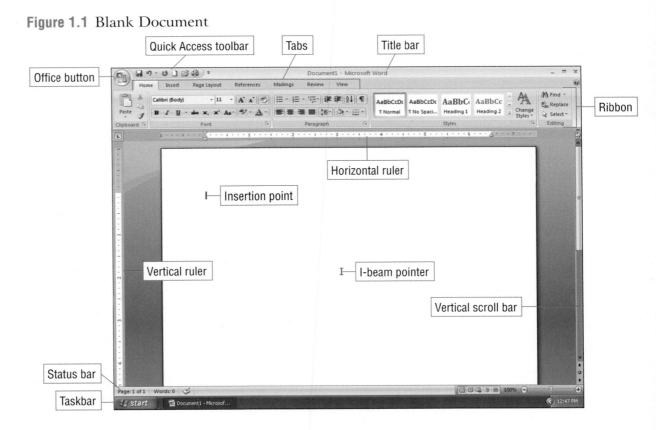

**Table 1.1** Microsoft Word Screen Features

| Feature | Description |
|---|---|
| Office button | Displays as a Microsoft Office logo and, when clicked, displays a list of options along with the most recently opened documents |
| Quick Access toolbar | Contains buttons for commonly used commands |
| Title bar | Displays document name followed by program name |
| Tabs | Contains commands and features organized into groups |
| Ribbon | Area containing the tabs and commands divided into groups |
| Horizontal ruler | Used to set margins, indents, and tabs |
| Vertical ruler | Used to set top and bottom margins |
| I-beam pointer | Used to move the insertion point or to select text |
| Insertion point | Indicates location of next character entered at the keyboard |
| Vertical scroll bar | Used to view various parts of the document |
| Status bar | Displays number of pages and words, View buttons, and the Zoom slider bar |

- **AutoCorrect:** Word contains a feature that automatically corrects certain words as you type them. For example, if you type the word *adn* instead of *and*, Word automatically corrects it when you press the spacebar after the word. AutoCorrect will also superscript the letters that follow an ordinal number. For example, if you type *2nd* and then press the spacebar or Enter key, Word will convert this ordinal number to $2^{nd}$.

- **Automatic Spell Checker:** By default, Word will automatically insert a red wavy line below words that are not contained in the Spelling dictionary or automatically corrected by AutoCorrect. This may include misspelled words, proper names, some terminology, and some foreign words. If you type a word not recognized by the Spelling dictionary, leave it as written if the word is correct. However, if the word is incorrect, you have two choices—you can delete the word and then type it correctly, or you can position the I-beam pointer on the word, click the right mouse button, and then click the correct spelling in the pop-up list.

- **Automatic Grammar Checker:** Word includes an automatic grammar checker. If the grammar checker detects a sentence containing a grammatical error, a green wavy line is inserted below the sentence. You can leave the sentence as written or position the mouse I-beam pointer on the sentence, click the *right* mouse button, and a pop-up list will display with possible corrections.

- **Spacing Punctuation:** Typically, Word uses Calibri as the default typeface, which is a proportional typeface. (You will learn more about typefaces in Chapter 2.) When typing text in a proportional typeface, space once (rather than twice) after end-of-sentence punctuation such as a period, question mark, or exclamation

**HINT**

A book icon displays in the Status bar. A check mark on the book indicates no spelling errors detected in the document by the spell checker, while an X in the book indicates errors. Double-click the book icon to move to the next error. If the book icon is not visible, right-click the Status bar and then click the *Spelling and Grammar Check* option at the pop-up list.

point, and after a colon. Proportional typeface is set closer together, and extra white space at the end of a sentence or after a colon is not needed.

- **Option Buttons:** As you insert and edit text in a document, you may notice an option button popping up in your text. The name and appearance of this option button varies depending on the action. If a word you type is corrected by AutoCorrect, if you create an automatic list, or if autoformatting is applied to text, the AutoCorrect Options button appears. Click this button to undo the specific automatic action. If you paste text in a document, the Paste Options button appears near the text. Click this button to display options for controlling how the pasted text is formatted.

- **AutoComplete:** Microsoft Word and other Office applications include an AutoComplete feature that inserts an entire item when you type a few identifying characters. For example, type the letters *Mond* and *Monday* displays in a ScreenTip above the letters. Press the Enter key or press F3 and Word inserts *Monday* in the document.

## Using the New Line Command

A Word document is based on a template that applies default formatting. Some basic formatting includes 1.15 line spacing and 10 points of spacing after a paragraph. Each time you press the Enter key, a new paragraph begins and 10 points of spacing is inserted after the paragraph. If you want to move the insertion point down to the next line without including the additional 10 points of spacing, use the New Line command, Shift + Enter.

Project **1a**  **Creating a Document**

1. Follow the instructions in this chapter to open Microsoft Word or check with your instructor for specific instructions.
2. At a blank document, type the information shown in Figure 1.2 with the following specifications:
   a. Correct any errors highlighted by the spell checker as they occur.
   b. Space once after end-of-sentence punctuation.
   c. After typing *Created:* press Shift + Enter to move the insertion point to the next line without adding 10 points of additional spacing.
   d. To insert the word *Thursday* located towards the end of the document, type Thur and then press F3. (This is an example of the AutoComplete feature.)
   e. To insert the word *December*, type Dece and then press the Enter key. (This is another example of the AutoComplete feature.)
   f. Press Shift + Enter after typing *December 9, 2010*.
   g. When typing the last line (the line containing the ordinal numbers), type the ordinal number text and AutoCorrect will automatically convert the letters in the ordinal numbers to superscript.
3. When you are finished typing the text, press the Enter key once.

## Figure 1.2 Project 1a

The first large computers made use of the decimal number system, in which numbers are indicated by the symbols 0 through 9. Engineers soon hit upon a much simpler system known as machine language for representing data with numbers.

Machine language uses binary numbers ("bi" means two), which are constructed solely of the symbols 0 and 1. The bit (0 or 1) is the smallest unit of data in the binary system. By itself, a bit is not very meaningful. However, a group of eight bits, or a byte, is significant because a byte contains enough possible combinations of zeros and ones to represent 256 separate characters.

Created:
Thursday, December 9, 2010
Note: The two paragraphs will become the 2nd and 3rd paragraphs of the 5th section.

# Saving a Document

Save a document if you want to use it in the future. You can use a variety of methods to save a document such as clicking the Save button on the Quick Access toolbar, clicking the Office button and then clicking *Save As* at the drop-down menu, or using the keyboard shortcut Ctrl + S. To save a document, click the Save button on the Quick Access toolbar. At the Save As dialog box shown in Figure 1.3, type the name of the document and then press Enter or click the Save button located in the lower right corner of the dialog box.

**QUICK STEPS**

**Save a Document**
1. Click Save button.
2. Type document name.
3. Click Save button.

**HINT**

Save a document approximately every 15 minutes or when interrupted.

Save

## Figure 1.3 Save As Dialog Box

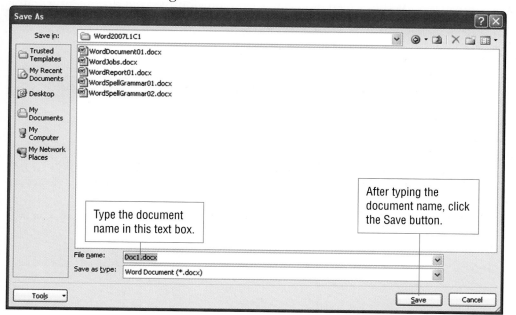

Type the document name in this text box.

After typing the document name, click the Save button.

## Naming a Document

Office button

Document names created in Word and other applications in the Office suite can be up to 255 characters in length, including drive letter and any folder names, and may include spaces. File names cannot include any of the following characters:

| | |
|---|---|
| forward slash (/) | question mark (?) |
| backslash (\) | quotation mark (") |
| greater than sign (>) | colon (:) |
| less than sign (<) | semicolon (;) |
| asterisk (*) | pipe symbol (\|) |

## Printing a Document

Quick Print

Many of the computer exercises you will be creating will need to be printed. A printing of a document on paper is referred to as ***hard copy*** and a document displayed in the screen is referred to as ***soft copy***. Send a document to the printer by clicking the Quick Print button on the Quick Access toolbar. This sends the document immediately to the printer. (If the Quick Print button does not display on the Quick Access toolbar, click the Customize Quick Access Toolbar button that displays at the right side of the toolbar and then click *Quick Print* at the drop-down list.) You can also print by clicking the Office button and then clicking *Print* at the drop-down list or by pressing the keyboard shortcut, Ctrl + P. This displays the Print dialog box. At this dialog box, click OK to send the document to the printer.

## Closing a Document

When you save a document it is saved on your storage medium and remains in the document screen. To remove the document from the screen, click the Office button and then click *Close* at the drop-down list or use the keyboard shortcut, Ctrl + F4. When you close a document, the document is removed and a blank screen displays. At this screen, you can open a previously saved document, create a new document, or exit the Word program.

---

Project **1b**  |  **Saving, Printing, and Closing a Document**

1. Save the document you created for Project 1a and name it **WordL1_C1_P1** (for Word Level 1, Chapter 1, Project 1) by completing the following steps:
   a. Click the Save button on the Quick Access toolbar.

Step 1a

b. At the Save As dialog box, type **WordL1_C1_P1** and then press Enter.

2. Print the document by clicking the Quick Print button on the Quick Access toolbar.

3. Close the document by clicking the Office button and then clicking *Close* at the drop-down list.

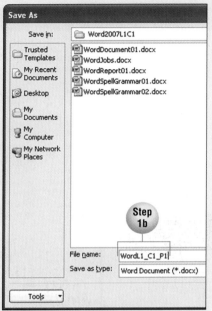

Step 2

Step 1b

**P**roject **2** **Save and Edit a Word Document**

You will open a document located in the Word2007L1C1 folder on your storage medium, add text to the document, and then save the document with a new name.

# Creating a New Document

When you close a document, a blank screen displays. If you want to create a new document, display a blank document. To do this, click the New button on the Quick Access toolbar or click the Office button and then click *New*. (If the New button does not display on the Quick Access toolbar, click the Customize Quick Access Toolbar button that displays at the right side of the toolbar and then click *New* at the drop-down list.) At the New Document dialog box, double-click the *Blank document* option. You can also open a new document using the keyboard shortcut, Ctrl + N.

New

# Opening a Document

After you save and close a document, you can open it at the Open dialog box shown in Figure 1.4. To display this dialog box, click the Open button on the Quick Access toolbar, click the Office button and then click *Open*, or use the keyboard shortcut, Ctrl + O. (If the Open button does not display on the Quick Access toolbar, click

**QUICK STEPS**

**Open a Document**
1. Click Office button.
2. Click *Open*.
3. Double-click document name.

Open

the Customize Quick Access Toolbar button that displays at the right side of the toolbar and then click *Open* at the drop-down list.) At the Open dialog box, double-click the document name. The most recently opened documents display in a list at the right side of the Office button drop-down menu. Click a document in the list to open the document.

**Figure 1.4** Open Dialog Box

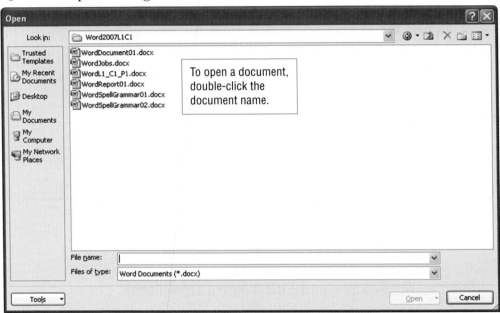

To open a document, double-click the document name.

## Project 2a    Opening a Document

1. Open the **WordJobs.docx** document by completing the following steps:
   a. Click the Open button on the Quick Access toolbar.
   b. At the Open dialog box, make sure the Word2007L1C1 folder on your storage medium is the active folder.
   c. Double-click *WordJobs.docx*.
2. With the insertion point positioned at the beginning of the document, type the text shown in Figure 1.5.

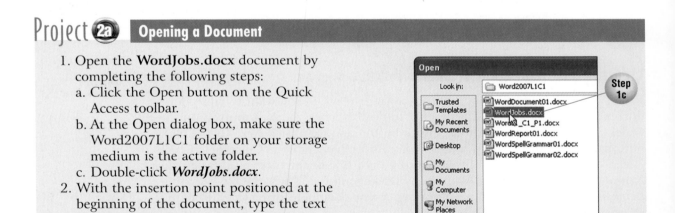

Step 1c

**Figure 1.5  Project 2a**

The majority of new jobs being created in the United States today involve daily work with computers. Computer-related careers include technical support jobs, sales and training, programming and applications development, network and database administration, and computer engineering.

# Saving a Document with Save As

If you open a previously saved document and want to give it a new name, use the *Save As* option from the Office button drop-down list rather than the *Save* option. When you click *Save As*, the Save As dialog box displays. At this dialog box, type the new name for the document and then press Enter.

# Exiting Word

When you are finished working with Word and have saved all necessary information, exit Word by clicking the Office button and then clicking the Exit Word button (located at the bottom right side of the drop-down list). You can also exit the Word program by clicking the Close button located in the upper right corner of the screen.

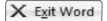

## Project 2b    Saving a Document with Save As

1. With **WordJobs.docx** open, save the document with a new name by completing the following steps:
   a. Click the Office button and then click *Save As*.
   b. At the Save As dialog box, type WordL1_C1_P2.
   c. Press Enter.
2. Print the document by clicking the Quick Print button on the Quick Access toolbar.
3. Close the document by pressing Ctrl + F4.

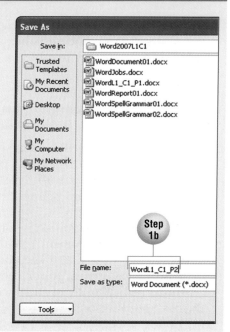

Step 1b

# Project ③ Scroll and Browse in a Document

**You will open a previously created document, save it with a new name, and then use scrolling and browsing techniques to move the insertion point to specific locations in the document.**

## Editing a Document

When editing a document, you may decide to insert or delete text. To edit a document, use the mouse, the keyboard, or the mouse combined with the keyboard to move the insertion point to specific locations in the document. To move the insertion point using the mouse, position the I-beam pointer where you want the insertion point located and then click the left mouse button.

You can also scroll in a document, which changes the text display but does not move the insertion point. Use the mouse with the *vertical scroll bar*, located at the right side of the screen, to scroll through text in a document. Click the up scroll arrow at the top of the vertical scroll bar to scroll up through the document and click the down scroll arrow to scroll down through the document. The scroll bar contains a scroll box that indicates the location of the text in the document screen in relation to the remainder of the document. To scroll up one screen at a time, position the arrow pointer above the scroll box (but below the up scroll arrow) and then click the left mouse button. Position the arrow pointer below the scroll box and click the left button to scroll down a screen. If you hold down the left mouse button, the action becomes continuous. You can also position the arrow pointer on the scroll box, hold down the left mouse button, and then drag the scroll box along the scroll bar to reposition text in the document screen. As you drag the scroll box along the vertical scroll bar in a longer document, page numbers display in a box at the right side of the document screen.

## Project ③ⓐ Scrolling in a Document

1. Open **WordReport01.docx** and then press the Enter key once. (This document is located in the Word2007L1C1 folder you copied to your storage medium.)
2. Save the document with Save As and name it **WordL1_C1_P3**.
3. Position the I-beam pointer at the beginning of the first paragraph and then click the left mouse button.
4. Click the down scroll arrow on the vertical scroll bar several times. (This scrolls down lines of text in the document.) With the mouse pointer on the down scroll arrow, hold down the left mouse button and keep it down until the end of the document displays.
5. Position the mouse pointer on the up scroll arrow and hold down the left mouse button until the beginning of the document displays.
6. Position the mouse pointer below the scroll box and then click the left mouse button. Continue clicking the mouse button (with the mouse pointer positioned below the scroll box) until the end of the document displays.

7. Position the mouse pointer on the scroll box in the vertical scroll bar. Hold down the left mouse button, drag the scroll box to the top of the vertical scroll bar, and then release the mouse button. (Notice that the document page numbers display in a box at the right side of the document screen.)
8. Click on the title at the beginning of the document. (This moves the insertion point to the location of the mouse pointer.)

## Moving the Insertion Point to a Specific Page

Along with scrolling options, Word also contains navigation buttons for moving the insertion point to specific locations. Navigation buttons display toward the bottom of the vertical scroll bar and include the Previous button, the Select Browse Object button, and the Next button. The full names of and the tasks completed by the Previous and Next buttons vary depending on the last navigation completed. Click the Select Browse Object button and a palette of browsing choices displays. You will learn more about the Select Browse Object button in the next section.

Previous

Next

Word includes a Go To option you can use to move the insertion point to a specific page within a document. To move the insertion point to a specific page, click the Find button arrow located in the Editing group in the Home tab and then click *Go To* at the drop-down list. At the Find and Replace dialog box with the Go To tab selected, type the page number in the *Enter page number* text box and then press Enter. Click the Close button to close the dialog box.

## Browsing in a Document

The Select Browse Object button located toward the bottom of the vertical scroll bar contains options for browsing through a document. Click this button and a palette of browsing choices displays. Use the options on the palette to move the insertion point to various features in a Word document. Position the arrow pointer on an option in the palette and the option name displays below the options. The options on the palette and the location of the options vary depending on the last function performed.

Select
Browse Object

## Moving the Insertion Point with the Keyboard

To move the insertion point with the keyboard, use the arrow keys located to the right of the regular keyboard. You can also use the arrow keys on the numeric keypad. If you use these keys, make sure Num Lock is off. Use the arrow keys together with other keys to move the insertion point to various locations in the document as shown in Table 1.2.

When moving the insertion point, Word considers a word to be any series of characters between spaces. A paragraph is any text that is followed by a stroke of the Enter key. A page is text that is separated by a soft or hard page break. If you open a previously saved document, you can move the insertion point to where the insertion point was last located when the document was closed by pressing Shift + F5.

**Table 1.2** Insertion Point Movement Commands

| To move insertion point | Press |
|---|---|
| One character left | Left Arrow |
| One character right | Right Arrow |
| One line up | Up Arrow |
| One line down | Down Arrow |
| One word to the left | Ctrl + Left Arrow |
| One word to the right | Ctrl + Right Arrow |
| To end of a line | End |
| To beginning of a line | Home |
| To beginning of current paragraph | Ctrl + Up Arrow |
| To beginning of next paragraph | Ctrl + Down Arrow |
| Up one screen | Page Up |
| Down one screen | Page Down |
| To top of previous page | Ctrl + Page Up |
| To top of next page | Ctrl + Page Down |
| To beginning of document | Ctrl + Home |
| To end of document | Ctrl + End |

## Project 3b  Moving the Insertion Point and Browsing in a Document

1. With **WordL1_C1_P3.docx** open, move the insertion point to page 3 by completing the following steps:
   a. Click the Find button arrow located in the Editing group in the Home tab and then click *Go To* at the drop-down list.
   b. At the Find and Replace dialog box with the Go To tab selected, type 3 in the *Enter page number* text box and then press Enter.
   c. Click the Close button to close the Find and Replace dialog box.
2. Click the Previous Page button located immediately above the Select Browse Object button on the vertical scroll bar. (This moves the insertion point to page 2.)

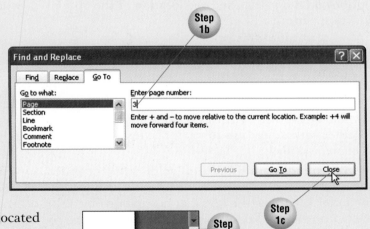

Step 1b

Step 1c

Step 2

3. Click the Previous Page button again. (This moves the insertion point to page 1.)
4. Click the Next Page button located immediately below the Select Browse Object button on the vertical scroll bar. (This moves the insertion point to the beginning of page 2.)

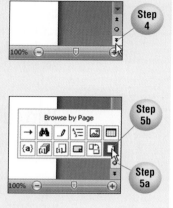

5. Move to the beginning of page 3 by completing the following steps:
   a. Click the Select Browse Object button.
   b. At the palette of browsing choices, click the last choice in the bottom row (*Browse by Page*). (This moves the insertion point to page 3.)
6. Press Ctrl + Home to move the insertion point to the beginning of the document.
7. Practice using the keyboard commands shown in Table 1.2 to move the insertion point within the document.
8. Close **WordL1_C1_P3.docx**.

 roject ④ **Insert and Delete Text**

**You will open a previously created document, save it with a new name, and then make editing changes to the document. The editing changes include selecting, inserting, and deleting text.**

## Inserting and Deleting Text

Editing a document may include inserting and/or deleting text. To insert text in a document, position the insertion point in the desired location and then type the text. Existing characters move to the right as you type the text. A number of options are available for deleting text. Some deletion commands are shown in Table 1.3.

**Table 1.3** Deletion Commands

| *To delete* | *Press* |
| --- | --- |
| Character right of insertion point | Delete key |
| Character left of insertion point | Backspace key |
| Text from insertion point to beginning of word | Ctrl + Backspace |
| Text from insertion point to end of word | Ctrl + Delete |

By default, text you type in a document is inserted in the document and existing text is moved to the right. If you want to type over something, you need to turn on the Overtype mode. With the Overtype mode on, anything you type will replace existing text. To turn on the Overtype mode, click the Office button and then click

the Word Options button located toward the bottom of the drop-down list. At the Word Options dialog box, click *Advanced* in the left panel. In the *Advanced options for working with Word.* section, insert a check mark in the *Use Overtype mode* check box if you want the Overtype mode always on in the document. Or, insert a check mark in the *Use the Insert key to control Overtype mode* check box if you want to use the Insert key to turn Overtype mode on and off. After making your selection, click the OK button located in the lower right corner of the dialog box.

## Selecting Text

You can use the mouse and/or keyboard to select a specific amount of text. Once selected, you can delete the text or perform other Word functions involving the selected text. When text is selected, it displays with a blue background as shown in Figure 1.6 and the Mini toolbar displays in a dimmed fashion and contains options for common tasks. Move the mouse pointer over the Mini toolbar and it becomes active. (You will learn more about the Mini toolbar in Chapter 2.)

**Figure 1.6** Selected Text and Mini Toolbar

## Selecting Text with the Mouse

Use the mouse to select a word, line, sentence, paragraph, or the entire document. Table 1.4 indicates the steps to follow to select various amounts of text. To select a specific amount of text such as a line or a paragraph, the instructions in the table tell you to click in the selection bar. The selection bar is the space located toward the left side of the document screen between the left edge of the page and the text. When the mouse pointer is positioned in the selection bar, the pointer turns into an arrow pointing up and to the right (instead of to the left).

To select an amount of text other than a word, sentence, or paragraph, position the I-beam pointer on the first character of the text to be selected, hold down the left mouse button, drag the I-beam pointer to the last character of the text to be selected, and then release the mouse button. You can also select all text between the current insertion point and the I-beam pointer. To do this, position the insertion point where you want the selection to begin, hold down the Shift key, click the I-beam pointer at the end of the selection, and then release the Shift key. To cancel a selection using the mouse, click anywhere in the document screen outside the selected text.

**HINT**
To select text vertically, hold down the Alt key while dragging the mouse.

**Table 1.4**  Selecting with the Mouse

| To select | Complete these steps using the mouse |
|---|---|
| A word | Double-click the word. |
| A line of text | Click in the selection bar to the left of the line. |
| Multiple lines of text | Drag in the selection bar to the left of the lines. |
| A sentence | Hold down the Ctrl key, then click anywhere in the sentence. |
| A paragraph | Double-click in the selection bar next to the paragraph or triple-click anywhere in the paragraph. |
| Multiple paragraphs | Drag in the selection bar. |
| An entire document | Triple-click in the selection bar. |

## Selecting Text with the Keyboard

To select a specific amount of text using the keyboard, turn on the Selection Mode by pressing the F8 function key. With the Selection Mode activated, use the arrow keys to select the desired text. If you want to cancel the selection, press the Esc key and then press any arrow key. You can customize the Status bar to display text indicating that the Selection Mode is activated. To do this, right-click any blank location on the Status bar and then click *Selection Mode* at the pop-up list. When you press F8 to turn on the Selection Mode, the words *Selection Mode* display on the Status bar. You can also select text with the commands shown in Table 1.5.

**HINT**
If text is selected, any character you type replaces the selected text.

Project 4a  **Editing a Document**

1. Open **WordDocument01.docx**. (This document is located in the Word2007L1C1 folder you copied to your storage medium.)
2. Save the document with Save As and name it **WordL1_C1_P4**.
3. Change the word *give* in the first sentence of the first paragraph to *enter*.
4. Change the second *to* in the first sentence to *into*.
5. Delete the words *means of* in the first sentence in the *QWERTY Keyboard* section.
6. Select the words *and use no cabling at all* and the period that follows located at the end of the last sentence in the first paragraph, and then press the Delete key.
7. Insert a period immediately following the word *signal*.

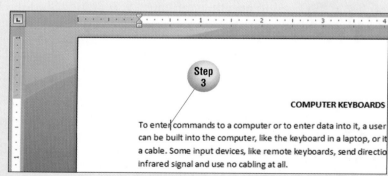

Step 3

COMPUTER KEYBOARDS

To enter commands to a computer or to enter data into it, a user can be built into the computer, like the keyboard in a laptop, or it a cable. Some input devices, like remote keyboards, send directio infrared signal and use no cabling at all.

8. Delete the heading line containing the text *QWERTY Keyboard* using the Selection Mode by completing the following steps:
   a. Position the insertion point immediately before the *Q* in *QWERTY*.
   b. Press F8 to turn on the Selection Mode.
   c. Press the Down Arrow key.
   d. Press the Delete key.
9. Complete steps similar to those in Step 8 to delete the heading line containing the text *DVORAK Keyboard*.
10. Begin a new paragraph with the sentence that reads *Keyboards have different physical appearances.* by completing the following steps:
    a. Position the insertion point immediately left of the *K* in *Keyboards* (the first word of the fifth sentence in the last paragraph).
    b. Press the Enter key.
11. Save **WordL1_C1_P4.docx**.

**Steps 8a–8c**

To enter commands into a computer device can be built into the computer computer by a cable. Some input dev means of an infrared signal.

QWERTY Keyboard

Keyboards can be external devices tha itself as they are in laptops. Most key the first six keys at the left of the first of mechanical typewriters to slow do

To enter commands into a computer or device can be built into the computer, li computer by a cable. Some input device means of an infrared signal.

Keyboards can be external devices that itself as they are in laptops. Most keybo the first six keys at the left of the first ro of mechanical typewriters to slow down

The DVORAK keyboard is an alternative commonly used keys are placed close to install software on a QWERTY keyboard keyboards is convenient especially whe

**Steps 10a–10b**

Keyboards have different physical appe that of a calculator, containing numbers "broken" into two pieces to reduce stra change the symbol or characters entere

**Table 1.5**  Selecting with the Keyboard

| To select | Press |
| --- | --- |
| One character to right | Shift + Right Arrow |
| One character to left | Shift + Left Arrow |
| To end of word | Ctrl + Shift + Right Arrow |
| To beginning of word | Ctrl + Shift + Left Arrow |
| To end of line | Shift + End |
| To beginning of line | Shift + Home |
| One line up | Shift + Up Arrow |
| One line down | Shift + Down Arrow |
| To beginning of paragraph | Ctrl + Shift + Up Arrow |
| To end of paragraph | Ctrl + Shift + Down Arrow |
| One screen up | Shift + Page Up |
| One screen down | Shift + Page Down |
| To end of document | Ctrl + Shift + End |
| To beginning of document | Ctrl + Shift + Home |
| Entire document | Ctrl + A or click Select button in Editing group and then Select All |

# Using the Undo and Redo Buttons

If you make a mistake and delete text that you did not intend to, or if you change your mind after deleting text and want to retrieve it, you can use the Undo or Redo buttons on the Quick Access toolbar. For example, if you type text and then click the Undo button, the text will be removed. You can undo text or commands. For example, if you add formatting such as bolding to text and then click the Undo button, the bolding is removed.

If you use the Undo button and then decide you do not want to reverse the original action, click the Redo button. For example, if you select and underline text and then decide to remove underlining, click the Undo button. If you then decide you want the underlining back on, click the Redo button. Many Word actions can be undone or redone. Some actions, however, such as printing and saving, cannot be undone or redone.

Word maintains actions in temporary memory. If you want to undo an action performed earlier, click the Undo button arrow. This causes a drop-down list to display. To make a selection from this drop-down list, click the desired action and the action, along with any actions listed above it in the drop-down list, is undone.

**HINT**
You cannot undo a save.

Undo

Redo

## Project 4b — Undoing and Redoing Deletions

1. With **WordL1_C1_P4.docx** open, delete the last sentence in the last paragraph using the mouse by completing the following steps:
   a. Position the I-beam pointer anywhere in the sentence that begins *All keyboards have modifier keys . . . .*
   b. Hold down the Ctrl key and then click the left mouse button.

> install software on a QWERTY keyboard that emulates a DVORAK keyboard. The ability to emulate other keyboards is convenient especially when working with foreign languages.
>
> Keyboards have different physical appearances. Many keyboards have a separate numeric keypad, like that of a calculator, containing numbers and mathematical operators. Some keyboards are sloped and "broken" into two pieces to reduce strain. All keyboards have modifier keys that enable the user to change the symbol or characters entered when a given key is pressed.

**Steps 1a–1b**

   c. Press the Delete key.
2. Delete the last paragraph by completing the following steps:
   a. Position the I-beam pointer anywhere in the last paragraph (the paragraph that reads *Keyboards have different physical appearances.*).
   b. Triple-click the left mouse button.
   c. Press the Delete key.
3. Undo the deletion by clicking the Undo button on the Quick Access toolbar.
4. Redo the deletion by clicking the Redo button on the Quick Access toolbar.
5. Select the first sentence in the second paragraph and then delete it.
6. Select the first paragraph in the document and then delete it.

7. Undo the two deletions by completing the following steps:
   a. Click the Undo button arrow.
   b. Click the *second* Clear listed in the drop-down list. (This will redisplay the first sentence in the second paragraph as well as displaying the first paragraph. The sentence will be selected.)
8. Click outside the sentence to deselect it.
9. Save, print, and then close **WordL1_C1_P4.docx**.

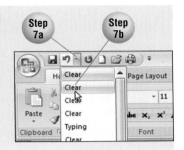

Step 7a   Step 7b

---

roject ⑤ **Complete a Spelling and Grammar Check**

**You will open a previously created document, save it with a new name, and then check the spelling and grammar in the document.**

## Checking the Spelling and Grammar in a Document ▬▬▬

Two tools for creating thoughtful and well-written documents include a spelling checker and a grammar checker. The spelling checker finds misspelled words and offers replacement words. It also finds duplicate words and irregular capitalizations. When you spell check a document, the spelling checker compares the words in your document with the words in its dictionary. If the spelling checker finds a match, it passes over the word. If a match is not found for the word, the spelling checker will stop, select the word, and offer replacements.

The grammar checker will search a document for errors in grammar, punctuation, and word usage. The spelling checker and the grammar check can help you create a well-written document, but do not replace the need for proofreading. To complete a spelling and grammar check, click the Review tab and then click the Spelling & Grammar button in the Proofing group. You can also begin spelling and grammar checking by pressing the keyboard shortcut, F7. As the spelling and grammar checker selects text, make a choice from some of the options in the Spelling and Grammar dialog box as shown in Table 1.6.

By default, a spelling and grammar check are both completed on a document. If you want to check only the spelling in a document and not the grammar, remove the check mark from the *Check grammar* check box located in the lower left corner of the Spelling and Grammar dialog box. When spell checking a document, you can temporarily leave the Spelling and Grammar dialog box, make corrections in the document, and then resume spell checking by clicking the Resume button.

**Table 1.6** Spelling and Grammar Dialog Box Buttons

| Button | Function |
|---|---|
| Ignore Once | During spell checking, skips that occurrence of the word; in grammar checking, leaves currently selected text as written |
| Ignore All | During spell checking, skips that occurrence of the word and all other occurrences of the word in the document |
| Ignore Rule | During grammar checking, leaves currently selected text as written and ignores the current rule for remainder of the grammar check |
| Add to Dictionary | Adds selected word to the main spelling check dictionary |
| Change | Replaces selected word in sentence with selected word in *Suggestions* list box |
| Change All | Replaces selected word in sentence with selected word in *Suggestions* list box and all other occurrences of the word |
| AutoCorrect | Inserts selected word and correct spelling of word in AutoCorrect dialog box |
| Explain | During grammar checking, displays grammar rule information about the selected text |
| Undo | Reverses most recent spelling and grammar action |
| Next Sentence | Accepts manual changes made to sentence and then continues grammar checking |
| Options | Displays a dialog box with options for customizing a spelling and grammar check |

Project 5  **Checking the Spelling and Grammar in a Document**

1. Open **WordSpellGrammar01.docx**.
2. Save the document with Save As and name it **WordL1_C1_P5**.
3. Click the Review tab.
4. Click the Spelling & Grammar button in the Proofing group.

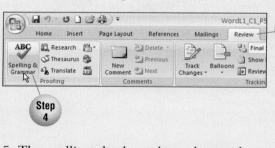

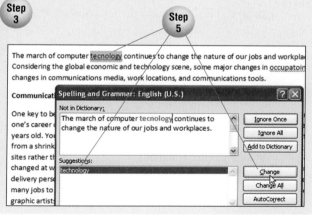

5. The spelling checker selects the word *tecnology*. The proper spelling is selected in the *Suggestions* list box, so click the Change button (or Change All button).

6. The spelling checker selects the word *occupatoins*. The proper spelling of the word is selected in the *Suggestions* list box, so click the Change button (or Change All button).

7. The grammar checker selects the sentence that begins *One key to being successful . . .* and displays *trends* and *a trend* in the *Suggestions* list box. Click *a trend* in the *Suggestions* list box and then click the Change button.

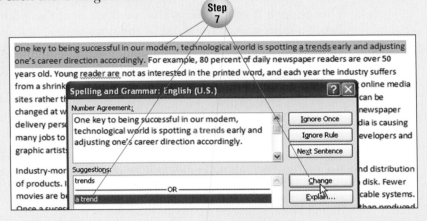

8. The grammar checker selects the sentence that begins *Young reader are not as interested . . .* and displays *reader is* and *readers are* in the *Suggestions* text box. Click the Explain button, read the information about subject-verb agreement that displays in the Word Help window, and then click the Close button located in the upper right corner of the Word Help window.

9. Click *readers are* in the *Suggestions* text box and then click the Change button.

10. The spelling checker selects *excelent*. The proper spelling is selected in the *Suggestions* list box, so click the Change button.

11. The grammar checker selects the sentence that begins *The number of printing and lithography job's is shrinking . . . .* Click the Explain button, read the information about plural or possessive that displays in the Word Help window, and then click the Close button located in the upper right corner of the Word Help window.

12. With *jobs* selected in the *Suggestions* list box, click the Change button.

13. The spelling checker selects the word *sucessful* and offers *successful* in the *Suggestions* text box. Since this word is misspelled in another location in the document, click the Change All button.

14. The spelling checker selects the word *telework*. This word is correct so click the Ingore All button.

15. The spelling checker selects the word *are* that is repeated twice. Click the Delete button to delete the word.

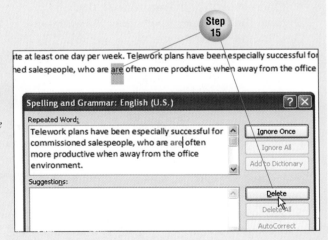

16. When the message displays telling you that the spelling and grammar check is complete, click the OK button.

17. Save, print, and then close **WordL1_C1_P5.docx**.

# Project ⑥ Use the Help Feature

You need to learn more about selecting text and saving a document so you decide to use Help to research these features.

## Using Help

Word's Help feature is an on-screen reference manual containing information about all Word features and commands. Word's Help feature is similar to the Windows Help and the Help features in Excel, PowerPoint, and Access. Get help by clicking the Microsoft Office Word Help button located in the upper right corner of the screen (a question mark in a circle) or by pressing the keyboard shortcut, F1. This displays the Word Help window. In this window, type a topic, feature, or question in the *Search* text box and then press Enter. Topics related to the search text display in the Help window. Click a topic that interests you. If the topic window contains a Show All hyperlink in the upper right corner, click this hyperlink and the information expands to show all help information related to the topic. When you click the Show All hyperlink, it becomes the Hide All hyperlink.

**QUICK STEPS**

**Use Help Feature**
1. Click Microsoft Office Word Help button.
2. Type topic, feature, or question.
3. Press Enter.
4. Click desired topic.

Help

## Project ⑥a  Using the Help Feature

1. At a blank document, click the Microsoft Office Word Help button located in the upper right corner of the screen.
2. At the Word Help window, type selecting text in the *Search* text box.

Step 1

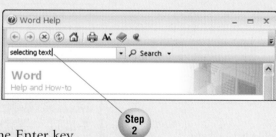

Step 2

3. Press the Enter key.
4. When the list of topics displays, click the Select text hyperlink.

Step 4

5. Click the <u>Show All</u> hyperlink that displays in the upper right corner of the window.
6. Read the information about selecting text.
7. Print the information by clicking the Print button located toward the top of the Word Help window.
8. At the Print dialog box, click the Print button.
9. Click the Close button to close the Word Help window.

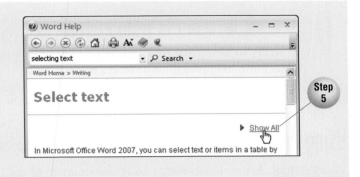

## Getting Help in a Dialog Box

Dialog boxes contain a Help button you can click to display the Word Help window that is specific to the dialog box. This button is located in the upper right corner of the dialog box and displays as a question mark inside a square. Click this button and the Word Help window displays with topics related to the dialog box.

**Project 6b    Getting Help in a Dialog Box**

1. At a blank document, click the Office button and then click *Save As* at the drop-down list.
2. At the Save As dialog box, click the Help button located in the upper right corner of the dialog box.
3. At the Word Help window, click the <u>Save As</u> hyperlink.
4. In the Save As list box, click *Microsoft Office Word*.
5. Read the information that displays about saving in Word and then click the Close button to close the Word Help window.
6. Close the Save As dialog box.

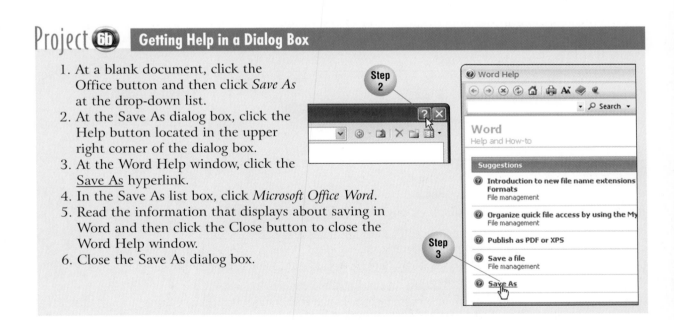

# CHAPTER summary

- Open Microsoft Word by clicking the Start button on the Taskbar, pointing to *All Programs*, pointing to *Microsoft Office*, and then clicking *Microsoft Office Word 2007*.

- The Office button displays as a Microsoft Office logo and, when clicked, displays a list of options and most recently opened documents.

- The Quick Access toolbar is located to the right of the Office button and contains buttons for commonly used commands.

- The Title bar is located to the right of the Quick Access toolbar and displays the document name followed by the program name.

- The ribbon area contains tabs with commands and options divided into groups.

- The insertion point displays as a blinking vertical line and indicates the position of the next character to be entered in the document.

- The mouse displays in the screen as an I-beam pointer or as an arrow pointing up and to the left.

- Use the vertical scroll bar to view various parts of the document.

- The Status bar displays the number of pages and words, View buttons, and the Zoom slider bar.

- Word automatically wraps text to the next line as you type information. Press the Enter key only to end a paragraph, create a blank line, or end a short line.

- Word contains a feature named AutoCorrect that automatically corrects certain words as they are typed.

- When typing text, the automatic spell checker feature inserts a red wavy line below words not contained in the Spelling dictionary, and the automatic grammar checker inserts a green wavy line below a sentence containing a grammatical error.

- The AutoComplete feature inserts an entire item when you type a few identifying characters and then press Enter or F3.

- Document names can contain a maximum of 255 characters, including the drive letter and folder names, and may include spaces.

- The insertion point can be moved throughout the document without interfering with text by using the mouse, the keyboard, or the mouse combined with the keyboard.

- You can move the insertion point by character, word, screen, or page, and from the first to the last character in a document. Refer to Table 1.2 for keyboard insertion point movement commands.

- The scroll box on the vertical scroll bar indicates the location of the text in the document in relation to the remainder of the document.

- Click the Select Browse Object button located at the bottom of the vertical scroll bar to display options for browsing through a document.

- You can delete text by character, word, line, several lines, or partial page using specific keys or by selecting text using the mouse or the keyboard.

- You can select a specific amount of text using the mouse or the keyboard. Refer to Table 1.4 for information on selecting with the mouse and refer to Table 1.5 for information on selecting with the keyboard.
- Use the Undo button on the Quick Access toolbar if you change your mind after typing, deleting, or formatting text and want to undo the action. Use the Redo button to redo something that had been undone with the Undo button.
- The spelling checker matches the words in your document with the words in its dictionary. If a match is not found, the word is selected and possible corrections are suggested. The grammar checker searches a document for errors in grammar, style, punctuation, and word usage. When a grammar error is detected, display information about the error by clicking the Explain button at the Spelling & Grammar dialog box.
- Word's Help feature is an on-screen reference manual containing information about all Word features and commands.
- Click the Microsoft Office Word Help button or press F1 to display the Word Help window. At this window, type a topic and then press Enter.
- Dialog boxes contain a Help button you can click to display the Word Help window with information specific to the dialog box.

# COMMANDS review

| FEATURE | RIBBON TAB, GROUP | BUTTON | QUICK ACCESS TOOLBAR | OFFICE BUTTON DROP-DOWN LIST | KEYBOARD SHORTCUT |
|---|---|---|---|---|---|
| Close document | | | | Close | Ctrl + F4 |
| Exit Word | | X | | Exit Word | |
| Find and Replace dialog box with Go To tab selected | Home, Editing | Find ▾, Go To | | | Ctrl + G |
| New blank document | | | 📄 | New, Blank document | Ctrl + N |
| Open dialog box | | | 📂 | Open | Ctrl + O |
| Print dialog box | | | | Print | Ctrl + P |
| Print document | | | 🖨 | Print, Quick Print | |
| Save document | | | 💾 | Save | Ctrl + S |
| Select document | Home, Editing | Select ▾ | | | Ctrl + A |
| Spelling and Grammar dialog box | Review, Proofing | ABC | | | F7 |
| Word Help window | | ❓ | | | F1 |

# CONCEPTS check

## Test Your Knowledge

**Completion:** In the space provided at the right, indicate the correct term, symbol, or command.

1. This toolbar contains the Save button. _____

2. This button displays in the upper left corner of the screen and displays with the Microsoft logo. _____

3. This is the area located toward the top of the screen that contains tabs with commands and options divided into groups. _____

4. This bar, located toward the bottom of the screen, displays number of pages and words, View buttons, and the Zoom slider bar. _____

5. This tab is selected by default. _____

6. This feature automatically corrects certain words as you type them. _____

7. This feature inserts an entire item when you type a few identifying characters and then press Enter or F3. _____

8. This is the keyboard shortcut to display the Print dialog box. _____

9. This is the keyboard shortcut to close a document. _____

10. This is the keyboard shortcut to display a new blank document. _____

11. Use this keyboard shortcut to move the insertion point to the beginning of the previous page. _____

12. Use this keyboard shortcut to move the insertion point to the end of the document. _____

13. Press this key on the keyboard to delete the character left of the insertion point. _____

14. Using the mouse, do this to select one word. _____

15. To select various amounts of text using the mouse, you can click in this bar. _____

16. Click this tab to display the Spelling & Grammar button in the Proofing group. _____

17. This is the keyboard shortcut to display the Word Help window. _____

# SKILLS check

*Demonstrate Your Proficiency*

## Assessment

### 1  TYPE AND EDIT A DOCUMENT ON FUZZY LOGIC

1. Open Word and then type the text in Figure 1.7. Correct any errors highlighted by the spell checker and space once after end-of-sentence punctuation.
2. Make the following changes to the document:
   a. Delete *AI* in the first sentence of the first paragraph and then insert *artificial intelligence*.
   b. Insert the words *for approximations and* between the words *allowing* and *incomplete* located in the first sentence of the first paragraph.
   c. Insert the words *or numerical* between the words *yes/no* and *information* in the second sentence of the first paragraph.
   d. Delete the words *hard to come by* in the last sentence of the first paragraph and replace with the word *rare*.
   e. Insert the letters *SQL* between the words *logic* and *database* in the last sentence of the second paragraph.
   f. Move the insertion point immediately left of the period at the end of the last sentence of the last paragraph, type a comma, and then insert the words *and trade shares on the Tokyo Stock Exchange*. Delete the word *and* before the words *automobile transmissions* in the last sentence.
   g. Join the first and second paragraphs.
   h. Delete the name *Marie Solberg* and then type your first and last names.
3. Save the document and name it **WordL1_C1_A1**.
4. Print and then close **WordL1_C1_A1.docx**.

## Assessment

### 2  CHECK THE SPELLING AND GRAMMAR OF A COMPUTER SOFTWARE DOCUMENT

1. Open **WordSpellGrammar02.docx**.
2. Save the document with Save As and name it **WordL1_C1_A2**.
3. Complete a spelling and grammar check on the document. You determine what to change and what to leave as written.
4. Insert the sentence *Wizards are small programs designed to assist users by automating tasks.* between the third and fourth sentences in the *User-Friendly System Software* section.
5. Move the insertion point to the end of the document, type your first and last names, press Shift + Enter, and then type the current date.
6. Save, print, and then close **WordL1_C1_A2.docx**.

*spell check <F7> on REVIEW menu*

**Figure 1.7 Assessment 1**

Fuzzy Logic

The fuzzy logic branch of AI attempts to model human reasoning by allowing incomplete input data. Instead of demanding precise yes/no information, fuzzy logic systems allow users to input "fuzzy" data. The terminology used by the system is deliberately vague and includes terms such as very probable, somewhat decreased, reasonable, or very slight. This is an attempt to simulate real-world conditions, where precise answers are hard to come by.

A fuzzy logic system attempts to work more naturally with the user by piecing together an answer in a manner similar to that used by a traditional expert system. Fuzzy logic database queries seem significantly more human than traditional queries.

Fuzzy logic systems are much more common in Japan than they are in the United States, where traditional expert systems and neural networks tend to be favored. In Japan, microprocessors specially designed by Toshiba and Hitachi to use fuzzy logic operate subways, consumer electronics, and automobile transmissions.

Created by Marie Solberg
Monday, September 27, 2010
Note: Please insert this information between the 4th and 5th sections.

## Assessment

## 3 CREATE A DOCUMENT DESCRIBING KEYBOARD SHORTCUTS

1. Click the Microsoft Office Word Help button, type keyboard shortcuts, and then press Enter.
2. At the Word Help window, click the Keyboard shortcuts for Microsoft Office Word hyperlink.
3. At the keyboard shortcut window, click the Show All hyperlink.
4. Read through the information in the Word Help window.
5. Create a document describing four keyboard shortcuts.
6. Save the document and name it **WordL1_C1_A3**.
7. Print and then close **WordL1_C1_A3.docx**.

# CASE study

## *Apply Your Skills*

**Part 1**

You are the assistant to Paul Brewster, the training coordinator at a medium-sized service-oriented business. You have been asked by Mr. Brewster to prepare a document for Microsoft Word users within the company explaining how to use the Save As command when saving a document rather than the Save command. Save the document and name it **WordL1_C1_CS_P1**. Print and then close the document.

**Part 2**

Mr. Brewster would like a document containing a brief summary of some basic Word commands for use in Microsoft Word training classes. He has asked you to prepare a document containing the following information:

- A brief explanation on how to move the insertion point to a specific page
- Keyboard shortcuts to move the insertion point to the beginning and end of a text line and beginning and end of a document
- Commands to delete text from the insertion point to the beginning of the word and from the insertion point to the end of the word
- Steps to select a word, a sentence, a paragraph, and an entire document using the mouse.
- Keyboard shortcut to select the entire document

Save the document and name it **WordL1_C1_CS_P2**. Print and then close the document.

**Part 3**

According to Mr. Brewster, the company is considering updating the Resources Department computers to Microsoft Office 2007. He has asked you to use the Internet to go to the Microsoft home page at www.microsoft.com and then use the search feature to find information on the system requirements for Office Professional Edition 2007. When you find the information, type a document that contains the Office Professional Edition 2007 system requirements for the computer and processor, memory, hard disk space, drives, and operating system. Save the document and name it **WordL1_C1_CS_P3**. Print and then close the document.

# CHAPTER 2

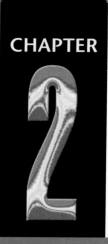

# Formatting Characters and Paragraphs

## PERFORMANCE OBJECTIVES

**Upon successful completion of Chapter 2, you will be able to:**

- Change the font and font effects
- Format selected text with buttons on the Mini toolbar
- Apply styles from Quick Styles sets
- Apply themes
- Change the alignment of text in paragraphs
- Indent text in paragraphs
- Increase and decrease spacing before and after paragraphs
- Repeat the last action
- Automate formatting with Format Painter
- Change line spacing in a document
- Reveal and compare formatting

**Tutorial 2.1**
Modifying Text Format
**Tutorial 2.2**
Other Formatting Features
**Tutorial 2.3**
Modifying and Comparing Text
Formatting

A Word document is based on a template that applies default formatting. Some of the default formats include 11-point Calibri, line spacing of 1.15, 10 points of spacing after each paragraph, and left-aligned text. The appearance of a document in the document screen and how it looks when printed is called the *format*. In this chapter, you will learn about character formatting that can include such elements as changing the typeface, type size, and typestyle as well as applying font effects such as bolding and italicizing. The Paragraph group in the Home tab includes buttons for applying formatting to paragraphs of text. In Word, a paragraph is any amount of text followed by the press of the Enter key. In this chapter, you will learn to apply paragraph formatting to text such as changing text alignment, indenting text, applying formatting with Format Painter, and changing line spacing.

*Note: Before beginning computer projects, copy to your storage medium the Word2007L1C2 subfolder from the Word2007L1 folder on the CD that accompanies this textbook and then make Word2007L1C2 the active folder.*

**You will open a document containing a glossary of terms, add additional text, and then format the document by applying character formatting.**

# Changing Fonts

The Font group shown in Figure 2.1 contains a number of buttons you can use to apply character formatting to text in a document. The top row contains buttons for changing the font and font size as well as buttons for increasing and decreasing the size of the font. The bottom row contains buttons for applying typestyles such as bold, italics, underlining, superscript, and subscript. You can remove character formatting (as well as paragraph formatting) applied to text by clicking the Clear Formatting button in the Font group. Remove only character formatting from selected text by pressing the keyboard shortcut, Ctrl + spacebar.

Clear Formatting

**Figure 2.1** Font Group Buttons

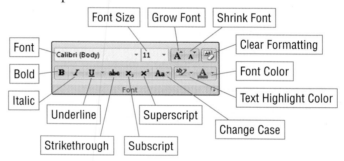

**HINT**

Change the default font by selecting the desired font at the Font dialog box, clicking the Default button, and then clicking Yes.

**HINT**

Use a serif typeface for text-intensive documents.

A Word document is based on a template that formats text in 11-point Calibri. You may want to change this default to some other font for such reasons as changing the mood of the document, enhancing the visual appeal, and increasing the readability of the text. A font consists of three elements—typeface, type size, and typestyle.

A typeface is a set of characters with a common design and shape and can be decorative or plain and either monospaced or proportional. Word refers to typeface as *font*. A monospaced typeface allots the same amount of horizontal space for each character while a proportional typeface allots a varying amount of space for each character. Proportional typefaces are divided into two main categories: *serif* and *sans serif*. A serif is a small line at the end of a character stroke. Consider using a serif typeface for text-intensive documents because the serifs help move the reader's eyes across the page. Use a sans serif typeface for headings, headlines, and advertisements.

Microsoft Word 2007 includes six new typefaces designed for extended on-screen reading. These typefaces include the default, Calibri, as well as Cambria, Candara, Consolas, Constantia, and Corbel. Calibri, Candara, and Corbel are sans serif typefaces; Cambria and Constantia are serif typefaces; and Consolas is monospaced. These six typefaces as well as some other popular typefaces are shown in Table 2.1.

**Table 2.1** Serif and Sans Serif Typefaces

| Serif Typefaces | Sans Serif Typefaces | Monospaced Typefaces |
|---|---|---|
| Cambria | Calibri | Consolas |
| Constantia | Candara | Courier |
| Times New Roman | Corbel | Letter Gothic |
| Bookman Old Style | Arial | |

Type size is generally set in proportional size. The size of proportional type is measured vertically in units called **points**. A point is approximately ½₂ of an inch—the higher the point size, the larger the characters. Within a typeface, characters may have a varying style. Type styles are divided into four main categories: regular, bold, italic, and bold italic.

You can use the Font button in the Font group to change the font and the Font Size button to change the size. When you select text and then click the Font button arrow, a drop-down gallery displays of font options. Hover your mouse pointer over a font option and the selected text in the document displays with the font applied. You can continue hovering your mouse pointer over different font options to see how the selected text displays in the specified font. The Font button drop-down gallery is an example of the **live preview** feature, which allows you to see how the font formatting affects your text without having to return to the document. The live preview feature is also available when you click the Font Size button arrow.

## Project ⓵ Changing the Font

1. Open **WordDocument02.docx**.
2. Save the document with Save As and name it **WordL1_C2_P1**.
3. Change the typeface to Cambria by completing the following steps:
   a. Select the entire document by pressing Ctrl + A. (You can also select all text in the document by clicking the Select button in the Editing group and then clicking *Select All* at the drop-down list.)
   b. Click the Font button arrow, scroll down the Font drop-down gallery until *Cambria* displays, and then hover the mouse pointer over *Cambria*. This displays a live preview of the text set in Cambria.
   c. Click the mouse button on *Cambria*.

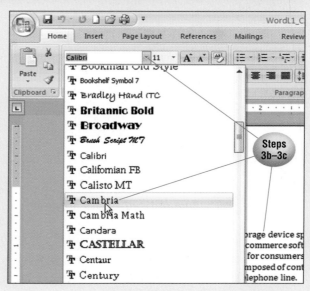

4. Change the type size to 14 by completing the following steps:
   a. With the text in the document still selected, click the Font Size button arrow.
   b. At the drop-down gallery that displays, hover the mouse pointer on *14* and look at the live preview of the text with 14 points applied.
   c. Click the left mouse button on *14*.
5. At the document screen, deselect the text by clicking anywhere in the document screen outside the selected text.
6. Change the type size and typeface by completing the following steps:
   a. Press Ctrl + A to select the entire document.
   b. Click three times on the Shrink Font button in the Font group. (This decreases the size to 10 points.)
   c. Click twice on the Grow Font button. (This increases the size of the font to 12 points.)
   d. Click the Font button arrow, scroll down the drop-down gallery, and then click *Constantia*. (The most recently used fonts display at the beginning of the document, followed by a listing of all fonts.)
7. Save **WordL1_C2_P1.docx**.

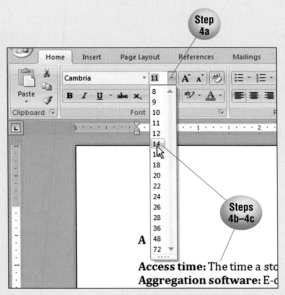

Step 4a

Steps 4b–4c

Access time: The time a sto
Aggregation software: E-c

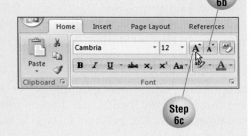

Step 6b

Step 6c

Bold

Italic

Underline

# Choosing a Typestyle

Apply a particular typestyle to text with the Bold, Italic, or Underline buttons in the bottom row in the Font group. You can apply more than one style to text. For example, you can bold and italicize the same text or apply all three styles to the same text.

Each of the three styles has traditional uses that you may find appropriate in your documents. Bold is often used to draw the reader's attention to important words to remember. In this text, for example, bold is used for file names in exercises. Italics typically are used to emphasize certain words or phrases within a sentence. In biology texts, they are used for genus and species names. In this text, you may have noticed italics are used to set apart the names of features in drop-down galleries. Underlining also serves to emphasize and set apart words or phrases, although most style manuals recommend using italics instead of underlines.

1. With **WordL1_C2_P1.docx** open, press Ctrl + Home to move the insertion point to the beginning of the document.
2. Type a heading for the document by completing the following steps:
   a. Press the Caps Lock key.
   b. Click the Bold button in the Font group. (This turns on bold.)
   c. Click the Underline button in the Font group. (This turns on underline.)
   d. Type GLOSSARY OF TERMS.
3. Press Ctrl + End to move the insertion point to the end of the document.
4. Type the text shown in Figure 2.2 with the following specifications:
   a. While typing the document, make the appropriate text bold as shown in the figure by completing the following steps:
      1) Click the Bold button in the Font group. (This turns on bold.)
      2) Type the text.
      3) Click the Bold button in the Font group. (This turns off bold.)
   b. While typing the document, italicize the appropriate text as shown in the figure by completing the following steps:
      1) Click the Italic button in the Font group.
      2) Type the text.
      3) Click the Italic button in the Font group.
5. After typing the text, press the Enter key twice.
6. Remove underlining from the title by selecting GLOSSARY OF TERMS and then clicking the Underline button in the Font group.
7. With the title GLOSSARY OF TERMS selected, change the font size to 14 points.
8. Save **WordL1_C2_P1.docx**.

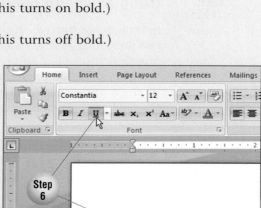

**Figure 2.2 Project 1b**

C

**Chip:** A thin wafer of *silicon* containing electronic circuitry that performs various functions, such as mathematical calculations, storage, or controlling computer devices.

**Cluster:** A group of two or more *sectors* on a disk, which is the smallest unit of storage space used to store data.

**Coding:** A term used by programmers to refer to the act of writing source code.

**Crackers:** A term coined by computer hackers for those who intentionally enter (or hack) computer systems to damage them.

## Choosing a Font Effect

Strikethrough

Subscript

Superscript

Change Case

ab

Text Highlight Color

A

Font Color

Apply font effects with some of the buttons in the bottom row in the Font group. Use the Strikethrough button to draw a line through selected text. This has a practical application in some legal documents in which deleted text must be retained in the document. Use the Subscript button to create text that is lowered slightly below the line such as the chemical formula $H_2O$. Use the Superscript button to create text that is raised slightly above the text line such as the mathematical equation four to the third power (written as $4^3$).

Change the case of text with the Change Case button drop-down list. Click the Change Case button and a drop-down list displays with the options *Sentence case*, *lowercase*, *UPPERCASE*, *Capitalize Each Word*, and *tOGGLE cASE*. You can also change the case of selected text with the keyboard shortcut, Shift + F3. Each time you press Shift + F3, selected text cycles through the case options.

The bottom row in the Font group contains two additional buttons—the Text Highlight Color button and the Font Color button. Use the Text Highlight Color button to highlight specific text in a document and use the Font Color button to change the color of text.

## Using Keyboard Shortcuts

Several of the buttons in the Font group have keyboard shortcuts. For example, you can press Ctrl + B to turn on bold or press Ctrl + I to turn on italics. Position the mouse pointer on a button and an enhanced ScreenTip displays with the name of the button; the keyboard shortcut, if any; a description of the action performed by the button; and sometimes access to the Word Help window. Table 2.2 identifies the keyboard shortcuts available for buttons in the Font group.

**Table 2.2** Font Button Keyboard Shortcuts

| Font Group Button | Keyboard Shortcut |
|---|---|
| Font | Ctrl + Shift + F |
| Font Size | Ctrl + Shift + P |
| Grow Font | Ctrl + Shift + > |
| Shrink Font | Ctrl + Shift + < |
| Bold | Ctrl + B |
| Italic | Ctrl + I |
| Underline | Ctrl + U |
| Subscript | Ctrl + = |
| Superscript | Ctrl + Shift + + |
| Change Case | Shift + F3 |

# Formatting with the Mini Toolbar

When you select text, the Mini toolbar displays in a dimmed fashion above the selected text. Hover the mouse pointer over the Mini toolbar and it becomes active. Click a button on the Mini toolbar to apply formatting to selected text.

## Project 1C    Applying Font Effects

1. With **WordL1_C2_P1.docx** open, move the insertion point to the beginning of the term *Chip*, press the Enter key, and then press the Up Arrow key. Type the text shown in Figure 2.3. Create the superscript numbers by clicking the Superscript button, typing the number, and then clicking the Superscript button.
2. Change the case of text by completing the following steps:
   a. Select the title *GLOSSARY OF TERMS*.
   b. Click the Change Case button in the Font group and then click *Capitalize Each Word* at the drop-down list.
3. Strike through text by completing the following steps:
   a. Select the words and parentheses *(or hack)* in the *Crackers* definition.
   b. Click the Strikethrough button in the Font group.

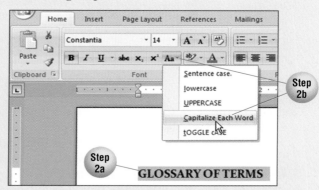

Step 2b

Step 2a

**GLOSSARY OF TERMS**

Step 3b

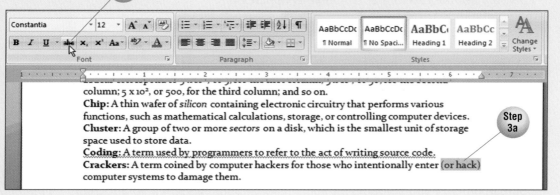

column; 5 x 10², or 500, for the third column; and so on.
**Chip:** A thin wafer of *silicon* containing electronic circuitry that performs various functions, such as mathematical calculations, storage, or controlling computer devices.
**Cluster:** A group of two or more *sectors* on a disk, which is the smallest unit of storage space used to store data.
**Coding:** A term used by programmers to refer to the act of writing source code.
**Crackers:** A term coined by computer hackers for those who intentionally enter (or hack) computer systems to damage them.

Step 3a

4. Change the font color by completing the following steps:
   a. Press Ctrl + A to select the entire document.
   b. Click the Font Color button arrow.
   c. Click the Dark Blue color (second color from *right* in the *Standard Colors* section) at the drop-down gallery.
   d. Click outside the selected area to deselect text.

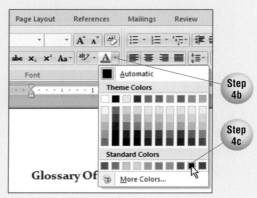

Step 4b

Step 4c

Glossary Of

5. Highlight text in the document by completing the following steps:
   a. Click the Text Highlight Color button in the Font group. (This causes the mouse pointer to display as an I-beam pointer with a pen attached.)
   b. Select the term *Beta-testing* and the definition that follows.

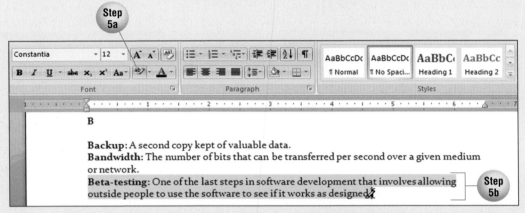

c. Click the Text Highlight Color button arrow and then click a green color (you decide which green).
   d. Select the term *Cluster* and the definition that follows.
   e. Click the Text Highlight Color button arrow and then click the yellow color that displays in the upper left corner of the drop-down gallery.
   f. Click the Text Highlight Color button to turn off highlighting.
6. Change the case of the title by selecting *Glossary Of Terms* and then pressing Shift + F3. (This changes the case of the title text to uppercase.)
7. Apply italic formatting using the Mini toolbar by completing the following steps:
   a. Select the text *one-stop shopping* located in the definition for the term *Aggregation software*. (When you select the text, the Mini toolbar displays.)
   b. Click the Italic button on the Mini toolbar.
   c. Select the word *bits* located in the definition for the term *Bandwidth* and then click the Italic button on the Mini toolbar.
8. Save **WordL1_C2_P1.docx**.

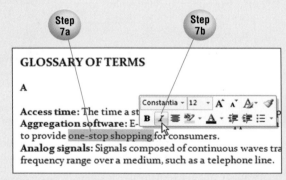

---

**Figure 2.3  Project 1c**

**Chinese abacus:** Pebbles strung on a rod inside a frame. Pebbles in the upper part of an abacus correspond to $5 \times 10^0$, or 5, for the first column; $5 \times 10^1$, or 50, for the second column; $5 \times 10^2$, or 500, for the third column; and so on.

# Changing Fonts at the Font Dialog Box

In addition to buttons in the Font group, you can use options at the Font dialog box shown in Figure 2.4 to change the typeface, type size, and typestyle of text as well as apply font effects. Display the Font dialog box by clicking the Font group dialog box launcher. The dialog box launcher is a small square containing a diagonal-pointing arrow that displays in the lower right corner of the Font group.

**QUICK STEPS**

**Change Font and Apply Effects**
1. Click Font group dialog box launcher.
2. Choose desired options at dialog box.
3. Click OK.

**Figure 2.4** Font Dialog Box

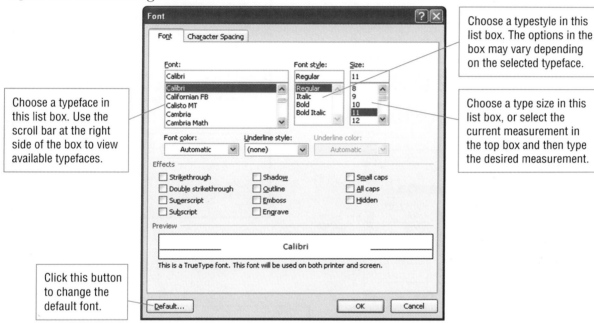

Choose a typestyle in this list box. The options in the box may vary depending on the selected typeface.

Choose a typeface in this list box. Use the scroll bar at the right side of the box to view available typefaces.

Choose a type size in this list box, or select the current measurement in the top box and then type the desired measurement.

Click this button to change the default font.

---

## Project 1d    Changing the Font at the Font Dialog Box

1. With **WordL1_C2_P1.docx** open, press Ctrl + End to move the insertion point to the end of the document. (Make sure the insertion point is positioned a double space below the last line of text.)
2. Type **Created by Susan Ashby** and then press the Enter key.
3. Type **Wednesday, February 17, 2010**.
4. Change the font to 13-point Times New Roman and the color to dark red by completing the following steps:
   a. Press Ctrl + A to select the entire document.
   b. Click the Font group dialog box launcher.

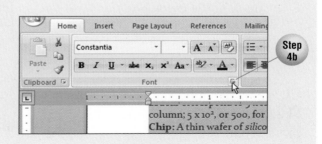

Step 4b

c. At the Font dialog box, click the down-pointing arrow at the right side of the *Font* list box to scroll down the list box and then click *Times New Roman*.

d. Click in the *Size* text box and then type **13**.

e. Click the down-pointing arrow at the right side of the *Font color* list box and then click a dark red color of your choosing at the color gallery.

f. Click OK to close the dialog box.

5. Double underline text by completing the following steps:

a. Select *Wednesday, February 17, 2010*.

b. Click the Font group dialog box launcher.

c. At the Font dialog box, click the down-pointing arrow at the right side of the *Underline style* option box and then click the double-line option at the drop-down list.

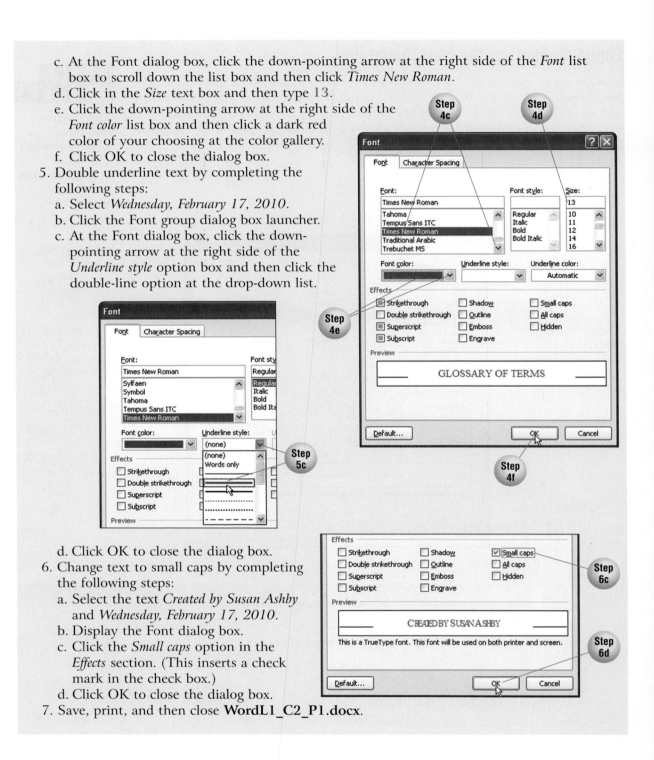

d. Click OK to close the dialog box.

6. Change text to small caps by completing the following steps:

a. Select the text *Created by Susan Ashby* and *Wednesday, February 17, 2010*.

b. Display the Font dialog box.

c. Click the *Small caps* option in the *Effects* section. (This inserts a check mark in the check box.)

d. Click OK to close the dialog box.

7. Save, print, and then close **WordL1_C2_P1.docx**.

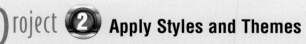

## Project ② Apply Styles and Themes

**You will open a document containing information on the life cycle of software, apply styles to text, and then change the Quick Styles set. You will also apply a theme and then change the theme colors and fonts.**

# Applying Styles from a Quick Styles Set

A Word document contains a number of predesigned formats grouped into style sets called Quick Styles. Four of the styles in the default Quick Styles set display in the Styles group in the Home tab. Display additional styles by clicking the More button that displays at the right side of the four styles. This displays a drop-down gallery of style choices. To apply a style, position the insertion point in the paragraph of text to which you want the style applied, click the More button at the right side of the styles in the Styles group, and then click the desired style at the drop-down gallery.

A Word document contains some default formatting including 10 points of spacing after paragraphs and a line spacing of 1.15. (You will learn more about these formatting options later in this chapter.) You can remove this default formatting as well as any character formatting applied to text in your document by applying the No Spacing style to your text. This style is located in the Styles group.

## Changing the Quick Styles Set

Word contains a number of Quick Styles sets containing styles you can use to apply formatting to a document. To change to a different Quick Styles set, click the Change Styles button in the Styles group in the Home tab and then point to Style Set. This displays a side menu with Quick Styles sets. Click the desired set and the style formatting changes for the styles in the set.

**QUICK STEPS**

**Apply a Style**
1. Position insertion point in paragraph of desired text.
2. Click More button in Styles group.
3. Click desired style.

**Change Quick Style Set**
1. Click Change Style button.
2. Point to Style Set.
3. Click desired set.

More

Change Styles

## Project 2a   Applying Quick Styles

1. Open **WordDocument05.docx**.
2. Save the document with Save As and name it **WordL1_C2_P2**.
3. Remove the 10 points of spacing after paragraphs and change the line spacing to 1 by completing the following steps:
   a. Press Ctrl + A to select the entire document.
   b. Click the No Spacing style in the Styles group in the Home tab.

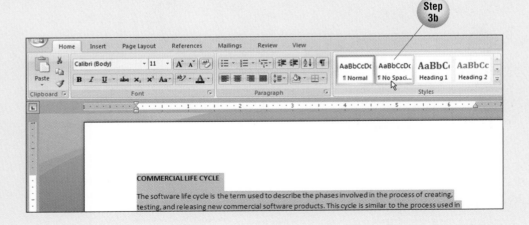

Step 3b

4. Position the insertion point on any character in the title *COMMERCIAL LIFE CYCLE* and then click the Heading 1 style that displays in the Styles group.

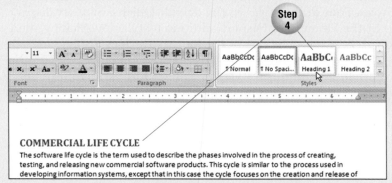

5. Position the insertion point on any character in the heading *Proposal and Planning* and then click the Heading 2 style that displays in the Styles group.

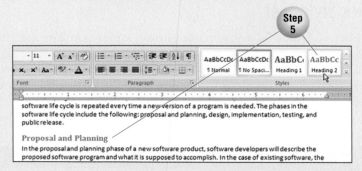

6. Position the insertion point on any character in the heading *Design* and then click the Heading 2 style in the Styles group.
7. Apply the Heading 2 style to the remaining headings (*Implementation*, *Testing*, and *Public Release and Support*).
8. Click the Change Styles button in the Styles group, point to *Style Set*, and then click *Modern*. (Notice how the Heading 1 and Heading 2 formatting changes.)

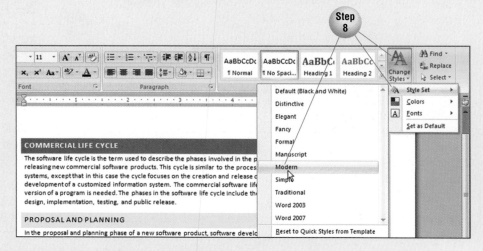

9. Save and then print **WordL1_C2_P2.docx**.

# Applying a Theme

Word provides a number of themes you can use to format text in your document. A theme is a set of formatting choices that include a color theme (a set of colors), a font theme (a set of heading and body text fonts), and an effects theme (a set of lines and fill effects). To apply a theme, click the Page Layout tab and then click the Themes button in the Themes group. At the drop-down gallery that displays, click the desired theme. You can hover the mouse pointer over a theme and the live preview feature will display your document with the theme formatting applied. With the live preview feature you can see how the theme formatting affects your document before you make your final choice. Applying a theme is an easy way to give your document a professional look.

**QUICK STEPS**

**Apply a Theme**
1. Click Page Layout tab.
2. Click Themes button.
3. Click desired theme.

## Project 2b    Applying a Theme to Text in a Document

1. With **WordL1_C2_P2.docx** open, click the Page Layout tab and then click the Themes button in the Themes group.
2. At the drop-down gallery, hover your mouse pointer over each theme and notice how the text formatting changes in your document.
3. Click the *Module* theme.
4. Save and then print **WordL1_C2_P2.docx**.

Step 1

Step 3

# Changing Themes

You can change a theme with the three buttons that display at the right side of the Themes button. A theme contains specific color formatting, which you can change with options from the Theme Colors button in the Themes group. Click this button and a drop-down gallery displays with named color schemes. The names of the color schemes correspond to the names of the themes. Each theme applies specific fonts, which you can change with options from the Theme Fonts button in the Themes group. Click this button and a drop-down gallery displays with font choices. Each font group in the drop-down gallery contains two choices. The first choice in the group is the font that is applied to headings and the second choice is the font that is applied to body text in the document. If you are formatting a document containing graphics with lines and fills, you can apply a specific theme effect with options at the Theme Effects drop-down gallery.

**QUICK STEPS**

**Change Theme Color**
1. Click Page Layout tab.
2. Click Theme Colors button.
3. Click desired theme color.

**Change Theme Fonts**
1. Click Page Layout tab.
2. Click Theme Fonts button.
3. Click desired theme font.

Theme Colors    Theme Fonts

Theme Effects

1. With **WordL1_C2_P2.docx** open, click the Theme Colors button in the Themes group and then click *Foundry* at the drop-down gallery. (Notice how the colors in the title and headings change.)
2. Click the Theme Fonts button and then click the *Civic* option. (Notice how the document text font changes.)

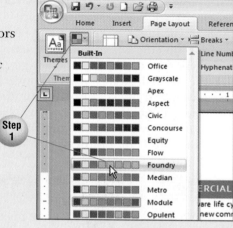

Step 1

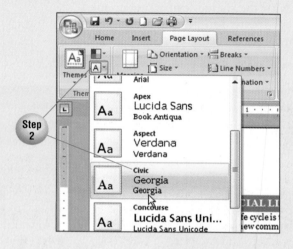

Step 2

3. Save, print, and then close **WordL1_C2_P2.docx**.

# Project 3   Apply Paragraph Formatting and Use Format Painter

You will open a report on intellectual property and fair use issues and then format the report by changing the alignment of text in paragraphs, applying spacing before and after paragraphs of text, and repeating the last formatting action.

## Changing Paragraph Alignment

By default, paragraphs in a Word document are aligned at the left margin and ragged at the right margin. Change this default alignment with buttons in the Paragraph group in the Home tab or with keyboard shortcuts as shown in Table 2.3.

You can change the alignment of text in paragraphs before you type the text or you can change the alignment of existing text. If you change the alignment before typing text, the alignment formatting is inserted in the paragraph mark. As you type text and press Enter, the paragraph formatting is continued. For example, if you click the Center button in the Paragraph group, type text for the first paragraph, and then press the Enter key, the center alignment formatting is still active and the insertion point displays centered between the left and right margins. To display the paragraph symbols in a document, click the Show/Hide ¶ button in the Paragraph

Center

Show/Hide

**Table 2.3** Paragraph Alignment Buttons and Keyboard Shortcuts

| To align text | Paragraph Group Button | Keyboard Shortcut |
|---|---|---|
| At the left margin | | Ctrl + L |
| Between margins | | Ctrl + E |
| At the right margin | | Ctrl + R |
| At the left and right margins | | Ctrl + J |

group. With the Show/Hide ¶ button active (displays with an orange background), nonprinting formatting symbols display such as the paragraph symbol ¶ indicating a press of the Enter key or a dot indicating a press of the spacebar.

To return paragraph alignment to the default (left-aligned), click the Align Text Left button in the Paragraph group. You can also return all paragraph formatting to the default with the keyboard shortcut, Ctrl + Q. This keyboard shortcut removes paragraph formatting from selected text. If you want to remove all formatting from selected text including character and paragraph formatting, click the Clear Formatting button in the Font group.

To change the alignment of existing text in a paragraph, position the insertion point anywhere within the paragraph. You do not need to select the entire paragraph. To change the alignment of several adjacent paragraphs in a document, select a portion of the first paragraph through a portion of the last paragraph. You do not need to select all of the text in the paragraphs.

Align Text Left

**H I N T**

Align text in a document so the message of the document can be followed and the page is attractive.

## Project 3a  Changing Paragraph Alignment

1. Open **WordReport03.docx**. (Some of the default formatting in this document has been changed.)
2. Save the document with Save As and name it **WordL1_C2_P3**.
3. Click the Show/Hide ¶ button in the Paragraph group in the Home tab to turn on the display of nonprinting characters.

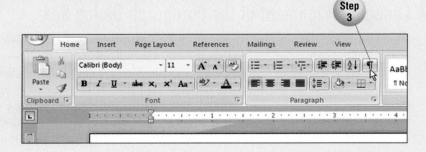

4. Press Ctrl + A to select the entire document and then change the alignment to Justify by clicking the Justify button in the Paragraph group in the Home tab.

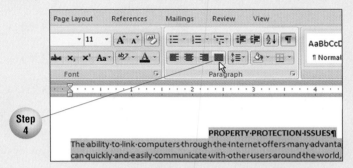

5. Press Ctrl + End to move the insertion point to the end of the document.
6. Press the Enter key once.
7. Press Ctrl + E to move the insertion point to the middle of the page.
8. Type **Prepared by Clarissa Markham**.
9. Press Shift + Enter and then type **Edited by Joshua Streeter**.

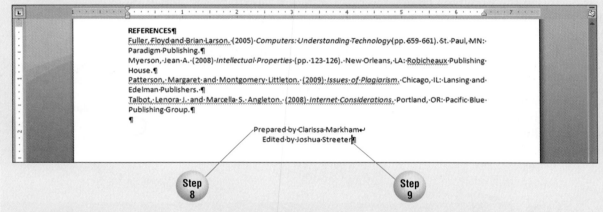

10. Click the Show/Hide ¶ button in the Paragraph group in the Home tab to turn off the display of nonprinting characters.
11. Save **WordL1_C2_P3.docx**.

## QUICK STEPS

**Change Paragraph Alignment**
Click desired alignment button in Paragraph group.
OR
1. Click Paragraph group dialog box launcher.
2. Click *Alignment* option down-pointing arrow.
3. Click desired alignment.
4. Click OK.

## Changing Alignment at the Paragraph Dialog Box

Along with buttons in the Paragraph group and keyboard shortcuts, you can also change paragraph alignment with the Alignment option at the Paragraph dialog box shown in Figure 2.5. Display this dialog box by clicking the Paragraph group dialog box launcher. At the Paragraph dialog box, click the down-pointing arrow at the right side of the *Alignment* option box. At the drop-down list that displays, click the desired alignment option and then click OK to close the dialog box.

**Figure 2.5** Paragraph Dialog Box with Alignment Options

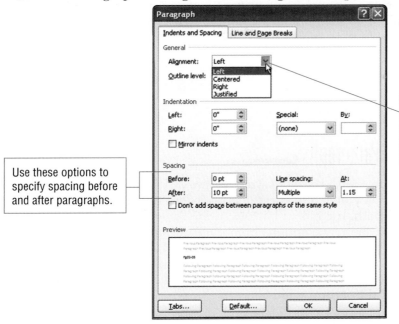

Change paragraph alignment by clicking this down-pointing arrow and then clicking the desired alignment at the drop-down list.

Use these options to specify spacing before and after paragraphs.

## Project 3b  Changing Paragraph Alignment at the Paragraph Dialog Box

1. With **WordL1_C2_P3.docx** open, change paragraph alignment by completing the following steps:
   a. Select the entire document.
   b. Click the Paragraph group dialog box launcher.
   c. At the Paragraph dialog box with the Indents and Spacing tab selected, click the down-pointing arrow at the right of the *Alignment* list box and then click *Left*.
   d. Click OK to close the dialog box.
   e. Deselect the text.

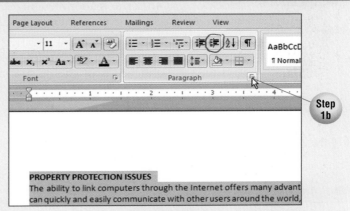

2. Change paragraph alignment by completing the following steps:
   a. Press Ctrl + End to move the insertion point to the end of the document.
   b. Position the insertion point on any character in the text *Prepared by Clarissa Markham*.
   c. Click the Paragraph group dialog box launcher.
   d. At the Paragraph dialog box with the Indents and Spacing tab selected, click the down-pointing arrow at the right of the *Alignment* list box and then click *Right*.

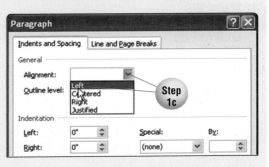

e. Click OK. (The line of text containing the name *Clarissa Markham* and the line of text containing the name *Joshua Streeter* are both aligned at the right since you used the New Line command, Shift + End, to separate the lines of text without creating a new paragraph.)

3. Save and then print **WordL1_C2_P3.docx**.

## Indenting Text in Paragraphs

**QUICK STEPS**

**Indent Text in Paragraph**
Drag indent marker(s) on Ruler.
OR
Press keyboard shortcut keys.
OR
1. Click Paragraph group dialog box launcher.
2. Insert measurement in *Left, Right,* and/or *By* text box.
3. Click OK.

View Ruler

By now you are familiar with the word wrap feature of Word, which ends lines and wraps the insertion point to the next line. To indent text from the left margin, the right margin, or both, use indent buttons in the Paragraph group, in the Page Layout tab, keyboard shortcuts, options from the Paragraph dialog box, markers on the Ruler, or use the Alignment button on the Ruler. Figure 2.6 identifies indent markers and the Alignment button on the Ruler. Refer to Table 2.4 for methods for indenting text in a document. To display the Ruler, click the View Ruler button located at the top of the vertical scroll bar.

One situation that may call for indented text is the use of a lengthy passage of quoted material. Suppose you are writing a report in which you quote a paragraph of text from a well known expert's book. Rather than using quotation marks to set off the paragraph, consider indenting it from both margins. This option creates a block of text that the reader recognizes instantly as being separate from the body of the report and therefore "new" or "different."

Another type of indent is a negative indent, which is referred to as an "outdent" because it moves the text out into the left margin. A negative indent is an additional option for highlighting, or calling special attention to, a section of writing.

**Figure 2.6** Ruler and Indent Markers

| Alignment Button | First Line Indent Marker |

Left Indent Marker     Hanging Indent Marker     Right Indent Marker

**Table 2.4** Methods for Indenting Text

| *Indent* | *Methods for Indenting* |
| --- | --- |
| First line of paragraph | • Press the Tab key. |
| | • Display Paragraph dialog box, click the down-pointing arrow to the right of the *Special* list box, click *First line*, and then click OK. |
| | • Drag the First Line Indent marker on the Ruler. |
| | • Click the Alignment button located at the left side of the Ruler until the First Line Indent button displays and then click on the Ruler at the desired location. |
| Text from left margin | • Click the Increase Indent button in the Paragraph group in the Home tab to increase the indent or click the Decrease Indent button to decrease the indent. |
| | • Insert a measurement in the *Indent Left* measurement button in the Paragraph group in the Page Layout tab. |
| | • Press Ctrl + M to increase the indent or press Ctrl + Shift + M to decrease the indent. |
| | • Display the Paragraph dialog box, type the desired indent measurement in the *Left* measurement box, and then click OK. |
| | • Drag the left indent marker on the Ruler. |
| Text from right margin | • Insert a measurement in the *Indent Right* measurement button in the Paragraph group in the Page Layout tab. |
| | • Display the Paragraph dialog box, type the desired indent measurement in the *Right* measurement box, and then click OK. |
| | • Drag the right indent marker on the Ruler. |
| All lines of text except the first (called a hanging indent) | • Press Ctrl + T. (Press Ctrl + Shift + T to remove hanging indent.) |
| | • Display the Paragraph dialog box, click the down-pointing arrow to the right of the *Special* list box, click *Hanging*, and then click OK. |
| | • Click the Alignment button located at the left side of the Ruler until the Hanging Indent button displays and then click on the Ruler at the desired location. |
| Text from both left and right margins | • Display the Paragraph dialog box, type the desired indent measurement in the *Left* measurement box, type the desired measurement in the *Right* measurement box, and then click OK. |
| | • Insert a measurement in the *Indent Right* and *Indent Left* measurement buttons in the Paragraph group in the Page Layout tab. |
| | • Drag the left indent marker on the Ruler; then drag the right indent marker on the Ruler. |

1. With **WordL1_C2_P3.docx** open, indent the first line of text in paragraphs by completing the following steps:

   a. Select the first two paragraphs of text in the document (the text after the title *PROPERTY PROTECTION ISSUES* and before the heading *Intellectual Property*.

   b. Position the mouse pointer on the First Line Indent marker on the Ruler, hold down the left mouse button, drag the marker to the 0.5-inch mark, and then release the mouse button.

   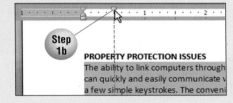

   **Step 1b**

   PROPERTY PROTECTION ISSUES
   The ability to link computers through
   can quickly and easily communicate v
   a few simple keystrokes. The conveni

   c. Select the paragraphs of text in the *Intellectual Property* section and then drag the First Line Indent marker on the Ruler to the 0.5-inch mark.

   d. Select the paragraphs of text in the *Fair Use* section, click the Alignment button located at the left side of the Ruler until the First Line Indent button displays, and then click on the Ruler at the 0.5-inch mark.

   **Step 1d**

   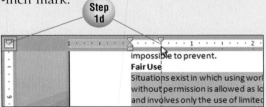

   impossible to prevent.
   **Fair Use**
   Situations exist in which using worl
   without permission is allowed as lc
   and involves only the use of limited

   e. Position the insertion point on any character in the paragraph of text below the *Intellectual Property Protection* heading, make sure the First Line Indent button displays in the Alignment button, and then click at the 0.5-inch mark on the Ruler.

2. Since the text in the second paragraph in the *Fair Use* section is a quote, you need to indent the text from the left and right margins by completing the following steps:

   a. Position the insertion point anywhere within the second paragraph in the *Fair Use* section (the paragraph that begins *[A] copyrighted work, including such . . .* ).

   b. Click the Paragraph group dialog box launcher.

   c. At the Paragraph dialog box, with the Indents and Spacing tab selected, select the current measurement in the *Left* measurement box and then type **0.5**.

   d. Select the current measurement in the *Right* measurement box and then type **0.5**.

   e. Click the down-pointing arrow at the right side of the *Special* list box and then click *(none)* at the drop-down list.

   f. Click OK or press Enter.

   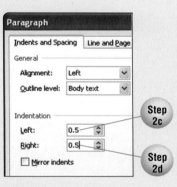

   **Step 2c**

   **Step 2d**

3. Create a hanging indent for the first paragraph in the *REFERENCES* section by positioning the insertion point anywhere in the first paragraph below *REFERENCES* and then pressing Ctrl + T.

4. Create a hanging indent for the second paragraph in the *REFERENCES* section by completing the following steps:

   a. Position the insertion point anywhere in the second paragraph in the *REFERENCES* section.

b. Make sure the Ruler is displayed. (If not, click the View Ruler button located at the top of the vertical scroll bar.)

c. Click the Alignment button located at the left side of the Ruler until the Hanging Indent button displays.

d. Click on the 0.5-inch mark on the Ruler.

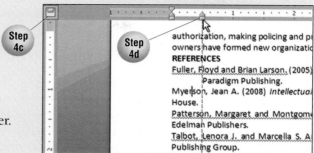

5. Create a hanging indent for the third and fourth paragraphs by completing the following steps:

a. Select a portion of the third and fourth paragraphs.

b. Click the Paragraph group dialog box launcher.

c. At the Paragraph dialog box with the Indents and Spacing tab selected, click the down-pointing arrow at the right side of the *Special* list box and then click *Hanging* at the drop-down list.

d. Click OK or press Enter.

6. Save **WordL1_C2_P3.docx**.

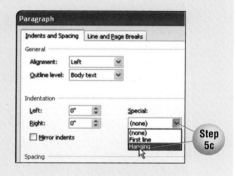

# Spacing Before and After Paragraphs

By default, Word applies 10 points of additional spacing after a paragraph. You can remove this spacing, increase or decrease the spacing, and insert spacing above the paragraph. To change spacing before or after a paragraph, use the Spacing Before and Spacing After measurement boxes located in the Paragraph group in the Page Layout tab, or the *Before* and/or *After* options at the Paragraph dialog box with the Indents and Spacing tab selected.

Spacing before or after a paragraph is part of the paragraph and will be moved, copied, or deleted with the paragraph. If a paragraph, such as a heading, contains spacing before it, and the paragraph falls at the top of a page, Word ignores the spacing.

Spacing before or after paragraphs is added in points and a vertical inch contains approximately 72 points. To add spacing before or after a paragraph you would click the Page Layout tab, select the current measurement in the *Spacing Before* or the *Spacing After* measurement box, and then type the desired number of points. You can also click the up- or down-pointing arrows at the right side of the *Spacing Before* and *Spacing After* measurement boxes to increase or decrease the amount of spacing.

**HINT**
Line spacing determines the amount of vertical space between lines while paragraph spacing determines the amount of space above or below paragraphs of text.

# Repeating the Last Action

If you apply formatting to text and then want to apply the same formatting to other text in the document, consider using the Repeat command. To use this command, apply the desired formatting, move the insertion point to the next location where you want the formatting applied, and then press the F4 function key or press Ctrl + Y.

**Repeat Last Action**
Press F4
OR
Press Ctrl + Y

1. With **WordL1_C2_P3.docx** open, add 6 points of spacing before and after each paragraph in the document by completing the following steps:
   a. Select the entire document.
   b. Click the Page Layout tab.
   c. Click once on the up-pointing arrow at the right side of the *Spacing Before* measurement box in the Paragraph group (this inserts *6 pt* in the box).
   d. Click once on the up-pointing arrow at the right side of the *Spacing After* measurement box in the Paragraph group (this inserts *6 pt* in the text box).

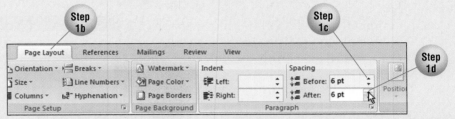

2. Add an additional 6 points of spacing above the headings by completing the following steps:
   a. Position the insertion point on any character in the heading *Intellectual Property* and then click once on the up-pointing arrow at the right side of the *Spacing Before* measurement box (this changes the measurement to *12 pt*).

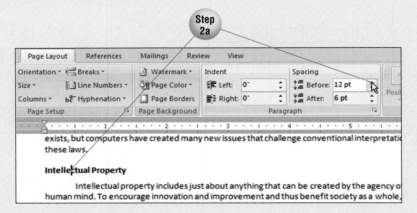

   b. Position the insertion point on any character in the heading *Fair Use* and then press F4 (this is the Repeat command).
   c. Position the insertion point on any character in the heading *Intellectual Property Protection* and then press F4.
   d. Position the insertion point on any character in the heading *REFERENCES* and then press Ctrl + Y (this is also the Repeat command).
3. Save **WordL1_C2_P3.docx**.

# Formatting with Format Painter

The Clipboard group in the Home tab contains a button for copying formatting and displays in the Clipboard group as a paintbrush. To use the Format Painter button, position the insertion point on a character containing the desired formatting, click the Format Painter button, and then select text to which you want the formatting applied. When you click the Format Painter button, the mouse I-beam pointer displays with a paintbrush attached. If you want to apply formatting a single time, click the Format Painter button once. If you want to apply the formatting in more than one location in the document, double-click the Format Painter button and then select text to which you want formatting applied. When you are finished, click the Format Painter button to turn it off. You can also turn off Format Painter by pressing the Esc key.

**Format with Format Painter**
1. Format text.
2. Double-click Format Painter button.
3. Select text.
4. Click Format Painter button.

Format Painter

## Project ③e  Formatting Headings with the Format Painter

1. With **WordL1_C2_P3.docx** open, click the Home tab.
2. Select the entire document and then change the font to 12-point Cambria.
3. Select the title *PROPERTY PROTECTION ISSUES*, click the Center button in the Paragraph group, and then change the font to 16-point Candara bold.
4. Apply 16-point Candara bold formatting to the *REFERENCES* heading by completing the following steps:
   a. Click on any character in the title *PROPERTY PROTECTION ISSUES*.
   b. Click once on the Format Painter button in the Clipboard group.

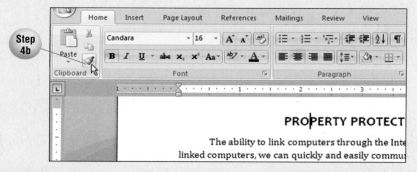

   c. Press Ctrl + End to move the insertion point to the end of the document and then select the heading *REFERENCES*. (This applies the 16-point Candara bold formatting and centers the text.)
5. With the insertion point positioned on any character in the heading *REFERENCES*, add an additional 6 points of spacing before the heading.
6. Select the heading *Intellectual Property* and then change the font to 14-point Candara bold.
7. Use the Format Painter button and apply 14-point Candara bold formatting to the other headings by completing the following steps:
   a. Position the insertion point on any character in the heading *Intellectual Property*.
   b. Double-click the Format Painter button in the Clipboard group.
   c. Using the mouse, select the heading *Fair Use*.

d. Using the mouse, select the heading *Intellectual Property Protection*.

e. Click once on the Format Painter button in the Clipboard group. (This turns off the feature.)

f. Deselect the heading.

8. Save **WordL1_C2_P3.docx**.

QUICK
STEPS

# Changing Line Spacing

**Change Line Spacing**
Click Line Spacing button
in Paragraph group, then
click desired option at
drop-down list.
OR
Press shortcut command
keys.
OR
1. Click Paragraph group
dialog box launcher.
2. Click *Line Spacing*
option down-pointing
arrow.
3. Click desired line
spacing option.
4. Click OK.
OR
1. Click Paragraph group
dialog box launcher.
2. Type line measurement
in *At* text box.
3. Click OK.

Line Spacing

The default line spacing for a document is 1.15. (The line spacing for the **WordReport03.docx** document, which you opened at the beginning of Project 3, had been changed to single.) In certain situations, Word automatically adjusts the line spacing. For example, if you insert a large character or object such as a graphic, Word increases the line spacing of that specific line. But you also may sometimes encounter a writing situation in which you decide to change the line spacing for a section or for the entire document.

Change line spacing using the Line Spacing button in the Paragraph group in the Home tab, with keyboard shortcuts, or with options from the Paragraph dialog box. Table 2.5 displays the keyboard shortcuts to change line spacing.

**Table 2.5** Line Spacing Keyboard Shortcuts

| *Press* | *To change line spacing to* |
|---------|------------------------------|
| Ctrl + 1 | single spacing |
| Ctrl + 2 | double spacing |
| Ctrl + 5 | 1.5 line spacing |

You can also change line spacing at the Paragraph dialog box with the *Line spacing* option or the *At* option. If you click the down-pointing arrow at the right side of the *Line spacing* option, a drop-down list displays with a variety of spacing options. For example, to change the line spacing to double you would click *Double* at the drop-down list. You can type a specific line spacing measurement in the *At* text box. For example, to change the line spacing to 1.75, type 1.75 in the *At* text box.

1. With **WordL1_C2_P3.docx** open, change the line spacing for all paragraphs to double spacing by completing the following steps:
   a. Select the entire document.
   b. Click the Line Spacing button located in the Paragraph group in the Home tab.
   c. Click *2.0* at the drop-down list.
2. With the entire document still selected, press Ctrl + 5. (This changes the line spacing to 1.5 line spacing.)
3. Change the line spacing to 1.3 using the Paragraph dialog box by completing the following steps:
   a. With the document still selected, click the Paragraph group dialog box launcher.
   b. At the Paragraph dialog box, make sure the Indents and Spacing tab is selected, click inside the *At* text box, and then type 1.3. (This text box is located to the right of the *Line spacing* list box.)
   c. Click OK or press Enter.
   d. Deselect the text.
4. Save, print, and then close **WordL1_C2_P3.docx**.

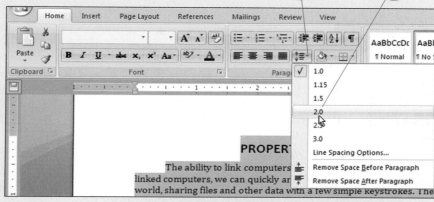

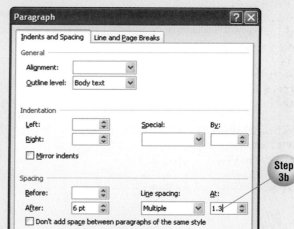

 **Project** **4** **Format Quiz Document**

You will open a document containing two problems to solve, reveal the formatting, compare the formatting, and make formatting changes.

# Revealing Formatting

Display formatting applied to specific text in a document at the Reveal Formatting task pane. The Reveal Formatting task pane displays font, paragraph, and section formatting applied to text where the insertion point is positioned or to selected text. Display the Reveal Formatting task pane with the keyboard shortcut Shift + F1.

Generally, a minus symbol precedes *Font* and *Paragraph* and a plus symbol precedes *Section* in the *Formatting of selected text* section of the Reveal Formatting task pane. Click the minus symbol to hide any items below a heading and click the plus symbol to reveal items. Some of the items below headings in the *Formatting of selected text* section are hyperlinks. Click a hyperlink and a dialog box displays with the specific option.

**Figure 2.7** Reveal Formatting Task Pane

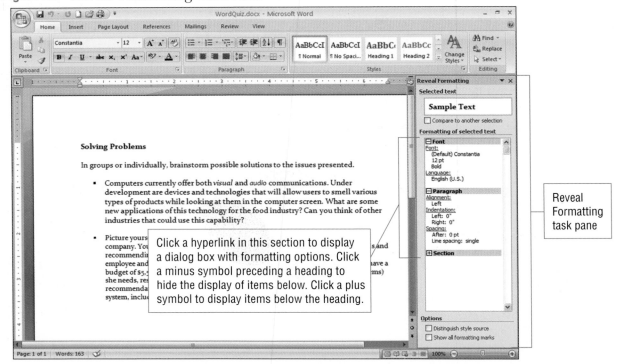

Click a hyperlink in this section to display a dialog box with formatting options. Click a minus symbol preceding a heading to hide the display of items below. Click a plus symbol to display items below the heading.

Reveal Formatting task pane

Project **4a**  **Revealing Formatting**

1. Open **WordQuiz.docx**.
2. Save the document with Save As and name it **WordL1_C2_P4**.
3. Press Shift + F1 to display the Reveal Formatting task pane.
4. Click anywhere in the heading *Solving Problems* and then notice the formatting information that displays in the Reveal Formatting task pane.
5. Click in the bulleted paragraph and notice the formatting information thast displays in the Reveal Formatting task pane.

# Comparing Formatting

Along with displaying formatting applied to text, you can use the Reveal Formatting task pane to compare formatting of two text selections to determine what formatting is different. To compare formatting, select the first instance of formatting to be compared, click the *Compare to another selection* check box, and then select the second instance of formatting to compare. Any differences between the two selections display in the *Formatting differences* list box.

**Compare Formatting**
1. Display Reveal Formatting task pane.
2. Click or select text.
3. Click *Compare to another selection* check box.
4. Click or select text.

## Project 4b   Comparing Formatting

1. With **WordL1_C2_P4.docx** open, make sure the Reveal Formatting task pane displays. If it does not, turn it on by pressing Shift + F1.
2. Select the first bulleted paragraph (the paragraph that begins *Computers currently offer both . . .* ).
3. Click the *Compare to another selection* check box to insert a check mark.
4. Select the second bulleted paragraph (the paragraph that begins *Picture yourself working in the . . .* ).
5. Determine the formatting differences by reading the information in the *Formatting differences* list box. (The list box displays *12 pt -> 11 pt* below the Font: hyperlink, indicating that the difference is point size.)
6. Format the second bulleted paragraph so it is set in 12-point size.
7. Click the *Compare to another selection* check box to remove the check mark.
8. Select the word *visual* that displays in the first sentence in the first bulleted paragraph.
9. Click the *Compare to another selection* check box to insert a check mark.
10. Select the word *audio* that displays in the first sentence of the first bulleted paragraph.
11. Determine the formatting differences by reading the information in the *Formatting differences* list box.
12. Format the word *audio* so it matches the formatting of the word *visual*.
13. Click the *Compare to another selection* check box to remove the check mark.
14. Close the Reveal Formatting task pane by clicking the Close button (contains an X) that displays in the upper right corner of the task pane.
15. Save, print, and then close **WordL1_C2_P4.docx**.

**Step 5**
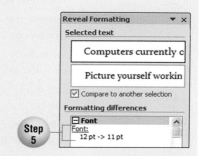

**Step 11**
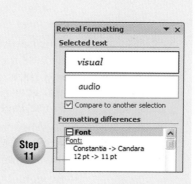

# CHAPTER summary

- The appearance of a document in the document screen and how it looks when printed is called the format.
- The top row in the Font group in the Home tab contains buttons for changing the font and font size. The bottom row contains buttons for applying typestyles and effects.
- A font consists of three parts: typeface, type size, and typestyle.
- A typeface (font) is a set of characters with a common design and shape. Typefaces are either monospaced, allotting the same amount of horizontal space to each character, or proportional, allotting a varying amount of space for each character. Proportional typefaces are divided into two main categories: serif and sans serif.
- Type size is measured in point size—the higher the point size, the larger the characters.
- A typestyle is a variation of style within a certain typeface. You can apply typestyle formatting with some of the buttons in the Font group.
- With some of the buttons in the Font group, you can apply font effects such as superscript, subscript, and strikethrough.
- Some buttons in the Font group contain keyboard shortcuts. Refer to Table 2.2 for a list of these shortcuts.
- The Mini toolbar automatically displays above selected text. Use buttons on this toolbar to apply formatting to selected text.
- With options at the Font dialog box, you can change the font, font size, and font style and apply specific effects. Display this dialog box by clicking the Font group dialog box launcher.
- A Word document contains a number of predesigned formats grouped into style sets called Quick Styles. Change to a different Quick Styles set by clicking the Change Styles button in the Styles group in the Home tab, pointing to Style Set, and then clicking the desired set.
- Word provides a number of themes, which are a set of formatting choices that include a color theme (a set of colors), a font theme (a set of heading and body text fonts), and an effects theme (a set of lines and fill effects). Apply a theme and change theme colors, fonts, and effects with buttons in the Themes group in the Page Layout tab.
- In Word, a paragraph is any amount of text followed by a paragraph mark (a stroke of the Enter key). Word inserts into the paragraph mark any paragraph formatting that is turned on.
- By default, paragraphs in a Word document are aligned at the left margin and ragged at the right margin. Change this default alignment with buttons in the Paragraph group, at the Paragraph dialog box, or with keyboard shortcuts.
- To turn on or off the display of nonprinting characters such as paragraph marks, click the Show/Hide ¶ button in the Paragraph group.

- Indent text in paragraphs with indent buttons in the Paragraph group in the Home tab, buttons in the Paragraph group in the Page Layout tab, keyboard shortcuts, options from the Paragraph dialog box, markers on the Ruler, or use the Alignment button on the Ruler. Refer to Table 2.4 for a description of the various indenting options.

- Increase and/or decrease spacing before and after paragraphs using the *Spacing Before* and *Spacing After* measurement boxes in the Paragraph group in the Page Layout tab, or using the *Before* and/or *After* options at the Paragraph dialog box.

- Repeat the last action by pressing the F4 function key or pressing Ctrl + Y.

- Use the Format Painter button in the Clipboard group in the Home tab to copy formatting already applied to text to different locations in the document.

- Change line spacing with the Line Spacing button in the Paragraph group in the Home tab, keyboard shortcuts, or options from the Paragraph dialog box.

- Display the Reveal Formatting task pane to display formatting applied to text. Use the *Compare to another selection* option in the task pane to compare formatting of two text selections to determine what formatting is different.

# COMMANDS review

| FEATURE | RIBBON TAB, GROUP | BUTTON | KEYBOARD SHORTCUT |
|---------|-------------------|--------|-------------------|
| Bold text | Home, Font | **B** | Ctrl + B |
| Center-align text | Home, Paragraph | | Ctrl + E |
| Change case of text | Home, Font | Aa | Shift + F3 |
| Change Quick Styles set | Home, Styles | | |
| Clear all formatting | Home, Font | | |
| Clear character formatting | | | Ctrl + spacebar |
| Clear paragraph formatting | | | Ctrl + Q |
| Decrease font size | Home, Font | A | Ctrl + < |
| Display nonprinting characters | Home, Paragraph | ¶ | Ctrl + * |
| Font | Home, Font | Calibri (Body) | |
| Font color | Home, Font | A | |
| Font dialog box | Home, Font | | Ctrl + Shift + F |
| Format Painter | Home, Clipboard | | Ctrl + Shift + C |

*continued*

| FEATURE | RIBBON TAB, GROUP | BUTTON | KEYBOARD SHORTCUT |
|---|---|---|---|
| Highlight text | Home, Font | [ab✐ ▾] | |
| Increase font size | Home, Font | [A▲] | Ctrl + > |
| Italicize text | Home, Font | [I] | Ctrl + I |
| Justify-align text | Home, Paragraph | [≡] | Ctrl + J |
| Left-align text | Home, Paragraph | [≡] | Ctrl + L |
| Line spacing | Home, Paragraph | [↕≡ ▾] | Ctrl + 1 (single) Ctrl + 2 (double) Ctrl + 5 (1.5) |
| Paragraph dialog box | Home, Paragraph | [▦] | |
| Repeat last action | | | F4 or Ctrl + Y |
| Reveal Formatting task pane | | | Shift + F1 |
| Right-align text | Home, Paragraph | [≡] | Ctrl + R |
| Spacing after paragraph | Page Layout, Paragraph | [↕≡ After: 0 pt ▲▼] | |
| Spacing before paragraph | Page Layout, Paragraph | [↕≡ Before: 0 pt ▲▼] | |
| Strikethrough text | Home, Font | [abc] | |
| Subscript text | Home, Font | [x₂] | Ctrl + = |
| Superscript text | Home, Font | [x²] | Ctrl + Shift + + |
| Theme Colors | Page Layout, Themes | [■ ▾] | |
| Theme Fonts | Page Layout, Themes | [A ▾] | |
| Themes | Page Layout, Themes | [Aa] | |
| Underline text | Home, Font | [U ▾] | Ctrl + U |

# CONCEPTS check

## Test Your Knowledge

**Completion:** In the space provided at the right, indicate the correct term, symbol, or command.

1. The Bold button is located in this group in the Home tab. _____

2. Click this button in the Font group to remove all formatting from selected text. _____

3. Proportional typefaces are divided into two main categories, serif and this.

_____

4. This is the keyboard shortcut to italicize selected text.

_____

5. This term refers to text that is raised slightly above the regular text line.

_____

6. This automatically displays above selected text.

_____

7. Click this to display the Font dialog box.

_____

8. A Word document contains a number of predesigned formats grouped into style sets called this.

_____

9. Apply a theme and change theme colors, fonts, and effects with buttons in the Themes group in this tab.

_____

10. This is the default paragraph alignment.

_____

11. Click this button in the Paragraph group to turn on the display of nonprinting characters.

_____

12. Return all paragraph formatting to normal with this keyboard shortcut.

_____

13. Click this button in the Paragraph group in the Home tab to align text at the right margin.

_____

14. In this type of paragraph, the first line of text remains at the left margin and the remaining lines of text are indented to the first tab.

_____

15. Repeat the last action by pressing F4 or with this keyboard shortcut.

_____

16. Use this button in the Clipboard group in the Home tab to copy formatting already applied to text to different locations in the document.

_____

17. Change line spacing to 1.5 with this keyboard shortcut.

_____

18. Press these keys to display the Reveal Formatting task pane.

_____

# SKILLS check
## *Demonstrate Your Proficiency*

## 1 APPLY CHARACTER FORMATTING TO A LEASE AGREEMENT DOCUMENT

1. Open **WordDocument03.docx**.
2. Save the document with Save As and name it **WordL1_C2_A1**.
3. Press Ctrl + End to move the insertion point to the end of the document and then type the text shown in Figure 2.8. Bold, italicize, and underline text as shown.
4. Select the entire document and then change the font to 12-point Candara.
5. Select and then bold *THIS LEASE AGREEMENT* located in the first paragraph.
6. Select and then bold *DOLLARS* located in the *Rent* section.
7. Select and then bold *DOLLARS* located in the *Damage Deposit* section.
8. Select and then italicize *12 o'clock midnight* in the *Term* section.
9. Select the title *LEASE AGREEMENT* and then change the font to 18-point Corbel and the font color to dark blue. (Make sure the title retains the bold formatting.)
10. Select the heading *Term*, change the font to 14-point Corbel, and apply small caps formatting. (Make sure the heading retains the bold formatting.)
11. Use Format Painter to change the formatting to small caps in 14-point Corbel for the remaining headings (*Rent, Damage Deposit, Use of Premises, Condition of Premises, Alterations and Improvements, Damage to Premises, Inspection of Premises, Default,* and *Late Charge*).
12. Save, print, and then close **WordL1_C2_A1.docx**.

### Figure 2.8 Assessment 1

**Inspection of Premises**

Lessor shall have the right at all reasonable times during the term of this Agreement to exhibit the Premises and to display the usual *for sale*, *for rent*, or *vacancy* signs on the Premises at any time within <u>forty-five</u> days before the expiration of this Lease.

**Default**

If Lessee fails to pay rent when due and the default continues for <u>seven</u> days thereafter, Lessor may declare the entire balance immediately due and payable and may exercise any and all rights and remedies available to Lessor.

**Late Charge**

In the event that any payment required to be paid by Lessee is not made by the 10th day of the month, Lessee shall pay to Lessor a *late fee* in the amount of **$50**.

## 2 APPLY STYLES, A QUICK STYLES SET, AND A THEME TO A HARDWARE TECHNOLOGY DOCUMENT

1. Open **WordDocument06.docx**.
2. Save the document with Save As and name it **WordL1_C2_A2**.
3. Apply the Heading 1 style to the title *ON THE HORIZON*.
4. Apply the Heading 2 style to the headings in the document (*Increased Optical Disk Storage Capacity, Improved Monitors, Holographic Storage*, and *Electronic Paper*).
5. Change the Quick Styles set to *Fancy*.
6. Apply the *Foundry* theme.
7. Change the theme colors to *Aspect*.
8. Change the theme fonts to *Flow*.
9. Highlight the second sentence in the *Increased Optical Disk Storage Capacity* section.
10. Highlight the second sentence in the *Holographic Storage* section.
11. Save, print, and then close **WordL1_C2_A2.docx**.

## 3 APPLY CHARACTER AND PARAGRAPH FORMATTING TO AN EMPLOYEE PRIVACY DOCUMENT

1. Open **WordDocument04.docx**.
2. Save the document with Save As and name it **WordL1_C2_A3**.
3. Move the insertion point to the beginning of the document and then type WORKPLACE PRIVACY centered.
4. Select text from the beginning of the first paragraph to the end of the document and then make the following changes:
   a. Change the line spacing to 1.5.
   b. Change the spacing after to 0 points.
   c. Indent the first line of each paragraph 0.5 inch.
   d. Change the alignment to Justify.
5. Move the insertion point to the end of the document and, if necessary, drag the First Line Indent marker on the Ruler back to 0″. Type the text shown in Figure 2.9. (Hang indent text as shown in Figure 2.9.)
6. Select the entire document and then change the font to Constantia.
7. Select the title *WORKPLACE PRIVACY* and then change the font to 14-point Calibri bold and the font color to dark red.
8. Apply the same formatting to the title *BIBLIOGRAPHY* that you applied to the title *WORKPLACE PRIVACY*.
9. Save, print, and then close **WordL1_C2_A3.docx**.

**Figure 2.9** **Assessment 3**

BIBLIOGRAPHY

Amaral, Howard G. (2009). *Privacy in the Workplace*, 2nd edition (pp. 103-

112). Denver, CO: Goodwin Publishing Group.

Cuevas, Roxanne A. (2007). *Employer and Employee Rights* (pp. 18-35). Los

Angeles, CA: North Ridge, Inc.

Forsyth, Stuart M. (2010). *Protecting Your Privacy* (pp. 23-31). San Francisco,

CA: Roosevelt & Carson Publishing.

# CASE study
## *Apply Your Skills*

**Part 1**

You work for your local chamber of commerce and are responsible for assisting the Office Manager, Teresa Alexander. Ms. Alexander would like to maintain consistency in articles submitted for publication in the monthly chamber newsletter. She wants you to explore various handwriting, decorative, and plain fonts. She would like you to choose two handwriting fonts, two decorative fonts, and two plain fonts and then prepare a document containing an illustration of each of these fonts. Save the document and name it **WordL1_C2_CS_P1**. Print and then close the document.

**Part 2**

Ms. Alexander has asked you to write a short article for the upcoming chamber newsletter. In the article, she would like you to describe an upcoming event at your school, a local college or university, or your local community. Effectively use at least two of the fonts you wrote about in the document you prepared for Case Study Part 1. Save the document and name it **WordL1_C2_CS_P2**. Print and then close the document.

**Part 3**

When preparing the monthly newsletter, additional fonts may be necessary. Ms. Alexander has asked you to research the steps needed to install new fonts on your computer. Use the Help feature to research the steps and then prepare a document listing the steps. Format the document with appropriate headings and fonts. Save the document and name it **WordL1_C2_CS_P3**. Print and then close the document.

# CHAPTER 3

# Customizing Paragraphs

## PERFORMANCE OBJECTIVES

**Upon successful completion of Chapter 3, you will be able to:**

- Apply numbering and bulleting formatting to text
- Insert paragraph borders and shading
- Apply custom borders and shading
- Sort paragraph text
- Set, clear, and move tabs on the Ruler and at the Tabs dialog box
- Cut, copy, and paste text in a document
- Copy and paste text between documents

**Tutorial 3.1**
Using Formatting Features
**Tutorial 3.2**
Copying and Moving Text

As you learned in Chapter 2, Word contains a variety of options for formatting text in paragraphs. In this chapter you will learn how to insert numbers and bullets in a document, how to apply borders and shading to paragraphs of text in a document, how to sort paragraphs of text, and how to manipulate tabs on the Ruler and at the Tabs dialog box. Editing some documents might include selecting and then deleting, moving, or copying text. You can perform this type of editing with buttons in the Clipboard group in the Home tab or with keyboard shortcuts.

*Note: Before beginning computer projects, copy to your storage medium the Word2007L1C3 subfolder from the Word2007L1 folder on the CD that accompanies this textbook and then make Word2007L1C3 the active folder.*

## Project 1 Format a Document on Computer Technology

You will open a document containing information on computer technology, type numbered text in the document, and apply numbering and bullet formatting to paragraphs in the document.

## Applying Numbering and Bullets

**QUICK STEPS**

**Type Numbered Paragraphs**
1. Type 1.
2. Press spacebar.
3. Type text.
4. Press Enter.

Automatically number paragraphs or insert bullets before paragraphs using buttons in the Paragraph group. Use the Bullets button to insert bullets before specific paragraphs and use the Numbering button to insert numbers.

## Numbering Paragraphs

**HINT**
Define new numbering by clicking the Numbering button arrow and then clicking Define New Number Format.

If you type 1., press the spacebar, type a paragraph of text, and then press the Enter key, Word indents the number approximately 0.25 inch and then hang indents the text in the paragraph approximately 0.5 inch from the left margin. Additionally, *2.* is inserted 0.25 inch from the left margin at the beginning of the next paragraph. Continue typing items and Word inserts the next number in the list. To turn off numbering, press the Enter key twice or click the Numbering button in the Paragraph group. (You can also remove all paragraph formatting from a paragraph, including automatic numbering, with the keyboard shortcut, Ctrl + Q. Remove all formatting including character and paragraph formatting from selected text by clicking the Clear Formatting button in the Font group.)

If you press the Enter key twice between numbered paragraphs, the automatic number is removed. To turn it back on, type the next number in the list (and the period) followed by a space, type the paragraph of text, and then press Enter. Word will automatically indent the number and hang indent the text.

Bullets

Numbering

When the AutoFormat feature inserts numbering and indents text, the AutoCorrect Options button displays. Click this button and a drop-down list displays with options for undoing and/or stopping the automatic numbering. An AutoCorrect Options button also displays when AutoFormat inserts automatic bulleting in a document. If you want to insert a line break without inserting a bullet or number, you do not need to turn off the automatic numbering/bulleting and then turn it back on again. Instead, simply press Shift + Enter to insert the line break.

## Project 1a — Typing Numbered Paragraphs

1. Open **WordDocument12.docx**.
2. Save the document with Save As and name it **WordL1_C3_P1**.
3. Press Ctrl + End to move the insertion point to the end of the document and then type the text shown in Figure 3.1. Bold and center the title *Technology Career Questions*. When typing the numbered paragraphs, complete the following steps:
   a. Type 1. and then press the spacebar.
   b. Type the paragraph of text and then press the Enter key. (This moves the insertion point down to the next line, inserts *2.* indented 0.25 inch from the left margin, and also indents the first paragraph of text approximately 0.5 inch from the left margin. Also, the AutoCorrect Options button displays. Use this button if you want to undo or stop automatic numbering.)
   c. Continue typing the remaining text. (Remember, you do not need to type the paragraph number and period—these are automatically inserted.)
   d. After typing the last question, press the Enter key twice. (This turns off paragraph numbering.)
4. Save **WordL1_C3_P1.docx**.

**Figure 3.1 Project 1a**

### Technology Career Questions

1. What is your ideal technical job?
2. Which job suits your personality?
3. Which is your first-choice certificate?
4. How does the technical job market look in your state right now? Is the job market wide open or are the information technology career positions limited?

If you do not want automatic numbering in a document, turn off the feature at the AutoCorrect dialog box with the AutoFormat As You Type tab selected as shown in Figure 3.2. To display this dialog box, click the Office button and then click the Word Options button that displays toward the bottom of the drop-down list. At the Word Options dialog box, click the *Proofing* option located in the left panel and then click the AutoCorrect Options button that displays in the *AutoCorrect options* section of the dialog box. At the AutoCorrect dialog box, click the AutoFormat As You Type tab and then click the *Automatic numbered lists* check box to remove the check mark. Click OK to close the AutoCorrect dialog box and then click OK to close the Word Options dialog box.

**Figure 3.2** AutoCorrect Dialog Box with AutoFormat As You Type Tab Selected

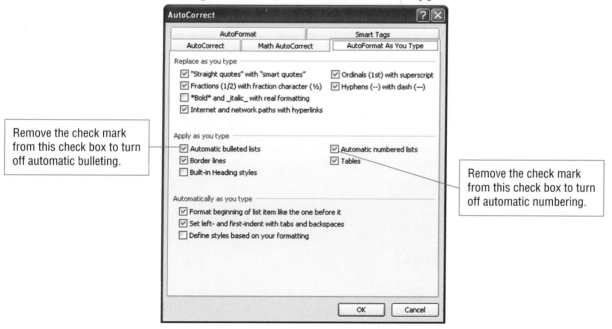

Remove the check mark from this check box to turn off automatic bulleting.

Remove the check mark from this check box to turn off automatic numbering.

**Create Numbered Paragraph**
1. Select text.
2. Click Numbering button.

You can also automate the creation of numbered paragraphs with the Numbering button in the Paragraph group. To use this button, type the text (do not type the number) for each paragraph to be numbered, select the paragraphs to be numbered, and then click the Numbering button in the Paragraph group. You can insert or delete numbered paragraphs in a document.

## Project 1b  Inserting Paragraph Numbering

1. With **WordL1_C3_P1.docx** open, apply numbers to paragraphs by completing the following steps:
   a. Select the five paragraphs of text in the *Technology Information Questions* section.
   b. Click the Numbering button in the Paragraph group.
2. Add the paragraph shown in Figure 3.3 between paragraphs 4 and 5 in the *Technology Information Questions* section by completing the following steps:
   a. Position the insertion point immediately to the right of the question mark at the end of the fourth paragraph.
   b. Press Enter.
   c. Type the paragraph shown in Figure 3.3.
3. Delete the second question (paragraph) in the *Technology Information Questions* section by completing the following steps:
   a. Select the text of the second paragraph (you will not be able to select the number).
   b. Press the Delete key.
4. Save **WordL1_C3_P1.docx**.

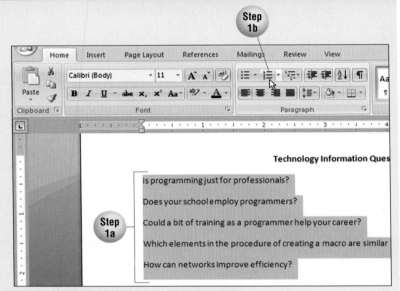

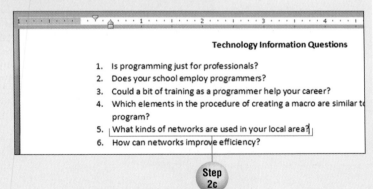

**Figure 3.3 Project 1b**

What kinds of networks are used in your local area?

# Bulleting Paragraphs

In addition to automatically numbering paragraphs, Word's AutoFormat feature will create bulleted paragraphs. You can also create bulleted paragraphs with the Bullets button in the Paragraph group. Figure 3.4 shows an example of bulleted paragraphs. Bulleted lists with hanging indents are automatically created when a paragraph begins with the symbol *, >, or -. Type one of the symbols, press the spacebar, type text, and then press Enter. The AutoFormat feature inserts a bullet approximately 0.25 inch from the left margin and indents the text following the bullet another 0.25 inch. The type of bullet inserted depends on the type of character entered. For example, if you use the asterisk (*) symbol, a round bullet is inserted and an arrow bullet is inserted if you type the greater than symbol (>). Like the numbering feature, you can turn off the automatic bulleting feature at the AutoCorrect dialog box with the AutoFormat As You Type tab selected.

**Figure 3.4** Bulleted Paragraphs

- This is a paragraph preceded by a bullet. A bullet indicates a list of items or topics.

- This is another paragraph preceded by a bullet. You can easily create bulleted paragraphs by typing certain symbols before the text or with the Bullets button in the Paragraph group.

## Project 1C   Typing Bulleted Paragraphs

1. With **WordL1_C3_P1.docx** open, press Ctrl + End to move the insertion point to the end of the document and then press the Enter key once.
2. Type the text shown in Figure 3.5. Bold and center the title *Technology Timeline: Computer Design*. Create the bulleted paragraphs by completing the following steps:
   a. With the insertion point positioned at the left margin of the first paragraph to contain a bullet, type the greater than symbol (>).
   b. Press the spacebar once.
   c. Type the text of the first bulleted paragraph.
   d. Press the Enter key once and then continue typing the text after the bullets.
3. After typing the last bulleted paragraph, press the Enter key twice (this turns off bullets).
4. Save **WordL1_C3_P1.docx**.

Figure 3.5  **Project 1c**

**Technology Timeline: Computer Design**

➤ 1937: Dr. John Atanasoff and Clifford Berry design and build the first electronic digital computer.

➤ 1958: Jack Kilby, an engineer at Texas Instruments, invents the integrated circuit, thereby laying the foundation for fast computers and large-capacity memory.

➤ 1981: IBM enters the personal computer field by introducing the IBM-PC.

➤ 2004: Wireless computer devices, including keyboards, mice, and wireless home networks, become widely accepted among users.

**QUICK STEPS**

**Create Bulleted Paragraphs**
1. Select text.
2. Click Bullets button.

You can also create bulleted paragraphs with the Bullets button in the Paragraph group. To create bulleted paragraphs using the Bullets button, type the text (do not type the bullet) of the paragraphs, select the paragraphs, and then click the Bullets button in the Paragraph group.

## Project 1d  Inserting Bullets Using the Bullets Button

1. With **WordL1_C3_P1.docx** open, insert bullets before the paragraphs of text in the *Technology Timeline: Computers in the Workplace* section by completing the following steps:
   a. Select the paragraphs of text in the *Technology Timeline: Computers in the Workplace* section.
   b. Click the Bullets button in the Paragraph group. (Word will insert the same arrow bullets that you inserted in Project 1c. Word keeps the same bullet formatting until you choose a different bullet.)

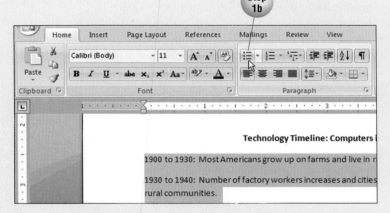

2. Save and then print **WordL1_C3_P1.docx**. (This document will print on two pages.)

# Inserting Paragraph Borders and Shading

Every paragraph you create in Word contains an invisible frame. You can apply a border to the frame around the paragraph. You can apply a border to specific sides of the paragraph or to all sides, you can customize the type of border lines, and you can add shading and fill to the border. Add borders and shading to paragraphs in a document using the Borders and Shading buttons in the Paragraph group or options from the Borders and Shading dialog box.

Borders

Shading

## Inserting Paragraph Borders

When a border is added to a paragraph of text, the border expands and contracts as text is inserted or deleted from the paragraph. You can create a border around a single paragraph or a border around selected paragraphs. One method for creating a border is to use options from the Borders button in the Paragraph group. Click the Borders button arrow and a drop-down list displays as shown in Figure 3.6.

**Figure 3.6** Borders Drop-down List

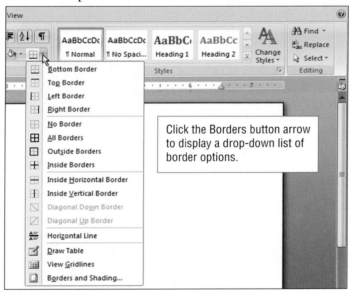

Click the Borders button arrow to display a drop-down list of border options.

At the drop-down list, click the option that will insert the desired border. For example, to insert a border at the bottom of the paragraph, click the *Bottom Border* option. Clicking an option will add the border to the paragraph where the insertion point is located. To add a border to more than one paragraph, select the paragraphs first and then click the desired option.

**QUICK STEPS**

**Apply Border**
1. Select text.
2. Click Borders button.

1. With **WordL1_C3_P1.docx** open, select text from the beginning of the title *Technology Timeline: Computer Design* through the four bulleted paragraphs of text below and then press the Delete key.
2. Insert an outside border to specific text by completing the following steps:
    a. Select text from the title *Technology Information Questions* through the five numbered paragraphs of text.
    b. In the Paragraph group, click the Borders button arrow.
    c. At the Borders drop-down list, click the *Outside Borders* option.

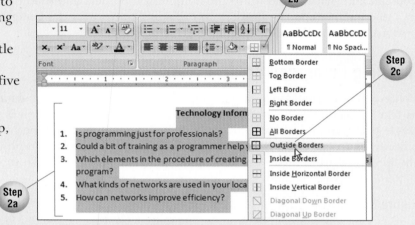

3. Select text from the title *Technology Timeline: Computers in the Workplace* through the six bulleted paragraphs of text and then click the Borders button in the Paragraph group. (The button will apply the border option that was previously selected.)
4. Select text from the title *Technology Career Questions* through the four numbered paragraphs of text below and then click the Borders button in the Paragraph group.
5. Save and then print **WordL1_C3_P1.docx**.

## Adding Paragraph Shading

**Apply Shading**
1. Select text.
2. Click Shading button.

With the Shading button in the Paragraph group you can add shading to text in a document. Select text you want to shade and then click the Shading button. This applies a background color behind the text. Click the Shading button arrow and a Shading drop-down gallery displays as shown in Figure 3.7.

**Figure 3.7** Shading Gallery

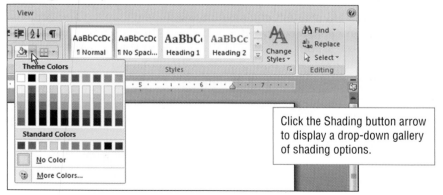

Click the Shading button arrow to display a drop-down gallery of shading options.

Paragraph shading colors display in themes in the drop-down gallery. Use one of the theme colors or click one of the standard colors that displays at the bottom of the gallery. Click the *More Colors* option and the Colors dialog box displays. At the Colors dialog box with the Standard tab selected, click the desired color or click the Custom tab and then specify a custom color.

## Project ⓫   Applying Shading to Paragraphs

1. With **WordL1_C3_P1.docx** open, apply paragraph shading and change border lines by completing the following steps:
   a. Position the insertion point on any character in the title *Technology Information Questions*.
   b. Click the Borders button arrow and then click *No Border* at the drop-down list.
   c. Click the Borders button arrow and then click *Bottom Border* at the drop-down list.
   d. Click the Shading button arrow and then click the *Purple, Accent 4, Lighter 60%* option.
2. Apply the same formatting to the other titles by completing the following steps:
   a. With the insertion point positioned on any character in the title *Technology Information Questions*, double-click the Format Painter button in the Clipboard group.
   b. Select the title *Technology Timeline: Computers in the Workplace*.
   c. Select the title *Technology Career Questions*.
   d. Click the Format Painter button in the Clipboard group.
3. Remove the paragraph border and apply shading to paragraphs by completing the following steps:
   a. Select the numbered paragraphs of text below the *Technology Information Questions* title.
   b. Click the Borders button arrow and then click *No Border* at the drop-down list.
   c. Click the Shading button arrow and then click the *Purple, Accent 4, Lighter 80%* option.

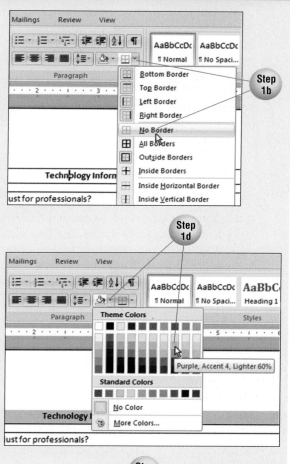

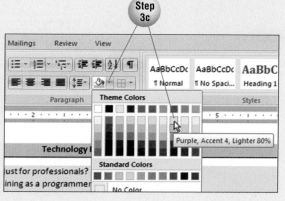

4. Select the bulleted paragraphs of text below the *Technology Timeline: Computers in the Workplace* title, click the Borders button, and then click the Shading button. (Clicking the Borders button will apply the previous border option, which was no border. Clicking the Shading button will apply the previous shading option, which was *Purple, Accent 4, Lighter 80%*.)
5. Select the numbered paragraphs of text below the *Technology Career Questions* title, click the Borders button, and then click the Shading button.
6. Save, print, and then close **WordL1_C3_P1.docx**.

## Project ② Customize a Document on Online Shopping

**You will open a document containing information on online shopping, apply and customize borders and shading, and then sort text in the document.**

## Customizing Borders and Shading

If you want to further customize paragraph borders and shading, use options at the Borders and Shading dialog box. Click the Borders tab and options display for customizing the border; click the Shading tab and shading options display. As you learned in a previous section, you can add borders to a paragraph with the Borders button in the Paragraph group. If you want to further customize borders, use options at the Borders and Shading dialog box with the Borders tab selected as shown in Figure 3.8. Display this dialog box by clicking the Borders button arrow and then clicking *Borders and Shading* at the drop-down list. At the Borders and Shading dialog box, specify the desired border, style, color, and width. Click the Shading tab and the dialog box displays with shading options as shown in Figure 3.9.

**Figure 3.8** Borders and Shading Dialog Box with the Borders Tab Selected

Click the sides, top, or bottom of this preview area to insert or remove a border.

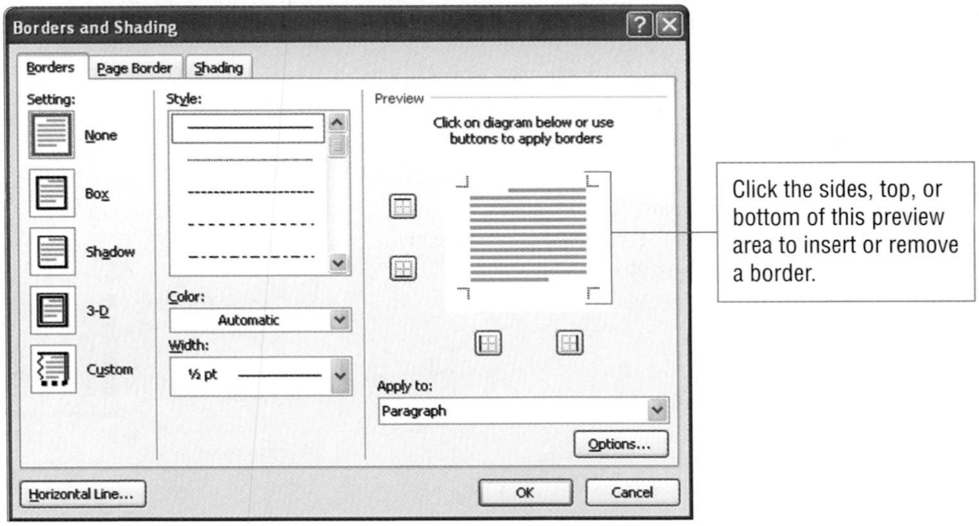

**Figure 3.9** Borders and Shading Dialog Box with the Shading Tab Selected

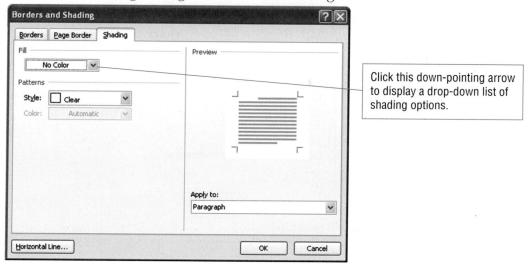

Click this down-pointing arrow to display a drop-down list of shading options.

## Project 2a  Adding Customized Border and Shading to a Document

1. Open **WordDocument13.docx**.
2. Save the document with Save As and name it
   **WordL1_C3_P2**.
3. Make the following changes to the document:
   a. Insert 12 points of space before and 6 points
      of space after the headings *Online Shopping,
      Advantages of Online Shopping, Online Shopping
      Venues, Online Shopping Safety Tips*, and
      *REFERENCES*. (Do this with the *Spacing
      Before* and *Spacing After* measurement boxes in
      the Page Layout tab.)
   b. Center the *REFERENCES* title.
4. Insert a custom border and add shading to a
   heading by completing the following steps:
   a. Move the insertion point to any character in
      the heading *Online Shopping*.
   b. Click the Borders button arrow and then click
      *Borders and Shading* at the drop-down list.
   c. At the Borders and Shading dialog box with
      the Borders tab selected, click the down-
      pointing arrow at the right side of the *Color*
      option box and then click the *Dark Blue* color
      in the *Standard Colors* section.

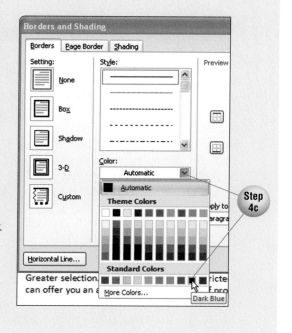

Step 4c

d. Click the down-pointing arrow at the right of the *Width* option box and then click *1 pt* at the drop-down list.

e. Click the top border of the box in the *Preview* section of the dialog box.

f. Click the down scroll arrow in the *Style* list box and then click the first thick/thin line.

g. Click the down-pointing arrow at the right side of the *Color* option box and then click the *Dark Blue* color in the *Standard Colors* section.

h. Click the bottom border of the box in the *Preview* section of the dialog box.

i. Click the Shading tab.

j. Click the down-pointing arrow at the right side of the *Fill* option box and then click *Olive Green, Accent 3, Lighter 60%*.

k. Click OK to close the dialog box.

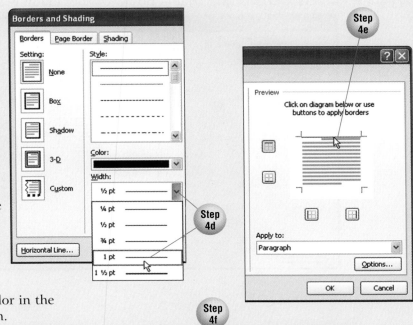

Step 4e

Step 4d

5. Use Format Painter to apply the same border and shading formatting to the remaining headings by completing the following steps:

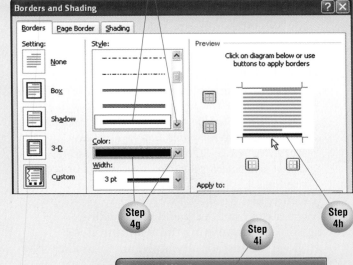

Step 4f

Step 4g

Step 4h

Step 4i

a. Position the insertion point on any character in the heading *Online Shopping*.

b. Double-click the Format Painter button in the Clipboard group in the Home tab.

c. Select the heading *Advantages of Online Shopping*.

d. Select the heading *Online Shopping Venues*.

e. Select the heading *Online Shopping Safety Tips*.

f. Click the Format Painter button once.

6. Move the insertion point to any character in the heading *Online Shopping* and then remove the 12 points of spacing above.

7. Save **WordL1_C3_P2.docx**.

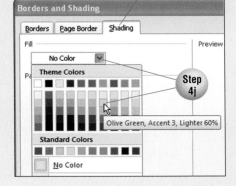

Step 4j

# Sorting Text in Paragraphs

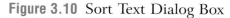

You can sort text arranged in paragraphs alphabetically by the first character. This character can be a number, symbol (such as $ or #), or letter. Type paragraphs you want to sort at the left margin or indented to a tab stop. Unless you select specific paragraphs for sorting, Word sorts the entire document.

To sort text in paragraphs, open the document. If the document contains text you do not want sorted, select the specific paragraphs. Click the Sort button in the Paragraph group and the Sort Text dialog box displays as shown in Figure 3.10. At this dialog box, click OK. If you select text and then display the dialog box the *Sort by* option is set at *Paragraph*. If the text you select is numbers, then *Numbers* displays in the Sort Text dialog box.

**Sort Paragraphs of Text**
1. Click Sort button.
2. Make any needed changes at Sort Text dialog box.
3. Click OK.

Sort

**Figure 3.10** Sort Text Dialog Box

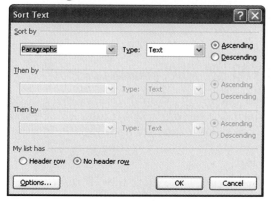

---

## Project  Sorting Paragraphs Alphabetically

1. With **WordL1_C3_P2.docx** open, sort the bulleted text alphabetically by completing the following steps:
   a. Select the bulleted paragraphs in the *Advantages of Online Shopping* section.
   b. Click the Sort button in the Paragraph group.
   c. At the Sort Text dialog box, make sure *Paragraphs* displays in the *Sort by* option box and the *Ascending* option is selected.
   d. Click OK.

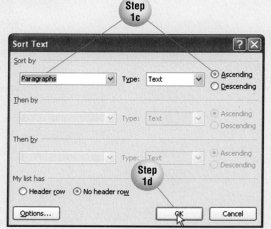

word Level 1

Customizing Paragraphs **81**

2. Sort the numbered paragraphs by completing the following steps:
   a. Select the numbered paragraphs in the *Online Shopping Safety Tips* section.
   b. Click the Sort button in the Paragraph group.
   c. Click OK at the Sort Text dialog box.
3. Follow steps similar to those in Step 1 or Step 2 to sort alphabetically the three paragraphs of text below the *REFERENCES* title.
4. Save, print, and then close **WordL1_C3_P2.docx**.

P roject ③ **Prepare a Document on Workshops and Training Dates**

**You will set and move tabs on the Ruler and at the Tabs dialog box and type tabbed text about workshops, training dates, and a table of contents.**

# Manipulating Tabs on the Ruler

When you work with a document, Word offers a variety of default settings such as margins and line spacing. One of these defaults is a left tab set every 0.5 inch. In some situations, these default tabs are appropriate; in others, you may want to create your own. Two methods exist for setting tabs. Tabs can be set on the Ruler or at the Tabs dialog box.

Use the Ruler to set, move, and delete tabs. If the Ruler is not visible, click the View Ruler button located at the top of the vertical scroll bar. The Ruler displays left tabs set every 0.5 inch. These default tabs are indicated by tiny vertical lines along the bottom of the Ruler. With a left tab, text aligns at the left edge of the tab. The other types of tabs that can be set on the Ruler are center, right, decimal, and bar. Use the Alignment button that displays at the left side of the Ruler to specify tabs. Each time you click the Alignment button, a different tab or paragraph alignment symbol displays. Table 3.1 shows the tab alignment button and what type of tab each will set.

**Table 3.1** Tab Alignment Symbols

| Alignment Button | Type of Tab |
|---|---|
| L | Left tab |
| ⊥ | Center tab |
| ⌐ | Right tab |
| ⊥ | Decimal tab |
| I | Bar tab |

# Setting Tabs

To set a left tab on the Ruler, make sure the left alignment symbol (see Table 3.1) displays in the Alignment button. Position the arrow pointer just below the tick mark (the marks on the Ruler) where you want the tab symbol to appear and then click the left mouse button. When you set a tab on the Ruler, any default tabs to the left are automatically deleted by Word. Set a center, right, decimal, or bar tab on the Ruler in a similar manner.

Before setting a tab on the Ruler, click the Alignment button at the left side of the Ruler until the appropriate tab symbol displays and then set the tab. If you change the tab symbol in the Alignment button, the symbol remains until you change it again or you exit Word. If you exit and then reenter Word, the tab symbol returns to the default of left tab.

If you want to set a tab at a specific measurement on the Ruler, hold down the Alt key, position the arrow pointer at the desired position, and then hold down the left mouse button. This displays two measurements on the Ruler. The first measurement displays the location of the arrow pointer on the Ruler in relation to the left margin. The second measurement is the distance from the location of the arrow pointer on the Ruler to the right margin. With the left mouse button held down, position the tab symbol at the desired location and then release the mouse button and the Alt key.

If you change tab settings and then create columns of text using the New Line command, Shift + Enter, the tab formatting is stored in the paragraph mark at the end of the columns. If you want to make changes to the tab settings for text in the columns, position the insertion point anywhere within the columns (all of the text in the columns does not have to be selected) and then make the changes.

**QUICK STEPS**

**Set Tabs on Ruler**
1. Click Alignment button on Ruler.
2. Click desired location on Ruler.

**HINT**
When setting tabs on the ruler, a dotted guideline displays to help align tabs.

**HINT**
Position the insertion point in any paragraph of text, and tabs for the paragraph appear on the Ruler.

## Project 3a — Setting Left, Center, and Right Tabs on the Ruler

1. At a new blank document, type WORKSHOPS centered and bolded as shown in Figure 3.11.
2. Press the Enter key and then return the paragraph alignment back to left and turn off bold.
3. Set a left tab at the 0.5-inch mark, a center tab at the 3.25-inch mark, and a right tab at the 6-inch mark by completing the following steps:
   a. Click the Show/Hide ¶ button in the Paragraph group in the Home tab to turn on the display of nonprinting characters.
   b. Make sure the Ruler is displayed. (If not, click the View Ruler button located at the top of the vertical scroll bar.)
   c. Make sure the left tab symbol displays in the Alignment button at the left side of the Ruler.
   d. Position the arrow pointer on the 0.5-inch mark on the Ruler and then click the left mouse button.

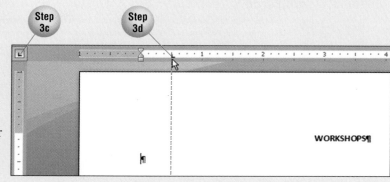

e. Position the arrow pointer on the Alignment button at the left side of the Ruler and then click the left mouse button until the center tab symbol displays (see Table 3.1).

f. Position the arrow pointer below the 3.25-inch mark on the Ruler. Hold down the Alt key and then the left mouse button. Make sure the first measurement on the Ruler displays as *3.25"* and then release the mouse button and the Alt key.

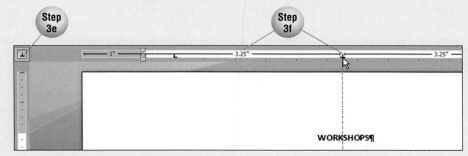

g. Position the arrow pointer on the Alignment button at the left side of the Ruler and then click the left mouse button until the right tab symbol displays (see Table 3.1).

h. Position the arrow pointer below the 6-inch mark on the Ruler. Hold down the Alt key and then the left mouse button. Make sure the first measurement on the Ruler displays as *6"* and then release the mouse button and the Alt key.

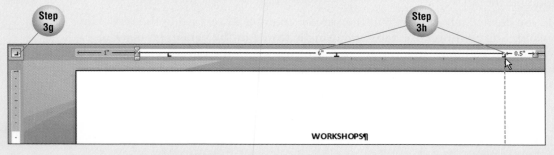

4. Type the text in columns as shown in Figure 3.11. Press the Tab key before typing each column entry and press Shift + Enter after typing the text in the third column.

5. After typing the last column entry, press the Enter key twice.

6. Press Ctrl + Q to remove paragraph formatting (tab settings).

7. Click the Show/Hide ¶ button to turn off the display of nonprinting characters.

8. Save the document and name it **WordL1_C3_P3**.

**Figure 3.11 Project 3a**

WORKSHOPS

| Title | Price | Date |
|---|---|---|
| Quality Management | $240 | Friday, February 5 |
| Staff Development | 229 | Friday, February 12 |
| Streamlining Production | 175 | Monday, March 1 |
| Managing Records | 150 | Tuesday, March 23 |
| Customer Service Training | 150 | Thursday, March 25 |
| Sales Techniques | 125 | Tuesday, April 6 |

## Moving Tabs

After a tab has been set on the Ruler, it can be moved to a new location. To move a tab, position the arrow pointer on the tab symbol on the Ruler, hold down the left mouse button, drag the symbol to the new location on the Ruler, and then release the mouse button.

## Deleting Tabs

To delete a tab from the Ruler, position the arrow pointer on the tab symbol you want deleted, hold down the left mouse button, drag the symbol down into the document, and then release the mouse button.

### Project 3b — Moving Tabs

1. With **WordL1_C3_P3.docx** open, position the insertion point on any character in the first entry in the tabbed text.
2. Position the arrow pointer on the left tab symbol at the 0.5-inch mark, hold down the left mouse button, drag the left tab symbol to the 1-inch mark on the Ruler, and then release the mouse button. ***Hint: Use the Alt key to help you precisely position the tab symbol.***

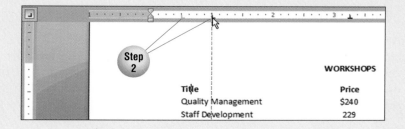

3. Position the arrow pointer on the right tab symbol at the 6-inch mark, hold down the left mouse button, drag the right tab symbol to the 5.5-inch mark on the Ruler, and then release the mouse button. ***Hint: Use the Alt key to help you precisely position the tab symbol.***
4. Save **WordL1_C3_P3.docx**.

## Manipulating Tabs at the Tabs Dialog Box

Use the Tabs dialog box shown in Figure 3.12 to set tabs at a specific measurement. You can also use the Tabs dialog box to set tabs with preceding leaders and clear one tab or all tabs. To display the Tabs dialog box, click the Paragraph group dialog box launcher. At the Paragraph dialog box, click the Tabs button located in the bottom left corner of the dialog box.

**Set Tabs at Tabs Dialog Box**
1. Click Paragraph group dialog box launcher.
2. Click Tabs button.
3. Specify tab positions, alignments, and leader options.
4. Click OK.

**Figure 3.12** Tabs Dialog Box

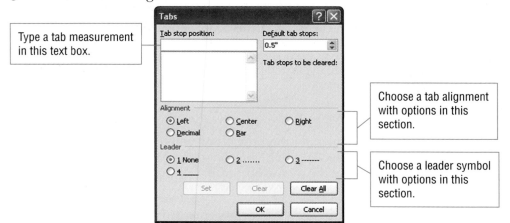

Type a tab measurement in this text box.

Choose a tab alignment with options in this section.

Choose a leader symbol with options in this section.

## Clearing Tabs

At the Tabs dialog box, you can clear an individual tab or all tabs. To clear all tabs, click the Clear All button. To clear an individual tab, specify the tab position, and then click the Clear button.

## Setting Tabs

At the Tabs dialog box, you can set a left, right, center, or decimal tab as well as a bar. (For an example of a bar tab, refer to Figure 3.13.) You can also set a left, right, center, or decimal tab with preceding leaders. To change the type of tab at the Tabs dialog box, display the dialog box and then click the desired tab in the Alignment section. Type the desired measurement for the tab in the *Tab stop position* text box.

## Project ③C   Setting Left Tabs and a Bar Tab at the Tabs Dialog Box

1. With **WordL1_C3_P3.docx** open, press Ctrl + End to move the insertion point to the end of the document.
2. Type the title TRAINING DATES bolded and centered as shown in Figure 3.13, press the Enter key, return the paragraph alignment back to left, and then turn off bold.
3. Display the Tabs dialog box and then set left tabs and a bar tab by completing the following steps:
   a. Click the Paragraph group dialog box launcher.
   b. At the Paragraph dialog box, click the Tabs button located in the lower left corner of the dialog box.
   c. Make sure *Left* is selected in the *Alignment* section of the dialog box.
   d. Type 1.75 in the *Tab stop position* text box.
   e. Click the Set button.
   f. Type 4 in the *Tab stop position* text box and then click the Set button.
   g. Type 3.25 in the *Tab stop position* text box, click *Bar* in the *Alignment* section, and then click the Set button.
   h. Click OK to close the Tabs dialog box.

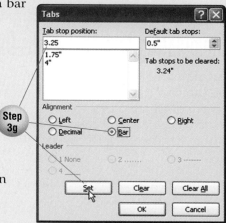

Step 3g

4. Type the text in columns as shown in Figure 3.13. Press the Tab key before typing each column entry and press Shift + Enter to end each line.
5. After typing *February 23*, complete the following steps:
   a. Press the Enter key.
   b. Clear tabs by displaying the Tabs dialog box, clicking the Clear All button, and then clicking OK.
   c. Press the Enter key.
6. Remove the 10 points of spacing after the last entry in the text by completing the following steps:
   a. Position the insertion point on any character in the *January 18* entry.
   b. Click the Page Layout tab.
   c. Click twice on the down-pointing arrow at the right side of the *Spacing After* measurement box. (This changes the measurement to *0 pt*.)
7. Save **WordL1_C3_P3.docx**.

**Figure 3.13  Project 3c**

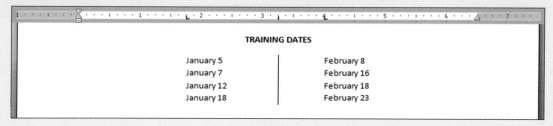

## Setting Leader Tabs

The four types of tabs can also be set with leaders. Leaders are useful in a table of contents or other material where you want to direct the reader's eyes across the page. Figure 3.14 shows an example of leaders. Leaders can be periods (.), hyphens (-), or underlines (_). To add leaders to a tab, click the type of leader desired in the *Leader* section of the Tabs dialog box.

Project **3d**  Setting a Left Tab and a Right Tab with Dot Leaders

1. With **WordL1_C3_P3.docx** open, press Ctrl + End to move the insertion point to the end of the document.
2. Type the title TABLE OF CONTENTS bolded and centered as shown in Figure 3.14.
3. Press the Enter key and then return the paragraph alignment back to left and turn off bold.
4. Set a left tab and a right tab with dot leaders by completing the following steps:
   a. Click the Paragraph group dialog box launcher.
   b. Click the Tabs button located in the lower left corner of the Paragraph dialog box.
   c. At the Tabs dialog box, make sure *Left* is selected in the *Alignment* section of the dialog box.
   d. With the insertion point positioned in the *Tab stop position* text box, type 1 and then click the Set button.

e. Type 5.5 in the *Tab stop position* text box.
f. Click *Right* in the *Alignment* section of the dialog box.
g. Click *2 ......* in the *Leader* section of the dialog box and then click the Set button.
h. Click OK to close the dialog box.
5. Type the text in columns as shown in Figure 3.14. Press the Tab key before typing each column entry and press Shift + Enter to end each line.
6. Save, print, and then close **WordL1_C3_P3.docx**.

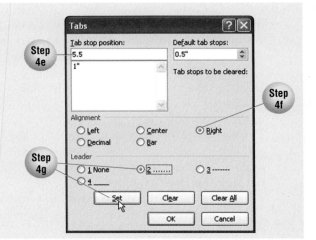

**Figure 3.14  Project 3d**

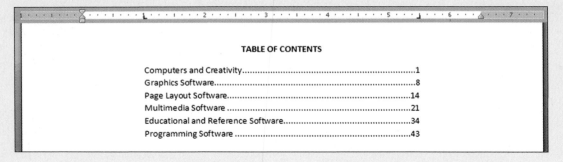

# Project ④ Move and Copy Text in a Document on Online Shopping Tips

You will open a document containing information on online shopping safety tips and then cut, copy, and paste text in the document.

## Cutting, Copying, and Pasting Text

When editing a document, you may need to delete specific text, move text to a different location in the document, and/or copy text to various locations in the document. You can complete these activities using buttons in the Clipboard group in the Home tab.

### Deleting Selected Text

Cut

Word offers different methods for deleting text from a document. To delete a single character, you can use either the Delete key or the Backspace key. To delete more than a single character, select the text, and then press the Delete key on the keyboard or click the Cut button in the Clipboard group. If you press the Delete key, the text is deleted permanently. (You can restore deleted text with the Undo button on the Quick Access toolbar.) The Cut button in the Clipboard group will remove the selected text from the document and insert it in the **Clipboard**. Word's Clipboard is a temporary area of memory. The Clipboard holds text while it is being moved or copied to a new location in the document or to a different document.

**HINT**

The Clipboard contents are deleted when the computer is turned off. Text you want to save permanently should be saved as a separate document.

## Cutting and Pasting Text

To move text to a different location in the document, select the text, click the Cut button in the Clipboard group, position the insertion point at the location where you want the text inserted, and then click the Paste button in the Clipboard group.

Paste

You can also move selected text with a shortcut menu. To do this, select the text and then position the insertion point inside the selected text until it turns into an arrow pointer. Click the *right* mouse button and then click *Cut* at the shortcut menu. Position the insertion point where you want the text inserted, click the *right* mouse button, and then click *Paste* at the shortcut menu. Keyboard shortcuts are also available for cutting and pasting text. Use Ctrl + X to cut text and Ctrl + V to insert text.

**QUICK STEPS**

**Move Selected Text**
1. Select text.
2. Click Cut button.
3. Move to desired location.
4. Click Paste button.

When selected text is cut from a document and inserted in the Clipboard, it stays in the Clipboard until other text is inserted in the Clipboard. For this reason, you can paste text from the Clipboard more than just once. For example, if you cut text to the Clipboard, you can paste this text in different locations within the document or other documents as many times as desired.

Project **4a**   **Moving Selected Text**

1. Open **WordDocument10.docx**.
2. Save the document with Save As and name it **WordL1_C3_P4**.
3. Move a paragraph by completing the following steps:
   a. Select the paragraph that begins with *Only buy at secure sites.* including the blank line below the paragraph.
   b. Click the Cut button in the Clipboard group in the Home tab.
   c. Position the insertion point at the beginning of the paragraph that begins with *Look for sites that follow ... .*
   d. Click the Paste button in the Clipboard group. (If the first and second paragraphs are not separated by a blank line, press the Enter key once.)
4. Following steps similar to those in Step 3, move the paragraph that begins with *Never provide your social security number.* so it is positioned before the paragraph that begins *Look for sites that follow privacy ...* and after the paragraph that begins *Only buy at secure sites.*.
5. Save **WordL1_C3_P4.docx**.

# Moving Text by Dragging with the Mouse

You can also use the mouse to move text. To do this, select text to be moved and then position the I-beam pointer inside the selected text until it turns into an arrow pointer. Hold down the left mouse button, drag the arrow pointer (displays with a gray box attached) to the location where you want the selected text inserted, and then release the button. If you drag and then drop selected text in the wrong location, immediately click the Undo button.

## Project 4b  Moving Text by Dragging with the Mouse

1. With **WordL1_C3_P4.docx** open, use the mouse to select the paragraph that begins with *Keep current with the latest Internet scams.* including the blank line below the paragraph.
2. Move the I-beam pointer inside the selected text until it becomes an arrow pointer.
3. Hold down the left mouse button, drag the arrow pointer (displays with a small gray box attached) so that the insertion point, which displays as a grayed vertical bar, is positioned at the beginning of the paragraph that begins with *Never provide your social security number.*, and then release the mouse button.

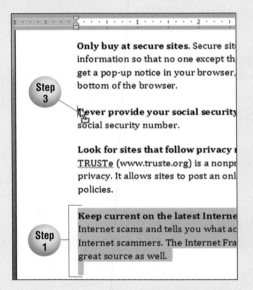

4. Deselect the text.
5. Save **WordL1_C3_P4.docx**.

# Using the Paste Options Button

Paste Options

When selected text is pasted, the Paste Options button displays in the lower right corner of the text. Click this button and a drop-down list displays as shown in Figure 3.15. Use options from this drop-down list to specify how you want information pasted in the document. By default, pasted text retains the formatting of the selected text. You can choose to match the formatting of the pasted text with the formatting where the text is pasted, paste only the text without retaining formatting, or apply a style to pasted text.

**Figure 3.15** Paste Options Button Drop-down List

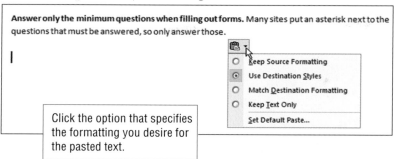

Click the option that specifies the formatting you desire for the pasted text.

## Project ④C  Using the Paste Options Button

1. With **WordL1_C3_P4.docx** open, open **WordParagraph01.docx**.
2. Select the paragraph of text in the document including the blank line below the paragraph and then click the Copy button in the Clipboard group.
3. Close **WordParagraph01.docx**.
4. Move the insertion point to the end of the document.
5. Click the Paste button in the Clipboard group.
6. Click the Paste Options button that displays at the end of the paragraph and then click the *Match Destination Formatting* option. (This changes the font so it matches the formatting of the other paragraphs in the document.)

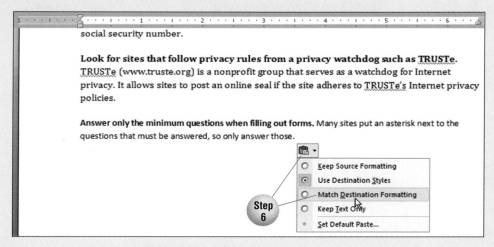

7. Save, print, and then close **WordL1_C3_P4.docx**.

roject **5** **Copy Text in a Staff Meeting Announcement**

You will copy and paste text in a document announcing a staff meeting for the Technical Support Team.

## Copying and Pasting Text

**Copy Selected Text**
1. Select text.
2. Click Copy button.
3. Move to desired location.
4. Click Paste button.

Copy

Copying selected text can be useful in documents that contain repetitive portions of text. You can use this function to insert duplicate portions of text in a document instead of retyping the text. After you have selected text, copy the text to a different location with the Copy and Paste buttons in the Clipboard group in the Home tab or using the mouse. You can also use the keyboard shortcut, Ctrl + C, to copy text.

To use the mouse to copy text, select the text and then position the I-beam pointer inside the selected text until it becomes an arrow pointer. Hold down the left mouse button and hold down the Ctrl key. Drag the arrow pointer (displays with a small gray box and a box containing a plus symbol) to the location where you want the copied text inserted (make sure the insertion point, which displays as a grayed vertical bar, is positioned in the desired location) and then release the mouse button and then the Ctrl key.

## Project **5a**    Copying Text

1. Open **WordBlock01.docx**.
2. Save the document with Save As and name it **WordL1_C3_P5**.
3. Copy the text in the document to the end of the document by completing the following steps:
   a. Select all of the text in the document and include one blank line below the text. ***Hint: Click the Show/Hide ¶ button to turn on the display of nonprinting characters. When you select the text, select one of the paragraph markers below the text.***
   b. Click the Copy button in the Clipboard group.
   c. Move the insertion point to the end of the document.
   d. Click the Paste button in the Clipboard group.
4. Copy the text again at the end of the document. To do this, position the insertion point at the end of the document, and then click the Paste button in the Clipboard group. (This inserts a copy of the text from the Clipboard.)
5. Save **WordL1_C3_P5.docx**.

1. With **WordL1_C3_P5.docx** open, select all of the text in the document using the mouse and include one blank line below the text. (Consider turning on the display of nonprinting characters.)
2. Move the I-beam pointer inside the selected text until it becomes an arrow pointer.
3. Hold down the Ctrl key and then the left mouse button. Drag the arrow pointer (displays with a box with a plus symbol inside) to the end of the document, release the mouse button, and then release the Ctrl key.

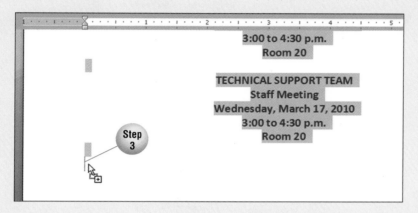

3:00 to 4:30 p.m.
Room 20

TECHNICAL SUPPORT TEAM
Staff Meeting
Wednesday, March 17, 2010
3:00 to 4:30 p.m.
Room 20

Step 3

4. Deselect the text.
5. Make sure all text fits on one page. If not, consider deleting any extra blank lines.
6. Save, print, and then close **WordL1_C3_P5.docx**.

# Project ⑥ Create a Contract Negotiations Document

You will use the Clipboard to copy and paste paragraphs to and from paragraphs in separate documents to create a contract negotiations document. You will also use the Paste Special dialog box to paste text in the contract negotiation document as unformatted text.

# Using the Clipboard

Use the Clipboard to collect and paste multiple items. You can collect up to 24 different items and then paste them in various locations. To display the Clipboard task pane, click the Clipboard group dialog box launcher located in the lower right corner of the Clipboard group. The Clipboard task pane displays at the left side of the screen in a manner similar to what you see in Figure 3.16.

**QUICK STEPS**

**Use Clipboard**
1. Click Clipboard group dialog box launcher.
2. Select and copy desired text.
3. Move to desired location.
4. Click desired option in Clipboard task pane.

**Figure 3.16** Clipboard Task Pane

Click this button to paste all of the Clipboard items into the document.

Click this button to clear all items from the Clipboard.

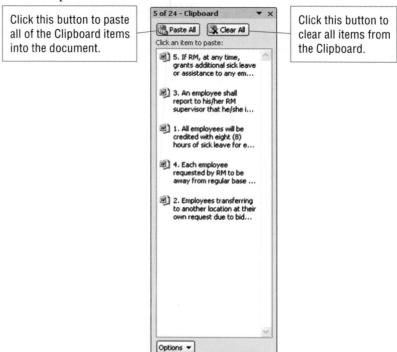

Select text or an object you want to copy and then click the Copy button in the Clipboard group. Continue selecting text or items and clicking the Copy button. To insert an item, position the insertion point in the desired location and then click the option in the Clipboard task pane representing the item. Click the Paste All button to paste all of the items in the Clipboard into the document. If the copied item is text, the first 50 characters display beside the button on the Clipboard task pane. When all desired items are inserted, click the Clear All button to remove any remaining items.

Project 6a **Collecting and Pasting Paragraphs of Text**

1. Open **WordContItems01.docx**.
2. Turn on the display of the Clipboard task pane by clicking the Clipboard group dialog box launcher. (If the Clipboard task pane list box contains any text, click the Clear All button located toward the top of the task pane.)
3. Select paragraph 1 in the document (the 1. is not selected) and then click the Copy button in the Clipboard group.
4. Select paragraph 3 in the document (the 3. is not selected) and then click the Copy button in the Clipboard group.
5. Close **WordContItems01.docx**.

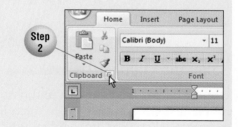

6. Paste the paragraphs by completing the following steps:
   a. Press Ctrl + N to display a new blank document. (If the Clipboard task pane does not display, click the Clipboard group dialog box launcher.)
   b. Type CONTRACT NEGOTIATION ITEMS centered and bolded.
   c. Press the Enter key, turn off bold, and return the paragraph alignment back to left.
   d. Click the Paste All button in the Clipboard task pane to paste both paragraphs in the document.
   e. Click the Clear All button in the Clipboard task pane.

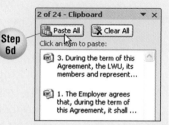

7. Open **WordContract01.docx**.
8. Select and then copy each of the following paragraphs:
   a. Paragraph 2 in the *Transfers and Moving Expenses* section.
   b. Paragraph 4 in the *Transfers and Moving Expenses* section.
   c. Paragraph 1 in the *Sick Leave* section.
   d. Paragraph 3 in the *Sick Leave* section.
   e. Paragraph 5 in the *Sick Leave* section.
9. Close **WordContract01.docx**.
10. Make sure the insertion point is positioned at the end of the document and then paste the paragraphs by completing the following steps:
    a. Click the button in the Clipboard task pane representing paragraph 2. (When the paragraph is inserted in the document, the paragraph number changes to 3.)
    b. Click the button in the Clipboard task pane representing paragraph 4.
    c. Click the button in the Clipboard task pane representing paragraph 3.
    d. Click the button in the Clipboard task pane representing paragraph 5.

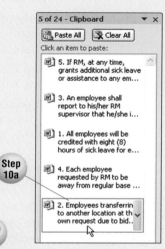

11. Click the Clear All button located toward the top of the Clipboard task pane.
12. Close the Clipboard task pane.
13. Save the document and name it **WordL1_C3_P6**.
14. Print and then close **WordL1_C3_P6.docx**.

# CHAPTER summary

- Number paragraphs with the Numbering button in the Paragraph group in the Home tab and insert bullets before paragraphs with the Bullets button.
- Remove all paragraph formatting from a paragraph by pressing the keyboard shortcut, Ctrl + Q, and remove all character and paragraph formatting by clicking the Clear Formatting button in the Font group.
- The AutoCorrect Options button displays when the AutoFormat feature inserts numbers. Click this button to display options for undoing and/or stopping automatic numbering.
- Bulleted lists with hanging indents are automatically created when a paragraph begins with *, >, or -. The type of bullet inserted depends on the type of character entered.
- You can turn off automatic numbering and bullets at the AutoCorrect dialog box with the AutoFormat As You Type tab selected.
- A paragraph created in Word contains an invisible frame and you can insert a border around this frame. Click the Border button arrow to display a drop-down list of border choices.
- Apply shading to text by clicking the Shading button arrow and then clicking the desired color at the drop-down gallery.
- Use options at the Borders and Shading dialog box with the Borders tab selected to add a customized border to a paragraph or selected paragraphs and use options with Shading tab selected to add shading or a pattern to a paragraph or selected paragraphs.
- With the Sort button in the Paragraph group in the Home tab, you can sort text arranged in paragraphs alphabetically by the first character, which includes numbers, symbols, or letters.
- By default, tabs are set every 0.5 inch. These settings can be changed on the Ruler or at the Tabs dialog box.
- Use the Alignment button at the left side of the Ruler to select a left, right, center, or decimal tab. When you set a tab on the Ruler, any default tabs to the left are automatically deleted.
- After a tab has been set on the Ruler, it can be moved or deleted using the mouse pointer.
- At the Tabs dialog box, you can set any of the four types of tabs as well as a bar tab at a specific measurement. You can also set tabs with preceding leaders and clear one tab or all tabs. Preceding leaders can be periods, hyphens, or underlines.
- Cut, copy, and paste text using buttons in the Clipboard group or with keyboard shortcuts.
- When selected text is pasted, the Paste Options button displays in the lower right corner of the text with options for specifying how you want information pasted in the document.
- With the Office Clipboard, you can collect up to 24 items and then paste them in various locations in a document.

# COMMANDS review

| FEATURE | RIBBON TAB, GROUP | BUTTON, OPTION | KEYBOARD SHORTCUT |
|---|---|---|---|
| Borders | Home, Paragraph | | |
| Borders and Shading dialog box | Home, Paragraph | , Borders and Shading | |
| Bullets | Home, Paragraph | | |
| Clear character and paragraph formatting | Home, Font | | |
| Clear paragraph formatting | | | Ctrl + Q |
| Clipboard task pane | Home, Clipboard | | |
| Copy text | Home, Clipboard | | Ctrl + C |
| Cut text | Home, Clipboard | | Ctrl + X |
| New Line command | | | Shift + Enter |
| Numbering | Home, Paragraph | | |
| Paragraph dialog box | Home, Paragraph | | |
| Paste text | Home, Clipboard | | Ctrl + V |
| Shading | Home, Paragraph | | |
| Sort Text dialog box | Home, Paragraph | | |
| Tabs dialog box | Home, Paragraph | , Tabs | |

# CONCEPTS check

## Test Your Knowledge

**Completion:** In the space provided at the right, indicate the correct term, symbol, or command.

1. The Numbering button is located in this group in the Home tab. _____

2. Automate the creation of bulleted paragraphs with this button in the Home tab. _____

3. This button displays when the AutoFormat feature inserts numbers. _____

4. You can turn off automatic numbering and bullets at the AutoCorrect dialog box with this tab selected.

        _____

5. Bulleted lists with hanging indents are automatically created when you begin a paragraph with the asterisk symbol (*), the hyphen (-), or this symbol.

        _____

6. The Borders button is located in this group in the Home tab.

        _____

7. Use options at this dialog box with the Borders tab selected to add a customized border to a paragraph or selected paragraphs.

        _____

8. Sort text arranged in paragraphs alphabetically by the first character, which includes numbers, symbols, or this.

        _____

9. By default, each tab is set apart from the other by this measurement.

        _____

10. This is the default tab type.

        _____

11. When setting tabs on the Ruler, choose the tab type with this button.

        _____

12. Tabs can be set on the Ruler or here.

        _____

13. This group in the Home tab contains the Cut, Copy, and Paste buttons.

        _____

14. To copy selected text with the mouse, hold down this key while dragging selected text.

        _____

15. With this task pane, you can collect up to 24 items and then paste the items in various locations in the document.

        _____

# SKILLS check

## Demonstrate Your Proficiency

## Assessment

### 1 APPLY PARAGRAPH FORMATTING TO A COMPUTER ETHICS DOCUMENT

1. Open **WordDocument07.docx**.
2. Save the document with Save As and name it **WordL1_C3_A1**.
3. Move the insertion point to the end of the document and then type the text shown in Figure 3.17.
4. Change the Quick Styles set to *Formal*.
5. Apply the Heading 1 style to the three headings in the document.
6. Apply the Paper theme.

7. Select the paragraphs of text in the *Computer Ethics* section and then apply numbering formatting.

8. Select the paragraphs of text in the *Technology Timeline* section and then apply bullet formatting.

9. Insert the following paragraph of text between paragraphs 2 and 3 in the *Computer Ethics* section: Find sources relating to the latest federal and/or state legislation on privacy protection.

10. Apply Blue-Gray, Accent 6, Lighter 60% paragraph shading to the three headings in the document.

11. Apply Blue-Gray, Accent 6, Lighter 80% paragraph shading to the numbered paragraphs in the *Computer Ethics* section and the bulleted paragraphs in the *Technology Timeline* and *ACLU Fair Electronic Monitoring Policy* sections.

12. Save, print, and then close **WordL1_C3_A1.docx**.

**Figure 3.17 Assessment 1**

### ACLU Fair Electronic Monitoring Policy

➢ Notice to employees of the company's electronic monitoring practices

➢ Use of a signal to let an employee know he or she is being monitored

➢ Employee access to all personal data collected through monitoring

➢ No monitoring of areas designed for the health or comfort of employees

➢ The right to dispute and delete inaccurate data

➢ A ban on the collection of data unrelated to work performance

➢ Restrictions on the disclosure of personal data to others without the employee's consent

## Assessment

## 2 TYPE TABBED TEXT AND APPLY FORMATTING TO A COMPUTER SOFTWARE DOCUMENT

1. Open **WordDocument14.docx**.

2. Save the document with Save As and name it **WordL1_C3_A2**.

3. Move the insertion point to the end of the document and then type the tabbed text as shown in Figure 3.18. Before typing the text in columns, set left tabs at the 0.75-inch, 2.75-inch, and 4.5-inch marks on the Ruler.

4. Apply the Heading 1 style to the three headings in the document (*Productivity Software*, *Personal-Use Software*, and *Software Training Schedule*).

5. Change the Quick Styles set to *Distinctive*.

6. Apply the Opulent theme.

7. Select the productivity software categories in the *Productivity Software* section (from *Word processing* through *Computer-aided design*) and then sort the text alphabetically.

8. With the text still selected, apply bullet formatting.

9. Select the personal-use software categories in the *Personal-Use Software* section (from *Personal finance software* through *Games and entertainment software*) and then sort the text alphabetically.

10. With the text still selected, apply bullet formatting.
11. Apply a single-line border to the top and a double-line border to the bottom of the three headings in the document and then apply paragraph shading of your choosing to each heading.
12. Select the text in columns and then move the tab symbols on the Ruler as follows:
    a. Move the tab at the 0.75-inch mark to the 1-inch mark.
    b. Move the tab at the 4.5-inch mark to the 4-inch mark.
13. Save, print, and then close **WordL1_C3_A2.docx**.

**Figure 3.18  Assessment 2**

| Software Training Schedule | | |
|---|---|---|
| Word | April 12 | 8:30 to 11:30 a.m. |
| PowerPoint | April 14 | 1:00 to 3:30 p.m. |
| Excel | May 11 | 8:30 to 11:30 a.m. |
| Access | May 13 | 1:00 to 3:30 p.m. |
| Outlook | May 18 | 8:30 to 11:30 a.m. |
| Vista | May 20 | 1:00 to 3:30 p.m. |

## Assessment

## 3  TYPE AND FORMAT A TABLE OF CONTENTS DOCUMENT

1. At a new blank document, type the document shown in Figure 3.19 with the following specifications:
   a. Change the font to 11-point Cambria.
   b. Bold and center the title as shown.
   c. Before typing the text in columns, display the Tabs dialog box and then set left tabs at the 1-inch mark and the 1.5-inch mark, and a right tab with dot leaders at the 5.5-inch mark.
2. Save the document and name it **WordL1_C3_A3**.
3. Print **WordL1_C3_A3.docx**.
4. Select the text in columns and then move the tab symbols on the Ruler as follows:
   a. Delete the left tab symbol that displays at the 1.5-inch mark.
   b. Set a new left tab at the 0.5-inch mark.
   c. Move the right tab at the 5.5-inch mark to the 6-inch mark.
5. Apply paragraph borders and shading of your choosing to enhance the visual appeal of the document.
6. Save, print, and then close **WordL1_C3_A3.docx**.

**Figure 3.19 Assessment 3**

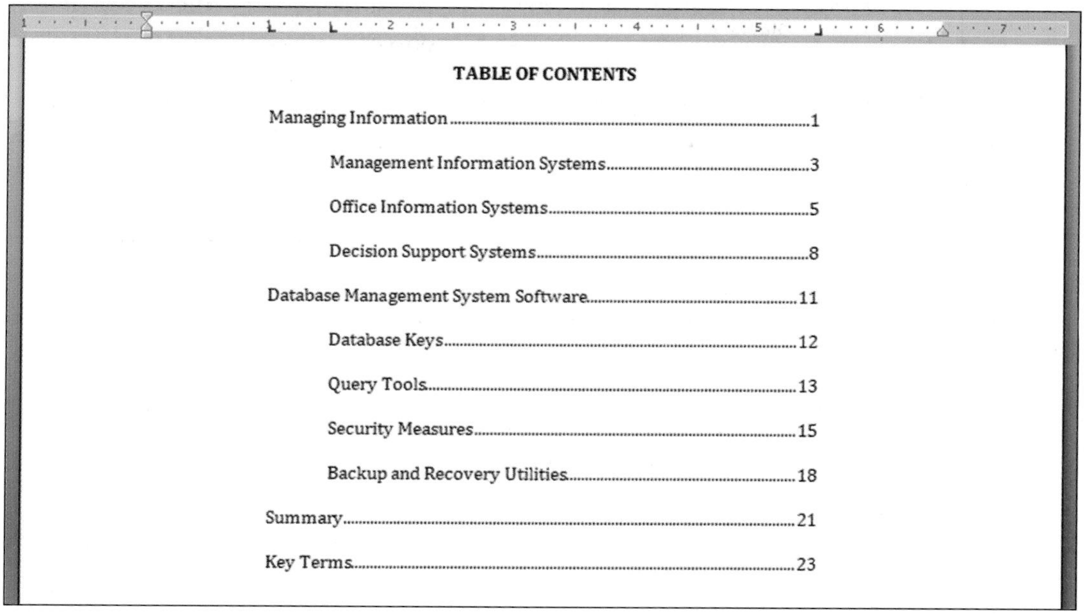

TABLE OF CONTENTS

Managing Information........................................1

Management Information Systems........................................3

Office Information Systems........................................5

Decision Support Systems........................................8

Database Management System Software........................................11

Database Keys........................................12

Query Tools........................................13

Security Measures........................................15

Backup and Recovery Utilities........................................18

Summary........................................21

Key Terms........................................23

## Assessment 4 FORMAT A BUILDING CONSTRUCTION AGREEMENT DOCUMENT

1. Open **WordAgreement02.docx**.
2. Save the document with Save As and name it **WordL1_C3_A4**.
3. Select and then delete the paragraph that begins *Supervision of Work*.
4. Select and then delete the paragraph that begins *Exclusions*.
5. Move the paragraph that begins *Financing Arrangements* above the paragraph that begins *Start of Construction*.
6. Open **WordDocument11.docx**.
7. Turn on the display of the Clipboard.
8. Select and then copy the first paragraph.
9. Select and then copy the second paragraph.
10. Select and then copy the third paragraph.
11. Close **WordDocument11.docx** without saving the changes.
12. With **WordL1_C3_A4.docx** open, paste the *Supervision* paragraph above the *Changes and Alterations* paragraph and match the destination formatting.
13. Paste the *Pay Review* paragraph above the *Possession of Residence* paragraph and match the destination formatting.
14. Clear all items from the Clipboard and then close the Clipboard.
15. Save, print, and then close **WordL1_C3_A4.docx**.

## Assessment 5 HYPHENATE WORDS IN A REPORT

1. In some Word documents, especially documents with left and right margins wider than 1 inch, the right margin may appear quite ragged. If the paragraph alignment is changed to justified, the right margin will appear even, but there

will be extra space added throughout the line. In these situations, hyphenating long words that fall at the end of the text line provides the document with a more balanced look. Use Word's Help feature to learn how to automatically hyphenate words in a document.

2. Open **WordReport01.docx**.
3. Save the document with Save As and name it **WordL1_C3_A5**.
4. Automatically hyphenate words in the document, limiting the consecutive hyphens to 2. ***Hint: Specify the number of consecutive hyphens at the Hyphenation dialog box.***
5. Save, print, and then close **WordL1_C3_A5.docx**.

# CASE study
## *Apply Your Skills*

**Part 1**

You are the assistant to Gina Coletti, manager of La Dolce Vita, an Italian restaurant. She has been working on updating and formatting the lunch menu. She has asked you to complete the menu by opening the **WordMenu.docx** document (located in the Word2007L1C3 folder), determining how the appetizer section is formatted, and then applying the same formatting to the *Soup and Salad*; *Sandwiches, Calzones and Burgers*; and *Individual Pizzas* sections. Save the document and name it **WordL1_C3_CS_P1**. Print and then close the document.

**Part 2**

Ms. Coletti has reviewed the completed menu and is pleased with the menu but wants to add a page border around the entire page to increase visual interest. Open **WordL1_C3_CS_P1.docx** and then save the document and name it **WordL1_C3_CS_P2**. Display the Borders and Shading dialog box with the Page Border tab selected and then experiment with the options available. Apply an appropriate page border to the menu (consider applying an art page border). Save, print, and then close **WordL1_C3_CS_P2.docx**.

**Part 3**

Each week, the restaurant offers daily specials. Ms. Coletti has asked you to open and format the text in the **WordMenuSpecials.docx** document. She has asked you to format the specials menu in a similar manner as the main menu but to make some changes to make it unique from the main menu. Apply the same page border to the specials menu document that you applied to the main menu document. Save the document and name it **WordL1_C3_CS_P3**. Print and then close the document.

**Part 4**

You have been asked by the head chef to research a new recipe for an Italian dish. Using the Internet, find a recipe that interests you and then prepare a Word document containing the recipe and ingredients. Use bullets before each ingredient and use numbering for each step in the recipe preparation. Save the document and name it **WordL1_C3_CS_P4**. Print and then close the document.

# Formatting Pages

## PERFORMANCE OBJECTIVES

Upon successful completion of Chapter 4, you will be able to:

- Change document views
- Navigate in a document with Document Map and Thumbnails
- Change margins, page orientation, and paper size in a document
- Format pages at the Page Setup dialog box
- Insert a page break, blank page, and cover page
- Insert page numbering
- Insert and edit predesigned headers and footers
- Insert a watermark, page color, and page border
- Find and replace text and formatting

**Tutorial 4.1**
Organizing Documents
**Tutorial 4.2**
Enhancing Documents
**Tutorial 4.3**
Searching within a Document

A document generally displays in Print Layout view. You can change this default view with buttons in the View area on the Status bar or with options in the View tab. Use the Document Map and Thumbnails features to navigate in a document. A Word document, by default, contains 1-inch top, bottom, left, and right margins. You can change these default margins with the Margins button in the Page Setup group in the Page Layout tab or with options at the Page Setup dialog box. You can insert a variety of features in a Word document including a page break, blank page, and cover page as well as page numbers, headers, footers, a watermark, page color, and page border. Use options at the Find and Replace dialog box to search for specific text or formatting and replace with other text or formatting.

*Note: Before beginning computer projects, copy to your storage medium the Word2007L1C4 subfolder from the Word2007L1 folder on the CD that accompanies this textbook and then make Word2007L1C4 the active folder.*

roject ❶ **Navigate in a Report on Computer Input and Output Devices**

You will open a document containing information on computer input and output devices, change document views, navigate in the document using Document Map and Thumbnails, and show and hide white space at the top and bottom of pages.

## Changing the View

By default a Word document displays in Print Layout view. This view displays the document on the screen as it will appear when printed. Other views are available such as Draft and Full Screen Reading. Change views with buttons in the View area on the Status bar or with options in the View tab. The buttons in the View area on the Status bar are identified in Figure 4.1. Along with the View buttons, the Status bar also contains a Zoom slider bar as shown in Figure 4.1. Drag the button on the Zoom slider bar to increase or decrease the size of display, or click the Zoom Out button to decrease size and click the Zoom In to increase size.

Figure 4.1 Viewing Buttons and Zoom Slider Bar

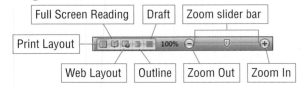

Zoom Out

Zoom In

Draft

Draft

## Displaying a Document in Draft View

Change to Draft view and the document displays in a format for efficient editing and formatting. At this view, margins and other features such as headers and footers do not display on the screen. Change to Draft view by clicking the Draft button in the View section on the Status bar or click the View tab and then click the Draft button in the Document Views group.

## Displaying a Document in Full Screen Reading View

Full Screen Reading

Full Screen Reading

The Full Screen Reading view displays a document in a format for easy viewing and reading. Change to Full Screen Reading view by clicking the Full Screen Reading button in the View section on the Status bar or by clicking the View tab and then clicking the Full Screen Reading button in the Document Views group.

Navigate in Full Screen Reading view using the keys on the keyboard as shown in Table 4.1. You can also navigate in Full Screen Reading view with options from the View Options button that displays toward the top right side of the screen or with the Next Screen and Previous Screen buttons located at the top of the window and also located at the bottom of each page.

You can customize the Full Screen Reading view with some of the options from the View Options drop-down list. Display this list by clicking the View Options button located in the upper right corner of the Full Screen Reading window.

**Table 4.1** Keyboard Commands in Full Screen Reading View

| Press this key | To complete this action |
| --- | --- |
| Page Down key or spacebar | Move to the next page or section |
| Page Up key or Backspace key | Move to the previous page or section |
| Right Arrow key | Move to next page |
| Left Arrow key | Move to previous page |
| Home | Move to first page in document |
| End | Move to last page in document |
| Esc | Return to previous view |

Project 1a    Changing Views

1. Open **WordReport05.docx**.
2. Click the Draft button located in the View section on the Status bar.
3. Using the mouse, drag the Zoom slider bar button to the left to decrease the size of the document display to approximately 60%. (The percentage displays at the left side of the Zoom Out button.)
4. Drag the Zoom slider bar button back to the middle until *100%* displays at the left side of the Zoom Out button.
5. Click the Print Layout button in the View section on the Status bar.
6. Click the Full Screen Reading button located in the View section on the Status bar.
7. Click the View Options button located toward the top of the viewing window and then click *Show Two Pages* at the drop-down list.

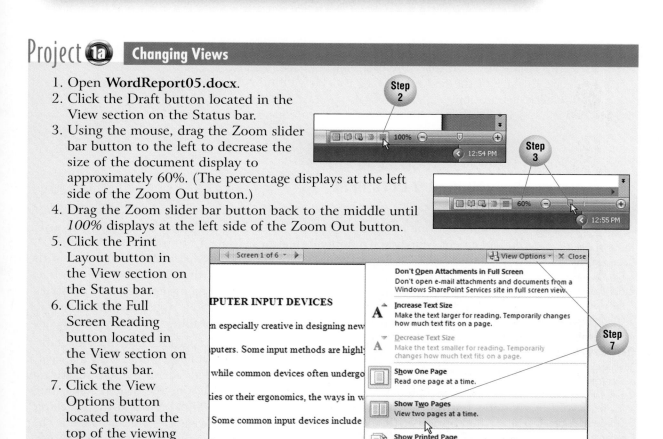

8. Click the Next Screen button to display the next two pages in the viewing window.

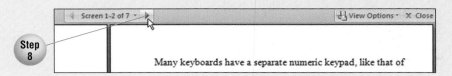

9. Click the Previous Screen button to display the previous two pages.
10. Click the View Options button located toward the top of the viewing window and then click *Show One Page* at the drop-down list.
11. Practice navigating using the actions shown in Table 4.1. (Try all of the actions in Table 4.1 except pressing the Esc key since that action will close Full Screen Reading view.)
12. Increase the size of the text by clicking the View Options button and then clicking the *Increase Text Size* option.

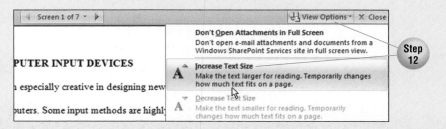

13. Press the Home key to display the first viewing page.
14. Decrease the size of the text by clicking the View Options button and then clicking the *Decrease Text Size* option.
15. Click the Close button located in the upper right corner of the screen.

## Navigating in a Document

**Navigate with Document Map**
1. Click View tab.
2. Click *Document Map* check box.
3. Click desired heading in navigation pane.

**Navigate with Thumbnails**
1. Click View tab.
2. Click *Thumbnails* check box.
3. Click desired thumbnail in navigation pane.

Word includes a number of features you can use to navigate in a document. Along with the navigating features you have already learned, you can also navigate using the Document Map and Thumbnails features. To navigate using the Document Map feature, click the View tab and then click the *Document Map* check box in the Show/Hide group. This displays a navigation pane at the left side of the screen as shown in Figure 4.2. Document Map displays any headings formatted with styles or text that looks like headings, such as short lines set in a larger type size. Navigate to a specific location in the document by clicking the heading in the navigation pane.

To navigate in a document using the Thumbnails feature, click the View tab and then click the Thumbnails check box in the Show/Hide group. This displays a thumbnail of each page in the navigation pane at the left side of the screen. You can switch between Thumbnails and Document Map by clicking the Switch Navigation Window button that displays at the top of the navigation pane and then clicking the desired option at the drop-down list. Close the navigation pane by clicking the *Thumbnails* check box to remove the check mark or by clicking the Close button located in the upper right corner of the pane.

**Figure 4.2** Navigation Pane

Switch Navigation Window button

Navigation pane

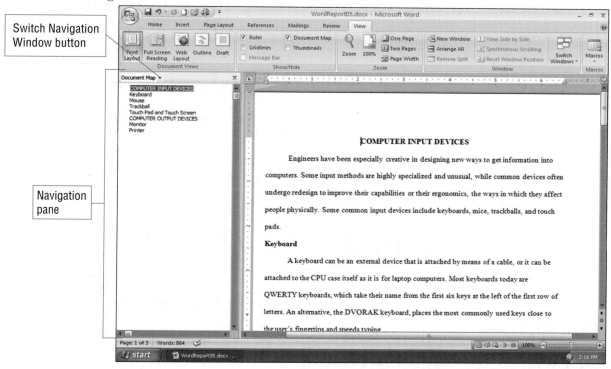

## Project 1b  Navigating Using Document Map

1. With **WordReport05.docx** open, click the View tab and then click the *Document Map* check box.
2. Click the *COMPUTER OUTPUT DEVICES* title that displays in the navigation pane.

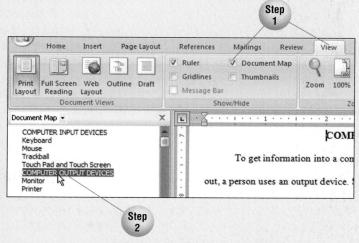

Step 1

Step 2

3. Click the *Keyboard* heading that displays in the navigation pane.
4. Click the *Document Map* check box to remove the check mark.

5. Click the *Thumbnails* check box in the Show/Hide group in the View tab.
6. Click the number 3 thumbnail in the navigation pane.
7. Click the number 1 thumbnail in the navigation pane.
8. Close the navigation pane by clicking the Close button located in the upper right corner of the navigation pane.

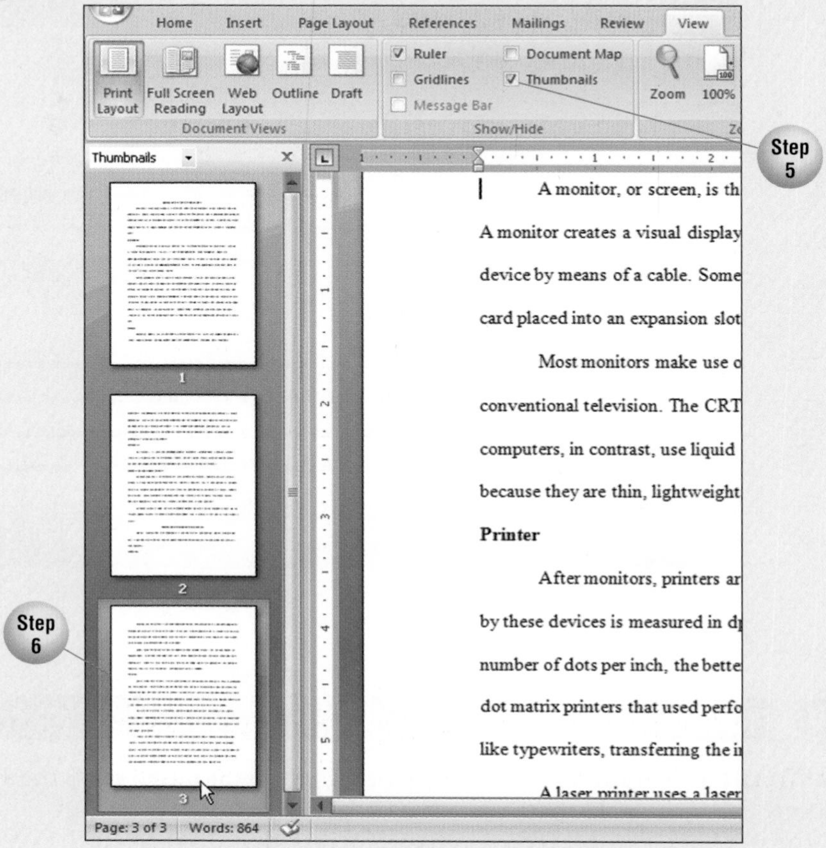


**QUICK STEPS**

**Hide White Space**
1. Position mouse pointer at top of page until pointer displays as *Hide White Space* icon.
2. Double-click left mouse button.

**Show White Space**
1. Position mouse pointer on thin line separating pages until pointer displays as *Show White Space* icon.
2. Double-click left mouse button.

## Hiding/Showing White Space in Print Layout View

In Print Layout view, a page displays as it will appear when printed including the white space at the top and bottom of the page representing the default margins. To save space on the screen in Print Layout view, you can remove the white space by positioning the mouse pointer at the top edge or bottom edge of a page or between pages until the pointer displays as the *Hide White Space* icon and then double-clicking the left mouse button. To redisplay the white space, position the mouse pointer on the thin, black line separating pages until the pointer turns into the *Show White Space* icon and then double-click the left mouse button.

## Project 1c   Hiding/Showing White Space

1. With **WordReport05.docx** open, make sure the document displays in Print Layout view.
2. Press Ctrl + Home to move the insertion point to the beginning of the document.
3. Hide the white spaces at the top and bottom of pages by positioning the mouse pointer at the top edge of the page until the pointer turns into the *Hide White Space* icon and then double-clicking the left mouse button.
4. Scroll through the document and notice the display of pages.
5. Redisplay the white spaces at the top and bottom of pages by positioning the mouse pointer on any thin, black, horizontal line separating pages until the pointer turns into the *Show White Space* icon and then double-clicking the left mouse button.

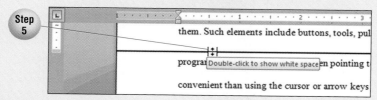

Step 3

6. Close **WordReport05.docx**.

---

## Project 2   Format a Document on Online Etiquette Guidelines

You will open a document containing information on guidelines for online etiquette and then change the margins, page orientation, and page size.

# Changing Page Setup

The Page Setup group in the Page Layout tab contains a number of options for affecting pages in a document. With options in the group you can perform such actions as changing margins, orientation, and page size and inserting page breaks. The Pages group in the Insert tab contains three buttons for inserting a page break, blank page, and cover page.

## Changing Margins

Change page margins with options at the Margins drop-down list as shown in Figure 4.3. To display this list, click the Page Layout tab and then click the Margins button in the Page Setup group. To change the margins, click one of the preset margins that display in the drop-down list. Be aware that most printers contain a required margin (between one-quarter and three-eighths inch) because printers cannot print to the edge of the page.

**QUICK STEPS**

**Change Margins**
1. Click Page Layout tab.
2. Click Margins button.
3. Click desired margin option.

Margins

**Figure 4.3** Margins Drop-down List

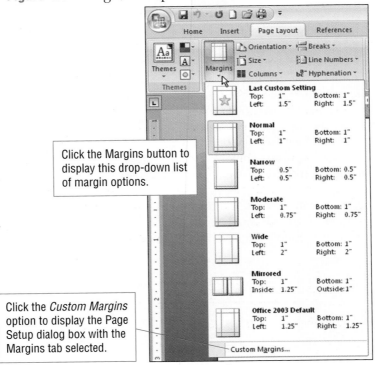

Click the Margins button to display this drop-down list of margin options.

Click the *Custom Margins* option to display the Page Setup dialog box with the Margins tab selected.

Project **2a**   **Changing Margins**

1. Open **WordNetiquette.docx**.
2. Save the document with Save As and name it **WordL1_C4_P2**.
3. Click the Page Layout tab.
4. Click the Margins button in the Page Setup group and then click the *Office 2003 Default* option.
5. Save **WordL1_C4_P2.docx**.

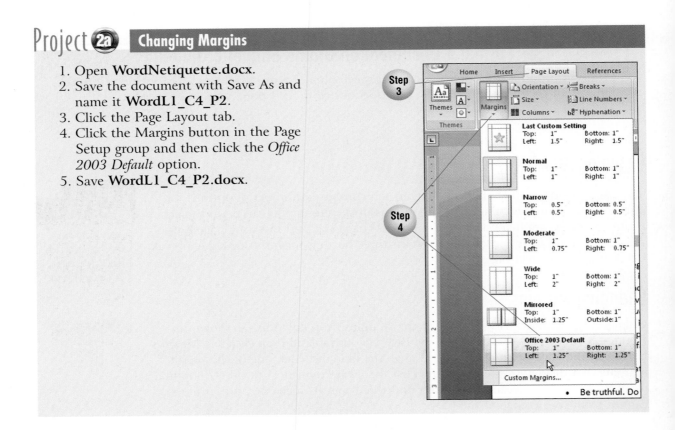

# Changing Page Orientation

Click the Orientation button in the Page Setup group in the Page Layout tab and two options display—*Portrait* and *Landscape*. At the portrait orientation, which is the default, the page is 11 inches tall and 8.5 inches wide. At the landscape orientation, the page is 8.5 inches tall and 11 inches wide. Change the page orientation and the page margins automatically change.

Can you picture some instances in which you might use a landscape orientation? Suppose you are preparing a company's annual report and you need to include a couple of tables that have several columns of text. If you use the default portrait orientation, the columns would need to be quite narrow, possibly so narrow that reading becomes difficult. Changing the orientation to landscape results in three more inches of usable space. Also, you are not committed to using landscape orientation for the entire document. You can use portrait and landscape in the same document. To do this, select the text, display the Page Setup dialog box, click the desired orientation, and change the *Apply to* option box to *Selected text*.

**QUICK STEPS**

**Change Page Orientation**
1. Click Page Layout tab.
2. Click Orientation button.
3. Click desired orientation.

## Project 2b    Changing Page Orientation

1. With **WordL1_C4_P2.docx** open, make sure the Page Layout tab is selected.
2. Click the Orientation button in the Page Setup group.
3. Click *Landscape* at the drop-down list.
4. Scroll through the document and notice how the text displays on the page in landscape orientation.
5. Save **WordL1_C4_P2.docx**.

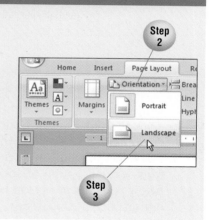

# Changing Page Size

By default, Word uses a page size of 8.5 inches wide and 11 inches tall. You can change this default setting with options at the Size drop-down list shown in Figure 4.4. Display this drop-down list by clicking the Size button in the Page Setup group in the Page Layout tab.

**QUICK STEPS**

**Change Page Size**
1. Click Page Layout tab.
2. Click Size button.
3. Click desired size option.

**Figure 4.4** Size Drop-down List

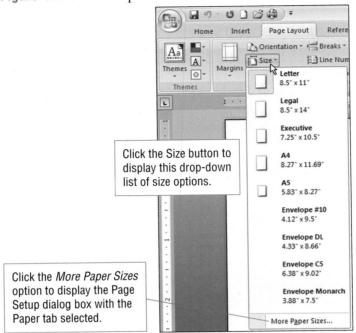

Click the Size button to display this drop-down list of size options.

Click the *More Paper Sizes* option to display the Page Setup dialog box with the Paper tab selected.

Project **2c**   **Changing Page Size**

1. With **WordL1_C4_P2.docx** open, make sure the Page Layout tab is selected.
2. Click the Orientation button in the Page Setup group and then click *Portrait* at the drop-down list. (This changes the orientation back to the default.)
3. Click the Size button in the Page Setup group.
4. Click the A5 option (displays with *5.83″ × 8.27″* below *A5*). If this option is not available, choose an option with a similar size.
5. Scroll through the document and notice how the text displays on the page.
6. Click the Size button and then click *Legal* (displays with *8.5″ × 14″* below *Legal*).
7. Scroll through the document and notice how the text displays on the page.
8. Click the Size button and then click *Letter* (displays with *8.5″ × 11″* below *Letter*). (This returns the size back to the default.)
9. Save **WordL1_C4_P2.docx**.

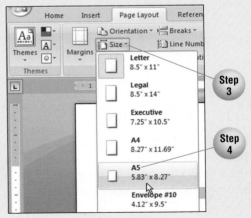

Step 3

Step 4

## Changing Margins at the Page Setup Dialog Box

The Margins button in the Page Setup group provides you with a number of preset margins. If these margins do not fit your needs, you can set specific margins at the Page Setup dialog box with the Margins tab selected as shown in Figure 4.5. Display this dialog box by clicking the Page Setup group dialog box launcher or by clicking the Margins button and then clicking *Custom Margins* at the bottom of the drop-down list.

To change margins, select the current measurement in the *Top*, *Bottom*, *Left*, or *Right* text box, and then type the new measurement. You can also increase a measurement by clicking the up-pointing arrow at the right side of the text box. Decrease a measurement by clicking the down-pointing arrow. As you make changes to the margin measurements at the Page Setup dialog box, the sample page in the *Preview* section illustrates the effects of the margin changes.

**QUICK STEPS**

**Change Margins at Page Setup Dialog Box**
1. Click Page Layout tab.
2. Click Page Setup group dialog box launcher.
3. Specify desired margins.
4. Click OK.

**Change Page Size at Page Setup Dialog Box**
1. Click Page Layout tab.
2. Click Size button.
3. Click *More Paper Sizes* at drop-down list.
4. Specify desired size.
5. Click OK.

**Figure 4.5** Page Setup Dialog Box with Margins Tab Selected

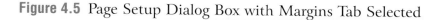
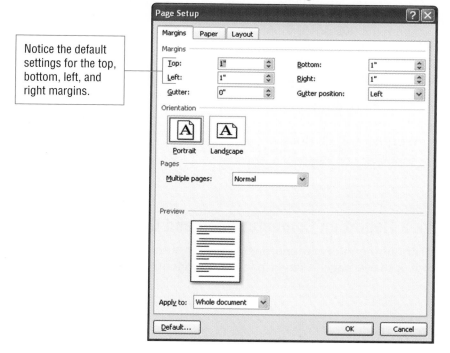

Notice the default settings for the top, bottom, left, and right margins.

## Changing Paper Size at the Page Setup Dialog Box

The Size button drop-down list contains a number of preset page sizes. If these sizes do not fit your needs, you can specify page size at the Page Setup dialog box with the Paper tab selected. Display this dialog box by clicking the Size button in the Page Setup group and then clicking *More Paper Sizes* that displays at the bottom of the drop-down list.

1. With **WordL1_C4_P2.docx** open, make sure the Page Layout tab is selected.
2. Click the Page Setup group dialog box launcher.
3. At the Page Setup dialog box with the Margins tab selected, click the down-pointing arrow at the right side of the *Top* text box until *0.5"* displays.
4. Click the down-pointing arrow at the right side of the *Bottom* text box until *0.5"* displays.
5. Select the current measurement in the *Left* text box and then type *0.75*.
6. Select the current measurement in the *Right* text box and then type *0.75*.
7. Click OK to close the dialog box.
8. Click the Size button in the Page Setup group and then click *More Paper Sizes* at the drop-down list.
9. At the Page Setup dialog box with the Paper tab selected, click the down-pointing arrow at the right side of the *Paper size* option and then click *A4* at the drop-down list.
10. Click OK to close the dialog box.
11. Scroll through the document and notice how the text displays on the page.
12. Click the Size button in the Page Setup group and then click *Letter* at the drop-down list.
13. Save, print, and then close **WordL1_C4_P2.docx**.

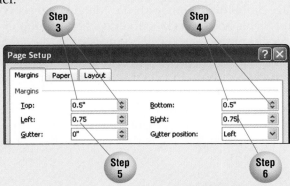

Step 3

Step 4

Step 5

Step 6

Step 9

Project **3**  **Customize a Report on Computer Input and Output Devices**

You will open a document containing information on computer input and output devices and then insert page breaks, a blank page, a cover page, and page numbering.

## Inserting a Page Break

With the default top and bottom margins of one inch, approximately nine inches of text print on the page. At approximately the ten-inch mark, Word automatically inserts a page break. You can insert your own page break in a document with the keyboard shortcut, Ctrl + Enter, or with the Page Break button in the Pages group in the Insert tab.

A page break inserted by Word is considered a *soft* page break and a page break inserted by you is considered a *hard* page break. Soft page breaks automatically adjust if you add or delete text from a document. A hard page break does not adjust and is therefore less flexible than a soft page break. If you add or delete text from a document with a hard page break, check the break to determine whether it is still in a desirable location. In Draft view, a hard page break displays as a row of dots with the words Page Break in the center. To delete a page break, position the insertion point immediately below the page break and then press the Backspace key or change to Draft view, position the insertion point on the page break, and then press the Delete key.

## Project 3a — Inserting Page Breaks

1. Open **WordReport05.docx**.
2. Save the document with Save As and name it **WordL1_C4_P3**.
3. Change the top margin by completing the following steps:
   a. Click the Page Layout tab.
   b. Click the Page Setup group dialog box launcher.
   c. At the Page Setup dialog box, click the Margins tab and then type 1.5 in the *Top* text box.
   d. Click OK to close the dialog box.

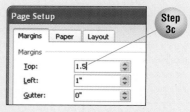
Step 3c

4. Insert a page break at the beginning of the heading *Mouse* by completing the following steps:
   a. Position the insertion point at the beginning of the heading *Mouse* (located toward the bottom of page 1).
   b. Click the Insert tab and then click the Page Break button in the Pages group.
5. Move the insertion point to the beginning of the title *COMPUTER OUTPUT DEVICES* (located at the bottom of page 2) and then insert a page break by pressing Ctrl + Enter.
6. Move the insertion point to the beginning of the heading *Printer* and then press Ctrl + Enter to insert a page break.

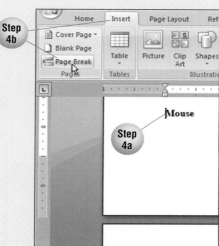
Step 4b
Step 4a

7. Delete the page break by completing the following steps:
   a. Click the Draft button in the view area on the Status bar.
   b. With the insertion point positioned at the beginning of the heading *Printer*, press the Backspace key. (This displays the page break in the document.)
   c. Press the Backspace key again to delete the page break.
   d. Click the Print Layout button in the view area of the Status bar.
8. Save **WordL1_C4_P3.docx**.

## Inserting a Blank Page

Click the Blank Page button in the Pages group in the Insert tab to insert a blank page at the position of the insertion point. This might be useful in a document where you want to insert a blank page for an illustration, graphic, or figure.

**QUICK STEPS**

**Insert Blank Page**
1. Click Insert tab.
2. Click Blank Page button.

Blank Page

## Inserting a Cover Page

**Insert Cover Page**
1. Click Insert tab.
2. Click Cover Page button.
3. Click desired cover page at drop-down list.

**HINT**

A cover page provides a polished and professional look to a document.

If you are preparing a document for distribution to others or you want to simply improve the visual appeal of your document, consider inserting a cover page. With the Cover Page button in the Pages group in the Insert tab, you can insert a predesigned and formatted cover page and then type personalized text in specific locations on the page. Click the Cover Page button and a drop-down list displays similar to the one shown in Figure 4.6. The drop-down list provides a visual representation of the cover page. Scroll through the list and then click the desired cover page.

A predesigned cover page contains location placeholders where you can enter specific information. For example, a cover page might contain the placeholder *[Type the document title]*. Click anywhere in the placeholder text and the placeholder text is selected. With the placeholder text selected, type the desired text. You can delete a placeholder by clicking anywhere in the placeholder text, clicking the placeholder tab, and then pressing the Delete key.

**Figure 4.6** Cover Page Drop-down List

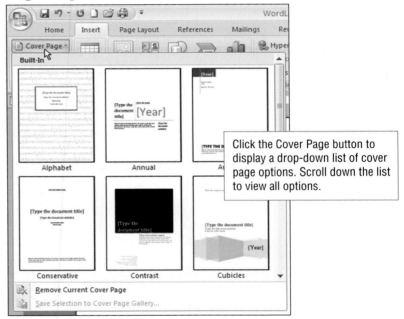

Click the Cover Page button to display a drop-down list of cover page options. Scroll down the list to view all options.

1. With **WordL1_C4_P3.docx** open, create a blank page by completing the following steps:
   a. Move the insertion point to the beginning of the heading *Touch Pad and Touch Screen* located on the second page.
   b. Click the Insert tab.
   c. Click the Blank Page button in the Pages group.
2. Insert a cover page by completing the following steps:
   a. Press Ctrl + Home to move the insertion point to the beginning of the document.
   b. Click the Cover Page button in the Pages group.
   c. At the drop-down list, scroll down and then click the *Motion* cover page.
   d. Click anywhere in the placeholder text *[Type the document title]* and then type **Computer Devices**.

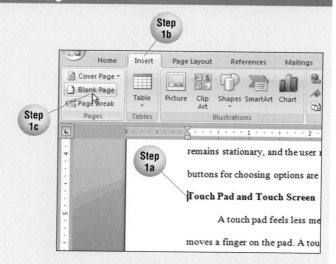

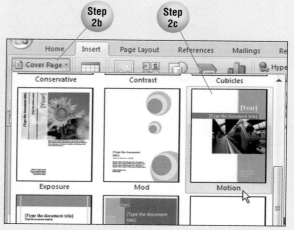

e. Click the placeholder text *[Year]*. Click the down-pointing arrow that displays at the right side of the placeholder and then click the Today button that displays at the bottom of the drop-down calendar.

f. Click anywhere in the placeholder text *[Type the company name]* and then type **Drake Computing**.

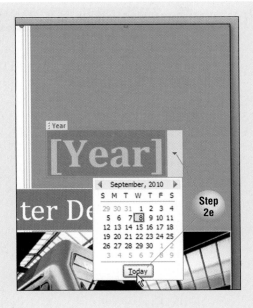

Step 2e

Step 2f

g. Click anywhere in the placeholder text *[Type the author name]* and then type your first and last names.

3. Remove the blank page you created in Step 1 by completing the following steps:

a. Move the insertion point to the beginning of page 5 immediately left of the heading *Touch Pad and Touch Screen*.

b. Click the Draft button in the View section on the Status bar.

c. Press the Backspace key until the heading *Touch Pad and Touch Screen* displays a double-space below the previous paragraph of text.

d. Click the Print Layout button in the View section on the Status bar.

4. Save **WordL1_C4_P3.docx**.

Step 3c

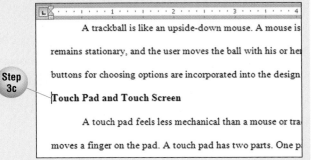

# Inserting Predesigned Page Numbering

Word, by default, does not print page numbers on a page. If you want to insert page numbering in a document, use the Page Number button in the Header & Footer group in the Insert tab. When you click the Page Number button, a drop-down list displays with options for specifying the page number location. Point to an option at this list and a drop-down list displays of predesigned page number formats. Scroll through the options in the drop-down list and then click the desired option. If you want to change the format of page numbering in a document, double-click the page number, select the page number text, and then apply the desired formatting. You can remove page numbering from a document by clicking the Page Number button and then clicking *Remove Page Numbers* at the drop-down list.

## Project 3C — Inserting Predesigned Page Numbering

1. With **WordL1_C4_P3.docx** open, insert page numbering by completing the following steps:
   a. Move the insertion point so it is positioned on any character in the title *COMPUTER INPUT DEVICES*.
   b. Click the Insert tab.
   c. Click the Page Number button in the Header & Footer group and then point to *Top of Page*.
   d. Scroll through the drop-down list and then click the *Brackets 2* option.

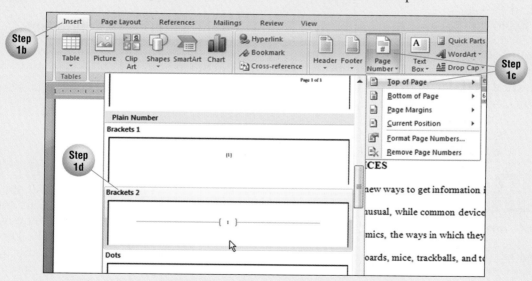

2. Double-click the document to make it active and then scroll through the document and notice the page numbering that displays at the top of each page except the cover page. (The cover page and text are divided by a section break, which you will learn more about in Chapter 5. Word considers the cover page as page 1 but does not include the numbering on the page.)

3. Remove the page numbering by clicking the Insert tab, clicking the Page Number button, and then clicking *Remove Page Numbers* at the drop-down list.

4. Click the Page Number button, point to *Bottom of Page*, scroll down the drop-down list and then click the *Circle* option.

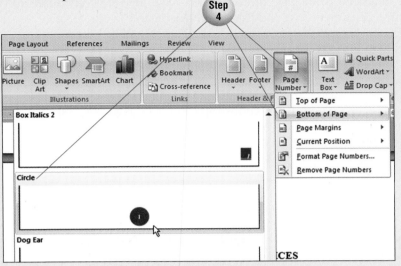

5. Save, print, and then close **WordL1_C4_P3.docx**.

P**roject** 4 **Add Elements to a Report on the Future of the Internet**

You will open a document containing information on the future of the Internet, insert a predesigned header and footer in the document, remove a header, and format and delete header and footer elements.

## Inserting Predesigned Headers and Footers

Text that appears at the top of every page is called a **header** and text that appears at the bottom of every page is referred to as a **footer**. Headers and footers are common in manuscripts, textbooks, reports, and other publications. Insert a predesigned header in a document by clicking the Insert tab and then clicking the Header button in the Header & Footer group. This displays the Header drop-down list as shown in Figure 4.7. At this list, click the desired predesigned header option and the header is inserted in the document. The header is visible in Print Layout view but not Draft view.

A predesigned header or footer may contain location placeholders where you can enter specific information. For example, a header might contain the placeholder *[Type the document title]*. Click anywhere in the placeholder text and all of the placeholder text is selected. With the placeholder text selected, type the desired text. You can delete a placeholder by clicking anywhere in the placeholder text, clicking the placeholder tab, and then pressing the Delete key.

**Figure 4.7** Header Drop-down List

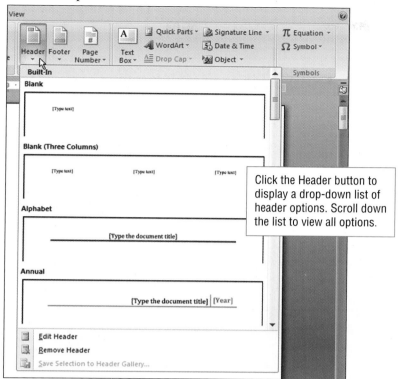

Click the Header button to display a drop-down list of header options. Scroll down the list to view all options.

## Project 4a  Inserting a Predesigned Header in a Document

1. Open **WordReport02.docx**.
2. Save the document with Save As and name it **WordL1_C4_P4**.
3. Make the following changes to the document:
   a. Select the entire document, change the line spacing to *2*, and then deselect the document.
   b. Change the Quick Styles set to *Formal*. (*Hint: Use the Changes Styles button in the Styles group in the Home tab.*)
   c. Apply the *Heading 1* style to the title *FUTURE OF THE INTERNET*.
   d. Apply the *Heading 2* style to the headings *Satellite Internet Connections, Second Internet, Internet Services for a Fee*, and *Internet in 2030*.
   e. Move the insertion point to the beginning of the heading *INTERNET IN 2030* (located at the bottom of page 2) and then insert a page break by clicking the Insert tab and then clicking the Page Break button in the Pages group.

4. Press Ctrl + Home to move the insertion point to the beginning of the document and then insert a header by completing the following steps:

   a. If necessary, click the Insert tab.

   b. Click the Header button in the Header & Footer group.

   c. Scroll to the bottom of the drop-down list that displays and then click *Tiles*.

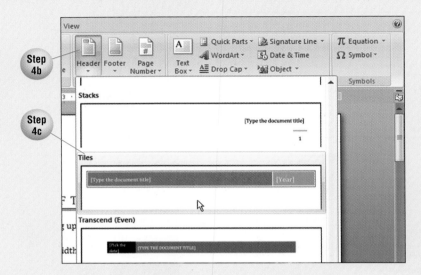

   d. Click anywhere in the placeholder text *[Type the document title]* and then type Future of the Internet.

   e. Click anywhere in the placeholder text *[Year]* and then type the current year.

   f. Double-click in the document text. (This makes the document text active and dims the header.)

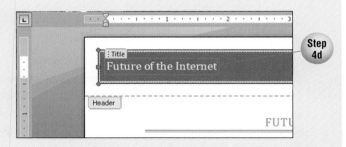

5. Scroll through the document to see how the header will print.

6. Save and then print **WordL1_C4_P4.docx**.

**Insert Predesigned Footer**
1. Click Insert tab.
2. Click Footer button.
3. Click desired option at drop-down list.
5. Type text in specific placeholders in footer.

Insert a predesigned footer in the same manner as inserting a header. Click the Footer button in the Header & Footer group in the Insert tab and a drop-down list displays similar to the Header drop-down list shown in Figure 4.7. Click the desired footer and the predesigned footer formatting is applied to the document.

## Removing a Header or Footer

Remove a header from a document by clicking the Insert tab and then clicking the Header button in the Header & Footer group. At the drop-down list that displays, click the *Remove Header* option. Complete similar steps to remove a footer.

1. With **WordL1_C4_P4.docx** open, press Ctrl + Home to move the insertion point to the beginning of the document.
2. Remove the header by clicking the Insert tab, clicking the Header button in the Header & Footer group, and then clicking the *Remove Header* option at the drop-down menu.

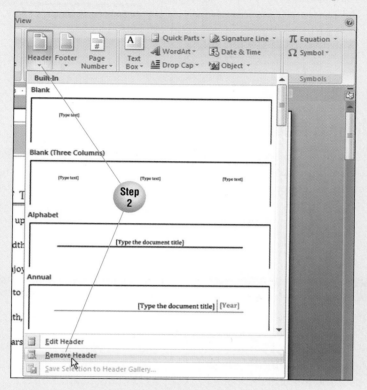

3. Insert a footer in the document by completing the following steps:
   a. Click the Footer button in the Header & Footer group.
   b. Click *Alphabet* at the drop-down list.

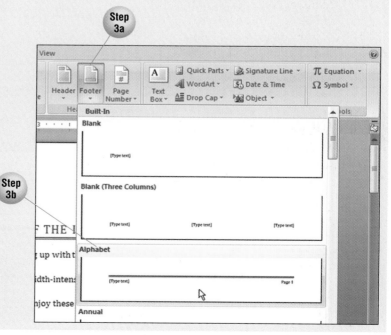

c. Click anywhere in the placeholder
   text *[Type text]* and then type
   **Future of the Internet**.
d. Double-click in the document text.
   (This makes the document text
   active and dims the footer.)
4. Scroll through the document to see
   how the footer will print.
5. Save and then print **WordL1_C4_P4.docx**.

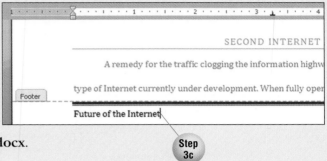

Step
3c

## Editing a Predesigned Header or Footer

Predesigned headers and footers contain elements such as page numbers and a
title. You can change the formatting of the element by clicking the desired
element and then applying the desired formatting. You can also select and then
delete an item.

## Project 4C   Formatting and Deleting Header and Footer Elements

1. With **WordL1_C4_P4.docx** open, remove the footer by clicking the Insert tab, clicking the
   Footer button, and then clicking *Remove Footer* at the drop-down list.
2. Insert and then format a header by completing the following steps:
a. Click the Header button in the Header & Footer group in the Insert tab, scroll in the
   drop-down list, and then click *Motion (Odd Page)*. (This header inserts the document title
   as well as the page number.)

Step
2a

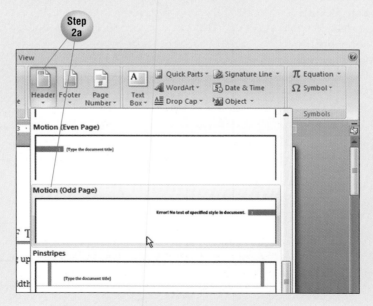

b. Delete the document title from the header by clicking anywhere in the text *FUTURE OF THE INTERNET*, selecting the text, and then pressing the Delete key.

c. Double-click in the document text.

3. Insert and then format a footer by completing the following steps:

a. Click the Insert tab.

b. Click the Footer button, scroll down the drop-down list, and then click *Motion (Odd Page)*.

c. Click on any character in the date that displays in the footer, select the date, and then type the current date.

d. Select the date, turn on bold, and then change the font size to 12.

e. Double-click in the document text.

4. Scroll through the document to see how the header and footer will print.

5. Save, print, and then close **WordL1_C4_P4.docx**.

## Project ⑤ Format a Report on Robots

**You will open a document containing information on the difficulties of creating a humanlike robot and then insert a watermark, change page background color, and insert a page border.**

# Formatting the Page Background

The Page Background group in the Page Layout tab contains three buttons for customizing a page background. Click the Watermark button and choose a predesigned watermark from a drop-down list. If a document is going to be viewed on-screen or on the Web, consider adding a page color. In Chapter 3, you learned how to apply borders and shading to text at the Borders and Shading dialog box. This dialog box also contains options for inserting a page border.

## Inserting a Watermark

A watermark is a lightened image that displays behind text in a document. Using watermarks is an excellent way to add visual appeal to a document. Word provides a number of predesigned watermarks you can insert in a document. Display these watermarks by clicking the Watermark button in the Page Background group in the Page Layout tab. Scroll through the list of watermarks and then click the desired option.

## Changing Page Color

Use the Page Color button in the Page Background group to apply background color to a document. This background color is intended for viewing a document on-screen or on the Web. The color is visible on the screen but does not print. Insert a page color by clicking the Page Color button and then clicking the desired color at the color palette.

**QUICK STEPS**

**Insert Watermark**
1. Click Page Layout tab.
2. Click Watermark button.
3. Click desired option at drop-down list.

**Change Page Color**
1. Click Page Layout tab.
2. Click Page Color button.
3. Click desired option at color palette.

1. Open **WordReport07.docx** and then save the document and name it **WordL1_C4_P5**.
2. Apply the Heading 1 style to the title *ROBOTS AS ANDROIDS* and the Heading 2 style to the five headings in the document.
3. Change the Quick Styles set to *Formal*.
4. Insert a page break at the beginning of the heading *Tactile Perception*.
5. Insert a watermark by completing the following steps:
   a. Move the insertion point to the beginning of the document.
   b. Click the Page Layout tab.
   c. Click the Watermark button in the Page Background group.
   d. At the drop-down list, click the *CONFIDENTIAL 1* option.

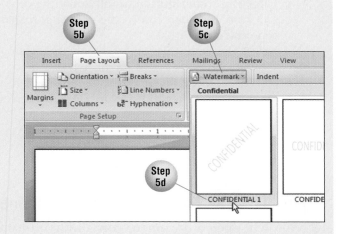

Step 5b

Step 5c

Step 5d

6. Scroll through the document and notice how the watermark displays behind the text.
7. Remove the watermark and insert a different one by completing the following steps:
   a. Click the Watermark button in the Page Background group and then click *Remove Watermark* at the drop-down list.
   b. Click the Watermark button and then click *DO NOT COPY 1* at the drop-down list.

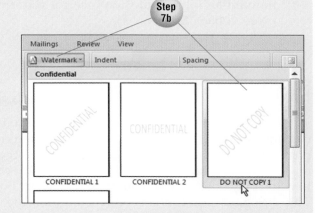

Step 7b

8. Scroll through the document and notice how the watermark displays.
9. Move the insertion point to the beginning of the document.
10. Click the Page Color button in the Page Background group and then click *Aqua, Accent 5, Lighter 80%* at the color palette.
11. Save **WordL1_C4_P5.docx**.

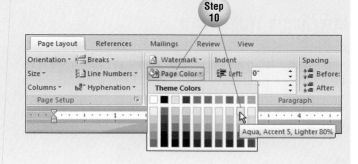

Step 10

# Inserting a Page Border

To improve the visual appeal of a document, consider inserting a page border. When you insert a page border in a multiple-page document, the border prints on each page. To insert a page border, click the Page Borders button in the Page Background group in the Page Layout tab. This displays the Borders and Shading dialog box with the Page Border tab selected as shown in Figure 4.8. At this dialog box, you can specify the border style, color, and width.

The dialog box contains an option for inserting a page border containing an image. To display the images available, click the down-pointing arrow at the right side of the *Art* list box. Scroll down the drop-down list and then click the desired image. (This feature may need to be installed the first time you use it.)

**Insert Page Border**
1. Click Page Layout tab.
2. Click Page Borders button.
3. Specify desired options at dialog box.

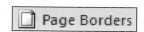

**Figure 4.8** Borders and Shading Dialog Box with Page Border Tab Selected

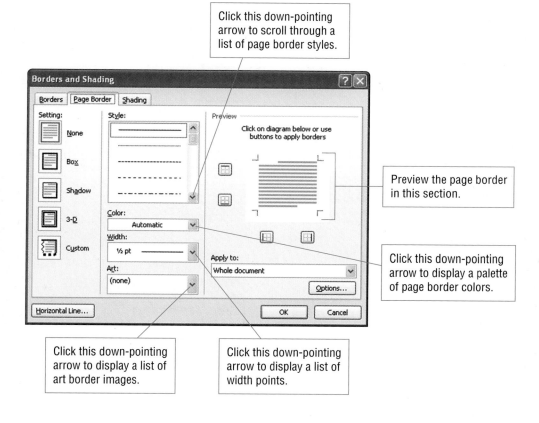

Click this down-pointing arrow to scroll through a list of page border styles.

Preview the page border in this section.

Click this down-pointing arrow to display a palette of page border colors.

Click this down-pointing arrow to display a list of art border images.

Click this down-pointing arrow to display a list of width points.

1. With **WordL1_C4_P5.docx** open, remove the page color by clicking the Page Color button in the Page Background group and then clicking *No Color* at the color palette.
2. Insert a page border by completing the following steps:
   a. Click the Page Borders button in the Page Background group in the Page Layout tab.
   b. Click the *Box* option in the *Setting* section.
   c. Scroll down the list of line styles in the *Style* list box until the end of the list displays and then click the third line from the end.
   d. Click the down-pointing arrow at the right of the *Color* list box and then click *Red, Accent 2, Darker 25%* at the color palette.
   e. Click OK to close the dialog box.

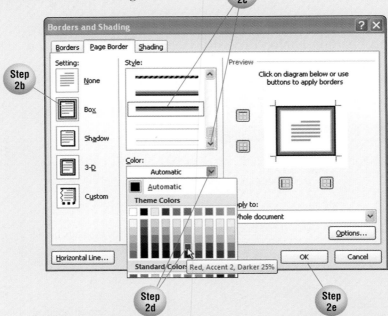

Step 2c

Step 2b

Step 2d

Step 2e

3. Save and then print **WordL1_C4_P5**.
4. Insert an image page border by completing the following steps:
   a. Click the Page Borders button in the Page Background group.
   b. Click the down-pointing arrow at the right side of the *Art* list box and then click the border image shown at the right.
   c. Click OK to close the dialog box.
5. Save, print, and then close **WordL1_C4_P5.docx**.

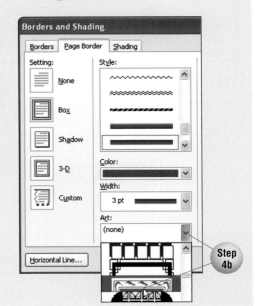

Step 4b

Project 6 Format a Lease Agreement Document

You will open a lease agreement document, search for specific text and replace it with other text, and then search for specific formatting and replace it with other formatting.

# Finding and Replacing Text and Formatting

With Word's Find feature you can search for specific characters or formatting. With the Find and Replace feature, you can search for specific characters or formatting and replace them with other characters or formatting. The Find button and the Replace button are located in the Editing group in the Home tab.

## Finding Text

With the Find feature, you can search a document for specific text. To use the Find feature, click the Find button in the Editing group in the Home tab or use the keyboard shortcut, Ctrl + F. This displays the Find and Replace dialog box with the Find tab selected as shown in Figure 4.9. Type the text you want to find in the *Find what* text box. Click the Find Next button and Word searches for and selects the first occurrence of the text in the document. Make corrections to the text if needed and then search for the next occurrence by clicking the Find Next button again. Click the Cancel button to close the Find and Replace dialog box.

QUICK STEPS

**Find Text**
1. Click Find button in Home tab.
2. Type search text.
3. Click Find Next button.

**Figure 4.9** Find and Replace Dialog Box with Find Tab Selected

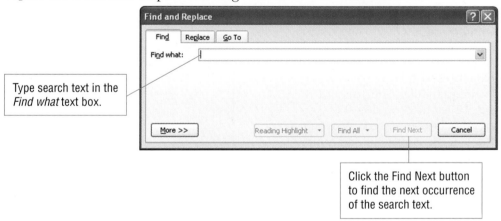

Type search text in the *Find what* text box.

Click the Find Next button to find the next occurrence of the search text.

# Highlighting Find Text

You can use the Find feature to highlight specific text in a document. This can help you easily scan a document for every occurrence of the specific text. To find and highlight text, click the Find button, type the text you want highlighted in the *Find what* text box, click the Reading Highlight button, and then click *Highlight All* at the drop-down list. All occurrences of the text in the document are highlighted. To remove highlighting, click the Reading Highlight button and then click *Clear Highlighting* at the drop-down list.

## Project 6a — Finding Text and Finding and Highlighting Text

1. Open **WordAgreement01.docx** and then save the document and name it **WordL1_C4_P6**.
2. Find all occurrences of *lease* by completing the following steps:
   a. Click the Find button in the Editing group in the Home tab.
   b. At the Find and Replace dialog box with the Find tab selected, type **lease** in the *Find what* text box.
   c. Click the Find Next button.

**Step 2b**

**Find and Replace**

Find | Replace | Go To

Find what: lease

More >>    Reading Highlight ▾    Find All ▾    Find Next    Cancel

**Step 2c**

   d. Continue clicking the Find Next button until a message displays telling you that Word has finished searching the document. At this message, click OK.
3. Highlight all occurrences of *Premises* in the document by completing the following steps:
   a. At the Find and Replace dialog box with the Find tab selected, select the text in the *Find what* text box and then type **Premises**.
   b. Click the Reading Highlight button and then click *Highlight All* at the drop-down list.
   c. Click in the document to make it active and then scroll through the document and notice the occurrences of highlighted text.
   d. Click in the dialog box to make it active.
   e. Click the Reading Highlight button and then click *Clear Highlighting* at the drop-down list.
4. Click the Close button to close the Find and Replace dialog box.

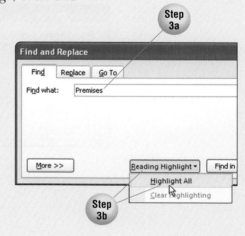

**Step 3a**

**Find and Replace**

Find | Replace | Go To

Find what: Premises

More >>    Reading Highlight ▾    Find in

Highlight All

Clear Highlighting

**Step 3b**

# Finding and Replacing Text

To find and replace text, click the Replace button in the Editing group in the Home tab or use the keyboard shortcut, Ctrl + H. This displays the Find and Replace dialog box with the Replace tab selected as shown in Figure 4.10. Type the text you want to find in the *Find what* text box, press the Tab key, and then type the replacement text.

**Figure 4.10** Find and Replace Dialog Box with the Replace Tab Selected

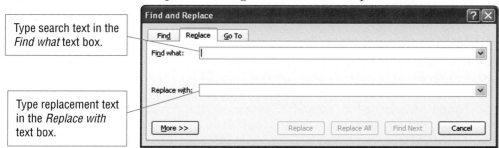

Type search text in the *Find what* text box.

Type replacement text in the *Replace with* text box.

**QUICK STEPS**

**Find and Replace Text**
1. Click Replace button in Home tab.
2. Type search text.
3. Press Tab key.
4. Type replace text.
5. Click Replace or Replace All button.

The Find and Replace dialog box contains several command buttons. Click the Find Next button to tell Word to find the next occurrence of the characters. Click the Replace button to replace the characters and find the next occurrence. If you know that you want all occurrences of the characters in the *Find what* text box replaced with the characters in the *Replace with* text box, click the Replace All button. This replaces every occurrence from the location of the insertion point to the beginning or end of the document (depending on the search direction). Click the Cancel button to close the Find and Replace dialog box.

**HINT**
If the Find and Replace dialog box is in the way of specific text, drag the dialog box to a different location.

## Project 6b  Finding and Replacing Text

1. With **WordL1_C4_P6.docx** open, make sure the insertion point is positioned at the beginning of the document.
2. Find all occurrences of *Lessor* and replace with *Tracy Hartford* by completing the following steps:
   a. Click the Replace button in the Editing group in the Home tab.
   b. At the Find and Replace dialog box with the Replace tab selected, type Lessor in the *Find what* text box.
   c. Press the Tab key to move the insertion point to the *Replace with* text box.
   d. Type Tracy Hartford.
   e. Click the Replace All button.

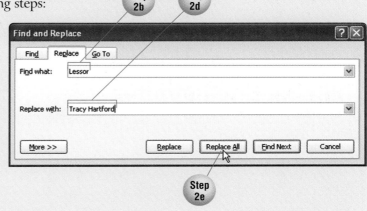

Step 2b

Step 2d

Step 2e

f. At the message *Word has completed its search of the document and has made 11 replacements*, click OK. (Do not close the Find and Replace dialog box.)

3. With the Find and Replace dialog box still open, complete steps similar to those in Step 2 to find all occurrences of *Lessee* and replace with *Michael Iwami*.

4. Close the Find and Replace dialog box.

5. Save **WordL1_C4_P6.docx**.

# Choosing Check Box Options

The Find and Replace dialog box contains a variety of check boxes with options you can choose for completing a search. To display these options, click the More button located at the bottom of the dialog box. This causes the Find and Replace dialog box to expand as shown in Figure 4.11. Each option and what will occur if it is selected is described in Table 4.2. To remove the display of options, click the Less button. (The Less button was previously the More button.) Note that if you make a mistake when replacing text, you can close the Find and Replace dialog box and then click the Undo button on the Quick Access toolbar.

**Figure 4.11** Expanded Find and Replace Dialog Box

Specify search options with options in this section.

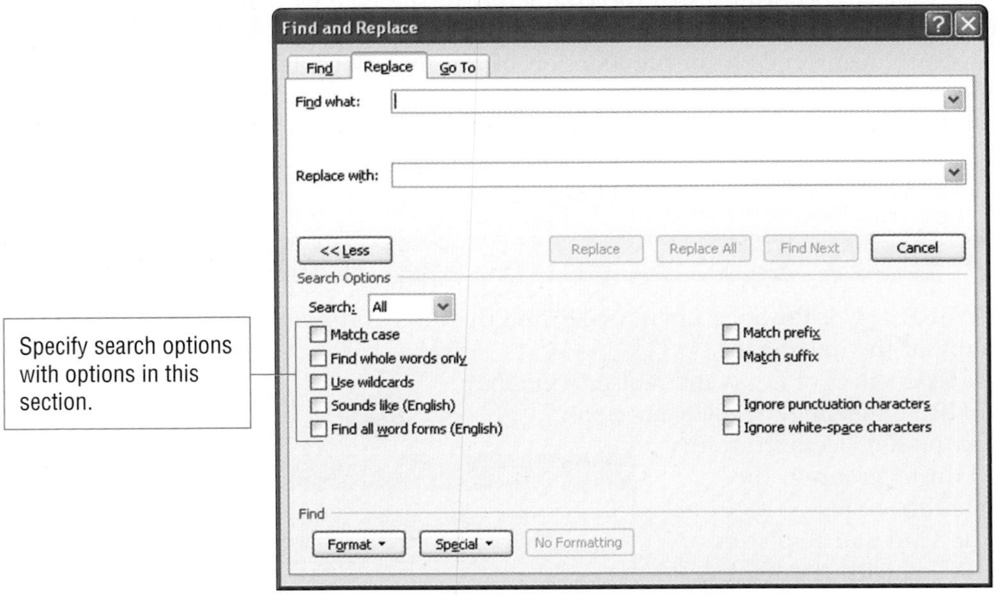

**Table 4.2** Options at the Expanded Find and Replace Dialog Box

| *Choose this option* | *To* |
|---|---|
| Match case | Exactly match the case of the search text. For example, if you search for *Book* and select the *Match case* option, Word will stop at *Book* but not *book* or *BOOK*. |
| Find whole words only | Find a whole word, not a part of a word. For example, if you search for *her* and did not select *Find whole words only*, Word would stop at *there*, *here*, *hers*, etc. |
| Use wildcards | Search for wildcards, special characters, or special search operators. |
| Sounds like | Match words that sound alike but are spelled differently such as *know* and *no*. |
| Find all word forms | Find all forms of the word entered in the *Find what* text box. For example, if you enter *hold*, Word will stop at *held* and *holding*. |
| Match prefix | Find only those words that begin with the letters in the *Find what* text box. For example, if you enter *per*, Word will stop at words such as *perform* and *perfect* but skip words such as *super* and *hyperlink*. |
| Match suffix | Find only those words that end with the letters in the *Find what* text box. For example, if you enter *ly*, Word will stop at words such as *accurately* and *quietly* but skip over words such as *catalyst* and *lyre*. |
| Ignore punctuation characters | Ignore punctuation within characters. For example, if you enter *US* in the *Find what* text box, Word will stop at *U.S.* |
| Ignore white space characters | Ignore spaces between letters. For example, if you enter *F B I* in the *Find what* text box, Word will stop at FBI. |

1. With **WordL1_C4_P6.docx** open, make sure the insertion point is positioned at the beginning of the document.
2. Find all word forms of the word *lease* and replace with *rent* by completing the following steps:
   a. Click the Replace button in the Editing group in the Home tab.
   b. At the Find and Replace dialog box with the Replace tab selected, type **lease** in the *Find what* text box.
   c. Press the Tab key and then type **rent** in the *Replace with* text box.
   d. Click the More button.
   e. Click the *Find all word forms* option. (This inserts a check mark in the check box.)
   f. Click the Replace All button.
   g. At the message telling you that Replace All is not recommended with Find All Word Forms, click OK.
   h. At the message *Word has completed its search of the document and has made 6 replacements*, click OK.
   i. Click the *Find all word forms* option to remove the check mark.

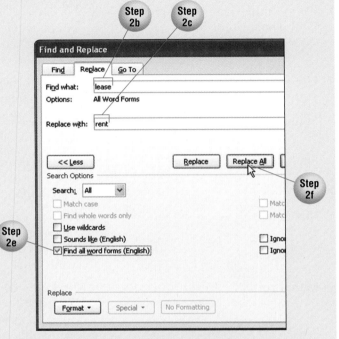

3. Find the word *less* and replace with the word *minus* and specify that you want Word to find only those words that end in *less* by completing the following steps:
   a. At the expanded Find and Replace dialog box, select the text in the *Find what* text box and then type **less**.
   b. Select the text in the *Replace with* text box and then type **minus**.
   c. Click the *Match suffix* check box to insert a check mark and tell Word to find only words that end in *less*.
   d. Click the Replace All button.

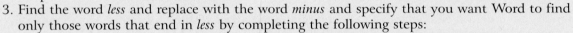

   e. At the message telling you that 2 replacements were made, click OK.
   f. Click the *Match suffix* check box to remove the check mark.
   g. Click the Less button.
   h. Close the Find and Replace dialog box.
4. Save **WordL1_C4_P6.docx**.

# Finding and Replacing Formatting

With options at the Find and Replace dialog box with the Replace tab selected, you can search for characters containing specific formatting and replace them with other characters or formatting. To specify formatting in the Find and Replace dialog box, click the More button and then click the Format button that displays toward the bottom of the dialog box. At the pop-up list that displays, identify the type of formatting you want to find.

## Project 6d  Finding and Replacing Fonts

1. With **WordL1_C4_P6.docx** open, move the insertion point to the beginning of the document.
2. Find text set in 12-point Candara bold dark red and replace it with text set in 14-point Calibri bold dark blue by completing the following steps:
   a. Click the Replace button in the Editing group.
   b. At the Find and Replace dialog box, press the Delete key. (This deletes any text that displays in the *Find what* text box.)
   c. Click the More button. (If a check mark displays in any of the check boxes, click the option to remove the check mark.)
   d. With the insertion point positioned in the *Find what* text box, click the Format button located toward the bottom of the dialog box and then click *Font* at the pop-up list.
   e. At the Find Font dialog box, change the Font to *Candara*, the Font style to *Bold*, the Size to *12*, and the Font color to *Dark Red* (first color option from the left in the *Standard Colors* section).
   f. Click OK to close the Find Font dialog box.
   g. At the Find and Replace dialog box, click inside the *Replace with* text box and then delete any text that displays.
   h. Click the Format button located toward the bottom of the dialog box and then click *Font* at the pop-up list.

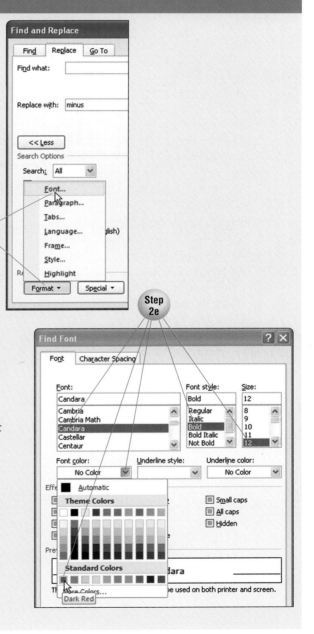

Step 2d

Step 2e

i. At the Replace Font dialog box, change the Font to *Calibri*, the Font style to *Bold*, the Size to *14*, and the Font color to *Dark Blue* (second color option from the right in the *Standard Colors* section).

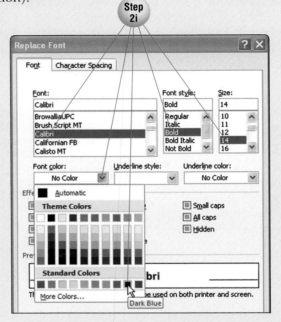

j. Click OK to close the Replace Font dialog box.

k. At the Find and Replace dialog box, click the Replace All button.

l. At the message telling you that the search of the document is complete and eight replacements were made, click OK.

m. Click in the *Find what* text box and then click the No Formatting button.

n. Click in the *Replace with* text box and then click the No Formatting button.

o. Click the Less button.

p. Close the Find and Replace dialog box.

3. Save, print, and then close **WordL1_C4_P6.docx**.

# CHAPTER summary

- You can change the document view with buttons in the View section on the Status bar or with options in the View tab.
- Print Layout is the default view, which can be changed to other views such as Draft view or Full Screen Reading view.
- The Draft view displays the document in a format for efficient editing and formatting.
- Use the Zoom slider bar to change the percentage of the display.
- Full Screen Reading view displays a document in a format for easy viewing and reading.
- Navigate in Full Screen Reading view using keys on the keyboard or with the Next and Previous buttons.
- Navigate in a document using the Document Map or Thumbnails features. Click the *Document Map* check box in the View tab or the *Thumbnails* check box and a navigation pane displays at the left side of the screen.
- In Print Layout view, you can remove the white space at the top and bottom of pages.
- By default, a Word document contains 1-inch top, bottom, left, and right margins. Change margins with preset margin settings at the Margins drop-down list or with options at the Page Setup dialog box with the Margins tab selected.
- The default page orientation is portrait, which can be changed to landscape with the Orientation button in the Page Setup group in the Page Layout tab.
- The default page size is 8.5 by 11 inches, which can be changed with options at the Size drop-down list or options at the Page Setup dialog box with the Paper tab selected.
- The page break that Word inserts automatically is a soft page break. A page break that you insert is a hard page break. Insert a page break with the Page Break button in the Pages group in the Insert tab or by pressing Ctrl + Enter.
- Insert a blank page in a document by clicking the Blank Page button in the Pages group in the Insert tab.
- Insert a predesigned and formatted cover page by clicking the Cover Page button in the Pages group in the Insert tab and then clicking the desired option at the drop-down list.
- Insert predesigned and formatted page numbering by clicking the Page Number button in the Header & Footer group in the Insert tab, specifying the desired location of page numbers, and then clicking the desired page numbering option.
- Text that appears at the top of every page is called a header and text that appears at the bottom of every page is called a footer.
- You can insert predesigned headers and footers in a document with the Header button and the Footer button in the Header & Footer group in the Insert tab.
- A header or footer displays in Print Layout view but will not display in Draft view.
- You can remove and/or edit predesigned headers and footers.

- A watermark is a lightened image that displays behind text in a document. Use the Watermark button in the Page Background group in the Page Layout tab to insert a watermark.
- Insert page color in a document with the Page Color button in the Page Background group. Page color is designed for viewing a document on-screen and does not print.
- Click the Page Borders button in the Page Background group and the Borders and Shading dialog box with the Page Border tab selected displays. Use options at this dialog box to insert a page border or an image page border in a document.
- Use the Find feature to search for specific characters or formatting. Use the Find and Replace feature to search for specific characters or formatting and replace with other characters or formatting.
- At the Find and Replace dialog box, click the Find Next button to find the next occurrence of the characters and/or formatting. Click the Replace button to replace the characters or formatting and find the next occurrence, or click the Replace All button to replace all occurrences of the characters or formatting.
- Click the More button at the Find and Replace dialog box to display additional options for completing a search.

# COMMANDS review

| FEATURE | RIBBON TAB, GROUP | BUTTON | KEYBOARD SHORTCUT |
|---|---|---|---|
| Blank page | Insert, Pages | Blank Page | |
| Borders and Shading dialog box with Page Border tab selected | Page Layout, Page Background | Page Borders | |
| Cover page | Insert, Pages | Cover Page | |
| Document Map | View, Show/Hide | ✓ Document Map | |
| Draft view | View, Document Views | | |
| Find and Replace dialog box with Find tab selected | Home, Editing | Find | Ctrl + F |
| Find and Replace dialog box with Replace tab selected | Home, Editing | Replace | Ctrl + H |
| Footer | Insert, Header & Footer | | |
| Full Screen Reading view | View, Document Views | | |
| Header | Insert, Header & Footer | | |
| Margins | Page Layout, Page Setup | | |
| Orientation | Page Layout, Page Setup | Orientation | |
| Page break | Insert, Pages | Page Break | Ctrl + Enter |
| Page color | Page Layout, Page Background | Page Color | |
| Page numbering | Insert, Header & Footer | | |
| Page Setup dialog box with Margins tab selected | Page Layout, Page Setup | , *Custom Margins;* or Page Setup group dialog box launcher | |
| Page Setup dialog box with Paper tab selected | Page Layout, Page Setup | Size , *More Paper Sizes* | |
| Page size | Page Layout, Page Setup | Size | |
| Print Layout view | View, Document Views | | |
| Thumbnails | View, Show/Hide | ✓ Thumbnails | |
| Watermark | Page Layout, Page Background | Watermark | |

# CONCEPTS check

## Test Your Knowledge

**Completion:** In the space provided at the right, indicate the correct term, symbol, or command.

1. This is the default measurement for the top, bottom, left, and right margins. _____

2. This view displays a document in a format for efficient editing and formatting. _____

3. This view displays a document in a format for easy viewing and reading. _____

4. The Document Map check box is located in this group in the View tab. _____

5. Insert a check mark in the *Document Map* or *Thumbnails* check box and this displays at the left side of the screen. _____

6. To remove white space, double-click this icon. _____

7. This is the default page orientation. _____

8. Set specific margins at this dialog box with the Margins tab selected. _____

9. Press these keys on the keyboard to insert a page break. _____

10. The Cover Page button is located in the Pages group in this tab. _____

11. Text that appears at the top of every page is called this. _____

12. A footer displays in Print Layout view, but not this view. _____

13. A lightened image that displays behind text in a document is called this. _____

14. The Page Borders button displays in this group in the Page Layout tab. _____

15. If you want to replace every occurrence of what you are searching for in a document, click this button at the Find and Replace dialog box. _____

16. Click this option at the Find and Replace dialog box if you are searching for a word and all of its forms. _____

# SKILLS check

## Demonstrate Your Proficiency

## 1 FORMAT A SOFTWARE LIFE CYCLE DOCUMENT AND CREATE A COVER PAGE

1. Open **WordDocument05.docx** and then save the document and name it **WordL1_C4_A1**.
2. Select the entire document, change the line spacing to 2, and then deselect the document.
3. Apply the Heading 1 style to the title of the document and apply the Heading 2 style to the headings in the document.
4. Change the Quick Styles set to *Fancy*.
5. Change the theme colors to *Flow*.
6. Insert a page break at the beginning of the heading *Testing*.
7. Move the insertion point to the beginning of the document and then insert the *Austere* cover page.
8. Insert the following text in the specified fields:
   a. Insert the current year in the *[Year]* placeholder.
   b. Insert your school's name in the *[Type the company name]* placeholder.
   c. If a name displays below your school's name, select the name and then type your first and last names.
   d. Insert *software life cycle* in the *[TYPE THE DOCUMENT TITLE]* placeholder (the placeholder will convert the text you type to all uppercase letters).
   e. Click the text below the document title, click the Abstract tab, and then press the Delete key twice.
9. Move the insertion point to any character in the title *COMMERCIAL LIFE CYCLE* and then insert the Box Italics 2 page numbering at the bottom of the pages (the page numbering will not appear on the cover page).
10. Save, print, and then close **WordL1_C4_A1.docx**.

## 2 FORMAT AN INTELLECTUAL PROPERTY REPORT AND INSERT HEADERS AND FOOTERS

1. Open **WordReport03.docx** and then save the document and name it **WordL1_C4_A2**.
2. Select the entire document and then change the line spacing to 2 and the font to 12-point Constantia.
3. Select text from the beginning of the first paragraph of text to just above the *REFERENCES* title located toward the end of the document and then indent the first line to 0.25 inch.
4. Apply the Heading 1 style to the titles *PROPERTY PROTECTION ISSUES* and *REFERENCES* (located toward the end of the document).
5. Apply the Heading 2 style to the headings in the document.
6. Change the Quick Styles set to *Distinctive*.
7. Center the *PROPERTY PROTECTION ISSUES* and *REFERENCES* titles.
8. Select and then hang indent the paragraphs below the *REFERENCES* title.

9. Insert a page break at the beginning of the *REFERENCES* title.
10. Move the insertion point to the beginning of the document and then insert the Exposure header. Type Property Protection Issues in the *[Type the document title]* placeholder and, if necessary, insert the current date in the *[Pick the date]* placeholder.
11. Insert the Pinstripes footer and type your first and last names in the *[Type text]* placeholder.
12. Save and then print **WordL1_C4_A2.docx**.
13. Remove the header and footer.
14. Insert the *Austere (Odd Page)* footer and then make the following changes:
    a. Delete the *[Type the company name]* placeholder.
    b. Select the text and page number in the footer and then change the font to 10-point Constantia bold.
15. Insert the DRAFT 1 watermark in the document.
16. Insert a page border of your choosing to the document.
17. Save, print, and then close **WordL1_C4_A2.docx**.

## Assessment

3 FORMAT A REAL ESTATE AGREEMENT

1. Open **WordContract02.docx** and then save the document and name it **WordL1_C4_A3**.
2. Find all occurrences of *BUYER* (matching the case) and replace with *James Berman*.
3. Find all occurrences of *SELLER* (matching the case) and replace with *Mona Trammell*.
4. Find all word forms of the word *buy* and replace with *purchase*.
5. Search for 14-point Tahoma bold formatting in dark red and replace with 12-point Times New Roman bold formatting in black.
6. Insert page numbers at the bottom of each page.
7. Save, print, and then close **WordL1_C4_A3.docx**.

# CASE study

## *Apply Your Skills*

You work for Citizens for Consumer Safety, a non-profit organization providing information on household safety. Your supervisor, Melinda Johansson, has asked you to attractively format a document on smoke detectors. She will be using the document as an informational handout during a presentation on smoke detectors. Open the document named **WordSmokeDetectors.docx** and then save the document and name it **WordL1_C4_CS_P1**. Apply a theme to the document and apply appropriate styles to the title and headings. Ms. Johansson has asked you to change the page orientation and then change the left and right margins to 1.5 inches. She wants the extra space at the left and right margins so audience members can write notes in the margins. Use the Help feature or experiment with the options in the Header & Footer Tools Design tab and figure out how to number pages on every page but the first page. Insert page numbering in the document that prints at the top right side of every page except the first page. Save, print, and then close **WordL1_C4_CS_P1.docx**.

After reviewing the formatted document on smoke detectors, Ms. Johansson has decided that she wants the document to print in the default orientation and she is not happy with the theme and style choices. She also noticed that the term "smoke alarm" should be replaced with "smoke detector." She has asked you to open and then format the original document. Open **WordSmokeDetectors.docx** and then save the document and name it **WordL1_C4_CS_P2**. Apply a theme to the document (other than the one you chose for Part 1) and apply styles to the title and headings. Search for all occurrences of *smoke alarm* and replace with *smoke detector*. Insert a cover page of your choosing and insert the appropriate information in the page. Use the Help feature or experiment with the options in the Header & Footer Tools Design tab and figure out how to insert an odd-page and even-page footer in a document. Insert an odd-page footer that prints the page number at the right margin and insert an even-page footer that prints the page number at the left margin. You do not want the footer to print on the cover page so make sure you position the insertion point below the cover page before inserting the footers. After inserting the footers in the document, you decide that they need to be moved down the page to create more space between the last line of text on a page and the footer. Use the Help feature or experiment with the options in the Header & Footer Tools Design tab to figure out how to move the footers down and then edit each footer so they display 0.3″ from the bottom of the page. Save, print, and then close **WordL1_C4_CS_P2.docx**.

**Part 3**

Ms. Johansson has asked you to prepare a document on infant car seats and car seat safety. She wants this informational car seat safety document available for distribution at a local community center. Use the Internet to find Web sites that provide information on child and infant car seats and car seat safety. Write a report on the information you find that includes at least the following information:

- Description of the types of car seats (such as rear-facing, convertible, forward-facing, built-in, and booster)
- Safety rules and guidelines
- Installation information
- Specific child and infant seat models
- Sites on the Internet that sell car seats
- Price ranges
- Internet sites providing safety information

Format the report using a theme and styles and include a cover page and headers and/or footers. Save the completed document and name it **WordL1_C4_CS_P3**. Print and then close the document.

# Editing and Formatting Documents

## ASSESSING proficiency

In this unit, you have learned to create, edit, save, and print Word documents. You also learned to format characters, paragraphs, and pages.

*Note: Before beginning unit assessments, copy to your storage medium the Word2007L1U1 subfolder from the Word2007L1 folder on the CD that accompanies this textbook and then make Word2007L1U1 the active folder.*

### Assessment 1 Format *Designing an Effective Web Site* Document

1. Open **WordDocument08.docx** and then save the document and name it **WordL1_U1_A1**.
2. Complete a spelling and grammar check.
3. Select from the paragraph that begins *Make your home page work for you.* through the end of the document and then apply bullet formatting.
4. Select and then bold the first sentence of each bulleted paragraph.
5. Apply paragraph border and shading to the document title.
6. Save and then print **WordL1_U1_A1.docx**.
7. Change the top, left, and right margins to 1.5 inches.
8. Select the bulleted paragraphs, change the paragraph alignment to justified, and then insert numbering.
9. Select the entire document and then change the font to 12-point Constantia.
10. Insert the text shown in Figure U1.1 after paragraph number 2. (The number 3. should be inserted preceding the text you type.)
11. Save, print, and then close **WordL1_U1_A1.docx**.

**Figure U1.1 Assessment 1**

**Avoid a cluttered look.** In design, less is more. Strive for a clean look to your pages, using ample margins and white space.

### Assessment 2 Format *Accumulated Returns* Document

1. Open **WordDocument09.docx** and then save the document and name it **WordL1_U1_A2**.
2. Select the entire document and then make the following changes:
   a. Click the No Spacing style.
   b. Change the line spacing to 1.5.
   c. Change the font to 12-point Cambria.
   d. Apply 6 points of spacing after paragraphs.

3. Select the title *TOTAL RETURN CHARTS*, change the font to 14-point Corbel bold, change the alignment to center, and apply paragraph shading of your choosing.
4. Bold the following text that appears at the beginning of the second through the fifth paragraphs:
   *Average annual total return:*
   *Annual total return:*
   *Accumulation units:*
   *Accumulative rates:*
5. Select the paragraphs of text in the body of the document (all paragraphs except the title) and then change the paragraph alignment to justified.
6. Select the paragraphs that begin with the bolded words, sort the paragraphs, and then indent the text 0.5 inch from the left margin.
7. Insert a watermark that prints *DRAFT* diagonally across the page.
8. Save, print, and then close **WordL1_U1_A2.docx**.

## Assessment 3 Format Computer Ethics Report

1. Open **WordReport04.docx** and then save the document and name it **WordL1_U1_A3**.
2. Apply the *Foundry* theme to the document.
3. Apply the Heading 1 style to the titles *FUTURE OF COMPUTER ETHICS* and *REFERENCES*.
4. Apply the Heading 2 style to the headings in the document.
5. Change the Quick Styles set to *Modern*.
6. Change the theme colors to *Opulent*.
7. Center the two titles (*FUTURE OF COMPUTER ETHICS* and *REFERENCES*).
8. Hang indent the paragraphs of text below the *REFERENCES* title.
9. Insert page numbering that prints at the bottom of each page.
10. Save, print, and then close **WordL1_U1_A3.docx**.

## Assessment 4 Set Tabs and Type Division Income Text in Columns

1. At a new blank document, type the text shown in Figure U1.2 with the following specifications:
   a. Bold and center the title as shown.
   b. You determine the tab settings for the text in columns.
   c. Select the entire document and then change the font to 12-point Arial.
2. Save the document and name it **WordL1_U1_A4**.
3. Print and then close **WordL1_U1_A4.docx**.

**Figure U1.2  Assessment 4**

### INCOME BY DIVISION

|  | 2007 | 2008 | 2009 |
|---|---|---|---|
| Public Relations | $14,375 | $16,340 | $16,200 |
| Database Services | 9,205 | 15,055 | 13,725 |
| Graphic Design | 18,400 | 21,790 | 19,600 |
| Technical Support | 5,780 | 7,325 | 9,600 |

## Assessment 5 Set Tabs and Type Table of Contents Text

1. At a new blank document, type the text shown in Figure U1.3 with the following specifications:
   a. Bold and center the title as shown.
   b. You determine the tab settings for the text in columns.
   c. Select the entire document, change the font to 12-point Bookman Old Style (or a similar serif typeface), and then change the line spacing to 1.5.
2. Save the document and name it **WordL1_U1_A5**.
3. Print and then close **WordL1_U1_A5.docx**.

**Figure U1.3 Assessment 5**

**TABLE OF CONTENTS**

Online Shopping........................................................ 2

Online Services.......................................................... 4

Peer-to-Peer Online Transactions.............................. 5

Transaction Payment Methods.................................. 8

Transaction Security and Encryption...................... 11

Establishing a Web Site.......................................... 14

## Assessment 6 Format Union Agreement Contract

1. Open **WordContract01.docx** and then save the document and name it **WordL1_U1_A6**.
2. Find all occurrences of *REINBERG MANUFACTURING* and replace with *MILLWOOD ENTERPRISES*.
3. Find all occurrences of *RM* and replace with *ME*.
4. Find all occurrences of *LABOR WORKER'S UNION* and replace with *SERVICE EMPLOYEE'S UNION*.
5. Find all occurrences of *LWU* and replace with *SEU*.
6. Select the entire document and then change the font to 12-point Cambria and the line spacing to double.
7. Select the numbered paragraphs in the *Transfers and Moving Expenses* section and change to bullets.
8. Select the numbered paragraphs in the *Sick Leave* section and change to bullets.
9. Change the page orientation to landscape and the top margin to 1.5″.
10. Save and then print **WordL1_U1_A6.docx**.
11. Change the page orientation to portrait and the left margin (previously the top margin) back to 1″.
12. Insert a footer that prints *Union Agreement* at the left margin and the page number at the right margin.

13. Insert a cover page of your choosing and insert *UNION AGREEMENT* as the document name and *Millwood Enterprises* as the company name. Include any additional information required by the cover page.
14. Save, print, and then close **WordL1_U1_A6.docx**.

### Assessment 7 Copy and Paste Text in Health Plan Document

1. Open **WordKeyLifePlan.docx** and then save the document and name it **WordL1_U1_A7**.
2. Open **WordDocument15.docx** and then turn on the display of the Clipboard task pane. Make sure the Clipboard is empty.
3. Copy to the Clipboard the heading *Plan Highlights* and the six paragraphs of text below the heading.
4. Copy to the Clipboard the heading *Plan Options* and the two paragraphs of text below the heading.
5. Copy to the Clipboard the heading *Quality Assessment* and the six paragraphs of text below the heading.
6. Close **WordDocument15.docx**.
7. With **WordL1_U1_A7.docx** open, display the Clipboard task pane.
8. Move the insertion point to the beginning of the *Provider Network* heading, paste the *Plan Options* item from the Clipboard, and match the destination formatting.
9. With the insertion point positioned at the beginning of the *Provider Network* heading, paste the *Plan Highlights* item from the Clipboard, and match the destination formatting.
10. Move the insertion point to the end of the document, paste the *Quality Assessment* item from the Clipboard, and match the destination formatting.
11. Clear the Clipboard and then close it.
12. Apply the Heading 1 style to the title, *KEY LIFE HEALTH PLAN*.
13. Apply the Heading 2 style to the headings in the document.
14. Change to a Quick Styles set of your choosing (other than the default).
15. Change to a theme of your choosing (other than the default).
16. Insert a page border of your choosing in the document.
17. Insert a header or footer of your choosing in the document.
18. Add a cover page of your choosing to the document.
19. Save, print, and then close **WordL1_U1_A7.docx**.

# WRITING activities

The following activities give you the opportunity to practice your writing skills along with demonstrating an understanding of some of the important Word features you have mastered in this unit. Use correct grammar, appropriate word choices, and clear sentence constructions. Follow the steps explained below to improve your writing skills.

# The Writing Process

**Plan:** Gather ideas, select which information to include, and choose the order in which to present the information.

**Checkpoints**

What is the purpose?

What information do the readers need in order to reach your intended conclusion?

**Write:** Following the information plan and keeping the reader in mind, draft the document using clear, direct sentences that say what you mean.

**Checkpoints**

What are the subpoints for each main thought?

How can you connect paragraphs so the reader moves smoothly from one idea to the next?

**Revise:** Improve what is written by changing, deleting, rearranging, or adding words, sentences, and paragraphs.

**Checkpoints**

Is the meaning clear?

Do the ideas follow a logical order?

Have you included any unnecessary information?

Have you built your sentences around strong nouns and verbs?

**Edit:** Check spelling, sentence construction, word use, punctuation, and capitalization.

**Checkpoints**

Can you spot any redundancies or clichés?

Can you reduce any phrases to an effective word (for example, change *the fact that* to *because*)?

Have you used commas only where there is a strong reason for doing so?

Did you proofread the document for errors that your spell checker cannot identify?

**Publish:** Prepare a final copy that could be reproduced and shared with others.

**Checkpoints**

Which design elements, for example, bolding and different fonts, would help highlight important ideas or sections?

Would charts or other graphics help clarify meaning?

### Activity 1 Write Hyphenation Steps and Hyphenate Computer Text in Health Plan Document

Use Word's Help feature to learn about hyphenating text in a document. Learn how to hyphenate text automatically as well as manually. Create a document that contains the following:

1. Include an appropriate title that is bolded and centered.
2. Write the steps required to automatically hyphenate text in a document.
3. Write the steps required to manually hyphenate text in a document.

Save the document and name it **WordL1_U1_Hyphen**. Print and then close **WordL1_U1_Hyphen.docx**. Open **WordL1_U1_A3.docx** and then save the document and name it **WordL1_U1_Act01**. Manually hyphenate text in the document. Save, print, and then close **WordL1_U1_Act01.docx**.

### Activity 2 Write Information on Customizing Spelling and Grammar

Use Word's Help feature to learn about grammar and style options. Learn about grammar options and what they detect and style options and what they detect. Also, learn how to set rules for grammar and style. Once you have determined this information, create a document describing at least two grammar options and at least two style options. Also include in this document the steps required to change the writing style from grammar only to grammar and style. Save the completed document and name it **WordL1_U1_Act02**. Print and then close **WordL1_U1_Act02.docx**.

### Research Business Desktop Computer Systems

You hold a part-time job at a local newspaper, *The Daily Chronicle*, where you conduct Internet research for the staff writers. Mr. Woods, the editor, has decided to purchase nine new desktop computers for the staff. He has asked you to identify at least three Macintosh PCs that can be purchased directly over the Internet, and he requests that you put your research and recommendations in writing. Mr. Woods is looking for solid, reliable, economical, and powerful desktop computers with good warranties and service plans. He has given you a budget of $1,300 per unit.

Search the Internet for three desktop Macintosh computer systems from three different manufacturers. Consider price, specifications (processor speed, amount of RAM, hard drive space, and monitor type and size), performance, warranties, and service plans when making your choice of systems. Print your research findings and include them with your report. (For helpful information on choosing a PC, read the article "Factors to Consider When Buying a PC," which is available in the Computer Concepts Resource Center at EMC/Paradigm's Web site. Go to www.emcp.com; click College Division and then click Resource Center for either *Computer Technology* or *Computers: Exploring Concepts*. Choose Student and then select the article under "Practical Tips for Computer Users.")

Using Word, write a brief report in which you summarize the capabilities and qualities of each of the three computer systems you recommend. Include a final paragraph detailing which system you suggest for purchase and why. If possible, incorporate user opinions and/or reviews about this system to support your decision. At the end of your report, include a table comparing the computer system. Format your report using the concepts and techniques you learned in Unit 1. Save the report and name it **WordL1_U1_InternetResearch**. Print and then close the file.

## Level 1

### Microsoft®
# word

## Unit 2: Enhancing and Customizing Documents

- ➤ Applying Formatting and Inserting Objects
- ➤ Maintaining Documents
- ➤ Creating Tables and SmartArt
- ➤ Merging Documents

# Benchmark Microsoft® Word 2007 Level 1

## Microsoft Certified Application Specialist Skills—Unit 2

| Reference No. | Skill | Pages |
|---|---|---|
| **1** | **Creating and Customizing Documents** | |
| 1.1 | Create and format documents | |
| 1.1.1 | Use document templates | 216-217 |
| 1.2 | Lay out documents | |
| 1.2.3 | Create and design the appearance of columns | 155-159 |
| **2** | **Formatting Content** | |
| 2.3 | Control pagination | |
| 2.3.2 | Create and revise sections | 154-155, 155-159 |
| **3** | **Working with Visual Content** | |
| 3.1 | Insert illustrations | |
| 3.1.1 | Create SmartArt graphics | 251-259 |
| 3.1.2 | Add pictures from files and clip art | 169-174 |
| 3.1.3 | Add shapes to a document | 177-184 |
| 3.2 | Format illustrations | |
| 3.2.1 | Change text wrapping style | 170-174 |
| 3.2.2 | Size, crop, scale, and rotate images | 170-174 |
| 3.2.4 | Apply contrast, brightness, and coloration | 169-172 |
| 3.2.5 | Include text in SmartArt graphics and shapes | 257-259 |
| 3.2.6 | Reduce picture file size | 169-172 |
| 3.3 | Format text graphically | |
| 3.3.1 | Add and edit WordArt | 184-185 |
| 3.3.2 | Create Pull Quotes | 175-177 |
| 3.3.3 | Create and revise drop caps | 162 |
| 3.4 | Insert and modify text boxes | |
| 3.4.1 | Create text boxes | 180-181 |
| 3.4.2 | Design the appearance of text boxes | 180-181 |
| 3.4.3 | Connect text boxes with a link | 182-183 |
| **4** | **Organizing Content** | |
| 4.2 | Use tables and lists to organize content | 225-229 |
| 4.2.1 | Convert text to tables and lists and convert tables to text | 247 |
| 4.2.2 | Sort text | 248 |
| 4.3 | Modify tables | |
| 4.3.1 | Format tables with Quick Styles | 229-230 |
| 4.3.2 | Change table properties and options | 234-236 |
| 4.3.3 | Combine and split table cells | 236-238 |
| 4.3.4 | Calculate numbers in tables | 249-251 |
| 4.3.5 | Modify cell contents direction and position | 243-244 |
| 4.5 | Merge documents and data sources | |
| 4.5.1 | Create a data source and a main document | 272-274, 275-276 |
| 4.5.2 | Complete a merge with form letters | 277, 283-285, 285-288 |
| 4.5.3 | Merge envelopes and labels | 278-280, 280-281 |
| **5** | **Reviewing Documents** | |
| 5.1 | Navigate documents | |
| 5.1.2 | Change window views | 201-205 |
| **6** | **Sharing and Securing Content** | |
| 6.1 | Prepare documents for sharing | |
| 6.1.1 | Save a document in different formats | 199-201 |

*Note:* The Level 1 and Level 2 texts each address approximately half of the Microsoft Certified Application Specialist skills. Complete coverage of the skills is offered in the combined Level 1 and Level 2 text titled *Benchmark Series Microsoft® Word 2007: Levels 1 and 2,* which has been approved as certified courseware and which displays the Microsoft Certified Application Specialist logo on the cover.

# Applying Formatting and Inserting Objects

## PERFORMANCE OBJECTIVES

Upon successful completion of Chapter 5, you will be able to:

- Insert section breaks
- Create and format text in columns
- Hyphenate words automatically and manually
- Create a drop cap
- Insert symbols, special characters, and the date and time
- Use the Click and Type feature
- Vertically align text
- Insert, format, and customize pictures, clip art images, text boxes, shapes, and WordArt

word Chapter 5

SNAP

Tutorial 5.1
Creating Presentable Documents
Tutorial 5.2
Using Additional Features

To apply page or document formatting to only a portion of the document, insert a section break. You can insert a continuous section break or a section break that begins a new page. A section break is useful when formatting text in columns. The hyphenation feature hyphenates words at the end of lines, creating a less ragged margin. Use buttons in the Text and Symbols groups in the Insert tab to insert symbols, special characters, and the date and time. With the Click and Type feature, you can position the insertion point at various locations in the document and change the paragraph alignment. Use the *Vertical alignment* option at the Page Setup dialog box with the Layout tab selected to align text vertically on the page. Along with these features, you will also learn how to increase the visual appeal of a document by inserting and customizing images such as pictures, clip art, text boxes, shapes, and WordArt.

*Note: Before beginning computer projects, copy to your storage medium the Word2007L1C5 subfolder from the Word2007L1 folder on the CD that accompanies this textbook and then make Word2007L1C5 the active folder.*

## Project 1  Format a Document on Computer Input Devices

You will format into columns text in a document on computer input devices, improve the readability of the document by hyphenating long words, and improve the visual appeal by inserting a drop cap.

# Inserting a Section Break

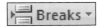

**Insert a Section Break**
1. Click Page Layout tab.
2. Click Breaks button.
3. Click section break type in drop-down list.

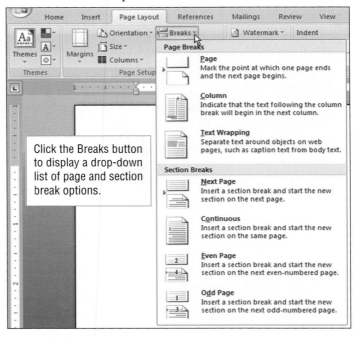

You can change the layout and formatting of specific portions of a document by inserting section breaks. For example, you can insert section breaks and then change margins for the text between the section breaks. If you want to format specific text in a document into columns, insert a section break.

Insert a section break in a document by clicking the Page Layout tab, clicking the Breaks button in the Page Setup group, and then clicking the desired option in the *Section Breaks* section of the drop-down list shown in Figure 5.1. You can insert a section break that begins a new page or a continuous section break that does not begin a new page. A continuous section break separates the document into sections but does not insert a page break. Click one of the other three options in the *Section Breaks* section of the Breaks drop-down list if you want to insert a section break that begins a new page.

**Figure 5.1** Breaks Button Drop-down List

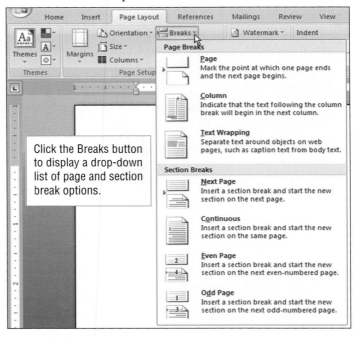

Click the Breaks button to display a drop-down list of page and section break options.

**HINT**

If you delete a section break, the text that follows the section break takes on the formatting of the text preceding the break.

A section break inserted in a document is not visible in Print Layout view. Click the Draft button and a section break displays in the document as a double row of dots with the words *Section Break* in the middle. Depending on the type of section break you insert, text follows *Section Break*. For example, if you insert a continuous section break, the words *Section Break (Continuous)* display in the middle of the row of dots. To delete a section break, change to Draft view, position the insertion point on the section break, and then press the Delete key.

# Project 1a  Inserting a Continuous Section Break

1. Open **WordDocument16.docx** and then save it and name it **WordL1_C5_P1**.
2. Insert a continuous section break by completing the following steps:
   a. Move the insertion point to the beginning of the *Keyboard* heading.
   b. Click the Page Layout tab.
   c. Click the Breaks button in the Page Setup group and then click *Continuous* in the *Section Breaks* section of the drop-down list.
3. Click the Draft button in the view area on the Status bar and then notice the section break that displays across the screen.
4. Click the Print Layout button in the view area on the Status bar.
5. With the insertion point positioned at the beginning of the *Keyboard* heading, change the left and right margins to 1.5 inches. (The margin changes affect only the text after the continuous section break.)
6. Save and then print **WordL1_C5_P1.docx**.

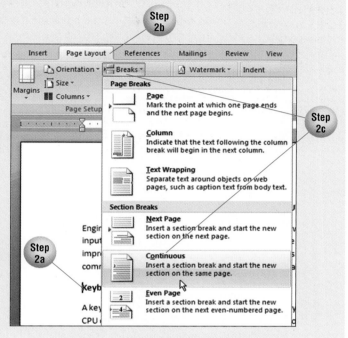

## Creating Columns

When preparing a document containing text, an important point to consider is the readability of the document. Readability refers to the ease with which a person can read and understand groups of words. The line length of text in a document can enhance or detract from the readability of text. If the line length is too long, the reader may lose his or her place on the line and have a difficult time moving to the next line below. To improve the readability of some documents such as newsletters or reports, you may want to set the text in columns. One common type of column is newspaper, which is typically used for text in newspapers, newsletters, and magazines. Newspaper columns contain text that flows up and down in the document.

Create newspaper columns with the Columns button in the Page Setup group in the Page Layout tab or with options from the Columns dialog box. The Columns button creates columns of equal width. Use the Columns dialog box to create columns with varying widths. A document can include as many columns as room available on the page. Word determines how many columns can be included on the page based on the page width, the margin widths, and the size and spacing of the columns. Columns must be at least one-half inch in width. Changes in columns affect the entire document or the section of the document in which the insertion point is positioned.

**QUICK STEPS**

**Create Columns**
1. Click Page Layout tab.
2. Click Columns button.
3. Click on desired number of columns.

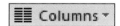

1. With **WordL1_C5_P1.docx** open, make sure the insertion point is positioned below the section break and then return the left and right margins to 1 inch.
2. Delete the section break by completing the following steps:
   a. Click the Draft button in the view area on the Status bar.
   b. Position the insertion point on the section break.

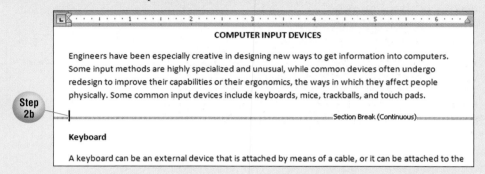

**COMPUTER INPUT DEVICES**

Engineers have been especially creative in designing new ways to get information into computers. Some input methods are highly specialized and unusual, while common devices often undergo redesign to improve their capabilities or their ergonomics, the ways in which they affect people physically. Some common input devices include keyboards, mice, trackballs, and touch pads.

Step 2b

Section Break (Continuous)

**Keyboard**

A keyboard can be an external device that is attached by means of a cable, or it can be attached to the

   c. Press the Delete key.
   d. Click the Print Layout button in the view area on the Status bar.
3. Move the insertion point to the beginning of the first paragraph of text in the document and then insert a continuous section break.
4. Format the text into columns by completing the following steps:
   a. Make sure the insertion point is positioned below the section break.
   b. Click the Page Layout tab.
   c. Click the Columns button in the Page Setup group.
   d. Click *Two* at the drop-down list.
5. Save **WordL1_C5_P1.docx**.

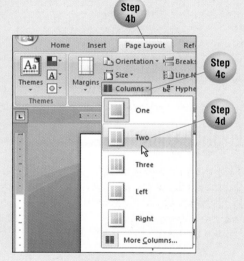

**Create Columns with Columns Dialog Box**
1. Click Page Layout tab.
2. Click Columns button.
3. Click *More Columns* at the drop-down list.
4. Specify column options.
5. Click OK.

## Creating Columns with the Columns Dialog Box

You can use the Columns dialog box to create newspaper columns that are equal or unequal in width. To display the Columns dialog box shown in Figure 5.2, click the Columns button in the Page Setup group of the Page Layout tab and then click *More Columns* at the drop-down list.

**Figure 5.2** Columns Dialog Box

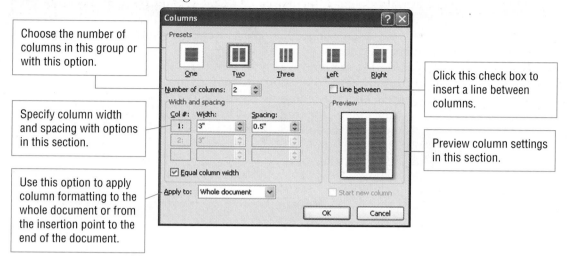

Choose the number of columns in this group or with this option.

Specify column width and spacing with options in this section.

Use this option to apply column formatting to the whole document or from the insertion point to the end of the document.

Click this check box to insert a line between columns.

Preview column settings in this section.

With options at the Columns dialog box you can specify the style and number of columns, enter your own column measurements, and create unequal columns. You can also insert a line between columns. By default, column formatting is applied to the whole document. With the *Apply to* option at the bottom of the Columns dialog box, you can change this from *Whole document* to *This point forward*. At the *This point forward* option, a section break is inserted and the column formatting is applied to text from the location of the insertion point to the end of the document or until other column formatting is encountered. The *Preview* section of the dialog box displays an example of how the columns will appear in your document.

## Removing Column Formatting

To remove column formatting using the Columns button, position the insertion point in the section containing columns, click the Page Layout tab, click the Columns button, and then click *One* at the drop-down list. You can also remove column formatting at the Columns dialog box by selecting the *One* option in the *Presets* section.

## Inserting a Column Break

When formatting text into columns, Word automatically breaks the columns to fit the page. At times, column breaks may appear in an undesirable location. You can insert a column break by positioning the insertion point where you want the column to end, clicking the Page Layout tab, clicking the Breaks button, and then clicking *Column* at the drop-down list.

HINT
You can also insert a column break with the keyboard shortcut, Ctrl + Shift + Enter.

1. With **WordL1_C5_P1.docx** open, delete the section break by completing the following steps:
   a. Click the Draft button in the view area on the Status bar.
   b. Position the insertion point on the section break and then press the Delete key.
   c. Click the Print Layout button in the view area on the Status bar.
2. Remove column formatting by clicking the Columns button in the Page Setup group in the Page Layout tab and then clicking *One* at the drop-down list.
3. Format text in columns by completing the following steps:
   a. Position the insertion point at the beginning of the first paragraph of text in the document.
   b. Click the Columns button in the Page Setup group and then click *More Columns* at the drop-down list.
   c. At the Columns dialog box, click *Two* in the *Presets* section.
   d. Click the down-pointing arrow at the right of the *Spacing* option box until 0.3″ displays.
   e. Click the *Line between* check box to insert a check mark.
   f. Click the down-pointing arrow at the right side of the *Apply to* option box and then click *This point forward* at the drop-down list.
   g. Click OK to close the dialog box.
4. Insert a column break by completing the following steps:
   a. Position the insertion point at the beginning of the *Mouse* heading.
   b. Click the Breaks button in the Page Setup group and then click *Column* at the drop-down list.

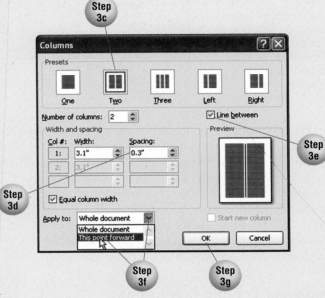

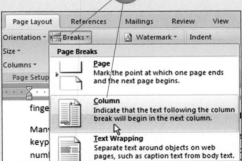

5. Save and then print **WordL1_C5_P1.docx**.

# Balancing Columns on a Page

In a document containing text formatted into columns, Word automatically lines up (balances) the last line of text at the bottom of each column, except the last page. Text in the first column of the last page may flow to the end of the page, while the text in the second column may end far short of the end of the page. You can balance columns by inserting a continuous section break at the end of the text.

## Project 1d    Formatting and Balancing Columns of Text

1. With **WordL1_C5_P1.docx** open, delete the column break by completing the following steps:
   a. Position the insertion point at the beginning of the *Mouse* heading.
   b. Click the Draft button in the view area on the Status bar.
   c. Position the insertion point on the column break.

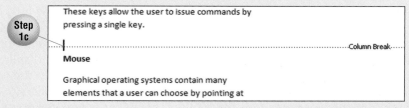

   d. Press the Delete key.
   e. Click the Print Layout button in the view area on the Status bar.
2. Select the entire document and then change the font to 12-point Constantia.
3. Move the insertion point to the end of the document and then balance the columns by clicking the Page Layout tab, clicking the Breaks button, and then clicking *Continuous* at the drop-down list.
4. Apply the Aqua, Accent 5, Lighter 60% paragraph shading to the title *COMPUTER INPUT DEVICES*.
5. Apply the Aqua, Accent 5, Lighter 80% paragraph shading to each of the headings in the document.
6. Insert page numbering that prints at the bottom of each page.
7. Save **WordL1_C5_P1.docx**.

# Hyphenating Words

In some Word documents, especially documents with left and right margins wider than 1 inch, or text set in columns, the right margin may appear quite ragged. To improve the display of text lines by making line lengths more uniform, consider hyphenating long words that fall at the end of a text line. When using the hyphenation feature, you can tell Word to hyphenate words automatically in a document or you can manually insert hyphens.

**Automatic Hyphenation**
1. Click Page Layout tab.
2. Click Hyphenation button.
3. Click *Automatic* at drop-down list.

**Manual Hyphenation**
1. Click Page Layout tab.
2. Click Hyphenation button.
3. Click *Manual* at drop-down list.
4. Click Yes or No to hyphenate indicated words.
5. When complete, click OK.

**H I N T**

Avoid dividing words at the ends of more than two consecutive lines.

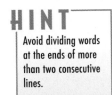

## Automatically Hyphenating Words

To automatically hyphenate words in a document, click the Page Layout tab, click the Hyphenation button in the Page Setup group, and then click *Automatic* at the drop-down list. Scroll through the document and check to see if hyphens display in appropriate locations within the words. If, after hyphenating words in a document, you want to remove all hyphens, immediately click the Undo button on the Quick Access toolbar. This must be done immediately after hyphenating since the Undo feature undoes only the last function.

## Manually Hyphenating Words

If you want to control where a hyphen appears in a word during hyphenation, choose manual hyphenation. To do this, click the Page Layout tab, click the Hyphenation button in the Page Setup group, and then click *Manual* at the drop-down list. This displays the Manual Hyphenation dialog box as shown in Figure 5.3. (The word in the *Hyphenate at* text box will vary.) At this dialog box, click Yes to hyphenate the word as indicated in the *Hyphenate at* text box; click No if you do not want the word hyphenated; or click Cancel to cancel hyphenation. You can also reposition the hyphen in the *Hyphenate at* text box. Word displays the word with syllable breaks indicated by a hyphen. The position where the word will be hyphenated displays as a blinking black bar. If you want to hyphenate at a different location in the word, position the blinking black bar where you want the hyphen and then click Yes. Continue clicking Yes or No at the Manual Hyphenation dialog box. Be careful with words ending in *-ed*. Several two-syllable words can be divided before that final syllable, for example, *noted*. However, one-syllable words ending in *-ed* should not be divided. An example is *served*. Watch for this type of occurrence and click No to cancel the hyphenation. At the hyphenation complete message, click OK.

**Figure 5.3** Manual Hyphenation Dialog Box

Click Yes to hyphenate the word at this location or move to a different syllable break and then click Yes.

Manual Hyphenation: English (U.S.)

Hyphenate at: er-go nom-ics

Yes    No    Cancel

1. With **WordL1_C5_P1.docx** open, hyphenate words automatically by completing the following steps:
   a. Press Ctrl + Home and then click the Page Layout tab.
   b. Click the Hyphenation button in the Page Setup group and then click *Automatic* at the drop-down list.

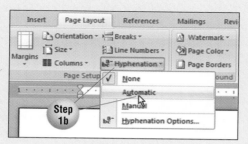

2. Scroll through the document and notice the automatic hyphenations.
3. Click the Undo button to remove the hyphens.
4. Manually hyphenate words by completing the following steps:
   a. Click the Hyphenation button in the Page Setup group and then click *Manual* at the drop-down list.

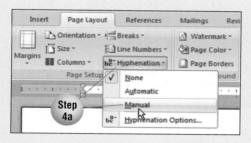

   b. At the Manual Hyphenation dialog box, make one of the following choices:
      • Click Yes to hyphenate the word as indicated in the *Hyphenate at* text box.
      • Move the hyphen in the word to a more desirable location, and then click Yes.
      • Click No if you do not want the word hyphenated.
   c. Continue clicking Yes or No at the Manual Hyphenation dialog box.
   d. At the hyphenation complete message, click OK.
5. Save **WordL1_C5_P1.docx**.

If you want to remove all hyphens in a document, immediately click the Undo button on the Quick Access toolbar. To delete a few, but not all, of the optional hyphens inserted during hyphenation, use the Find and Replace dialog box. To do this, you would display the Find and Replace dialog box with the Replace tab selected, insert an optional hyphen symbol in the *Find what* text box (to do this, click the More button, click the Special button and then click *Optional Hyphen* at the pop-up list), and make sure the *Replace with* text box is empty. Complete the find and replace, clicking the Replace button to replace the hyphen with nothing or clicking the Find Next button to leave the hyphen in the document.

# Creating a Drop Cap

**QUICK STEPS**

**Create Drop Cap**
1. Click Insert tab.
2. Click Drop Cap button.
3. Click desired type in drop-down list.

A≡ Drop Cap ▾

Use a drop cap to enhance the appearance of text. A drop cap is the first letter of the first word of a paragraph that is set into a paragraph, as shown below. Drop caps identify the beginning of major sections or parts of a document. Create a drop cap with the Drop Cap button in the Text group in the Insert tab. You can choose to set the drop cap in the paragraph or in the margin. At the Drop Cap dialog box, you can specify a font, the numbers of lines you want the letter to drop, and the distance you want the letter positioned from the text of the paragraph. You can drop cap the first word by selecting the word first and then clicking the Drop Cap button.

D rop caps look best when set in a paragraph containing text set in a proportional font. Here is an example of a drop cap.

## Project 1f — Inserting Drop Caps

1. With **WordL1_C5_P1.docx** open, create a drop cap by completing the following steps:
   a. Position the insertion point on the first word of the first paragraph of text (*Engineers*).
   b. Click the Insert tab.
   c. Click the Drop Cap button in the Text group.
   d. Click *In margin* at the drop-down gallery.
2. Looking at the drop cap, you decide that you do not like it in the margin and want it to be a little smaller. To change the drop cap, complete the following steps:
   a. With the E in the word *Engineers* selected, click the Drop Cap button in the Text group and then click *None* at the drop-down gallery.
   b. Click the Drop Cap button and then click *Drop Cap Options* at the drop-down gallery.
   c. At the Drop Cap dialog box, click *Dropped* in the *Position* section.
   d. Change the font to Times New Roman.
   e. Change the *Lines to drop* option to *2*.
   f. Click OK to close the dialog box.
   g. Click outside the drop cap to deselect it.
3. Save **WordL1_C5_P1.docx**.

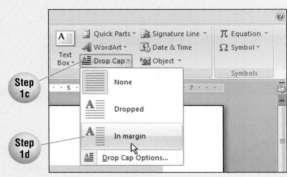

Step 1c

Step 1d

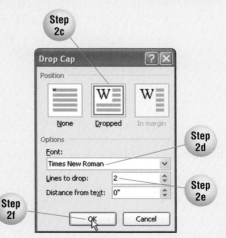

Step 2c

Step 2d

Step 2e

Step 2f

# Inserting Symbols and Special Characters

You can use the Symbol button in the Insert tab to insert special symbols in a document. Click the Symbol button in the Symbols group in the Insert tab and a drop-down list displays with the most recently inserted symbols along with a *More Symbols* option. Click one of the symbols that displays in the list to insert it in the document or click the *More Symbols* option to display the Symbol dialog box as shown in Figure 5.4. At the Symbol dialog box, double-click the desired symbol, and then click Close; or click the desired symbol, click the Insert button, and then click Close.

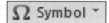
**Figure 5.4** Symbol Dialog Box with Symbols Tab Selected

Use the *Font* option to select the desired set of characters.

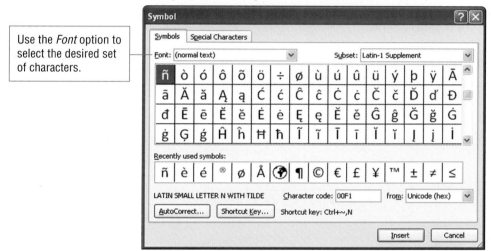

At the Symbol dialog box with the Symbols tab selected, you can change the font with the *Font* option. When you change the font, different symbols display in the dialog box. Click the Special Characters tab at the Symbol dialog box and a list of special characters displays along with keyboard shortcuts to create the special character.

## Project 1g    Inserting Symbols and Special Characters

1. With **WordL1_C5_P1.docx** open, press Ctrl + End to move the insertion point to the end of the document.
2. Press the Enter key once, type **Prepared by:**, and then press the spacebar once.
3. Type the first name **Matthew**.
4. Insert the last name *Viña* by completing the following steps:
   a. Type **Vi**.
   b. Click the Symbol button in the Symbols group in the Insert tab.
   c. Click *More Symbols* at the drop-down list.

d. At the Symbol dialog box, make sure the *Font* option displays as *(normal text)* and then double-click the ñ symbol (first symbol from the left in the twelfth row).

e. Click the Close button.

f. Type a.

5. Press Shift + Enter.

6. Insert the keyboard symbol (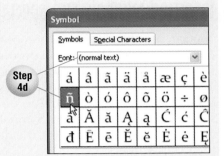) by completing the following steps:

a. Click the Symbol button and then click *More Symbols*.

b. At the Symbol dialog box, click the down-pointing arrow at the right side of the *Font* option and then click *Wingdings* at the drop-down list. (You will need to scroll down the list to display this option.)

c. Double-click 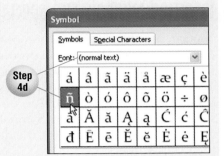 (eighth symbol from the left in the second row).

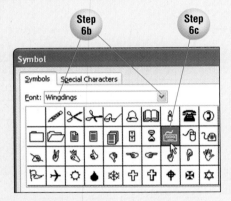

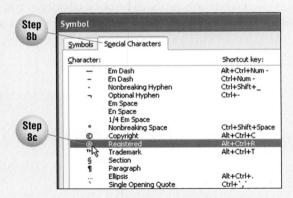

d. Click the Close button.

7. Type SoftCell Technologies.

8. Insert the registered trademark symbol (®) by completing the following steps:

a. Click the Symbol button and then click *More Symbols*.

b. At the Symbol dialog box, click the Special Characters tab.

c. Double-click the ® symbol (tenth option from the top).

d. Click the Close button.

e. Press Shift + Enter.

9. Select the keyboard symbol (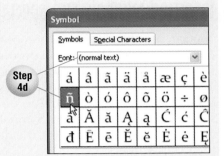) and then change the font size to 18.

10. Save WordL1_C5_P1.docx.

# Inserting the Date and Time

Use the Date & Time button in the Text group in the Insert tab to insert the current date and time in a document. Click this button and the Date and Time dialog box displays as shown in Figure 5.5 (your date will vary from what you see in the figure). At the Date and Time dialog box, click the desired date and/or time format in the *Available formats* list box.

**Insert Date and Time**
1. Click Insert tab.
2. Click Date and Time button.
3. Click option in list box.
4. Click OK.

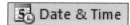

**Figure 5.5** Date and Time Dialog Box

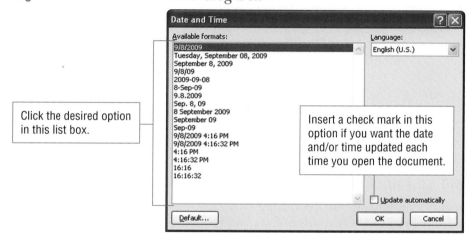

Click the desired option in this list box.

Insert a check mark in this option if you want the date and/or time updated each time you open the document.

If the *Update automatically* check box does not contain a check mark, the date and/or time are inserted in the document as normal text that you can edit in the normal manner. You can also insert the date and/or time as a field. The advantage to inserting the date or time as a field is that the field can be updated with the Update Field keyboard shortcut, F9. Insert a check mark in the *Update automatically* check box to insert the data and/or time as a field. You can also insert the date as a field using the keyboard shortcut Alt + Shift + D, and insert the time as a field with the keyboard shortcut Alt + Shift + T.

## Project 1h  Inserting the Date and Time

1. With **WordL1_C5_P1.docx** open, press Ctrl + End and make sure the insertion point is positioned below the company name.
2. Insert the current date by completing the following steps:
   a. Click the Date & Time button in the Text group in the Insert tab.

b. At the Date and Time dialog box, click the third option from the top in the *Available formats* group.

c. Click in the *Update automatically* check box to insert a check mark.

d. Click OK to close the dialog box.

3. Press Shift + Enter.

4. Insert the current time by pressing Alt + Shift + T.

5. Save **WordL1_C5_P1.docx**.

6. Update the time by clicking the time and then pressing F9.

7. Save, print, and then close **WordL1_C5_P1.docx**.

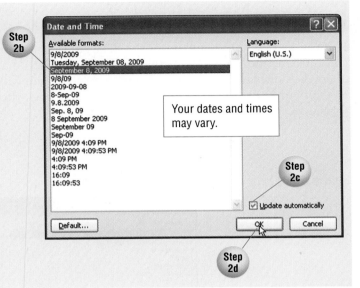

Step 2b

Your dates and times may vary.

Step 2c

Step 2d

---

# Project 2  Create an Announcement about Supervisory Training

**You will create an announcement about upcoming supervisory training and use the click and type feature to center and right align text. You will vertically center the text on the page and insert and format a picture to add visual appeal to the announcement.**

## Using the Click and Type Feature

Word contains a click and type feature you can use to position the insertion point at a specific location and alignment in the document. This feature allows you to position one or more lines of text as you write (type), rather than typing the text and then selecting and reformatting the text, which requires multiple steps.

To use click and type, make sure the document displays in Print Layout view and then hover the mouse pointer at the location where you want the insertion point positioned. As you move the mouse pointer, you will notice that the pointer displays with varying horizontal lines representing the alignment. Double-click the mouse button and the insertion point is positioned at the location of the mouse pointer. Turn off the click and type feature by clicking the Office button and then clicking Word Options. Click the Advanced option in the left panel, click the *Enable click and type* check box to remove the check mark, and then click OK.

If the horizontal lines do not display next to the mouse pointer when you double-click the mouse button, a left tab is set at the position of the insertion point. If you want to change the alignment and not set a tab, make sure the horizontal lines display near the mouse pointer before double-clicking the mouse.

## Project 2a  Using Click and Type

1. At a blank document, create the centered text shown in Figure 5.6 by completing the following steps:
   a. Position the I-beam pointer between the left and right margins at about the 3.25-inch mark on the horizontal ruler and the top of the vertical ruler.
   b. When the center alignment lines display below the I-beam pointer, double-click the left mouse button.

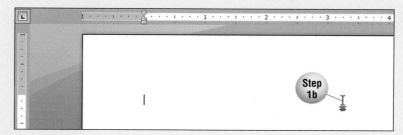

   c. Type the centered text shown in Figure 5.6. Press Shift + Enter to end each text line.
2. Change to right alignment by completing the following steps:
   a. Position the I-beam pointer near the right margin at approximately the 1.5-inch mark on the vertical ruler until the right alignment lines display at the left side of the I-beam pointer.
   b. Double-click the left mouse button.
   c. Type the right-aligned text shown in Figure 5.6. Press Shift + Enter to end the text line.
3. Select the centered text and then change the font to 14-point Candara bold and the line spacing to double.
4. Select the right-aligned text, change the font to 10-point Candara bold, and then deselect the text.
5. Save the document and name it **WordL1_C5_P2**.

**Figure 5.6  Project 2a**

SUPERVISORY TRAINING

Maximizing Employee Potential

Wednesday, February 10, 2010

Training Center

9:00 a.m. to 3:30 p.m.

Sponsored by

Cell Systems

# Vertically Aligning Text

Text in a Word document is aligned at the top of the page by default. You can change this alignment with the *Vertical alignment* option at the Page Setup dialog box with the Layout tab selected as shown in Figure 5.7. Display this dialog box by clicking the Page Layout tab, clicking the Page Setup group dialog box launcher, and then clicking the Layout tab at the Page Setup dialog box.

**Figure 5.7** Page Setup Dialog Box with Layout Tab Selected

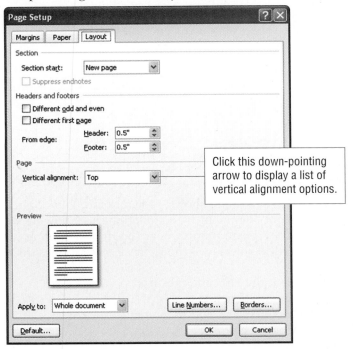

Click this down-pointing arrow to display a list of vertical alignment options.

**Vertically Align Text**
1. Click Page Layout tab.
2. Click Page Setup dialog box launcher.
3. Click Layout tab.
4. Click desired alignment.
5. Click OK.

The *Vertical alignment* option from the Page Setup dialog box contains four choices—*Top, Center, Justified,* and *Bottom.* The default setting is *Top,* which aligns text at the top of the page. Choose *Center* if you want text centered vertically on the page. The *Justified* option will align text between the top and the bottom margins. The *Center* option positions text in the middle of the page vertically, while the *Justified* option adds space between paragraphs of text (not within) to fill the page from the top to bottom margins. If you center or justify text, the text does not display centered or justified on the screen in the Draft view, but it does display centered or justified in the Print Layout view. Choose the *Bottom* option to align text in the document vertically along the bottom of the page.

**Vertically Centering Text**

1. With **WordL1_C5_P2.docx** open, click the Page Layout tab and then click the Page Setup group dialog box launcher.
2. At the Page Setup dialog box, click the Layout tab.
3. Click the down-pointing arrow at the right side of the *Vertical alignment* option box and then click *Center* at the drop-down list.
4. Click OK to close the dialog box.
5. Save and then print **WordL1_C5_P2.docx**.

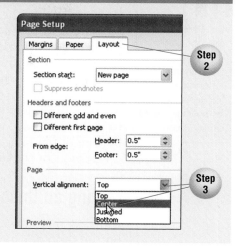

# Inserting an Image

You can insert an image such as a picture or clip art in a Word document with buttons in the Illustrations group in the Insert tab. Click the Picture button to display the Insert Picture dialog box where you can specify the desired picture file or click the Clip Art button and then choose from a variety of images available at the Clip Art task pane. When you insert a picture or a clip art image in a document, the Picture Tools Format Tab displays as shown in Figure 5.8.

**Figure 5.8** Picture Tools Format Tab

# Customizing and Formatting an Image

With options in the Adjust group in the Picture Tools Format tab you can recolor the picture or clip art image and change the brightness and contrast of the image. You can also reset the picture or clip art back to its original color or change to a different image. Use the Compress Pictures button to compress the size of the image file. Word provides predesigned styles you can apply to your image. These styles are available in the Picture Styles group along with buttons for changing the image border and applying effects to the image. Use options in the Arrange group to position the image on the page, specify text wrapping in relation to the image, align the image with other objects in the document, and rotate the image. Use the Crop button in the Size group to remove any unnecessary parts of the image and specify the image size with the *Shape Height* and *Shape Width* measurement boxes.

## Sizing an Image

You can change the size of an image with the *Shape Height* and *Shape Width* measurement boxes in the Size group in the Picture Tools Format tab or with the sizing handles that display around the selected image. To change size with a sizing handle, position the mouse pointer on a sizing handle until the pointer turns into a double-headed arrow and then hold down the left mouse button. Drag the sizing handle in or out to decrease or increase the size of the image and then release the mouse button. Use the middle sizing handles at the left or right side of the image to make the image wider or thinner. Use the middle sizing handles at the top or bottom of the image to make the image taller or shorter. Use the sizing handles at the corners of the image to change both the width and height at the same time.

## Moving an Image

Move an image to a specific location on the page with options from the Position button drop-down gallery. The Position button is located in the Arrange group in the Picture Tools Format tab. When you choose an option at the Position button drop-down gallery, the image is moved to the specified location on the page and square text wrapping is applied to the image.

You can also move the image by dragging it to the desired location. Before dragging an image, you must first choose a text wrapping style by clicking the Text Wrapping button in the Arrange group and then clicking the desired wrapping style at the drop-down list. After choosing a wrapping style, move the image by positioning the mouse pointer on the image border until the arrow pointer turns into a four-headed arrow. Hold down the left mouse button, drag the image to the desired position, and then release the mouse button. To help precisely position an image, consider turning on gridlines. Do this by clicking the Align button in the Arrange group in the Picture Tools Format tab and then clicking *Show Gridlines*.

Rotate the image by positioning the mouse pointer on the green, round rotation handle until the pointer displays as a circular arrow. Hold down the left mouse button, drag in the desired direction, and then release the mouse button.

## Inserting a Picture

**Insert Picture**
1. Click Insert tab.
2. Click Picture button.
3. Double-click desired picture in Insert Picture dialog box.

To insert a picture in a document, click the Insert tab and then click the Picture button in the Illustrations group. At the Insert Picture dialog box, navigate to the folder containing the desired picture and then double-click the picture. Use buttons in the Picture Tools Format tab to format and customize the picture. You can insert a picture from a Web page by opening the Web page, opening a Word document, and then dragging the picture from the Web page to the document. If the picture is linked, the link (rather than the image) will display in your document.

1. With **WordL1_C5_P2.docx** open, return the vertical alignment back to *Top* by completing the following steps:
   a. Click the Page Layout tab.
   b. Click the Page Setup group dialog box launcher.
   c. At the Page Setup dialog box, click the Layout tab.
   d. Click the down-pointing arrow at the right side of the *Vertical alignment* option box and then click *Top* at the drop-down list.
   e. Click OK to close the dialog box.
2. Select and then delete the text *Sponsored by* and the text *Cell Systems*.
3. Select the remaining text and change the line spacing to single.
4. Move the insertion point to the beginning of the document and then press the Enter key until the first line of text displays at approximately the 3-inch mark on the vertical ruler.
5. Insert a picture by completing the following steps:
   a. Click the Insert tab.
   b. Click the Picture button in the Illustrations group.
   c. At the Insert Picture dialog box, navigate to your Word2007L1C5 folder.
   d. Double-click **Mountain.jpg** in the list box.
6. Crop the picture by completing the following steps:
   a. Click the Crop button in the Size group.
   b. Position the mouse pointer on the bottom, middle crop handle (displays as a short black line) until the pointer turns into the crop tool (displays as a small, black T).
   c. Hold down the left mouse button, drag up to just below the mountain as shown at the right, and then release the mouse button.
   d. Click the Crop button in the Size group to turn off the feature.

Step 6c

Maximizing Employee

7. Increase the size of the picture by clicking in the *Shape Width* measurement box, typing 5, and then pressing Enter.
8. Move the picture behind the text by clicking the Text Wrapping button in the Arrange group and then clicking *Behind Text* at the drop-down list.

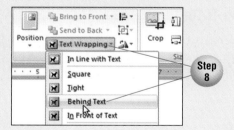

Step 8

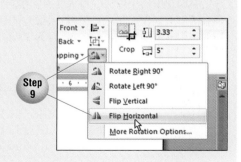

Step 9

9. Rotate the image by clicking the Rotate button in the Arrange group and then clicking *Flip Horizontal* at the drop-down list.

10. Change the picture color by clicking the Recolor button in the Adjust group and then clicking the second option from the left in the Light Variations section (*Accent color 1 Light*).

11. After looking at the coloring you decide to return to the original color by clicking the Recolor button in the Adjust group and then clicking the option in the *No Recolor* section.

12. Click the Brightness button in the Adjust group and then click *+10%* at the drop-down gallery.

13. Click the Contrast button in the Adjust group and then click *-10%* at the drop-down gallery.

14. Apply a picture style by clicking the More button at the right side of the picture styles and then clicking *Soft Edge Rectangle* (first image from the left in the second row).

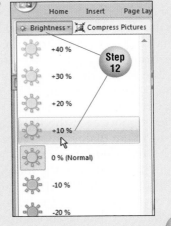

15. Compress the picture by completing the following steps:
    a. Click the Compress Pictures button in the Adjust group.
    b. At the Compress Pictures dialog box, click the *Apply to selected pictures only* check box to insert a check mark.
    c. Click OK.

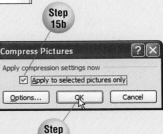

16. Position the mouse pointer on the border of the selected picture until the pointer turns into a four-headed arrow and then drag the picture so it is positioned behind the text.

17. Click outside the picture to deselect it.

18. Save, print, and then close **WordL1_C5_P2.docx**.

# Project ③ Customize a Report on Robots

**You will open a report on robots and then add visual appeal to the report by inserting and formatting a clip art image and a built-in text box.**

## Inserting a Clip Art Image

Microsoft Office includes a gallery of media images you can insert in a document such as clip art, photographs, and movie images, as well as sound clips. To insert an image in a Word document, click the Insert tab and then click the Clip Art button in the Illustrations group. This displays the Clip Art task pane at the right side of the screen as shown in Figure 5.9.

**Figure 5.9** Clip Art Task Pane

Type the search word or topic in this text box.

Use this option to specify where to search.

Use this option to specify the type of files for which you are searching.

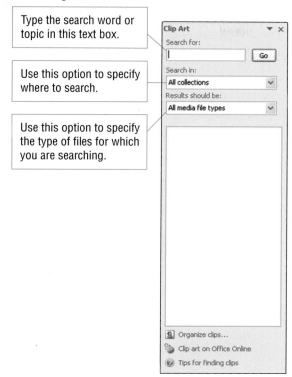

To view all picture, sound, and motion files, make sure the *Search for* text box in the Clip Art task pane does not contain any text and then click the Go button. When the desired image is visible, click the image to insert it in the document. Use buttons in the Picture Tools Format tab shown in Figure 5.8 to format and customize the clip art image.

By default (unless it has been customized), the Clip Art task pane looks for all media images and sound clips found in all locations. You can narrow the search to specific locations and to specific images. The *Search in* option at the Clip Art task pane has a default setting of *All collections*. This can be changed to *My Collections*, *Office Collections*, and *Web Collections*. The *Results should be* option has a default setting of *All media file types*. Click the down-pointing arrow at the right side of this option to display media types. To search for a specific media type, remove the check mark before all options at the drop-down list but the desired type. For example, if you are searching only for photograph images, remove the check mark before Clip Art, Movies, and Sounds.

If you are searching for specific images, click in the *Search for* text box, type the desired topic, and then click the Go button. For example, if you want to find images related to business, click in the *Search for* text box, type business, and then click the Go button. Clip art images related to *business* display in the viewing area of the task pane. If you are connected to the Internet, Word will search for images at the Office Online Web site matching the topic.

**QUICK STEPS**

**Insert Clip Art Image**
1. Click Insert tab.
2. Click Clip Art button.
3. Type search word or topic.
4. Press Enter.
5. Click desired image.

**HINT**
You can drag a clip art image from the Clip Art task pane to your document.

1. Open **WordReport07.docx** and then save the document and name it **WordL1_C5_P3**.
2. Apply the Heading 1 style to the title *ROBOTS AS ANDROIDS* and apply the Heading 2 style to the headings in the document.
3. Change the Quick Styles set to *Modern*. **Hint: Do this with the Change Styles button in the Styles group in the Home tab.**
4. Insert a clip art image by completing the following steps:
   a. Move the insertion point so it is positioned at the beginning of the first paragraph of text (the sentence that begins *Robotic factories are increasingly . . .* ).
   b. Click the Insert tab.
   c. Click the Clip Art button in the Illustrations group.
   d. At the Clip Art task pane, select any text that displays in the *Search for* text box, type **computer**, and then press Enter.
   e. Click the computer image in the list box as shown at the right.
   f. Close the Clip Art task pane by clicking the Close button (contains an X) located in the upper right corner of the task pane.

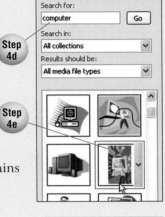

Step 4d

Step 4e

5. Crop the clip art image by completing the following steps:
   a. Click the Crop button in the Size group.
   b. Position the mouse pointer on the top middle crop handle (displays as a short black line) until the pointer turns into the crop tool.
   c. Hold down the left mouse button, drag down to just above the top of the computer as shown at the right, and then release the mouse button.
   d. Click the Crop button in the Size group to turn off the feature.
6. Decrease the size of the picture by clicking in the *Shape Height* measurement box, typing 1.3, and then pressing Enter.
7. Change the text wrapping by clicking the Text Wrapping button in the Arrange group and then clicking *Square* at the drop-down list.
8. Rotate the image by clicking the Rotate button in the Arrange group and then clicking *Flip Horizontal* at the drop-down list.
9. Change the picture color by clicking the Recolor button in the Adjust group and then clicking the second option from the left in the Light Variations section (*Accent color 1 Light*).
10. Click the Picture Effects button in the Picture Styles group, point to *Shadow*, and then click the *Offset Diagonal Bottom Left* option (last option in the top row of the *Outer* section).
11. Position the mouse pointer on the border of the selected picture until the pointer turns into a four-headed arrow and then drag the picture so it is positioned as shown at the right.
12. Click outside the clip art image to deselect it.
13. Save **WordL1_C5_P3.docx**.

ROBOTS AS ANDROID

Step 5c

where tolerance of repetitive

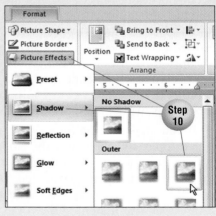

Step 10

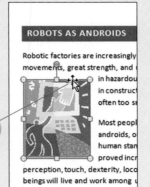

ROBOTS AS ANDROIDS

Robotic factories are increasingly movements, great strength, and in hazardou in constru often too s

Most peopl androids, o human stan proved incr

perception, touch, dexterity, loco beings will live and work among

**VISUAL PERCEPTION**

Step 11

# Inserting and Customizing a Pull Quote

Use a pull quote in a document such as an article to attract attention. A pull quote is a quote from an article that is "pulled out" and enlarged and positioned in an attractive location on the page. Some advantages of pull quotes are that they reinforce important concepts, summarize your message, and break up text blocks to make them easier to read. If you use multiple pull quotes in a document, keep them in order to ensure clear comprehension for readers.

**Inserting Pull Quote**
1. Click Insert tab.
2. Click Text Box button.
3. Click desired pull quote.

You can insert a pull quote in a document with a predesigned built-in text box. Display the available pull quote built-in text boxes by clicking the Insert tab and then clicking the Text Box button in the Text group. Click the desired pull quote from the drop-down list that displays and the built-in text box is inserted in the document. Type the quote inside the text box and then format the text and/or customize the text box. Use buttons in the Text Box Tools Format tab shown in Figure 5.10 to format and customize the built-in text box.

**Figure 5.10** Text Box Tools Format Tab

With options in the Text group in the Text Box Tools Format tab, you can draw a text box, change text direction in a text box, and link text boxes. Apply predesigned styles to a text box with options in the Text Box Styles group. You can also change the shape, shape fill, and shape outline. Add and customize shadows and 3-D effects with options in the Shadow Effects and 3-D Effects groups. Use options in the Arrange group to position the text box on the page, specify text wrapping in relation to the text box, align the text box with other objects in the document, and rotate the text box. Specify the image size with the *Shape Height* and *Shape Width* measurement boxes in the Size group.

1. With **WordL1_C5_P3.docx** open, click the Insert tab.
2. Click the Text Box button in the Text group.
3. Scroll down the drop-down list and then click the *Contrast Quote* option.

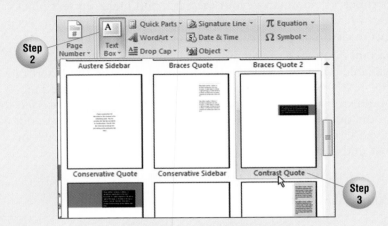

4. Type the following text in the text box: "The task of creating a humanlike body has proved incredibly difficult."
5. Click the More button at the right side of the Text Box Styles group.

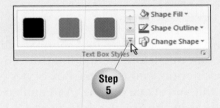

6. Click the blue *Diagonal Gradient - Accent 1* option at the drop-down gallery (second option from the left in the sixth row).
7. Click the Shadow Effects button in the Shadow Effects group and then click the *Shadow Style 5* option in the *Drop Shadow* section (first option from the left in the second row).

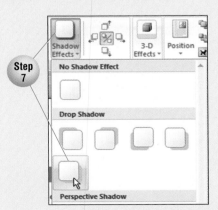

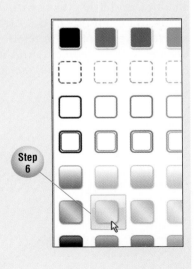

8. Position the mouse pointer on the border of the selected text box until the pointer turns into a four-headed arrow and then drag the text box so it is positioned as shown below.

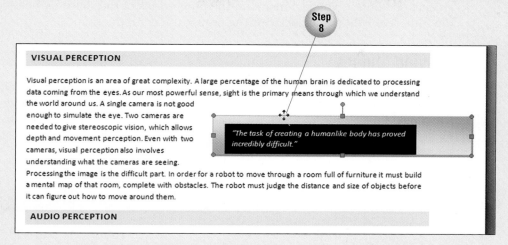

9. Save, print, and then close **WordL1_C5_P3.docx**.

# Project ④ Prepare a Company Flyer

**You will prepare a company flyer by inserting and customizing shapes, text boxes, and WordArt.**

# Drawing Shapes

Use the Shapes button in the Insert tab to draw shapes in a document including lines, basic shapes, block arrows, flow chart shapes, callouts, stars, and banners. Click a shape and the mouse pointer displays as crosshairs (plus sign). Position the crosshairs where you want the shape to begin, hold down the left mouse button, drag to create the shape, and then release the mouse button. This inserts the shape in the document and also displays the Drawing Tools Format tab shown in Figure 5.11. Use buttons in this tab to change the shape, apply a style to the shape, arrange the shape, and change the size of the shape. This tab contains many of the same options and buttons as the Picture Tools Format tab and the Text Box Tools Format tab.

**QUICK STEPS**

**Draw a Shape**
1. Click Insert tab.
2. Click Shapes button.
3. Click desired shape at drop-down list.
4. Drag in document screen to create shape.

**Figure 5.11** Drawing Tools Format Tab

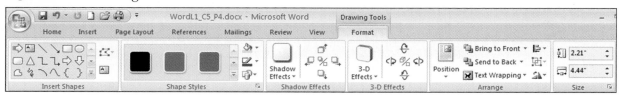

To draw a square, choose the Rectangle shape and then hold down the Shift key while drawing the shape. To draw a circle, choose the Oval shape and then hold down the Shift key while drawing the shape.

If you choose a shape in the *Lines* section of the drop-down list, the shape you draw is considered a *line drawing*. If you choose an option in the other sections of the drop-down list, the shape you draw is considered an *enclosed object*. When drawing an enclosed object, you can maintain the proportions of the shape by holding down the Shift key while dragging with the mouse to create the shape.

## Copying Shapes

To copy a shape, select the shape and then click the Copy button in the Clipboard group in the Home tab. Position the insertion point at the location where you want the copied image and then click the Paste button. You can also copy a selected shape by holding down the Ctrl key while dragging the shape to the desired location.

## Project 4a  Drawing Arrow Shapes

1. At a blank document, press the Enter key twice and then draw an arrow shape by completing the following steps:
   a. Click the Insert tab.
   b. Click the Shapes button in the Illustrations group and then click the *Striped Right Arrow* shape in the *Block Arrows* section.

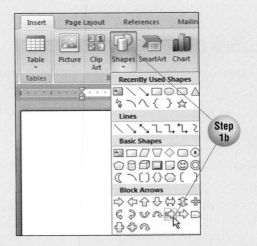

   c. Position the mouse pointer (displays as crosshairs) in the document at approximately the 1-inch mark on the horizontal ruler and the 0.5-inch mark on the vertical ruler.
   d. Hold down the Shift key and the left mouse button, drag to the right until the tip of the arrow is positioned at approximately the 5.5-inch mark on the horizontal ruler, and then release the mouse button and the Shift key.
2. Format the arrow by completing the following steps:
   a. Click in the *Shape Height* measurement box in the Size group, type 2.4, and then press Enter.
   b. Click in the *Shape Width* measurement box in the Size group, type 4.5, and then press Enter.

c. Click the More button at the right side of the Shape Styles group and then click the green *Linear Up Gradient - Accent 3* option at the drop-down gallery (fourth option from the left in the fifth row).

d. Click the 3-D Effects button in the 3-D Effects group and then click *3-D Style 6* in the *Perspective* section.

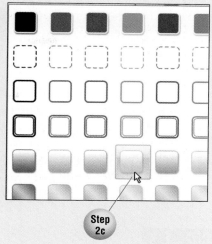
Step 2c

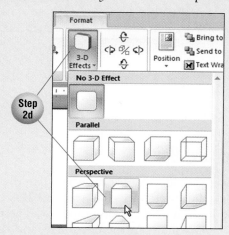
Step 2d

e. Click the 3-D Effects button, point to *3-D Color*, and then click the *Olive Green, Accent 3, Darker 50%* color.

3. Copy the arrow by completing the following steps:
   a. With the insertion point positioned in the arrow (mouse pointer displays with four-headed arrow attached), hold down the Ctrl key.
   b. Drag down until the outline of the copied arrow displays just below the top arrow, release the mouse button, and then release the Ctrl key.
   c. Copy the arrow again by holding down the Ctrl key and then dragging the outline of the copied arrow just below the second arrow.

4. Flip the middle arrow by completing the following steps:
   a. Click the middle arrow to select it.
   b. Click the Rotate button in the Arrange group and then click *Flip Horizontal* at the drop-down gallery.

5. Insert text in the top arrow by completing the following steps:
   a. Click the top arrow.
   b. Click the Edit Text button in the Insert Shapes group in the Drawing Tools Format tab.
   c. Click the Home tab.
   d. Change the font size to 16, turn on bold, and then change the font color to Olive Green, Accent 3, Darker 50%.

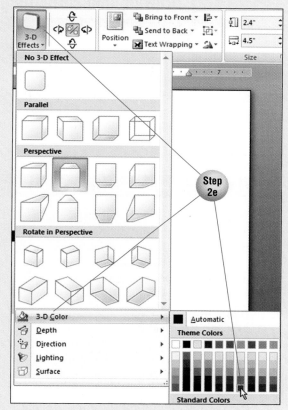
Step 2e

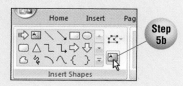
Step 5b

e. Click the Center button in the Paragraph group.
f. Type Financial.
g. Click the Text Box Tools Format tab.
h. Click the Text Direction button in the Text group.
6. Complete steps similar to those in Step 5 to insert the word *Direction* in the middle arrow. (Click twice on the Text Direction button to insert *Direction* in the tip of the arrow.)
7. Complete steps similar to those in Step 5 to insert the word *Retirement* in the bottom arrow.
8. Save the document and name it **WordL1_C5_P4**.
9. Print the document.

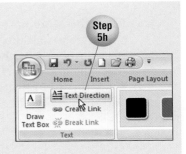

## Drawing and Formatting a Text Box

You can use the built-in text boxes provided by Word or you can draw your own text box. To draw a text box, click the Insert tab, click the Text Box button in the Text group, and then click *Draw Text Box* at the drop-down list. The mouse pointer displays as crosshairs. Position the crosshairs in the document and then drag to create the text box. When a text box is selected, the Text Box Tools Format tab displays as shown in Figure 5.11. Use buttons in this tab to format text boxes in the same manner as formatting built-in text boxes.

## Project 4b    Inserting a Text Box in a Shape

1. With **WordL1_C5_P4.docx** open, delete the bottom arrow by completing the following steps:
   a. Click the bottom arrow. (This displays a border around the arrow.)
   b. Position the mouse pointer on the border (displays with four-headed arrow attached) and then click the left mouse button.
   c. Press the Delete key.
2. Insert a shape below the two arrows by completing the following steps:
   a. Click the Insert tab.
   b. Click the Shapes button in the Illustrations group and then click the *Bevel* shape in the *Basic Shapes* section.
   c. Scroll down the document to display the blank space below the bottom arrow.
   d. Position the mouse pointer (displays as crosshairs) in the document at approximately the 1-inch mark on the horizontal ruler and the 6.5-inch mark on the vertical ruler and then click the left mouse button. (This inserts a bevel shape in the document.)

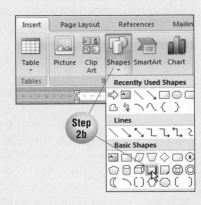

3. Format the shape by completing the following steps:
   a. Click in the *Shape Height* measurement box in the Size group, type 1.7, and then press Enter.
   b. Click in the *Shape Width* measurement box in the Size group, type 4.5, and then press Enter.
   c. Click the More button at the right side of the Shape Styles group and then click the *Linear Up Gradient - Accent 3* option at the drop-down gallery (fourth option from the left in the fifth row).
   d. Click the Shape Outline button arrow in the Shape Styles group and then click the *Olive Green, Accent 3, Darker 50%* color at the drop-down gallery.

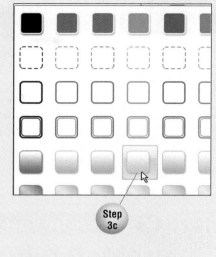

Step
3c

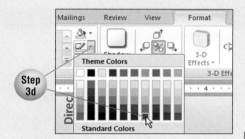

Step
3d

4. Insert a text box inside the shape by completing the following steps:
   a. Click the Insert tab.
   b. Click the Text Box button in the Text group and then click *Draw Text Box* at the drop-down list.
   c. Click inside the bevel shape.

Step
4c

5. Format the text box by completing the following steps:
   a. Click in the *Shape Width* measurement box in the Size group, type 3.5, and then press Enter.
   b. Drag the text box so it is centered inside the bevel shape.
   c. Click the Shape Fill button arrow in the Text Box Styles group and then click *No Fill* at the drop-down gallery.
   d. Click the Shape Outline button arrow in the Text Box Styles group and then click *No Outline* at the drop-down gallery.

6. Insert text inside the text box by completing the following steps:
   a. With the text box selected, click the Home tab.
   b. Change the font size to 24 points, turn on bold, and change the font color to Olive Green, Accent 3, Darker 50%.
   c. Click the Center button in the Paragraph group.
   d. Change the line spacing to 1.
   e. Type Retirement Financial Consulting. (Your shape and text box should appear as shown at the right.)

7. Save and then print **WordL1_C5_P4.docx**.

Step
6e

Retirement Financial
Consulting

# Linking Text Boxes

You can create several text boxes and then have text flow from one text box to another by linking the text boxes. To do this, draw the desired text boxes and then select the first text box you want in the link. Click the Create Link button in the Text group in the Text Box Tools Format tab and the mouse pointer displays with a link image attached. Click an empty text box to link it with the selected text box. To break a link between two boxes, select the first text box in the link, click the Break Link button in the Text group, and then click the linked text box. When you break a link, all of the text is placed in the selected text box.

## Project 4C    Linking Text Boxes

1. With **WordL1_C5_P4.docx** open, delete the text in the arrow shapes by completing the following steps:
   a. Click *Financial* located in the top arrow.
   b. Drag through *Financial* to select it. (You will need to drag down to select the word since the word displays vertically rather than horizontally.)
   c. Press the Delete key.
   d. Click *Direction* in the bottom arrow.
   e. Select *Direction* and then press the Delete key.
2. Draw a text box inside the top arrow by completing the following steps:
   a. Click the Insert tab.
   b. Click the Text Box button in the Text group and then click *Draw Text Box* at the drop-down list.
   c. Draw a text box inside the top arrow.

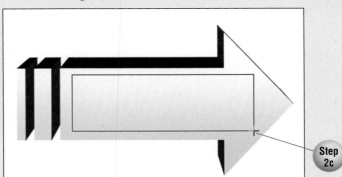

Step 1b

Step 2c

3. Format the text box by completing the following steps:
   a. Change the height measurement to *1″* and the width measurement to *3″*.
   b. Click the Shape Fill button arrow and then click *No Fill*.
   c. Click the Shape Outline button arrow and then click *No Outline*.
   d. Make sure the text box is centered in the arrow.
4. Copy the text box to the bottom arrow.
5. Click the text box in the top arrow to select it.

6. Link the top text box with the text box in the second arrow by clicking the Create Link button in the Text group and then clicking the text box in the second arrow.
7. With the top text box selected, make the following changes:
   a. Click the Home tab.
   b. Change the font size to 16 points, the font color to Olive Green, Accent 3, Darker 50%, and turn on bold.
   c. Change the line spacing to single.
   d. Click the Center button in the Paragraph group.
   e. Type Miller-Callahan Financial Services can help you plan for retirement and provide you with information to determine your financial direction. (The text will flow to the text box in the bottom arrow.)
8. Save **WordL1_C5_P4.docx**.

## Selecting Objects

When a document contains a number of objects you may need to select multiple objects and then perform tasks such as formatting, moving, or aligning the objects. To select multiple objects, click the Select button in the Editing group in the Home tab and then click *Select Objects* at the drop-down list. Using the mouse, draw a border around the objects you want to select. When you click *Select Objects* at the drop-down list, the option in the drop-down list becomes active and the mouse arrow at the left side of the option displays with an orange background. To turn off object selecting, click the Select button and then click *Select Objects*. (This removes the orange background from the mouse arrow at the left side of the option.)

**QUICK STEPS**

**Select Objects**
1. Click Select button.
2. Click *Select Objects*.
3. Draw border around objects to select.

## Project 4d   Selecting, Moving, and Aligning Objects

1. With **WordL1_C5_P4.docx** open, select the beveled shape and text box inside the shape by completing the following steps:
   a. Click the Zoom Out button located at the left side of the Zoom slider bar until 60% displays at the left side of the button.
   b. Click the Home tab.
   c. Click the Select button in the Editing group and then click *Select Objects* at the drop-down list.

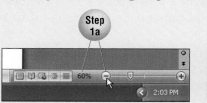
Step 1a

Step 1c

   d. Using the mouse, draw a border around the bevel shape. (When you release the mouse button, the shape is selected as well as the text box inside the shape.)

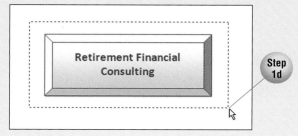
Step 1d

e. Position the mouse pointer on the border of the selected shape until the pointer displays as a four-headed arrow and then drag the shape down so the bottom of the shape is positioned at approximately the 8.5-inch mark on the vertical ruler.

f. Click outside the selected objects.

2. Select and move the arrows by completing the following steps:

a. Using the mouse, draw a border around the two arrows. (When you release the mouse button the arrows are selected as well as the text boxes in the arrows.)

b. Drag the arrows down so they are positioned just above the bevel shape.

c. Click outside the selected objects.

3. Select and then align all of the objects by completing the following steps:

a. Using the mouse, draw a border around the two arrows and the bevel shape.

b. Click the Drawing Tools Format tab.

c. Click the Align button in the Arrange group and then click *Align Center* at the drop-down list.

d. Click outside the selected objects.

e. Turn off object selecting by clicking the Select button in the Editing group and then clicking *Select Objects* at the drop-down list.

4. Save **WordL1_C5_P4.docx**.

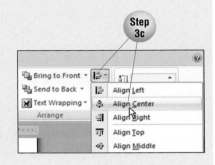

Step 3c

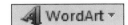

QUICK STEPS

**Create WordArt Text**
1. Click Insert tab.
2. Click WordArt button.
3. Click desired WordArt style.
4. Type WordArt text.
5. Click OK.

## Creating and Modifying WordArt Text

Use the WordArt feature to distort or modify text to conform to a variety of shapes. Consider using WordArt to create a company logo, letterhead, flier title, or heading. Insert WordArt in a document by clicking the Insert tab, clicking the WordArt button in the Text group, and then clicking the desired WordArt style at the drop-down list. Type the WordArt text at the Edit WordArt text dialog box and then click OK. You can also change the WordArt font and font size at the Edit WordArt Text dialog box.

You can customize WordArt with options and buttons in the WordArt Tools Format tab as shown in Figure 5.12. This tab displays when WordArt is selected in a document. With options and buttons at the WordArt Tools Format tab you can edit WordArt and change spacing, apply a WordArt style, change the shape fill and outline, apply shadow and 3-D effects, and arrange and size the WordArt.

**Figure 5.12** WordArt Tools Format Tab

1. With **WordL1_C5_P4.docx** open, press Ctrl + Home to move the insertion point to the beginning of the document.

2. Insert WordArt by completing the following steps:
   a. Click the Insert tab.
   b. Click the WordArt button in the Text group and then click *WordArt style 15* at the drop-down list.
   c. Type Miller-Callahan Financial Services in the Edit WordArt Text box and then click OK.

Step 2b

3. Format the WordArt text by completing the following steps:
   a. Click in the *Shape Height* measurement box, type 1, and then press Enter.
   b. Click in the *Shape Width* measurement box, type 6.5, and then press Enter.
   c. Click the Position button in the Arrange group and then click the middle option in the top row of the *With Text Wrapping* section (the option named *Position Top Center with Square Text Wrapping*).

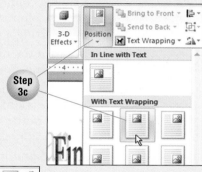

Step 3c

   d. Click the Shadow Effects button in the Shadow Effects group and then click *Shadow Style 2* at the drop-down gallery (second option from the left in the top row of the *Drop Shadow* section).

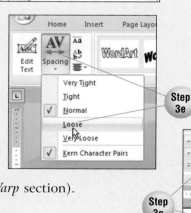

Step 3d

   e. Click the Spacing button in the Text group and then click *Loose* at the drop-down list.
   f. Click the Shape Outline button arrow in the WordArt Styles group and then click the *Olive Green, Accent 3, Darker 50%* option.
   g. Click the Change WordArt Shape button in the WordArt Styles group and then click *Can Up* (third shape from the left in the top row of the *Warp* section).

Step 3e

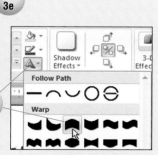

Step 3g

4. Return the display to 100%.
5. Click outside the WordArt to deselect it.
6. Make sure that all of the objects fit on one page. Consider deleting blank lines between shapes to make sure all of the objects fit on the page.
7. Save, print, and then close **WordL1_C5_P4.docx**.

# CHAPTER summary

- Insert a section break in a document to apply formatting to a portion of a document. You can insert a continuous section break or a section break that begins a new page. View a section break in Draft view since section breaks are not visible in Print Layout view.

- Set text in columns to improve readability of documents such as newsletters or reports. Format text in columns using the Columns button in the Page Setup group in the Page Layout tab or with options at the Columns dialog box.

- Remove column formatting with the Columns button in the Page Layout tab or at the Columns dialog box. Balance column text on the last page of a document by inserting a continuous section break at the end of the text.

- Improve the display of text lines by hyphenating long words that fall at the end of the line. You can automatically or manually hyphenate words in a document.

- To enhance the appearance of text, use drop caps to identify the beginning of major sections or parts of a paragraph. Create drop caps with the Drop Cap button in the Text group in the Insert tab.

- Insert symbols with options at the Symbol dialog box with the Symbols tab selected and insert special characters with options at the Symbol dialog box with the Special Characters tab selected.

- Click the Date & Time button in the Text group in the Insert tab to display the Date and Time dialog box. Insert the date or time with options at this dialog box or with keyboard shortcuts. If the date or time is inserted as a field, update the field with the Update Field key, F9.

- Use the click and type feature to center, right-align, and left-align text.

- Vertically align text in a document with the *Vertical alignment* option at the Page Setup dialog box with the Layout tab selected.

- Insert an image such as a picture or clip art with buttons in the Illustrations group in the Insert tab.

- Customize and format an image with options and buttons in the Picture Tools Format tab. Size an image with the *Shape Height* and *Shape Width* measurement boxes in the Picture Tools Format tab or with the sizing handles that display around the selected image.

- Move an image with options from the Position button drop-down gallery located in the Picture Tools Format tab or by choosing a text wrapping style and then moving the image by dragging it with the mouse.

- To insert a picture, click the Insert tab, click the Picture button, navigate to the desired folder at the Insert Picture dialog box, and then double-click the picture.

- To insert a clip art image, click the Insert tab, click the Clip Art button, and then click the desired image in the Clip Art task pane.

- Insert a pull quote in a document with a built-in text box by clicking the Insert tab, clicking the Text Box button, and then clicking the desired built-in text box at the drop-down list.

- Draw shapes in a document by clicking the Shapes button in the Illustrations group in the Insert tab, clicking the desired shape at the drop-down list, and then dragging in the document to draw the shape. Customize a shape with options at the Drawing Tools Format tab. Copy a shape by holding down the Ctrl key while dragging the selected shape.

- Draw a text box by clicking the Text Box button in the Text group in the Insert tab, clicking *Draw Text Box* at the drop-down list, and then clicking in the document or dragging in the document. Customize a text box with buttons at the Text Box Tools Format tab.

- Link drawn text boxes with the Create Link button in the Text group in the Text Box Tools Format tab. Break a link with the Break Link button in the Text group.

- Use WordArt to distort or modify text to conform to a variety of shapes. Customize WordArt with options at the WordArt Tools Format tab.

# COMMANDS review

| FEATURE | RIBBON TAB, GROUP | BUTTON | OPTION | KEYBOARD SHORTCUT |
|---------|-------------------|--------|--------|-------------------|
| Continuous section break | Page Layout, Page Setup | Breaks ▾ | Continuous | |
| Columns dialog box | Page Layout, Page Setup | Columns ▾ | More Columns | |
| Columns | Page Layout, Page Setup | Columns ▾ | | |
| Hyphenate words automatically | Page Layout, Page Setup | Hyphenation ▾ | Automatic | |
| Manual Hyphenation dialog box | Page Layout, Page Setup | Hyphenation ▾ | Manual | |
| Drop cap | Insert, Text | Drop Cap ▾ | | |
| Symbol dialog box | Insert, Symbols | Ω Symbol ▾ | | |
| Date and Time dialog box | Insert, Text | Date & Time | | |
| Insert date | | | | Alt + Shift + D |
| Insert time | | | | Alt + Shift + T |
| Update field | | | | F9 |
| Page Setup dialog box | Page Layout, Page Setup | ◻ | | |
| Insert Picture dialog box | Insert, Illustrations | ◻ | | |
| Clip Art task pane | Insert, Illustrations | ◻ | | |
| Pull quote (Built-in text box) | Insert, Text | A◻ | | |
| Shapes | Insert, Illustrations | ◻ | | |
| Text box | Insert, Text | A◻ | Draw Text Box | |
| Link text box | Text Box Tools Format, Text | Create Link | | |
| Select objects | Home, Editing | Select ▾ | Select Objects | |
| WordArt | Insert, Text | WordArt ▾ | | |

# CONCEPTS check

## Test Your Knowledge

**Completion:** In the space provided at the right, indicate the correct term, symbol, or command.

1. View a section break in this view.

2. Format text into columns with the Columns button located in this group in the Page Layout tab.

3. Balance column text on the last page of a document by inserting this type of break at the end of the text.

4. The first letter of the first word of a paragraph that is set into a paragraph is called this.

5. The Symbol button is located in this tab.

6. This is the keyboard shortcut to insert the current date.

7. Use this feature to position the insertion point at a specific location and alignment in a document.

8. Vertically align text with the *Vertical alignment* option at the Page Setup dialog box with this tab selected.

9. Insert an image in a document with buttons in this group in the Insert tab.

10. Customize and format an image with options and buttons in this tab.

11. Size an image with the sizing handles that display around the selected image or with these boxes in the Picture Tools Format tab.

12. Click the Picture button in the Insert tab and this dialog box displays.

13. Click the Clip Art button in the Insert tab and this displays at the right side of the screen.

14. This is the term for a quote that is enlarged and positioned in an attractive location on the page.

15. Format text boxes with options and buttons in this tab.

16. The Shapes button is located in this tab.

17. To copy a selected shape, hold down this key while dragging the shape.    _____

18. Link text boxes using this button in the Text group.    _____

19. To select multiple objects in a document, click the Select button in the Editing group in the Home tab and then click this option.    _____

20. Use this feature to distort or modify text to conform to a variety of shapes.    _____

# SKILLS check
## Demonstrate Your Proficiency

## Assessment

### 1 ADD VISUAL APPEAL TO A REPORT ON THE FUTURE OF THE INTERNET

1. Open **WordReport02.docx** and then save the document and name it **WordL1_C5_A1**.
2. Remove the first line indent by selecting text from the beginning of the first paragraph of text to the end of the document and then dragging the First Line Indent marker on the horizontal ruler to the 0″ mark.
3. Apply the Heading 1 style to the title of the report and apply the Heading 2 style to the headings in the report.
4. Change the Quick Styles set to *Formal*.
5. Format the text from the first paragraph to the end of the document into two columns with 0.4 inches between columns.
6. Select the title *FUTURE OF THE INTERNET* and then change the font size to 16 points, increase the spacing after the title to 12 points and, if necessary center-align the title.
7. Balance the text on the second page.
8. Insert a clip art image related to *satellite*. (Choose the clip art image that is available with Word and does not require downloading. This clip art image is blue and black and contains a satellite and a person holding a telephone and a briefcase.)
9. Make the following customizations to the clip art image:
   a. Change the height to 1.3″.
   b. Apply tight text wrapping.
   c. Recolor the clip art image to Accent color 6 Dark.
   d. Change the brightness to +10%.
   e. Drag the image so it is positioned at the left margin in the *Satellite Internet Connections* section.
10. Insert the *Alphabet Quote* built-in text box and then make the following customizations:
    a. Type the following text in the text box: "A remedy for the traffic clogging the information highway is Internet2."

b. Select the text and then change the font size to 12 and change the line spacing to 1.15.

c. Apply the Linear Up Gradient - Accent 6 style to the text box (last option in the fifth row of the Text Box Styles drop-down gallery).

d. Apply a shadow effect of your choosing to the text box.

e. Drag the box so it is positioned above the SATELLITE INTERNET CONNECTIONS heading in the first column, below the SECOND INTERNET heading in the second column, and centered between the left and right margins.

11. Press Ctrl + End to move the insertion point to the end of the document. (The insertion point will be positioned below the continuous section break you inserted on the second page to balance the columns of text.)

12. Change back to one column.

13. Press the Enter key twice and then create a shape of your choosing and make the following customizations:

a. Recolor the shape to match the color formatting in the document or the built-in text box.

b. Position the shape centered between the left and right margins.

c. Make any other changes to enhance the visual appeal of the shape.

d. Draw a text box inside the shape.

e. Remove the shape fill and the shape outline.

f. Type the following text inside the text box: &#10148;Felicité Compagnie&#10174;. Insert the &#10148; and &#10174; symbols at the Symbol dialog box with the Wingdings font selected. Insert the é symbol at the Symbol dialog box with the *(normal text)* font selected.

g. Insert the current date below &#10148;*Felicité Compagnie*&#10174; and insert the current time below the date.

h. Select and then center the text in the text box.

14. Manually hyphenate the document (do not hyphenate headings or proper names).

15. Create a drop cap with the first letter of the word *The* that begins the first paragraph of text.

16. Save, print, and then close **WordL1_C5_A1.docx**.

## Assessment

# 2 CREATE A SALES MEETING ANNOUNCEMENT

1. Create an announcement about an upcoming sales meeting with the following specifications:

a. Insert the company name *Inlet Development Company* as WordArt text.

b. Insert the following text in the document:
   National Sales Meeting
   Northwest Division
   Ocean View Resort
   August 23 through 25, 2010

c. Insert the picture named **Ocean.jpg** and size and position the picture behind the text.

d. Make any formatting changes to the WordArt, text, and picture to enhance the visual appeal of the document.

2. Save the announcement document and name it **WordL1_C5_A2**.

3. Print and then close **WordL1_C5_A2.docx**.

# CASE study
## *Apply Your Skills*

**Part 1**

You work for Honoré Financial Services and have been asked by the office manager, Jason Monroe, to prepare an information newsletter. Mr. Monroe has asked you open the document named **WordBudget.docx** and then format it into columns. You determine the number of columns and any additional enhancements to the columns. He also wants you to proofread the document and correct any spelling and grammatical errors. Save the completed newsletter and name it **WordL1_C5_CS_P1** and then print the newsletter. When Mr. Monroe reviews the newsletter, he decides that it needs additional visual appeal. He wants you to insert visual elements in the newsletter such as WordArt, clip art, a built-in text box, and/or a drop cap. Save **WordL1_C5_CS_P1.docx** and then print and close the document.

**Part 2**

Honoré Financial Services will be offering a free workshop on Planning for Financial Success. Mr. Monroe has asked you to prepare an announcement containing information on the workshop. You determine what to include in the announcement such as the date, time, location, and so forth. Enhance the announcement by inserting a picture or clip art and by applying formatting such as font, paragraph alignment, and borders. Save the completed document and name it **WordL1_C5_CS_P2**. Print and then close the document.

**Part 3**

Honoré Financial Services has adopted a new slogan and Mr. Monroe has asked you to create a shape with the new slogan inside. Experiment with the shadow and 3-D effects available at the Text Box Tools Format tab and then create a shape and enhance the shape with shadow and/or 3-D effects. Insert the new Honoré Financial Services slogan "Retirement Planning Made Easy" in the shape. Include any additional enhancements to improve the visual appeal of the shape and slogan. Save the completed document and name it **WordL1_C5_CS_P3**. Print and then close the document.

**Part 4**

Mr. Monroe has asked you to prepare a document containing information on teaching children how to budget. Use the Internet to find Web sites and articles that provide information on how to teach children to budget their money. Write a synopsis of the information you find and include at least four suggestions on how to teach children to manage their money. Format the text in the document into newspaper columns. Add additional enhancements to improve the appearance of the document. Save the completed newsletter and name it **WordL1_C5_CS_P4**. Print and then close the document.

# CHAPTER 6

# Maintaining Documents

## PERFORMANCE OBJECTIVES

Upon successful completion of Chapter 6, you will be able to:

- Create and rename a folder
- Select, delete, copy, move, rename, and print documents
- Save documents in different file formats
- Open, close, arrange, split, maximize, minimize, and restore documents
- Insert a file into an open document
- Print specific pages and sections in a document
- Print multiple copies of a document
- Print envelopes and labels
- Create a document using a Word template

**Tutorial 6.1**
Managing Folders and Multiple Documents
**Tutorial 6.2**
Printing Documents

Almost every company that conducts business maintains a filing system. The system may consist of documents, folders, and cabinets; or it may be a computerized filing system where information is stored on the computer's hard drive or other storage medium. Whatever type of filing system a business uses, daily maintenance of files is important to a company's operation. In this chapter, you will learn to maintain files (documents) in Word, including such activities as creating additional folders and copying, moving, and renaming documents. You will also learn how to create and print documents, envelopes, and labels and create a document using a Word template.

*Note: Before beginning computer projects, copy to your storage medium the Word2007L1C6 subfolder from the Word2007L1 folder on the CD that accompanies this textbook and then make Word2007L1C6 the active folder.*

roject **1** Manage Documents

You will perform a variety of file management tasks including creating and renaming a folder; selecting and then deleting, copying, cutting, pasting, and renaming documents; deleting a folder; and opening, printing, and closing a document.

# Maintaining Documents

Many file (document) management tasks can be completed at the Open dialog box (and some at the Save As dialog box). These tasks can include copying, moving, printing, and renaming documents; opening multiple documents; and creating a new folder and renaming a folder.

**QUICK STEPS**

**Create a Folder**
1. Display Open dialog box.
2. Click Create New Folder button.
3. Type folder name.
4. Press Enter.

Create New Folder

Up One Level

Back

## Creating a Folder

In Word, documents are grouped logically and placed in *folders*. The main folder on a storage medium is called the *root folder* and you can create additional folders within the root folder. At the Open or Save As dialog box, documents display in the list box preceded by a document icon 📄 and folders are preceded by a folder icon 📁. Create a new folder by clicking the Create New Folder button located on the dialog box toolbar. At the New Folder dialog box, type a name for the folder, and then press Enter. The new folder becomes the active folder. A folder name can contain a maximum of 255 characters. Numbers, spaces, and symbols can be used in the folder name, except those symbols explained in Chapter 1 in the "Naming a Document" section.

If you want to make the previous folder the active folder, click the Up One Level button on the dialog box toolbar. Clicking this button changes to the folder that is up one level from the current folder. After clicking the Up One Level button, the Back button becomes active. Click this button and the previously active folder becomes active again. You can also use the keyboard shortcut, Alt + 2, to move up one level and make the previous folder active.

## Project 1a    Creating a Folder

1. Create a folder named *Correspondence* on your storage medium by completing the following steps:
   a. Display the Open dialog box and open the Word2007L1C6 folder on your storage medium.
   b. Click the Create New Folder button located on the dialog box toolbar.
   c. At the New Folder dialog box, type **Correspondence**.
   d. Click OK or press Enter. (The Correspondence folder is now the active folder.)

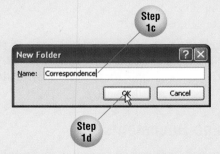

2. Change back to the Word2007L1C6 folder by clicking the Up One Level button on the dialog box toolbar.

# Renaming a Folder

As you organize your files and folders, you may decide to rename a folder. Rename a folder using the Tools button in the Open or Save As dialog box or using a shortcut menu. To rename a folder using the Tools button, display the Open or Save As dialog box, click the folder you want to rename, click the Tools button located in the lower left corner of the dialog box, and then click *Rename* at the drop-down list. This selects the folder name and inserts a border around the name. Type the new name for the folder and then press Enter. To rename a folder using a shortcut menu, display the Open dialog box, right-click the folder name in the list box, and then click *Rename* at the shortcut menu. Type a new name for the folder and then press Enter.

**Rename a Folder**
1. Display Open dialog box.
2. Right-click folder.
3. Click *Rename*.
4. Type new name.
5. Press Enter.

## Project 1b  Renaming a Folder

1. With the Open dialog box open, right-click the *Correspondence* folder name in the dialog box list box.
2. Click *Rename* at the shortcut menu.
3. Type Documents and then press Enter.

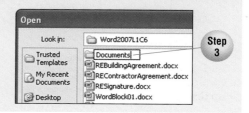

# Selecting Documents

You can complete document management tasks on one document or selected documents. To select one document, display the Open dialog box, and then click the desired document. To select several adjacent documents (documents that display next to each other), click the first document, hold down the Shift key, and then click the last document. To select documents that are not adjacent, click the first document, hold down the Ctrl key, click any other desired documents, and then release the Ctrl key.

# Deleting Documents

At some point, you may want to delete certain documents from your storage medium or any other drive or folder in which you may be working. To delete a document, display the Open or Save As dialog box, select the document, and then click the Delete button on the dialog box toolbar. At the dialog box asking you to confirm the deletion, click Yes. To delete a document using a shortcut menu, right-click the document name in the list box, click *Delete* at the shortcut menu, and then click Yes at the confirmation dialog box.

**Delete Folder/ Document**
1. Display Open dialog box.
2. Click folder or document name.
3. Click Delete button.
4. Click Yes.

Delete

**HINT**
Remember to empty the Recycle Bin on a regular basis.

# Deleting to the Recycle Bin

Documents deleted from the hard drive are automatically sent to the Windows Recycle Bin. If you accidentally delete a document to the Recycle Bin, it can be easily restored. To free space on the drive, empty the Recycle Bin on a periodic basis. Restoring a document from or emptying the contents of the Recycle Bin is completed at the Windows desktop (not in Word). To display the Recycle Bin, minimize the Word window, and then double-click the *Recycle Bin* icon located on the Windows desktop. At the Recycle Bin, you can restore file(s) and empty the Recycle Bin.

1. Open **WordDocument04.docx** and then save the document and name it **WordL1_C6_P1**.
2. Close **WordL1_C6_P1.docx**.
3. Delete **WordL1_C6_P1.docx** by completing the following steps:
   a. Display the Open dialog box.
   b. Click *WordL1_C6_P1.docx* to select it.
   c. Click the Delete button on the dialog box toolbar.

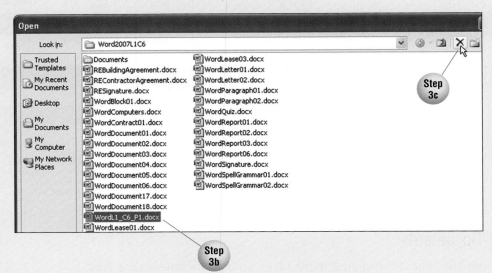

   d. At the question asking if you want to delete **WordL1_C6_P1.docx**, click Yes.
4. Delete selected documents by completing the following steps:
   a. At the Open dialog box, click *WordReport01.docx*.
   b. Hold down the Shift key and then click *WordReport03.docx*.
   c. Position the mouse pointer on a selected document and then click the *right* mouse button.
   d. At the shortcut menu that displays, click *Delete*.
   e. At the question asking if you want to delete the items, click Yes.
5. Open **WordDocument01.docx** and then save the document and name it **Keyboards**.
6. Save a copy of the **Keyboards.docx** document in the Documents folder by completing the following steps. (If your system does not contain this folder, check with your instructor to determine if another folder is available for you to use.)
   a. With **Keyboards.docx** open, click the Office button and then click *Save As*.
   b. At the Save As dialog box, double-click the *Documents* folder located at the beginning of the list box (folders are listed before documents).
   c. Click the Save button located in the lower right corner of the dialog box.
7. Close **Keyboards.docx**.
8. Display the Open dialog box and then click the Up One Level button to return to the Word2007L1C6 folder.

# Copying and Moving Documents

You can copy a document to another folder without opening the document first. To do this, use the Copy and Paste options from a shortcut menu at the Open or Save As dialog box. You can copy a document or selected documents into the same folder. When you do this, Word names the document(s) "Copy of xxx" (where *xxx* is the current document name). You can copy one document or selected documents into the same folder.

Remove a document from one folder and insert it in another folder using the Cut and Paste options from the shortcut menu at the Open dialog box. To do this, display the Open dialog box, position the arrow pointer on the document to be removed (cut), click the *right* mouse button, and then click *Cut* at the shortcut menu. Change to the desired folder, position the arrow pointer in a white area in the list box, click the *right* mouse button, and then click *Paste* at the shortcut menu.

**QUICK STEPS**

**Copy Documents**
1. Display Open dialog box.
2. Right-click document name.
3. Click *Copy*.
4. Navigate to desired folder.
5. Right-click blank area.
6. Click *Paste*.

## Project ⑩ Copying Documents

1. At the Open dialog box with Word2007L1C6 the active folder, copy a document to another folder by completing the following steps:
   a. Position the arrow pointer on **WordDocument02.docx**, click the *right* mouse button, and then click *Copy* at the shortcut menu.
   b. Change to the Documents folder by double-clicking *Documents* at the beginning of the list box.
   c. Position the arrow pointer in any white area (not on a document name) in the list box, click the *right* mouse button, and then click *Paste* at the shortcut menu.
2. Change back to the Word2007L1C6 folder by clicking the Up One Level button located on the dialog box toolbar.
3. Copy several documents to the Documents folder by completing the following steps:
   a. Click once on **WordDocument01.docx**. (This selects the document.)
   b. Hold down the Ctrl key, click **WordDocument04.docx**, click **WordDocument05.docx**, and then release the Ctrl key.
   c. Position the arrow pointer on one of the selected documents, click the *right* mouse button, and then click *Copy* at the shortcut menu.
   d. Double-click the *Documents* folder.
   e. Position the arrow pointer in any white area in the list box, click the *right* mouse button, and then click *Paste* at the shortcut menu.
4. Click the Up One Level button to return to the Word2007L1C6 folder.
5. Move **WordQuiz.docx** to the Documents folder by completing the following steps:
   a. Position the arrow pointer on **WordQuiz.docx**, click the *right* mouse button, and then click *Cut* at the shortcut menu.
   b. Double-click *Documents* to make it the active folder.
   c. Position the arrow pointer in the white area in the list box, click the *right* mouse button, and then click *Paste* at the shortcut menu.
6. Click the Up One Level button to return to the Word2007L1C6 folder.

# Renaming Documents

At the Open dialog box, use the *Rename* option from the Tools drop-down list to give a document a different name. The *Rename* option changes the name of the document and keeps it in the same folder. To use Rename, display the Open dialog box, click once on the document to be renamed, click the Tools button, and then click *Rename* at the drop-down list. This causes a black border to surround the document name and the name to be selected. Type the desired name and then press Enter. You can also rename a document by right-clicking the document name at the Open dialog box and then clicking *Rename* at the shortcut menu. Type the desired name for the document and then press the Enter key.

## Project 1e  Renaming Documents

1. Rename a document located in the Documents folder by completing the following steps:
   a. At the Open dialog box with the Word2007L1C6 folder open, double-click the *Documents* folder to make it active.
   b. Click once on **WordDocument04.docx** to select it.
   c. Click the Tools button located in the lower left corner of the dialog box.
   d. Click *Rename* at the drop-down list.
   e. Type **Privacy.docx** and then press the Enter key.
2. Click the Up One Level button to return to the Word2007L1C6 folder.

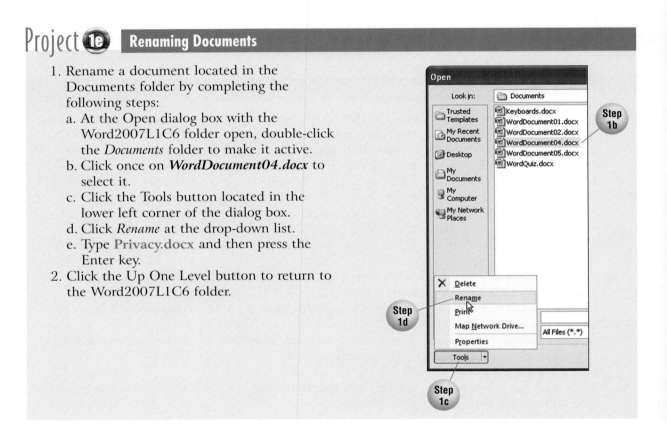

# Deleting a Folder

As you learned earlier in this chapter, you can delete a document or selected documents. Delete a folder and all its contents in the same manner as deleting a document.

## Project  Deleting a Folder

1. At the Open dialog box, click the *Documents* folder to select it.
2. Click the Delete button on the dialog box toolbar.

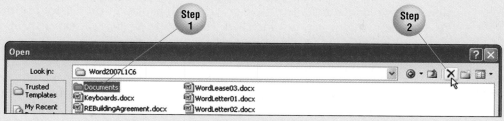

3. At the question asking if you want to remove the folder and its contents, click Yes.

# Opening and Printing Multiple Documents

To open more than one document, select the documents in the Open dialog box, and then click the Open button. You can also open multiple documents by positioning the arrow pointer on one of the selected documents, clicking the *right* mouse button, and then clicking *Open* at the shortcut menu. Up to this point, you have opened a document and then printed it. With the *Print* option from the Tools drop-down list or the *Print* option from the shortcut menu at the Open dialog box, you can print a document or several documents without opening them.

**HINT**
Open a recently opened document by clicking the Office button and then clicking the document in the drop-down list.

## Project  Opening and Printing Multiple Documents

1. Select **WordDocument01.docx**, **WordDocument02.docx**, **WordDocument03.docx**, and **WordDocument04.docx**.
2. Click the Open button located toward the lower right corner of the dialog box.
3. Close the open documents.
4. Display the Open dialog box and then select **WordDocument03.docx** and **WordDocument04.docx**.
5. Click the Tools button located in the lower left corner of the dialog box.
6. Click *Print* at the drop-down list.

# Saving a Document in a Different Format

When you save a document, the document is automatically saved as a Word document. If you need to share a document with someone who is using a different Word processing program or a different version of Word, you can save the document in another format. You can also save a Word document as a Web page, in rich text format, as plain text, or in PDF format. To save a document with a different format, display the Save As dialog box, click the down-pointing arrow at the right side of the *Save as type* option, and then click the desired format at the drop-down list.

**HINT**
A file's format is indicated by a three- or four-letter extension after the file name.

You can also save a document in a different format with the *Save As* option at the Office button drop-down list. Click the Office button, point to *Save As*, and a side menu displays with options for saving a document in the default format, saving the document as a template, in Office 97 to 2003 format as well as PDF format.

**QUICK STEPS**

**Save Document in Different Format**
1. Open document.
2. Click Office button, *Save As*.
3. Click *Save as type* option.
4. Click desired type.
5. Click Save button.

The portable document format (PDF) was developed by Adobe Systems and is a format that captures all of the elements of a file as an electronic image. You can view a PDF file on any application on any computer, making this format the most widely used for transferring files to other users. Before saving a file in PDF format, you must install an add-in download from the Microsoft Web site. If the add-in download is installed, *PDF or XPS* will display in the Office button Save As side menu and if it is not installed, *Find add-ins for other file formats* will display. To download the add-in, click the *Find add-ins for other file formats* option and then follow the steps in the Word Help window.

When you click the *PDF or XPS* option at the Save As side menu, the Save As dialog box displays with *PDF (*.pdf)* specified as the *Save as type* option. At this dialog box, type a name in the *File name* text box and then click the Publish button. By default, the file will open in PDF format in Adobe Reader. The Adobe Reader application is designed to view your file. You will be able to navigate in the file but you will not be able to make any changes to the file. You can open a PDF file in your browser window by clicking the File option on the browser menu bar and then clicking *Open*. At the Open dialog box, browse to the appropriate folder and then double-click the desired file. You may need to change the *Files of type* option to *All Files*.

The Open dialog box generally displays only Word documents, which are documents containing the *.docx* extension. If you want to display all files, display the Open dialog box, click the down-pointing arrow at the right side of the *Files of type* option, and then click *All Files (*.*)* at the drop-down list.

## Project 1h   Saving a Document in Different Formats

1. Open **WordDocument18.docx**.
2. Click the Office button, point to *Save As*, and then click *Word 97-2003 Document* at the side menu.
3. At the Save As dialog box, check to make sure that the *Save as type* option displays as *Word 97-2003 Document (*.doc)* and then type WordDocument18in2003format.
4. Click the Save button.
5. Save the document in PDF file format by completing the following steps:
   a. Click the Office button, point to *Save As*, and then click *PDF or XPS* in the side menu. (If this option does not display, the PDF add-in has not been installed.)
   b. At the Save As dialog box with the *Save as type* option set at *PDF (*.pdf)*, click the Publish button.
6. Scroll through the document in Adobe Reader.
7. Close Adobe Reader by clicking the Close button located in the upper right corner of the window.
8. Save the document as plain text by completing the following steps:
   a. Click the Office button and then click *Save As*.
   b. At the Save As dialog box, type WordDocument18PlainText in the *File name* text box.

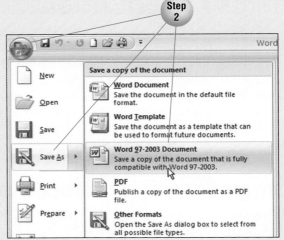

c. Click the down-pointing arrow at the right side of the *Save as type* option, scroll down the drop-down list, and then click *Plain Text (\*.txt)*.

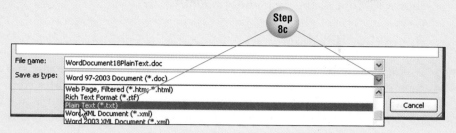

Step
8c

File name: WordDocument18PlainText.doc

Save as type: Word 97-2003 Document (\*.doc)

Web Page, Filtered (\*.htm; \*.html)
Rich Text Format (\*.rtf)
Plain Text (\*.txt)
Word XML Document (\*.xml)
Word 2003 XML Document (\*.xml)

Cancel

d. Click the Save button.
e. At the File Conversion dialog box, click OK.
9. Close the document.
10. Display the Open dialog box and, if necessary, display all files. To do this, click the down-pointing arrow at the right side of the *Files of type* option, and then click *All Files (\*.\*)* at the drop-down list. (This displays all files containing any extension.)
11. Double-click **WordDocument18PlainText.txt** in the list box. (If a File Conversion dialog box displays, click OK. Notice that the character and margin formatting has been removed from the document.)
12. Close the document.
13. Display the Open dialog box, change the *Files of type* option to *Word Documents (\*.docx)*, and then close the dialog box.

Project ② **Manage Multiple Documents**

**You will work with windows by arranging, maximizing, restoring, and minimizing windows; move selected text between split windows; compare formatting of documents side by side; print specific text, pages, and multiple copies; and create and modify document properties.**

# Working with Windows

You can open multiple documents and move the insertion point between the documents. You can also move and copy information between documents or compare the contents of documents. The maximum number of documents that you can have open at one time depends on the memory of your computer system and the amount of data in each document. When you open a new window, it is placed on top of the original window. Once multiple windows are open, you can resize the windows to see all or a portion of them on the screen.

When a document is open, a button displays on the Taskbar. This button represents the open document and contains a document icon, and the document name. (Depending on the length of the document name and the size of the button, not all of the name may be visible.) Another method for determining what documents are open is to click the View tab and then click the Switch Windows button in the Window group. The document name that displays in the list with

**HINT**
Press Ctrl + F6 to switch between open documents.

**HINT**
Press Ctrl + W or Ctrl + F4 to close the active document window.

the check mark in front of it is the **active** document. The active document is the document containing the insertion point. To make one of the other documents active, click the document name. If you are using the keyboard, type the number shown in front of the desired document.

## Arranging Windows

**Arrange Windows**
1. Open documents.
2. Click View tab.
3. Click Arrange All.

If you have more than one document open, you can arrange them so a portion of each document displays. The portions that display are the titles (if present) and opening paragraphs of each document. Seeing this information is helpful if you are preparing a report that needs to incorporate key ideas from several documents.

To arrange a group of open documents, click the View tab and then click the Arrange All button in the Window group. Figure 6.1 shows a document screen with four documents open that have been arranged.

**Figure 6.1** Arranged Documents

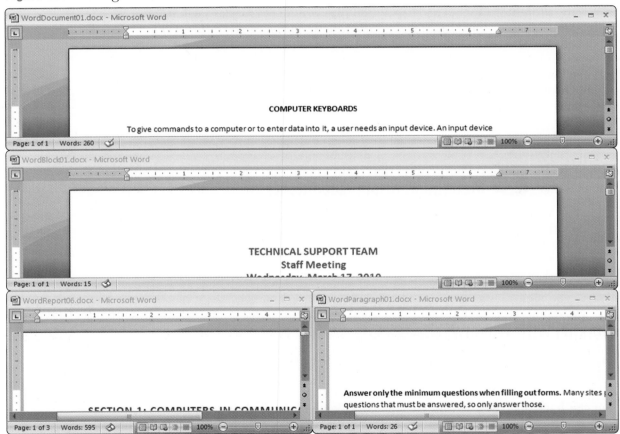

## Maximizing, Restoring, and Minimizing Documents

Minimize  Maximize

Use the Maximize and Minimize buttons in the active document window to change the size of the window. The Maximize button is the button in the upper right corner of the active document immediately to the left of the Close button. (The Close button is the button containing the *X*.) The Minimize button is located immediately to the left of the Maximize button.

If you arrange all open documents and then click the Maximize button in the active document, the active document expands to fill the document screen. In addition, the Maximize button changes to the Restore button. To return the active document back to its size before it was maximized, click the Restore button. If you click the Minimize button in the active document, the document is reduced and a button displays on the Taskbar representing the document. To maximize a document that has been minimized, click the button on the Taskbar representing the document.

Restore

## Project 2a — Arranging, Maximizing, Restoring, and Minimizing Windows

*Note: If you are using Word on a network system that contains a virus checker, you may not be able to open multiple documents at once. Continue by opening each document individually.*

1. Open the following documents: **WordBlock01.docx**, **WordDocument01.docx**, **WordParagraph01.docx**, and **WordReport06.docx**.
2. Arrange the windows by clicking the View tab and then clicking the Arrange All button in the Window group.
3. Make **WordDocument01.docx** the active document by positioning the arrow pointer on the title bar for **WordDocument01.docx** and then clicking the left mouse button.
4. Close **WordDocument01.docx**.
5. Make **WordParagraph01.docx** active and then close it.
6. Make **WordReport06.docx** active and minimize it by clicking the Minimize button in the upper right corner of the active window.
7. Maximize **WordBlock01.docx** by clicking the Maximize button at the right side of the Title bar. (The Maximize button is the button at the right side of the Title bar, immediately left of the Close button.)
8. Close **WordBlock01.docx**.
9. Restore **WordReport06.docx** by clicking the button on the Taskbar representing the document.
10. Maximize **WordReport06.docx**.

Step 7

Step 9

## Splitting a Window

You can divide a window into two *panes*, which is helpful if you want to view different parts of the same document at one time. You may want to display an outline for a report in one pane, for example, and the portion of the report that you are editing in the other. The original window is split into two panes that extend horizontally across the screen.

Split a window by clicking the View tab and then clicking the Split button in the Window group. This causes a wide gray line to display in the middle of the screen and the mouse pointer to display as a double-headed arrow pointing up and down with a small double line between. Move this double-headed arrow pointer up or down, if desired, by dragging the mouse or by pressing the up- and/or down-pointing arrow keys on the keyboard. When the double-headed arrow is positioned at the desired location in the document, click the left mouse button or press the Enter key.

You can also split the window with the split bar. The split bar is the small gray horizontal bar above the up scroll arrow on the vertical scroll bar. To split the window with the split bar, position the arrow pointer on the split bar until it turns

**QUICK STEPS**

**Split Window**
1. Open document.
2. Click View tab.
3. Click Split button.
OR
Drag split bar.

 Split

into a short double line with an up- and down-pointing arrow. Hold down the left mouse button, drag the double-headed arrow into the document screen to the location where you want the window split, and then release the mouse button. With the window split, you may decide you want to move certain objects or sections of text. Do this by selecting the desired object or text and then dragging and dropping it across the split bar.

When a window is split, the insertion point is positioned in the bottom pane. To move the insertion point to the other pane with the mouse, position the I-beam pointer in the other pane, and then click the left mouse button. To remove the split line from the document, click the View tab and then click the Remove Split button in the Window group. You can also double-click the split bar or drag the split bar to the top or bottom of the screen.

## Project 2b   Moving Selected Text between Split Windows

1. With **WordReport06.docx** open, save the document with Save As and name it **WordL1_C6_P2**.
2. Click the View tab and then click the Split button in the Window group.
3. With the split line displayed in the middle of the document screen, click the left mouse button.

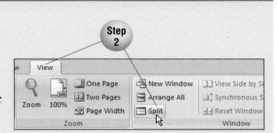

4. Move the first section below the second section by completing the following steps:
   a. Click the Home tab.
   b. Select the *SECTION 1: COMPUTERS IN COMMUNICATION* section from the title to right above *SECTION 2: COMPUTERS IN ENTERTAINMENT*.
   c. Click the Cut button in the Clipboard group in the Home tab.
   d. Position the arrow pointer at the end of the document in the bottom window pane and then click the left mouse button.
   e. Click the Paste button in the Clipboard group in the Home tab.
   f. Change the number in the two titles to *SECTION 1: COMPUTERS IN ENTERTAINMENT* and *SECTION 2: COMPUTERS IN COMMUNICATION*.
5. Remove the split from the window by clicking the View tab and then clicking the Remove Split button in the Window group.
6. If the Section 2 title displays at the bottom of the first page, move the insertion point to the beginning of the title and then press Ctrl + Enter to insert a page break.
7. Save **WordL1_C6_P2.docx**.

## Viewing Documents Side by Side

**QUICK STEPS**

**View Side by Side**
1. Open two documents.
2. Click View tab.
3. Click View Side by Side.

If you want to compare the contents of two documents, open both documents, click the View tab, and then click the View Side by Side button in the Window group. Both documents are arranged in the screen side by side as shown in Figure 6.2. By default synchronous scrolling is active. With this feature active, scrolling in one document causes the same scrolling to occur in the other document. This feature is useful in situations where you want to compare text, formatting, or other features between documents. If you want to scroll in one document and not the other, click the Synchronous Scrolling button in the Window group in the View tab to turn it off.

**Figure 6.2** Viewing Documents Side by Side

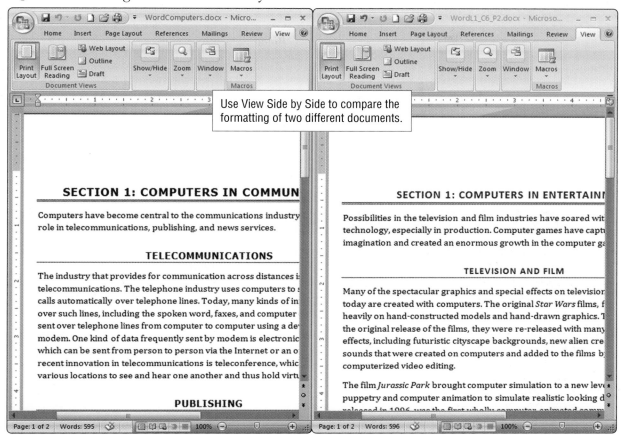

Use View Side by Side to compare the formatting of two different documents.

## Project 2c  Viewing Documents Side by Side

1. With **WordL1_C6_P2.docx** open, open **WordComputers.docx**.
2. Click the View tab and then click the View Side by Side button in the Window group.

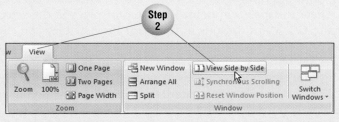

Step 2

3. Scroll through both documents simultaneously. Notice the difference between the two documents. (The title and headings are set in a different font and color.) Select and then format the title and headings in **WordL1_C6_P2.docx** so they match the formatting in **WordComputers.docx**.
4. Save **WordL1_C6_P2.docx**.
5. Make **WordComputers.docx** the active document and then close it.

**QUICK STEPS**

**Insert a File**
1. Open document.
2. Click Insert tab.
3. Click Object button arrow.
4. Click *Text from File*.
5. Navigate to desired folder.
6. Double-click document name.

# Inserting a File

If you want to insert the contents of one document into another, use the Object button in the Text group in the Insert tab. Click the Object button arrow and then click *Text from File* and the Insert File dialog box displays. This dialog box contains similar features as the Open dialog box. Navigate to the desired folder and then double-click the document you want to insert in the open document.

## Project 2d    Inserting a File

1. With **WordL1_C6_P2.docx** open, move the insertion point to the end of the document.
2. Insert a file into the open document by completing the following steps:
   a. Click the Insert tab.
   b. Click the Object button arrow in the Text group.
   c. Click *Text from File* at the drop-down list.
   d. At the Insert File dialog box, navigate to the Word2007L1C6 folder and then double-click *WordDocument17.docx*.
3. Check the formatting of the inserted text and format it to match the formatting of the original text.
4. Save **WordL1_C6_P2.docx**.

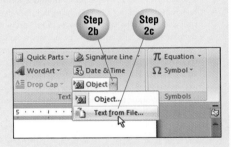

Step 2b    Step 2c

# Previewing a Document

**HINT**

View the positioning of elements on a page in Print Preview.

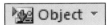

Before printing a document, you may want to view the document as it will appear when printed. To do this, display the document in Print Preview by clicking the Office button, pointing to the *Print* option, and then clicking *Print Preview*. The page where the insertion point is located displays in the screen in a manner similar to Figure 6.3. With options in the Print Preview tab, you can send the document to the printer, change the page setup, change the zoom display, and customize the preview window. Viewing a document in Print Preview is especially useful for making sure that a letter is positioned attractively on the page. For example, use Print Preview to help you center letters vertically, which means allowing equal space above and below the beginning and end of the letter.

**Figure 6.3** Document in Print Preview

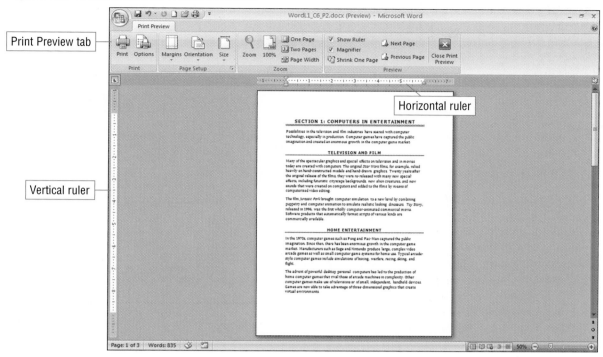

Print Preview tab

Horizontal ruler

Vertical ruler

## Project 2e  Previewing the Document

1. With **WordL1_C6_P2.docx** open, press Ctrl + Home to move the insertion point to the beginning of the document.
2. Preview the document by clicking the Office button, pointing to the *Print* option, and then clicking *Print Preview*.
3. Click the Two Pages button in the Zoom group in the Print Preview tab. (This displays the first two pages in the document.)

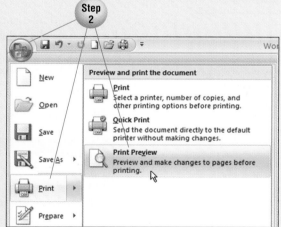

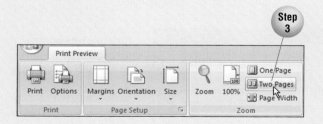

4. Click the Next Page button in the Preview group. (This displays the third page.)
5. Click the Previous Page button in the Preview group. (This redisplays the first two pages.)
6. Click the One Page button in the Zoom group.
7. Change the page orientation by clicking the Orientation button in the Page Setup group and then clicking *Landscape* at the drop-down list.

word Level 1

Maintaining Documents  **207**

8. After looking at the page in landscape orientation, you decide to return to portrait orientation. To do this, click the Orientation button in the Page Setup group and then click *Portrait* at the drop-down list.
9. Change margins by completing the following steps:
   a. Click the Margins button in the Page Setup group and then click *Custom Margins* at the drop-down list.
   b. At the Page Setup dialog box with the Margins tab selected, change the top margin to 1.25″.
   c. Click OK to close the dialog box.
10. Change the Zoom by completing the following steps:
    a. Click the Zoom button in the Zoom group.
    b. At the Zoom dialog box, click the *75%* option.
    c. Click OK to close the dialog box.
    d. After viewing the document in 75% view, click the Zoom button.
    e. At the Zoom dialog box, click the *Whole page* option.
    f. Click OK to close the dialog box.
11. Click the Close Print Preview button.
12. Save **WordL1_C6_P2.docx**.

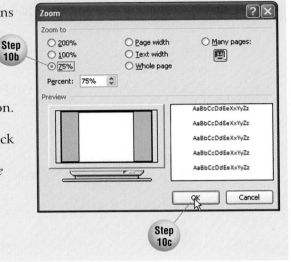

Step 10b

Step 10c

## Printing Documents

**HINT**

Save a document before printing it.

In Chapter 1, you learned to print at the Print dialog box the document displayed in the document screen. By default, one copy of all pages of the currently open document prints. With options at the Print dialog box, you can specify the number of copies to print and also specific pages for printing. To display the Print dialog box shown in Figure 6.4, click the Office button and then click *Print* or press Ctrl + P.

**Figure 6.4** Print Dialog Box

Make sure the correct printer displays here.

Click the down-pointing arrow to display a list of installed printers.

Click this button to set options for the selected printer such as paper size, layout, orientation, paper source, and paper quality.

Specify the amount of text to print with options in this section of the dialog box.

Print multiple copies of a document by increasing this number.

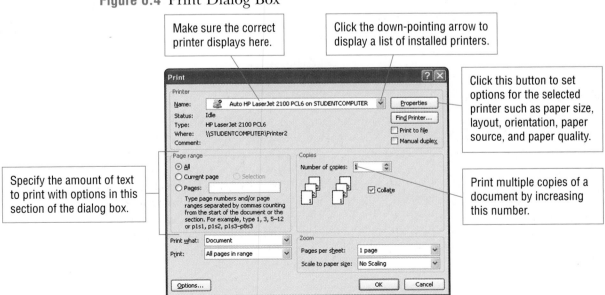

# Printing Specific Text or Pages

The *Page range* section of the Print dialog box contains settings you can use to specify the amount of text you want printed. At the default setting of *All*, all pages of the current document are printed. Choose the *Current page* option to print the page where the insertion point is located. If you want to select and then print a portion of the document, choose the *Selection* option at the Print dialog box. This prints only the text that has been selected in the current document. (This option is dimmed unless text is selected in the document.)

With the *Pages* option, you can identify a specific page, multiple pages, and/or a range of pages. If you want specific multiple pages printed, use a comma (,) to indicate *and* and use a hyphen (-) to indicate *through*. For example, to print pages 2 and 5, you would type 2,5 in the *Pages* text box. To print pages 6 through 10, you would type 6-10.

## Project 2⃣ Printing Specific Text and Pages

1. With **WordL1_C6_P2.docx** open, select the heading *Television and Film* and the two paragraphs that follow it.
2. Press Ctrl + P.
3. At the Print dialog box, click the *Selection* option in the *Page range* section.
4. Click OK.
5. Press Ctrl + Home to move the insertion point to the beginning of the document.
6. Click the Office button and then click *Print*.
7. At the Print dialog box, click the *Pages* option in the *Page range* section.
8. Type 1-2 in the *Pages* text box.
9. Click OK.

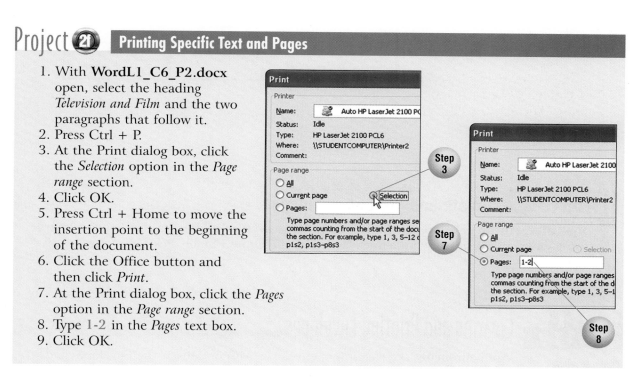

## Printing Multiple Copies

If you want to print more than one copy of a document, use the *Number of copies* option from the Print dialog box. If you print several copies of a document containing multiple pages, Word prints the pages in the document collated. For example, if you print two copies of a three-page document, pages 1, 2, and 3 are printed, and then the pages are printed a second time. Printing pages collated is helpful but takes more printing time. To speed up the printing time, you can tell Word *not* to print the pages collated. To do this, remove the check mark from the *Collate* option at the Print dialog box. With the check mark removed, Word will print all copies of the first page, and then all copies of the second page, and so on.

## Project 2g  Printing Multiple Copies of a Specific Page

1. With **WordL1_C6_P2.docx** open, press Ctrl + P.
2. Type 2 in the *Number of copies* text box.
3. Click the *Pages* option in the *Page range* section.
4. Type 1,3.
5. Click the *Collate* check box in the *Copies* section to remove the check mark.
6. Click OK.
7. Close **WordL1_C6_P2.docx**.

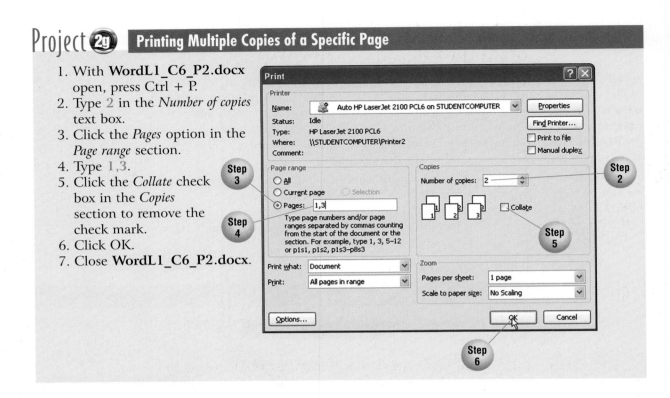

## Project 3  Create and Print an Envelope

You will create an envelope document and type the return address and delivery address using envelope addressing guidelines issued by the United States Postal Service.

**Create Envelope**
1. Click Mailings tab.
2. Click Envelopes button.
3. Type delivery address.
4. Click in *Return address* text box.
5. Type return address.
6. Click Add to Document button or Print button.

## Creating and Printing Envelopes

Word automates the creation of envelopes with options at the Envelopes and Labels dialog box with the Envelopes tab selected as shown in Figure 6.5. Display this dialog box by clicking the Mailings tab and then clicking the Envelopes button in the Create group. At the dialog box, type the delivery address in the *Delivery address* text box and the return address in the *Return address* text box. You can send the envelope directly to the printer by clicking the Print button or insert the envelope in the current document by clicking the Add to Document button.

**Figure 6.5** Envelopes and Labels Dialog Box with Envelopes Tab Selected

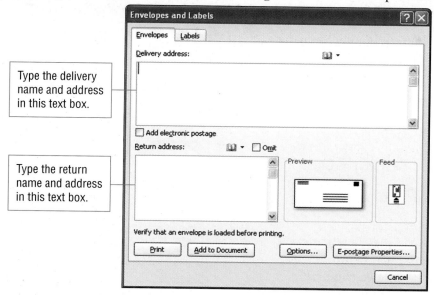

Type the delivery name and address in this text box.

Type the return name and address in this text box.

If you enter a return address before printing the envelope, Word will display the question *Do you want to save the new return address as the default return address?* At this question, click Yes if you want the current return address available for future envelopes. Click No if you do not want the current return address used as the default. If a default return address displays in the *Return address* section of the dialog box, you can tell Word to omit the return address when printing the envelope. To do this, click the *Omit* check box to insert a check mark.

The Envelopes and Labels dialog box contains a *Preview* sample box and a *Feed* sample box. The *Preview* sample box shows how the envelope will appear when printed and the *Feed* sample box shows how the envelope should be inserted into the printer.

When addressing envelopes, consider following general guidelines issued by the United States Postal Service (USPS). The USPS guidelines suggest using all capital letters with no commas or periods for return and delivery addresses. Figure 6.6 shows envelope addresses following the USPS guidelines. Use abbreviations for street suffixes (such as *ST* for *STREET* and *AVE* for *Avenue*). For a complete list of address abbreviations, visit the www.emcp.net/usps site and then search for *Official USPS Abbreviations*.

Project ③ **Printing an Envelope**

1. At a blank document, create an envelope that prints the delivery address and return address shown in Figure 6.6. Begin by clicking the Mailings tab.
2. Click the Envelopes button in the Create group.

3. At the Envelopes and Labels dialog box with the Envelopes tab selected, type the delivery address shown in Figure 6.6 (the one containing the name *GREGORY LINCOLN*). (Press the Enter key to end each line in the name and address.)

4. Click in the *Return address* text box. (If any text displays in the *Return address* text box, select and then delete it.)

5. Type the return address shown in Figure 6.6 (the one containing the name *WENDY STEINBERG*). (Press the Enter key to end each line in the name and address.)

6. Click the Add to Document button.

7. At the message *Do you want to save the new return address as the default return address?*, click No.

8. Save the document and name it **WordL1_C6_P3**.

9. Print and then close **WordL1_C6_P3.docx**. *Note: Manual feed of the envelope may be required. Please check with your instructor.*

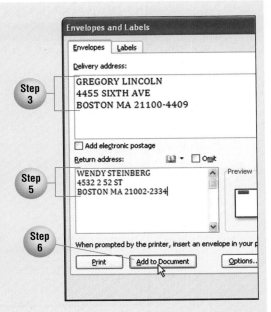

**Figure 6.6** **Project 3**

WENDY STEINBERG
4532 S 52 ST
BOSTON MA 21002-2334

GREGORY LINCOLN
4455 SIXTH AVE
BOSTON MA 21100-4409

roject ④ **Create and Print an Envelope and Mailing Labels**
You will open a letter document and then create an envelope using the inside address of the letter and then create mailing labels containing the inside address.

If you open the Envelopes and Labels dialog box in a document containing a name and address (the name and address lines must end with a press of the Enter key and not Shift + Enter), the name and address are automatically inserted in the *Delivery address* section of the dialog box. To do this, open a document containing a name and address and then display the Envelopes and Labels dialog box. The name and address are inserted in the *Delivery address* section as they appear in the letter and may not conform to the USPS guidelines. The USPS guidelines for addressing envelopes are only suggestions, not requirements.

## Project ④a Creating an Envelope in an Existing Document

1. Open **WordLetter01.docx**.
2. Click the Mailings tab.
3. Click the Envelopes button in the Create group.
4. At the Envelopes and Labels dialog box (with the Envelopes tab selected), make sure the delivery address displays properly in the *Delivery address* section.
5. If any text displays in the *Return address* section, insert a check mark in the *Omit* check box (located to the right of the *Return address* option). (This tells Word not to print the return address on the envelope.)
6. Click the Print button.

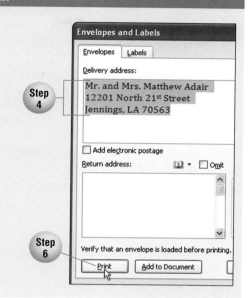

Step 4

Step 6

# Creating and Printing Labels

Use Word's labels feature to print text on mailing labels, file labels, disk labels, or other types of labels. Word includes a variety of predefined formats for labels that can be purchased at an office supply store. To create a sheet of mailing labels with the same name and address using the default options, click the Labels button in the Create group in the Mailings tab. At the Envelopes and Labels dialog box with the Labels tab selected as shown in Figure 6.7, type the desired address in the *Address* text box. Click the New Document button to insert the mailing label in a new document or click the Print button to send the mailing label directly to the printer.

**QUICK STEPS**

**Create Labels**
1. Click Mailings tab.
2. Click Labels button.
3. Type desired address(es).
4. Click New Document button or Print button.

Labels

**Figure 6.7** Envelopes and Labels Dialog Box with Labels Tab Selected

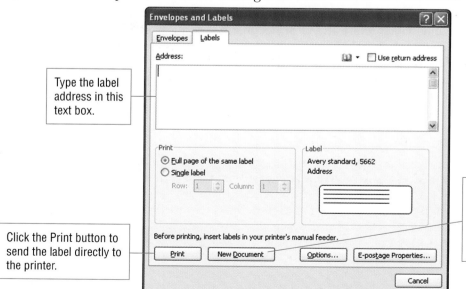

Type the label address in this text box.

Click the Print button to send the label directly to the printer.

Click the New Document button to insert the mailing label in a new document.

1. With **WordLetter01.docx** open, create mailing labels with the delivery address. Begin by clicking the Mailings tab.
2. Click the Labels button in the Create group.
3. At the Envelopes and Labels dialog box with the Labels tab selected, make sure the delivery address displays properly in the *Address* section.
4. Click the New Document button.
5. Save the mailing label document and name it **WordL1_C6_P4.docx**.
6. Print and then close **WordL1_C6_P4.docx**.
7. Close **WordLetter01.docx**.

Step 3

Step 4

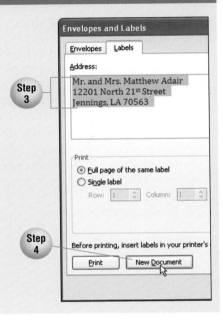

P roject **5**  Create Mailing Labels

You will create mailing labels containing varying names and addresses.

If you open the Envelopes and Labels dialog box with the Labels tab selected in a document containing a name and address, the name and address are automatically inserted in the *Address* section of the dialog box. To enter different names in each of the mailing labels, start at a clear document screen, display the Envelopes and Labels dialog box with the Labels tab selected, and then click the New Document button. The Envelopes and Labels dialog box is removed from the screen and the document screen displays with label forms. The insertion point is positioned in the first label form. Type the name and address in this label and then press the Tab key to move the insertion point to the next label. Pressing Shift + Tab will move the insertion point to the preceding label.

# Changing Label Options

Click the Options button at the Envelopes and Labels dialog box with the Labels tab selected and the Label Options dialog box displays as shown in Figure 6.8. At the Label Options dialog box, choose the type of printer, the desired label product, and the product number. This dialog box also displays information about the selected label such as type, height, width, and paper size. When you select a label, Word automatically determines label margins. If, however, you want to customize these default settings, click the Details button at the Label Options dialog box.

**Figure 6.8** Label Options Dialog Box

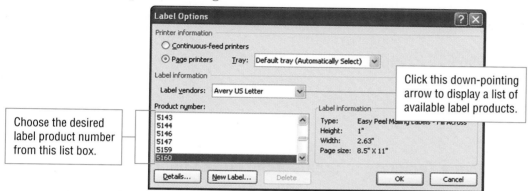

Click this down-pointing arrow to display a list of available label products.

Choose the desired label product number from this list box.

## Project 5  Creating Customized Mailing Labels

1. At a blank document, click the Mailings tab.
2. Click the Labels button in the Create group.
3. At the Envelopes and Labels dialog box with the Labels tab selected, click the Options button.
4. At the Label Options dialog box, click the down-pointing arrow at the right side of the *Label vendors* option and then click *Avery US Letter* at the drop-down list.
5. Scroll down the *Product number* list box and then click *5160*.
6. Click OK or press Enter.
7. At the Envelopes and Labels dialog box, click the New Document button.
8. At the document screen, type the first name and address shown in Figure 6.9 in the first label.
9. Press the Tab key twice to move the insertion point to the next label and then type the second name and address shown in Figure 6.9.

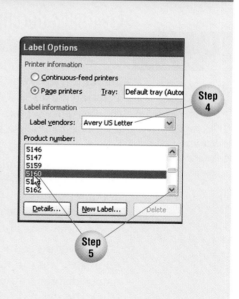

Step 4

Step 5

10. Continue in this manner until all names and addresses in Figure 6.9 have been typed.
11. Save the document and name it **WordL1_C6_P5**.
12. Print and then close **WordL1_C6_P5.docx**.
13. At the blank document, close the document without saving changes.

---

**Figure 6.9 Project 5**

| | | |
|---|---|---|
| DAVID LOWRY | MARCELLA SANTOS | KEVIN DORSEY |
| 12033 S 152 ST | 394 APPLE BLOSSOM | 26302 PRAIRIE DR |
| HOUSTON TX 77340 | FRIENDSWOOD TX 77533 | HOUSTON TX 77316 |
| | | |
| AL AND DONNA SASAKI | JACKIE RHYNER | MARK AND TINA ELLIS |
| 1392 PIONEER DR | 29039 107 AVE E | 607 FORD AVE |
| BAYTOWN TX 77903 | HOUSTON TX 77302 | HOUSTON TX 77307 |

---

# Project ⑥ Use a Template to Create a Business Letter

You will use a letter template provided by Word to create a business letter.

## Creating a Document Using a Template

**QUICK STEPS**

**Create Document using a Template**
1. Click Office button, New.
2. Click *Installed Templates.*
3. Double-click desired template.

Word includes a number of template documents formatted for specific uses. Each Word document is based on a template document with the Normal template the default. With Word templates, you can easily create a variety of documents such as letters, faxes, and awards, with specialized formatting. Templates are available in the *Templates* section of the New Document dialog box. You can choose an installed template or choose from a variety of templates available online.

To create a document based on a template, display the New Document dialog box, click the *Installed Templates* option in the *Templates* section, and then double-click the desired template in the *Installed Templates* list box. This causes a template document to open that contains formatting as well as specific locations where you enter text. Locations for personalized text display in placeholders. Click the placeholder text and then type the personalized text.

If you are connected to the Internet, Microsoft offers a number of predesigned templates you can download. Templates are grouped into categories and the category names display in the *Microsoft Office Online* section of the New Document dialog box. Click the desired template category in the list box and available templates display at the right. Click the desired template and then click the Download button.

1. Click the Office button and then click *New* at the drop-down list.
2. At the New Document dialog box, display available templates by clicking *Installed Templates* in the *Templates* section.
3. Scroll through the list of installed templates and then double-click the **Equity Letter** template.

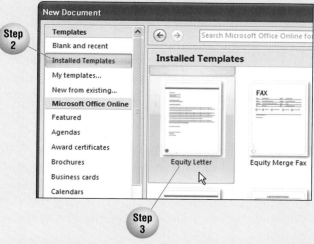

Step 2

Step 3

4. At the letter document, click the placeholder text *[Pick the date]*, click the down-pointing arrow at the right side of the placeholder, and then click the Today button located at the bottom of the calendar.
5. Click in the name that displays below the date, select the name, and then type your first and last names.
6. Click the placeholder text *[Type the sender company name]* and then type Sorenson Funds.
7. Click the placeholder text *[Type the sender company address]*, type 4400 Jackson Avenue, press the Enter key, and then type Seattle, WA 98021.
8. Click the placeholder text *[Type the recipient name]* and then type Ms. Jennifer Gonzalez.
9. Click the placeholder text *[Type the recipient address]*, type 12990 California Avenue, press the Enter key, and then type Seattle, WA 98022.
10. Click the placeholder text *[Type the salutation]* and then type Dear Ms. Gonzalez:.
11. Insert a file in the document by completing the following steps:
    a. Click anywhere in the three paragraphs of text in the body of the letter and then click the Delete key.
    b. Click the Insert tab.
    c. Click the Object button arrow in the Text group and then click *Text from File* at the drop-down list.
    d. At the Insert File dialog box, navigate to the Word2007L1C6 folder on your storage medium and then double-click **WordLetter02.docx**.
12. Click the placeholder text *[Type the closing]* and then type Sincerely,.
13. Delete one blank line above Sincerely.
14. Click the placeholder text *[Type the sender title]* and then type Financial Consultant.
15. Save the document and name it **WordL1_C6_P6**.
16. Print and then close **WordL1_C6_P6.docx**.

# CHAPTER summary

- Group Word documents logically into folders. Create a new folder at the Open or Save As dialog box.
- You can select one or several documents at the Open dialog box. Copy, move, rename, delete, print, or open a document or selected documents.
- Use the *Cut*, *Copy*, and *Paste* options from the Open dialog box shortcut menu to move or copy a document from one folder to another.
- Delete documents and/or folders with the Delete button on the Open or Save As dialog box toolbar or the *Delete* option from the shortcut menu.
- You can open multiple documents and print multiple documents at the Open dialog box.
- Save a document in a different format with the *Save As* side menu at the Office button drop-down list or with the *Save as type* option at the Save As dialog box.
- Move among the open documents by clicking the button on the Taskbar representing the desired document, or by clicking the View tab, clicking the Switch Windows button in the Window group, and then clicking the desired document name.
- View a portion of all open documents by clicking the View tab and then clicking the Arrange All button in the Window group.
- Use the Minimize, Maximize, and Restore buttons located in the upper right corner of the window to reduce or increase the size of the active window.
- Divide a window into two panes by clicking the View tab and then clicking the Split button in the Window group. This enables you to view different parts of the same document at one time.
- View the contents of two open documents side by side by clicking the View tab, and then clicking the View Side by Side button in the Window group.
- Insert a document into the open document by clicking the Insert tab, clicking the Object button arrow, and then clicking *Text from File* at the drop-down list. At the Insert File dialog box, double-click the desired document.
- Preview a document to display how the document will appear when printed. Use options and buttons in the Print Preview tab to customize the view and to format text in the document.
- Customize a print job with options at the Print dialog box. Use the *Page range* section to specify the amount of text you want printed; use the *Pages* option to identify a specific page, multiple pages, and/or a range of pages for printing; and use the *Number of copies* option to print more than one copy of a document.
- With Word's envelope feature you can create and print an envelope at the Envelopes and Labels dialog box with the Envelopes tab selected.
- If you open the Envelopes and Labels dialog box in a document containing a name and address (with each line ending with a press of the Enter key), that information is automatically inserted in the *Delivery address* text box in the dialog box.
- Use Word's labels feature to print text on mailing labels, file labels, disk labels, or other types of labels.
- Word includes a number of template documents you can use to create a variety of documents. Display the list of template documents by clicking the Office button and then clicking *New* at the drop-down list.

# COMMANDS review

| FEATURE | RIBBON TAB, GROUP | BUTTON | OPTION | KEYBOARD SHORTCUT |
|---|---|---|---|---|
| Open dialog box | | | | Ctrl + O |
| Save As dialog box | | | Save As | |
| Print dialog box | | | Print | Ctrl + P |
| Arrange all documents | View, Window | Arrange All | | |
| Minimize document | | | | |
| Maximize document | | | | |
| Restore | | | | |
| Split window | View, Window | Split | | |
| View documents side by side | View, Window | View Side by Side | | |
| Insert file | Insert, Text | Object | Text from File | |
| Preview document | | | Print, Print Preview | |
| Envelopes and Labels dialog box with Envelopes tab selected | Mailings, Create | | | |
| Envelopes and Labels dialog box with Labels tab selected | Mailings, Create | | | |
| New Document dialog box | | | New | |

# CONCEPTS check

## Test Your Knowledge

**Completion:** In the space provided at the right, indicate the correct term, command, or number.

1. Create a new folder with this button at the Open or Save As dialog box.

2. Click this button at the Open dialog box to make the previous folder active.

3. Using the mouse, select nonadjacent documents at the Open dialog box by holding down this key while clicking the desired documents.

_____

4. Documents deleted from the hard drive are automatically sent to this bin.

_____

5. Copy a document to another folder without opening the document with the *Copy* option and this option from the Open dialog box shortcut menu.

_____

6. Save a document in a different file format with this option at the Save As dialog box.

_____

7. Click this button in the Window group in the View tab to arrange all open documents so a portion of each document displays.

_____

8. Click this button and the active document fills the editing window.

_____

9. Click this button to reduce the active document to a button on the Taskbar.

_____

10. To display documents side by side, click this button in the Window group in the View tab.

_____

11. Display the Insert File dialog box by clicking the Object button arrow in the Insert tab and then clicking this option.

_____

12. Display a document in this view to determine how a document will appear when printed.

_____

13. Type this in the *Pages* text box in the *Page range* section of the Print dialog box to print pages 3 through 6 of the open document.

_____

14. Type this in the *Pages* text box in the *Page range* section of the Print dialog box to print page 4 and 9 of the open document.

_____

15. The Envelopes button is located in the Create group in this tab.

_____

16. Click the *Installed Templates* option at this dialog box to display a list of templates.

_____

# SKILLS check
## *Demonstrate Your Proficiency*

## 1 MANAGE DOCUMENTS

1. Display the Open dialog box with Word2007L1C6 the active folder and then create a new folder named *CheckingTools*.
2. Copy (be sure to copy and not cut) all documents that begin with *WordSpellGrammar* into the CheckingTools folder.
3. With the CheckingTools folder as the active folder, rename **WordSpellGrammar01.docx** to **Technology.docx**.
4. Rename **WordSpellGrammar02.docx** to **Software.docx**.
5. Make Word2007L1C6 the active folder.
6. Delete the CheckingTools folder and all documents contained within it.
7. Open **WordBlock01.docx**, **WordLease03.docx**, and **WordDocument04.docx**.
8. Make **WordLease03.docx** the active document.
9. Make **WordBlock01.docx** the active document.
10. Arrange all of the windows.
11. Make **WordDocument04.docx** the active document and then minimize it.
12. Minimize the remaining documents.
13. Restore **WordBlock01.docx**.
14. Restore **WordLease03.docx**.
15. Restore **WordDocument04.docx**.
16. Maximize and then close **WordBlock01.docx** and then maximize and close **WordDocument04.docx**.
17. Maximize **WordLease03.docx** and then save the document and name it **WordL1_C6_A1**.
18. Open **WordDocument18.docx**.
19. View the **WordL1_C6_A1.docx** document and **WordDocument18.docx** document side by side.
20. Scroll through both documents simultaneously and notice the formatting differences between the title and headings in the two documents. Change the font size and apply shading to the title and headings in **WordL1_C6_A1.docx** to match the font size and shading of the title and headings in **WordDocument18.docx**.
21. Make **WordDocument18.docx** active and then close it.
22. Save **WordL1_C6_A1.docx**.
23. Move the insertion point to the end of the document and then insert the document named **WordParagraph02.docx**.
24. Apply formatting to the inserted text so it matches the formatting of the original text.
25. If the heading, *Condition of Premises*, displays at the bottom of page 1, insert a page break at the beginning of the heading.
26. Move the insertion point to the end of the document and then insert the document named **WordSignature.docx**.
27. Save, print, and then close **WordL1_C6_A1.docx**.

## Assessment

### 2 CREATE AN ENVELOPE

1. At a blank document, create an envelope with the text shown in Figure 6.10.
2. Save the envelope document and name it **WordL1_C6_A2**.
3. Print and then close **WordL1_C6_A2.docx**.

**Figure 6.10 Assessment 2**

DR ROSEANNE HOLT
21330 CEDAR DR
LOGAN UT 84598

GENE MIETZNER
4559 CORRIN AVE
SMITHFIELD UT 84521

## Assessment

### 3 CREATE MAILING LABELS

1. Create mailing labels with the names and addresses shown in Figure 6.11. Use a label option of your choosing. (You may need to check with your instructor before choosing an option.)
2. Save the document and name it **WordL1_C6_A3**.
3. Print and then close **WordL1_C6_A3.docx**.
4. At the clear document screen, close the document screen without saving changes.

**Figure 6.11 Assessment 3**

| | | |
|---|---|---|
| SUSAN LUTOVSKY | JIM AND PAT KIEL | IRENE HAGEN |
| 1402 MELLINGER DR | 413 JACKSON ST | 12930 147TH AVE E |
| FAIRHOPE OH 43209 | AVONDALE OH 43887 | CANTON OH 43296 |
| | | |
| VINCE KILEY | LEONARD KRUEGER | HELGA GUNDSTROM |
| 14005 288TH S | 13290 N 120TH | PO BOX 3112 |
| CANTON OH 43287 | CANTON OH 43291 | AVONDALE OH 43887 |

## 4  PREPARE A FAX

1. Open the Equity fax template from the New Document dialog box and then insert the following information in the specified fields.
   To: Frank Gallagher
   From: (your first and last names)
   Fax: (206) 555-9010
   Pages: 3
   Phone: (206) 555-9005
   Date: (insert current date)
   Re: Consultation Agreement
   CC: Jolene Yin
   Insert an X in the *For Review* check box
   Comments: Please review the Consultation Agreement and advise me of any legal issues.
2. Save the fax document and name it **WordL1_C6_A4**.
3. Print and then close the document.

## 5  SAVE A DOCUMENT AS A WEB PAGE

1. Experiment with the *Save as type* option at the Save As dialog box and figure out how to save a document as a single file Web page.
2. Open **WordComputers.docx**, display the Save As dialog box, and then change the save as type to a single file Web page. Click the Change Title button that displays in the Save As dialog box. At the Set Page Title dialog box, type Computers in Communication and Entertainment and then close the dialog box. Click the Save button in the Save As dialog box and at the message telling you that some features are not supported by Web browsers, click the Continue button.
3. Close the WordComputers.mht file.
4. Open your Web browser and then open the WordComputers.mht file.
5. Close WordComputers.mht and then close your Web browser.

# CASE study
## *Apply Your Skills*

**Part 1**

You are the office manager for the real estate company, Macadam Realty, and have been asked by the senior sales associate, Lucy Hendricks, to organize contract forms into a specific folder. Create a new folder named *RealEstate* and then copy into the folder documents that begin with the letters "RE." Ms. Hendricks has also asked you to prepare mailing labels for Macadam Realty. Include the name,

Macadam Realty, and the address 100 Third Street, Suite 210, Denver, CO 80803, on the labels. Use a decorative font for the label and make the *M* in *Macadam* and the *R* in *Realty* larger and more pronounced than surrounding text. ***Hint: Format text in the label by selecting text, right-clicking in the selected text, and then choosing the desired option at the shortcut menu.*** Save the completed document and name it **WordL1_C6_CS_P1**. Print and then close the document.

Part 2

One of your responsibilities is to format contract forms. Open the document named **REContractorAgreement.docx** and then save it and name it **WordL1_C6_CS_P2**. The sales associate has asked you to insert signature information at the end of the document and so you decide to insert at the end of the document the file named **RESignature.docx**. With **WordL1_C6_CS_P2.docx** still open, open **REBuildingAgreement.docx**. Format the **WordL1_C6_CS_P2.docx** document so it is formatted in a manner similar to the **REBuildingAreement.docx** document. Consider the following when specifying formatting: margins, fonts, and paragraph shading. Save, print, and then close **WordL1_C6_CS_P2.docx**. Close **REBuildingAgreement.docx**.

Part 3

Help

As part of the organization of contracts, Ms. Hendricks has asked you to insert document properties for the **REBuildingAgreement.docx** and **WordL1_C6_CS_P2.docx** documents. Use the Help feature to learn how to insert document properties. With the information you learn from the Help feature, open each of the two documents separately and then insert document properties in the following fields (you determine the information to type): *Author* (type your first and last names), *Title*, *Subject*, *Keywords*, and *Category*. Print the document properties for each document (change the *Print what* option at the Print dialog box to *Document properties*). Save each document with the original name and close the documents.

Part 4

www

A client of the real estate company, Anna Hurley, is considering purchasing several rental properties and has asked for information on how to locate real estate rental forms. Using the Internet, locate at least three Web sites that offer real estate rental forms. Write a letter to Anna Hurley at 2300 South 22$^{nd}$ Street, Denver, CO 80205. In the letter, list the Web sites you found and include information on which site you thought offered the most resources. Also include in the letter that Macadam Realty is very interested in helping her locate and purchase rental properties. Save the document and name it **WordL1_C6_CS_P4**. Create an envelope for the letter and add it to the letter document. Save, print, and then close **WordL1_C6_CS_P4.docx**. (You may need to manually feed the envelope in the printer.)

# CHAPTER 7

# Creating Tables and SmartArt

## PERFORMANCE OBJECTIVES

Upon successful completion of Chapter 7, you will be able to:

- Create, edit, and format a table
- Change the table design and layout
- Sort text in a table
- Perform calculations on data in a table
- Create and format a SmartArt diagram
- Create and format a SmartArt organizational chart

word Chapter 7

SNAP

Tutorial 7.1
Using Tables
Tutorial 7.2
Working with Charts

Some Word data can be organized in a table, which is a combination of columns and rows. With the Tables feature, you can insert data in columns and rows. This data can consist of text, values, and formulas. In this chapter you will learn how to create and format a table and insert and format data in the table. Word includes a SmartArt feature that provides a number of predesigned diagrams and organizational charts. Use this feature to create and then customize a diagram or organizational chart.

*Note: Before beginning computer projects, copy to your storage medium the Word2007L1C7 subfolder from the Word2007L1 folder on the CD that accompanies this textbook and then make Word2007L1C7 the active folder.*

## Project 1 Create and Format Tables with Company Information

You will create a table containing contact information and another containing information on plans offered by the company. You will then change the design and layout of both tables.

## Creating a Table

Use the Tables feature to create boxes of information called *cells*. A cell is the intersection between a row and a column. A cell can contain text, characters, numbers, data, graphics, or formulas. Create a table by clicking the Insert tab,

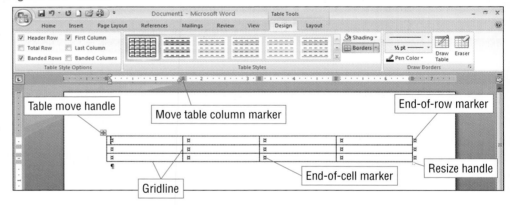

**QUICK STEPS**

**Create a Table**
1. Click Insert tab.
2. Click Table button.
3. Drag to create desired number of columns and rows.
4. Click mouse button.
OR
1. Click Insert tab.
2. Click Table button.
3. Click *Insert Table*.
4. Specify number of columns and rows.
5. Click OK.

clicking the Table button, dragging down and to the right until the correct number of rows and columns displays, and then clicking the mouse button. You can also create a table with options at the Insert Table dialog box. Display this dialog box by clicking the Table button in the Tables group in the Insert tab and then clicking *Insert Table* at the drop-down list.

Figure 7.1 shows an example of a table with four columns and three rows. Various parts of the table are identified in Figure 7.1 such as the gridlines, move table column marker, end-of-cell marker, end-of-row marker, and the resize handle. In a table, nonprinting characters identify the end of a cell and the end of a row. To view these characters, click the Show/Hide ¶ button in the Paragraph group in the Home tab. The end-of-cell marker displays inside each cell and the end-of-row marker displays at the end of a row of cells. These markers are identified in Figure 7.1.

When you create a table, the insertion point is located in the cell in the upper left corner of the table. Cells in a table contain a cell designation. Columns in a table are lettered from left to right, beginning with *A*. Rows in a table are numbered from top to bottom beginning with *1*. The cell in the upper left corner of the table is cell A1. The cell to the right of A1 is B1, the cell to the right of B1 is C1, and so on.

**Figure 7.1** Table

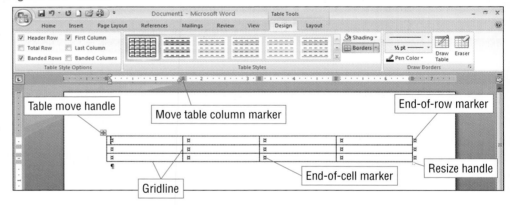

**HINT**
You can create a table within a table, creating a *nested* table.

When the insertion point is positioned in a cell in the table, move table column markers display on the horizontal ruler. These markers represent the end of a column and are useful in changing the width of columns. Figure 7.1 identifies a move table column marker.

**HINT**
Pressing the Tab key in a table moves the insertion point to the next cell. Pressing Ctrl + Tab moves the insertion point to the next tab within a cell.

## Entering Text in Cells

With the insertion point positioned in a cell, type or edit text. Move the insertion point to other cells with the mouse by clicking in the desired cell. If you are using the keyboard, press the Tab key to move the insertion point to the next cell or press Shift + Tab to move the insertion point to the previous cell.

If the text you type does not fit on one line, it wraps to the next line within the same cell. Or, if you press Enter within a cell, the insertion point is moved to the next line within the same cell. The cell vertically lengthens to accommodate the text, and all cells in that row also lengthen. Pressing the Tab key in a table causes the insertion point to move to the next cell in the table. If you want to move the insertion point to a tab stop within a cell, press Ctrl + Tab. If the insertion point is located in the last cell of the table and you press the Tab key, Word adds another row to the table. Insert a page break within a table by pressing Ctrl + Enter. The page break is inserted between rows, not within.

## Moving the Insertion Point within a Table

To move the insertion point to a different cell within the table using the mouse, click in the desired cell. To move the insertion point to different cells within the table using the keyboard, refer to the information shown in Table 7.1.

**Table 7.1** Insertion Point Movement within a Table Using the Keyboard

| To move the insertion point | Press these keys |
|---|---|
| To next cell | Tab |
| To preceding cell | Shift + Tab |
| Forward one character | Right Arrow key |
| Backward one character | Left Arrow key |
| To previous row | Up Arrow key |
| To next row | Down Arrow key |
| To first cell in the row | Alt + Home |
| To last cell in the row | Alt + End |
| To top cell in the column | Alt + Page Up |
| To bottom cell in the column | Alt + Page Down |

## Project 1a  Creating a Table

1. At a blank document, turn on bold, and then type the title CONTACT INFORMATION shown in Figure 7.2.
2. Turn off bold and then press the Enter key.
3. Create the table shown in Figure 7.2. To do this, click the Insert tab, click the Table button in the Tables group, drag down and to the right until the number above the grid displays as *3x5*, and then click the mouse button.
4. Type the text in the cells as indicated in Figure 7.2. Press the Tab key to move to the next cell or press Shift + Tab to move to the preceding cell. (If you accidentally press the Enter key within a cell, immediately press the Backspace key. Do not press Tab after typing the text in the last cell. If you do, another row is inserted in the table. If this happens, immediately click the Undo button on the Quick Access toolbar.)
5. Save the table and name it **WordL1_C7_P1**.

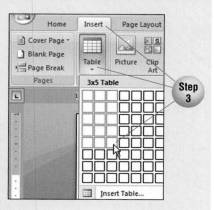

**Figure 7.2  Project 1a**

**CONTACT INFORMATION**

| Maggie Rivera | First Trust Bank | (203) 555-3440 |
|---|---|---|
| Regina Stahl | United Fidelity | (301) 555-1221 |
| Justin White | Key One Savings | (360) 555-8966 |
| Les Cromwell | Madison Trust | (602) 555-4900 |
| Cecilia Nordyke | American Financial | (509) 555-3995 |

You can also create a table with options at the Insert Table dialog box shown in Figure 7.3. To display this dialog box, click the Insert tab, click the Table button in the Tables group, and then click *Insert Table*. At the Insert Table dialog box, enter the desired number of columns and rows and then click OK.

**Figure 7.3**  Insert Table Dialog Box

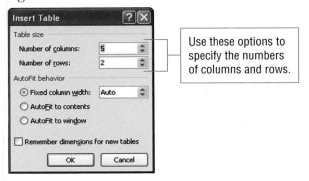

Use these options to specify the numbers of columns and rows.

## Project 1b  Creating a Table with the Insert Table Dialog Box

1. With **WordL1_C7_P1.docx** open, press Ctrl + End to move the insertion point below the table.
2. Press the Enter key twice.
3. Turn on bold and then type the title OPTIONAL PLAN PREMIUM RATES shown in Figure 7.4.
4. Turn off bold and then press the Enter key.
5. Click the Insert tab, click the Table button in the Tables group, and then click *Insert Table* at the drop-down list.
6. At the Insert Table dialog box, type 3 in the *Number of columns* text box. (The insertion point is automatically positioned in this text box.)
7. Press the Tab key (this moves the insertion point to the *Number of rows* option) and then type 5.
8. Click OK.
9. Type the text in the cells as indicated in Figure 7.4. Press the Tab key to move to the next cell or press Shift + Tab to move to the preceding cell. To indent the text in cells B2 through B5 and cells C2 through C5, press Ctrl + Tab to move the insertion to a tab within cells and then type the text.
10. Save **WordL1_C7_P1.docx**.

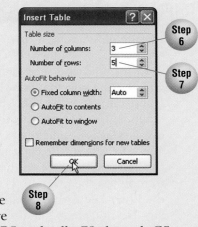

Step 6

Step 7

Step 8

## Figure 7.4 Project 1b

**OPTIONAL PLAN PREMIUM RATES**

| Waiting Period | Plan 2010 Employees | Basic Plan Employees |
|----------------|---------------------|----------------------|
| 60 days | 0.79% | 0.67% |
| 90 days | 0.59% | 0.49% |
| 120 days | 0.35% | 0.30% |
| 180 days | 0.26% | 0.23% |

# Changing the Table Design

When you create a table, the Table Tools Design tab is selected and the tab contains a number of options for enhancing the appearance of the table as shown in Figure 7.5. With options in the Table Styles group, apply a predesigned style that applies color and border lines to a table. Maintain further control over the predesigned style formatting applied to columns and rows with options in the Table Style Options group. For example, if your table contains a total column, you would insert a check mark in the *Total Row* option. Apply additional design formatting to cells in a table with the Shading and Borders buttons in the Table Styles group. Draw a table or draw additional rows and/or columns in a table by clicking the Draw Table button in the Draw Borders group. Click this button and the mouse pointer turns into a pencil. Drag in the table to create the desired columns and rows. Click the Eraser button and the mouse pointer turns into an eraser. Drag through the column and/or row lines you want to erase in the table.

**HINT**
Draw a freeform table by clicking the Insert tab, clicking the Table button, and then clicking the *Draw Table* option. Drag in the document to create the table.

Draw Table    Eraser

## Figure 7.5 Table Tools Design Tab

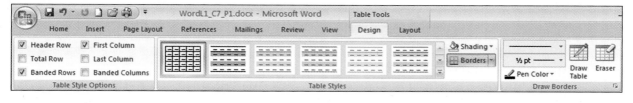

# Project 1c    Applying Table Styles

1. With **WordL1_C7_P1.docx** open, click in any cell in the top table.
2. Apply a table style by completing the following steps:

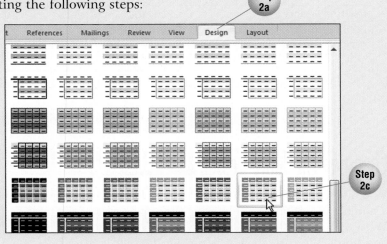

Step 2a

Step 2c

   a. Click the Table Tools Design tab.
   b. Click the More button at the right side of the table styles in the Table Styles group.
   c. Click the *Medium Grid 3 - Accent 5* style (second table style from the *right* in the tenth row in the *Built-in* section).
3. After looking at the table, you realize that the first row is not a header row and the first column should not be formatted differently than the other columns. To format the first row and first column in the same manner as the other rows and columns, click the *Header Row* check box and the *First Column* check box in the Table Style Options to remove the check marks.

Step 3

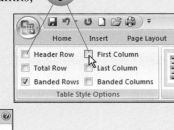

4. Click in any cell in the bottom table, apply the Dark List - Accent 5 table style (second option from the *right* in the eleventh row in the Built-in section), and then remove the check mark from the *First Column* check box.
5. Add color borders to the top table by completing the following steps:

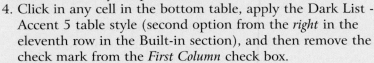

   a. Click in any cell in the top table.
   b. Click the Pen Color button arrow in the Draw Borders group and then click the *Orange, Accent 6, Darker 50%* color.

Step 5b

   c. Click the Line Weight button in the Draw Borders group and then click *1 ½ pt* at the drop-down list. (When you choose a line weight, the Draw Table button is automatically activated.)

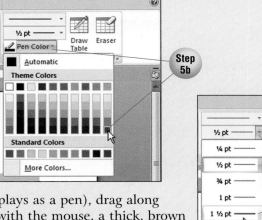

Step 5c

   d. Using the mouse (mouse pointer displays as a pen), drag along each side of the table. (As you drag with the mouse, a thick, brown border line is inserted. If you make a mistake or the line does not display as you intended, click the Undo button and then continue drawing along each side of the table.)
6. Drag along each side of the bottom table.
7. Click the Line Weight button in the Draw Borders group and then click *1 pt* at the drop-down list.
8. Drag along the row boundary separating the first row from the second row in the bottom table.
9. Click the Draw Table button to turn off the feature.
10. Save **WordL1_C7_P1.docx**.

# Selecting Cells

You can apply formatting to an entire table or to specific cells, rows, or columns in a table. To identify cells for formatting, select the specific cells using the mouse or the keyboard.

## Selecting in a Table with the Mouse

Use the mouse pointer to select a cell, row, column, or an entire table. Table 7.2 describes methods for selecting a table with the mouse. The left edge of each cell, between the left column border and the end-of-cell marker or first character in the cell, is called the *cell selection bar*. When you position the mouse pointer in the cell selection bar, it turns into a small, black arrow pointing up and to the right. Each row in a table contains a *row selection bar*, which is the space just to the left of the left edge of the table. When you position the mouse pointer in the row selection bar, the mouse pointer turns into an arrow pointing up and to the right.

**Table 7.2**  Selecting in a Table with the Mouse

| To select this | Do this |
|---|---|
| A cell | Position the mouse pointer in the cell selection bar at the left edge of the cell until it turns into a small, black arrow pointing up and to the right and then click the left mouse button. |
| A row | Position the mouse pointer in the row selection bar at the left edge of the table until it turns into an arrow pointing up and to the right and then click the left mouse button. |
| A column | Position the mouse pointer on the uppermost horizontal gridline of the table in the appropriate column until it turns into a short, black down-pointing arrow and then click the left mouse button. |
| Adjacent cells | Position the mouse pointer in the first cell to be selected, hold down the left mouse button, drag the mouse pointer to the last cell to be selected, and then release the mouse button. |
| All cells in a table | Click the table move handle; or position the mouse pointer in any cell in the table, hold down the Alt key, and then double-click the left mouse button. You can also position the mouse pointer in the row selection bar for the first row at the left edge of the table until it turns into an arrow pointing up and to the right, hold down the left mouse button, drag down to select all rows in the table, and then release the left mouse button. |
| Text within a cell | Position the mouse pointer at the beginning of the text and then hold down the left mouse button as you drag the mouse across the text. (When a cell is selected, the cell background color changes to blue. When text within cells is selected, only those lines containing text are selected.) |

## Selecting in a Table with the Keyboard

In addition to the mouse, you can also use the keyboard to select specific cells within a table. Table 7.3 displays the commands for selecting specific amounts of a table.

**Table 7.3** Selecting in a Table with the Keyboard

| To select | Press |
|---|---|
| The next cell's contents | Tab |
| The preceding cell's contents | Shift + Tab |
| The entire table | Alt + 5 (on numeric keypad with Num Lock off) |
| Adjacent cells | Hold down Shift key, then press an arrow key repeatedly. |
| A column | Position insertion point in top cell of column, hold down Shift key, then press down-pointing arrow key until column is selected. |

If you want to select only text within cells, rather than the entire cell, press F8 to turn on the Extend mode and then move the insertion point with an arrow key. When a cell is selected, the cell background color changes to blue. When text within a cell is selected, only those lines containing text are selected.

## Project 10  Selecting and Formatting Cells in a Table

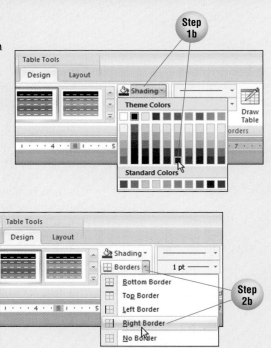

Step 1b

Step 2b

1. With **WordL1_C7_P1.docx** open, apply shading to a row by completing the following steps:
   a. Position the mouse pointer in the row selection bar at the left edge of the first row in the bottom table until the pointer turns into an arrow pointing up and to the right and then click the left mouse button. (This selects the entire first row of the bottom table.)
   b. Click the Shading button arrow in the Table Styles group and then click the *Red, Accent 2, Darker 50%* color.
2. Apply a border line to a column by completing the following steps:
   a. Position the mouse pointer on the uppermost horizontal gridline of the first column in the bottom table until the pointer turns into a short, down-pointing arrow and then click the left mouse button.
   b. Click the Borders button arrow and then click *Right Border* at the drop-down list. (This inserts a 1 point dark orange border line at the right side of the column.)

3. Complete steps similar to those in Step 2 to insert a border line at the right side of the second column.
4. Apply italic formatting to a column by completing the following steps:
   a. Position the insertion point in the first cell of the first row in the top table.
   b. Hold down the Shift key and then press the Down Arrow key four times. (This should select all cells in the first column.)
   c. Press Ctrl + I.
5. Save **WordL1_C7_P1.docx.**

# Changing Table Layout

To further customize a table, consider changing the table layout by inserting or deleting columns and rows and specifying cell alignments. Change table layout with options at the Table Tools Layout tab shown in Figure 7.6. Use options and buttons in the tab to select specific cells, delete and insert rows and columns, merge and split cells, specify cell height and width, sort data in cells, and insert a formula.

**HINT**

Some table layout options are available at a shortcut menu that can be viewed by right-clicking a table.

**Figure 7.6** Table Tools Layout Tab

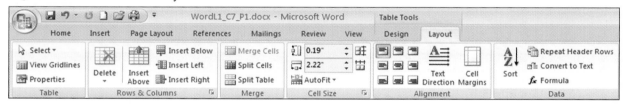

## Selecting with the Select Button

Along with selecting cells with the keyboard and mouse, you can also select specific cells with the Select button in the Table group in the Table Tools Layout tab. To select with this button, position the insertion point in the desired cell, column, or row and then click the Select button. At the drop-down list that displays, specify what you want to select—the entire table or a column, row, or cell.

# Inserting and Deleting Rows and Columns

With buttons in the Rows & Columns group in the Table Tools Layout tab, you can insert a row or column and delete a row or column. Click the button in the group that inserts the row or column in the desired location such as above, below, to the left, or to the right. Add a row to the bottom of a table by positioning the insertion point in the last cell and then pressing the Tab key. To delete a table, row, or column, click the Delete button and then click the option identifying what you want to delete. If you make a mistake while formatting a table, immediately click the Undo button on the Quick Access toolbar.

## Project 1e  Selecting, Inserting, and Deleting Columns and Rows

1. With **WordL1_C7_P1.docx** open, select a column and apply formatting by completing the following steps:
   a. Click in any cell in the first column in the top table.
   b. Click the Table Tools Layout tab.
   c. Click the Select button in the Table group and then click *Select Column* at the drop-down list.

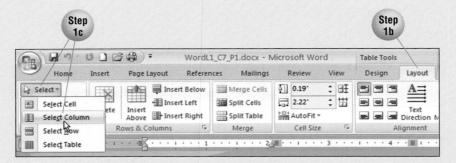

   d. With the first column selected, press Ctrl + I to remove italics and then press Ctrl + B to apply bold formatting.
2. Select a row and apply formatting by completing the following steps:
   a. Click in any cell in the first row in the bottom table.
   b. Click the Select button in the Table group and then click *Select Row* at the drop-down list.
   c. With the first row selected in the bottom table, press Ctrl + I to apply italic formatting.
3. Insert a new row in the bottom table and type text in the new cells by completing the following steps:
   a. Click in the cell containing the text *60 days*.

b. Click the Insert Above button in the Rows & Columns group.

c. Type **30 days** in the first cell of the new row, type **0.85%** in the middle cell of the new row (make sure you press Ctrl + Tab before typing the text), and type **0.81%** in the third cell of the new row (make sure you press Ctrl + Tab before typing the text).

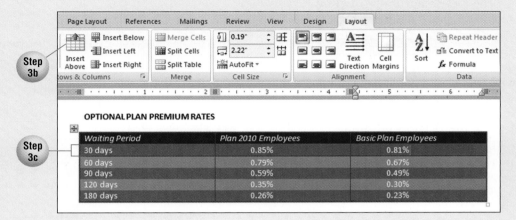

4. Insert three new rows in the top table and type text in the new cells by completing the following steps:

a. Select the three rows of cells that begin with the names *Regina Stahl*, *Justin White*, and *Les Cromwell*.

b. Click the Insert Below button in the Rows & Columns group.

c. Type the following text in the new cells:

| | | |
|---|---|---|
| Teresa Getty | Meridian Bank | (503) 555-9800 |
| Michael Vazquez | New Horizon Bank | (702) 555-2435 |
| Samantha Roth | Cascade Mutual | (206) 555-6788 |

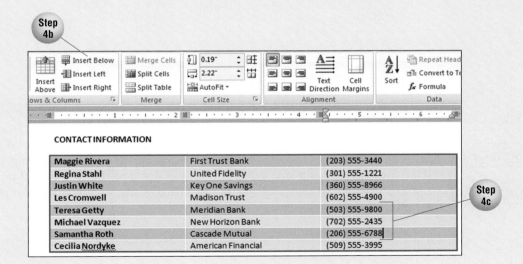

5. Delete a row by completing the
   following steps:
   a. Click in the cell containing the
      name *Les Cromwell*.
   b. Click the Delete button in the Rows
      & Columns group and then click
      *Delete Rows* at the drop-down list.
6. Insert a new column and type text in
   the new cells by completing the
   following steps:
   a. Click in the cell containing the
      text *First Trust Bank*.
   b. Click the Insert Left button in
      the Rows & Columns group.
   c. Type the following text in the
      news cells:

   | | | |
   |---|---|---|
   | B1 | = | Vice President |
   | B2 | = | Loan Officer |
   | B3 | = | Account Manager |
   | B4 | = | Branch Manager |
   | B5 | = | President |
   | B6 | = | Vice President |
   | B7 | = | Regional Manager |

7. Save **WordL1_C7_P1.docx**.

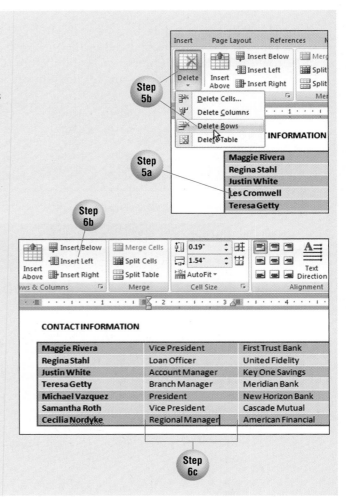

## Merging and Splitting Cells and Tables

Click the Merge Cells button in the Merge group in the Table Tools Layout tab to merge selected cells and click the Split Cells button to split the currently active cell. When you click the Split Cells button, the Split Cells dialog box displays where you specify the number of columns or rows into which you want to split the active cell. If you want to split one table into two tables, position the insertion point in a cell in the row that you want to be the first row in the new table and then click the Split Table button.

1. With **WordL1_C7_P1.docx** open, insert a new row and merge cells in the row by completing the following steps:
   a. Click in the cell containing the text *Waiting Period* (located in the bottom table).
   b. Click the Insert Above button in the Rows & Columns group.
   c. With all of the cells in the new row selected, click the Merge Cells button in the Merge group.
   d. Type OPTIONAL PLAN PREMIUM RATES and then press Ctrl + E to center-align the text in the cell. (The text you type will be italicized.)

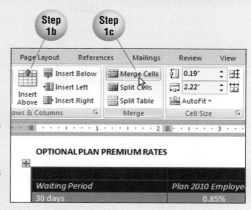

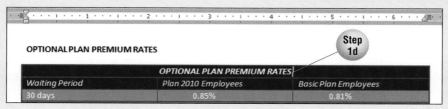

2. Select and then delete the text *OPTIONAL PLAN PREMIUM RATES* that displays above the bottom table.
3. Insert rows and text in the top table and merge cells by completing the following steps:
   a. Click in the cell containing the text *Maggie Rivera*.
   b. Click the Table Tools Layout tab.
   c. Click the Insert Above button twice. (This inserts two rows at the top of the table.)
   d. With the cells in the top row selected, click the Merge Cells button in the Merge group.
   e. Type **CONTACT INFORMATION, NORTH** and then press Ctrl + E to change the paragraph alignment to center.
   f. Type the following text in the four cells in the new second row.

   Name    Title    Company    Telephone

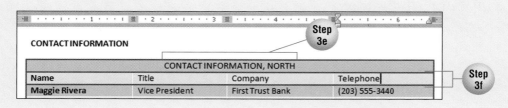

4. Apply heading formatting to the new top row by completing the following steps:
   a. Click the Table Tools Design tab.
   b. Click the *Header Row* check box in the Table Style Options dialog box.
5. Select and then delete the text *CONTACT INFORMATION* that displays above the top table.
6. Split a cell by completing the following steps:
   a. Click in the cell containing the telephone number *(360) 555-8966*.
   b. Click the Table Tools Layout tab.

c. Click the Split Cells button in the Merge group.

d. At the Split Cells dialog box, click OK. (The telephone number will wrap to a new line. You will change this in the next project.)

e. Click in the new cell.

f. Type x453 in the new cell. If AutoCorrect automatically capitalizes the *x*, hover the mouse pointer over the *X* until the AutoCorrect Options button displays. Click the AutoCorrect Options button and then click *Undo Automatic Capitalization* or click *Stop Auto-capitalizing First Letter of Table Cells*.

| Telephone | |
|---|---|
| (203) 555-3440 | |
| (301) 555-1221 | |
| (360) 555-8966 | x453 |
| (503) 555-9800 | |

Step 6f

7. Split the cell containing the telephone number *(206) 555-6788* and then type x2310 in the new cell. (If necessary, make the *x* lowercase.)

8. Split the top table into two tables by completing the following steps:

a. Click in the cell containing the name *Teresa Getty*.

b. Click the Split Table button in the Merge group.

c. Click in the cell containing the name *Teresa Getty* (in the first row of the new table).

d. Click the Insert Above button.

e. With the new row selected, click the Merge Cells button.

f. Type CONTACT INFORMATION, SOUTH in the new row and then press Ctrl + E to center-align the text.

9. Draw a dark orange border at the bottom of the top table and the top of the middle table by completing the following steps:

a. Click the Table Tools Design tab.

b. Click the Line Weight button in the Draw Borders group and then click *1 ½ pt* at the drop-down list. (This activates the Draw Table button.)

c. Using the mouse (pointer displays as a pen), drag along the bottom border of the top table.

d. Drag along the top border of the middle table.

e. Click the Draw Table button to turn it off.

10. Save and then print **WordL1_C7_P1.docx**.

11. Delete the middle table by completing the following steps:

a. Click in any cell in the middle table.

b. Click the Table Tools Layout tab.

c. Click the Delete button in the Rows & Columns group and then click *Delete Table* at the drop-down list.

12. Save **WordL1_C7_P1.docx**.

## Customizing Cell Size

Distribute Rows

Distribute Columns

When you create a table, column width and row height are equal. You can customize the width of columns or height of rows with buttons in the Cell Size group in the Table Tools Layout tab. Use the *Table Row Height* measurement box to increase or decrease the height of rows and use the *Table Column Width* measurement box to increase or decrease the width of columns. The Distribute Rows button will distribute equally the height of selected rows and the Distribute Columns button will distribute equally the width of selected columns.

You can also change column width using the move table column markers on the horizontal ruler or by using the table gridlines. To change column width using the horizontal ruler, position the mouse pointer on a move table column marker until it turns into a left and right arrow, and then drag the marker to the desired position. Hold down the Shift key while dragging a table column marker and the horizontal ruler remains stationary while the table column marker moves. Hold down the Alt key while dragging a table column marker and measurements display on the horizontal ruler. To change column width using gridlines, position the arrow pointer on the gridline separating columns until the insertion point turns into a left and right arrow with a vertical line between and then drag the gridline to the desired position. If you want to see the column measurements on the horizontal ruler as you drag a gridline, hold down the Alt key.

Adjust row height in a manner similar to adjusting column width. You can drag the adjust table row marker on the vertical ruler or drag the gridline separating rows. Hold down the Alt key while dragging the adjust table row marker or the row gridline and measurements display on the vertical ruler.

Use the AutoFit button in the Cell Size group to make the column widths in a table automatically fit the contents. To do this, position the insertion point in any cell in the table, click the AutoFit button in the Cell Size group, and then click *AutoFit Contents* at the drop-down list.

## Project 1g  Changing Column Width and Row Height

1. With **WordL1_C7_P1.docx** open, change the width of the first column in the top table by completing the following steps:
   a. Click in the cell containing the name *Maggie Rivera*.
   b. Position the mouse pointer on the move table column marker that displays just right of the 1.5-inch marker on the horizontal ruler until the pointer turns into an arrow pointing left and right.
   c. Hold down the Shift key and then the left mouse button.
   d. Drag the marker to the 1.25-inch mark, release the mouse button and then release the Shift key.
2. Complete steps similar to those in Step 1 to drag the move table column marker that displays just right of the 3-inch mark on the horizontal ruler to the 2.5-inch mark. (Make sure the text *Account Manager* in the second column does not wrap to the next line. If it does, slightly increase the width of the column.)
3. Change the width of the third column in the top table by completing the following steps:
   a. Position the mouse pointer on the gridline separating the third and fourth columns until the pointer turns into a left- and right-pointing arrow with a vertical double line between.
   b. Hold down the Alt key and then the left mouse button, drag the gridline to the left until the measurement for the third column on the horizontal ruler displays as *1.4"*, and then release the Alt key and then the mouse button.

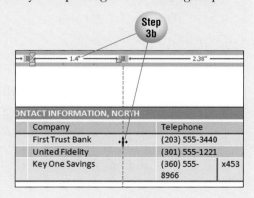

4. Position the mouse pointer on the gridline that separates the telephone number *(360) 555-8966* from the extension *x453* and then drag the gridline to the 5.25-inch mark on the horizontal ruler.
5. Drag the right border of the top table to the 5.75-inch marker on the horizontal ruler.
6. Autofit the columns in the bottom table by completing the following steps:
   a. Click in any cell in the bottom table.
   b. Click the AutoFit button in the Cell Size group and then click *AutoFit Contents* at the drop-down list.
7. Increase the height of the first row in the bottom table by completing the following steps:
   a. Make sure the insertion point is located in one of the cells in the bottom table.
   b. Position the mouse pointer on the top adjust table row marker on the vertical ruler.
   c. Hold down the left mouse button and hold down the Alt key.
   d. Drag the adjust table row marker down until the first row measurement on the vertical ruler displays as *0.36"*, release the mouse button and then the Alt key.
8. Increase the height of the first row in the top table by completing the following steps:
   a. Click in any cell in the top table.
   b. Position the arrow pointer on the gridline that displays at the bottom of the top row until the arrow pointer turns into an up- and down-pointing arrow with a vertical double line between.
   c. Hold down the left mouse button and then hold down the Alt key.
   d. Drag the gridline down until the first row measurement on the vertical ruler displays as *0.36"* and release the mouse button and then the Alt key.
9. Save **WordL1_C7_P1.docx**.

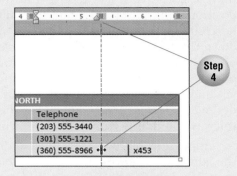

Step 4

Step 6b

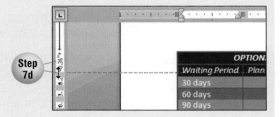

Step 7d

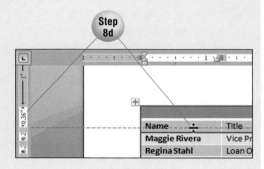

Step 8d

## Changing Cell Alignment

The Alignment group in the Table Tools Layout tab contains a number of buttons for specifying the horizontal and vertical alignment of text in cells. The buttons contain a visual representation of the alignment and you can also hover the mouse pointer over a button to determine the alignment.

## Project 1h  Aligning Text in Cells

Step 2

1. With **WordL1_C7_P1.docx** open, click in the top cell in the top table (the cell containing the title *CONTACT INFORMATION, NORTH*).
2. Click the Align Center button in the Alignment group in the Table Tools Layout tab.
3. Format and align text in the second row in the table by completing the following steps:
   a. Select the second row.
   b. Press Ctrl + B (this turns off bold for the entry in the first cell) and then press Ctrl + B again (this turns on bold for all entries in the second row).
   c. Click the Align Top Center button in the Alignment group.
4. Click in the top cell in the bottom table and then click the Align Center button in the Alignment group.
5. Save, print, and then close **WordL1_C7_P1.docx**.

## Project 2  Create and Format Tables with Employee Information

You will create and format a table containing information on the names and departments of employees of Tri-State Products and also insert a table containing additional information on employees and then format the table.

## Changing Cell Margin Measurements

By default, cells in a table contain specific margin settings. Top and bottom margins in a cell have a default measurement of *0″* and left and right margins have a default setting of *0.08″*. Change these default settings with options at the Table Options dialog box shown in Figure 7.7. Display this dialog box by clicking the Cell Margins button in the Alignment group in the Table Tools Layout tab. Use the options in the *Default cell margins* section to change the top, bottom, left, and/or right cell margin measurements.

Cell Margins

**Figure 7.7** Table Options Dialog Box

Use options in this section to increase and/or decrease margin measurements in cells.

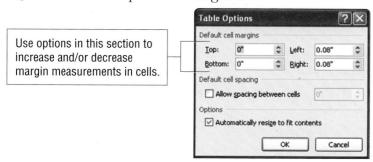

 **Properties**

Changes to cell margins will affect all cells in a table. If you want to change the cell margin measurements for one cell or for selected cells, position the insertion point in the cell or select the desired cells, and then click the Properties button in the Table group in the Table Tools Layout tab. (You can also click the Cell Size group dialog box launcher.) At the Table Properties dialog box that displays, click the Cell tab and then the Options button that displays in the lower right corner of the dialog box. This displays the Cell Options dialog box shown in Figure 7.8.

**Figure 7.8** Cell Options Dialog Box

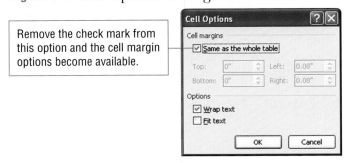

Remove the check mark from this option and the cell margin options become available.

Before setting the new cell margin measurements, remove the check mark from the *Same as the whole table* option. With the check mark removed from this option, the cell margin options become available. Specify the new cell margin measurements and then click OK to close the dialog box.

## Project 2a  Changing Cell Margin Measurements

1. Open **WordTable01.docx** and then save the document and name it **WordL1_C7_P2**.
2. Change the top and bottom margins for all cells in the table by completing the following steps:
   a. Position the insertion point in any cell in the table and then click the Table Tools Layout tab.
   b. Click the Cell Margins button in the Alignment group.
   c. At the Table Options dialog box, change the *Top* and *Bottom* measurements to *0.05"*.
   d. Click OK to close the Table Options dialog box.
3. Change the top and bottom cell margin measurements for the first row of cells by completing the following steps:
   a. Select the first row of cells (the cells containing *Name* and *Department*).
   b. Click the Properties button in the Table group.
   c. At the Table Properties dialog box, click the Cell tab.
   d. Click the Options button.
   e. At the Cell Options dialog box, remove the check mark from the *Same as the whole table* option.
   f. Change the *Top* and *Bottom* measurements to *0.1"*.
   g. Click OK to close the Cell Options dialog box.
   h. Click OK to close the Table Properties dialog box.

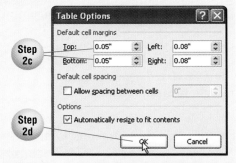

Step 2c

Step 2d

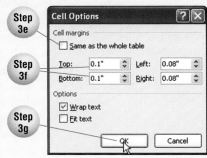

Step 3e

Step 3f

Step 3g

4. Change the left cell margin measurement for specific cells by completing the following steps:
   a. Select all rows in the table *except* the top row.
   b. Click the Cell Size group dialog box launcher.
   c. At the Table Properties dialog box, click the Cell tab.
   d. Click the Options button.
   e. At the Cell Options dialog box, remove the check mark from the *Same as the whole table* option.
   f. Change the *Left* measurement to *0.3"*.
   g. Click OK to close the Cell Options dialog box.
   h. Click OK to close the Table Properties dialog box.
5. Save **WordL1_C7_P2.docx**.

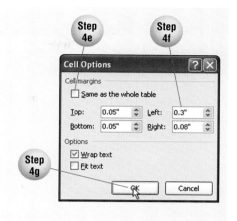

## Changing Cell Direction

Change the direction of text in a cell using the Text Direction button in the Alignment group in the Table Tools Layout tab. Each time you click the Text Direction button, the text rotates in the cell 90 degrees.

## Changing Table Alignment

By default, a table aligns at the left margin. Change this alignment with options at the Table Properties dialog box with the Table tab selected as shown in Figure 7.9. To change the alignment, click the desired alignment option in the Alignment section of the dialog box.

**Figure 7.9** Table Properties Dialog Box with Table Tab Selected

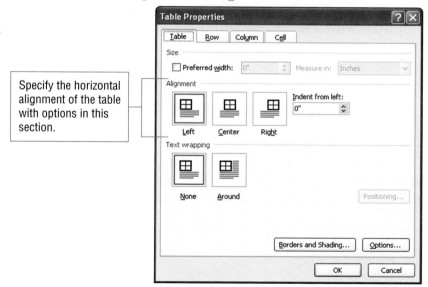

Specify the horizontal alignment of the table with options in this section.

1. With **WordL1_C7_P2.docx** open, insert a new column and change text direction by completing the following steps:
   a. Click in any cell in the first column.
   b. Click the Insert Left button in the Rows & Columns group.
   c. With the cells in the new column selected, click the Merge Cells button in the Merge group.
   d. Type **Tri-State Products**.
   e. Click the Align Center button in the Alignment group.
   f. Click twice on the Text Direction button in the Alignment group.
   g. With *Tri-State Products* selected, click the Home tab, and then increase the font size to *16*.
2. Autofit the contents by completing the following steps:
   a. Click in any cell in the table.
   b. Click the Table Tools Layout tab.
   c. Click the AutoFit button in the Cell Size group and then click the *AutoFit Contents* at the drop-down list.
3. Change the table alignment by completing the following steps:
   a. Click the Properties button in the Table group in the Table Tools Layout tab.
   b. At the Table Properties dialog box, click the Table tab.
   c. Click the *Center* option in the *Alignment* section.
   d. Click OK.
4. Select the two cells containing the text *Name* and *Department* and then click the Align Center button in the Alignment group.
5. Save **WordL1_C7_P2.docx**.

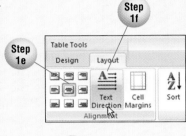

Step 1f

Step 1e

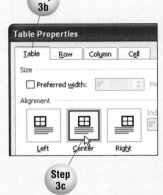

Step 3b

Step 3c

## Changing Table Size with the Resize Handle

When you hover the mouse pointer over a table, a resize handle displays in the lower right corner of the table. The resize handle displays as a small, white square. Drag this resize handle to increase and/or decrease the size and proportion of the table.

## Moving a Table

Position the mouse pointer in a table and a table move handle displays in the upper left corner. Use this handle to move the table in the document. To move a table, position the mouse pointer on the table move handle until the pointer turns into a four-headed arrow, hold down the left mouse button, drag the table to the desired position, and then release the mouse button.

1. With **WordL1_C7_P2.docx** open, insert a table into the current document by completing the following steps:
   a. Press Ctrl + End to move the insertion point to the end of the document and then press the Enter key.
   b. Click the Insert tab.
   c. Click the Object button arrow in the Text group and then click *Text from File* at the drop-down list.
   d. At the Insert File dialog box, navigate to the Word2007L1C7 folder and then double-click *WordTable02.docx*.
2. Autofit the bottom table by completing the following steps:
   a. Click in any cell in the bottom table.
   b. Click the Table Tools Layout tab.
   c. Click the AutoFit button in the Cell Size group and then click *AutoFit Contents* at the drop-down list.
3. Format the bottom table by completing the following steps:
   a. Click the Table Tools Design tab.
   b. Click the More button that displays at the right side of the Table Styles group and then click the *Medium Shading 1 - Accent 2* style (third style from the left in the fourth row of the *Built-In* section).

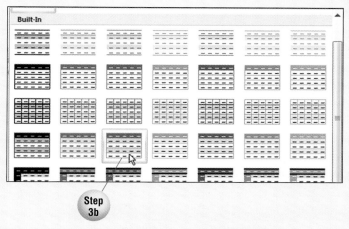

Step 3b

   c. Click the First Column check box to remove the check mark.
   d. Select the first and second rows, click the Table Tools Layout tab, and then click the Align Center button in the Alignment group.
   e. Select the second row and then press Ctrl + B to turn on bold.

4. Resize the bottom table by completing the following steps:
   a. Position the mouse pointer on the resize handle located in the lower right corner of the top table.
   b. Hold down the left mouse button, drag down and to the right until the width and height of the table increases approximately one inch, and then release the mouse button.

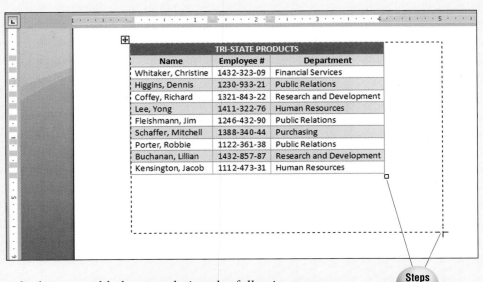

Steps
4a–4b

5. Move the bottom table by completing the following steps:
   a. Hover the mouse pointer over the bottom table.
   b. Position the mouse pointer on the table move handle until the pointer displays with a four-headed arrow attached.
   c. Hold down the left mouse button, drag the table so it is positioned equally between the left and right margins, and then release the mouse button.

Step
5c

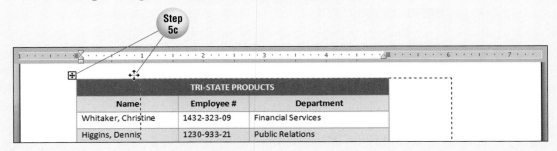

6. Select the cells in the column below the heading *Employee #* and then click the Align Top Center button in the Alignment group.
7. Save **WordL1_C7_P2.docx**.

# Converting Text to a Table

You can create a table and then enter data in the cells or you can create the data and then convert it to a table. To convert text to a table, type the text and separate it with a separator character such as a comma or tab. The separator character identifies where you want text divided into columns. To convert text, select the text, click the Insert tab, click the Table button in the Tables group, and then click *Convert Text to Table* at the drop-down list.

# Converting a Table to Text

You can convert a table to text by positioning the insertion point in any cell of the table, clicking the Table Tools Layout tab, and then clicking the Convert to Text button in the Data group. At the Convert Table to Text dialog box, specify the desired separator and then click OK.

**QUICK STEPS**

**Convert Text to Table**
1. Select text.
2. Click Insert tab.
3. Click Table button.
4. Click *Convert Text to Table*.

**Convert Table to Text**
1. Position insertion point in any cell of table.
2. Click Table Tools Layout tab.
3. Click *Convert to Text*.
4. Specify desired separator at Convert Table to Text dialog box.
5. Click OK.

## Project 2f    Converting Text to a Table

1. With **WordL1_C7_P2.docx** open, press Ctrl + End to move the insertion point to the end of the document and then press the Enter key until the insertion point is positioned approximately a double space below the bottom table.
2. Insert the document named **WordList01.docx** into the current document.
3. Convert the text to a table by completing the following steps:
   a. Select the text you just inserted.
   b. Click the Insert tab.
   c. Click the Table button in the Tables group and then click *Convert Text to Table* at the drop-down list.
   d. At the Convert Text to Table dialog box, type 2 in the *Number of columns* text box.
   e. Click the *AutoFit to contents* option in the *AutoFit behavior* section.
   f. Click the *Commas* option in the *Separate text at* section.
   g. Click OK.
4. Select and merge the cells in the top row (the row containing the title *TRI-STATE PRODUCTS* and then change the alignment to Center.
5. Apply the Medium Shading 1 - Accent 2 style (third style from the left in the fourth row of the *Built-In* section) and remove the check mark from the *First Column* check box in the Table Style Options group in the Table Tools Design tab.
6. Drag the table so it is centered and positioned below the table above.
7. Apply the Medium Shading 1 - Accent 2 style to the top table. Increase the width of the columns so the text *TRI-STATE PRODUCTS* is visible and the text in the second and third columns displays on one line.
8. If necessary, drag the table so it is centered and positioned above the middle table. Make sure the three tables fit on one page.
9. Save, print, and then close **WordL1_C7_P2.docx**.

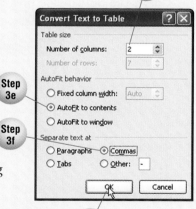

Step 3d

Step 3e

Step 3f

Step 3g

# Project ③ Sort and Calculate Sales Data

**You will sort data in tables on Tri-State Products sales and then insert formulas to calculate total sales, average sales, and top sales.**

## Sorting Text in a Table

With the Sort button in the Data group in the Table Tools Layout tab, you can sort text in selected cells in a table in ascending alphabetic or numeric order. To sort text, select the desired rows in the table and then click the Sort button in the Data group. At the Sort dialog box, specify the column containing the text on which you want to sort, and then click OK.

## Project ③ₐ   Sorting Text in a Table

1. Open **WordTable03.docx** and then save the document and name it **WordL1_C7_P3**.
2. Sort text in the top table by completing the following steps:
   a. Select all of the rows containing names (from *Novak, Diana* through *Sogura, Jeffrey*).
   b. Click Table Tools Layout tab.
   c. Click the Sort button in the Data group.
   d. At the Sort dialog box, click OK. (This sorts the last names in the first column in alphabetical order.)

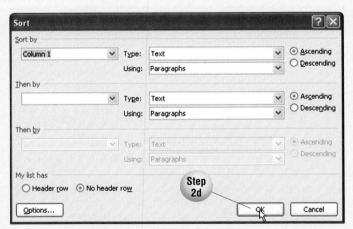

3. After looking at the table, you decide to sort by 2009 Sales. To do this, complete the following steps:
   a. With the rows still selected, click the Sort button in the Data group.
   b. At the Sort dialog box, click the down-pointing arrow at the right side of the *Sort by* option box and then click *Column 2* at the drop-down list.
   c. Click OK.
   d. Deselect the rows.
4. Save **WordL1_C7_P3.docx**.

# Performing Calculations in a Table

You can use the Formula button in the Data group in the Table Tools Layout tab to insert formulas that calculate data in a table. Numbers in cells in a table can be added, subtracted, multiplied, and divided. In addition, you can calculate averages, percentages, and minimum and maximum values. You can calculate data in a Word table, but for complex calculations use an Excel worksheet.

To perform a calculation on data in a table, position the insertion point in the cell where you want the result of the calculation inserted and then click the Formula button in the Data group in the Table Tools Layout tab. This displays the Formula dialog box shown in Figure 7.10. At this dialog box, accept the default formula that displays in the *Formula* text box or type the desired calculation, and then click OK.

**Figure 7.10** Formula Dialog Box

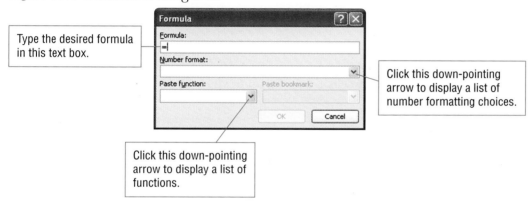

Type the desired formula in this text box.

Click this down-pointing arrow to display a list of number formatting choices.

Click this down-pointing arrow to display a list of functions.

You can use four basic operators when writing a formula including the plus sign (+) for addition, the minus sign (hyphen) for subtraction, the asterisk (*) for multiplication, and the forward slash (/) for division. If a calculation contains two or more operators, Word calculates from left to right. If you want to change the order of calculation, use parentheses around the part of the calculation to be performed first.

In the default formula, the **SUM** part of the formula is called a *function*. Word provides other functions you can use to write a formula. These functions are available with the *Paste function* option in the Formula dialog box. For example, you can use the AVERAGE function to average numbers in cells.

Specify the numbering format with the *Number format* option at the Formula dialog box. For example, if you are calculating money amounts, you can specify that the calculated numbers display with no numbers or two numbers following the decimal point.

# Project 3D  Inserting Formulas

1. With **WordL1_C7_P3.docx** open, insert a formula by completing the following steps:
   a. Click in cell B9 (the empty cell located immediately below the cell containing the amount *$623,214*).
   b. Click the Table Tools Layout tab.
   c. Click the Formula button in the Data group.
   d. At the Formula dialog box, make sure *=SUM(ABOVE)* displays in the *Formula* option box.
   e. Click the down-pointing arrow at the right side of the *Number format* option box and then click *#,##0* at the drop-down list (top option in the list).
   f. Click OK to close the Formula dialog box.
   g. At the table, type a dollar sign ($) before the number just inserted in cell B9.

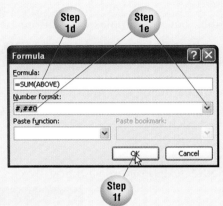

Step 1d

Step 1e

Step 1f

2. Complete steps similar to those in Steps 1c through 1g to insert a formula in cell C9 (the empty cell located immediately below the cell containing the amount *$635,099*).
3. Complete steps similar to those in Steps 1c through 1g to insert in the bottom table formulas that calculate totals. Insert formulas in the cells in the *Total* row and *Total* column. When inserting formulas in cells F3 through F6, you will need to change the formula to *=SUM(LEFT)*.
4. Insert a formula that calculates the average of amounts by completing the following steps:
   a. Click in cell B10 in the top table. (Cell B10 is the empty cell immediately right of the cell containing the word *Average*.)
   b. Click the Formula button in the Data group.
   c. At the Formula dialog box, delete the formula in the *Formula* text box *except* the equals sign.
   d. With the insertion point positioned immediately right of the equals sign, click the down-pointing arrow at the right side of the *Paste function* option box and then click *AVERAGE* at the drop-down list.
   e. With the insertion point positioned between the left and right parentheses, type **B2:B8**. (When typing cell designations in a formula, you can type either uppercase or lowercase letters.)

Step 4e

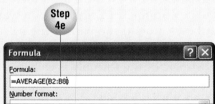

   f. Click the down-pointing arrow at the right side of the *Number format* option box and then click *#,##0* at the drop-down list (top option in the list).
   g. Click OK to close the Formula dialog box.
   h. Type a dollar sign ($) before the number just inserted in cell B10.
5. Complete steps similar to those in Steps 4b through 4h to insert a formula in cell C10 in the top table that calculates the average of cells C2 through C8.

6. Complete steps similar to those in Steps 4b through 4h to insert a formula in cell B7 in the bottom table that calculates the average of cells B2 through B5. Complete similar steps to insert in cell C7 the average of cells C2 through C5; insert in cell D7 the average of cells D2 through D5; insert in cell E7 the average of cells E2 through E5; and insert in cell F7 the average of cells F2 through F5.

7. Insert a formula that calculates the maximum number by completing the following steps:

   a. Click in cell B11 in the top table (the empty cell immediately right of the cell containing the word *Top Sales*).

   b. Click the Formula button in the Data group.

   c. At the Formula dialog box, delete the formula in the *Formula* text box *except* the equals sign.

   d. With the insertion point positioned immediately right of the equals sign, click the down-pointing arrow at the right side of the *Paste function* option box and then click *MAX* at the drop-down list. (You will need to scroll down the list to display the *MAX* option.)

   e. With the insertion point positioned between the left and right parentheses, type **B2:B8**.

   f. Click the down-pointing arrow at the right side of the *Number format* option box and then click *#,##0* at the drop-down list (top option in the list).

   g. Click OK to close the Formula dialog box.

   h. Type a dollar sign ($) before the number just inserted in cell B11.

Step 7d

8. Complete steps similar to those in Steps 7b through 7h to insert the maximum number in cell C11.

9. Apply formatting to each table to enhance the visual appeal of the tables.

10. Save, print, and then close **WordL1_C7_P3.docx**.

## Project ④ Prepare and Format a Diagram

You will prepare a process diagram identifying steps in the production process and then apply formatting to enhance the diagram.

# Creating SmartArt

With Word's SmartArt feature you can insert diagrams and organizational charts in a document. SmartArt offers a variety of predesigned diagrams and organizational charts that are available at the Choose a SmartArt Graphic dialog box shown in Figure 7.11. At this dialog box, *All* is selected in the left panel and all available predesigned diagrams display in the middle panel.

**HINT**

Use SmartArt to communicate your message and ideas in a visual manner.

SmartArt

**Figure 7.11** Choose a SmartArt Graphic Dialog Box

Double-click the desired SmartArt graphic in this panel.

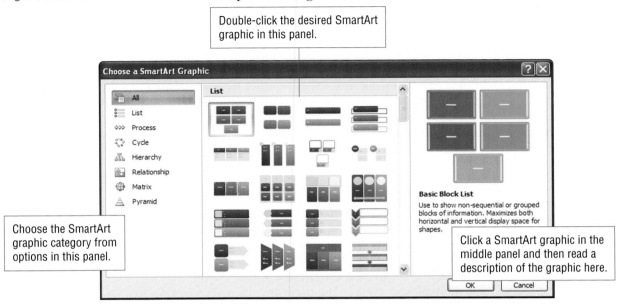

Choose the SmartArt graphic category from options in this panel.

Click a SmartArt graphic in the middle panel and then read a description of the graphic here.

# Inserting and Formatting a SmartArt Diagram

**Insert a SmartArt Diagram**
1. Click Insert tab.
2. Click SmartArt button.
3. Double-click desired diagram.

Predesigned diagrams display in the middle panel of the Choose a SmartArt Graphic dialog box. Use the scroll bar at the right side of the middle panel to scroll down the list of diagram choices. Click a diagram in the middle panel and the name of the diagram displays in the right panel along with a description of the diagram type. SmartArt includes diagrams for presenting a list of data; showing data processes, cycles, and relationships; and presenting data in a matrix or pyramid. Double-click a diagram in the middle panel of the dialog box and the diagram is inserted in the document.

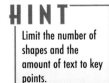

Limit the number of shapes and the amount of text to key points.

When you double-click a diagram at the dialog box, the diagram is inserted in the document and a text pane displays at the left side of the diagram. You can type text in the diagram in the text pane or directly in the diagram. Apply design formatting to a diagram with options at the SmartArt Tools Design tab shown in Figure 7.12. This tab is active when the diagram is inserted in the document. With options and buttons in this tab you add objects, change the diagram layout, apply a style to the diagram, and reset the diagram back to the original formatting.

**Figure 7.12** SmartArt Tools Design Tab

1. At a blank document, insert the diagram shown in Figure 7.13 by completing the following steps:

   a. Click the Insert tab.

   b. Click the SmartArt button in the Illustrations group.

   c. At the Choose a SmartArt Graphic dialog box, click *Process* in the left panel and then double-click the *Alternating Flow* diagram (last option in the top row).

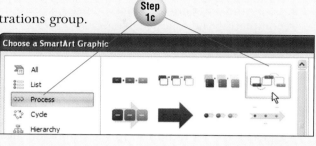

Step
1c

   d. If a *Type your text here* text pane does not display at the left side of the diagram, click the Text Pane button in the Create Graphic group to display the pane.

   e. With the insertion point positioned after the top bullet in the *Type your text here* text pane, type **Design**.

   f. Click *[Text]* that displays below *Design* and then type **Mock-up**.

   g. Continue clicking occurrences of *[Text]* and typing text so the text pane displays as shown at the right.

   h. Close the text pane by clicking the Close button (contains an X) that displays in the upper right corner of the pane. (You can also click the Text Pane button in the Create Graphic group.)

2. Change the diagram colors by clicking the Change Colors button in the SmartArt Styles group and then clicking the first option in the *Colorful* section (*Colorful – Accent Colors*).

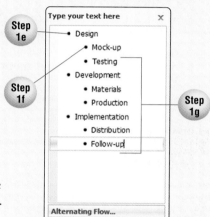

Step
1e

Step
1f

Step
1g

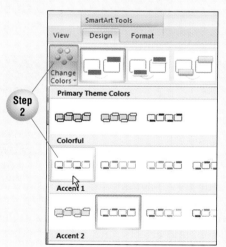

Step
2

3. Apply a style by clicking the More button that displays at the right side of the SmartArt Styles group and then clicking the second option from the left in the top row of the *3-D* section (*Inset*).
4. Copy the diagram and then change the layout by completing the following steps:
   a. Click inside the diagram border but outside of any shapes.
   b. Click the Home tab and then click the Copy button in the Clipboard group.
   c. Press Ctrl + End, press the Enter key once, and then press Ctrl + Enter to insert a page break.
   d. Click the Paste button in the Clipboard group.
   e. Click the bottom diagram.
   f. Click the SmartArt Tools Design tab.
   g. Click the middle layout (*Continuous Block Process*) in the Layouts group.
   h. Click outside the diagram to deselect it.
5. Save the document and name it **WordL1_C7_P4**.

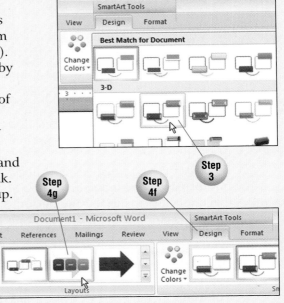

**Step 3**

**Step 4g**

**Step 4f**

### Figure 7.13 **Project 4a**

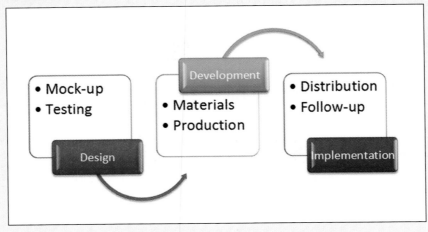

Apply formatting to a diagram with options at the SmartArt Tools Format tab shown in Figure 7.14. With options and buttons in this tab you can change the size and shape of objects in the diagram; apply shape styles and WordArt styles; change the shape fill, outline, and effects; and arrange and size the diagram.

### Figure 7.14  SmartArt Tools Format Tab

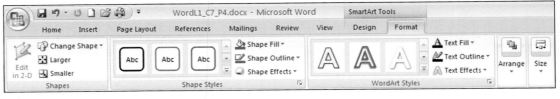

# Arranging and Moving a SmartArt Diagram

Before moving a SmartArt diagram, you must select a text wrapping style. Select a text wrapping style with the Arrange button in the SmartArt Tools Format tab. Click the Arrange button, click the Position button, and then click the desired position at the drop-down gallery. You can also choose a text wrapping by clicking the Arrange button, clicking Text Wrapping, and then clicking the desired wrapping style at the drop-down list. Move the diagram by positioning the arrow pointer on the diagram border until the pointer turns into a four-headed arrow, holding down the left mouse button, and then dragging the diagram to the desired location. Nudge selected shape(s) with the up, down, left, or right arrow keys on the keyboard.

## Project 4h — Formatting Diagrams

1. With **WordL1_C7_P4.docx** open, format shapes by completing the following steps:
   a. Click the diagram on the first page to select it (light turquoise border surrounds the diagram).
   b. Click the SmartArt Tools Format tab.
   c. In the diagram, click the rectangle shape containing the word *Design*.
   d. Hold down the Shift key and then click the shape containing the word *Development*.
   e. With the Shift key still down, click the shape containing the word *Implementation*. (All three shapes should now be selected.)
   f. Click the Change Shape button in the Shapes group.
   g. Click the seventh shape from the left in the second row of the *Block Arrows* section (the Pentagon shape).
   h. With the shapes still selected, click the Larger button in the Shapes group.
   i. With the shapes still selected, click the Shape Outline button arrow in the Shape Styles group and then click the red color *Red, Accent 2*.

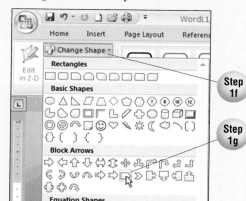

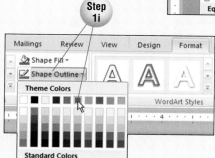

j. Click inside the diagram border but outside any shape. (This deselects the shapes but keeps the diagram selected.)

2. Change the size of the diagram by completing the following steps:
   a. Click the Size button located at the right side of the tab.
   b. Click in the *Height* measurement box, type 4, and then press Enter.

3. Position the diagram by completing the following steps:
   a. Click the Arrange button located toward the right side of the tab.
   b. Click the Position button.
   c. Click the middle option in the second row of the *With Text Wrapping* section (the *Position in Middle Center with Square Text Wrapping* option).

4. Format the bottom diagram by completing the following steps:
   a. Press Ctrl + End to move to the end of the document and then click in the bottom diagram to select it.
   b. Hold down the Shift key and then click each of the three shapes.
   c. Click the More button at the right side of the styles in the WordArt Styles group.
   d. Click the last WordArt style in the lower right corner of the drop-down gallery (*Fill - Accent 1, Metal Bevel, Reflection*).

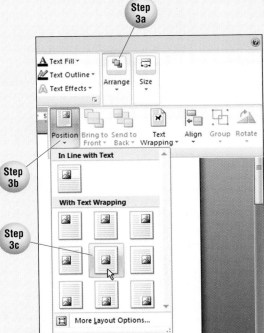

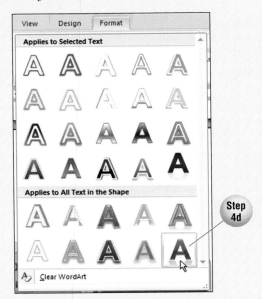

e. Click the Text Outline button arrow in the WordArt Styles group and then click the light blue color in the *Standard Colors* section (the seventh color from the left).

f. Click the Text Effects button in the WordArt Styles group, point to *Glow* at the drop-down list, and then click the last option in the top row.

g. Click inside the diagram border but outside any shape.

5. Arrange the diagram by clicking the Arrange button, clicking the Position button, and then clicking the middle option in the second row of the *With Text Wrapping* section (the *Position in Middle Center with Square Text Wrapping* option).

6. Save, print, and then close **WordL1_C7_P4.docx**.

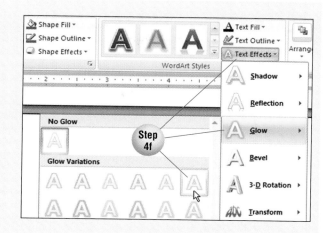

Step 4f

# Project 5   Prepare and Format a Company Organizational Chart

**You will prepare an organizational chart for a company and then apply formatting to enhance the visual appeal of the organizational chart.**

## Creating an Organizational Chart with SmartArt

If you need to visually illustrate hierarchical data, consider creating an organizational chart with a SmartArt option. To display organizational chart SmartArt options, click the Insert tab and then click the SmartArt button in the Illustrations group. At the Choose a SmartArt Graphic dialog box, click *Hierarchy* in the left panel. Organizational chart options display in the middle panel of the dialog box. Double-click the desired organizational chart and the chart is inserted in the document. Type text in a diagram by selecting the shape and then typing text in the shape or you can type text in the *Type your text here* window that displays at the left side of the diagram. Format a SmartArt organizational chart with options and buttons in the SmartArt Tools Design tab similar to the one shown in Figure 7.12 and the SmartArt Tools Format tab similar to the one shown in Figure 7.14.

**QUICK STEPS**

**Insert an Organizational Chart**
1. Click Insert tab.
2. Click SmartArt button.
3. Click *Hierarchy*.
4. Double-click desired organizational chart.

1. At a blank document, create the organizational chart shown in Figure 7.15. To begin, click the Insert tab.
2. Click the SmartArt button in the Illustrations group.
3. At the Choose a SmartArt Graphic dialog box, click *Hierarchy* in the left panel of the dialog box and then double-click the first option in the middle panel, *Organization Chart*.

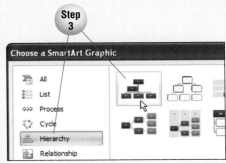

Step 3

4. If a *Type your text here* window displays at the left side of the organizational chart, close the pane by clicking the Text Pane button in the Create Graphic group.
5. Delete one of the boxes in the organizational chart by clicking the border of the box in the lower right corner to select it and then pressing the Delete key. (Make sure that the selection border that surrounds the box is a solid line and not a dashed line. If a dashed line displays, click the box border again. This should change it to a solid line.)
6. With the bottom right box selected, click the Add Shape button arrow and then click the *Add Shape Below* option.

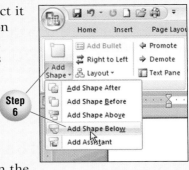

Step 6

7. Click *[Text]* in the top box, type **Blaine Willis**, press the Enter key, and then type **President**. Click in each of the remaining boxes and type the text as shown in Figure 7.15.
8. Click the More button located at the right side of the styles in the SmartArt Styles group and then click the *Inset* style in the *3-D* section (second option from the left in the top row of the *3-D* section).
9. Click the Change Colors button in the SmartArt Styles group and then click the *Colorful Range - Accent Colors 4 to 5* in the *Colorful* section (fourth option from the left in the *Colorful* row).

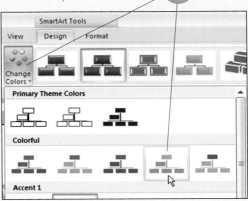

Step 9

10. Click the SmartArt Tools Format tab.
11. Click the tab (displays with a right- and left-pointing triangle) that displays at the left side of the diagram border. (This displays the *Type your text here* window.)
12. Using the mouse, select the text that displays in the *Type your text here* window.
13. Click the Change Shape button in the Shapes group and then click the *Round Same Side Corner Rectangle* option (second option from the *right* in the top row).
14. Click the Shape Outline button arrow in the Shape Styles group and then click the dark blue color (second color from the *right* in the *Standard Colors* section).

Step 13

15. Click the Size button located at the right side of the tab and then change the height to 4″ and the width to 6.5″.
16. Click outside the chart to deselect it.
17. Save the document and name it **WordL1_C7_P5**.
18. Print and then close the document.

Figure 7.15 **Project 5**

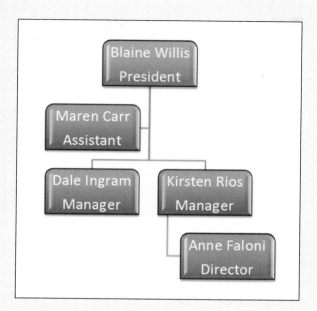

# CHAPTER summary

- Use the Tables feature to create columns and rows of information. Create a table with the Table button in the Tables group in the Insert tab or with options at the Insert Table dialog box.
- A cell is the intersection between a row and a column. The lines that form the cells of the table are called gridlines. Columns in a table are lettered from left to right beginning with *A*. Rows are numbered from top to bottom beginning with *1*.
- Move the insertion point to cells in a document using the mouse by clicking in the desired cell or use the keyboard commands shown in Table 7.1.
- Change the table design with options and buttons in the Table Tools Design tab.
- Refer to Table 7.2 for a list of mouse commands for selecting specific cells in a table.
- Refer to Table 7.3 for a list of keyboard commands for selecting specific cells in a table.
- Change the layout of a table with options and buttons in the Table Tools Layout tab.
- You can select a table, column, row, or cell using the Select button in the Table group in the Table Tools Layout tab.
- Insert and delete columns and rows with buttons in the Rows & Columns group in the Table Tools Layout tab.
- Merge selected cells with the Merge Cells button and split cells with the Split Cells button, both located in the Merge group in the Table Tools Layout tab.
- Change column width and row height using the height and width measurement boxes in the Cell Size group in the Table Tools Layout tab; by dragging move table column markers on the horizontal ruler, adjust table row markers on the vertical ruler, gridlines in the table; or with the AutoFit button in the Cell Size group.
- Change alignment of text in cells with buttons in the Alignment group in the Table Tools Layout tab.
- Change cell margins with options in the Table Options dialog box.
- Change text direction in a cell with the Text Direction button in the Alignment group.
- Change the table alignment at the Table Properties dialog box with the Table tab selected.
- You can use the resize handle to change the size of the table and use the table move handle to move the table.
- Convert text to a table with the *Convert Text to Table* option at the Table button drop-down list. Convert a table to text with the Convert to Text button in the Data group in the Table Tools Layout tab.
- Sort selected rows in a table with the Sort button in the Data group.
- Perform calculations on data in a table by clicking the Formula button in the Data group in the Table Tools Layout tab and then specifying the formula and number format at the Formula dialog box.

- Use the SmartArt feature to insert predesigned diagrams and organizational charts in a document. Click the SmartArt button in the Insert tab to display the Choose a SmartArt Graphic dialog box.
- Format a SmartArt diagram or organizational chart with options and buttons in the SmartArt Tools Design tab and the SmartArt Tools Format tab.
- To move a SmartArt diagram, first choose a position or a text wrapping style with the Arrange button in the SmartArt Tools Format tab.

# COMMANDS review

| FEATURE | RIBBON TAB, GROUP | BUTTON | OPTION |
|---|---|---|---|
| Table | Insert, Tables | | |
| Insert Table dialog box | Insert, Tables | | Insert Table |
| Draw table | Table Tools Design, Draw Borders | | |
| Insert column left | Table Tools Layout, Rows & Columns | Insert Left | |
| Insert column right | Table Tools Layout, Rows & Columns | Insert Right | |
| Insert row above | Table Tools Layout, Rows & Columns | | |
| Insert row below | Table Tools Layout, Rows & Columns | Insert Below | |
| Delete table | Table Tools Layout, Rows & Columns | | Delete Table |
| Delete row | Table Tools Layout, Rows & Columns | | Delete Rows |
| Delete column | Table Tools Layout, Rows & Columns | | Delete Columns |
| Merge cells | Table Tools Layout, Merge | Merge Cells | |
| Split cells dialog box | Table Tools Layout, Merge | Split Cells | |
| AutoFit table contents | Table Tools Layout, Cell Size | AutoFit | |
| Cell alignment | Table Tools Layout, Alignment | | |
| Table Options dialog box | Table Tools Layout, Alignment | | |
| Cell direction | Table Tools Layout, Alignment | | |
| Convert text to table | Insert, Tables | | Convert Text to Table |
| Convert table to text | Table Tools Layout, Data | Convert to Text | |

*continued*

| FEATURE | RIBBON TAB, GROUP | BUTTON | OPTION |
|---|---|---|---|
| Sort text in table | Table Tools Layout, Data | A↓ Z | |
| Formula dialog box | Table Tools Layout, Data | $f_x$ Formula | |
| Choose a SmartArt Graphic dialog box | Insert, Illustrations | | |

# CONCEPTS check

## Test Your Knowledge

Completion: In the space provided at the right, indicate the correct term, command, or number.

1. The Table button is located in this tab.  _____

2. This is another name for the lines that form the cells of the table.  _____

3. Use this keyboard shortcut to move the insertion point to the previous cell.  _____

4. Use this keyboard shortcut to move the insertion point to a tab within a cell.  _____

5. This tab contains table styles you can apply to a table.  _____

6. Click this button in the Table Tools Layout tab to insert a column at the left side of the column containing the insertion point.  _____

7. Insert and delete columns and rows with buttons in this group in the Table Tools Layout tab.  _____

8. One method for changing column width is dragging this on the horizontal ruler.  _____

9. Use this button in the Cell Size group to make the column widths in a table automatically fit the contents.  _____

10. Change the table alignment at this dialog box with the Table tab selected.  _____

11. Hover the mouse pointer over a table and this displays in the lower right corner of the table.  _____

12. Position the mouse pointer in a table and this displays in the upper left corner.  _____

13. Display the Formula dialog box by clicking the Formula button in this group in the Table Tools Layout tab.

_____

14. The SmartArt button is located in this tab.

_____

15. Click the SmartArt button and this dialog box displays.

_____

16. If you need to visually illustrate hierarchical data, consider creating this with the SmartArt feature.

_____

# SKILLS check
## *Demonstrate Your Proficiency*

### Assessment

## 1 CREATE AND FORMAT A PROPERTY REPLACEMENT COSTS TABLE

1. At a blank document, create the table shown in Figure 7.16 with the following specifications:
   a. Create a table with two columns and eight rows.
   b. Merge the cells in the top row and then change the alignment to Align Center.
   c. Type the text in the cells as shown in Figure 7.16.
   d. Right-align the cells containing the money amounts as well as the blank line below the last amount (cells B2 through B8).
   e. Autofit the contents of the cells.
   f. Apply the Light List – Accent 4 table style.
   g. Remove the check mark from the *First Column* check box.
   h. Draw a green (Olive Green, Accent 3, Darker 25%) 1½ pt border around the table.
   i. Change the font size to 14 for the text in cell A1.
   j. Use the resize handle located in the lower right corner of the table and increase the width and height of the table by approximately one inch.
2. Click in the *Accounts receivable* cell and insert a row below. Type **Equipment** in the new cell at the left and type **$83,560** in the new cell at the right.
3. Insert a formula in cell B9 that sums the amounts in cell B2 through B8. (Insert a dollar sign before the amount in cell B9.)
4. Save the document and name it **WordL1_C7_A1**.
5. Print and then close **WordL1_C7_A1.docx**.

**Figure 7.16 Assessment 1**

| PROPERTY Replacement Costs | |
|---|---|
| Business personal property | $1,367,340 |
| Earnings and expenses | $945,235 |
| Domestic and foreign transit | $123,400 |
| Accounts receivable | $95,460 |
| Legal liability | $75,415 |
| Computer coverage | $53,098 |
| Total | |

## Assessment

## 2 FORMAT A TABLE CONTAINING TRANSPORTATION SERVICE INFORMATION

1. Open **WordTable04.docx** and then save the document and name it **WordL1_C7_A2**.
2. Format the table so it appears as shown in Figure 7.17.
3. Position the table in the middle of the page.
4. Save, print, and then close **WordL1_C7_A2.docx**.

**Figure 7.17 Assessment 2**

| | Service | Telephone |
|---|---|---|
| Metro Area Transportation Services | **Langley City Transit** | |
| | Subway and bus information | (507) 555-3049 |
| | Service status hotline | (507) 555-4123 |
| | Travel information | (507) 555-4993 |
| | **Valley Rail Road** | |
| | Railway information | (202) 555-2300 |
| | Status hotline | (202) 555-2343 |
| | Travel information | (202) 555-2132 |
| | **Mainline Bus** | |
| | Bus routes | (507) 555-6530 |
| | Emergency hotline | (507) 555-6798 |
| | Travel information | (507) 555-7542 |
| | **Village Travel Card** | |
| | Village office | (507) 555-1232 |
| | Card inquiries | (507) 555-1930 |

# 3 CREATE AND FORMAT A COMPANY DIAGRAM

1. At a blank document, create the SmartArt diagram shown in Figure 7.18 with the following specifications:
   a. Use the Titled Matrix diagram.
   b. Apply the Colorful - Accent Colors SmartArt style.
   c. Type all of the text shown in Figure 7.18.
   d. Select all of the text and then apply the Gradient Fill - Accent 4, Reflection WordArt style.
2. Save the document and name it **WordL1_C7_A3**.
3. Print and then close **WordL1_C7_A3.docx**.

**Figure 7.18  Assessment 3**

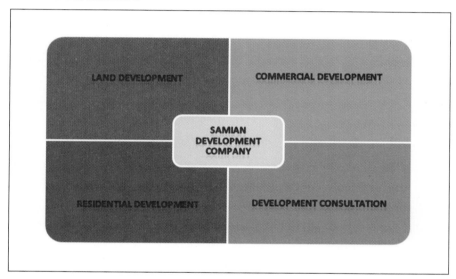

# 4 CREATE AND FORMAT A COMPANY ORGANIZATIONAL CHART

1. At a blank document, create the organizational chart shown in Figure 7.19 with the following specifications:
   a. Use the Hierarchy organizational chart.
   b. Select the top text box and insert a shape above.
   c. Select the top right text box and then add a shape below.
   d. Type the text shown in the organizational chart in Figure 7.19.
   e. Apply the Colorful Range - Accent Colors 2 to 3 option.
   f. Increase the height to 4.5″ and the width to 6.5″.
   g. Position the organizational chart in the middle of the page.
2. Save the document and name it **WordL1_C7_A4**.
3. Print and then close **WordL1_C7_A4.docx**.

**Figure 7.19  Assessment 4**

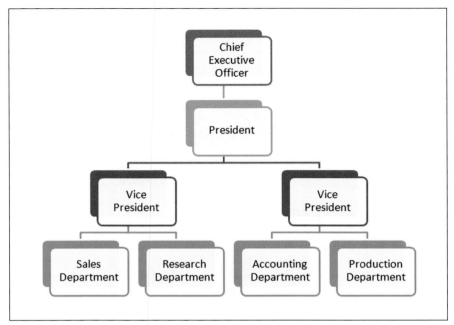

## Assessment

### 5   INSERT FORMULAS IN A TABLE

1. In this chapter, you learned how to insert formulas in a table. Experiment with writing formulas (consider using the Help feature or other reference) and then open **WordTable05.docx**. Save the document and name it **WordL1_C7_A5**.
2. Format the table so it appears as shown in Figure 7.20.
3. Insert a formula in cell B13 that sums the amounts in cells B6 through B12. Complete similar steps to insert a formula in cell C13, D13, and E13.
4. Insert a formula in cell B14 that subtracts the amount in B4 from the amount in B13. *(Hint: The formula should look like this:* =(B4-B13).*)* Complete similar steps to insert a formula in cells C14, D14, and E14.
5. Save, print, and then close **WordL1_C7_A5.docx**.

**Figure 7.20  Assessment 5**

| TRI-STATE PRODUCTS | | | | |
|---|---|---|---|---|
| **Financial Analysis** | | | | |
| | **2007** | **2008** | **2009** | **2010** |
| **Revenue** | $1,450,348 | $1,538,239 | $1,634,235 | $1,523,455 |
| **Expenses** | | | | |
| Facilities | $250,220 | $323,780 | $312,485 | $322,655 |
| Materials | $93,235 | $102,390 | $87,340 | $115,320 |
| Payroll | $354,390 | $374,280 | $380,120 | $365,120 |
| Benefits | $32,340 | $35,039 | $37,345 | $36,545 |
| Marketing | $29,575 | $28,350 | $30,310 | $31,800 |
| Transportation | $4,492 | $5,489 | $5,129 | $6,349 |
| Miscellaneous | $4,075 | $3,976 | $4,788 | $5,120 |
| Total | | | | |
| **Net Revenue** | | | | |

# CASE study
## *Apply Your Skills*

**Part 1**

You have recently been hired as an accounting clerk for a landscaping business, Landmark Landscaping, which has two small offices in your city. The accounting clerk prior to you kept track of monthly sales using Word, and the manager would prefer that you continue using that application. Open the file named **WordMonthlySales.docx** and then save the document and name it **WordL1_C7_CS_P1**. After reviewing the information, you decide that a table would be a better way of maintaining and displaying the data. Convert the data to a table and modify its appearance so that it is easy to read and understand. Insert a total row at the bottom of the table and then insert formulas to sum the totals in the columns containing amounts. Apply formatting to the table to enhance the visual appeal. Determine a color theme for the table and then continue that same color theme when preparing other documents for Landmark Landscaping. Save, print, and then close the document.

The president of Landmark Landscaping has asked you to prepare an organizational chart for the company that will become part of the company profile. Use a SmartArt organizational chart and create a chart with the following company titles (in the order shown below):

| President | | |
|---|---|---|
| **Westside Manager** | | **Eastside Manager** |
| Landscape Architect | Landscape Director | Landscape Architect | Landscape Director |
| | Assistant | | Assistant |

Format the organizational chart to enhance the visual appeal and apply colors that match the color scheme you chose for the company in Part 1. Save the document and name it **WordL1_C7_CS_P2**. Print and then close the document.

As part of the company profile, the president of the company would like to include a diagram that represents the services offered by the company and use the diagram as a company marketing tool. Use SmartArt to create a diagram that contains the following services: Maintenance Contracts, Planting Services, Landscape Design, and Landscape Consultation. Format the diagram to enhance the visual appeal and apply colors that match the color scheme you chose for the company in Part 1. Save the document and name it **WordL1_C7_CS_P3**. Print and then close the document.

Since the SmartArt feature is new and others in the company will need training on the feature, the office manager has started a training document with information on using SmartArt. He has asked you to add information on keyboard shortcuts for working with shapes. Use the Help feature to learn about the keyboard shortcuts available for working with shapes and then create a table and insert the information in the table. Format the table to enhance the visual appeal and apply colors that match the color scheme you chose for the company in Part 1. Save the document and name it **WordL1_C7_CS_P4**. Print and then close the document.

One of the landscape architects has asked you to prepare a table containing information on trees that need to be ordered next month. She would also like to have you include the Latin name for the trees since this is important when ordering. Create a table that contains the common name of the tree, the Latin name, the number required, and the price per tree as shown in Figure 7.21. Use the Internet (or any other resource available to you) to find the Latin name of each tree listed in Figure 7.21. Create a column in the table that multiplies the number of trees required by the price and include this formula for each tree. Format and enhance the table so it is attractive and easy to read. Save the document and name it **WordL1_C7_CS_P5**. Print and then close the document.

**Figure 7.21** **Case Study, Part 5**

Douglas Fir, 15 required, $1.99 per tree
White Elm, 10 required, $2.49 per tree
Western Hemlock, 10 required, $1.89 per tree
Red Maple, 8 required, $6.99 per tree
Ponderosa Pine, 5 required, $2.69 per tree

# CHAPTER 8

# Merging Documents

## PERFORMANCE OBJECTIVES

Upon successful completion of Chapter 8, you will be able to:

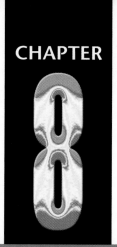

- Create and merge letters, envelopes, labels, and a directory
- Create custom fields for a merge
- Edit main documents and data source files
- Input text during a merge

**Tutorial 8.1**
Using Mail Merge

Word includes a Mail Merge feature you can use to create customized letters, envelopes, labels, directories, e-mail messages, and faxes. The Mail Merge feature is useful for situations where you need to send the same letter to a number of people and create an envelope for each letter. Use Mail Merge to create a main document that contains a letter, envelope, or other data and then merge the main document with a data source. In this chapter, you will use Mail Merge to create letters, envelopes, labels, and directories.

*Note: Before beginning computer projects, copy to your storage medium the Word2007L1C8 subfolder from the Word2007L1 folder in the CD that accompanies this textbook and then make Word2007L1C8 the active folder.*

## Project  Merge Letters to Customers

You will create a data source file and a letter main document, and then merge the main document with the records in the data source file.

## Completing a Merge

Use buttons and options in the Mailings tab shown in Figure 8.1 to complete a merge. A merge generally takes two files—the *data source* file and the *main document*. The main document contains the standard text along with fields identifying where variable information is inserted during the merge. The data source file contains the variable information that will be inserted in the main document.

**Figure 8.1** Mailings Tab

Use the Start Mail Merge button in the Mailings tab to identify the type of main document you want to create and use the Select Recipients button to create a data source file or to specify an existing data source file. You can also use the Mail Merge Wizard to guide you through the merge process. Start the wizard by clicking the Mailings tab, clicking the Start Mail Merge button, and then clicking *Step by Step Mail Merge Wizard*.

## Creating a Data Source File

**QUICK STEPS**

**Create Data Source File**
1. Click Mailings tab.
2. Click Select Recipients button.
3. Click *Type New List* in drop-down list.
4. Type data in predesigned or custom fields.
5. Click OK.

Before creating a data source file, determine what type of correspondence you will be creating and the type of information you will need to insert in the correspondence. Word provides predetermined field names you can use when creating the data source file. Use these field names if they represent the data you are creating. Variable information in a data source file is saved as a *record*. A record contains all of the information for one unit (for example, a person, family, customer, client, or business). A series of fields makes one record, and a series of records makes a data source file.

Create a data source file by clicking the Select Recipients button in the Start Mail Merge group in the Mailings tab and then clicking *Type New List* at the drop-down list. At the New Address List dialog box shown in Figure 8.2, use the predesigned fields offered by Word and type the required data or edit the fields by deleting and/or inserting custom fields and then typing the data. Note that fields in the main document correspond to the column headings in the data source file. When all records have been entered, click OK. At the Save Address List dialog box, navigate to the desired folder, type a name for the data source file, and then click OK. Word saves a data source file as an Access database. You do not need Access on your computer to complete a merge with a data source file.

**Figure 8.2** New Address List Dialog Box

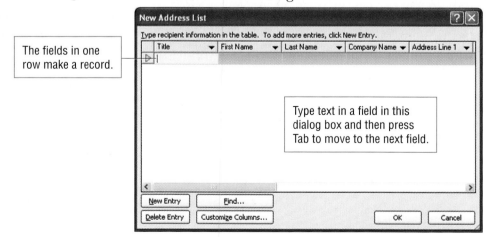

1. At a blank document, click the Mailings tab.
2. Click the Start Mail Merge button in the Start Mail Merge group and then click *Letters* at the drop-down list.
3. Click the Select Recipients button in the Start Mail Merge group and then click *Type New List* at the drop-down list.

4. At the New Address List dialog box, Word provides you with a number of predesigned fields. Delete the fields you do not need by completing the following steps:
   a. Click the Customize Columns button.
   b. At the Customize Address List dialog box, click *Company Name* to select it and then click the Delete button.

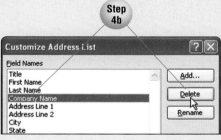

   c. At the message asking if you are sure you want to delete the field, click the Yes button.
   d. Complete steps similar to those in 4b and 4c to delete the following fields:
      *Country or Region*
      *Home Phone*
      *Work Phone*
      *E-mail Address*
5. Insert a custom field by completing the following steps:
   a. At the Customize Address List box, click the Add button.
   b. At the Add Field dialog box, type **Fund** and then click OK.
   c. Click the OK button to close the Customize Address List dialog box.

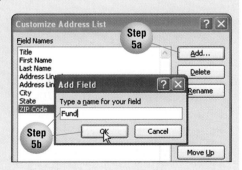

6. At the New Address List dialog box, enter the information for the first client shown in Figure 8.3 by completing the following steps:
   a. Click in the *Title* text box.
   b. Type **Mr.** and then press the Tab key. (This moves the insertion point to the *First Name* field. You can also press Shift + Tab to move to the previous field.)
   c. Type **Kenneth** and then press the Tab key.
   d. Type **Porter** and then press the Tab key.
   e. Type **7645 Tenth Street** and then press the Tab key.
   f. Type **Apt. 314** and then press the Tab key.
   g. Type **New York** and then press the Tab key.
   h. Type **NY** and then press the Tab key.
   i. Type **10192** and then press the Tab key.
   j. Type **Mutual Investment Fund** and then press the Tab key. (This makes the New Entry button active.)

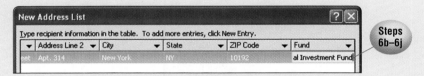

Steps
6b–6j

   k. With the insertion point positioned in the *Title* field, complete steps similar to those in 6b through 6j to enter the information for the three other clients shown in Figure 8.3.
7. After entering all of the information for the last client in Figure 8.3 (Mrs. Wanda Houston), click the OK button located in the bottom right corner of the New Address List dialog box.
8. At the Save Address List dialog box, navigate to the Word2007L1C8 folder on your storage medium, type **WordL1_C8_P1_DS** in the *File name* text box, and then click the Save button.

### Figure 8.3 **Project 1a**

| | | | | | |
|---|---|---|---|---|---|
| Title | = | Mr. | Title | = | Ms. |
| First Name | = | Kenneth | First Name | = | Carolyn |
| Last Name | = | Porter | Last Name | = | Renquist |
| Address Line 1 | = | 7645 Tenth Street | Address Line 1 | = | 13255 Meridian Street |
| Address Line 2 | = | Apt. 314 | Address Line 2 | = | (leave this blank) |
| City | = | New York | City | = | New York |
| State | = | NY | State | = | NY |
| Zip Code | = | 10192 | Zip Code | = | 10435 |
| Fund | = | Mutual Investment Fund | Fund | = | Quality Care Fund |
| | | | | | |
| Title | = | Dr. | Title | = | Mrs. |
| First Name | = | Amil | First Name | = | Wanda |
| Last Name | = | Ranna | Last Name | = | Houston |
| Address Line 1 | = | 433 South 17th | Address Line 1 | = | 566 North 22nd Avenue |
| Address Line 2 | = | Apt. 17-D | Address Line 2 | = | (leave this blank) |
| City | = | New York | City | = | New York |
| State | = | NY | State | = | NY |
| Zip Code | = | 10322 | Zip Code | = | 10634 |
| Fund | = | Priority One Fund | Fund | = | Quality Care Fund |

# Creating a Main Document

When you begin a mail merge, you specify the type of main document you are creating. After creating and typing the records in the data source file, type the main document. Insert in the main document fields identifying where you want the variable information inserted when the document is merged with the data source file. Use buttons in the Write & Insert Fields group to insert fields and field blocks in the main document.

Insert all of the fields required for the inside address of a letter with the Address Block button in the Write & Insert Fields group. Click this button and the Insert Address Block dialog box displays with a preview of how the fields will be inserted in the document to create the inside address; the dialog box also contains buttons and options for customizing the fields. Click OK and the «AddressBlock» field is inserted in the document. The «AddressBlock» field is an example of a composite field that groups a number of fields together.

Click the Greeting Line button and the Insert Greeting Line dialog box displays with options for customizing how the fields are inserted in the document to create the greeting line. When you click OK at the dialog box the «GreetingLine» composite field is inserted in the document.

If you want to insert an individual field from the data source file, click the Insert Merge Field button. This displays the Insert Merge Field dialog box with a list of fields from the data source file. Click the Insert Merge Field button arrow and a drop-down list displays containing the fields in the data source file. If you want merged data formatted, you can format the merge fields at the main document.

Address Block

Greeting Line

Insert Merge Field

## Project 1b  Creating a Main Document

1. At the blank document, create the letter shown in Figure 8.4. Begin by clicking the No Spacing style in the Styles group in the Home tab.
2. Press the Enter key six times and then type February 23, 2010.
3. Press the Enter key five times and then insert the address fields by completing the following steps:
   a. Click the Mailings tab and then click the Address Block button in the Write & Insert Fields group.
   b. At the Insert Address Block dialog box, click the OK button.
   c. Press the Enter key twice.
4. Insert the greeting line fields by completing the following steps:
   a. Click the Greeting Line button in the Write & Insert Fields group.
   b. At the Insert Greeting Line dialog box, click the down-pointing arrow at the right of the option box containing the comma (the box to the right of the box containing *Mr. Randall*).
   c. At the drop-down list that displays, click the colon.

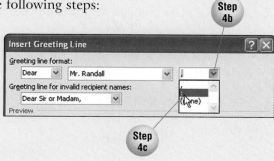

Step 4b

Step 4c

d. Click OK to close the Insert Greeting Line dialog box.

e. Press the Enter key twice.

5. Type the letter to the point where «Fund» displays and then insert the «Fund» field by clicking the Insert Merge Field button arrow and then clicking *Fund* at the drop-down list.

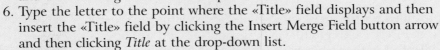
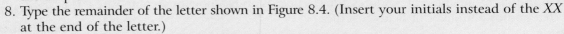

6. Type the letter to the point where the «Title» field displays and then insert the «Title» field by clicking the Insert Merge Field button arrow and then clicking *Title* at the drop-down list.

7. Press the spacebar and then insert the «Last_Name» field by clicking the Insert Merge Field button arrow and then clicking *Last_Name* at the drop-down list.

8. Type the remainder of the letter shown in Figure 8.4. (Insert your initials instead of the *XX* at the end of the letter.)

9. Save the document and name it **WordL1_C8_P1_MD**.

**Figure 8.4  Project 1b**

February 23, 2010

«AddressBlock»

«GreetingLine»

McCormack Funds is lowering its expense charges beginning May 1, 2010. The reductions in expense charges mean that more of your account investment performance in the «Fund» is returned to you, «Title» «Last_Name». The reductions are worth your attention because most of our competitors' fees have gone up.

Lowering expense charges is noteworthy because before the reduction, McCormack expense deductions were already among the lowest, far below most mutual funds and variable annuity accounts with similar objectives. At the same time, services for you, our client, will continue to expand. If you would like to discuss this change, please call us at (212) 555-2277. Your financial future is our main concern at McCormack.

Sincerely,

Jodie Langstrom
Director, Financial Services

XX:WordL1_C8_P1_MD.docx

# Previewing a Merge

To view how the main document will appear when merged with the first record in the data source file, click the Preview Results button in the Mailings tab. You can view the main document merged with other records by using the navigation buttons in the Preview Results group. This group contains the buttons First Record, Previous Record, Go to Record, Next Record, and Last Record. Click the button that will display the main document merged with the desired record. Viewing the merged document before printing is helpful to ensure that the merged data is correct. To use the Go to Record button, click the button, type the number of the desired record, and then press Enter. Turn off the preview feature by clicking the Preview Results button.

Preview Results

First Record   Last Record

Previous Record   Next Record

# Merging Documents

To complete the merge, click the Finish & Merge button in the Finish group in the Mailings tab. At the drop-down list that displays, you can choose to merge the records and create a new document, send the merged documents directly to the printer, or send the merged documents by e-mail.

    To merge the documents and create a new document with the merged records, click the Finish & Merge button and then click *Edit Individual Documents* at the drop-down list. At the Merge to New Document dialog box, make sure *All* is selected in the *Merge records* section and then click OK. This merges the records in the data source file with the main document and inserts the merged documents in a new document. You can also display the Merge to New Document dialog box by pressing Alt + Shift + N. Press Alt + Shift + M to display the Merge to Printer dialog box.

**QUICK STEPS**

**Merge Documents**
1. Click Finish & Merge button.
2. Click *Edit Individual Documents* at drop-down list.
3. Make sure *All* is selected in Merge to New Document dialog box.
4. Click OK.

Finish & Merge

---

## Project 1C — Merging the Main Document with the Data Source File

1. With **WordL1_C8_P1_MD.docx** open, preview the main document merged with the first record in the data source file by clicking the Preview Results button in the Mailings tab.
2. Click the Next Record button to view the main document merged with the second record in the data source file.
3. Click the Preview Results button to turn it off.
4. Click the Finish & Merge button in the Finish group and then click *Edit Individual Documents* at the drop-down list.
5. At the Merge to New Document dialog box, make sure *All* is selected, and then click OK.
6. Save the merged letters and name the document **WordL1_C8_P1_Ltrs**.
7. Print **WordL1_C8_P1_Ltrs.docx**. (This document will print four letters.)
8. Close **WordL1_C8_P1_Ltrs.docx**.
9. Save and then close **WordL1_C8_P1_MD.docx**.

Step 1

Step 2

Step 4

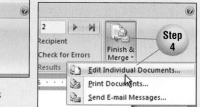

## Merging Envelopes

If you create a letter as a main document and then merge it with a data source file, more than likely you will need properly addressed envelopes in which to send the letters. To prepare an envelope main document that is merged with a data source file, click the Mailings tab, click the Start Mail Merge button, and then click *Envelopes* at the drop-down list. This displays the Envelope Options dialog box as shown in Figure 8.5. At this dialog box, specify the desired envelope size, make any other changes, and then click OK.

**Figure 8.5** Envelope Options Dialog Box

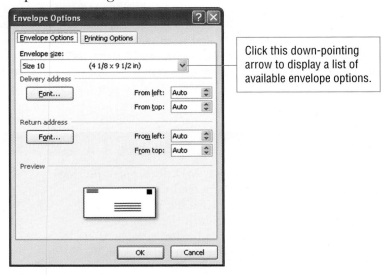

Click this down-pointing arrow to display a list of available envelope options.

The next step in the envelope merge process is to create the data source file or identify an existing data source file. To identify an existing data source file, click the Select Recipients button in the Start Mail Merge group and then click *Use Existing List* at the drop-down list. At the Select Data Source dialog box, navigate to the folder containing the desired data source file and then double-click the file.

With the data source file attached to the envelope main document, the next step is to insert the appropriate fields. Click in the envelope in the approximate location where the recipient's address will appear and a box with a dashed blue border displays. Click the Address Block button in the Write & Insert Fields group and then click OK at the Insert Address Block dialog box.

1. At a blank document, click the Mailings tab.
2. Click the Start Mail Merge button in the Start Mail Merge group and then click *Envelopes* at the drop-down list.
3. At the Envelope Options dialog box, make sure the envelope size is 10 and then click OK.
4. Click the Select Recipients button in the Start Mail Merge group and then click *Use Existing List* at the drop-down list.
5. At the Select Data Source dialog box, navigate to the Word2007L1C8 folder on your storage medium and then double-click the data source file named **WordL1_C8_P1_DS.mdb**.
6. Click in the approximate location in the envelope document where the recipient's address will appear. (This causes a box with a dashed blue border to display. If you do not see this box, try clicking in a different location on the envelope.)

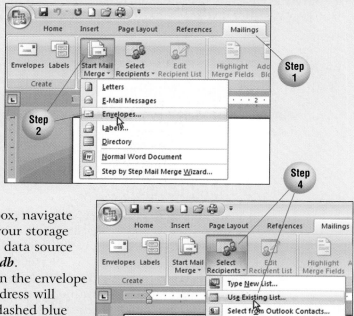

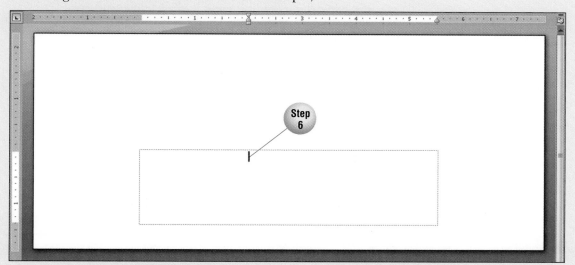

7. Click the Address Block button in the Write & Insert Fields group.
8. At the Insert Address Block dialog box, click the OK button.
9. Click the Preview Results button to see how the envelope appears merged with the first record in the data source file.
10. Click the Preview Results button to turn it off.
11. Click the Finish & Merge button in the Finish group and then click *Edit Individual Documents* at the drop-down list.
12. At the Merge to New Document dialog box, make sure *All* is selected and then click OK.
13. Save the merged envelopes and name the document **WordL1_C8_P2_Envs**.
14. Print **WordL1_C8_P2_Envs.docx**. (This document will print four envelopes.)

15. Close **WordL1_C8_P2_Envs.docx**.
16. Save the envelope main document and name it **WordL1_C8_P2_MD**.
17. Close **WordL1_C8_P2_MD.docx**.

# Project 3 Merge Mailing Labels

You will use Mail Merge to prepare mailing labels with customer names and addresses.

## Merging Labels

Create mailing labels for records in a data source file in much the same way that you create envelopes. Click the Start Mail Merge button and then click *Labels* at the drop-down list. This displays the Label Options dialog box as shown in Figure 8.6. Make sure the desired label is selected and then click OK to close the dialog box. The next step is to create the data source file or identify an existing data source file. With the data source file attached to the label main document, insert the appropriate fields and then complete the merge.

**Figure 8.6** Label Options Dialog Box

## Project 3 Merging Mailing Labels

1. At a blank document, click the Mailings tab.
2. Click the Start Mail Merge button in the Start Mail Merge group and then click *Labels* at the drop-down list.

3. At the Label Options dialog box, complete the following steps:
   a. If necessary, click the down-pointing arrow at the right side of the *Label vendors* option and then click *Avery US Letter* at the drop-down list. (If this product vendor is not available, choose a vendor name that offers labels that print on a full page.)
   b. Scroll in the *Product number* list box and then click *5160*. (If this option is not available, choose a label number that prints labels in two or three columns down a full page.)
   c. Click OK to close the dialog box.

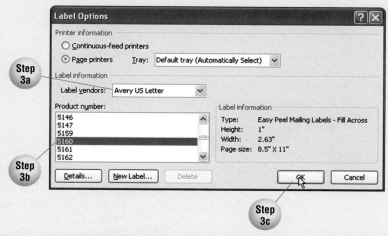

4. Click the Select Recipients button in the Start Mail Merge group and then click *Use Existing List* at the drop-down list.
5. At the Select Data Source dialog box, navigate to the Word2007L1C8 folder on your storage medium and then double-click the data source file named **WordL1_C8_P1_DS.mdb**.
6. At the labels document, click the Address Block button in the Write & Insert Fields group.
7. At the Insert Address Block dialog box, click the OK button. (This inserts «AddressBlock» in the first label. The other labels contain the «Next Record» field.)
8. Click the Update Labels button in the Write & Insert Fields group. (This adds the «AddressBlock» field after each «Next Record» field in the second and subsequent labels.)
9. Click the Preview Results button to see how the labels appear merged with the records in the data source file.
10. Click the Preview Results button to turn it off.
11. Click the Finish & Merge button in the Finish group and then click *Edit Individual Documents* at the drop-down list.
12. At the Merge to New Document dialog box, make sure *All* is selected, and then click OK.
13. Format the labels by completing the following steps:
    a. Click the Table Tools Layout tab.
    b. Click the Select button in the Table group and then click *Select Table*.
    c. Click the Align Center Left button in the Alignment group.
    d. Click the Home tab and then click the Paragraph group dialog box launcher.
    e. At the Paragraph dialog box, click the up-pointing arrow at the right of *Before* and also at the right of *After* to change the measurement to 0″. Click the up-pointing arrow at the right of the *Inside* option to change the measurement to 0.3″ and then click OK.
14. Save the merged labels and name the document **WordL1_C8_P3_Labels**.
15. Print and then close **WordL1_C8_P3_Labels.docx**.
16. Save the label main document and name it **WordL1_C8_P3_MD**.
17. Close **WordL1_C8_P3_MD.docx**.

# Project 4 Merge a Directory

You will use Mail Merge to prepare a directory list containing customer names and type of funds.

## Merging a Directory

When merging letters, envelopes, or mailing labels, a new form is created for each record. For example, if the data source file merged with the letter contains eight records, eight letters are created. If the data source file merged with a mailing label contains twenty records, twenty labels are created. In some situations, you may want merged information to remain on the same page. This is useful, for example, when creating a list such as a directory or address list.

Begin creating a merged directory by clicking the Start Mail Merge button and then clicking *Directory*. Create or identify an existing data source file and then insert the desired fields in the directory document. You may want to set tabs to insert text in columns.

## Project 4 | Merging a Directory

1. At a blank document, click the Mailings tab.
2. Click the Start Mail Merge button in the Start Mail Merge group and then click *Directory* at the drop-down list.
3. Click the Select Recipients button in the Start Mail Merge group and then click *Use Existing List* at the drop-down list.
4. At the Select Data Source dialog box, navigate to the Word2007L1C8 folder on your storage medium and then double-click the data source file named *WordL1_C8_P1_DS.mdb*.
5. At the document screen, set left tabs at the 1-inch mark, the 2.5-inch mark, and the 4-inch mark on the Ruler and then press the Tab key. (This moves the insertion point to the tab set at the 1-inch mark.)

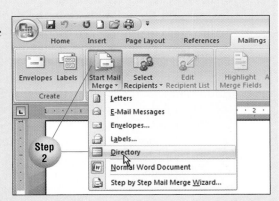

6. Click the Insert Merge Field button arrow and then click *Last_Name* at the drop-down list.
7. Press the Tab key to move the insertion point to the 2.5-inch mark.
8. Click the Insert Merge Field button arrow and then click *First_Name* at the drop-down list.
9. Press the Tab key to move the insertion point to the 4-inch mark.
10. Click the Insert Merge Field button arrow and then click *Fund* at the drop-down list.
11. Press the Enter key once.
12. Click the Finish & Merge button in the Finish group and then click *Edit Individual Documents* at the drop-down list.
13. At the Merge to New Document dialog box, make sure *All* is selected, and then click OK. (This merges the fields in the document.)
14. Press Ctrl + Home, press the Enter key once, and then press the Up Arrow key once.

15. Press the Tab key, turn on bold, and then type Last Name.
16. Press the Tab key and then type First Name.
17. Press the Tab key and then type Fund.

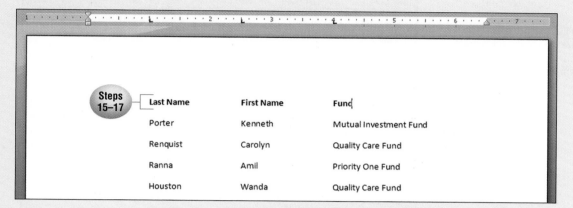

18. Save the directory document and name it **WordL1_C8_P4_Directory**.
19. Print and then close the document.
20. Close the directory main document without saving it.

## Editing a Data Source File

**Edit Data Source File**
1. Open main document.
2. Click Mailings tab.
3. Click Edit Recipient List button.
4. Make desired changes at Mail Merge Recipients dialog box.
5. Click OK.

Edit a main document in the normal manner. Open the document, make the required changes, and then save the document. Since a data source is actually an Access database file, you cannot open it in the normal manner. Open a data source file for editing using the Edit Recipient List button in the Start Mail Merge group in the Mailings tab. When you click the Edit Recipient List button, the Mail Merge Recipients dialog box displays as shown in Figure 8.7. Select or edit records at this dialog box.

 roject **5** **Select Records and Merge Mailing Labels**

You will use Mail Merge to prepare mailing labels with names and addresses of customers living in Baltimore.

## Selecting Specific Records

All of the records in the Mail Merge Recipients dialog box contain a check mark before the first field. If you want to select specific records, remove the check mark from those records you do not want included in a merge. In this way you can select and then merge specific records in the data source file with the main document.

**Figure 8.7** Mail Merge Recipients Dialog Box

Select specific records by removing the check marks from those records you do not want included in the merge.

## Project 5 Selecting Records and Merging Mailing Labels

1. At a blank document, create mailing labels for customers living in Baltimore. Begin by clicking the Mailings tab.
2. Click the Start Mail Merge button in the Start Mail Merge group and then click *Labels* at the drop-down list.
3. At the Label Options dialog box, make sure *Avery US Letter* displays in the *Label products* option box, and *5160* displays in the *Product number* list box, and then click OK.
4. Click the Select Recipients button in the Start Mail Merge group and then click *Use Existing List* at the drop-down list.
5. At the Select Data Source dialog box, navigate to the Word2007L1C8 folder on your storage medium and then double-click the data source file named ***LFSClients.mdb***.
6. Click the Edit Recipient List button in the Start Mail Merge group.
7. At the Mail Merge Recipients dialog box, complete the following steps:

   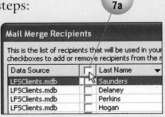
   **Step 7a**

   a. Click the check box located immediately left of the *Last Name* field column heading to remove the check mark. (This removes all of the check marks from the check boxes.)
   b. Click the check box immediately left of each of the following last names: *Saunders, Perkins, Grenwald, Dutton, Fernandez*, and *Stahl*. (These are the customers that live in Baltimore.)
   c. Click OK to close the dialog box.
8. At the labels document, click the Address Block button in the Write & Insert Fields group.
9. At the Insert Address Block dialog box, click the OK button.
10. Click the Update Labels button in Write & Insert Fields group.
11. Click the Preview Results button and then click the Next Record button to display each of the labels and make sure only those customers living in Baltimore display.
12. Click the Preview Results button to turn it off.
13. Click the Finish & Merge button in the Finish group and then click *Edit Individual Documents* at the drop-down list.

14. At the Merge to New Document dialog box, make sure *All* is selected, and then click OK.
15. Format the labels by completing the following steps:
    a. Click the Table Tools Layout tab.
    b. Click the Select button in the Table group and then click *Select Table*.
    c. Click the Align Center Left button in the Alignment group.
    d. Click the Home tab and then click the Paragraph group dialog box launcher.
    e. At the Paragraph dialog box, click the up-pointing arrow at the right of *Before* and also at the right of *After* to change the measurement to 0″. Click the up-pointing arrow at the right of the *Inside* option to change the measurement to 0.3″ and then click OK.
16. Save the merged labels and name the document **WordL1_C8_P5_Labels**.
17. Print and then close **WordL1_C8_P5_Labels.docx**.
18. Close the main labels document without saving it.

# Project ⑥ Edit Records in a Data Source File

You will edit records in a data source file and then use Mail Merge to prepare a directory with the edited records that contains customer names, telephone numbers, and cell phone numbers.

## Editing Records

A data source file may need editing on a periodic basis to add or delete customer names, update fields, insert new fields, or delete existing fields. To edit a data source file, click the Edit Recipient List button in the Start Mail Merge group. At the Mail Merge Recipients dialog box, click the data source file name in the *Data Source* list box and then click the Edit button that displays below the list box. This displays the Edit Data Source dialog box shown in Figure 8.8. At this dialog box you can add a new entry, delete an entry, find a particular entry, and customize columns.

**Figure 8.8** Edit Data Source Dialog Box

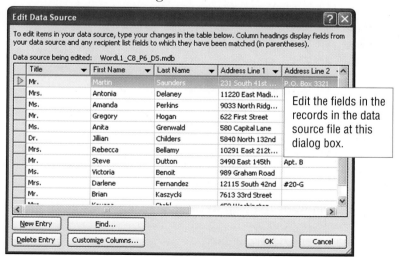

1. Make a copy of the **LFSClients.mdb** file by completing the following steps:
   a. Display the Open dialog box and make Word2007L1C8 the active folder.
   b. If necessary, change the *Files of type* option to *All Files (\*.\*)*.
   c. Right-click on the **LFSClients.mdb** file and then click *Copy* at the shortcut menu.
   d. Position the mouse pointer in a white portion of the Open dialog box list box (outside of any file name), click the right mouse button, and then click *Paste* at the shortcut menu. (This inserts a copy of the file in the dialog box list box and names the file **Copy of LFSClients.mdb**.)
   e. Right-click on the file name **Copy of LFSClients.mdb** and then click *Rename* at the shortcut menu.
   f. Type **WordL1_C8_P6_DS.mdb** and then press Enter.
   g. Close the Open dialog box.
2. At a blank document, click the Mailings tab.
3. Click the Select Recipients button and then click *Use Existing List* from the drop-down list.
4. At the Select Data Source dialog box, navigate to the Word2007L1C8 folder on your storage medium and then double-click the data source file named **WordL1_C8_P6_DS.mdb**.
5. Click the Edit Recipient List button in the Start Mail Merge group.
6. At the Mail Merge Recipients dialog box, click **WordL1_C8_P6_DS.mdb** that displays in the *Data Source* list box and then click the Edit button.
7. Delete the record for Steve Dutton by completing the following steps:
   a. Click the square that displays at the beginning of the row for *Mr. Steve Dutton*.
   b. Click the Delete Entry button.

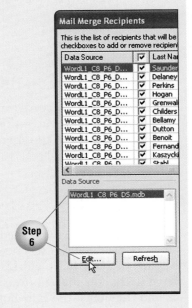

Step 6

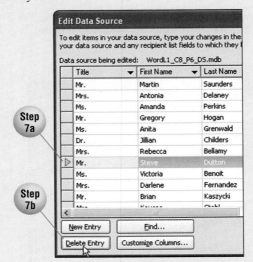

Step 7a

Step 7b

   c. At the message asking if you want to delete the entry, click the Yes button.
8. Insert a new record by completing the following steps:
   a. Click the New Entry button in the dialog box.

b. Type the following text in the new record in the specified fields:

    Title = Ms.
    First Name = Jennae
    Last Name = Davis
    Address Line 1 = 3120 South 21st
    Address Line 2 = (none)
    City = Rosedale
    State = MD
    ZIP Code = 20389
    Home Phone = 410-555-5774

9. Insert a new field and type text in the field by completing the following steps:
   a. At the Edit Data Source dialog box, click the Customize Columns button.
   b. At the message asking if you want to save the changes made to the data source file, click Yes.
   c. At the Customize Address List dialog box, click *ZIP Code* in the *Field Names* list box. (A new field is inserted below the selected field.)
   d. Click the Add button.
   e. At the Add Field dialog box, type **Cell Phone** and then click OK.
   f. You decide that you want the *Cell Phone* field to display after the *Home Phone* field. To move the *Cell Phone* field, make sure it is selected and then click the Move Down button.
   g. Click OK to close the Customize Address List dialog box.
   h. At the Edit Data Source dialog box, scroll to the right to display the *Cell Phone* field (last field in the file) and then type the following cell phone numbers (after typing each cell phone number, except the last number, press the Down Arrow key to make the next cell below active):

Step 9d

Step 9c

Step 9e

    Record 1 = 410-555-1249
    Record 2 = 413-555-3492
    Record 3 = 410-555-0695
    Record 4 = 410-555-9488
    Record 5 = 413-555-1200
    Record 6 = 410-555-7522
    Record 7 = 410-555-8833
    Record 8 = 413-555-9378
    Record 9 = 410-555-4261
    Record 10 = 410-555-9944
    Record 11 = 413-555-2321
    Record 12 = 410-555-9435

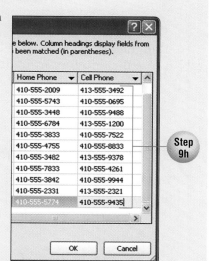

Step 9h

   i. Click OK to close the Edit Data Source dialog box.
   j. At the message asking if you want to update the recipient list and save changes, click Yes.
   k. At the Mail Merge Recipients dialog box, click OK.
10. Create a directory by completing the following steps:
   a. Click the Start Mail Merge button and then click *Directory* at the drop-down list.
   b. At a blank document, set left tabs on the horizontal ruler at the 1-inch mark, the 3-inch mark, and the 4.5-inch mark.
   c. Press the Tab key (this moves the insertion point to the first tab set at the 1-inch mark).

d. Click the Insert Merge Field button arrow and then click *Last_Name* at the drop-down list.

e. Type a comma and then press the spacebar.

f. Click the Insert Merge Field button arrow and then click *First_Name* at the drop-down list.

g. Press the Tab key, click the Insert Merge Field button arrow, and then click *Home_Phone* at the drop-down list.

h. Press the Tab key, click the Insert Merge Field button arrow, and then click *Cell_Phone* at the drop-down list.

i. Press the Enter key once.

j. Click the Finish & Merge button in the Finish group and then click *Edit Individual Documents* at the drop-down list.

k. At the Merge to New Document dialog box, make sure *All* is selected and then click OK. (This merges the fields in the document.)

11. Press Ctrl + Home, press the Enter key once, and then press the Up Arrow key once.

12. Press the Tab key, turn on bold, and then type Name.

13. Press the Tab key and then type Home Phone.

14. Press the Tab key and then type Cell Phone.

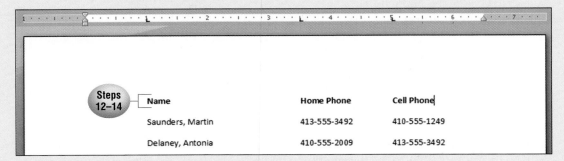

15. Save the directory document and name it **WordL1_C8_P6_Directory**.

16. Print and then close the document.

17. Close the directory main document without saving it.

# Project 7 Add Fill-in Fields to a Main Document

You will edit a form letter and insert sales representative contact information during a merge.

## Inputting Text during a Merge

Word's Merge feature contains a large number of Word fields you can insert in a main document. In this chapter, you will learn about the *Fill-in* field that is used for information input at the keyboard during a merge. For more information on the other Word fields, please refer to the on-screen help.

Situations may arise in which you do not need to keep all variable information in a data source file. For example, variable information that changes on a regular basis might include a customer's monthly balance, a product price, and so on. Word lets you input variable information into a document during the merge using the keyboard. A Fill-in field is inserted in a main document by clicking the Rules button in the Write & Insert Fields group in the Mailings tab and then clicking *Fill-in* at the drop-down list. This displays the Insert Word Field: Fill-in dialog box shown in Figure 8.9. At this dialog box, type a short message indicating what should be entered at the keyboard and then click OK. At the Microsoft Word dialog box with the message you entered displayed in the upper left corner, type text you want to display in the document and then click OK. When the Fill-in field or fields are added, save the main document in the normal manner. A document can contain any number of Fill-in fields.

**Insert Fill-in Field in Main Document**
1. Click Mailings tab.
2. Click Rules button.
3. Click *Fill-in* at drop-down list.
4. Type prompt text.
5. Click OK.
6. Type text to be inserted in document.
7. Click OK.

**Figure 8.9** Insert Word Field: Fill-in Dialog Box

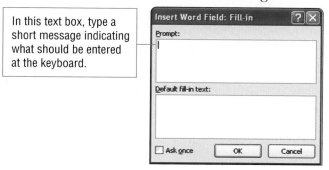

In this text box, type a short message indicating what should be entered at the keyboard.

When you merge the main document with the data source file, the first record is merged with the main document and the Microsoft Word dialog box displays with the message you entered displayed in the upper left corner. Type the required information for the first record in the data source file and then click the OK button. Word displays the dialog box again. Type the required information for the second record in the data source file and then click OK. Continue in this manner until the required information has been entered for each record in the data source file. Word then completes the merge.

Project ⑦ **Adding Fill-in Fields to a Main Document**

1. Open the document named **WordL1_C8_P1_MD.docx** (at the message asking if you want to continue, click Yes) and then save the document and name it **WordL1_C8_P7_MD**.
2. Change the second paragraph in the body of the letter to the paragraph shown in Figure 8.10. Insert the first Fill-in field (representative's name) by completing the following steps:
   a. Click the Mailings tab.
   b. Click the Rules button in the Write & Insert Fields group and then click *Fill-in* at the drop-down list.

Step 2b

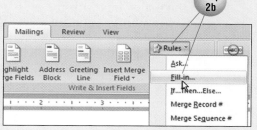

c. At the Insert Word Field: Fill-in dialog box, type **Insert rep name** in the *Prompt* text box and then click OK.

d. At the Microsoft Office Word dialog box with *Insert rep name* displayed in the upper left corner, type **(representative's name)** and then click OK.

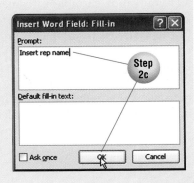

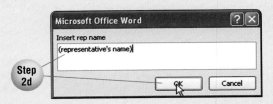

3. Complete steps similar to those in Step 2 to insert the second Fill-in field (phone number), except type **Insert phone number** in the *Prompt* text box at the Insert Word Field: Fill-in dialog box and type **(phone number)** at the Microsoft Word dialog box.

4. Save **WordL1_C8_P7_MD.docx**.

5. Merge the main document with the data source file by completing the following steps:

   a. Click the Finish & Merge button and then click *Edit Individual Documents* at the drop-down list.

   b. At the Merge to New Document dialog box, make sure *All* is selected, and then click OK.

   c. When Word merges the main document with the first record, a dialog box displays with the message *Insert rep name* and the text *(representative's name)* selected. At this dialog box, type **Marilyn Smythe** and then click OK.

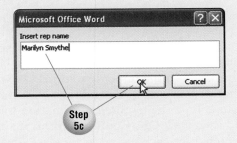

   d. At the dialog box with the message *Insert phone number* and *(phone number)* selected, type **(646) 555-8944** and then click OK.

   e. At the dialog box with the message *Insert rep name*, type **Anthony Mason** (over *Marilyn Smythe*) and then click OK.

   f. At the dialog box with the message *Insert phone number*, type **(646) 555-8901** (over the previous number) and then click OK.

   g. At the dialog box with the message *Insert rep name*, type **Faith Ostrom** (over *Anthony Mason*) and then click OK.

   h. At the dialog box with the message *Insert phone number*, type **(646) 555-8967** (over the previous number) and then click OK.

   i. At the dialog box with the message *Insert rep name*, type **Thomas Rivers** (over *Faith Ostrom*) and then click OK.

   j. At the dialog box with the message *Insert phone number*, type **(646) 555-0793** (over the previous number) and then click OK.

6. Save the merged document and name it **WordL1_C8_P7_Ltrs**.

7. Print and then close **WordL1_C8_P7_Ltrs.docx**.

8. Save and then close **WordL1_C8_P7_MD.docx**.

**Figure 8.10  Project 7**

Lowering expense charges is noteworthy because before the reduction, McCormack expense deductions were already among the lowest, far below most mutual funds and variable annuity accounts with similar objectives. At the same time, services for you, our client, will continue to expand. If you would like to discuss this change, please call our service representative, **(representative's name)**, at **(phone number)**.

# CHAPTER summary

- Use the Mail Merge feature to create letters, envelopes, labels, directories, e-mail messages, and faxes, all with personalized information.
- Generally, a merge takes two documents—the data source file containing the variable information and the main document containing standard text along with fields identifying where variable information is inserted during the merge process.
- Variable information in a data source file is saved as a record. A record contains all of the information for one unit. A series of fields makes one record, and a series of records makes a data source file.
- A data source file is saved as an Access database but you do not need Access on your computer to complete a merge with a data source.
- You can use predesigned fields when creating a data source file or you can create your own custom field at the Customize Address List dialog box.
- Use the Address Block button in the Write & Insert Fields group in the Mailings tab to insert all of the fields required for the inside address of a letter. This inserts the «AddressBlock» field, which is considered a composite field because it groups a number of fields together.
- Click the Greeting Line button in the Write & Insert Fields group in the Mailings tab to insert the «GreetingLine» composite field in the document.
- Click the Insert Merge Field button arrow in the Write & Insert Fields group in the Mailings tab to display a drop-down list of fields contained in the data source file.
- Click the Preview Results button in the Mailings tab to view the main document merged with the first record in the data source. Use the navigation buttons in the Preview Results group in the Mailings tab to display the main document merged with the desired record.
- Click the Finish & Merge button in the Mailings tab to complete the merge.
- Select specific records for merging by inserting or removing check marks from the desired records in the Mail Merge Recipients dialog box. Display this dialog box by clicking the Edit Recipient List button in the Mailings tab.
- Edit specific records in a data source file at the Edit Data Source dialog box. Display this dialog box by clicking the Edit Recipient List button in the Mailings tab, clicking the desired data source file name in the *Data Source* list box, and then clicking the Edit button.
- Use the Fill-in field in a main document to insert variable information at the keyboard during a merge.

# COMMANDS review

| FEATURE | RIBBON TAB, GROUP | BUTTON, OPTION |
|---------|-------------------|----------------|
| New Address List dialog box | Mailings, Start Mail Merge | , Type New List |
| Letter main document | Mailings, Start Mail Merge | , Letters |
| Envelopes main document | Mailings, Start Mail Merge | , Envelopes |
| Labels main document | Mailings, Start Mail Merge | , Labels |
| Directory main document | Mailings, Start Mail Merge | , Directory |
| Preview merge results | Mailings, Preview Results | |
| Mail Merge Recipients dialog box | Mailings, Start Mail Merge | |
| Address Block field | Mailings, Write & Insert Fields | |
| Greeting Line field | Mailings, Write & Insert Fields | |
| Insert merge fields | Mailings, Write & Insert Fields | |
| Fill-in merge field | Mailings, Write & Insert Fields | Rules ▾ , Fill-in |

# CONCEPTS check

## Test Your Knowledge

**Completion:** In the space provided at the right, indicate the correct term, command, or number.

1. A merge generally takes two files—a data source file and this. _____

2. This term refers to all of the information for one unit in a data source file. _____

3. Create a data source file by clicking this button in the Mailings tab and then clicking *Type New List* at the drop-down list. _____

4. A data source file is saved as this type of file. _____

5. Create your own custom fields in a data source file with options at this dialog box. _____

6. Use this button in the Mailings tab to insert all of the required fields for the inside address in a letter. _____

7. The «GreetingLine» field is considered this type of field because it includes all of the fields required for the greeting line. _____

8. Click this button in the Mailings tab to display the first record merged with the main document. _____

9. To complete a merge, click this button in the Finish group in the Mailings tab. _____

10. Select specific records in a data source file by inserting or removing check marks from the records in this dialog box. _____

11. Use this field to insert variable information at the keyboard during a merge. _____

# SKILLS check

## *Demonstrate Your Proficiency*

## Assessment

### 1 PREPARE AND MERGE LETTERS, ENVELOPES, AND LABELS

1. Look at the information shown in Figure 8.11 and Figure 8.12.
2. Use the Mail Merge feature to prepare four letters using the information shown in the figures. Name the data source file **WordL1_C8_A1_DS**, name the main document **WordL1_C8_A1_MD**, and name the merged letters document **WordL1_C8_A1_Ltrs**.
3. Print and then close **WordL1_C8_A1_Ltrs.docx**. Save and then close **WordL1_C8_A1_MD.docx**.
4. Create an envelope main document and merge it with the **WordL1_C8_A1_DS.mdb** data source file. Save the merged envelopes document and name it **WordL1_C8_A1_Envs**. Print and then close document. Close the envelope main document without saving it.
5. Use the Mail Merge feature to prepare mailing labels for the names and addresses in the **WordL1_C8_A1_DS.mdb** data source file.
6. Save the merged labels document and name it **WordL1_C8_A1_Labels**. Print and then close the document.
7. Close the labels main document without saving it.

**Figure 8.11  Assessment 1**

Mr. Tony Benedetti
1315 Cordova Road
Apt. 402
Santa Fe, NM 87505
Home Phone: 505-555-0489

Ms. Theresa Dusek
12044 Ridgway Drive
(leave this blank)
Santa Fe, NM 87505
Home Phone: 505-555-1120

Mrs. Mary Arguello
2554 Country Drive
#105
Santa Fe, NM 87504
Home Phone: 505-555-7663

Mr. Preston Miller
120 Second Street
(leave this blank)
Santa Fe, NM 87505
Home Phone: 505-555-3551

**Figure 8.12  Assessment 1**

May 6, 2010

«AddressBlock»

«GreetingLine»

The Cordova Children's Community Center is a nonprofit agency providing educational and recreational activities to children in the Cordova community. We are funded by donations from the community and rely on you and all of our volunteers to provide quality care and services to our children. As a member of our outstanding volunteer team, we are inviting you to attend our summer volunteer open house on Saturday, May 22, at the community center from 1:00 to 4:30 p.m. We want to honor you and our other volunteers for your commitment to children so please plan to attend so we can thank you in person.

The Center's summer volunteer session begins Tuesday, June 1, and continues through August 31. According to our volunteer roster, you have signed up to volunteer during the summer session. Throughout the summer we will be offering a variety of services to our children including tutoring, creative art classes, recreational activities, and a science camp. At the open house, you can sign up for the specific area or areas in which you want to volunteer. We look forward to seeing you at the open house and during the upcoming summer session.

Sincerely,

Andy Amura
Volunteer Coordinator

XX:WordL1_C8_A1_MD.docx

# 2 EDIT AND MERGE LETTERS

1. Open **WordL1_C8_A1_MD.docx** (at the message asking if you want to continue, click Yes) and then save the main document and name it **WordL1_C8_A2_MD**.
2. Edit the **WordL1_C8_A1_DS.mdb** data source file by making the following changes:
   a. Display the record for Ms. Theresa Dusek and then change the address from *12044 Ridgway Drive* to *1390 Fourth Avenue*.
   b. Display the record for Mr. Preston Miller and change the home phone number from *505-555-3551* to *505-555-1289*.
   c. Delete the record for Mrs. Mary Arguello.
   d. Insert a new record with the following information:
      Mr. Cesar Rivera
      3201 East Third Street
      Santa Fe, NM 87505
      505-555-6675
3. At the main document, edit the second sentence of the second paragraph so it reads as follows (insert a *Fill-in* field for the *(number of hours)* shown in the sentence below):
      According to our volunteer roster, you have signed up to volunteer for *(number of hours)* during the summer session.
4. Merge the main document with the data source file and type the following text for each of the records:
      Record 1 = four hours a week
      Record 2 = six hours a week
      Record 3 = twelve hours a week
      Record 4 = four hours a week
5. Save the merged document and name it **WordL1_C8_A2_Ltrs**.
6. Print and then close **WordL1_C8_A2_Ltrs.docx**.
7. Save and then close **WordL1_C8_A2_MD.mdb**.

# CASE study

## *Apply Your Skills*

**Part 1**

You are the office manager for Freestyle Extreme, a sporting goods store that specializes in snowboarding and snow skiing equipment and supplies. The store has two branches, one on the east side of town and the other on the west side. One of your job responsibilities is to send letters to customers letting them know about sales, new equipment, and upcoming events. Next month, both stores are having a sale and all snowboard and snow skiing supplies will be 15% off the regular price. Create a data source file that contains the following customer information: first name, last name, address, city, state, ZIP code, and branch. Add six customers to the data source file and indicate that three usually shop at the East branch and the other three usually shop at the West branch. Create a letter as a main document that includes information about the upcoming sale. The letter should contain at least two paragraphs and, in addition to the information on the sale, might include information about the store, snowboarding, and/or snow skiing. Save the data source file with the name **WordL1_C8_CS_DS**, save the main document with the name **WordL1_C8_CS_P1_MD**, and save the merged document with the name **WordL1_C8_CS_P1_Ltrs**. Create envelopes for the six merged letters and name the merged envelope document **WordL_C8_CS_P1_Envs**. Do not save the envelope main document. Print the merged letters document and the merged envelopes document.

A well-known extreme snowboarder will be visiting both branches of the store to meet with customers and sign autographs. Use the Help feature to learn how to insert an If . . . Then . . . Else merge field in a document and then create a letter that includes the name of the extreme snowboarder (you determine the name), the time, which is 1:00 p.m. to 4:30 p.m., and any additional information that might interest the customer. Also include in the letter an If . . . Then . . . Else merge field that will insert *Wednesday, September 22* if the customer's Branch is *East* and will insert *Thursday, September 23* if the Branch is *West*. Add visual appeal to the letter by inserting a picture, clip art image, WordArt, or any other feature that will attract the reader's attention. Save the letter main document and name it **WordL1_C8_CS_P2_MD**. Merge the letter main document with the **WordL1_C8_CS_DS.mdb** data source. Save the merged letters document and name it **WordL1_C8_CS_P2_AnnLtrs**. Print the merged letters document.

The store owner wants to try selling shorter skis known as "snow blades" or "skiboards." He has asked you to research the shorter skis and identify one type and model to sell only at the West branch of the store. If the model sells well, he will consider selling it at the East branch at a future time. Prepare a main document letter that describes the new snow blade or skiboard that the West branch is selling. Include information about pricing and tell customers that the new item is being offered at a 40% discount if purchased within the next week. Merge the letter main document with the **WordL1_C8_CS_DS.mdb** data source file and include only those customers that shop at the West branch. Save the merged letters document and name it **WordL1_C8_CS_P3_Ltrs**. Print the merged letters document. Save the letter main document and name it **WordL1_C8_CS_P3_MD**. Print and then close the main document

# Enhancing and Customizing Documents

## ASSESSING proficiency

In this unit, you have learned to format text into columns; insert, format, and customize objects to enhance the visual appeal of a document; manage files, print envelopes and labels, and create documents using templates; create and edit tables; visually represent data in SmartArt diagrams and organizational charts; and use Mail Merge to create letters, envelopes, labels, and directions.

*Note: Before beginning unit assessments, copy to your storage medium the Word2007L1U2 subfolder from the Word2007L1 folder on the CD that accompanies this textbook and then make Word2007L1U2 the active folder.*

### Assessment 1  Format a Technology Occupations Document

1. Open **WordReport09.docx** and then save the document and name it **WordL1_U2_A1**.
2. Move the insertion point to the beginning of the heading *Telecommuting* and then insert the file named **WordDocument19.docx**.
3. Apply the Heading 1 style to the title and the Heading 2 style to the headings in the document.
4. Change the Quick Styles set to *Formal*.
5. Insert a continuous section break at the beginning of the first paragraph of text (the paragraph that begins *The march of computer technology . . .* ).
6. Format the text below the section break into two newspaper columns.
7. Balance the columns on the second page.
8. Insert a pull quote of your choosing on the first page of the document that includes the text *"As the future of wireless unfolds, many new jobs will emerge as well."*
9. Create a drop cap with the first letter of the first word *The* that begins the first paragraph of text and make the drop cap two lines in height.
10. Manually hyphenate words in the document.
11. Insert page numbering that prints at the bottom of each page (you determine the page number formatting).
12. Save, print, and then close **WordL1_U2_A1.docx**.

### Assessment 2  Create a Workshop Flyer

1. Create the flyer shown in Figure U2.1 with the following specifications:
   a. Insert the WordArt shape with WordArt style 15 and then customize the WordArt by changing the shadow effect to Shadow Style 1, the shape to Deflate Bottom, and increasing the width of the WordArt to 6.5″ and the height to 1″.

b. Type the text shown in the figure set in 22-point Calibri bold and center the text.

c. Insert the clip art image shown in the figure (use the keyword *buildings* to find the clip art) and then change the wrapping style to *Square*. Position and size the image as shown in the figure.

2. Save the document and name it **WordL1_U2_A2**.

3. Print and then close **WordL1_U2_A2.docx**.

**Figure U2.1 Assessment 2**

## Assessment 3 Create a Staff Meeting Announcement

1. Create the announcement shown in Figure U2.2 with the following specifications:

a. Use the *Hexagon* shape in the *Basic Shapes* section of the Shapes drop-down list to create the shape.

b. Apply the Diagonal Gradient - Accent 5 style to the shape.

c. Apply the 3-D Style 2 located in the *Parallel* group in the 3-D Effects drop-down list.

d. Insert a text box in the shape.

e. Display the Home tab and then click the No Spacing style in the Styles group.

f. Insert the text shown in Figure U2.2. Insert the clock as a symbol (in the *Wingdings* font) and insert the ñ as a symbol (in the *(normal text)* font).

g. Increase the size of the shape and text so they display as shown in Figure U2.2.

2. Save the completed document and name it **WordL1_U2_A3**.

3. Print and then close **WordL1_U2_A3.docx**.

**Figure U2.2  Assessment 3**

## Assessment 4  Create a River Rafting Flyer

1. At a blank document, insert the picture named **River.jpg**. (Insert the picture using the Picture button.)
2. Crop out a portion of the trees at the left and right and a portion of the hill at the top.
3. Change the brightness to *+20%*.
4. Specify that the picture should wrap behind text.
5. Insert the text *River Rafting Adventures* on one line, *Salmon River, Idaho* on the next line, and *1-888-555-3322* on the third line.
6. Increase the size of the picture so it is easier to see and the size of the text so it is easier to read. Center the text and position it on the picture on top of the river so the text is readable.
7. Save the document and name it **WordL1_U2_A4**.
8. Print and then close **WordL1_U2_A4.docx**.

## Assessment 5  Create an Envelope

1. At a blank document, create an envelope with the text shown in Figure U2.3.
2. Save the envelope document and name it **WordL1_U2_A5**.
3. Print and then close **WordL1_U2_A5.docx**.

**Figure U2.3  Assessment 5**

Mrs. Eileen Hebert
15205 East 42nd Street
Lake Charles, LA 71098

Mr. Earl Robicheaux
1436 North Sheldon Street
Jennings, LA 70542

## Assessment 6  Create Mailing Labels

1. Create mailing labels with the name and address for Mrs. Eileen Hebert shown in Figure U2.3 using a label vendor and product of your choosing.
2. Save the document and name it **WordL1_U2_A6**.
3. Print and then close **WordL1_U2_A6.docx**.

## Assessment 7  Create and Format a Table with Software Training Information

1. At a blank document, create the table shown in Figure U2.4. Format the table and the text in a manner similar to what is shown in Figure U2.4.
2. Insert a formula in B8 that totals the numbers in cells B4 through B7.
3. Insert a formula in C8 that totals the numbers in cells C4 through C7.
4. Save the document and name it **WordL1_U2_A7**.
5. Print and then close **WordL1_U2_A7.docx**.

**Figure U2.4  Assessment 7**

| TRI-STATE PRODUCTS | | |
|---|---|---|
| Computer Technology Department Microsoft® Office 2007 Training | | |
| **Application** | **# Enrolled** | **# Completed** |
| Access 2007 | 20 | 15 |
| Excel 2007 | 62 | 56 |
| PowerPoint 2007 | 40 | 33 |
| Word 2007 | 80 | 72 |
| Total | | |

## Assessment 8  Create and Format a Table Containing Training Scores

1. Open **WordTable06.docx** and then save the document and name it **WordL1_U2_A8**.
2. Insert formulas that calculate the averages in the appropriate row and column. (When writing the formulas, change the *Number format* option to *0*.)
3. Autofit the contents of the table.
4. Apply a table style of your choosing to the table.
5. Appy any other formatting to improve the visual appeal of the table.
6. Save, print, and then close **WordL1_U2_A8.docx**.

## Assessment 9 Create an Organizational Chart

1. Use SmartArt to create an organizational chart for the following text (in the order displayed). Apply formatting to enhance the visual appeal of the organizational chart.
2. Save the completed document and name it **WordL1_U2_A9**.
3. Print and then close **WordL1_U2_A9.docx**.

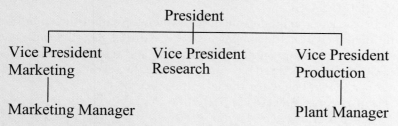

## Assessment 10 Create a SmartArt Diagram

1. At a blank document, create the WordArt and diagram shown in Figure U2.5 with the following specifications:
   a. Insert the WordArt shape with WordArt style 11 and then customize the WordArt by changing the shape to Can Up and increasing the width to 6.5″ and the height to 1″.
   b. Create the diagram using the Vertical Picture Accent List diagram. Click the picture icon that displays in the top circle and then insert the picture named **Seagull.jpg** located in the Word2007L1U2 folder. Insert the same picture in the other two circles. Type the text in each rectangle shape as shown in Figure U2.5.
2. Save the document and name it **WordL1_U2_A10**.
3. Print and then close **WordL1_U2_A10.docx**.

**Figure U2.5  Assessment 10**

## Assessment 11 Merge and Print Letters

1. Look at the information shown in Figure U2.6 and Figure U2.7. Use the Mail Merge feature to prepare six letters using the information shown in the figures. When creating the letter main document, insert Fill-in fields in place of the *(coordinator name)* and *(telephone number)* text. Create the data source file with the text shown in Figure U2.6 and name the file **WordL1_U2_DS**.

2. Create the letter main document with the information shown in Figure U2.7 and then merge the document with the **WordL1_U2_DS.mdb** data source file. When merging, enter the first name and telephone number shown below for the first three records and enter the second name and telephone number shown below for the last three records.

   Jeff Greenswald  (813) 555-9886
   Grace Ramirez  (813) 555-9807

3. Save the merged letters document and name it **WordL1_U2_Letters**. Print and then close the document.

4. Save the main document and name it **WordL1_U2_MD** and then close the document.

### Figure U2.6 Assessment 11

Mrs. Antonio Mercado
3241 Court G
Tampa, FL 33623

Ms. Alexandria Remick
909 Wheeler South
Tampa, FL 33620

Mr. Curtis Iverson
10139 93rd Court South
Tampa, FL 33654

Ms. Kristina Vukovich
1120 South Monroe
Tampa, FL 33655

Mr. Minh Vu
9302 Lawndale Southwest
Tampa, FL 33623

Mrs. Holly Bernard
8904 Emerson Road
Tampa, FL 33620

**Figure U2.7  Assessment 11**

December 12, 2009

«AddressBlock»

«GreetingLine»

Sound Medical is switching hospital care in Tampa to St. Jude's Hospital beginning
January 1, 2010. As mentioned in last month's letter, St. Jude's Hospital was selected
because it meets our requirements for high-quality, customer-pleasing care that is
also affordable and accessible. Our physicians look forward to caring for you in this
new environment.

Over the past month, staff members at Sound Medical have been working to make
this transition as smooth as possible. Surgeries planned after January 1 are being
scheduled at St. Jude's Hospital. Mothers delivering babies any time after January 1
are receiving information about delivery room tours and prenatal classes available at
St. Jude's. Your Sound Medical doctor will have privileges at St. Jude's and will
continue to care for you if you need to be hospitalized.

You are a very important part of our patient family, «Title» «Last_Name», and we
hope this information is helpful. If you have any additional questions or concerns,
please call your Sound Medical health coordinator, (coordinator name), at
(telephone number), between 8:00 a.m. and 4:30 p.m.

Sincerely,

Jody Tiemann
District Administrator

XX:WordL1_U2_MD.docx

## Assessment 12 **Merge and Print Envelopes**

1. Use the Mail Merge feature to prepare envelopes for the letters created in
   Assessment 11.
2. Specify **WordL1_U2_DS.mdb** as the data source document.
3. Save the merged envelopes document and name the document
   **WordL1_U2_Envs**.
4. Print and then close **WordL1_U2_Envs.docx**.
5. Do not save the envelope main document.

# WRITING activities

The following activities give you the opportunity to practice your writing skills along with demonstrating an understanding of some of the important Word features you have mastered in this unit. Use correct grammar, appropriate word choices, and clear sentence constructions.

### Activity 1  Compose a Letter to  Volunteers

You are an employee for the City of Greenwater and are responsible for coordinating volunteers for the city's Safe Night program. Compose a letter to the volunteers listed below and include the following information in the letter:

- Safe Night event scheduled for Saturday, June 19, 2010.
- Volunteer orientation scheduled for Thursday, May 20, 2010, at 7:30 p.m. At the orientation, participants will learn about the types of volunteer positions available and the work schedule.

Include any additional information in the letter, including a thank you to the volunteers. Use the Mail Merge feature to create a data source with the names and addresses that is attached to the main document, which is the letter to the volunteers. Save the merged letters as **WordL1_U2_Act01** and then print the letters.

| | |
|---|---|
| Mrs. Laura Reston<br>376 Thompson Avenue<br>Greenwater, OR 99034 | Mr. Matthew Klein<br>7408 Ryan Road<br>Greenwater, OR 99034 |
| Ms. Cecilia Sykes<br>1430 Canyon Road<br>Greenwater, OR 99034 | Mr. Brian McDonald<br>8980 Union Street<br>Greenwater, OR 99034 |
| Mr. Ralph Emerson<br>1103 Highlands Avenue<br>Greenwater, OR 99034 | Mrs. Nola Alverez<br>598 McBride Street<br>Greenwater, OR 99034 |

### Activity 2  Create a Business Letterhead

You have just opened a new mailing and shipping business and need letterhead stationery. Create a letterhead for your company in a header and/or footer. Use Word's Help feature to learn about creating a header that only displays and prints on the first page. Create the letterhead in a header that displays and prints only on the first page and include *at least* one of the following: a clip art image, a picture, a shape, a text box, and/or WordArt. Include the following information in the header:

Global Mailing
4300 Jackson Avenue
Toronto, ON M4C 3X4
(416) 555-0095
www.emcp.net/globalmailing

Save the completed letterhead and name it **WordL1_U2_Act02**. Print and then close the document.

## INTERNET research

### Create a Flyer on an Incentive Program

The owner of Evergreen Travel is offering an incentive to motivate travel consultants to increase travel bookings. The incentive is a sales contest with a grand prize of a one-week paid vacation to Cancun, Mexico. The owner has asked you to create a flyer that will be posted on the office bulletin board that includes information about the incentive program and some information about Cancun. Create this flyer using information about Cancun that you find on the Internet. Include a photo you find on a Web site (make sure it is not copyrighted) or include a clip art image representing travel. Include any other information or object to add visual appeal to the flyer. Save the completed flyer and name it **WordL1_U2_InternetResearch**. Print and then close the document.

## JOB study

### Develop Recycling Program Communications

The Chief Operating Officer of Harrington Engineering has just approved your draft of the company's new recycling policy (see the file named **WordRecyclingPolicy.docx** located in the Word2007L1U2 folder) with a note that you need to add some statistics on national average costs of recycling, which you can locate on the Internet. Edit the draft and prepare a final copy of the policy along with a memorandum to all employees describing the new guidelines. To support the company's energy resources conservation effort, you will send hard copies of the new policy to the Somerset Recycling Program president and to directors of Somerset Chamber of Commerce.

Using the concepts and techniques you learned in this unit, prepare the following documents:

- Format the recycling policy manual, including a cover page, appropriate headers and footers, and page numbers. Add at least one graphic and one diagram where appropriate. Format the document using a Quick Styles set and styles. Save the manual and name it **WordL1_U2_JobStudyManual**. Print the manual.

- Download a memo template from the Microsoft Online Web site and then create a memo from Susan Gerhardt, Chief Operating Officer of Harrington Engineering to all employees introducing the new recycling program. Copy the *Procedure* section of the recycling policy manual into the memo where appropriate. Include a table listing five employees who will act as Recycling Coordinators at Harrington Engineering (make up the names). Add columns for the employees' department names and their telephone extensions. Save the memo and name it **WordL1_U2_JobStudyMemo**. Print the memo.

- Write a letter to the President of the Somerset Recycling Program, William Elizondo, enclosing a copy of the recycling policy manual. Add a notation indicating copies with enclosures were sent to all members of the Somerset Chamber of Commerce. Save the letter and name it **WordL1_U2_JobStudyLetter**. Print the letter.

- Create mailing labels (see Figure U2.8). Save the labels and name the file **WordL1_U2_JobStudyLabels**. Print the file.

**Figure U2.8 Mailing Labels**

William Elizondo, President
Somerset Recycling Program
700 West Brighton Road
Somerset, NJ 55123

Paul Schwartz
Somerset Chamber of Commerce
45 Wallace Road
Somerset, NJ 55123

Ashley Crighton
Somerset Chamber of Commerce
45 Wallace Road
Somerset, NJ 55123

Carol Davis
Somerset Chamber of Commerce
45 Wallace Road
Somerset, NJ 55123

Robert Knight
Somerset Chamber of Commerce
45 Wallace Road
Somerset, NJ 55123

## A

Abbreviations: address, 211
Active documents, 201–202
Addition: table calculations and plus sign (+) operator for, 251
Address Block button: in Write & Insert Fields group, 296
Address Block field, 297
Addresses: United States Postal Service guidelines for, 211
Alignment. *See also* Margins
  of cells, 263
  of cells, changing, 242
  changing, at Paragraph dialog box, 50–52
  of objects, 183–184
  of paragraphs, changing, 48–50
  of tables, changing, 245–246
  of text, 186
  vertical, 168
Alignment button, 63, 82, 83, 96
Alignment group, 242, 262
Alignment option: at Paragraph dialog box, 50
Alphabetical sorting: of paragraphs, 81–82
Arithmetic operations: on numbers in table cells, 251
Arrange All button: in Window group, 202, 219
Arrow bullets, 73
Arrow keys, 17
Arrow shapes: drawing, 178–180
Art list box, 128
Asterisk (*) operator: performing calculations in a table and, 251
Asterisk (*) symbol: in bulleted paragraphs, 73
AutoComplete feature, 10, 29
AutoCorrect dialog box, 96
  with AutoFormat As You Type tab selected, 71, 73
AutoCorrect feature, 9, 29
AutoCorrect Options button, 10, 70, 96
AutoFit button, 262
  in Cell Size group, 241

AutoFit table contents feature, 263
AutoFormat feature, 70, 96
  bulleted paragraphs and, 73
AVERAGE function: for averaging numbers in cells, 251
Averages: calculating, 251

## B

Backgrounds: formatting, 126–129
Backspace key, 88
Banners: drawing, 177
Bar tab
  setting at Tabs dialog box, 86–87
  setting on Ruler, 83
Binary numbers, 11
Bits, 11
Blank Page button, 116, 140
Blank pages: inserting, 103, 109, 116, 118–119, 138, 140
Bold button
  in Font group, 38
  keyboard shortcut with, 40
Bold italic type style, 37
Bold text, 35, 63
Bold type style, 37
Borders, 126
  around paragraphs, 75, 76, 96
  customizing, 78–80
Borders and Shading dialog box, 96, 97, 126
  with Borders tab selected, 78
  with Page Border tab selected, 128, 140
  with Shading tab selected, 79
Borders button, 97
  in Paragraph group, 78
  in Table Styles group, 231
Borders gallery, 75
Bottom alignment option, 168
Bottom margins: in cells, 243
Break Link button, 187
  in Text group, 182
Breaks button: in Page Setup group, 154
Brightness: changing in images, 169
Browsing: in document, 17, 18–19

Built-in text boxes: inserting, 176–177
Bulleted lists: with hanging indents, 96
Bulleted paragraphs, 73
  typing, 73–74
Bullets
  inserting before paragraphs, 70
  inserting with Bullets button, 74
Bullets button, 70, 97
  inserting bullets with, 74
  in Paragraph group, 73
Bytes, 11

## C

Calculations: performing in tables, 251–252
Calibri typeface: as default typeface in Word, 10, 35, 36
Callouts: drawing, 177
Cambria typeface, 36
Candara typeface, 36
Capitalization: irregular, 24
Case of text: changing, 40
Cell alignment: changing, 242
Cell direction: changing, 245
Cell margins: changing, 243–245, 262
Cell Margins button, 243
Cell Options dialog box, 244
Cells
  alignment of, 263
  alignment of text in, 243
  defined, 227
  direction of, 263
  merging, 263
  merging and splitting, 238
  selecting, 233, 262
  selecting and formatting, in a table, 234–235
  text entered into, 228–229
Cell size: customizing, 240–241
Cell Size group: in Table Tools Layout tab, 240
Center alignment option, 168
Center-align text, 63
Center tabs: setting on Ruler, 83–84
Change Case button, 40
  keyboard shortcut with, 40
Character formatting, 35
  applying to text as you type, 39

clearing, 97
removing, 36, 49
Characters: searching for, 130
Check box options: choosing, 133
Chemical formulas: subscripts in, 40
Choose a SmartArt Graphic dialog box, 253, 254, 264
Clear All button, 94
Clear Formatting button: in Font group, 36, 70
Click and Type feature, 153, 186
using, 166–167
Clip Art button, 186
Clip art images: inserting, 169, 172–174, 186
Clip Art task pane, 169, 172, 173, 188
Clipboard, 89, 96
using, 93–94
Clipboard group, 57, 69
cutting, copying, and pasting text with, 88
Clipboard task pane, 93, 94, 97
Close button, 15
Closing documents, 12–13, 30
Collate option: at Print dialog box, 209
Color
page, 126, 127, 139, 140
paragraph shading, 77
Color formatting: in themes, 47
Colors dialog box, 77
Color theme, 46, 62
Column breaks: inserting, 157
Column formatting: removing, 157, 186
Columns
balancing of, on a page, 159
creating, 155
creating, with Columns dialog box, 156–157
deleting, 263
formatting, at Columns dialog box, 158
formatting text in, 156, 186
newspaper, 155
selecting, 262
selecting, inserting and deleting, 236–238
Columns button, 155, 186, 188
removing column formatting with, 157
Columns dialog box, 155, 186, 188

columns created with, 156–157
formatting columns at, 158
Column text: balancing, 186
Column width: changing, 240, 241–242, 262
Compare to another selection check box, 61
Compress Pictures button, 169
Consolas typeface, 36
Constantia typeface, 36
Continuous section breaks, 188
inserting, 154, 155, 186
Contrast: changing in images, 169
Convert Text to Table option: at Table button drop-down list, 262
Convert to Text button: in Data group, 249
Copy button: in Clipboard group, 92, 94, 178
Copying
documents, 194, 197
shapes, 178, 187
text, 96, 97
Copy option
copying and moving documents with, 197
from Open dialog box shortcut, 219
Corbel typeface, 36
Cover Page button, 116, 138, 140
Cover Page drop-down list, 117
Cover pages, 103
inserting, 109, 116–119, 138, 140
Create Link button, 182, 187
Create New Folder button, 194
Crop button, 169
Current page option: at Print dialog box, 209
Customize Address List dialog box, 296
Customized mailing labels: creating, 216
Customize Quick Access Toolbar button, 12, 13, 14
Customizing
cell size, 240–241
Full Screen Reading view, 105
images, 169, 186
paragraphs, 69–102
pictures, 171–172

pull quotes, 175
shapes, 187
Status bar, 21
themes, 47, 48
WordArt, 187
Cut button, 88
Cut option: from Open dialog box shortcut, 219
Cutting text, 89

## D

Data source file, 273, 296
creating, 274, 275–276
editing, 287, 289
editing records in, 290–293
merging main document with, 281
Date and time: inserting, 165–166, 188
Date and Time dialog box, 165, 186, 188
Date & Time button, 165, 186
Decimal tab: setting on Ruler, 83
Deleted text: restoring, 88
Delete key, 88
Deleting
documents, 195, 196, 219
folders, 198–199
header and footer elements, 125
rows and columns, 236–238
selected text from document, 88
tables, 263
tabs, 85, 96
text, 16, 19–20, 29
undoing and redoing, 23–24
Deletion commands, 19
Delivery address section: of Envelopes and Labels dialog box, 212
Delivery address text box: at Envelopes and Labels dialog box, 210, 219
Details button: at Label Options dialog box, 215
Diagrams: predesigned, 254
Dialog boxes
getting help in, 28
Help button in, 30
Directories: merging, 286–287
Directory main document, 297
Distribute Columns button, 240
Distribute Rows button, 240

Line Spacing button: in
    Paragraph group, 58, 63
Linking: text boxes, 182–183,
    187, 188
Live preview feature, 37, 47
Logos: WordArt and, 184

## M

Machine language, 11
Mailing labels, 213
    creating, 214
    customized, 216
    merging, 284–285,
        288–289
Mailings tab, 274
Mail Merge feature, 273, 296
Mail Merge Recipients dialog
    box, 288, 289, 296, 297
Main document, 273, 296
    creating, 277–279
    fill-in fields in, 294–295,
        296
    merging with data source
        file, 281
    Word fields in, 293
Manual Hyphenation dialog
    box, 160, 161, 188
Margins, 49, 140. *See also*
    Alignment
    changing, 110–111, 138
    changing, at Page Setup
        dialog box, 113–114, 115
    default, changing, 103
    indenting text from, 52
    preset, 113
Margins button: in Page Setup
    group, 103, 113
Margins drop-down list, 110
Mathematical equations:
    superscripts in, 40
Maximize button, 202, 219,
    220
Maximum values: calculating,
    251
Media images: inserting,
    172–174
Merge Cells button, 238, 262
Merge feature, 293
Merge fields: inserting, 297
Merge results: previewing, 297
Merges
    completing, 273–274
    inputting text during,
        293–294
    previewing, 280
Merging
    cells, 263

cells and tables, 238
directories, 286–287
documents, 280
envelopes, 281–282
mailing labels, 284–285,
    288–289
selected cells, 262
Microsoft Office 2007, 8
Microsoft Office Word Help
    button, 27
Microsoft Word 2007
    clear document screen in, 8
    exiting, 15, 30
    new typefaces in, 36
    opening, 8, 29
    screen features, 9
Minimize button, 202–203,
    219, 220
Minimum values: calculating,
    251
Mini toolbar
    formatting with, 41, 62
    selected text and, 20
Minus sign (-) operator:
    performing calculations in
    a table and, 251
Misspelled words, 24
Monospaced typefaces, 36, 62
More button, 133, 139
Motion files: viewing, 173
Mouse
    copying text with, 93
    moving insertion point
        with, 16
    moving text by dragging
        with, 90
    selecting cells in a table
        with, 233
    text selected with, 20–21,
        29, 30
Move table column marker: in
    table, 228
Moving
    documents, 194, 197
    SmartArt diagrams, 257,
        263
    tables, 246–248, 262
Multiple copies: printing, 209
Multiple documents
    opening, 199
    printing, at Open dialog
        box, 199
Multiple-page documents: page
    borders in, 128
Multiplication: table
    calculations and asterisk
    (*) operator for, 251

## N

Names/naming
    documents, 12, 29
    folders, 194
Navigation, 103
    in documents, 106–108,
        138
    in Full Screen Reading view,
        104
Navigation buttons, 17
Navigation pane, 107
New Address List dialog box,
    274, 275, 297
New blank document, 30
New button: on Quick Access
    toolbar, 13
New Document dialog box, 13,
    217, 220
New Folder dialog box, 194
New Line command, 10, 83, 97
Newspaper columns: creating,
    155
Next button, 17
Next Record button, 280
Nonprinting characters:
    displaying, 63
Normal template, 217
No Spacing style, 45
Numbered paragraphs: typing,
    70–71
Number format option: at
    Formula dialog box, 252
Numbering
    applying, 70–72
    automatic, in document, 71
    automatic, turning off, 96
    paragraphs, 96
Numbering button, 97
Numbering button: in
    Paragraph group, 70, 72,
        96
Number of copies option: at
    Print dialog box, 209
Numbers in table cells:
    arithmetic operations on,
        251
Num Lock, 17

## O

Object button, 206
Objects
    selecting, 188
    selecting, moving, and
        aligning, 183–184
Office button, 9, 29
Open dialog box, 220

creating new folders at, 194, 219

displaying, 13, 14

file management tasks and, 194

printing multiple documents at, 199

renaming documents at, 198

Option buttons, 10

Options button: at Envelopes and Labels dialog box, 215

Organizational charts
creating and formatting, 260
creating with SmartArt, 259

Orientation, 140

Orientation button: in Page Setup group, 111

Overtype mode: turning on, 19–20

## P

Page background: formatting, 126–129

Page Background group, 126

Page borders, 103
inserting, 128–129, 139

Page Borders button, 128, 139, 140

Page Break button: in Pages group, 115

Page breaks
hard, 116
inserting, 103, 109, 115–116, 138, 140
soft, 116

Page color, 103
changing, 126
inserting, 127, 139, 140

Page Color button, 126, 139

Page Number button, 120

Page numbers, 103
inserting, 140
predesigned, inserting, 120–121, 138

Page orientation, 140
changing, 111–112

Page range section: of Print dialog box, 209

Pages
columns balanced on, 159
removing multiple copies of, 210
specific, printing, 209

Page setup: changing, 109

Page Setup dialog box, 103, 188
with Layout tab selected, 168
margins changed at, 113–114, 115
with Margins tab selected, 114, 140
paper size changed at, 114–115
with Paper tab selected, 140

Page Setup group, 109

Page size, 140
changing, 112–113, 138

Panes: splitting windows into, 203, 219

Paper size: changing at Page Setup dialog box, 114–115

Paragraph alignment
buttons and commands, 49
changing, 48–50

Paragraph borders: inserting, 75

Paragraph dialog box, 53, 64, 97
with alignment options, 51
changing alignment at, 50–52
changing line spacing at, 58
changing paragraph alignment at, 51–52

Paragraph formatting, 62
clearing, 63, 97
removing, 36, 49, 96

Paragraph group, 70
in Home tab, 35
indent buttons in, 52

Paragraph numbering: inserting, 72

Paragraphs
alphabetical sorting of, 81–82
borders around, 96
bulleting, 73
bullets inserted before, 70
customizing, 69–102
customizing borders and shading in, 78–80
increasing/decreasing spacing before and after, 63
indenting, 54–55
indenting text in, 52–53, 63
numbering, 70, 96
shading added to, 75, 76–78
sorting text in, 81–82

spacing before and after, 55, 56, 64
in Word, 35

Paragraph symbols: displaying in documents, 49

Parentheses: order of calculation and use of, 251

Paste button, 92

Paste function option: in Formula dialog box, 251

Paste option
copying and moving documents with, 197
from Open dialog box shortcut, 219

Paste Options button, 10, 96
drop-down list, 91
using, 90–91

Pasting
paragraphs of text, 94–95
text, 89, 92, 96, 97

Percentages: calculating, 251

Periods (.): leaders as, 87, 96

Picture button, 169

Pictures: inserting, 169, 170–172, 186

Picture Styles group, 169

Picture Tools Format tab, 169, 186

Placeholders
for predesigned cover pages, 117
for predesigned headers or footers, 121

Plus sign (+) operator: performing calculations in a table and, 251

Points, 37
within vertical inches, 55

Point size, 62

Portrait orientation, 111, 138

Position button, 170

Position button drop-down gallery, 186

Predefined labels, 213

Predesigned footers
inserting, 121, 123, 138
inserting, removing header and, 124–125
removing, 138

Predesigned headers
inserting, 121–123, 138
removing, 138

Predesigned page numbering: inserting, 120–121, 138

Predesigned watermarks, 126

# Microsoft® excel

## Making Excel Work for You!

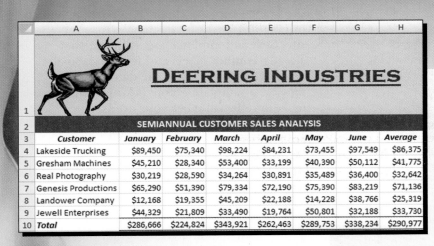

| | | | | | | | |
|---|---|---|---|---|---|---|---|
| **DEERING INDUSTRIES** | | | | | | | |
| **SEMIANNUAL CUSTOMER SALES ANALYSIS** | | | | | | | |
| *Customer* | *January* | *February* | *March* | *April* | *May* | *June* | *Average* |
| Lakeside Trucking | $89,450 | $75,340 | $98,224 | $84,231 | $73,455 | $97,549 | $86,375 |
| Gresham Machines | $45,210 | $28,340 | $53,400 | $33,199 | $40,390 | $50,112 | $41,775 |
| Real Photography | $30,219 | $28,590 | $34,264 | $30,891 | $35,489 | $36,400 | $32,642 |
| Genesis Productions | $65,290 | $51,390 | $79,334 | $72,190 | $75,390 | $83,219 | $71,136 |
| Landower Company | $12,168 | $19,355 | $45,209 | $22,188 | $14,228 | $38,766 | $25,319 |
| Jewell Enterprises | $44,329 | $21,809 | $33,490 | $19,764 | $50,801 | $32,188 | $33,730 |
| **Total** | $286,666 | $224,824 | $343,921 | $262,463 | $289,753 | $338,234 | $290,977 |

Tracking and analyzing numerical data is a large component of the daily activity in today's workplace. Microsoft Excel 2007 is a popular choice among individuals and companies for organizing, analyzing, and presenting numerical information.

## Organizing Information

Numbers are the foundation of every business transaction. Think about all of the numbers that the owner of a retail operation needs to organize to record customer purchases: account numbers, stock numbers, quantities, sale price, cost price, taxes, total due, amount received—just to name a few. Now consider a different scenario in which the manager of an apple orchard wants to track the volume of apples produced by each of 10 hybrids, along with the associated costs, in order to identify which hybrid apple trees are the most cost-effective. Factors to consider might include the number of apples produced weekly plus the costs of seed, fertilizer, general maintenance, and so on. These are just two examples of the type of information management for which you could use Excel.

Formula bar

Column header

Active cell

Row header

Spreadsheet software organizes data in columns and rows—an electronic version of an accountant's ledger—only with a lot more power and versatility. In Microsoft Excel, information is organized by creating column and row *headers*, also called headings or labels. Numbers, called *values*, are entered below and beside the headers and then formulas are created to perform calculations. The completed document is referred to as a *worksheet*. The potential uses for an application like Excel are only limited by your imagination—any type of document that can be set up in the column/row format is a candidate for an Excel worksheet.

Not sure how to set up the information you want to track? Go to Office Online and browse the templates at the Microsoft Web site. Several templates are available that already contain labels and formulas, so all you have to do is fill in the data. You can preview a template before downloading it to make sure it will meet your needs. The templates site is updated continually, so keep checking for new additions.

# Analyzing Information

The true power of Excel lies in its ability to analyze information at the click of a mouse. Once you have created a worksheet, you can play the *what-if* game. For example, suppose you work in the sales department of a construction company and have used Excel to set up a worksheet that tracks sales quotas. You can use Excel's calculating and protecting features to answer questions: What kind of sales increase could we achieve if we added four more salespeople who each sold an average of the total current sales? What if we increase the existing sales quotas by 20 percent? Whenever you change a value in a worksheet, Excel automatically recalculates other values that are dependent on the number you changed. In an instant, you have your answer.

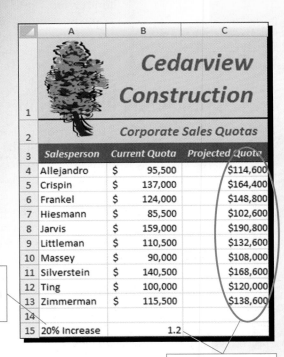

What would be the projected sales quotas with a 20% increase?

Answer appears as soon as you change the percentage.

Excel includes several predefined formulas, called *functions*, that make the task of constructing complex worksheets easier to manage. So math is not your favorite subject? Not a problem with Excel's Insert Function dialog box, which helps you build a formula by prompting you with explanations for each parameter.

Use the sorting and filtering in Excel to help you analyze the data in various arrangements. With the click of a button, you can rearrange the order of the worksheet to sort in ascending or descending order by a single column or by multiple columns. By filtering records, you can reduce the data you are viewing by temporarily hiding rows that do not meet your criteria. For example, in a workplace scenario, you might want to view only those clients that owe the company less than $500.

Original worksheet

**Real Photography**

Invoices

| Invoice # | Client # | Service | Date | Amount | Tax | Amount Due |
|---|---|---|---|---|---|---|
| 1199 | 03-288 | Development | 9/11/2010 | $ 95.00 | 0.0% | $ 95.00 |
| 1326 | 04-325 | Sports Portraits | 9/3/2010 | $ 750.00 | 8.5% | $ 813.75 |
| 1320 | 04-325 | Sports Portraits | 9/7/2010 | $ 750.00 | 8.5% | $ 813.75 |
| 1270 | 04-789 | Family Portraits | 9/8/2010 | $ 560.00 | 8.8% | $ 609.28 |
| 1345 | 05-335 | Development | 9/8/2010 | $ 400.00 | 0.0% | $ 400.00 |
| 1144 | 05-335 | Development | 9/15/2010 | $ 140.00 | 0.0% | $ 140.00 |
| 1302 | 10-226 | Wedding Portraits | 9/14/2010 | $ 2,250.00 | 8.5% | $ 2,441.25 |
| 1233 | 10-455 | Sports Portraits | 9/10/2010 | $ 600.00 | 8.5% | $ 651.00 |
| 1230 | 10-788 | Family Portraits | 9/1/2010 | $ 450.00 | 8.5% | $ 488.25 |
| 1277 | 11-005 | Business Portrait | 9/14/2010 | $ 225.00 | 8.8% | $ 244.80 |
| 1438 | 11-279 | Wedding Portraits | 9/1/2010 | $ 1,075.00 | 8.8% | $ 1,169.60 |
| 1129 | 11-279 | Development | 9/2/2010 | $ 225.00 | 0.0% | $ 225.00 |
| 1355 | 11-279 | Development | 9/4/2010 | $ 350.00 | 0.0% | $ 350.00 |
| 1198 | 11-325 | Wedding Portraits | 9/4/2010 | $ 875.00 | 8.5% | $ 949.38 |

Records sorted by Invoice #

**Real Photography**

Invoices

| Invoice # | Client # | Service | Date | Amount | Tax | Amount Due |
|---|---|---|---|---|---|---|
| 1129 | 11-279 | Development | 9/2/2010 | $ 225.00 | 0.0% | $ 225.00 |
| 1144 | 05-335 | Development | 9/15/2010 | $ 140.00 | 0.0% | $ 140.00 |
| 1198 | 11-325 | Wedding Portraits | 9/4/2010 | $ 875.00 | 8.5% | $ 949.38 |
| 1199 | 03-288 | Development | 9/11/2010 | $ 95.00 | 0.0% | $ 95.00 |
| 1230 | 10-788 | Family Portraits | 9/1/2010 | $ 450.00 | 8.5% | $ 488.25 |
| 1233 | 10-455 | Sports Portraits | 9/10/2010 | $ 600.00 | 8.5% | $ 651.00 |
| 1270 | 04-789 | Family Portraits | 9/8/2010 | $ 560.00 | 8.8% | $ 609.28 |
| 1277 | 11-005 | Business Portrait | 9/14/2010 | $ 225.00 | 8.8% | $ 244.80 |
| 1302 | 10-226 | Wedding Portraits | 9/14/2010 | $ 2,250.00 | 8.5% | $ 2,441.25 |
| 1320 | 04-325 | Sports Portraits | 9/7/2010 | $ 750.00 | 8.5% | $ 813.75 |
| 1326 | 04-325 | Sports Portraits | 9/3/2010 | $ 750.00 | 8.5% | $ 813.75 |
| 1345 | 05-335 | Development | 9/8/2010 | $ 400.00 | 0.0% | $ 400.00 |
| 1355 | 11-279 | Development | 9/4/2010 | $ 350.00 | 0.0% | $ 350.00 |
| 1438 | 11-279 | Wedding Portraits | 9/1/2010 | $ 1,075.00 | 8.8% | $ 1,169.60 |

**Real Photog**

Records filtered to display amounts less than $500.00

Invoices

| Invoice | Client # | Service | Date | Amoun | Ta | Amount Du |
|---|---|---|---|---|---|---|
| 1199 | 03-288 | Development | 9/11/2010 | $ 95.00 | 0.0% | $ 95.00 |
| 1345 | 05-335 | Development | 9/8/2010 | $ 400.00 | 0.0% | $ 400.00 |
| 1144 | 05-335 | Development | 9/15/2010 | $ 140.00 | 0.0% | $ 140.00 |
| 1230 | 10-788 | Family Portraits | 9/1/2010 | $ 450.00 | 8.5% | $ 488.25 |
| 1277 | 11-005 | Business Portrait | 9/14/2010 | $ 225.00 | 8.8% | $ 244.80 |
| 1129 | 11-279 | Development | 9/2/2010 | $ 225.00 | 0.0% | $ 225.00 |
| 1355 | 11-279 | Development | 9/4/2010 | $ 350.00 | 0.0% | $ 350.00 |

excel Lev

# Presenting Information

With information already structured in columns and rows, the task of interpreting the results is already simplified. Add some color and other rich text enhancements to draw the reader's attention to important titles, totals, or other results and you have just made the process even easier! Add clip art, photographs, or other media to a worksheet using the Clip Art task pane.

Since a picture is worth a thousand words, why not use Excel's charting capabilities to turn those numbers into a chart—a pictorial representation that enables a reader to more easily distinguish the impact of the differences between columns of numbers. Excel can render both two-dimensional and three-dimensional charts in several chart types, a sampling of which are: column, bar, line, pie, area, radar, doughnut, and scatter.

Knowing how to use Excel is a prerequisite for many jobs in our information-driven economy. Creating worksheets in Microsoft Excel 2007 is as simple as one, two, three—set up the column and row headings, enter the data, and create the formulas. Within a short period of time, you will *excel* at creating, editing, and formatting worksheets!

### Corporate Sales

| | North America | South America | Europe | Asia |
|---|---|---|---|---|

*Corporate Sales chart showing values from $0 to $1,800,000 for years 2008, 2009, and 2010.*

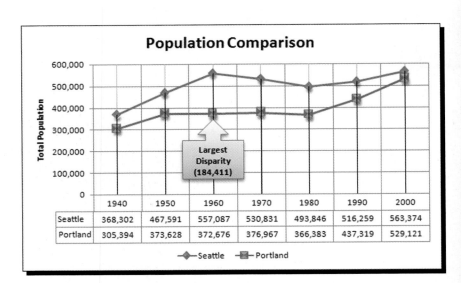

### Population Comparison

| | 1940 | 1950 | 1960 | 1970 | 1980 | 1990 | 2000 |
|---|---|---|---|---|---|---|---|
| Seattle | 368,302 | 467,591 | 557,087 | 530,831 | 493,846 | 516,259 | 563,374 |
| Portland | 305,394 | 373,628 | 372,676 | 376,967 | 366,383 | 437,319 | 529,121 |

Largest Disparity (184,411)

— Seattle   — Portland

Microsoft®

# excel

## Unit 1:    Preparing and Formatting a Worksheet

➤ Preparing an Excel Workbook

➤ Inserting Formulas in a Worksheet

➤ Formatting an Excel Worksheet

➤ Enhancing a Worksheet

Excel

## Benchmark Microsoft® Excel 2007 Level 1

### Microsoft Certified Application Specialist Skills—Unit 1

| Reference No. | Skill | Pages |
|---|---|---|
| **1** | **Creating and Manipulating Data** | |
| 1.1 | Insert data using AutoFill | |
| 1.1.1 | Fill a series | 16-19 |
| 1.1.2 | Copy a series | 21 |
| 1.4 | Change worksheet views | |
| 1.4.1 | Change views within a single window | 79-80, 115-116 |
| **2** | **Formatting Data and Content** | |
| 2.1 | Format worksheets | |
| 2.1.1 | Use themes to format worksheets | 81-82 |
| 2.1.4 | Format worksheet backgrounds | 118 |
| 2.2 | Insert and modify rows and columns | |
| 2.2.1 | Insert and delete cells, rows, and columns | 71-74 |
| 2.2.2 | Format rows and columns | 75-78 |
| 2.2.3 | Hide and unhide rows and columns | 96-98 |
| 2.2.4 | Modify row height and column width | 68-71 |
| 2.3 | Format cells and cell content | |
| 2.3.1 | Apply number formats | 51-52, 82-84 |
| 2.3.3 | Apply and modify cell styles | 25-26 |
| 2.3.4 | Format text in cells | 75-78, 85-87 |
| 2.3.6 | Merge and split cells | 76-78 |
| 2.3.7 | Add and remove cell borders | 91-93 |
| **3** | **Creating and Modifying Formulas** | |
| 3.1 | Reference data in formulas | |
| 3.1.1 | Create formulas that use absolute and relative cell references | 56-59 |
| 3.2 | Summarize data using a formula | |
| 3.2.1 | Use SUM, COUNT, COUNTA, AVERAGE, MIN, and MAX | 43-49 |
| 3.8 | Display and print formulas | 49 |
| **5** | **Collaborating and Securing Data** | |
| 5.5 | Set print options for printing data, worksheets, and workbooks | |
| 5.5.1 | Define the area of a worksheet to be printed | 120-121 |
| 5.5.2 | Insert and move a page break | 114-116 |
| 5.5.3 | Set margins | 110-112 |
| 5.5.4 | Add and modify headers and footers | 121-123 |
| 5.5.5 | Change the orientation of a worksheet | 112-113 |
| 5.5.6 | Scale worksheet content to fit a printed page | 117-118 |

Note: The Level 1 and Level 2 texts each address approximately half of the Microsoft Certified Application Specialist skills. Complete coverage of the skills is offered in the combined Level 1 and Level 2 text titled *Benchmark Series Microsoft® Excel 2007: Levels 1 and 2*, which has been approved as certified courseware and which displays the Microsoft Certified Application Specialist logo on the cover.

# Preparing an Excel Workbook

## PERFORMANCE OBJECTIVES

**Upon successful completion of Chapter 1, you will be able to:**

- Identify the various elements of an Excel workbook
- Create, save, and print a workbook
- Enter data in a workbook
- Edit data in a workbook
- Insert a formula using the Sum button
- Apply predesigned formatting to cells in a workbook
- Use the Help feature

excel Chapter 1

**Tutorial 1.1**
Creating an Excel Workbook

Many companies use a spreadsheet for numerical and financial data and to analyze and evaluate information. An Excel spreadsheet can be used for such activities as creating financial statements, preparing budgets, managing inventory, and analyzing cash flow. In addition, numbers and values can be easily manipulated to create "what if" situations. For example, using a spreadsheet, a person in a company can ask questions such as "What if the value in this category is decreased? How would that change affect the department budget?" Questions like these can be easily answered in an Excel spreadsheet. Change the value in a category and Excel will recalculate formulas for the other values. In this way, a spreadsheet can be used not only for creating financial statements or budgets, but also as a planning tool.

*Note: Before beginning computer projects, copy to your storage medium the Excel2007L1C1 subfolder from the Excel2007L1 folder on the CD that accompanies this textbook. Steps on how to copy a folder are presented on the inside of the back cover of this textbook. Do this every time you start a chapter's projects.*

## roject ① Prepare a Worksheet with Employee Information

You will create a worksheet containing employee information, edit the contents, and then save and close the workbook.

# Creating a Worksheet

Open Excel by clicking the Start button at the left side of the Taskbar, pointing to *All Programs*, pointing to *Microsoft Office*, and then clicking *Microsoft Office Excel 2007*. (Depending on your operating system, these steps may vary.) When Excel is open, you are presented with a blank worksheet like the one shown in Figure 1.1. The elements of a blank Excel worksheet are described in Table 1.1.

**Figure 1.1** Blank Excel Worksheet

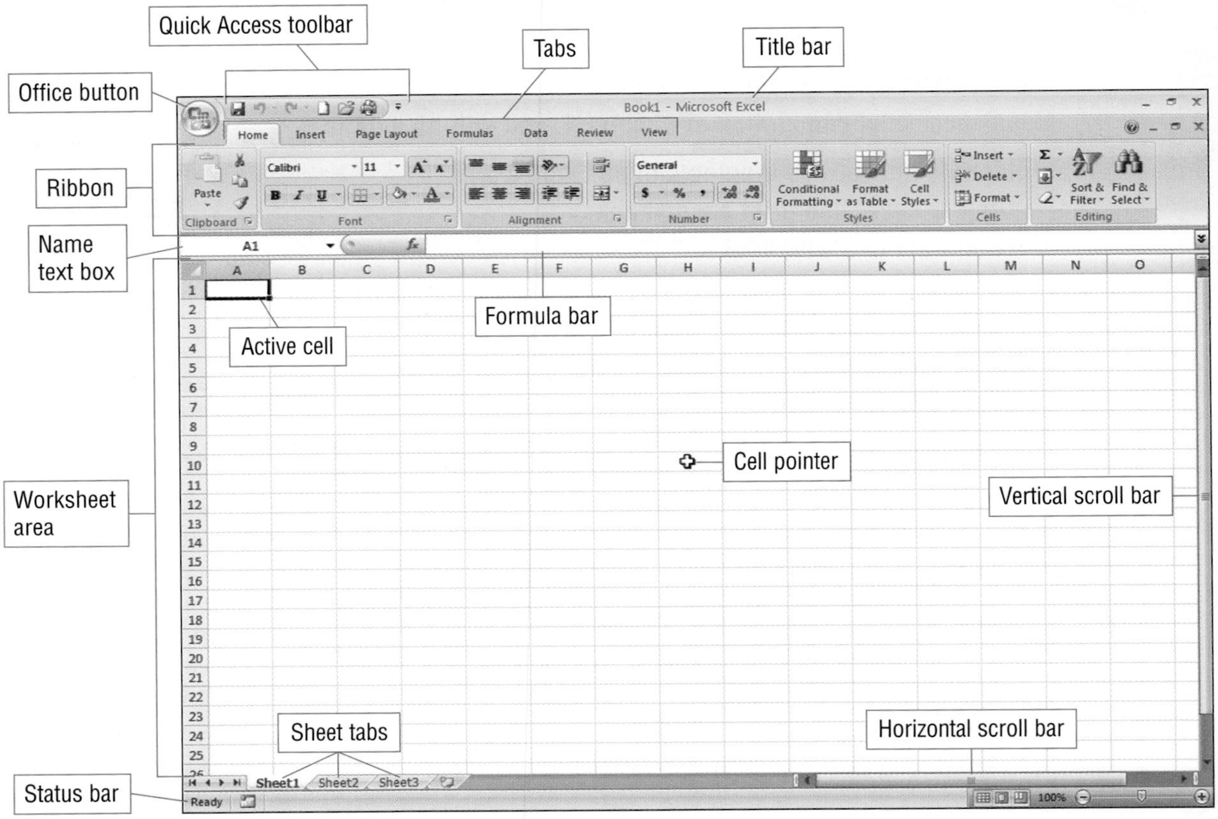

A file created in Excel is referred to as a ***workbook***. An Excel workbook consists of individual worksheets (or *sheets*) like the sheets of paper in a notebook. Notice the tabs located toward the bottom of the Excel window that are named *Sheet1*, *Sheet2*, and so on. The area containing the gridlines in the Excel window is called the ***worksheet area***. Figure 1.2 identifies the elements of the worksheet area. Create a worksheet in the worksheet area that will be saved as part of a workbook. Columns in a worksheet are labeled with letters of the alphabet and rows are numbered.

**Table 1.1** Elements of an Excel Worksheet

| Feature | Description |
|---------|-------------|
| Office button | Displays as a Microsoft Office logo and, when clicked, displays a list of options along with the most recently opened workbooks |
| Quick Access toolbar | Contains buttons for commonly-used commands |
| Title bar | Displays workbook name followed by program name |
| Tab | Contains commands and features organized into groups |
| Ribbon | Area containing the tabs and commands divided into groups |
| Name box | Displays cell address (also called the cell reference) and includes the column letter and row number |
| Formula bar | Provides information about active cell; enter and edit formulas in this bar |
| Scroll bars | Use vertical and horizontal scroll bars to navigate within a worksheet |
| Sheet tab | Displays towards bottom of screen and identifies current worksheet |
| Status bar | Displays information about worksheet and active cell, view buttons, and Zoom slider bar |

**Figure 1.2** Elements of a Worksheet Area

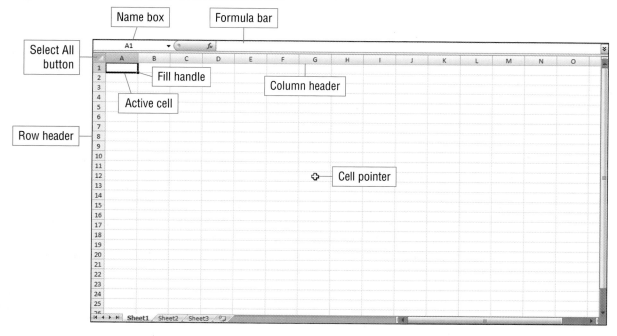

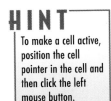
The horizontal and vertical lines that define the cells in the worksheet area are called *gridlines*. When a cell is active (displays with a black border), the *cell address*, also called the *cell reference*, displays in the *Name box*. The cell reference includes the column letter and row number. For example, if the first cell of the worksheet is active, the cell reference *A1* displays in the Name box. A thick black border surrounds the active cell.

## Entering Data in a Cell

Enter data such as a heading, number, or value in a cell. To enter data in a cell, make the desired cell active and then type the data. To make the next cell active, press the Tab key. Table 1.2 displays additional commands for making a specific cell active.

**Table 1.2** Commands for Making a Specific Cell Active

| *To make this cell active* | *Press* |
|---|---|
| Cell below current cell | Enter |
| Cell above current cell | Shift + Enter |
| Next cell | Tab |
| Previous cell | Shift + Tab |
| Cell at beginning of row | Home |
| Next cell in the direction of the arrow | Up, Down, Left, or Right Arrow keys |
| Last cell in worksheet | Ctrl + End |
| First cell in worksheet | Ctrl + Home |
| Cell in next window | Page Down |
| Cell in previous window | Page Up |
| Cell in window to right | Alt + Page Down |
| Cell in window to left | Alt + Page Up |

Another method for making a specific cell active is to use the Go To feature. To use this feature, click the Find & Select button in the Editing group in the Home tab and then click Go To. At the Go To dialog box, type the cell reference in the *Reference* text box, and then click OK.

When you are ready to type data into the active cell, check the Status bar. The word *Ready* should display at the left side. As you type data, the word *Ready* changes to *Enter*. Data you type in a cell displays in the cell as well as in the Formula bar. If the data you type is longer than the cell can accommodate, the data overlaps the next cell to the right (it does not become a part of the next cell—it simply overlaps it). You will learn how to change column widths to accommodate data later in this chapter.

If the data you enter in a cell consists of text and the text does not fit into the cell, it overlaps the next cell. If, however, you enter a number in a cell, specify it as a number (rather than text) and the number is too long to fit in the cell, Excel changes the display of the number to number symbols *(###)*. This is because Excel does not want you to be misled by a number when you see only a portion of it in the cell.

Along with the keyboard, you can use the mouse to make a specific cell active. To make a specific cell active with the mouse, position the mouse pointer, which displays as a white plus sign (called the **cell pointer**), on the desired cell, and then click the left mouse button. The cell pointer displays as a white plus sign when positioned in a cell in the worksheet and displays as an arrow pointer when positioned on other elements of the Excel window such as options in tabs or scroll bars.

Scroll through a worksheet using the horizontal and/or vertical scroll bars. Scrolling shifts the display of cells in the worksheet area, but does not change the active cell. Scroll through a worksheet until the desired cell is visible and then click the desired cell.

# Saving a Workbook

Save an Excel workbook, which may consist of a worksheet or several worksheets, by clicking the Save button on the Quick Access toolbar or by clicking the Office button and then clicking *Save* at the drop-down list. At the Save As dialog box, type a name for the workbook in the *File name* text box and then press Enter or click the Save button. A workbook file name can contain up to 255 characters, including drive letter and any folder names, and can include spaces. Note that you cannot give a workbook the same name in first uppercase and then lowercase letters. Also, some symbols cannot be used in a file name such as:

| | |
|---|---|
| forward slash (/) | question mark (?) |
| backslash (\) | quotation mark (") |
| greater than sign (>) | colon (:) |
| less than sign (<) | semicolon (;) |
| asterisk (*) | pipe symbol ( \| ) |

To save an Excel workbook in the Excel2007L1C1 folder on your storage medium, display the Save As dialog box and then click the down-pointing arrow at the right side of the *Save in* option box. At the drop-down list that displays, click the drive representing your storage medium and then double-click Excel2007L1C1 in the list box.

**Save a Workbook**
1. Click Save button.
2. Type workbook name.
3. Press Enter.

**HINT**
Ctrl + S is the keyboard command to save a document.

Save

Office button

## Project 1a — Creating and Saving a Workbook

1. Open Excel by clicking the Start button on the Taskbar, pointing to *All Programs*, pointing to *Microsoft Office*, and then clicking *Microsoft Office Excel 2007*. (Depending on your operating system, these steps may vary.)

2. At the Excel worksheet that displays, create the worksheet shown in Figure 1.3 by completing the following steps:
   a. Press the Enter key once to make cell A2 the active cell.
   b. With cell A2 active (displays with a thick black border), type **Employee**.
   c. Press the Tab key. (This makes cell B2 active.)
   d. Type **Location** and then press the Tab key. (This makes cell C2 active.)
   e. Type **Benefits** and then press the Enter key to move the insertion point to cell A3.
   f. With cell A3 active, type the name **Avery**.
   g. Continue typing the data shown in Figure 1.3. (For commands for making specific cells active, refer to Table 1.2.)

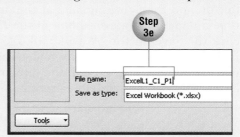

3. After typing the data shown in the cells in Figure 1.3, save the workbook by completing the following steps:
   a. Click the Save button on the Quick Access toolbar.
   b. At the Save As dialog box, click the down-pointing arrow to the right of the *Save in* option.
   c. From the drop-down list that displays, click the letter representing your storage medium.
   d. Double-click the Excel2007L1C1 folder that displays in the list box.
   e. Select the text in the *File name* text box and then type **ExcelL1_C1_P1** (for Excel Level 1, Chapter 1, Project 1).
   f. Press the Enter key or click the Save button.

**Figure 1.3  Project 1a**

|   | A | B | C | D |
|---|---|---|---|---|
| 1 |   |   |   |   |
| 2 | Employee | Location | Benefits |   |
| 3 | Avery |   |   |   |
| 4 | Connors |   |   |   |
| 5 | Estrada |   |   |   |
| 6 | Juergens |   |   |   |
| 7 | Mikulich |   |   |   |
| 8 | Talbot |   |   |   |
| 9 |   |   |   |   |

## Editing Data in a Cell

Edit data being typed in a cell by pressing the Backspace key to delete the character to the left of the insertion point or pressing the Delete key to delete the character to the right of the insertion point. To change the data in a cell, click the cell once to make it active and then type the new data. When a cell containing data is active, anything typed will take the place of the existing data.

If you want to edit only a portion of the data in a cell, double-click the cell. This makes the cell active, moves the insertion point inside the cell, and displays the word *Edit* at the left side of the Status bar. Move the insertion point using the arrow keys or the mouse and then make the needed corrections. If you are using the keyboard, you can press the Home key to move the insertion point to the first character in the cell or Formula bar, or press the End key to move the insertion point to the last character.

When you are finished editing the data in the cell, be sure to change out of the Edit mode. To do this, make another cell active. You can do this by pressing Enter, Tab, or Shift + Tab. You can also change out of the Edit mode and return to the Ready mode by clicking another cell or clicking the Enter button on the Formula bar.

If the active cell does not contain data, the Formula bar displays only the cell reference (by column letter and row number). As you type data, the two buttons shown in Figure 1.4 display on the Formula bar to the right of the Name box. Click the Cancel button to delete the current cell entry. You can also delete the cell entry by pressing the Delete key. Click the Enter button to indicate that you are finished typing or editing the cell entry. When you click the Enter button on the Formula bar, the word *Enter* (or *Edit*) located at the left side of the Status bar changes to *Ready*.

Cancel

Enter

**Figure 1.4** Buttons on the Formula Bar

Cancel    Enter

A1

## Project 1b  Editing Data in a Cell

1. With **ExcelL1_C1_P1.xlsx** open, double-click cell A7 (contains *Mikulich*).
2. Move the insertion point immediately left of the *k* and then type a **c**. (This changes the spelling to *Mickulich*.)
3. Click once in cell A4 (contains *Connors*), type **Bryant**, and then press the Tab key. (Clicking only once allows you to type over the existing data.)
4. Edit cell C2 by completing the following steps:
   a. Click the Find & Select button in the Editing group in the Home tab and then click *Go To* at the drop-down list.
   b. At the Go To dialog box, type **C2** in the *Reference* text box, and then click OK.
   c. Type **Classification** (over *Benefits*).
5. Click once in any other cell.
6. Click the Save button on the Quick Access toolbar to save the workbook again.

Step 4b

Quick Print

# Printing a Workbook

Click the Quick Print button on the Quick Access toolbar to print the active worksheet. If the Quick Print button does not display on the Quick Access toolbar, click the Customize Quick Access Toolbar button that displays at the right side of the toolbar and then click *Quick Print* at the drop-down list. You can also print a worksheet by clicking the Office button, pointing to the *Print* option, and then clicking *Quick Print* at the side menu.

# Closing a Workbook

Close Window

To close an Excel workbook, click the Office button and then click *Close* at the drop-down list. You can also close a workbook by clicking the Close Window button located toward the upper right corner of the screen. Position the mouse pointer on the button and a ScreenTip displays with the name *Close Window*.

# Exiting Excel

✕ Exit Excel

Close

To exit Excel, click the Close button that displays in the upper right corner of the screen. The Close button contains an X and if you position the mouse pointer on the button a ScreenTip displays with the name *Close*. You can also exit Excel by clicking the Office button and then clicking the Exit Excel button located at the bottom of the drop-down list.

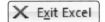

**QUICK STEPS**

**Print a Workbook**
Click Quick Print button.
OR
1. Click Office button, *Print*.
2. Click OK.

**Close a Workbook**
Click Office button, *Close*.
OR
Click Close Window button.

**Exit Excel**
Click Close button.
OR
Click Office button, Exit Excel.

# Using Automatic Entering Features

Excel contains several features that help you enter data into cells quickly and efficiently. These features include ***AutoComplete***, which automatically inserts data in a cell that begins the same as a previous entry; ***AutoCorrect***, which automatically corrects many common typographical errors; and ***AutoFill***, which will automatically insert words, numbers, or formulas in a series.

# Using AutoComplete and AutoCorrect

The AutoComplete feature will automatically insert data in a cell that begins the same as a previous entry. If the data inserted by AutoComplete is the data you want in the cell, press Enter. If it is not the desired data, simply continue typing the correct data. This feature can be very useful in a worksheet that contains repetitive data entries. For example, consider a worksheet that repeats the word *Payroll*. The second and subsequent times this word is to be inserted in a cell, simply typing the letter *P* will cause AutoComplete to insert the entire word.

The AutoCorrect feature automatically corrects many common typing errors. To see what symbols and words are in the AutoCorrect feature, click the Office button and then click Excel Options located in the lower right corner of the drop-down list. At the Excel Options dialog box, click *Proofing* in the left panel and then click the AutoCorrect Options button located in the right panel. This displays the AutoCorrect dialog box with the AutoCorrect tab selected as shown in Figure 1.5 with a list box containing the replacement data.

**Figure 1.5** AutoCorrect Dialog Box with AutoCorrect Tab Selected

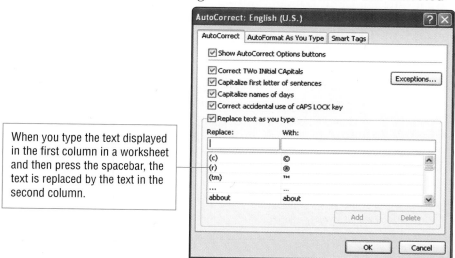

When you type the text displayed in the first column in a worksheet and then press the spacebar, the text is replaced by the text in the second column.

At the AutoCorrect dialog box, type the text shown in the first column in the list box and the text in the second column is inserted in the cell. Along with symbols, the AutoCorrect dialog box contains commonly misspelled words and common typographical errors.

## Project 1c  Inserting Data in Cells with AutoComplete

1. With **ExcelL1_C1_P1.xlsx** open make cell A1 active.
2. Type the text in cell A1 as shown in Figure 1.6. Insert the ® symbol by typing (r). (AutoCorrect will change (r) to ®.)
3. Type the remaining text in the cells. When you type the **W** in *West* in cell B5, the AutoComplete feature will insert *West*. Accept this by pressing the Enter key. (Pressing the Enter key accepts *West* and also makes the cell below active.) Use the AutoComplete feature to enter *West* in B6 and B8 and *North* in cell B7. Use AutoComplete to enter the second and subsequent occurrences of *Salaried* and *Hourly*.
4. Click the Save button on the Quick Access toolbar.
5. Print **ExcelL1_C1_P1.xlsx** by clicking the Quick Print button on the Quick Access toolbar. (The gridlines will not print.) If the Quick Print button does not display on the Quick Access toolbar, click the Customize Quick Access Toolbar button that displays at the right side of the toolbar and then click *Quick Print* at the drop-down list.
6. Close the workbook by clicking the Close Window button (contains an X) that displays in the upper right corner of screen. (Make sure you click the Close Window button and not the Close button.)

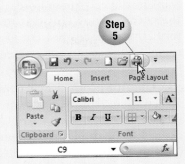

Step 5

Step 6

**Figure 1.6  Project 1c**

|   | A | B | C | D |
|---|---|---|---|---|
| 1 | Team Net® | | | |
| 2 | Employee | Location | Classification | |
| 3 | Avery | West | Hourly | |
| 4 | Bryant | North | Salaried | |
| 5 | Estrada | West | Salaried | |
| 6 | Juergens | West | Salaried | |
| 7 | Mickulich | North | Hourly | |
| 8 | Talbot | West | Hourly | |
| 9 | | | | |

## Project 2  Open and Format a Workbook and Insert Formulas

You will open an existing workbook, insert formulas to find the sum and averages of numbers and apply predesigned formatting with table and cell styles.

## Using AutoFill

When a cell is active, a thick black border surrounds it and a small black square displays in the bottom right corner of the border. This black square is called the AutoFill *fill handle* (see Figure 1.2). With the fill handle, you can quickly fill a range of cells with the same data or with consecutive data. For example, suppose you need to insert the year 2010 in a row or column of cells. To do this quickly, type 2010 in the first cell, position the mouse pointer on the fill handle, hold down the left mouse button, drag across the cells in which you want the year inserted, and then release the mouse button.

You can also use the fill handle to insert a series in a row or column of cells. For example, suppose you are creating a worksheet with data for all of the months in the year. Type January in the first cell, position the mouse pointer on the fill handle, hold down the left mouse button, drag down or across to 11 more cells, and then release the mouse button. Excel automatically inserts the other 11 months in the year in the proper order. When using the fill handle, the cells must be adjacent. Table 1.3 identifies the sequence inserted in cells by Excel when specific data is entered.

**Table 1.3** AutoFill Fill Handle Series

| Enter this data (Commas represent data in separate cells.) | And the fill handle will insert this sequence in adjacent cells |
| --- | --- |
| January | February, March, April, and so on . . . |
| Jan | Feb, Mar, Apr, and so on . . . |
| Jan 08, Jan 09 | Jan-10, Jan-11, Jan-12, and so on . . . |
| Monday | Tuesday, Wednesday, Thursday, and so on . . . |
| Product 1 | Product 2, Product 3, Product 4, and so on . . . |
| Qtr 1 | Qtr 2, Qtr 3, Qtr 4 |
| 2, 4 | 6, 8, 10, and so on . . . |

Certain sequences, such as *2, 4* and *Jan 08, Jan 09*, require that both cells be selected before using the fill handle. If only the cell containing *2* is active, the fill handle will insert *2*s in the selected cells. The list in Table 1.3 is only a sampling of what the fill handle can do. You may find a variety of other sequences that can be inserted in a worksheet using the fill handle.

An Auto Fill Options button displays when you fill cells with the fill handle. Click this button and a list of options displays for filling the cells. By default, data and formatting are filled in each cell. You can choose to fill only the formatting in the cells or fill only the data without the formatting.

**HINT**
If you do not want a series to increment, hold down the Ctrl key while dragging the fill handle.

Auto Fill Options

# Opening a Workbook

Open an Excel workbook by displaying the Open dialog box and then double-clicking the desired workbook name. Display the Open dialog box by clicking the Open button on the Quick Access toolbar or clicking the Office button and then clicking *Open* at the drop-down list. If the Open button does not display on the Quick Access toolbar, click the Customize Quick Access Toolbar button that displays at the right side of the toolbar and then click *Open* at the drop-down list. You can also use the keyboard shortcut Ctrl + O to display the Open dialog box.

## Project 2a    Inserting Data in Cells with the Fill Handle

1. Open **ExcelC01Project02.xlsx**. (This workbook is located in the Excel2007L1C1 folder on your storage medium.)
2. Save the workbook with Save As and name it **ExcelL1_C1_P2**.
3. Add data to cells as shown in Figure 1.7. Begin by making cell B1 active and then typing *January*.
4. Position the mouse pointer on the fill handle for cell B1, hold down the left mouse button, drag across to cell G1, and then release the mouse button.
5. Type a sequence and then use the fill handle to fill the remaining cells by completing the following steps:
   a. Make cell A2 active and then type *Year 1*.
   b. Make cell A3 active and then type *Year 3*.
   c. Select cells A2 and A3 by positioning the mouse pointer in cell A2, holding down the left mouse button, dragging down to cell A3, and then releasing the mouse button.
   d. Drag the fill handle for cell A3 to cell A5. (This inserts *Year 5* in cell A4 and *Year 7* in cell A5.)
6. Use the fill handle to fill adjacent cells with a number but not the formatting by completing the following steps:
   a. Make cell B2 active. (This cell contains *100* with bold formatting.)
   b. Drag the fill handle for cell B2 to cell E2. (This inserts *100* in cells C2, D2, and E2.)
   c. Click the Auto Fill Options button that displays at the bottom right of the selected cells.
   d. Click the *Fill Without Formatting* option at the drop-down list.

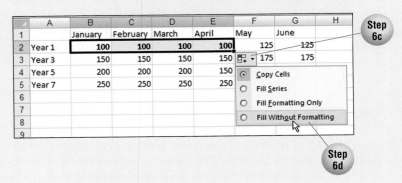

Step 6c

Step 6d

7. Use the fill handle to apply formatting only by completing the following steps:
   a. Make cell B2 active.
   b. Drag the fill handle to cell B5.
   c. Click the Auto Fill Options button and then click *Fill Formatting Only* at the drop-down list.
8. Make cell A10 active and then type Qtr 1.
9. Drag the fill handle for cell A10 to cell A13.
10. Save **ExcelL1_C1_P2.xlsx**.

| | A | B | C | D | E | |
|---|---|---|---|---|---|---|
| 1 | | January | February | March | April | |
| 2 | Year 1 | **100** | 100 | 100 | 10 | |
| 3 | Year 3 | **100** | 150 | 150 | 15 | |
| 4 | Year 5 | **100** | 200 | 200 | 15 | |
| 5 | Year 7 | **100** | 250 | 250 | 25 | **Step 7c** |
| 6 | | | | | | |
| 7 | | | ⦿ Copy Cells | | | |
| 8 | | | ○ Fill Series | | | |
| 9 | | | ○ Fill Formatting Only | | | |
| 10 | | $5,500 | ○ Fill Without Formatting | | | |
| 11 | | $6,000 | | | | |

**Figure 1.7  Project 2a**

| | A | B | C | D | E | F | G | H |
|---|---|---|---|---|---|---|---|---|
| 1 | | January | February | March | April | May | June | |
| 2 | Year 1 | **100** | 100 | 100 | 100 | 125 | 125 | |
| 3 | Year 3 | **150** | 150 | 150 | 150 | 175 | 175 | |
| 4 | Year 5 | **200** | 200 | 200 | 150 | 150 | 150 | |
| 5 | Year 7 | **250** | 250 | 250 | 250 | 250 | 250 | |
| 6 | | | | | | | | |
| 7 | | | | | | | | |
| 8 | | | | | | | | |
| 9 | | | | | | | | |
| 10 | Qtr 1 | $5,500 | $6,250 | $7,000 | $8,500 | $5,500 | $4,500 | |
| 11 | Qtr 2 | $6,000 | $7,250 | $6,500 | $9,000 | $4,000 | $5,000 | |
| 12 | Qtr 3 | $4,500 | $8,000 | $6,000 | $7,500 | $6,000 | $5,000 | |
| 13 | Qtr 4 | $6,500 | $8,500 | $7,000 | $8,000 | $5,500 | $6,000 | |
| 14 | | | | | | | | |

# Inserting Formulas

Excel is a powerful decision-making tool containing data that can be manipulated to answer "what if" situations. Insert a formula in a worksheet and then manipulate the data to make projections, answer specific questions, and use as a planning tool. For example, the manager of a department might use an Excel worksheet to prepare a department budget and then determine the impact on the budget of hiring a new employee or increasing the volume of production.

Insert a formula in a worksheet to perform calculations on values. A formula contains a mathematical operator, value, cell reference, cell range, and a function. Formulas can be written that add, subtract, multiply, and/or divide values. Formulas can also be written that calculate averages, percentages, minimum and maximum values, and much more. Excel includes a Sum button in the Editing group in the Home tab that inserts a formula to calculate the total of a range of cells.

## Using the Sum Button to Add Numbers

You can use the Sum button in the Editing group in the Home tab to insert a formula. The Sum button adds numbers automatically with the SUM function. Make active the cell in which you want to insert the formula (this cell should be empty) and then click the Sum button. Excel looks for a range of cells containing numbers above the active cell. If no cell above contains numbers, then Excel looks to the left of the active cell. Excel suggests the range of cells to be added. If the

**Insert Formula Using Sum Button**
1. Click in desired cell.
2. Click Sum button.
3. Check range identified and make changes if necessary.
4. Press Enter.

You can use the keyboard shortcut, Alt + = to insert the SUM function in the cell.

Sum

suggested range is not correct, drag through the desired range with the mouse, and then press Enter. You can also just double-click the Sum button and this will insert the SUM function with the range Excel chooses.

## Project 2b — Adding Values with the Sum Button

1. With **ExcelL1_C1_P2.xlsx** open, make cell A6 active and then type Total.
2. Make cell B6 active and then calculate the sum of cells by clicking the Sum button in the Editing group in the Home tab.
3. Excel inserts the formula =*SUM(B2:B5)* in cell B6. This is the correct range of cells, so press Enter.

**Step 2**

**Step 3**

4. Make cell C6 active and then click the Sum button in the Editing group.
5. Excel inserts the formula =*SUM(C2:C5)* in cell C6. This is the correct range of cells, so press Enter.
6. Make cell D6 active.
7. Double-click the Sum button. (This inserts the formula =*SUM(D2:D5)* in cell D6 and inserts the sum *700*.)
8. Insert the sum in cells E6, F6, and G6.
9. Save **ExcelL1_C1_P2.xlsx**.

## QUICK STEPS

**Insert Average Formula Using Sum Button**
1. Click in desired cell.
2. Click Sum button arrow.
3. Click *Average*.
4. Check range identified and make changes if necessary.
5. Press Enter.

## Using the Sum Button to Average Numbers

A common function in a formula is the AVERAGE function. With this function, a range of cells is added together and then divided by the number of cell entries. The AVERAGE function is available on the Sum button. Click the Sum button arrow and a drop-down list displays with a number of common functions.

## Using the Fill Handle to Copy a Formula

In a worksheet, you may want to insert the same basic formula in other cells. In a situation where a formula is copied to other locations in a worksheet, use a *relative cell reference*. Copy a formula containing relative cell references and the cell references change. For example, if you enter the formula =*SUM(A2:C2)* in cell D2 and then copy it relatively to cell D3, the formula in cell D3 displays as =*SUM(A3:C3)*. You can use the fill handle to copy a formula relatively in a worksheet. To do this, position the mouse pointer on the fill handle until the mouse pointer turns into a thin black cross. Hold down the left mouse button, drag and select the desired cells, and then release the mouse button.

## Project 2c — Inserting the AVERAGE Function and Copying a Formula Relatively

1. With **ExcelL1_C1_P2.xlsx** open, make cell A14 active, and then type Average.
2. Insert the average of cells B10 through B13 by completing the following steps:
   a. Make cell B14 active.
   b. Click the Sum button arrow and then click *Average* at the drop-down list.
   c. Excel inserts the formula =*AVERAGE(B10:B13)* in cell B14. This is the correct range of cells, so press Enter.
3. Copy the formula relatively to cells C14 through G14 by completing the following steps:
   a. Make cell B14 active.
   b. Position the mouse pointer on the fill handle, hold down the left mouse button, drag across to cell G14, and then release the mouse button.

**Step 2b**

Σ ▾ A ▾
Σ  Sum
   Average
   Count Numbers
   Max
   Min
   More Functions...

🔁 Insert ▾
🔁 Delete ▾
📋 Format ▾
   Cells

| M |

| 9  |         |        |        |        |        |        |        |
|----|---------|--------|--------|--------|--------|--------|--------|
| 10 | Qtr 1   | $5,500 | $6,250 | $7,000 | $8,500 | $5,500 | $4,500 |
| 11 | Qtr 2   | $6,000 | $7,250 | $6,500 | $9,000 | $4,000 | $5,000 |
| 12 | Qtr 3   | $4,500 | $8,000 | $6,000 | $7,500 | $6,000 | $5,000 |
| 13 | Qtr 4   | $6,500 | $8,500 | $7,000 | $8,000 | $5,500 | $6,000 |
| 14 | Average | $5,625 | $7,500 | $6,625 | $8,250 | $5,250 | $5,125 |
| 15 |         |        |        |        |        |        |  |

**Step 3b**

4. Save **ExcelL1_C1_P2.xlsx**.

## Selecting Cells

You can use a variety of methods for formatting cells in a worksheet. For example, you can change the alignment of data in cells or rows or add character formatting. To identify the cells that are to be affected by the formatting, select the specific cells.

## Selecting Cells Using the Mouse

Select specific cells in a worksheet using the mouse or select columns or rows. Methods for selecting cells using the mouse display in Table 1.4.

Selected cells, except the active cell, display with a light blue background (this may vary) rather than a white background. The active cell is the first cell in the selection block and displays in the normal manner (white background with black data). Selected cells remain selected until you click a cell with the mouse or press an arrow key on the keyboard.

**Table 1.4** Selecting with the Mouse

| To select this | Do this |
|---|---|
| Column | Position the cell pointer on the column header (a letter) and then click the left mouse button. |
| Row | Position the cell pointer on the row header (a number) and then click the left mouse button. |
| Adjacent cells | Drag with mouse to select specific cells. |
| Nonadjacent cells | Hold down the Ctrl key while clicking column header, row header, or specific cells. |
| All cells in worksheet | Click Select All button (refer to Figure 1.2). |

## Selecting Cells Using the Keyboard

You can use the keyboard to select specific cells within a worksheet. Table 1.5 displays the commands for selecting specific cells.

**Table 1.5** Selecting Cells Using the Keyboard

| To select | Press |
|---|---|
| Cells in direction of arrow key | Shift + arrow key |
| To beginning of row | Shift + Home |
| To beginning of worksheet | Shift + Ctrl + Home |
| To last cell in worksheet containing data | Shift + Ctrl + End |
| An entire column | Ctrl + spacebar |
| An entire row | Shift + spacebar |
| An entire worksheet | Ctrl + A or Ctrl + Shift + spacebar |

## Selecting Data within Cells

The selection commands presented select the entire cell. You can also select specific characters within a cell. To do this with the mouse, position the cell pointer in the desired cell, and then double-click the left mouse button. Drag with the I-beam pointer through the data you want selected. Data selected within a cell displays in white with a black background. If you are using the keyboard to select data in a cell, hold down the Shift key, and then press the arrow key that moves the insertion point in the desired direction. Data the insertion point passes through will be selected. You can also press F8 to turn on the Extend Selection mode, move the insertion point in the desired direction to select the data, and then press F8 to turn off the Extend Selection mode. When the Extend Selection mode is on, the words *Extend Selection* display toward the left side of the Status bar.

# Formatting with Predesigned Styles

An Excel worksheet contains default formatting. For example, letters and words are aligned at the left of a cell, numbers are aligned at the right, and data is set in 11-point Calibri. Excel provides predesigned styles you can use to apply formatting to cells in a worksheet. Apply table formatting styles with the Format as Table button or the Cell Styles button, both located in the Styles group in the Home tab.

## Formatting with Table Styles

Apply table formatting styles to selected cells in a worksheet using the Format as Table button in the Styles group in the Home tab. When you select cells and then click the Format as Table button, a drop-down list displays as shown in Figure 1.8. Click the desired table style and the Format As Table dialog box displays. Click OK at this dialog box and the formatting is applied to the selected cells. Excel also inserts filtering arrows in each cell in the first row of selected cells. The filtering arrows do not print. You can turn off the display of the filtering arrows by clicking the Data tab and then clicking the Filter button in the Sort & Filter group. You will learn more about these filtering arrows in a later chapter.

**Apply Table Formatting**
1. Select desired cells.
2. Click Format as Table button.
3. Click desired table style.
4. Click OK at Format As Table dialog box.

**Figure 1.8** Format as Table Drop-down List

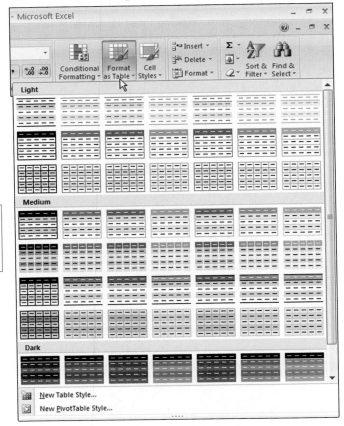

Choose an option at this drop-down list to apply predesigned formatting to selected cells in a worksheet.

## Project 2d  Formatting Cells with Table Styles

1. With **ExcelL1_C1_P2.xlsx** open, apply a table style to specific cells by completing the following steps:
   a. Select cells A1 through G6.
   b. Click the Format as Table button in the Styles group in the Home tab.
   c. At the drop-down list, click the *Table Style Light 9* option (second style option from the left in the second row in the *Light* section).

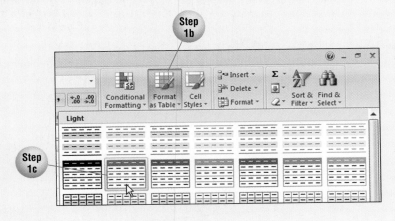

Step 1b

Step 1c

d. At the Format As Table dialog box, click OK. (Excel inserts filtering arrows in the cells in the first row.)

2. Select cells A10 through G14 and then apply the Table Style Light 11 style (fourth style option from the left in the second row in the *Light* section). At the Format As Table dialog box, click OK.

3. Save **ExcelL1_C1_P2.xlsx**. (Excel inserts a row with filtering arrows.)

Step 1d

# Formatting with Cell Styles

In some worksheets, you may want to highlight or accentuate certain cells. You can apply formatting to a cell or selected cells with cell styles. Click the Cell Styles button in the Styles group in the Home tab and a drop-down gallery of style options displays as shown in Figure 1.9. Hover your mouse pointer over a style option and the cell or selected cells display with the style formatting applied. You can hover your mouse over different style options to see how the style formatting affects the cell or selected cells. The Cell Styles button drop-down gallery is an example of the *live preview* feature, which allows you to see how the style formatting affects cells in your worksheet without having to return to the worksheet.

**QUICK STEPS**

**Apply Cell Style**
1. Select desired cell(s).
2. Click Cell Styles button.
3. Click desired style option.

Cell Styles ▾

**Figure 1.9** Cell Styles Drop-down Gallery

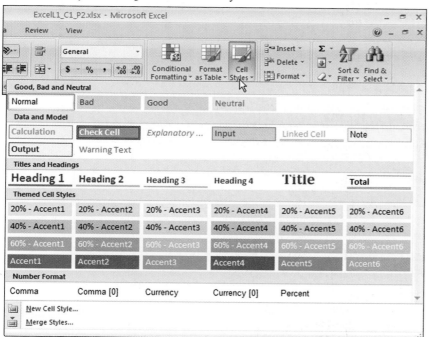

Choose an option at this drop-down gallery to apply a predesigned style to a cell or selected cells in a worksheet.

1. With **ExcelL1_C1_P2.xlsx** open, select cells B2 through G6.
2. Click the Cell Styles button in the Styles group in the Home tab.
3. At the drop-down gallery, hover your mouse over style options to see how the style formatting affects the selected cells.
4. Click the *Currency [0]* option (fourth option from the left in the *Number Format* section).

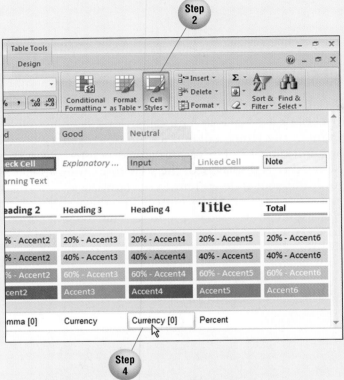

5. Select cells B6 through G6.
6. Click the Cell Styles button and then click the *Total* option (the last option in the *Titles and Headings* section).

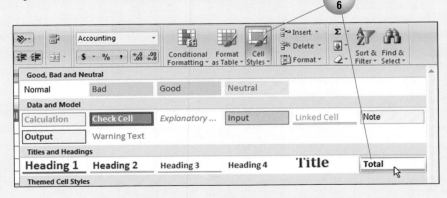

7. Select cells B15 through G15 and then apply the Total cell style.
8. Save, print, and then close **ExcelL1_C1_P2.xlsx**.

# Project 3 Use the Help Feature

You will use the Help feature to learn more about entering data in cells and selecting text and saving a workbook. You will also customize Help to search for information offline and for Excel training.

## Using Help

Excel's Help feature is an on-screen reference manual containing information about Excel features. Excel's Help feature is similar to the Windows Help and the Help features in Word, PowerPoint, and Access. Get help by clicking the Microsoft Office Excel Help button located in the upper right corner of the screen (a question mark in a circle) or by pressing the keyboard shortcut, F1. This displays the Excel Help window. In this window, type a topic, feature, or question in the *Search* text box and then press Enter. Topics related to the search text display in the Help window. Click a topic that interests you. If the topic window contains a <u>Show All</u> hyperlink in the upper right corner, click this hyperlink and the information expands to show all help information related to the topic. When you click the <u>Show All</u> hyperlink, it becomes the <u>Hide All</u> hyperlink.

## Project 3a Using the Help Feature

1. At a blank worksheet, click the Microsoft Office Excel Help button located in the upper right corner of the screen.
2. At the Excel Help window, type enter data in cells in the *Search* text box.
3. Press the Enter key.
4. When the list of topics displays, click the *Enter data manually in worksheet cells* hyperlink.
5. Click the <u>Show All</u> hyperlink that displays in the upper right corner of the window.

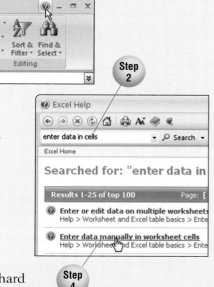

Step 1

Step 2

Step 4

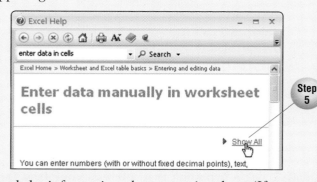

Step 5

6. Read the information about entering data. (If you want a hard copy of the Help text, click the Print button located toward the top of the Excel Help window, and then click the Print button at the Print dialog box.)
7. Click the Close button to close the Excel Help window.

## Getting Help in a Dialog Box

Dialog boxes contain a Help button you can click to display help in the Excel Help window that is specific to the dialog box. This button is located in the upper right corner of the dialog box and displays as a question mark inside a circle. Click this button and the Excel Help window displays with topics related to the dialog box.

## Getting Help on a Button

When you position the mouse pointer on a button, a ScreenTip displays with information about the button. Some button ScreenTips display with the message "Press F1 for more help." that is preceded by an image of the Help button. With the ScreenTip visible, press the F1 function key and the Excel Help window opens and displays information about the specific button.

Project 3D ▸ **Getting Help in a Dialog Box and Button ScreenTip**

1. At a blank worksheet, click the Office button and then click *Save As* at the drop-down list.
2. At the Save As dialog box, click the Help button located in the upper right corner of the dialog box.
3. At the Excel Help window, click the *Save As* hyperlink.
4. In the Save As list box, click *Microsoft Office Excel*.
5. Read the information that displays about saving in Excel and then click the Close button to close the Excel Help window.
6. Close the Save As dialog box.
7. Position the mouse pointer on the Office button until the ScreenTip displays and then press F1.

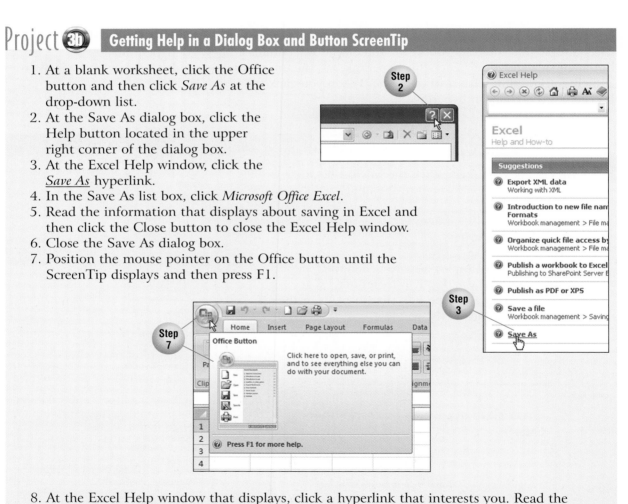

8. At the Excel Help window that displays, click a hyperlink that interests you. Read the information and then close the Excel Help window.

# Customizing Help

By default, the Excel Help feature will search for an Internet connection and, if one is found, display help resources from Office Online. If you are connected online to help resources, the message "Connected to Office Online" displays in the lower right corner of the Excel Help window. If you are not connected to the Internet, the message displays as "Offline."

Office Online provides additional help resources such as training and templates. To view the resources, display the Excel Help window and then click the down-pointing arrow at the right side of the Search button. This displays a drop-down list similar to the one shown in Figure 1.10. Generally, the *All Excel* option in the *Content from Office Online* is selected. If you want to search only the Help resources available with your computer (offline), click the *Excel Help* option in the *Content from this computer* section. To access Office Online training, click the *Excel Training* option in the *Content from Office Online* section, type a training topic in the *Search* text box, and then click OK.

**Figure 1.10** Excel Help Search Drop-down List

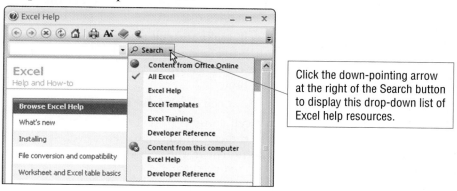

Click the down-pointing arrow at the right of the Search button to display this drop-down list of Excel help resources.

## Project 3c  Customizing Help

1. At a blank worksheet, click the Microsoft Office Excel Help button located toward the upper right corner of the screen.
2. Click the down-pointing arrow at the right side of the Search button in the Excel Help window.
3. At the drop-down list that displays, click *Excel Help* in the *Content from this computer* section.
4. Click in the *Search* text box, type **formulas** in the *Search* text box, and then press Enter.
5. Click a hyperlink that interests you and then read the information that displays.
6. Click the down-pointing arrow at the right side of the Search button and then click *Excel Training* in the *Content from Office Online* section.
7. Click in the *Search* text box (this will select *formulas*) and then press Enter.
8. Click the hyperlink of a training about formulas that interests you.
9. After completing the training, close Internet Explorer and then close the Excel Help window.

Step 2

Step 3

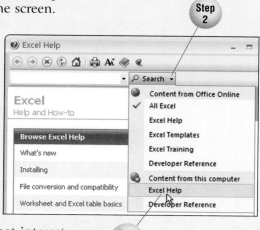

# CHAPTER summary

- Use an Excel spreadsheet to create financial statements, prepare budgets, manage inventory, and analyze cash flow. Numbers and values can be easily manipulated in an Excel spreadsheet to answer "what if" questions.
- A file created in Excel is called a workbook. A workbook consists of individual worksheets. The intersection of columns and rows in a worksheet is referred to as a cell.
- An Excel window contains the following elements: Office button, Quick Access toolbar, Title bar, tabs, ribbon, Name box, Formula bar, scroll bars, sheet tabs, and Status bar.
- The horizontal and vertical lines that define cells in the worksheet area are called gridlines.
- When the insertion point is positioned in a cell, the cell name (also called the cell reference) displays in the Name box located at the left side of the Formula bar. The cell name includes the column letter and row number.
- To enter data in a cell, make the cell active and then type the data. To move the insertion point to the next cell, press the Tab key. To move the insertion point to the previous cell, press Shift + Tab. For other insertion point movement commands, refer to Table 1.2.
- Data being entered in a cell displays in the cell as well as in the Formula bar.
- If data entered in a cell consists of text (letters) and the text does not fit into the cell, it overlaps the cell to the right. However, if the data being entered are numbers and do not fit in the cell, the numbers are changed to number symbols (###).
- Save a workbook by clicking the Save button on the Quick Access toolbar or by clicking the Office button and then clicking *Save* at the drop-down list.
- To replace data in a cell, click the cell once and then type the new data. To edit data within a cell, double-click the cell and then make necessary changes.
- Print a workbook by clicking the Quick Print button on the Quick Access toolbar or by clicking the Office button, pointing to the *Print* option, and then clicking *Quick Print*.
- Close a workbook by clicking the Close Window button located in the upper right corner of the screen or by clicking the Office button and then clicking *Close* at the drop-down list.
- Exit Excel by clicking the Close button located in the upper right corner of the screen or by clicking the Office button and then clicking the Exit Excel button.
- The AutoComplete feature will automatically insert a previous entry if the character or characters being typed in a cell match a previous entry.
- The AutoCorrect feature corrects many common typographical errors.
- Use the AutoFill fill handle to fill a range of cells with the same or consecutive data.
- Open a workbook by clicking the Open button on the Quick Access toolbar or by clicking the Office button and then clicking the *Open* option at the drop-down list. At the Open dialog box, double-click the desired workbook.
- Use the Sum button in the Editing group in the Home tab to find the total or average of data in columns or rows.

- Select all cells in a column by clicking the column header. Select all cells in a row by clicking the row header. Select all cells in a worksheet by clicking the Select All button located immediately to the left of the column headers.
- To select cells with the mouse, refer to Table 1.4; to select cells using the keyboard, refer to Table 1.5.
- Use options from the Format as Table button drop-down gallery to apply predesigned table styles to selected cells.
- Use options from the Cell Styles button drop-down gallery to apply predesigned styles to a cell or selected cells.
- Excel's Help feature is an on-screen reference manual containing information about Excel features.
- Click the Microsoft Office Excel Help button or press F1 to display the Excel Help window. At this window, type a topic and then press Enter.
- Dialog boxes contain a Help button you can click to display the Excel Help window with information specific to the dialog box. The ScreenTip for some buttons displays with a message telling you to press F1. Press F1 and the Excel Help window opens with information about the button.
- Customize Help with options from the Search button drop-down list in the Excel Help window.

# COMMANDS review

| FEATURE | RIBBON TAB, GROUP | BUTTON | QUICK ACCESS TOOLBAR | OFFICE BUTTON DROP-DOWN LIST | KEYBOARD SHORTCUT |
|---|---|---|---|---|---|
| Close workbook | | [X] | | Close | Ctrl + F4 |
| Exit Excel | | [X] | | Exit Excel | |
| Go To dialog box | Home, Editing | [icon], Go To | | | Ctrl + G |
| Excel Help window | | [?] | | | F1 |
| Open workbook | | | [icon] | Open | Ctrl + O |
| Print workbook | | | [icon] | Print, Quick Print | |
| Save workbook | | | [icon] | Save | Ctrl + S |
| Format as Table drop-down list | Home, Styles | [icon] | | | |
| Cell Styles drop-down gallery | Home, Styles | [icon] | | | |
| Sum button drop-down list | Home, Editing | [Σ ▾] | | | |

# CONCEPTS check

## Test Your Knowledge

**Completion:** In the space provided at the right, indicate the correct term, symbol, or command.

1. Columns in a worksheet are labeled with this.                                    _____

2. Rows in a worksheet are labeled with this.                                       _____

3. The horizontal and vertical lines that define the cells in a worksheet area are referred to as this.                                       _____

4. Press this key on the keyboard to move the insertion point to the next cell.                                                       _____

5. Press these keys on the keyboard to move the insertion point to the previous cell.                                                _____

6. If a number entered in a cell is too long to fit inside the cell, the number is changed to this.                                     _____

7. Data being typed in a cell displays in the cell as well as here.                 _____

8. This is the name of the small black square that displays in the bottom right corner of the active cell.                            _____

9. To select nonadjacent columns using the mouse, hold down this key on the keyboard while clicking the column headers.              _____

10. Use this button in the Editing group in the Home tab to insert a formula in a cell.                                              _____

11. With this function, a range of cells is added together and then divided by the number of cell entries.                           _____

12. Click this button in the worksheet area to select all of the cells in the table.                                                  _____

13. This feature allows you to see how style formatting affects cells in your worksheet without having to return to the worksheet.    _____

14. Press this function key to display the Excel Help window.                       _____

# SKILLS check

*Demonstrate Your Proficiency*

## Assessment

**1 CREATE AND FORMAT A WORKSHEET WITH A TABLE STYLE**

1. Create the worksheet shown in Figure 1.11.
2. Select cells A1 through C5 and then apply the Table Style Medium 3 table style.
3. Save the workbook and name it **ExcelL1_C1_A1**.
4. Print and then close **ExcelL1_C1_A1.xlsx**.

**Figure 1.11 Assessment 1**

| | A | B | C | D |
|---|---|---|---|---|
| 1 | Expense | Original | Current | |
| 2 | Labor | 97000 | 98500 | |
| 3 | Material | 129000 | 153000 | |
| 4 | Permits | 1200 | 1350 | |
| 5 | Tax | 1950 | 2145 | |
| 6 | | | | |

## Assessment

**2 CREATE A WORKSHEET USING AUTOCOMPLETE**

1. Create the worksheet shown in Figure 1.12. To create the © symbol in cell A1, type (c). Type the misspelled words as shown and let the AutoCorrect feature correct the spelling. Use the AutoComplete feature to insert the second occurrence of *Category*, *Available*, and *Balance*.
2. Apply a table style of your choosing to cells A1 through B7. (Excel inserts a row with filtering arrows.)
3. Save the workbook and name it **ExcelL1_C1_A2**.
4. Print and then close **ExcelL1_C1_A2.xlsx**.

**Figure 1.12 Assessment 2**

| | A | B | C |
|---|---|---|---|
| 1 | Premiere Plan© | | |
| 2 | Plan A | Catagory | |
| 3 | | Availalbe | |
| 4 | | Balence | |
| 5 | Plan B | Category | |
| 6 | | Available | |
| 7 | | Balance | |
| 8 | | | |

## 3  CREATE A WORKSHEET USING THE FILL HANDLE

1. Create the worksheet shown in Figure 1.13. Type Monday in cell B2 and then use the fill handle to fill in the remaining days of the week. Use the fill handle to enter other repetitive data.
2. Apply a table style of your choosing to cells A1 through F4.
3. Save the workbook and name it **ExcelL1_C1_A3**.
4. Print and then close **ExcelL1_C1_A3.xlsx**.

**Figure 1.13  Assessment 3**

| | A | B | C | D | E | F | G |
|---|---|---|---|---|---|---|---|
| 1 | CAPITAL INVESTMENTS | | | | | | |
| 2 | | Monday | Tuesday | Wednesday | Thursday | Friday | |
| 3 | Budget | 350 | 350 | 350 | 350 | 350 | |
| 4 | Actual | 310 | 425 | 290 | 375 | 400 | |
| 5 | | | | | | | |

## 4  INSERT FORMULAS IN A WORKSHEET

1. Open **ExcelC01Assessment04.xlsx** and then save the workbook and name it **ExcelL1_C1_A4**.
2. Insert a formula in cell B15 that totals the amounts in cells B4 through B14.
3. Use the fill handle to copy relatively the formula in cell B15 to cell C15.
4. Insert a formula in cell D4 that finds the average of cells B4 and C4.
5. Use the fill handle to copy relatively the formula in cell D4 down to cells D5 through D14.
6. Save, print, and then close **ExcelL1_C1_A4.xlsx**.

## 5  USE HELP FEATURE TO LEARN ABOUT SCROLLING

1. Use the Help feature to learn more about how to scroll within an Excel worksheet.
2. Read and then print the information provided by Help.
3. Create a worksheet containing the information. Set this up as a worksheet with two columns (cells will contain only text—not numbers). Create a title for the worksheet.
4. Select the cells in your worksheet containing data and then apply a table style to the cells.
5. Save the completed workbook and name it **ExcelL1_C1_A5**.
6. Print and then close **ExcelL1_C1_A5.xlsx**.

# CASE study

## Apply Your Skills

You are the office manager for Deering Industries. One of your responsibilities is creating a monthly calendar containing information on staff meetings, training, and due dates for time cards. Open **DeeringCalendar.xlsx** and then insert the following information:

- Insert the text **September, 2010** in cell A2.
- Insert the days of the week (*Sunday, Monday, Tuesday, Wednesday, Thursday, Friday*, and *Saturday*) in cells A3 through G3.
- Insert the number *1* in cell D4, number *2* in cell E4, number *3* in cell F4, and number *4* in cell G4.
- Insert in the calendar the remaining numbers of the days (numbers 5-11 in cells A6 through G6, numbers 12 through 18 in cells A8 through G8, numbers 19 through 25 in cells A10 through G10, and numbers 26 through 30 in cells A12 through E12).
- Excel training will be held Thursday, September 2, from 9-11 a.m. Insert this information in cell E5. (Insert the text on two lines by typing Excel Training, pressing Alt + Enter to move the insertion point to the next line, and then typing 9-10 a.m.)
- A staff meeting is held the second and fourth Monday of each month from 9-10 a.m. Insert this information in cell B9 and cell B13.
- Time cards are due the first and third Fridays of the month. Insert in cells F5 and F9 information indicating that time cards are due.
- A production team meeting is scheduled for Tuesday, September 21, from 1-3 p.m. Insert this information in cell C11.

Save the workbook and name it **ExcelL1_C1_CS_P1**. Print and then close the workbook.

The manager of the Purchasing Department has asked you to prepare a worksheet containing information on quarterly purchases. Open **DeeringExpenditures.xlsx** and then insert the data as shown in Figure 1.14. After typing the data, insert in the appropriate cells formulas to calculate averages and totals. Save the workbook and name it **ExcelL1_C1_CS_P2**. Print and then close the workbook.

**Figure 1.14 Case Study Part 2**

| | A | B | C | D | E | F | G |
|---|---|---|---|---|---|---|---|
| 1 | | | | **DEERING INDUSTRIES** | | | |
| 2 | | **PURCHASING DEPARTMENT - EXPENDITURES** | | | | | |
| 3 | **Category** | **1st Qtr.** | **2nd Qtr.** | **3rd Qtr.** | **4th Qtr.** | **Average** | |
| 4 | Supplies | $ 645.75 | $ 756.25 | $ 534.78 | $ 78,950.00 | | |
| 5 | Equipment | $ 4,520.55 | $ 10,789.35 | $ 3,825.00 | $ 12,890.72 | | |
| 6 | Furniture | $ 458.94 | $ 2,490.72 | $ 851.75 | $ 743.20 | | |
| 7 | Training | $ 1,000.00 | $ 250.00 | $ 1,200.00 | $ 800.00 | | |
| 8 | Software | $ 249.00 | $ 1,574.30 | $ 155.45 | $ 3,458.70 | | |
| 9 | Total | | | | | | |
| 10 | | | | | | | |

**Part 3**

The manager of the Purchasing Department has asked you to prepare a note to the finances coordinator, Jennifer Strauss. In Word, type a note to Jennifer Strauss explaining that you have prepared an Excel worksheet with the Purchasing Department expenditures. You are including the cells from the worksheet containing the expenditure information. In Excel, open **ExcelL1_C1_CS_P2.xlsx**, copy cells A3 through F9, and then paste them in the Word document. Make any corrections to the table so the information is readable. Save the document and name it **WordExcelL1_C1_CS_P3**. Print and then close the document. Close **ExcelL1_C1_CS_P3.xlsx**.

**Part 4**

You will be ordering copy machines for several departments in the company and decide to research prices. Using the Internet, find three companies that sell copiers and write down information on different copier models. Open **DeeringCopiers.xlsx** and then type the company, model number, and price in the designated cells. Save the completed workbook and name it **ExcelL1_C1_CS_P4**. Print and then close **ExcelL1_C1_CS_P4.xlsx**.

# CHAPTER

# Inserting Formulas in a Worksheet

## PERFORMANCE OBJECTIVES

**Upon successful completion of Chapter 2, you will be able to:**

- Write formulas with mathematical operators
- Type a formula in the Formula bar
- Copy a formula
- Use the Insert Function feature to insert a formula in a cell
- Write formulas with the AVERAGE, MAX, MIN, COUNT, PMT, FV, DATE, NOW, and IF functions
- Create an absolute and mixed cell reference

**Tutorial 2.1**
Inserting and Editing Formulas
**Tutorial 2.2**
Working with Cell References

Excel is a powerful decision-making tool containing data that can be manipulated to answer "what if" situations. Insert a formula in a worksheet and then manipulate the data to make projections, answer specific questions, and use as a planning tool. For example, the owner of a company might prepare a worksheet on production costs and then determine the impact on company revenues if production is increased or decreased.

Insert a formula in a worksheet to perform calculations on values. A formula contains a mathematical operator, value, cell reference, cell range, and a function. Formulas can be written that add, subtract, multiply, and/or divide values. Formulas can also be written that calculate averages, percentages, minimum and maximum values, and much more. As you learned in Chapter 1, Excel includes a Sum button in the Editing group in the Home tab that inserts a formula to calculate the total of a range of cells and also includes some commonly used formulas. Along with the Sum button, Excel includes a Formulas tab that offers a variety of functions to create formulas.

*Note: Before beginning computer projects, copy to your storage medium the Excel2007L1C2 subfolder from the Excel2007L1 folder on the CD that accompanies this textbook and make Excel2007L1C2 the active folder.*

# Project ① Insert Formulas in a Worksheet

**You will open a worksheet containing data and then insert formulas to calculate differences, salaries, and percentages of budgets.**

## Writing Formulas with Mathematical Operators

**HINT**

After typing a formula in a cell, press the Enter key, the Tab key, Shift + Tab, or click the Enter button on the Formula bar.

As you learned in Chapter 1, the Sum button in the Editing group in the Home tab creates the formula for you. You can also write your own formulas using mathematical operators. Commonly used mathematical operators and their functions are displayed in Table 2.1. When writing your own formula, begin the formula with the equals (=) sign. For example, to create a formula that divides the contents of cell B2 by the contents of cell C2 and inserts the result in cell D2, you would make D2 the active cell and then type =B2/C2.

**Table 2.1** Mathematical Operators

| Operator | Function |
|----------|----------------|
| + | Addition |
| - | Subtraction |
| * | Multiplication |
| / | Division |
| % | Percent |
| ^ | Exponentiation |

If a formula contains two or more operators, Excel uses the same order of operations used in algebra. From left to right in a formula, this order, called the *order of operations*, is: negations (negative number—a number preceded by -) first, then percents (%), then exponentiations (^), followed by multiplications (*), divisions (/), additions (+), and finally subtractions (-). If you want to change the order of operations, use parentheses around the part of the formula you want calculated first.

### Copying a Formula with Relative Cell References

In many worksheets, the same basic formula is used repetitively. In a situation where a formula is copied to other locations in a worksheet, use a ***relative cell reference***. Copy a formula containing relative cell references and the cell references change. For example, if you enter the formula *=SUM(A2:C2)* in cell D2 and then copy it relatively to cell D3, the formula in cell D3 displays as *=SUM(A3:C3)*. (Additional information on cell references is discussed later in this chapter in the "Using an Absolute Cell Reference in a Formula" section.)

To copy a formula relatively in a worksheet, use the Fill button or the fill handle (you used the fill handle to copy a formula in Chapter 1). To use the Fill button, select the cell containing the formula as well as the cells to which you want the formula copied and then click the Fill button in the Editing group in the Home tab. At the Fill drop-down list, click the desired direction. For example, if you are copying the formula down cells, click the *Down* option.

**QUICK STEPS**

**Copy Relative Formula**
1. Insert formula in cell.
2. Select cell containing formula and all cells you want to contain formula.
3. Click Fill button.
4. Click desired direction.

---

## Project 1a — Finding Differences by Inserting and Copying a Formula

1. Open **ExcelC02Project01.xlsx**.
2. Save the workbook with Save As and name it **ExcelL1_C2_P1**.
3. Insert a formula by completing the following steps:
   a. Make cell D3 active.
   b. Type the formula **=C3-B3**.
   c. Press Enter.
4. Copy the formula to cells D4 through D10 by completing the following steps:
   a. Select cells D3 through D10.
   b. Click the Fill button in the Editing group in the Home tab and then click *Down* at the drop-down list.
5. Save **ExcelL1_C2_P1.xlsx**.
6. With the worksheet open, make the following changes to cell contents:
   B4: Change *$48,290* to *46425*
   C6: Change *$61,220* to *60000*
   B8: Change *$55,309* to *57415*
   B9: Change *$12,398* to *14115*
7. Save **ExcelL1_C2_P1.xlsx**.

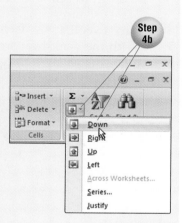

Step 4b

# Copying Formulas with the Fill Handle

Use the fill handle to copy a formula up, down, left, or right within a worksheet. To use the fill handle, insert the desired data in the cell (text, value, formula, etc.). With the cell active, position the mouse pointer on the fill handle until the mouse pointer turns into a thin, black cross. Hold down the left mouse button, drag and select the desired cells, and then release the mouse button. If you are dragging a cell containing a formula, a relative version of the formula is copied to the selected cells.

**HINT**
Use the fill handle to copy a relative version of a formula.

1. With **ExcelL1_C2_P1.xlsx** open, insert a formula by completing the following steps:
   a. Make cell D15 active.
   b. Click in the Formula bar text box and then type **=C15*B15**.
   c. Click the Enter button on the Formula bar.
2. Copy the formula to cells D16 through D20 by completing the following steps:
   a. Make sure cell D15 is the active cell.
   b. Position the mouse pointer on the fill handle that displays at the lower right corner of cell D15 until the pointer turns into a thin, black cross.
   c. Hold down the left mouse button, drag down to cell D20, and then release the mouse button.
3. Save **ExcelL1_C2_P1.xlsx**.
4. With the worksheet still open, make the following changes to cell contents:
   B16: Change *20* to *28*
   C17: Change *$18.75* to *19.10*
   B19: Change *15* to *24*
5. Save **ExcelL1_C2_P1.xlsx**.

Step 1c

Step 1b

DATE  ✕ ✓ *fx*  =C15*B15

Enter

## Highland Construction

| | A | B | C | D |
|---|---|---|---|---|
| 1 | | | | |
| 2 | Customer | Actual | Planned | Difference |
| 3 | Sellar Corporation | $30,349.00 | $34,109.00 | $3,760.00 |
| 4 | Main Street Photos | $46,425.00 | $48,100.00 | $1,675.00 |
| 5 | Sunset Automotive | $34,192.00 | $32,885.00 | -$1,307.00 |
| 6 | Linstrom Enterprises | $63,293.00 | $60,000.00 | -$3,293.00 |
| 7 | Morcos Media | $29,400.00 | $30,500.00 | $1,100.00 |
| 8 | Green Valley Optics | $57,415.00 | $58,394.00 | $979.00 |
| 9 | Detailed Designs | $14,115.00 | $13,100.00 | -$1,015.00 |
| 10 | Arrowstar Company | $87,534.00 | $86,905.00 | -$629.00 |
| 11 | | | | |
| 12 | | | | |
| 13 | | | | |
| 14 | Name | Hours | Rate | Salary |
| 15 | Carolyn Bentley | 35 | $23.15 | =C15*B15 |
| 16 | Lindon Cassini | 20 | $19.00 | |

| | A | B | C | D |
|---|---|---|---|---|
| 13 | | | | |
| 14 | Name | Hours | Rate | Salary |
| 15 | Carolyn Bentley | 35 | $23.15 | $810.25 |
| 16 | Lindon Cassini | 20 | $19.00 | $380.00 |
| 17 | Michelle DeFord | 40 | $18.75 | $750.00 |
| 18 | Javier Farias | 24 | $16.45 | $394.80 |
| 19 | Deborah Gould | 15 | $11.50 | $172.50 |
| 20 | William Jarman | 15 | $11.50 | $172.50 |
| 21 | | | | |
| 22 | | | | |

Step 2c

## Writing a Formula by Pointing

**Write Formula by Pointing**
1. Click cell that will contain formula.
2. Type equals sign.
3. Click cell you want to reference in formula.
4. Type desired mathematical operator.
5. Click next cell reference.

In Project 1a and Project 1b, you wrote formulas using cell references such as =C3-B3. Another method for writing a formula is to "point" to the specific cells that are to be part of the formula. Creating a formula by pointing is more accurate than typing the cell reference since a mistake can happen when typing the cell reference.

To write a formula by pointing, click the cell that will contain the formula, type the equals sign to begin the formula, and then click the cell you want to reference in the formula. This inserts a moving border around the cell and also changes the mode from Enter to Point. (The word *Point* displays at the left side of the Status bar.) Type the desired mathematical operator and then click the next cell reference. Continue in this manner until all cell references are specified and then press the Enter key. This ends the formula and inserts the result of the calculation of the formula in the active cell. When writing a formula by pointing, you can also select a range of cells you want included in a formula.

1. With **ExcelL1_C2_P1.xlsx** open, enter a formula by pointing that calculates the percentage of actual budget by completing the following steps:
   a. Make cell D25 active.
   b. Type the equals sign.
   c. Click cell C25. (This inserts a moving border around the cell and the mode changes from Enter to Point.)
   d. Type the forward slash symbol (/).
   e. Click cell B25.

| | A | B | C | D | E |
|---|---|---|---|---|---|
| 22 | | | | | |
| 23 | | | | | |
| 24 | Expense | Actual | Budget | % of Actual | |
| 25 | Salaries | $126,000.00 | $124,000.00 | =C25/B25 | |
| 26 | Commissions | $58,000.00 | $54,500.00 | | |
| 27 | Media space | $8,250.00 | $10,100.00 | | |
| 28 | Travel expenses | $6,350.00 | $6,000.00 | | |
| 29 | Dealer display | $4,140.00 | $4,500.00 | | |
| 30 | Payroll taxes | $2,430.00 | $2,200.00 | | |
| 31 | Telephone | $1,450.00 | $1,500.00 | | |
| 32 | | | | | |

Steps 1a–1e

| | C | D | E |
|---|---|---|---|
| | Budget | % of Actual | |
| | $124,000.00 | 98% | |
| | $54,500.00 | 94% | |
| | $10,100.00 | 122% | |
| | $6,000.00 | 94% | |
| | $4,500.00 | 109% | |
| | $2,200.00 | 91% | |
| | $1,500.00 | 103% | |

Step 2

   f. Make sure the formula looks like this =C25/B25 and then press Enter.
2. Make cell D25 active, position the mouse pointer on the fill handle, drag down to cell D31, and then release the mouse button.
3. Save **ExcelL1_C2_P1.xlsx**.

## Using the Trace Error Button

As you are working in a worksheet, you may occasionally notice a button pop up near the active cell. The general term for this button is *smart tag*. The display of the smart tag button varies depending on the action performed. In Project 1d, you will insert a formula that will cause a smart tag button, named the Trace Error button, to appear. When the Trace Error button appears, a small dark green triangle also displays in the upper left corner of the cell. Click the Trace Error button and a drop-down list displays with options for updating the formula to include specific cells, getting help on the error, ignoring the error, editing the error in the Formula bar, and completing an error check. In Project 1d, two of the formulas you insert return the desired results. You will click the Trace Error button, read information on what Excel perceives as the error, and then tell Excel to ignore the error.

Trace Error

1. With **ExcelL1_C2_P1.xlsx** open, enter a formula by pointing that computes the percentage of equipment down time by completing the following steps:
   a. Make cell B45 active.
   b. Type the equals sign followed by the left parenthesis (=().
   c. Click cell B37. (This inserts a moving border around the cell and the mode changes from Enter to Point.)
   d. Type the minus symbol (-).
   e. Click cell B43.
   f. Type the right parenthesis followed by the forward slash ()/).
   g. Click cell B37.
   h. Make sure the formula looks like this =(B37-B43)/B37 and then press Enter.

2. Make cell B45 active, position the mouse pointer on the fill handle, drag across to cell G45, and then release the mouse button.

3. Enter a formula by dragging through a range of cells by completing the following steps:
   a. Click in cell B46 and then click the Sum button in the Editing group in the Home tab.
   b. Select cells B37 through D37.
   c. Click the Enter button on the Formula bar. (This inserts *7,260* in cell B46.)

4. Click in cell B47 and then complete steps similar to those in Step 3 to create a formula that totals hours available from April through June (cells E37 through G37). (This inserts *7,080* in cell B47.)

5. Click in cell B46 and notice the Trace Error button that displays. Complete the following steps to read about the error and then tell Excel to ignore the error:
   a. Click the Trace Error button.
   b. At the drop-down list that displays, click the *Help on this error* option.
   c. Read the information that displays in the Excel Help window and then close the window.

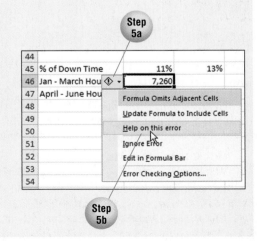

Steps 1a–1g

Step 3c

Step 5a

Step 5b

d. Click the Trace Error button again and then click *Ignore Error* at the drop-down list.

6. Remove the dark green triangle from cell B47 by completing the following steps:
   a. Click in cell B47.
   b. Click the Trace Error button and then click *Ignore Error* at the drop-down list.

7. Save, print, and then close **ExcelL1_C2_P1.xlsx**.

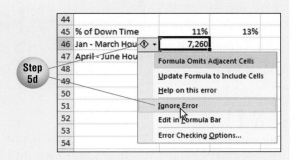

| | | | |
|---|---|---|---|
| 44 | | | |
| 45 | % of Down Time | 11% | 13% |
| 46 | Jan - March Hou | 7,260 | |
| 47 | April - June Hou | | |
| 48 | | | |
| 49 | | | |
| 50 | | | |
| 51 | | | |
| 52 | | | |
| 53 | | | |
| 54 | | | |

Step 5d

Formula Omits Adjacent Cells
Update Formula to Include Cells
Help on this error
Ignore Error
Edit in Formula Bar
Error Checking Options...

# Project ② Insert Formulas with Statistical Functions

**You will use the AVERAGE function to determine average test scores, use the MINIMUM and MAXIMUM functions to determine lowest and highest averages, use the COUNT function to count number of students taking a test, and display formulas in a cell rather than the result of the formula.**

## Inserting Formulas with Functions

In Project 2a in Chapter 1, you used the Sum button to insert the formula *=SUM(B2:B5)* in a cell. The beginning section of the formula, *=SUM*, is called a *function*, which is a built-in formula. Using a function takes fewer keystrokes when creating a formula. For example, the *=SUM* function saved you from having to type each cell to be included in the formula with the plus (+) symbol between cell entries.

Excel provides other functions for writing formulas. A function operates on what is referred to as an *argument*. An argument may consist of a constant, a cell reference, or another function (referred to as a nested function). In the formula *=SUM(B2:B5)*, the cell range *(B2:B5)* is an example of a cell reference argument. An argument may also contain a *constant*. A constant is a value entered directly into the formula. For example, if you enter the formula *=SUM(B3:B9,100)*, the cell range *B3:B9* is a cell reference argument and *100* is a constant. In this formula, 100 is always added to the sum of the cells. If a function is included in an argument within a function, it is called a *nested function*. (You will learn about nested functions later in this chapter.)

When a value calculated by the formula is inserted in a cell, this process is referred to as *returning the result*. The term *returning* refers to the process of calculating the formula and the term *result* refers to inserting the value in the cell.

You can type a function in a cell in a worksheet or you can use the Insert Function button on the Formula bar or in the Formulas tab to help you write the formula. Figure 2.1 displays the Formulas tab. The Formulas tab provides the Insert Function button as well as other buttons for inserting functions in a worksheet. The Function Library group in the Formulas tab contains a number of buttons for inserting functions from a variety of categories such as Financial, Logical, Text, and Date & Time.

Insert Function

Figure 2.1  Formulas Tab

Click the Insert Function button on the Formula bar or in the Formulas tab and the Insert Function dialog box displays as shown in Figure 2.2. At the Insert Function dialog box, the most recently used functions display in the *Select a function* list box. You can choose a function category by clicking the down-pointing arrow at the right side of the *Or select a category* list box and then clicking the desired category at the drop-down list. Use the *Search for a function* option to locate a specific function.

Figure 2.2  Insert Function Dialog Box

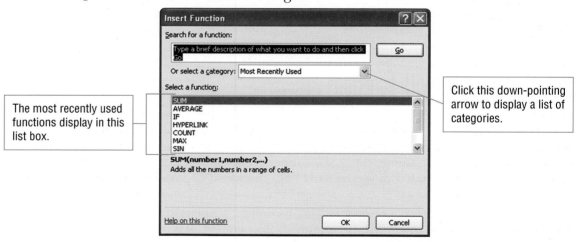

With the desired function category selected, choose a function in the *Select a function* list box and then click OK. This displays a Function Arguments palette like the one shown in Figure 2.3. At this palette, enter in the *Number1* text box the range of cells you want included in the formula, enter any constants that are to be included as part of the formula, or enter another function. After entering a range of cells, a constant, or another function, click the OK button. You can include more than one argument in a function. If the function you are creating contains more than one argument, press the Tab key to move the insertion point to the *Number2* text box, and then enter the second argument. If you need to display a specific cell or cells behind the function palette, move the palette by clicking and dragging it.

**Figure 2.3** Example Function Arguments Palette

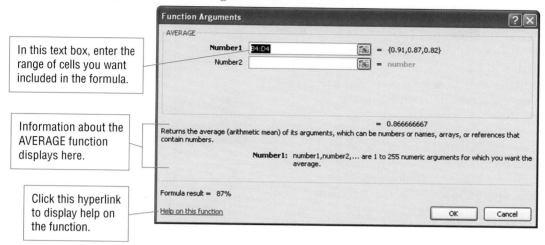

In this text box, enter the range of cells you want included in the formula.

Information about the AVERAGE function displays here.

Click this hyperlink to display help on the function.

Excel includes over 200 functions that are divided into 11 different categories including *Financial, Date & Time, Math & Trig, Statistical, Lookup & Reference, Database, Text, Logical, Information, Engineering,* and *Cube.* Clicking the Sum button in the Function Library group in the Formulas tab or the Editing group in the Home tab automatically adds numbers with the SUM function. The SUM function is included in the *Math & Trig* category. In some projects in this chapter, you will write formulas with functions in other categories including *Statistical, Financial, Date & Time,* and *Logical.*

Excel includes the Formula AutoComplete feature that displays a drop-down list of functions. To use this feature, click in the desired cell or click in the Formula bar text box, type the equals sign (=), and then type the first letter of the desired function. This displays a drop-down list with functions that begin with the letter. Double-click the desired function, enter the cell references, and then press Enter.

## Writing Formulas with Statistical Functions

In this section, you will learn to write formulas with the statistical functions AVERAGE, MAX, MIN, and COUNT. The AVERAGE function returns the average (arithmetic mean) of the arguments. The MAX function returns the largest value in a set of values and the MIN function returns the smallest value in a set of values. Use the COUNT function to count the number of cells that contain numbers within the list of arguments.

### *Finding Averages*

A common function in a formula is the AVERAGE function. With this function, a range of cells is added together and then divided by the number of cell entries. In Project 2a you will use the AVERAGE function, which will add all of the test scores for a student and then divide that number by the total number of tests. You will use the Insert Function button to simplify the creation of the formula containing an AVERAGE function.

One of the advantages to using formulas in a worksheet is the ability to easily manipulate data to answer certain questions. In Project 2a you will learn the impact of retaking certain tests on the final average score.

1. Open **ExcelC02Project02.xlsx**.
2. Save the workbook with Save As and name it **ExcelL1_C2_P2**.
3. Use the Insert Function button to find the average of test scores by completing the following steps:
   a. Make cell E4 active.
   b. Click the Insert Function button on the Formula bar.
   c. At the Insert Function dialog box, click the down-pointing arrow at the right side of the *Or select a category* list box and then click *Statistical* at the drop-down list.
   d. Click *AVERAGE* in the *Select a function* list box.
   e. Click OK.
   f. At the Function Arguments palette, make sure *B4:D4* displays in the *Number1* text box. (If not, type **B4:D4** in the *Number1* text box.)
   g. Click OK.
4. Copy the formula by completing the following steps:
   a. Make sure cell E4 is active.
   b. Position the mouse pointer on the fill handle until the pointer turns into a thin black cross.
   c. Hold down the left mouse button, drag down to cell E16, and then release the mouse button.
5. Save and then print **ExcelL1_C2_P2.xlsx**.
6. After viewing the averages of test scores, you notice that a couple of people have a low average. You decide to see what happens to the average score if students make up tests where they scored the lowest. You decide that a student can score a maximum of 70% on a retake of the test. Make the following changes to test scores to see how the changes will affect the test average.

   B9: Change *50* to *70*
   C9: Change *52* to *70*
   D9: Change *60* to *70*
   B10: Change *62* to *70*
   B14: Change *0* to *70*
   D14: Change *0* to *70*
   D16: Change *0* to *70*

7. Save and then print **ExcelL1_C2_P2.xlsx**. (Compare the test averages for Teri Fisher-Edwards, Stephanie Flanery, Claude Markovits, and Douglas Pherson to see what the effect of retaking the tests has on their final test averages.)

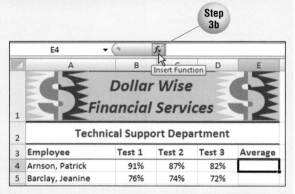

Step 3b

| Employee | Test 1 | Test 2 | Test 3 | Average |
|---|---|---|---|---|
| Arnson, Patrick | 91% | 87% | 82% | |
| Barclay, Jeanine | 76% | 74% | 72% | |

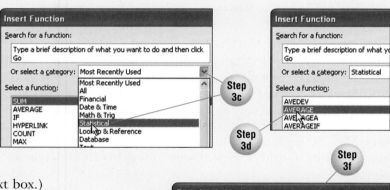

Step 3c

Step 3d

Step 3f

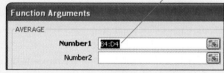

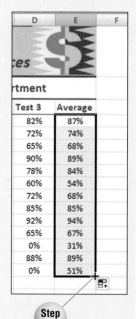

| Test 3 | Average |
|---|---|
| 82% | 87% |
| 72% | 74% |
| 65% | 68% |
| 90% | 89% |
| 78% | 84% |
| 60% | 54% |
| 72% | 68% |
| 85% | 85% |
| 92% | 94% |
| 65% | 67% |
| 0% | 31% |
| 88% | 89% |
| 0% | 51% |

Step 4c

When a formula such as the AVERAGE formula you inserted in a cell in Project 2a calculates cell entries, it ignores certain cell entries. The AVERAGE function will ignore text in cells and blank cells (not zeros). For example, in the worksheet containing test scores, a couple of cells contained a *0%* entry. This entry was included in the averaging of the test scores. If you did not want that particular test to be included in the average, enter text in the cell such as *N/A* (for *not applicable*) or leave the cell blank.

## Finding Maximum and Minimum Values

The MAX function in a formula returns the maximum value in a cell range and the MIN function returns the minimum value in a cell range. As an example, you could use the MAX and MIN functions in a worksheet containing employee hours to determine which employee worked the most number of hours and which worked the least. In a worksheet containing sales commissions, you could use the MAX and MIN functions to determine the salesperson who earned the most commission dollars and the one who earned the least.

Insert a MAX and MIN function into a formula in the same manner as an AVERAGE function. In Project 2b, you will use the Formula AutoComplete feature to insert the MAX function in cells to determine the highest test score average and the Insert Function button to insert the MIN function to determine the lowest test score average.

Project **2b**    **Finding Maximum and Minimum Values in a Worksheet**

1. With **ExcelL1_C2_P2.xlsx** open, type the following in the specified cells:
   A19: Highest Test Average
   A20: Lowest Test Average
   A21: Average of All Tests
2. Insert a formula to identify the highest test score average by completing the following steps:
   a. Make cell B19 active.
   b. Type =M. (This displays the Formula AutoComplete list.)
   c. Double-click *MAX* in the Formula AutoComplete list.
   d. Type E4:E16) and then press Enter.
3. Insert a formula to identify the lowest test score average by completing the following steps:
   a. Make cell B20 active.
   b. Click the Insert Function button on the Formula bar.
   c. At the Insert Function dialog box, make sure *Statistical* is selected in the *Or select a category* list box, and then click *MIN* in the *Select a function* list box. (You will need to scroll down the list to display *MIN*.)
   d. Click OK.
   e. At the Function Arguments palette, type E4:E16 in the *Number1* text box.
   f. Click OK.

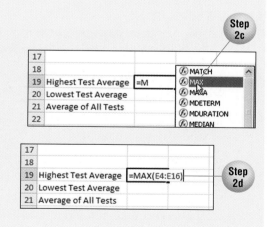

4. Insert a formula to determine the average of all test scores by completing the following steps:
   a. Make cell B21 active.
   b. Click the Formulas tab.
   c. Click the Insert Function button in the Function Library group.
   d. At the Insert Function dialog box, make sure *Statistical* is selected in the *Or select a category* list box and then click *AVERAGE* in the *Select a function* list box.
   e. Click OK.
   f. At the Function Arguments palette, type **E4:E16** in the *Number1* text box, and then click OK.
5. Save and then print **ExcelL1_C2_P2.xlsx**.
6. Change the *70%* values (which were previously *0%*) in cells B14, D14, and D16 to *N/A*. (This will cause the average of test scores for Claude Markovits and Douglas Pherson to increase and will change the minimum number and average of all test scores.)
7. Save and then print **ExcelL1_C2_P2.xlsx**.

## Counting Numbers in a Range

Use the COUNT function to count the numeric values in a range. For example, in a range of cells containing cells with text and cells with numbers, you can count how many cells in the range contain numbers. In Project 2c, you will use the COUNT function to specify the number of students taking Test 2 and Test 3. In the worksheet, the cells containing the text N/A are not counted by the COUNT function.

Project **2c**   **Counting the Number of Students Taking Tests**

1. With **ExcelL1_C2_P2.xlsx** open, make cell A22 active.
2. Type **Test 2 Completed**.
3. Make cell B22 active.
4. Insert a formula counting the number of students who have taken Test 2 by completing the following steps:
   a. With cell B22 active, click in the Formula bar text box.
   b. Type **=C**.
   c. At the Formula AutoComplete list that displays, scroll down the list until *COUNT* displays and then double-click *COUNT*.
   d. Type **C4:C16)** and then press Enter.
5. Count the number of students who have taken Test 3 by completing the following steps:
   a. Make cell A23 active.
   b. Type **Test 3 Completed**.

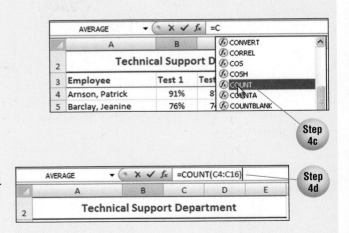

c. Make cell B23 active.

d. Click the Insert Function button on the Formula bar.

e. At the Insert Function dialog box, make sure *Statistical* is selected in the *Or select a category* list box.

f. Scroll down the list of functions in the *Select a function* list box until *COUNT* is visible and then double-click *COUNT*.

g. At the formula palette, type D4:D16 in the *Value1* text box, and then click OK.

6. Save and then print **ExcelL1_C2_P2.xlsx**.

7. Add test scores by completing the following steps:

a. Make cell B14 active and then type 68.

b. Make cell D14 active and then type 70.

c. Make cell D16 active and then type 55.

d. Press Enter.

8. Save and then print **ExcelL1_C2_P2.xlsx**.

## Displaying Formulas

In some situations, you may need to display the formulas in a worksheet rather than the results of the formula. You may want to turn on formulas for auditing purposes or check formulas for accuracy. Display all formulas in a worksheet rather than the results by pressing Ctrl + ` (this is the grave accent). Press Ctrl + ` to turn off the display of formulas.

Project **2d** **Displaying Formulas**

1. With **ExcelL1_C2_P2.xlsx** open, make cell A3 active.

2. Press Ctrl + ` to turn on the display of formulas.

3. Print the worksheet with the formulas.

4. Press Ctrl + ` to turn off the display of formulas.

5. Save and then close **ExcelL1_C2_P2.xlsx**.

 roject **3** **Insert Formulas with Financial and Date and Time Functions**

You will use the PMT financial function to calculate payments and the FV function to find the future value of an investment. You will also use the DATE function to return the serial number for a date and the NOW function to insert the current date and time as a serial number.

## Writing Formulas with Financial Functions

In this section, you will learn to write formulas with the financial functions PMT and FV. The PMT function calculates the payment for a loan based on constant payments and a constant interest rate. Use the FV function to return the future value of an investment based on periodic, constant payments and a constant interest rate.

## Finding the Periodic Payments for a Loan

*Rate = X%/12 (months)*

*Pv = amt borrowed as a Negative number*

*Fv = 0 (paid off)*

The PMT function finds the periodic payment for a loan based on constant payments and a constant interest rate. The PMT function contains the arguments Nper, Pv, Fv, and Type. The Nper argument is the number of payments that will be made to an investment or loan, Pv is the current value of amounts to be received or paid in the future, Fv is the value of a loan or investment at the end of all periods, and Type determines whether calculations will be based on payments made in arrears (at the end of each period) or in advance (at the beginning of each period).

## Project 3a    Calculating Payments

1. Open **ExcelC02Project03.xlsx**.
2. Save the workbook with Save As and name it **ExcelL1_C2_P3**.
3. The owner of Real Photography is interested in purchasing a new developer and needs to determine monthly payments on three different models. Insert a formula that calculates monthly payments and then copy that formula by completing the following steps:
   a. Make cell E5 active.
   b. Click the Formulas tab.
   c. Click the Financial button in the Function Library group, scroll down the drop-down list until *PMT* displays, and then click *PMT*.
   d. At the Function Arguments palette, type **C5/12** in the *Rate* text box. (This tells Excel to divide the interest rate by 12 months.)
   e. Press the Tab key. (This moves the insertion point to the *Nper* text box).
   f. Type **D5**. (This is the total number of months in the payment period.)
   g. Press the Tab key. (This moves the insertion point to the *Pv* text box.)
   h. Type **-B5**. (Excel displays the result of the PMT function as a negative number since the loan represents a negative cash flow to the borrower. Insert a minus sign before *B5* to show the monthly payment as a positive number rather than a negative number.)
   i. Click OK. (This closes the palette and inserts the monthly payment of *$316.98* in cell E7.)
   j. Copy the formula in cell E5 down to cells E6 and E7.
4. Insert a formula in cell F5 that calculates the total amount of the payments by completing the following steps:
   a. Make cell F5 active.
   b. Type **=E5*D5** and then press Enter.
   c. Make cell F5 active and then copy the formula down to cells F6 and F7.
5. Insert a formula in cell G5 that calculates the total amount of interest paid by completing the following steps:
   a. Make cell G5 active.
   b. Type **=F5-B5** and then press Enter.
   c. Make cell G5 active and then copy the formula down to cells G6 and G7.
6. Save **ExcelL1_C2_P3.xlsx**.

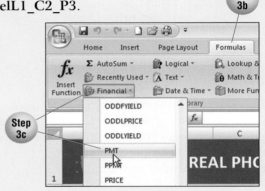

**Step 3b** / **Step 3c** / **Step 3d** / **Step 3f** / **Step 3h**

| | Rate | C5/12 | | = 0.007083333 |
| --- | --- | --- | --- | --- |
| | Nper | D5 | | = 60 |
| | Pv | -B5 | | = -15450 |
| | Fv | | | = number |
| | Type | | | = number |

| Monthly Payments | Total Payments | Total Interest |
| --- | --- | --- |
| $316.98 | $ 19,018.82 | $ 3,568.82 |
| $615.39 | $ 36,923.60 | $ 6,928.60 |
| $711.92 | $ 42,715.42 | $ 8,015.42 |

**Step 5c**

## Finding the Future Value of a Series of Payments

The FV function calculates the future value of a series of equal payments or an annuity. Use this function to determine information such as how much money can be earned in an investment account with a specific interest rate and over a specific period of time.

### Project 3b  Finding the Future Value of an Investment

1. Make sure **ExcelL1_C2_P3.xlsx** is open.
2. The owner of Real Photography has decided to save money to purchase a new developer and wants to compute how much money can be earned by investing the money in an investment account that returns 9% annual interest. The owner determines that $1,200 per month can be invested in the account for three years. Complete the following steps to determine the future value of the investment account by completing the following steps:
   a. Make cell B15 active.
   b. Click the Financial button in the Function Library group in the Formulas tab.
   c. At the drop-down list that displays, scroll down the list until *FV* is visible and then click *FV*.
   d. At the Function Arguments palette, type B12/12 in the *Rate* text box.
   e. Press the Tab key.
   f. Type B13 in the *Nper* text box.
   g. Press the Tab key.
   h. Type B14 in the *Pmt* text box.
   i. Click OK. (This closes the palette and also inserts the future value of $49,383.26 in cell B15.)
3. Save and then print **ExcelL1_C2_P3.xlsx**.
4. The owner decides to determine the future return after two years. To do this, change the amount in cell B13 from *36* to *24* and then press Enter. (This recalculates the future investment amount in cell B15.)
5. Save and then print **ExcelL1_C2_P3.xlsx**.

**Step 2d**

**Step 2f**

**Step 2h**

**Function Arguments**

FV

| | | |
|---|---|---|
| Rate | B12/12 | = 0.0075 |
| Nper | B13 | = 36 |
| Pmt | B14| | = -1200 |
| Pv | | = number |
| Type | | = number |

**Step 4**

| 10 | | |
|---|---|---|
| 11 | **Future Value of Investment** | |
| 12 | Rate | 9% |
| 13 | Number of Months | 24 |
| 14 | Monthly Payment | $ (1,200.00) |
| 15 | Future Value | $31,426.16 |
| 16 | | |

## Writing Formulas with Date and Time Functions

In this section, you will learn to write formulas with the date and time functions NOW and DATE. The NOW function returns the serial number of the current date and time. The DATE function returns the serial number that represents a particular date. Excel can make calculations using dates because the dates are represented as serial numbers. To calculate a date's serial number, Excel counts the days since the beginning of the twentieth century. The date serial number for January 1, 1900, is 1. The date serial number for January 1, 2000, is 36,526. To access the DATE and NOW functions, click the Date & Time button in the Function Library group in the Formulas tab.

**HINT**
Ctrl + ; is the keyboard shortcut to insert the current date in the active cell.

Date & Time ▾

1. Make sure **ExcelL1_C2_P3.xlsx** is open.
2. Certain cells in this worksheet establish overdue dates for Real Photography accounts. Enter a formula in cell D20 that returns the serial number for the date March 17, 2010, by completing the following steps:
   a. Make cell D20 active.
   b. Click the Formulas tab.
   c. Click the Date & Time button in the Function Library group.
   d. At the drop-down list that displays, click *DATE*.
   e. At the Function Arguments palette, type **2010** in the *Year* text box.
   f. Press the Tab key and then type **03** in the *Month* text box.
   g. Press the Tab key and then type **17** in the *Day* text box.
   h. Click OK.

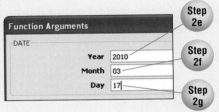

3. Complete steps similar to those in Step 2 to enter the following dates as serial numbers in the specified cells:

    D21 = March 24, 2010
    D22 = March 31, 2010
    D23 = April 7, 2010

4. Enter a formula in cell F20 that inserts the due date (the purchase date plus the number of days in the *Terms* column) by completing the following steps:
   a. Make cell F20 active.
   b. Type **=D20+E20** and then press Enter.
   c. Make cell F20 active and then copy the formula down to cells F21, F22, and F23.

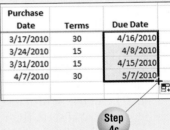

5. Make cell A26 active and then type your name.
6. Insert the current date and time as a serial number by completing the following steps:
   a. Make cell A27 active.
   b. Click the Date & Time button in the Function Library group in the Formulas tab and then click *NOW* at the drop-down list.
   c. At the Function Arguments palette telling you that the function takes no argument, click OK.
7. Save, print, and then close **ExcelL1_C2_P3.xlsx**.

# Project 4 Insert Formulas with the IF Logical Function

**You will use the IF logical function to calculate sales bonuses, determine letter grades based on test averages, and identify discounts and discount amounts.**

## Writing a Formula with the IF Logical Function

The IF function is considered a *conditional function*. With the IF function you can perform conditional tests on values and formulas. A question that can be answered with true or false is considered a *logical test*. The IF function makes a logical test and then performs a particular action if the answer is true and another action if the answer is false.

For example, an IF function can be used to write a formula that calculates a salesperson's bonus as 10% if the quota of $100,000 is met or exceeded, and zero if the quota is less than $100,000. That formula would look like this: *=IF(quota=>100000,quota\*0.1,0)*. The formula contains three parts—the condition or logical test *IF(quota=>100000)*, action taken if the condition or logical test is true *(quota\*0.1)*, and the action taken if the condition or logical test is false *(0)*. Commas separate the condition and the actions. In the bonus formula, if the quota is equal to or greater than $100,000, then the quota is multiplied by 10%. If the quota is less than $100,000, then the bonus is zero.

In Project 4a, you will write a formula with cell references rather than cell data. The formula in Project 4a is *=IF(C5>B5,C5\*0.15,0)*. In this formula the condition or logical test is whether or not the number in cell C5 is greater than the number in cell B5. If the condition is true and the number is greater, then the number in cell C5 is multiplied by 0.15 (providing a 15% bonus). If the condition is false and the number in cell C5 is less than the number in cell B5, then nothing happens (no bonus). Notice how commas are used to separate the logical test from the actions.

## Editing a Formula

Edit a formula by making active the cell containing the formula and then editing the formula in the cell or in the Formula bar text box. After editing the formula, press Enter or click the Enter button on the Formula bar and Excel will recalculate the result of the formula.

Enter

## Project 4a  Writing a Formula with an IF Function and Editing the Formula

1. Open **ExcelC02Project04.xlsx**.
2. Save the workbook with Save As and name it **ExcelL1_C2_P4**.
3. Write a formula with the IF function by completing the following steps. (The formula will determine if the quota has been met and, if it has, will insert the bonus [15% of the actual sales]. If the quota has not been met, the formula will insert a zero.)
   a. Make cell D5 active.
   b. Type **=IF(C5>B5,C5\*0.15,0)** and then press Enter.
   c. Make cell D5 active and then use the fill handle to copy the formula to cells D6 through D10.
4. Print the worksheet.
5. Revise the formula so it will insert a 25% bonus if the quota has been met by completing the following steps:
   a. Make cell D5 active.
   b. Click in the Formula bar, edit the formula so it displays as **=IF(C5>B5,C5\*0.25,0)**, and then click the Enter button on the Formula bar.
   c. Copy the formula down to cells D6 through D10.
6. Save and then print **ExcelL1_C2_P4.xlsx**.

| partment | | |
|---|---|---|
| **Actual Sales** | | **Bonus** |
| $ 103,295.00 | $ | 15,494.25 |
| $ 129,890.00 | $ | - |
| $ 133,255.00 | $ | 19,988.25 |
| $ 94,350.00 | $ | 14,152.50 |
| $ 167,410.00 | $ | 25,111.50 |
| $ 109,980.00 | $ | - |

Step 3c

Step 5b

=IF(C5>B5,C5*0.25,0)

| | Bonus |
|---|---|
| $ | 25,823.75 |
| $ | - |
| $ | 33,313.75 |
| $ | 23,587.50 |
| $ | 41,852.50 |
| $ | - |

Step 5c

| NOW | | | =IF(C5>B5,C5*0.25,0) |
|---|---|---|---|
| | A | B | IF(logical_test, [value_if_true], [v |

### Capstan Marine Produ

| | | | | |
|---|---|---|---|---|
| 1 | | | | |
| 2 | | | | |
| 3 | | Sales Department | | |
| 4 | Salesperson | Quota | Actual Sales | Bonus |
| 5 | Allejandro | $ 95,500.00 | $ 103,295.00 | :5>B5,C5*0.25,0 |
| 6 | Crispin | $ 137,000.00 | $ 129,890.00 | $ - |

## Writing a Nested IF Condition

In Project 4a, the IF function had only two possible actions—the actual sales times 15% or a zero. In a formula where more than two actions are required, use nested IF functions. For example, in Project 4b, you will write a formula with IF conditions that has four possible actions—a letter grade of A, B, C, or D. When writing nested IF conditions, insert symbols such as commas, quotation marks, and parentheses in the proper locations. If you want an IF condition to insert text, insert quotation marks before and after the text. The formula you will be writing in Project 4b is shown below.

$$=IF(E16>89,"A",IF(E16>79,"B",IF(E16>69,"C",IF(E16>59, "D"))))$$

This formula begins with the condition *=IF(E16>89, "A",*. If the number in cell E16 is greater than 89, then the condition is met and the grade of A is returned. The formula continues with a nested condition, *IF(E16>79, "B",*. If the number in cell E16 does not meet the first condition (greater than 89), then Excel looks to the next condition—is the number in cell E16 greater than 79? If it is, then the grade of B is inserted in cell E16. The formula continues with another nested condition, *IF(E16>69, "C",*. If the number in cell E16 does not match the first condition, Excel looks to the second condition, and if that condition is not met, then Excel looks to the third condition. If the number in cell E16 is greater than 69, then the grade of C is inserted in cell E16. The final nested condition is *IF(E16>59, "D"*. If the first three conditions are not met but this one is, then the grade of D is inserted in cell E16. The four parentheses at the end of the formula end each condition in the formula.

## Project 4b — Writing a Formula with Nested IF Conditions

1. With **ExcelL1_C2_P4.xlsx** open, insert a formula to average the scores by completing the following steps:
   a. Make cell E16 active.
   b. Type **=AVERAGE(B16:D16)** and then press Enter.
   c. Make cell E16 active and then copy the formula down to cells E17 through E20.
2. Insert a formula with nested IF conditions by completing the following steps:
   a. Make cell F16 active.
   b. Type **=IF(E16>89,"A",IF(E16>79,"B",IF(E16>69,"C",IF(E16>59,"D"))))** and then press Enter.

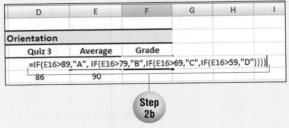

Step 2b

c. Make cell F16 active and then use the fill handle to copy the formula down to cells F17 through F20.

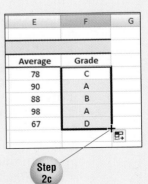

Step 2c

3. Save **ExcelL1_C2_P4.xlsx**.

As you typed the formula with nested IF conditions in Step 2b of Project 4b, did you notice that the parentheses were different colors? Each color represents a condition. The four right parentheses at the end of the formula ended each of the conditions and each matched in color a left parenthesis. If an average in column E in **ExcelL1_C2_P4.xlsx** is less than 59, the nested formula inserts *FALSE* in the cell. If you want the formula to insert a letter grade, such as *F*, instead of *FALSE*, include another nested IF condition in the formula. Up to 64 levels of functions can be nested.

You can use the IF function from the Logical button drop-down list in the Function Library in the Formulas tab to write an IF statement. The IF statement you write using the IF function from the Logical button checks whether a condition is met and returns one value if the condition is met and another if the condition is not met. For example, in Project 4c you will insert an IF statement that identifies whether or not a part receives a discount. Parts that sell for more than $499 receive a discount and parts that sell for less do not. If the condition is met (the amount is greater than $499), then the statement will return a *YES* and if the condition is not met, the statement will return a *NO*.

In Project 4c, you will type the second IF statement in the cell rather than using the IF function from the Logical button drop-down list. The IF statement you write will reduce the price by five percent for parts that sell from $500 up to $749, seven percent for parts that sell from $750 up to $999, and ten percent for parts that sell for at least $1,000.

Project ④c    **Writing IF Statements Identifying Discounts and Discount Amounts**

1. With **ExcelL1_C2_P4.xlsx** open, insert an IF statement by completing the following steps:
   a. Make cell C26 active.
   b. Click the Logical button in the Function Library group in the Formulas tab and then click IF at the drop-down list.
   c. At the Function Arguments palette, type **B26>499** in the *Logic_test* text box.
   d. Press the Tab key to move the insertion point to the *Value_if_true* text box and then type **YES**.
   e. Press the Tab key to move the insertion point to the *Value_if_false* text box and then type **NO**.
   f. Click OK to close the Function Arguments palette.
2. Copy the formula in cell C26 down to cells C27 through C38.
3. Make cell D26 active.
4. Insert the following IF statement in the cell:
   =IF(B26>999,B26*0.1,IF(B26>749,B26*0.07,IF(B26>499,B26*0.05,IF(B26>0,"N/A"))))
5. Copy the formula in cell D26 down to cells D27 through D38.
6. Save, print, and then close **ExcelL1_C2_P4.xlsx**.

Step 1c     Step 1d

Function Arguments

IF

| Logical_test | B26>499 | | = TRUE |
| Value_if_true | "YES" | | = "YES" |
| Value_if_false | NO | | = |

Step 1e

# Project 5 — Insert Formulas Using Absolute and Mixed Cell References

You will insert a formula containing an absolute cell reference that determines the effect on earnings with specific increases, insert a formula with multiple absolute cell references that determine the weighted average of scores, and use mixed cell references to determine simple interest.

## Using Absolute and Mixed Cell References in Formulas

A reference identifies a cell or a range of cells in a worksheet and can be relative, absolute, or mixed. Relative cell references refer to cells relative to a position in a formula. Absolute references refer to cells in a specific location. When a formula is copied, a relative cell reference adjusts while an absolute cell reference remains constant. A mixed cell reference does both—either the column remains absolute and the row is relative or the column is relative and the row is absolute. Distinguish between relative, absolute, and mixed cell references using the dollar sign ($). Type a dollar sign before the column and/or row cell reference in a formula to specify that the column or row is an absolute cell reference.

## Using an Absolute Cell Reference in a Formula

In this chapter you have learned to copy a relative formula. For example, if the formula =SUM(A2:C2) in cell D2 is copied relatively to cell D3, the formula changes to =SUM(A3:C3). In some situations, you may want a formula to contain an absolute cell reference, which always refers to a cell in a specific location. In Project 5a, you will add a column for projected job earnings and then perform "what if" situations using a formula with an absolute cell reference. To identify an absolute cell reference, insert a $ symbol before the row and the column. For example, the absolute cell reference C12 would be typed as $C$12 in a formula.

## Project 5a — Inserting and Copying a Formula with an Absolute Cell Reference

1. Open **ExcelC02Project05.xlsx**.
2. Save the workbook with Save As and name it **ExcelL1_C2_P5**.
3. Determine the effect on actual job earnings with a 20% increase by completing the following steps:
   a. Make cell C3 active, type the formula =B3*$B$12, and then press Enter.
   b. Make cell C3 active and then use the fill handle to copy the formula to cells C4 through C10.
4. Save and then print **ExcelL1_C2_P5.xlsx**.

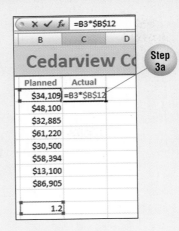

Step 3a

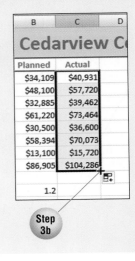

Step 3b

5. With the worksheet still open, determine the effect on actual job earnings with a 10% decrease by completing the following steps:
   a. Make cell B12 active.
   b. Type **0.9** and then press Enter.
6. Save and then print the **ExcelL1_C2_P5.xlsx**.
7. Determine the effects on actual job earnings with a 10% increase. (To do this, type **1.1** in cell B12.)
8. Save and then print **ExcelL1_C2_P5.xlsx**.

| | $f_x$ | |
|---|---|---|
| | **B** | **C** |
| | **Cedarview** | |
| | Planned | Actual |
| | $34,109 | $30,698 |
| | $48,100 | $43,290 |
| | $32,885 | $29,597 |
| | $61,220 | $55,098 |
| | $30,500 | $27,450 |
| | $58,394 | $52,555 |
| | $13,100 | $11,790 |
| | $86,905 | $78,215 |
| | | |
| | 0.9 | |

Step 5b

In Project 5a, you created a formula with one absolute cell reference. You can also create a formula with multiple absolute cell references. For example, in Project 5b you will create a formula that contains both relative and absolute cell references to determine the average of training scores based on specific weight percentages.

## Project 5b  Inserting and Copying a Formula with Multiple Absolute Cell References

1. With **ExcelL1_C2_P5.xlsx** open, insert the following formulas:
   a. Insert a formula in cell B23 that averages the percentages in cells B17 through B22.
   b. Copy the formula in cell B23 to the right to cells C23 and D23.
2. Insert a formula that determines the weighted average of training scores by completing the following steps:
   a. Make cell E17 active.
   b. Type the following formula:
      =$B$24*B17+$C$24*C17+$D$24*D17
   c. Press the Enter key.
   d. Copy the formula in cell E17 down to cells E18 through E22.
3. Save and then print the **ExcelL1_C2_P5.xlsx**.
4. With the worksheet still open, determine the effect on weighted training scores if the weighted values change by completing the following steps:
   a. Make cell B24 active, type **30**, and then press Enter.
   b. Make cell D24 active, type **40**, and then press Enter.
5. Save and then print **ExcelL1_C2_P5.xlsx**.

| 15 | | Employee Training | | | |
|---|---|---|---|---|---|
| 16 | Name | Plumbing | Electrical | Carpentry | Weighted Average |
| 17 | Allesandro | 76% | 80% | 84% | 89% |
| 18 | Ellington | 66% | 72% | 64% | 73% |
| 19 | Goodman | 90% | 88% | 94% | 100% |
| 20 | Huntington | 76% | 82% | 88% | 91% |
| 21 | Kaplan-Downing | 90% | 84% | 92% | 98% |
| 22 | Larimore | 58% | 62% | 60% | 66% |
| 23 | Training Averages | 76% | 78% | 80% | |
| 24 | Training Weights | 30% | 30% | 50% | |
| 25 | | | | | |

Step 4a

# Using a Mixed Cell Reference in a Formula

The formula you created in Step 3a in Project 5a contained a relative cell reference (B3) and an absolute cell reference ($B$12). A formula can also contain a mixed cell reference. In a mixed cell reference either the column remains absolute and the row is relative or the column is relative and the row is absolute. In Project 5c you will insert a number of formulas, two of which will contain mixed cell references. You will insert the formula =E29*E$26 to calculate withholding tax and =E29*H$36 to calculate Social Security tax. The dollar sign before the rows indicates that the row is an absolute cell reference.

Project **5c** **Determining Payroll Using Formulas with Absolute and Mixed Cell References**

1. With **ExcelL1_C2_P5.xlsx** open, make cell E29 active and then insert the following formula containing mixed cell references:
    =(B29*C29+(B29*$B$36*D29))
2. Copy the formula in cell E29 down to cells E30 through E34.
3. Make cell F29 active and then insert the following formula that calculates the amount of withholding tax:
    =E29*E$36
4. Copy the formula in cell F29 down to cells F30 through F34.
5. Make cell G29 active and then insert the following formula that calculates the amount of Social Security tax:
    =E29*H$36
6. Copy the formula in cell G29 down to cells G30 through G34.
7. Make cell H29 active and then insert the following formula that calculates net pay:
    =E29-(F29+G29)
8. Copy the formula in cell H29 down to cells H30 through H34.
9. Save **ExcelL1_C2_P5.xlsx**.

As you learned in Project 5c, a formula can contain a mixed cell reference. In a mixed cell reference either the column remains absolute and the row is relative or the column is relative and the row is absolute. In Project 5d, you will create the formula =$A41*B$40. In the first cell reference in the formula, $A41, the column is absolute and the row is relative. In the second cell reference, B$40, the column is relative and the row is absolute. The formula containing the mixed cell references allows you to fill in the column and row data using only one formula.

Identify an absolute or mixed cell reference by typing a dollar sign before the column and/or row reference or press the F4 function key to cycle through the various cell references. For example, type =A41 in a cell, press F4, and the cell reference changes to =$A$41. Press F4 again and the cell reference changes to =A$41. The next time you press F4, the cell reference changes to =$A41 and press it again to change the cell reference back to =A41.

1. With **ExcelL1_C2_P5.xlsx** open, make cell B41 the active cell and then insert a formula containing mixed cell references by completing the following steps:
   a. Type =A41 and then press the F4 function key three times. (This changes the cell reference to *$A41*.)
   b. Type *B40 and then press the F4 function key twice. (This changes the cell reference to *B$40*.)
   c. Make sure the formula displays as =*$A41*B$40* and then press Enter.

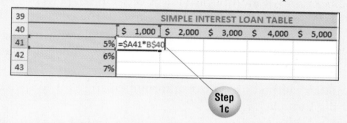

Step 1c

2. Copy the formula to the right by completing the following steps:
   a. Make cell B41 active and then use the fill handle to copy the formula right to cell F41.

| 39 | | SIMPLE INTEREST LOAN TABLE | | | | | |
|---|---|---|---|---|---|---|---|
| 40 | | $ 1,000 | $ 2,000 | $ 3,000 | $ 4,000 | $ 5,000 | |
| 41 | 5% | $ 50 | $ 100 | $ 150 | $ 200 | $ 250 | |
| 42 | 6% | | | | | | |
| 43 | 7% | | | | | | |

Step 2a

   b. With cells B41 through F41 selected, use the fill handle to copy the formula down to cell F51.

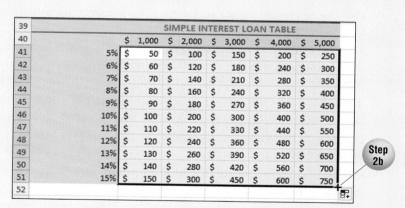

Step 2b

3. Save, print, and then close **ExcelL1_C2_P5.xlsx**. (This worksheet will print on two pages.)

# CHAPTER summary

- Type a formula in a cell and the formula displays in the cell as well as in the Formula bar. If cell entries are changed, a formula will automatically recalculate the values and insert the result in the cell.

- Create your own formula with commonly used operators such as addition (+), subtraction (-), multiplication (*), division (/), percent (%), and exponentiation (^). When writing a formula, begin with the equals (=) sign.

- Copy a formula to other cells in a row or column with the Fill button in the Editing group in the Home tab or with the fill handle that displays in the bottom right corner of the active cell.

- Another method for writing a formula is to point to specific cells that are part of the formula.

- If Excel detects an error in a formula, a Trace Error button appears and a dark green triangle displays in the upper left corner of the cell containing the formula.

- Excel includes over 200 functions that are divided into eleven categories. Use the Insert Function feature to create formulas using built-in functions.

- A function operates on an argument, which may consist of a cell reference, a constant, or another function. When a value calculated by a formula is inserted in a cell, this is referred to as returning the result.

- The AVERAGE function returns the average (arithmetic mean) of the arguments. The MAX function returns the largest value in a set of values, and the MIN function returns the smallest value in a set of values. The COUNT function counts the number of cells containing numbers within the list of arguments.

- Use the keyboard shortcut, Ctrl + ` (grave accent) to turn on the display of formulas in a worksheet.

- The PMT function calculates the payment for a loan based on constant payments and a constant interest rate. The FV function returns the future value of an investment based on periodic, constant payments and a constant interest rate.

- The NOW function returns the serial number of the current date and time and the DATE function returns the serial number that represents a particular date.

- Use the IF function, considered a conditional function, to perform conditional tests on values and formulas.

- Use nested IF functions in a formula where more than two actions are required.

- A reference identifies a cell or a range of cells in a worksheet and can be relative, absolute, or mixed. Identify an absolute cell reference by inserting a $ symbol before the column and row. Cycle through the various cell reference options by typing the cell reference and then pressing F4.

# COMMANDS review

| FEATURE | RIBBON TAB, GROUP | BUTTON | KEYBOARD SHORTCUT |
|---|---|---|---|
| SUM function | Home, Editing OR Formulas, Function Library | Σ AutoSum ▾ | Alt + = |
| Insert Function dialog box | Formulas, Function Library | *fx* | Shift + F3 |
| Display formulas | | | Ctrl + ` |

# CONCEPTS check
## Test Your Knowledge

**Completion:** In the space provided at the right, indicate the correct term, symbol, or command.

1. When typing a formula, begin the formula with this sign. _____

2. This is the operator for division that is used when writing a formula. _____

3. This is the operator for multiplication that is used when writing a formula. _____

4. This is the name of the small black box located at the bottom right corner of a cell that can be used to copy a formula to adjacent cells. _____

5. A function operates on this, which may consist of a constant, a cell reference, or other function. _____

6. This function returns the largest value in a set of values. _____

7. This is the keyboard shortcut to display formulas in a worksheet. _____

8. This function finds the periodic payment for a loan based on constant payments and a constant interest rate. _____

9. This function returns the serial number of the current date and time. _____

10. This function is considered a conditional function. _____

11. To identify an absolute cell reference, type this symbol before the column and row.

_____

12. Suppose that cell B2 contains the budgeted amount and cell C2 contains the actual amount. Write the formula (including the IF conditions) that would insert the word *under* if the actual amount was less than the budgeted amount and insert the word *over* if the actual amount was greater than the budgeted amount.

_____

# SKILLS check
## *Demonstrate Your Proficiency*

## Assessment

### 1 INSERT AVERAGE, MAX, AND MIN FUNCTIONS

1. Open **ExcelC02Assessment01.xlsx**.
2. Save the workbook with Save As and name it **ExcelL1_C2_A1**.
3. Use the AVERAGE function to determine the monthly sales (cells H4 through H9).
4. Total each monthly column including the Average column (cells B10 through H10).
5. Use the MAX function to determine the highest monthly total (for cells B4 through G9) and insert the amount in cell B11.
6. Use the MIN function to determine the lowest monthly total (for cells B4 through G9) and insert the amount in cell B12.
7. Save, print, and then close **ExcelL1_C2_A1.xlsx**.

## Assessment

### 2 INSERT PMT FUNCTION

1. Open **ExcelC02Assessment02.xlsx**.
2. Save the workbook with Save As and name it **ExcelL1_C2_A2**.
3. The manager of Clearline Manufacturing is interested in refinancing a loan for either $125,000 or $300,000 and wants to determine the monthly payments, total payments, and total interest paid. Insert a formula with the following specifications:
   a. Make cell E5 active.
   b. Use the Insert Function button on the Formula bar to insert a formula using the PMT function. At the formula palette, enter the following:
      Rate =   C5/12
      Nper=   D5
      Pv   =   -B5
   c. Copy the formula in cell E5 down to cells E6 through E8.
4. Insert a formula in cell F5 that multiplies the amount in E5 by the amount in D5.

5. Copy the formula in cell F5 down to cells F6 through F8.
6. Insert a formula in cell G5 that subtracts the amount in B5 from the amount in F5. (The formula is =F5-B5.)
7. Copy the formula in cell G5 down to cells G6 through G8.
8. Save, print, and then close **ExcelL1_C2_A2.xlsx**.

## Assessment

# 3  INSERT FV FUNCTION

1. Open **ExcelC02Assessment03.xlsx**.
2. Save the workbook with Save As and name it **ExcelL1_C2_A3**.
3. Make the following changes to the worksheet:
   a. Change the percentage in cell B3 from *9%* to *10%*.
   b. Change the number in cell B4 from *36* to *60*.
   c. Change the amount in cell B5 from *($1,200)* to *-500*.
   d. Use the FV function to insert a formula that calculates the future value of the investment. ***Hint: For help with the formula, refer to Project 3b.***
4. Save, print, and then close **ExcelL1_C2_A3.xlsx**.

## Assessment

# 4  WRITE IF STATEMENT FORMULAS

1. Open **ExcelC02Assessment04.xlsx**.
2. Save the workbook with Save As and name it **ExcelL1_C2_A4**.
3. Insert a formula in cell C4 that contains an IF statement with the following details:

   If the contents of cell B4 are greater than 150000, then insert the word Platinum.
   If the contents of cell B4 are greater than 100000, then insert the word Gold.
   If the contents of cell B4 are greater than 75000, then insert the word Silver.
   If the contents of cell B4 are greater than 0 (zero), then insert the word Bronze.

   When writing the IF statement, make sure you insert quotes around the words *Platinum*, *Gold*, *Silver*, and *Bronze*. Copy the formula in cell C4 down to cell C14.
4. Insert a formula in cell D4 that contains in IF statement with the following details:

   If the content of cell C4 is Bronze, then insert the word None.
   If the content of cell C4 is Silver, then insert $3,000.
   If the content of cell C4 is Gold, then insert $5,000.
   If the content of cell C4 is Platinum, then insert $10,000.

   When writing the IF statement, you will need to insert quotes around the words *Platinum*, *Gold*, *Silver*, *Bronze*, and *None* as well as the amounts *$3,000*, *$5,000*, and *$10,000*. Copy the formula in cell D4 down to cell D14.
5. Save and then print **ExcelL1_C2_A4.xlsx**.

6. Display the formulas in the worksheet.
7. Print **ExcelL1_C2_A4.xlsx**.
8. Turn off the display of the formulas.
9. Save and then close **ExcelL1_C2_A4.xlsx**.

## Assessment

## 5 WRITE FORMULAS WITH ABSOLUTE CELL REFERENCES

1. Open **ExcelC02Assessment05.xlsx**.
2. Save the workbook with Save As and name it **ExcelL1_C2_A5**.
3. Make the following changes to the worksheet:
   a. Insert a formula using an absolute reference to determine the projected quotas at 10% of the current quotas.
   b. Save and then print **ExcelL1_C2_A5.xlsx**.
   c. Determine the projected quotas at 15% of the current quota by changing cell A15 to *15% Increase* and cell B15 to *1.15*.
   d. Save and then print **ExcelL1_C2_A5.xlsx**.
   e. Determine the projected quotas at 20% of the current quota.
4. Save, print, and then close **ExcelL1_C2_A5.xlsx**.

## Assessment

## 6 USE HELP TO LEARN ABOUT EXCEL OPTIONS

1. Learn about specific options in the Excel Options dialog box by completing the following steps:
   a. Display the Excel Options dialog box by clicking the Office button and then clicking the Excel Options button that displays in the lower right corner of the drop-down list.
   b. At the Excel Options dialog box, click the *Advanced* option located in the left panel.
   c. Click the Help button that displays in the upper right corner of the dialog box, read the information that displays about advanced features, and then close the Excel Help window.
   d. Write down the check box options available in the *Display options for this workbook* section and the *Display options for this worksheet* section of the dialog box and identify whether or not the check box contains a check mark. (Record only check box options and ignore buttons and options preceded by circles.)
2. With the information you wrote down about the options, create an Excel spreadsheet with the following information:
   a. In column C, type each option you wrote down. (Include an appropriate heading.)
   b. In column B, insert an X in the cell that precedes any option that contains a check mark in the check box. (Include an appropriate heading.)
   c. In column A, write a formula with the IF function that inserts the word ON in the cell if the cell in column B contains an X and inserts the word OFF if it does not (the cell is blank). (Include an appropriate heading.)
   d. Apply formatting to improve the visual appeal of the worksheet.

3. Save the workbook and name it **ExcelL1_C2_A6**.
4. Turn on the display of formulas.
5. Print the worksheet.
6. Turn off the display of formulas.
7. Save, print, and then close **ExcelL1_C2_A6.xlsx**.

# CASE study

## *Apply Your Skills*

**Part 1**

You are a loan officer for Dollar Wise Financial Services and work in the department that specializes in home loans. You have decided to prepare a sample home mortgage worksheet to show prospective clients. This sample home mortgage worksheet will show the monthly payments on variously priced homes with varying interest rates. Open the **DollarWise.xlsx** worksheet and then complete the home mortgage worksheet by inserting the following formulas:

- Since many homes in your area sell for at least $400,000, you decide to add that amount to the worksheet with a 5%, 10%, 15%, and 20% down payment.
- In column C, insert a formula that determines the down payment amount.
- In column D, insert a formula that determines the loan amount.
- In column G, insert a formula using the PMT function (the monthly payment will display as a negative number).

Save the worksheet and name it **ExcelL1_C2_CS_P1**.

**Part 2**

If home buyers put down less than twenty percent of the home's purchase price, mortgage insurance is required. With **ExcelL1_C2_C1.xlsx** open, insert an IF statement in the cells in column H that inserts the word "No" if the percentage in column B is equal to or greater than 20% or inserts the word "Yes" if the percentage in column B is less than 20%. Save and then print **ExcelL1_C2_CS_P1.xlsx**.

**Part 3**

Interest rates fluctuate on a regular basis. Using the resources available to you, determine a current interest rate in your area. Delete the interest rate of 7% in the Dollar Wise worksheet and insert the interest rate for your area. Save and then print **ExcelL1_C2_CS_P1.xlsx**.

**Part**

**4**

When a client is required to purchase mortgage insurance, you would like to provide information to the client concerning this insurance. Use the Help feature to learn about creating hyperlinks in Excel. Locate a helpful Web site that specializes in private mortgage insurance. Create a hyperlink in the worksheet that will display the Web site. Save, print, and then close **ExcelL1_C2_CS_P1.xlsx**.

**Part**

**5**

Once a loan has been approved and finalized, a letter is sent to the client explaining the details of the loan. Use a letter template in Word to create a letter that is sent to the client. Copy and link the information in the **ExcelL1_C2_CS_P1.xlsx** worksheet to the client letter. Save the letter document and name it **WordDollarWiseLetter**. Print and then close **WordDollarWiseLetter.docx**.

# CHAPTER 3

# Formatting an Excel Worksheet

## PERFORMANCE OBJECTIVES

**Upon successful completion of Chapter 3, you will be able to:**

- Change column widths
- Change row heights
- Insert rows and columns in a worksheet
- Delete cells, rows, and columns in a worksheet
- Clear data in cells
- Apply formatting to data in cells
- Apply formatting to selected data using the Mini toolbar
- Preview a worksheet
- Apply a theme and customize the theme font and color
- Format numbers
- Repeat the last action
- Automate formatting with Format Painter
- Hide and unhide rows and columns

excel Chapter 3

Tutorial 3.1
Working with Excel
Tutorial 3.2
Enhancing the Appearance of a
Worksheet

The appearance of a worksheet on the screen and how it looks when printed is called the *format*. In Chapter 1, you learned how to apply formatting to a table with the Format as Table button in the Styles group in the Home tab and apply formatting to a cell or selected cells with the Cell Styles button. Other types of formatting you may want to apply to a worksheet include changing column width and row height; applying character formatting such as bold, italics, and underlining; specifying number formatting; inserting and deleting rows and columns; and applying borders, shading, and patterns to cells. You can also apply formatting to a worksheet with a theme. A theme is a set of formatting choices that include colors and fonts.

*Note: Before beginning computer projects, copy to your storage medium the Excel2007L1C3 subfolder from the Excel2007L1 folder on the CD that accompanies this textbook and then make Excel2007L1C3 the active folder.*

# Project ① Format a Product Pricing Worksheet

**You will open a workbook containing a worksheet with product pricing data, and then format the worksheet by changing column widths and row heights, inserting and deleting rows and columns, deleting rows and columns, and clearing data in cells. You will also apply font and alignment formatting to data in cells and then preview the worksheet.**

## Changing Column Width

Columns in a worksheet are the same width by default. In some worksheets you may want to change column widths to accommodate more or less data. You can change column width using the mouse on column boundaries or at a dialog box.

### Changing Column Width Using Column Boundaries

You can use the mouse to change the width of a column or selected columns. For example, to change the width of column B, you would position the mouse pointer on the blue boundary line between columns B and C in the column header until the mouse pointer turns into a double-headed arrow pointing left and right and then drag the boundary to the right to increase the size or to the left to decrease the size.

You can change the width of selected adjacent columns at the same time. To do this, select the columns and then drag one of the column boundaries within the selected columns. As you drag the boundary the column width changes for all selected columns. To select adjacent columns, position the cell pointer on the first desired column header (the mouse pointer turns into a black, down-pointing arrow), hold down the left mouse button, drag the cell pointer to the last desired column header, and then release the mouse button.

As a column boundary is being dragged, the column width displays in a box above the mouse pointer. The column width number that displays represents the average number of characters in the standard font that can fit in a cell.

A column width in an existing worksheet can be adjusted to fit the longest entry in the column. To automatically adjust a column width to the longest entry, position the cell pointer on the column boundary at the right side of the column and then double-click the left mouse button.

**HINT**
To change the width of all columns in a worksheet, click the Select All button and then drag a column boundary to the desired position.

## Project ①a  Changing Column Width Using a Column Boundary

1. Open **ExcelC03Project01.xlsx**.
2. Save the workbook with Save As and name it **ExcelL1_C3_P1**.
3. Insert a formula in cell D2 that multiplies the price in cell B2 with the number in cell C2. Copy the formula in cell D2 down to cells D3 through D14.

4. Change the width of column D by completing the following steps:
   a. Position the mouse pointer on the column boundary in the column header between columns D and E until it turns into a double-headed arrow pointing left and right.
   b. Hold down the left mouse button, drag the column boundary to the right until *Width: 11.00 (82 pixels)* displays in the box, and then release the mouse button.

| D16 | | | fx | Width: 11.00 (82 pixels) | |
|---|---|---|---|---|---|
| | A | B | C | D | E | F |
| 1 | Product # | Price | Number | Total | | |
| 2 | 240-490-B | $ 85.75 | 7 | $ 600.25 | | |

**Step 4b**

5. Make cell D15 active and then insert the sum of cells D2 through D14.
6. Change the width of columns A and B by completing the following steps:
   a. Select columns A and B. To do this, position the cell pointer on the column A header, hold down the left mouse button, drag the cell pointer to the column B header, and then release the mouse button.
   b. Position the cell pointer on the column boundary between columns A and B until it turns into a double-headed arrow pointing left and right.
   c. Hold down the left mouse button, drag the column boundary to the right until *Width: 10.14 (76 pixels)* displays in the box, and then release the mouse button.

| A1 | Width: 10.14 (76 pixels) | fx | Product # |
|---|---|---|---|
| | A | B | C | D |
| 1 | Product # | Price | Number | Total |
| 2 | 240-490-B | $ 85.75 | 7 | $ 600.25 |
| 3 | 1203-3422 | $ 20.99 | 15 | $ 314.85 |

**Step 6c**

7. Adjust the width of column C to accommodate the longest entry in the column by completing the following steps:
   a. Position the cell pointer on the column boundary between columns C and D until it turns into a double-headed arrow pointing left and right.
   b. Double-click the left mouse button.
8. Save **ExcelL1_C3_P1.xlsx**.

# Changing Column Width at the Column Width Dialog Box

At the Column Width dialog box shown in Figure 3.1, you can specify a column width number. Increase the column width number to make the column wider or decrease the column width number to make the column narrower.

To display the Column Width dialog box, click the Format button in the Cells group in the Home tab and then click *Column Width* at the drop-down list. At the Column Width dialog box, type the number representing the average number of characters in the standard font that you want to fit in the column, and then press Enter or click OK.

**Figure 3.1** Column Width Dialog Box

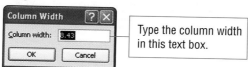

Type the column width in this text box.

**QUICK STEPS**

**Change Column Width**
Drag column boundary line.
OR
Double-click column boundary.
OR
1. Click Format button.
2. Click *Column Width* at drop-down list.
3. Type desired width.
4. Click OK.

Format

1. With **ExcelL1_C3_P1.xlsx** open, change the width of column A by completing the following steps:
   a. Make any cell in column A active.
   b. Click the Format button in the Cells group in the Home tab and then click *Column Width* at the drop-down list.
   c. At the Column Width dialog box, type 12.75 in the *Column width* text box.
   d. Click OK to close the dialog box.
2. Make any cell in column B active and then change the width of column B to *12.75* by completing steps similar to those in Step 1.
3. Make any cell in column C active and then change the width of column C to *8* by completing steps similar to those in Step 1.
4. Save **ExcelL1_C3_P1.xlsx**.

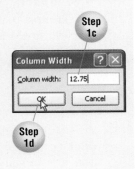

Step 1c

Step 1d

**QUICK STEPS**

## Changing Row Height

**Change Row Height**
Drag row boundary line.
OR
1. Click Format button.
2. Click *Row Height* at drop-down list.
3. Type desired height.
4. Click OK.

Row height can be changed in much the same manner as column width. For example, you can change the row height using the mouse on a row boundary, or at the Row Height dialog box. Change row height using a row boundary in the same manner as you learned to change column width. To do this, position the cell pointer on the boundary between rows in the row header until it turns into a double-headed arrow pointing up and down, hold down the left mouse button, drag up or down until the row is the desired height, and then release the mouse button.

The height of selected rows that are adjacent can be changed at the same time. (The height of nonadjacent rows will not all change at the same time.) To do this, select the rows and then drag one of the row boundaries within the selected rows. As the boundary is being dragged the row height changes for all selected rows.

As a row boundary is being dragged, the row height displays in a box above the mouse pointer. The row height number that displays represents a point measurement. A vertical inch contains approximately 72 points. Increase the point size to increase the row height; decrease the point size to decrease the row height.

At the Row Height dialog box shown in Figure 3.2, you can specify a row height number. To display the Row Height dialog box, click the Format button in the Cells group in the Home tab and then click *Row Height* at the drop-down list.

**HINT**

To change the height of all rows in a worksheet, click the Select All button and then drag a row boundary to the desired position.

**Figure 3.2** Row Height Dialog Box

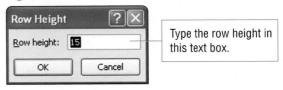

Type the row height in this text box.

1. With **ExcelL1_C3_P1.xlsx** open, change the height of row 1 by completing the following steps:
   a. Position the cell pointer in the row header on the row boundary between rows 1 and 2 until it turns into a double-headed arrow pointing up and down.
   b. Hold down the left mouse button, drag the row boundary down until *Height: 19.50 (26 pixels)* displays in the box, and then release the mouse button.
2. Change the height of rows 2 through 14 by completing the following steps:
   a. Select rows 2 through 14. To do this, position the cell pointer on the number 2 in the row header, hold down the left mouse button, drag the cell pointer to the number 14 in the row header, and then release the mouse button.
   b. Position the cell pointer on the row boundary between rows 2 and 3 until it turns into a double-headed arrow pointing up and down.
   c. Hold down the left mouse button, drag the row boundary down until *Height: 16.50 (22 pixels)* displays in the box, and then release the mouse button.
3. Change the height of row 15 by completing the following steps:
   a. Make cell A15 active.
   b. Click the Format button in the Cells group in the Home tab and then click *Row Height* at the drop-down list.
   c. At the Row Height dialog box, type **20** in the *Row height* text box, and then click OK.
4. Save **ExcelL1_C3_P1.xlsx**.

Step 1b

Step 2c

Step 3c

# Inserting/Deleting Cells, Rows, and Columns

New data may need to be included in an existing worksheet. For example, a row or several rows of new data may need to be inserted into a worksheet, or data may need to be removed from a worksheet.

## Inserting Rows

After you create a worksheet, you can add (insert) rows to the worksheet. Insert a row with the Insert button in the Cells group in the Home tab or with options at the Insert dialog box. By default, a row is inserted above the row containing the active cell. To insert a row in a worksheet, select the row below where the row is to be inserted, and then click the Insert button. If you want to insert more than one row, select the number of rows in the worksheet that you want inserted and then click the Insert button.

**HINT**

When you insert rows in a worksheet, all references affected by the insertion are automatically adjusted.

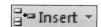

**Insert Row**
Click Insert button.
OR
1. Click Insert button arrow.
2. Click *Insert Sheet Rows* at drop-down list.
OR
1. Click Insert button arrow.
2. Click *Insert Cells*.
3. Click *Entire row* in dialog box.
4. Click OK.

You can also insert a row by making a cell active in the row below where the row is to be inserted, clicking the Insert button arrow, and then clicking *Insert Sheet Rows*. Another method for inserting a row is to click the Insert button arrow and then click *Insert Cells*. This displays the Insert dialog box as shown in Figure 3.3. At the Insert dialog box, click *Entire row*. This inserts a row above the active cell.

**Figure 3.3** Insert Dialog Box

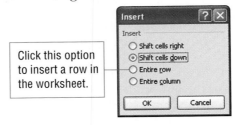

Click this option to insert a row in the worksheet.

## Project 1d    Inserting Rows

1. With **ExcelL1_C3_P1.xlsx** open, insert two rows at the beginning of the worksheet by completing the following steps:
   a. Make cell A1 active.
   b. Click the Insert button arrow in the Cells group in the Home tab.
   c. At the drop-down list that displays, click *Insert Sheet Rows*.
   d. With cell A1 active, click the Insert button arrow and then click *Insert Sheet Rows* at the drop-down list.

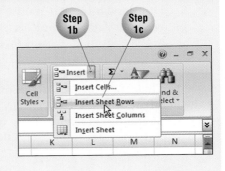

Step 1b        Step 1c

2. Type the text Capstan Marine Products in cell A1.
3. Make cell A2 active and then type Purchasing Department.
4. Change the height of row 1 to *42.00 (56 pixels)*.
5. Change the height of row 2 to *21.00 (28 pixels)*.
6. Insert two rows by completing the following steps:
   a. Select rows 7 and 8 in the worksheet.
   b. Click the Insert button in the Cells group in the Home tab.

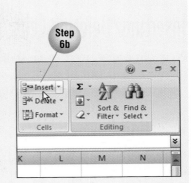

Step 6b

7. Type the following data in the specified cells (you do not need to type the dollar sign in cells containing money amounts):

   A7 = 855-495
   B7 = 42.75
   C7 = 5
   A8 = ST039
   B8 = 12.99
   C8 = 25

8. Make D6 the active cell and then use the fill handle to copy the formula down to cells D7 and D8.
9. Save **ExcelL1_C3_P1.xlsx**.

# Inserting Columns

Insert columns in a worksheet in much the same way as rows. Insert a column with options from the Insert button drop-down list or with options at the Insert dialog box. By default, a column is inserted immediately to the left of the column containing the active cell. To insert a column in a worksheet, make a cell active in the column immediately to the right of where the new column is to be inserted, click the Insert button arrow and then click *Insert Sheet Columns* at the drop-down list. If you want to insert more than one column, select the number of columns in the worksheet that you want inserted, click the Insert button arrow and then click *Insert Sheet Columns*.

You can also insert a column by making a cell active in the column immediately to the right of where the new column is to be inserted, clicking the Insert button arrow, and then clicking *Insert Cells* at the drop-down list. This causes the Insert dialog box to display. At the Insert dialog box, click *Entire column*. This inserts an entire column immediately to the left of the active cell.

Excel includes an especially helpful and time-saving feature related to inserting columns. When you insert columns in a worksheet, all references affected by the insertion are automatically adjusted.

**Insert Column**
Click Insert button.
OR
1. Click Insert button arrow.
2. Click *Insert Sheet Columns* at drop-down list.
OR
1. Click Insert button arrow.
2. Click *Insert Cells*.
3. Click *Entire column*.
4. Click OK.

## Project 1e    Inserting a Column

1. With **ExcelL1_C3_P1.xlsx** open, insert a column by completing the following steps:
   a. Click in any cell in column A.
   b. Click the Insert button arrow in the Cells group in the Home tab and then click *Insert Sheet Columns* at the drop-down list.
2. Type the following data in the specified cell:

   | A3  | = | Company           |
   |-----|---|-------------------|
   | A4  | = | RD Manufacturing  |
   | A8  | = | Smithco, Inc.     |
   | A11 | = | Sunrise Corporation |
   | A15 | = | Geneva Systems    |

3. Make cell A1 active and then adjust the width of column A to accommodate the longest entry.
4. Insert another column by completing the following steps:
   a. Make cell B1 active.
   b. Click the Insert button arrow and then click *Insert Cells* at the drop-down list.
   c. At the Insert dialog box, click *Entire column*.
   d. Click OK.
5. Type **Date** in cell B3 and then press Enter.
6. Save **ExcelL1_C3_P1.xlsx**.

# Deleting Cells, Rows, or Columns

You can delete specific cells in a worksheet or rows or columns in a worksheet. To delete a row, select the row and then click the Delete button in the Cells group in the Home tab. To delete a column, select the column and then click the Delete button. Delete a specific cell by making the cell active, clicking the Delete button arrow, and then clicking *Delete Cells* at the drop-down list. This displays the Delete dialog box shown in Figure 3.4. At the Delete dialog box, specify what you want deleted, and then click OK. You can also delete adjacent cells by selecting the cells and then displaying the Delete Cells dialog box.

**Figure 3.4** Delete Dialog Box

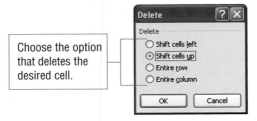

Choose the option that deletes the desired cell.

Clear

# Clearing Data in Cells

If you want to delete cell contents but not the cell, make the cell active or select desired cells and then press the Delete key. A quick method for clearing the contents of a cell is to right-click the cell and then click *Clear Contents* at the shortcut menu. Another method for deleting cell contents is to make the cell active or select desired cells, click the Clear button in the Editing group in the Home tab, and then click *Clear Contents* at the drop-down list.

With the options at the Clear button drop-down list you can clear the contents of the cell or selected cells as well as formatting and comments. Click the *Clear Formats* option to remove formatting from cells or selected cells while leaving the data. You can also click the *Clear All* option to clear the contents of the cell or selected cells as well as the formatting.

Project **1f**    **Deleting and Clearing Rows in a Worksheet**

1. With **ExcelL1_C3_P1.xlsx** open, delete column B in the worksheet by completing the following steps:
   a. Click in any cell in column B.
   b. Click the Delete button arrow in the Cells group in the Home tab and then click *Delete Sheet Columns* at the drop-down list.
2. Delete row 5 by completing the following steps:
   a. Select row 5.
   b. Click the Delete button in the Cells group.

Step 1b

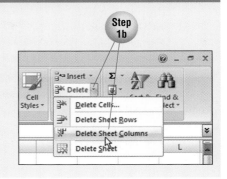

3. Clear row contents by completing the following steps:
   a. Select rows 7 and 8.
   b. Click the Clear button in the Editing group in the Home tab and then click *Clear Contents* at the drop-down list.

4. Type the following data in the specified cell:

   | | | |
   |---|---|---|
   | A7 | = | Ray Enterprises |
   | B7 | = | S894-T |
   | C7 | = | 4.99 |
   | D7 | = | 30 |
   | B8 | = | B-3448 |
   | C8 | = | 25.50 |
   | D8 | = | 12 |

| | | | | | | | |
|---|---|---|---|---|---|---|---|
| 6 | | | 855-495 | $ | 42.75 | 5 | $ 213.75 |
| 7 | Ray Enterprises | | S894-T | $ | 4.99 | 30 | |
| 8 | | | B-3448 | $ | 25.50 | 12 | |
| 9 | | | 43-GB-39 | $ | 45.00 | 20 | $ 900.00 |

5. Make cell E6 active and then copy the formula down to cells E7 and E8.
6. Save **ExcelL1_C3_P1.xlsx**.

# Applying Formatting

With many of the groups in the Home tab you can apply formatting to text in the active cells or selected cells. Use buttons in the Font group to apply font formatting to text and use buttons in the Alignment group to apply alignment formatting to text.

## Applying Font Formatting

You can apply a variety of formatting to cells in a worksheet with buttons in the Font group in the Home tab. With buttons in the Font group shown in Figure 3.5, you can change the font, font size, and font color; bold, italicize, and underline data in cells; change the text color; and apply a border or add fill to cells.

**Figure 3.5** Font Group

Use buttons in the font group to apply formatting to cells or data in cells.

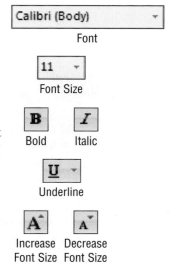

Font

Font Size

Bold    Italic

Underline

Increase   Decrease
Font Size  Font Size

Use the Font button in the Font group to change the font of text in a cell and use the Font Size button to specify size for the text. Apply bold formatting to text in a cell with the Bold button, italic formatting with the Italic button, and underlining with the Underline button.

Click the Increase Font Size button and the text in the active cell or selected cells increases from 11 points to 12 points. Click the Increase Font Size button again and the font size increases to 14. Each additional time you click the button, the font size increases by two points. Click the Decrease Font Size button and text in the active cell or selected cells decreases in point size.

**Border**

**Fill Color**

**Font Color**

With the Borders button in the Font group, you can insert a border on any or all sides of the active cell or any or all sides of selected cells. The name of the button changes depending on the most recent border applied to a cell or selected cells. Use the Fill Color button to insert color in the active cell or in selected cells. With the Font Color button, you can change the color of text within a cell.

## Formatting with the Mini Toolbar

Double-click in a cell and then select data within the cell and the Mini toolbar displays in a dimmed fashion above the selected data. Hover the mouse pointer over the Mini toolbar and it becomes active. The Mini toolbar contains buttons for applying font formatting such as font, font size, and font color as well as bold and italic formatting. Click a button on the Mini toolbar to apply formatting to selected text.

## Applying Alignment Formatting

**Merge & Center**

**Orientation**

**Wrap Text**

The alignment of data in cells depends on the type of data entered. Enter words or text combined with numbers in a cell and the text is aligned at the left edge of the cell. Enter numbers in a cell and the numbers are aligned at the right side of the cell. Use options in the Alignment group to align text at the left, center, or right side of the cell; align text at the top, center, or bottom of the cell; increase and/or decrease the indent of text; and change the orientation of text in a cell. Click the Merge & Center button to merge selected cells and center data within the merged cells. If you have merged cells and want to split them again, select the cells and then click the Merge & Center button.

Click the Orientation button to rotate data in a cell. Click the Orientation button and a drop-down list displays with options for rotating text in a cell. If data typed in a cell is longer than the cell, it overlaps the next cell to the right. If you want data to remain in a cell and wrap to the next line within the same cell, click the Wrap Text button in the Alignment group.

Project **1g**  |  **Applying Font and Alignment Formatting**

1. With **ExcelL1_C3_P1.xlsx** open, make cell B1 active and then click the Wrap Text button in the Alignment group in the Home tab. (This wraps the company name within the cell.)
2. Make cell B2 active and then click the Wrap Text button.
3. Instead of wrapping text within cells, you decide to spread out the text over several cells and vertically align text in cells by completing the following steps:
   a. Select cells A1 through E1.
   b. Click the Merge & Center button in the Alignment group in the Home tab.
   c. Click the Middle Align button in the Alignment group.
   d. Select cells A2 through E2, click the Merge & Center button, and then click the Middle Align button.

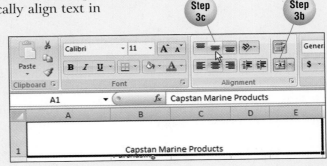

4. Rotate text in the third row by completing the following steps:
   a. Select cells A3 through E3.
   b. Click the Orientation button in the Alignment group and then click *Angle Counterclockwise* at the drop-down list.
   c. After looking at the rotated text, you decide to return the orientation back to the horizontal by clicking the Undo button on the Quick Access toolbar.

5. Change the font, font size, and font color for text in specific cells by completing the following steps:
   a. Make cell A1 active.
   b. Click the Font button arrow in the Font group in the Home tab, scroll down the drop-down gallery, and then click *Bookman Old Style*.

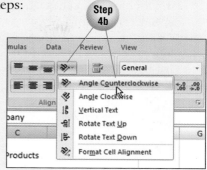

Step 4b

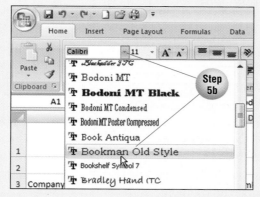

Step 5b

   c. Click the Font Size button arrow in the Font group and then click *22* at the drop-down gallery.
   d. Click the Font Color button arrow and then click *Dark Blue* in the *Standard* section of the drop-down color palette.

6. Make cell A2 active and then complete steps similar to those in Step 5 to change the font to Bookman Old Style, the font size to 16, and the font color to Dark Blue.

7. Select cells A3 through E3 and then click the Center button in the Alignment group.

8. With cells A3 through E3 still selected, click the Bold button in the Font group and then click the Italic button.

9. Select cells A3 through E18 and then change the font to Bookman Old Style.

10. Apply formatting to selected data using the Mini toolbar by completing the following steps:
    a. Double-click cell A4.
    b. Select the letters *RD*. (This displays the dimmed Mini toolbar above the selected word.)
    c. Click the Increase Font Size button on the Mini toolbar.

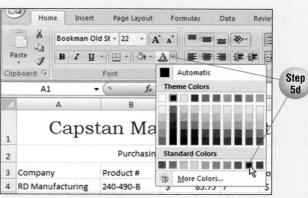

Step 5d

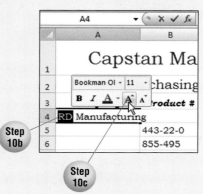

Step 10b

Step 10c

d. Double-click cell A14.

e. Select the word *Geneva* and then click the Italic button on the Mini toolbar.

11. Adjust columns A through E to accommodate the longest entry in each column.

12. Select cells D4 through D17 and then click the Center button in the Alignment group.

13. Add a double-line bottom border to cell A2 by completing the following steps:

a. Make cell A2 active.

b. Click the Borders button arrow in the Font group in the Home tab.

c. Click the *Bottom Double Border* option at the drop-down list.

14. Add a single-line bottom border to cells A3 through E3 by completing the following steps:

a. Select cells A3 through E3.

b. Click the Borders button arrow and then click the *Bottom Border* option.

15. Apply fill color to specific cells by completing the following steps:

a. Select cells A1 through E3.

b. Click the Fill Color button arrow in the Font group.

c. Click the *Aqua, Accent 5, Lighter 80%* color option.

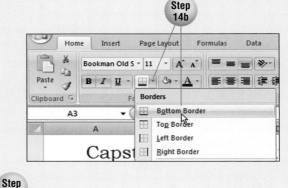

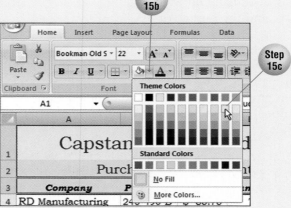

16. Save **ExcelL1_C3_P1.xlsx**.

# Previewing a Worksheet

Before printing a worksheet, consider previewing it to see how it will appear when printed. To preview a worksheet, click the Office button, point to the *Print* option, and then click the *Print Preview* option. You can also display a worksheet in Print Preview by clicking the Preview button that displays in the lower left corner of the Print dialog box. A document displays in Print Preview as it will appear when printed. Figure 3.6 displays the **ExcelL1_C3_P1.xlsx** worksheet in Print Preview. Notice that the gridlines in the worksheet do not print.

**Figure 3.6** Worksheet in Print Preview

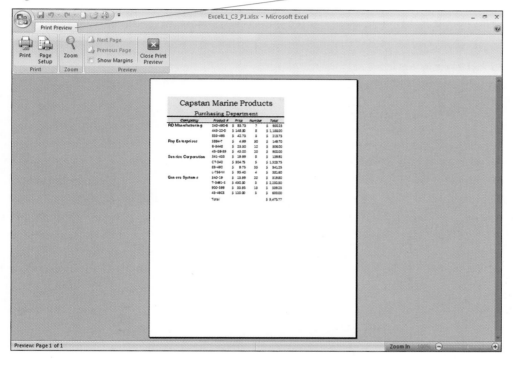

To zoom in on the worksheet, position the mouse pointer (displays as a magnifying glass) in the worksheet text and then click the left mouse button. You can also click the Zoom In option located at the left slide of the Zoom slider bar located at the right side of the Status bar (lower right corner of the Excel window). Click the Print button in the Print Preview tab to send the worksheet to the printer. Click the Page Setup button in the Print Preview tab and the Page Setup dialog box displays with options for changing the paper size and orientation of the page. Insert a check mark in the *Show Margins* check box and margin boundary lines display around the worksheet. Insert a check mark in the *Show Margins* check box and you can change worksheet margins by dragging margin borders. Close Print Preview by clicking the Close Print Preview button.

**Preview a Worksheet**
1. Click Office button.
2. Point to *Print.*
3. Click *Print Preview.*

## Changing the Zoom Setting

In Print Preview, you can zoom in on the worksheet and make the display bigger. You can also change the size of worksheet display in Normal view using the Zoom slider bar that displays at the right side of the Status bar. To change the percentage of display, drag the button on the Zoom slider bar to increase or decrease the percentage of display. You can also click the Zoom Out button located at the left side of the slider bar to decrease the percentage of display or click the Zoom In button located at the right side of the slider bar to increase the percentage of display.

Project **1h**   **Previewing a Worksheet**

1. With **ExcelL1_C3_P1.xlsx** open, click the Office button, point to the *Print* option, and then click the *Print Preview* option.
2. At the print preview screen, click in the worksheet. (This increases the display of the worksheet cells.)
3. After viewing the worksheet, click the Close Print Preview button.
4. At the worksheet, drag the button on the Zoom slider bar to the right until the zoom displays as 190%. (The percentage amount displays at the left side of the slider.)
5. After viewing the worksheet at 190% display, click the Zoom Out button located at the left side of the slider until the display percentage is 100%.

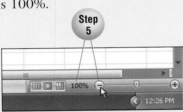

6. Save, print, and then close **ExcelL1_C3_P1.xlsx**.

## Project ② Apply a Theme to a Payroll Worksheet

You will open a workbook containing a worksheet with payroll information and then insert text, apply formatting to cells and cell contents, apply a theme, and then change the theme font and colors.

# Applying a Theme

Excel provides a number of themes you can use to format text and cells in a worksheet. A theme is a set of formatting choices that include a color theme (a set of colors), a font theme (a set of heading and body text fonts), and an effects theme (a set of lines and fill effects). To apply a theme, click the Page Layout tab and then click the Themes button in the Themes group. At the drop-down gallery that displays, click the desired theme. Position the mouse pointer over a theme and the *live preview* feature will display the worksheet with the theme formatting applied. With the live preview feature you can see how the theme formatting affects your worksheet before you make your final choice.

**HINT**

Apply a theme to give your worksheet a professional look.

## Project ② Applying a Theme

1. Open **ExcelC03Project02.xlsx** and then save it and name it **ExcelL1_C3_P2**.
2. Make G4 the active cell and then insert a formula that calculates the amount of Social Security tax (multiply the gross pay amount in E4 with the Social Security rate in cell H11 [you will need to use the mixed cell reference H$11 when writing the formula]).
3. Copy the formula in cell G4 down to cells G5 through G9.
4. Make H4 the active cell and then insert a formula that calculates the net pay (gross pay minus withholding and Social Security tax).
5. Automatically adjust the width of column H.
6. Copy the formula in H4 down to cells H5 through H9.
7. Increase the height of row 1 to 36.00.
8. Make A1 the active cell, click the Middle Align button in the Alignment group, click the Font Size button arrow and click *18* at the drop-down list, and then click the Bold button.
9. Type Stanton & Barnett Associates in cell A1.
10. Select cells A2 through H3 and then click the Bold button in the Font group.
11. Apply a theme and customize the font and colors by completing the following steps:
    a. Click the Page Layout tab.
    b. Click the Themes button in the Themes group and then click *Aspect* at the drop-down gallery. (You might want to point the mouse to various themes to see how the theme formatting affects the worksheet).

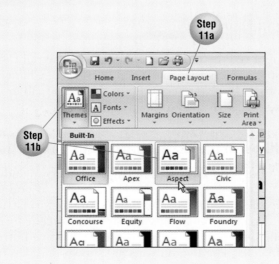

Step 11a

Step 11b

c. Click the Colors button in the Themes group and then click *Flow* at the drop-down gallery.
d. Click the Fonts button in the Themes group, scroll down the drop-down gallery, and then click *Opulent*.

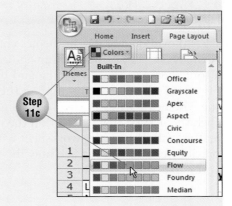

Step 11c

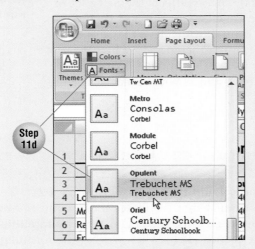

Step 11d

12. Select columns A through H and then adjust the width of the columns to accommodate the longest entries.
13. Save, print, and then close **ExcelL1_C3_P2.xlsx**.

roject **3**  **Format an Invoices Worksheet**

You will open a workbook containing an invoice worksheet and apply number formatting to numbers in cells.

## Formatting Numbers

Numbers in a cell, by default, are aligned at the right and decimals and commas do not display unless they are typed in the cell. Change the format of numbers with buttons in the Number group in the Home tab or with options at the Format Cells dialog box with the Number tab selected.

### Formatting Numbers Using Number Group Buttons

Format symbols you can use to format numbers include a percent sign (%), a comma (,), and a dollar sign ($). For example, if you type the number *$45.50* in a cell, Excel automatically applies Currency formatting to the number. If you type *45%*, Excel automatically applies the Percent formatting to the number. The Number group in the Home tab contains five buttons you can use to format numbers in cells. The five buttons are shown and described in Table 3.1.

**Table 3.1** Number Formatting Buttons on Formatting Toolbar

| | Click this button | To do this |
|---|---|---|
| **$** ▾ | Accounting Number Format | Add a dollar sign, any necessary commas, and a decimal point followed by two decimal digits, if none are typed; right-align number in cell |
| **%** | Percent Style | Multiply cell value by 100 and display result with a percent symbol; right-align number in cell |
| **,** | Comma Style | Add any necessary commas and a decimal point followed by two decimal digits, if none are typed; right-align number in cell |
| **←.0/.00** | Increase Decimal | Increase number of decimal places displayed after decimal point in selected cells |
| **.00/→.0** | Decrease Decimal | Decrease number of decimal places displayed after decimal point in selected cells |

Specify the formatting for numbers in cells in a worksheet before typing the numbers, or format existing numbers in a worksheet. The Increase Decimal and Decrease Decimal buttons in the Number group in the Home tab will change decimal places for existing numbers only.

Increase  Decrease
Decimal   Decimal

The Number group in the Home tab also contains the Number Format button. Click the Number Format button arrow and a drop-down list displays of common number formats. Click the desired format at the drop-down list to apply the number formatting to the cell or selected cells.

| General | ▾ |
|---|---|

Number Format

## Project 3a     Formatting Numbers with Buttons in the Number Group

1. Open **ExcelC03Project03.xlsx**.
2. Save the workbook with Save As and name it **ExcelL1_C3_P3**.
3. Make the following changes to column widths:
   a. Change the width of column C to 17.00.
   b. Change the width of column D to 10.00.
   c. Change the width of column E to 7.00.
   d. Change the width of column F to 12.00.
4. Select row 1 and then click the Insert button in the Cells group.
5. Change the height of row 1 to 42.00.
6. Select cells A1 through F1 and then make the following changes:
   a. Click the Merge & Center button in the Alignment group.
   b. With cell A1 active, change the font size to 24 points.
   c. Click the Fill Color button arrow in the Font group and then click *Olive Green, Accent 3, Lighter 80%*.

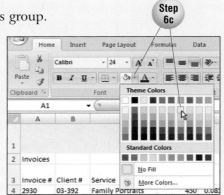

Step 6c

d. Click the Borders button arrow in the Font group and then click the *Top and Thick Bottom Border* option.

e. With cell A1 active, type **REAL PHOTOGRAPHY** and then press Enter.

7. Change the height of row 2 to 24.00.

8. Select cells A2 through F2 and then make the following changes:

a. Click the Merge & Center button in the Alignment group.

b. With cell A2 active, change the font size to 18.

c. Click the Fill Color button in the Font group. (This will fill the cell with light green color.)

d. Click the Borders button arrow in the Font group and then click the *Bottom Border* option.

9. Make the following changes to row 3:

a. Change the height of row 3 to 18.00.

b. Select cells A3 through F3, click the Bold button in the Font group, and then click the Center button in the Alignment group.

c. With the cells still selected, click the Borders button arrow and then click the *Bottom Border* option.

10. Make the following number formatting changes:

a. Select cells E4 through E16 and then click the *Percent Style* button in the Number group.

b. With the cells still selected, click once on the Increase Decimal button in the Number group. (The percent numbers should contain one decimal place.)

Step 6d

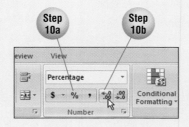

Step 10a

Step 10b

c. Select cells A4 through B16.

d. Click the Number Format button arrow, scroll down the drop-down list, and then click *Text*.

e. With A4 through B16 still selected, click the Center button in the Alignment group.

11. Save **ExcelL1_C3_P3.xlsx**.

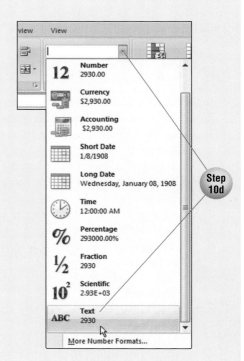

Step 10d

# Formatting Numbers Using the Format Cells Dialog Box

Along with buttons in the Number group, you can format numbers with options at the Format Cells dialog box with the Number tab selected as shown in Figure 3.7. Display this dialog box by clicking the Number group dialog box launcher or by clicking the Number Format button arrow and then clicking *More Number Formats* at the drop-down list. The left side of the dialog box displays number categories with a default category of *General*. At this setting no specific formatting is applied to numbers except right-aligning numbers in cells. The other number categories are described in Table 3.2.

**Figure 3.7** Format Cells Dialog Box with Number Tab Selected

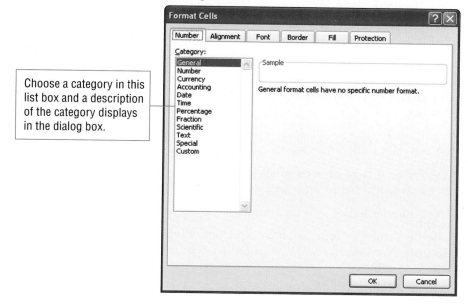

Choose a category in this list box and a description of the category displays in the dialog box.

**Table 3.2** Number Categories at the Format Cells Dialog Box

| Click this category | To apply this number formatting |
|---|---|
| Number | Specify number of decimal places and whether or not a thousand separator should be used; choose the display of negative numbers; right-align numbers in cell. |
| Currency | Apply general monetary values; dollar sign is added as well as commas and decimal points, if needed; right-align numbers in cell. |
| Accounting | Line up the currency symbol and decimal points in a column; add dollar sign and two digits after a decimal point; right-align numbers in cell. |
| Date | Display date as date value; specify the type of formatting desired by clicking an option in the *Type* list box; right-align date in cell. |
| Time | Display time as time value; specify the type of formatting desired by clicking an option in the *Type* list box; right-align time in cell. |
| Percentage | Multiply cell value by 100 and display result with a percent symbol; add decimal point followed by two digits by default; number of digits can be changed with the *Decimal places* option; right-align number in cell. |
| Fraction | Specify how fraction displays in cell by clicking an option in the *Type* list box; right-align fraction in cell. |
| Scientific | Use for very large or very small numbers. Use the letter *E* to tell Excel to move a decimal point a specified number of positions. |
| Text | Treat number in cell as text; number is displayed in cell exactly as typed. |
| Special | Choose a number type, such as Zip Code, Phone Number, or Social Security Number in the *Type* option list box; useful for tracking list and database values. |
| Custom | Specify a numbering type by choosing an option in the *Type* list box. |

Project ③b **Formatting Numbers at the Format Cells Dialog Box**

1. With **ExcelL1_C3_P3.xlsx** open, make cell F4 active and then insert the following formula: =(D4*E4)+D4.
2. Make cell F4 active and then copy the formula down to cells F5 through F16.
3. Change number formatting by completing the following steps:
   a. Select cells D4 through D16.
   b. Click the Number group dialog box launcher.

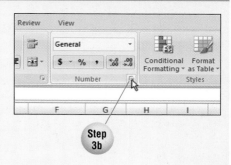

Step 3b

c. At the Format Cells dialog box with the Number tab selected, click *Accounting* in the *Category* section.

d. Make sure a *2* displays in the *Decimal places* option box and a dollar sign *$* displays in the *Symbol* option box.

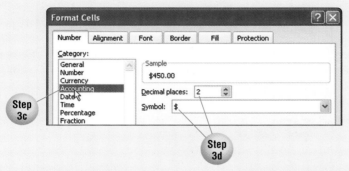

e. Click OK.

4. Apply Accounting formatting to cells F4 through F16 by completing steps similar to those in Step 3.

5. Save, print, and then close **ExcelL1_C3_P3.xlsx**.

 roject ④ **Format a Company Budget Worksheet**

**You will open a workbook containing a company budget worksheet and then apply formatting to cells with options at the Format Cells dialog box, use the Format Painter to apply formatting, and hide and unhide rows and columns in the worksheet.**

# Formatting Cells Using the Format Cells Dialog Box

In the previous section, you learned how to format numbers with options at the Format Cells dialog box with the Number tab selected. This dialog box contains a number of other tabs you can select to format cells.

## Aligning and Indenting Data

You can align and indent data in cells using buttons in the Alignment group in the Home tab or with options at the Format Cells dialog box with the Alignment tab selected as shown in Figure 3.8. Display this dialog box by clicking the Alignment group dialog box launcher.

**Figure 3.8** Format Cells Dialog Box with Alignment Tab Selected

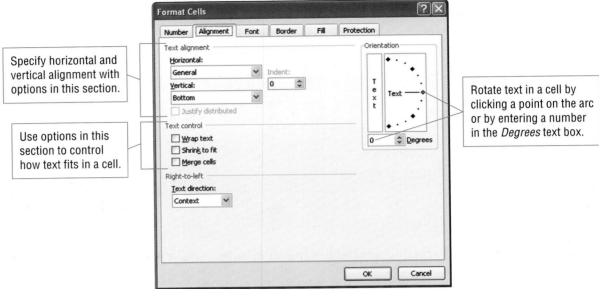

Specify horizontal and vertical alignment with options in this section.

Use options in this section to control how text fits in a cell.

Rotate text in a cell by clicking a point on the arc or by entering a number in the *Degrees* text box.

In the *Orientation* section, you can choose to rotate data. A portion of the *Orientation* section shows points on an arc. Click a point on the arc to rotate the text along that point. You can also type a rotation degree in the *Degrees* text box. Type a positive number to rotate selected text from the lower left to the upper right of the cell. Type a negative number to rotate selected text from the upper left to the lower right of the cell.

If data typed in a cell is longer than the cell, it overlaps the next cell to the right. If you want data to remain in a cell and wrap to the next line within the same cell, click the *Wrap text* option in the *Text control* section of the dialog box. Click the *Shrink to fit* option to reduce the size of the text font so all selected data fits within the column. Use the *Merge cells* option to combine two or more selected cells into a single cell.

If you want to enter data on more than one line within a cell, enter the data on the first line and then press Alt + Enter. Pressing Alt + Enter moves the insertion point to the next line within the same cell.

Project 4a  **Aligning and Rotating Data in Cells**

1. Open **ExcelC03Project04.xlsx**.
2. Save the workbook with Save As and name it **ExcelL1_C3_P4**.
3. Make the following changes to the worksheet:
   a. Insert a new row at the beginning of the worksheet.
   b. Change the height of row 1 to 66.00.
   c. Merge and center cells A1 through E1.
   d. Type **Harris & Briggs** in cell A1 and then press Alt + Enter. (This moves the insertion point down to the next line in the same cell.)
   e. Type **Construction** and then press Enter.
   f. With cell A2 active, type **Preferred**, press Alt + Enter, type **Customer**, and then press Enter.

g. Change the width of column A to 20.00.
h. Change the width of column B to 7.00.
i. Change the width of columns C, D, and E to 10.00.
4. Change number formatting for specific cells by completing the following steps:
   a. Select cells C3 through E11.
   b. Click the Number group dialog box launcher.
   c. At the Format Cells dialog box with the Number tab selected, click *Accounting* in the *Category* section.
   d. Click the down-pointing arrow at the right side of the *Decimal places* option until *0* displays.
   e. Make sure a dollar sign *$* displays in the *Symbol* option box.
   f. Click OK.

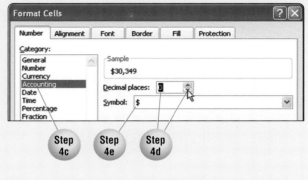

5. Make cell E3 active and then insert a formula that subtracts the *Planned* amount from the *Actual* amount. Copy this formula down to cells E4 through E11.
6. Change the orientation of data in cells by completing the following steps:
   a. Select cells B2 through E2.
   b. Click the Alignment group dialog box launcher.
   c. At the Format Cells dialog box with the Alignment tab selected, select *0* in the *Degrees* text box and then type *45*.
   d. Click OK.
7. Change the vertical alignment of text in cells by completing the following steps:
   a. Select cells A1 through E2.
   b. Click the Alignment group dialog box launcher.
   c. At the Format Cells dialog box with the Alignment tab selected, click the down-pointing arrow at the right side of the *Vertical* alignment option.
   d. Click *Center* at the drop-down list.
   e. Click OK.

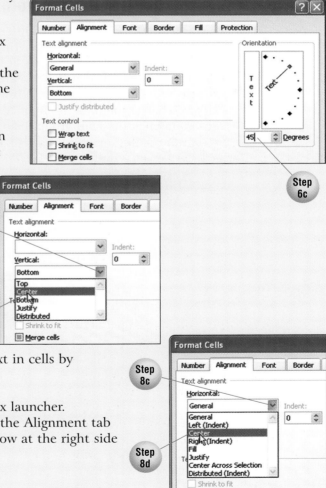

8. Change the horizontal alignment of text in cells by completing the following steps:
   a. Select cells A2 through E2.
   b. Click the Alignment group dialog box launcher.
   c. At the Format Cells dialog box with the Alignment tab selected, click the down-pointing arrow at the right side of the *Horizontal* alignment option.
   d. Click *Center* at the drop-down list.
   e. Click OK.

9. Change the horizontal alignment and indent of
   text in cells by completing the following steps:
   a. Select cells B3 through B11.
   b. Click the Alignment group dialog box launcher.
   c. At the Format Cells dialog box with the
      Alignment tab selected, click the down-pointing
      arrow at the right side of the *Horizontal*
      alignment option and then click *Right (Indent)* at
      the drop-down list.
   d. Click once on the up-pointing arrow at the right
      side of the *Indent* option box (this displays *1* in
      the box).
   e. Click OK.
10. Save **ExcelL1_C3_P4.xlsx**.

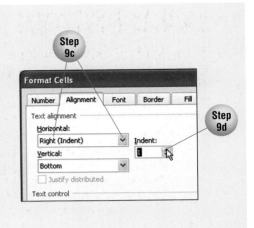

## Changing the Font at the Format Cells Dialog Box

As you learned earlier in this chapter, the Font group in the Home tab contains
buttons for applying font formatting to data in cells. You can also change the
font for data in cells with options at the Format Cells dialog box with the Font tab
selected as shown in Figure 3.9. At the Format Cells dialog box with the Font
tab selected, you can change the font, font style, font size, and font color. You
can also change the underlining method and add effects such as superscript and
subscript. Click the Font group dialog box launcher to display this dialog box.

**Figure 3.9** Format Cells Dialog Box with Font Tab Selected

1. With **ExcelL1_C3_P4.xlsx** open, change the font and font color by completing the following steps:
   a. Select cells A1 through E11.
   b. Click the Font group dialog box launcher.
   c. At the Format Cells dialog box with the Font tab selected, click *Garamond* in the *Font* list box (you will need to scroll down the list to make this font visible).
   d. Click *12* in the *Size* list box.
   e. Click the down-pointing arrow at the right of the *Color* option box.
   f. At the palette of color choices that displays, click the *Dark Red* color (first color option from the left in the *Standard Colors* section).
   g. Click OK to close the dialog box.
2. Make cell A1 active and then change the font to 24-point Garamond bold.
3. Select cells A2 through E2 and then apply bold formatting.
4. Save and then print **ExcelL1_C3_P4.xlsx**.

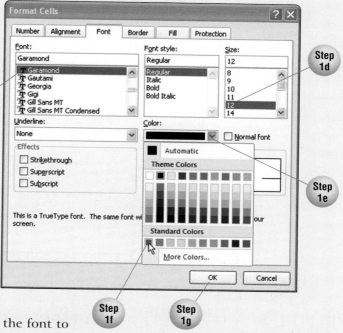

## Adding Borders to Cells

The gridlines that display in a worksheet do not print. As you learned earlier in this chapter, you can use the Borders button in the Font group to add borders to cells that will print. You can also add borders to cells with options at the Format Cells dialog box with the Border tab selected as shown in Figure 3.10. Display this dialog box by clicking the Borders button arrow in the Font group and then clicking *More Borders* at the drop-down list.

With options in the *Presets* section, you can remove borders with the *None* option, add only outside borders with the *Outline* option, or click the *Inside* option to add borders to the inside of selected cells. In the *Border* section of the dialog box, specify the side of the cell or selected cells to which you want to apply a border. Choose the style of line desired for the border with the options that display in the *Style* list box. Add color to border lines with choices from the color palette that displays when you click the down-pointing arrow located at the right side of the *Color* option box.

**QUICK STEPS**

**Add Borders to Cells**
1. Select cells.
2. Click Borders button arrow.
3. Click desired border.
OR
1. Select cells.
2. Click Borders button arrow.
3. Click *More Borders*.
4. Use options in dialog box to apply desired border.
5. Click OK.

Figure 3.10 Format Cells Dialog Box with Border Tab Selected

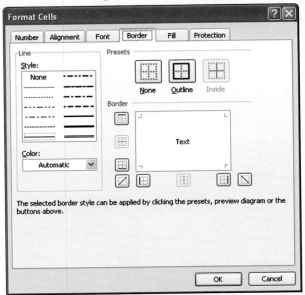

## Project 4C — Adding Borders to Cells

1. With **ExcelL1_C3_P4.xlsx** open, remove the 45 degrees orientation you applied in Project 4a by completing the following steps:
   a. Select cells B2 through E2.
   b. Click the Alignment group dialog box launcher.
   c. At the Format Cells dialog box with the Alignment tab selected, select *45* in the *Degrees* text box and then type 0.
   d. Click OK.

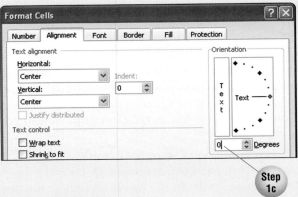

Step 1c

2. Change the height of row 2 to 33.00.
3. Add a thick, dark red border line to cells by completing the following steps:
   a. Select cells A1 through E11 (cells containing data).
   b. Click the Border button arrow in the Font group and then click the *More Borders* option at the drop-down list.

c. At the Format Cells dialog box with the Border tab selected, click the down-pointing arrow at the right side of the *Color* option and then click *Dark Red* at the color palette (first color option from the left in the *Standard Colors* section).

d. Click the thick single line option located in the second column (sixth option from the top) in the *Style* option box in the *Line* section.

e. Click the *Outline* option in the *Presets* section.

f. Click OK.

4. Add a border above and below cells by completing the following steps:

a. Select cells A2 through E2.

b. Click the Border button arrow in the Font group and then click *More Borders* at the drop-down list.

c. At the Format Cells dialog box with the Border tab selected, make sure the color is Dark Red.

d. Make sure the thick single line option (sixth option from the top in the second column) is selected in the *Style* option box in the *Line* section.

e. Click the top border of the sample cell in the *Border* section of the dialog box.

f. Click the double-line option (bottom option in the second column) in the *Style* option box.

g. Click the bottom border of the sample cell in the *Border* section of the dialog box.

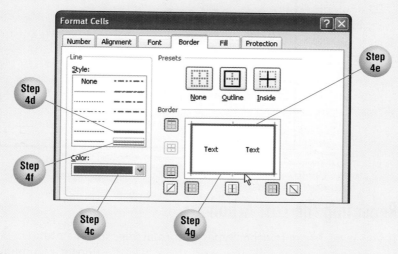

h. Click OK.

5. Save **ExcelL1_C3_P4.xlsx**.

# Adding Fill and Shading to Cells

**Add Shading to Cells**
1. Select cells.
2. Click Fill Color button arrow.
3. Click desired color.
OR
1. Select cells.
2. Click Format button.
3. Click *Format Cells* at drop-down list.
4. Click Fill tab.
5. Use options in dialog box to apply desired shading.
6. Click OK.

To enhance the visual display of cells and data within cells, consider adding fill and/or shading to cells. As you learned earlier in this chapter, you can add fill color to cells with the Fill Color button in the Font group. You can also add fill color and/or shading to cells in a worksheet with options at the Format Cells dialog box with the Fill tab selected as shown in Figure 3.11. Display the Format Cells dialog box by clicking the Format button in the Cells group and then clicking *Format Cells* at the drop-down list. You can also display the dialog box by clicking the Font group, Alignment group, or Number group dialog box launcher. At the Format Cells dialog box, click the Fill tab.

Choose a fill color for a cell or selected cells by clicking a color choice in the *Color* palette. To add shading to a cell or selected cells, click the Fill Effects button, and then click the desired shading style at the Fill Effects dialog box.

**Figure 3.11** Format Cells Dialog Box with Fill Tab Selected

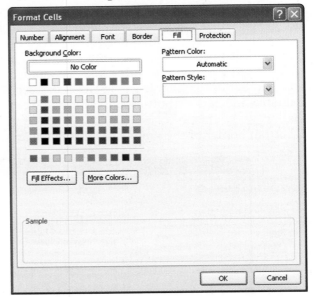

# Repeating the Last Action

**QUICK STEPS**

**Repeat Last Action**
1. Apply formatting.
2. Move to desired location.
3. Press F4 or Ctrl + Y.

If you want to apply other types of formatting, such as number, border, or shading formatting to other cells in a worksheet, use the Repeat command by pressing F4 or Ctrl + Y. The Repeat command repeats the last action performed.

1. With **ExcelL1_C3_P4.xlsx** open, add fill color to cell A1 and repeat the formatting by completing the following steps:
   a. Make cell A1 active.
   b. Click the Format button in the Cells group and then click *Format Cells* at the drop-down list.
   c. At the Format Cells dialog box, click the Fill tab.
   d. Click a light purple color in the *Color* section (click the eighth color from the left in the second row).

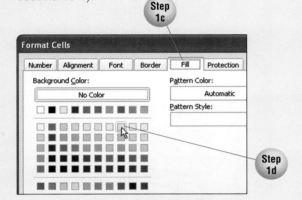

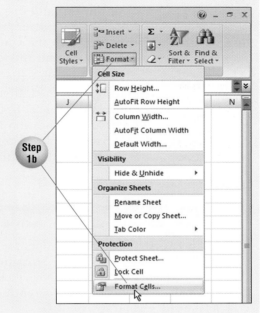

   e. Click OK.
   f. Select cells A2 through E2 and then press the F4 function key. (This repeats the light purple fill.)
2. Select row 2, insert a new row, and then change the width of the new row to 12.00.
3. Add shading to cells by completing the following steps:
   a. Select cells A2 through E2.
   b. Click the Format button in the Cells group and then click *Format Cells* at the drop-down list.
   c. At the Format Cells dialog box, if necessary, click the Fill tab.
   d. Click the Fill Effects button.
   e. At the Fill Effects dialog box, click the down-pointing arrow at the right side of the *Color 2* option box and then click *Purple, Accent 4* (eighth color from the left in the top row).
   f. Click *Horizontal* in the *Shading styles* section of the dialog box.
   g. Click OK to close the Fill Effects dialog box.
   h. Click OK to close the Format Cells dialog box.

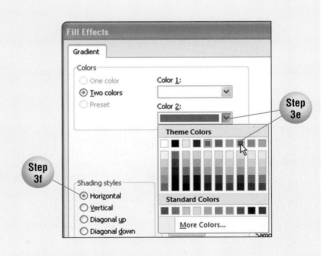

4. Save **ExcelL1_C3_P4.xlsx**.

**Format with Format Painter**
1. Select cells with desired formatting.
2. Double-click Format Painter button.
3. Select cells.
4. Click Format Painter button.

Format Painter

# Formatting with Format Painter

The Clipboard group in the Home tab contains a button you can use to copy formatting to different locations in the worksheet. This button is the Format Painter button and displays in the Clipboard group as a paintbrush. To use the Format Painter button, make a cell or selected cells active that contain the desired formatting, click the Format Painter button, and then click the cell or selected cells to which you want the formatting applied.

When you click the Format Painter button, the mouse pointer displays with a paintbrush attached. If you want to apply formatting a single time, click the Format Painter button once. If, however, you want to apply the character formatting in more than one location in the worksheet, double-click the Format Painter button. If you have double-clicked the Format Painter button, turn off the feature by clicking the Format Painter button once.

## Project 4e — Formatting with Format Painter

1. With **ExcelL1_C3_P4.xlsx** open, select cells A5 through E5.
2. Click the Font group dialog box launcher.
3. At the Format Cells dialog box, click the Fill tab.
4. Click the light green color (seventh color from the left in the second row).
5. Click OK to close the dialog box.
6. Use Format Painter to "paint" formatting to rows by completing the following steps:
   a. With A5 through E5 selected, double-click the Format Painter button in the Clipboard group.
   b. Select cells A7 through E7.
   c. Select cells A9 through E9.
   d. Select cells A11 through E11.
   e. Turn off Format Painter by clicking the Format Painter button in the Clipboard group.
7. Save and then print **ExcelL1_C3_P4.xlsx**.

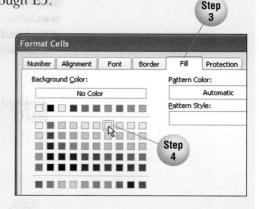

# Hiding and Unhiding Columns/Rows

**HINT**

Set the column width to zero and the column is hidden. Set the row height to zero and the row is hidden.

If a worksheet contains columns and/or rows of sensitive data or data that you are not using or do not want to view, consider hiding the columns and/or rows. To hide columns in a worksheet, select the columns to be hidden, click the Format button in the Cells group in the Home tab, point to *Hide & Unhide*, and then click *Hide Columns*. To hide selected rows, click the Format button in the Cells group, point to *Hide & Unhide*, and then click *Hide Rows*. To make a hidden column visible, select the column to the left and the column to the right of the hidden column, click the Format button in the Cells group, point to *Hide & Unhide*, and then click *Unhide Columns*. To make a hidden row visible, select the row above and the row below the hidden row, click the Format button in the Cells group, point to *Hide & Unhide*, and then click *Unhide Rows*.

If the first row or column is hidden, use the Go To feature to make the row or column visible. To do this, click the Find & Select button in the Editing group in the Home tab and then click *Go To* at the drop-down list. At the Go To dialog box, type **A1** in the *Reference* text box, and then click OK. At the worksheet, click the Format button in the Cells group, point to *Hide & Unhide*, and then click *Unhide Columns* or click *Unhide Rows*.

You can also unhide columns or rows using the mouse. If a column or row is hidden, the light blue boundary line in the column or row header displays as a slightly thicker blue line. To unhide a column, position the mouse pointer on the slightly thicker blue line that displays in the column header until the mouse pointer changes to left- and right-pointing arrows with a double line between. (Make sure the mouse pointer displays with two lines between the arrows. If a single line displays, you will simply change the size of the visible column.) Hold down the left mouse button, drag to the right until the column displays at the desired width, and then release the mouse button. Unhide a row in a similar manner. Position the mouse pointer on the slightly thicker blue line in the row header until the mouse pointer changes to up- and down-pointing arrows with a double line between. Drag down to display the row and then release the mouse button. If two or more adjacent columns or rows are hidden, you will need to unhide each column or row separately.

**Hide Columns**
1. Select columns.
2. Click Format button.
3. Point to *Hide & Unhide*.
4. Click *Hide Columns*.

**Hide Rows**
1. Select rows.
2. Click Format button.
3. Point to *Hide & Unhide*.
4. Click *Hide Rows*

## Project ④ Hiding/Unhiding Columns and Rows

1. With **ExcelL1_C3_P4.xlsx** open, hide the row for Linstrom Enterprises and the row for Summit Services by completing the following steps:
   a. Click the row 7 header to select the entire row.
   b. Hold down the Ctrl key and then click the row 11 header to select the entire row.
   c. Click the Format button in the Cells group in the Home tab, point to *Hide & Unhide*, and then click *Hide Rows*.

2. Hide the column containing the planned amounts by completing the following steps:
   a. Click cell D3 to make it the active cell.
   b. Click the Format button in the Cells group, point to *Hide & Unhide*, and then click *Hide Columns*.

3. Save and then print **ExcelL1_C3_P4.xlsx**.

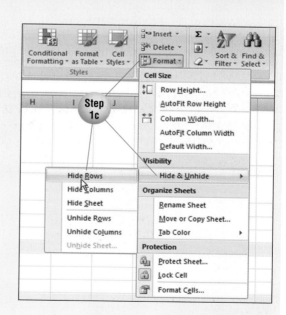

4. Unhide the rows by completing the following steps:
   a. Select rows 6 through 12.
   b. Click the Format button in the Cells group, point to *Hide & Unhide*, and then click *Unhide Rows*.
   c. Click in cell A4.

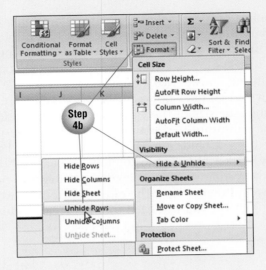

5. Unhide column D by completing the following steps:
   a. Position the mouse pointer on the thicker blue line that displays between columns C and E in the column header until the pointer turns into arrows pointing left and right with a double line between.
   b. Hold down the left mouse button, drag to the right until *Width: 12.57 (93 pixels)* displays in a box above the mouse pointer, and then release the mouse button.

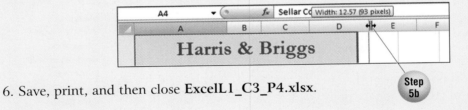

6. Save, print, and then close **ExcelL1_C3_P4.xlsx**.

# CHAPTER summary

- Change column width using the mouse on column boundaries or with options at the Column Width dialog box.

- To automatically adjust a column to accommodate the longest entry in the column, double-click the column header boundary on the right.

- Change row height using the mouse on row boundaries or with options at the Row Height dialog box.

- Insert a row in a worksheet with the Insert button in the Cells group in the Home tab or with options at the Insert dialog box.

- Insert a column in a worksheet with the Insert button in the Cells group or with options at the Insert dialog box.

- Delete a specific cell by clicking the Delete button arrow and then clicking *Delete Cells* at the drop-down list. At the Delete dialog box, specify if you want to delete just the cell or an entire row or column.

- Delete a selected row(s) or column(s) by clicking the Delete button in the Cells group.

- Delete cell contents by pressing the Delete key or clicking the Clear button in the Editing group and then clicking *Clear Contents* at the drop-down list.

- Apply font formatting with buttons in the Font group in the Home tab.

- Use the Mini toolbar to apply font formatting to selected data in a cell.

- Apply alignment formatting with buttons in the Alignment group in the Home tab.

- Preview a worksheet by clicking the Office button, pointing to *Print*, and then clicking *Print Preview*.

- Change the size of the worksheet display with the Zoom button in the Print Preview tab or with the Zoom slider bar that displays at the right side of the Status bar.

- Use the Themes button in the Themes group in the Page Layout tab to apply a theme to cells in a worksheet that applies formatting such as color, font, and effects. Use the other buttons in the Themes group to customize the theme.

- Format numbers in cells with the Accounting Number Format, Percent Style, Comma Style, Increase Decimal, and Decrease Decimal buttons in the Number group in the home tab. You can also apply number formatting with options at the Format Cells dialog box with the Number tab selected.

- Apply formatting to cells in a worksheet with options at the Format Cells dialog box. This dialog box includes the following tabs for formatting cells: Number, Alignment, Font, Border, and Fill.

- Press F4 or Ctrl + Y to repeat the last action performed.

- Use the Format Painter button in the Clipboard group in the Home tab to apply formatting to different locations in a worksheet.

- Hide selected columns or rows in a worksheet by clicking the Format button in the Cells group in the Home tab, pointing to *Hide & Unhide*, and then clicking *Hide Columns* or *Hide Rows*.

- To make a hidden column visible, select the column to the left and right, click the Format button in the Cells group, point to *Hide & Unhide*, and then click *Unhide Columns*.
- To make a hidden row visible, select the row above and below, click the Format button in the Cells group, point to *Hide & Unhide*, and then click *Unhide Rows*.

# COMMANDS review

| FEATURE | RIBBON TAB, GROUP | BUTTON | KEYBOARD SHORTCUT |
|---|---|---|---|
| Format | Home, Cells | Format | |
| Insert cells, rows, columns | Home, Cells | Insert | |
| Delete cells, rows, columns | Home, Cells | Delete | |
| Clear cell or cell contents | Home, Editing | | |
| Font | Home, Font | Calibri | |
| Font size | Home, Font | 11 | |
| Increase Font Size | Home, Font | A | |
| Decrease Font Size | Home, Font | A | |
| Bold | Home, Font | B | Ctrl + B |
| Italic | Home, Font | I | Ctrl + I |
| Underline | Home, Font | U | Ctrl + U |
| Borders | Home, Font | | |
| Fill Color | Home, Font | | |
| Font Color | Home, Font | A | |
| Top Align | Home, Alignment | | |
| Middle Align | Home, Alignment | | |
| Bottom Align | Home, Alignment | | |
| Orientation | Home, Alignment | | |
| Align Text Left | Home, Alignment | | |

*continued*

| FEATURE | RIBBON TAB, GROUP | BUTTON | KEYBOARD SHORTCUT |
|---|---|---|---|
| Center | Home, Alignment | | |
| Align Text Right | Home, Alignment | | |
| Decrease Indent | Home, Alignment | | Ctrl + Alt + Shift + Tab |
| Increase Indent | Home, Alignment | | Ctrl + Alt + Tab |
| Wrap Text | Home, Alignment | | |
| Merge & Center | Home, Alignment | | |
| Print Preview | | , Print, Print Preview | Ctrl + F2 |
| Themes | Page Layout, Themes | | |
| Number Format | Home, Number | General | |
| Accounting Number Format | Home, Number | $ | |
| Percent Style | Home, Number | % | Ctrl + Shift + % |
| Increase Decimal | Home, Number | | |
| Decrease Decimal | Home, Number | | |
| Format Painter | Home, Clipboard | | |
| Repeat | | | F4 or Ctrl + Y |

# CONCEPTS check

## Test Your Knowledge

**Completion:** In the space provided at the right, indicate the correct term, symbol, or command.

1. To automatically adjust a column width to accommodate the longest entry in the cell, do this with the mouse on the column boundary.

2. By default, a column is inserted in this direction from the column containing the active cell.

3. To delete a row, select the row and then click the Delete button in this group in the Home tab.

4. With the options at this button drop-down list, you can clear the contents of the cell or selected cells.

_____

5. Use this button to insert color in the active cell or selected cells.

_____

6. By default, numbers are aligned at this side of a cell.

_____

7. Click this button to merge selected cells and center data within the merged cells.

_____

8. Select data in a cell and this displays in a dimmed fashion above the selected text.

_____

9. Click this button in the Alignment group in the Home tab to rotate data in a cell.

_____

10. Use this bar, located at the right side of the Status bar, to zoom the display of the worksheet.

_____

11. The Themes button is located in this tab.

_____

12. If you type a number with a dollar sign, such as $50.25, Excel automatically applies this formatting to the number.

_____

13. If you type a number with a percent sign, such as 25%, Excel automatically applies this formatting to the number.

_____

14. Align and indent data in cells using buttons in the Alignment group in the Home tab or with options at this dialog box with the Alignment tab selected.

_____

15. You can repeat the last action performed with the command Ctrl + Y or pressing this function key.

_____

16. The Format Painter button is located in this group in the Home tab.

_____

17. To hide a column, select the column, click this button in the Cells group in the Home tab, point to *Hide & Unhide*, and then click *Hide Columns*.

_____

# SKILLS check
## Demonstrate Your Proficiency

## Assessment

### 1 FORMAT A SALES AND BONUSES WORKSHEET

1. Open **ExcelC03Assessment01.xlsx**.
2. Save the workbook with Save As and name it **ExcelL1_C3_A1**.
3. Change the width of columns as follows:

   | | | |
   |---|---|---|
   | Column A | = | 14.00 |
   | Columns B - E | = | 10.00 |
   | Column F | = | 6.00 |

4. Select row 2 and then insert a new row.
5. Merge and center cells A2 through F2.
6. Type Sales Department in cell A2 and then press Enter.
7. Increase the height of row 1 to 33.00.
8. Increase the height of row 2 to 21.00.
9. Increase the height of row 3 to 18.00.
10. Make the following formatting changes to the worksheet:
    a. Make cell A1 active, change the font size to 18 points, and turn on bold.
    b. Make cell A2 active, change the font size to 14 points, and turn on bold.
    c. Select cells A3 through F3, click the Bold button in the Font group, and then click the Center button in the Alignment group.
    d. Select cells A1 through F3, change the vertical alignment to Middle Align.
    e. Select cells B4 through E11 and then change the number formatting to Accounting with 0 decimal places and a dollar sign.
11. Insert the following formulas in the worksheet:
    a. Insert a formula in D4 that adds the amounts in B4 and C4. Copy the formula down to cells D5 through D11.
    b. Insert a formula in E4 that averages the amounts in B4 and C4. Copy the formula down to cells E5 through E11.
    c. Insert an IF statement in cell F4 that says that if the amount in cell E4 is greater than 74999, then insert the word "Yes" and if the amount is less than 75000, then insert the word "No." Copy this formula down to cells F5 through F11.
12. Make the following changes to the worksheet:
    a. Select cells F4 through F11 and then click the Center button in the Alignment group.
    b. Add a double-line border around cells A1 through F11.
    c. Select cells A1 and A2 and then apply a light orange fill color.
    d. Select cells A3 through F3 and apply an orange fill color.
13. Save and then print the worksheet.
14. Apply the Verve theme to the worksheet.
15. Save, print, and then close **ExcelL1_C3_A1.xlsx**.

## Assessment

## 2 FORMAT AN OVERDUE ACCOUNTS WORKSHEET

1. Open **ExcelC03Assessment02.xlsx**.
2. Save the workbook with Save As and name it **ExcelL1_C3_A2**.
3. Change the width of columns as follows:

   | | | |
   |---|---|---|
   | Column A | = | 21.00 |
   | Column B | = | 10.00 |
   | Column C | = | 10.00 |
   | Column D | = | 12.00 |
   | Column E | = | 7.00 |
   | Column F | = | 12.00 |

4. Make cell A1 active and then insert a new row.
5. Merge and center cells A1 through F1.
6. Type Compass Corporation in cell A1 and then press Enter.
7. Increase the height of row 1 to 42.00.
8. Increase the height of row 2 to 24.00.
9. Make the following formatting changes to the worksheet:
   a. Select cells A1 through F11 and then change the font to 10-point Bookman Old Style.
   b. Make cell A1 active, change the font size to 24 points, and turn on bold.
   c. Make cell A2 active, change the font size to 18 points, and turn on bold.
   d. Select cells A3 through F3, click the Bold button in the Font group and then click the Center button in the Alignment group.
   e. Select cells A1 through F3, click the Middle Align button in the Alignment group.
   f. Select cells B4 through C11 and then click the Center button in the Alignment group.
   g. Select cells E4 through E11 and then click the Center button in the Alignment group.
10. Use the DATE function in the following cells to enter a formula that returns the serial number for the following dates:

    | | | |
    |---|---|---|
    | D4 | = | September 1, 2010 |
    | D5 | = | September 3, 2010 |
    | D6 | = | September 8, 2010 |
    | D7 | = | September 22, 2010 |
    | D8 | = | September 15, 2010 |
    | D9 | = | September 30, 2010 |
    | D10 | = | October 6, 2010 |
    | D11 | = | October 13, 2010 |

11. Enter a formula in cell F4 that inserts the due date (the purchase date plus the number of days in the Terms column). Copy the formula down to cells F5 through F11.
12. Apply the following borders and fill color:
    a. Add a thick line border around cells A1 through F11.
    b. Make cell A2 active and then add a double-line border at the top and bottom of the cell.
    c. Select cells A3 through F3 and then add a single line border to the bottom of the cells.
    d. Select cells A1 and A2 and then apply a light blue fill color.
13. Save, print, and then close **ExcelL1_C3_A2.xlsx**.

## Assessment

# 3 FORMAT A SUPPLIES AND EQUIPMENT WORKSHEET

1. Open **ExcelC03Assessment03.xlsx**.
2. Save the workbook with Save As and name it **ExcelL1_C3_A3**.
3. Select cells A1 through D19 and then change the font to Garamond and the font color to dark blue.
4. Select and then merge and center cells A1 through D1.
5. Select and then merge and center cells A2 through D2.
6. Make cell A1 active and then change the font size to 22 points and turn on bold.
7. Make cell A2 active and then change the font size to 12 points and turn on bold.
8. Change the height of row 1 to 36.00.
9. Change the height of row 2 to 21.00.
10. Change the width of column A to 15.00.
11. Select cells A3 through A17, turn on bold, and then click the Wrap Text button in the Alignment group.
12. Select cells A1 and A2 and then click the Middle Align button in the Alignment group.
13. Make cell B3 active and then change the number formatting to Currency with no decimal places.
14. Select cells C6 through C19 and then change the number formatting to Percentage with one decimal place.
15. Automatically adjust the width of column B.
16. Make cell D6 active and then type a formula that multiplies the absolute cell reference $B$3 with the percentage in cell C6. Copy the formula down to cells D7 through D19.
17. With cells D6 through D19 selected, change the number formatting to Currency with no decimal places.
18. Make cell D8 active and then clear the cell contents. Use the Repeat command, F4, to clear the contents from cells D11, D14, and D17.
19. Add light green fill color to the following cells: A1, A2, A5–D5, A8–D8, A11–D11, A14–D14, and A17–D17.
20. Add borders and/or shading of your choosing to enhance the visual appeal of the worksheet.
21. Save, print, and then close **ExcelL1_C3_A3.xlsx**.

## Assessment

# 4 FORMAT A FINANCIAL ANALYSIS WORKSHEET

1. Use the Help feature to learn how to use the shrink to fit option to show all data in a cell (with an option at the Format Cells dialog box with the Alignment tab selected).
2. Open **ExcelC03Assessment04.xlsx**.
3. Save the workbook with Save As and name it **ExcelL1_C3_A4**.
4. Make cell B9 active and then insert a formula that averages the percentages in cells B3 through B8. Copy the formula to the right to cells C9 and D9.

5. Select cells B3 through D9, display the Format Cells dialog box with the Alignment tab selected, change the horizontal alignment to Right (Indent) and the indent to *2*, and then close the dialog box.
6. Select cells A1 through D9 and then change the font size to 14.
7. Select cells B2 through D2 and then change the orientation to 45 degrees.
8. With cells B2 through D2 still selected, shrink the font size to show all data in the cells.
9. Save, print, and then close **ExcelL1_C3_A4.xlsx**.

# CASE study
## *Apply Your Skills*

**Part 1**

You are the office manager for HealthWise Fitness Center and you decide to prepare an Excel worksheet that displays the various plans offered by the health club. In this worksheet, you want to include yearly dues for each plan as well as quarterly and monthly payments. Open the **HealthWise.xlsx** workbook and then save it and name it **ExcelL1_C3_CS_P1A**. Make the following changes to the worksheet:

- Select cells B3 through D8 and then change the number formatting to Accounting with two decimal places and a dollar sign.
- Make cell B3 active and then insert *500.00*.
- Make cell B4 active and then insert a formula that adds the amount in B3 with the product (multiplication) of B3 multiplied by 10%. (The formula should look like this: **=B3+(B3*10%)**. The Economy plan is the base plan and each additional plan costs 10% more than the previous plan.)
- Copy the formula in cell B4 down to cells B5 through B8.
- Insert a formula in cell C3 that divides the amount in cell B3 by 4 and then copy the formula down to cells C4 through C8.
- Insert a formula in cell D3 that divides the amount in cell B3 by 12 and then copy the formula down to cells D4 through D8.
- Apply formatting to enhance the visual display of the worksheet.

Save and print the completed worksheet.

With **ExcelL1_C3_CS_P1A.xlsx** open, save the workbook with Save As and name it **ExcelL1_C3_CS_P1B**, and then make the following changes:

- You have been informed that the base rate for yearly dues has increased from $500.00 to $600.00. Change this amount in cell B3 of the worksheet.
- If clients are late with their quarterly or monthly dues payments, a late fee is charged. You decide to add the late fee information to the worksheet. Insert a new column to the right of Column C. Type Late Fees in cell D2 and also in cell F2.
- Insert a formula in cell D3 that multiplies the amount in C3 by 5%. Copy this formula down to cells D4 through D8.
- Insert a formula in cell F3 that multiplies the amount in E3 by 7%. Copy this formula down to cells F4 through F8. If necessary, change the number formatting for cells F3 through F8 to Accounting with two decimal places and a dollar sign.
- Apply any additional formatting to enhance the visual display of the worksheet.

Save, print, and then close **ExcelL1_C3_CS_P1B.xlsx**.

**Part 2**

Prepare a payroll sheet for the employees of the fitness center and include the following information:

HealthWise Fitness Center
Weekly Payroll

| Employee | Hourly Wage | Hours | Weekly Salary | Benefits |
|---|---|---|---|---|
| Heaton, Kelly | $26.50 | 40 | | |
| Severson, Joel | $25.00 | 40 | | |
| Turney, Amanda | $20.00 | 15 | | |
| Walters, Leslie | $19.65 | 30 | | |
| Overmeyer, Jean | $18.00 | 20 | | |
| Haddon, Bonnie | $16.00 | 20 | | |
| Baker, Grant | $15.00 | 40 | | |
| Calveri, Shannon | $12.00 | 15 | | |
| Dugan, Emily | $10.50 | 10 | | |
| Joyner, Daniel | $10.50 | 10 | | |
| Lee, Alexander | $10.50 | 10 | | |

Insert a formula in the *Weekly Salary* column that multiplies the hourly wage by the number of hours. Insert an IF statement in the *Benefits* column that states that if the number in the *Hours* column is greater than 19, then insert "Yes" and if the number is less than 20, then insert "No." Apply formatting to enhance the visual display of the worksheet. Save the workbook and name it **ExcelL1_C3_CS_P2**. Print **ExcelL1_C3_CS_P2.xlsx**. Press Ctrl + ` to turn on the display of formulas, print the worksheet, and then press Ctrl + ` to turn off the display of formulas.

Make the following changes to the worksheet:

* Change the hourly wage for Amanda Turney to $22.00.
* Increase the hours for Emily Dugan to 20.
* Remove the row for Grant Baker.
* Insert a row between Jean Overmeyer and Bonnie Haddon and then type the following information in the cells in the new row: Employee: Tonya McGuire; Hourly Wage: $17.50; Hours: 15.

Save and then print **ExcelL1_C3_CS_P2.xlsx**. Press Ctrl + ` to turn on the display of formulas and then print the worksheet. Press Ctrl + ` to turn off the display of formulas and then save and close **ExcelL1_C3_CS_P2.xlsx**.

**Part 3**

Your boss is interested in ordering new equipment for the health club. She is interested in ordering three elliptical machines, three recumbent bikes, and three upright bikes. She has asked you to use the Internet to research models and prices for this new equipment. She then wants you to prepare a worksheet with the information. Using the Internet, search for the following equipment:

* Search for elliptical machines for sale. Locate two different models and, if possible, find at least two companies that sell each model. Make a note of the company names, model numbers, and prices.

- Search for recumbent bikes for sale. Locate two different models and, if possible, find at least two companies that sell each model. Make a note of the company names, model numbers, and prices.
- Search for upright bikes for sale. Locate two different models and, if possible, find at least two companies that sell each model. Make a note of the company names, model numbers, and prices.

Using the information you found on the Internet, prepare an Excel worksheet with the following information:

- Equipment name
- Equipment model
- Price
- A column that multiplies the price by the number required (which is 3).

Include the fitness center name, HealthWise Fitness Center, and any other information you determine is necessary to the worksheet. Apply formatting to enhance the visual display of the worksheet. Save the workbook and name it **ExcelL1_C3_CS_P3**. Print and then close **ExcelL1_C3_CS_P3.xlsx**.

Part 4

When a prospective client contacts HealthWise about joining, you send a letter containing information about the fitness center, the plans offered, and the dues amounts. Use a letter template in Word to create a letter to send to a prospective client (you determine the client's name and address). Copy the cells in **ExcelL1_C3_CS_P1B.xlsx** containing data and paste them into the body of the letter. Make any formatting changes to make the data readable. Save, print, and then close the letter.

CHAPTER

# Enhancing a Worksheet

4

# PERFORMANCE OBJECTIVES

**Upon successful completion of Chapter 4, you will be able to:**

- Change worksheet margins
- Center a worksheet horizontally and vertically on the page
- Insert a page break in a worksheet
- Print gridlines and row and column headings
- Set and clear a print area
- Insert headers and footers
- Customize print jobs
- Complete a spelling check on a worksheet
- Find and replace data and cell formatting in a worksheet
- Sort data in cells in ascending and descending order
- Filter a list using AutoFilter
- Plan and create a worksheet

excel Chapter 4

**Tutorial 4.1**
Printing Worksheets
**Tutorial 4.2**
Finding, Sorting, and Filtering
Data

Excel contains features you can use to enhance and control the formatting of a worksheet. In this chapter, you will learn how to change worksheet margins, orientation, size, and scale; print column and row titles; print gridlines; and center a worksheet horizontally and vertically on the page. You will also learn how to complete a spell check on text in a worksheet, find and replace specific data and formatting in a worksheet, sort and filter data, and plan and create a worksheet.

*Note: Before beginning computer projects, copy to your storage medium the Excel2007L1C4 subfolder from the Excel2007L1 folder on the CD that accompanies this textbook and make Excel2007L1C4 the active folder.*

# $P$roject ① Format a Yearly Budget Worksheet

You will format a yearly budget worksheet by inserting formulas; changing margins, page orientation, and page size; inserting a page break; printing column headings on multiple pages; scaling data to print on one page; inserting a background picture; inserting headers and footers; and identifying a print area and customizing print jobs.

## Formatting a Worksheet Page

**QUICK STEPS**

**Change Worksheet Margins**
1. Click Page Layout tab.
2. Click Margins button.
3. Click desired predesigned margin.

OR

1. Click Page Layout tab.
2. Click Margins button.
3. Click *Custom Margins* at drop-down list.
4. Change the top, left, right, and/or bottom measurements.
5. Click OK.

An Excel worksheet contains default page formatting. For example, a worksheet contains left and right margins of 0.7 inch and top and bottom margins of 0.75 inch, a worksheet prints in portrait orientation, and the worksheet page size is 8.5 inches by 11 inches. These default settings as well as additional options can be changed and/or controlled with options in the Page Layout tab.

## Changing Margins

The Page Setup group in the Page Layout tab contains buttons for changing margins, the page orientation and size, as well as buttons for establishing a print area, inserting a page break, applying a picture background, and printing titles.

Change the worksheet margins by clicking the Margins button in the Page Setup group in the Page Layout tab. This displays a drop-down list of predesigned margin choices. If one of the predesigned choices is what you want to apply to the worksheet, click the option. If you want to customize margins, click the *Custom Margins* option at the bottom of the Margins drop-down list. This displays the Page Setup dialog box with the Margins tab selected as shown in Figure 4.1.

**Figure 4.1** Page Setup Dialog Box with Margins Tab Selected

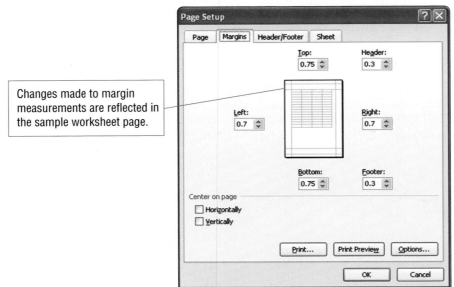

Changes made to margin measurements are reflected in the sample worksheet page.

A worksheet page showing the cells and margins displays in the dialog box. As you increase or decrease the top, bottom, left, or right margin measurements, the sample worksheet page reflects the change. You can also increase or decrease the measurement from the top of the page to the header with the *Header* option or the measurement from the footer to the bottom of the page with the *Footer* option. (You will learn about headers and footers later in this chapter.)

**QUICK STEPS**

**Center Worksheet Horizontally/Vertically**
1. Click Page Layout tab.
2. Click *Custom Margins* at drop-down list.
3. Click *Horizontally* option and/or click *Vertically* option.
4. Click OK.

## Centering a Worksheet Horizontally and/or Vertically

By default, worksheets print in the upper left corner of the page. You can center a worksheet on the page by changing the margins; however, an easier method for centering a worksheet is to use the *Horizontally* and/or *Vertically* options that display at the bottom of the Page Setup dialog box with the Margins tab selected. If you choose one or both of these options, the worksheet page in the preview section displays how the worksheet will print on the page.

**Project 1a — Changing Margins and Horizontally and Vertically Centering a Worksheet**

1. Open **ExcelC04Project01.xlsx**.
2. Save the workbook with Save As and name it **ExcelL1_C4_P1**.
3. Insert the following formulas in the worksheet:
   a. Insert formulas in column N, rows 5 through 10 that sum the totals for each income item.
   b. Insert formulas in row 11, columns B through N that sum the income as well as the total for all income items.
   c. Insert formulas in column N, rows 14 through 19 that sum the totals for each expense item.
   d. Insert formulas in row 20, columns B through N that sum the expenses as well as the total of expenses.
   e. Insert formulas in row 21, columns B through N that subtract the total expenses from the income. (To begin the formula, make cell B21 active and then type the formula =B11-B20. Copy this formula to columns C through N.)
4. Click the Page Layout tab.
5. Click the Margins button in the Page Setup group and then click *Custom Margins* at the drop-down list.

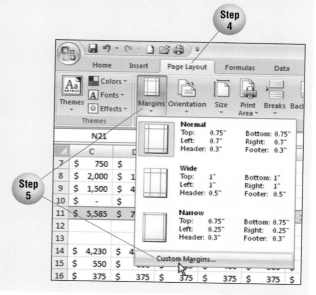

6. At the Page Setup dialog box with the Margins tab selected, click the up-pointing arrow at the right side of the *Top* text box until *3.5* displays.
7. Click the up-pointing arrow at the right side of the *Bottom* text box until *1.5* displays.
8. Preview the worksheet by clicking the Print Preview button located toward the bottom of the Page Setup dialog box. The worksheet appears to be a little low on the page so you decide to horizontally and vertically center it by completing the following steps:
   a. Click the Close Print Preview button.
   b. Click the Margins button in the Page Setup group and then click *Custom Margins* at the drop-down list.
   c. At the Page Setup dialog box with the Margins tab selected, change the *Top* and *Bottom* measurements to *1*.
   d. Click the *Horizontally* option. (This inserts a check mark.)
   e. Click the *Vertically* option. (This inserts a check mark.)
   f. Click OK to close the dialog box.
9. Save **ExcelL1_C4_P1.xlsx**.

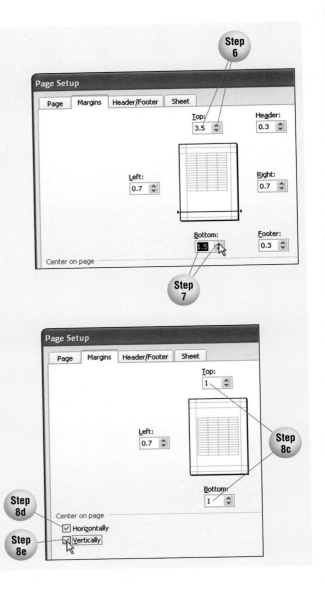

## Changing Page Orientation

**Change Page Orientation**
1. Click Page Layout tab.
2. Click Orientation button.
3. Click desired orientation at drop-down list.

Click the Orientation button in the Page Setup group and a drop-down list displays with two choices, *Portrait* and *Landscape*. The two choices are represented by sample pages. A sample page that is taller than it is wide shows how the default orientation (*Portrait*) prints data on the page. The other choice, *Landscape*, will rotate the data and print it on a page that is wider than it is tall.

# Changing the Page Size

An Excel worksheet page size, by default, is set at 8.5 × 11 inches. You can change this default page size by clicking the Size button in the Page Setup group. At the drop-down list that displays, notice that the default setting is *Letter* and the measurement *8.5" × 11"* displays below *Letter*. This drop-down list also contains a number of page sizes such as *Executive*, *Legal*, and a number of envelope sizes.

## Project 1b  Changing Page Orientation and Size

1. With **ExcelL1_C4_P1.xlsx** open, click the Orientation button in the Page Setup group in the Page Layout tab and then click *Landscape* at the drop-down list.

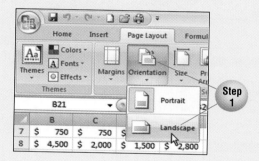

2. Click the Size button in the Page Setup group and then click *Legal* at the drop-down list.

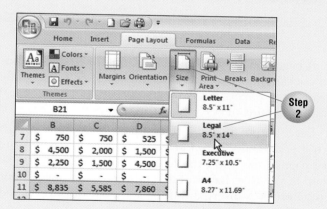

3. Preview the worksheet by clicking the Office button, pointing to *Print*, and then clicking *Print Preview*. After viewing the worksheet in Print Preview, click the Close Print Preview button.
4. Save **ExcelL1_C4_P1.xlsx**.

# Inserting and Removing Page Breaks

The default left and right margins of 0.7 inch allow approximately 7 inches of cells across the page (8.5 inches minus 1.4 inches equals 7.1 inches). If a worksheet contains more than 7 inches of cells across the page, a page break is inserted in the worksheet and the remaining columns are moved to the next page. A page break displays as a broken line along cell borders. Figure 4.2 shows the page break in **ExcelL1_C4_P1.xlsx**.

**Figure 4.2** Page Break

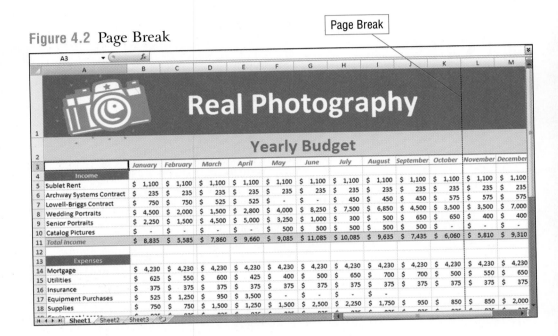

Page Break

**Insert Page Break**
1. Select column or row.
2. Click Page Layout tab.
3. Click Breaks button.
4. Click *Insert Page Break* at drop-down list.

Breaks

A page break also displays horizontally in a worksheet. By default, a worksheet can contain approximately 9.5 inches of cells vertically down the page. This is because the paper size is set by default at 11 inches. With the default top and bottom margins of 0.75 inch, this allows 9.5 inches of cells to print on one page.

Excel automatically inserts a page break in a worksheet. You can insert your own if you would like more control over what cells print on a page. To insert your own page break, select the column or row, click the Breaks button in the Page Setup group in the Page Layout tab, and then click *Insert Page Break* at the drop-down list. A page break is inserted immediately left of the selected column or immediately above the selected row.

If you want to insert both a horizontal and vertical page break at the same time, make a cell active, click the Breaks button in the Page Setup group and then click *Insert Page Break*. This causes a horizontal page break to be inserted immediately above the active cell, and a vertical page break to be inserted at the left side of the active cell. To remove a page break, select the column or row or make the desired cell active, click the Breaks button in the Page Setup group, and then click *Remove Page Break* at the drop-down list.

The page break automatically inserted by Excel may not be visible initially in a worksheet. One way to display the page break is to preview the worksheet. When you close Print Preview, the page break will display in the worksheet.

# Displaying a Worksheet in Page Break Preview

Excel provides a page break view that displays worksheet pages and page breaks. To display this view, click the Page Break Preview button located in the view area at the right side of the Status bar or click the View tab and then click the Page Break Preview button in the Workbook Views group. This causes the worksheet to display similar to the worksheet shown in Figure 4.3. The word *Page* along with the page number is displayed in gray behind the cells in the worksheet. A solid blue line indicates a page break inserted by Excel and a dashed blue line indicates a page break inserted manually.

You can move the page break by positioning the arrow pointer on the blue line, holding down the left mouse button, dragging the line to the desired location, and then releasing the mouse button. To return to the Normal view, click the Normal button in the view area on the Status bar or click the View tab and then click the Normal button in the Workbook Views group.

Page Break Preview

Normal

**Figure 4.3** Worksheet in Page Break Preview

Adjust page break by dragging page break to desired location.

## Project 1C  Inserting a Page Break in a Worksheet

1. With **ExcelL1_C4_P1.xlsx** open, click the Size button in the Page Setup group in the Page Layout tab and then click *Letter* at the drop-down list.
2. Click the Margins button and then click *Custom Margins* at the drop-down list.
3. At the Page Setup dialog box with the Margins tab selected, click *Horizontally* to remove the check mark, click *Vertically* to remove the check mark, and then click OK to close the dialog box.
4. Insert a page break between columns I and J by completing the following steps:
   a. Select column J.
   b. Click the Breaks button in the Page Setup group and then click *Insert Page Break* at the drop-down list. Click in any cell in column I.

Step 4b

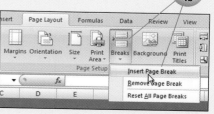

5. View the worksheet in Page Break Preview by completing the following steps:

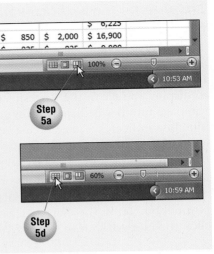

Step
5a

Step
5d

   a. Click the Page Break Preview button located in the view area on the Status bar. (If a welcome message displays, click OK.)

   b. View the pages and page breaks in the worksheet.

   c. You decide to include the first six months of the year on one page. To do this, position the arrow pointer on the vertical blue line, hold down the left mouse button, drag the line to the left so it is positioned between columns G and H, and then release the mouse button.

   d. Click the Normal button located in the view area on the Status bar.

6. Save **ExcelL1_C4_P1.xlsx**.

## Printing Column and Row Titles on Multiple Pages

Print
Titles

Columns and rows in a worksheet are usually titled. For example, in **ExcelL1_C4_P1.xlsx**, column titles include *Income*, *Expenses*, *January*, *February*, *March*, and so on. Row titles include the income and expenses categories. If a worksheet prints on more than one page, having column and/or row titles printing on each page can be useful. To do this, click the Print Titles button in the Page Setup group in the Page Layout tab. This displays the Page Setup dialog box with the Sheet tab selected as shown in Figure 4.4.

**Figure 4.4** Page Setup Dialog Box with Sheet Tab Selected

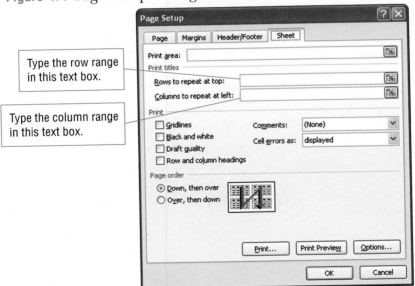

Type the row range in this text box.

Type the column range in this text box.

At the Page Setup dialog box with the Sheet tab selected, specify the range of row cells you want to print on every page in the *Rows to repeat at top* text box. Type a cell range using a colon. For example, if you want cells A1 through J1 to print on every page, you would type **A1:J1** in the *Rows to repeat at top* text box. Type the range of column cells you want to print on every page in the *Columns to repeat at left* text box. To make rows and columns easier to identify on the printed page, specify that row and/or column headings print on each page.

**Print Column and Row Titles**

1. Click Page Layout tab.
2. Click Print Titles button.
3. Type row range in *Rows to repeat at top* option.
4. Type column range in *Columns to repeat at left* option.
5. Click OK.

## Project 1d  Printing Column Titles on Each Page of a Worksheet

1. With **ExcelL1_C4_P1.xlsx** open, click the Page Layout tab and then click the Print Titles button in the Page Setup group.
2. At the Page Setup dialog box with the Sheet tab selected, click in the *Columns to repeat at left* text box.
3. Type **A1:A21**.

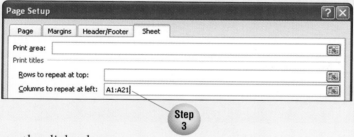

4. Click OK to close the dialog box.
5. Save, preview, and then print **ExcelL1_C4_P1.xlsx**.

## Scaling Data

With buttons in the Scale to Fit group in the Page Layout tab, you can adjust the printed output by a percentage to fit the number of pages specified. For example, if a worksheet contains too many columns to print on one page, click the down-pointing arrow at the right side of the *Width* box in the Scale to Fit group in the Page Layout tab and then click *1 page*. This causes the data to shrink so all columns display and print on one page.

## Project 1e  Scaling Data to Fit on One Page

1. With **ExcelL1_C4_P1.xlsx** open, click the down-pointing arrow at the right side of the *Width* box in the Scale to Fit group in the Page Layout tab.
2. At the drop-down list that displays, click the *1 page* option.

Step 1

Step 2

3. Preview the worksheet to make sure it displays on one page.
4. Save and then print **ExcelL1_C4_P1.xlsx**.

## Inserting a Background Picture

**Insert Background Picture**
1. Click Page Layout tab.
2. Click Background button.
3. Navigate to desired picture and double-click picture.

With the Background button in the Page Setup group in the Page Layout tab you can insert a picture as a background to the worksheet. The picture displays only on the screen and does not print. To insert a picture, click the Background button in the Page Setup group. At the Sheet Background dialog box navigate to the folder containing the desired picture and then double-click the picture. To remove the picture from the worksheet, click the Delete Background button.

## Project 1f  Inserting a Background Picture

1. With **ExcelL1_C4_P1.xlsx** open, change the scaling back to the default by completing the following steps:
   a. Click the down-pointing arrow at the right side of the *Width* box in the Scale to Fit group and then click *Automatic* at the drop-down list.
   b. Click the up-pointing arrow at the right side of the *Scale* measurement box until *100%* displays in the box.
2. Remove titles from printing on second and subsequent pages by completing the following steps:
   a. Click the Print Titles button in the Page Setup group.
   b. At the Page Setup dialog box with the Sheet tab selected, select the text that displays in the *Columns to repeat at left* text box and then press the Delete key.
   c. Click OK to close the dialog box.
3. Insert a background picture by completing the following steps:
   a. Click the Background button in the Page Setup group.
   b. At the Sheet Background dialog box, navigate to the Excel2007L1C4 folder, and then double-click **Mountain.jpg**.

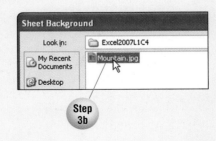

Step 3b

4. Preview the worksheet. (Notice that the picture does not display in Print Preview.)
5. Remove the picture by clicking the Delete Background button in the Page Setup group.
6. Save **ExcelL1_C4_P1.xlsx**.

# Printing Gridlines and Row and Column Headings

By default, the gridlines that create the cells in a worksheet and the row numbers and column letters do not print. The Sheet Options group in the Page Layout tab contain check boxes for gridlines and headings. The *View* check boxes for Gridlines and Headings contain check marks. At these settings, gridlines and row and column headings display on the screen but do not print. If you want them to print, insert check marks in the *Print* check boxes. Complex worksheets may be easier to read with the gridlines printed.

You can also control the display and printing of gridlines and headings with options at the Page Setup dialog box with the Sheet tab selected. Display this dialog box by clicking the Sheet Options dialog box launcher. To print gridlines and headings, insert check marks in the check boxes located in the *Print* section of the dialog box. The *Print* section contains two additional options—*Black and white* and *Draft quality*. If you are printing with a color printer, you can print the worksheet in black and white by inserting a check mark in the *Black and white* check box. Insert a check mark in the *Draft* option if you want to print a draft of the worksheet. With this option checked, some formatting such as shading and fill are not printed.

**QUICK STEPS**

**Print Gridlines**
1. Click Page Layout tab.
2. Click *Print* check box in Gridlines section in Sheet Options group.
OR
1. Click Page Layout tab.
2. Click Sheet Options dialog box launcher.
3. Click *Gridlines* option.
4. Click OK.

**Print Row and Column Headings**
1. Click Page Layout tab.
2. Click *Print* check box in Headings section in Sheet Options group.
OR
1. Click Page Layout tab.
2. Click Sheet Options dialog box launcher.
3. Click *Row and column headings* option.
4. Click OK.

## Project 1g  Printing Gridlines and Row and Column Headings

1. With **ExcelL1_C4_P1.xlsx** open, click in the *Print* check box below Gridlines in the Sheet Options group to insert a check mark.
2. Click in the *Print* check box below Headings in the Sheet Options group to insert a check mark.

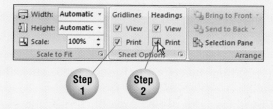

Step 1

Step 2

3. Click the Margins button in the Page Setup group and then click *Custom Margins* at the drop-down list.
4. At the Page Setup dialog box with the Margins tab selected, click in the *Horizontally* check box to insert a check mark.
5. Click in the *Vertically* check box to insert a check mark.
6. Click OK to close the dialog box.
7. Save, preview, and then print **ExcelL1_C4_P1.xlsx**.
8. Click in the *Print* check box below Headings in the Sheet Options group to remove the check mark.
9. Click in the *Print* check box below Gridlines in the Sheet Options group to remove the check mark.
10. Save **ExcelL1_C4_P1.xlsx**.

# Printing a Specific Area of a Worksheet

With the Print Area button in the Page Setup group in the Page Layout tab you can select and print specific areas in a worksheet. To do this, select the cells you want to print, click the Print Area button in the Page Setup group in the Page Layout tab, and then click *Set Print Area* at the drop-down list. This inserts a border around the selected cells. Click the Quick Print button on the Quick Access toolbar and the cells within the border are printed.

You can specify more than one print area in a worksheet. To do this, select the first group of cells, click the Print Area button in the Page Setup group, and then click *Set Print Area*. Select the next group of cells, click the Print Area button, and then click *Add to Print Area*. Clear a print area by clicking the Print Area button in the Page Setup group and then clicking *Clear Print Area* at the drop-down list.

Each area specified as a print area will print on a separate page. If you want nonadjacent print areas to print on the same page, consider hiding columns and/or rows in the worksheet to bring the areas together.

## Project 1h  Printing Specific Areas

1. With **ExcelL1_C4_P1.xlsx** open, print the first half expenses by completing the following steps:
   a. Select cells A3 through G21.
   b. Click the Print Area button in the Page Setup group in the Page Layout tab and then click *Set Print Area* at the drop-down list.

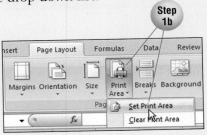

   c. With the border surrounding the cells A3 through G21, click the Quick Print button on the Quick Access toolbar.
   d. Clear the print area by clicking the Print Area button in the Page Setup group and then clicking *Clear Print Area* at the drop-down list.
2. Suppose you want to print the income and expenses information as well as the totals for the month of April. To do this, hide columns and select a print area by completing the following steps:
   a. Select columns B through D.
   b. Click the Home tab.
   c. Click the Format button in the Cells group, point to *Hide & Unhide*, and then click *Hide Columns*.
   d. Click the Page Layout tab.
   e. Select cells A3 through E21. (Columns A and E are now adjacent.)
   f. Click the Print Area button in the Page Setup group and then click *Set Print Area* at the drop-down list.

3. Click the Quick Print button on the Quick Access toolbar.
4. Clear the print area by making sure cells A3 through E21 are selected, clicking the Print Area button in the Page Setup group, and then clicking *Clear Print Area* at the drop-down list.
5. Unhide the columns by completing the following steps:
   a. Click the Home tab.
   b. Select columns A and E (these columns are adjacent).
   c. Click the Format button in the Cells group, point to *Hide & Unhide*, and then click *Unhide Columns*.
   d. Deselect the text by clicking in any cell containing data in the worksheet.
6. Save **ExcelL1_C4_P1.xlsx**.

# Inserting Headers/Footers

Text that prints at the top of each worksheet page is called a ***header*** and text that prints at the bottom of each worksheet page is called a ***footer***. You can create a header and/or footer with the Header & Footer button in the Text group in the Insert tab, in Page Layout View, or with options at the Page Setup dialog box with the Header/Footer tab selected.

To create a header with the Header & Footer button, click the Insert tab and then click the Header & Footer button in the Text group. This displays the worksheet in Page Layout view and displays the Header & Footer Tools Design tab. Use buttons in this tab, shown in Figure 4.5, to insert predesigned headers and/or footers or insert header and footer elements such as the page number, date, time, path name, and file name. You can also create a different header or footer on the first page of the worksheet or create a header or footer for even pages and another for odd pages.

QUICK STEPS

**Insert a Header or Footer**
1. Click Insert tab.
2. Click Header & Footer button.
3. Click Header button and then click predesigned header or click Footer button and then click predesigned footer.
OR
1. Click Insert tab.
2. Click Header & Footer button.
3. Click desired header or footer elements.

HINT
Close the header or footer pane by clicking in the worksheet or pressing Esc.

**Figure 4.5** Header & Footer Tools Design Tab

1. With **ExcelL1_C4_P1.xlsx** open, create a header by completing the following steps:
   a. Click the Insert tab.
   b. Click the Header & Footer button in the Text group.

c. Click the Header button located at the
   left side of the Header & Footer Tools
   Design tab and then click *Page 1,
   ExcelL1_C4_P1.xlsx* at the drop-down
   list. (This inserts the page number in
   the middle header box and the workbook
   name in the right header box.)
2. Click in any cell in the worksheet
   containing data.
3. Click the Normal view button located in
   the view area on the Status bar.
4. Save **ExcelL1_C4_P1.xlsx**.

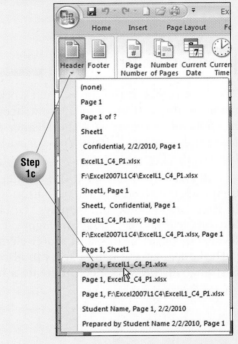

You also can insert a header and/or footer by switching to Page Layout view.
In Page Layout view, the top of the worksheet page displays with the text *Click
to add header*. Click this text and the insertion point is positioned in the middle
header box. Type the desired header in this box or click in the left box or the right
box and then type the header. Create a footer in a similar manner. Scroll down
the worksheet until the bottom of the page displays and then click the text *Click
to add footer*. Type the footer in the center footer box or click the left or right box
and then type the footer.

Project **1j**    **Inserting a Footer and Modifying a Header in a Worksheet**

1. With **ExcelL1_C4_P1.xlsx** open, click the Page Layout button located in the view area on the Status bar.
2. Scroll down the worksheet until the text *Click to add footer* displays and then click the text.

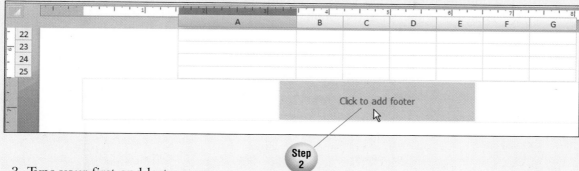

Step 2

3. Type your first and last names.
4. Click in the left footer box and then click the Current Date button in the Header & Footer Elements group in the Header & Footer Tools Design tab.
5. Click in the right footer box and then click the Current Time button in the Header & Footer Elements group.
6. Click in a cell in the worksheet.
7. Save and then print **ExcelL1_C4_P1.xlsx**.
8. Modify the header by completing the following steps:
   a. Scroll to the beginning of the worksheet and display the header text.
   b. Click the page number in the middle header box. (This displays the Header & Footer Tools Design tab, changes the header to a field, and selects the field.)
   c. Press the Delete key to delete the header.
   d. Click the header text that displays in the right header box and then press the Delete key.
   e. Insert the page number by clicking the Page Number button in the Header & Footer Elements group.
   f. Click in the left header box and then click the File Name button in the Header & Footer Elements group.

Step 8f

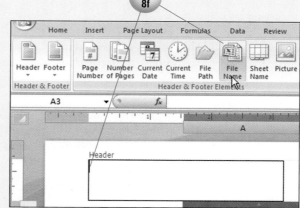

9. Click in any cell in the worksheet containing data.
10. Click the Normal button in the view area on the Status bar.
11. Preview the worksheet to determine how the header and footer print on each page.
12. Save and then print **ExcelL1_C4_P1.xlsx**.

# Customizing Print Jobs

The Print dialog box provides options for customizing a print job. Display the Print dialog box shown in Figure 4.6 by clicking the Office button and then clicking *Print* at the drop-down list or by pressing the keyboard shortcut Ctrl + P. Use options at the Print dialog box to print a specific range of cells, selected cells, or multiple copies of a workbook.

**Figure 4.6** Print Dialog Box

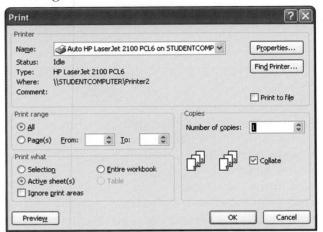

At the Print dialog box, the currently selected printer name displays in the *Name* option box. If other printers are installed, click the down-pointing arrow at the right side of the *Name* option box to display a list of printers.

The *Active sheet(s)* option in the *Print what* section is selected by default. At this setting, the currently active worksheet will print. If you want to print an entire workbook that contains several worksheets, click *Entire workbook* in the *Print what* section. Click the *Selection* option in the *Print what* section to print the currently selected cells.

If you want more than one copy of a worksheet or workbook printed, change the desired number of copies with the *Number of copies* option in the *Copies* section. If you want the copies collated, make sure the *Collate* check box in the *Copies* section contains a check mark.

A worksheet within a workbook can contain more than one page. If you want to print specific pages of a worksheet within a workbook, click *Page(s)* in the *Print range* section, and then specify the desired page numbers in the *From* and *To* text boxes.

If you want to preview the worksheet before printing, click the Preview button that displays at the bottom left corner of the dialog box. This displays the worksheet as it will appear on the printed page. After viewing the worksheet, click the Close Print Preview button that displays at the right side of the Print Preview tab.

 **Project 1k** **Printing Specific Cells in a Worksheet**

1. With **ExcelL1_C4_P1.xlsx** open, print selected cells by completing the following steps:
   a. Select cells A3 through G11.
   b. Click the Office button and then click *Print* at the drop-down list.
   c. At the Print dialog box, click *Selection* in the *Print what* section.
   d. Click OK.
2. Close **ExcelL1_C4_P1.xlsx**.

**Project 2** **Format a May Sales and Commissions Worksheet**

You will format a sales commission worksheet by inserting a formula, completing a spelling check, and finding and replacing data and cell formatting.

# Completing a Spelling Check

Excel includes a spelling checker you can use to check the spelling of text in a worksheet. Before checking the spelling in a worksheet, make the first cell active. The spell checker checks the worksheet from the active cell to the last cell in the worksheet that contains data.

To use the spelling checker, click the Review tab and then click the Spelling button. Figure 4.7 displays the Spelling dialog box. At this dialog box, you can click a button to tell Excel to ignore a word or you can replace a misspelled word with a word from the *Suggestions* list box.

**Complete a Spelling Check**
1. Click Review tab.
2. Click Spelling button.
3. Replace or ignore selected words.

**HINT**

Customize spell checking options at the Excel Options dialog box with Proofing selected.

**Figure 4.7** Excel Spelling Dialog Box

The word in the worksheet not found in the spell check dictionary displays here.

Suggested spellings display in the *Suggestions* list box.

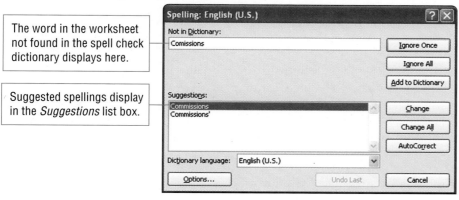

# Using Undo and Redo

## HINT

Ctrl + Z is the keyboard shortcut to undo a command.

Undo

Redo

Excel includes an Undo button on the Quick Access toolbar that will reverse certain commands or delete the last data typed in a cell. For example, if you apply an autoformat to selected cells in a worksheet and then decide you want the autoformatting removed, click the Undo button on the Quick Access toolbar. If you decide you want the autoformatting back again, click the Redo button on the Quick Access toolbar.

Excel maintains actions in temporary memory. If you want to undo an action performed earlier, click the down-pointing arrow at the right side of the Undo button and a drop-down list displays containing the actions performed on the worksheet. Click the desired action at the drop-down list. Any actions preceding a chosen action are also undone. You can do the same with the Redo drop-down list. Multiple actions must be undone or redone in sequence.

## Project 2a   Spell Checking and Formatting a Worksheet

1. Open **ExcelC04Project02.xlsx**.
2. Save the workbook with Save As and name it **ExcelL1_C4_P2**.
3. Complete a spelling check on the worksheet by completing the following steps:
   a. Make sure cell A1 is the active cell.
   b. Click the Review tab.
   c. Click the Spelling button.
   d. Click the Change button as needed to correct misspelled words in the worksheet. (When the spell checker stops at proper names *Pirozzi*, *Valona*, and *Yonemoto*, click the Ignore All button.)
   e. At the message telling you the spelling check is completed, click OK.

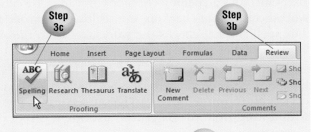

Step 3c

Step 3b

4. Make cell G4 active and then insert a formula that multiplies the sale price by the commission percentage. Copy the formula down to cells G5 through G26.
5. Make cell G27 active and then insert the sum of cells G4 through G26.
6. Apply a theme by clicking the Page Layout button, clicking the Themes button, and then clicking *Civic* at the drop-down gallery.
7. After looking at the worksheet with the Civic theme applied, you decide you want to return to the original formatting. To do this, click the Undo button on the Quick Access toolbar.
8. You realize that copying the formula in cell G4 down to cells G5 through G26 caused the yellow fill to be removed from certain cells and you decide to insert the shading. To do this, complete the following steps:
   a. Make cell G5 active.
   b. Click the Home tab.

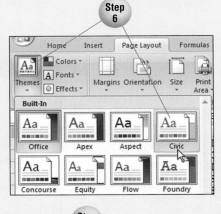

Step 6

Step 7

c. Click the Fill Color button arrow and then click *More Colors* at the drop-down gallery.

d. At the Colors dialog box with the Standard tab selected, click the yellow color as shown at the right.

e. Click OK to close the dialog box.

f. Make cell G7 active and then press F4 (the Repeat command).

g. Use F4 to apply yellow shading to cells G9, G11, G13, G15, G17, G19, G21, G23, and G25.

9. Save **ExcelL1_C4_P2.xlsx**.

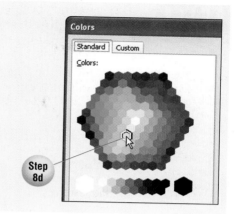

**Step 8d**

# Finding and Replacing Data in a Worksheet

Excel provides a Find feature you can use to look for specific data and either replace it with nothing or replace it with other data. This feature is particularly helpful in a large worksheet with data you want to find quickly. Excel also includes a find and replace feature. Use this to look for specific data in a worksheet and replace it with other data.

To find specific data in a worksheet, click the Find & Select button located in the Editing group in the Home tab and then click *Find* at the drop-down list. This displays the Find and Replace dialog box with the Find tab selected as shown in Figure 4.8. Type the data you want to find in the *Find what* text box and then click the Find Next button. Continue clicking the Find Next button to move to the next occurrence of the data. If the Find and Replace dialog box obstructs your view of the worksheet, use the mouse pointer on the title bar to drag the box to a different location.

**QUICK STEPS**

**Find Data**
1. Click Find & Select button.
2. Click *Find* at drop-down list.
3. Type data in *Find what* text box.
4. Click Find Next button.

Find & Select

**Figure 4.8** Find and Replace Dialog Box with Find Tab Selected

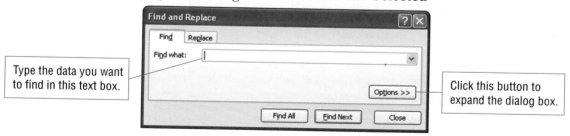

Type the data you want to find in this text box.

Click this button to expand the dialog box.

**QUICK STEPS**

**Find and Replace Data**
1. Click Find & Select button.
2. Click *Replace* at drop-down list.
3. Type data in *Find what* text box.
4. Type data in *Replace with* text box.
5. Click Replace button or Replace All button.

To find specific data in a worksheet and replace it with other data, click the Find & Select button in the Editing group in the Home tab and then click *Replace* at the drop-down list. This displays the Find and Replace dialog box with the Replace tab selected as shown in Figure 4.9. Enter the data for which you are looking in the *Find what* text box. Press the Tab key or click in the *Replace with* text box and then enter the data that is to replace the data in the *Find what* text box.

**Figure 4.9** Find and Replace Dialog Box with Replace Tab Selected

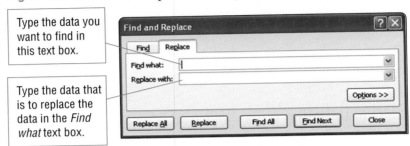

Type the data you want to find in this text box.

Type the data that is to replace the data in the *Find what* text box.

Click the Find Next button to tell Excel to find the next occurrence of the data. Click the Replace button to replace the data and find the next occurrence. If you know that you want all occurrences of the data in the *Find what* text box replaced with the data in the *Replace with* text box, click the Replace All button. Click the Close button to close the Replace dialog box.

Display additional find and replace options by clicking the Options button. This expands the dialog box as shown in Figure 4.10. By default, Excel will look for any data that contains the same characters as the data in the *Find what* text box, without concern for the characters before or after the entered data. For example, in Project 2b, you will be looking for sale prices of $450,000 and replacing with $475,000. If you do not specify to Excel that you want to find cells that contain only *450000*, Excel will stop at any cell containing *450000*. In this example, Excel would stop at a cell containing *$1,450,000* or a cell containing *$2,450,000*. To specify that the only data that should be contained in the cell is what is entered in the *Find what* text box, click the Options button to expand the dialog box, and then insert a check mark in the *Match entire cell contents* check box.

**Figure 4.10** Expanded Find and Replace Dialog Box

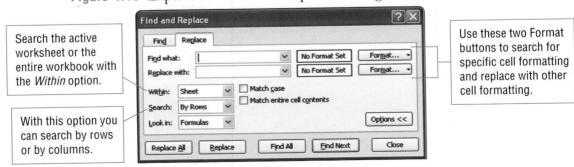

Search the active worksheet or the entire workbook with the *Within* option.

With this option you can search by rows or by columns.

Use these two Format buttons to search for specific cell formatting and replace with other cell formatting.

If the *Match case* option is active (contains a check mark), Excel will look for only that data that exactly matches the case of the data entered in the *Find what* text box. Remove the check mark from this check box if you do not want Excel to find exact case matches. Excel will search in the current worksheet. If you want Excel to search an entire workbook, change the *Within* option to *Workbook*. Excel, by default, searches by rows in a worksheet. You can change this to *By Columns* with the *Search* option.

## Project 2b    Finding and Replacing Data

1. With **ExcelL1_C4_P2.xlsx** open, find all occurrences of *Land* in the worksheet and replace with *Acreage* by completing the following steps:
   a. Click the Find & Select button in the Editing group in the Home tab and then click *Replace* at the drop-down list.
   b. At the Find and Replace dialog box with the Replace tab selected, type Land in the *Find what* text box.
   c. Press the Tab key (this moves the insertion point to the *Replace with* text box).
   d. Type Acreage.
   e. Click the Replace All button.
   f. At the message telling you that four replacements were made, click OK.
   g. Click the Close button to close the Find and Replace dialog box.

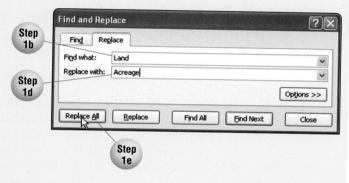

2. Find all occurrences of *$450,000* and replace with *$475,000* by completing the following steps:
   a. Click the Find & Select button in the Editing group and then click *Replace* at the drop-down list.
   b. At the Find and Replace dialog box with the Replace tab selected, type 450000 in the *Find what* text box.
   c. Press the Tab key.
   d. Type 475000.
   e. Click the Options button to display additional options. (If additional options already display, skip this step.)
   f. Click the *Match entire cell contents* option to insert a check mark in the check box.
   g. Click Replace All.
   h. At the message telling you that two replacements were made, click OK.
   i. At the Find and Replace dialog box, click the *Match entire cell contents* option to remove the check mark.
   j. Click the Close button to close the Find and Replace dialog box.
3. Save **ExcelL1_C4_P2.xlsx**.

# Finding and Replacing Cell Formatting

Use the Format buttons at the expanded Find and Replace dialog box (see Figure 4.10) to search for specific cell formatting and replace with other formatting. Click the down-pointing arrow at the right side of the Format button and a drop-down list displays. Click the *Format* option and the Find Format dialog box displays with the Number, Alignment, Font, Border, Fill, and Protection tabs. Specify formatting at this dialog box. Click the *Choose Format From Cell* option and the mouse pointer displays with a pointer tool attached. Click in the cell containing the desired formatting and the formatting displays in the *Preview* box to the left of the Format button. Click the *Clear Find Format* option and any formatting in the *Preview* box is removed.

Project 2c    **Finding and Replacing Cell Formatting**

1. With **ExcelL1_C4_P2.xlsx** open, search for light turquoise fill color and replace with a purple fill color by completing the following steps:
   a. Click the Find & Select button in the Editing group and then click *Replace* at the drop-down list.
   b. At the Find and Replace dialog box with the Replace tab selected, make sure the dialog box is expanded. (If not, click the Options button.)
   c. Select and then delete any text that displays in the *Find what* text box.
   d. Select and then delete any text that displays in the *Replace with* text box.
   e. Make sure the boxes immediately preceding the two Format buttons display with the text *No Format Set*. (If not, click the down-pointing arrow at the right of the Format button, and then click the *Clear Find Format* option at the drop-down list. Do this for each Format button.)
   f. Click the top Format button.
   g. At the Find Format dialog box, click the Fill tab.
   h. Click the More Colors button.
   i. At the Colors dialog box with the Standard tab selected, click the light turquoise color shown at the right.
   j. Click OK to close the Colors dialog box.
   k. Click OK to close the Find Format dialog box.
   l. Click the bottom Format button.
   m. At the Replace Format dialog box with the Fill tab selected, click the purple color shown at the right.
   n. Click OK to close the dialog box.
   o. At the Find and Replace dialog box, click the Replace All button.
   p. At the message telling you that ten replacements were made, click OK.

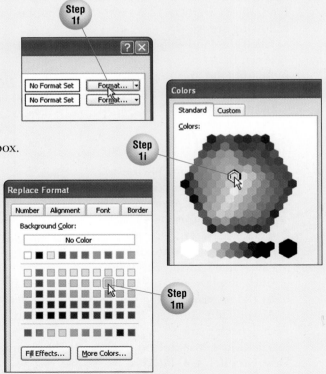

2. Search for yellow fill color and replace with a green fill color by completing the following steps:

   a. At the Find and Replace dialog box, click the top Format button.

   b. At the Find Format dialog box, click the Fill tab.

   c. Click the More Colors button.

   d. At the Colors dialog box with the Standard tab selected, click the yellow color as shown at the right.

   e. Click OK to close the Colors dialog box.

   f. Click OK to close the Find Format dialog box.

   g. Click the bottom Format button.

   h. At the Replace Format dialog box with the Fill tab selected, click the green color shown at the right.

   i. Click OK to close the dialog box.

   j. At the Find and Replace dialog box, click the Replace All button.

   k. At the message telling you that 78 replacements were made, click OK.

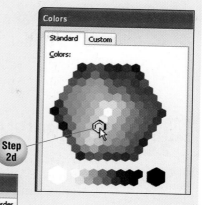

Step 2d

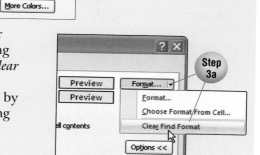

Step 2h

3. Search for 11-point Calibri formatting and replace with 10-point Arial formatting by completing the following steps:

   a. With the Find and Replace dialog box open, clear formatting from the top Format button by clicking the down-pointing arrow and then clicking the *Clear Find Format* option at the drop-down list.

   b. Clear formatting from the bottom Format button by clicking the down-pointing arrow and then clicking *Clear Replace Format.*

   c. Click the top Format button.

   d. At the Find Format dialog box, click the Font tab.

   e. Click *Calibri* in the *Font* list box (you may need to scroll down the list to display this typeface).

   f. Click *11* in the *Size* text box.

   g. Click OK to close the dialog box.

   h. Click the bottom Format button.

   i. At the Replace Format dialog box with the Font tab selected, click *Arial* in the *Font* list box (you may need to scroll down the list to display this typeface).

   j. Click *10* in the *Size* list box.

   k. Click OK to close the dialog box.

   l. At the Find and Replace dialog box, click the Replace All button.

   m. At the message telling you that 174 replacements were made, click OK.

   n. At the Find and Replace dialog box, remove formatting from both Format buttons.

   o. Click the Close button to close the Find and Replace dialog box.

4. Save, print, and then close **ExcelL1_C4_P2.xlsx**.

# Project ③ Format a Billing Worksheet

You will insert a formula in a weekly billing worksheet and then sort and filter specific data in the worksheet.

**QUICK STEPS**

**Sort Data**
1. Select cells.
2. Click Sort & Filter button.
3. Click desired sort option at drop-down list.

## Sorting Data

Excel is primarily a spreadsheet program, but it also includes some basic database functions. With a database program, you can alphabetize information or arrange numbers numerically. Data can be sorted by columns in a worksheet. Sort data in a worksheet with the Sort & Filter button in the Editing group in the Home tab.

To sort data in a worksheet, select the cells containing data you want to sort, click the Sort & Filter button in the Editing group and then click the option representing the desired sort. The sort option names vary depending on the data in selected cells. For example, if the first column of selected cells contains text, the sort options in the drop-down list display as *Sort A to Z* and *Sort Z to A*. If the selected cells contain dates, the sort options in the drop-down list display as *Sort Oldest to Newest* and *Sort Newest to Oldest* and if the cells contain numbers or values, the sort options display as *Sort Smallest to Largest* and *Sort Largest to Smallest*. If you select more than one column in a worksheet, Excel will sort the data in the first selected column.

**HINT**

If you are not satisfied with the results of the sort, immediately click the Undo button.

## Project ③ᵃ  Sorting Data

1. Open **ExcelC04Project03.xlsx** and save it and name it **ExcelL1_C4_P3**.
2. Insert a formula in cell F4 that multiplies the rate by the hours. Copy the formula down to cells F5 through F29.
3. Sort the data in the first column in descending order by completing the following steps:
   a. Make cell A4 active.
   b. Click the Sort & Filter button in the Editing group.
   c. Click the *Sort Largest to Smallest* option at the drop-down list.
4. Sort in ascending order by clicking the Sort & Filter button and then clicking *Sort Smallest to Largest* at the drop-down list.
5. Save and then print **ExcelL1_C4_P3.xlsx**.

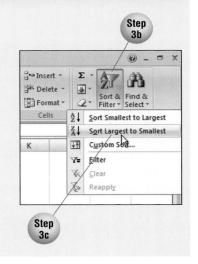

Step 3b

Step 3c

## Completing a Custom Sort

If you want to sort data in a column other than the first column, use the Sort dialog box. If you select just one column in a worksheet, click the Sort & Filter button, and then click the desired sort option, only the data in that column is sorted. If this data is related to data to the left or right of the data in the sorted column, that relationship is broken. For example, if you sort cells C4 through C29 in **ExcelL1_C4_P3.xlsx**, the client number, treatment, hours, and total would no longer match the date.

Use the Sort dialog box to sort data and maintain the relationship of all cells. To sort using the Sort dialog box, select the cells you want sorted, click the Sort & Filter button, and then click *Custom Sort*. This displays the Sort dialog box shown in Figure 4.11.

The data displayed in the *Sort by* option box will vary depending on what you have selected. Generally, the data that displays is the title of the first column of selected cells. If the selected cells do not have a title, the data may display as *Column A*. Use this option to specify what column you want sorted. Using the Sort dialog box to sort data in a column maintains the relationship of the data.

**QUICK STEPS**

**Complete Custom Sort**
1. Select cells.
2. Click Sort & Filter button.
3. Click *Custom Sort* at drop-down list.
4. Specify options at Sort dialog box.
5. Click OK.

**Figure 4.11** Sort Dialog Box

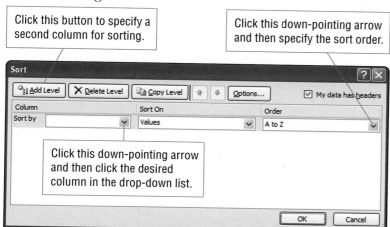

Click this button to specify a second column for sorting.

Click this down-pointing arrow and then specify the sort order.

Click this down-pointing arrow and then click the desired column in the drop-down list.

**Project 3b** Sorting Data Using the Sort Dialog Box

1. With **ExcelL1_C4_P3.xlsx** open, sort the rates in cells E4 through E29 in ascending order and maintain the relationship to the other data by completing the following steps:
   a. Select cells A3 through F29.
   b. Click the Sort & Filter button and then click *Custom Sort*.
   c. At the Sort dialog box, click the down-pointing arrow at the right of the *Sort by* option box, and then click *Rate* at the drop-down list.
   d. Click the down-pointing arrow at the right of the *Order* option box and then click *Largest to Smallest* at the drop-down list.
   e. Click OK to close the Sort dialog box.
   f. Deselect the cells.

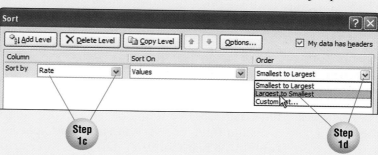

Step 1c

Step 1d

2. Save and then print **ExcelL1_C4_P3.xlsx**.
3. Sort the dates in ascending order (oldest to newest) by completing steps similar to those in Step 1.
4. Save and then print **ExcelL1_C4_P3.xlsx**.

# Sorting More Than One Column

When sorting data in cells, you can sort in more than one column. For example, in Project 3c you will be sorting the date from oldest to newest and then sorting client numbers from lowest to highest. In this sort, the dates are sorted first and then client numbers are sorted in ascending order within the same date.

To sort in more than one column, select all columns in the worksheet that need to remain relative and then display the Sort dialog box. At the Sort dialog box, specify the first column you want sorted in the *Sort by* option box, click the *Add Level* button, and then specify the second column in the first *Then by* option box. In Excel, you can sort on multiple columns. Add additional *Then by* option boxes by clicking the *Add Level* button.

## Project 3c — Sorting Data in Two Columns

1. With **ExcelL1_C4_P3.xlsx** open, select cells A3 through F29.
2. Click the Sort & Filter button and then click *Custom Sort*.
3. At the Sort dialog box, click the down-pointing arrow at the right side of the *Sort by* option box, and then click *Date* in the drop-down list.
4. Make sure *Oldest to Newest* displays in the *Order* option box.
5. Click the *Add Level* button.
6. Click the down-pointing arrow at the right of the first *Then by* option box and then click *Client #* in the drop-down list.
7. Click OK to close the dialog box.
8. Deselect the cells.
9. Save and then print **ExcelL1_C4_P3.xlsx**.

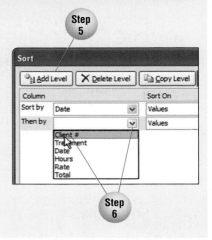

Step 5

Step 6

## QUICK STEPS

**Filter a List**
1. Select cells.
2. Click Filter & Sort button.
3. Click *Filter* at drop-down list.
4. Click down-pointing arrow of heading to filter.
5. Click desired option at drop-down list.

## Filtering Data

You can place a restriction, called a *filter*, on data in a worksheet to isolate temporarily specific data. To turn on filtering, make a cell containing data active, click the Filter & Sort button in the Editing group in the Home tab, and then click *Filter* at the drop-down list. This turns on filtering and causes a filter arrow to appear in each column label in the worksheet as shown in Figure 4.12. You do not need to select before turning on filtering because Excel automatically searches for column labels in a worksheet.

To filter data in a worksheet, click the filter arrow in the heading you want to filter. This causes a drop-down list to display with options to filter all records, create a custom filter, or select an entry that appears in one or more of the cells in the column. When you filter data, the filter arrow changes to a funnel icon. The funnel icon indicates that rows in the worksheet have been filtered. To turn off filtering, click the Sort & Filter button and then click *Filter*.

If a column contains numbers, click the filter arrow, point to *Number Filters*, and a side menu displays with options for filtering numbers. For example, you can filter numbers that are equal to, greater than, or less than a number you specify; filter the top ten numbers; and filter numbers that are above or below a specified number.

**Figure 4.12** Filtering Data

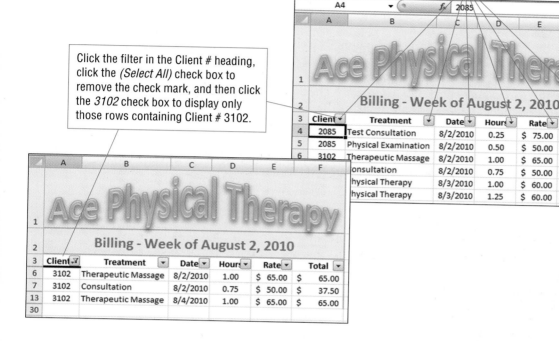

Turn on the filter feature and filter arrows display in column headings.

Click the filter in the Client # heading, click the *(Select All)* check box to remove the check mark, and then click the *3102* check box to display only those rows containing Client # 3102.

## Project 3d — Filtering Data

1. With **ExcelL1_C4_P3.xlsx** open, click in cell A4.
2. Turn on filtering by clicking the Sort & Filter button in the Editing group in the Home tab and then clicking *Filter* at the drop-down list.
3. Filter and then print rows for client number 3102 by completing the following steps:
   a. Click the filter arrow in the *Client #* heading.
   b. Click the *(Select All)* check box to remove the check mark.
   c. Scroll down the list box and then click *3102* to insert a check mark in the check box.
   d. Click OK.
   e. Print the worksheet by clicking the Quick Print button on the Quick Access toolbar.
4. Redisplay all rows containing data by completing the following steps:
   a. Click the funnel icon in the *Client #* heading.
   b. Click the *(Select All)* check box to insert a check mark (this also inserts a check mark for all items in the list).
   c. Click OK.

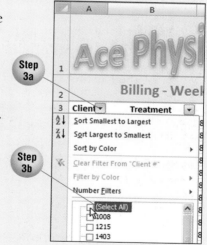

Step 3a

Step 3b

5. Filter and then print a list of clients receiving physical therapy by completing the following steps:
   a. Click the filter arrow in the *Treatment* heading.
   b. Click the *(Select All)* check box.
   c. Click the *Physical Therapy* check box.
   d. Click OK.
   e. Click the Quick Print button on the Quick Access toolbar.
6. Redisplay all rows containing data by completing the following steps:
   a. Click the funnel icon in the *Treatment* heading.
   b. Click the *(Select All)* check box to insert a check mark (this also inserts a check mark for all items in the list).
   c. Click OK.
7. Display the top two highest rates by completing the following steps:
   a. Click the filter arrow in the *Rate* heading.
   b. Point to *Number Filters* and then click *Top 10* at the side menu.
   c. At the Top 10 AutoFilter dialog box, select the *10* that displays in the middle text box and then type *2*.
   d. Click OK to close the dialog box.
   e. Click the Quick Print button on the Quick Access toolbar.
8. Redisplay all rows containing data by completing the following steps:
   a. Click the funnel icon in the *Rate* heading.
   b. Click the *(Select All)* check box to insert a check mark (this also inserts a check mark for all items in the list).
   c. Click OK.

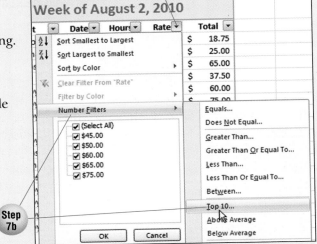

9. Display totals greater than $60 by completing the following steps:
   a. Click the filter arrow in the *Total* heading.
   b. Point to *Number Filters* and then click *Greater Than*.
   c. At the Custom AutoFilter dialog box, type *60* and then click OK.

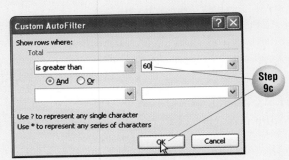

   d. Click the Quick Print button on the Quick Access toolbar.
10. Turn off the filtering feature by clicking the Sort & Filter button and then clicking *Filter* at the drop-down list.
11. Save and then close **ExcelL1_C4_P3.xlsx**.

# Project 4 Plan and Create a Worksheet

You will use steps presented to plan a worksheet and then create, save, print, and then close the worksheet.

## Planning a Worksheet

The worksheets you have worked with so far basically have already been planned. If you need to plan a worksheet yourself, some steps you can follow are listed below. These are basic steps—you may think of additional steps or additional information to help you plan a worksheet.

- **Step 1: Identify the purpose of the worksheet.** The more definite you are about your purpose, the easier organizing your data into an effective worksheet will be. Consider things such as the purpose of the worksheet, the intended audience, the desired output or results, and the data required.

- **Step 2: Design the worksheet.** To do this, you need to determine how the data is to be organized, the titles of columns and rows, and how to emphasize important information. Designing the worksheet also includes determining any calculations that need to be performed.

- **Step 3: Create a sketch of the worksheet.** A diagram or sketch can help create a logical and well-ordered worksheet. With a sketch, you can experiment with alternative column and row configurations and titles and headings. When creating a sketch, start with the heading or title of the worksheet, which should provide a quick overview of what the data represents in the worksheet. Determine appropriate column and row titles that clearly identify the data.

- **Step 4: Enter the data in the worksheet.** Type the data in the worksheet, including the worksheet title, column titles, row titles, and data within cells. Enter any required formulas into the worksheet and then format the worksheet to make it appealing and easy to read.

- **Step 5: Test the worksheet data.** After preparing the worksheet and inserting any necessary formulas, check the data to be sure that the calculations are performed correctly. Consider verifying the formula results by completing the formula on a calculator.

## Project 4 Planning and Creating a Worksheet

1. Look at the data shown in Figure 4.13. (The first paragraph is simply a description of the data—do not include this in the worksheet.) After reviewing the data, complete the following steps:
   a. Create a sketch of how you think the worksheet should be organized.
   b. Create a worksheet from the sketch. (Be sure to include the necessary formula to calculate the total costs.)
   c. Apply formatting to enhance the appearance of the worksheet.
2. Save the workbook and name it **ExcelL1_C4_P4**.
3. Print and then close **ExcelL1_C4_P4.xlsx**.

## Figure 4.13  Project 4

The following data itemizes budgeted direct labor hours and dollars by department for planning purposes. This data is prepared quarterly and sent to the plant manager and production manager.

DIRECT LABOR BUDGET

|  | Labor Rate | Total Hours | Total Costs |
|---|---|---|---|
| **April** | | | |
| Assembly | 12.75 | 723 | |
| Electronics | 16.32 | 580 | |
| Machining | 27.34 | 442 | |
| **May** | | | |
| Assembly | 12.75 | 702 | |
| Electronics | 16.32 | 615 | |
| Machining | 27.34 | 428 | |
| **June** | | | |
| Assembly | 12.75 | 694 | |
| Electronics | 16.32 | 643 | |
| Machining | 27.34 | 389 | |

# CHAPTER summary

- The Page Setup group in the Page Layout tab contains buttons for changing margins, page orientation and size, and buttons for establishing a print area, inserting page break, applying a picture background, and printing titles.

- The default left and right margins are 0.7 inch and the default top and bottom margins are 0.75 inch. Change these default margins with the Margins button in the Page Setup group in the Page Layout tab.

- Display the Page Setup dialog box with the Margins tab selected by clicking the Margins button and then clicking *Custom Margins* at the drop-down list.

- Center a worksheet on the page with the *Horizontally* and *Vertically* options at the Page Setup dialog box with the Margins tab selected.

- Click the Orientation button in the Page Setup group in the Page Layout tab to display the two orientation choices—*Portrait* and *Landscape*.

- Insert a page break by selecting the column or row, clicking the Breaks button in the Page Setup group in the Page Layout tab, and then clicking *Insert Page Break* at the drop-down list.

- To insert both a horizontal and vertical page break at the same time, make a cell active, click the Breaks button, and then click *Insert Page Break* at the drop-down list.

- Display a worksheet in page break preview by clicking the Page Break Preview button in the view area on the Status bar or clicking the View tab and then clicking the Page Break Preview button.

- Use options at the Page Setup dialog box with the Sheet tab selected to specify that you want column or row titles to print on each page. Display this dialog box by clicking the Print Titles button in the Page Setup group in the Page Layout tab.

- Use options in the Scale to Fit group in the Page Layout tab to scale data to fit on a specific number of pages.

- Use the Background button in the Page Setup group in the Page Layout tab to insert a worksheet background picture. A background picture displays on the screen but does not print.

- Use options in the Sheet Options group in the Page Layout tab to specify if you want gridlines and headings to view and/or print.

- Specify a print area by selecting the desired cells, clicking the Print Area button in the Page Setup group in the Page Layout tab and then clicking *Set Print Area* at the drop-down list. Add another print area by selecting the desired cells, clicking the Print Area button, and then clicking *Add to Print Area* at the drop-down list.

- Create a header and/or footer with the Header & Footer button in the Text group in the Insert tab, in Page Layout view, or with options at the Page Setup dialog box with the Header/Footer tab selected.

- Customize print jobs with options at the Print dialog box.

- To check spelling in a worksheet, click the Review tab and then click the Spelling button.

- Click the Undo button on the Quick Access toolbar to reverse the most recent action and click the Redo button to redo a previously reversed action.
- Use options at the Find and Replace dialog box with the Find tab selected to find specific data and/or formatting in a worksheet.
- Use options at the Find and Replace dialog box with the Replace tab selected to find specific data and/or formatting and replace with other data and/or formatting.
- Sort data in a worksheet with options from the Sort & Filter button in the Editing group in the Home tab.
- Create a custom sort with options at the Sort dialog box. Display this dialog box by clicking the Sort & Filter button and then clicking *Custom Sort* at the drop-down list.
- Use the filter feature to temporarily isolate specific data. Turn on the filter feature by clicking the Sort & Filter button in the Editing group in the Home tab and then clicking *Filter* at the drop-down list. This inserts filter arrows in each column label. Click a filter arrow and then use options at the drop-down list that displays to specify the filter data.
- Plan a worksheet by completing these basic steps: identify the purpose of the worksheet, design the worksheet, create a sketch of the worksheet, enter the data in the worksheet, and test the worksheet data.

# COMMANDS review

| FEATURE | RIBBON TAB, GROUP | BUTTON, OPTION | KEYBOARD SHORTCUT |
|---------|-------------------|----------------|-------------------|
| Margins | Page Layout, Page Setup | | |
| Page Setup dialog box with Margins tab selected | Page Layout, Page Setup | , Custom Margins | |
| Orientation | Page Layout, Page Setup | | |
| Size | Page Layout, Page Setup | | |
| Insert page break | Page Layout, Page Setup | , Insert Page Break | |
| Remove page break | Page Layout, Page Setup | , Remove Page Break | |
| Page Break Preview | View, Workbook Views | | |
| Page Setup dialog box with Sheet tab selected | Page Layout, Page Setup | | |
| Scale width | Page Layout, Scale to Fit | Width: Automatic | |
| Scale height | Page Layout, Scale to Fit | Height: Automatic | |
| Scale | Page Layout, Scale to Fit | Scale: 100% | |
| Background picture | Page Layout, Page Setup | | |
| Print Area | Page Layout, Page Setup | | |
| Header and footer | Insert, Text | | |
| Page Layout view | View, Workbook Views | | |
| Spelling | Review, Proofing | | F7 |
| Find and Replace dialog box with Find tab selected | Home, Editing | , Find | Ctrl + F |
| Find and Replace dialog box with Replace tab selected | Home, Editing | , Replace | Ctrl + H |
| Sort data | Home, Editing | | |
| Filter data | Home, Editing | | |

# CONCEPTS check

## Test Your Knowledge

**Completion:** In the space provided at the right, indicate the correct term, symbol, or command.

1. This is the default left and right margin measurement.  _____

2. This is the default top and bottom margin measurement.  _____

3. The Margins button is located in this tab.  _____

4. By default, a worksheet prints in this orientation on a page.  _____

5. Click the Print Titles button in the Page Setup group in the Page Layout tab and the Page Setup dialog box displays with this tab selected.  _____

6. Use options in this group in the Page Layout tab to adjust the printed output by a percentage to fit the number of pages specified.  _____

7. Use this button in the Page Setup group in the Page Layout tab to select and print specific areas in a worksheet.  _____

8. Click the Header & Footer button in the Text group in the Insert tab and the worksheet displays in this view.  _____

9. This tab contains options for formatting and customizing a header and/or footer.  _____

10. Click this tab to display the Spelling button.  _____

11. The Undo and Redo buttons are located on this toolbar.  _____

12. Click this button in the Find and Replace dialog box to expand the dialog box.  _____

13. Use these two buttons at the expanded Find and Replace dialog box to search for specific cell formatting and replace with other formatting.  _____

14. Use this button in the Home tab to sort data in a worksheet.  _____

15. Use this feature to isolate temporarily a specific data in a worksheet.  _____

# SKILLS check
## *Demonstrate Your Proficiency*

### Assessment

## 1 FORMAT A DATA ANALYSIS WORKSHEET

1. Open **ExcelC04Assessment01.xlsx**.
2. Save the workbook with Save As and name it **ExcelL1_C4_A1**.
3. Make the following changes to the worksheet:
   a. Insert a formula in cell H4 that averages the amounts in cells B4 through G4.
   b. Copy the formula in cell H4 down to cells H5 through H9.
   c. Insert a formula in cell B10 that adds the amounts in cells B4 through B9.
   d. Copy the formula in cell B10 over to cells C10 through H10. (Click the AutoFill Options button and then click *Fill With Formatting* at the drop-down list.)
   e. Change the orientation of the worksheet to landscape.
   f. Change the top margin to 3 inches and the left margin to 1.5 inches.
4. Save and then print **ExcelL1_C4_A1.xlsx**.
5. Make the following changes to the worksheet:
   a. Change the top margin to 1 inch and the left margin to 0.7 inch.
   b. Change the orientation back to portrait.
   c. Horizontally and vertically center the worksheet on the page.
   d. Scale the worksheet so it fits on one page.
6. Save, print, and then close **ExcelL1_C4_A1.xlsx**.

### Assessment

## 2 FORMAT A TEST RESULTS WORKSHEET

1. Open **ExcelC04Assessment02.xlsx**.
2. Save the workbook with Save As and name it **ExcelL1_C4_A2**.
3. Make the following changes to the worksheet.
   a. Insert a formula in cell N4 that averages the test scores in cells B4 through M4.
   b. Copy the formula in cell N4 down to cells N5 through N21.
   c. Type Average in cell A22.
   d. Insert a formula in cell B22 that averages the test scores in cells B4 through B21.
   e. Copy the formula in cell B22 across to cells C22 through N22.
   f. Insert a page break between columns G and H.
4. View the worksheet in Page Break Preview.
5. Change back to the Normal view.
6. Specify that the column row titles (A3 through A22) are to print on each page.
7. Create a header that prints the page number at the right side of the page.
8. Create a footer that prints your name at the left side of the page and the workbook file name at the right side of the page.
9. Save and then print the worksheet.
10. Set a print area for cells N4 through N22 and then print the cells.
11. Clear the print area.
12. Save and then close **ExcelL1_C4_A2.xlsx**.

## Assessment

### 3 FORMAT AN EQUIPMENT RENTAL WORKSHEET

1. Open **ExcelC04Assessment03.xlsx**.
2. Save the workbook with Save As and name it **ExcelL1_C4_A3**.
3. Insert a formula in cell H3 that multiplies the rate in cell G3 by the hours in cell F3. Copy the formula in cell H3 down to cells H4 through H16.
4. Insert a formula in cell H17 that sums the amounts in cells H3 through H16.
5. Complete the following find and replaces:
   a. Find all occurrences of cells containing *75* and replace with *90*.
   b. Find all occurrences of cells containing *55* and replace with *60*.
   c. Find all occurrences of *Barrier Concrete* and replace with *Lee Sand and Gravel*.
   d. Find all occurrences of 11-point Calibri and replace with 10-point Cambria.
6. Insert a header that prints the date at the left side of the page and the time at the right side of the page.
7. Insert a footer that prints your name at the left side of the page and the workbook name at the right side of the page.
8. Print the worksheet horizontally and vertically centered on the page.
9. Save and then close **ExcelL1_C4_A3.xlsx**.

## Assessment

### 4 FORMAT AN INVOICES WORKSHEET

1. Open **ExcelC04Assessment04.xlsx**.
2. Save the workbook with Save As and name it **ExcelL1_C4_A4**.
3. Search for the light green fill (the lightest fill in the worksheet that fills cells in every other row beginning with row 5) and replace it with no fill. (Do this at the Find and Replace dialog box with the Replace tab selected.)
4. Insert a formula in G4 that multiplies the amount in E4 with the percentage in F4 and then adds the product to cell E4. (If you write the formula correctly, the result in G4 will display as *$488.25*.)
5. Copy the formula in cell G4 down to cells G5 through G17.
6. Complete a spelling check on the worksheet.
7. Find all occurrences of *Picture* and replace with *Portrait*. (Do not type a space after *Picture* or *Portrait* because you want to find occurrences that end with an "s.")
8. Sort the records by invoice number in ascending order (smallest to largest).
9. Sort the records by client number in ascending order (A to Z) and then by date in ascending order (oldest to newest).
10. Insert a footer in the worksheet that prints your name at the left side of the page and the current date at the right side of the page.
11. Center the worksheet horizontally and vertically on the page.
12. Save and then print **ExcelL1_C4_A4.xlsx**.
13. Select cells A3 through G3 and then turn on the filter feature and complete the following filters:
    a. Filter and then print a list of rows containing client number 11-279.

b. Filter and then print a list of rows containing the top three highest amounts due.

c. Filter and then print a list of rows containing amounts due that are less than $500.

14. Save and then close **ExcelL1_C4_A4.xlsx**.

## Assessment

## 5 CREATE A WORKSHEET CONTAINING SORT ORDER INFORMATION

1. Use Excel's Help feature and learn about the default sort order. After reading and printing the information presented, create a worksheet containing a summary of the information. Create the worksheet with the following features:

a. Create a title for the worksheet.

b. Set the data in cells in a serif typeface and change the data color.

c. Add borders to the cells (you determine the border style).

d. Add a color shading to cells (you determine the color—make it complementary to the data color).

e. Create a footer that prints your name at the left margin and the file name at the right margin.

2. Save the workbook and name it **ExcelL1_C4_A5**.

3. Print and then close **ExcelL1_C4_A5.xlsx**.

# CASE study

## Part 1

### Apply Your Skills

You are the sales manager for Macadam Realty. You decide that you want to display sample mortgage worksheets in the reception area display rack. Open the **MacadamMortgages.xlsx** workbook, save it with Save As and name it **ExcelL1_C4_CS_P1A**, and then add the following information and make the following changes:

- In column C, insert a formula that determines the down payment amount.
- In column D, insert a formula that determines the loan amount.
- In column G, insert a formula using the PMT function (enter the *Pv* as a negative).
- Insert the date and time as a header and your name and the workbook name (**ExcelL1_C4_CS_P1A.xlsx**) as a footer.
- Find 11-point Calibri formatting and replace with 11-point Candara formatting.
- Scale the worksheet so it prints on one page.

Save and then print **ExcelL1_C4_CS_P1A.xlsx**. After looking at the printed worksheet, you decide that you need to make the following changes:

- Sort the *Price of Home* column from smallest to largest.
- Change the percentage amount in column E from 6% to 7%.
- Shade the cells in row 4 in the light yellow color that matches the fill in cell A2. Copy this shading to every other row of cells in the worksheet (stopping at row 46).

Save the edited worksheet with Save As and name it **ExcelL1_C4_CS_P1B**. Edit the footer to reflect the workbook name change (from *ExcelL1_C4_CS_P1A.xlsx* to *ExcelL1_C4_CS_P1B.xlsx*). Save, print and then close **ExcelL1_C4_CS_P1B.xlsx**. (Make sure the worksheet prints on one page.)

**Part 2**

You are preparing for a quarterly sales meeting during which you will discuss retirement issues with the sales officers. You want to encourage them to consider opening an Individual Retirement Account (IRA) to supplement the retirement contributions made by Macadam Realty. You have begun an IRA worksheet but need to complete it. Open **MacadamIRA.xlsx** and then save it with Save As and name it **ExcelL1_C4_CS_P2A**. Make the following changes to the worksheet:

- Insert in cell C6 a formula that calculates the future value of an investment. Use the FV function to write the formula. You must use absolute and mixed cell references for the formula. When entering the *Rate* (percentage), the column letter is variable but the row number is fixed; when entering the *Nper* (years), the column letter is fixed but the row number is variable; and when entering the *Pmt* (the contribution amount), both the column letter and row number are absolute.
- Copy the formula in cell C6 down to cells C7 through C19. Copy the formula in cell C6 across to cells D6 through K6. Continue in this manner until the amounts are entered in all the appropriate cells.
- Select and then merge and center cells A6 through A19. Type the text **Number of Years** and then rotate the text up. Make sure the text is centered in the merged cell. Apply 12-point Calibri bold formatting to the text.
- Adjust the column widths so all text is visible in the cells.
- Change the page orientation to landscape.
- Vertically and horizontally center the worksheet.
- Include a header that prints the page number and insert a footer that prints your name.

Save the worksheet and then print it so that the row titles print on both pages. After looking at the worksheet, you decide to make the following changes:

- Remove the header containing the page number.
- Edit the footer so the date prints at the left margin and your name prints at the right margin.
- Scale the worksheet so it prints on one page.

Save the workbook and name it **ExcelL1_C4_CS_P2B** and then print the worksheet. Change the amount in cell D3 to *$2,500* and then print the worksheet again. Change the amount in cell D3 to *$3,000* and then print the worksheet again. Save and then close **ExcelL1_C4_CS_P2B.xlsx**.

**Part 3**

You have clients living in Canada that are interested in purchasing real estate in the United States. For those clients, you like to keep a conversion worksheet available. Using the Internet, search for the MS MoneyCentral Investor Currency Rates site. Determine the current currency exchange rate for Canada and then create a worksheet with the following specifications:

- Apply formatting that is similar to the formatting in the worksheets you worked with in the first two parts of the case study.
- Create the following columns:
  - Column for home price in American dollars.
  - Column for home price in Canadian dollars.
  - Column for amount of down payment.
  - Column for loan total.
  - Column for monthly payment.
- In the column for home prices, insert home amounts beginning with $100,000, incrementing every $50,000, and ending with $1,000,000.
- Insert a formula in the home price in the Canadian dollars column that displays the home price in Canadian dollars.
- Insert a formula in the down payment column that multiplies the Canadian home price by 20%.
- Insert a formula in the loan total column that subtracts the down payment from the Canadian home price.
- Insert a formula in the monthly payment column that determines the monthly payment using the PMT function. Use 6% as the rate (be sure to divide by 12 months), 360 as the number of payments, and the loan amount as a negative as the present value.
- Apply any other formatting you feel necessary to improve the worksheet.

Save the completed workbook and name it **ExcelL1_C4_CS_P3**. Display formulas and then print the worksheet. Redisplay the formulas and then save and close the workbook.

**Part 4**

After working with the commissions worksheet, you decide to maintain the information in an Access table. Before importing the information to an Access table, open **MacadamCommissions.xlsx** and then save the workbook with Save As and name it **ExcelL1_C4_CS_P4**. Insert a formula in G4 that multiplies the sale price by the commission percentage. Copy the formula down to cells G5 through G24. Insert a formula in cell G25 that totals the commissions and then adjust the column width so the entire total is visible. Select cells A3 through G25 and then save the selected cells in a separate workbook named **ExcelMacadamComm**. Create a database in Access named **Macadam** and then import the **ExcelMacadamComm.xlsx** Excel workbook as an Access table. Save the database and print the newly imported table.

# Preparing and Formatting a Worksheet

# ASSESSING proficiency

In this unit, you have learned to create, save, print, edit, and format Excel worksheets; create and insert formulas; and enhance worksheets with features such as headers and footers, page numbering, sorting, and filtering.

*Note: Before beginning computer assessments, copy to your storage medium the Excel2007L1U1 subfolder from the Excel2007L1 folder on the CD that accompanies this textbook and then make Excel2007L1U1 the active folder.*

## Assessment 1 Create Sales Bonuses Workbook

1. Create the Excel worksheet shown in Figure U1.1. Format the cells as you see them in the figure. Format the money amounts in Accounting format with no decimal places.
2. Insert an IF statement in cell C4 that inserts *7%* if B4 is greater than 99999 and inserts *5%* if B4 is less than 100000.
3. Format the number in cell C4 so it displays as a percentage with no decimal places. Copy the formula in cell C4 down to cells C5 through C11.
4. Insert a formula in cell D4 that multiplies the amount in B4 with the percentage in cell C4. Copy the formula in D4 down to cells D5 through D11.
5. Insert a footer that contains your first and last names and the current date.
6. Print the worksheet horizontally and vertically centered on the page.
7. Save the workbook and name it **ExcelL1_U1_A1**.
8. Close **ExcelL1_U1_A1.xlsx**.

**Figure U1.1 Assessment 1**

| | A | B | C | D | E |
|---|---|---|---|---|---|
| 1 | **Capstan Marine Products** | | | | |
| 2 | | **Sales Department** | | | |
| 3 | **Salesperson** | **Sales** | **Bonus** | **Bonus Amount** | |
| 4 | Allejandro, Eduardo | $ 105,345 | | | |
| 5 | Crispin, Juliette | $ 96,345 | | | |
| 6 | Frankel, Hayden | $ 89,234 | | | |
| 7 | Hiesmann, Denae | $ 120,455 | | | |
| 8 | Jarvis, Robert | $ 131,095 | | | |
| 9 | Littleman, Marcus | $ 99,850 | | | |
| 10 | Weisen, George | $ 103,125 | | | |
| 11 | Schoenfeld, Allie | $ 78,495 | | | |
| 12 | | | | | |

## Assessment 2 Format Equipment Purchase Plan Workbook

1. Open **ExcelU01Assessment02.xlsx** and then save the workbook and name it **ExcelL1_U1_A2**.
2. The owner of Hilltop Equipment Rental is interested in purchasing a new tractor and needs to determine monthly payments on three different models. Insert a formula in cell E4 that uses the PMT function to calculate monthly payments. Copy the formula down to cells E5 and E6.
3. Insert a formula in cell F4 that multiplies the amount in E4 by the amount in D4.
4. Copy the formula in cell F4 down to cells F5 and F6.
5. Insert a formula in cell G4 that subtracts the amount in B4 from the amount in F4.
6. Copy the formula in cell G4 down to cells G5 and G6.
7. Change the vertical alignment of cell A2 to Middle Align.
8. Change the vertical alignment of cells A3 through G3 to Bottom Align.
9. Save, print, and then close **ExcelL1_U1_A2.xlsx**.

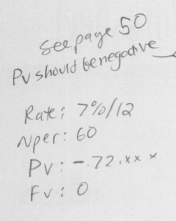

See page 50
Pv should be negative

Rate: 7%/12
Nper: 60
Pv: -.72.xx ×
Fv: 0

## Assessment 3 Format Accounts Due Workbook

1. Open **ExcelU01Assessment03.xlsx** and then save the workbook and name it **ExcelL1_U1_A3**.
2. Using the DATE function, enter a formula in each of the specified cells that returns the serial number for the specified date:

| | | |
|---|---|---|
| C4 | = | **October 26, 2010** |
| C5 | = | **October 27, 2010** |
| C6 | = | **October 27, 2010** |
| C7 | = | **October 29, 2010** |
| C8 | = | **November 3, 2010** |
| C9 | = | **November 5, 2010** |
| C10 | = | **November 5, 2010** |
| C11 | = | **November 12, 2010** |
| C12 | = | **November 12, 2010** |

3. Enter a formula in cell E4 that inserts the due date (date of service plus the number of days in the *Terms* column).
4. Copy the formula in cell E4 down to cells E5 through E12.
5. Make cell A14 active and then type your name.
6. Make cell A15 active and then use the NOW function to insert the current date as a serial number.
7. Save, print, and then close **ExcelL1_U1_A3.xlsx**.

## Assessment 4 Format First Quarter Sales Workbook

1. Open **ExcelU01Assessment04.xlsx** and then save the workbook and name it **ExcelL1_U1_A4**.
2. Insert a formula in cell E4 that totals the amounts in B4, C4, and D4. Copy the formula in cell E4 down to cells E5 through E18.
3. Insert an IF statement in cell F4 that inserts *10%* if E4 is greater than 99999 and inserts *7%* if E4 is greater than 49999 and inserts *5%* if E4 is greater than 24999 and inserts *0%* if E4 is greater than 0.
4. Make sure the result of the IF formula displays in cell F4 as a percentage with no decimal points and then copy the formula down to cells F5 through F18.

5. Select cells A5 through F5 and then insert the same yellow fill as cell A2. Apply the same yellow fill to cells A7 through F7, A9 through F9, A11 through F11, A13 through F13, A15 through F15, and cells A17 through F17.

6. Insert a footer that prints your name at the left, the current date at the middle, and the current time at the right.

7. Print the worksheet horizontally and vertically centered on the page.

8. Save, print, and then close **ExcelL1_U1_A4.xlsx**.

## Assessment 5 Format Weekly Payroll Workbook

1. Open **ExcelU01Assessment05.xlsx** and then save the workbook and name it **ExcelL1_U1_A5**.

2. Insert a formula in cell E4 that multiplies the hourly wage by the hours and then adds that to the multiplication of the hourly wage by the overtime pay rate (1.5) and then overtime hours. (Use parentheses in the formula and use an absolute cell reference for the overtime pay rate (1.5). Refer to Chapter 2, Project 5c.) Copy the formula down to cells E5 through E17.

3. Insert a formula in cell F4 that multiplies the gross pay by the withholding tax rate (W/H Rate). (Use a mixed cell reference for the cell containing the withholding rate. Refer to Chapter 2, Project 5c.) Copy the formula down to cells F5 through F17.

4. Insert a formula in cell G4 that multiplies the gross pay by the Social Security rate (SS Rate). (Use a mixed cell reference for the cell containing the Social Security rate. Refer to Chapter 2, Project 5c.) Copy the formula down to cells G5 through G17.

5. Insert a formula in cell H4 that adds together the Social Security tax and the withholding tax and subtracts that from the gross pay. Copy the formula down to cells H5 through H17.

6. Sort the employee last names alphabetically in ascending order (A to Z).

7. Center the worksheet horizontally and vertically on the page.

8. Insert a footer that prints your name at the left side of the page and the worksheet name at the right side of the page.

9. Save, print, and then close **ExcelL1_U1_A5.xlsx**.

## Assessment 6 Format Customer Sales Analysis Workbook

1. Open **ExcelU01Assessment06.xlsx** and then save the workbook and name it **ExcelL1_U1_A6**.

2. Insert formulas and drag down formulas to complete the worksheet.

3. Change the orientation to landscape.

4. Insert a header that prints the page number at the right side of the page.

5. Insert a footer that prints your name at the right side of the page.

6. Horizontally and vertically center the worksheet on the page.

7. Specify that the column headings in cells A3 through A9 print on both pages.

8. Save, print, and then close **ExcelL1_U1_A6.xlsx**.

## Assessment 7 Format Invoices Workbook

1. Open **ExcelU01Assessment07.xlsx** and then save the workbook and name it **ExcelL1_U1_A7**.

2. Insert a formula in cell G4 that multiplies the amount in E4 by the percentage in F4 and then adds that total to the amount in E4. (Use parentheses in this formula.)

3. Copy the formula in cell G4 down to cells G5 through G18.

4. Find all occurrences of cells containing *11-279* and replace with *10-005*.
5. Find all occurrences of cells containing *8.5* and replace with *9.0*.
6. Search for the Calibri font and replace with the Candara font (do not specify a type size so that Excel replaces all sizes of Calibri with Candara).
7. Print **ExcelL1_U1_A7.xlsx**.
8. Filter and then print a list of rows containing only the client number *04-325*. (After printing, return the list to *(All)*.)
9. Filter and then print a list of rows containing only the service *Development*. (After printing, return the list to *(All)*.)
10. Filter and then print a list of rows containing the top three highest totals in the *Amount Due* column. (After printing, turn off the filter feature.)
11. Save and then close **ExcelL1_U1_A7.xlsx**.

# WRITING activities

The following activities give you the opportunity to practice your writing skills along with demonstrating an understanding of some of the important Excel features you have mastered in this unit. Use correct grammar, appropriate word choices, and clear sentence construction.

## Activity 1 Plan and Prepare Orders Summary Workbook

Plan and prepare a worksheet with the information shown in Figure U1.2. Apply formatting of your choosing to the worksheet either with a cell or table style or with formatting at the Format Cells dialog box. Save the completed worksheet and name it **ExcelL1_U1_Act01**. Print and then close **ExcelL1_U1_Act01.xlsx**.

**Figure U1.2 Activity 1**

Prepare a weekly summary of orders taken that itemizes the products coming into the company and the average order size.

The products and average order size include:

Black and gold wall clock—$2,450 worth of orders, average order size of $125
Traveling alarm clock—$1,358 worth of orders, average order size of $195
Water-proof watch—$890 worth of orders, average order size of $90
Dashboard clock—$2,135 worth of orders, average order size of $230
Pyramid clock—$3,050 worth of orders, average order size of $375
Gold chain watch—$755 worth of orders, average order size of $80

In the worksheet, total the amount ordered and also calculate the average weekly order size. Sort the data in the worksheet by the order amount in descending order.

## Activity 2 Prepare Depreciation Workbook

Assets within a company, such as equipment, can be depreciated over time. Several methods are available for determining the amount of depreciation such as the straight-line depreciation method, fixed-declining balance method, and the double-declining method. Use Excel's Help feature to learn about two depreciation methods—straight-line and double-declining depreciation. After reading about the two methods, create an Excel worksheet with the following information:

- An appropriate title
- A heading for straight-line depreciation
- The straight-line depreciation function
- The name and a description for each straight-line depreciation function argument category
- A heading for double-declining depreciation
- The double-declining depreciation function
- The name and a description for each double-declining depreciation function argument category

Apply formatting of your choosing to the worksheet. Save the completed workbook and name it **ExcelL1_U1_Act02**. Print the worksheet horizontally and vertically centered on the page. Close **ExcelL1_U1_Act02.xlsx**.

## Activity 3 Insert Straight-Line Depreciation Formula

Open **ExcelU01Activity03.xlsx** and then save the workbook and name it **ExcelL1_U1_Act03**. Insert the function to determine straight-line depreciation in cell E3. Copy the formula down to cells E4 through E10. Apply formatting of your choosing to the worksheet. Print the worksheet horizontally and vertically centered on the page. Save and then close **ExcelL1_U1_Act03.xlsx**.

**Optional:** Briefly research the topic of straight-line and double-declining depreciation to find out why businesses depreciate their assets. What purpose does it serve? Locate information about the topic on the Internet or in your school library. Then use Word 2007 to write a half-page, single-spaced report explaining the financial reasons for using depreciation methods. Save the document and name it **ExcelL1_U1_Act03Report**. Print and then close the document.

## Create a Travel Planning Worksheet

Make sure you are connected to the Internet. Use a search engine of your choosing to look for information on traveling to a specific country that interests you. Find sites that provide cost information for airlines, hotels, meals, entertainment, and car rentals. Create a travel planning worksheet for the country that includes the following:

- appropriate title
- appropriate headings
- airline costs

- hotel costs (off-season and in-season rates if available)
- estimated meal costs
- entertainment costs
- car rental costs

Save the completed workbook and name it **ExcelL1_U1_Act04**. Print and then close the workbook.

# Level 1

# Microsoft® excel

## Unit 2: Enhancing the Display of Workbooks

➤ Moving Data within and between Workbooks

➤ Maintaining Workbooks

➤ Creating a Chart in Excel

➤ Adding Visual Interest to Workbooks

# Benchmark Microsoft® Excel 2007 Level 1

## Microsoft Certified Application Specialist Skills—Unit 2

| Reference No. | Skill | Pages |
|---|---|---|
| **1** | **Creating and Manipulating Data** | |
| 1.3 | Modify cell contents and formats | |
| 1.3.1 | Cut, copy, and paste data and cell contents | 158-164, 181-182 |
| 1.4 | Change worksheet views | |
| 1.4.1 | Change views within a single window | 171-174 |
| 1.4.2 | Split windows | 171-174 |
| 1.4.3 | Open and arrange new windows | 177-180 |
| 1.5 | Manage worksheets | |
| 1.5.1 | Copy worksheets | 167-168, 207-208 |
| 1.5.2 | Reposition worksheets within workbooks | 167-168 |
| 1.5.3 | Rename worksheets | 167-168 |
| 1.5.4 | Hide and unhide worksheets | 169-170 |
| 1.5.5 | Insert and delete worksheets | 164-166 |
| **2** | **Formatting Data and Content** | |
| 2.1 | Format worksheets | |
| 2.1.3 | Add color to worksheet tabs | 167-168 |
| 2.1.4 | Format worksheet backgrounds | 291-292 |
| 2.3 | Format cells and cell content | |
| 2.3.8 | Insert, modify, and remove hyperlinks | 275-277 |
| **4** | **Presenting Data Visually** | |
| 4.1 | Create and format charts | |
| 4.1.1 | Select appropriate data sources for charts | 239-243 |
| 4.1.2 | Select appropriate chart types to represent data sources | 243-245 |
| 4.1.3 | Format charts using Quick Styles | 246-248, 257-259 |
| 4.2 | Modify charts | |
| 4.2.1 | Add and remove chart elements | 249-253 |
| 4.2.2 | Move and size charts | 241-243, 260-261 |
| 4.2.3 | Change chart types | 243-245 |
| 4.4 | Insert and modify illustrations | |
| 4.4.1 | Insert and modify pictures from files (not clip art files) | 255-256, 288-289 |
| 4.4.2 | Insert and modify SmartArt graphics | 292-297 |
| 4.4.3 | Insert and modify shapes | 284-287 |
| **5** | **Collaborating and Securing Data** | |
| 5.1 | Manage changes to workbooks | |
| 5.1.2 | Insert, display, modify, and delete comments | 222-226 |
| 5.4 | Save workbooks | |
| 5.4.1 | Save workbooks for use in a previous version of Excel | 211-212 |
| 5.4.2 | Using the correct format, save a workbook as a template, a Web page, a macro-enabled document, or another appropriate format | 213-214, 272-274 |

Note: The Level 1 and Level 2 texts each address approximately half of the Microsoft Certified Application Specialist skills. Complete coverage of the skills is offered in the combined Level 1 and Level 2 text titled *Benchmark Series Microsoft® Excel 2007: Levels 1 and 2,* which has been approved as certified courseware and which displays the Microsoft Certified Application Specialist logo on the cover.

# Moving Data within and between Workbooks

## PERFORMANCE OBJECTIVES

Upon successful completion of Chapter 5, you will be able to:

- Create a workbook with multiple worksheets
- Move, copy, and paste cells within a worksheet
- Split a worksheet into windows and freeze panes
- Name a range of cells and use a range in a formula
- Open multiple workbooks
- Arrange, size, and move workbooks
- Copy and paste data between workbooks
- Link data between worksheets
- Link worksheets with a 3-D reference
- Copy and paste a worksheet between programs

excel Chapter 5

**Tutorial 5.1**
Managing Worksheets and Workbooks
**Tutorial 5.2**
Working with Multiple Worksheets

Up to this point, the workbooks in which you have been working have consisted of only one worksheet. In this chapter, you will learn to create a workbook with several worksheets and complete tasks such as copying and pasting data within and between worksheets. Moving and pasting or copying and pasting selected cells in and between worksheets is useful for rearranging data or for saving time. You will also work with multiple workbooks and complete tasks such as arranging, sizing, and moving workbooks, and opening and closing multiple workbooks.

*Note: Before beginning computer projects, copy to your storage medium the Excel2007L1C5 subfolder from the Excel2007L1 folder on the CD that accompanies this textbook and then make Excel2007L1C5 the active folder.*

roject ① **Manage Data in a Multiple-Worksheet Account Workbook**

You will open an account workbook containing three worksheets and then move, copy, and paste data between the worksheets. You will also hide and unhide worksheets, and format and print multiple worksheets in the workbook.

# Creating a Workbook with Multiple Worksheets

An Excel workbook can contain multiple worksheets. You can create a variety of worksheets within a workbook for related data. For example, a workbook may contain a worksheet for the expenses for each salesperson in a company and another worksheet for the monthly payroll for each department within the company. Another example is recording sales statistics for each quarter in individual worksheets within a workbook.

By default, a workbook contains three worksheets named *Sheet1*, *Sheet2*, and *Sheet3*. (Later in this chapter, you will learn how to change these default names.) Display various worksheets in the workbook by clicking the desired tab.

## Project 1a  Displaying Worksheets in a Workbook

1. Open **ExcelC05Project01.xlsx** and then save the workbook and name it **ExcelL1_C5_P1**.
2. This workbook contains three worksheets. Display the various worksheets by completing the following steps:
   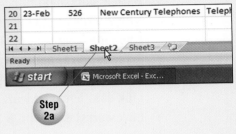
   Step 2a

   a. Display the second worksheet by clicking the Sheet2 tab that displays immediately above the Status bar.
   b. Display the third worksheet by clicking the Sheet3 tab that displays immediately above the Status bar.
   c. Return to the first worksheet by clicking the Sheet1 tab.
3. Make the following changes to worksheets in the workbook:
   a. Click the Sheet2 tab and then change the column width for columns E, F, and G to 11.00.
   b. Click the Sheet3 tab and then change the column width for columns E, F, and G to 11.00.
   c. Click the Sheet1 tab to display the first worksheet.
4. Save **ExcelL1_C5_P1.xlsx**.

# Cutting, Copying, and Pasting Selected Cells

Situations may arise where you need to move cells to a different location within a worksheet, or you may need to copy repetitive data in a worksheet. You can perform these actions by selecting cells and then using the Cut, Copy, and/or Paste buttons in the Clipboard group in the Home tab. You can also perform these actions with the mouse.

## Moving Selected Cells

Cut

Paste

You can move selected cells and cell contents in a worksheet and between worksheets. Move selected cells with the Cut and Paste buttons in the Clipboard group in the Home tab or by dragging with the mouse.

To move selected cells with buttons in the Home tab, select the cells and then click the Cut button in the Clipboard group. This causes a moving dashed line border (called a marquee) to display around the selected cells. Click the cell where you want the first selected cell inserted and then click the Paste button in the Clipboard group. If you change your mind and do not want to move the selected cells, press the Esc key to remove the moving dashed line border or double-click in any cell.

To move selected cells with the mouse, select the cells and then position the mouse pointer on any border of the selected cells until the pointer turns into an arrow pointer with a four-headed arrow attached. Hold down the left mouse button, drag the outline of the selected cells to the desired location, and then release the mouse button.

**QUICK STEPS**

**Move and Paste Cells**
1. Select cells.
2. Click Cut button.
3. Click desired cell.
4. Click Paste button.

**HINT**
Ctrl + X is the keyboard shortcut to cut selected data. Ctrl + V is the keyboard shortcut to paste data.

## Project 1b    Moving Selected Cells

1. With **ExcelL1_C5_P1.xlsx** open, you realize that the sublet rent deposit was recorded on the wrong day. The correct day is January 11. To move the cells containing information on the deposit, complete the following steps:
   a. Make cell A13 active and then insert a row. (The new row should display above the row containing information on *Rainer Suppliers*.)
   b. Select cells A7 through F7.
   c. Click the Cut button in the Clipboard group in the Home tab.

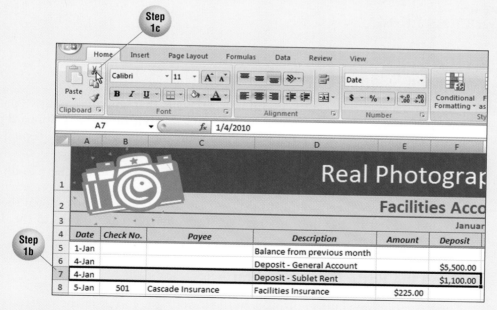

   d. Click cell A13 to make it active.
   e. Click the Paste button in the Clipboard group.

f. Change the date of the deposit from January 4 to January 11.

g. Select row 7 and then delete it.

2. Click the Sheet2 tab and then complete steps similar to those in Step 1 to move the sublet deposit row so it is positioned above the *Rainier Suppliers* row and below the *Clear Source* row. Change the date of the deposit to February 11 and make sure you delete row 7.

3. Move cells using the mouse by completing the following steps:

a. Click the Sheet3 tab.

b. Make cell A13 active and then insert a new row.

c. Using the mouse, select cells A7 through F7.

d. Position the mouse pointer on any boundary of the selected cells until it turns into an arrow pointer with a four-headed arrow attached.

e. Hold down the left mouse button, drag the outline of the selected cells to row 13, and then release the mouse button.

| | Date | Check No. | Payee | Description | Amount | Deposit |
|---|---|---|---|---|---|---|
| 4 | | | | | | |
| 5 | 1-Mar | | | Balance from previous month | | |
| 6 | 1-Mar | | | Deposit - General Account | | $5,500.00 |
| 7 | 1-Mar | | | Deposit - Sublet Rent | | $1,100.00 |
| 8 | 2-Mar | 527 | | | | |
| 9 | 3-Mar | 528 | | | | |
| 10 | 3-Mar | 529 | | | | |
| 11 | 8-Mar | 530 | Stationery Plus | Paper Supplies | $113.76 | |
| 12 | 9-Mar | 531 | Clear Source | Developer Supplies | $251.90 | |
| 13 | | | | | | |
| 14 | 10-Mar | 532 | Rainier S[A13:F13] | Camera Supplies | $119.62 | |
| 15 | 11-Mar | 533 | A1 Wedding Supplies | Photo Albums | $323.58 | |

Step 3c

Step 3e

f. Change the date of the deposit to March 10.

g. Delete row 7.

4. Save **ExcelL1_C5_P1.xlsx**.

**QUICK STEPS**

**Copy and Paste Cells**
1. Select cells.
2. Click Copy button.
3. Click desired cell.
4. Click Paste button.

**HINT**
Ctrl + C is the keyboard shortcut to copy selected data.

Copy

Paste Options

## Copying Selected Cells

Copying selected cells can be useful in worksheets that contain repetitive data. To copy cells, select the cells, and then click the Copy button in the Clipboard group in the Home tab. Click the cell where you want the first selected cell copied and then click the Paste button in the Clipboard group.

You can also copy selected cells using the mouse and the Ctrl key. To do this, select the cells you want to copy and then position the mouse pointer on any border around the selected cells until it turns into an arrow pointer. Hold down the Ctrl key and the left mouse button, drag the outline of the selected cells to the desired location, release the left mouse button, and then release the Ctrl key.

## Using the Paste Options Button

The Paste Options button displays in the lower right corner of the pasted cell(s) when you paste a cell or cells. Hover the mouse over this button until it displays with a down-pointing arrow and then click the left mouse button. This causes a drop-down list to display as shown in Figure 5.1. With the options from this list you can specify what you want pasted. You can specify that you want to keep source formatting or use destination themes or destination formatting. You can also keep the column widths of the source worksheet.

**Figure 5.1** Paste Options Button Drop-down List

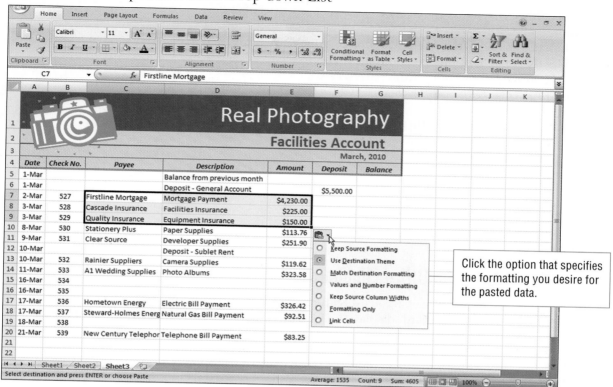

Click the option that specifies the formatting you desire for the pasted data.

## Project ⑩ Copying Selected Cells in a Worksheet

1. With **ExcelL1_C5_P1.xlsx** open, make Sheet2 active.
2. Select cells C7 through E9.
3. Click the Copy button in the Clipboard group in the Home tab.

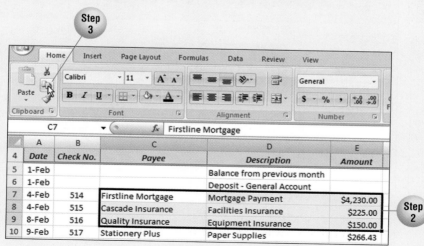

Step 3

Step 2

4. Make Sheet3 active.
5. Make cell C7 active.
6. Click the Paste button in the Clipboard group.
7. Click the Paste Options button that displays in the lower right corner of the pasted cells and then click *Keep Source Column Widths* at the drop-down list.
8. Make Sheet2 active and then press the Esc key to remove the moving marquee.
9. Save **ExcelL1_C5_P1.xlsx**.

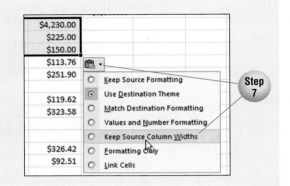

Step 7

**QUICK STEPS**

**Copy and Paste Multiple Items**
1. Click Clipboard group dialog box launcher.
2. Select desired cells.
3. Click Copy button.
4. Continue selecting desired cells and then clicking the Copy button.
5. Make active the desired cell.
6. Click item in Clipboard task pane that you want inserted in the worksheet.
7. Continue pasting desired items from the Clipboard task pane.

# Using the Office Clipboard

Use the Office Clipboard feature to collect and paste multiple items. To use the Office Clipboard, display the Clipboard task pane by clicking the Clipboard group dialog box launcher. This button is located in the lower right corner of the Clipboard group in the Home tab. The Clipboard task pane displays at the left side of the screen in a manner similar to what you see in Figure 5.2.

**Figure 5.2** Clipboard Task Pane

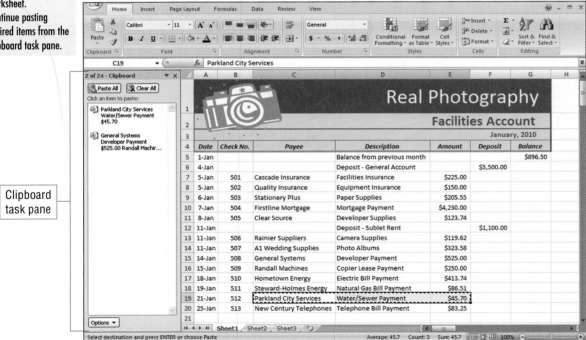

Clipboard task pane

Select data or an object you want to copy and then click the Copy button in the Clipboard group. Continue selecting text or items and clicking the Copy button. To insert an item, position the insertion point in the desired location and then click the item in the Clipboard task pane. If the copied item is text, the first 50 characters display. When all desired items are inserted, click the Clear All button to remove any remaining items. Sometimes, you may have a situation in which you want to copy all of the selected items to a single location. If so, position the insertion point in the desired location and then click the Paste All button in the Clipboard task pane.

## Project 10 — Copying and Pasting Cells Using the Office Clipboard

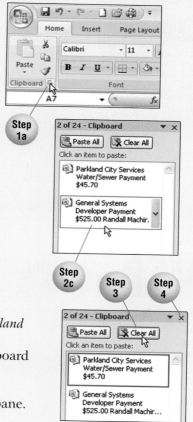

1. With **ExcelL1_C5_P1.xlsx** open, select cells for copying by completing the following steps:
   a. Display the Clipboard task pane by clicking the Clipboard group dialog box launcher. (If the Clipboard contains any copied data, click the Clear All button.)
   b. Click the Sheet1 tab.
   c. Select cells C15 through E16.
   d. Click the Copy button in the Clipboard group.
   e. Select cells C19 through E19.
   f. Click the Copy button in the Clipboard group.
2. Paste the copied cells by completing the following steps:
   a. Click the Sheet2 tab.
   b. Make cell C15 active.
   c. Click the item in the Clipboard task pane representing *General Systems Developer*.
   d. Click the Sheet3 tab.
   e. Make C15 active.
   f. Click the item in the Clipboard task pane representing *General Systems Developer*.
   g. Make cell C19 active.
   h. Click the item in the Clipboard task pane representing *Parkland City Services*.
3. Click the Clear All button located toward the top of the Clipboard task pane.
4. Close the Clipboard task pane by clicking the Close button (contains an X) located in the upper right corner of the task pane.
5. Save **ExcelL1_C5_P1.xlsx**.

## Pasting Values Only

When you copy and then paste a cell containing a value as well as a formula, the Paste Options button contains the options shown in Figure 5.1 as well as the additional option *Values Only*. Click this option if you want to copy only the value and not the formula.

Project **1e** **Copying and Pasting Values**

1. With **ExcelL1_C5_P1.xlsx** open, make Sheet1 active.
2. Make cell G6 active, insert the formula =(F6-E6)+G5, and then press Enter.
3. Copy the formula in cell G6 down to cells G7 through G20.
4. Copy the final balance amount from Sheet1 to Sheet2 by completing the following steps:
   a. Make cell G20 active.
   b. Click the Copy button in the Clipboard group.
   c. Click the Sheet2 tab.
   d. Make cell G5 active and then click the Paste button in the Clipboard group.
   e. Hover the mouse over the Paste Options button until the button displays with a down-pointing arrow and then click the left mouse button.
   f. At the drop-down list, click the *Values Only* option. (This inserts the value and not the formula.)

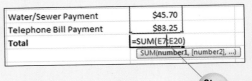

| February, 2010 | |
|---|---|
| **Deposit** | **Balance** |
| ◈ | #VALUE! |
| $5,500.00 | |

Step 4e

Paste Options:
○ Keep Source Formatting
◉ Use Destination Theme
○ Match Destination Formatting
○ Values Only
○ Values and Number Formatting
○ Values and Source Formatting
○ Keep Source Column Widths
○ Formatting Only
○ Link Cells

$1,100.00    Step 4f

5. Make cell G6 active, insert a formula that determines the balance, and then copy the formula down to cells G7 through G20.
6. Copy the amount in cell G20 and then paste the value only into cell G5 in Sheet3.
7. With Sheet3 active, make cell G6 active, insert a formula that determines the balance, and then copy the formula down to cells G7 through G20.
8. Save **ExcelL1_C5_P1.xlsx**.

**QUICK STEPS**

**Insert Worksheet**
Click Insert Worksheet tab.
OR
Press Shift + F11.

## Inserting a Worksheet

A workbook, by default, contains three worksheets. You can insert additional worksheets in a workbook. To do this, click the Insert Worksheet tab located to the right of the Sheet3 tab. This inserts a new worksheet labeled *Sheet4* at the right of the Sheet3 tab. You can also press Shift + F11 to insert a new worksheet. Or, you can insert a worksheet by clicking the Insert button arrow in the Cells group in the Home tab and then clicking *Insert Sheet*.

Project **1f** **Inserting a Worksheet**

1. With **ExcelL1_C5_P1.xlsx** open, make the following changes:
   a. Make Sheet1 active.
   b. Make cell D21 active, turn on bold, and then type Total.
   c. Make cell E21 active and then click once on the Sum button located in the Editing group in the Home tab. (This inserts the formula =SUM(E13:E20).)
   d. Change the formula to =SUM(E7:E20) and then press Enter.

| Water/Sewer Payment | $45.70 |
|---|---|
| Telephone Bill Payment | $83.25 |
| **Total** | =SUM(E7:E20) |
| | SUM(number1, [number2], ...) |

Step 1d

e. Make cell F21 active and then click once on the Sum button in the Editing group. (This inserts the formula =SUM(F12:F20).)

  f. Change the formula to =SUM(F6:F20) and then press Enter.

2. Make Sheet2 active and then complete the steps in Step 1 to insert the totals of the *Amount* and *Deposit* columns.

3. Make Sheet3 active and then complete the steps in Step 1 to insert the totals of the *Amount* and *Deposit* columns.

4. Insert a new worksheet by clicking the Insert Worksheet tab located to the right of the Sheet3 tab.

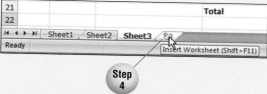

Step 4

5. Make Sheet1 active, copy cells A1 through G3, make Sheet4 active (with cell A1 active), and then paste the cells. (When copying the cells, position the cell pointer to the right of the image, make sure the pointer displays as a white plus symbol, and then drag to select the cells.)

6. Make the following changes to the worksheet:

  a. Make cell A3 active and then type **First Quarter Summary, 2010**.

  b. Change the width of column A to 20.00.

  c. Change the width of columns B, C, and D to 12.00.

  d. Select cells B4 through D4, click the Bold button in the Font group in the Home tab, and then click the Center button in the Alignment group.

  e. Select cells B5 through D7 and then change the number formatting to Currency with two decimal places and include the dollar sign symbol.

  f. Type the following text in the specified cells:

  B4  =  January
  C4  =  February
  D4  =  March
  A5  =  Checks Amount
  A6  =  Deposit Amount
  A7  =  End-of-month Balance

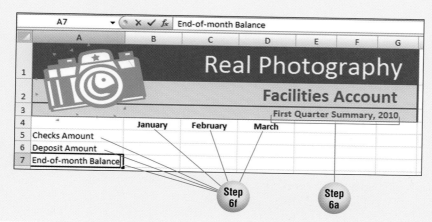

Step 6f

Step 6a

7. Copy a value by completing the following steps:
   a. Make Sheet1 active.
   b. Make cell E21 active and then click the Copy button in the Clipboard group in the Home tab.
   c. Make Sheet4 active.
   d. Make cell B5 active and then click the Paste button in the Clipboard group.
   e. Click the Paste Options button and then click *Values Only* at the drop-down list.

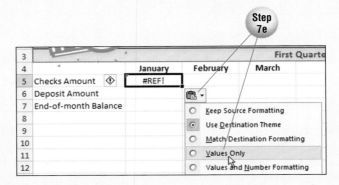

   f. Make Sheet1 active.
   g. Press the Esc key to remove the moving marquee.
   h. Make cell F21 active and then click the Copy button.
   i. Make Sheet4 active.
   j. Make cell B6 active and then click the Paste button.
   k. Click the Paste Options button and then click *Values Only* at the drop-down list.
   l. Make Sheet1 active.
   m. Press the Esc key to remove the moving marquee.
   n. Make cell G20 active and then click the Copy button.
   o. Make Sheet4 active.
   p. Make cell B7 active and then click the Paste button.
   q. Click the Paste Options button and then click *Values Only* at the drop-down list.
8. Complete steps similar to those in Step 7 to insert amounts and balances for February and March.
9. Save **ExcelL1_C5_P1.xlsx**.

# Managing Worksheets

Right-click a sheet tab and a shortcut menu displays as shown in Figure 5.3 with the options for managing worksheets. For example, remove a worksheet by clicking the *Delete* option. Move or copy a worksheet by clicking the *Move or Copy* option. Clicking this option causes a Move or Copy dialog box to display where you specify before what sheet you want to move or copy the selected sheet. By default, Excel names worksheets in a workbook *Sheet1, Sheet2, Sheet3,* and so on. To rename a worksheet, click the *Rename* option (this selects the default sheet name) and then type the desired name.

**Figure 5.3** Sheet Tab Shortcut Menu

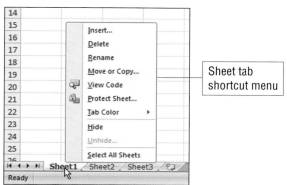

Sheet tab shortcut menu

In addition to the shortcut menu options, you can use the mouse to move or copy worksheets. To move a worksheet, position the mouse pointer on the worksheet tab, hold down the left mouse button (a page icon displays next to the mouse pointer), drag the page icon to the desired position, and then release the mouse button. For example, to move Sheet2 tab after Sheet3 tab you would position the mouse pointer on the Sheet2 tab, hold down the left mouse button, drag the page icon so it is positioned after the Sheet3 tab, and then release the mouse button. To copy a worksheet, hold down the Ctrl key while dragging the sheet tab.

Use the *Tab Color* option at the shortcut menu to apply a color to a worksheet tab. Right-click a worksheet tab, point to *Tab Color* at the shortcut menu, and then click the desired color at the color palette.

**QUICK STEPS**

**Move or Copy a Worksheet**
1. Right-click sheet tab.
2. Click *Move or Copy.*
3. At Move or Copy dialog box, click desired worksheet name in *Before sheet* list box.
4. Click OK.
OR
Drag worksheet tab to the desired position (to copy, hold down Ctrl key while dragging).

**HINT**

Use the tab scroll buttons, located to the left of the sheet tabs, to bring into view any worksheet tabs not currently visible.

**QUICK STEPS**

**Recolor Sheet Tab**
1. Right-click sheet tab.
2. Point to *Tab Color.*
3. Click desired color at color palette.

1. With **ExcelL1_C5_P1.xlsx** open, move Sheet4 by completing the following steps:
   a. Right-click Sheet4 and then click *Move or Copy* at the shortcut menu.

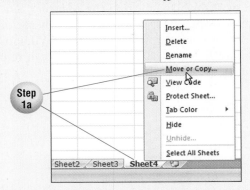

Step 1a

   b. At the Move or Copy dialog box, make sure *Sheet1* is selected in the *Before sheet* section, and then click OK.

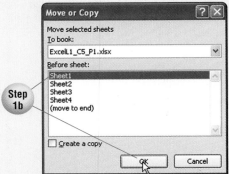

Step 1b

2. Rename Sheet4 by completing the following steps:
   a. Right-click the Sheet4 tab and then click *Rename*.
   b. Type **Summary** and then press Enter.

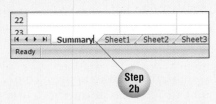

Step 2b

3. Complete steps similar to those in Step 2 to rename Sheet1 to *January*, Sheet2 to *February*, and Sheet3 to *March*.
4. Change the color of the Summary sheet tab by completing the following steps:
   a. Right-click the Summary sheet tab.
   b. Point to *Tab Color* at the shortcut menu.
   c. Click a red color of your choosing at the color palette.
5. Follow steps similar to those in Step 4 to change the January sheet tab to a blue color, the February sheet tab to a purple color, and the March sheet tab to a green color.
6. Save **ExcelL1_C5_P1.xlsx**.

## Hiding a Worksheet in a Workbook

In a workbook containing multiple worksheets, you can hide a worksheet that may contain sensitive data or data you do not want to display or print with the workbook. To hide a worksheet in a workbook, click the Format button in the Cells group in the Home tab, point to *Hide & Unhide*, and then click *Hide Sheet*. You can also hide a worksheet by right-clicking a worksheet tab and then clicking the *Hide* option at the shortcut menu. To make a hidden worksheet visible, click the Format button in the Cells group, point to *Hide & Unhide*, and then click *Unhide Sheet*, or right-click a worksheet tab and then click *Unhide* at the shortcut menu. At the Unhide dialog box shown in Figure 5.4, double-click the name of the hidden worksheet you want to display.

**QUICK STEPS**

**Hide a Worksheet**
1. Click Format button.
2. Point to *Hide & Unhide*.
3. Click *Hide Sheet*.
OR
1. Right-click worksheet tab.
2. Click *Hide* at shortcut menu.

**Unhide a Worksheet**
1. Click Format button.
2. Point to *Hide & Unhide*.
3. Click *Unhide Sheet*.
4. Double-click desired hidden worksheet in Unhide dialog box.
OR
1. Right-click worksheet tab.
2. Click *Unhide* at shortcut menu.
3. Double-click desired hidden worksheet in Unhide dialog box.

**Figure 5.4** Unhide Dialog Box

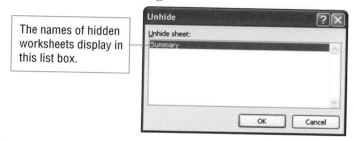

The names of hidden worksheets display in this list box.

**HINT**
If the *Hide* option is unavailable, the workbook is protected from change.

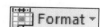

## Formatting Multiple Worksheets

When you apply formatting to a worksheet, such as changing margins, orientation, or inserting a header or footer, and so on, the formatting is applied only to the active worksheet. If you want formatting to apply to multiple worksheets in a workbook, select the tabs of the desired worksheets and then apply the formatting. For example, if a workbook contains three worksheets and you want to apply formatting to the first and second worksheets only, select the tabs for the first and second worksheets and then apply the formatting.

To select adjacent worksheet tabs, click the first tab, hold down the Shift key, and then click the last tab. To select nonadjacent worksheet tabs, click the first tab, hold down the Ctrl key, and then click any other tabs you want selected.

1. With **ExcelL1_C5_P1.xlsx** open, hide the Summary worksheet by completing the following steps:
   a. Click the Summary tab.
   b. Click the Format button in the Cells group in the Home tab, point to *Hide & Unhide*, and then click *Hide Sheet*.

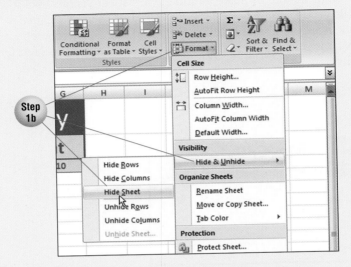

Step 1b

2. Unhide the worksheet by completing the following steps:
   a. Click the Format button in the Cells group, point to *Hide & Unhide*, and then click *Unhide Sheet*.
   b. At the Unhide dialog box, make sure *Summary* is selected and then click OK.

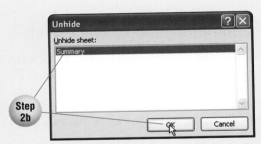

Step 2b

3. Insert a header for each worksheet by completing the following steps:
   a. Click the Summary tab.
   b. Hold down the Shift key and then click the March tab. (This selects all four tabs.)
   c. Click the Insert tab.
   d. Click the Header & Footer button in the Text group.
   e. Click the Header button in the Header & Footer group in the Header & Footer Tools Design tab and then click the option at the drop-down list that prints your name at the left side of the page, the page number in the middle, and the date at the right side of the page.
4. With all the sheet tabs selected, horizontally and vertically center each worksheet on the page. *Hint: Do this at the Page Setup dialog box with the Margins tab selected.*
5. With all of the sheet tabs still selected, change the page orientation to landscape. *Hint: Do this with the Orientation button in the Page Layout tab.*
6. Save **ExcelL1_C5_P1.xlsx**.

# Printing a Workbook Containing Multiple Worksheets

By default, Excel prints the currently displayed worksheet. If you want to print all worksheets in a workbook, display the Print dialog box by clicking the Office button and then clicking *Print*. At the Print dialog box, click *Entire workbook* in the *Print what* section, and then click OK. You can also print specific worksheets in a workbook by selecting the tabs of the worksheets you want to print.

**QUICK STEPS**

**Print all Worksheets in a Workbook**
1. Click Office button, *Print.*
2. Click *Entire workbook.*
3. Click OK.

## Project ① Printing All Worksheets in a Workbook

1. With **ExcelL1_C5_P1.xlsx** open, click the Office button and then click *Print*.
2. At the Print dialog box, click the *Entire workbook* option in the *Print what* section.
3. Click OK.
4. Close **ExcelL1_C5_P1.xlsx**.

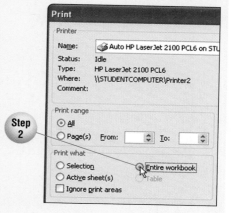

## Project ② Write Formulas Using Ranges in an Equipment Usage Workbook

You will open an equipment usage workbook and then split the window and edit cells. You will also name ranges and then use the range names to write formulas in the workbook.

# Splitting a Worksheet into Windows and Freezing and Unfreezing Panes

In some worksheets, not all cells display at one time in the worksheet area (such as ExcelC05Project02.xlsx). When working in worksheets with more cells than can display at one time, you may find splitting the worksheet window into panes helpful. Split the worksheet window into panes with the Split button in the Window group in the View tab or with the split bars that display at the top of the vertical scroll bar and at the right side of the horizontal scroll bar. Figure 5.5 identifies these split bars.

**QUICK STEPS**

**Split a Worksheet**
1. Click View tab.
2. Click Split button.
OR
Drag horizontal and/or vertical split bars.

**Figure 5.5** Split Bars

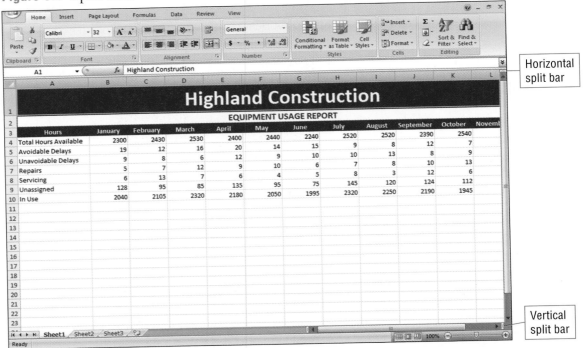

Highland Construction

EQUIPMENT USAGE REPORT

| Hours | January | February | March | April | May | June | July | August | September | October | Novemb |
|---|---|---|---|---|---|---|---|---|---|---|---|
| Total Hours Available | 2300 | 2430 | 2530 | 2400 | 2440 | 2240 | 2520 | 2520 | 2390 | 2540 | |
| Avoidable Delays | 19 | 12 | 16 | 20 | 14 | 15 | 9 | 8 | 12 | 7 | |
| Unavoidable Delays | 9 | 8 | 6 | 12 | 9 | 10 | 10 | 13 | 8 | 9 | |
| Repairs | 5 | 7 | 12 | 9 | 10 | 6 | 7 | 8 | 10 | 13 | |
| Servicing | 6 | 13 | 7 | 6 | 4 | 5 | 8 | 3 | 12 | 6 | |
| Unassigned | 128 | 95 | 85 | 135 | 95 | 75 | 145 | 120 | 124 | 112 | |
| In Use | 2040 | 2105 | 2320 | 2180 | 2050 | 1995 | 2320 | 2250 | 2190 | 1945 | |

Horizontal split bar

Vertical split bar

**HINT**

Restore a split window by double-clicking anywhere on the split bar that divides the panes.

To split a window with the split bar located at the top of the vertical scroll bar, position the mouse pointer on the split bar until it turns into a double-headed arrow with a short double line in the middle. Hold down the left mouse button, drag down the thick gray line that displays until the pane is the desired size, and then release the mouse button. Split the window vertically with the split bar at the right side of the horizontal scroll bar.

To split a worksheet window with the Split button, click the View tab, and then click the Split button. This causes the worksheet to split into four window panes as shown in Figure 5.6. The windows are split by thick, light blue lines (with a three-dimensional look). To remove a split from a worksheet click the Split button to deactivate it or drag the split bars to the upper left corner of the worksheet.

**Figure 5.6** Split Window

| Hours | January | February | March | April | May | June | July | August | September | October | Novem |
|---|---|---|---|---|---|---|---|---|---|---|---|
| | | | | **Highland Construction** | | | | | | | |
| | | | | EQUIPMENT USAGE REPORT | | | | | | | |
| Total Hours Available | 2300 | 2430 | 2530 | 2400 | 2440 | 2240 | 2520 | 2520 | 2390 | 2540 | |
| Avoidable Delays | 19 | 12 | 16 | 20 | 14 | 15 | 9 | 8 | 12 | 7 | |
| Unavoidable Delays | 9 | 8 | 6 | 12 | 9 | 10 | 10 | 13 | 8 | 9 | |
| Repairs | 5 | 7 | 12 | 9 | 10 | 6 | 7 | 8 | 10 | 13 | |
| Servicing | 6 | 13 | 7 | 6 | 4 | 5 | 8 | 3 | 12 | 6 | |
| Unassigned | 128 | 95 | 85 | 135 | 95 | 75 | 145 | 120 | 124 | 112 | |
| In Use | 2040 | 2105 | 2320 | 2180 | 2050 | 1995 | 2320 | 2250 | 2190 | 1945 | |

A window pane will display the active cell. As the insertion point is moved through the pane, another active cell with a blue background may display. This additional active cell displays when the insertion point passes over one of the light blue lines that creates the pane. As you move through a worksheet, you may see both active cells—one with a normal background and one with a blue background. If you make a change to the active cell, the change is made in both. If you want only one active cell to display, freeze the window panes by clicking the Freeze Panes button in the Window group in the View tab and then clicking *Freeze Panes* at the drop-down list. You can maintain the display of column headings while editing or typing text in cells by clicking the Freeze Panes button and then clicking *Freeze Top Row*. Maintain the display of row headings by clicking the Freeze Panes button and then clicking *Freeze First Column*. Unfreeze window panes by clicking the Freeze Panes button and then clicking *Unfreeze Panes* at the drop-down list.

Using the mouse, you can move the thick, light blue lines that divide the window into panes. To do this, position the mouse pointer on the line until the pointer turns into a double-headed arrow with a double line in the middle. Hold down the left mouse button, drag the outline of the light blue line to the desired location, and then release the mouse button. If you want to move both the horizontal and vertical lines at the same time, position the mouse pointer on the intersection of the thick, light blue lines until it turns into a four-headed arrow. Hold down the left mouse button, drag the thick, light blue lines in the desired direction, and then release the mouse button.

1. Open **ExcelC05Project02.xlsx** and then save the workbook and name it **ExcelL1_C5_P2**.
2. Make sure cell A1 is active and then split the window by clicking the View tab and then clicking the Split button in the Window group. (This splits the window into four panes.)
3. Drag the vertical light blue line by completing the following steps:
   a. Position the mouse pointer on the vertical split line until the pointer turns into a double-headed arrow pointing left and right with a double-line between.
   b. Hold down the left mouse button, drag to the left until the vertical light blue line is immediately to the right of the first column, and then release the mouse button.
4. Freeze the window panes by clicking the Freeze Panes button in the Window group in the View tab and then clicking *Freeze Panes* at the drop-down list.
5. Make cell L4 active and then type the following data in the specified cells:

| | | | | |
|---|---|---|---|---|
| L4 | = | 2310 | M4 | = | 2210 |
| L5 | = | 12 | M5 | = | 5 |
| L6 | = | 5 | M6 | = | 7 |
| L7 | = | 9 | M7 | = | 8 |
| L8 | = | 11 | M8 | = | 12 |
| L9 | = | 95 | M9 | = | 120 |
| L10 | = | 2005 | M10 | = | 1830 |

6. Unfreeze the window panes by clicking the Freeze Panes button and then clicking *Unfreeze Panes* at the drop-down list.
7. Remove the panes by clicking the Split button in the Window group to deactivate it.
8. Save **ExcelL1_C5_P2.xlsx**.

## Working with Ranges

**Name a Range**
1. Select cells.
2. Click in Name box.
3. Type range name.
4. Press Enter.

A selected group of cells is referred to as a *range*. A range of cells can be formatted, moved, copied, or deleted. You can also name a range of cells and then move the insertion point to the range or use a named range as part of a formula.

To name a range, select the cells, and then click in the Name box located at the left of the Formula bar. Type a name for the range (do not use a space) and then press Enter. To move the insertion point to a specific range and select the range, click the down-pointing arrow at the right side of the Name box and then click the range name.

You can also name a range using the Define Name button in the Formulas tab. To do this, click the Formulas tab and then click the Define Name button in the Defined Names group. At the New Name dialog box, type a name for the range and then click OK.

You can use a range name in a formula. For example, if a range is named *Profit* and you want to insert the average of all cells in the *Profit* range, you would make the desired cell active and then type =AVERAGE(Profit). You can use a named range in the current worksheet or in another worksheet within the workbook.

HINT

Another method for moving to a range is to click the Find & Select button in the Editing group in the Home tab and then click *Go To*. At the Go To dialog box, double-click the range name.

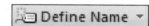

## Project 2h Naming a Range and Using a Range in a Formula

1. With **ExcelL1_C5_P2.xlsx** open, click the Sheet2 tab and then type the following text in the specified cells:

   | A1 | = | EQUIPMENT USAGE REPORT |
   | A2 | = | Yearly Hours |
   | A3 | = | Avoidable Delays |
   | A4 | = | Unavoidable Delays |
   | A5 | = | Total Delay Hours |
   | A6 | = | (leave blank) |
   | A7 | = | Repairs |
   | A8 | = | Servicing |
   | A9 | = | Total Repair/Servicing Hours |

   Step 1

2. Make the following formatting changes to the worksheet:
   a. Automatically adjust the width of column A.
   b. Center and bold the text in cells A1 and A2.
3. Select a range of cells in worksheet 1, name the range, and use it in a formula in worksheet 2 by completing the following steps:
   a. Click the Sheet1 tab.
   b. Select cells B5 through M5.
   c. Click in the Name box located to the left of the Formula bar.
   d. Type adhours (for Avoidable Delays Hours) and then press Enter.
   e. Click the Sheet2 tab.
   f. Make cell B3 active.
   g. Type the equation =SUM(adhours) and then press Enter.

   Step 3d

   Step 3g

4. Click the Sheet1 tab and then complete the following steps:
   a. Select cells B6 through M6.
   b. Click the Formulas tab.
   c. Click the Define Name button in the Defined Names group.

d. At the New Name dialog box, type **udhours** and then click OK.

e. Make worksheet 2 active, make cell B4 active, and then insert the equation *=SUM(udhours)*.

5. Make worksheet 1 active and then complete the following steps:

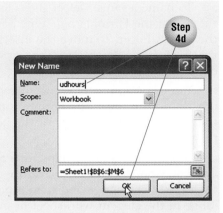

Step 4d

a. Select cells B7 through M7 and then name the range *rhours*.

b. Make worksheet 2 active, make cell B7 active, and then insert the equation *=SUM(rhours)*.

c. Make worksheet 1 active.

d. Select cells B8 through M8 and then name the range *shours*.

e. Make worksheet 2 active, make cell B8 active, and then insert the equation *=SUM(shours)*.

6. With worksheet 2 still active, make the following changes:

a. Make cell B5 active.

b. Double-click the Sum button in the Editing group in the Home tab.

c. Make cell B9 active.

d. Double-click the Sum button in the Editing group in the Home tab.

7. Make worksheet 1 active and then move to the range *adhours* by clicking the down-pointing arrow at the right side of the Name box and then clicking *adhours* at the drop-down list.

8. Select both sheet tabs, change the orientation to landscape, scale the contents to fit on one page (in Page Layout tab, change width to *1 page*), and insert a custom footer with your name, page number, and date.

9. Print both worksheets in the workbook.

10. Save and then close **ExcelL1_C5_P2.xlsx**.

Step 7

---

roject ③ **Arrange, Size, and Copy Data between Workbooks**

**You will open, arrange, hide, unhide, size, and move multiple workbooks. You will also copy cells from one workbook and paste in another workbook.**

## Working with Windows

You can open multiple workbooks in Excel and arrange the open workbooks in the Excel window. With multiple workbooks open, you can cut and paste or copy and paste cell entries from one workbook to another using the same techniques discussed earlier in this chapter with the exception that you activate the destination workbook before executing the Paste command.

# Opening Multiple Workbooks

With multiple workbooks open, you can move or copy information between workbooks or compare the contents of several workbooks. When you open a new workbook, it is placed on top of the original workbook. Once multiple workbooks are opened, you can resize the workbooks to see all or a portion of them on the screen.

Open multiple workbooks at one time at the Open dialog box. If workbooks are adjacent, display the Open dialog box, click the first workbook name to be opened, hold down the Shift key, and then click the last workbook name to be opened. If the workbooks are nonadjacent, click the first workbook name to be opened and then hold down the Ctrl key while clicking the remaining desired workbook names. Release the Shift key or the Ctrl key and then click the Open button.

To see what workbooks are currently open, click the View tab and then click the Switch Windows button in the Window group. The names of the open workbooks display in a drop-down list and the workbook name preceded by a check mark is the active workbook. To make one of the other workbooks active, click the desired workbook name at the drop-down list.

Switch Windows ▾

# Arranging Workbooks

If you have more than one workbook open, you can arrange the workbooks at the Arrange Windows dialog box shown in Figure 5.7. To display this dialog box, open several workbooks, and then click the Arrange All button in the Window group in the View tab. At the Arrange Windows dialog box, click *Tiled* to display a portion of each open workbook. Figure 5.8 displays four tiled workbooks.

**QUICK STEPS**

**Arrange Workbooks**
1. Click View tab.
2. Click Arrange All button.
3. At Arrange Windows dialog box, click desired arrangement.
4. Click OK.

Arrange All

**Figure 5.7** Arrange Windows Dialog Box

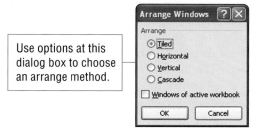

Use options at this dialog box to choose an arrange method.

**Figure 5.8** Tiled Workbooks

Choose the *Horizontal* option at the Arrange Windows dialog box and the open workbooks display across the screen. The *Vertical* option displays the open workbooks up and down the screen. The last option, *Cascade*, displays the Title bar of each open workbook. Figure 5.9 shows four cascaded workbooks.

The option you select for displaying multiple workbooks depends on which part of the workbooks is most important to view simultaneously. For example, the tiled workbooks in Figure 5.8 allow you to view the company logos and the first few rows and columns of each workbook.

**Figure 5.9** Cascaded Workbooks

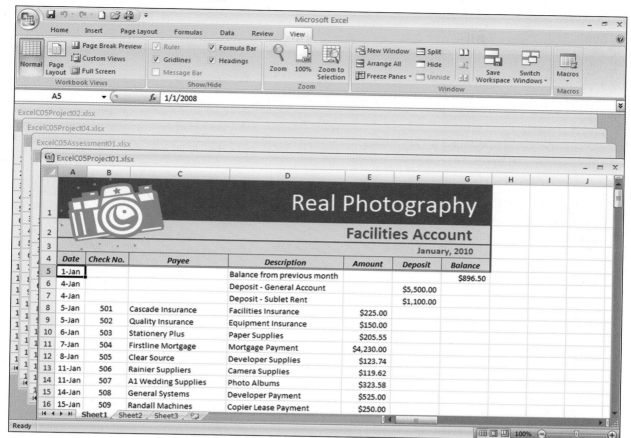

## Hiding/Unhiding Workbooks

With the Hide button in the Window group in the View tab, you can hide the active workbook. If a workbook has been hidden, redisplay the workbook by clicking the Unhide button in the Window group in the View tab. At the Unhide dialog box, make sure the desired workbook is selected in the list box, and then click OK.

**Project ③a    Opening, Arranging, and Hiding/Unhiding Workbooks**

1. Open several workbooks at the same time by completing the following steps:
   a. Display the Open dialog box.
   b. Click the workbook named ***ExcelC05Project01.xlsx***.
   c. Hold down the Ctrl key, click ***ExcelC05Project02.xlsx***, click ***ExcelC05Project04.xlsx***, and click ***ExcelC05Assessment01.xlsx***.
   d. Release the Ctrl key and then click the Open button in the dialog box.

2. Make **ExcelC05Assessment01.xlsx** the active workbook by clicking the View tab, clicking the Switch Windows button in the Window group, and then clicking *4* at the drop-down list.

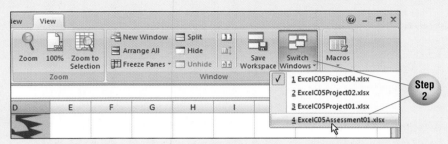

3. Make **ExcelC05Project01.xlsx** the active workbook by clicking the Switch Windows button and then clicking ***ExcelC05Project01.xlsx*** at the drop-down list.
4. Tile the workbooks by completing the following steps:
   a. Click the Arrange All button in the Window group in the View tab.
   b. At the Arrange Windows dialog box, make sure *Tiled* is selected and then click OK.

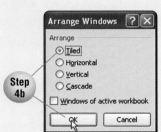

5. Tile the workbooks horizontally by completing the following steps:
   a. Click the Arrange All button.
   b. At the Arrange Windows dialog box, click *Horizontal*.
   c. Click OK.
6. Cascade the workbooks by completing the following steps:
   a. Click the Arrange All button.
   b. At the Arrange Windows dialog box, click *Cascade*.
   c. Click OK.
7. Hide and unhide workbooks by completing the following steps:
   a. Make sure **ExcelC05Project01.xlsx** is the active workbook (displays on top of the other workbooks).
   b. Click the Hide button in the Window group in the View tab.
   c. Make sure **ExcelC05Assessment01.xlsx** is the active workbook (displays on top of the other workbooks).
   d. Click the Hide button.
   e. Click the Unhide button.
   f. At the Unhide dialog box, click ***ExcelC05Project01.xlsx*** in the list box, and then click OK.

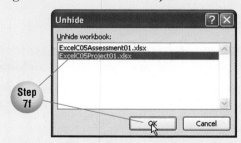

   g. Click the Unhide button.
   h. At the Unhide dialog box, make sure **ExcelC05Assessment01.xlsx** is selected in the list box and then click OK.
8. Close all of the open workbooks without saving changes.

## Sizing and Moving Workbooks

You can use the Maximize and Minimize buttons located in the upper right corner of the active workbook to change the size of the window. The Maximize button is the button in the upper right corner of the active workbook immediately to the left of the Close button. (The Close button is the button containing the *X*.) The Minimize button is located immediately to the left of the Maximize button.

Maximize    Minimize

Close    Restore

If you arrange all open workbooks and then click the Maximize button in the active workbook, the active workbook expands to fill the screen. In addition, the Maximize button changes to the Restore button. To return the active workbook back to its size before it was maximized, click the Restore button.

Clicking the Minimize button causes the active workbook to be reduced and positioned as a button on the Taskbar. In addition, the Minimize button changes to the Restore button. To maximize a workbook that has been reduced, click the button on the Taskbar representing the workbook.

---

## Project 3b — Minimizing, Maximizing, and Restoring Workbooks

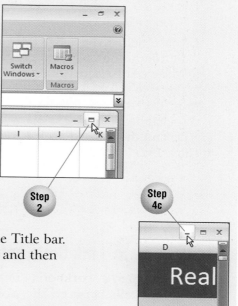

Step 2

Step 4c

Real

1. Open **ExcelC05Project01.xlsx**.
2. Maximize **ExcelC05Project01.xlsx** by clicking the Maximize button at the right side of the workbook Title bar. (The Maximize button is the button at the right side of the Title bar, immediately to the left of the Close button.)
3. Open **ExcelC05Project02.xlsx** and **ExcelC05Project03.xlsx**.
4. Make the following changes to the open workbooks:
   a. Tile the workbooks.
   b. Make **ExcelC05Project01.xlsx** the active workbook (Title bar displays with a light blue background [the background color may vary depending on how Windows is customized]).
   c. Minimize **ExcelC05Project01.xlsx** by clicking the Minimize button that displays at the right side of the Title bar.
   d. Make **ExcelC05Project02.xlsx** the active workbook and then minimize it.
   e. Minimize **ExcelC05Project03.xlsx**.
5. Close all workbooks.

---

# Moving, Copying, and Pasting Data

With more than one workbook open, you can move, copy, and/or paste data from one workbook to another. To move, copy, and/or paste data between workbooks, use the cutting and pasting options you learned earlier in this chapter, together with the information about windows in this chapter.

1. Open **ExcelC05Project03.xlsx**.
2. If you just completed Project 3b, click the Maximize button so the worksheet fills the entire worksheet window.
3. Save the workbook and name it **ExcelL1_C5_P3**.
4. With **ExcelL1_C5_P3.xlsx** open, open **ExcelC05Deering.xlsx**.
5. Select and then copy text from **ExcelC05Deering.xlsx** to **ExcelL1_C5_P3.xlsx** by completing the following steps:
   a. With **ExcelC05Deering.xlsx** the active workbook, select cells A3 through D10.
   b. Click the Copy button in the Clipboard group in the Home tab.
   c. Click the button on the Taskbar representing **ExcelL1_C5_P3.xlsx**.

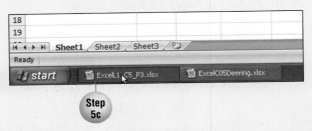

Step 5c

Step 5d

   d. Make cell A8 the active cell and then click the Paste button in the Clipboard group in the Home tab.
   e. Make cell E7 active and then drag the fill handle down to cell E15.
6. Print **ExcelL1_C5_P3.xlsx** horizontally and vertically centered on the page.
7. Save and then close **ExcelL1_C5_P3.xlsx**.
8. Close **ExcelC05Deering.xlsx**.

Project 4    **Link Cells between Quarterly Expenses Worksheets**

You will open a workbook containing worksheets with quarterly expenses data and then link cells between the worksheets.

## Linking Data between Worksheets

You may want to create a link between worksheets or workbooks with data in cells in related workbooks or workbooks containing multiple worksheets. When data is linked, a change made in a linked cell is automatically made to the other cells in the link. You can make links with individual cells or with a range of cells.

Linking cells between worksheets creates what is called a *dynamic link*. Dynamic links are useful in worksheets or workbooks that need to maintain consistency and control over critical data. The worksheet that contains the original data is called the *source* worksheet and the worksheet relying on the source worksheet for the data in the link is called the *dependent* worksheet.

To create a link, make active the cell containing the data to be linked (or select the cells), and then click the Copy button in the Clipboard group in the Home tab. Make active the worksheet where you want to paste the cell or cells, click the Paste button arrow, and then click *Paste Link* at the drop-down list. When a change is made to the cell or cells in the source worksheet, the change is automatically made to the linked cell or cells in the dependent worksheet. You can also create a link by clicking the Paste button, clicking the Paste Options button, and then clicking the *Link Cells* option.

You can also link cells with options at the Paste Special dialog box. Display this dialog box by clicking the Paste button arrow and then clicking *Paste Special* at the drop-down list. At the Paste Special dialog box, specify what in the cell you want to copy and what operators you want to include and then click the Paste Link button.

**QUICK STEPS**

**Link Data between Worksheets**
1. Select cells.
2. Click Copy button.
3. Click desired worksheet tab.
4. Click in desired cell.
5. Click Paste button arrow.
6. Click *Paste Link* at drop-down list.

## Project 4 — Linking Cells between Worksheets

1. Open **ExcelC05Project04.xlsx** and then save the workbook and name it **ExcelL1_C5_P4**.
2. Link cells in the first quarter worksheet to the other three worksheets by completing the following steps:
   a. Select cells C4 through C10.
   b. Click the Copy button in the Clipboard group in the Home tab.
   c. Click the 2nd Qtr. tab.
   d. Make cell C4 active.
   e. Click the Paste button arrow and then click *Paste Link* at the drop-down list.
   f. Click the 3rd Qtr. tab.
   g. Make cell C4 active.
   h. Click the Paste button.
   i. Click the Paste Options button that displays in the lower right corner of the pasted cell and then click *Link Cells* at the drop-down list.
   j. Click the 4th Qtr. tab.
   k. Make cell C4 active.
   l. Click the Paste button arrow and then click *Paste Link*.
   m. Click the 1st Qtr. tab and then press the Esc key to remove the moving marquee.

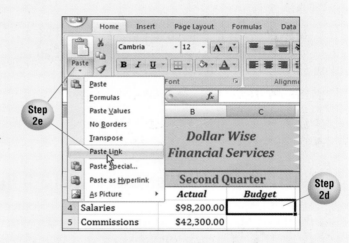

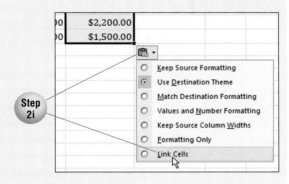

3. Insert a formula in all worksheets that subtracts the Budget amount from the Variance amount by completing the following steps:

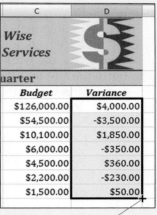

   a. Make sure the first quarter worksheet displays.
   b. Hold down the Shift key and then click the 4th Qtr. tab. (This selects all four tabs.)
   c. Make cell D4 active and then insert the formula =C4-B4.
   d. Copy the formula in cell D4 down to cells D5 through D10.
   e. Click the 2nd Qtr. tab and notice that the formula was inserted and copied in this worksheet.
   f. Click the other worksheet tabs and notice the formula.
   g. Click the 1st Qtr. tab.

Step 3d

4. With the first quarter worksheet active, make the following changes to some of the linked cells:

   C4: Change $126,000 to 128,000
   C5: Change $54,500 to 56,000
   C9: Change $2,200 to 2,400

5. Click the 2nd Qtr. tab and notice that the values in cells C4, C5, and C9 automatically changed (because they are linked to the first quarter worksheet).
6. Click the 3rd Qtr. tab and notice that the values in cells C4, C5, and C9 automatically changed.
7. Click the 4th Qtr. tab and notice that the values in cells C4, C5, and C9 automatically changed.
8. Save **ExcelL1_C5_P4.xlsx** and then print all the worksheets in the workbook.
9. Close **ExcelL1_C5_P4.xlsx**.

## Project 5   Link Worksheets with 3-D References

You will open a workbook containing worksheets with quarterly sales data and then link the sales data in the worksheets with a 3-D reference.

## Linking Worksheets with a 3-D Reference

In multiple worksheet workbooks, you can use a 3-D reference to analyze data in the same cell or range of cells. A 3-D reference includes the cell or range of cells, preceded by a range of worksheet names. For example, you can add all of the values contained in cells in B2 through B5 in worksheets 1 and 2 in a workbook using a 3-D reference. To do this, you would complete these basic steps:

Use for ch.6
Assess.# 2

   1. Make active the cell where you want to enter the function.
   2. Type =SUM( and then click the Sheet1 tab.
   3. Hold down the Shift key and then click the Sheet2 tab.
   4. Select cells B2 through B5 in the worksheet.
   5. Type ) (this is the closing parenthesis that ends the formula) and then press Enter.

# Project ⑤ Linking Worksheets with a 3-D Reference

1. Open **ExcelC05Project05.xlsx** and then save the workbook and name it **ExcelL1_C5_P5**.
2. Make sure Sales 2007 is the active worksheet.
3. Make the following changes to the Sales 2007 worksheet:
   a. Make cell B12 active.
   b. Click the Center button in the Alignment group and then click the Bold button in the Font group.
   c. Type *January Sales* and then press Alt + Enter.
   d. Type *2007-2009* and then press Enter.
4. Link the Sales 2007, Sales 2008, and Sales 2009 worksheets with a 3-D reference by completing the following steps:
   a. With cell B13 active, type =SUM(.
   b. Hold down the Shift key, click the Sales 2009 sheet tab, and then release the Shift key. (This selects all three sheet tabs.)
   c. Select cells B5 through B10.
   d. Type ) and then press Enter.

type at top of screen

| | FIRST-QUARTER SALES - 2007 | | | | | |
|---|---|---|---|---|---|---|
| 3 | | | | | | |
| 4 | Customer | January | | February | | March |
| 5 | Lakeside Trucking | $ | 84,231 | $ | 73,455 | $ | 97,549 |
| 6 | Gresham Machines | $ | 33,199 | $ | 40,390 | $ | 50,112 |
| 7 | Real Photography | $ | 30,891 | $ | 35,489 | $ | 36,400 |
| 8 | Genesis Productions | $ | 72,190 | $ | 75,390 | $ | 83,219 |
| 9 | Landower Company | $ | 22,188 | $ | 14,228 | $ | 38,766 |
| 10 | Jewell Enterprises | $ | 19,764 | $ | 50,801 | $ | 32,188 |
| 11 | | | | | | |
| 12 | | January Sales 2007-2009 | | | | |
| 13 | | =SUM('Sales 2007:Sales 2009'!B5:B10) | | | | |
| 14 | | | | | | |

Steps 4a–4d

5. Complete steps similar to those in Step 3 to add *February Sales 2007-2009* (on two lines) in cell C12 and complete steps similar to those in Step 4 to insert the formula with the 3-D reference in cell C13. (Select cells C5 through C10.)
6. Complete steps similar to those in Step 3 to add *March Sales 2007-2009* (on two lines) in cell D12 and complete steps similar to those in Step 4 to insert the formula with the 3-D reference in cell D13. (Select cells D5 through D10.)
7. Save the workbook.
8. Print only the Sales 2007 worksheet.
9. Close **ExcelL1_C5_P5.xlsx**.

# Project ⑥ Copy and Paste a Worksheet in a Word Document

You will copy cells in a worksheet and paste the cells in a Word letter document. You will then edit some of the data in cells in the Word document.

# Copying and Pasting a Worksheet between Programs

Microsoft Office is a suite that allows integration, which is the combining of data from two or more programs into one file. Integration can occur by copying and pasting data between programs. The program containing the data to be copied is called the *source* program and the program where the data is pasted is called the *destination* program. For example, you can create a worksheet in Excel and then copy it to a Word document. The steps to copy and paste between programs are basically the same as copying and pasting within the same program.

When copying data between worksheets or from one program to another, you can copy and paste, copy and link, or copy and embed the data. Consider the following when choosing a method for copying data:

- Copy data in the source program and paste it in the destination program when the data will not need to be edited.
- Copy data in the source program and then link it in the destination program when the data is updated regularly in the source program and you want the update reflected in the destination program.
- Copy data in the source program and then embed it in the destination program when the data will be edited in the destination program (with the tools of the source program).

Earlier in this chapter, you copied and pasted cells within and between worksheets and you also copied and linked cells between worksheets. You can also copy and link data between programs. Copy and embed data using options at the Paste Special dialog box. In Project 6, you will copy cells in a worksheet and then embed the cells in a Word document. With the worksheet embedded in a Word document, double-click the worksheet and Excel tools display in the document for editing the worksheet.

## Project 6   Copying and Pasting a Worksheet into a Word Document

1. Open the Word program and then open **WordC05_Letter01.docx**.
2. Save the document and name it **WordExcelL1_C5_P6**.
3. With **WordExcelL1_C5_P6.docx** open, make Excel the active program.
4. Open **ExcelC05Project06.xlsx** and then save the workbook and name it **ExcelL1_C5_P6**.
5. Copy the worksheet to the letter by completing the following steps:
   a. Select cells A1 through D8.
   b. Click the Copy button in the Clipboard group in the Home tab.
   c. Click the button on the Taskbar representing the Word document **WordExcelL1_C5_P6.docx**.
   d. Position the insertion point on the blank line below the first paragraph of text in the body of the letter.
   e. Click the Paste button arrow in the Clipboard group in the Home tab and then click *Paste Special* at the drop-down list.
   f. At the Paste Special dialog box, click *Microsoft Office Excel Worksheet Object* in the *As* list box, and then click OK.

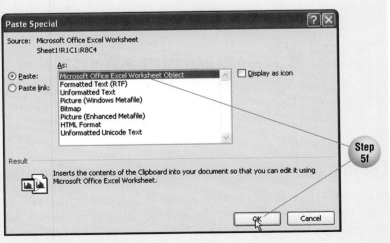

Step 5f

6. Edit a few of the cells in the worksheet by completing the following steps:
   a. Double-click anywhere in the worksheet. (This displays the Excel ribbon for editing.)
   b. Click in each of the following cells and make the change indicated:
      B6: Change *196%* to *110%*.
      C6: Change *190%* to *104%*.
      D6: Change *187%* to *101%*.

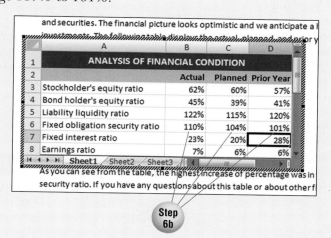

Step
6b

   c. Click outside the worksheet to remove the Excel tools (and deselect the worksheet).
7. Save, print, and then close **WordExcelL1_C5_P6.docx**.
8. Exit Word.
9. With Excel the active program, close **ExcelL1_C5_P6.xlsx**.

# CHAPTER summary

- An Excel workbook, by default, contains three worksheets. Click a worksheet tab to display the worksheet.
- Move selected cells and cell contents in and between worksheets using the Cut, Copy, and Paste buttons in the Clipboard group in the Home tab or by dragging with the mouse.
- Move selected cells with the mouse by dragging the outline of the selected cells to the desired position.
- Copy selected cells with the mouse by holding down the Ctrl key and the left mouse button, dragging the outline of the selected cells to the desired location, releasing the left mouse button, and then releasing the Ctrl key.
- When pasting data, use the Paste Options button to specify what you want pasted. Click the Paste Options button and a drop-down list displays with options to specify that you want to keep source formatting, use destination themes, use destination formatting, or keep the column widths of the source worksheet. If you are pasting a cell containing a value as well as a formula, the Paste Options button drop-down list also includes the *Values Only* option.
- Use the Clipboard task pane to collect and paste data within and between worksheets and workbooks. Display the Clipboard task pane by clicking the Clipboard group dialog box launcher.
- Insert a worksheet in a workbook by clicking the Insert Worksheet tab located to the right of the Sheet3 tab or pressing Shift + F11.
- Perform maintenance activities, such as deleting and renaming, on worksheets within a workbook by clicking the *right* mouse button on a sheet tab and then clicking the desired option at the shortcut menu.
- You can use the mouse to move or copy worksheets. To move a worksheet, drag the worksheet tab with the mouse. To copy a worksheet, hold down the Ctrl key and then drag the worksheet tab with the mouse.
- Use the *Tab Color* option at the sheet tab shortcut menu to apply a color to a worksheet tab.
- Hide and unhide a worksheet by clicking the Format button in the Cells group and then clicking the desired option at the drop-down list, or by right-clicking the worksheet tab and then clicking the desired option at the shortcut menu.
- Manage more than one worksheet at a time by first selecting the worksheets. Use the mouse together with the Shift key to select adjacent worksheet tabs and use the mouse together with the Ctrl key to select nonadjacent worksheet tabs.
- If you want formatting to apply to multiple worksheets in a workbook, select the tabs of the desired worksheets and then apply the formatting.
- To print all worksheets in a workbook, click *Entire workbook* in the *Print what* section of the Print dialog box. You can also print specific worksheets by selecting the tabs of the worksheets you want to print.
- Split the worksheet window into panes with the Split button in the Window group in the View tab or with the split bars on the horizontal and vertical scroll bars.

- To remove a split from a worksheet, click the Split button to deactivate it or drag the split bars to the upper left corner of the worksheet.

- Freeze window panes by clicking the Freeze Panes button in the Window group in the View tab and then clicking *Freeze Panes* at the drop-down list. Unfreeze window panes by clicking the Freeze Panes button and then clicking *Unfreeze Panes* at the drop-down list.

- A selected group of cells is referred to as a range. A range can be named and used in a formula. Name a range by typing the name in the Name box located to the left of the Formula bar or at the New Name dialog box.

- To open multiple workbooks that are adjacent, display the Open dialog box, click the first workbook, hold down the Shift key, click the last workbook, and then click the Open button. If workbooks are nonadjacent, click the first workbook, hold down the Ctrl key, click the desired workbooks, and then click the Open button.

- To see a list of open workbooks, click the View tab and then click the Switch Windows button in the Window group.

- Arrange multiple workbooks in a window with options at the Arrange Windows dialog box.

- Hide the active workbook by clicking the Hide button and unhide a workbook by clicking the Unhide button in the Window group in the View tab.

- Click the Maximize button located in the upper right corner of the active workbook to make the workbook fill the entire window area. Click the Minimize button to shrink the active workbook to a button on the Taskbar. Click the Restore button to return the workbook to its previous size.

- You can move, copy, and/or paste data between workbooks.

- Copy and then link data if you make changes in the source worksheet and you want the changes reflected in the destination worksheet. The worksheet containing the original data is called the source worksheet and the worksheet relying on the source worksheet for data in the link is called the dependent worksheet.

- Copy and link data using the Paste Special dialog box or the *Link Cells* option at the Paste Options button drop-down list.

- You can copy data from a file in one program (called the source program) and paste the data into a file in another program (called the destination program).

- Use a 3-D reference to analyze data in the same cell or range of cells.

- You can copy and then paste, link, or embed data between programs in the Office suite. Integrating is the combining of data from two or more programs in the Office suite.

# COMMANDS review

| FEATURE | RIBBON TAB, GROUP | BUTTON, OPTION | KEYBOARD SHORTCUT |
|---|---|---|---|
| Cut selected cells | Home, Clipboard | ✄ | Ctrl + X |
| Copy selected cells | Home, Clipboard | | Ctrl + C |
| Paste selected cells | Home, Clipboard | | Ctrl + V |
| Clipboard task pane | Home, Clipboard | | |
| Insert worksheet | | | Shift + F11 |
| Hide worksheet | Home, Cells | Format ▾ , Hide & Unhide, Hide Sheet | |
| Unhide worksheet | Home, Cells | Format ▾ , Hide & Unhide, Unhide Sheet | |
| Split window into pane | View, Window | Split | |
| Freeze window panes | View, Window | Freeze Panes ▾ , Freeze Panes | |
| Unfreeze window panes | View, Window | Freeze Panes ▾ , Unfreeze Panes | |
| New Name dialog box | Formulas, Defined Names | Define Name ▾ | |
| Arrange Windows dialog box | View, Window | Arrange All | |
| Maximize window | | | |
| Restore | | | |
| Minimize window | | | |
| Paste Special dialog box | Home, Clipboard | , Paste Special | |

# CONCEPTS check

## Test Your Knowledge

**Completion:** In the space provided at the right, indicate the correct term, symbol, or command.

1. By default, a workbook contains this number of worksheets. _____

2. To copy selected cells with the mouse, hold down this key while dragging the outline of the selected cells to the desired location. _____

3. The Cut, Copy, and Paste buttons are located in this group in the Home tab. _____

4. This button displays in the lower right corner of pasted cells. _____

5. Use this task pane to collect and paste multiple items. _____

6. Click this tab to insert a new worksheet. _____

7. Click this option at the sheet tab shortcut menu to apply a color to a worksheet tab. _____

8. To select adjacent worksheet tabs, click the first tab, hold down this key, and then click the last tab. _____

9. To select nonadjacent worksheet tabs, click the first tab, hold down this key, and then click any other tabs you want selected. _____

10. Click this option in the *Print what* section of the Print dialog box to print all worksheets in a workbook. _____

11. The Split button is located in this tab. _____

12. Display the Arrange Windows dialog box by clicking this button in the Window group in the View tab. _____

13. Click this button to make the active workbook expand to fill the screen. _____

14. Click this button to reduce the active workbook to a button on the Taskbar. _____

15. When copying and pasting data between programs, the program containing the original data is called this. _____

# SKILLS check
*Demonstrate Your Proficiency*

## Assessment

### 1 COPY AND PASTE DATA BETWEEN WORKSHEETS IN A SALES WORKBOOK

1. Open **ExcelC05Assessment01.xlsx** and then save the workbook and name it **ExcelL1_C5_A1**.
2. Turn on the display of the Clipboard task pane, click the Clear All button to clear any content, and then complete the following steps:
   a. Select and copy cells A7 through C7.
   b. Select and copy cells A10 through C10.
   c. Select and copy cells A13 through C13.
   d. Display the second worksheet, make cell A7 active, and then paste the *Avalon Clinic* cells.
   e. Make cell A10 active and then paste the *Stealth Media* cells.
   f. Make A13 active and then paste the *Danmark Contracting* cells.
   g. Make the third worksheet active and then complete similar steps to paste the cells in the same location as the second worksheet.
   h. Clear the contents of the Clipboard task pane and then close the task pane.
3. Change the name of the Sheet1 tab to *2007 Sales*, the name of the Sheet2 tab to *2008 Sales*, and the name of the Sheet3 tab to *2009 Sales*.
4. Change the color of the 2007 Sales tab to blue, the color of the 2008 Sales tab to green, and the color of the 2009 Sales tab to yellow.
5. Display the 2007 Sales worksheet, select all three tabs, and then insert a formula in cell D4 that sums the amounts in cells B4 and C4. Copy the formula in cell D4 down to cells D5 through D14.
6. Make cell D15 active and then insert a formula that sums the amounts in cells D4 through D14.
7. Insert a footer on all three worksheets that prints your name at the left side and the current date at the right.
8. Save, print, and then close **ExcelL1_C5_A1.xlsx**.

## Assessment

### 2 COPY, PASTE, AND FORMAT WORKSHEETS IN AN INCOME STATEMENT WORKBOOK

1. Open **ExcelC05Assessment02.xlsx** and then save the workbook and name it **ExcelL1_C5_A2**.
2. Copy cells A1 through B17 in Sheet1 and paste them into Sheet2. (Click the Paste Options button and then click *Keep Source Column Widths* at the drop-down list.)
3. Make the following changes to the Sheet2 worksheet:
   a. Adjust the row heights so they match the heights in the Sheet1 worksheet.
   b. Change the month from *January* to *February*.
   c. Change the amount in B4 to *97,655*.
   d. Change the amount in B5 to *39,558*.
   e. Change the amount in B11 to *1,105*.

4. Select both sheet tabs and then insert the following formulas:
   a. Insert a formula in B6 that subtracts the Cost of Sales from the Sales Revenue (=B4-B5).
   b. Insert a formula in B16 that sums the amounts in B8 through B15.
   c. Insert a formula in B17 that subtracts the Total Expenses from the Gross Profit (=B6-B16).
5. Change the name of the Sheet1 tab to *January* and the name of the Sheet2 tab to *February*.
6. Change the color of the January tab to blue and the color of the February tab to red.
7. Insert a custom footer on both worksheets that prints your name at the left side, the date in the middle, and the file name at the right side.
8. Save, print, and then close **ExcelL1_C5_A2.xlsx**.

## Assessment

## 3 FREEZE AND UNFREEZE WINDOW PANES IN A TEST SCORES WORKBOOK

1. Open **ExcelC05Assessment03.xlsx** and then save the workbook and name it **ExcelL1_C5_A3**.
2. Make cell A1 active and then split the window by clicking the View tab and then clicking the Split button in the Window group. (This causes the window to split into four panes.)
3. Drag both the horizontal and vertical gray lines up and to the left until the horizontal gray line is immediately below the second row and the vertical gray line is immediately to the right of the first column.
4. Freeze the window panes.
5. Add two rows immediately above row 18 and then type the following text in the specified cells:

| | | | | | | |
|---|---|---|---|---|---|---|
| A18 | = | Nauer, Sheryl | | A19 | = | Nunez, James |
| B18 | = | 75 | | B19 | = | 98 |
| C18 | = | 83 | | C19 | = | 96 |
| D18 | = | 85 | | D19 | = | 100 |
| E18 | = | 78 | | E19 | = | 90 |
| F18 | = | 82 | | F19 | = | 95 |
| G18 | = | 80 | | G19 | = | 93 |
| H18 | = | 79 | | H19 | = | 88 |
| I18 | = | 82 | | I19 | = | 91 |
| J18 | = | 92 | | J19 | = | 89 |
| K18 | = | 90 | | K19 | = | 100 |
| L18 | = | 86 | | L19 | = | 96 |
| M18 | = | 84 | | M19 | = | 98 |

6. Insert a formula in cell N3 that averages the percentages in cells B3 through M3 and then copy the formula down to cells N4 through N22.
7. Unfreeze the window panes.
8. Remove the split.
9. Save the worksheet and then print it in landscape orientation.
10. Close **ExcelL1_C5_A3.xlsx**.

## Assessment

# 4   CREATE, COPY, PASTE, AND FORMAT CELLS IN AN EQUIPMENT USAGE WORKBOOK

1. Create the worksheet shown in Figure 5.10 (change the width of column A to 21.00).
2. Save the workbook and name it **ExcelL1_C5_A4**.
3. With **ExcelL1_C5_A4.xlsx** open, open **ExcelC05Project02.xlsx**.
4. Select and copy the following cells from **ExcelC05Project02.xlsx** to **ExcelL1_C5_A4.xlsx**:
   a. Copy cells A4 through G4 in **ExcelC05Project02.xlsx** and paste them into **ExcelL1_C5_A4.xlsx** beginning with cell A12.
   b. Copy cells A10 through G10 in **ExcelC05Project02.xlsx** and paste them into **ExcelL1_C5_A4.xlsx** beginning with cell A13.
5. With **ExcelL1_C5_A4.xlsx** the active workbook, make cell A1 active and then apply the following formatting:
   a. Change the height of row 1 to 25.50.
   b. Change the font size of the text in cell A1 to 14 points.
   c. Insert Olive Green, Accent 3, Lighter 60% fill color to cell A1.
6. Select cells A2 through G2 and then insert Olive Green, Accent 3, Darker 50% fill color.
7. Select cells B2 through G2 and then change to right alignment, change the text color to white, and turn on italics.
8. Select cells A3 through G3 and then insert Olive Green, Accent 3, Lighter 80% fill color.
9. Select cells A7 through G7 and then insert Olive Green, Accent 3, Lighter 80% fill color.
10. Select cells A11 through G11 and then insert Olive Green, Accent 3, Lighter 80% fill color.
11. Change the orientation to landscape.
12. Print the worksheet centered horizontally and vertically on the page.
13. Save and then close **ExcelL1_C5_A4.xlsx**.
14. Close **ExcelC05Project02.xlsx** without saving the changes.

**Figure 5.10**   **Assessment 4**

| | A | B | C | D | E | F | G | H |
|---|---|---|---|---|---|---|---|---|
| 1 | | EQUIPMENT USAGE REPORT | | | | | | |
| 2 | | January | February | March | April | May | June | |
| 3 | Machine #12 | | | | | | | |
| 4 | Total Hours Available | 2300 | 2430 | 2530 | 2400 | 2440 | 2240 | |
| 5 | In Use | 2040 | 2105 | 2320 | 2180 | 2050 | 1995 | |
| 6 | | | | | | | | |
| 7 | Machine #25 | | | | | | | |
| 8 | Total Hours Available | 2100 | 2240 | 2450 | 2105 | 2390 | 1950 | |
| 9 | In Use | 1800 | 1935 | 2110 | 1750 | 2215 | 1645 | |
| 10 | | | | | | | | |
| 11 | Machine #30 | | | | | | | |
| 12 | | | | | | | | |

# Assessment

## 5 LINK WORKSHEETS IN A SALES WORKBOOK WITH 3-D REFERENCES

1. Open **ExcelC05Assessment05.xlsx** and then save the workbook and name it **ExcelL1_C5_A5**.
2. Change the color of the Sales 2007 tab to purple, the color of the Sales 2008 tab to blue, and the color of the Sales 2009 tab to green.
3. Make the following changes to the workbook:
   a. Make Sales 2007 the active worksheet.
   b. Select columns B, C, and D and then change the width to 16.00.
   c. Insert the heading *Average January Sales 2007-2009* (on multiple lines) in cell B11, centered and bolded.
   d. Insert a formula in cell B12 with a 3-D reference that averages the total in cells B4 through B9 in the Sales 2007, Sales 2008, and Sales 2009 worksheets.
   e. Insert the heading *Average February Sales 2007-2009* (on multiple lines) in cell C11, centered and bolded.
   f. Insert a formula in cell C12 with a 3-D reference that averages the total in cells C4 through C9 in the Sales 2007, Sales 2008, and Sales 2009 worksheets.
   g. Insert the heading *Average March Sales 2007-2009* (on multiple lines) in cell D11, centered and bolded.
   h. Insert a formula in cell D12 with a 3-D reference that averages the total in cells D4 through D9 in the Sales 2007, Sales 2008, and Sales 2009 worksheets.
4. Save the workbook and then print only the Sales 2007 worksheet.
5. Close **ExcelL1_C5_A5.xlsx**.

## 6 LINK DATA BETWEEN A WORD LETTER AND AN EXCEL WORKSHEET

1. Use Excel's Help feature to learn about linking data between programs.
2. After locating and reading the information on linking, open the Word program and then open **WordC05_Letter02.docx**.
3. Save the document and name it **WordExcelL1_C5_A6**.
4. Make Excel the active program and then open **ExcelC05Assessment06.xlsx**.
5. Save the workbook with Save As and name it **ExcelL1_C5_A6**.
6. In column G, insert a formula using the PMT function.
7. Save and then print the worksheet.
8. Select cells A2 through G10 and then copy and link the cells to **WordExcelL1_C5_A6.docx** (between the two paragraphs in the body of the letter).
9. Save, print, and then close **WordExcelL1_C5_A6.docx**.
10. Click the button on the Taskbar representing the Excel workbook **ExcelL1_C5_A6.xlsx** and then change the percentages in cells E3 through E6 to 7.5% and the percentages in cells E7 through E10 to 8.5%.
11. Save, print, and then close **ExcelL1_C5_A6.xlsx**.
12. Make Word the active program and then open **WordExcelL1_C5_A6.docx**.
13. At the message that displays, click Yes.
14. Save, print, and then close **WordExcelL1_C5_A6.docx**.
15. Exit Word.

# CASE study
## Apply Your Skills

**Part 1**

You are an administrator for Gateway Global, an electronics manufacturing corporation. You are gathering information on money spent on supplies and equipment purchases. You have gathered information for the first quarter of the year and decide to create a workbook containing worksheets for monthly information. To do this, create a worksheet that contains the following information:

- Company name is Gateway Global.
- Create the title *January Expenditures*.
- Create the following columns:

| Department | Supplies | Equipment | Total |
|---|---|---|---|
| Production | $25,425 | $135,500 | |
| Research and Development | $50,000 | $125,000 | |
| Technical Support | $14,500 | $65,000 | |
| Finance | $5,790 | $22,000 | |
| Sales and Marketing | $35,425 | $8,525 | |
| Facilities | $6,000 | $1,200 | |
| Total | | | |

- Insert a formula in the *Total* column that sums the amounts in the *Supplies* and *Equipment* columns and insert a formula in the *Total* row that sums the Supplies amounts, Equipment amounts, and Total amounts.
- Apply formatting such as fill color, borders, font color, and shading to enhance the visual appeal of the worksheet.

After creating and formatting the worksheet, complete the following:

- Copy the worksheet data to Sheet2 and then to Sheet3.
- Make the following changes to data in Sheet2:
  - Change *January Expenditures* to *February Expenditures*.
  - Change the Production Department Supplies amount to *$38,550* and the Equipment amount to *$88,500*.
  - Change the Technical Support Department Equipment amount to *$44,250*.
  - Change the Finance Department Supplies amount to *$7,500*.
- Make the following changes to data in Sheet3:
  - Change *January Expenditures* to *March Expenditures*.
  - Change the Research and Development Department Supplies amount to *$65,000* and the Equipment amount to *$150,000*.
  - Change the Technical Support Department Supplies amount to *$21,750* and the Equipment amount to *$43,525*.
  - Change the Facilities Department Equipment amount to *$18,450*.

Create a new worksheet that summarizes the Supplies and Equipment totals for January, February, and March. Apply the same formatting to the worksheet as applied to the other three. Change the tab name for Sheet1 to *Jan. Expenditures*, the tab name for Sheet2 to *Feb. Expenditures*, the tab name for Sheet3 to *Mar. Expenditures*, and the tab name for Sheet4 to *Qtr. Summary*. Change the color of each tab (you determine the colors).

Insert a footer that prints your name at the left side of each worksheet and the current date at the right side of each worksheet. Save the workbook and name it **ExcelL1_C5_CS_P1**. Print all the worksheets in the workbook and then close the workbook.

**Part 2**

Employees of Gateway Global have formed two intramural co-ed softball teams and you have volunteered to keep statistics for the players. Open **ExcelGGStats.xlsx** and then make the following changes to both worksheets in the workbook:

- Insert a formula that calculates a player's batting average (Hits divided by At Bats).
- Insert a formula that calculates a player's on-base percentage (Walks + Hits divided by At Bats plus Walks). Make sure you insert parentheses in the formula.
- Insert the company name.
- Apply formatting to enhance the visual appeal of the worksheets.
- Horizontally and vertically center the worksheets.
- Insert a footer that prints on both worksheets and prints your name at the left side of the worksheet and the date at the right of the worksheet.

Using Help, learn how to apply conditional formatting to data in a worksheet. Select both worksheets and then apply conditional formatting that inserts red fill and changes text color to dark red for cells in the *Batting Average* column with an average over .400. Save the workbook and name it **ExcelL1_C5_CS_P2**. Print and then close **ExcelL1_C5_CS_P2.xlsx**.

**Part 3**

Many of the suppliers for Gateway Global are international and use different length, weight, and volume measurements. The purchasing manager has asked you to prepare a conversion chart in Excel that displays conversion tables for length, weight, volume, and temperature. Use the Internet to locate conversion tables for length, weight, and volume. When preparing the workbook, create a worksheet with the following information:

- Include the following length conversions:
  - 1 inch  to centimeters
  - 1 foot to centimeters
  - 1 yard to meters
  - 1 mile to kilometers
- Include the following weight conversions:
  - 1 ounce to grams
  - 1 pound to kilograms
  - 1 ton to metric tons
- Include the following volume conversions:
  - 1 fluid ounce to milliliters
  - 1 pint to liters
  - 1 quart to liters
  - 1 gallon to liters

Locate a site on the Internet that provides the formula for converting Fahrenheit temperatures to Celsius temperatures and then create another worksheet in the workbook with the following information:

- Insert Fahrenheit temperatures beginning with zero, continuing to 100, and incrementing by 5 (for example, 0, 5, 10, 15, and so on).
- Insert a formula that converts the Fahrenheit temperature to a Celsius temperature.

Include the company name, Gateway Global, in both worksheets. Apply additional formatting to improve the visual appeal of both worksheets. Rename both sheet names and apply a color to each tab (you determine the names and colors). Save the workbook and name it **ExcelL1_C5_CS_P3**. Print both worksheets centered horizontally and vertically on the page and then close **ExcelL1_C5_CS_P3.xlsx**.

**Part**
**4**

Open Microsoft Word and then create a letterhead document that contains the company name *Gateway Global*, the address (you decide the address including street address, city, state, and ZIP code or street address, city, province, and postal code), and the telephone number (you determine the telephone number). Apply formatting to improve the visual display of the letterhead. Save the document and name it **WordGGLtrhd**. Save the document again with Save As and name it **WordL1_C5_CS_P4A**. In Excel, open **ExcelL1_C5_CS_P3.xlsx**. In the first worksheet, copy the cells containing data and then paste them in **WordL1_C5_CS_P4A.docx** using Paste Special. Save, print, and then close **WordL1_C5_CS_P4A.docx**. In Word, open **WordGGLtrd.docx**. Save the document with Save As and name it **WordL1_C5_CS_P4B**. In Excel, make the worksheet active that contains the Fahrenheit conversion information, copy the cells containing data, and then paste them in the Word document using Paste Special. Save, print, and then close **WordL1_C5_CS_P4B.docx**. Close Microsoft Word and then, in Excel, close **ExcelL1_C5_CS_P3.xlsx**.

# CHAPTER

# Maintaining Workbooks

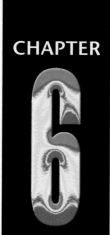

## PERFORMANCE OBJECTIVES

**Upon successful completion of Chapter 6, you will be able to:**

- Create and rename a folder
- Delete workbooks and folders
- Copy and move workbooks within and between folders
- Copy, move, and rename worksheets within a workbook
- Save a workbook in a variety of formats
- Maintain consistent formatting with styles
- Use comments for review and response
- Create financial forms using templates

**Tutorial 6.1**
Managing Folders and
Workbooks
**Tutorial 6.2**
Advanced Formatting Techniques

Once you have been working with Excel for a period of time you will have accumulated several workbook files. Workbooks should be organized into folders to facilitate fast retrieval of information. Occasionally you should perform file maintenance activities such as copying, moving, renaming, and deleting workbooks to ensure the workbook list in your various folders is manageable. You will learn these file management tasks in this chapter along with creating and applying styles, inserting and printing comments, and using Excel templates to create a workbook.

*Note: Before beginning computer projects, copy to your storage medium the Excel2007L1C6 subfolder from the Excel2007L1 folder on the CD that accompanies this textbook and then make Excel2007L1C6 the active folder.*

## Project ① Manage Workbooks

You will perform a variety of file management tasks including creating and renaming a folder; selecting and then deleting, copying, cutting, pasting, and renaming workbooks; deleting a folder; and opening, printing, and closing a workbook.

# Maintaining Workbooks

You can complete many workbook management tasks at the Open and Save As dialog boxes. These tasks can include copying, moving, printing, and renaming workbooks; opening multiple workbooks; and creating and renaming a new folder. Some file maintenance tasks such as creating a folder and deleting files are performed by using buttons on the Open dialog box or Save As dialog box toolbar. Figure 6.1 displays the Open dialog box toolbar buttons.

**Figure 6.1** Open Dialog Box Toolbar Buttons

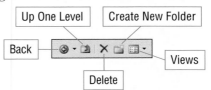

## Creating a Folder

**Create a Folder**
1. Click Office button, *Open*.
2. Click Create New Folder button.
3. Type folder name.
4. Press Enter.

In Excel, you should logically group and store workbooks in folders. For example, you could store all of the workbooks related to one department in one folder with the department name being the folder name. You can create a folder within a folder (called a ***subfolder***). If you create workbooks for a department by individuals, each individual name could have a subfolder within the department folder. The main folder on a disk or drive is called the root folder. You create additional folders as branches of this root folder.

At the Open or Save As dialog boxes, workbook file names display in the list box preceded by a workbook icon and a folder name displays preceded by a folder icon. Create a new folder by clicking the Create New Folder button located on the dialog box toolbar at the Open dialog box or Save As dialog box. At the New Folder dialog box shown in Figure 6.2, type a name for the folder in the *Name* text box, and then click OK or press Enter. The new folder becomes the active folder.

**HINT**

Change the default folder with the *Default file location* option at the Excel Options dialog box with Save selected.

If you want to make the previous folder the active folder, click the Up One Level button on the dialog box toolbar. After clicking the Up One Level button, the Back button becomes active. Click this button and the previously active folder becomes active again.

A folder name can contain a maximum of 255 characters. Numbers, spaces, and symbols can be used in the folder name, except those symbols explained in Chapter 1 in the "Saving a Workbook" section.

Create New Folder

Up One Level

**Figure 6.2** New Folder Dialog Box

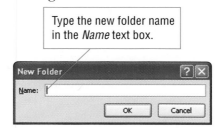

1. Create a folder named *Payroll* on your storage medium. To begin, display the Open dialog box.
2. Double-click the *Excel2007L1C6* folder name to make it the active folder.
3. Click the Create New Folder button (located on the dialog box toolbar).
4. At the New Folder dialog box, type **Payroll**.
5. Click OK. (The Payroll folder is now the active folder.)

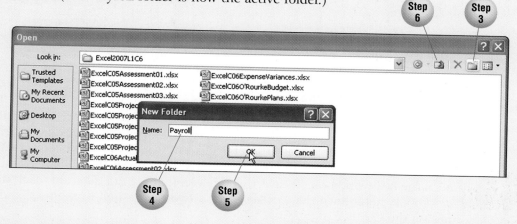

6. Click the Up One Level button on the dialog box toolbar to change back to the Excel2007L1C6 folder.

## Renaming a Folder

As you organize your files and folders, you may decide to rename a folder. Rename a folder using the Tools button in the Open dialog box or using a shortcut menu. To rename a folder using the Tools button, display the Open dialog box, click in the list box the folder you want to rename, click the Tools button located in the lower left corner of the dialog box, and then click *Rename* at the drop-down list. This selects the folder name and inserts a border around the name. Type the new name for the folder and then press Enter. To rename a folder using a shortcut menu, display the Open dialog box, right-click the folder name in the list box, and then click *Rename* at the shortcut menu. Type a new name for the folder and then press Enter.

A tip to remember when you are organizing files and folders is to be sure that your system is set up to display all of the files in a particular folder and not just the Excel files, for example. You can display all files in a folder by changing the *Files of type* option at the Open dialog box to *All Files (\*.\*)*.

### QUICK STEPS

**Rename a Folder**
1. Click Office button, *Open*.
2. Click desired folder.
3. Click Tools button, *Rename*.
4. Type new name.
5. Press Enter.
OR
1. Click Office button, *Open*.
2. Right-click folder name.
3. Click *Rename*.
4. Type new name.
5. Press Enter.

## Project 1b    Renaming a Folder

1. At the Open dialog box, right-click the *Payroll* folder name in the Open dialog box list box.
2. Click *Rename* at the shortcut menu.
3. Type Finances and then press Enter.

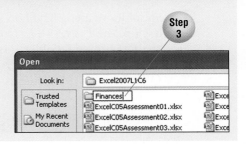

## Selecting Workbooks

You can complete workbook management tasks on one workbook or selected workbooks. To select one workbook, display the Open dialog box, and then click the desired workbook. To select several adjacent workbooks (workbooks that display next to each other), click the first workbook, hold down the Shift key, and then click the last workbook. To select workbooks that are not adjacent, click the first workbook, hold down the Ctrl key, click any other desired workbooks, and then release the Ctrl key.

**Delete Workbook/ Folder**
1. Click Office button, *Open.*
2. Click workbook or folder name.
3. Click Delete button.
4. Click Yes.

Delete

## Deleting Workbooks and Folders

At some point, you may want to delete certain workbooks from your storage medium or any other drive or folder in which you may be working. To delete a workbook, display the Open or Save As dialog box, select the workbook, and then click the Delete button on the dialog box toolbar. At the dialog box asking you to confirm the deletion, click Yes. To delete a workbook using a shortcut menu, display the Open dialog box, right-click the workbook name in the list box, and then click *Delete* at the shortcut menu. Click Yes at the confirmation dialog box.

## Deleting to the Recycle Bin

Workbooks deleted from the hard drive are automatically sent to the Windows Recycle Bin. You can easily restore a deleted workbook from the Recycle Bin. To free space on the drive, empty the Recycle Bin on a periodic basis. Restoring a workbook from or emptying the contents of the Recycle Bin is completed at the Windows desktop (not in Excel). To display the Recycle Bin, minimize the Excel window, and then double-click the *Recycle Bin* icon located on the Windows desktop. At the Recycle Bin, you can restore file(s) and empty the Recycle Bin.

## Project 1c    Selecting and Deleting Workbooks

1. At the Open dialog box, open **ExcelC05Project01.xlsx** (located in the Excel2007L1C6 folder).
2. Save the workbook with Save As and name it **ExcelL1_C6_P1**.
3. Close **ExcelL1_C6_P1.xlsx**.

4. Delete **ExcelL1_C6_P1.xlsx** by completing the following steps:
   a. Display the Open dialog box with Excel2007L1C6 the active folder.
   b. Click *ExcelL1_C6_P1.xlsx* to select it.
   c. Click the Delete button on the dialog box toolbar.

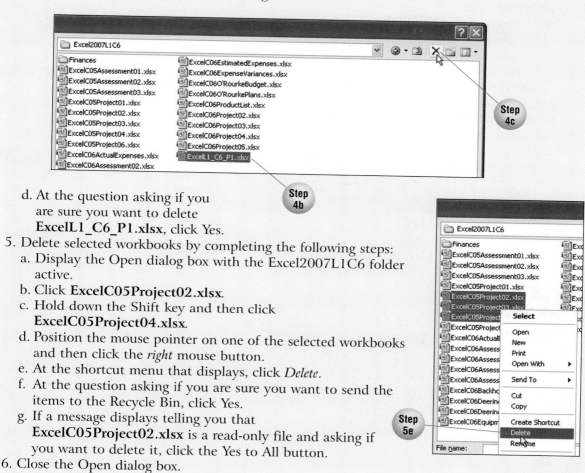

   d. At the question asking if you are sure you want to delete **ExcelL1_C6_P1.xlsx**, click Yes.
5. Delete selected workbooks by completing the following steps:
   a. Display the Open dialog box with the Excel2007L1C6 folder active.
   b. Click **ExcelC05Project02.xlsx**.
   c. Hold down the Shift key and then click **ExcelC05Project04.xlsx**.
   d. Position the mouse pointer on one of the selected workbooks and then click the *right* mouse button.
   e. At the shortcut menu that displays, click *Delete*.
   f. At the question asking if you are sure you want to send the items to the Recycle Bin, click Yes.
   g. If a message displays telling you that **ExcelC05Project02.xlsx** is a read-only file and asking if you want to delete it, click the Yes to All button.
6. Close the Open dialog box.

# Copying Workbooks

In previous chapters, you have been opening a workbook from your storage medium and saving it with a new name in the same location. This process makes an exact copy of the workbook, leaving the original on your storage medium. You have been copying workbooks and saving the new workbook in the same folder as the original workbook. You can also copy a workbook into another folder.

1. Open **ExcelC05Assessment01.xlsx**.
2. Save the workbook with Save As and name it **TotalSales**. (Make sure Excel2007L1C6 is the active folder.)
3. Save a copy of the **TotalSales.xlsx** workbook in the Finances folder you created in Project 1a by completing the following steps:
   a. With **TotalSales.xlsx** open, display the Save As dialog box.
   b. At the Save As dialog box, change to the Finances folder. To do this, double-click *Finances* at the beginning of the list box (folders are listed before workbooks).
   c. Click the Save button located in the lower right corner of the dialog box.
4. Close **TotalSales.xlsx**.
5. Change back to the Excel2007L1C6 folder by completing the following steps:
   a. Display the Open dialog box.
   b. Click the Up One Level button located on the dialog box toolbar.

Step 5b

   c. Close the Open dialog box.

**Copy a Workbook**
1. Click Office button, *Open.*
2. Right-click workbook name.
3. Click *Copy.*
4. Navigate to desired folder.
5. Right-click white area in list box.
6. Click *Paste.*

You can copy a workbook to another folder without opening the workbook first. To do this, use the *Copy* and *Paste* options from a shortcut menu at the Open (or Save As) dialog box. You can also copy a workbook or selected workbooks into the same folder. When you do this, Excel names the workbook(s) "Copy of xxx" (where *xxx* is the current workbook name). You can copy one workbook or selected workbooks into the same folder.

1. Copy **ExcelC05Assessment02.xlsx** to the Finance folder. To begin, display the Open dialog box with the Excel2007L1C6 folder active.
2. Position the arrow pointer on **ExcelC05Assessment02.xlsx**, click the right mouse button, and then click *Copy* at the shortcut menu.
3. Change to the Finance folder by double-clicking *Finances* at the beginning of the list box.
4. Position the arrow pointer in any white area (not on a workbook name) in the list box, click the right mouse button, and then click *Paste* at the shortcut menu.
5. Change back to the Excel2007L1C6 folder by clicking the Up One Level button located on the dialog box toolbar.
6. Close the Open dialog box.

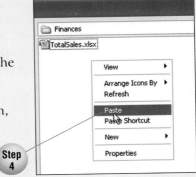

Step 4

## Sending Workbooks to a Different Drive or Folder

Copy workbooks to another folder or drive with the *Copy* and *Paste* options from the shortcut menu at the Open or Save As dialog box. With the *Send To* option, you can send a copy of a workbook to another drive or folder. To use this option, position the arrow pointer on the workbook you want copied, click the *right* mouse button, point to *Send To* (this causes a side menu to display), and then click the desired drive or folder.

## Cutting and Pasting a Workbook

You can remove a workbook from one folder and insert it in another folder using the *Cut* and *Paste* options from the shortcut menu at the Open dialog box. To do this, display the Open dialog box, position the arrow pointer on the workbook to be removed (cut), click the *right* mouse button, and then click *Cut* at the shortcut menu. Change to the desired folder or drive, position the arrow pointer in a white area in the list box, click the *right* mouse button, and then click *Paste* at the shortcut menu.

**Move a Workbook**
1. Click Office button, *Open.*
2. Right-click workbook name.
3. Click *Cut.*
4. Navigate to desired folder.
5. Right-click white area in list box.
6. Click *Paste.*

### Project 1f  Cutting and Pasting a Workbook

1. Move a workbook to a different folder. To begin, display the Open dialog box with the Excel2007L1C6 folder active.
2. Position the arrow pointer on **ExcelC05Project06.xlsx**, click the right mouse button, and then click *Cut* at the shortcut menu.
3. Double-click *Finances* to make it the active folder.
4. Position the arrow pointer in the white area in the list box, click the right mouse button, and then click *Paste* at the shortcut menu.
5. If a Confirm File Move dialog box displays asking if you are sure you want to move the file, click Yes. (This dialog box usually does not appear when you cut and paste. Since the files you copied from your student CD-ROM are read-only files, this warning message appears.)
6. Click the Up One Level button to make the Excel2007L1C6 folder the active folder.

## Renaming Workbooks

At the Open dialog box, use the *Rename* option from the Tools button drop-down list or the shortcut menu to give a workbook a different name. The *Rename* option changes the name of the workbook and keeps it in the same folder. To use *Rename*, display the Open dialog box, click once on the workbook to be renamed, click the Tools button located in the lower left corner of the dialog box, and then click *Rename*. This causes a thin black border to surround the workbook name and the name to be selected. Type the new name and then press Enter.

You can also rename a workbook by right-clicking the workbook name at the Open dialog box and then clicking *Rename* at the shortcut menu. Type the new name for the workbook and then press the Enter key.

**QUICK STEPS**

**Rename Workbook**
1. Click Office button, *Open.*
2. Click desired workbook.
3. Click Tools button, *Rename.*
4. Type new name.
5. Press Enter.
OR
1. Click Office button, *Open.*
2. Right-click workbook name.
3. Click *Rename.*
4. Type new name.
5. Press Enter.

## Project 1g  Renaming a Workbook

1. Rename a workbook located in the Finances folder. To begin, make sure the Open dialog box displays with Excel2007L1C6 the active folder.
2. Double-click *Finances* to make it the active folder.
3. Click once on **ExcelC05Project06.xlsx** to select it.
4. Click the Tools button that displays in the lower left corner of the dialog box.
5. Click *Rename* at the drop-down list.
6. Type Analysis.xlsx and then press the Enter key.
7. If a message displays asking if you are sure you want to change the name of the read-only file, click Yes.
8. Complete steps similar to those in Steps 3 through 6 to rename **ExcelC05Assessment02.xlsx** to *SoftwareTests.xlsx*.
9. Click the Up One Level button.

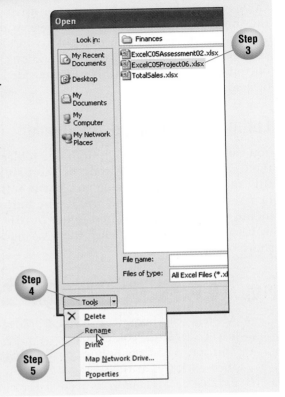

## Deleting a Folder and Its Contents

As you learned earlier in this chapter, you can delete a workbook or selected workbooks. In addition to workbooks, you can delete a folder and all of its contents. Delete a folder in the same manner as you delete a workbook.

## Project 1h  Deleting a Folder and Its Contents

1. Delete the Finances folder and its contents. To begin, make sure the Open dialog box displays with the Excel2007L1C6 folder active.
2. Right-click on the *Finances* folder.
3. Click *Delete* at the shortcut menu.
4. At the Confirm Folder Delete dialog box, click Yes.
5. If the Confirm File Delete dialog box displays, click the Yes to All button.

## Printing Workbooks

Up to this point, you have opened a workbook and then printed it. With the *Print* option from the Tools button drop-down list or the *Print* option from the shortcut menu at the Open dialog box, you can print a workbook or several workbooks without opening them.

## Project 1i Printing Workbooks

1. At the Open dialog box with the Excel2007L1C6 folder active, select *ExcelC05Assessment01.xlsx* and *ExcelC05Assessment02.xlsx*.
2. Click the Tools button located in the lower left corner of the dialog box.
3. Click *Print* at the drop-down list.

## Project 2 Copy and Move Worksheets into an Equipment Rental Workbook

You will open an equipment rental workbook, open two other workbooks containing equipment rental information, and then copy and move worksheets between the workbooks.

# Managing Worksheets

You can move or copy individual worksheets within the same workbook or to another existing workbook. Exercise caution when moving sheets since calculations or charts based on data on a worksheet might become inaccurate if you move the worksheet. To make a duplicate of a worksheet in the same workbook, hold down the Ctrl key and then drag the worksheet tab to the desired position.

## Copying a Worksheet to Another Workbook

To copy a worksheet to another existing workbook, open both the source and the destination workbooks. Right-click the sheet tab and then click *Move or Copy* at the shortcut menu. At the Move or Copy dialog box shown in Figure 6.3, select the destination workbook name from the *To book* drop-down list, select the worksheet that you want the copied worksheet placed before in the *Before sheet* list box, click the *Create a copy* check box, and then click OK.

**QUICK STEPS**

**Copy a Worksheet to Another Workbook**
1. Right-click desired sheet tab.
2. Click *Move or Copy*.
3. Select desired destination workbook.
4. Select desired worksheet location.
5. Click *Create a copy* check box.
6. Click OK.

**Figure 6.3** Move or Copy Dialog Box

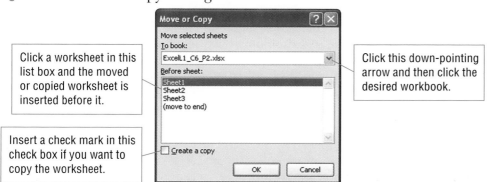

Click a worksheet in this list box and the moved or copied worksheet is inserted before it.

Click this down-pointing arrow and then click the desired workbook.

Insert a check mark in this check box if you want to copy the worksheet.

## Project 2a · Copying a Worksheet to Another Workbook

1. Open **ExcelC06Project02.xlsx** and then save the workbook and name it **ExcelL1_C6_P2**.
2. With **ExcelL1_C6_P2.xlsx** open, open **ExcelC06Equipment.xlsx**.
3. Copy the Front Loader worksheet by completing the following steps:
   a. With **ExcelC06Equipment.xlsx** the active workbook, right-click the Front Loader tab and then click *Move or Copy* at the shortcut menu.
   b. Click the down-pointing arrow next to the *To book* option box and then click **ExcelL1_C6_P2.xlsx** at the drop-down list.
   c. Click *Sheet2* in the *Before sheet* list box.
   d. Click the *Create a copy* check box to insert a check mark.
   e. Click OK. (Excel switches to the **ExcelL1_C6_P2.xlsx** workbook and inserts the copied Front Loader worksheet between Sheet1 and Sheet2.)
4. Complete steps similar to those in Step 3 to copy the Tractor worksheet to the **ExcelL1_C6_P2.xlsx** workbook. (Insert the Tractor worksheet between Front Loader and Sheet2.)
5. Complete steps similar to those in Step 3 to copy the Forklift worksheet to the **ExcelL1_C6_P2.xlsx** workbook. (Insert the Forklift worksheet between Tractor and Sheet2.)
6. Save **ExcelL1_C6_P2.xlsx**.
7. Make **ExcelC06Equipment.xlsx** the active workbook and then close it.

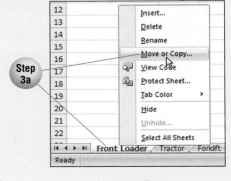

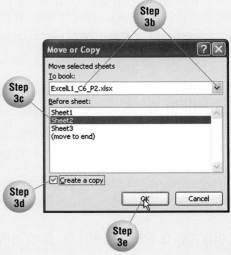

**QUICK STEPS**

**Move a Worksheet to another Workbook**
1. Right-click desired sheet tab.
2. Click *Move or Copy.*
3. Select desired destination workbook.
4. Select desired worksheet location.
5. Click OK.

## Moving a Worksheet to Another Workbook

To move a worksheet to another existing workbook, open both the source and the destination workbooks. Make active the sheet you want to move in the source workbook, right-click the sheet tab and then click *Move or Copy* at the shortcut menu. At the Move or Copy dialog box shown in Figure 6.3, select the destination workbook name from the *To book* drop-down list, select the worksheet that you want the worksheet placed before in the *Before sheet* list box, and then click OK. If you need to reposition a worksheet tab, drag the tab to the desired position.

Be careful when moving a worksheet to another workbook file. If formulas exist in the workbook that depend on the contents of the cells in the worksheet that is moved, they will no longer calculate properly.

1. With **ExcelL1_C6_P2.xlsx** open, open **ExcelC06Backhoe.xlsx**.
2. Move Sheet1 from **ExcelC06Backhoe.xlsx** to **ExcelL1_C6_P2.xlsx** by completing the following steps:

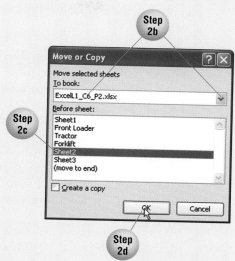

   a. With **ExcelC06Backhoe.xlsx** the active workbook, right-click the Sheet1 tab and then click *Move or Copy* at the shortcut menu.
   b. Click the down-pointing arrow next to the *To book* option box and then click **ExcelL1_C6_P2.xlsx** at the drop-down list.
   c. Click *Sheet2* in the *Before sheet* list box.
   d. Click OK.
3. Make **ExcelC06Backhoe.xlsx** the active workbook and then close it without saving the changes.
4. With **ExcelL1_C6_P2.xlsx** open, make the following changes:
   a. Delete Sheet2 and Sheet3 tabs. (These worksheets are blank.)
   b. Rename Sheet1 to *Equipment Hours*.
   c. Rename Sheet1 (2) to *Backhoe*.
5. Create a range for the Forklift total hours available by completing the following steps:
   a. Click the Front Loader tab.
   b. Select cells B4 through E4.
   c. Click in the Name box.
   d. Type *FrontLoaderHours*.

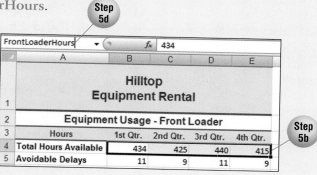

   e. Press Enter.
6. Complete steps similar to those in Step 5 to create the following ranges:
   a. In the Front Loader worksheet, create a range with cells B10 through E10 and name it *FrontLoaderHoursInUse*.
   b. Click the Tractor tab and then create a range with cells B4 through E4 and name it *TractorHours* and create a range with cells B10 through E10 and name it *TractorHoursInUse*.
   c. Click the Forklift tab and then create a range with cells B4 through E4 and name it *ForkliftHours* and create a range with cells B10 through E10 and name it *ForkliftHoursInUse*.
   d. Click the Backhoe tab and then create a range with cells B4 through E4 and name it *BackhoeHours* and create a range with cells B10 through E10 and name it *BackhoeHoursInUse*.

7. Click the EquipmentHours tab to make it the active worksheet and then insert a formula that inserts the total hours for the Front Loader by completing the following steps:

   a. Make cell C4 active.

   b. Type =SUM(Fr.

   c. When you type *Fr* a drop-down list displays with the Front Loader ranges. Double-click *FrontLoaderHours*.

   d. Type ) (the closing parenthesis).

   e. Press Enter.

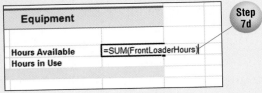

Step 7b

Step 7c

Step 7d

8. Complete steps similar to those in Step 7 to insert ranges in the following cells:

   a. Make cell C5 active and then insert a formula that inserts the total in-use hours for the Front Loader.

   b. Make cell C8 active and then insert a formula that inserts the total hours available for the Tractor.

   c. Make cell C9 active and then insert a formula that inserts the total in-use hours for the Tractor.

   d. Make cell C12 active and then insert a formula that inserts the total hours available for the Forklift.

   e. Make cell C13 active and then insert a formula that inserts the total in-use hours for the Forklift.

   f. Make cell C16 active and then insert a formula that inserts the total hours available for the Backhoe.

   g. Make cell C17 active and then insert a formula that inserts the total in-use hours for the Backhoe.

9. Make the following changes to specific worksheets:

   a. Click the Front Loader tab and then change the number in cell E4 from *415* to *426* and change the number in cell C6 from *6* to *14*.

   b. Click the Forklift tab and then change the number in cells E4 from *415* to *426* and change the number in cell D8 from *4* to *12*.

10. Select all of the worksheet tabs and then create a footer that prints your name at the left side of each worksheet, the page number in the middle, and the current date at the right side of each worksheet.

11. Save, print, and then close **ExcelL1_C6_P2.xlsx**.

# P roject ③ Save Workbooks in Various Formats

You will open a workbook and then save it in a previous version of Excel, in text format, and in PDF format.

# Saving a Workbook in a Different Format

When you save a workbook, the workbook is automatically saved as an Excel workbook with the *.xlsx* file extension. If you need to share a workbook with someone who is using a different version of Excel, or someone who will open it in an application other than Excel, save the workbook in another format. You can also save an Excel workbook as a Web page and in text format. Save a workbook in a different format with options from the Office button Save As side menu or with the *Save as type* option at the Save As dialog box.

## Saving a Workbook in a Previous Version of Excel

If you create workbooks that others will open in a previous version of Excel, consider saving the workbook in the Excel 97-2003 format. If you save a workbook in a previous version, the workbook name displays in the title bar followed by the words *[Compatibility Mode]*. In this mode, some Excel 2007 features may not be available.

You can save a workbook in a previous version with the Office button Save As side menu or with the *Save as type* option at the Save As dialog box. To save using the side menu, click the Office button, point to the *Save As* option, and then click *Excel 97-2003 Workbook* at the side menu as shown in Figure 6.4. At the Save As dialog box, type the name for the workbook, and then click the Save button. Note also that some file formats save the active worksheet and others save the entire workbook. If you want to save a specific worksheet, hide the other worksheets and then save.

**QUICK STEPS**

**Save Workbook in Different Format**
1. Click Office button.
2. Point to *Save As*.
3. Click desired format type.
4. Type name for workbook.
5. Click Save button.
OR
1. Click Office button, *Save As*.
2. Type name for workbook.
3. Click down-pointing arrow at right of *Save as type* option box.
4. Click desired type in drop-down list.
5. Click Save button.

**Figure 6.4** Save As Side Menu

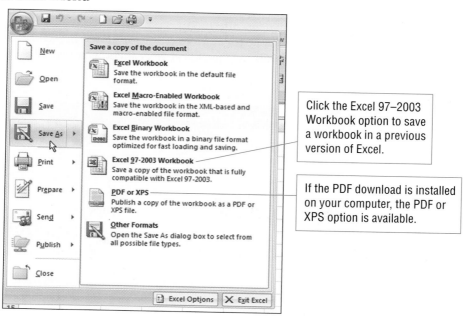

Click the Excel 97–2003 Workbook option to save a workbook in a previous version of Excel.

If the PDF download is installed on your computer, the PDF or XPS option is available.

Project **3a**   **Saving a Workbook in a Previous Version of Excel**

1. Open **ExcelC06Project03.xlsx**.
2. Click the Office button, point to the *Save As* option, and then click the *Excel 97-2003 Workbook* option that displays in the side menu.
3. At the Save As dialog box with the *Save as type* option changed to *Excel 97-2003 Workbook (*.xls)*, type ExcelL1_C6_P3_xlsformat in the *File name* text box and then press Enter.

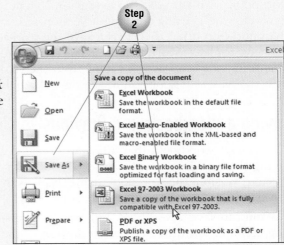

Step 2

Step 3

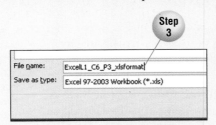

4. At the Compatibility Checker dialog box, click Continue.
5. Close **ExcelL1_C6_P3_xlsformat.xls**.
6. Open **ExcelL1_C6_P3_xlsformat.xls** and then notice that *[Compatibility Mode]* displays after the workbook title at the top of the screen.
7. Close **ExcelL1_C6_P3_xlsformat.xls**.

## Saving a Workbook in Text Format

Along with the Save As side menu, you can also save workbooks in different formats with options at the *Save as type* drop-down list at the Save As dialog box. In Project 3b, you will save an Excel worksheet as a text file with tab delimiters.

Project **3b**   **Saving a Workbook in Text Format**

1. Open **ExcelC06Project03.xlsx**.
2. Click the Office button and then click *Save As*.
3. At the Save As dialog box, type ExcelL1_C6_P3tab in the *File name* text box.
4. Click the down-pointing arrow at the right side of the *Save as type* list box and then click *Text (Tab delimited) (*.txt)* at the drop-down list. (You will need to scroll down the list box to display this option.)

Step 3

Step 4

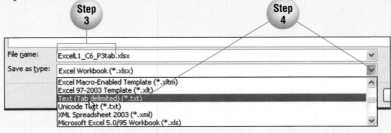

5. Click the Save button.
6. At the message telling you that the selected file type does not support workbooks that contain multiple worksheets, click OK.
7. At the message telling you that the file may contain features that are not compatible with Text (Tab delimited) and asking if you want to keep the workbook in the format, click Yes.
8. Close the workbook. (At the message asking if you want to save the changes, click Yes. At the message asking if you want to keep the workbook in the format, click Yes.)
9. Open Microsoft Word.
10. Display the Open dialog box, change the *Files of type* to *All Files (\*.\*)* and then open **ExcelL1_C6_P3tab.txt**.
11. Close **ExcelL1_C6_P3tab.txt** and then exit Word.

## Saving in PDF Format

The portable document format (PDF) was developed by Adobe Systems and is a format that captures all of the elements of a file as an electronic image. You can view a PDF file on any application on any computer making this format the most widely used for transferring files to other users. A workbook saved in PDF format is printer friendly and most, if not all, of the workbook's original appearance is maintained.

Before saving an Excel workbook in PDF format, you must install an add-in download from the Microsoft Web site. To determine whether or not the download is installed, click the Office button and then point to the *Save As* option. If the add-in is installed, you will see the option *PDF or XPS* in the side menu with the following text below the option: *Publish a copy of the document as a PDF or XPS file.* If the add-in is not downloaded, you will see the option *Find add-ins for other file formats* in the side menu with the following text below the option: *Learn about add-ins to save to other formats such as PDF or XPS.*

If the add-in is not downloaded and you want to download it, click the *Find add-ins for other file formats* option at the side menu. This displays the Excel Help window with information on how to download the add-in. The steps in Project 3c assume that the PDF add-in is downloaded and installed and available on your computer. Before completing Project 3c, check with your instructor.

When you click the *PDF or XPS* option at the Save As side menu, the Save As dialog box displays with *PDF (\*.pdf)* specified as the *Save as type* option. At this dialog box, type a name in the *File name* text box and then click the Publish button. By default, the workbook will open in PDF format in Adobe Reader. The Adobe Reader application is designed to view your workbook. You will be able to navigate in the workbook but you will not be able to make any changes to the workbook. After viewing the workbook in Adobe Reader, click the Close button located in the upper right corner of the Adobe Reader window. This closes the workbook and also closed Adobe Reader.

You can open your PDF file in Adobe Reader or in your browser window. To open a PDF workbook in your browser window, click File on the browser Menu bar and then click *Open*. (If the Menu bar is not visible, click the Tools button located in the upper right corner of the window and then click *Menu Bar* at the drop-down list.) At the Open dialog box, browse to the folder containing your PDF workbook and then double-click the workbook. You may need to change the *Files of type* option to *All Files (\*.\*)*.

1. Open **ExcelC06Project03.xlsx**.
2. Save the workbook in PDF file format by completing the following steps:
   a. Click the Office button and then point to the *Save As* option.
   b. Click *PDF or XPS* in the side menu. (If this option does not display, the PDF add-in download has not been installed.)

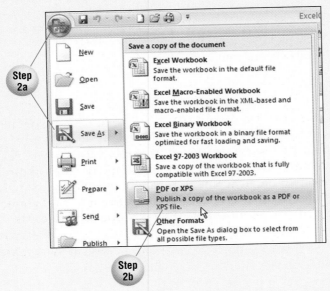

Step 2a

Step 2b

   c. At the Save As dialog box with the *Save as type* option set at *PDF (\*.pdf)*, click the Publish button.

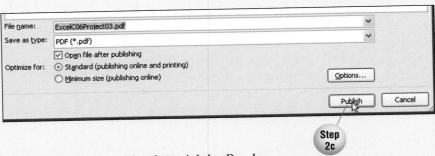

Step 2c

3. Scroll through the workbook in Adobe Reader.
4. Click the Close button located in the upper right corner of the window to close Adobe Reader.
5. Close **ExcelC06Project03.xlsx**.

 **roject** **4** **Create and Apply Styles to a Payroll Workbook**

You will open a payroll workbook, define styles and apply styles and then modify the styles. You will also copy the styles to another workbook and then apply the styles in the new workbook.

# Formatting with Cell Styles

In Chapter 1 you learned how to apply formatting to cells with the Cell Styles button in the Styles group in the Home tab. A style is a predefined set of formatting attributes such as font, font size, alignment, borders, shading, and so forth. You can apply the styles from the Cell Styles drop-down gallery or create your own style. Using a style to apply formatting has several advantages. A style helps to ensure consistent formatting from one worksheet to another. Once you define all attributes for a particular style, you do not have to redefine them again. If you need to change the formatting, change the style and all cells formatted with that style automatically reflect the change.

## Defining a Cell Style

Two basic methods are available for defining your own cell style. You can define a style with formats already applied to a cell or you can display the Style dialog box, click the Format button, and then choose formatting options at the Format Cells dialog box. Styles you create are only available in the workbook in which they are created. To define a style with existing formatting, select the cell or cells containing the desired formatting, click the Cell Styles button in the Styles group in the Home tab, and then click the *New Cell Style* option located toward the bottom of the drop-down gallery. At the Style dialog box, shown in Figure 6.5, type a name for the new style in the *Style name* text box, and then click OK to close the dialog box.

**QUICK STEPS**

**Define a Cell Style with Existing Formatting**
1. Select cell containing formatting.
2. Click Cell Styles button.
3. Click *New Cell Style*.
4. Type name for new style.
5. Click OK.

**Define a Style**
1. Click in a blank cell.
2. Click Cell Styles button.
3. Click *New Cell Style*.
4. Type name for new style.
5. Click Format button.
6. Choose formatting options.
7. Click OK to close Format Cells dialog box.
8. Click OK to close Style dialog box.

**HINT**
Cell styles are based on the workbook theme.

**Figure 6.5** Style Dialog Box

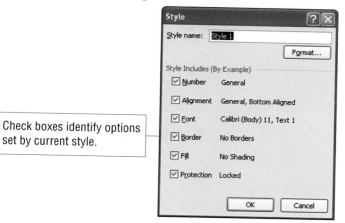

Check boxes identify options set by current style.

## Project 4a  Defining a Style

1. Open **ExcelC06Project04.xlsx** and then save the workbook and name it **ExcelL1_C6_P4**.
2. Make Sheet1 the active worksheet and then insert the necessary formulas to calculate gross pay, withholding tax amount, Social Security tax amount, and net pay. *Hint: Refer to Project 5c in Chapter 2 for assistance.*
3. Make Sheet2 the active worksheet and then insert a formula that calculates the amount due.

4. Make Sheet3 the active worksheet and then insert a formula in the *Due Date* column that inserts the purchase date plus the number of days in the *Terms* column. ***Hint: Refer to Project 3c in Chapter 2 for assistance.***

5. Define a style named *C06Title* with the formatting in cell A1 by completing the following steps:

    a. Make *Sheet1* active and then make cell A1 active.

    b. Click the Cell Styles button in the Styles group in the Home tab and then click the *New Cell Style* option located toward the bottom of the drop-down gallery.

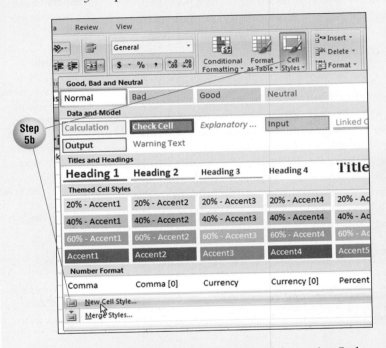

Step 5b

Step 5c

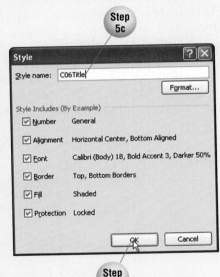

Step 5d

    c. At the Style dialog box, type **C06Title** in the *Style name* text box.

    d. Click OK.

6. Save **ExcelL1_C6_P4.xlsx**.

## QUICK STEPS

**Apply a Style**
1. Select cells.
2. Click Cell Styles button.
3. Click desired style at drop-down gallery.

## Applying a Style

To apply a style, select the cells you want to format, click the Cell Styles button in the Styles group, and then click the desired style at the drop-down gallery. The styles you create display at the top of the drop-down gallery.

# Project 4b Applying a Style

1. With **ExcelL1_C6_P4.xlsx** open, apply the C06Title style to cell A1 by completing the following steps:
   a. Make sure cell A1 is the active cell. (Even though cell A1 is already formatted, the style has not been applied to it. Later, you will modify the style and the style must be applied to the cell for the change to affect it.)
   b. Click the Cell Styles button in the Styles group in the Home tab.
   c. Click the *C06Title* style in the *Custom* section located toward the top of the drop-down gallery.

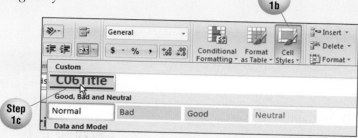

Step 1b

Step 1c

2. Apply the C06Title style to other cells by completing the following steps:
   a. Click the Sheet2 tab.
   b. Make cell A1 active.
   c. Click the Cell Styles button in the Styles group and then click the *C06Title* style at the drop-down gallery. (Notice that the style did not apply the row height formatting. The style applies only cell formatting.)
   d. Click the Sheet3 tab.
   e. Make cell A1 active.
   f. Click the Cell Styles button and then click the *C06Title* style at the drop-down gallery.
   g. Click the Sheet1 tab.
3. Save **ExcelL1_C6_P4.xlsx**.

In addition to defining a style based on cell formatting, you can also define a new style without first applying the formatting. To do this, you would display the Style dialog box, type a name for the new style, and then click the Format button. At the Format Cells dialog box, apply any desired formatting and then click OK to close the dialog box. At the Style dialog box, remove the check mark from any formatting that you do not want included in the style and then click OK to close the Style dialog box.

# Project 4c Defining a Style without First Applying Formatting

1. With **ExcelL1_C6_P4.xlsx** open, define a new style named *C06Subtitle* without first applying the formatting by completing the following steps:
   a. With Sheet1 active, click in any empty cell.
   b. Click the Cell Styles button in the Styles group and then click *New Cell Style* at the drop-down gallery.

c. At the Style dialog box, type **C06Subtitle** in the *Style name* text box.

d. Click the Format button in the Style dialog box.

e. At the Format Cells dialog box, click the Font tab.

f. At the Format Cells dialog box with the Font tab selected, change the font to Candara, the font style to bold, the size to 12, and the color to white.

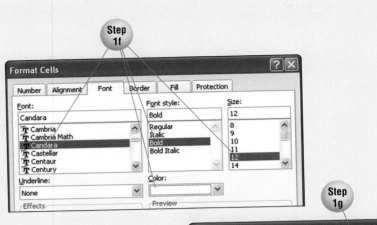

g. Click the Fill tab.

h. Click the bottom color in the green column as shown at the right.

i. Click the Alignment tab.

j. Change the Horizontal alignment to Center.

k. Click OK to close the Format Cells dialog box.

l. Click OK to close the Style dialog box.

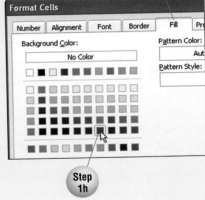

2. Apply the C06Subtitle style by completing the following steps:

a. Make cell A2 active.

b. Click the Cell Styles button and then click the *C06Subtitle* style located toward the top of the drop-down gallery in the *Custom* section.

c. Click the Sheet2 tab.

d. Make cell A2 active.

e. Click the Cell Styles button and then click the *C06Subtitle* style.

f. Click the Sheet3 tab.

g. Make cell A2 active.

h. Click the Cell Styles button and then click the *C06Subtitle* style.

i. Click the Sheet1 tab.

3. Apply the following predesigned cell styles:

a. Select cells A3 through G3.

b. Click the Cell Styles button and then click the *Heading 3* style at the drop-down gallery.

c. Select cells A5 through G5.

d. Click the Cell Styles button and then click the *20% - Accent3* style.

e. Apply the 20% - Accent3 style to cells A7 through G7 and cells A9 through G9.

f. Click the Sheet2 tab.

g. Select cells A3 through F3 and then apply the Heading 3 style.

h. Select cells A5 through F5 and then apply the 20% - Accent3 style.

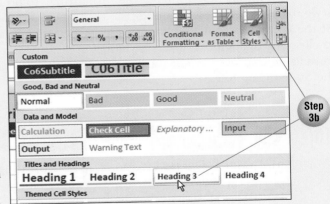

i. Apply the 20% - Accent3 style to every other row of cells (A7 through F7, A9 through F9, and so on, finishing with A17 through F17).

j. Click the Sheet3 tab.

k. Select cells A3 through F3 and then apply the Heading 3 style.

l. Apply the 20% - Accent3 style to A5 through F5, A7 through F7, and A9 through F9.

4. Make Sheet2 active and then change the height of row 1 to 36.00 (48 pixels).

5. Make Sheet3 active and then change the height of row 1 to 36.00 (48 pixels).

6. Make Sheet1 active.

7. Save **ExcelL1_C6_P4.xlsx** and then print only the first worksheet.

## Modifying a Style

One of the advantages to formatting with a style is that you can modify the formatting of the style and all cells formatted with that style automatically reflect the change. You can modify a style you create or one of the predesigned styles provided by Word. When you modify a predesigned style, only the style in the current workbook is affected. If you open a blank workbook, the cell styles available are the default styles.

To modify a style, click the Cell Styles button in the Styles group in the Home tab and then right-click the desired style at the drop-down gallery. At the shortcut menu that displays, click *Modify*. At the Style dialog box, click the Format button. Make the desired formatting changes at the Format Cells dialog box and then click OK. Click OK to close the Style dialog box and any cells formatted with the specific style are automatically updated.

**QUICK STEPS**

**Modify a Style**
1. Click Cell Styles button.
2. Right-click desired style at drop-down gallery.
3. Click *Modify*.
4. Click Format button.
5. Make desired formatting changes.
6. Click OK to close Format Cells dialog box.
7. Click OK to close Style dialog box.

## Project 4d    Modifying Styles

1. With **ExcelL1_C6_P4.xlsx** open, modify the C06Title style by completing the following steps:

   a. Click in any empty cell.

   b. Click the Cell Styles button in the Styles group.

   c. At the drop-down gallery, right-click on the *C06Title* style located toward the top of the gallery in the *Custom* section, and then click Modify.

   d. At the Style dialog box, click the Format button.

   e. At the Format Cells dialog box, click the Font tab, and then change the font to Candara.

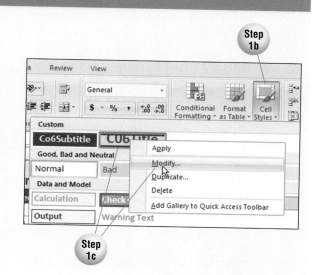

f. Click the Alignment tab.
g. Click the down-pointing arrow to the right of the *Vertical* option box, and then click *Center* at the drop-down list.
h. Click the Fill tab.
i. Click the light turquoise fill color as shown at the right.
j. Click OK to close the Format Cells dialog box.
k. Click OK to close the Style dialog box.

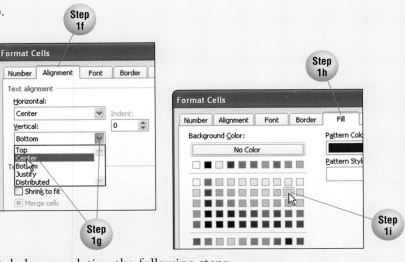

Step 1f

Step 1h

Step 1g

Step 1i

2. Modify the C06Subtitle style by completing the following steps:
   a. Click in any empty cell.
   b. Click the Cell Styles button in the Styles group.
   c. At the drop-down gallery, right-click on the *C06Subtitle* style located toward the top of the gallery in the *Custom* section, and then click *Modify*.
   d. At the Style dialog box, click the Format button.
   e. At the Format Cells dialog box, click the Font tab, and then change the font to Calibri.
   f. Click the Fill tab.
   g. Click the dark turquoise fill color as shown at the right.
   h. Click OK to close the Format Cells dialog box.
   i. Click OK to close the Style dialog box.

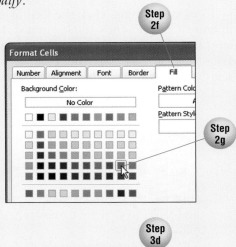

Step 2f

Step 2g

3. Modify the predefined 20% - Accent3 style by completing the following steps:
   a. Click the Cell Styles button in the Styles group.
   b. At the drop-down gallery, right-click on the *20% - Accent3* style and then click *Modify*.
   c. At the Style dialog box, click the Format button.
   d. At the Format Cells dialog box, click the Fill tab.
   e. Click the light turquoise fill color as shown at the right.
   f. Click OK to close the Format Cells dialog box.
   g. Click OK to close the Style dialog box.

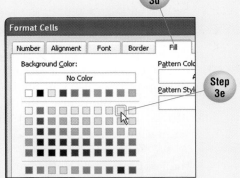

Step 3d

Step 3e

4. Click each sheet tab and notice the formatting changes made by the modified styles.
5. Change the name of Sheet1 to *Weekly Payroll*, the name of Sheet2 to *Invoices*, and the name of Sheet3 to *Overdue Accounts*.
6. Apply a different color to each of the three worksheet tabs.
7. Save and then print all the worksheets in **ExcelL1_C6_P4.xlsx**.

# Copying Styles to Another Workbook

Styles you define are saved with the workbook in which they are created. You can, however, copy styles from one workbook to another. To do this, open the workbook containing the styles you want to copy and open the workbook into which you want to copy the styles. Click the Cell Styles button in the Styles group in the Home tab, and then click the *Merge Styles* option located at the bottom of the drop-down gallery. At the Merge Styles dialog box shown in Figure 6.6, double-click the name of the workbook that contains the styles you want to copy, and then click OK.

**Figure 6.6** Merge Styles Dialog Box

**QUICK STEPS**

**Copy Styles to Another Workbook**
1. Open workbook containing desired styles.
2. Click Cell Styles button.
3. Click *Merge Styles* option.
4. Double-click name of workbook that contains styles you want to copy.

**Remove a Style**
1. Select cells formatted with style you want removed.
2. Click Cell Styles button.
3. Click *Normal* at drop-down gallery.

**Delete a Style**
1. Click Cell Styles button.
2. Right-click desired style to delete.
3. Click *Delete* at shortcut menu.

# Removing a Style

If you apply a style to text and then decide you do not want the formatting applied, return the formatting to Normal, which is the default formatting. To do this, select the cells formatted with the style you want to remove, click the Cell Styles button, and then click *Normal* at the drop-down gallery.

> **HINT**
> The Undo command will not reverse the effects of the Merge Styles dialog box.

# Deleting a Style

To delete a style, click the Cell Styles button in the Styles group in the Home tab. At the drop-down gallery that displays, right-click the style you want to delete, and then click *Delete* at the shortcut menu. Formatting applied by the deleted style is removed from cells in the workbook.

> **HINT**
> You cannot delete the Normal style.

Project 4e **Copying and Removing Styles**

1. With **ExcelL1_C6_P4.xlsx** open, open **ExcelC06O'RourkePlans.xlsx**.
2. Save the workbook with Save As and name it **ExcelL1_C6_P4b**.

3. Copy the styles in **ExcelL1_C6_P4.xlsx** into **ExcelL1_C6_P4b.xlsx** by completing the following steps:
   a. Click the Cell Styles button in the Styles group in the Home tab.
   b. Click the *Merge Styles* option located toward the bottom of the drop-down gallery.
   c. At the Merge Styles dialog box, double-click **ExcelL1_C6_P4.xlsx** in the *Merge styles from* list box.
   d. At the message that displays asking if you want to merge styles that have the same names, click Yes.

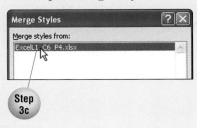

Step 3c

4. Apply the C06Title style to cell A1 and the C06Subtitle style to cell A2.
5. Increase the height of row 1 to 36.00 (48 pixels).
6. Insert the required formulas in the workbook. ***Hint: Refer to Project 3a of Chapter 2 for assistance.***
7. If neccessary, adjust column widths so all text is visible in cells.
8. Save, print, and then close **ExcelL1_C6_P4b.xlsx**.
9. Close **ExcelL1_C6_P4.xlsx**.

## Project ⑤ Insert, Modify, and Print Comments in an Equipment Rental Workbook

You will open an equipment rental workbook and then insert, edit, delete and print comments.

**Insert a Comment**
1. Click in desired cell.
2. Click Review tab.
3. Click New Comment button.
4. Type comment.
OR
1. Right-click desired cell.
2. Click *Insert Comment*.
3. Type comment.

**HINT**
You can resize and/or move overlapping comments.

New Comment

## Inserting Comments

If you want to make comments in a worksheet, or if a reviewer wants to make comments in a worksheet prepared by someone else, insert a comment. A comment is useful for providing specific instructions, identifying critical information, or for multiple individuals reviewing the same worksheet to insert comments. Some employees in a company may be part of a ***workgroup***, which is a networked collection of computers sharing files, printers, and other resources. In a workgroup, you may collaborate with coworkers on a specific workbook. Comments provide a method for reviewing the workbook and responding to others in the workgroup.

### Inserting a Comment

Insert a comment by clicking the Review tab and then clicking the New Comment button in the Comments group. This displays a color shaded box with the user's name inside. Type the desired information or comment in this comment box and then click outside the comment box. A small, red triangle appears in the upper right corner of a cell containing a comment. You can also insert a comment by right-clicking a cell and then clicking *Insert Comment* at the shortcut menu.

# Displaying a Comment

Hover the mouse over a cell containing a comment and the comment box displays. You can also display comments by right-clicking the cell containing a comment and then clicking *Show/Hide Comments* at the shortcut menu. Turn on the display of all comments by clicking the Show All Comments button in the Comments group in the Review tab. Turn on the display of an individual comment by making the cell active and then clicking the Show/Hide Comment button in the Comments group in the Review tab. Hide the display of an individual comment by clicking the same button. Move to comments in a worksheet by clicking the Next or Previous buttons in the Comments group in the Review tab.

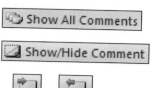

## Project 5a  Inserting and Displaying Comments

1. Open **ExcelC06Project05.xlsx**.
2. Save the workbook with Save As and name it **ExcelL1_C6_P5**.
3. Insert a formula in cell H3 that multiplies the rate by the hours and then copy the formula down to cells H4 through H16. (When you copy the formula, click the Auto Fill Options button and then click *Fill Without Formatting* at the drop-down list.)
4. Make cell H17 active and then insert a formula that sums the amounts in cells H3 through H16.
5. Insert a comment by completing the following steps:
   a. Click cell F3 to make it active.
   b. Click the Review tab.
   c. Click the New Comment button in the Comments group.
   d. In the comment box, type **Bill Lakeside Trucking for only 7 hours for the backhoe and front loader on May 1.**
   e. Click outside the comment box.
6. Insert another comment by completing the following steps:
   a. Click cell C6 to make it active.
   b. Click the New Comment button in the Comments group.
   c. In the comment box, type **I think Country Electrical has changed their name to Northwest Electrical.**
   d. Click outside the comment box.

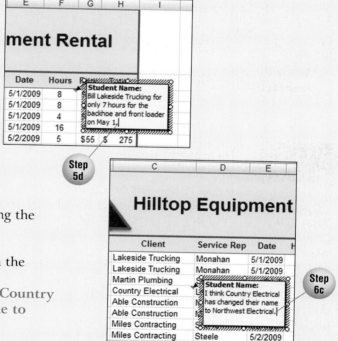

7. Assume that more than one person is reviewing and commenting on this worksheet. Change the user name and then insert additional comments by completing the following steps:

a. Click the Office button and then click the Excel Options button located toward the bottom of the drop-down list.

b. At the Excel Options dialog box make sure *Popular* is selected in the left panel.

c. Select the current name in the *User name* text box (remember the name you are selecting) and then type Jean Coen.

d. Click OK to close the dialog box.

e. Click cell D11 to make it active.

f. Click the New Comment button in the Comments group.

g. In the comment box, type This rental should be credited to Monahan instead of Leuke.

h. Click outside the comment box.

i. Click cell G11 to make it active.

j. Click the New Comment button in the Comments group.

k. In the comment box, type The hourly rental for the pressure sprayer is $25.

l. Click outside the comment box.

8. Complete steps similar to those in Steps 7a through 7d to return the user name back to the original name (the name that displayed before you changed it to *Jean Coen*).

9. Click the Show All Comments button to turn on the display of all comments.

10. Save **ExcelL1_C6_P5.xlsx**.

## HINT

Display the document in Print Preview to view how comments will print.

## Printing a Comment

By default, comments do not print. If you want comments to print, use the *Comments* option at the Page Setup dialog box with the Sheet tab selected. Display this dialog box by clicking the Page Layout tab, clicking the Page Setup group dialog box launcher, and then clicking the Sheet tab. Click the down-pointing arrow at the right side of the *Comments* option box. At the drop-down list that displays, choose *At end of sheet* to print comments on the page after cell contents, or choose the *As displayed on sheet* option to print the comments in the comment box in the worksheet.

1. With **ExcelL1_C6_P5.xlsx** open, click the Page Layout tab.
2. Click the Orientation button in the Page Setup group and then click *Landscape* at the drop-down list.
3. Click the Page Setup group dialog box launcher.
4. At the Page Setup dialog box, click the Sheet tab.
5. Click the down-pointing arrow at the right side of the *Comments* option box and then click *As displayed on sheet*.
6. Click the Print button that displays toward the bottom of the dialog box and then click OK at the Print dialog box.
7. Turn off the display of comments by clicking the Review tab and then clicking the Show All Comments button.
8. Save **ExcelL1_C6_P5.xlsx**.

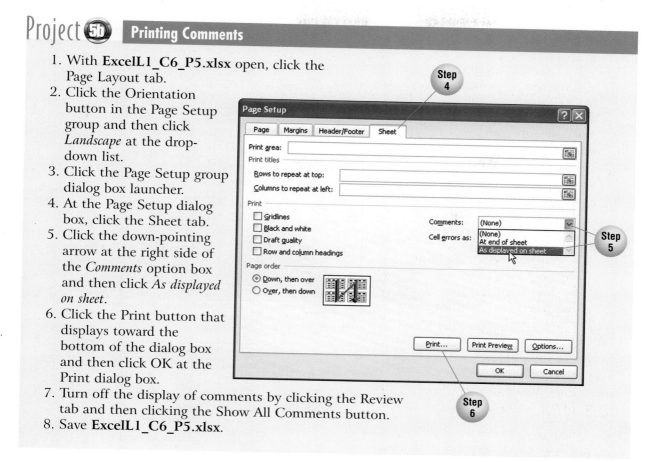

## Editing a Comment

To edit a comment, click the cell containing the comment and then click the Edit Comment button in the Comments group in the Review tab. (The New Comment button changes to the Edit Comment button when the active cell contains a comment.) You can also edit a comment by right-clicking the cell containing the comment and then clicking *Edit Comment* at the shortcut menu.

## Deleting a Comment

Cell comments exist in addition to data in a cell. Deleting data in a cell does not delete the comment. To delete a comment, click the cell containing the comment and then click the Delete button in the Comments group in the Review tab. You can also delete a comment by right-clicking the cell containing the comment and then clicking *Delete Comment* at the shortcut menu.

1. With **ExcelL1_C6_P5.xlsx** open, display comments by completing the following steps:
   a. Click cell A3 to make it the active cell.
   b. Click the Review tab.
   c. Click the Next button in the Comments group.
   d. Read the comment and then click the Next button.
   e. Continue clicking the Next button until a message displays telling you that Microsoft Excel has reached the end of the workbook and asking if you want to continue reviewing from the beginning of the workbook. At this message, click the Cancel button.
   f. Click outside the comment box.

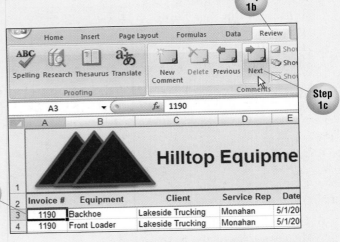

2. Edit a comment by completing the following steps:
   a. Click cell D11 to make it active.
   b. Click the Edit Comment button.
   c. Edit the comment so it displays as *This rental should be credited to Steele instead of Leuke.*

3. Delete a comment by completing the following steps:
   a. Click cell C6 to make it active.
   b. Click the Delete button in the Comments group.

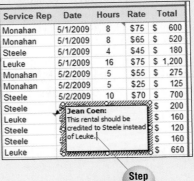

4. Respond to the comments by making the following changes:
   a. Change the contents of F3 from *8* to *7*.
   b. Change the contents of F4 from *8* to *7*.
   c. Change the contents of D11 from *Leuke* to *Steele*.
   d. Change the contents of G11 from *$20* to *$25*.

5. Print the worksheet and the comments by completing the following steps:
   a. Click the Page Layout tab.
   b. Click the Page Setup group dialog box launcher.
   c. At the Page Setup dialog box, click the Sheet tab.
   d. Click the down-pointing arrow at the right side of the *Comments* option and then click *At end of sheet*.
   e. Click the Print button that displays toward the bottom of the dialog box.
   f. At the Print dialog box, click OK. (The worksheet will print on one page and the comments will print on a second page.)

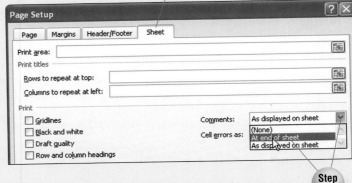

6. Save and then close **ExcelL1_C6_P5.xlsx**.

# Project 6 Create a Billing Statement Workbook Using a Template

You will open a Billing Statement template provided by Excel, add data, save it as an Excel workbook, and then print the workbook.

## Using Excel Templates

Excel has included a number of *template* worksheet forms formatted for specific uses. For example, Excel has provided template forms for a balance sheet, billing statement, loan amortization, sales invoice, and timecard. To view the templates available, click the Office button and then click *New* at the drop-down list. At the New Workbook dialog box shown in Figure 6.7, click the *Installed Templates* option in the *Templates* section. This displays the installed templates in the middle panel of the dialog box. Note that the first time you download a template, Microsoft checks to determine if you are using a genuine Office product.

**QUICK STEPS**

**Use an Excel Template**
1. Click Office button, *New*.
2. Click *Installed Templates* option.
3. Double-click desired template.

Figure 6.7 New Workbook Dialog Box

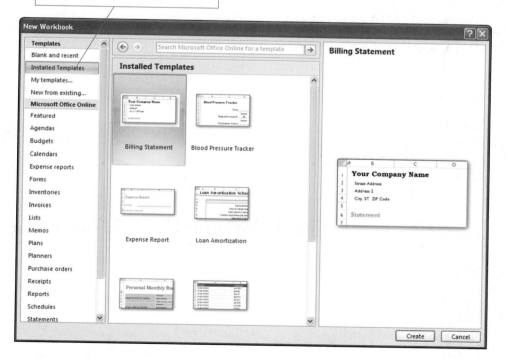

Click the *Installed Templates* option to display available templates.

## Entering Data in a Template

Templates contain unique areas where information is entered at the keyboard. For example, in the Billing Statement template shown in Figure 6.8, you enter information such as the customer name, address, and telephone number, and also the date, time, description, amount, payment, and balance of items. To enter information in the appropriate location, position the mouse pointer (white plus sign) in the location where you want to type data and then click the left mouse button. After typing the data, click the next location. You can also move the insertion point to another cell using the commands learned in Chapter 1. For example, press the Tab key to make the next cell active, press Shift + Tab to make the previous cell active.

**Figure 6.8** Billing Statement Template

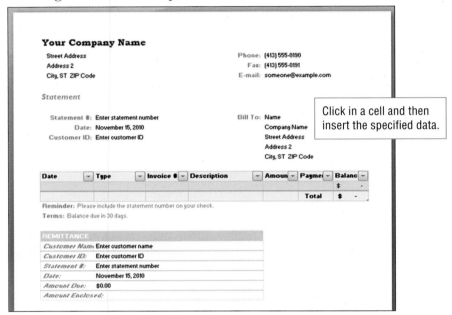

Click in a cell and then insert the specified data.

## Project 6 — Preparing a Billing Statement Using a Template

1. Click the Office button and then click *New* at the drop-down list.
2. At the New Workbook dialog box, click the *Installed Templates* option in the *Templates* section.
3. Double-click the *Billing Statement* template in the *Installed Templates* section of the dialog box.

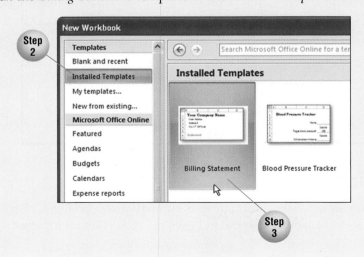

Step 2

Step 3

4. With cell B1 active, type IN-FLOW SYSTEMS.
5. Click the text *Street Address* (cell B2) and then type 320 Milander Way.
6. Click in the specified location (cell) and then type the text indicated:
    *Address 2* (cell B3) = P.O. Box 2300
    *City, ST ZIP Code* (cell B4) = Boston, MA 02188
    *Phone* (cell F2) = (617) 555-3900
    *Fax* (cell F3) = (617) 555-3945
    *Statement #* (cell C8) = 5432
    *Customer ID* (cell C10) = 25-345
    *Name* (cell F8) = Aidan Mackenzie
    *Company Name* (cell F9) = Stanfield Enterprises
    *Street Address* (cell F10) = 9921 South 42nd Avenue
    *Address 2* (cell F11) = P.O. Box 5540
    *City, ST ZIP Code* (cell F12) = Boston, MA 02193
    *Date* (cell B15) = (insert current date in numbers as ##/##/####)
    *Type* (cell C15) = System Unit
    *Invoice #* (cell D15) = 7452
    *Description* (cell E15) = Calibration Unit
    *Amount* (cell F15) = 950
    *Payment* (cell G15) = 200
    *Customer Name* (cell C21) = Stanfield Enterprises
    *Amount Enclosed* (C26) = 750

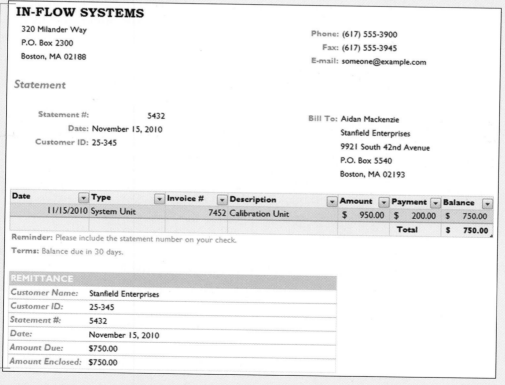

7. Save the completed invoice and name it **ExcelL1_C6_P6**.
8. Print and then close **ExcelL1_C6_P6.xlsx**.

# CHAPTER summary

- Perform file management tasks such as copying, moving, printing, and renaming workbooks and creating a new folder and renaming a folder at the Open or Save As dialog boxes.
- Create a new folder by clicking the Create New Folder button located on the dialog box toolbar at the Open dialog box or Save As dialog box.
- Rename a folder with the *Rename* option from the Tools button drop-down list or with a shortcut menu.
- To select adjacent workbooks in the Open dialog box, click the first workbook, hold down the Shift key, and then click the last workbook. To select nonadjacent workbooks, click the first workbook, hold down the Ctrl key, and then click any desired workbooks.
- To delete a workbook, use the Delete button on the Open or Save As dialog box toolbar, the *Delete* option at the Tools button drop-down list, or with a shortcut menu option.
- Workbooks deleted from the hard drive are automatically sent to the Windows Recycle Bin where they can be restored or permanently deleted.
- Create a copy of an existing workbook by opening the workbook and then using the *Save As* command to assign the workbook a different file name.
- Use the *Copy* and *Paste* options from the shortcut menu at the Open (or Save As) dialog box to copy a workbook from one folder to another folder or drive.
- When you copy a workbook into the same folder from which it originates, Excel names the duplicated workbook(s) "Copy of xxx" (where *xxx* is the original workbook name).
- Use the *Send To* option from the shortcut menu to send a copy of a workbook to another drive or folder.
- Remove a workbook from a folder or drive and insert it in another folder or drive using the *Cut* and *Paste* options from the shortcut menu.
- Use the *Rename* option from the Tools button drop-down list or the shortcut menu to give a workbook a different name.
- Print multiple workbooks by selecting the desired workbooks at the Print dialog box, clicking the Tools button, and then clicking *Print* at the drop-down list.
- To move or copy a worksheet to another existing workbook, open both the source and the destination workbook and then open the Move or Copy dialog box.
- Save a workbook in a different format with options from the Office button Save As side menu or with the *Save as type* option at the Save As dialog box. Click the down-pointing arrow at the right side of the *Save as type* option and a drop-down list displays with the available formats.
- Automate the formatting of cells in a workbook by defining and then applying styles. A style is a predefined set of formatting attributes.
- A style helps to ensure consistent formatting from one worksheet to another. All formatting attributes for a particular style are defined only once. Define a style with formats already applied to a cell or display the Style dialog box, click the Format button, and then choose formatting options at the Format Cells dialog box.

- To apply a style, select the desired cells, click the Cell Styles button in the Styles group in the Home tab, and then click the desired style at the drop-down gallery.

- Modify a style and all cells to which the style is applied automatically reflect the change. To modify a style, click the Cell Styles button in the Styles group in the Home tab, right-click the desired style, and then click *Modify* at the shortcut menu.

- Styles are saved in the workbook in which they are created. Styles can be copied, however, to another workbook. Do this with options at the Merge Styles dialog box.

- Insert comments in a worksheet to provide specific instructions, identify critical information, review a workbook, and respond to others in a workgroup about the workbook.

- Insert, display, edit, and delete comments using buttons in the Comments group in the Review tab.

- By default, comments do not print. To print comments, display the Page Setup dialog box with the Sheet tab selected, and then choose the printing location with the *Comments* option.

- Excel provides preformatted templates for creating forms such as a balance sheet, billing statement, loan amortization, sales invoice, and timecard. Display the available templates by clicking the *Installed Templates* option in the *Templates* section of the New Workbook dialog box.

- Templates contain unique areas where information is entered at the keyboard. These areas vary depending on the template.

# COMMANDS review

| FEATURE | RIBBON TAB, GROUP | BUTTON, OPTION | OFFICE BUTTON DROP-DOWN LIST | KEYBOARD SHORTCUT |
|---|---|---|---|---|
| Open dialog box | | | Open | Ctrl + O |
| Save As dialog box | | | Save As | Ctrl + S |
| Print dialog box | | | Print | Ctrl + P |
| Save in PDF format | | | Save As, PDF or XPS | |
| Style dialog box | Home, Styles | , New Cell Style | | |
| Merge Styles dialog box | Home, Styles | , Merge Styles | | |
| Insert comment | Review, Comments | | | Shift + F2 |
| Display all comments | Review, Comments | Show All Comments | | |
| Delete comment | Review, Comments | | | |
| Display next comment | Review, Comments | | | |
| Display previous comment | Review, Comments | | | |
| New Workbook dialog box | | | New | |

# CONCEPTS check

## Test Your Knowledge

**Completion:** In the space provided at the right, indicate the correct term, symbol, or command.

1. Perform file management tasks such as copying, moving, or deleting workbooks with options at the Open dialog box or this dialog box.

_____

2. Click this button on the Open dialog box toolbar to display the folder that is up a level from the current folder.

_____

3. At the Open dialog box, hold down this key while selecting nonadjacent workbooks.

_____

4. Workbooks deleted from the hard drive are automatically sent to this location.

_____

5. Click the down-pointing arrow at the right side of this option at the Save As dialog box to display a drop-down list of available workbook formats.

_____

6. If the PDF format is installed, this option for saving a workbook in PDF file format displays at the Office button Save As side menu.

_____

7. The Cell Styles button is located in this group in the Home tab.

_____

8. Click the *New Cell Style* option at the Cell Styles button drop-down gallery and this dialog box displays.

_____

9. A style you create displays in this section of the Cell Styles button drop-down gallery.

_____

10. Copy styles from one workbook to another with options at this dialog box.

_____

11. This displays in the upper right corner of a cell containing a comment.

_____

12. The New Comment button is located in the Comments group in this tab.

_____

13. Print comments by choosing the desired printing location with the *Comments* option at the Page Setup dialog box with this tab selected.

_____

14. Click this button in the Comments group to display all comments in the worksheet.

_____

15. Click this option at the New Workbook dialog box to display available templates.

_____

# SKILLS check

## Demonstrate Your Proficiency

### Assessment

## 1 MANAGE WORKBOOKS

1. Display the Open dialog box with Excel2007L1C6 the active folder.
2. Create a new folder named *O'Rourke* in the Excel2007L1C6 folder.
3. Copy **ExcelC06O'RourkeBudget.xlsx**, **ExcelC06O'RourkePlans.xlsx**, and **ExcelC06Project04.xlsx** to the O'Rourke folder.
4. Display the contents of the O'Rourke folder and then rename **ExcelC06O'RourkeBudget.xlsx** to **EquipmentBudget.xlsx**.
5. Rename **ExcelC06O'RourkePlans.xlsx** to **PurchasePlans.xlsx** in the O'Rourke folder.
6. Change the active folder back to Excel2007L1C6.
7. Delete all of the workbooks in the Excel2007L1C6 folder that begin with *ExcelC05*.
8. Close the Open dialog box.

### Assessment

## 2 MOVE AND COPY WORKSHEETS BETWEEN SALES ANALYSIS WORKBOOKS

1. Open **ExcelC06Assessment02.xlsx**.
2. Save the workbook with Save As and name it **ExcelL1_C6_A2**.
3. Rename Sheet1 to *1st Qtr.*
4. Rename Sheet2 to *Yearly Summary*.
5. Move the Yearly Summary sheet before the 1st Qtr. sheet.
6. Open **ExcelC06DeeringQtrs.xlsx**.
7. Rename Sheet1 to *2nd Qtr.* and then copy it to **ExcelL1_C6_A2.xlsx** (following the 1st Qtr. worksheet).
8. Make **ExcelC06DeeringQtrs.xlsx** active, rename Sheet2 to *3rd Qtr.* and then copy it to **ExcelL1_C6_A2.xlsx** (following the 2nd Qtr. worksheet).
9. Make **ExcelC06DeeringQtrs.xlsx** active and then close it without saving the changes.
10. Open **ExcelC06DeeringFourthQtr.xlsx**.
11. Rename Sheet1 to *4th Qtr.* and then move it to **ExcelL1_C6_A2.xlsx** (following the 3rd Qtr. worksheet).
12. Make **ExcelC06DeeringFourthQtr.xlsx** active and then close it without saving the changes.
13. With **ExcelL1_C6_A2.xlsx** active, make the following changes:
    a. Make 1st Qtr. the active worksheet and then insert a formula to calculate the averages and another to calculate the totals. (Use the Auto Fill Options button to fill without formatting.)
    b. Make 2nd Qtr. the active worksheet and then insert a formula to calculate the averages and another to calculate the totals. (Use the Auto Fill Options button to fill without formatting.)

c. Make 3rd Qtr. the active worksheet and then insert a formula to calculate the averages and another to calculate the totals. (Use the Auto Fill Options button to fill without formatting.)

d. Make 4th Qtr. the active worksheet and then insert a formula to calculate the averages and another to calculate the totals. (Use the Auto Fill Options button to fill without formatting.)

e. Make Yearly Summary the active worksheet and then insert a formula that inserts in cell B4 the average of the amounts in cell E4 for the 1st Qtr., 2nd Qtr., 3rd Qtr., and 4th Qtr. worksheets.
*← use steps on pages 184–185*

f. Copy the formula in cell B4 down to cells B5 through B9.

g. Make cell B10 active and then insert a formula that calculates the total of cells B4 through B9.
*Type closing parenthesis ")" at top of screen (Do Not click Back to sheet 1)*

14. Delete the Sheet3 tab.

15. Insert a footer on all worksheets that prints your name at the left, the page number in the middle, and the current date at the right.

16. Horizontally and vertically center the worksheets.

17. Save and then print all of the worksheets in **ExcelL1_C6_A2.xlsx**.

18. Close **ExcelL1_C6_A2.xlsx**.

## Assessment

# 3 DEFINE AND APPLY STYLES TO A PROJECTED EARNINGS WORKBOOK

1. At a blank worksheet, define a style named *C06Heading* that contains the following formatting:
   a. 14-point Cambria bold in dark blue color
   b. Horizontal alignment of Center
   c. Top and bottom border in a dark red color
   d. Light purple fill

2. Define a style named *C06Subheading* that contains the following formatting:
   a. 12-point Cambria bold in dark blue color
   b. Horizontal alignment of Center
   c. Top and bottom border in dark red color
   d. Light purple fill

3. Define a style named *C06Column* that contains the following formatting:
   a. 12-point Cambria in dark blue color
   b. Light purple fill

4. Save the workbook and name it **ExcelL1_C6_A3_Styles**.

5. With **ExcelL1_C6_A3_Styles.xlsx** open, open **ExcelC06Assessment03.xlsx**.

6. Save the workbook with Save As and name it **ExcelL1_C6_A3**.

7. Make cell C6 active and then insert a formula that multiplies the content of cell B6 with the amount in cell B3. (When writing the formula, identify cell B3 as an absolute reference.) Copy the formula down to cells C7 through C17.

8. Copy the styles from **ExcelL1_C6_A3_Styles.xlsx** into **ExcelL1_C6_A3.xlsx**. *Hint: Do this at the Merge Styles dialog box.*

9. Apply the following styles:
   a. Select cells A1 and A2 and then apply the C06Heading style.
   b. Select cells A5 through C5 and then apply the C06Subheading style.
   c. Select cells A6 through A17 and then apply the C06Column style.

10. Save the workbook again and then print **ExcelL1_C6_A3.xlsx**.

11. With **ExcelL1_C6_A3.xlsx** open, modify the following styles:
    a. Modify the C06Heading style so it changes the font color to dark purple (instead of dark blue), changes the vertical alignment to Center, and inserts a top and bottom border in dark purple (instead of dark red).
    b. Modify the C06Subheading style so it changes the font color to dark purple (instead of dark blue) and inserts a top and bottom border in dark purple (instead of dark red).
    c. Modify the C06Column style so it changes the font color to dark purple (instead of dark blue). Leave all of the other formatting attributes.
12. Save the workbook and then print **ExcelL1_C6_A3.xlsx**.
13. Close **ExcelL1_C6_A3.xlsx** and then close **ExcelL1_C6_A3_Styles.xlsx** without saving the changes.

## Assessment

### 4  INSERT, DELETE AND PRINT COMMENTS IN A TRAVEL WORKBOOK

1. Open **ExcelC06Asessment04.xlsx**.
2. Save the workbook with Save As and name it **ExcelL1_C6_A4.xlsx**.
3. Insert the following comments in the specified cells:

    | | | |
    |---|---|---|
    | B7 | = | Should we include Sun Valley, Idaho, as a destination? |
    | B12 | = | Please include the current exchange rate. |
    | G8 | = | What other airlines fly into Aspen, Colorado? |

4. Save **ExcelL1_C6_A4.xlsx**.
5. Turn on the display of all comments.
6. Print the worksheet in landscape orientation with the comments as displayed on the worksheet.
7. Turn off the display of all comments.
8. Delete the comment in cell B12.
9. Print the worksheet again with the comments printed at the end of the worksheet. (The comments will print on a separate page from the worksheet.)
10. Save and then close **ExcelL1_C6_A4.xlsx**.

## Assessment

### 5  APPLY CONDITIONAL FORMATTING TO A SALES WORKBOOK

1. Use Excel Help files to learn more about conditional formatting.
2. Open **ExcelC06Assessment05.xlsx** and then save the workbook and name it **ExcelL1_C6_A5**.
3. Select cells D5 through D19 and then use conditional formatting to display the amounts as data bars.
4. Insert a footer that prints your name, a page number, and the current date.
5. Save, print, and then close **ExcelL1_C6_A5.xlsx**.

# CASE study

## Apply Your Skills

**Part 1**

You are the office manager for Leeward Marine and you decide to consolidate into one workbook worksheets containing information on expenses. Copy **ExcelC06EstimatedExpenses.xlsx**, **ExcelC06ActualExpenses.xlsx**, and **ExcelC06ExpenseVariances.xlsx** into one workbook. Apply appropriate formatting to numbers and insert necessary formulas. Include the company name, Leeward Marine, in each worksheet. Create styles and apply the styles to cells in each worksheet to maintain consistent formatting. Rename and recolor the three worksheet tabs (you determine the names and colors). Save the workbook and name it **ExcelC06LeewardExpenses**.

**Part 2**

As you look at the information in each worksheet in the **ExcelC06LeewardExpenses.xlsx** workbook, you decide that the information should be summarized for easy viewing. Include a new worksheet in the workbook that summarizes each category in Employee Costs, Facilities Costs, and Marketing Costs by estimated costs, actual costs, and expense variances. Insert formulas in the summary worksheet that insert the appropriate totals from each of the three other worksheets. Insert an appropriate header or footer in the workbook. Scale the worksheets so each print on one page. Save, print (all of the worksheets in the workbook), and then close **ExcelC06LeewardExpenses.xlsx**.

**Part 3**

You are not happy with the current product list form so you decide to look at template forms available at the Microsoft online site. Display the New Workbook dialog box and then download the Product price list template located in the *Lists* category. Open **ExcelC06ProductList.xlsx** and then copy the product information into the Produce price list template. Insert the following company information as required by the template:

Leeward Marine
4500 Shoreline Drive,
Ketchikan, AK 99901
(907) 555-2200
(907) 555-2595 (fax)
www.emcp.com/leewardmarine

Format the product list form with formatting similar to the formatting you applied to the **ExcelC06LeewardExpenses.xlsx** workbook. Save the completed products list form and name it **ExcelC06ProductsList**. Print and then close the workbook.

You need to print a number of copies of the product list and you want the company letterhead to print at the top of the page. You decide to use the letterhead you created in Word and copy the product list information from Excel into the Word letterhead document. To do this, open Word and then open the document named **LeewardMarineLtrhd.docx**. Open **ExcelC06ProductList.xlsx** and then copy the cells containing data and paste them into the Word letterhead document using *Paste Special*. When the product list information is pasted into the Word document, apply blue font color to the data in the cells. Apply any other formatting you think will enhance the cells in the document. Save the Word document with *Save As* and name it **WordC06ProductList**. Print and then close **WordC06ProductList.docx** and then close **ExcelC06ProductList.xlsx**.

# Creating a Chart in Excel

## PERFORMANCE OBJECTIVES

**Upon successful completion of Chapter 7, you will be able to:**

- **Create a chart with data in an Excel worksheet**
- **Size, move, and delete charts**
- **Print a selected chart and print a worksheet containing a chart**
- **Preview a chart**
- **Choose a chart style, layout, and formatting**
- **Change chart location**
- **Insert, move, size, and delete chart labels, shapes, and pictures**

**Tutorial 7.1**
Creating and Formatting Charts

In the previous Excel chapters, you learned to create data in worksheets. While a worksheet does an adequate job of representing data, you can present some data more visually by charting the data. A chart is sometimes referred to as *graph* and is a picture of numeric data. In this chapter, you will learn to create and customize charts in Excel.

*Note: Before beginning computer projects, copy to your storage medium the Excel2007L1C7 subfolder from the Excel2007L1 folder on the CD that accompanies this textbook and then make Excel2007L1C7 the active folder.*

## Project  Create a Quarterly Sales Column Chart

You will open a workbook containing quarterly sales data and then use the data to create a column chart. You will decrease the size of the chart, move it to a different location in the worksheet and then make changes to sales numbers.

## Creating a Chart

In Excel, create a chart with buttons in the Charts group in the Insert tab as shown in Figure 7.1. With buttons in the Charts group you can create a variety of charts such as a column chart, line chart, pie chart, and much more. Excel provides 11

basic chart types as described in Table 7.1. To create a chart, select cells in a worksheet that you want to chart, click the Insert tab, and then click the desired chart button in the Charts group. At the drop-down gallery that displays, click the desired chart style. You can also create a chart by selecting the desired cells and then pressing Alt + F1. This keyboard shortcut, by default, inserts the data in a 2-D column chart (unless the default chart type has been changed).

**Figure 7.1** Chart Group Buttons

These buttons display in the Insert tab and you can use them to create a variety of charts.

**Table 7.1** Types of Charts

| Chart | Description |
|---|---|
| Area | An Area chart emphasizes the magnitude of change, rather than time and the rate of change. It also shows the relationship of parts to a whole by displaying the sum of the plotted values. |
| Bar | A Bar chart shows individual figures at a specific time, or shows variations between components but not in relationship to the whole. |
| Bubble | A Bubble chart compares sets of three values in a manner similar to a scatter chart, with the third value displayed as the size of the bubble marker. |
| Column | A Column chart compares separate (noncontinuous) items as they vary over time. |
| Doughnut | A Doughnut chart shows the relationship of parts of the whole. |
| Line | A Line chart shows trends and change over time at even intervals. It emphasizes the rate of change over time rather than the magnitude of change. |
| Pie | A Pie chart shows proportions and relationships of parts to the whole. |
| Radar | A Radar chart emphasizes differences and amounts of change over time and variations and trends. Each category has its own value axis radiating from the center point. Lines connect all values in the same series. |
| Stock | A Stock chart shows four values for a stock—open, high, low, and close. |
| Surface | A Surface chart shows trends in values across two dimensions in a continuous curve. |
| XY (Scatter) | A Scatter chart either shows the relationships among numeric values in several data series or plots the interception points between $x$ and $y$ values. It shows uneven intervals of data and is commonly used in scientific data. |

# Sizing, Moving, and Deleting a Chart

When you create a chart, the chart is inserted in the same worksheet as the selected cells. Figure 7.2 displays the worksheet and chart you will create in Project 1a. The chart is inserted in a box which you can size and/or move in the worksheet.

To size the worksheet, position the mouse pointer on the four dots located in the middle of the border you want to size until the pointer turns into a two-headed arrow, hold down the left mouse button, and then drag to increase or decrease the size of the chart. To increase or decrease the height and width of the chart at the same time, position the mouse pointer on the three dots that display in a chart border corner until the pointer displays as a two-headed arrow, hold down the left mouse button, and then drag to the desired size. To increase or decrease the size of the chart and maintain the proportions of the chart, hold down the Shift key while dragging a chart corner border.

To move the chart, make sure the chart is selected (light turquoise box displays around the chart), position the mouse pointer on a border until it turns into a four-headed arrow, hold down the left mouse button, and then drag to the desired position.

**HINT**
Hide rows or columns that you do not want to chart.

**Figure 7.2** Project 1a Chart

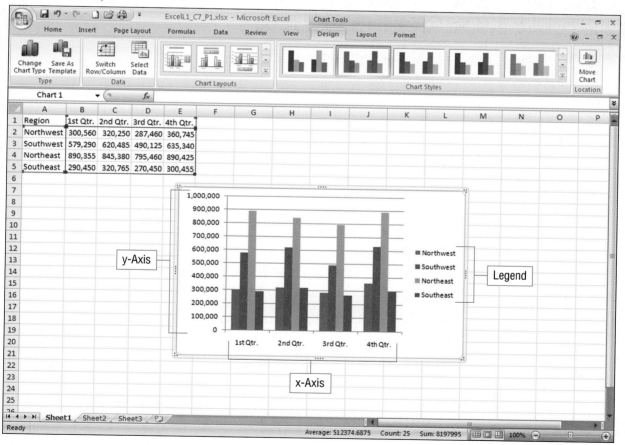

# Editing Data

The cells you select to create the chart are linked to the chart. If you need to change data for a chart, edit the data in the desired cell and the corresponding section of the chart is automatically updated.

## Project (1a) Creating a Chart

1. Open **ExcelC07Project01.xlsx** and then save the workbook and name it **ExcelL1_C7_P1**.
2. Select cells A1 through E5.
3. Press Alt + F1.
4. Slightly increase the size of the chart and maintain the proportions of the chart by completing the following steps:
   a. Position the mouse pointer on the bottom right corner of the chart border until the pointer turns into a two-headed arrow pointing diagonally.
   b. Hold down the Shift key and then hold down the left mouse button.
   c. Drag out approximately one-half inch and then release the mouse button and then the Shift key.

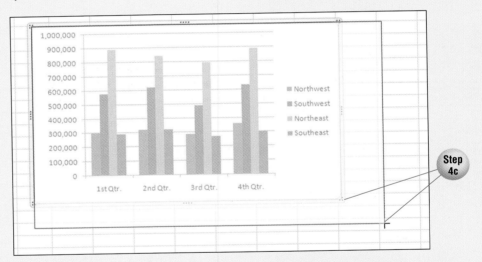

Step
4c

5. Move the chart below the cells containing data by completing the following steps:
   a. Make sure the chart is selected (light turquoise border surrounds the chart).

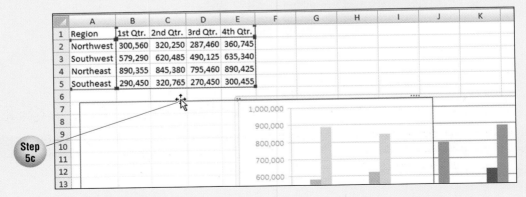

Step
5c

b. Position the mouse pointer on the chart border until the pointer turns into a four-headed arrow.

c. Hold down the left mouse button, drag the chart so it is positioned below the cells containing data, and then release the mouse button.

6. Make the following changes to the specified cells:
   a. Make cell B2 active and then change *300,560* to *421,720*.
   b. Make cell C2 active and then change *320,250* to *433,050*.
   c. Make cell D2 active and then change *287,460* to *397,460*.
   d. Make cell E2 active and then change *360,745* to *451,390*.

7. Save **ExcelL1_C7_P1.xlsx**.

## Printing Only the Chart

In a worksheet containing data in cells as well as a chart, you can print only the chart. To do this, click the chart to select it and then display the Print dialog box. At the Print dialog box, *Selected Chart* will automatically be selected in the *Print what* section. Click OK to print only the selected chart.

## Previewing a Chart

Preview a chart by clicking the Office button, pointing to the *Print* option, and then clicking *Print Preview*. After previewing the chart, click the Close Preview button, or print the worksheet by clicking the Print button in the Print Preview tab.

Project **1b**  **Previewing and Printing the Chart**

1. With **ExcelL1_C7_P1.xlsx** open, make sure the chart displays.
2. Preview the chart by completing the following steps:
   a. Click the Office button.
   b. Point to the *Print* option.
   c. Click *Print Preview*.
   d. After viewing the chart in Print Preview, click the Close Print Preview button.
3. Print the worksheet by clicking the Quick Print button in the Quick Access toolbar.
4. Save and then close **ExcelL1_C7_P1.xlsx**.

Project **2**  **Create a Technology Purchases Bar Chart and Column Chart**

You will open a workbook containing technology purchases data by department and then create a bar chart with the data. You will then change the chart type, layout, and style and move the chart to a new sheet.

# Changing the Chart Design

When you insert a chart in a worksheet, the Chart Tools Design tab displays as shown in Figure 7.3. With options in this tab, you can change the chart type, specify a different layout or style for the chart, and change the location of the chart so it displays in a separate worksheet.

**Figure 7.3** Chart Tools Design Tab

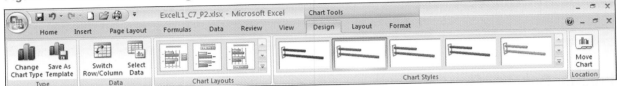

**QUICK STEPS**

**Change Chart Type and Style**
1. Make the chart active.
2. Click Chart Tools Design tab.
3. Click Change Chart Type button.
4. Click desired chart type.
5. Click desired chart style.
6. Click OK.

## Choosing a Custom Chart Style

The chart feature offers a variety of preformatted custom charts and offers varying styles for each chart type. You can choose a chart style with buttons in the Charts group by clicking a chart button and then choosing from the styles offered at the drop-down list. You can also choose a chart style with the Change Chart Type button in the Chart Tools Design tab. Click this button and the Change Chart Type dialog box displays as shown in Figure 7.4. Click the desired chart type in the panel at the left side of the dialog box and then click the desired chart style at the right. If you create a particular chart type on a regular basis, you may want to set that chart type as the default. To do this, click the Set as Default Chart button in the Change Chart Type dialog box.

**Figure 7.4** Change Chart Type Dialog Box

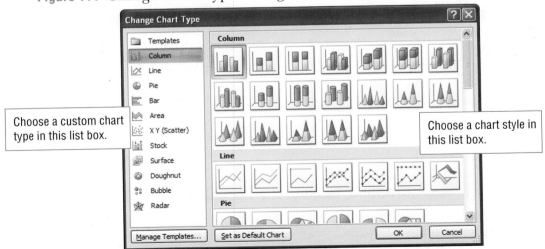

Choose a custom chart type in this list box.

Choose a chart style in this list box.

# Changing the Data Series

A data series is information represented on the chart by bars, lines, columns, pie slices, and so on. When Excel creates a chart, the data in the first column (except the first cell) is used to create the x-axis (the information along the bottom of the chart) and the data in the first row (except the first cell) is used to create the legend. You can switch the data in the axes by clicking the Switch Row/Column button in the Data group in the Chart Tools Design tab. This moves the data on the x-axis to the y-axis and the y-axis data to the x-axis.

QUICK STEPS

**Change Chart Data Series**
1. Make the chart active.
2. Click Chart Tools Design tab.
3. Click Switch Row/Column button.

Switch Row/Column

## Project 2a · Creating a Chart and Changing the Design

1. Open **ExcelC07Project02.xlsx** and then save the workbook and name it **ExcelL1_C7_P2**.
2. Create a bar chart by completing the following steps:
   a. Select cells A3 through B9.
   b. Click the Insert tab.
   c. Click the Bar button in the Charts group.
   d. Click the first option from the left in the *Cylinder* section (*Clustered Horizontal Cylinder*).
3. With the chart selected and the Chart Tools Design tab displayed, change the data series by clicking the Switch Row/Column button located in the Data group.

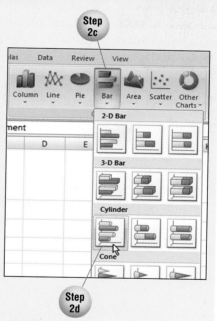

Step 2c

Step 2d

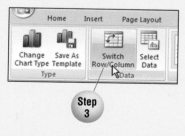

Step 3

4. Change the chart type and style by completing the following steps:
   a. Click the Change Chart Type button located in the Type group.
   b. At the Change Chart Type dialog box, click the *Column* option in the left panel.
   c. Click the *3-D Cylinder* option in the *Column* section (fourth chart style from the left in the second row of the *Column* section).
   d. Click OK to close the Change Chart Type dialog box.
5. Save **ExcelL1_C7_P2.xlsx**.

Step 4b

Step 4c

## Changing Chart Layout and Style

**HINT**

Click the Save As Template button in the Type group in the Chart Tools Design tab to save the formatting and layout of the current chart as a template you can use to create future charts.

The Chart Tools Design tab contains options for changing the chart layout and style. The Chart Layouts group in the tab contains preformatted chart layout options. Click the More button (contains an underline and a down-pointing arrow) to display a drop-down list of layout options. Hover the mouse pointer over an option and a ScreenTip displays with the option name. You can also scroll through layout options by clicking the up-pointing arrow or the down-pointing arrow located at the right side of the Chart Layouts group.

Use options in the Chart Styles group to apply a particular style of formatting to a chart. Click the More button located at the right side of the Chart Styles group to display a drop-down list with all the style options or click the up-pointing or down-pointing arrow at the right of the group to scroll through the options.

## Changing Chart Location

**QUICK STEPS**

**Change Chart Location**
1. Make the chart active.
2. Click Chart Tools Design tab.
3. Click Move Chart button.
4. Click *New Sheet* option.
5. Click OK.

Move Chart

Create a chart and the chart is inserted in the currently open worksheet as an embedded object. You can change the location of a chart with the Move Chart button in the Location group. Click this button and the Move Chart dialog box displays as shown in Figure 7.5. Click the *New sheet* option to move the chart to a new sheet within the workbook. Excel automatically names the sheet *Chart1*. Click the down-pointing arrow at the right side of the *Object in* option box and then click the desired location. The drop-down list will generally display the names of the worksheets within the open workbook. You can use the keyboard shortcut, F11, to create a default chart type (usually a column chart) and Excel automatically inserts the chart in a separate sheet.

If you have moved a chart to a separate sheet, you can move it back to the original sheet or move it to a different sheet within the workbook. To move a chart to a sheet, click the Move Chart button in the Location group in the Chart Tools Design tab. At the Move Chart dialog box, click the down-pointing arrow at the right side of the *Object in* option and then click the desired sheet at the drop-down list. Click OK and the chart is inserted in the specified sheet as an object that you can move, size, and format.

**Figure 7.5** Move Chart Dialog Box

Click the *New sheet* option to insert the chart in a separate sheet.

To move the chart to a different sheet, click this down-pointing arrow and then click the desired sheet.

> **Move Chart**
>
> Choose where you want the chart to be placed:
>
> ○ New sheet: | Chart1
>
> ● Object in: | Sheet1 ▾
>
> OK      Cancel

# Deleting a Chart

Delete a chart created in Excel by clicking once in the chart to select it and then pressing the Delete key. If you move a chart to a different worksheet in the workbook and then delete the chart, the chart is deleted but not the worksheet. To delete the chart as well as the worksheet, position the mouse pointer on the Chart1 tab, click the *right* mouse button, and then click *Delete* at the shortcut menu. At the message box telling you that selected sheets will be permanently deleted, click Delete.

**QUICK STEPS**

**Delete a Chart**
1. Click once in chart.
2. Press Delete key.
OR
1. Right-click chart tab.
2. Click Cut.

## Project 2b   Changing Chart Layout, Style, and Location

1. With **ExcelL1_C7_P2.xlsx** open, make sure the Chart Tools Design tab displays. (If it does not, make sure the chart is selected and then click the Chart Tools Design tab.)
2. Change the chart type by completing the following steps:
   a. Click the Change Chart Type button in the Type tab.
   b. Click *3-D Clustered Column* (fourth column style from the left in the top row).
   c. Click OK to close the dialog box.
3. Change the chart layout by clicking the *Layout 1* option in the Chart Layouts group (first option from the left). This layout inserts the words *Chart Title* at the top of the chart.
4. Change the chart style by clicking the More button located at the right side of the Chart Styles group and the clicking *Style 34* (second option from the left in the fifth row).

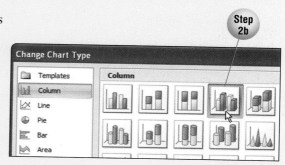

Step 2b

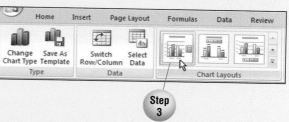

Step 3

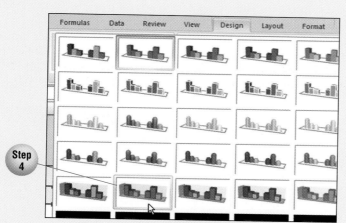

Step 4

5. Move the chart to a new location by completing the following steps:
   a. Click the Move Chart button in the Location group.
   b. At the Move Chart dialog box, click the *New sheet* option and then click OK. (The chart is inserted in a worksheet named *Chart1*.)
6. Save **ExcelL1_C7_P2.xlsx**.
7. Print the Chart1 worksheet containing the chart.
8. Move the chart from Chart1 to Sheet2 by completing the following steps:
   a. Make sure Chart1 is the active sheet and that the chart is selected (not an element in the chart).
   b. Make sure the Chart Tools Design tab is active.
   c. Click the Move Chart button in the Location group.
   d. At the Move Chart dialog box, click the down-pointing arrow at the right side of the *Object in* option and then click *Sheet2* at the drop-down list.

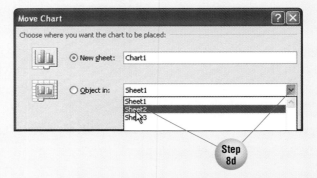

   e. Click OK.
9. Increase the size of the chart and maintain the proportions by completing the following steps:
   a. Click inside the chart but outside any chart elements. (This displays a light turquoise border around the chart.)
   b. Hold down the Shift key.
   c. Position the mouse pointer on the upper left border corner until the pointer turns into a double-headed arrow pointing diagonally.
   d. Hold down the left mouse button, drag left approximately one inch and then release the mouse button and then the Shift key.
   e. Display the worksheet in Print Preview to determine if the chart will print on one page. If the chart does not fit on the page, close Print Preview and then decrease the size of the chart until it fits on one page.
10. Change amounts in Sheet1 by completing the following steps:
    a. Click Sheet1.
    b. Make cell B4 active and then change the number from *$33,500* to *$12,750*.
    c. Make cell B9 active and then change the number from *$19,200* to *$5,600*.
    d. Make cell A2 active.
    e. Click the Sheet2 tab and notice that the chart displays the updated amounts.
11. Print the active worksheet (Sheet2).
12. Save and then close **ExcelL1_C7_P2.xlsx**.

roject **3** **Create a Population Comparison Bar Chart**

You will open a workbook containing population comparison data for Seattle and Portland and then create a bar chart with the data. You will also add chart labels and shapes and move, size, and delete labels/shapes.

# Changing the Chart Layout

Customize the layout of labels in a chart with options in the Chart Tools Layout tab as shown in Figure 7.6. With buttons in this tab, you can change the layout and/or insert additional chart labels. Certain chart labels are automatically inserted in a chart including a chart legend and labels for the x-axis and y-axis. Add chart labels to an existing chart with options in the Labels group in the Chart Tools Layout tab. In addition to chart labels, you can also insert shapes, pictures, and/or clip art and change the layout of 3-D chart labels.

**Figure 7.6** Chart Tools Layout Tab

# Inserting, Moving, and Deleting Chart Labels

Certain chart labels are automatically inserted in a chart, including a chart legend and labels for the x-axis and y-axis. The legend identifies which data series is represented by which data marker. Insert additional chart labels with options in the Labels group in the Chart Tools Layout tab. For example, click the Chart Title button in the Labels group and a drop-down list displays with options for inserting a chart title in a specific location in the chart.

You can move and/or size a chart label. To move a chart label, click the label to select it and then move the mouse pointer over the border line until the pointer turns into a four-headed arrow. Hold down the left mouse button, drag the label to the desired location, and then release the mouse button. To size a chart label, use the sizing handles that display around the selected label to increase or decrease the size. To delete a chart label, click the label to select it and then press the Delete key. You can also delete a label by right-clicking the label and then clicking *Delete* at the shortcut menu.

**QUICK STEPS**

**Add Chart Labels**
1. Make the chart active.
2. Click Chart Tools Layout tab.
3. Click desired chart labels button.
4. Choose desired option at drop-down list.

1. Open **ExcelC07Project03.xlsx** and then save the workbook and name it **ExcelL1_C7_P3**.
2. Create a Bar chart by completing the following steps:
   a. Select cells A2 through H4.
   b. Click the Insert tab.
   c. Click the Bar button in the Charts group and then click the *Clustered Horizontal Cylinder* option in the *Cylinder* section.
3. Change to a Line chart by completing the following steps:
   a. Click the Change Chart Type button in the Type group.
   b. At the Change Chart Type dialog box, click *Line* located at the left side of the dialog box.
   c. Click the *Line with Markers* option in the *Line* section (fourth option from the left).

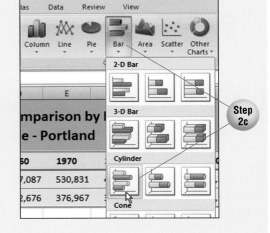

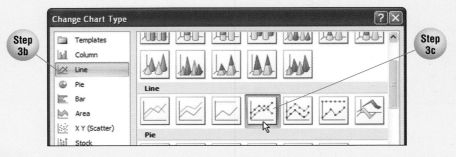

   d. Click OK to close the Change Chart Type dialog box.
4. Click the More button in the Chart Styles group in the Chart Tools Design tab and then click *Style 18* at the drop-down gallery (second option from left in the third row).

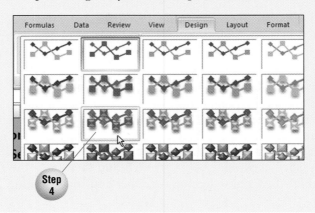

5. Change the layout of the chart by completing the following steps:
   a. Click the Chart Tools Layout tab.
   b. Click the Legend button in the Labels group.
   c. At the drop-down list, click the *Show Legend at Bottom* option.

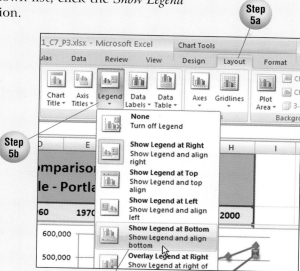

d. Click the Chart Title button in the Labels group.
e. At the drop-down list, click the *Above Chart* option.
f. Select the text *Chart Title* located in the chart title text box and then type **Population Comparison**.

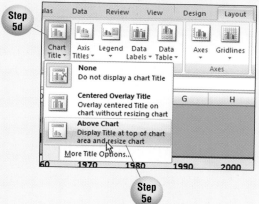

6. Insert an x-axis title by completing the following steps:
   a. Click the Axis Titles button, point to the *Primary Horizontal Axis Title* option at the drop-down list, and then click *Title Below Axis* at the side menu.

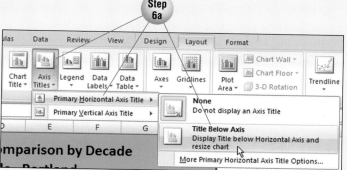

b. Select the text *Axis Title* located in the title text box and then type **Decades**.

7. Insert a y-axis title by completing the following steps:
   a. Click the Axis Titles button, point to the *Primary Vertical Axis Title* option at the drop-down list, and then click *Rotated Title* at the side menu. (This inserts a rotated title at the left side of the chart containing the text *Axis Title*).

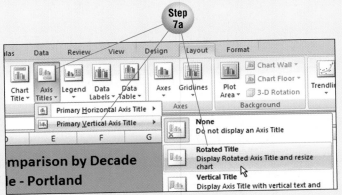

   b. Select the text *Axis Title* located in the axis title text box and then type Total Population.
8. Click the Gridlines button in the Axes group, point to *Primary Vertical Gridlines*, and then click the *Major & Minor Gridlines* option at the side menu.

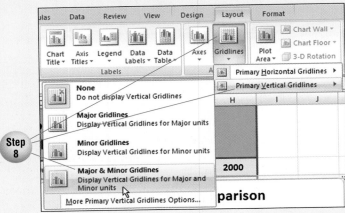

9. Click the Data Table button in the Labels group and then click the *Show Data Table* option. (This inserts cells toward the bottom of the chart containing cell data.)
10. Click the Lines button in the Analysis group and then click *Drop Lines* at the drop-down list.

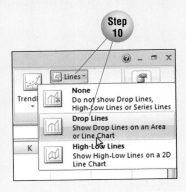

11. Drag the bottom right corner of the chart border to increase the size by approximately one inch.
12. Drag the chart so it is positioned below the data in cells but not overlapping the data.
13. Click the x-axis title (*Decades*) to select the title text box and then drag the box so it is positioned as shown below.

Step 13

14. Print only the selected chart.
15. Delete the horizontal axis title by clicking the axis title *Decades* and then pressing the Delete key.
16. Save **ExcelL1_C7_P3.xlsx**.

## Inserting Shapes

The Insert group in the Chart Tools Layout tab contains three buttons with options for inserting shapes or images in a chart. Click the Shapes button in the Insert group and a drop-down list displays with a variety of shape options as shown in Figure 7.7. Click the desired shape at the drop-down list and the mouse pointer turns into a thin, black plus symbol. Drag with this pointer symbol to create the shape in the chart. The shape is inserted in the chart with default formatting. You can change this formatting with options in the Drawing Tools Format tab. This tab contains many of the same options as the Chart Tools Format tab. For example, you can insert a shape, apply a shape or WordArt style, and arrange and size the shape.

## Moving, Sizing, and Deleting Shapes

Move, size, and delete shapes in the same manner as moving, sizing, and deleting chart elements. To move a shape, select the shape, position the mouse pointer over the border line until the pointer turns into a four-headed arrow. Hold down the left mouse button, drag the shape to the desired location, and then release the mouse button. To size a shape, select the shape and then use the sizing handles that display around the shape to increase or decrease the size. Delete a selected shape by clicking the Delete key or right-clicking the shape and then clicking *Cut* at the shortcut menu.

**Insert Shape**
1. Make the chart active.
2. Click Chart Tools Layout tab.
3. Click Shapes button.
4. Click desired shape at drop-down list.
5. Drag pointer symbol to create shape in chart.

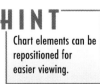
Shapes

**HINT**
Chart elements can be repositioned for easier viewing.

**Figure 7.7** Shapes Button Drop-down List

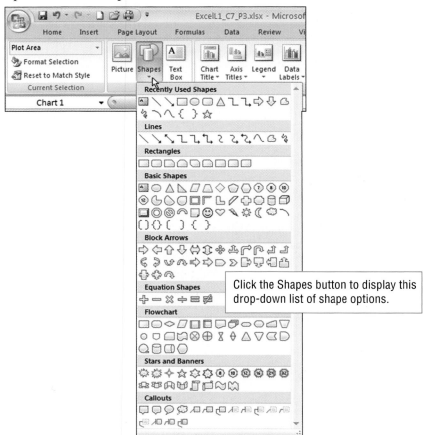

Click the Shapes button to display this drop-down list of shape options.

Project **3D** | **Inserting and Customizing a Shape**

1. With **ExcelL1_C7_P3.xlsx** open, make sure the Chart Tools Layout tab displays.
2. Create a shape similar to the shape shown in Figure 7.8. Begin by clicking the Shapes button in the Insert group.
3. Click the *Up Arrow Callout* shape in the *Block Arrows* section (last shape in the second row).
4. Drag in the chart to create the shape.

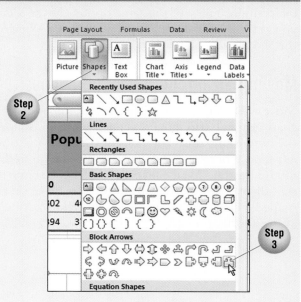

Step 2

Step 3

5. Click the More button in the Shapes Styles group (located at the right side of the three shapes) and then click *Subtle Effect - Accent 1* at the drop-down gallery.

6. With the shape selected, use the sizing handles around the shape to increase and/or decrease the size so it displays as shown in Figure 7.8.

7. Type **Largest Disparity** in the shape box, press Enter, and then type **(184,411)**.

8. Select the text you just typed and then complete the following steps:
   a. Click the Home tab.
   b. Click the Center button in the Alignment group.
   c. Click the Bold button in the Font group.
   d. Click the Font Size button arrow and then click *10*.

9. With the shape selected, drag the shape so it is positioned as shown in Figure 7.8.

10. Save **ExcelL1_C7_P3.xlsx**.

Figure 7.8 **Project 3b Chart**

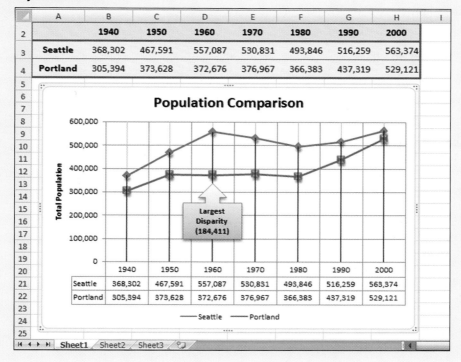

# Inserting Images

Click the Picture button in the Insert group in the Chart Tools Layout tab and the Insert Picture dialog box displays. If you have a picture or image file saved in a folder, navigate to the desired folder and then double-click the file name. This inserts the picture or image in the chart. Drag the picture or image to the desired position in the chart and use the sizing handles to change the size.

## Project 3c  Inserting a Picture in a Chart

1. With **ExcelL1_C7_P3.xlsx** open, make sure the chart is selected and then click the Chart Tools Layout tab.
2. Insert the company logo by completing the following steps:
   a. Click the Picture button in the Insert group.
   b. At the Insert Picture dialog box, navigate to the Excel2007L1C7 folder on your storage medium and then double-click *WELogo.jpg* in the list box.

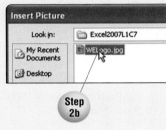

Step 2b

3. With the logo image inserted in the chart, use the sizing handles to decrease the size of the image and then move the image so it displays in the upper left corner of the chart area as shown in Figure 7.9.
4. Print only the selected chart.
5. Save and then close **ExcelL1_C7_P3.xlsx**.

## Figure 7.9  Project 3c Chart

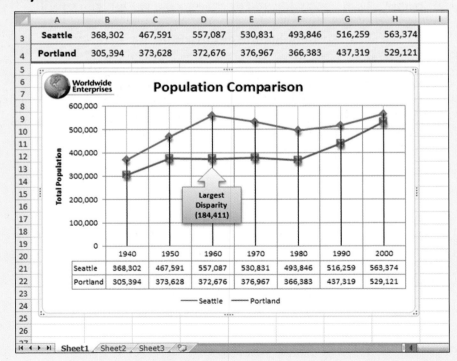

# Project 4 Create a Costs Percentage Pie Chart

You will open a workbook containing percentage of costs for company departments and then create a pie chart with the data. You will apply formatting to the chart and then move the chart to a new worksheet.

# Changing the Chart Formatting

Customize the format of the chart and chart elements with options in the Chart Tools Format tab as shown in Figure 7.10. With buttons in the Current Selection group you can identify a specific element in the chart and then apply formatting to that element. You can also click the Reset to Match Style button in the Current Selection group to return the formatting of the chart back to the original layout.

**Figure 7.10** Chart Tools Format Tab

With options in the Shape Styles group, you can apply formatting styles to specific elements in a chart. Identify the desired element either by clicking the element to select it or by clicking the down-pointing arrow at the right side of the Chart Elements button in the Current Selection group and then clicking the desired element name at the drop-down list. With the chart element specified, apply formatting by clicking a style button in the Shape Styles group. You can also apply a style from a drop-down gallery. Display this gallery by clicking the More button located at the right side of the shape styles. Click the up-pointing or the down-pointing arrow at the right of the shape styles to cycle through the available style options.

**HINT**
Apply a WordArt style to make numbers stand out.

Chart Area

Chart Elements

1. Open **ExcelC07Project04.xlsx** and then save the workbook and name it **ExcelL1_C7_P4**.

2. Create the pie chart as shown in Figure 7.11 by completing the following steps:
   a. Select cells A3 through B10.
   b. Click the Insert tab.
   c. Click the Pie button in the Charts group and then click the first pie option in the *2-D Pie* section.

3. Click the More button located at the right side of the Chart Styles group.

4. At the drop-down gallery, click the *Style 32* option (last option in the fourth row).

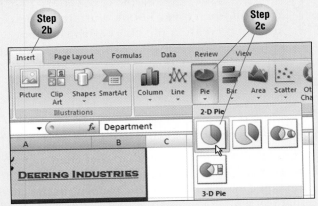

Step 2b
Step 2c

Step 4

5. Click the Chart Tools Layout tab.

6. Insert data labels by clicking the Data Labels button in the Labels group and then clicking *Outside End* at the drop-down list.

7. Format chart elements by completing the following steps:
   a. Click the Chart Tools Format tab.
   b. Click the down-pointing arrow at the right side of the Chart Elements button in the Current Selection group and then click *Legend* at the drop-down list.
   c. Click the More button in the Shape Styles group and then click the last option in the fourth row (*Subtle Effect - Accent 6*).
   d. Click the down-pointing arrow at the right side of the Chart Elements button in the Current Selection group and then click *Chart Title*.

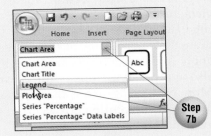

Step 7b

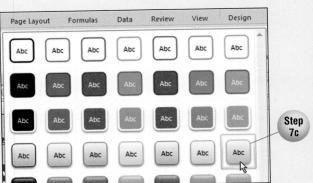

Step 7c

e. Click the More button at the right side of the WordArt styles in the WordArt Styles group and then click the *Gradient Fill - Accent 6, Inner Shadow* (second option from the left in the fourth row).

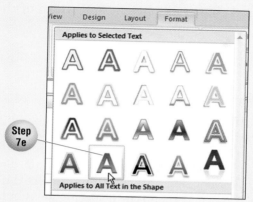

Step 7e

8. Insert the chart in a new sheet by completing the following steps:
   a. With the chart selected, click the Chart Tools Design tab.
   b. Click the Move Chart button in the Location group.
   c. At the Move Chart dialog box, click the *New sheet* option.
   d. Click OK.
9. Print only the worksheet containing the chart.
10. Save and then close **ExcelL1_C7_P4.xlsx**.

**Figure 7.11  Project 4**

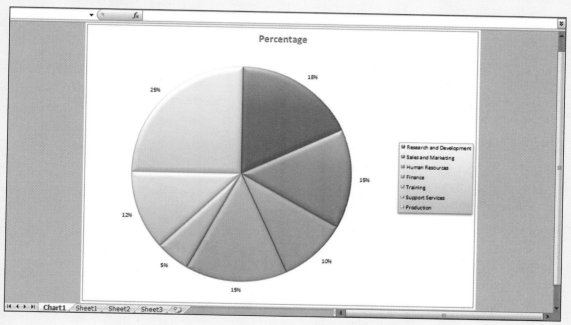

# $P$roject ⑤ Create a Regional Sales Column Chart

You will create a column chart using regional sales data, change the layout of the chart, apply formatting, and change the height and width of the chart.

**Change Chart Height and/or Width**
1. Make the chart active.
2. Click Chart Tools Format tab.
3. Insert desired height and/or width with *Shape Height* and/or *Shape Width* text boxes.

## Changing the Chart Height and Width

You can size a chart by selecting the chart and then dragging a sizing handle. You can also size a chart to specific measurements with the *Shape Height* and *Shape Width* measurement boxes in the Size group in the Chart Tools Format tab. Change the height or width by clicking the up- or down-pointing arrows that display at the right side of the button or select the current measurement in the measurement box and then type a specific measurement.

## $P$roject ⑤ | Changing the Height and Width of a Chart

1. Open **ExcelC07Project05.xlsx**.
2. Save the workbook with Save As and name it **ExcelL1_C7_P5**.
3. Create a Column chart by completing the following steps:
   a. Select cells A3 through B8.
   b. Click the Insert tab.
   c. Click the Column button in the Charts group.
   d. Click the *3-D Clustered Column* option (first option in the *3-D Column* section).
   e. Click the Switch Row/Column button located in the Data group to change the data series.
   f. Click the *Layout 1* option in the Chart Layouts group (first option from the left in the group).
   g. Select the text *Chart Title* and then type Northeast Regional Sales.
   h. Click the More button located at the right side of the Chart Styles group and then click *Style 32* at the drop-down gallery (last option in fourth row).

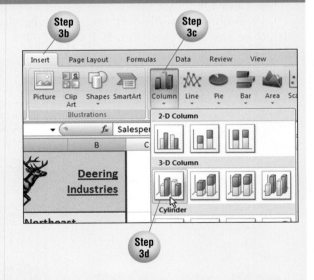

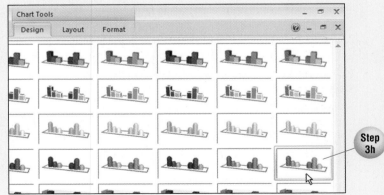

4. Change a series color by completing the following steps:
   a. Click the Chart Tools Format tab.
   b. Click the down-pointing arrow at the right side of the Chart Elements button and then click *Series "Newman, Jared"* at the drop-down list.

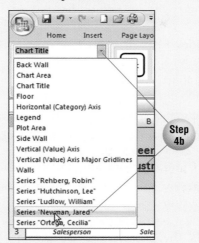

Step
4b

   c. Click the Shape Fill button arrow in the Shape Styles group and then click the dark red color *Red, Accent 2, Darker 25%*.

Step
4c

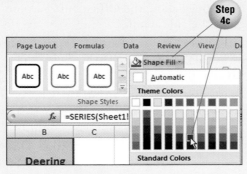

5. Change a series color by completing the following steps:
   a. With the Chart Tools Format tab active, click the down-pointing arrow at the right side of the Chart Elements button and then click *Series "Hutchinson, Lee"* at the drop-down list.
   b. Click the Shape Fill button arrow in the Shape Styles group and then click the dark green color *Olive Green, Accent 3, Darker 25%*.
6. Drag the chart down below the cells containing data.
7. Click the Chart Tools Format tab.
8. Click in the *Shape Height* measurement box in the Size group and then type 3.8.
9. Click the up-pointing arrow at the right side of the *Shape Width* measurement box in the Size group until 5.5 displays in the text box.
10. Print only the chart.
11. Save and then close **ExcelL1_C7_P5.xlsx**.

Step
8

Step
9

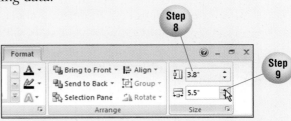

# CHAPTER summary

- Create a chart with data in an Excel worksheet. A chart is a visual presentation of data.
- Excel provides 11 basic chart types: Area, Bar, Bubble, Column, Doughnut, Line, Pyramid, Radar, Stock, Surface, and XY (Scatter).
- To create a chart, select cells containing data you want to chart, click the Insert tab, and then click the desired chart button in the Charts group.
- A chart you create is inserted in the same worksheet as the selected cells.
- You can increase or decrease the size of a chart by positioning the mouse pointer on the four dots located in the middle of each border line or the three dots at each corner, and then dragging to the desired size.
- Move a chart by positioning the mouse pointer on the chart border until it turns into a four-headed arrow and then dragging with the mouse.
- Data in cells used to create the chart are linked to the chart. If you change the data in cells, the chart reflects the changes.
- Print by selecting the chart and then displaying the Print dialog box. At the Print dialog box, make sure *Selected Chart* is selected and then click OK.
- Preview a chart by clicking the Office button, pointing to *Print*, and then clicking *Print Preview* at the side menu.
- When you insert a chart in a worksheet, the Chart Tools Design tab is active. Use options in this tab to change the chart type, specify a different layout or style, and change the location of the chart.
- Choose a chart style with buttons in the Charts group in the Insert tab or at the Change Chart Type dialog box. Display this dialog box by clicking the Change Chart Type button in the Type group in the Chart Tools Design tab.
- The Chart Layouts group in the Chart Tools Design tab contains preformatted chart layout options. Use options in the Chart Styles group to apply a particular style of formatting to a chart.
- By default, a chart is inserted in the active worksheet. You can move the chart to a new sheet within the workbook with the *New sheet* option at the Move Chart dialog box. Display this dialog box by clicking the Move Chart button in the Location group in the Chart Tools Design tab.
- To delete a chart in a worksheet, click the chart to select it, and then press the Delete key. To delete a chart created in a separate sheet, position the mouse pointer on the chart tab, click the *right* mouse button, and then click Delete.
- Use options in the Chart Tools Layout tab to change the layout and/or insert additional chart labels, shapes, pictures, or clip art images.
- Insert additional chart labels with options in the Labels group in the Chart Tools Layout tab.
- Use buttons in the Insert group in the Chart Tools Layout tab to insert shapes, pictures, or text boxes.
- To move a chart label, click the label to select it and then drag the label with the mouse. To delete a label, click the label and then press the Delete key.

- Use options in the Chart Tools Format tab to customize the format of the chart and chart elements.
- Change the chart size by dragging the chart sizing handles or by entering a measurement in the *Shape Height* and *Shape Width* measurement boxes in the Size group in the Chart Tools Format tab.

# COMMANDS review

| FEATURE | RIBBON TAB, GROUP | BUTTON, OPTION | KEYBOARD SHORTCUT |
|---------|-------------------|----------------|-------------------|
| Default chart in worksheet | | | Alt + F1 |
| Default chart in separate sheet | | | F11 |
| Change Chart Type dialog box | Chart Tools Design, Type | | |
| Move Chart dialog box | Chart Tools Design, Location | | |
| Shapes button drop-down list | Chart Tools Layout, Insert | | |
| Insert Picture dialog box | Chart Tools Layout, Insert | | |

# CONCEPTS check

## Test Your Knowledge

**Completion:** In the space provided at the right, indicate the correct term, symbol, or command.

1. This is the keyboard shortcut to create a chart with the default chart type.

   _____

2. This type of chart shows proportions and relationships of parts to the whole.

   _____

3. The Charts group contains buttons for creating charts and is located in this tab.

   _____

4. When you create a chart, the chart is inserted in this location by default.

   _____

5. Select a chart in a worksheet, display the Print dialog box, and this option is automatically selected in the *Print what* section.

   _____

6. When Excel creates a chart, the data in the first row (except the first cell) is used to create this.

   _____

7. Click the Picture button in the Chart Tools Layout tab and this dialog box displays.

   _____

8. Click this option at the Move Chart dialog box to move the chart to a separate sheet.

   _____

9. Use buttons in the Insert group in this tab to insert shapes, pictures, or text boxes.

   _____

10. Change the chart size by entering measurements in these text boxes in the Size group in the Chart Tools Format tab.

    _____

# SKILLS check

## Demonstrate Your Proficiency

**Assessment**

## 1 CREATE A COMPANY SALES COLUMN CHART

1. Open **ExcelC07Assessment01.xlsx** and then save the workbook and name it **ExcelL1_C7_A1**.
2. Select cells A3 through C15 and then create a Column chart with the following specifications:
   a. Choose the *3-D Clustered Column* chart at the Chart button drop-down list.
   b. At the Chart Tools Design tab, click the *Layout 3* option in the Chart Layouts group.
   c. Change the chart style to *Style 26*.
   d. Select the text *Chart Title* and then type Company Sales.
   e. Move the location of the chart to a new sheet.
3. Print only the worksheet containing the chart.
4. Save and then close **ExcelL1_C7_A1.xlsx**.

**Assessment**

## 2 CREATE QUARTERLY DOMESTIC AND FOREIGN SALES BAR CHART

1. Open **ExcelC07Assessment02.xlsx** and then save the workbook and name it **ExcelL1_C7_A2**.
2. Select cells A3 through E5 and then create a Bar chart with the following specifications:
   a. Click the *Clustered Bar in 3-D* option at the Bar button drop-down list.
   b. At the Chart Tools Design tab choose the *Layout 2* option in the Chart Layouts group.
   c. Choose the *Style 23* option in the Chart Styles group.
   d. Select the text *Chart Title*, type Quarterly Sales, and then click in the chart but outside any chart elements.
   e. Display the Chart Tools Layout tab and then insert primary vertical minor gridlines. (Do this with the Gridlines button.)
   f. Display the Chart Tools Format tab and then apply to the chart the *Subtle Effect - Accent 3* option in the Shape Styles group.
   g. Select the *Domestic* series (using the Chart Elements button) and then apply a purple fill (Purple, Accent 4, Darker 25%) using the Shape Fill button in the Shape Styles group.
   h. Select the Foreign series and then apply a dark aqua fill (Aqua, Accent 5, Darker 25%) using the Shape Fill button in the Shape Styles group.
   i. Select the chart title and then apply the *Gradient Fill - Accent 6, Inner Shadow* option with the WordArt Styles button.
   j. Increase the height of the chart to 4 inches and the width to 6 inches.
   k. Move the chart below the cells containing data and make sure the chart fits on the page with the data. (**Hint: Display the worksheet in Print Preview.**)
3. Print only the worksheet.
4. Save and then close **ExcelL1_C7_A2.xlsx**.

## 3 CREATE AND FORMAT A CORPORATE SALES COLUMN CHART

1. Open **ExcelC07Assessment03.xlsx** and then save the workbook and name it **ExcelL1_C7_A3**.
2. Create a column chart and format the chart so it displays as shown in Figure 7.12.
3. Print only the worksheet containing the chart.
4. Save and then close **ExcelL1_C7_A3.xlsx**.

**Figure 7.12 Assessment 3**

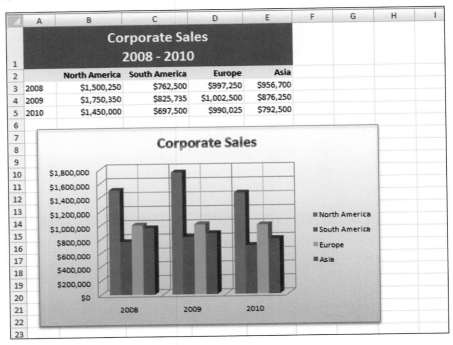

## 4 CREATE A FUNDS ALLOCATIONS PIE CHART

1. At a blank worksheet, create a worksheet with the following data:

Fund Allocations

| Fund | Percentage |
|---|---|
| Annuities | 23% |
| Stocks | 42% |
| Bonds | 15% |
| Money Market | 20% |

2. Using the data above, create a pie chart as a separate worksheet with the following specifications:
   a. Create a title for the pie chart.
   b. Add data labels to the chart.
   c. Add any other enhancements that will improve the visual presentation of the data.

3. Save the workbook and name it **ExcelL1_C7_A4**.
4. Print only the sheet containing the chart.
5. Close **ExcelL1_C7_A4.xlsx**.

## Assessment

# 5 CREATE AN ACTUAL AND PROJECTED SALES CHART

1. Open **ExcelC07Assessment05.xlsx** and then save the workbook and name it **ExcelL1_C7_A5**.
2. Look at the data in the worksheet and then create a chart to represent the data. Add a title to the chart and add any other enhancements to improve the visual display of the chart.
3. Save the workbook and then print the chart.
4. Close **ExcelL1_C7_A5.xlsx**.

## Assessment

# 6 CREATE AN ATTENDANCE SCATTER CHART

1. Use Excel's Help feature to learn more about chart types and then create a worksheet with the data shown in Figure 7.13. Create a scatter chart from the data in a separate sheet and create an appropriate title for the chart. Use the DATE function to enter the dates in the first column and enter the current year for the date.
2. Save the completed workbook and name it **ExcelL1_C7_A6**.
3. Print both sheets of the workbook (the sheet containing the data in cells and the sheet containing the chart).
4. Close **ExcelL1_C7_A6.xlsx**.

**Figure 7.13  Assessment 6**

### HIGHLAND PARK ATTENDANCE

| Week | Projected | Actual |
|---|---|---|
| July 1 | 35,000 | 42,678 |
| July 8 | 33,000 | 41,065 |
| July 15 | 30,000 | 34,742 |
| July 22 | 28,000 | 29,781 |
| July 29 | 28,000 | 26,208 |

# CASE study
## *Apply Your Skills*

Part
1

You are an administrator for Dollar Wise Financial Services and you need to prepare charts indicating home loan and commercial loan amounts for the past year. Use the information below to prepare two charts in Excel. You determine the type and style of chart and the layout and formatting of the chart. Insert a shape in the Commercial Loans chart that contains the text *All-time High* and points to the second quarter amount (*$6,785,250*).

Home Loans
1$^{st}$ Qtr. = $2,675,025
2$^{nd}$ Qtr. = $3,125,750
3$^{rd}$ Qtr. = $1,975,425
4$^{th}$ Qtr. = $875,650

Commercial Loans
1$^{st}$ Qtr. = $5,750,980
2$^{nd}$ Qtr. = $6,785,250
3$^{rd}$ Qtr. = $4,890,625
4$^{th}$ Qtr. = $2,975,900

Save the workbook containing the two charts and name it **ExcelL1_C7_CS_P1**. Print only the two charts and then close **ExcelL1_C7_CS_P1.xlsx**.

Part
2

You need to present information on the budget for the company. You have the dollar amounts and need to convert the amounts to a percentage of the entire budget. Use the information below to calculate the percentage of the budget for each item and then create a pie chart with the information. You determine the chart style, layout, and formatting.

Total Budget: $6,000,000

| | | |
|---|---|---|
| Building Costs | = | $720,000 |
| Salaries | = | $2,340,000 |
| Benefits | = | $480,000 |
| Advertising | = | $840,000 |
| Marketing | = | $600,000 |
| Client Expenses | = | $480,000 |
| Equipment | = | $420,000 |
| Supplies | = | $120,000 |

Save the workbook containing the pie chart and name it **ExcelL1_C7_CS_P2**. Print only the chart and then close **ExcelL1_C7_CS_P2.xlsx**.

One of your clients owns a number of stocks and you like to prepare a daily chart of the stocks' high, low, and close price. Use the Help feature to learn about stock charts and then create a stock chart with the following information (the company stock symbols are fictitious):

|       | IDE     | POE     | QRR     |
|-------|---------|---------|---------|
| High  | $23.75  | $18.55  | $34.30  |
| Low   | $18.45  | $15.00  | $31.70  |
| Close | $19.65  | $17.30  | $33.50  |

Save the workbook containing the stock chart and name it **ExcelL1_C7_CS_P3**. Print only the chart and then close **ExcelL1_C7_CS_P3.xlsx**.

You need to prepare information on mortgage rates for a community presentation. You decide to include the information on mortgage rates in a chart for easy viewing. Use the Internet to search for historical data on the national average for mortgage rates. Determine the average mortgage rate for a 30-year FRM (fixed-rate mortgage) for each January and July beginning with the year 2005 and continuing to the current year. Also include the current average rate. Use this information to create the chart. Save the workbook and name it **ExcelL1_C7_CS_P4**. Print only the chart and then close **ExcelL1_C7_CS_P4.xlsx**.

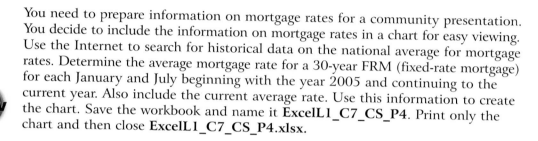

You will be presenting information at an upcoming meeting on the information in the previous challenges for which you created a chart. You decide to include the charts in a PowerPoint presentation so you can display the charts on a screen while presenting. Open PowerPoint and then open the presentation named **ExcelC07Presentation.pptx**. Copy the chart you created in Part 1 to the second slide, copy the chart for Part 2 into the third slide, and then copy the chart for Part 4 into the fourth slide. Increase the size of the charts to better fill the slides. Save the presentation and name it **PPL1_C7_CS_P5**. Print the three slides containing charts. Close **PPL1_C7_CS_P5.pptx**.

# Adding Visual Interest to Workbooks

## PERFORMANCE OBJECTIVES

Upon successful completion of Chapter 8, you will be able to:

- Save a workbook as a Web page
- Create and modify a hyperlink
- Insert symbols and special characters
- Insert, size, move, and format a clip art image
- Draw, format, and copy shapes
- Insert, size, move, and format a picture image
- Insert, format, and type text in a text box
- Insert a picture image as a watermark
- Insert and format SmartArt diagrams
- Insert and format WordArt

**Tutorial 8.1**
Using Web-Based Features
**Tutorial 8.2**
Adding Graphic Elements

You can save an Excel workbook as a Web page and then view it in a Web browser. You can also insert hyperlinks in a workbook that connect to a Web site or to another workbook. Microsoft Excel includes a variety of features that you can use to enhance the visual appeal of a workbook. Some methods for adding visual appeal that you will learn in this chapter include inserting and modifying clip art images, shapes, pictures, text boxes, SmartArt, and WordArt.

*Note: Before beginning computer projects, copy to your storage medium the Excel2007L1C8 subfolder from the Excel2007L1 folder on the CD that accompanies this textbook and make Excel2007L1C8 the active folder.*

## Project ① Save a Travel Workbook as a Web Page

You will open a travel destinations workbook and then save the workbook as a single page Web page. You will also create hyperlinks in the Web page that link you to sites on the Internet.

# Creating a Web Page

You can save an Excel workbook as a Web page and then view it in the default Web browser software. You can also insert hyperlinks in the Web page to jump to other workbooks or sites on the Internet with additional information pertaining to the workbook content.

**Save Workbook as
Single File Web Page**
1. Click Office button,
   *Save As.*
2. Change *Save as type*
   option to *Single File
   Web Page (*.mht;
   *.mhtml).*
3. Type name in *File name*
   text box.
4. Click Save button.

## Saving a Workbook as a Web Page

You can save the entire workbook, a worksheet, or a single item in a worksheet. Save a workbook as a Web page by changing the *Save as type* option at the Save As dialog box. You can save the data in the workbook as a single Web page or as a conventional Web page. If you choose the *Single File Web Page (*.mht; *.mhtml)* option, all data in the workbook such as graphics and other supplemental data is saved in a single Web file. If you choose the *Web Page (*.htm; *.html)* option, Excel creates additional files for supplemental data and saves the files in a subfolder.

When you choose a Web page option at the *Save as type* drop-down list, the Save As dialog box changes as shown in Figure 8.1. At this dialog box, specify which part of the workbook you want published and if you want to add a title to the Web page. Click the Publish button and the Publish as Web Page dialog box appears as shown in Figure 8.2. This dialog box contains advanced options for publishing a Web page.

**HINT**

Web pages are files containing special formatting codes written in HTML (Hypertext Markup Language).

**Figure 8.1** Save As Dialog Box

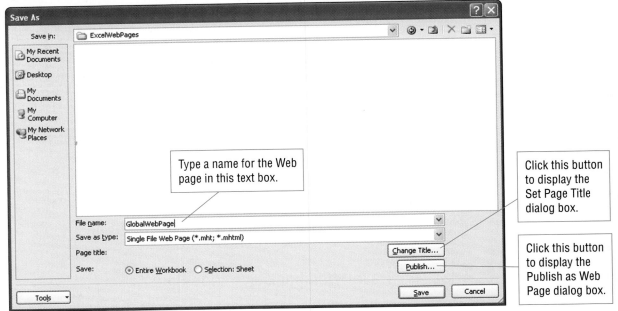

Type a name for the Web page in this text box.

Click this button to display the Set Page Title dialog box.

Click this button to display the Publish as Web Page dialog box.

**Figure 8.2** Publish as Web Page Dialog Box

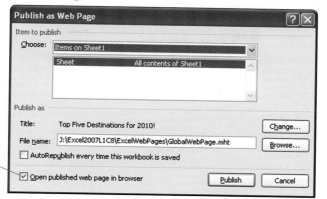

Insert a check mark in this check box if you want the worksheet to automatically display in the default Web browser.

## Project 1a  Saving a Workbook as a Web Page

1. Create a folder named *ExcelWebPages* within the Excel2007L1C8 folder on your storage medium.
2. Open **ExcelC08Project01.xlsx** and then save the workbook with Save As and name it **ExcelL1_C8_P1**.
3. Click the Office button and then click *Save As*.
4. At the Save As dialog box, double-click *ExcelWebPages* in the list box.
5. Click the down-pointing arrow at the right side of the *Save as type* list box and then click *Single File Web Page (*.mht; *.mhtml)* at the drop-down list.
6. Select the text in the *File name* text box and then type **GlobalWebPage**.
7. Click the Change Title button.

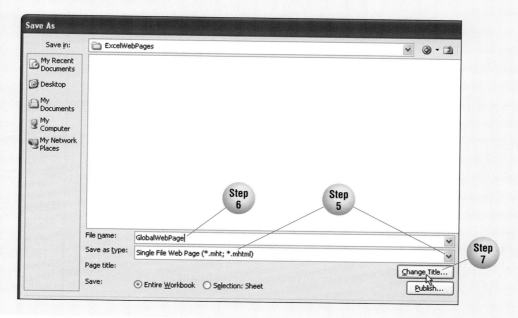

8. At the Set Page Title dialog box, type Top Five Destinations for 2010! in the *Page title* text box and then click OK.
9. At the Save As dialog box, click the Publish button.
10. At the Publish as Web Page dialog box, click the *Open published web page in browser* option to insert a check mark.
11. Click the Publish button. (This automatically displays the worksheet in your default Web browser.)

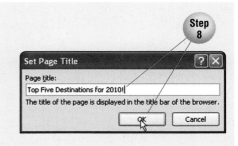

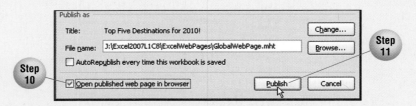

12. After viewing your Web page, close the Web page browser.
13. Save and then close **ExcelL1_C8_P1.xlsx**.

## Opening a Workbook in Internet Explorer

Another method for opening a workbook saved as a Web page is to open Internet Explorer, click the File option on the Menu bar, and then click *Open* at the drop-down list. At the Open dialog box, click the Browse button. At the Microsoft Internet Explorer dialog box, navigate to the folder containing the saved Web page and then double-click the Web page file.

## Project 1b  Opening the Web Page in Internet Explorer

1. Open Internet Explorer.
2. Click File in the Menu bar and then click *Open* at the drop-down list. (If the Menu bar is not visible, click the Tools button and then click *Menu Bar*.)
3. At the Open dialog box, click the Browse button.
4. At the Microsoft Internet Explorer dialog box, navigate to the ExcelWebPages folder and then double-click *GlobalWebPage.mht*.
5. Click OK at the Open dialog box.
6. After viewing the Web page in Internet Explorer, close **GlobalWebPage.mht**.
7. Close Internet Explorer.

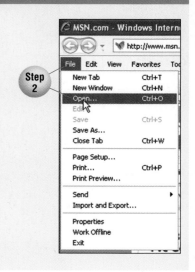

# Creating Hyperlinks

A hyperlink is text or an object that you click to go to a different file, an HTML page on the Internet, or an HTML page on an intranet. Create a hyperlink in an Excel worksheet by typing the address of an existing Web page such as *www.emcp.com*. By default, the automatic formatting of hyperlinks is turned on and the Web address is formatted as a hyperlink (text is underlined and the color changes to blue). (You can turn off the automatic formatting of hyperlinks at the AutoCorrect dialog box. Display this dialog box by clicking the Office button, clicking the Excel Options button, and then clicking *Proofing* in the left panel of the Excel Options dialog box. Click the AutoCorrect Options button to display the AutoCorrect dialog box. At this dialog box, click the AutoFormat As You Type tab and then remove the check mark from the *Internet and network paths with hyperlinks* check box.)

You can also create a customized hyperlink by clicking the desired cell in a workbook, clicking the Insert tab, and then clicking the Hyperlink button in the Links group. At the Insert Hyperlink dialog box shown in Figure 8.3, type the file name or Web site address in the *Address* text box and then click OK. You can also use the *Look in* option to browse to the desired folder and file and then double-click the file name. To link to the specified file or Web page, position the mouse pointer (white plus symbol) on the hyperlink until the mouse pointer displays as a hand and then click the left mouse button.

**QUICK STEPS**

**Create Hyperlink**
1. Click desired cell.
2. Click Insert tab.
3. Click Hyperlink button.
4. Type Web address or file name.
5. Click OK.

## HINT
Ctrl + K is the keyboard shortcut to display the Insert Hyperlink dialog box.

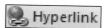

**Figure 8.3** Insert Hyperlink Dialog Box

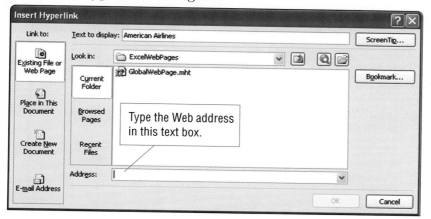

## Project 1c | Creating Hyperlinks

1. Display the Open dialog box and then double-click *GlobalWebPage.mht*.
2. Create a hyperlink so that clicking *American Airlines* displays the American Airlines Web page by completing the following steps:
   a. Click cell G10 (this is the cell containing *American Airlines*).
   b. Click the Insert tab.
   c. Click the Hyperlink button in the Links group.

d. At the Insert Hyperlink dialog box, type www.aa.com in the *Address* text box. (The *http://* is automatically inserted in the address.)

e. Click OK. (This changes the color of the *American Airlines* text and also adds underlining to the text.)

f. Repeat Steps 2c through 2e in cell G13.

3. Complete steps similar to those in Step 2 to create a hyperlink from *Northwest Airlines* to the URL *www.nwa.com* in cells G11 and G12.

4. Complete steps similar to those in Step 2 to create a hyperlink from *Air Canada* to the URL *www.aircanada.ca* in cell G14.

5. Click the Save button on the Quick Access toolbar. At the compatibility dialog box, click Yes.

6. Jump to the hyperlinked sites by completing the following steps:

a. Make sure you are connected to the Internet.

b. Position the mouse pointer on one of the <u>American Airlines</u> hyperlinks until the mouse pointer turns into a hand and then click the left mouse button.

c. When the American Airlines Web page displays, scroll through the page, and then click a hyperlink that interests you.

d. After looking at this next page, click File and then *Exit*.

e. At the **GlobalWebPage.mht** workbook, click the <u>Air Canada</u> hyperlink.

f. At the Air Canada Web page, click the hyperlink to see their site displayed in English.

g. After viewing the Air Canada page, click File and then *Exit*.

h. At the **GlobalWebPage.mht** workbook, click one of the <u>Northwest</u> hyperlinks.

i. At the Northwest Airlines Web page, click a link that interests you.

j. After viewing the Northwest Airlines page, click File and then *Exit*.

7. Change the orientation to landscape.

8. Save **GlobalWebPage.mht** and click Yes at the compatibility dialog box.

9. Print and then close **GlobalWebPage.mht**.

---

# Project 2 Insert a Hyperlink in a Company Sales Workbook

You will open a company sales workbook and then create a hyperlink that links you to another Excel workbook.

**Edit Hyperlink**
1. Right-click hyperlink.
2. Click *Edit Hyperlink*.
3. Make desired changes.
4. Click OK.

## Creating a Hyperlink to an Excel Worksheet

In Project 1c, you created hyperlinks from an Excel workbook to sites on the Web. You can also insert hyperlinks in a workbook that link to other Excel workbooks or files in other programs in the Office suite. In Project 2, you will create a hyperlink that displays another Excel workbook.

You can modify or change hyperlink text or the hyperlink destination. To do this, right-click the hyperlink, and then click *Edit Hyperlink*. At the Edit Hyperlink dialog box, make any desired changes and then close the dialog box. The Edit Hyperlink dialog box contains the same options as the Insert Hyperlink dialog box.

**HINT**
Deactivate a hyperlink by right-clicking the hyperlink and then clicking *Remove Hyperlink* at the shortcut menu.

## Project ② Creating and Modifying a Hyperlink to an Excel Worksheet

1. Open **ExcelC08Project02.xlsx**.
2. Save the workbook with Save As and name it **ExcelL1_C8_P2**.
3. Create a hyperlink that will display **ExcelC08Sales.xlsx** by completing the following steps:
   a. Make cell A12 active.
   b. Type Semiannual Sales and then press Enter.
   c. Click cell A12 to make it the active cell.
   d. Click the Insert tab.
   e. Click the Hyperlink button in the Links group.
   f. At the Insert Hyperlink dialog box, click the down-pointing arrow at the right side of the *Look in* option and then navigate to the Excel2007L1C8 folder on your storage medium.
   g. Double-click **ExcelC08Sales.xlsx**. (This closes the Insert Hyperlink dialog box and displays the *Semiannual Sales* text as a hyperlink in the workbook.)
4. Display **ExcelC08Sales.xlsx** by clicking the Semiannual Sales hyperlink.
5. Close **ExcelC08Sales.xlsx**.
6. Print **ExcelL1_C8_P2.xlsx**.
7. Modify the hyperlink text in **ExcelL1_C8_P2.xlsx** by completing the following steps:
   a. Position the mouse pointer on the Semiannual Sales hyperlink, click the *right* mouse button, and then click *Edit Hyperlink*.
   b. At the Edit Hyperlink dialog box, select the text *Semiannual Sales* in the *Text to display* text box and then type Customer Sales Analysis.
   c. Click OK.
8. Click the Customer Sales Analysis hyperlink.
9. Close **ExcelC08Sales.xlsx**.
10. Save, print, and then close **ExcelL1_C8_P2.xlsx**.

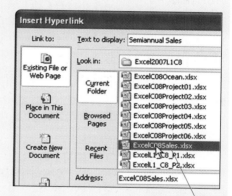

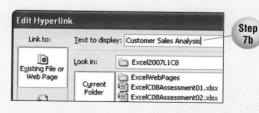

# Project ③ Insert a Clip Art Image and Shapes in a Financial Analysis Workbook

You will open a financial analysis workbook and then insert, move, size, and format a clip art image in the workbook. You will also insert an arrow shape, type and format text in the shape, and then copy the shape.

**QUICK STEPS**

**Insert Symbol**
1. Click in desired cell.
2. Click the Insert tab.
3. Click Symbol button.
4. Double-click desired symbol.
5. Click Close.

**Insert Special Character**
1. Click in desired cell.
2. Click Insert tab.
3. Click Symbol button.
4. Click Special Characters tab.
5. Double-click desired special character.
6. Click Close.

## Inserting Symbols and Special Characters

You can use the Symbol button in the Insert tab to insert special symbols in a worksheet. Click the Symbol button in the Text group in the Insert tab and the Symbol dialog box displays as shown in Figure 8.4. At the Symbol dialog box, double-click the desired symbol, and then click Close; or click the desired symbol, click the Insert button, and then click Close. At the Symbol dialog box with the Symbols tab selected, you can change the font with the *Font* option. When you change the font, different symbols display in the dialog box. Click the Special Characters tab at the Symbol dialog box and a list of special characters displays along with keyboard shortcuts to create the special character.

**HINT**

You can increase and/or decrease the size of the Symbol dialog box by positioning the mouse pointer on the lower right corner until the pointer displays as a two-headed arrow and then dragging with the mouse.

Ω
Symbol

**Figure 8.4** Symbol Dialog Box with Symbols Tab Selected

Use the *Font* option to select the desired set of characters.

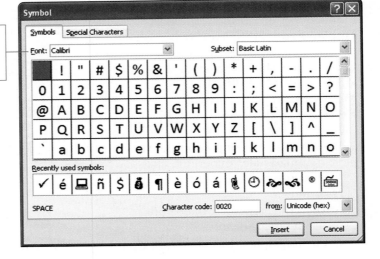

1. Open **ExcelC08Project03.xlsx** and then save the workbook and name it **ExcelL1_C8_P3**.
2. Insert a symbol by completing the following steps:
   a. Double-click cell A2.
   b. Delete the *e* that displays at the end of *Qualite*.
   c. With the insertion point positioned immediately right of the *t* in *Qualit*, click the Insert tab.
   d. Click the Symbol button in the Text group.
   e. At the Symbol dialog box, scroll down the list box and then click the *é* symbol (ninth symbol from the left in the eleventh row).
   f. Click the Insert button and then click the Close button.

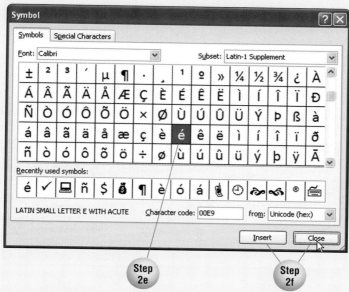

Step 2e

Step 2f

3. Insert a special character by completing the following steps:
   a. With cell A2 selected and in Edit mode, move the insertion point so it is positioned immediately right of *Group*.
   b. Click the Symbol button in the Text group.
   c. At the Symbol dialog box, click the Special Characters tab.
   d. Double-click the ® symbol (tenth option from the top).
   e. Click the Close button.

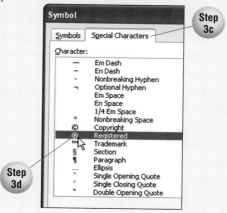

Step 3c

Step 3d

4. Insert a symbol by completing the following steps:
  a. With cell A2 selected and in Edit mode, move the insertion point so it is positioned immediately left of the *Q* in *Qualité*.
  b. Click the Symbol button in the Text group.
  c. At the Symbol dialog box, click the down-pointing arrow at the right side of the *Font* option box and then click *Wingdings* at the drop-down list. (You will need to scroll down the list to display this option.)
  d. Click the ❖ symbol (seventh option from the left in the sixth row).
  e. Click the Insert button and then click the Close button.

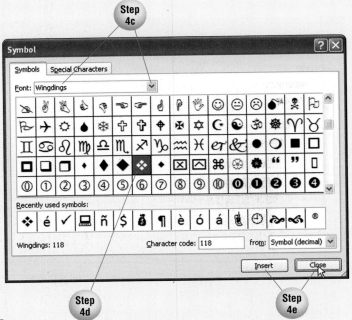

Step 4c

Step 4d

Step 4e

5. Click in cell A3.
6. Save **ExcelL1_C8_P3.xlsx**.

# Inserting an Image

You can insert an image such as a picture or clip art in an Excel workbook with buttons in the Illustrations group in the Insert tab. Click the Picture button to display the Insert Picture dialog box where you can specify the desired picture file, or click the Clip Art button and then choose from a variety of images available at the Clip Art task pane. When you insert a picture or a clip art image in a worksheet, the Picture Tools Format Tab displays as shown in Figure 8.5.

**Figure 8.5** Picture Tools Format Tab

## Customizing and Formatting an Image

With options in the Adjust group in the Picture Tools Format tab you can recolor the picture or clip art image and change the brightness and contrast of the image. You can also reset the picture or clip art back to its original color or change to a different image. Use the Compress Pictures button to compress the size of the image file. Apply predesigned styles with options in the Picture Styles group. Use options in the Arrange group to position the image on the page, specify text wrapping in relation to the image, align the image with other objects in the worksheet, and rotate the image. Use the Crop button in the Size group to remove any unnecessary parts of the image and specify the image size with the *Shape Height* and *Shape Width* measurement boxes.

## Sizing and Moving an Image

You can change the size of an image with the *Shape Height* and *Shape Width* measurement boxes in the Size group in the Picture Tools Format tab or with the sizing handles that display around the selected image. To change size with a sizing handle, position the mouse pointer on a sizing handle until the pointer turns into a double-headed arrow and then hold down the left mouse button. Drag the sizing handle in or out to decrease or increase the size of the image and then release the mouse button. Use the middle sizing handles at the left or right side of the image to make the image wider or thinner. Use the middle sizing handles at the top or bottom of the image to make the image taller or shorter. Use the sizing handles at the corners of the image to change both the width and height at the same time. Hold down the Shift key while dragging a sizing handle to maintain the proportions of the image.

Move an image by positioning the mouse pointer on the image border until the pointer displays with a four-headed arrow attached. Hold down the left mouse button, drag the image to the desired position, and then release the mouse button. Rotate the image by positioning the mouse pointer on the green, round rotation handle until the pointer displays as a circular arrow. Hold down the left mouse button, drag in the desired direction, and then release the mouse button.

> **HINT**
> You can use arrow keys on the keyboard to move a selected object. To move the image in small increments, hold down the Ctrl key while pressing one of the arrow keys.

## Inserting a Clip Art Image

Microsoft Office includes a gallery of media images you can insert in a worksheet such as clip art, photographs, and movie images, as well as sound clips. To insert an image in a worksheet, click the Insert tab and then click the Clip Art button in the Illustrations group. This displays the Clip Art task pane at the right side of the screen as shown in Figure 8.6.

> **QUICK STEPS**
>
> **Insert Clip Art Image**
> 1. Click Insert tab.
> 2. Click Clip Art button.
> 3. Type desired word or topic in *Search for* text box.
> 4. Click Go button or press Enter.
> 5. Click desired image.

**Figure 8.6** Clip Art Task Pane

Type in this text box the word or topic for which you are searching.

Use these options to specify where to search and the media types.

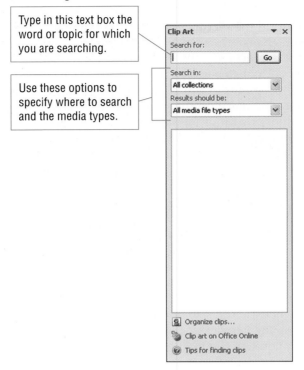

To view all picture, sound, and motion files, make sure the *Search for* text box in the Clip Art task pane does not contain any text and then click the Go button. When the desired image is visible, click the image to insert it in the worksheet. Use buttons in the Picture Tools Format tab shown in Figure 8.5 to format and customize the clip art image.

By default (unless it has been customized), the Clip Art task pane looks for all media images and sound clips found in all locations. You can narrow the search to specific locations and to specific images. The *Search in* option at the Clip Art task pane has a default setting of *All collections*. This can be changed to *My Collections*, *Office Collections*, and *Web Collections*. The *Results should be* option has a default setting of *Selected media file types*. Click the down-pointing arrow at the right side of this option to display media types. To search for a specific media type, remove the check mark before all options at the drop-down list but the desired type. For example, if you are searching only for photograph images, remove the check mark before Clip Art, Movies, and Sound.

If you are searching for specific images, click in the *Search for* text box, type the desired topic, and then click the Go button. For example, if you want to find images related to business, click in the *Search for* text box, type business, and then click the Go button. Clip art images related to *business* display in the viewing area of the task pane. If you are connected to the Internet, Word will search for images at the Office Online Web site matching the topic.

## Project (3b) Inserting an Image

1. With **ExcelL1_C8_P3.xlsx** open, insert a clip art image by completing the following steps:
   a. Click the Insert tab.
   b. Click the Clip Art button in the Illustrations group.
   c. At the Clip Art task pane, click the down-pointing arrow at the right side of the *Results should be* option box and then click the *Photographs*, *Movies*, and *Sounds* check boxes at the drop-down list to remove the check marks. Click in the task pane to remove the drop-down list.

   d. Select any text that displays in the *Search for* text box, type stock market, and then press Enter.
   e. Click the image in the list box as shown at the right. (If you are not connected to the Internet and this image is not available, click a similar image.)
   f. Click the down-pointing at the right side of the *Results should be* option box and then click the *Photographs*, *Movies*, and *Sounds* check boxes at the drop-down list to insert check marks.
   g. Close the Clip Art task pane by clicking the Close button (contains an X) located in the upper right corner of the task pane.
2. Size and move the clip art image by completing the following steps:
   a. Click in the *Shape Width* measurement box, type 2.52, and then press Enter.

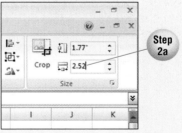

b. Position the mouse pointer on a border of the clip art image until the mouse pointer displays with a four-headed arrow attached. Hold down the left mouse button, drag the upper left corner of the clip art image so it is positioned in the upper left corner of cell A1, and then release the mouse button.

c. Change the height of the clip art image by positioning the mouse pointer on the bottom middle sizing handle until the mouse pointer displays as a double-headed arrow pointing up and down. Hold down the left mouse button, drag up until the bottom of the clip art image is aligned with the bottom of cell A1, and then release the mouse button.

3. Click outside the clip art image to deselect it.

4. Save **ExcelL1_C8_P3.xlsx**.

## Inserting a Shape

**Insert Shape**
1. Click Insert tab.
2. Click Shapes button.
3. Click desired shape at drop-down list.
4. Drag in worksheet to create shape.

In Chapter 7, you learned how to insert shapes in a chart. With the Shapes button in the Illustrations group in the Insert tab, you can also insert shapes in a worksheet. Use the Shapes button in the Insert tab to draw shapes in a worksheet including lines, basic shapes, block arrows, flow chart shapes, callouts, stars, and banners. Click a shape and the mouse pointer displays as crosshairs (plus sign). Position the crosshairs where you want the shape to begin, hold down the left mouse button, drag to create the shape, and then release the mouse button. This inserts the shape in the worksheet and also displays the Drawing Tools Format tab shown in Figure 8.7. Use buttons in this tab to change the shape, apply a style to the shape, arrange the shape, and change the size of the shape.

If you choose a shape in the *Lines* section of the drop-down list, the shape you draw is considered a *line drawing*. If you choose an option in the other sections of the drop-down list, the shape you draw is considered an *enclosed object*. When drawing an enclosed object, you can maintain the proportions of the shape by holding down the Shift key while dragging with the mouse to create the shape. You can type text in an enclosed object and then use buttons in the WordArt Styles group to format the text.

**Figure 8.7** Drawing Tools Format Tab

# Copying Shapes

If you have drawn or inserted a shape, you may want to copy it to other locations in the worksheet. To copy a shape, select the shape and then click the Copy button in the Clipboard group in the Home tab. Position the insertion point at the location where you want the copied image and then click the Paste button. You can also copy a selected shape by holding down the Ctrl key while dragging the shape to the desired location.

**QUICK STEPS**

**Copy Shape**
1. Click in shape to select it.
2. Click Copy button.
3. Position insertion point in desired location.
4. Click Paste button.
OR
1. Click in shape to select.
2. Hold down Ctrl key.
3. Drag shape to desired location.

## Project 3c  Drawing Arrow Shapes

1. With **ExcelL1_C8_P3.xlsx** open, create the tallest arrow shown in Figure 8.8 by completing the following steps:
   a. Click the Insert tab.
   b. Click the Shapes button and then click the *Up Arrow* shape (third option from the left in the top row of the *Block Arrows* section).
   c. Position the mouse pointer (displays as a thin, black cross) near the upper left corner of cell D1, hold down the left mouse button, drag down and to the right to create the shape as shown below, and then release the mouse button.

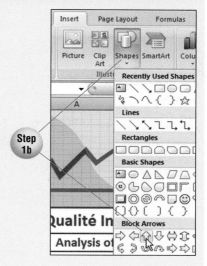

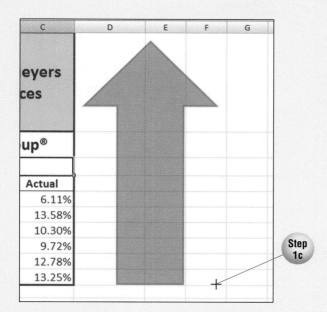

   d. Click in the *Shape Height* measurement box and then type 3.9.
   e. Click in the *Shape Width* measurement box, type 2.2, and then press Enter.

f. If necessary, drag the arrow so it is positioned as shown in Figure 8.8. (To drag the arrow, position the mouse pointer on the border of the selected arrow until the pointer turns into a four-headed arrow, hold down the left mouse button, drag the arrow to the desired position, and then release the mouse button.)

g. Click the More button at the right side of the shapes in the Shape Styles group and then click the *Intense Effect - Accent 1* option (second option from the left in the bottom row).

h. Click the Shape Effects button in the Shape Styles group, point to *Glow*, and then click the last option in the bottom row (*Accent color 6, 18 pt glow*).

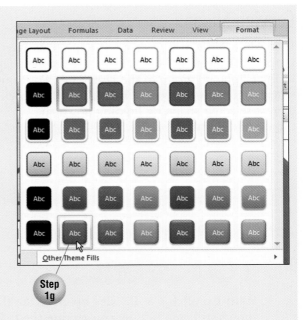

Step 1g

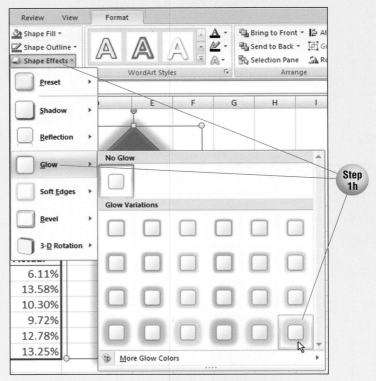

Step 1h

2. Insert text in the arrow shape by completing the following steps:
   a. With the arrow shape selected, type **McGuire Mutual Shares 5.33%**.
   b. Select the text you just typed (*McGuire Mutual Shares 5.33%*).

c. Click the More button at the right side of the styles in the WordArt Styles group and then click the second option from the left in the second row (*Fill - None, Outline - Accent 6, Glow - Accent 6*).

d. Click the Home tab.

e. Click the Top Align button in the Alignment group.

3. With the arrow selected, copy the arrow by completing the following steps:

a. Hold down the Ctrl key.

b. Position the mouse pointer on the arrow border until the pointer displays with a square box and plus symbol attached.

c. Hold down the left mouse button and drag to the right so the outline of the arrow is positioned at the right side of the existing arrow.

d. Release the mouse button and then release the Ctrl key.

4. Format the second arrow by completing the following steps:

a. With the second arrow selected, click the Drawing Tools Format tab.

b. Click in the *Shape Height* measurement box and then type 2.

c. Click in the *Shape Width* measurement box, type 1.7, and then press Enter

d. Select the text *McGuire Mutual Shares 5.33%* and then type **SR Linus Fund 0.22%**.

e. Drag the arrow so it is positioned as shown in Figure 8.8.

5. Change the orientation to landscape. (Make sure the cells containing data and the arrows will print on the same page.)

6. Save, print, and then close **ExcelL1_C8_P3.xlsx**.

**Figure 8.8  Project 3c**

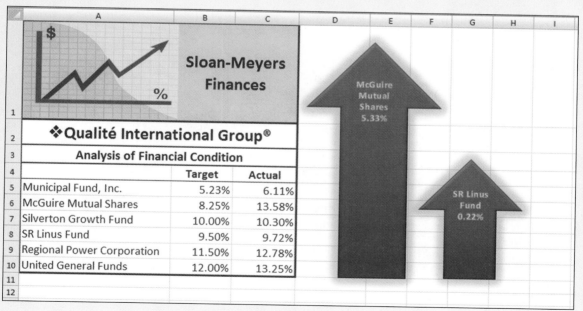

roject 4  **Insert a Picture and Text Box in a Division Sales Workbook**

You will open a division sales workbook and then insert, move, and size a picture.
You will also insert a text box and then format the text.

**Insert Picture**
1. Click Insert tab.
2. Click Picture button.
3. Navigate to desired folder.
4. Double-click desired picture.

## Inserting a Picture

To insert a picture in a worksheet, click the Insert tab and then click the Picture button in the Illustrations group. At the Insert Picture dialog box, navigate to the folder containing the desired picture and then double-click the picture. Use buttons in the Picture Tools Format tab to format and customize the picture.

Project 4a  **Inserting and Customizing a Picture**

1. Open **ExcelC08Project04.xlsx** and then save the workbook and name it **ExcelL1_C8_P4**.
2. Make the following changes to the bird clip art image:
   a. Click the bird clip art image to select it.
   b. Click the Picture Tools Format tab.
   c. Click the Rotate button in the Arrange group and then click *Flip Horizontal* at the drop-down list.

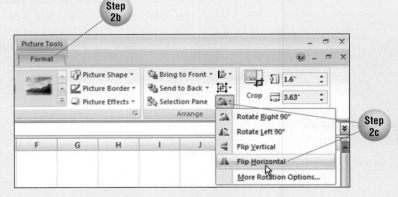

   d. Click the Recolor button in the Adjust group and then click the *Black and White* option in the *Color Modes* section.

e. Click in the *Shape Height* measurement box and then type 0.6.

f. Click in the *Shape Width* measurement box, type 1.3, and then press Enter.

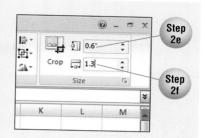

Step 2e

Step 2f

3. Insert and format a picture by completing the following steps:

a. Click in cell A1 outside of the bird image.

b. Click the Insert tab.

c. Click the Picture button in the Illustrations group.

d. At the Insert Picture dialog box, navigate to the Excel2007L1C8 folder on your storage medium and then double-click *Ocean.jpg*.

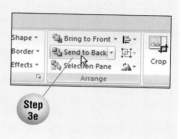

e. With the picture selected, click the Send to Back button in the Arrange group in the Picture Tools Format tab.

f. Use the sizing handles that display around the picture image to move and size it so it fills cell A1 as shown in Figure 8.9.

g. Click the bird clip art image and then drag the image so it is positioned as shown in Figure 8.9.

Step 3e

4. Save **ExcelL1_C8_P4.xlsx**.

## Drawing and Formatting a Text Box

Use the Text Box button in the Insert tab to draw a text box in a worksheet. To draw a text box, click the Insert tab and then click the Text Box button in the Text group. This causes the mouse pointer to display as a thin, down-pointing arrow. Position the arrow in the worksheet and then drag to create the text box. When a text box is selected, the Drawing Tools Format tab displays with options for customizing the text box.

Click a text box to select it and a dashed border and sizing handles display around the text box. If you want to delete the text box, click the text box border again to change the dashed border lines to solid border lines and then press the Delete key.

**QUICK STEPS**

**Draw Text Box**
1. Click Insert tab.
2. Click Text Box button.
3. Drag in worksheet to create text box.

A
Text Box

## Project 4b  Inserting and Formatting a Text Box

1. With **ExcelL1_C8_P4.xlsx** open, draw a text box by completing the following steps:

a. Click the Insert tab.

b. Click the Text Box button in the Text group.

c. Drag in cell A1 to draw a text box the approximate size and shape shown at the right.

Step 1c

2. Format the text box by completing the
following steps:
   a. Make sure the Drawing Tools Format tab
   is active.
   b. Click the Shape Fill button arrow in the
   Shape Styles group and then click *No Fill*
   at the drop-down gallery.
   c. Click the Shape Outline button arrow in
   the Shape Styles group and then click *No
   Outline* at the drop-down gallery.
3. Insert text in the text box by completing the
following steps:
   a. With the text box selected, click the
   Home tab.

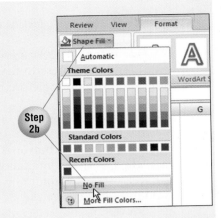

Step 2b

   b. Click the Font button arrow and then click *Lucida Calligraphy* at the drop-down gallery.
   (You will need to scroll down the gallery to display this font.)
   c. Click the Font Size button arrow and then click *32* at the drop-down gallery.
   d. Click the Font Color button arrow and then click *White, Background 1* (first option in the
   first row in the *Theme Colors* section).
   e. Type Seabird Productions.
4. Move the text box so the text is positioned in cell A1 as shown in Figure 8.9. If necessary,
move the bird clip art image. (To move the bird image, you may need to move the text box
so you can select the image. Move the text box back to the desired location after moving
the bird image.)
5. Save, print, and then close **ExcelL1_C8_P4.xlsx**.

**Figure 8.9** **Projects 4a and 4b**

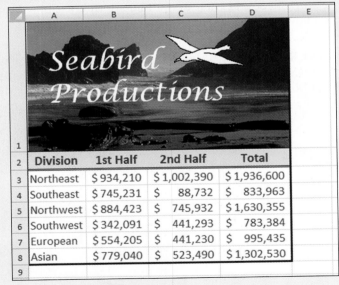

| | Division | 1st Half | 2nd Half | Total |
|---|---|---|---|---|
| 3 | Northeast | $ 934,210 | $ 1,002,390 | $ 1,936,600 |
| 4 | Southeast | $ 745,231 | $ 88,732 | $ 833,963 |
| 5 | Northwest | $ 884,423 | $ 745,932 | $ 1,630,355 |
| 6 | Southwest | $ 342,091 | $ 441,293 | $ 783,384 |
| 7 | European | $ 554,205 | $ 441,230 | $ 995,435 |
| 8 | Asian | $ 779,040 | $ 523,490 | $ 1,302,530 |

roject **5** **Insert a Watermark in an Equipment Usage Workbook**

You will open an equipment usage report workbook and then insert a picture watermark that prints on both pages of the worksheet.

# Inserting a Picture as a Watermark

A watermark is a lightened image that displays behind data in a file. You can create a watermark in a Word document but the watermark functionality is not available in Excel. You can, however, insert a picture in a header or footer and then resize and format the picture to display behind each page of the worksheet.

To create a picture watermark in a worksheet, click the Insert tab and then click the Header & Footer button in the Text group. With the worksheet in Print Layout view, click the Picture button in the Header & Footer Elements group in the Header & Footer Tools Design tab. At the Insert Picture dialog box, navigate to the desired folder and then double-click the desired picture. This inserts &[Picture] in the header. Resize and format the picture by clicking the Format Picture button in the Header & Footer Elements group. Use options at the Format Picture dialog box with the Size tab selected to specify the size of the picture and use options in the dialog box with the Picture tab selected to specify brightness and contrast.

**Insert Picture as Watermark**
1. Click Insert tab.
2. Click Header & Footer button.
3. Click Picture button.
4. Navigate to desired folder.
5. Double-click desired picture.

Project **5** **Inserting a Picture as a Watermark**

1. Open **ExcelC08Project05.xlsx** and then save the workbook and name it **ExcelL1_C8_P5**.
2. Insert a picture as a watermark by completing the following steps:
   a. Click the Insert tab.
   b. Click the Header & Footer button in the Text group.
   c. Click the Picture button in the Header & Footer Elements group in the Header & Footer Tools Design tab.
   d. At the Insert Picture dialog box, navigate to the Excel2007L1C8 folder on your storage medium and then double-click **Olympics.jpg**.
   e. Click the Format Picture button in the Header & Footer Elements group.
   f. At the Format Picture dialog box with the Size tab selected, click the *Lock aspect ratio* in the *Scale* section to remove the check mark.
   g. Select the current measurement in the *Height* measurement box in the *Size and rotate* section and then type 10.
   h. Select the current measurement in the *Width* measurement box in the *Size and rotate* section and then type 7.5.

Step 2c

Step 2g

Step 2h

Step 2f

i. Click the Picture tab.
j. At the Format Picture dialog box with the Picture tab selected, select the current percentage number in the *Brightness* option box in the *Image control* section and then type 75.
k. Select the current percentage number in the *Contrast* option box and then type 25.
l. Click OK to close the Format Picture dialog box.
3. Click in the worksheet.
4. Display the worksheet in Print Preview to view how the image will print on page 1 and page 2 and then close Print Preview.
5. Save, print, and then close **ExcelL1_C8_P5.xlsx**. (If you are printing on a laser printer, the text may not print in the worksheet. Check with your instructor before printing this worksheet.)

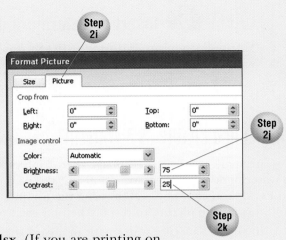

# Project 6  Insert and Format Diagrams in a Company Sales Workbook

You will open a workbook that contains two company sales worksheets. You will insert and format a cycle diagram in one worksheet and insert and format a relationship diagram in the other. You will also create and format WordArt text.

## Inserting a SmartArt Diagram

Excel includes the SmartArt feature you can use to insert diagrams and organizational charts in a worksheet. SmartArt offers a variety of predesigned diagrams and organizational charts that are available at the Choose a SmartArt Graphic dialog box shown in Figure 8.10. Display this dialog box by clicking the Insert tab and then clicking the SmartArt button in the Illustrations group. At the dialog box, *All* is selected in the left panel and all available predesigned diagrams display in the middle panel. Use the scroll bar at the right side of the middle panel to scroll down the list of diagram choices. Click a diagram in the middle panel and the name of the diagram displays in the right panel along with a description of the diagram type. SmartArt includes diagrams for presenting a list of data; showing data processes, cycles, and relationships; and presenting data in a matrix or pyramid. Double-click a diagram in the middle panel of the dialog box and the diagram is inserted in the worksheet.

SmartArt

**Figure 8.10** Choose a SmartArt Graphic Dialog Box

Double-click the desired SmartArt graphic in this panel.

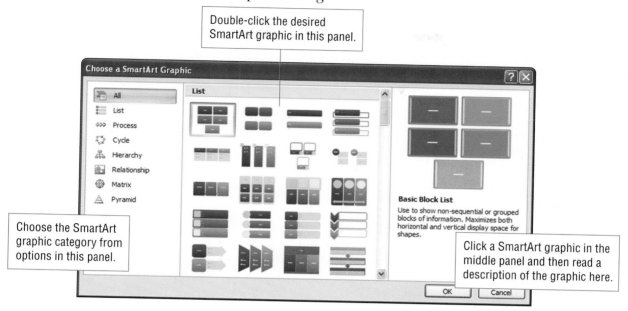

Choose the SmartArt graphic category from options in this panel.

Click a SmartArt graphic in the middle panel and then read a description of the graphic here.

# Entering Data in a Diagram

Some diagrams are designed to include text. You can type text in a diagram by selecting the shape and then typing text in the shape or you can display a text pane and then type text in the pane. Display the text pane by clicking the Text Pane button in the Create Graphic group in the SmartArt Tools Design tab. Turn off the display of the pane by clicking the Text Pane button or by clicking the Close button that displays in the upper right corner of the text pane.

# Sizing, Moving, and Deleting a Diagram

Increase or decrease the size of a diagram by dragging the diagram border. Increase or decrease the width of the diagram by positioning the mouse pointer on the set of four dots that displays in the middle of the left and right borders until the pointer turns into a left- and right-pointing arrow, hold down the left mouse button and then drag the border to the desired size. Increase or decrease the height of the diagram in a similar manner using the set of four dots that displays in the middle of the top and bottom borders. To increase or decrease both the height and the width of the diagram, drag one of the sets of three dots that displays in each corner of the border.

To move a diagram, select the diagram and then position the mouse pointer on the diagram border until the pointer turns into a four-headed arrow. Hold down the left mouse button, drag the diagram to the desired position, and then release the mouse button. Delete a diagram by selecting the diagram and then pressing the Delete key.

1. Open **ExcelC08Project06.xlsx** and then save the workbook and name it **ExcelL1_C8_P6**.
2. Create the diagram shown in Figure 8.11. To begin, click the Insert tab.
3. Click the SmartArt button in the Illustrations group.
4. At the Choose a SmartArt Graphic dialog box, click *Cycle* in the left panel.
5. Double-click *Radial Cycle* as shown at the right.
6. If the text pane is not open, click the Text Pane button in the Create Graphic group. (The text pane will display at the left side of the diagram.)
7. With the insertion point positioned after the top bullet in the text pane, type **Evergreen Products**.
8. Click the *[Text]* box below *Evergreen Products* and then type **Seattle**.
9. Click the next *[Text]* box and then type **Olympia**.
10. Click the next *[Text]* box and then type **Portland**.
11. Click the next *[Text]* box and then type **Spokane**.
12. Click the Text Pane button to turn off the display of the text pane.
13. Drag the diagram so it is positioned as shown in Figure 8.11. To drag the diagram, position the mouse pointer on the diagram border until the pointer turns into a four-headed arrow. Hold down the left mouse button, drag the diagram to the desired position, and then release the mouse button.
14. Increase or decrease the size of the diagram so it displays as shown in Figure 8.11. Use the sets of dots on the diagram border to drag the border to the desired size.
15. Save **ExcelL1_C8_P6.xlsx**.

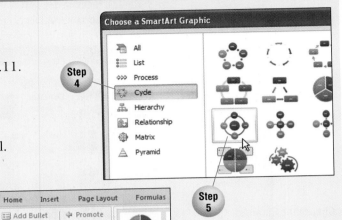

Step 4

Step 5

Step 6

Steps 7–11

## HINT

To restore the SmartArt default layout and color, click the Reset Graphic button in the Reset group in the SmartArt Tools Design tab.

## Changing the Diagram Design

When you double-click a diagram at the dialog box, the diagram is inserted in the worksheet and the SmartArt Tools Design tab is active. With options and buttons in this tab, you can add objects, change the diagram layout, apply a style to the diagram, and reset the diagram back to the original formatting.

1. With **ExcelL1_C8_P6.xlsx** open, make sure the SmartArt Tools Design tab is active and the *Spokane* circle shape is selected.
2. Click the Right to Left button in the Create Graphic group. (This switches *Olympia* and *Spokane*.)
3. Click the More button located at the right side of the SmartArt Styles group and then click the *Polished* option at the drop-down list (first option from the left in the top row of the *3-D* section).

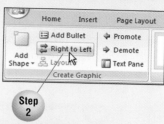

**Step 2**

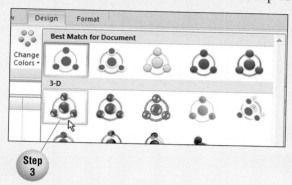

**Step 3**

4. Click the Change Colors button in the SmartArt Styles group and then click the fourth option from the left in the *Accent 3* section (*Gradient Loop - Accent 3*).
5. Click outside the diagram to deselect it.
6. Change the orientation to landscape. (Make sure the diagram fits on the first page.)
7. Save **ExcelC1_C8_P6.xlsx** and then print the Total Sales worksheet.

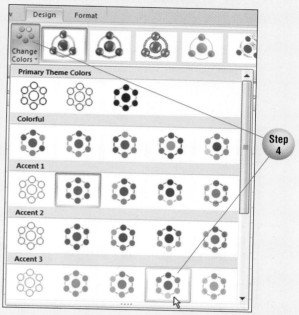

**Step 4**

**Figure 8.11** **Projects 6a and 6b**

|   | A | B | C | D | E | F | G | H | I |
|---|---|---|---|---|---|---|---|---|---|
| 1 | **Evergreen Products** | | | | | | | | |
| 2 | 2010 Company Sales | | | | | | | | |
| 3 | Division | First Half | Second Half | Total Sales | | | | | |
| 4 | Seattle | $1,250,360 | $1,345,200 | $2,595,560 | | | | | |
| 5 | Spokane | $905,250 | $987,550 | $1,892,800 | | | | | |
| 6 | Portland | $1,125,000 | $1,200,500 | $2,325,500 | | | | | |
| 7 | Olympia | $705,610 | $789,450 | $1,495,060 | | | | | |
| 8 | Total | $3,986,220 | $4,322,700 | $8,308,920 | | | | | |
| 9 | | | | | | | | | |

## Changing the Diagram Formatting

Click the SmartArt Tools Format tab and options display for formatting a diagram. Use buttons in this tab to insert and customize shapes; apply a shape quick style; customize shapes; insert WordArt quick styles; and specify the position, alignment, rotation, wrapping style, height, and width of the diagram.

**Project 6c** — Changing the Diagram Formatting

1. With **ExcelL1_C8_P6.xlsx** open, click the Seattle Sales worksheet tab.
2. Create the diagram shown in Figure 8.12. To begin, click the Insert tab and then click the SmartArt button in the Illustrations group.
3. At the Choose a SmartArt Graphic dialog box, click *Relationship* in the left panel and then double-click *Gear* in the middle panel.

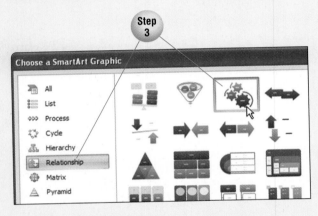

4. Click *[Text]* that appears in the bottom gear and then type **Quality Products**.
5. Click *[Text]* that appears in the left gear and then type **Customized Plans**.
6. Click *[Text]* that appears in the top gear and then type **Exemplary Service**.
7. Click the More button that displays at the right side of the SmartArt Styles group and then click the *Inset* option (second option from the left in the top row of the *3-D* section).
8. Click the Change Colors button in the SmartArt Styles group and then click the third option from the left in the *Accent 3* section (*Gradient Range - Accent 3*).
9. Click the SmartArt Tools Format tab.

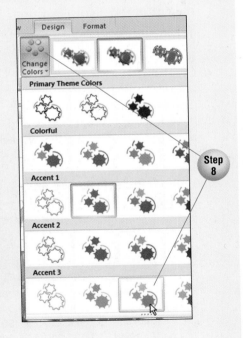

10. Click the Size button located at the right side of the tab.
11. Click in the *Height* text box and then type 3.75.
12. Click in the *Width* text box, type 5.25, and then press Enter.

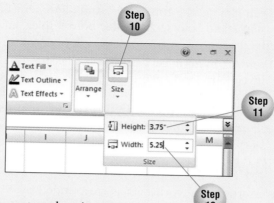

13. Click the bottom gear to select it.
14. Click the Shape Fill button arrow in the Shape Styles group and then click the bottom dark green color (*Olive Green, Accent 3, Darker 50%*) that displays in the *Theme Colors* section.
15. Click the top gear to select it.
16. Click the Shape Fill button arrow and then click the dark green color (*Olive Green, Accent 3, Darker 25%*) that displays in the *Theme Colors* section.
17. Change the orientation to landscape.
18. Move the diagram so it fits on the first page and displays as shown in Figure 8.12.
19. Save **ExcelL1_C8_P6.xlsx** and then print the Seattle Sales worksheet.

**Figure 8.12 Project 6c**

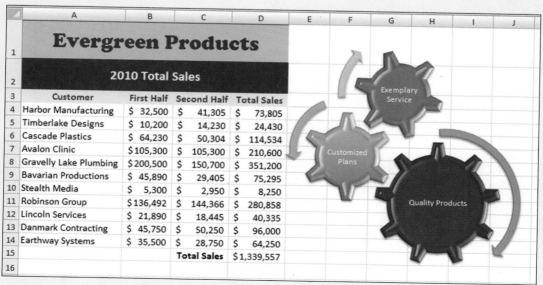

# Creating WordArt

**Create WordArt**
1. Click Insert tab.
2. Click WordArt button.
3. Click desired WordArt style at drop-down list.
4. Type desired text.

With the WordArt application, you can distort or modify text to conform to a variety of shapes. This is useful for creating company logos and headings. With WordArt, you can change the font, style, and alignment of text. You can also use different fill patterns and colors, customize border lines, and add shadow and three-dimensional effects.

To insert WordArt in an Excel worksheet, click the Insert tab, click the WordArt button in the Text group, and then click the desired option at the drop-down list. This displays *Your Text Here* inserted in the worksheet in the WordArt option you selected at the gallery. Type the desired text and then use the buttons on the Drawing Tools Format tab to format the WordArt.

## HINT

To remove WordArt style from text and retain the text, click the More button in the WordArt Styles group in the Drawing Tools Format tab and then click *Clear WordArt*.

## Sizing and Moving WordArt

WordArt text inserted in a worksheet is surrounded by white sizing handles. Use the white sizing handles to change the height and width of the WordArt text. To move WordArt text, position the arrow pointer on the border of the WordArt until the pointer displays with a four-headed arrow attached. Hold down the left mouse button, drag the outline of the WordArt text box to the desired position, and then release the mouse button. When you change the shape of the WordArt text, the WordArt border displays with a purple diamond shape. Use this shape to change the slant of the WordArt text.

Project 6d  **Inserting and Formatting WordArt**

1. With **ExcelL1_C8_P6.xlsx** open, click the Total Sales worksheet tab.
2. Make cell A1 active and then press the Delete key. (This removes the text from the cell.)
3. Increase the height of row 1 to 136.50.
4. Click the Insert tab.
5. Click the WordArt button in the Text group and then click the last option in the top row (*Fill - Accent 3, Outline - Text 2*).

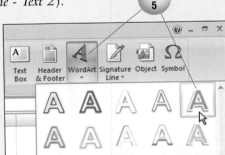

Step 5

6. Type Evergreen, press the Enter key, and then type Products.
7. Position the mouse pointer on the WordArt border until the pointer displays with a four-headed arrow attached and then drag the WordArt inside cell A1.

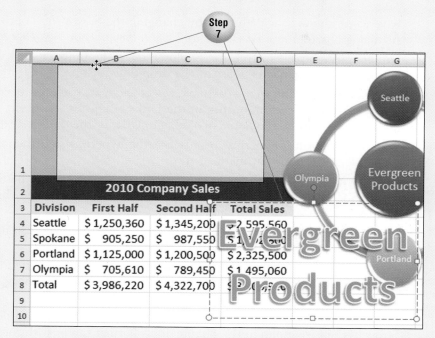

8. Click the Text Fill button arrow in the WordArt Styles group and then click the dark green color (*Olive Green, Accent 3, Darker 25%*).
9. Click the Text Outline button arrow in the WordArt Styles group and then click the dark green color (*Olive Green, Accent 3, Darker 50%*).
10. Resize the chart and position it so it prints on one page with the data.
11. Click the Seattle Sales worksheet tab and then complete steps similar to those in Steps 2 through 10 to insert *Evergreen Products* as WordArt.
12. Save **ExcelL1_C8_P6.xlsx** and then print both worksheets.
13. Close **ExcelL1_C8_P6.xlsx**.

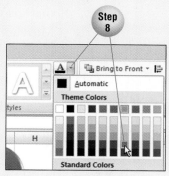

# CHAPTER summary

- Save a workbook as a Web page by changing the *Save as type* option at the Save As dialog box to *Single File Web Page (*.mht; *.mhtml)* or *Web Page (*.htm; *.html)*.

- To open a Web page in Internet Explorer, open the browser, click File on the Menu bar, and then click *Open* at the drop-down list.

- To create a hyperlink in a workbook, select the text, click the Insert tab, and then click the Hyperlink button in the Links group. At the Insert Hyperlink dialog box, type the file name or Web site URL in the *Address* text box.

- To modify or edit a hyperlink, right-click the hyperlink and then click *Edit Hyperlink* at the shortcut menu.

- Insert symbols with options at the Symbol dialog box with the Symbols tab or the Special Characters tab selected. Click the Insert tab and then click the Symbol button to display the dialog box.

- With buttons in the Illustrations group in the Insert tab, you can insert a picture, clip art image, shapes, or a SmartArt diagram.

- When you insert a picture or clip art image in a worksheet, the Picture Tools Format tab is active and includes options for adjusting the image, applying preformatted styles, and arranging and sizing the image.

- Change the size of an image with the *Shape Height* and *Shape Width* measurement boxes in the Size group in the Picture Tools Format tab or with the sizing handles that display around the selected image.

- Move an image by positioning the mouse pointer on the image border until the pointer displays with a four-headed arrow attached and then drag the image to the desired location.

- Delete a selected image by pressing the Delete key.

- Rotate an image by positioning the mouse pointer on the green rotation handle until the pointer displays as a circular arrow and then dragging in the desired direction.

- Insert an image in a workbook with options at the Clip Art task pane. Display this task pane by clicking the Insert tab and then clicking the Clip Art button in the Illustrations group.

- With options at the Clip Art task pane, you can narrow the search for images to specific locations and to specific images.

- To draw shapes in a workbook, click the Insert tab, click the Shapes button in the Illustrations group, and then click the desired shape at the drop-down list. Drag in the worksheet to draw the shape. To maintain the proportions of the shape, hold down the Shift key while dragging in the worksheet.

- Copy a shape with the Copy and Paste buttons in the Clipboard group in the Home tab or by holding down the Ctrl key while dragging the shape.

- You can type text in an enclosed drawn object.

- To insert a picture in a worksheet, click the Insert tab and then click the Picture button in the Illustrations group. At the Insert Picture dialog box, navigate to the desired folder and then double-click the file name.

- Draw a text box in a worksheet by clicking the Insert tab, clicking the Text Box button in the Text group and then dragging in the worksheet. Use options at the Drawing Tools Format tab to format and customize the text box.
- A watermark is a lightened image that displays behind data in a file. You can create a picture watermark in a worksheet by inserting a picture in a header or footer and then changing the size and formatting of the picture.
- Insert a SmartArt diagram in a worksheet by clicking the Insert tab, clicking the SmartArt button in the Illustrations group, and then double-clicking the desired diagram at the Choose a SmartArt Graphic dialog box. Customize a diagram with options in the SmartArt Tools Design tab or the SmartArt Tools Format tab.
- Use WordArt to create, distort, modify, and/or conform text to a variety of shapes. Insert WordArt in a worksheet by clicking the Insert tab, clicking the WordArt button in the Text group, and then clicking the desired option at the drop-down list.
- Customize WordArt text with options in the Drawing Tools Format tab.
- Size WordArt using the sizing handles that display around selected WordArt text and move selected WordArt by dragging it to the desired location using the mouse.

# COMMANDS review

| FEATURE | RIBBON TAB, GROUP | BUTTON | KEYBOARD SHORTCUT |
|---|---|---|---|
| Insert Hyperlink dialog box | Insert, Links | | Ctrl + K |
| Symbol dialog box | Insert, Text | | |
| Clip Art task pane | Insert, Illustrations | | |
| Shapes drop-down list | Insert, Illustrations | | |
| Insert Picture dialog box | Insert, Illustrations | | |
| Text box | Insert, Text | | |
| Choose a SmartArt Graphic dialog box | Insert, Illustrations | | |
| WordArt drop-down list | Insert, Text | | |

# CONCEPTS check

## Test Your Knowledge

**Completion:** In the space provided at the right, indicate the correct term, symbol, or command.

1. Change the *Save as type* option at the Save As dialog box to this to save the open workbook as a single Web page.

2. Click the Insert tab and then click the Hyperlink button and this dialog box displays.

3. The Symbol button is located in this tab.

4. The *Font* option is available at the Symbol dialog box with this tab selected.

5. Insert a picture, clip art image, shape, or SmartArt diagram with buttons in this group in the Insert tab.

6. When you insert a picture or clip art image in a worksheet, this tab is active.

7. Maintain the proportions of the image by holding down this key while dragging a sizing handle.

8. To move an image, position the mouse pointer on the image border until the mouse pointer displays with this attached and then drag the image to the desired location.

9. To copy a shape, hold down this key while dragging the shape.

10. When you draw a text box in a worksheet and then release the mouse button, this tab is active.

11. This term refers to a lightened image that displays behind data in a file.

12. Click the SmartArt button in the Illustrations group in the Insert tab and this dialog box displays.

# SKILLS check
## Demonstrate Your Proficiency

## 1 INSERT A TEXT BOX IN AND SAVE A BOOK CLUB WORKBOOK AS A WEB PAGE

1. Display the Open dialog box with Excel2007L1C8 the active folder.
2. Open **ExcelC08Assessment01.xlsx** and then save the workbook and name it **ExcelL1_C8_A1**.
3. Draw a text box at the right side of the Books Galore clip art image with the following specifications:
   a. Change the height to 1.7" and the width to 2.7".
   b. Remove the text box outline.
   c. Click the Middle Align button and the Center button in the Alignment group in the Home tab.
   d. Change the font to 32-point Forte and change the font color to blue.
   e. Type Book of the Month Club News, 2010 in the text box.
4. Change the orientation to landscape.
5. Save and then print **ExcelL1_C8_A1.xlsx**.
6. Save **ExcelL1_C8_A1.xlsx** as a single Web page in the ExcelWebPages folder (you created this folder in Project 8a) on your storage medium and name it **BooksGaloreWebPage**.
7. Open Internet Explorer and then open **BooksGaloreWebPage.mht**.
8. Close Internet Explorer.
9. Print **BooksGaloreWebPage.mht** in landscape orientation.
10. Select E12 and hyperlink it to *www.microsoft.com*.
11. Select E13 and hyperlink it to *www.symantec.com*.
12. Select E14 and hyperlink it to *www.nasa.gov*.
13. Select E15 and hyperlink it to *www.cnn.com*.
14. Make sure you are connected to the Internet and then click the hyperlink to NASA.
15. Jump to a link from the NASA Web page that interests you.
16. Print the page you viewed from NASA and then close the browser application window.
17. Jump to each of the remaining links in the Web page. At each Web page, jump to a link that interests you, print the page, and then close the browser application window.
18. Save (click Yes at the compatibility dialog box) and then close **BooksGaloreWebPage.mht**.

## 2 INSERT A CLIP ART IMAGE AND WORDART IN AN EQUIPMENT PURCHASE WORKBOOK

1. Open **ExcelC08Assessment02.xlsx** and then save the workbook and name it **ExcelL1_C8_A2**.
2. Insert a formula in cell E4 using the PMT function that calculates monthly payments. *Hint: Refer to Chapter 2, Project 3a.*
3. Copy the formula in cell E4 down to cells E5 and E6.
4. Insert a formula in cell F4 that calculates the total amount of the payments. *Hint: Refer to Chapter 2, Project 3a.*
5. Copy the formula in cell F4 down to cells F5 and F6.
6. Insert a formula in cell G4 that calculates to the total amount of interest paid. *Hint: Refer to Chapter 2, Project 3a.*
7. Copy the formula in cell G4 down to cells G5 and G6.
8. Increase the height of row 1 to 75.00.
9. Delete *BAYSIDE TRAVEL* in cell A1.
10. Insert the clip art image shown in Figure 8.13 (search for this clip art by searching only for clip art images [remove check marks from *Photographs, Movies,* and *Sound*] and typing travel in the *Search for* text box). If this clip art image is not available, choose another image related to travel. (Before closing the Clip Art task pane, reinsert check marks in the *Photographs, Movies,* and *Sound* check boxes at the *Results should be* option drop-down list.)
11. Size and move the clip art image so it is positioned as shown in Figure 8.13.
12. Insert the company name as WordArt as shown in Figure 8.13 with the following specifications:
    a. Create the WordArt with the second option from the left in the bottom row of the WordArt drop-down list (*Fill - Accent 6, Warm Matte Bevel*).
    b. Select the WordArt text, click the Text Fill button arrow in the WordArt Styles group, and then click the light blue color (in the *Standard Colors* section) at the drop-down gallery.
13. Change the worksheet orientation to landscape
14. Save, print, and then close **ExcelL1_C8_A2.xlsx**.

**Figure 8.13 Assessment 2**

| | A | B | C | D | E | F | G | H |
|---|---|---|---|---|---|---|---|---|
| 1 | | | **Bayside Travel** | | | | | |
| 2 | | | | Equipment Purchase Plans | | | | |
| 3 | Equipment | Purchase Price | Interest Rate | Term in Months | Monthly Payments | Total Payments | Total Interest | |
| 4 | Photocopier, Model C120 | $ 8,500.00 | 8.80% | 60 | | | | |
| 5 | Photocopier, Model C150 | $12,750.00 | 8.80% | 60 | | | | |
| 6 | Photocopier, Model C280 | $19,250.00 | 8.80% | 60 | | | | |
| 7 | | | | | | | | |

## 3   INSERT AND FORMAT SHAPES IN A COMPANY SALES WORKBOOK

1. Open **ExcelC08Assessment03.xlsx** and then save the workbook and name it **ExcelL1_C8_A3**.
2. In cell A1, type Mountain, press Alt + Enter, and then type Systems.
3. Select *Mountain Systems* and then change the font to 24-point Calibri bold.
4. Change the horizontal alignment of cell A1 to left and the vertical alignment to center.
5. Display the Format Cells dialog box with the Alignment tab selected and then change the *Indent* measurement to *1*. **Hint: Display the Format Cells dialog box by clicking the Alignment group dialog box launcher in the Home tab.**
6. Click outside cell A1.
7. Use the *Isosceles Triangle* shape located in the *Basic Shapes* section of the Shapes drop-down palette to draw a triangle as shown in Figure 8.14.
8. Copy the triangle three times. Add green fill, dark green outline color, and a shadow effect of your choosing to the triangles so they appear in a similar manner to the triangles in Figure 8.14. Position the triangles as shown in the figure.
9. Save, print, and then close **ExcelL1_C8_A3.xlsx**.

**Figure 8.14**   **Assessment 3**

| | A | B | C | D | E |
|---|---|---|---|---|---|
| 1 | Mountain Systems | | | | |
| 2 | FIRST-QUARTER SALES - 2010 | | | | |
| 3 | Customer | January | February | March | |
| 4 | Lakeside Trucking | $ 84,231 | $ 73,455 | $ 97,549 | |
| 5 | Gresham Machines | $ 33,199 | $ 40,390 | $ 50,112 | |
| 6 | Real Photography | $ 30,891 | $ 35,489 | $ 36,400 | |
| 7 | Genesis Productions | $ 72,190 | $ 75,390 | $ 83,219 | |
| 8 | Landower Company | $ 22,188 | $ 14,228 | $ 38,766 | |
| 9 | Jewell Enterprises | $ 19,764 | $ 50,801 | $ 32,188 | |
| 10 | *Total* | $ 262,463 | $ 289,753 | $ 338,234 | |
| 11 | | | | | |

## 4   INSERT AND FORMAT A SMARTART DIAGRAM IN A SALES WORKBOOK

1. Open **ExcelC08Assessment04.xlsx** and then save the workbook and name it **ExcelL1_C8_A4**.
2. Change the orientation to landscape.
3. Insert a pyramid shape at the right side of the worksheet data using the *Basic Pyramid* SmartArt diagram and insert the following information in the pyramid:
   a. In the bottom shape, type Red Level, press Enter, and then type $25,000 - $49,999.

b. In the middle shape, type **Blue Level**, press Enter, and then type $50,000 - $99,999.

c. In the top shape, type **Gold Level**, press Enter, and then type $100,000+.

d. Change the font size and/or move the text so the text displays in each shape.

e. Change the color of the shapes to match the color level.

f. If necessary, change the color of the text inside the shapes so it is easy to read.

g. Size and/or move the diagram so it displays attractively at the right side of the worksheet data. (Make sure the entire diagram will print on the same page as the worksheet data.)

4. Save, print, and then close **ExcelL1_C8_A4.xlsx**.

## Assessment

### 5 APPLY CONDITIONAL FORMATTING TO CELLS IN A SALES WORKBOOK

1. Using the Help feature, learn about applying conditional formatting to numbers in cells that match a specific range.

2. Open **ExcelL1_C8_A4.xlsx** and then save the workbook and name it **ExcelL1_C8_A5**.

3. Using the conditional formatting feature, apply the following formatting to amounts in the *Total* column:

a. Apply red color formatting to numbers between $25,000 and $49,999.

b. Apply blue color formatting to numbers between $50,000 and $99,999.

c. Apply gold color formatting to numbers between $100,000 and $500,000.

4. Save, print, and then close **ExcelL1_C8_A5.xlsx**.

# CASE study

## *Apply Your Skills*

**Part 1**

You are the office manager for Ocean Truck Sales and are responsible for maintaining a spreadsheet of the truck and SUV inventory. Open **ExcelC08Ocean.xlsx** and then save the workbook and name it **ExcelL1_C8_CS_P1**. Apply formatting to improve the appearance of the worksheet and insert at least one clip art image (related to "truck" or "ocean"). Save **ExcelL1_C8_CS_P1.xlsx** and then print the worksheet.

**Part 2**

You have been asked to save the inventory worksheet as a Web page for viewing online and also to insert hyperlinks to various sites. With **ExcelL1_C8_CS_P1.xlsx** open, locate at least one financial institution in your area that will finance an automobile and then insert in the worksheet a hyperlink to that site. Locate another site that provides information on book value of a used automobile and then insert in the worksheet a hyperlink to that site. Save the workbook as a single Web page with the name **ExcelC08OceanWebPage**. Open your Internet browser and then open the Web page. Click each hyperlink to make sure it takes you to the proper Web site. Close your Internet browser and then close **ExcelC08OceanWebPage.mht**.

Open **ExcelL1_C8_CS_P1.xlsx** and then save it with Save As and name it **ExcelL1_C8_CS_P3**. You make the inventory workbook available to each salesperson at the beginning of the week. For easier viewing, you decide to divide the workbook into two worksheets with one worksheet containing all Ford vehicles and the other worksheet containing all Chevrolet vehicles. Rename the worksheet tabs to reflect the contents. Sort each worksheet by price from the most expensive to the least expensive. The owner offers incentives each week to help motivate the sales force. Insert in the first worksheet a SmartArt diagram of your choosing that contains the following information:

> Small-sized truck = $100
> 2WD Regular Cab = $75
> SUV 4x4 = $50

Copy the diagram in the first worksheet and then paste it into the second worksheet. Change the orientation to landscape and then save, print, and close **ExcelL1_C8_CS_P3.xlsx**.

As part of your weekly duties, you need to post the incentive diagram in various locations throughout the company. You decide to insert the diagram in PowerPoint for easy printing. Open **ExcelL1_C8_CS_P3.xlsx** and then open PowerPoint. Change the slide layout in PowerPoint to Blank. Copy the diagram in the first worksheet and paste it into the PowerPoint blank slide. Increase and/or move the diagram so it better fills the slide. Print the slide and then close PowerPoint without saving the presentation. Close **ExcelL1_C8_CS_P3.xlsx**.

# Maintaining and Enhancing Workbooks

# ASSESSING proficiency

In this unit, you have learned how to work with multiple windows; move, copy, link, and paste data between workbooks and applications; create and customize charts with data in a worksheet; save a workbook as a Web page; insert hyperlinks; and insert and customize pictures, clip art images, shapes, SmartArt diagrams, and WordArt.

*Note: Before beginning computer assessments, copy to your storage medium the Excel2007L1U2 subfolder from the Excel2007L1 folder on the CD that accompanies this textbook and then make Excel2007L1U2 the active folder.*

**Assessment 1 Copy and Paste Data and Insert WordArt in a Training Scores Workbook**

1. Open **ExcelU02Assessment01.xlsx** and then save the workbook and name it **ExcelL1_U2_A1**.
2. Delete row 15 (the row for *Kwieciak, Kathleen*).
3. Insert a formula in cell D4 that averages the percentages in cells B4 and C4.
4. Copy the formula in cell D4 down to cells D5 through D20.
5. Make cell A22 active, turn on bold, and then type Highest Averages.
6. Display the Clipboard task pane and make sure it is empty.
7. Select and then copy each of the following rows (individually): row 7, 10, 14, 16, and 18.
8. Make cell A23 active and then paste row 14 (the row for *Jewett, Troy*).
9. Make cell A24 active and then paste row 7 (the row for *Cumpston, Kurt*).
10. Make cell A25 active and then paste row 10 (the row for *Fisher-Edwards, Theresa*).
11. Make cell A26 active and then paste row 16 (the row for *Mathias, Caleb*).
12. Make cell A27 active and then paste row 18 (the row for *Nyegaard, Curtis*).
13. Click the Clear All button in the Clipboard task pane and then close the task pane.
14. Insert in cell A1 the text *Roseland* as WordArt. Format the WordArt text to add visual appeal to the worksheet.
15. Save, print, and then close **ExcelL1_U2_A1.xlsx**.

## Assessment 2 Manage Multiple Worksheets in a Projected Earnings Workbook

1. Open **ExcelU02Assessment02.xlsx** and then save the workbook and name it **ExcelL1_U2_A2**.
2. Delete *Roseland* in cell A1. Open **ExcelL1_U2_A1.xlsx** and then copy the *Roseland* WordArt text and paste it into cell A1 in **ExcelL1_U2_A2.xlsx**. If necessary, increase the height of row 1 to accommodate the WordArt text.
3. Notice the fill color in cells in **ExcelL1_U2_A1.xlsx** and then apply the same fill color to cells of data in **ExcelL1_U2_A2.xlsx**. Close **ExcelL1_U2_A1.xlsx**.
4. Select cells A1 through C11 and then copy and paste the cells to Sheet2 keeping the source column widths.
5. With Sheet2 displayed, make the following changes:
   a. Increase the height of row 1 to accommodate the WordArt text.
   b. Delete the contents of cell B2.
   c. Change the contents of the following cells:
      A6: Change *January* to *July*
      A7: Change *February* to *August*
      A8: Change *March* to *September*
      A9: Change *April* to *October*
      A10: Change *May* to *November*
      A11: Change *June* to *December*
      B6: Change *8.30%* to *8.10%*
      B8: Change *9.30%* to *8.70%*
6. Make Sheet1 active and then copy cell B2 and paste link it to cell B2 in Sheet2.
7. Rename Sheet1 to *First Half* and rename Sheet2 to *Second Half*.
8. Make the First Half worksheet active and then determine the effect on projected monthly earnings if the projected yearly income is increased by 10% by changing the number in cell B2 to *$1,480,380*.
9. Save the workbook (two worksheets) again and then print both worksheets of the workbook so they are horizontally and vertically centered on each page.
10. Determine the effect on projected monthly earnings if the projected yearly income is increased by 20% by changing the number in cell B2 to *$1,614,960*.
11. Save the workbook again and then print both worksheets of the workbook so they are horizontally and vertically centered on each page.
12. Close **ExcelL1_U2_A2.xlsx**.

## Assessment 3 Create Charts in Worksheets in a Sales Totals Workbook

1. Open **ExcelU02Assessment03** and then save the workbook and name it **ExcelL1_U2_A3**.
2. Insert the heading **Average Sales 2008-2010** (on multiple lines) in cell A13.
3. Insert a formula in cell B13 with a 3-D reference that averages the total in cells B4 through B11 in Sheet1, Sheet2, and Sheet3.
4. Insert a formula in cell C13 with a 3-D reference that averages the total in cells C4 through C11 in Sheet1, Sheet2, and Sheet3.
5. Rename Sheet1 to *2008 Sales*, rename Sheet2 to *2009 Sales*, and rename Sheet3 to *2010 Sales*.
6. Make the 2008 Sales worksheet active, select cells A3 through C11 and create a column chart. Click the Switch Row/Column button at the Chart Tools Design tab. Apply formatting to increase the visual appeal of the chart. Drag the chart below the worksheet data. (Make sure the chart fits on the page.)

7. Make the 2009 Sales worksheet active and then create the same type of chart you created in Step 6.
8. Make the 2010 Sales worksheet active and then create the same type of chart you created in Step 6.
9. Save the workbook and then print the entire workbook.
10. Close **ExcelL1_U2_A3.xlsx**.

## Assessment 4 **Create and Format a Line Chart**

1. Type the following information in a worksheet:

   | Country | Total Sales |
   |---------|-------------|
   | Denmark | $85,345 |
   | Finland | $71,450 |
   | Norway | $135,230 |
   | Sweden | $118,895 |

2. Using the data just entered in the worksheet, create a line chart with the following specifications:
   a. Apply a chart style of your choosing.
   b. Insert major and minor primary vertical gridlines.
   c. Insert drop lines. (Do this with the Lines button in the Analysis group in the Chart Tools Layout tab.)
   d. Apply any other formatting to improve the visual appeal of the chart.
   e. Move the chart to a new sheet.
3. Save the workbook and name it **ExcelL1_U2_A4**.
4. Print only the sheet containing the chart.
5. Change the line chart to a bar chart of your choosing.
6. Save the workbook and then print only the sheet containing the chart.
7. Close **ExcelL1_U2_A4.xlsx**.

## Assessment 5 **Create and Format a Pie Chart**

1. Open **ExcelU02Assessment05.xlsx** and then save the workbook and name it **ExcelL1_U2_A5**.
2. Create a pie chart as a separate sheet with the data in cells A3 through B10. You determine the type of pie. Include an appropriate title for the chart and include percentage labels.
3. Print only the sheet containing the chart.
4. Save and then close **ExcelL1_U2_A5.xlsx**.

## Assessment 6 **Insert a Text Box in and Save a Travel Workbook as a Web Page**

1. Open **ExcelU02Assessment06.xlsx** and then save the workbook and name it **ExcelL1_U2_A6**.
2. Insert a text box in the workbook with the following specifications:
   a. Draw the text box at the right side of the clip art image.
   b. Remove the fill in the text box and the outline around the text box.
   c. Type Call 1-888-555-1288 for last-minute vacation specials!
   d. Select the text and then change the font to 20-point Bradley Hand ITC in blue color and turn on bold.
   e. Size and position the text box so it appears visually balanced with the travel clip art image.
3. Make sure you are connected to the Internet and then search for sites that might be of interest to tourists for each of the cities in the worksheet. Write down the URL for the best Web page you find for each city.

4. Create a hyperlink for each city to jump to the URL you wrote down in Step 3. (Select the hyperlink text in each cell and change the font size to 18 points.)
5. Save **ExcelL1_U2_A6.xlsx** and then print the worksheet.
6. Create a new folder named TravelWebPages in the Excel2007L1U2 folder.
7. Save **ExcelL1_U2_A6.xlsx** as a single file Web page in the TravelWebPages folder with the following specifications:
   a. Name the Web page **TravelAdvantageWebPage**.
   b. Change the title to *Winter Getaway Destinations!*
8. Open Internet Explorer and then open **TravelAdvantageWebPage.mht**.
9. Test the hyperlinks to make sure you entered the URLs correctly by clicking each hyperlink and then closing the Web browser.
10. Close **TravelAdvantageWebPage.mht** and then close Internet Explorer.
11. Save and then close **ExcelL1_U2_A6.xlsx**.

### Assessment 7 Insert Clip Art Image and Smart Diagram in a Projected Quotas Workbook

1. Open **ExcelU02Assessment07.xlsx** and then save the workbook and name it **ExcelL1_U2_A7**.
2. Insert a formula in cell C3 using an absolute reference to determine the projected quotas at 10% of the current quotas.
3. Copy the formula in cell C3 down to cells C4 through C12.
4. Insert a clip art image in row 1 related to money. You determine the size and position of the clip art image. If necessary, increase the height of the row.
5. Apply the following conditional formatting to the values in cells C3 through C12:
   Apply green color to values from $50,000 to $99,999.
   Apply blue color to values from $100,000 to $149,999.
   Apply red color to values from $150,000 to $200,000.
6. Insert a SmartArt diagram at the right side of the chart that contains three shapes. Insert the quota ranges in the shapes as identified in Step 5 and apply color fill to match the conditional formatting. (For example, type $50,000 to $99,999 in a shape and then apply green fill color to the shape.)
7. Change the orientation to landscape and make sure the diagram fits on the page.
8. Save, print, and then close **ExcelL1_U2_A7.xlsx**.

### Assessment 8 Insert Symbol, Clip Art, and Comments in a Sales Workbook

1. Open **ExcelU02Assessment08.xlsx** and then save the workbook and name it **ExcelL1_U2_A8**.
2. Delete the text *Landower Company* and then type Económico in the cell. (Use the Symbol dialog box to insert ó.)
3. Insert a new row at the beginning of the worksheet.
4. Select and then merge cells A1 through D1.
5. Increase the height of row 1 to approximately 100.50.
6. Insert the text *Custom Interiors* as WordArt in cell A1. You determine the formatting of the WordArt. Move and size the WordArt so it fits in cell A1.
7. Insert the following comments in the specified cells:
   D4 = Increase amount to $100,000.
   A5 = Change the name to Gresham Technology.
   A9 = Decrease amounts for this company by 5%.

8. Turn on the display of all comments.
9. Print the worksheet with the comments as displayed on the worksheet.
10. Turn off the display of all comments.
11. Delete the comment in A5.
12. Print the worksheet again with the comments printed at the end of the worksheet. (The comments will print on a separate page from the worksheet.)
13. Save and then close **ExcelL1_U2_A8.xlsx**.

## Assessment 9  Insert and Format a Shape in a Budget Workbook

1. Open **ExcelU02Assessment09.xlsx** and then save the workbook and name it **ExcelL1_U2_A9**.
2. Make the following changes to the worksheet so it displays as shown in Figure U2.1:
   a. Select and then merge cells A1 through D1.
   b. Add fill to the cells as shown in Figure U2.1.
   c. Increase the height of row 1 to the approximate size shown in Figure U2.1.
   d. Insert the text **SOLAR ENTERPRISES** in cell A1 set in 20-point Calibri bold, center and middle aligned, and set in aqua (Aqua, Accent 5, Darker 25%).
   e. Insert the sun shape (located in the *Basic Shapes* section of the Shapes button drop-down list). Apply orange shape fill and change the shape outline to aqua (Aqua, Accent 5, Darker 25%)
3. Save, print, and then close **ExcelL1_U2_A9.xlsx**.

**Figure U2.1 Assessment 9**

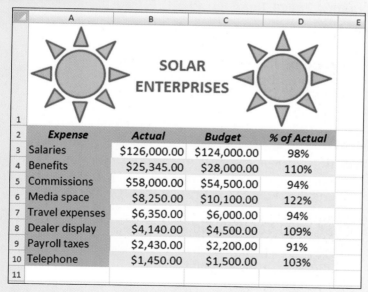

# WRITING activities

The following activities give you the opportunity to practice your writing skills along with demonstrating an understanding of some of the important Excel features you have mastered in this unit. Use correct grammar, appropriate word choices, and clear sentence constructions.

## Activity 1 Prepare a Projected Budget

You are the accounting assistant in the financial department of McCormack Funds and you have been asked to prepare a yearly proposed department budget. The total amount for the department is $1,450,000. You are given the percentages for the proposed budget items, which are: Salaries, 45%; Benefits, 12%; Training, 14%; Administrative Costs, 10%; Equipment, 11%; and Supplies, 8%. Create a worksheet with this information that shows the projected yearly budget, the budget items in the department, the percentage of the budget, and the amount for each item. After the worksheet is completed, save the workbook and name it **ExcelL1_U2_Act01**. Print and then close the workbook.

**Optional:** Using Word 2007, write a memo to the McCormack Funds Finance Department explaining that the proposed annual department budget is attached for their review. Comments and suggestions are to be sent to you within one week. Save the file and name it **ExcelL1_U2_Act01_Memo**. Print and then close the file.

## Activity 2 Create a Travel Tours Bar Chart

Prepare a worksheet in Excel for Carefree Travels that includes the following information:

### Scandinavian Tours

| Country | Tours Booked |
|---------|--------------|
| Norway  | 52           |
| Sweden  | 62           |
| Finland | 29           |
| Denmark | 38           |

Use the information in the worksheet to create and format a bar chart as a separate sheet. Save the workbook and name it **ExcelL1_U2_Act02**. Print only the sheet containing the chart and then close **ExcelL1_U2_Act02.xlsx**.

## Activity 3 Prepare a Ski Vacation Worksheet

Prepare a worksheet for Carefree Travels that advertises a snow skiing trip. Include the following information in the announcement:

- At the beginning of the worksheet, create a company logo that includes the company name *Carefree Travels* and a clip art image related to travel.
- Include the heading *Whistler Ski Vacation Package* in the worksheet.
- Include the following below the heading:
  - Round-trip air transportation: $395
  - Seven nights' hotel accommodations: $1,550
  - Four all-day ski passes: $425

- ○ Compact rental car with unlimited mileage: $250
- ○ Total price of the ski package: (calculate the total price)
- Include the following information somewhere in the worksheet:
  - ○ Book your vacation today at special discount prices.
  - ○ Two-for-one discount at many of the local ski resorts.

Save the workbook and name it **ExcelL1_U2_Act03**. Print and then close **ExcelL1_U2_Act03.xlsx**.

## Find Information on Excel Books and Present the Data in a Worksheet

Locate two companies on the Internet that sell new books. At the first new book company site, locate three books on Microsoft Excel. Record the title, author, and price for each book. At the second new book company site, locate the same three books and record the prices. Create an Excel worksheet that includes the following information:

- Name of each new book company
- Title and author of the three books
- Prices for each book from the two book company sites

Create a hyperlink for each book company to the URL on the Internet. Then save the completed workbook and name it **ExcelL1_U2_InternetResearch**. Print and then close the workbook.

## Create a Customized Time Card for a Landscaping Company

You are the manager of a landscaping company and are responsible for employee time cards. Locate the time card template that is available with *Installed Templates* selected in the New Workbook dialog box. Use the template to create a customized time card for your company. With the template open, delete the Company Name that displays in the middle header pane. Insert additional blank rows to increase the spacing above the Employee row. Insert a clip art image related to landscaping or gardening and position and size it attractively in the form. Include a text box with the text Lawn and Landscaping Specialists inside the box. Format, size, and position the text attractively in the form. Fill in the form for the current week with the following employee information:

Employee = Jonathan Holder
Address = 12332 South 152$^{nd}$ Street, Baton Rouge, LA 70804
Manager = (Your name)
Employee phone = (225) 555-3092
Employee e-mail = None

Regular hours = 8 hours for Monday, Tuesday, Wednesday, and Thursday
Overtime = 2 hours on Wednesday
Sick hours = None
Vacation = 8 hours on Friday
Rate per hour = $20.00
Overtime pay = $30.00

Save the completed form and name it **ExcelL1_U2_JobStudy**. Print and then close **ExcelL1_U2_JobStudy.xlsx**.

# INDEX

Microsoft®

# access

## Making Access Work for You

Each of us interacts with a database more often than we realize. Did you use a bank machine to get some cash today? Did you search the library's catalog for a book that you need? Did you browse an online retail catalog or flip through the pages of a printed catalog? If you did any of these activities, you were accessing and/or updating a database. Any time you look for something by accessing an organized file system you are probably using a database. Microsoft Access is the database management system included with Microsoft Office.

## Organizing Information

Information in a database is organized into a collection of *tables* that can be related to each other for purposes of exchanging data. Each table is broken down into a series of columns (called *fields*) and rows (called *records*). If you are familiar with a spreadsheet program such as Excel, you will be comfortable viewing a datasheet in Access. Much thought is put into the design of a database and its tables since all of the data a business collects in a database must

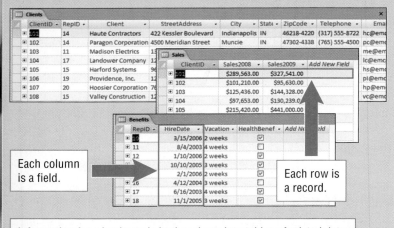

Each column is a field.

Each row is a record.

Information for a business is broken down into tables of related data. In this example, Client information is in a separate table from Benefit information and Sales information.

be organized into logical groups. Defining a *relationship* between two tables enables data from more than one table to be shared or exchanged for viewing, updating, or reporting purposes. Access allows for three kinds of relationships that can be created: one-to-one, one-to-many, and many-to-many.

Records within tables can be sorted and filtered numerous ways to allow the data to be reorganized to suit many needs. Sorting by one column and by multiple columns is accomplished with just a few mouse clicks. Temporarily hide records that

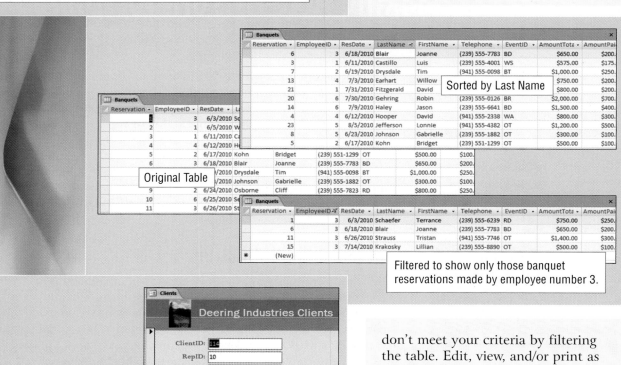

Sorted by Last Name

Original Table

Filtered to show only those banquet reservations made by employee number 3.

The form is a more user-friendly interface to the table to which it is associated.

don't meet your criteria by filtering the table. Edit, view, and/or print as required and then redisplay the remaining records. Forms allow those using a database to interact with the table by viewing and updating only one record at a time. Large tables clutter the screen, overwhelming the user with data and requiring scrolling to view all of the fields. Creating a form solves this problem by presenting the table data in a more user-friendly interface. Additional explanatory text can be added to forms, providing information about using the form or following particular business practices.

# Analyzing Information

Databases store a wealth of data that can be extracted in various ways. A *query* is one method for extracting information from tables. A basic query might simply list fields from several tables in one datasheet. This method is shown in the adjacent screen captures, where individual fields from three tables are selected for viewing in one datasheet. In more complex queries, data can be selected for viewing based on meeting a single criterion or multiple criteria, and calculations can be performed on fields.

For more sophisticated analysis, tables can be grouped and then filtered on more than one field. Open a table or query and then switch to PivotTable View or PivotChart View. Access has simplified the task of creating pivot tables and pivot charts by incorporating a drag and drop technique in the view. Interact with the pivot table or pivot chart by clicking one of the filter arrows, selecting or deselecting the items you want to view, and then clicking OK. The data in the view is instantly updated to reflect the new settings.

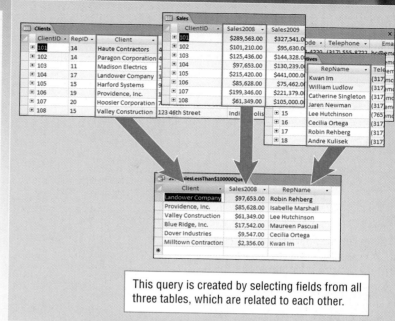

This query is created by selecting fields from all three tables, which are related to each other.

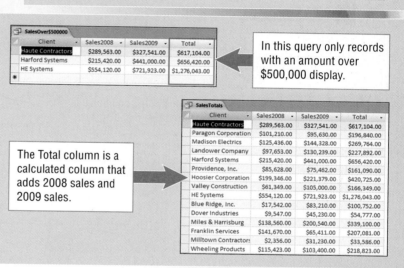

In this query only records with an amount over $500,000 display.

The Total column is a calculated column that adds 2008 sales and 2009 sales.

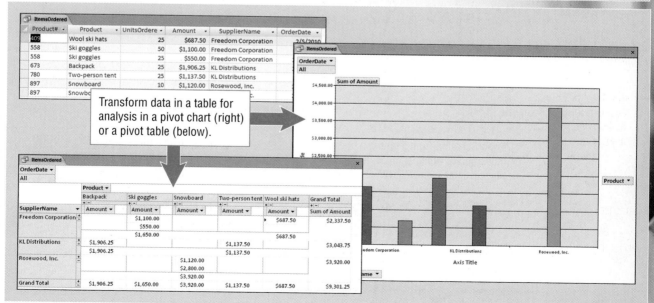

Transform data in a table for analysis in a pivot chart (right) or a pivot table (below).

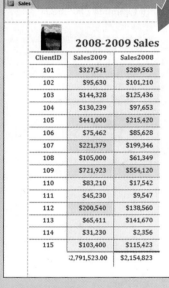

Create a report to produce high-quality output.

2008-2009 Sales

| ClientID | Sales2009 | Sales2008 |
|---|---|---|
| 101 | $327,541 | $289,563 |
| 102 | $95,630 | $101,210 |
| 103 | $144,328 | $125,436 |
| 104 | $130,239 | $97,653 |
| 105 | $441,000 | $215,420 |
| 106 | $75,462 | $85,628 |
| 107 | $221,379 | $199,346 |
| 108 | $105,000 | $61,349 |
| 109 | $721,923 | $554,120 |
| 110 | $83,210 | $17,542 |
| 111 | $45,230 | $9,547 |
| 112 | $200,540 | $138,560 |
| 113 | $65,411 | $141,670 |
| 114 | $31,230 | $2,356 |
| 115 | $103,400 | $115,423 |
| | ;2,791,523.00 | $2,154,823 |

Page 1 of 1

Report with conditional formatting that displays amounts over $199,999 with green shading and amounts under $200,000 with red shading.

# Presenting Information

Having critical business information stored electronically and the ability to easily extract specific data from the database is a valuable asset to a business. However, there are still times when a printed report is a necessity. Reports in Access are used to create professional-looking, high-quality output. Reports can be grouped and sorted and can include calculations. Access includes the Report Wizard, which can be used to create a report such as the one shown at the left by choosing the table or query for the source data, specifying a group or sort order, and choosing from predefined styles and layouts. Once the report is generated, you can easily modify its design by moving, resizing, adding, or deleting objects, changing the layout or sort order, adding a calculation, applying gridlines, and so on.

Having a well designed database that is easy to update and maintain is a necessity for most businesses. Microsoft Access is a database management system that is easy to learn and use. In just a few pages, you will be exploring the world of databases and learning how to access the technology that drives business success.

Report created from a query that displays Indianapolis and Muncie sales over $75,000.

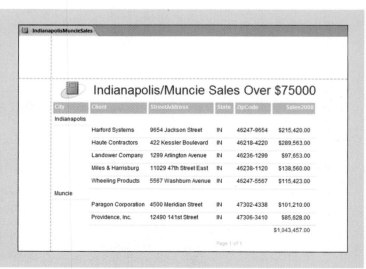

**Level 1**

Microsoft®

# access

## Unit 1: Creating Tables and Queries

➤ Creating Database Tables

➤ Creating Relationships between Tables

➤ Modifying and Managing Tables

➤ Performing Queries

## Benchmark Microsoft® Access 2007 Level 1

### Microsoft Certified Application Specialist Skills—Unit 1

| Reference No. | Skill | Pages |
|---|---|---|
| **1** | **Structuring a Database** | |
| 1.2 | Define and print table relationships | |
| 1.2.1 | Create relationships | 35-46 |
| 1.2.2 | Modify relationships | 40-50 |
| 1.2.3 | Print table relationships | 43, 46 |
| 1.3 | Add, set, change, or remove primary keys | |
| 1.3.1 | Define and modify primary keys | 37-40 |
| **2** | **Creating and Formatting Database Elements** | |
| 2.1 | Create databases | |
| 2.1.2 | Create blank databases | 8, 13-21 |
| 2.2 | Create tables | |
| 2.2.1 | Create custom tables in Design view | 13-21 |
| 2.3 | Modify tables | |
| 2.3.1 | Modify table properties | 66-70 |
| 2.3.5 | Summarize table data by adding a Total row | 70-72 |
| 2.4 | Create fields and modify field properties | |
| 2.4.1 | Create commonly used fields | 13-19 |
| 2.4.2 | Modify field properties | 70-76 |
| **3** | **Entering and Modifying Data** | |
| 3.1 | Enter, edit, and delete records | 26-28, 49-50 |
| 3.3 | Find and replace data | 84-86 |
| **4** | **Creating and Modifying Queries** | |
| 4.1 | Create queries | 99-105 |
| 4.1.1 | Create queries based on single tables | 99-105 |
| 4.1.2 | Create queries based on more than one table | 105-128 |
| 4.1.4 | Create crosstab queries | 121-123 |
| 4.2 | Modify queries | |
| 4.2.4 | Create calculated fields in queries | 116-118 |
| 4.2.6 | Create sum, average, min/max, and count queries | 118-121 |
| **5** | **Presenting and Sharing Data** | |
| 5.1 | Sort data | |
| 5.1.1 | Sort data within tables | 80-81 |
| 5.1.2 | Sort data within queries | 108-109 |
| 5.6 | Print database objects | 80-81 |
| **6** | **Managing and Maintaining Databases** | |
| 6.1 | Perform routine database operations | |
| 6.1.2 | Back up databases | 86-89 |
| 6.1.3 | Compact and repair databases | 87-89 |
| 6.2 | Manage databases | |
| 6.2.2 | Configure database options | 11-12 |

*Note:* The Level 1 and Level 2 texts each address approximately half of the Microsoft Certified Application Specialist skills. Complete coverage of the skills is offered in the combined Level 1 and Level 2 text titled *Benchmark Series Microsoft® Access 2007: Levels 1 and 2,* which has been approved as certified courseware and which displays the Microsoft Certified Application Specialist logo on the cover.

# CHAPTER 1

# Creating Database Tables

## PERFORMANCE OBJECTIVES

**Upon successful completion of Chapter 1, you will be able to:**

- Open and close objects in a database
- Design a table
- Determine fields and assign data types in a table
- Enter data in a table
- Open, save, print, and close a table
- Add and delete records in a table

access Chapter 1

SNAP

**Tutorial 1.1**
Organizing Data in a Database
Table

Managing information in a company is an integral part of operating a business. Information can come in a variety of forms, such as data about customers, including names, addresses, and telephone numbers; product data; purchasing and buying data; information on services performed for customers or clients; and much more. Most companies today manage data using a database management system software program. Microsoft Office Professional includes a database management system software program named *Access*. With Access, you can organize, store, maintain, retrieve, sort, and print all types of business data.

As an example of how Access might be used to manage data in an office, suppose a bookstore decides to send a mailer to all customers who have purchased a certain type of book in the past month (such as autobiographies). The bookstore uses Access and maintains data on customers, such as names, addresses, types of books purchased, and types of books ordered. With this data in Access, the manager of the bookstore can easily select those customers who have purchased or ordered autobiographies in the past month and send a mailer announcing a visit by an author who has written a recently-published autobiography. The bookstore could also use the information to determine what types of books have been ordered by customers in the past few months and use this information to determine what inventory to purchase.

Use the information in a database to perform a wide variety of functions. This chapter contains just a few ideas. With a properly designed and maintained database management system, a company can operate smoothly with logical, organized, and useful information. The Access program displays in the Start pop-up menu preceded by a picture of a key. The key symbolizes the importance of managing and maintaining data to a company's survival and success.

*Note: Before beginning computer projects, copy to your storage medium the Access 2007L1C1 subfolder from the Access2007L1 folder on the CD that accompanies this textbook. Steps on how to copy a folder are presented on the inside of the back cover of this textbook. Do this every time you start a chapter's projects.*

## Project 1 Explore an Access Database

**You will open a database and open and close objects in the database including tables, queries, and forms.**

## Exploring a Database

A database is comprised of a series of objects such as tables, forms, reports, and queries that you use to enter, manage, view, and print data. Data in a database is organized into tables, which contain information for related items such as customers, employees, orders, and products. To view the various objects in a database, you will open a previously created database and then navigate in the database and open various objects.

To open a previously created database, click the Start button on the Taskbar, point to *All Programs*, point to *Microsoft Office*, and then click *Microsoft Office Access 2007*. (These steps may vary depending on your operating system and/or system configuration.) This displays the *Getting Started with Microsoft Office Access* screen shown in Figure 1.1. This screen is divided into three sections. Use the *Template Categories* section at the left to preview and download database templates. Start a new database by clicking the Blank Database button in the *New Blank Database* section and open an existing database by clicking a database name in the *Open Recent Database* section.

### Opening and Closing a Database

**HINT**

Only one database can be open at a time.

Office button

To open a database, click the file name located in the *Open Recent Database* section of the *Getting Started with Microsoft Office Access* screen or click the Office button and then click *Open* at the drop-down list. At the Open dialog box, navigate to the desired folder and then double-click the desired database name in the list box. When you open a database, the Access screen displays as shown in Figure 1.2. Refer to Table 1.1 for a description of the Access screen elements. To close a database, click the Office button and then click *Close Database* at the drop-down list. To exit Access, click the Close button that displays in the upper right corner of the screen, or click the Office button and then click the Exit Access button that displays in the lower right corner of the drop-down list.

**Figure 1.1** Getting Started with Microsoft Office Access Screen

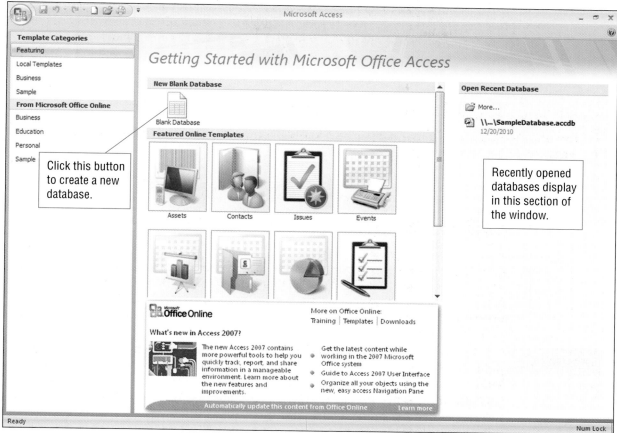

**Table 1.1** Access Screen Elements

| Feature | Description |
|---------|-------------|
| Office button | Displays as a Microsoft Office logo and, when clicked, displays a list of options along with the most recently opened databases |
| Quick Access toolbar | Contains buttons for commonly-used commands |
| Title bar | Displays database name followed by program name |
| Tabs | Contains commands and features organized into groups |
| Ribbon | Area containing the tabs and commands divided into groups |
| Message bar | Displays security alerts if the database you open contains potentially unsafe content |
| Navigation pane | Displays names of objects within database grouped by categories |
| Work area | Area in screen where opened objects display |
| Status bar | Displays number of pages and words, View buttons, and the Zoom slider bar |

**Figure 1.2** Access Screen

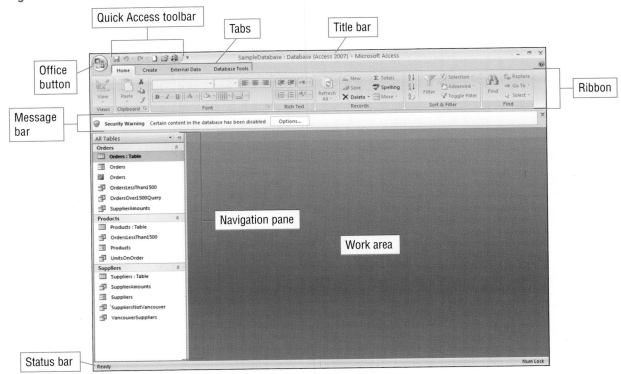

Security features in Access 2007 cause a message bar to display a security alert message below the ribbon. This message displays when you open an Access 2007 database outside of a trusted location (a list of drives and folder names stored in the Trust Center dialog box). If you know that the database is virus-free, click the Options button in the Message bar. At the Microsoft Office Security Options dialog box that displays, click the *Enable this content* option and then click OK. The Message bar closes when you identify the database as a trusted source.

The Navigation pane at the left side of the Access screen displays the objects that are contained in the database. Some common objects found in a database include tables, forms, reports, and queries. Refer to Table 1.2 for a description of these four types of objects.

**Table 1.2** Database Objects

| Object | Description |
|--------|-------------|
| Table | Organizes data in fields (columns) and rows (records). A database must contain at least one table. The table is the base upon which other objects are created. |
| Query | Used to display data from a table or related tables that meets a conditional statement and/or to perform calculations. For example, display only those records in which the city is Vancouver. |
| Form | Allows fields and records to be presented in a different layout than the datasheet. Used to facilitate data entry and maintenance. |
| Report | Prints data from tables or queries. |

# Opening and Closing Objects

Database objects display in the Navigation pane. Control what displays in the pane by clicking the Menu bar at the top of the Navigation pane and then clicking the desired option at the drop-down list. For example, to display a list of all saved objects in the database, click the *Object Type* option at the drop-down list. This view displays the objects grouped by type—Tables, Queries, Forms, and Reports. To open an object, double-click the object in the Navigation pane. The object opens in the work area and a tab displays with the object name at the left side of the object.

To view more of an object, consider closing the Navigation pane by clicking the Shutter Bar Open/Close button located in the upper right corner of the pane. Click the button again to open the Navigation pane.

You can open more than one object in the work area. Each object opens with a visible tab. You can navigate to objects by clicking the object tab. To close an object, click the Close button that displays at the right side of the work area.

**HINT**

Hide the Navigation pane by clicking the button in the upper right corner of the pane (called the Shutter Bar Open/Close Button) or by pressing F11.

Close Object

## Project 1   Opening and Closing a Database and Objects

1. Open Access by clicking the Start button on the Taskbar, pointing to *All Programs*, pointing to *Microsoft Office*, and then clicking *Microsoft Office Access 2007*. (These steps may vary.)
2. At the Getting Started with Microsoft Office Access screen, click the Office button and then click *Open* at the drop-down list.
3. At the Open dialog box, navigate to the Access2007L1C1 folder on your storage medium and then double-click the database ***SampleDatabase.accdb***.
4. Click the Options button in the Message bar.
5. At the Microsoft Office Security Options dialog box, click *Enable this content* and then click OK.
6. Click the Navigation pane Menu bar and then click *Object Type* at the drop-down list. (This option displays the objects grouped by type—Tables, Queries, Forms, and Reports.)
7. Double-click *Suppliers* in the *Tables* section of the Navigation pane. This opens the Suppliers table in the work area as shown in Figure 1.3. The fields in the table display in the top row of the table and some of the field names are not completely visible.
8. Close the Suppliers table by clicking the Close button in the upper right corner of the work area.
9. Double-click *OrdersLessThan1500* in the *Queries* section of the Navigation pane. A query displays data that meets a conditional statement and this query displays orders that meet the criterion of being less than $1,500.

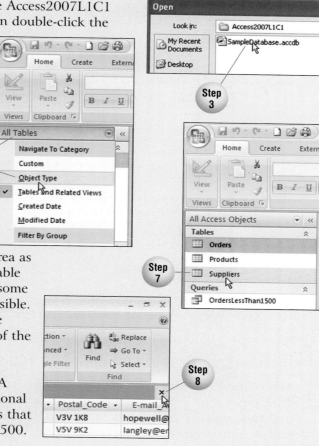

10. Close the query by clicking the Close button in the upper right corner of the work area.
11. Double-click the *SuppliersNotVancouver* query in the Navigation pane and notice that the query displays information about suppliers that are not located in Vancouver.
12. Click the Close button in the work area.
13. Double-click *Orders* in the *Forms* section of the Navigation pane. This displays an order form. A form is used to view and edit data in a table one record at a time.
14. Click the Close button in the work area.
15. Double-click *Orders* in the *Reports* section of the Navigation pane. This displays a report with information about orders and order amounts.
16. Close the Navigation pane by clicking the Shutter Bar Open/Close Button located in the upper right corner of the pane.
17. After viewing the report, click the button again to open the Navigation pane.
18. Click the Close button in the work area.
19. Close the database by clicking the Office button and then clicking *Close Database* at the drop-down list.
20. Exit Access by clicking the Close button (contains an X) that displays in the upper right corner of the screen.

**Figure 1.3** Open Suppliers Table

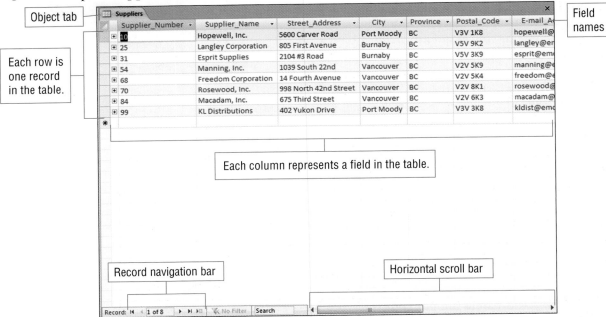

## Project ② Create and Maintain Tables

You will create tables for a Premium database by determining the field names and data types and then entering records in the tables. You will change the page layout and field widths and then print the tables; you will also maintain tables by adding and deleting records.

# Organizing Data in a Table

Data is not very useful to a company if it is not organized in a logical manner. Organizing data in a manageable and logical manner allows the data to be found and used for a variety of purposes. As mentioned earlier, the information in a database is organized into tables. A table contains information for related items such as customers, suppliers, inventory, or human resources broken down into individual units of information. Creating a new table generally involves determining fields, assigning a data type to each field, modifying properties, designating the primary key, and naming the table. This process is referred to as defining the table structure.

**HINT**
Organize data in tables to minimize or eliminate duplication.

## Determining Fields

Microsoft Access is a database management system software program that allows you to design, create, input, maintain, manipulate, sort, and print data. Access is considered a relational database in which you organize data in related tables. In this chapter, you will be creating tables as part of a database, and learn how to relate tables in Chapter 2.

**HINT**
A database table contains fields that describe a person, customer, client, object, place, idea, or event.

The first step in creating a table is to determine the fields. A field is one piece of information about a person, a place, or an item. For example, one field could be a customer's name, another field could be a customer's address, and another a customer number. All fields for one unit, such as a customer, are considered a record. For example, in Project 2a, a record is all of the information pertaining to one employee of Premium Health Services. A collection of records becomes a table.

When designing a table, determine fields for information to be included on the basis of how you plan to use the data. When organizing fields, be sure to consider not only current needs for the data but also any future needs. For example, a company may need to keep track of customer names, addresses, and telephone numbers for current mailing lists. In the future, the company may want to promote a new product to customers who purchase a specific type of product. For this situation, a field that identifies product type must be included in the database. When organizing fields, consider all potential needs for the data but also try to keep the fields logical and manageable.

After deciding what data you want included in a table, you need to determine field names. Consider the following guidelines when naming fields in a table:

- Each field must contain a unique name.
- The name should describe the contents of the field.
- A field name can contain up to 64 characters.
- A field name can contain letters, numbers, spaces, and symbols except the period (.), comma (,), exclamation point (!), square brackets ([]), and grave accent (`).
- A field name cannot begin with a space.

In Project 2a, you will create a table containing information on employees of a medical corporation. The fields in this table and the names you will give to each field are shown in Figure 1.4.

Figure 1.4 Field Information and Names for Project 2a

| Employee Information | Field Name |
|---|---|
| ID number | *Emp#* |
| Last name | *LastName* |
| First name | *FirstName* |
| Middle initial | *MI* |
| Street address | *StreetAddress* |
| City | *City* |
| State | *State* |
| ZIP code | *ZipCode* |
| Department code | *DeptCode* |
| Date of hire | *HireDate* |
| Supplemental health insurance | *Yes/No* |

## Assigning a Data Type to Fields

**HINT**

Assign a data type for each field that determines the values that can be entered for the field.

Part of the process of designing a table includes specifying or assigning a data type to each field. The data type specifies the type of data you can enter in a field. Assigning a data type to fields helps maintain and manage the data and helps identify for anyone entering information in the field what type of data is expected. The data types you will use in fields in this chapter include *Text*, *Date/Time*, and *Yes/No*.

Assign the Text data type to a field where text will be entered such as names, addresses, and numbers that do not require calculations, such as telephone numbers, Social Security numbers, and ZIP codes. You can store up to 255 characters in the text data field with 255 as the default. Assign the Date/Time data type to a field where a date and/or time will be entered. You will assign the data types and field sizes shown in Figure 1.5 when you create a table in Project 2a.

Figure 1.5 Data Types for Project 2a

| Field Name | Data Type |
|---|---|
| *Emp#* | Text (Field Size = 5) |
| *LastName* | Text (Field Size = 30) |
| *FirstName* | Text (Field Size = 30) |
| *MI* | Text (Field Size = 2) |
| *StreetAddress* | Text (Field Size = 30) |
| *City* | Text (Field Size = 20) |
| *State* | Text (Field Size = 2) |
| *ZipCode* | Text (Field Size = 5) |
| *DeptCode* | Text (Field Size = 2) |
| *HireDate* | Date/Time |
| *SuppIns* | Yes/No |

Data entered for some fields in Project 2a, such as *ZipCode,* will be numbers. These numbers, however, are not values and will not be used in calculations. This is why they are assigned the data type of Text (rather than Number or Currency).

When assigning a field size, consider the data that will be entered in the field, and then shorten or lengthen (up to the maximum number) the number to accommodate any possible entries. For the *FirstName* field or the *LastName* field, for example, shortening the number to 30 would be appropriate, ensuring that all names would fit in the field. The two-letter state abbreviation will be used in the *State* field, so the number of characters is changed to 2.

## Creating a Table

When you create a new blank database, the database opens and a blank table displays in the work area in Datasheet view. Datasheet view is used primarily for entering data. To specify fields and identify data types for your table, you need to change to Design view. To do this, click the View button that displays in the Views group in the Home tab or the Table Tools Datasheet tab. Before switching to Design view, you must save the table. At the Save As dialog box, type a name for the table and then press Enter or click OK and the table displays in Design view as shown in Figure 1.6.

**Create a Table**
1. Click Create tab.
2. Click Table button.
3. Click View button.
4. Type name for table.
5. Press Enter or click OK.
6. Type field names, specify types, and include descriptions.

**Figure 1.6** Table in Design View

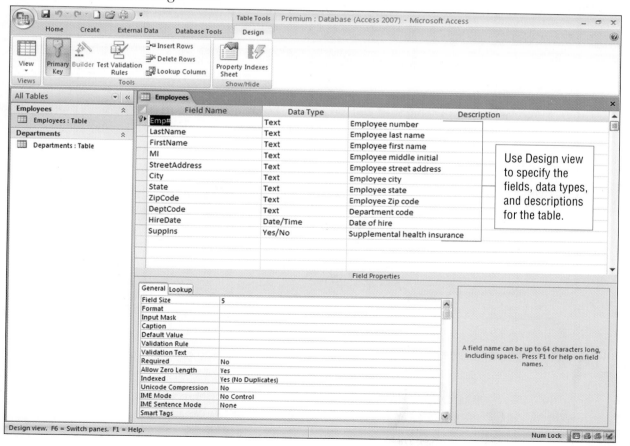

Save

By default, Access provides the *ID* field as the first field in the record and assigns the AutoNumber data type to the field. You can use the *ID* field or type your own field name. Accept the *ID* field name or type a new name and then press the Tab key. This moves the insertion point to the *Data Type* column. In this column, accept the data type or click the down-pointing arrow at the right side of the data type text and then click the desired data type at the drop-down list. Press the Tab key to move the insertion point to the *Description* column and then type a description for the field that specifies what should be entered in the field. Continue typing field names, assigning a data type to each field, and typing a description of all fields. When the table design is complete, save the table by clicking the Save button on the Quick Access toolbar or by clicking the Office button and then clicking *Save* at the drop-down list. Click the View button in the Views group in the Table Tools Design tab to switch to Datasheet view and enter records or click the Close button in the work area to close the table.

At the Table window shown in Figure 1.6, field names are entered, data types are assigned, and descriptions are typed. When assigning a data type, Access displays information in the bottom portion of the window in a section with the General tab selected. Information in this section can be changed to customize a data type for a field. For example, you can specify that only a maximum of two characters can be entered in the *MI* field.

A database can contain more than one table. Tables containing related data are saved in the same database. In Project 2a, you will create a table named Employees that is part of the database named Premium. In Project 2b, you will create another table as part of the Premium database that includes payroll information.

## Project **2a**  Creating an Employee Table

1. Open Access by clicking the Start button on the Taskbar, pointing to *All Programs*, pointing to *Microsoft Office*, and then clicking *Microsoft Office Access 2007*. (These steps may vary.)
2. At the Getting Started with Microsoft Office Access screen, click the Blank Database button in the *New Blank Database* section.
3. Click the folder icon located at the right side of the *File Name* text box in the *Blank Database* section.

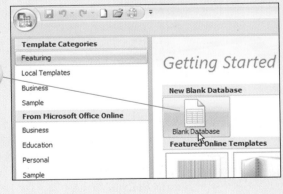

Step 2

Step 3

4. At the File New Database dialog box, navigate to the drive where your storage medium is located, type **Premium** in the *File name* text box, and then press Enter.

5. At the Getting Started with Microsoft Office Access screen, click the Create button located below the *File Name* text box in the *Blank Database* section.

6. At the Database window, change to Design view by clicking the View button in the Views group in the Home tab.

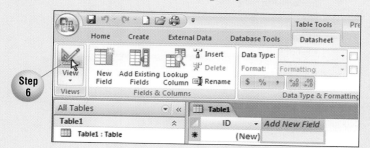

7. At the Save As dialog box, type **Employees** in the *Table Name* text box and then click OK.

8. In the table, type the fields shown in Figure 1.7 by completing the following steps:
   a. Type **Emp#** in the *Field Name* text box and then press the Tab key.
   b. Change the *Data Type* to *Text* by clicking the down-pointing arrow located in the *Data Type* box and then clicking *Text* at the drop-down list.
   c. Change the field size from the default of 255 to 5. To do this, select *255* that displays after *Field Size* in the *Field Properties* section of the window and then type 5.

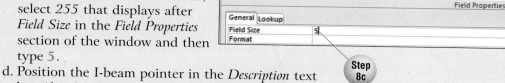

   d. Position the I-beam pointer in the *Description* text box (for the *Emp#*) and then click the left mouse button. Type **Employee number** in the *Description* text box and then press Tab.
   e. Type **LastName** in the *Field Name* text box and then press Tab.
   f. Change the field size to 30 and then click in the *Description* text box for the *LastName* field. Type **Employee last name** and then press Tab.
   g. Type **FirstName** in the *Field Name* text box and then press Tab.
   h. Change the field size to 30 and then click in the *Description* text box for the *FirstName* field. Type **Employee first name** and then press Tab.
   i. Continue typing the field names, data types, and descriptions as shown in Figure 1.7. Identify the following sizes: *MI* = 2, *StreetAddress* = 30, *City* = 20, *State* = 2, *ZipCode* = 5, and *DeptCode* = 2. (Refer to Figure 1.5.) To change the data type for the *HireDate* field, click the down-pointing arrow after *Text* and then click *Date/Time* at the drop-down list. To change the data type for the *SuppIns* field, click the down-pointing arrow after *Text* and then click *Yes/No* at the drop-down list.

9. When all of the fields are entered, save the table by clicking the Save button on the Quick Access toolbar.

10. Close the Employees table by clicking the Close button located at the upper right corner of the datasheet.

## Figure 1.7 Project 2a

| Field Name | Data Type | Description |
|---|---|---|
| 🔑 Emp# | Text | Employee number |
| LastName | Text | Employee last name |
| FirstName | Text | Employee first name |
| MI | Text | Employee middle initial |
| StreetAddress | Text | Employee street address |
| City | Text | Employee city |
| State | Text | Employee state |
| ZipCode | Text | Employee Zip code |
| DeptCode | Text | Department code |
| HireDate | Date/Time | Date of hire |
| SuppIns | Yes/No | Supplemental health insurance |

**HINT**

The active database is saved automatically on a periodic basis and also when you make another record active, close the table, or close the database.

✕ E**x**it Access

Access automatically saves an open (or active) database on a periodic basis and also when the database is closed. If you are working with a database that is saved on a removable storage medium, never remove the storage medium while the database is open because Access saves the database periodically. If the storage medium is not available when Access tries to save it, problems will be encountered and you run the risk of damaging the database. Exit (close) Access by clicking the Close button located in the upper right corner of the Access Title bar (contains an *X*) or by clicking the Office button and then clicking the Exit Access button located in the bottom right corner of the drop-down list.

The Employees table contains a *DeptCode* field. This field will contain a two-letter code identifying the department within the company. In Project 2b, you will create a table named Departments containing only two fields—the department code and the department name. Establishing a department code decreases the amount of data entered in the Employees table. For example, in an employee record, you type a two-letter code identifying the employee department rather than typing the entire department name. Imagine the time this saves when entering hundreds of employee records. This is an example of the power of a relational database.

## Project 2b  Creating a Department Table

1. At the Premium : Database window, create a new table in Design view. To do this, click the Create tab and then click the Table button in the Tables group.
2. At the Table1 window, click the View button in the Views group.
3. At the Save As dialog box, type Departments and then press Enter.
4. Type the fields shown in Figure 1.8 by completing the following steps:
   a. Type DeptCode in the *Field Name* text box and then press Tab.
   b. Click the down-pointing arrow after *AutoNumber* and then click *Text*.
   c. Change the field size to 2 and then click in the *Description* text box for the *DeptCode* field.
   d. Type Department code in the *Description* text box and then press the Tab key.

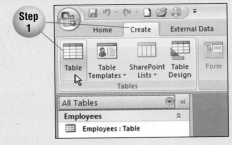

e. Type Department in the *Field Name* text box and then press Tab.

f. Change the field size to 30 and then click in the *Description* text box for the *Department* field.

g. Type Department name in the *Description* text box.

5. When all of the fields are entered, click the Save button on the Quick Access toolbar.

6. Close the Departments table by clicking the Close button located in the upper right corner of the table.

**Figure 1.8  Project 2b**

| Field Name | Data Type | Description |
|---|---|---|
| DeptCode | Text | Department code |
| Department | Text | Department name |

# Entering Data in a Table

Enter data in a table in a database in Datasheet view. A table datasheet displays the contents of a table in rows and columns in the same manner as a Word table or Excel worksheet. Each row in a datasheet represents one record. In the Employees table of the Premium database, one record will contain the information for one employee.

When you type data for the first field in the record, another row of cells is automatically inserted below the first row. Type the data for the first record, pressing Tab to move the insertion point to the next field or pressing Shift + Tab to move the insertion point to the previous field. The description you typed for each field when creating the table displays at the left side of the Access Status bar.

If you assigned the Yes/No data type to a field, a square displays in the field. You can leave this square empty or insert a check mark. If the field is asking a yes/no question, an empty box signifies "No" and a box with a check mark signifies "Yes." If the field is asking for a true/false answer, an empty box signifies "False" and a box with a check mark signifies "True." This field can also have an on/off response. An empty box signifies "Off" and a box with a check mark signifies "On." To insert a check mark in the box, tab to the field and then press the spacebar.

As you enter data in fields, the description you typed for each field displays at the left side of the Status bar. The descriptions help identify to the person entering data in the table what data is expected.

**QUICK STEPS**

**Enter Data in a Table**
1. Open database.
2. Double-click table name.
3. Make sure table displays in Datasheet view.
4. Type data in fields.

1. At the Premium : Database window, double-click *Employees : Table* in the Navigation pane.
2. At the Employees window, type the following data for five records in the specified fields. (Press Tab to move the insertion point to the next field or press Shift + Tab to move the insertion point to the previous field. When typing data, not all of the data may be visible. You will adjust column widths in a later project. For the *SuppIns* field, press the spacebar to insert a check mark indicating "Yes" and leave the check box blank indicating "No.")

Step 1

| | | |
|---|---|---|
| *Emp#* | = | 21043 |
| *LastName* | = | Brown |
| *FirstName* | = | Leland |
| *MI* | = | C. |
| *StreetAddress* | = | 112 Kansas Avenue |
| *City* | = | Missoula |
| *State* | = | MT |
| *ZipCode* | = | 84311 |
| *DeptCode* | = | PA |
| *HireDate* | = | 11/5/2007 |
| *SuppIns* | = | *Yes (Insert a check mark)* |

| | | |
|---|---|---|
| *Emp#* | = | 19034 |
| *LastName* | = | Guenther |
| *FirstName* | = | Julia |
| *MI* | = | A. |
| *StreetAddress* | = | 215 Bridge West |
| *City* | = | Lolo |
| *State* | = | MT |
| *ZipCode* | = | 86308 |
| *DeptCode* | = | MS |
| *HireDate* | = | 2/15/2005 |
| *SuppIns* | = | *No (Leave blank)* |

| | | |
|---|---|---|
| *Emp#* | = | 27845 |
| *LastName* | = | Oaklee |
| *FirstName* | = | Thomas |
| *MI* | = | E. |
| *StreetAddress* | = | 2310 Keating Road |
| *City* | = | Missoula |
| *State* | = | MT |
| *ZipCode* | = | 84325 |
| *DeptCode* | = | HR |
| *HireDate* | = | 6/8/2009 |
| *SuppIns* | = | *No (Leave blank)* |

| | | |
|---|---|---|
| *Emp#* | = | 08921 |
| *LastName* | = | Avery |

```
FirstName       =   Michael
MI              =   W.
StreetAddress   =   23155 Neadham Avenue
City            =   Florence
State           =   MT
ZipCode         =   85901
DeptCode        =   PA
HireDate        =   11/5/2006
SuppIns         =   Yes (Insert a check mark)

Emp#            =   30091
LastName        =   Latora
FirstName       =   Gina
MI              =   M.
StreetAddress   =   13221 138th Street
City            =   Missoula
State           =   MT
ZipCode         =   84302
DeptCode        =   HR
HireDate        =   9/16/2010
SuppIns         =   No (Leave blank)
```

3. After typing the data, save the table by clicking the Save button on the Quick Access toolbar.
4. Close the Employees table by clicking the Close button located in the upper right corner of the work area.
5. At the Premium : Database window, double-click *Departments : Table* in the Navigation pane.
6. At the Departments window, type the following data for four departments in the specified fields (press Tab to move the insertion point to the next field or press Shift + Tab to move the insertion point to the previous field):

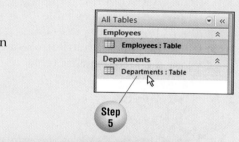

Step 5

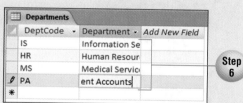

Step 6

```
DeptCode        =   IS
DepartmentName  =   Information Services

DeptCode        =   HR
DepartmentName  =   Human Resources

DeptCode        =   MS
DepartmentName  =   Medical Services

DeptCode        =   PA
DepartmentName  =   Patient Accounts
```

7. After typing the data, save the table by clicking the Save button on the Quick Access toolbar.
8. Close the Departments table by clicking the Close button located in the upper right corner of the table in the work area.

# Printing a Table

**QUICK STEPS**

**Print a Table**
1. Open database.
2. Open table.
3. Click Quick Print button.

Quick Print

Customize Quick Access Toolbar

Various methods are available for printing data in a table. One method for printing is to open the table and then click the Quick Print button on the Quick Access toolbar. If the Quick Print button is not visible on the Quick Access toolbar, click the Customize Quick Access Toolbar button that displays at the right side of the toolbar and then click *Quick Print* at the drop-down list.

When you click the Quick Print button, the information is sent directly to the printer without any formatting changes. In some fields created in the Employees table, this means that you would not be able to see all printed text in a field if all of the text did not fit in the field. For example, when typing the data in Project 2c, did you notice that the *StreetAddress* data was longer than the field column could accommodate? You can change the table layout to ensure that all data is visible. You will first print the Employees and Departments tables with the default settings, learn about changing the layout, and then print the tables again.

## Project 2d    Printing the Employees and Departments Tables with the Default Settings

1. Open the Employees table.
2. Click the Quick Print button on the Quick Access toolbar. (The table will print on two pages.)
3. Close the Employees table.
4. Open the Departments table.
5. Click the Quick Print button on the Quick Access toolbar.
6. Close the Departments table.

Step 2

Look at the printing of the Employees table and notice how the order of records displays differently in the printing (and in the table) than the order in which the records were typed. Access automatically sorted the records by employee number in ascending order. Access automatically sorted the records in the Departments table alphabetically by department name. You will learn more about sorting later in this chapter.

## Previewing a Table

**QUICK STEPS**

**Preview a Table**
1. Click Office button.
2. Point to *Print*.
3. Click *Print Preview*.

Before printing a table, you may want to display the table in Print Preview to determine how the table will print on the page. To display a table in Print Preview, click the Office button, point to *Print*, and then click *Print Preview*. This displays the table as it will appear when printed as well as the Print Preview tab as shown in Figure 1.9.

**Figure 1.9** Print Preview

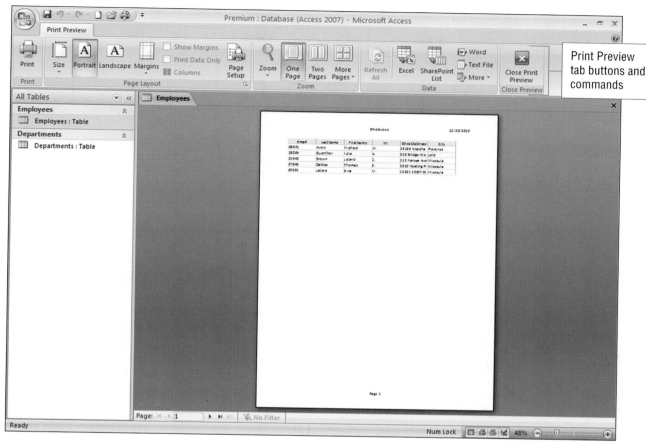

Print Preview tab buttons and commands

# Changing Page Layout

The Employees table printed on two pages in portrait orientation with default margins. You can change page orientation and page margins with options in the Page Layout group in Print Preview. By default, Access prints a table in standard page size that is 8.5 inches wide and 11 inches tall. Click the Size button in the Page Layout group and a drop-down list displays with options for changing the page size to legal size, executive size, envelope size, and so on.

Access prints a page in Portrait orientation by default. At this orientation, the page is 8.5 inches wide and 11 inches tall. You can change this orientation to landscape, which makes the page 11 inches wide and 8.5 inches tall. The orientation buttons are located in the Page Layout group. Access uses default top, bottom, left, and right margins of 1 inch. Change these default margins by clicking the Margins button in the Page Layout group and then clicking one of the predesigned margin options.

You can also change page layout with options at the Page Setup dialog box shown in Figure 1.10. To display this dialog box, click the Page Setup button in the Page Layout group. You can also display the dialog box by clicking the Page Layout group dialog box launcher.

QUICK STEPS

**Display Page Setup Dialog Box**
1. Click Office button, *Print, Print Preview.*
2. Click Page Setup button.
OR
1. Click Office button, *Print, Print Preview.*
2. Click Page Layout group dialog box launcher.

Size

Margins

Page Setup

**Figure 1.10** Page Setup Dialog Box with Print Options Tab Selected

Enter measurements in these text boxes to change page margins.

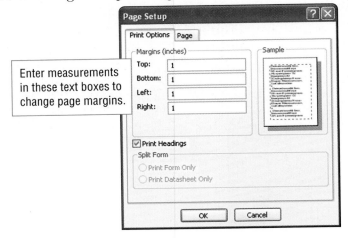

At the Page Setup dialog box with the Print Options tab selected, notice that the default margins are 1 inch. Change these defaults by typing a different number in the desired margin text box. By default, the table name prints at the top center of the page. For example, when you printed the Employees table, *Employees* printed at the top of the page along with the current date (printed at the right side of the page). *Page 1* also printed at the bottom of the page. If you do not want the name of the table and the date as well as the page number printed, remove the check mark from the *Print Headings* option at the Page Setup dialog box with the Print Options tab selected.

Change the table orientation at the Page Setup dialog box with the Page tab selected as shown in Figure 1.11. To change to landscape orientation, click *Landscape*. You can also change the paper size with options in the *Paper* section of the dialog box and specify the printer with options in the *Printer for (table name)* section of the dialog box.

**Figure 1.11** Page Setup Dialog Box with Page Tab Selected

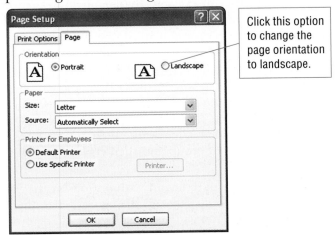

Click this option to change the page orientation to landscape.

# Changing Field Width

In the printing of the Employees table, not all of the data is visible in the *StreetAddress* field. You can remedy this situation by changing the width of the fields. Automatically adjust one field (column) in a table to accommodate the longest entry in the field by positioning the arrow pointer on the column boundary at the right side of the column until it turns into a double-headed arrow pointing left and right with a line between and then double-clicking the left mouse button. Automatically adjust adjacent columns by selecting the columns first and then double-clicking on a column boundary.

**QUICK STEPS**

**Changing Field Width**
1. Open table in Datasheet view.
2. Drag column boundary to desired position.

**HINT**

Automatically adjust column widths in an Access table in the same manner as adjusting column widths in an Excel worksheet.

## Project 2e    Changing Page Layout and Printing the Employees Table

1. Open the Employees table.
2. Display the table in Print Preview by clicking the Office button, pointing to *Print*, and then clicking *Print Preview*.
3. Change the page orientation by clicking the Landscape button in the Page Layout group in the Print Preview tab.
4. Change margins by completing the following steps:
   a. Click the Page Setup button in the Page Layout group in the Print Preview tab.
   b. At the Page Setup dialog box with the Print Options tab selected, select *1* in the *Top* text box and then type *2*.
   c. Select *1* in the *Left* text box and then type *0.5*.
   d. Select *1* in the *Right* text box and then type *0.5*.
   e. Click OK to close the dialog box.
5. Click the Close Print Preview button.
6. Automatically adjust columns in the table to accommodate the longest entry by completing the following steps:
   a. Position the arrow pointer on the *Emp#* field name (the arrow pointer turns into a down-pointing black arrow).
   b. Hold down the left mouse button, drag the arrow pointer to the *ZipCode* field name, and then release the mouse button.

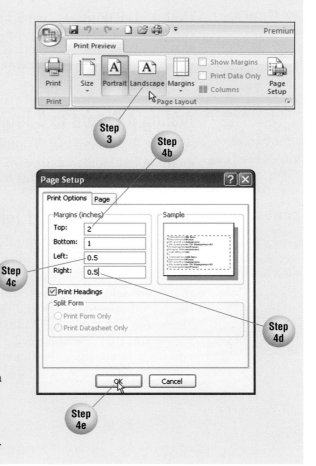

c. Position the arrow pointer on one of the column boundaries until it turns into a double-headed arrow pointing left and right with a line between and then double-click the left mouse button.

d. Click in any entry in the *ZipCode* column.

e. Drag the scroll box on the horizontal scroll bar to the right so the remaining fields (*DeptCode*, *HireDate*, and *SuppIns*) are visible.

f. Position the arrow pointer on the *DepCode* field name until the pointer turns into a down-pointing black arrow.

g. Hold down the left mouse button and then drag to the *SuppIns* field.

h. Double-click a column boundary between two of the selected columns.

i. Drag the scroll box to the left on the horizontal scroll bar so the *Emp#* field name displays.

j. Click in any entry in the *Emp#* field.

7. Send the table to the printer by clicking the Quick Print button on the Quick Access toolbar.

| Step 6c |
| --- |

| Employees | | |
| --- | --- | --- |
| Emp# | LastName | FirstName |
| 08921 | Avery | Michael |
| 19034 | Guenther | Julia |
| 21043 | Brown | Leland |
| 27845 | Oaklee | Thomas |
| 30091 | Latora | Gina |
| * | | |

## Maintaining a Table

**QUICK STEPS**

**Add a Record to a Table**
1. Open table in Datasheet view.
2. Click New button in Records group.
OR
1. Open table in Datasheet view.
2. Press Ctrl + Shift + +.

**Delete a Record from a Table**
1. Open table in Datasheet view.
2. Click Delete button arrow in Records group.
3. Click *Delete Record* at drop-down list.
4. Click Yes.

Once a table is created, more than likely it will require maintenance. For example, newly hired employees will need to be added to the Employees table. A system may be established for deleting an employee record when an employee leaves the company. The type of maintenance required on a table is related to the type of data stored in the table.

## Adding a Record to a Table

Add a new record to an existing table by clicking the New button in the Records group in the Home tab or with the keyboard shortcut Ctrl + Shift + +. Type the data in the appropriate fields in the new record.

## Deleting a Record in a Table

To delete an existing record in a table, select the row containing the record by clicking in the record selector bar. The record selector bar is the light blue area that displays at the left side of a record. When the mouse pointer is positioned in the record selector bar, the pointer turns into a black, right-pointing arrow. With the record selected, click the Delete button arrow in the Records group in the Home tab and then click *Delete Record* at the drop-down list. A message displays telling you that you will not be able to undo the delete operation and asking if you want to continue. At this message, click Yes.

## Project ㉑ Adding and Deleting Records in the Employees Table

1. With the Employees table open, add two new records to the table by completing the following steps:
   a. With the Home tab selected, click the New button in the Records group.

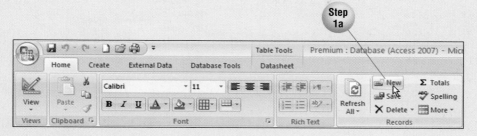

Step 1a

   b. Type the following data in the specified fields:

| | | |
|---|---|---|
| Emp# | = | 30020 |
| LastName | = | Pang |
| FirstName | = | Eric |
| MI | = | R. |
| StreetAddress | = | 15512 Country Drive |
| City | = | Lolo |
| State | = | MT |
| ZipCode | = | 86308 |
| DeptCode | = | IS |
| HireDate | = | 8/15/2009 |
| SuppIns | = | Yes (Insert a check mark) |

   c. Click the New button in the Records group (or just press the Tab key).
   d. Type the following data in the specified fields:

| | | |
|---|---|---|
| Emp# | = | 30023 |
| LastName | = | Zajac |
| FirstName | = | Elizabeth |
| MI | = | A. |
| StreetAddress | = | 423 Corrin Avenue |
| City | = | Missoula |
| State | = | MT |
| ZipCode | = | 84325 |
| DeptCode | = | HR |
| HireDate | = | 8/15/2007 |
| SuppIns | = | Yes (Insert a check mark) |

2. Delete a record in the table by completing the following steps:
   a. Select the row containing the record for Julia Guenther by clicking in the record selector bar that displays at the left side of the record. (When the mouse pointer is positioned in the record selector bar it turns into a black, right-pointing arrow.)

b. Click the Delete button arrow in the Records group and then click *Delete Record* at the drop-down list.

c. At the message telling you that you will not be able to undo the delete operation and asking if you want to continue, click Yes.

3. Click the Save button again on the Quick Access toolbar to save the Employees table.

4. Print the Employees table by completing the following steps:
   a. Click the Office button, point to *Print*, and then click *Print Preview*.
   b. In Print Preview, click the Landscape button in the Page Layout group.
   c. Click the Margins button in the Page Layout group and then click *Normal* at the drop-down list.
   d. Click the Print button at the left side of the Print Preview tab.
   e. Click OK at the Print dialog box.

5. Click the Close Print Preview button.

6. Save and then close the Employees table.

7. Close the **Premium.accdb** database.

# CHAPTER summary

- Microsoft Access is a database management system software program that will organize, store, maintain, retrieve, sort, and print all types of business data.

- Open a database by double-clicking the file name in the *Open Recent Database* section of the Getting Started with Microsoft Office Access screen. You can also open a database by double-clicking the desired database at the Open dialog box. Display this dialog box by clicking the Open button on the Quick Access toolbar or clicking the Microsoft Office button and then clicking *Open* at the drop-down list.

- Organize data in Access in related tables in a database.

- The first step in organizing data for a table is determining fields. A field is one piece of information about a person, place, or item. All fields for one unit, such as an employee or customer, are considered a record.

- A field name should be unique and describe the contents of the field. It can contain up to 64 characters including letters, numbers, spaces, and some symbols.

- Part of the process of designing a table is assigning a data type to each field, which helps maintain and manage data and helps identify what type of data is expected for the field.

- When assigning a data type, you can assign a specific field size to a field.

- Access automatically saves a database on a periodic basis and also when the database is closed.

- Enter data in a table in Datasheet view. Type data in a field, pressing the Tab key to move to the next field or pressing Shift + Tab to move to the previous field.

- Print a table by opening the table and then clicking the Quick Print button on the Quick Access toolbar.

- Change margins in a table with the Margins button in the Page Layout group in the Print Preview tab or with options at the Page Setup dialog box with the Print Options tab selected.

- Change the paper size with the Size button in the Page Layout group in the Print Preview tab or with the *Size* option at the Page Setup dialog box with the Page tab selected.

- Click the Landscape button in the Page Layout group in the Print Preview tab to change the page orientation or with options in the *Orientation* section of the Page Layout dialog box with the Page tab selected.

- Adjust field widths in a table in the same manner as column widths in an Excel worksheet. Double-click a column boundary to automatically adjust the width to accommodate the longest entry.

- Maintaining a table can include adding and/or deleting records.

# COMMANDS review

| FEATURE | RIBBON TAB, GROUP | BUTTON | QUICK ACCESS TOOLBAR | OFFICE BUTTON DROP-DOWN LIST | KEYBOARD SHORTCUT |
|---|---|---|---|---|---|
| Open dialog box | | | | Open | Ctrl + O |
| Close database | | | | Close Database | |
| Design view | Home, Views | OR | | | |
| Datasheet view | Home, Views | OR | | | |
| Save database | | | | Save | Ctrl + S |
| Save As dialog box | | | | Save As | |
| Print table | | | | | |
| Print Preview | | | | Print, Print Preview | |
| Portrait orientation | Print Preview, Page Layout | | | | |
| Landscape orientation | Print Preview, Page Layout | | | | |
| Page Setup dialog box | Print Preview, Page Layout | | | | |
| Margins | Print Preview, Page Layout | | | | |
| Add record | Home, Records | New | | | Ctrl + Shift + + |
| Delete record | Home, Records | X Delete ▾ | | | |

# CONCEPTS check

## Test Your Knowledge

**Completion:** For each description, indicate the correct term, symbol, or number.

1. This toolbar contains buttons for commonly used commands.  _____

2. This displays the names of objects within a database grouped by categories.  _____

3. All fields for one unit, such as an employee or customer, are considered to be this.

_____

4. In a field assigned the Yes/No data type, a check mark in the box in the field asking a yes/no question signifies this.

_____

5. This view is used in a table to define field names and assign data types.

_____

6. Use this view to enter data in fields.

_____

7. Change to landscape orientation by clicking the Landscape button in this group in the Print Preview tab.

_____

8. Add a new record to a table in this view.

_____

9. The Delete button is located in this group in the Home tab.

_____

10. Click this to select the row.

_____

# SKILLS check
## *Demonstrate Your Proficiency*

## Assessment

## 1 CREATE AN ORDERS TABLE IN A HEALTHPLUS DATABASE

1. Use Access to create a database for a store that sells vitamins and other health aids. The table you create will keep track of what vitamins are ordered for the store. (This table assumes that the database includes at least two other tables—one table containing information on suppliers and the other containing information on products. You will learn more about how tables are related in Chapter 2.) Use the name of the store, HealthPlus, as the database name, and name the table *Orders*. Create the following fields in the Orders table and assign the data type shown (you determine the Description):

| Field Name | | Data Type |
|---|---|---|
| *OrderNumber* | = | Text (field size = 3) |
| *ProductCode* | = | Text (field size = 2) |
| *SupplierNumber* | = | Text (field size = 2) |
| *DateOfOrder* | = | Date/Time |
| *AmountOfOrder* | = | Currency |

2. Save the table.
3. Change to Datasheet view and then enter the following data:

```
OrderNumber        =   214
ProductCode        =   MT
SupplierNumber     =   10
DateOfOrder        =   4/5/2010
AmountOfOrder      =   $875.50


OrderNumber        =   223
ProductCode        =   PA
SupplierNumber     =   27
DateOfOrder        =   4/6/2010
AmountOfOrder      =   $1,005.45


OrderNumber        =   241
ProductCode        =   GS
SupplierNumber     =   10
DateOfOrder        =   4/8/2010
AmountOfOrder      =   $441.95


OrderNumber        =   259
ProductCode        =   AV
SupplierNumber     =   18
DateOfOrder        =   4/8/2010
AmountOfOrder      =   $772.00
```

4. Automatically adjust the width of fields.
5. Save, print, and then close the Orders table.


## Assessment

## 2  ADD RECORDS TO THE ORDERS TABLE

1. With the **HealthPlus.accdb** database open, open the Orders table and then add the following records (remember to do this in Datasheet view):

```
OrderNumber        =   262
ProductCode        =   BC
SupplierNumber     =   27
DateOfOrder        =   4/9/2010
AmountOfOrder      =   $258.65


OrderNumber        =   265
ProductCode        =   VC
SupplierNumber     =   18
DateOfOrder        =   4/13/2010
AmountOfOrder      =   $1,103.45
```

2. Delete the record for order number 241.
3. Print the table with a top margin of 2 inches.
4. Close the Orders table.

# 3 CREATE A SUPPLIERS TABLE

1. With the **HealthPlus.accdb** database open, create a new table named Suppliers with the following fields and assign the data type shown (you determine the Description):

   | **Field Name** | | **Data Type** |
   |---|---|---|
   | *SupplierNumber* | = | Text (field size = 2) |
   | *SupplierName* | = | Text (field size = 20) |
   | *StreetAddress* | = | Text (field size = 30) |
   | *City* | = | Text (field size = 20) |
   | *State* | = | Text (field size = 2) |
   | *ZipCode* | = | Text (field size = 10) |

2. After creating and saving the table with the fields shown above, enter the following data in the table (remember to do this in Datasheet view):

   | *SupplierNumber* | = | 10 |
   |---|---|---|
   | *SupplierName* | = | VitaHealth, Inc. |
   | *StreetAddress* | = | 12110 South 23rd |
   | *City* | = | San Diego |
   | *State* | = | CA |
   | *ZipCode* | = | 97432-1567 |

   | *SupplierNumber* | = | 18 |
   |---|---|---|
   | *SupplierName* | = | Mainstream Supplies |
   | *StreetAddress* | = | 312 Evergreen Building |
   | *City* | = | Seattle |
   | *State* | = | WA |
   | *ZipCode* | = | 98220-2791 |

   | *SupplierNumber* | = | 21 |
   |---|---|---|
   | *SupplierName* | = | LaVerde Products |
   | *StreetAddress* | = | 121 Vista Road |
   | *City* | = | Phoenix |
   | *State* | = | AZ |
   | *ZipCode* | = | 86355-6014 |

   | *SupplierNumber* | = | 27 |
   |---|---|---|
   | *SupplierName* | = | Redding Corporation |
   | *StreetAddress* | = | 554 Ninth Street |
   | *City* | = | Portland |
   | *State* | = | OR |
   | *ZipCode* | = | 97466-3359 |

3. Automatically adjust the width of fields.
4. Save the Suppliers table.
5. Change the page orientation to landscape and then print the table.
6. Close the Suppliers table.
7. Close the **HealthPlus.accdb** database.

# CASE study

## *Apply Your Skills*

**Part 1**

You are the manager of Miles Music, a small music store that specializes in CDs, DVDs, and Laserdiscs. Recently, the small store has increased its volume of merchandise, requiring better organization and easier retrieval of information. You decide to create a database named *MilesMusic* that contains two tables. Name one table *Inventory* and include fields that identify the category of music, the name of the CD or DVD, the name of the performer or band, and the media type (such as CD or DVD). Create a second table named *Category* that includes a short abbreviation for a category (such as R for Rap, A for Alternative, and C for Country). When entering records in the Inventory table, enter the category abbreviation you established in the Category table (rather than the entire category name). Enter at least eight records in the Inventory table and identify at least five categories of music. Print the Inventory and Category tables.

**Part 2**

As part of the maintenance of the database, you need to delete and add records as items are sold or orders are received. Delete two records from the Inventory table and then add three additional records. Print the Inventory table and then close the **MilesMusic.accdb** database.

**Part 3**

In Microsoft Word, create a document that describes the tables you created in the **MilesMusic.accdb** database. In the document, specify the fields in each table, the data types assigned to each field, and the field size (if appropriate). Apply any formatting to the document to enhance the visual appeal and then save the document and name it **Access_C1_CS_P3**. Print and then close **Access_C1_CS_P3.docx**.

# CHAPTER 2

# Creating Relationships between Tables

## PERFORMANCE OBJECTIVES

**Upon successful completion of Chapter 2, you will be able to:**

- **Create a database table with a primary key and a foreign key**
- **Create a one-to-many relationship between tables**
- **Create a one-to-one relationship between tables**
- **Display related records in a subdatasheet**

**Tutorial 2.1**
Working with Tables and Relationships

Access is a relational database program that allows you to create tables that have a relation or connection to each other within the same database. In Chapter 1, you created a table containing information on employees and another containing department information. With Access, you can connect these tables through a common field that appears in both tables.

In this chapter you will learn how to identify a primary key field in a table that is unique to that table. In Access, data can be divided into logical groupings in tables for easier manipulation and management. Duplicate information is generally minimized in tables in the same database. A link or relationship, however, should connect the tables. In this chapter, you will define primary keys and define relationships between tables.

*Note: Before beginning computer projects, copy the Access2007L1C2 subfolder from the Access2007L1 folder on the CD that accompanies this textbook to your storage medium and make Access2007L1C2 the active folder.*

## Project 1 Establish Relationships between Tables

You will specify primary keys in tables, establish one-to-many and one-to-one relationships between tables, specify referential integrity, and print the relationships. You will also edit and delete a relationship and display records in a datasheet.

# Creating Related Tables

Generally, a database management system fits into one of two categories—either a file management system (also sometimes referred to as a *flat file database*) or a relational database management system. In a file management system, data is stored without indexing and sequential processing. This type of system lacks flexibility in manipulating data and requires the same data to be stored in more than one place.

In a relational database management system, like Access, relationships are defined between sets of data allowing greater flexibility in manipulating data and eliminating data redundancy (entering the same data in more than one place). In projects in this chapter, you will define relationships between tables in the insurance company database. Because these tables will be related, information on a client does not need to be repeated in a table on claims filed. If you used a file management system to maintain insurance records, you would need to repeat the client information for each claim filed.

## Determining Relationships

Taking time to plan a database is extremely important. Creating a database with related tables takes even more consideration. You need to determine how to break down the required data and what tables to create to eliminate redundancies. One idea to help you determine the necessary tables in a database is to think of the word "about." For example, an insurance company database will probably need a table "about" clients, another "about" the type of coverage, another "about" claims, and so on. A table should be about only one subject, such as a client, customer, department, or supplier.

**Figure 2.1** SouthwestInsurance.accdb Tables

**Clients table**
ClientNumber
Client
StreetAddress
City
State
ZipCode

**Insurance table**
LicenseNumber
ClientNumber
InsuranceCode
UninsuredMotorist

**Claims table**
ClaimNumber
ClientNumber
LicenseNumber
DateOfClaim
AmountOfClaim

**Coverage table**
InsuranceCode
TypeOfInsurance

Along with deciding on the necessary tables for a database, you also need to determine the relationship between tables. The ability to relate, or "join," tables is part of what makes Access a relational database system. Figure 2.1 illustrates the tables and fields that either are or will become part of the SouthwestInsurance.accdb database. Notice how each table is about only one subject—clients, type of insurance, claims, or coverage.

Some fields such as *ClientNumber*, *LicenseNumber*, and *InsuranceCode* appear in more than one table. These fields are used to create a relationship between tables. For example, in Project 1b you will create a relationship between the Clients table and the Insurance table with the *ClientNumber* field.

Creating relationships between tables tells Access how to bring the information in the database back together again. With relationships defined, you can bring information together to create queries, forms, and reports. (You will learn about these features in future chapters.)

**HINT**
Access uses a primary key to associate data from multiple tables.

## Creating a Primary Field

Before creating a relationship between tables, you need to define the primary key in a table. In a table, at least one field must be unique so that one record can be distinguished from another. A field (or several fields) with a unique value is considered a ***primary key***. When a primary key is defined, Access will not allow duplicate values in the primary field. For example, the *ClientNumber* field in the Clients table must contain a unique number (you would not assign the same client number to two different clients). If you define this as the primary key field, Access will not allow you to type the same client number in two different records.

In a field specified as a primary key, Access expects a value in each record in the table. This is referred to as ***entity integrity***. If a value is not entered in a field, Access actually enters a null value. A null value cannot be given to a primary key field. Access will not let you close a database containing a primary field with a null value.

To define a field as a primary key, open the table and then change to Design view. Position the insertion point somewhere in the row containing the field you want to identify as the primary key and then click the Primary Key button in the Tools group. An image of a key is inserted at the beginning of the row identified as the primary key field. To define more than one field as a primary key, select the rows containing the fields you want as primary keys and then click the Primary Key button in the Tools group.

**Specify a Primary Key**
1. Open table in Design view.
2. Click desired field.
3. Click Primary Key button.
4. Click Save button.

**HINT**
You must enter a value in the primary key field in every record.

Primary Key

## Creating a Foreign Key

A primary key field in one table may be a foreign key in another. For example, if you define the *ClientNumber* field in the Clients table as the primary key, the *ClientNumber* field in the Insurance table will then be considered a ***foreign key***. The primary key field and the foreign key field form a relationship between the two tables. In the Clients table, each entry in the *ClientNumber* field will be unique (it is the primary key), but the same client number may appear more than once in the *ClientNumber* field in the Insurance table (such as a situation where a client has insurance on more than one vehicle). Each table in Figure 2.1 contains a unique field that will be defined as the primary key. Figure 2.2 identifies the primary keys and also foreign keys.

**Figure 2.2** Primary and Foreign Keys

**Clients table**
ClientNumber *(primary key)*
Client
StreetAddress
City
State
ZipCode

**Insurance table**
LicenseNumber *(primary key)*
ClientNumber *(foreign key)*
InsuranceCode *(foreign key)*
UninsuredMotorist

**Claims table**
ClaimNumber *(primary key)*
ClientNumber *(foreign key)*
LicenseNumber *(foreign key)*
DateOfClaim
AmountOfClaim

**Coverage table**
InsuranceCode *(primary key)*
TypeOfInsurance

In Project 1a, you will create another table for the SouthwestInsurance.accdb database, enter data, and then define primary keys for the tables. In the section following Project 1a, you will learn how to create relationships between the tables.

## Project 1a  Creating a Table and Defining Primary Keys

1. Display the Open dialog box and make the Access2007L1C2 folder on your storage medium the active folder.
2. Open the **SouthwestInsurance.accdb** database.
3. At the SouthwestInsurance : Database window, create a new table by completing the following steps:
   a. Click the Create tab.
   b. Click the Table button in the Tables group.
   c. At the Table window, click the View button in the Views group in the Table Tools Datasheet tab.
   d. At the Save As dialog box, type Insurance in the *Table Name* text box and then press Enter or click OK.
   e. Type the fields, assign the data types, and type the descriptions as shown below (for assistance, refer to Chapter 1, Project 1a):

   | Field Name | Data Type | Description |
   |---|---|---|
   | *LicenseNumber* | Text (Field Size = 7) | Vehicle license number |
   | *ClientNumber* | Text (Field Size = 4) | Client number |
   | *InsuranceCode* | Text (Field Size = 1) | Insurance code |
   | *UninsuredMotorist* | Yes/No | Uninsured motorist coverage |

4. Click the Save button on the Quick Access toolbar.
5. Notice the key that displays at the left side of the *LicenseNumber* field identifying the field as a primary key.
6. Close the Insurance table by clicking the Close button located in the upper right corner of the window.

7. Define primary keys for the other tables in the database by completing the following steps:
   a. At the SouthwestInsurance : Database window, double-click *Claims* in the Navigation pane.
   b. With the Claims table open, click the View button to switch to Design view.
   c. Click anywhere in the text *ClaimNumber* and then click the Primary Key button in the Tools group.

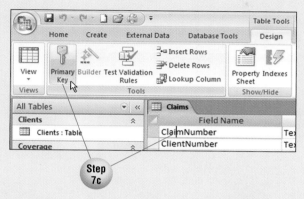

d. Click the Save button on the Quick Access toolbar.
e. Close the Claims table.
f. At the SouthwestInsurance : Database window, double-click *Clients* in the Navigation pane.
g. With the Clients table open, click the View button to switch to Design view.
h. Click anywhere in the text *ClientNumber* and then click the Primary Key button in the Tools group.

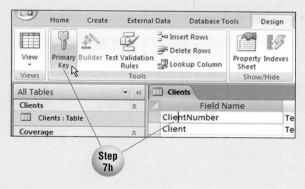

i. Click the Save button on the Quick Access toolbar.
j. Close the Clients table.
k. At the SouthwestInsurance : Database window, double-click *Coverage* in the Navigation pane.
l. With the Coverage table open, click the View button to switch to Design view.
m. Click anywhere in the text *InsuranceCode* and then click the Primary Key button in the Tools group.

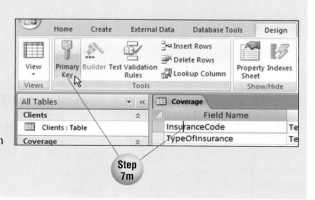

n. Click the Save button on the Quick Access toolbar.

o. Close the Coverage table.

8. Open the Insurance table and then type the following data in the specified fields. (If the *Uninsured Motorist* field is Yes, insert a check mark in the field by pressing the spacebar. If the field is No, leave the check box blank.)

| | | |
|---|---|---|
| LicenseNumber | = | 341 VIT |
| ClientNumber | = | 3120 |
| InsuranceCode | = | F |
| UninsuredMotorist | = | Yes |
| | | |
| LicenseNumber | = | 776 ERU |
| ClientNumber | = | 9383 |
| InsuranceCode | = | F |
| UninsuredMotorist | = | No |
| | | |
| LicenseNumber | = | 984 CWS |
| ClientNumber | = | 7335 |
| InsuranceCode | = | L |
| UninsuredMotorist | = | Yes |
| | | |
| LicenseNumber | = | 877 BNN |
| ClientNumber | = | 4300 |
| InsuranceCode | = | L |
| UninsuredMotorist | = | Yes |
| | | |
| LicenseNumber | = | 310 YTV |
| ClientNumber | = | 3120 |
| InsuranceCode | = | F |
| UninsuredMotorist | = | Yes |

**Insurance**

| LicenseNum ▾ | ClientNumb ▾ | InsuranceCo ▾ | UninsuredM ▾ | Add New Field |
|---|---|---|---|---|
| 341 VIT | 3120 | F | ☑ | |
| 776 ERU | 9383 | F | ☐ | |
| 984 CWS | 7335 | L | ☑ | |
| 877 BNN | 4300 | L | ☑ | |
| 310 YTV | 3120 | F | ☑ | |
| * | | | ☐ | |

Step 8

9. Save and then close the Insurance table.

# HINT

Defining a relationship between tables is one of the most powerful features of a relational database management system.

## Establishing a Relationship between Tables

In Access, one table can be related to another, which is generally referred to as performing a ***join***. When tables with a common field are joined, data can be extracted from both tables as if they were one large table. Another reason for relating tables is to ensure the integrity of the data. For example, in Project 1b, you will create a relationship between the Clients table and the Claims table. The relationship that is established will ensure that a client cannot be entered in the Claims table without first being entered in the Clients table. This ensures that a claim is not processed on a person who is not a client of the insurance company. This type of relationship is called a one-to-many relationship, which means that one record in the Clients table will match zero, one, or many records in the Claims table.

In a one-to-many relationship, the table containing the "one" is referred to as the ***primary table*** and the table containing the "many" is referred to as the ***related table***. Access follows a set of rules known as ***referential integrity***, which enforces consistency between related tables. These rules are enforced when data is updated in related tables. The referential integrity rules ensure that a record added to a related table has a matching record in the primary table.

**HINT**

Use the Table Analyzer Wizard to analyze your tables and restructure them to better conform to relational theory. Start the wizard by clicking the Database Tools tab and then clicking the Analyze Table button.

## Creating a One-to-Many Relationship

A relationship is specified between existing tables in a database. To create a one-to-many relationship, open the database containing the tables to be related. Click the Database Tools tab and then click the Relationships button in the Show/Hide group. This displays the Show Table dialog box, as shown in Figure 2.3. At the Show Table dialog box, each table that will be related must be added to the Relationships window. To do this, click the first table name to be included and then click Add. Continue in this manner until all necessary table names have been added to the Relationships window and then click the Close button.

**Figure 2.3** Show Table Dialog Box

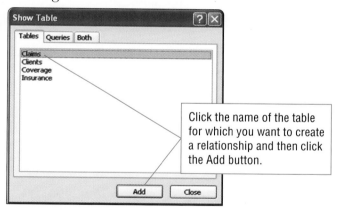

Click the name of the table for which you want to create a relationship and then click the Add button.

At the Relationships window, such as the one shown in Figure 2.4, use the mouse to drag the common field from the primary table (the "one") to the related table (the "many"). This causes the Edit Relationships dialog box to display as shown in Figure 2.5. At the Edit Relationships dialog box, check to make sure the correct field name displays in the *Table/Query* and *Related Table/Query* list boxes and the relationship type at the bottom of the dialog box displays as *One-To-Many*.

**Figure 2.4** Relationships Window

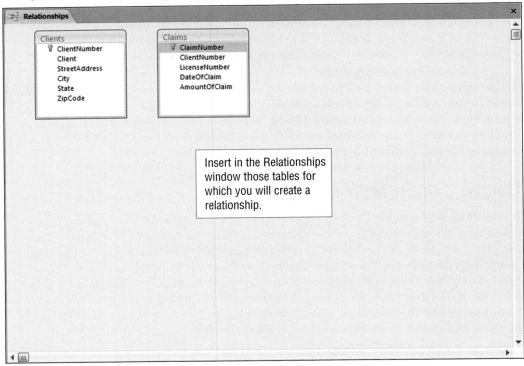

Insert in the Relationships window those tables for which you will create a relationship.

**Figure 2.5** Edit Relationships Dialog Box

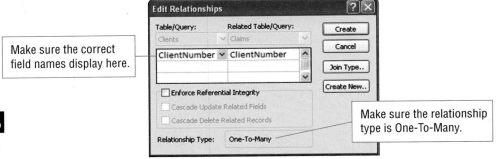

Make sure the correct field names display here.

Make sure the relationship type is One-To-Many.

**QUICK STEPS**

**Create a One-to-Many Relationship**
1. Click Database Tools tab.
2. Click Relationships button.
3. At Show Table dialog box, add tables to be related.
4. At Relationships window, drag "one" field from primary table to "many" field in related table.
5. At Edit Relationships dialog box, enforce referential integrity.
6. Click Create button.
7. Click Save button.

Specify the relationship options by choosing *Enforce Referential Integrity*, as well as *Cascade Update Related Fields* and/or *Cascade Delete Related Records*. Click the Create button. This causes the Edit Relationships dialog box to close and the Relationships window to display showing the relationship between the tables.

In Figure 2.6, the Clients table displays with a black line attached along with the number *1* (signifying the "one" side of the relationship). The black line is connected to the Claims table along with the infinity symbol ∞ (signifying the "many" side of the relationship). The black line, called the ***join line***, is thick at both ends if the enforce referential integrity option has been chosen. If this option is not chosen, the line is thin at both ends. Click the Save button on the Quick Access toolbar to save the relationship. Close the Relationships window by clicking the Close button located in the upper right corner of the window.

**Figure 2.6** One-to-Many Relationship

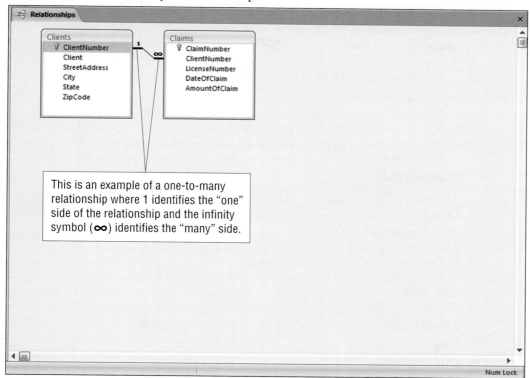

This is an example of a one-to-many relationship where 1 identifies the "one" side of the relationship and the infinity symbol (∞) identifies the "many" side.

## Specifying Referential Integrity

Choose *Enforce Referential Integrity* at the Edit Relationships dialog box to ensure that the relationships between records in related tables are valid. Referential integrity can be set if the field from the primary table is a primary key and the related fields have the same data type. When referential integrity is established, a value for the primary key must first be entered in the primary table before it can be entered in the related table.

If you select only *Enforce Referential Integrity* and the related table contains a record, you will not be able to change a primary key value in the primary table. You will not be able to delete a record in the primary table if its key value equals a foreign key value in the related table. If you choose *Cascade Update Related Fields*, you will be able to change a primary key value in the primary table and Access will automatically update the matching value in the related table. Choose *Cascade Delete Related Records* and you will be able to delete a record in the primary table and Access will delete any related records in the related table.

## Printing Relationships

You can print a report displaying the relationships between tables. To do this, display the Relationships window and then click the Relationship Report button in the Tools group. This displays the Relationships report in Print Preview. Click the Print button in the Print group in the Print Preview tab. After printing the relationships report, click the Close button that displays at the right side of the Relationships window.

**HINT**
Referential integrity ensures that a record exists in the "one" table before the record can be entered in the "many" table.

**QUICK STEPS**

**Print Database Relationships**
1. Click Database Tools tab.
2. Click Relationships button.
3. Click Relationships Report button.
4. Click Print button.
5. Click OK at Print dialog box.
6. Click Close button.

Relationship Report

Print

# Relating Tables in the SouthwestInsurance Database

The SouthwestInsurance.accdb database contains the four tables shown in Figure 2.1. Each table contains data about something—clients, insurance, claims, and coverage. You can relate these tables so that data can be extracted from more than one table as if they were all one large table. The relationships between the tables are identified in Figure 2.7.

**Figure 2.7** Relationships between SouthwestInsurance Tables

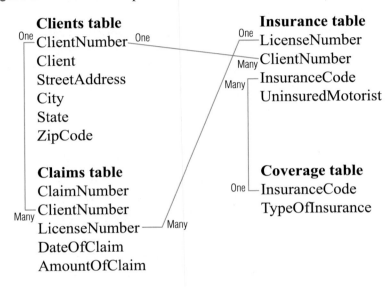

Relate the tables shown in Figure 2.7 so you can extract information from more than one table. For example, you can design a report about claims that contains information on claims as well as information on the clients submitting the claims.

## Project 1b · Creating a One-to-Many Relationship between the Client and Claims Tables

1. With the **SouthwestInsurance.accdb** database open, click the Database Tools tab and then click the Relationships button in the Show/Hide group.

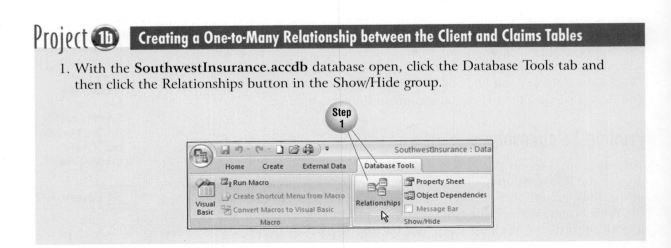

2. At the Show Table dialog box, add the Clients and Claims tables to the Relationships window by completing the following steps:
   a. Click *Clients* in the list box and then click Add.
   b. Click *Claims* in the list box and then click Add.
3. Click the Close button to close the Show Table dialog box.
4. At the Relationships window, drag the *ClientNumber* field from the Clients table to the Claims table by completing the following steps:
   a. Position the arrow pointer on the *ClientNumber* field that displays in the Clients table.
   b. Hold down the left mouse button, drag the arrow pointer (with a field icon attached) to the *ClientNumber* field in the *Claims* table, and then release the mouse button. (This causes the Edit Relationships dialog box to display.)

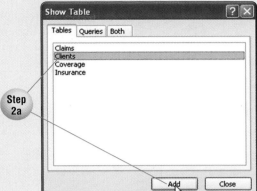

Step
2a

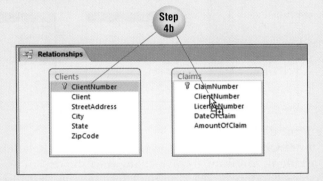

Step
4b

5. At the Edit Relationships dialog box, make sure *ClientNumber* displays in the *Table/Query* and *Related Table/Query* list boxes and the relationship type at the bottom of the dialog box displays as *One-To-Many*.
6. Enforce the referential integrity of the relationship by completing the following steps:
   a. Click *Enforce Referential Integrity*. (This makes the other two options available.)
   b. Click *Cascade Update Related Fields*.
   c. Click *Cascade Delete Related Records*.
7. Click the Create button. (This causes the Edit Relationships dialog box to close and the Relationships window to display showing a thick black line connecting Clients to Claims. At the Clients side, a *1* will appear and an infinity symbol ∞ will display at the Claims side of the thick black line.)

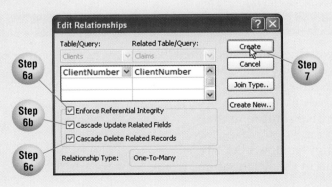

Step
6a

Step
6b

Step
6c

Step
7

8. Click the Save button on the Quick Access toolbar to save the relationship.
9. Print the relationships by completing the following steps:
   a. At the Relationships window, click the Relationship Report button in the Tools group. (This displays the Relationships report in Print Preview.)
   b. Click the Print button in the Print group.

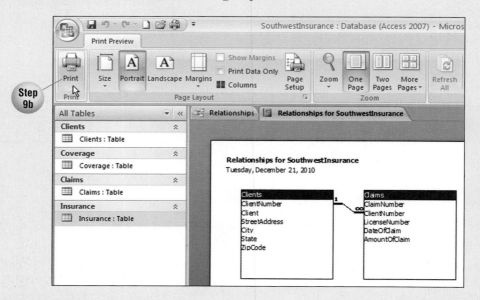

   c. Click OK at the Print dialog box.
   d. Click the Close button that displays at the right side of the Relationships window.
   e. At the message asking if you want to save changes to the design of the report, click No.
10. Close the Relationships window by clicking the Close button that displays at the right side of the Relationships window.

Once a relationship has been established between tables, clicking the Relationships button causes the Relationships window to display (rather than the Show Table dialog box). To create additional relationships, click the Database Tools tab, click the Relationships button in the Show/Hide group, and then click the Show Table button in the Relationships group. This displays the Show Table dialog box where you can specify the tables you need for creating another relationship.

## Project 1c  Creating Additional One-to-Many Relationships in a Database

1. With the **SouthwestInsurance.accdb** database open, create another one-to-many relationship between the Clients table and the Insurance table. Begin by clicking the Database Tools tab.
2. Click the Relationships button in the Show/Hide group.
3. At the Relationships window, click the Show Table button in the Relationships group.

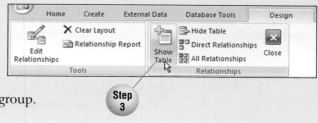

4. At the Show Table dialog box, click *Insurance* in the list box, and then click the Add button. (You do not need to add the Clients table because it was added in Project 1b.)
5. Click the Close button to close the Show Table dialog box.
6. At the Relationships window, drag the *ClientNumber* field from the Clients table to the Insurance table by completing the following steps:
   a. Position the arrow pointer on the *ClientNumber* field that displays in the Clients table.
   b. Hold down the left mouse button, drag the arrow pointer (with a field icon attached) to the *ClientNumber* field in the Insurance table, and then release the mouse button. (This causes the Edit Relationships dialog box to display.)

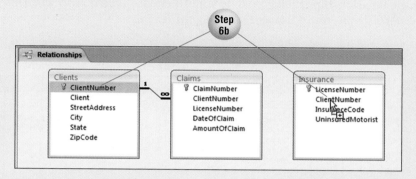

Step 6b

7. At the Edit Relationships dialog box, make sure *ClientNumber* displays in the *Table/Query* and *Related Table/Query* list boxes and the relationship type at the bottom of the dialog box displays as *One-To-Many*.
8. Enforce the referential integrity of the relationship by completing the following steps:
   a. Click *Enforce Referential Integrity*. (This makes the other two options available.)
   b. Click *Cascade Update Related Fields*.
   c. Click *Cascade Delete Related Records*.
9. Click the Create button. (This causes the Edit Relationships dialog box to close and the Relationships window to display showing a thick black line connecting Clients to Insurance. At the Clients side, a *1* will appear and an infinity symbol ∞ will display at the Insurance side of the thick black line.)

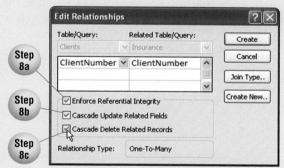

Step 8a

Step 8b

Step 8c

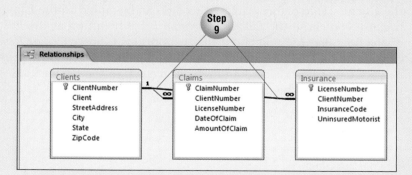

Step 9

10. Click the Save button on the Quick Access toolbar to save the relationship.

11. With the Relationships window still open, create the following one-to-many relationships by completing steps similar to those in Steps 3 through 10:
   a. Create a relationship between *LicenseNumber* in the Insurance table and the Claims table. (*LicenseNumber* in the Insurance table is the "one" and *LicenseNumber* in the Claims table is the "many.") At the Edit Relationships dialog box, be sure to choose *Enforce Referential Integrity*, *Cascade Update Related Fields*, and *Cascade Delete Related Records*.
   b. Add the Coverage table to the Relationships window and then create a relationship between *InsuranceCode* in the Coverage table and the Insurance table. (*InsuranceCode* in the Coverage table is the "one" and *InsuranceCode* in the Insurance table is the "many." At the Edit Relationships dialog box, be sure to choose *Enforce Referential Integrity*, *Cascade Update Related Fields*, and *Cascade Delete Related Records*.

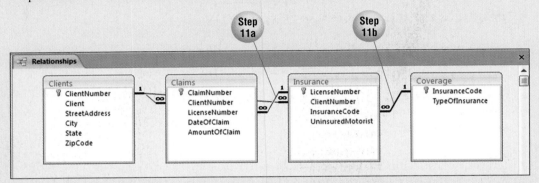

12. Click the Save button on the Quick Access toolbar.
13. Print the relationships by completing the following steps:
   a. At the Relationships window, click the Relationship Report button in the Tools group. (This displays the Relationships report in Print Preview.)
   b. Click the Print button in the Print group and then click OK at the Print dialog box.
   c. Click the Close button that displays at the right side of the Relationships window.
   d. At the message asking if you want to save changes to the design of the report, click No.
14. Close the Relationships window by clicking the Close button that displays at the right side of the Relationships window.

   In the relationship established in Project 1b, a record must first be added to the Clients table before a related record can be added to the Claims table. This is because you chose the *Enforce Referential Integrity* option at the Edit Relationships dialog box. Because you chose the two options *Cascade Update Related Fields* and *Cascade Delete Related Records*, records in the Clients table (the primary table) can be updated and/or deleted and related records in the Claims table (related table) will automatically be updated or deleted.

1. With the **SouthwestInsurance.accdb** database open, open the Clients table.
2. Change two client numbers in the Clients database (Access will automatically change it in the Claims table) by completing the following steps:
   a. Make sure the Clients window displays in Datasheet view.
   b. Click once in the *ClientNumber* field for Paul Vuong containing the number *4300*.
   c. Change the number from *4300* to *4308*.
   d. Click once in the *ClientNumber* field for Vernon Cook containing the number *7335*.
   e. Change the number from *7335* to *7325*.
   f. Click the Save button on the Quick Access toolbar.
   g. Close the Clients table.
   h. Open the Claims table. (Notice that the client numbers for Vernon Cook and Paul Vuong automatically changed.)
   i. Close the Claims table.

3. Open the Clients table, make sure the table displays in Datasheet view, and then add the following records at the end of the table:

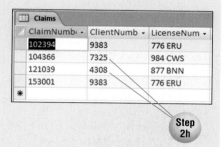

| ClientNumber | = | 5508 |
|---|---|---|
| Client | = | Martina Bentley |
| StreetAddress | = | 6503 Taylor Street |
| City | = | Scottsdale |
| State | = | AZ |
| ZipCode | = | 85889 |

| ClientNumber | = | 2511 |
|---|---|---|
| Client | = | Keith Hammond |
| StreetAddress | = | 21332 Janski Road |
| City | = | Glendale |
| State | = | AZ |
| ZipCode | = | 85310 |

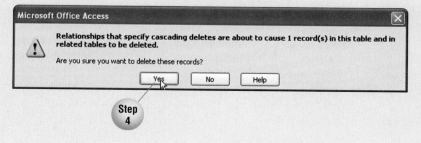

Step 3

4. With the Clients table still open, delete the record for Elaine Hueneka. At the message telling you that relationships that specify cascading deletes are about to cause records in this table and related tables to be deleted, click Yes.

**Microsoft Office Access**

⚠ Relationships that specify cascading deletes are about to cause 1 record(s) in this table and in related tables to be deleted.

Are you sure you want to delete these records?

[ Yes ] [ No ] [ Help ]

Step 4

5. Save, print, and then close the Clients table.
6. Open the Insurance table, make sure the table displays in Datasheet view, and then add the following records at the end of the table:

        *LicenseNumber*   =   422 RTW
        *ClientNumber*   =   5508
        *InsuranceCode*   =   L
        *UninsuredMotorist*   =   Yes

        *LicenseNumber*   =   130 YWR
        *ClientNumber*   =   5508
        *InsuranceCode*   =   F
        *UninsuredMotorist*   =   No

        *LicenseNumber*   =   795 GRT
        *ClientNumber*   =   2511     **Step 6**
        *InsuranceCode*   =   L
        *UninsuredMotorist*   =   Yes

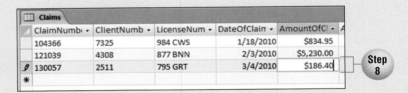

**Insurance**

| | LicenseNum | ClientNumb | InsuranceCo | UninsuredM | A |
|---|---|---|---|---|---|
| ⊞ | 310 YTV | 3120 | F | ☑ | |
| ⊞ | 341 VIT | 3120 | F | ☑ | |
| ⊞ | 877 BNN | 4308 | L | ☑ | |
| ⊞ | 984 CWS | 7325 | L | ☑ | |
| ⊞ | 422 RTW | 5508 | L | ☑ | |
| ⊞ | 130 YWR | 5508 | F | ☐ | |
| ⊞ | 795 GRT | 2511 | L | ☑ | |
| * | | | | ☐ | |

7. Save, print, and then close the Insurance table.
8. Open the Claims table, make sure the table displays in Datasheet view, and then add the following record:
    *ClaimNumber*   =   130057
    *ClientNumber*   =   2511
    *LicenseNumber*   =   795 GRT
    *DateOfClaim*   =   3/4/2010
    *AmountOfClaim*   =   $186.40

**Claims**

| | ClaimNumb | ClientNumb | LicenseNum | DateOfClaim | AmountOfCl | A |
|---|---|---|---|---|---|---|
| | 104366 | 7325 | 984 CWS | 1/18/2010 | $834.95 | |
| | 121039 | 4308 | 877 BNN | 2/3/2010 | $5,230.00 | |
| ⌀ | 130057 | 2511 | 795 GRT | 3/4/2010 | $186.40 | |
| * | | | | | | |

**Step 8**

9. Save and then print the Claims table.
10. With the Claims table still open, try to enter a record for a client who has not been entered in the Clients table by completing the following steps (Access will not allow this because of the one-to-many relationship that was established in Project 1b):
    a. Add the following record to the Claims table:
        *ClaimNumber*   =   201221
        *ClientNumber*   =   5824
        *LicenseNumber*   =   640 TRS
        *DateOfClaim*   =   3/11/2010
        *AmountOfClaim*   =   $895.25
    b. Click the Close button to close the Claims table. This causes a message to display telling you that the record cannot be added or changed because a related record is required in the Clients table. At this message, click OK.
    c. A message displays warning you that Access cannot save the table, that closing the object will cause the changes to be made, and asking if you want to close the database object. At this warning, click Yes.

# Editing and Deleting a Relationship

You can make changes to a relationship that has been established between tables. The relationship can also be deleted. To edit a relationship, open the database containing the tables with the relationship, click the Database Tools tab, and then click the Relationships button in the Show/Hide group. This displays the Relationships window with the related tables displayed in boxes. Click the Edit Relationships button located in the Tools group to display the Edit Relationships dialog box such as the one shown in Figure 2.5, where you can change the current relationship. You can also display the Edit Relationships dialog box by positioning the arrow pointer on the thin portion of one of the black lines that connects the related tables and then clicking the *right* mouse button. This causes a shortcut menu to display. At this shortcut menu, click the left mouse button on Edit Relationship.

To delete a relationship between tables, display the related tables in the Relationships window. Position the arrow pointer on the thin portion of the black line connecting the related tables and then click the *right* mouse button. At the shortcut menu that displays, click the left mouse button on Delete. At the message asking if you are sure you want to permanently delete the selected relationship from your database, click Yes.

## Creating a One-to-One Relationship

You can create a one-to-one relationship between tables in which each record in the first table matches only one record in the second table and one record in the second table matches only one record in the first table. A one-to-one relationship is not as common as a one-to-many relationship since the type of information used to create the relationship can be stored in one table. A one-to-one relationship can be helpful in a situation where you divide a table with many fields into two tables.

## Project 1e   Creating Tables and Defining a One-to-One Relationship

1. With the **SouthwestInsurance.accdb** database open, create a new table by completing the following steps:
   a. Click the Create tab.
   b. Click the Table button in the Tables group.
   c. At the Table window, click the View button in the Views group in the Table Tools Datasheet tab.
   d. At the Save As dialog box, type Assignments in the *Table Name* text box and then press Enter or click OK.
   e. Type the fields, assign the data types, and type the descriptions as shown below (for assistance, refer to Chapter 1, Project 1a):

   | Field Name | Data Type | Description |
   | --- | --- | --- |
   | *ClientNumber* | Text (Field Size = 4) | Client number |
   | *AgentNumber* | Text (Field Size = 3) | Agent number |

2. Make sure a key displays at the left side of the *ClientNumber* field and then click the Save button on the Quick Access toolbar.

3. Click the View button to change to Datasheet view and then type the following in the specified fields:

| ClientNumber | 2511 | ClientNumber | 2768 |
|---|---|---|---|
| AgentNumber | 210 | AgentNumber | 142 |
| ClientNumber | 3120 | ClientNumber | 3976 |
| AgentNumber | 173 | AgentNumber | 210 |
| ClientNumber | 4308 | ClientNumber | 5231 |
| AgentNumber | 245 | AgentNumber | 173 |
| ClientNumber | 5508 | ClientNumber | 7325 |
| AgentNumber | 245 | AgentNumber | 142 |

4. Save, print, and then close the Assignments table.
5. At the SouthwestInsurance : Database window, create a new table by completing the following steps:
    a. Click the Create tab.
    b. Click the Table button in the Tables group.
    c. At the Table window, click the View button in the Views group in the Table Tools Datasheet tab.
    d. At the Save As dialog box, type Agents in the *Table Name* text box and then press Enter or click OK.
    e. Type the fields, assign the data types, and type the descriptions as shown below (for assistance, refer to Chapter 1, Project 2a):

| Field Name | Data Type | Description |
|---|---|---|
| AgentNumber | Text (Field Size = 3) | Agent number |
| FirstName | Text (Field Size = 20) | Agent first name |
| LastName | Text (Field Size = 20) | Agent last name |
| Telephone | Text (Field Size = 12) | Agent phone number |
| Email | Text (Field Size = 30) | Agent e-mail address |

6. Make sure a key displays at the left side of the *AgentNumber* field and then click the Save button on the Quick Access toolbar.
7. Click the View button to change to Datasheet view and then type the following in the specified fields:

| AgentNumber | 142 | AgentNumber | 173 |
|---|---|---|---|
| FirstName | James | FirstName | Tamara |
| LastName | Moriyama | LastName | Sadler |
| Telephone | 602-555-2676 | Telephone | 602-555-2698 |
| Email | jmoriyama@emcp.net | Email | tsadler@emcp.net |
| AgentNumber | 210 | AgentNumber | 245 |
| FirstName | Phillip | FirstName | Dayton |
| LastName | Cowans | LastName | Hubbard |
| Telephone | 602-555-2683 | Telephone | 602-555-2644 |
| Email | pcowans@emcp.net | Email | dhubbard@emcp.net |

8. Automatically adjust the width of columns.

9. Save, print, and then close the Agents table.
10. Create a one-to-one relationship between the Assignments table and the Clients table by completing the following steps:
   a. Click the Database Tools tab.
   b. Click the Relationships button in the Show/Hide group.
   c. At the Relationships window, click the Show Table button in the Relationships group.
   d. At the Show Table dialog box, click *Assignments* in the list box, and then click the Add button.
   e. Click the Close button to close the Show Table dialog box.
   f. At the Relationships window, drag the *ClientNumber* field from the Assignments table to the *ClientNumber* field in the Clients table.

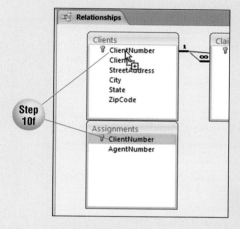

   g. At the Edit Relationships dialog box, make sure *ClientNumber* displays in the *Table/Query* and *Related Table/Query* list boxes and the relationship type at the bottom of the dialog box displays as *One-To-One*.

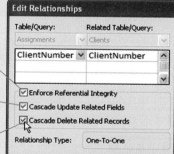

   h. Enforce the referential integrity of the relationship by completing the following steps:
      1) Click *Enforce Referential Integrity*. (This makes the other two options available.)
      2) Click *Cascade Update Related Fields*.
      3) Click *Cascade Delete Related Records*.
   i. Click the Create button. (This causes the Edit Relationships dialog box to close and the Relationships window to display showing a thick black line connecting the *ClientNumber* field in the Assignments and Clients tables.
   j. Click the Save button on the Quick Access toolbar to save the relationship.
11. Create a one-to-many relationship between the Assignments table and the Agents table by completing the following steps:
   a. With the Relationships window open, click the Show Table button in the Relationships group.
   b. At the Show Table dialog box, click *Agents* in the list box and then click the Add button.
   c. Click the Close button to close the Show Table dialog box.

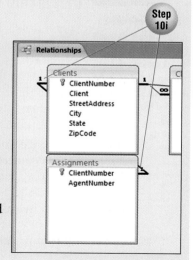

d. At the Relationships window, drag the *AgentNumber* field from the Agents table to the *AgentNumber* field in the Assignments table.
e. At the Edit Relationships dialog box, make sure *AgentNumber* displays in the *Table/Query* and *Related Table/Query* list boxes and the relationship type at the bottom of the dialog box displays as *One-To-Many*.
f. Enforce the referential integrity of the relationship by completing the following steps:
   1) Click *Enforce Referential Integrity*. (This makes the other two options available.)
   2) Click *Cascade Update Related Fields*.
   3) Click *Cascade Delete Related Records*.
g. Click the Create button.
h. Click the Save button on the Quick Access toolbar to save the relationship.

12. Print the relationships by completing the following steps:
a. At the Relationships window, click the Relationship Report button in the Tools group. (This displays the Relationships report in Print Preview.)
b. Click the Print button in the Print group.
c. Click OK at the Print dialog box.
d. Click the Close button that displays at the right side of the Relationships window.
e. At the message asking if you want to save changes to the design of the report, click No.

13. Close the Relationships window by clicking the Close button that displays at the right side of the Relationships window.

**Relationships**

| Clients | Claims |
| --- | --- |
| ClientNumber | ClaimNumber |
| Client | ClientNumber |
| StreetAddress | LicenseNumber |
| City | DateOfClaim |
| State | AmountOfClaim |
| ZipCode | |

| Assignments | Agents |
| --- | --- |
| ClientNumber | AgentNumber |
| AgentNumber | FirstName |
| | LastName |
| | Telephone |
| | Email |

**Step 11d**

**QUICK STEPS**

## Displaying Related Records in a Subdatasheet

**Display Subdatasheet**
1. Open table in Datasheet view.
2. Click expand indicator at left of desired record.
3. At Insert Subdatasheet dialog box, click desired table.
4. Click OK.

When a relationship is established between tables, you can view and edit fields in related tables with a subdatasheet. Figure 2.8 displays the Clients table with the subdatasheet displayed for the client Keith Hammond. The subdatasheet displays the fields in the Insurance table related to Keith Hammond. Use this subdatasheet to view information and also to edit information in the Clients table as well as the Insurance table. Changes made to fields in a subdatasheet affect the table and any related table.

Access automatically inserts plus symbols (referred to as *expand indicators*) before each record in a table that is joined to another table by a one-to-many relationship. Click the expand indicator and, if the table is related to only one other table, a subdatasheet containing fields from the related table displays below the record as shown in Figure 2.8. To remove the subdatasheet, click the minus sign (referred to as the *collapse indicator*) preceding the record. (The plus symbol turns into the minus symbol when a subdatasheet displays.)

**Figure 2.8** Table with Subdatasheet Displayed

Subdatasheet

| ClientNumb ▾ | Client ▾ | StreetAddress ▾ | City ▾ | State ▾ | ZipCode ▾ |
|---|---|---|---|---|---|
| ⊟ 2511 | Keith Hammon | 21332 Janski Road | Glendale | AZ | 85310 |

| ClaimNumb ▾ | LicenseNum ▾ | DateOfClain ▾ | AmountOfCl ▾ | Add New Field |
|---|---|---|---|---|
| 130057 | 795 GRT | 3/4/2010 | $186.40 | |
| ✱ | | | | |

| ⊞ 2768 | Marcus LeVign | 15676 North 32nd | Phoenix | AZ | 86231 |
| ⊞ 3120 | Spenser Winte | 12304 132nd Street | Glendale | AZ | 85310 |
| ⊞ 3976 | Joely Lindhal | 8809 South 142nd Stre | Scottsdale | AZ | 85230 |
| ⊞ 4308 | Paul Vuong | 3451 South Varner | Glendale | AZ | 85901 |
| ⊞ 5231 | Helena Myersc | 9032 45th Street East | Phoenix | AZ | 86203 |
| ⊞ 5508 | Martina Bentle | 6503 Taylor Street | Scottsdale | AZ | 85889 |
| ⊞ 7325 | Vernon Cook | 1230 South Mesa | Phoenix | AZ | 86201 |

If a table has more than one relationship defined, clicking the expand indicator will display the Insert Subdatasheet dialog box shown in Figure 2.9. At this dialog box, click the desired table in the Tables list box and then click OK. You can also display the Insert Subdatasheet dialog box by clicking the More button in the Records group in the Home tab, pointing to *Subdatasheet*, and then clicking *Subdatasheet*.

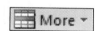

You can display subdatasheets for all records by clicking the More button, pointing to *Subdatasheet*, and then clicking *Expand All*. Remove all subdatasheets by clicking the More button, pointing to *Subdatasheet*, and then clicking *Collapse All*.

**Figure 2.9** Insert Subdatasheet Dialog Box

If a table is related to two or more tables, specify the desired subdatasheet at the Subdatasheet dialog box. If you decide to display a different subdatasheet, remove the subdatasheet first before selecting the next subdatasheet. Do this by clicking the More button, pointing to *Subdatasheet*, and then clicking *Remove*.

1. With the **SouthwestInsurance.accdb** database open, open the Clients table.
2. Display a subdatasheet by completing the following steps:
    a. Click the expand indicator (plus symbol) that displays at the left side of the first row (the row for Keith Hammond).
    b. At the Insert Subdatasheet dialog box, click *Claims* in the list box and then click OK.

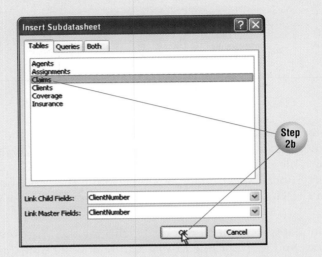

Step 2b

3. Remove the subdatasheet by clicking the collapse indicator (minus sign) that displays at the left side of the record for Keith Hammond.
4. Display subdatasheets for all of the records by clicking the More button in the Records group, pointing to *Subdatasheet*, and then clicking *Expand All*.

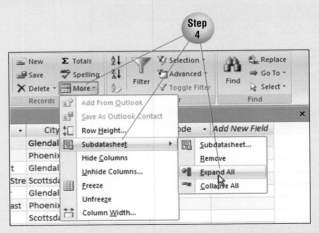

Step 4

5. Remove the display of all subdatasheets by clicking the More button, pointing to *Subdatasheet*, and then clicking *Collapse All*.
6. Remove the connection between Clients and Claims by clicking the More button, pointing to *Subdatasheet*, and then clicking *Remove*.

7. Suppose that the client, Vernon Cook, has moved to a new address and purchased insurance for a new car. Display the Insurance subdatasheet and make changes to fields in the Clients table and the Insurance table by completing the following steps:

a. Click the expand indicator (plus symbol) that displays at the left side of the *Vernon Cook* record.

b. At the Insert Subdatasheet dialog box, click *Insurance* in the list box and then click OK.

c. Change his street address from *1230 South Mesa* to *22135 Cactus Drive*.

d. Change his ZIP code from *86201* to *85344*.

e. Add the following information in the second row in the Insurance subdatasheet:

| | | |
|---|---|---|
| *LicenseNumber* | = | 430 DWT |
| *InsuranceCode* | = | F |
| *UninsuredMotorist* | = | *Yes* |

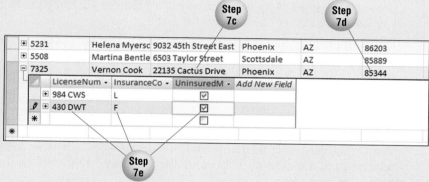

Step 7c

Step 7d

Step 7e

f. Click the Save button on the Quick Access toolbar.

g. Close the Clients table.

8. Open the Clients table, print it, and then close it.

9. Open the Insurance table, print it, and then close it.

10. Close the **SouthwestInsurance.accdb** database.

# CHAPTER summary

- Access is a relational database software program in which you can create tables that have a relation or connection to one another.
- When planning a table, take time to determine how to break down the required data and what relationships will need to be defined to eliminate data redundancies.
- In a table at least one field must be unique so that one record can be distinguished from another. A field with a unique value is considered a primary key.
- In a field defined as a primary key, duplicate values are not allowed in the primary field and Access also expects a value in each record in the primary key field.
- Define a primary key field with the Primary Key button in the Tools group.
- A primary key field included in another table is referred to as a foreign key. Unlike a primary key field, a foreign key field can contain duplicate data.
- In Access, you can relate a table to another by performing a join. When tables that have a common field are joined, you can extract data from both tables as if they were one large table.
- You can create a one-to-many relationship between tables in a database. In this relationship, a record must be added to the "one" table before it can be added to the "many" table.
- You can create a one-to-one relationship between tables in which each record in the first table matches only one record in the second table and one record in the second table matches only one record in the first table.
- You can edit or delete a relationship between tables.
- To print a relationship, display the Relationships window, click the Relationship Report button in the Tools group, and then click the Print button in the Print Preview tab.
- When a relationship is established between tables, you can view and edit fields in related tables with a subdatasheet.
- To display a subdatasheet for a record, click the expand indicator (plus symbol) that displays at the left side of the record. To display subdatasheets for all records, click the More button in the Reports group in the Home tab, point to *Subdatasheet*, and then click *Expand All*.
- Display the Insert Subdatasheet dialog box by clicking the More button in the Reports group in the Home tab, pointing to *Subdatasheet*, and then clicking *Subdatasheet*.
- Turn off the display of a subdatasheet by clicking the collapse indicator (minus symbol) at the beginning of a record. To turn off the display of subdatasheets for all records, click the More button, point to *Subdatasheet*, and then click *Collapse All*.

# COMMANDS review

| FEATURE | RIBBON TAB, GROUP | BUTTON, OPTION |
|---------|-------------------|----------------|
| Primary key | Table Tools Design, Tools | 🔑 |
| Relationships window | Database Tools, Show/Hide | |
| Edit Relationships window | Relationship Tools Design, Tools | |
| Show Table dialog box | Relationship Tools Design, Relationships | |
| Relationship report window | Relationship Tools Design, Tools | 🗐 Relationship Report |
| Insert Subdatasheet dialog box | Home, Records | More ▾, Subdatasheet, Subdatasheet |

# CONCEPTS check

## Test Your Knowledge

**Completion:** For each description, indicate the correct term, symbol, or character.

1. A primary key field must contain unique data while this type of key field can contain duplicate data.

2. In Access, one table can be related to another, which is generally referred to as performing this.

3. In a one-to-many relationship, the table containing the "one" is referred to as this.

4. In a one-to-many relationship, the table containing the "many" is referred to as this.

5. In a one-to-many relationship, Access follows a set of rules that enforces consistency between related tables and is referred to as this.

6. In related tables, this symbol displays near the black line next to the related table.

7. The black line that connects related tables is referred to as this.

8. Establish this type of relationship between tables in which each record in the first table matches only one record in the second table and one record in the second table matches only one record in the first table.

_____

9. The plus symbol that displays at the beginning of a record in a related table with a subdatasheet displayed is referred to as this.

_____

10. The minus symbol that displays at the beginning of a record in a related table with a subdatasheet displayed is referred to as this.

_____

11. Display subdatasheets for all records by clicking the More button, pointing to *Subdatasheet*, and then clicking this option.

_____

# SKILLS check
## *Demonstrate Your Proficiency*

### Assessment

**1** **CREATE AUTHORS, BOOKS, AND CATEGORIES TABLES IN A MYBOOKS DATABASE**

1. Use Access to create a database for keeping track of books. Name the database *MyBooks*. Create a table named *Authors* that includes the following fields (you determine the data type, field size, and description):

    **Field Name**
    *AuthorNumber* (primary key)
    *FirstName*
    *LastName*
    *MiddleInitial*

2. After creating the table with the fields shown above and defining the primary key, save the table. Switch to Datasheet view and then enter the following data in the table:

    | | | |
    |---|---|---|
    | *AuthorNumber* | = | 1 |
    | *FirstName* | = | Branson |
    | *LastName* | = | Walters |
    | *MiddleInitial* | = | A. |
    | | | |
    | *AuthorNumber* | = | 2 |
    | *FirstName* | = | Christiana |
    | *LastName* | = | Copeland |
    | *MiddleInitial* | = | M. |
    | | | |
    | *AuthorNumber* | = | 3 |
    | *FirstName* | = | Shirley |
    | *LastName* | = | Romero |
    | *MiddleInitial* | = | E. |

```
AuthorNumber    =    4
FirstName       =    Jeffrey
LastName        =    Fiedler
MiddleInitial   =    R.
```

3. Automatically adjust the width of columns.
4. Save, print, and then close the Authors table.
5. With the **MyBooks.accdb** database open, create another table named *Books* with the following fields (you determine the data type, field size, and description):
   **Field Name**
   *ISBN* (primary key)
   *AuthorNumber*
   *Title*
   *CategoryCode*
   *Price*
6. After creating the table with the fields shown above and defining the primary key, save the table. Switch to Datasheet view and then enter the following data in the table:

```
ISBN            =    12-6543-9008-7
AuthorNumber    =    4
Title           =    Today's Telecommunications
CategoryCode    =    B
Price           =    $34.95


ISBN            =    09-5225-5466-6
AuthorNumber    =    2
Title           =    Marketing in the Global Economy
CategoryCode    =    M
Price           =    $42.50


ISBN            =    23-9822-7645-0
AuthorNumber    =    1
Title           =    International Business Strategies
CategoryCode    =    B
Price           =    $45.00


ISBN            =    08-4351-4890-3
AuthorNumber    =    3
Title           =    Technological Advances
CategoryCode    =    B
Price           =    $36.95
```

7. Automatically adjust the width of columns (to accommodate the longest entry).
8. Save, print, and then close the Books table.
9. Create another table named *Categories* with the following fields (you determine the data type, field size, and description):
   **Field Name**
   *CategoryCode* (primary key)
   *Category*

10. After creating the table with the fields shown above and defining the primary key, save the table. Switch to Datasheet view and then enter the following data in the table:

CategoryCode = B
Category = Business

CategoryCode = M
Category = Marketing

11. Save, print, and then close the Categories table.

## Assessment

## 2 CREATE RELATIONSHIPS BETWEEN TABLES

1. With the **MyBooks.accdb** database open, create the following relationships:
   a. Create a one-to-many relationship with the *AuthorNumber* field in the Authors table the "one" and the *AuthorNumber* field in the Books table the "many." (At the Edit Relationships dialog box, choose *Enforce Referential Integrity*, *Cascade Update Related Fields*, and *Cascade Delete Related Records*.)
   b. Create a one-to-many relationship with the *CategoryCode* field in the Categories table the "one" and the *CategoryCode* field in the Books table the "many." (At the Edit Relationships dialog box, choose *Enforce Referential Integrity*, *Cascade Update Related Fields*, and *Cascade Delete Related Records*.)
2. Print the relationships.
3. After creating, saving, and printing the relationships, add the following record to the Authors table:
   AuthorNumber = 5
   FirstName = Glenna
   LastName = Zener-Young
   MiddleInitial = A.
4. Adjust the column width for the *LastName* field.
5. Save, print, and then close the Authors table.
6. Add the following records to the Books table:

ISBNNumber = 23-8931-0084-7
AuthorNumber = 2
Title = Practical Marketing Strategies
Category = M
Price = $28.50

ISBNNumber = 87-4009-7134-6
AuthorNumber = 5
Title = Selling More
Category = M
Price = $40.25

7. Save, print, and then close the Books table.
8. Close the **MyBooks.accdb** database.

## Apply Your Skills

**Part 1**

You are the owner of White Gloves Cleaning, a small housekeeping and cleaning service for residences and businesses. Since your business is continuing to grow, you decide to manage your records electronically instead of on paper. Create a database named **WhiteGloves** that contains three tables. Create a table named *Clients* that includes fields for a client number; name; address; city, state, ZIP code, contact person, location number, and rate number. Create another table named *Locations* that includes a location number field and a location field. Create a third table named *Rates* that includes a rate number field and a rates field.

In the Locations table, create the following:

| Location number | Location |
|---|---|
| 1 | Residence |
| 2 | Business |
| 3 | Construction Site |

In the Rates table, create the following:

| Rate number | Rate |
|---|---|
| 1 | $15.00 |
| 2 | $25.00 |
| 3 | $40.00 |

Assign primary keys in each table and then create a one-to-many relationship with the *Location number* field in the Locations table the "one" and the *Location number* field in the Clients the "many." Create another one-to-many relationship with the *Rate number* field in the Rates table the "one" and the *Rate number* field in the Clients table the "many." Save and then print the relationships.

Enter six records in the Clients table. Specify that the location number for two records is 1 (residence) and the rate is 1 ($15.00). Specify that the location number for two records is 2 (business) and the rate is 2 ($25.00). Specify that the location number for two records is 3 (construction site) and the rate is 3 ($40.00). Save and print each table (print the Clients table in landscape orientation) and then close the **WhiteGloves.accdb** database.

**Part 2**

Your business is growing and you have been hired to provide cleaning services to one additional business and one additional construction company. Add the appropriate information in the fields in the Clients table. One of your clients has cancelled services with your company so delete a client of your choosing from the Clients table. Print the Clients table. You have raised your hourly rates for cleaning a residence to $20.00. Make this change to the Rates table. Print the Rates table.

In Microsoft Word, create a document that describes the tables, fields, and relationships you created in the WhiteGloves database. In the document, specify the fields in each table, the data types assigned to each field, the field size (if appropriate), and describe the one-to-many relationships you created. Apply formatting to the document to enhance the visual appeal and then save the document and name it **Access_C2_CS_P3**. Print and then close **Access_C2_CS_P3.docx**.

# CHAPTER 3

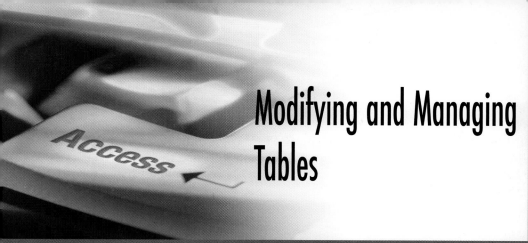

# Modifying and Managing Tables

## PERFORMANCE OBJECTIVES

**Upon successful completion of Chapter 3, you will be able to:**

- Modify a table by adding, deleting, or moving fields
- Assign a default value and validate a field entry
- Insert a Total row
- Use the Input Mask Wizard and the Lookup Wizard
- Complete a spelling check on data in a table
- Find specific records in a table
- Find specific data in a table and replace with other data
- Backup a database
- Compact and repair a database
- Use the Help feature

**Tutorial 3.1**
Managing a Database Table
**Tutorial 3.2**
Backing Up and Compacting
Databases

An Access database requires maintenance to keep the database up to date. Maintenance might include modifying the table by inserting or deleting fields, defining values and validating field entries, inserting a Total row, using wizards to identify data type, and sorting data in tables. In this chapter, you will learn how to modify tables as well as how to use the spelling checker to find misspelled words in a table and how to use the find and replace feature to find specific records in a table or find specific data in a table and replace with other data. As you continue working with a database, consider compacting and repairing the database to optimize performance and back up the database to protect your data from accidental loss or hardware failure. Microsoft Office contains an on-screen reference manual containing information on features and commands for each program within the suite. In this chapter, you will learn to use the Help feature to display information about Access.

*Note: Before beginning computer projects, copy the Access2007L1C3 subfolder from the Access2007L1 folder on the CD that accompanies this textbook to your storage medium and make Access2007L1C3 the active folder.*

# Project 1 Manage Data and Define Data Types

You will modify tables by adding and deleting fields, assign data types and default values to fields, validate field entries, insert a total row, and use the Input Mask Wizard and the Lookup Wizard. You will also move fields in a table and sort records in ascending and descending order.

## Modifying a Table

Maintaining a table involves adding and/or deleting records as needed. It can also involve adding, moving, changing, or deleting fields in the table. Modify the structure of the table in Datasheet view or Design view. In Datasheet view, click the Table Tools Datasheet tab and then use options in the Fields & Columns group to insert or delete fields. To display a table in Design view, open the table, and then click the View button in the Views group in the Home tab. You can also change to Design view by clicking the View button arrow and then clicking *Design View* at the drop-down list or by clicking the Design View button located in the View area at the right side of the Status bar.

In Design view, *Field Name*, *Data Type*, and *Description* display at the top of the window and *Field Properties* displays toward the bottom of the window. In Design view, you can add fields, remove fields, and change the order of fields. When you switch to Design view, the Table Tools Design tab displays as shown in Figure 3.1. Use buttons in this tab to insert and delete rows and perform a variety of other tasks.

**Figure 3.1** Table Tools Design Tab

**HINT**

Use options in the Data Type & Formatting group in the Table Tools Datasheet tab to set the data type.

### Adding a Field

Situations change within a company, and a table must be flexible to accommodate changes that occur with new situations. Adding a field is a change that may need to be made to an existing table. For example, more information may be required to manage the data or an additional field may be needed for accounting purposes.

You can add a new field in Datasheet view or in Design view. One method for creating a new field is to simply type new records into a blank table or in the *Add New Field* column that displays at the right side of the last field in the table. Access sets a data type for each new field you type based on the type of data entered. For example, a column that contains dates is automatically assigned the Date/Time data type. You can also insert a new field by clicking the Table Tools Datasheet tab and then clicking the Insert button in the Fields & Columns group.

To add a row for a new field in Design view, position the insertion point on any text in the row that will be located immediately *below* the new field and then click the Insert Rows button in the Tools group in the Table Tools Design tab or position the insertion point on any text in the row that will be immediately *below* the new field, click the *right* mouse button, and then click *Insert Rows*. If you insert a row for a new field and then change your mind, immediately click the Undo button on the Quick Access toolbar.

## Deleting a Field

Delete a field in a table and all data entered in that field is also deleted. When a field is deleted, it cannot be undone with the Undo button. Delete a field only if you are sure you really want it and the data associated with it completely removed from the table.

To delete a field in Datasheet view, click in any entry in the field you want to delete, click the Table Tools Datasheet tab, and then click the Delete button in the Fields & Columns group. To delete a field in Design view, click in the record selector bar at the left side of the row you want to delete and then click the Delete Rows button in the Tools group. At the message asking if you want to permanently delete the field and all of the data in the field, click Yes.

## Assigning Data Type

In Chapter 1, you created tables and assigned data types of *Text*, *Date/Time*, or *Yes/No*. Access includes these data types as well as additional types as described in Table 3.1. Assign a data type with the *Data Type* column in Design view.

**QUICK STEPS**

**Add a Field to a Table**
1. Open table in Design view.
2. Click in row that will follow the new field.
3. Click Insert Rows button.

**Delete a Field from a Table**
1. Open table in Design view.
2. Click in row to be deleted.
3. Click Delete Rows button.
4. Click Yes.

Undo

**Table 3.1** Data Types

| Data type | Description |
| --- | --- |
| Text | Alphanumeric data up to 255 characters in length, such as a name, address, or value such as a telephone number or Social Security number that it used as an identifier and not for calculating. |
| Memo | Alphanumeric data up to 64,000 characters in length. |
| Number | Positive or negative values that can be used in calculations. Do *not* use for value that will calculate monetary amounts (see Currency). |
| Date/Time | Use this type to ensure dates and times are entered and sorted properly. |
| Currency | Values that involve money. Access will not round off during calculations. |
| AutoNumber | Access automatically numbers each record sequentially (incrementing by 1) when you begin typing a new record. |
| Yes/No | Data in the field will be either Yes or No, True or False, or On or Off. |
| OLE Object | Used to embed or link objects created in other Office applications. |
| Hyperlink | Field that will store a hyperlink such as a URL. |
| Attachment | Use this data type to add file attachments to a record such as a Word document or an Excel workbook. |
| Lookup Wizard | Use the Lookup Wizard to enter data in the field from another existing table or display a list of values in a drop-down list from which the user chooses. |

# Project 1a  Modifying a Table

1. In Access, display the Open dialog box with the drive active containing your storage medium and Access2007L1C3 the active folder.
2. Open the **MedSafeClinic.accdb** database.
3. At the MedSafeClinic : Database window, double-click the *Products* table to open it.
4. Insert a new field by completing the following steps:
   a. Click in the empty field below the *Add New Field* column heading.
   b. Type 50 and then press the Down Arrow key on your keyboard.
   c. Type 50 and then press the Down Arrow key.
   d. Type 125 and then press the Down Arrow key.
   e. Type 100 and then press the Down Arrow key.
   f. Type 150 and then press the Down Arrow key.
   g. Type 100 and then press the Down Arrow key.

| UnitsInStock ▾ | Field1 ▾ | Add New Field |
|---|---|---|
| 63 | 50 | |
| 38 | 50 | |
| 144 | 125 | |
| 57 | 100 | |
| 122 | 150 | |
| 78 | 100 | |

Steps 4b–4g

5. Click the View button to switch to Design view and notice that Access automatically selected the Number data type for the new field you created. Modify the field by completing the following steps:
   a. Select *Field1* that displays in the *Field Name* column and then type ReorderLevel.
   b. Click in the *Description* text box for the *ReorderLevel* field and then type Reorder level number.

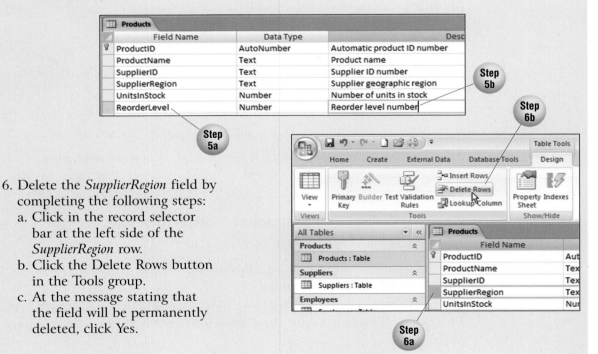

| Field Name | Data Type | Desc |
|---|---|---|
| ProductID | AutoNumber | Automatic product ID number |
| ProductName | Text | Product name |
| SupplierID | Text | Supplier ID number |
| SupplierRegion | Text | Supplier geographic region |
| UnitsInStock | Number | Number of units in stock |
| ReorderLevel | Number | Reorder level number |

Step 5a

Step 5b

Step 6b

6. Delete the *SupplierRegion* field by completing the following steps:
   a. Click in the record selector bar at the left side of the *SupplierRegion* row.
   b. Click the Delete Rows button in the Tools group.
   c. At the message stating that the field will be permanently deleted, click Yes.

Step 6a

7. Insert a new field by completing the following steps:
   a. Click on any character in the *ReorderLevel* field name.
   b. Click the Insert Rows button in the Tools group.
   c. With the insertion point positioned in the new blank field in the *Field Name* column, type UnitsOnOrder.
   d. Press the Tab key.
   e. Click the down-pointing arrow at the right side of the Text box and then click *Number* at the drop-down list.
   f. Press the Tab key and then type Number of units on order.

Step 7b

Step 7a

8. Insert a new field by completing the following steps:
   a. Click on any character in the *ReorderLevel* field name.
   b. Click the Insert Rows button in the Tools group.
   c. With the insertion point positioned in the new blank field in the *Field Name* column, type UnitPrice.
   d. Press the Tab key.
   e. Click the down-pointing arrow at the right side of the Text box and then click *Currency* at the drop-down list.
   f. Press the Tab key and then type Unit price.
9. Click the Save button on the Quick Access toolbar to save the modified table.
10. Click the View button to switch to Datasheet view and then enter the following information in the specified fields:

| UnitsOnOrder | UnitPrice |
|---|---|
| 0 | 12.50 |
| 50 | 24.00 |
| 0 | 5.70 |
| 100 | 9.90 |
| 150 | 4.50 |
| 100 | 10.00 |

11. Click the Save button on the Quick Access toolbar.
12. Display the table in Print Preview, change the orientation to landscape, and then print the table.
13. Close Print Preview and close the Products table.
14. Define a one-to-many relationship between the Suppliers and the Products tables by completing the following steps:
   a. Click the Database Tools tab and then click the Relationships button in the Show/Hide group.
   b. At the Show Table dialog box, click *Suppliers* in the list box and then click Add.
   c. Click *Products* in the list box and then click Add.
   d. Click the Close button to close the Show Table dialog box.
   e. At the Relationships window, drag the *SupplierID* field from the Suppliers table to the *SupplierID* field in the Products table.
   f. At the Edit Relationships dialog box, click *Enforce Referential Integrity*, click *Cascade Update Related Fields*, and then click *Cascade Delete Related Records*.
   g. Click the Create button.

15. Click the Save button on the Quick Access toolbar to save the relationship.
16. Print the relationships by completing the following steps:
    a. At the Relationships window, click the Relationship Report button in the Tools group. (This displays the Relationships report in Print Preview.)
    b. Click the Print button in the Print group.
    c. Click OK at the Print dialog box.
    d. Click the Close button that displays at the right side of the Relationships window.
    e. At the message asking if you want to save changes to the design of the report, click No.
17. Close the Relationships window by clicking the Close button that displays at the right side of the Relationships window.

## Assigning a Default Value

In Design view, the available field properties that display in the lower half of the work area vary depending on the data type of the active field. You can use a field property to control how the field displays or how the field interacts with data. For example, you have been using the *Field Size* option in the Field Properties section to limit the numbers of characters allowed when entering data in the field. If most records are likely to contain the same field value, use the *Default Value* property to insert the most common field entry. In Project 1b, you will insert a health insurance field with a Yes/No data type. Since most employees sign up for health insurance benefits, you will set the default value for the field as *Yes*. If you add a new field that contains a default value to an existing table, the existing records will not reflect the default value, only new records entered in the table.

**QUICK STEPS**

**Insert a Total Row**
1. Open table in Datasheet view.
2. Click Totals button.
3. Click in Total row.
4. Click down-pointing arrow that appears.
5. Click desired function at drop-down list.

## Validating Field Entries

Use the *Validation Rule* property to enter a statement containing a conditional test that is checked each time data is entered into a field. When data is entered that fails to satisfy the conditional test, Access does not accept the entry and displays an error message. By entering a conditional statement in the *Validation Rule* property that checks each entry against the acceptable range, you can reduce errors. Enter in the *Validation Text* property the content of the error message that you want to display.

## Inserting a Total Row

A new feature in Access 2007 is the ability to add a total row to a datasheet and then choose from a list of functions to add or to find the average, maximum, minimum, count, standard deviations, or variance result in a numeric column. To insert a total row, click the Totals button in the Records group in the Home tab. Access adds a row to the bottom of the datasheet with the label *Total* at the left. Click in the Total row, click the down-pointing arrow that appears, and then click the desired function at the drop-down list.

**HINT**

The Total row option provides a number of aggregate functions which are functions that calculate values across a range of data.

# Project 1b  Assigning a Default Value, Validating an Entry, and Inserting Total Row

1. With the **MedSafeClinic.accdb** database open, open the Employees table.
2. Insert a new field by completing the following steps:
   a. Click the View button to switch to Design view.
   b. Click in the empty field immediately below the *Salary* field in the *Field Name* column and then type **HealthIns**.
   c. Press the Tab key.
   d. Click the down-pointing arrow at the right side of the Text box and then click *Yes/No* at the drop-down list.
   e. Select the current entry in the *Default Value* field property box and then type **Yes**.

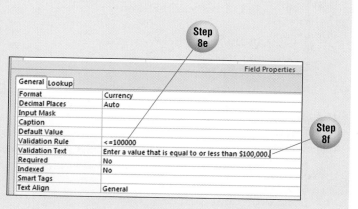

   f. Click in the field in the *Description* column for the *HealthIns* field and then type **Employee signed up for health insurance benefits**.
3. Click the Save button on the Quick Access toolbar.
4. Click the View button to switch to Datasheet view. (Notice that the *HealthIns* check box for existing records does not contain a check mark [the default value] but the check box in the new record contains a check mark.)
5. Enter the following new records:

   | | | | | |
   |---|---|---|---|---|
   | ID# | 265 | | ID# | 199 |
   | FirstName | Randy | | FirstName | Kristen |
   | LastName | Lewandowski | | LastName | Ridgway |
   | Ext | 3217 | | Ext | 2122 |
   | Salary | 29000 | | Salary | 33550 |
   | HealthIns | (Press Tab to accept default) | | HealthIns | (Press Tab to accept default) |

6. Click in each of the existing *HealthIns* check boxes to insert a check mark except the check box for *Chris Weaver*.
7. Save the Employees table.
8. Insert a new field by completing the following steps:
   a. Click the View button to switch to Design view.
   b. Click in the empty field immediately below the *HealthIns* field in the *Field Name* column and then type **LifeIns**.
   c. Press the Tab key.
   d. Click the down-pointing arrow at the right side of the Text box and then click *Currency* at the drop-down list.
   e. Click in the *Validation Rule* property box, type **<=100000**, and then press Enter.
   f. With the insertion point positioned in the *Validation Text* property box, type **Enter a value that is equal to or less than $100,000**.

g. Click in the box in the *Description* column for the *LifeIns* field and then type Optional life insurance amount.

9. Click the Save button on the Quick Access toolbar. Since the validation rule was created *after* data was entered into the table, Access displays a warning message indicating that some data may not be valid. At this message, click No.

10. Click the View button to switch to Datasheet view.

11. Click in the first empty field in the *LifeIns* column, type 200000, and then press the Down Arrow key.

12. Access inserts the error message telling you to enter an amount that is equal to or less than $100,000. At this error message, click OK.

13. Edit the amount in the field so it displays as 100000 and then press the Down Arrow key.

14. Type the following entries in the remaining fields in the *LifeIns* column:

    25000
    0
    50000
    50000
    0
    100000
    50000
    25000

15. Save the Employees table.

16. Insert a Total row and insert a function by completing the following steps:

a. In Datasheet view, click the Totals button in the Records group in the Home tab.

Step 16a

b. Click in the blank field in the *Salary* column in the Total row.

c. Click the down-pointing arrow at the left side of the field and then click *Average* at the drop-down list.

d. Click in any other field.

e. Save and then print the Employees table.

f. Click in the field containing the salary average amount.

g. Click the down-pointing arrow at the left side of the field and then click *Sum* at the drop-down list.

h. Click in any other field.

17. Save, print, and then close the Employees table.

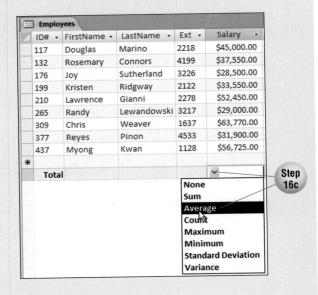

Step 16c

# Using the Input Mask Wizard

For some fields, you may want to control the data entered in the field. For example, in a *ZipCode* field, you may want the nine-digit ZIP code entered (rather than the five-digit ZIP code); or you may want the three-digit area code included in a telephone number. Use the *Input Mask* field property to set a pattern for how data is entered in a field. An input mask ensures that data in records conforms to a standard format. Access includes an Input Mask Wizard that guides you through creating an input mask.

Use the Input Mask Wizard when assigning a data type to a field. After specifying the *Field Size* in the *Field Properties* section in Design view, click in the Input Mask box. Run the Input Mask Wizard by clicking the Build button (button containing three black dots) that appears to the right of the Input Mask box. This displays the first Input Mask Wizard dialog box as shown in Figure 3.2. In the Input Mask list box, choose which input mask you want your data to look like and then click the Next button. At the second Input Mask Wizard dialog box as shown in Figure 3.3, specify the appearance of the input mask and the desired placeholder character and then click the Next button. At the third Input Mask Wizard dialog box, specify whether you want the data stored with or without the symbol in the mask and then click the Next button. At the fourth dialog box, click the Finish button.

**QUICK STEPS**

**Use Input Mask**
1. Open table in Design view.
2. Type text in *Field Name* column.
3. Press Tab key.
4. Click Save button.
5. Click in Input Mask box.
6. Click Build button.
7. At first Input Mask Wizard, click desired option.
8. Click Next.
9. At second Input Mask Wizard dialog box, make any desired changes.
10. Click Next.
11. At third Input Mask dialog box, make any desired changes.
12. Click Next.
13. Click Finish.

**HINT**

An input mask is a set of characters that control what you can and cannot enter in a field.

Build

**Figure 3.2** First Input Mask Wizard Dialog Box

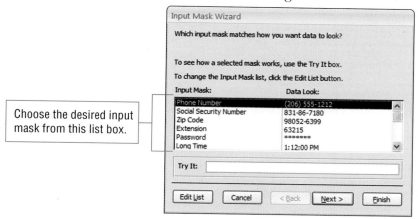

Choose the desired input mask from this list box.

**Figure 3.3** Second Input Mask Wizard Dialog Box

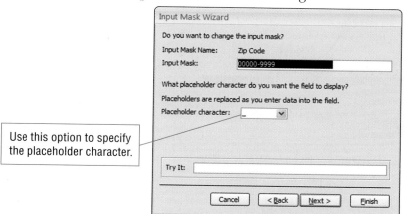

Use this option to specify the placeholder character.

Project **1c** **Inserting a Field with an Input Mask**

1. With the **MedSafeClinic.accdb** database open, open the Suppliers table.
2. Create a new *ZipCode* field with an Input Mask by completing the following steps:
   a. Click the View button in the Views group.
   b. Click anywhere in the text *Email* that displays in the *Field Name* column.
   c. Click the Insert Rows button in the Tools group.

**Step 2c**

   d. With the insertion point positioned in the new blank field in the *Field Name* column, type **ZipCode**.
   e. Press the Tab key. (This moves the insertion point to the *Data Type* column.)
   f. Select *255* that displays in the *Field Size* text box in the *Field Properties* section of the window and then type **10**.
   g. Click the Save button to save the table. (You must save the table before using the Input Mask Wizard.)
   h. Click in the *Input Mask* box in the *Field Properties* section of the window.
   i. Click the Build button (button containing three black dots) that displays to the right of the *Input Mask* box.

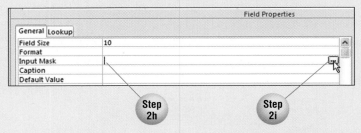

**Step 2h**   **Step 2i**

   j. At the first Input Mask Wizard dialog box, click *Zip Code* in the *Input Mask* list box and then click the Next button.

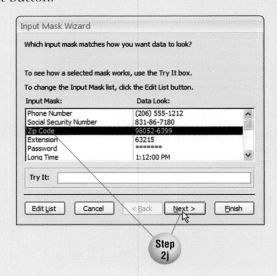

**Step 2j**

k. At the second Input Mask Wizard dialog box, click the Next button.
l. At the third Input Mask Wizard dialog box, click the *With the symbols in the mask, like this* option.

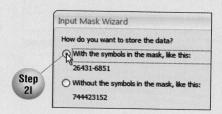

Step 2l

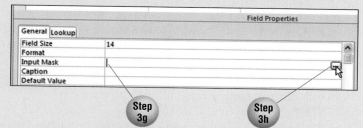

Step 2k

m. Click the Next button.
n. At the fourth Input Mask Wizard dialog box, click the Finish button.
o. Click in the *Description* column in the *ZipCode* row and then type Supplier nine-digit Zip code.
3. Create a new *Telephone* field with an Input Mask by completing the following steps:
   a. Click anywhere in the text *Email* that displays in the *Field Name* column.
   b. Click the Insert Rows button in the Tools group.
   c. With the insertion point positioned in the new blank field in the *Field Name* column, type Telephone.
   d. Press the Tab key. (This moves the insertion point to the *Data Type* column.)
   e. Select *255* that displays in the *Field Size* text box in the *Field Properties* section of the window and then type 14.
   f. Click the Save button to save the table. (You must save the table before using the Input Mask Wizard.)
   g. Click in the Input Mask box in the *Field Properties* section of the window.
   h. Click the Build button (button containing three black dots) that displays to the right of the Input Mask box.

Step 3g    Step 3h

   i. At the first Input Mask Wizard dialog box, make sure *Phone Number* is selected in the *Input Mask* list box and then click the Next button.

Step 3i

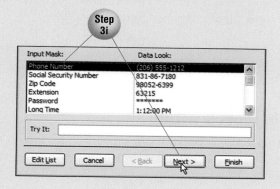

j. At the second Input Mask Wizard dialog box, click the down-pointing arrow at the right side of the *Placeholder character* box and then click # at the drop-down list.

k. Click the Next button.

l. At the third Input Mask Wizard dialog box, click the *With the symbols in the mask, like this* option.

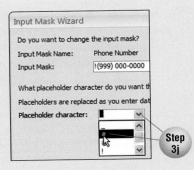

**Step 3j**

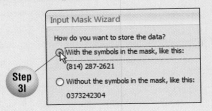

**Step 3l**

m. Click the Next button.

n. At the fourth Input Mask Wizard dialog box, click the Finish button.

o. Click in the *Description* column in the *Telephone* row and then type **Supplier telephone number**.

p. Click the Save button on the Quick Access toolbar.

4. Add ZIP codes for the records in the Suppliers table by completing the following steps:

a. Click the View button to switch to Datasheet view.

b. Click in the field containing *LA* (immediately left of the new blank field below *ZipCode*) and then press the Tab key.

c. Type **303239089** and then press the Down Arrow key. (This moves the insertion point to the next blank field in the *ZipCode* column. The Input Mask automatically inserts a hyphen between 30323 and 9089.)

| City | State | ZipCode | Telephone |
|------|-------|---------|-----------|
| Baton Rouge | LA | 30323-9089 | |
| Tampa | FL | | |
| Atlanta | GA | | |
| Atlanta | GA | | |
| Little Rock | AR | | |
| | | | |

**Step 4c**

d. Type **303542487** and then press the Down Arrow key.

e. Type **303573652** and then press the Down Arrow key.

f. Type **303654311** and then press the Down Arrow key.

g. Type **303253499**.

5. Add telephone numbers for the records in the Suppliers table by completing the following steps:

a. Click in the field containing the ZIP code *30323-9089* and then press the Tab key.

b. Type **2255557454** and then press the Down Arrow key. (The Input Mask automatically inserts the parentheses, spaces, and hyphens in the telephone numbers.)

c. Type **8135553495** and then press the Down Arrow key.

d. Type **4045557732** and then press the Down Arrow key.

e. Type **4045550926** and then press the Down Arrow key.

f. Type **5015554509**.

6. Save, print, and then close the Suppliers table.

## Using the Lookup Wizard

Like the Input Mask Wizard, you can use the Lookup Wizard to control the data entered in a field. Use the Lookup Wizard to confine the data entered into a field to a specific list of items. For example, in Project 1d you will use the Lookup Wizard to restrict the new *EmpCategory* field to one of three choices — *Salaried, Hourly,* and *Temporary*. When the user clicks in the field in the datasheet, a down-pointing arrow displays. The user clicks this down-pointing arrow to display a drop-down list of available entries and then clicks the desired item.

Use the Lookup Wizard when assigning a data type to a field. Click in the *Data Type* text box and then click the down-pointing arrow that displays at the right side of the box. At the drop-down list that displays, click *Lookup Wizard*. This displays the first Lookup Wizard dialog box as shown in Figure 3.4. At this dialog box, indicate that you want to enter the field choices by clicking the *I will type in the values that I want* option, and then click the Next button. At the second Lookup Wizard dialog box shown in Figure 3.5, click in the blank text box below *Col1* and then type the first choice. Press the Tab key and then type the second choice. Continue in this manner until all desired choices are entered and then click the Next button. At the third Lookup Wizard dialog box, make sure the proper name displays in the *What label would you like for your lookup column?* text box and then click the Finish button.

**QUICK STEPS**

**Use Lookup Wizard**
1. Open table in Design view.
2. Type text in *Field Name* column.
3. Press Tab key.
4. Click down-pointing arrow.
5. Click *Lookup Wizard*.
6. At first Lookup Wizard dialog box, make desired changes.
7. Click Next.
8. At second Lookup Wizard dialog box, click in blank text box.
9. Type desired text.
10. Press Tab key.
11. Continue typing text and pressing Tab until all desired text is entered.
12. Click Next.
13. Click Finish.

**HINT**
You can activate the Lookup Wizard by clicking the Lookup Column button in the Table Tools Datasheet tab.

**Figure 3.4** First Lookup Wizard Dialog Box

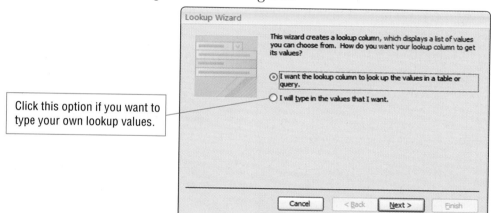

Click this option if you want to type your own lookup values.

**Figure 3.5** Second Lookup Wizard Dialog Box

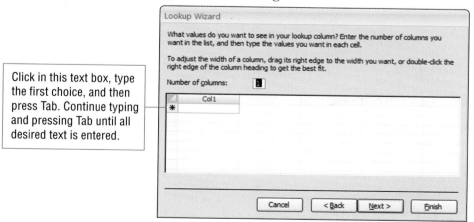

Click in this text box, type the first choice, and then press Tab. Continue typing and pressing Tab until all desired text is entered.

1. With the **MedSafeClinic.accdb** database open, open the Employees table.
2. Add the field *EmpCategory* and use the Lookup Wizard to specify field choices by completing the following steps:
   a. Click the View button to change to Design view.
   b. Click on any character in the *Ext* data in the *Field Name* column.
   c. Click the Insert Rows button in the Tools group.
   d. With the insertion point positioned in the new blank field in the *Field Name* column, type **EmpCategory**.
   e. Press the Tab key. (This moves the insertion point to the *Data Type* column.)
   f. Click the down-pointing arrow at the right side of the text box and then click *Lookup Wizard* at the drop-down list.
   g. At the first Lookup Wizard dialog box, click the *I will type in the values that I want* option and then click the Next button.

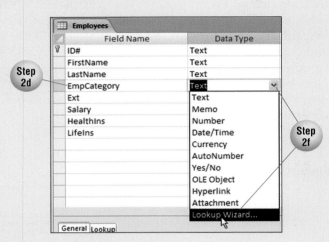

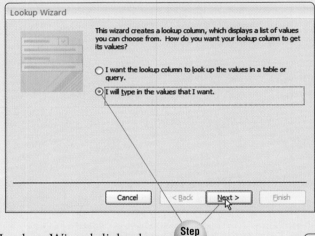

   h. At the second Lookup Wizard dialog box, click in the blank text box below *Col1*, type **Salaried**, and then press the Tab key.
   i. Type **Hourly** and then press the Tab key.
   j. Type **Temporary**.
   k. Click the Next button.
   l. At the third Lookup Wizard dialog box, click the Finish button.
   m. Press the Tab key and then type **Employee category** in the *Description* column.
3. Click the Save button on the Quick Access toolbar.

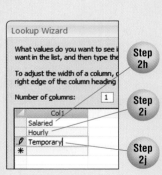

4. Insert information in the *EmpCategory* for the records by completing the following steps:
   a. Click the View button to switch to Datasheet view.
   b. Click in the first blank field below the new *EmpCategory* field.
   c. Click the down-pointing arrow at the right side of the field and then click *Hourly* at the drop-down list.

Step 4c

   d. Click in the next blank field in the *EmpCategory*, click the down-pointing arrow, and then click *Salaried* at the drop-down list.
   e. Continue entering information in the *EmpCategory* by completing similar steps. Choose the following in the specified record:

   | | |
   |---|---|
   | Third record | Hourly |
   | Fourth record | Salaried |
   | Fifth record | Temporary |
   | Sixth record | Hourly |
   | Seventh record | Salaried |
   | Eighth record | Temporary |
   | Ninth record | Hourly |

5. Save and then print the Employees table in landscape orientation.

## Moving a Field

You can move a field in a table to a different location. To do this, open the table and then change to Design view. Click in the record selector bar at the left side of the row you want to move. With the row selected, position the arrow pointer in the record selector bar at the left side of the selected row until the pointer turns into the normal arrow pointer (white arrow pointing up and to the left). Hold down the left mouse button, drag the arrow pointer with the gray square attached until a thick black line displays in the desired position, and then release the mouse button.

**QUICK STEPS**

**Move a Field**
1. Open table in Design view.
2. Select row to be moved.
3. Drag selected row to new position.

## Project 1e    Moving Fields in Tables

1. With the Employees table open, click the View button to switch to Design view.
2. Move the *EmpCategory* field immediately below the *Ext* field by completing the following steps:
   a. Click in the record selector bar at the left side of the *EmpCategory* field to select the row.
   b. Position the arrow pointer in the record selector bar of the selected row until it turns into the normal arrow pointer (white arrow pointing up and to the left).
   c. Hold down the left mouse button, drag the arrow pointer with the gray square attached until a thick black line displays below the *Ext* field, and then release the mouse button.

Step 2c

3. Click the Save button on the Quick Access toolbar.
4. Click the View button to switch to Datasheet view.
5. Print the table in landscape orientation.
6. Close the Employees table.
7. Open the Products table and then move the *ReorderLevel* field by completing the following steps:
   a. Click the View button to switch to Design view.
   b. Select the row containing the *ReorderLevel* field.
   c. Position the arrow pointer on the blue button at the left side of the selected row until the pointer turns into the normal arrow pointer (white arrow pointing up and to the left).
   d. Hold down the left mouse button, drag the arrow pointer below the *UnitsOnOrder* field, and then release the mouse button.

| Products | |
|---|---|
| Field Name | Data Type |
| ProductID | AutoNumber |
| ProductName | Text |
| SupplierID | Text |
| UnitsInStock | Number |
| UnitsOnOrder | Number |
| UnitPrice | Currency |
| ReorderLevel | Number |

Step 7d

8. Click the Save button on the Quick Access.
9. Click the View button to switch to Datasheet view.
10. Print the Products table in landscape orientation.
11. Close the Products table.

**QUICK STEPS**

**Sort Records**
1. Open table in Datasheet view.
2. Click in field in desired column.
3. Click Ascending button or Descending button.

**Print Selected Records**
1. Open table and select records.
2. Click Office button, *Print*.
3. Click *Selected Record(s)*.
4. Click OK.

Ascending

Descending

## Sorting Records

The Sort & Filter group in the Home tab contains two buttons you can use to sort data in records. Click the Ascending button to sort from lowest to highest on the field where the insertion point is located or click the Descending button to sort from highest to lowest.

## Printing Specific Records

If you click the Quick Print button on the Quick Access toolbar, all of the records in the selected or open table are printed. If you want to print specific records in a table, select the records and then display the Print dialog box by clicking the Office button and then clicking *Print* at the drop-down list. At the Print dialog box, click the *Selected Records* option in the *Print Range* section and then click OK. To select specific records, display the table in Datasheet view, click the record selector of the first record and then drag to select the desired records. The record selector is the light blue square that displays at the left side of the record. When you position the mouse pointer on the record selector, the pointer turns into a right-pointing black arrow.

## Project 1f  Sorting and Printing Records in the Employees Table

1. With the **MedSafeClinic.accdb** database open, open the Employees table.
2. With the table in Datasheet view, sort records in ascending alphabetical order by completing the following steps:
   a. Click any last name in the table.
   b. Click the Ascending button in the Sort & Filter group in the Home tab.

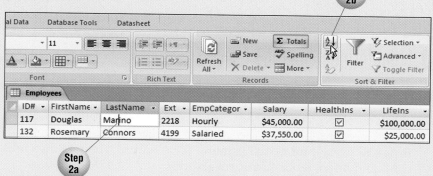

Step 2b

Step 2a

   c. Print the Employees table in landscape orientation.
3. Sort records in descending order (highest to lowest) by employee ID number by completing the following steps:
   a. Click on any number in the *ID#* field.
   b. Click the Descending button in the Sort & Filter group.

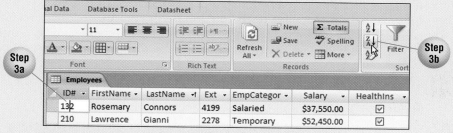

Step 3a

Step 3b

   c. Print the Employees table in landscape orientation.
4. Sort and print selected records of the salaried employees by completing the following steps:
   a. Click any entry in the *EmpCategory* field.
   b. Remove the Totals row by clicking the Totals button in the Records group in the Home tab.
   c. Click the Ascending button in the Sort & Filter group.
   d. Position the mouse pointer on the record selector of the first salaried employee, hold down the mouse button, and then drag to select the three records of salaried employees.
   e. Click the Office button and then click *Print* at the drop-down list.
   f. At the Print dialog box, click the *Selected Record(s)* option in the *Print Range* section.
   g. Click OK.
5. Click the Save button on the Quick Access toolbar.
6. Close the Employees table and then close the **MedSafeClinic.accdb** database.

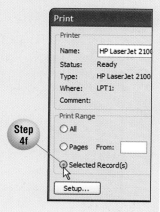

Step 4f

You will complete a spelling check on data in tables and find data and replace it with other data in tables. You will also back up a database and compact and repair a database.

## QUICK STEPS

**Completing a Spelling Check**

**Complete a Spelling Check**
1. Open table in Datasheet view.
2. Click Spelling button.
3. Change or ignore spelling as needed.
4. Click OK.

### HINT
You can also begin spell checking with the keyboard shortcut F7.

The spelling checker feature in Access finds misspelled words and offers replacement words. It also finds duplicate words and irregular capitalizations. When you spell check an object in a database such as a table, the spelling checker compares the words in your table with the words in its dictionary. If a match is found, the word is passed over. If no match is found for the word, the spelling checker selects the word and offers replacement suggestions.

To complete a spelling check, open the desired table in Datasheet view and then click the Spelling button in the Records group in the Home tab. If the spelling checker does not find a match for a word in your table, the Spelling dialog box displays with replacement options. Figure 3.6 displays the Spelling dialog box with the word *Montain* selected and possible replacements displayed in the *Suggestions* list box. At the Spelling dialog box, you can choose to ignore the word (for example, if the spelling checker has selected a proper name), change to one of the replacement options, or add the word to the dictionary or AutoCorrect feature. You can also complete a spelling check on other objects in a database such as a query, form, or report. (You will learn about these objects in future chapters.)

**Figure 3.6** Spelling Dialog Box

The spelling checker selects this word in the table and offers these suggestions.

| Spelling: English (U.S.) | | ? X |
| --- | --- | --- |
| Not In Dictionary: | | |
| Montain | | Ignore 'SupplierName' Field |
| Suggestions: | | |
| Mountain | | Ignore · Ignore All |
| Contain | | |
| Montaigne | | Change · Change All |
| Mountains | | |
| | | Add · AutoCorrect |
| Dictionary Language: | English (U.S.) | |
| Options... | | Undo Last · Cancel |

1. Open the **MedSafeClinic.accdb** database.
2. Open the Suppliers table.
3. In Datasheet view, add the following record at the end of the table. (Type the misspelled words as shown below. You will correct the spelling in a later step.)

   *SupplierID* = 6
   *SupplierName* = Blue Montain Supplies
   *Address* = 9550 Unaversity Avenue
   *City* = Little Rock
   *State* = AR
   *ZipCode* = 322093412
   *Telephone* = 5015554400
   *Email* = bluem@emcp.net

**Step 3**

| | SupplierID ▾ | SupplierName ▾ | Address ▾ | City ▾ | State ▾ | ZipCode ▾ | Telephone ▾ |
|---|---|---|---|---|---|---|---|
| ⊞ | 1 | Robicheaux Suppliers | 3200 Linden Drive | Baton Rouge | LA | 30323-9089 | (225) 555-745 |
| ⊞ | 2 | Quality Medical Supplies | 211 South Fourth Avenue | Tampa | FL | 30354-2487 | (813) 555-349 |
| ⊞ | 3 | Peachtree Medical Supplies | 764 Harmon Way | Atlanta | GA | 30357-3652 | (404) 555-773 |
| ⊞ | 4 | Lafferty Company | 12031 Ruston Way | Atlanta | GA | 30365-4311 | (404) 555-092 |
| ⊞ | 5 | National Products | 2192 Second Street | Little Rock | AR | 30325-3499 | (501) 555-450 |
| ⊞ | 6 | Blue Montain Supplies | 9550 Unaversity Avenue | Little Rock | AR | 72209-3412 | (501) 555-440 |

4. Save the Suppliers table.
5. Click in the first entry in the *SupplierID* column.
6. Click the Spelling button in the Records group in the Home tab.
7. The spelling checker selects the name *Robicheaux*. This is a proper name, so click the Ignore button to tell the spelling checker to leave the name as written.

**Step 7**

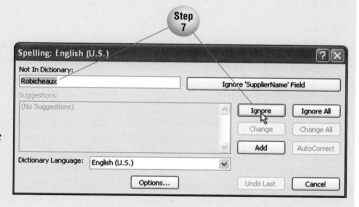

8. The spelling checker selects *Montain*. The proper spelling (*Mountain*) is selected in the *Suggestions* list box, so click the Change button.
9. The spelling checker selects *Unaversity*. The proper spelling (*University*) is selected in the *Suggestions* list box, so click the Change button.
10. At the message telling you that the spelling check is complete, click the OK button.

**Step 8**

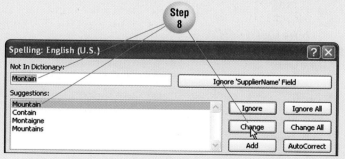

# Finding and Replacing Data

**Find Data**
1. Open table in Datasheet view.
2. Click Find button.
3. Type data in *Find What* text box.
4. Click Find Next button.
5. Continue clicking Find Next button until entire table is searched.

If you need to find a specific entry in a field in a table, consider using options at the Find and Replace dialog box with the Find tab selected as shown in Figure 3.7. Display this dialog box by clicking the Find button in the Find group in the Home tab. At the Find and Replace dialog box, enter the data for which you are searching in the *Find What* text box. By default, Access will look in the specific column where the insertion point is positioned. Click the Find Next button to find the next occurrence of the data or click the Cancel button to remove the Find and Replace dialog box.

**H I N T**

Press Ctrl + F to display the Find and Replace dialog box with the Find tab selected.

Find

**Figure 3.7** Find and Replace Dialog Box with Find Tab Selected

Enter the data for which you are searching in this text box.

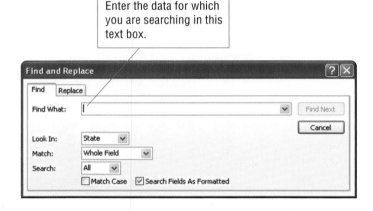

**Find and Replace Data**
1. Open table in Datasheet view.
2. Click Replace button.
3. Type find data in *Find What* text box.
4. Type replace data in *Replace With* text box.
5. Click Find Next button.
6. Click Replace button or Find Next button.

The *Look In* option defaults to the column where the insertion point is positioned. You can choose to look in the entire table by clicking the down-pointing arrow at the right side of the option and then clicking the table name at the drop-down list. The *Match* option has a default setting of *Whole Field*. You can change this to *Any Part of Field* or *Start of Field*. The *Search* option has a default setting of *All*, which means that Access will search all data in a specific column. This can be changed to *Up* or *Down*. If you want to find data that contains specific uppercase and lowercase letters, insert a check mark in the *Match Case* check box. By default, Access will search fields as they are formatted.

You can use the Find and Replace dialog box with the Replace tab selected to search for specific data and replace with other data. Display this dialog box by clicking the Replace button in the Find group in the Home tab.

**H I N T**

Press Ctrl + H to display the Find and Replace dialog box with the Replace tab selected.

1. With the Suppliers table open, find any records containing the two-letter state abbreviation *GA* by completing the following steps:
   a. Click in the first entry in the *State* column.
   b. Click the Find button in the Find group in the Home tab.

Step
1b

Step
1a

c. At the Find and Replace dialog box with the Find tab selected, type **GA** in the *Find What* text box.
d. Click the Find Next button. (Access finds and selects the first occurrence of *GA*. If the Find and Replace dialog box covers the data, drag the dialog box to a different location on the screen.)

Step
1c

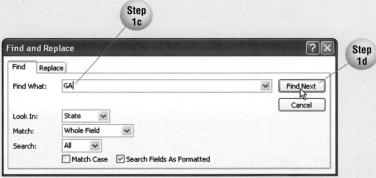

Step
1d

e. Continue clicking the Find Next button until a message displays telling you that Access has finished searching the records. At this message, click OK.
f. Click the Cancel button to close the Find and Replace dialog box.
2. Suppose Quality Medical Supplies has changed its telephone number. Complete the following steps to find the current telephone number and replace it with the new telephone number:
   a. Click in the first entry in the *Telephone* column.
   b. Click the Replace button in the Find group.

c. At the Find and Replace dialog box with the Replace tab selected, type (813) 555-3495 in the *Find What* text box.

d. Press the Tab key. (This moves the insertion point to the *Replace With* text box.)

e. Type (813) 555-9800 in the *Replace With* text box.

f. Click the Find Next button.

g. When Access selects the telephone number *(813) 555-3495*, click the Replace button.

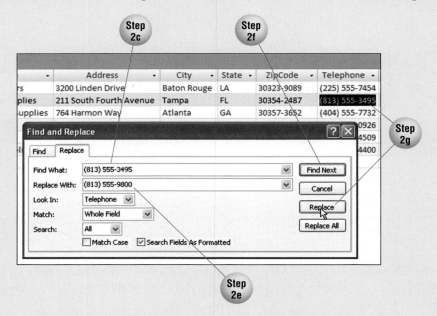

h. Click the Cancel button to close the Find and Replace dialog box.

3. Save the Suppliers table.

4. Display the table in Print Preview, change the page orientation to landscape, change the margins to *Normal*, and then print the table.

5. Close the Suppliers table.

QUICK STEPS

## Backing Up a Database

**Back Up Database**
1. Open database.
2. Click Office button, *Manage, Back Up Database*.
3. Navigate to desired folder or drive.
4. Type file name.
5. Click Save button.

Back up a database on a consistent basis to protect the data in the database from accidental loss or from any hardware failure. To back up a database, click the Office button, point to *Manage*, and then click *Back Up Database*. At the Save As dialog box, navigate to the desired folder or drive, type a name for the database, and then press Enter or click the Save button.

# Compacting and Repairing a Database

To optimize performance of your database, compact and repair the database on a consistent basis. As you work with a database, data in the database can become fragmented causing the amount of space the database takes on the storage medium or in the folder to be larger than necessary.

To compact and repair a database, open the database, click the Office button, point to *Manage*, and then click *Compact and Repair Database*. As the database is compacting and repairing, a message displays on the Status bar indicating the progress of the procedure. When the procedure is completed, close the database.

You can tell Access to compact and repair a database each time you close the database. To do this, click the Office button and then click the Access Options button located in the lower right corner of the drop-down list. At the Access Options dialog box, click *Current Database* in the left panel. This displays the Access Options dialog box as shown in Figure 3.8. Click the *Compact on Close* option to insert a check mark and then click OK to close the window.

**QUICK STEPS**

**Compact and Repair Database**
1. Open database.
2. Click Office button, Manage, Compact and Repair Database.

**HINT**
Before compacting and repairing a database in a multi-user environment, make sure that no other user has the database open.

**Figure 3.8** Access Options Dialog Box with *Current Database* Selected

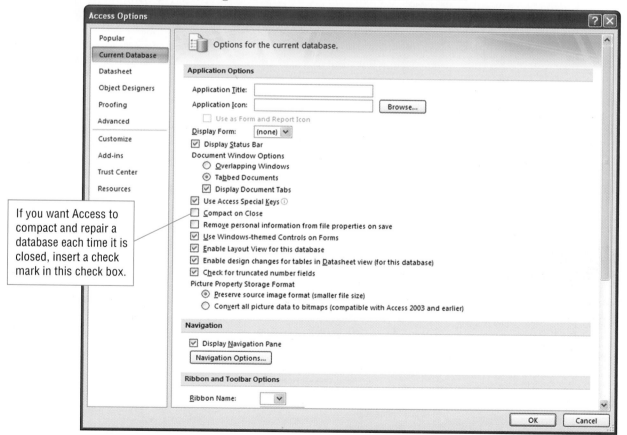

If you want Access to compact and repair a database each time it is closed, insert a check mark in this check box.

1. With the **MedSafeClinic,accdb** database open, create a backup of the database by completing the following steps:
   a. Click the Office button, point to *Manage*, and then click *Back Up Database*.
   b. At the Save As dialog box, type **MSCBackup10-01-2010** in the *File name* text box. (This file name assumes that the date is October 1, 2010. You do not have to use the date in the file name but it does help when using the backup feature to archive databases.)
   c. Click the Save button.

Step 1b

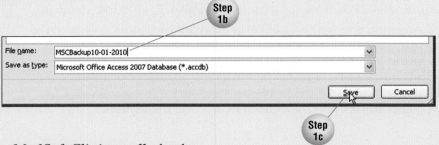

Step 1c

2. Close the **MedSafeClinic.accdb** database.
3. Determine the current size of the **MedSafeClinic.accdb** database (to compare to the size after compacting and repairing) by completing the following steps:
   a. Click the Open button on the Quick Access toolbar.
   b. At the Open dialog box, click the down-pointing arrow at the right side of the Views button and then click *Details* at the drop-down list.
   c. Display the drive (or folder) where your **MedSafeClinic.accdb** database is located and then check the size of the database.
   d. Close the Open dialog box.
4. Compact and repair the **MedSafeClinic.accdb** database by completing the following steps:
   a. Open the **MedSafeClinic.accdb** database.
   b. Click the Office button, point to *Manage*, and then click *Compact and Repair Database*.

Step 3b

Step 4b

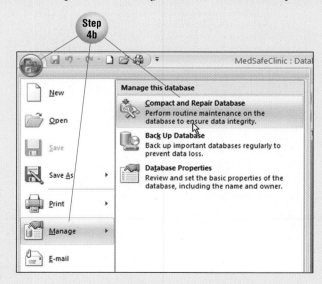

c. When the compact and repair procedure is completed, close the **MedSafeClinic.accdb** database.

5. Determine the size of the compacted and repaired **MedSafeClinic.accdb** database by completing the following steps:

a. Click the Open button on the Quick Access toolbar.

b. At the Open dialog box, make sure the details display in the list box and then look at the size of the **MedSafeClinic.accdb** database and compare this size to the previous size. (Notice that the size of the compacted and repaired **MedSafeClinic.accdb** database is approximately the same size as the **MSCBackup10-01-2010.accdb** database. The backup database was automatically compacted and repaired when saved.)

c. Return the display to a list by clicking the down-pointing arrow at the right side of the Views button and then clicking *List* at the drop-down list.

6. Close the Open dialog box.

# Project ③ Use Access Help

You will use the Access Help feature to display information on creating an input mask and performing diagnostic tests.

# Using Help

The Access Help feature is an on-screen reference manual containing information about all Access features and commands. The Access Help feature is similar to the Windows Help and the Help features in Word, PowerPoint, and Excel. Get help by clicking the Microsoft Office Access Help button located in the upper right corner of the screen (the button containing a question mark) or by pressing F1. This displays the Access Help window shown in Figure 3.9.

**QUICK STEPS**

**Use Help Feature**
1. Click Microsoft Office Access Help button.
2. Type topic, feature, or question.
3. Press Enter.
4. Click desired topic.

**HINT**
Press F1 to display the Access Help window.

Help

**Figure 3.9** Access Help Window

Type in this text box the word, topic, or phrase on which you want help.

Project ③ **Getting Help**

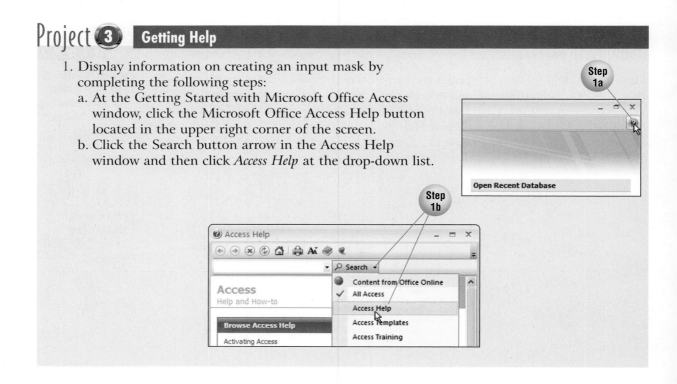

1. Display information on creating an input mask by completing the following steps:
   a. At the Getting Started with Microsoft Office Access window, click the Microsoft Office Access Help button located in the upper right corner of the screen.
   b. Click the Search button arrow in the Access Help window and then click *Access Help* at the drop-down list.

c. Click in the *Search* text box.

d. Type **input mask** and then press the Enter key.

e. Click the *Create an input mask to enter field or control values in a specific format* option that displays in the Help window.

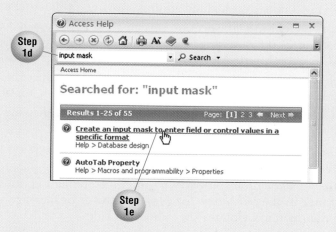

f. Read the information on creating an input mask.

2. Find information on performing diagnostic tests by completing the following steps:

a. Select the text *input mask* that displays in the *Search* text box.

b. Type **diagnostic test** and then press Enter.

c. Click the *Diagnose and repair crashing Office programs by using Office Diagnostics* option.

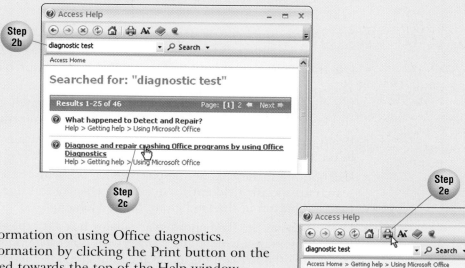

d. Read the information on using Office diagnostics.

e. Print the information by clicking the Print button on the toolbar located towards the top of the Help window.

f. At the Print dialog box, click the Print button.

3. Close the Help window by clicking the Close button located in the upper right corner of the window.

# CHAPTER summary

- Modifying a table can include adding, moving, or deleting a field.
- Add a new field in Datasheet or Design view. Type new records in a blank database or in the *Add New Field* column or add a row for a new field in Design view. Click the Insert Rows button in the Tools group to insert a new field.
- To delete a field, display the table in Design view, select the record you want deleted, and then click the Delete Rows button. Click Yes at the message.
- Select a row by clicking the record selector bar that displays at the left side of the row.
- Use the *Default Value* property in the *Field Properties* section to insert the most common field entry.
- Use the *Validation Rule* property to enter a statement containing a conditional test. Enter in the *Validation Text* property the error message you want to display if the data entered violates the validation rule.
- Click the Totals button in the Records group in the Home tab and Access inserts a row at the bottom of the datasheet with the label *Total* at the left. Click the down-pointing arrow in the Total row and then click the desired function at the drop-down list.
- Use the Input Mask Wizard to set a pattern for how data is entered in a field.
- Use the Lookup Wizard to confine data entered in a field to a specific list of items.
- Sort records in a table in ascending order with the Ascending button in the Sort & Filter group or in descending order with the Descending button.
- Use the spelling checker to find misspelled words in a table.
- The spelling checker compares the words in a table with words in its dictionary. If a match is found, the word is passed over. If no match is found, the spelling checker will select the word and offer possible replacements.
- Begin the spelling checker by clicking the Spelling button in the Records group in the Home tab.
- Use options at the Find and Replace dialog box with the Find tab selected to search for specific field entries in a table. Display this dialog box by clicking the Find button in the Find group in the Home tab.
- Use options at the Find and Replace dialog box with the Replace tab selected to search for specific data and replace with other data. Display this dialog box by clicking the Replace button in the Find group in the Home tab.
- Back up a database on a consistent basis to protect the data in the database from accidental loss or from any hardware failure. To back up a database, click the Office button, point to *Manage*, and then click *Back Up Database*.
- Compact and repair a database to optimize the performance of the database. Compact and repair a database by clicking the Office button, pointing to *Manage*, and then clicking *Compact and Repair Database*.
- Display the Access Help window by clicking the Microsoft Office Access Help button located in the upper right corner of the screen.

# COMMANDS review

| FEATURE | RIBBON TAB, GROUP | BUTTON, OPTION | KEYBOARD SHORTCUT |
|---|---|---|---|
| Add field | Table Tools Design, Tools | Insert Rows | |
| Delete field | Table Tools Design, Tools | Delete Rows | |
| Sort records ascending | Home, Sort & Filter | A Z ↓ | |
| Sort records descending | Home, Sort & Filter | Z A ↓ | |
| Spelling checker | Home, Records | ABC Spelling | F7 |
| Find and Replace dialog box with Find tab selected | Home, Find | 🔍 | Ctrl + F |
| Find and Replace dialog box with Replace tab selected | Home, Find | ab/ac Replace | Ctrl + H |
| Back up database | | , Manage, Back Up Database | |
| Compare and repair database | | , Manage, Compact and Repair Database | |
| Access Help window | | ? | F1 |

# CONCEPTS check

## Test Your Knowledge

**Completion:** For each description, indicate the correct term, symbol, or character.

1. Select a row by clicking this bar that displays at the left side of the row. _____

2. If most records are likely to contain the same field value, use this property to insert the most common field entry. _____

3. Use this property to enter a statement containing a conditional test that is checked each time data is entered into a field. _____

4. Use this wizard to set a pattern for how data is entered in a field. _____

5. Use this wizard to confine data entered in a field to a specific list of items. _____

6. The Ascending and Descending sort buttons are located in this group in the Home tab. _____

7. The Spelling button is located in this group in the Home tab. _____

8. This is the keyboard shortcut to begin spell checking. _____

9. Use options at the Find and Replace dialog box with this tab selected to search for specific data and replace with other data. _____

10. To back up a database, click the Office button, point to this option, and then click *Back Up Database*. _____

11. Perform this action on a database to optimize the performance of the database. _____

12. This is the keyboard shortcut to display the Access Help window. _____

# SKILLS check

*Demonstrate Your Proficiency*

## Assessment

## 1 CREATE TABLES AND RELATIONSHIPS BETWEEN TABLES IN A LAFFERTYCOMPANY DATABASE

1. Create a database named *LaffertyCompany* that contains two tables. Create the first table and name it *MarketingEmployees* and include the following fields (make sure the *EmpID* is identified as the primary key):

| Field Name | Data Type |
|---|---|
| EmpID | Text (field size = 4) |
| FirstName | Text (field size = 20) |
| MiddleName | Text (field size = 20) |
| LastName | Text (field size = 30) |
| Status | Text (field size = 20; assign a default value of *Full-time*) |
| HireDate | Date/Time (use the Input Mask to control the date so it is entered as a short date) |
| Vacation | Text (field size = 10; use the Lookup Wizard to confine the field entry to one of three entries: *0 weeks*, *2 weeks*, or *3 weeks* |

2. Type the following data or choose a field entry in the specified fields:

| | | | | |
|---|---|---|---|---|
| EmpID | 1002 | | EmpID | 3192 |
| FirstName | Samantha | | FirstName | Ralph |
| MiddleName | Lee | | MiddleName | Edward |
| LastName | Murray | | LastName | Sorrell |
| Status | Full-time | | Status | Full-time |
| HireDate | 06/15/2005 | | HireDate | 11/04/2006 |
| Vacation | 3 weeks | | Vacation | 3 weeks |
| | | | | |
| EmpID | 1799 | | EmpID | 2217 |
| FirstName | Brandon | | FirstName | Leland |
| MiddleName | Michael | | MiddleName | John |
| LastName | Perrault | | LastName | Nitsche |
| Status | Full-time | | Status | Part-time |
| HireDate | 03/12/2007 | | HireDate | 09/05/2008 |
| Vacation | 2 weeks | | Vacation | 0 weeks |
| | | | | |
| EmpID | 1340 | | EmpID | 1877 |
| FirstName | Jack | | FirstName | Immanuel |
| MiddleName | Ryan | | MiddleName | Nolan |
| LastName | McCleary | | LastName | Shandra |
| Status | Full-time | | Title | Part-time |
| HireDate | 07/01/2007 | | HireDate | 08/01/2009 |
| Vacation | 2 weeks | | Vacation | 0 weeks |

3. Complete a spelling check on the table. (Assume proper names are spelled correctly.)
4. Adjust the column widths.
5. Save the MarketingEmployees table.
6. Change the orientation to landscape and then print the table.
7. Close the MarketingEmployees table.
8. Create the second table and name it *Expenses* and include the following fields (make sure the *Item#* field is identified as the primary key):

| Field Name | Data Type |
|---|---|
| *Item#* | AutoNumber |
| *EmpID* | Text (field size = 4) |
| *Expense* | Text (field size = 30) |
| *Amount* | Currency (Type a condition in the *Validation Rule* property that states the entry must be $500 or less. Type an error message in the *Validation Text* property box.) |
| *DateSubmitted* | Date/Time (Use the Input Mask to control the date so it is entered as a short date.) |

9. Type the following data or choose a field entry in the specified fields (Access automatically inserts a number in the *Item#* field):

| | | | |
|---|---|---|---|
| *EmpID* | 3192 | *EmpID* | 1799 |
| *Expense* | Brochures | *Expense* | Marketing Conference |
| *Amount* | $245.79 | *Amount* | $500.00 |
| *DateSubmitted* | 02/01/2010 | *DateSubmitted* | 02/08/2010 |
| | | | |
| *EmpID* | 3192 | *EmpID* | 1340 |
| *Expense* | Business Cards | *Expense* | Marketing Conference |
| *Amount* | $150.00 | *Amount* | $500.00 |
| *DateSubmitted* | 02/10/2010 | *DateSubmitted* | 02/10/2010 |
| | | | |
| *EmpID* | 1799 | *EmpID* | 1340 |
| *Expense* | Supplies | *Expense* | Reference Material |
| *Amount* | $487.25 | *Amount* | $85.75 |
| *DateSubmitted* | 02/14/2010 | *DateSubmitted* | 02/15/2010 |

10. Complete a spelling check on the table.
11. Adjust the column widths.
12. Save, print, and then close the Expenses table.
13. Create a one-to-many relationship where *EmpID* in the MarketingEmployees table is the "one" and *EmpID* in the Expenses table is the "many."
14. Print the relationship and then close the relationships report window and the relationships window.

## 2 MODIFY A TABLE AND FIND AND REPLACE DATA IN A TABLE

1. With the **LaffertyCompany.accdb** database open, open the MarketingEmployees table and then make the following changes:
    a. Delete the *MiddleName* field.
    b. Insert a *Title* field between *LastName* and *Status*. (You determine the data type and description.)
    c. Move the *Status* field below the *HireDate* field.
    d. In Datasheet view, add the data to the *Title* field as specified below:

    | EmpID | Title |
    |-------|-------|
    | 1002 | Manager |
    | 3192 | Assistant Manager |
    | 1799 | Manager |
    | 2217 | Assistant |
    | 1340 | Assistant |
    | 1877 | Assistant |

2. Save the MarketingEmployees table.
3. Find all occurrences of *Manager* and replace with *Director*. **Hint: Position the insertion point in the first entry in the** Title **column and then display the Find and Replace dialog box. At the dialog box, change the** Match **option to Any Part of Field.**
4. Find all occurrences of *Assistant* and replace with *Associate*.
5. Save and then print the table in landscape orientation with *Normal* margins.
6. Close the MarketingEmployees table.
7. Open the Expenses table, insert a Total row in the table, and then calculate the sum of the expenses.
8. Save, print, and then close the Expenses table.
9. Close the **LaffertyCompany.accdb** database.

# CASE study
## *Apply Your Skills*

**Part 1**

You work for Sunrise Enterprises and your supervisor has asked you to create a database with information about clients and sales representatives. Create a database named *Sunrise* that contains two tables. Create a table named *Representatives* that includes fields for representative ID number, representative name, representative telephone number (use the Input Mask Wizard), insurance plan (use the Lookup Wizard and include four options: *Platinum*, *Premium*, *Standard*, and *None*) and yearly bonus (type a condition in the *Validation Rule* property that states the entry must be between $2,000 and $10,000 and type an error message in the *Validation Text* property box). Make sure the representative ID number is the primary key in the table. In Datasheet view, enter seven records in the table. Insert a total row and then sum the bonus amounts. Save, print, and then close the table.

Create a second table in the **Sunrise.accdb** database named *Clients* that includes fields for company ID number, representative ID number (the same field you created in the Representative table) company name, address, city, state, ZIP code (use the Input Mask Wizard and specify a nine digit ZIP code), telephone number (use the Input Wizard), and type of business (specify that *Wholesaler* is the default value). Make sure that the company ID number is identified as the primary key. In Datasheet view, enter at least five companies. Make sure you use representative ID numbers in the Clients table that match numbers in the Representative table. Identify that one of the clients is a *"Retailer"* rather than a *"Wholesaler."* Save, print, and then close the table.

**Part 2**

Create a one-to-many relationship with the representative ID number in the Representatives table as the "one" and the representative ID number in the Clients table as the "many." Save and then print the relationship.

**Part 3**

Open the Representatives table and then reverse the order of the yearly bonus and the insurance plan fields. Save, print, and then close the table. Open the Clients table and then reverse the order of the telephone number and type of business fields. Save, print, and then close the table.

**Part 4**

In Microsoft Word, create a document that describes three situations where you would use the Lookup Wizard, three situations where you would assign a default value to a field, and three situations where you would write a conditional statement for a field. Apply any formatting to the document to enhance the visual appeal and then save the document and name it **Access_C3_CS_P4**. Print and then close **Access_C3_CS_P4.docx**.

# Performing Queries

## PERFORMANCE OBJECTIVES

**Upon successful completion of Chapter 4, you will be able to:**

- **Design a query to extract specific data from a table**
- **Use the Simple Query Wizard to extract specific data from a table**
- **Modify a query**
- **Design queries with Or and And criteria**
- **Create a calculated field**
- **Use aggregate functions in queries**
- **Create crosstab, duplicate, and unmatched queries**

access Chapter 4

**Tutorial 4.1**
Extracting Specific Data
**Tutorial 4.2**
Performing Advanced Queries
and Filtering Records

One of the primary uses of a database is to extract specific information from the database. A company might need to know such information as: How much inventory is currently on hand? What products have been ordered? What accounts are past due? What customers live in a particular city? You can extract this type of information from a table by completing a query. You will learn how to perform a variety of queries on information in tables in this chapter.

*Note: Before beginning computer projects, copy the Access2007L1C4 subfolder from the Access2007L1 folder on the CD that accompanies this textbook to your storage medium and make Access2007L1C4 the active folder.*

roject **1** Design Queries

You will design and run a number of queries including queries with fields from one table and queries with fields from more than one table. You will also use the Simple Query Wizard to design queries.

## Performing Queries

Being able to extract (pull out) specific data from a table is one of the most important functions of a database. Extracting data in Access is referred to as performing a query. The word *query* means to ask a question. Access provides several methods for performing a query. You can design your own query, use a simple query wizard, or use complex query wizards. In this chapter, you will learn to design your own query; use the Simple Query Wizard; use aggregate functions in a query; and use the Crosstab, Find Duplicates, and Unmatched Query Wizards.

## Designing a Query

Designing a query consists of identifying the table from which you are gathering data, the field or fields from which the data will be drawn, and the criteria for selecting the data. To design a query and perform the query, open a database, click the Create tab, and then click the Query Design button in the Other group. This displays a query window in the work area and also displays the Show Table dialog box as shown in Figure 4.1.

Query Design

**Figure 4.1** Query Window with Show Table Dialog Box

Query design grid

Click the table you want included in the query and then click the Add button.

Click the table in the Show Table list box that you want included in the query and then click the Add button or double-click the desired table. Add any other tables required for the query. When all tables have been added, click the Close button. In the query window, click the down-pointing arrow at the right of the first *Field* text box in the query design grid and then click the desired field from the drop-down list. Figure 4.2 displays a sample query window.

**Figure 4.2** Query Window

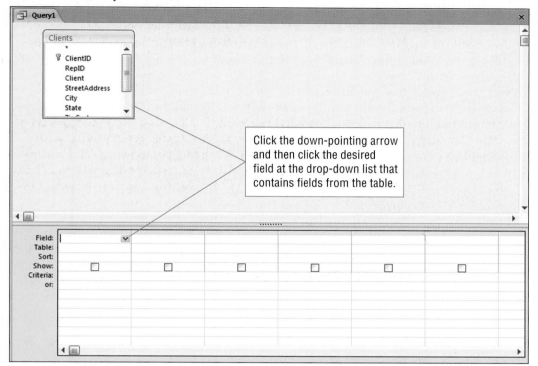

Click the down-pointing arrow and then click the desired field at the drop-down list that contains fields from the table.

To establish a criterion, click inside the *Criteria* text box in the column containing the desired field name in the query design grid and then type the criterion. With the fields and criteria established, click the Run button in the Results group in the Query Tools Design tab. Access searches the specified tables for records that match the criteria and then displays those records in the query results datasheet. If you plan to use the query in the future, save the query and name it. If you do not need the query again, close the query results datasheet without saving it.

You can click the down-pointing arrow at the right side of a *Field* text box and then click the desired field at the drop-down list. You can also double-click a field in a table and it is inserted in the first available *Field* text box in the query design grid. As an example, suppose you wanted to find out how many purchase orders were issued on a specific date. To do this, you would double-click *PurchaseOrderID* in the table (this inserts *PurchaseOrderID* in the first *Field* text box in the query design grid) and then double-click *OrderDate* in the table (this inserts *OrderDate* in the second *Field* text box in the query design grid). In this example, both fields are needed so the purchase order ID is displayed along with the specific order date. After inserting fields, you would then insert the criterion. The criterion for this example would be something like *#1/15/2010#*. After you insert the criterion, click the Run button in the Results group and the results of the query display in the query results datasheet.

A third method for inserting a field in the query design grid is to drag a field from the table to the desired field in the query design grid. To do this, position the mouse pointer on the desired field in the table, hold down the left mouse button, drag to the desired *Field* text box in the query design grid, and then release the mouse button.

**HINT**

Insert fields in the *Field* text boxes in the query design grid in the order in which you want the fields to display in the query results datasheet.

Run

# Establishing Query Criteria

**Establish Query Criterion**
1. At query window, click in desired *Criteria* text box in query design grid.
2. Type criterion and then press Enter.
3. Click Run button.

A query does not require that specific criteria are established. In the example described on the previous page, if the criterion for the date was not included, the query would "return" (*return* is the term used for the results of the query) all Purchase Order numbers with the dates. While this information may be helpful, you could easily find this information in the table. The value of performing a query is to extract specific information from a table. To do this, you must insert a criterion like the one described in the example.

Access makes writing a criterion fairly simple because it inserts the necessary symbols in the criterion. If you type a city such as *Indianapolis* in the *Criteria* text box and then press Enter, Access changes the criterion to *"Indianapolis"*. The quotation marks are inserted by Access and are necessary for the query to run properly. You can either let Access put the proper symbols in the *Criteria* text box, or you can type the criterion with the symbols. Table 4.1 shows some criteria examples including what is typed and what is returned.

**Table 4.1** Criteria Examples

| *Typing this criteria* | *Returns this* |
| --- | --- |
| "Smith" | Field value matching *Smith* |
| "Smith" or "Larson" | Field value matching either *Smith* or *Larson* |
| Not "Smith" | Field value that is not *Smith* (the opposite of "Smith") |
| "S*" | Field value that begins with *S* and ends in anything |
| "*s" | Field value that begins with anything and ends in *s* |
| "[A-D]*" | Field value that begins with *A* through *D* and ends in anything |
| #01/01/2010# | Field value matching the date 01/01/2010 |
| <#04/01/2010# | Field value less than (before) 04/01/2010 |
| >#04/01/2010# | Field value greater than (after) 04/01/2010 |
| Between #01/01/2010 And #03/31/2010 | Any date between 01/01/2010 and 03/31/2010 |

**HINT**

Access inserts quotation marks around text criteria and the pound symbol around date criteria.

In Table 4.1, notice the quotation marks surrounding field values (such as "Smith"). If you do not type the quotation marks when typing the criterion, Access will automatically insert them. The same is true for the pound symbol (#). If you do not type the pound symbol around a date, Access will automatically insert the symbols. Access automatically inserts the correct symbol when you press the Enter key after typing the query criteria.

In the criteria examples, the asterisk was used as a wild card indicating any character. This is consistent with many other software applications where the asterisk is used as a wildcard character. Two of the criteria examples in Table 4.1 use the less than and greater than symbols. You can use these symbols for fields containing numbers, values, dates, amounts, and so forth. In the next several projects, you will be designing queries to extract specific information from different tables in databases.

## Project 1a  Performing Queries on Tables

1. Display the Open dialog box with Access2007L1C4 on your storage medium the active folder.
2. Open the **Deering.accdb** database.
3. Create the following relationships:
    a. Create a one-to-one relationship where the *ClientID* field in the Clients table is the "one" and the *ClientID* field in the Sales table is the "one."
    b. Create a one-to-one relationship where the *RepID* field in the Representatives table is the "one" and the *RepID* field in the Benefits table is the "one."
    c. Create a one-to-many relationship where the *RepID* field in the Representatives table is the "one" and the *RepID* field in the Clients table is the "many."
    d. Create a one-to-many relationship where the *QuotaID* field in the Quotas table is the "one" and the *QuotaID* field in the Representatives table is the "many."
4. Save, print, and then close the relationships report and relationships window.
5. Extract records of those clients located in Indianapolis by completing the following steps:
    a. Click the Create tab.
    b. Click the Query Design button in the Other group.

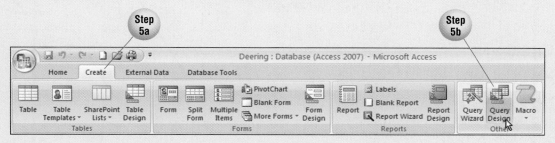

Step 5a

Step 5b

c. At the Show Table dialog box with the Tables tab selected (see Figure 4.1), click *Clients* in the list box, click the Add button, and then click the Close button.
d. Insert fields from the table to *Field* text boxes in the query design grid by completing the following steps:
    1) Click the down-pointing arrow located at the right of the first *Field* text box in the query design grid and then click *Client* in the drop-down list.

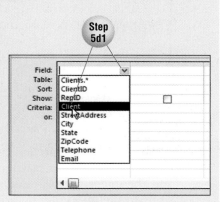

Step 5d1

2) Click inside the next *Field* text box (to the right of *Client*) in the query design grid, click the down-pointing arrow, and then click *StreetAddress* in the drop-down list.

3) Click inside the next *Field* box (to the right of *StreetAddress*), click the down-pointing arrow, and then click *City* in the drop-down list.

4) Click inside the next *Field* box (to the right of *City*), click the down-pointing arrow, and then click *State* in the drop-down list.

5) Click inside the next *Field* box (to the right of *State*), click the down-pointing arrow, and then select *ZipCode* in the drop-down list.

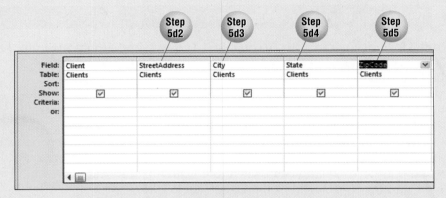

e. Insert the criterion text telling Access to display only those suppliers located in Indianapolis by completing the following steps:

1) Click in the *Criteria* text box in the *City* column in the query design grid. (This positions the insertion point inside the text box.)

2) Type **Indianapolis** and then press Enter. (This changes the criterion to "Indianapolis").

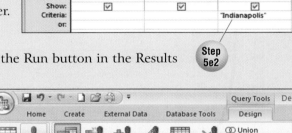

f. Return the results of the query by clicking the Run button in the Results group. (This displays the results in the query results datasheet.)

g. Save the results of the query by completing the following steps:

1) Click the Save button on the Quick Access toolbar.

2) At the Save As dialog box, type **IndianapolisQuery** and then press Enter or click OK.

h. Print the query results datasheet by clicking the Quick Print button on the Quick Access toolbar.

i. Close IndianapolisQuery.

6. Extract those records with quota identification numbers higher than 2 by completing the following steps:

a. Click the Create tab and then click the Query Design button in the Other group.

b. Double-click *Representatives* in the Show Table list box and then click the Close button.

c. In the query window, double-click *RepName* (this inserts the field in the first *Field* text box in the query design grid).

d. Double-click *QuotaID* (this inserts the field in the second *Field* text box in the query design grid).

e. Insert the query criterion by completing the following
   steps:
   1) Click in the *Criteria* text box in the *QuotaID* column
      in the query design grid.
   2) Type >2 and then press Enter. (Access will
      automatically insert quotation marks around 2 since
      the data type for the field is set at *Text* [rather than *Number*].)

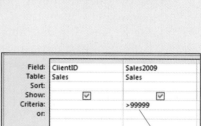

Step
6e2

f. Return the results of the query by clicking the Run button in the
   Results group.
g. Save the query and name it *QuotaIDGreaterThanTwoQuery*.
h. Print and then close the query.

7. Extract those 2009 sales greater than $99,999 by completing the following steps:
   a. Click the Create tab and then click the Query Design button.
   b. Double-click *Sales* in the Show Table dialog box and then click the Close button.
   c. At the query window, double-click *ClientID* (this inserts the field in the first *Field* text
      box in the query design grid).
   d. Insert the *Sales2009* field in the second *Field* text box.
   e. Insert the query criterion by completing the following steps:
      1) Click in the *Criteria* text box in the *Sales2009*
         column in the query design grid.
      2) Type >99999 and then press Enter. (Access will not
         insert quotation marks around *99999* since the field
         is identified as *Currency*.)

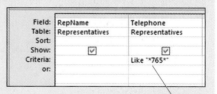

Step
7e2

   f. Return the results of the query by clicking the Run
      button in the Results group.
   g. Save the query and name it *2009SalesOver$99999Query*.
   h. Print and then close the query.

8. Extract records of those representatives with a telephone number that begins with the 765
   area code by completing the following steps:
   a. Click the Create tab and then click the Query Design button.
   b. Double-click *Representatives* in the Show Table dialog box and then click the Close button.
   c. Insert the *RepName* field in the first *Field* text box.
   d. Insert the *Telephone* field in the second *Field* text box.
   e. Insert the query criterion by completing the following
      steps:
      1) Click in the *Criteria* text box in the *Telephone* column.
      2) Type *765* and then press Enter.
   f. Return the results of the query by clicking the Run button in the Results group.
   g. Save the query and name it *RepsWith765AreaCodeQuery*.
   h. Print and then close the query.

Step
8e2

In Project 1a, you performed several queries on specific tables. A query can
also be performed on fields from more than one table. In Project 1b, you will be
performing queries on related tables. As mentioned earlier, one method for inserting
fields in the query design grid is to drag the field from the table to the desired
*Field* text box.

1. With the **Deering.accdb** database open, extract information on representatives hired between March of 2006 and November of 2006 and include the representative's name by completing the following steps:

   a. Click the Create tab and then click the Query Design button.

   b. Double-click *Representatives* in the Show Table dialog box.

   c. Double-click *Benefits* in the Show Table dialog box list box and then click the Close button.

   d. At the query window, position the mouse pointer on the *RepName* field in the Representatives table, hold down the left mouse button, drag to the first *Field* text box in the query design grid,

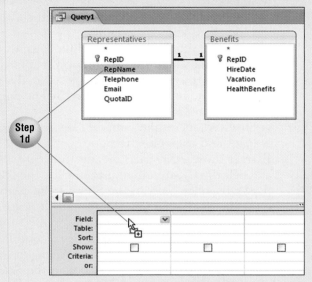

Step **1d**

   and then release the mouse button. (This inserts the field in the *Field* text box.)

   e. Drag the *HireDate* field from the Benefits table to the second *Field* text box.

   f. Insert the query criterion by completing the following steps:

   1) Click in the *Criteria* text box in the *HireDate* column.

   2) Type **Between 3/1/2006 And 11/30/2006** and then press Enter. (Make sure you type zeros and not capital *O*s.)

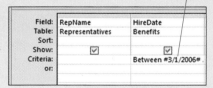

Step **1f2**

   g. Return the results of the query by clicking the Run button in the Results group.

   h. Save the query and name it *MarToNov2006HiresQuery*.

   i. Print and then close the query.

2. Extract records of those representatives who were hired in 2004 by completing the following steps:

   a. Click the Create tab and then click the Query Design button.

   b. Double-click *Representatives* in the Show Table dialog box.

   c. Double-click *Benefits* in the Show Table dialog box and then click the Close button.

   d. At the query window, drag the *RepID* field from the Representatives table to the first *Field* text box in the query design grid.

   e. Drag the *RepName* field from the Representatives table to the second *Field* text box.

   f. Drag the *HireDate* field from the Benefits table to the third *Field* text box.

   g. Insert the query criterion by completing the following steps:

   1) Click in the *Criteria* text box in the *HireDate* column.

   2) Type **\*2004** and then press Enter.

   | Field: | RepID | RepName | HireDate |
   |---|---|---|---|
   | Table: | Representatives | Representatives | Benefits |
   | Sort: | | | |
   | Show: | ☑ | ☑ | ☑ |
   | Criteria: | | | Like "*2004" |
   | or: | | | |

   Step **2g2**

   h. Return the results of the query by clicking the Run button in the Results group.

   i. Save the query and name it *RepsHiredIn2004Query*.

   j. Print and then close the query.

3. Suppose you need to determine 2008 and 2009 sales for a company but you can only remember that the company name begins with *Blue*. Create a query that finds the company and identifies the sales by completing the following steps:

  a. Click the Create tab and then click the Query Design button.

  b. Double-click *Clients* in the Show Table dialog box.

  c. Double-click *Sales* in the Show Table dialog box and then click the Close button.

  d. At the query window, insert the *ClientID* field in the Clients table in the first *Field* text box in the query design grid.

  e. Insert the *Client* field in the Clients table in the second *Field* text box.

  f. Insert the *Sales2008* field from the Sales table in the third *Field* text box.

  g. Insert the *Sales2009* field from the Sales table in the fourth *Field* text box.

  h. Insert the query criterion by completing the following steps:

    1) Click in the *Criteria* text box in the *Client* column.

    2) Type **Blue\*** and then press Enter.

Step 3h2

  i. Return the results of the query by clicking the Run button in the Results group.

  j. Save the query and name it *BlueRidgeSalesQuery*.

  k. Print and then close the query.

4. Close the **Deering.accdb** database.

5. Display the Open dialog box with Access2007L1C4 on your storage medium the active folder.

6. Open the **OutdoorOptions.accdb** database.

7. Extract information on products ordered between February 15 and February 28, 2010, and include the supplier's name by completing the following steps:

  a. Click the Create tab and then click the Query Design button.

  b. Double-click *Products* in the Show Table dialog box.

  c. Double-click *Orders* in the Show Table dialog box and then click the Close button.

  d. At the query window, insert the *Product#* field from the Products table in the first *Field* text box.

  e. Insert the *Product* field from the Products table in the second *Field* text box.

  f. Insert the *OrderDate* field from the Orders table in the third *Field* list box.

  g. Insert the query criterion by completing the following steps:

    1) Click in the *Criteria* text box in the *OrderDate* column.

    2) Type **Between 2/15/2010 And 2/28/2010** and then press Enter. (Make sure you type zeros and not capital *O*s.)

| Field: | Product# | Product | OrderDate |
|---|---|---|---|
| Table: | Products | Products | Orders |
| Sort: | | | |
| Show: | ☑ | ☑ | ☑ |
| Criteria: | | | Between #2/15/2010# |
| or: | | | |

Step 7g2

  h. Return the results of the query by clicking the Run button in the Results group.

  i. Save the query and name it *Feb15-28OrdersQuery*.

  j. Print and then close the query.

## Sorting Fields in a Query

**Sort Fields in Query**
1. At query window, click in *Sort* text box in query design grid.
2. Click down arrow in *Sort* text box.
3. Click *Ascending* or *Descending*.

When designing a query, you can specify the sort order of a field or fields. Click inside one of the columns in the *Sort* text box and a down-pointing arrow displays at the right of the field. Click this down-pointing arrow and a drop-down list displays with the choices *Ascending*, *Descending*, and *(not sorted)*. Click Ascending to sort from lowest to highest or click Descending to sort from highest to lowest.

## Project 1c  Performing a Query on Related Tables and Sorting in Ascending Order

1. With the **OutdoorOptions.accdb** database open, extract information on orders less than $1,500 by completing the following steps:
   a. Click the Create tab and then click the Query Design button.
   b. Double-click *Products* in the Show Table dialog box.
   c. Double-click *Orders* in the Show Table dialog box and then click the Close button.
   d. At the query window, insert the *Product#* field from the Products table in the first *Field* text box.
   e. Insert the *Supplier#* field from the Products table in the second *Field* text box.
   f. Insert the *UnitsOrdered* field from the Orders table in the third *Field* text box.
   g. Insert the *Amount* field from the Orders table in the fourth *Field* text box.
   h. Insert the query criterion by completing the following steps:
      1) Click in the *Criteria* text box in the *Amount* column.
      2) Type *<1500* and then press Enter. (Make sure you type zeros and not capital Os.)

| Field: | Product# | Supplier# | UnitsOrdered | Amount |
|---|---|---|---|---|
| Table: | Products | Products | Orders | Orders |
| Sort: | | | | |
| Show: | ☑ | ☑ | ☑ | ☑ |
| Criteria: | | | | <1500 |
| or: | | | | |

**Step 1h2**

   i. Sort the *Amount* field values from lowest to highest by completing the following steps:
      1) Click in the *Sort* text box in the *Amount* column. (This causes a down-pointing arrow to display at the right side of the text box.)
      2) Click the down-pointing arrow at the right side of the *Sort* text box and then click *Ascending*.
   j. Return the results of the query by clicking the Run button in the Results group.
   k. Save the query and name it *OrdersLessThan$1500Query*.
   l. Print and then close the query.
2. Close the **OutdoorOptions.accdb** database.
3. Open the **Deering.accdb** database.

**Step 1i1**

**Step 1i2**

4. Extract information on sales below $100,000 for 2008 by completing the following steps:
   a. Click the Create tab and then click the Query Design button.
   b. Double-click *Clients* in the Show Table dialog box.
   c. Double-click *Sales* in the list Show Table dialog box.
   d. Double-click *Representatives* in the Show Table dialog box and then click the Close button.
   e. At the query window, insert the *Client* field from the Clients table in the first *Field* text box.
   f. Insert the *Sales2008* field from the Sales table in the second *Field* text box.
   g. Insert the *RepName* field from the Representatives table in the third *Field* text box.
   h. Insert the query criterion by completing the following steps:
      1) Click in the *Criteria* text box in the *Sales2008* column.
      2) Type <100000 and then press Enter. (Make sure you type zeros and not capital *O*s.)
   i. Sort the *Sales2008* field values from highest to lowest by completing the following steps:
      1) Click in the *Sort* text box in the *Sales2008* column. (This causes a down-pointing arrow to display at the right side of the text box.)
      2) Click the down-pointing arrow at the right side of the *Sort* text box and then click *Descending*.
   j. Return the results of the query by clicking the Run button in the Results group.
   k. Save the query and name it *2008SalesLessThan$100000Query*.
   l. Print and then close the query.

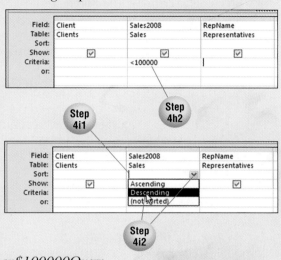

## Modifying a Query

You can modify a saved query. For example, suppose after designing the query that displays the 2008 sales that are less than $100,000, you decide that you want to find sales for 2009 that are less than $100,000. Rather than designing a new query, open the existing query, make any needed changes, and then run the query.

To modify an existing query, double-click the query in the Navigation pane (this displays the query in Datasheet view). Click the View button to display the query in Design view. Make the desired changes and then click the Run button in the Results group. Click the Save button on the Quick Access toolbar to save the query with the same name. If you want to save the query with a new name, click the Office button and then click Save As. At the Save As dialog box, type a name for the query and then press Enter.

If your database contains a number of queries, you can group and display them in the Navigation pane. To do this, click the down-pointing arrow in the Navigation pane Menu bar and then click *Object Type* at the drop-down list. This displays objects grouped in categories such as *Tables* and *Queries*.

**Modify a Query**
1. Double-click query in Navigation pane.
2. Click View button.
3. Make desired changes to query.
4. Click Run button.
5. Click Save button.

**HINT**
Save time designing a query by modifying an existing query.

1. With the **Deering.accdb** database open, find the sales less than $100,000 for 2009 by completing the following steps:

   Step 1a

   a. Change the display of objects in the Navigation pane by clicking the down-pointing arrow in the Navigation pane Menu bar and then clicking *Object Type* at the drop-down list.
   b. Double-click the *2008SalesLessThan$100000Query* in the *Queries* section of the Navigation pane.
   c. Click the View button in the Views group to switch to Design view.
   d. Click in the *Field* text box containing the text *Sales2008*.
   e. Click the down-pointing arrow that displays at the right side of the *Field* text box and then click *Sales2009* at the drop-down list.

   Step 1e

   f. Click the Run button in the Results group.

2. Save the query with a new name by completing the following steps:
   a. Click the Office button and then click Save As.
   b. At the Save As dialog box, type **2009SalesLessThan$100000Query** and then press Enter.

   Step 2b

   c. Print and then close the query.

3. Modify an existing query and find employees with three weeks of vacation by completing the following steps:
   a. Double-click the *MarToNov2006HiresQuery*.
   b. Click the View button in the Views group to switch to Design view.
   c. Click in the *Field* text box containing the text *HireDate*.
   d. Click the down-pointing arrow that displays at the right side of the *Field* text box and then click *Vacation* at the drop-down list.
   e. Select the current text in the *Criteria* text box in the *Vacation* column, type **3 weeks**, and then press Enter.

   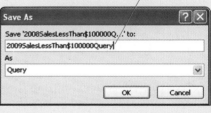

   Step 3e

   f. Click the Run button in the Results group.

4. Save the query with a new name by completing the following steps:
   a. Click the Office button and then click Save As.
   b. At the Save As dialog box, type **RepsWith3WeekVacationsQuery** and then press Enter.
   c. Print and then close the query.

# Designing Queries with *Or* and *And* Criteria

**HINT**
You can design a query that combines *And* and *Or* statements.

The query design grid contains an *Or* row you can use to design a query that instructs Access to display records that match either of the two criteria. For example, to display a list of employees with three weeks of vacation *or* four weeks of vacation, you would type 3 weeks in the *Criteria* text box for the *Vacation* field and then type 4 weeks in the field immediately below *3 weeks* in the *Or* row. Other examples include finding clients that live in *Muncie* or *Lafayette* or finding representatives with a quota of *1* or *2*.

You can also select records by entering criteria statements into more than one *Criteria* field. Multiple criteria all entered in the same row becomes an *And* statement where each criterion must be met for Access to select the record. For example, you could search for clients in the Indianapolis area with sales greater than $100,000.

## Project 1e — Designing Queries with *Or* and *And* Criteria

1. With the **Deering.accdb** database open, modify an existing query and find employees with three weeks or four weeks of vacation by completing the following steps:
   a. Double-click the *RepsWith3WeekVacationsQuery*.
   b. Click the View button in the Views group to switch to Design view.
   c. Click in the empty field below "*3 weeks*" in the *Or* row, type 4 weeks, and then press Enter.

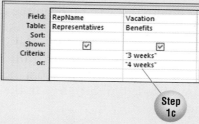

Step 1c

   d. Click the Run button in the Results group.
2. Save the query with a new name by completing the following steps:
   a. Click the Office button and then click Save As.
   b. At the Save As dialog box, type RepsWith3Or4WeekVacationsQuery and then press Enter.
   c. Print and then close the query.
3. Design a query that finds records of clients in the Indianapolis area with sales over $100,000 for 2008 and 2009 by completing the following steps:
   a. Click the Create tab and then click the Query Design button.
   b. Double-click *Clients* in the Show Table dialog box.
   c. Double-click *Sales* in the Show Table dialog box and then click the Close button.
   d. At the query window, insert the *Client* field from the Clients table in the first *Field* text box.
   e. Insert the *City* field from the Clients table in the second *Field* text box.
   f. Insert the *Sales2008* field from the Sales table in the third *Field* text box.
   g. Insert the *Sales2009* field from the Sales table in the fourth *Field* text box.

h. Insert the query criteria by completing the following steps:
   1) Click in the *Criteria* text box in the *City* column.
   2) Type **Indianapolis** and then press Enter.
   3) With the insertion point positioned in the *Criteria* text box in the *Sales2008* column, type **>100000** and then press Enter.
   4) With the insertion point positioned in the *Criteria* text box in the *Sales2009* column, type **>100000** and then press Enter.

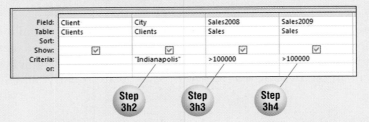

| Field: | Client | City | Sales2008 | Sales2009 |
|---|---|---|---|---|
| Table: | Clients | Clients | Sales | Sales |
| Sort: | | | | |
| Show: | ☑ | ☑ | ☑ | ☑ |
| Criteria: | | "Indianapolis" | >100000 | >100000 |
| or: | | | | |

Step 3h2    Step 3h3    Step 3h4

i. Click the Run button in the Results group.
j. Save the query and name it **IndianapolisSalesOver$100000**.
k. Print and then close the query.

## Performing a Query with the Simple Query Wizard

Query Wizard

The Simple Query Wizard provided by Access guides you through the steps for preparing a query. To use this wizard, open the database, click the Create tab, and then click the Query Wizard button in the Other group. At the New Query dialog box, make sure *Simple Query Wizard* is selected in the list box and then click the OK button. At the first Simple Query Wizard dialog box, shown in Figure 4.3, specify the table(s) in the *Tables/Queries* option box. After specifying the table, insert the fields you want included in the query in the *Selected Fields* list box, and then click the Next button.

**Figure 4.3** First Simple Query Wizard Dialog Box

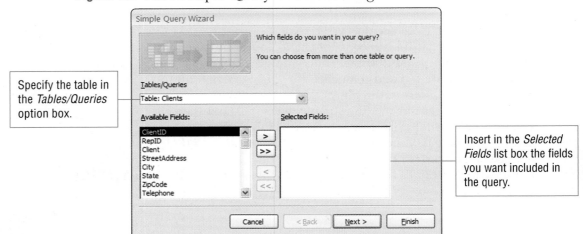

Specify the table in the *Tables/Queries* option box.

Insert in the *Selected Fields* list box the fields you want included in the query.

At the second Simple Query Wizard dialog box, specify whether you want a detail or summary query, and then click the Next button. At the third (and last) Simple Query Wizard dialog box, shown in Figure 4.4, type a name for the completed query or accept the name provided by the wizard. At this dialog box, you can also specify that you want to open the query to view the information or modify the query design. If you want to extract specific information, be sure to choose the *Modify the query design* option. After making any necessary changes, click the Finish button.

**QUICK STEPS**

**Create a Query with Simple Query Wizard**
1. Click Create tab.
2. Click Query Wizard button.
3. Make sure *Simple Query Wizard* is selected in list box and then click OK.
4. Follow query steps.

**Figure 4.4** Last Simple Query Wizard Dialog Box

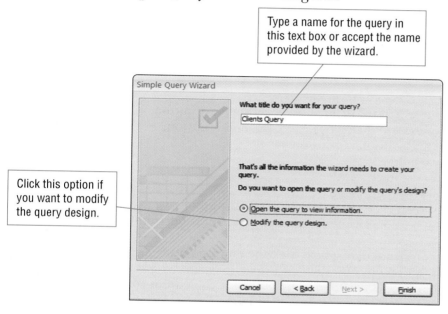

Type a name for the query in this text box or accept the name provided by the wizard.

Click this option if you want to modify the query design.

If you do not modify the query design in the last Simple Query Wizard dialog box, the query displays all records for the fields identified in the first Simple Query Wizard dialog box. In Project 1f you will perform a query without modifying the design, and in Project 1g you will modify the query design.

## Project 1f Performing a Query with the Simple Query Wizard

1. With the **Deering.accdb** database open, click the Create tab and then click the Query Wizard button in the Other group.
2. At the New Query dialog box, make sure *Simple Query Wizard* is selected in the list box and then click OK.
3. At the first Simple Query Wizard dialog box, click the down-pointing arrow at the right of the *Tables/Queries* option box and then click *Table: Clients*. (You will need to scroll up the list to display this table.)

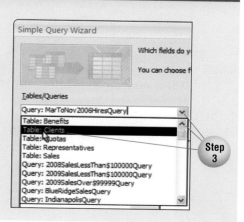

Step 3

4. With *ClientID* selected in the *Available Fields* list box, click the button containing the greater than symbol. (This inserts the *ClientID* field in the *Selected Fields* list box.)
5. Click *Client* in the *Available Fields* list box and then click the button containing the greater than symbol.
6. Click the down-pointing arrow at the right of the *Tables/Queries* option box and then click *Table: Sales*.
7. Click *Sales2008* in the *Available Fields* list box and then click the button containing the greater than symbol.
8. With *Sales2009* selected in the *Available Fields* list box, click the button containing the greater than symbol.

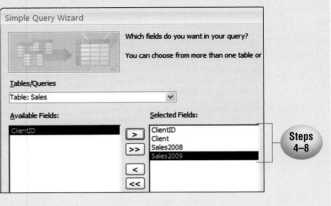

Steps 4–8

9. Click the Next button.
10. At the second Simple Query Wizard dialog box, click the Next button.
11. At the last Simple Query Wizard dialog box, click the Finish button.
12. When the results of the query display, print the results.
13. Close the Clients Query window.
14. Close the **Deering.accdb** database.
15. Open the **OutdoorOptions.accdb** database.
16. Click the Create tab and then click the Query Wizard button.
17. At the New Query dialog box, make sure *Simple Query Wizard* is selected in the list box and then click OK.
18. At the first Simple Query Wizard dialog box, click the down-pointing arrow at the right side of the *Tables/Queries* option box and then click *Table: Suppliers*.
19. With *Supplier#* selected in the *Available Fields* list box, click the button containing the greater than symbol. (This inserts the *Supplier#* field in the *Selected Fields* list box.)
20. With *SupplierName* selected in the *Available Fields* list box, click the button containing the greater than symbol.
21. Click the down-pointing arrow at the right of the *Tables/Queries* option box and then click *Table: Orders*.
22. Click *Product#* in the *Available Fields* list box and then click the button containing the greater than symbol.
23. Click *Amount* in the *Available Fields* list box and then click the button containing the greater than symbol.

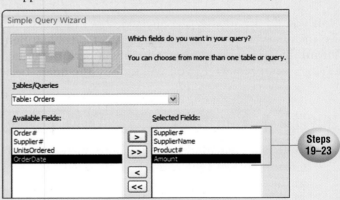

Steps 19–23

24. Click the Next button.
25. At the second Simple Query Wizard dialog box, click the Next button.
26. At the last Simple Query Wizard dialog box, click the Finish button.
27. When the results of the query display, print the results.
28. Close the query window.

To extract specific information when using the Simple Query Wizard, tell the wizard that you want to modify the query design. This displays the query window with the query design grid where you can insert query criteria.

## Project 1g — Performing and Modifying a Query with the Simple Query Wizard

1. With the **OutdoorOptions.accdb** database open, click the Create tab and then click the Query Wizard button.
2. At the New Query dialog box, make sure *Simply Query Wizard* is selected and then click OK.
3. At the first Simple Query Wizard dialog box, click the down-pointing arrow at the right side of the *Tables/Queries* option box and then click *Table: Suppliers*.
4. Insert the following fields in the *Selected Fields* list box:
   - *SupplierName*
   - *StreetAddress*
   - *City*
   - *Province*
   - *PostalCode*
5. Click the Next button.
6. At the second Simple Query Wizard dialog box, select the current text in the *What title do you want for your query?* text box and then type SuppliersNotVancouver.
7. Click the *Modify the query design* option and then click the Finish button.
8. At the query window, complete the following steps:
   a. Click in the *Criteria* text box in the *City* column in the query design grid.
   b. Type Not Vancouver and then press Enter.
9. Specify that the fields are to be sorted in ascending order by postal code by completing the following steps:
   a. Click in the *Sort* text box in the *PostalCode* column. (You may need to scroll to see this column.)
   b. Click the down-pointing arrow that displays at the right side of the text box and then click *Ascending*.

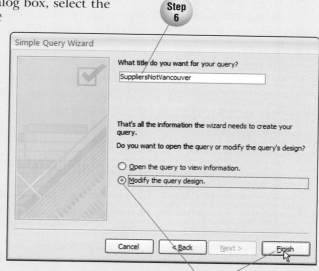

| Field: | [SupplierName] | [StreetAddress] | [City] | [Province] | [PostalCode] |
|---|---|---|---|---|---|
| Table: | Suppliers | Suppliers | Suppliers | Suppliers | Suppliers |
| Sort: | | | | | |
| Show: | ☑ | ☑ | ☑ | ☑ | Ascending |
| Criteria: | | | Not "Vancouver" | | Descending |
| or: | | | | | (not sorted) |

Step 8b

Step 9b

10. Click the Run button in the Results group. (This displays suppliers that are not located in Vancouver and displays the records sorted by PostalCode in ascending order.)
11. Save, print, and then close the query.
12. Close the **OutdoorOptions.accdb** database.
13. Open the **Deering.accdb** database.
14. Click the Create tab and then click the Query Wizard button.
15. At the New Query dialog box, make sure *Simply Query Wizard* is selected and then click OK.
16. At the first Simple Query Wizard dialog box, click the down-pointing arrow at the right of the *Tables/Queries* option box and then click *Table: Clients*. (You will need to scroll up the list to display this table.)
17. Insert the following fields in the *Selected Fields* list box:
    Client
    StreetAddress
    City
    State
    ZipCode
18. Click the Next button.

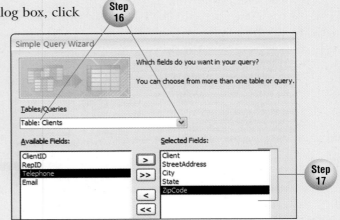

Step 16

Step 17

19. At the second Simple Query Wizard dialog box, select the current text in the *What title do you want for your query?* text box and then type IndianapolisClients.
20. Click the *Modify the query design* option and then click the Finish button.
21. At the query window, complete the following steps:
    a. Click in the *Criteria* text box in the *City* column.
    b. Type Indianapolis and then press Enter.
22. Click the Run button in the Results group. (This displays clients located in Indianapolis.)
23. Save, print, and then close the query.

## Creating a Calculated Field

In Chapter 3, you learned how to insert a total row in a datasheet and then choose from a list of functions. You can also calculate values using a calculated control that uses a mathematical equation to determine the contents that display in the control object. In a query, you can insert a calculated field that performs mathematical equations by inserting a calculated field in the *Fields* text box. To insert a calculated field, click in the desired *Field* text box, type the desired field name followed by a colon, and then type the equation. For example, to add 2008 sales amounts with 2009 sales, you would type Total:[Sales2008]+[Sales2009] in the *Field* text box.

Project **1h**    **Creating a Calculated Field in a Query**

1. With the **Deering.accdb** database open, click the Create tab and then click the Query Wizard button in the Other group.
2. With *Simple Query Wizard* selected in the New Query dialog box, click OK.

3. At the first Simple Query Wizard dialog box, click the down-pointing arrow at the right of the *Tables/Queries* option box, and then click *Table: Clients*. (You will need to scroll up the list to display this table.)

4. Insert the *Client* field in the *Selected Fields* list box.

5. Click the down-pointing arrow at the right of the *Tables/Queries* option box, click *Table: Sales*, and then insert the following fields in the *Selected Fields* list box:
   Sales2008
   Sales2009

6. Click the Next button.

7. At the second Simple Query Wizard dialog box, click the Next button.

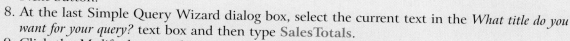

8. At the last Simple Query Wizard dialog box, select the current text in the *What title do you want for your query?* text box and then type **SalesTotals**.

9. Click the *Modify the query design* option and then click the Finish button.

10. At the query window, insert a calculated field that calculates the total sales for 2008 and 2009 for each client by completing the following steps:
    a. Click in the fourth *Field* text box.
    b. Type **Total:[Sales2008]+[Sales2009]** and then press Enter.

| Field: | Client | Sales2008 | Sales2009 | Total: [Sales2008]+[Sa |
|---|---|---|---|---|
| Table: | Clients | Sales | Sales | |
| Sort: | | | | |
| Show: | ☑ | ☑ | ☑ | ☑ |
| Criteria: | | | | |
| or: | | | | |

Step 10b

11. Click the Run button in the Results group. (All records will display with the total of the 2008 and 2009 sales.)

12. Save, print, and then close the query.

13. Close the **Deering.accdb** database.

14. Open the **OutdoorOptions.accdb** database.

15. Click the Create tab and then click the Query Wizard button in the Other group.

16. With the *Simple Query Wizard* option selected in the New Query dialog box, click OK.

17. At the first Simple Query Wizard dialog box, select *Table: Suppliers* in the *Tables/Queries* option box.

18. Insert the *SupplierName* field in the *Selected Fields* list box.

19. Click the down-pointing arrow at the right of the *Tables/Queries* option box, click *Table: Orders*, and then insert the following fields in the *Selected Fields* list box:
    Order#
    UnitsOrdered
    Amount

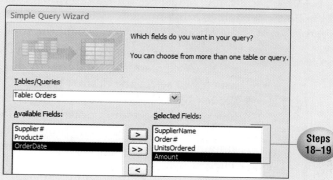

20. Click the Next button.

21. At the second Simple Query Wizard dialog box, click the Next button.
22. At the last Simple Query Wizard dialog box, select the current text in the *What title do you want for your query?* text box and then type **UnitPrices**.
23. Click the *Modify the query design* option and then click the Finish button.
24. At the query window, insert a calculated field that calculates the unit price by completing the following steps:
    a. Click in the fifth *Field* text box in the query design grid.
    b. Type **UnitPrice: [Amount]\*[UnitsOrdered]** and then press Enter.

| Field: | SupplierName | Order# | UnitsOrdered | Amount | UnitPrice: [Amount]*[U |
|---|---|---|---|---|---|
| Table: | Suppliers | Orders | Orders | Orders | |
| Sort: | | | | | |
| Show: | ☑ | ☑ | ☑ | ☑ | ☑ |
| Criteria: | | | | | |
| or: | | | | | |

Step 24b

25. Click the Run button in the Results group. (All records will display with the unit price calculated for each order.)
26. Save, print, and then close the query.
27. Close the **OutdoorOptions.accdb** database.

# Project 2 Create Aggregate Functions, Crosstab, Find Duplicates, and Find Unmatched Queries

You will create an aggregate functions query that determines the total, average, minimum, and maximum order amounts and determine total and average order amounts grouped by supplier. You will also use the Crosstab, Find Duplicates, and Find Unmatched query wizards to design queries.

## Designing Queries with Aggregate Functions

You can include an aggregate function such as Sum, Avg, Min, Max, or Count in a query to calculate statistics from numeric field values of all the records in the table. When an aggregate function is used, Access displays one row in the query results datasheet with the formula result for the function used. For example, in a table with a numeric field containing the annual salary amounts, you could use the Sum function to calculate the total of all salary amount values.

To display the aggregate function list, click the Totals button in the Show/Hide group. Access adds a Total row to the design grid with a drop-down list from which you select the desired function. Access also inserts the words *Group By* in the list box. Click the down-pointing arrow and then click the desired aggregate function from the drop-down list. In Project 2a, you will create a query in Design view and use aggregate functions to find the total of all sales, the average sales amount, the maximum and the minimum sales, and the total number of sales. The completed query will display as shown in Figure 4.5. Access automatically chooses the column heading names.

**Figure 4.5** Query Results for Project 2a

Access automatically determined the column heading names.

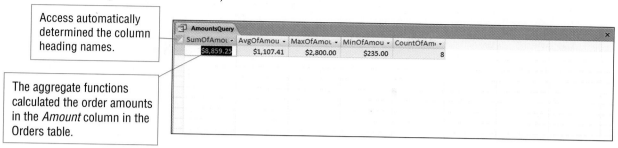

The aggregate functions calculated the order amounts in the *Amount* column in the Orders table.

## Project 2a  Using Aggregate Functions in a Query

1. Open the **OutdoorOptions.accdb** database.
2. Determine the total, average, minimum, and maximum order amounts as well as the total number of orders. To begin, click the Create tab and then click the Query Design button in the Other group.
3. At the Show Table dialog box, make sure *Orders* is selected in the list box, click the Add button, and then click the Close button.
4. Drag the *Amount* field to the first, second, third, fourth, and fifth *Field* text boxes.

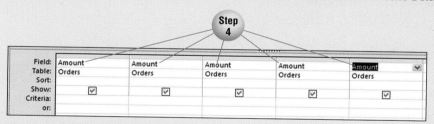

5. Click the Totals button in the Show/Hide group. (This adds a *Total* row to the design grid between *Table* and *Sort* with the default option of *Group By*.)
6. Specify a Sum function for the first *Group By* list box by completing the following steps:
   a. Click in the first *Group By* list box in the *Total* row.
   b. Click the down-pointing arrow that displays at the right side of the list box.
   c. Click *Sum* at the drop-down list.

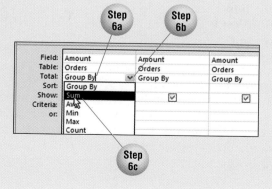

7. Complete steps similar to those in Step 6 to insert *Avg* in the second *Group By* list box in the *Total* row.
8. Complete steps similar to those in Step 6 to insert *Max* in the third *Group By* list box in the *Total* row.
9. Complete steps similar to those in Step 6 to insert *Min* in the fourth *Group By* list box in the *Total* row.
10. Complete steps similar to those in Step 6 to insert *Count* in the fifth *Group By* list box in the *Total* row.

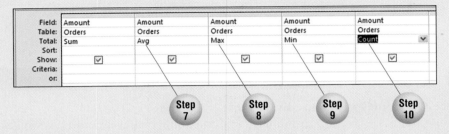

| Field: | Amount | Amount | Amount | Amount | Amount |
|---|---|---|---|---|---|
| Table: | Orders | Orders | Orders | Orders | Orders |
| Total: | Sum | Avg | Max | Min | Count |
| Sort: | | | | | |
| Show: | ☑ | ☑ | ☑ | ☑ | ☑ |
| Criteria: | | | | | |
| or: | | | | | |

Step 7  Step 8  Step 9  Step 10

11. Click the Run button in the Results group. (Notice the headings that Access chooses for the columns.)
12. Save the query and name it *AmountsQuery*.
13. Automatically adjust the widths of the columns.
14. Print and then close the query.

Using the *Group By* option in the Total drop-down list you can add a field to the query upon which you want Access to group records for statistical calculations. For example, to calculate the total of all orders for a specific supplier, add the *Supplier#* field to the design grid with the Total set to *Group By*. In Project 2b, you will create a query in Design view and use aggregate functions to find the total of all order amounts and the average order amounts grouped by the supplier number.

## Project ② Using Aggregate Functions and Grouping Records

1. With the **OutdoorOptions.accdb** database open, determine the total and average order amounts for each supplier. To begin, click the Create tab and then click the Query Design button.
2. At the Show Table dialog box, make sure *Orders* is selected in the list box and then click the Add button.
3. Click *Suppliers* in the list box, click the Add button, and then click the Close button.
4. Insert the *Amount* field from the Orders table list box to the first *Field* text box.
5. Insert the *Amount* field from the Orders table list box to the second *Field* text box.
6. Insert the *Supplier#* field from the Orders table list box to the third *Field* text box.
7. Insert the *SupplierName* field from the Suppliers table to the fourth *Field* text box.

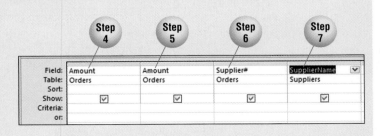

Step 4  Step 5  Step 6  Step 7

| Field: | Amount | Amount | Supplier# | SupplierName |
|---|---|---|---|---|
| Table: | Orders | Orders | Orders | Suppliers |
| Sort: | | | | |
| Show: | ☑ | ☑ | ☑ | ☑ |
| Criteria: | | | | |
| or: | | | | |

8. Click the Totals button in the Show/Hide group.
9. Click in the first *Group By* list box in the *Total* row, click the down-pointing arrow, and then click *Sum* at the drop-down list.
10. Click in the second *Group By* list box in the *Total* row, click the down-pointing arrow, and then click *Avg* at the drop-down list.
11. Make sure *Group By* displays in the third and fourth *Group By* list boxes.

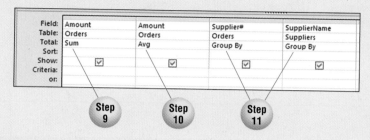

| Field: | Amount | Amount | Supplier# | SupplierName |
|---|---|---|---|---|
| Table: | Orders | Orders | Orders | Suppliers |
| Total: | Sum | Avg | Group By | Group By |
| Sort: | | | | |
| Show: | ☑ | ☑ | ☑ | ☑ |
| Criteria: | | | | |
| or: | | | | |

Step 9     Step 10     Step 11

12. Click the Run button in the Results group.
13. Save the query and name it *SupplierAmountsQuery*.
14. Print and then close the query.

# Creating a Crosstab Query

A crosstab query calculates aggregate functions such as Sum and Avg in which field values are grouped by two fields. A wizard is included that guides you through the steps to create the query. The first field selected causes one row to display in the query results datasheet for each group. The second field selected displays one column in the query results datasheet for each group. A third field is specified which is the numeric field to be summarized. The intersection of each row and column holds a value which is the result of the specified aggregate function for the designated row and column group.

Create a crosstab query from fields in one table. If you want to include fields from more than one table, you must first create a query containing the desired fields, and then create the crosstab query. For example, in Project 2c, you will create a new query that contains fields from each of the three tables in the OutdoorOptions.accdb database. Using this query, you will use the Crosstab Query Wizard to create a query that summarizes the order amounts by supplier name and by product ordered. Figure 4.6 displays the results of that crosstab query. The first column displays the supplier names, the second column displays the total of amounts for each supplier, and the remaining columns display the amounts by suppliers for specific items.

QUICK STEPS

Create a Crosstab Query
1. Click Create tab.
2. Click Query Wizard button.
3. Double-click *Crosstab Query Wizard*.
4. Complete wizard steps.

**Figure 4.6** Crosstab Query Results for Project 2c

In this query, the order amounts are grouped by supplier name and by individual product.

**OrdersBySupplierByProduct**

| SupplierName | Total Of Amc | Backpack | Ski goggles | Snowboard | Two-person | Wool ski hat |
|---|---|---|---|---|---|---|
| Freedom Corpc | $1,787.50 | | $1,100.00 | | | $687.50 |
| KL Distribution | $3,043.75 | $1,906.25 | | | $1,137.50 | |
| Rosewood, Inc | $2,800.00 | | | $2,800.00 | | |

## Project 2c  Creating a Crosstab Query

1. With the **OutdoorOptions.accdb** database open, create a query containing fields from the three tables by completing the following steps:
   a. Click the Create tab and then click the Query Design button.
   b. At the Show Table dialog box with *Orders* selected in the list box, click the Add button.
   c. Double-click *Products* in the Show Table dialog box.
   d. Double-click *Suppliers* in the list box and then click the Close button.
   e. Insert the following fields to the specified *Field* text boxes:
      1) From the Orders table, insert the *Product#* field to the first *Field* text box.
      2) From the Products table, insert the *Product* field to the second *Field* text box.
      3) From the Orders table, insert the *UnitsOrdered* field to the third *Field* text box.
      4) From the Orders table, insert the *Amount* field to the fourth *Field* text box.
      5) From the Suppliers table, insert the *SupplierName* field to the fifth *Field* text box.
      6) From the Orders table, insert the *OrderDate* field to the sixth *Field* text box.

Step 1e

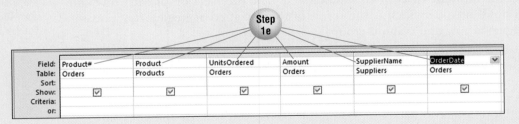

| Field: | Product# | Product | UnitsOrdered | Amount | SupplierName | OrderDate |
|---|---|---|---|---|---|---|
| Table: | Orders | Products | Orders | Orders | Suppliers | Orders |
| Sort: | | | | | | |
| Show: | ☑ | ☑ | ☑ | ☑ | ☑ | ☑ |
| Criteria: | | | | | | |
| or: | | | | | | |

   f. Click the Run button to run the query.
   g. Save the query and name it *ItemsOrdered*.
   h. Close the query.
2. Create a crosstab query that summarizes the orders by supplier name and by product ordered by completing the following steps:
   a. Click the Create tab and then click the Query Wizard button.
   b. At the New Query dialog box, double-click *Crosstab Query Wizard* in the list box.

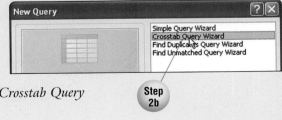

New Query

- Simple Query Wizard
- Crosstab Query Wizard
- Find Duplicates Query Wizard
- Find Unmatched Query Wizard

Step 2b

c. At the first Crosstab Query Wizard dialog box, click the *Queries* option in the *View* section and then click *Query: ItemsOrdered* in the list box.

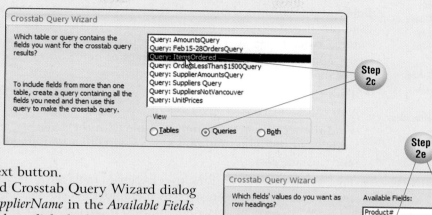

Step 2c

Step 2e

d. Click the Next button.
e. At the second Crosstab Query Wizard dialog box, click *SupplierName* in the *Available Fields* list box and then click the button containing the greater than (>) symbol. (This inserts *SupplierName* in the *Selected Fields* list box and specifies that you want *SupplierName* for the row headings.)
f. Click the Next button.
g. At the third Crosstab Query Wizard dialog box, click *Product* in the list box. (This specifies that you want *Product* for the column headings.)
h. Click the Next button.
i. At the fourth Crosstab Query Wizard dialog box, click *Amount* in the *Fields* list box and click *Sum* in the *Functions* list box.

Step 2g

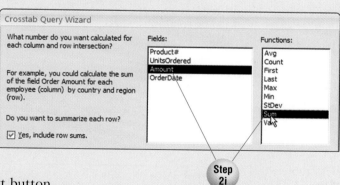

Step 2i

j. Click the Next button.
k. At the fifth Crosstab Query Wizard dialog box, select the current text in the *What do you want to name your query?* text box and then type OrdersBySupplierByProduct.
l. Click the Finish button.
3. Change the orientation to landscape and then print the query.
4. Close the OrdersBySupplierByProduct query.

Step 2k

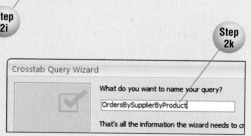

# Creating a Find Duplicates Query

Use the find duplicates query to search a specified table or query for duplicate field values within a designated field or fields. Create this type of query, for example, if you suspect a record, such as a product record has inadvertently been entered twice under two different product numbers. A find duplicates query has many applications. A few other examples of how you can use a find duplicates query include:

- Find the records in an Orders table with the same customer number so that you can identify your loyal customers.
- Find the records in a Customers table with the same last name and mailing address so that you send only one mailing to a household to save on printing and postage costs.
- Find the records in an EmployeeExpenses table with the same employee number so that you can see which employee is submitting the most claims.

Access provides the Find Duplicates Query Wizard that builds the select query based on the selections made in a series of dialog boxes. To use this wizard, open the desired table, click the Create tab, and then click the Query Wizard button. At the New Query dialog box, double-click *Find Duplicates Query Wizard* in the list box, and then complete the steps provided by the wizard.

In Project 2d, you will assume that you have been asked to update the address for a supplier in the OutdoorOptions.accdb database. Instead of updating the address, you create a new record. You will then use the Find Duplicates Query wizard to find duplicate field values in the Suppliers table.

## Project 2d  Creating a Find Duplicates Query

1. With the **OutdoorOptions.accdb** database open, double-click the *Suppliers: Table* option located in the *Suppliers* section of the Navigation pane.
2. Add the following record to the table:

   | | |
   |---|---|
   | *Supplier#* | 29 |
   | *SupplierName* | Langley Corporation |
   | *StreetAddress* | 805 First Avenue |
   | *City* | Burnaby |
   | *Province* | BC |
   | *PostalCode* | V5V 9K2 |
   | *Email* | lc@emcp.net |

3. Close the Suppliers table.
4. Use the Find Duplicates Query wizard to find any duplicate supplier names by completing the following steps:

   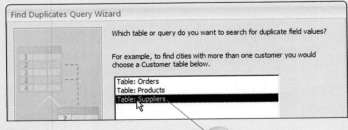

   Step 4c

   a. Click the Create tab and then click the Query Wizard button.
   b. At the New Query dialog box, double-click *Find Duplicates Query Wizard*.
   c. At the first wizard dialog box, click *Table: Suppliers* in the list box.
   d. Click the Next button.

e. At the second wizard dialog box, click *SupplierName* in the *Available fields* list box and then click the button containing the greater than (>) symbol. (This moves the *SupplierName* field to the *Duplicate-value fields* list box.)

f. Click the Next button.

g. At the third wizard dialog box, click the button containing the two greater than (>>) symbols. (This moves all the fields to the *Additional query fields* list box. You are doing this because if you find a duplicate supplier name, you want to view all the fields to determine which record is accurate.)

h. Click the Next button.

i. At the fourth (and last) wizard dialog box, type **DuplicateSuppliers** in the *What do you want to name your query?* text box.

j. Click the Finish button.

k. Change the orientation to landscape and then print the DuplicateSuppliers query.

5. As you look at the query results, you realize that an inaccurate record was entered for Langley so you decide to delete one of the records. To do this, complete the following steps:

a. With the DuplicateSuppliers query open, click in the record selector bar next to the first record (the one with a Supplier# of *29*). (This selects the entire row.)

b. Click the Home tab and then click the Delete button in the Records group.

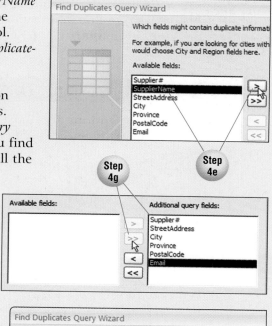

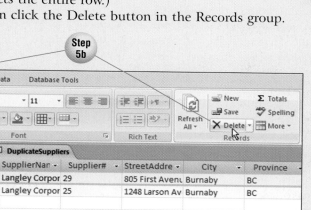

c. At the message asking you to confirm, click the Yes button.

d. Close the DuplicateSuppliers query.

6. Change the street address for Langley Corporation by completing the following steps:

a. Double-click the *Suppliers: Table* option located in the *Suppliers* section of the Navigation pane.

b. With the Suppliers table open in Datasheet view, change the address for Langley Corporation from *1248 Larson Avenue* to *805 First Avenue*. Leave the other fields as displayed.

c. Close the *Suppliers* table.

In Project 2d, you used the Find Duplicates Query Wizard to find records containing the same field. In Project 2e, you will use the Find Duplicates Query Wizard to find information on the suppliers you order from the most. You could use this information to negotiate for better prices or to ask for discounts.

## Project 2e    Finding Duplicate Orders

1. With the **OutdoorOptions.accdb** database open, create a query with the following fields (in the order shown) from the specified tables:

| | |
|---|---|
| *Order#* | Orders table |
| *Supplier#* | Orders table |
| *SupplierName* | Suppliers table |
| *Product#* | Orders table |
| *UnitsOrdered* | Orders table |
| *Amount* | Orders table |
| *OrderDate* | Orders table |

2. Run the query.
3. Save the query with the name *SupplierOrders* and then close the query.
4. Use the Find Duplicates Query Wizard to find the suppliers you order from the most by completing the following steps:

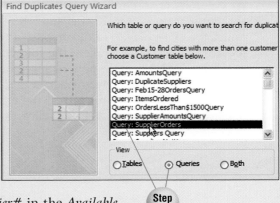

   a. Click the Create tab and then click the Query Wizard tab.
   b. At the New Query dialog box, double-click *Find Duplicates Query Wizard*.
   c. At the first wizard dialog box, click *Queries* in the *View* section, and then click *Query: SupplierOrders*. (You may need to scroll down the list to display this query.)

   **Step 4c**

   d. Click the Next button.
   e. At the second wizard dialog box, click *Supplier#* in the *Available fields* list box and then click the button containing the greater than (>) symbol.
   f. Click the Next button.
   g. At the third wizard dialog box, click the button containing the two greater than (>>) symbols. (This moves all the fields to the *Additional query fields* list box.)
   h. Click the Next button.
   i. At the fourth (and last) wizard dialog box, type **DuplicateSupplierOrders** in the *What do you want to name your query?* text box.
   j. Click the Finish button.
   k. Change the orientation to landscape and then print the DuplicateSupplierOrders query.

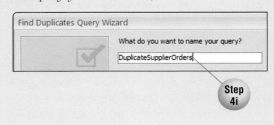

   **Step 4i**

5. Close the query.

# Creating an Unmatched Query

Create a find unmatched query to compare two tables and produce a list of the records in one table that have no matching record in the other related table. This type of query is useful to produce lists such as customers who have never placed an order or an invoice with no payment record. Access provides the Find Unmatched Query Wizard that builds the select query by guiding you through a series of dialog boxes.

In Project 2f, you will use the Find Unmatched Query Wizard to find all products that have no units on order. This information is helpful because it indicates which products are not selling and might need to be discontinued or returned. To use the Find Unmatched Query Wizard, click the Create tab and then click the Query Wizard button in the Other group. At the New Query dialog box, double-click *Find Unmatched Query Wizard* in the list box and then follow the wizard steps.

**QUICK STEPS**

**Create an Unmatched Query**
1. Click Create tab.
2. Click Query Wizard button.
3. Double-click *Find Unmatched Query Wizard*.
4. Complete wizard steps.

## Project 2f  Creating a Find Unmatched Query

1. With the **OutdoorOptions.accdb** database open, use the Find Unmatched Query Wizard to find all products that do not have any units on order by completing the following steps:
   a. Click the Create tab and then click the Query Wizard button.
   b. At the New Query dialog box, double-click *Find Unmatched Query Wizard*.
   c. At the first wizard dialog box, click *Table: Products* in the list box. (This is the table containing the fields you want to see in the query results.)
   d. Click the Next button.
   e. At the second wizard dialog box, make sure *Table: Orders* is selected in the list box. (This is the table containing the related records.)
   f. Click the Next button.
   g. At the third wizard dialog box, make sure *Product#* is selected in the *Fields in 'Products'* list box and in the *Fields in 'Orders'* list box.

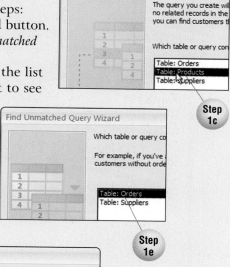

Step 1c

Step 1e

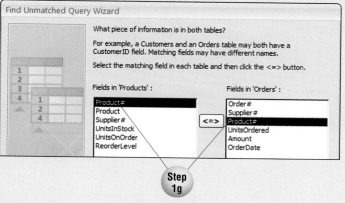

Step 1g

   h. Click the Next button.

i. At the fourth wizard dialog box, click the button containing the two greater than symbols (>>) to move all fields from the *Available fields* list box to the *Selected fields* list box.

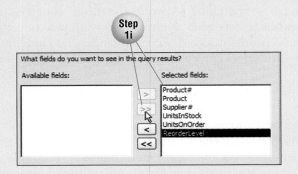

Step
1i

j. Click the Next button.
k. At the fifth wizard dialog box, click the Finish button. (Let the wizard determine the query name: *Products Without Matching Orders*.)
2. Print and then close the Products Without Matching Orders query.
3. Close the **OutdoorOptions.accdb** database.

# CHAPTER summary

- Being able to extract specific information is one of the most important functions of a database. Data can be extracted from an Access database by performing a query, which can be accomplished by designing a query or using a query wizard.

- Designing a query consists of identifying the table, the field or fields from which the data will be drawn, and the criteria for selecting the data.

- During the designing of a query, write the criterion (or criteria) for extracting the specific data. Access inserts any necessary symbols in the criterion when the Enter key is pressed.

- In a criterion, quotation marks surround field values and pound symbols (#) surround dates. Use the asterisk (*) as a wildcard symbol.

- You can perform a query on fields within one table or on fields from related tables.

- When designing a query, you can specify the sort order of a field or fields.

- You can modify an existing query. To do this, double-click the query in the Navigation pane, click the View button to display the query in Design view, make the desired changes, and then click the Run button.

- Enter criterion in the *Or* row in the query design grid to instruct Access to display records that match either of the two criteria.

- Multiple criteria entered in the *Criteria* row in the query design grid become an *And* statement where each criterion must be met for Access to select the record.

- The Simple Query Wizard guides you through the steps for preparing a query. You can modify a query you create with the wizard.

- You can insert a calculated field in a *Field* text box when designing a query.

- Include an aggregate function such as Sum, Avg, Min, Max, or Count to calculate statistics from numeric field values. Click the Totals button in the Show/Hide group to display the aggregate function list.

- Use the *Group By* option in the Total drop-down list to add a field to a query upon which you want Access to group records for statistical calculations.

- Create a crosstab query to calculate aggregate functions such as Sum and Avg in which fields are grouped by two fields. Create a crosstab query from fields in one table. If you want to include fields from more than one table, create a query first, and then create the crosstab query.

- Use the find duplicates query to search a specified table or query for duplicate field values within a designated field or fields.

- Create a find unmatched query to compare two tables and produce a list of the records in one table that have no matching record in the other related table.

# COMMANDS review

| FEATURE | RIBBON TAB, GROUP | BUTTON, OPTION |
|---------|-------------------|----------------|
| Query design window | Create, Other | |
| Run query | Query Tools Design, Results | |
| New Query dialog box | Create, Other | |
| Simple Query Wizard | Create, Other | , Simple Query Wizard |
| Add Total row to query design | Query Tools Design, Show/Hide | Σ |
| Crosstab Query Wizard | Create, Other | , Crosstab Query Wizard |
| Find Duplicates Query Wizard | Create, Other | , Find Duplicates Query Wizard |
| Find Unmatched Query Wizard | Create, Other | , Find Unmatched Query Wizard |

# CONCEPTS check

## Test Your Knowledge

**Completion:** For each description, indicate the correct term, symbol, or command.

1. The Query Design button is located in the Other group in this tab.

2. Click the Query Design button and the query window displays with this dialog box open.

3. To establish a criterion for the query, click in this text box in the column containing the desired field name and then type the criterion.

4. This is the term used for the results of the query.

5. This is the symbol Access automatically inserts around a date when writing a criterion for the query.

6. Use this symbol to indicate a wildcard character when writing a query criterion.

7. This is the criterion you would type to return field values greater than $500.

8. This is the criterion you would type to return field values that begin with the letter *L*.

   _____

9. This is the criterion you would type to return field values that are not in Oregon.

   _____

10. You can sort a field in a query in ascending order or this order.

    _____

11. Enter a criterion in this row in the query design grid to instruct Access to display records that match either of the two criteria.

    _____

12. This wizard guides you through the steps for preparing a query.

    _____

13. This type of query calculates aggregate functions in which field values are grouped by two fields.

    _____

14. Use this type of query to compare two tables and produce a list of the records in one table that have no matching record in the other related table.

    _____

# SKILLS check
## *Demonstrate Your Proficiency*

## Assessment

### 1  DESIGN QUERIES IN A LEGALSERVICES DATABASE

1. Display the Open dialog box with Access2007L1C4 on your storage medium the active folder.
2. Design a query that extracts records from the Billing table with the following specifications:
   a. Include the fields *Billing#*, *ClientID*, and *Category* in the query.
   b. Extract those records with the *SE* category.
   c. Save the query and name it *SECategoryBillingQuery*.
   d. Print and then close the query.
3. Design a query that extracts records from the Billing table with the following specifications:
   a. Include the fields *Billing#*, *ClientID*, and *Date*.
   b. Extract those records in the *Date* field with dates between 6/8/2010 and 6/10/2010.
   c. Save the query and name it *June8-10BillingQuery*.
   d. Print and then close the query.

4. Design a query that extracts records from the Clients table with the following specifications:
   a. Include the fields *FirstName*, *LastName*, and *City*.
   b. Extract those records with any city other than Kent in the *City* field.
   c. Save the query and name it *ClientsNotInKentQuery*.
   d. Print and then close the query.

5. Design a query that extracts information from two tables with the following specifications:
   a. Include the fields *Billing#*, *ClientID*, *Date*, and *Rate#* from the Billing table.
   b. Include the field *Rate* from the Rates table.
   c. Extract those records with a rate number greater than 2.
   d. Save the query and name it *RateGreaterThan2Query*.
   e. Print and then close the query.

6. Design a query that extracts information from three tables with the following specifications:
   a. Include the field *Attorney* from the Attorneys table.
   b. Include the fields *FirstName* and *LastName* from the Clients table.
   c. Include the fields *AttorneyID*, *Date,* and *Hours* from the Billing table.
   d. Extract those records with an *AttorneyID* of 12.
   e. Save the query and name it *Attorney12Query*.
   f. Print and then close the query.

7. Design a query that extracts records from four tables with the following specifications:
   a. Add the Attorneys, Billing, Rates, and Clients tables to the query window.
   b. Insert the *Attorney* field from the Attorneys table to the first *Field* text box.
   c. Insert the *AttorneyID* field from the Billing table to the second *Field* text box.
   d. Insert the *Rate#* field from the Billing table to the third *Field* text box.
   e. Insert the *Rate* field from the Rates table to the fourth *Field* text box.
   f. Insert the *FirstName* field from the Clients table to the fifth *Field* text box.
   g. Insert the *LastName* field from the Clients table to the sixth *Field* text box.
   h. Extract those records with an *AttorneyID* of 17 and a *Rate#* of 4.
   i. Run the query.
   j. Save the query and name it *Attorney17Rate4*.
   k. Print and then close the query.

# Assessment

## 2 USE THE SIMPLE QUERY WIZARD AND DESIGN QUERIES

1. With **LegalServices.accdb** database open, use the Simple Query Wizard to extract specific information from three tables with the following specifications:
   a. At the first Simple Query Wizard dialog box, include the following fields:
      From Attorneys table: *AttorneyID* and *Attorney*
      From Categories table: *CategoryName*
      From Billing table: *Hours*
   b. At the second Simple Query Wizard dialog box, click Next.
   c. At the third Simple Query Wizard dialog box, click the *Modify the query design* option, and then click the Finish button.
   d. At the query window, insert *14* in the *Criteria* text box in the *AttorneyID* column.
   e. Run the query.

f. Save the query with the default name.

g. Print and then close the query.

2. Create a query in Design view with the Billing table with the following specifications:

  a. Insert the *Hours* field from the Billing table to the first, second, third, and fourth *Field* text boxes.

  b. Click the Totals button in the Show/Hide group.

  c. Insert *Sum* in the first *Group By* list box in the *Total* row.

  d. Insert *Min* in the second *Group By* list box in the *Total* row.

  e. Insert *Max* in the third *Group By* list box in the *Total* row.

  f. Insert *Count* in the fourth *Group By* list box in the *Total* row.

  g. Run the query.

  h. Save the query and name it *HoursAmountQuery*.

  i. Automatically adjust the widths of the columns.

  j. Print and then close the query.

3. Create a query in Design view with the following specifications:

  a. Add the Attorneys table and the Billing table to the query window.

  b. Insert the *Attorney* field from the Attorneys table to the first *Field* text box.

  c. Insert the *AttorneyID* field from the Billing table to the second *Field* text box.

  d. Insert the *Hours* field from the Billing table to the third *Field* text box.

  e. Click the Totals button in the Show/Hide group.

  f. Insert *Sum* in the third *Group By* list box in the *Hours* column (in the *Total* row).

  g. Run the query.

  h. Save the query and name it *AttorneyHours*.

  i. Print and then close the query.

4. Create a query in Design view with the following specifications:

  a. Add the Attorneys, Clients, Categories, and Billing tables to the query window.

  b. Insert the *Attorney* field from the Attorneys table to the first *Field* text box.

  c. Insert the *ClientID* field from the Clients table to the second *Field* text box.

  d. Insert the *CategoryName* field from the Categories table to the third *Field* text box.

  e. Insert the *Hours* field from the Billing table to the fourth *Field* text box.

  f. Run the query.

  g. Save the query and name it *AttorneyClientHours*.

  h. Print and then close the query.

## Assessment

## 3   CREATE A CROSSTAB QUERY AND USE THE FIND DUPLICATES AND FIND UNMATCHED QUERY WIZARDS

1. With the **LegalServices.accdb** database open, create a crosstab query that summarizes the hours by attorney by category with the following specifications:

  a. At the first Crosstab Query Wizard dialog box, click the *Queries* option in the *View* section, and then click *Query: AttorneyClientHours* in the list box.

  b. At the second Crosstab Query Wizard dialog box, click *Attorney* in the *Available Fields* list box and then click the button containing the greater than (>) symbol.

  c. At the third Crosstab Query Wizard dialog box, click *CategoryName* in the list box.

  d. At the fourth Crosstab Query Wizard dialog box, click *Hours* in the *Fields* list box and click *Sum* in the *Functions* list box.

e. At the fifth Crosstab Query Wizard dialog box, type **HoursByAttorneyByCategory** in the *What do you want to name your query?* text box.

f. Print the query in landscape orientation and then close the query.

2. Use the Find Duplicates Query Wizard to find those clients with the same last name with the following specifications:

a. At the first wizard dialog box, click *Table: Clients* in the list box.

b. At the second wizard dialog box, click *LastName* in the *Available fields* list box and then click the button containing the greater than (>) symbol.

c. At the third wizard dialog box, click the button containing the two greater than (>>) symbols.

d. At the fourth wizard dialog box, name the query *DuplicateLastNames*.

e. Print the query in landscape orientation and then close the query.

3. Use the Find Unmatched Query Wizard to find all clients who do not have any billing hours with the following specifications:

a. At the first wizard dialog box, click *Table: Clients* in the list box.

b. At the second wizard dialog box, click *Table: Billing* in the list box.

c. At the third wizard dialog box, make sure *ClientID* is selected in the *Fields in 'Products'* list box and in the *Fields in 'Orders'* list box.

d. At the fourth wizard dialog box, click the button containing the two greater than symbols (>>) to move all fields from the *Available fields* list box to the *Selected fields* list box.

e. At the fifth wizard dialog box, click the Finish button. (Let the wizard determine the query name: *Clients Without Matching Billing*.)

4. Print the query in landscape orientation and then close the Clients Without Matching Billing query.

5. Close the **LegalServices.accdb** database.

## Assessment

## 4 DESIGN AND HIDE FIELDS IN A QUERY

1. You can use the check boxes in the query design grid *Show* row to show or hide fields in the query. Experiment with these check boxes and then open the **LegalServices.accdb** database and design the following query:

a. At the Show Table dialog box, add the Billing table, the Clients table, and the Rates table.

b. At the query window, insert the following fields to *Field* text boxes:

Clients table:
  *FirstName*
  *LastName*
Billing table:
  *Hours*
Rates table:
  *Rate*

c. Insert in the fifth *Field* text box the calculated field *Total:*[Hours]*[Rate].

d. Hide the *Hours* and the *Rate* fields.

e. Run the query.

f. Save the query and name it *ClientBillingQuery*.

g. Print and then close the query.

2. Close the **LegalServices.accdb** database.

# CASE study

## *Apply Your Skills*

**Part 1**

You work for the Skyline Restaurant in Fort Myers, Florida. Your supervisor is reviewing the restaurant operations and has asked for a number of query reports. Before running queries, you realize that the tables in the restaurant database, **Skyline.accdb**, are not related. Open the **Skyline.accdb** database and then create the following relationships:

| **Field Name** | **"One" Table** | **"Many" Table** |
| --- | --- | --- |
| EmployeeID | Employees | Banquets |
| Item# | Inventory | Orders |
| SupplierID | Suppliers | Orders |
| EventID | Events | Banquets |

Save and then print the relationships.

**Part 2**

As part of the review of the restaurant records, your supervisor has asked you for the following information. Create a separate query for each bulleted item listed below and save, name, and print the queries (you determine the name).

- Suppliers in Fort Myers (include supplier identification number, supplier name, and telephone number)
- Suppliers that are not located in Fort Myers (include supplier identification number, supplier name, and telephone number)
- Employees hired in 2007 (include employee identification number, first and last names, and hire date)
- Wedding receptions booked in the banquet room (include the reservation identification number; reservation date; and last name, first name, and telephone number of the person making the reservation)
- Banquet reservations booked between 6/15/2010 and 6/30/2010 (include reservation identification number; reservation date; and last name, first name, and telephone number of the person making the reservation)
- Banquet reservations that have not been confirmed (include reservation identification number and first name, last name, and telephone number)
- Names of employees that are signed up for health insurance (include employee first and last names)
- Items ordered from supplier number 4 (include the item number, item, supplier name, and supplier telephone number)
- Banquet room reserved by someone whose last name begins with "Wie" (include the first and last names of the employee who booked the reservation and the first and last names and telephone number of the person making the reservation)
- A query that inserts a calculated field that calculates the total of the number of units ordered by the unit price (information located in the Orders table) for all orders for supplier number 2

**Part 3**

Design at least three additional queries that require fields from at least two tables. Run the queries and then save and print the queries. In Microsoft Word, write the query information and include specific information about each query and format the document to enhance the visual appeal. Save the document and name it **Access_C4_CS_P3**. Print and then close **Access_C4_CS_P3.docx**.

# Creating Tables and Queries

# ASSESSING proficiency

In this unit, you have learned to design, create, and modify tables and to create one-to-many relationships and one-to-one relationships between tables. You also learned how to perform queries on data in tables.

*Note: The Student Resources CD does not include an Access Level 1, Unit 1 subfolder of files because no data files are required for the Unit 1 assessments. You will create all of the files yourself. Before beginning the assessments, create a folder called Access2007L1U1 for the new files.*

## Assessment 1 Create Tables in a Cornerstone Catering Database

1. Use Access to create tables for Cornerstone Catering. Name the database **Cornerstone**. Create a table named *Employees* that includes the following fields (you determine the field name, data type, field size, and description):

    *Employee#* (primary key)
    *FirstName*
    *LastName*
    *CellPhone* (Consider using the Input Mask Wizard for this field.)

2. After creating the table, switch to Datasheet view and then enter the following data in the appropriate fields:

    *Employee#:* 10
    *FirstName:* Erin
    *LastName:* Jergens
    *CellPhone:* (505) 555-3193

    *Employee#:* 14
    *FirstName:* Mikio
    *LastName:* Ogami
    *CellPhone:* (505) 555-1087

    *Employee#:* 19
    *FirstName:* Martin
    *LastName:* Vaughn
    *CellPhone:* (505) 555-4461

    *Employee#:* 21
    *FirstName:* Isabelle
    *LastName:* Baptista
    *CellPhone:* (505) 555-4425

    *Employee#:* 24
    *FirstName:* Shawn
    *LastName:* Kettering
    *CellPhone:* (505) 555-3885

    *Employee#:* 26
    *FirstName:* Madison
    *LastName:* Harris
    *CellPhone:* (505) 555-2256

3. Automatically adjust the column widths.
4. Save, print, and then close the Employees table.

5. Create a table named *Plans* that includes the following fields:
    *PlanCode* (primary key)
    *Plan*
6. After creating the table, switch to Datasheet view and then enter the following data in the appropriate fields:

*PlanCode:* A             *PlanCode:* B
*Plan:* Sandwich Buffet      *Plan:* Cold Luncheon Buffet

*PlanCode:* C             PlanCode: D
*Plan:* Hot Luncheon Buffet    *Plan:* Combination Dinner

7. Automatically adjust the column widths.
8. Save, print, and then close the Plans table.
9. Create a table named *Prices* that includes the following fields:
    *PriceCode* (primary key)
    *PricePerPerson* (identify this data type as Currency)
10. After creating the table, switch to Datasheet view and then enter the following data in the appropriate fields:

*PriceCode:* 1                 *PriceCode:* 2
*PricePerPerson:* $11.50     *PricePerPerson:* $12.75

*PriceCode:* 3                 *PriceCode:* 4
*PricePerPerson:* $14.50     *PricePerPerson:* $16.00

*PriceCode:* 5
*PricePerPerson:* $18.50

11. Automatically adjust the column widths.
12. Save, print, and then close the Prices table.
13. Create a table named *Clients* that includes the following fields:
    *Client#* (primary key)
    *ClientName*
    *StreetAddress*
    *City*
    *State*
    *ZipCode*
    *Telephone* (Consider using the Input Mask Wizard for this field.)
14. After creating the table, switch to Datasheet view and then enter the following data in the appropriate fields:

*Client#:* 104                      *Client#:* 155
*ClientName:* Sarco Corporation     *ClientName:* Creative Concepts
*StreetAddress:* 340 Cordova Road   *StreetAddress:* 1026 Market Street
*City:* Santa Fe                   *City:* Los Alamos
*State:* NM                      *State:* NM
*ZipCode:* 87510                *ZipCode:* 87547
*Telephone:* (505) 555-3880     *Telephone:* (505) 555-1200

Client#: 218
ClientName: Allenmore Systems
StreetAddress: 7866 Second Street
City: Espanola
State: NM
ZipCode: 87535
Telephone: (505) 555-3455

Client#: 286
ClientName: Sol Enterprises
StreetAddress: 120 Cerrillos Road
City: Santa Fe
State: NM
ZipCode: 87560
Telephone: (505) 555-7700

15. Automatically adjust the column widths and change the orientation to landscape.
16. Save, print, and then close the Clients table.
17. Create a table named *Events* that includes the following fields:
    Event# (primary key; identify this data type as AutoNumber)
    Client#
    Employee#
    DateOfEvent (identify this data type as Date/Time)
    PlanCode
    PriceCode
    NumberOfPeople (identify this data type as Number)
18. After creating the table, switch to Datasheet view and then enter the following data in the appropriate fields:

Event#: (AutoNumber)
Client#: 218
Employee#: 14
DateOfEvent: 7/1/2010
PlanCode: B
PriceCode: 3
NumberOfPeople: 250

Event#: (AutoNumber)
Client#: 104
Employee#: 19
DateOfEvent: 7/2/2010
PlanCode: D
PriceCode: 5
NumberOfPeople: 120

Event#: (AutoNumber)
Client#: 155
Employee#: 24
DateOfEvent: 7/8/2010
PlanCode: A
PriceCode: 1
NumberOfPeople: 300

Event#: (AutoNumber)
Client#: 286
Employee#: 10
DateOfEvent: 7/9/2010
PlanCode: C
PriceCode: 4
NumberOfPeople: 75

Event#: (AutoNumber)
Client#: 218
Employee#: 14
DateOfEvent: 7/10/2010
PlanCode: C
PriceCode: 4
NumberOfPeople: 50

Event#: (AutoNumber)
Client#: 104
Employee#: 10
DateOfEvent: 7/12/2010
PlanCode: B
PriceCode: 3
NumberOfPeople: 30

19. Automatically adjust the column widths and change the orientation to landscape.
20. Save, print, and then close the Events table.

## Assessment 2 Create Relationships between Tables

1. With the **Cornerstone.accdb** database open, create the following one-to-many relationships:
   a. *Client#* in the Clients table is the "one" and *Client#* in the Events table is the "many."
   b. *Employee#* in the Employees table is the "one" and *Employee#* in the Events table is the "many."
   c. *PlanCode* in the Plans table is the "one" and *PlanCode* in the Events table is the "many."
   d. *PriceCode* in the Prices table is the "one" and *PriceCode* in the Events table is the "many."
2. Save and then print the relationships.

## Assessment 3 Modify Tables

1. With the **Cornerstone.accdb** database open, open the Plans table in Datasheet view and then add the following record at the end of the table:
   *PlanCode:* E
   *Plan:* Hawaiian Luau Buffet
2. Save, print, and then close the Plans table.
3. Open the Events table in Datasheet view and then add the following record at the end of the table:
   *Event#:* (AutoNumber)
   *Client#:* 104
   *Employee#:* 21
   *Date:* 7/16/2010
   *PlanCode:* E
   *PriceCode:* 5
   *NumberOfPeople:* 125
4. Save, print (in landscape orientation), and then close the Events table.

## Assessment 4 Design Queries

1. With the **Cornerstone.accdb** database open, create a query to extract records from the Events table with the following specifications:
   a. Include the fields *Client#*, *DateOfEvent*, and *PlanCode*.
   b. Extract those records with a PlanCode of C.
   c. Save the query and name it *PlanCodeC*.
   d. Print and then close the query.
2. Extract records from the Clients table with the following specifications:
   a. Include the fields *ClientName*, *City*, and *Telephone*.
   b. Extract those records with a city of Santa Fe.
   c. Save the query and name it *SantaFeClients*.
   d. Print and then close the query.
3. Extract information from two tables with the following specifications:
   a. From the Clients table, include the fields *ClientName* and *Telephone*.
   b. From the Events table, include the fields *DateOfEvent*, *PlanCode*, and *NumberOfPeople*.
   c. Extract those records with a date between July 10 and July 25, 2010.
   d. Save the query and name it *July10-25Events*.
   e. Print and then close the query.

## Assessment 5 Design a Query with a Calculated Field Entry

1. With the **Cornerstone.accdb** database open, create a query in Design view with the Events table and the Prices table and insert the following fields to the specified locations:
   a. Insert *Event#* from the Events table to the first *Field* text box.
   b. Insert *DateOfEvent* from the Events table to the second *Field* text box.
   c. Insert *NumberOfPeople* from the Events table to the third *Field* text box.
   d. Insert *PricePerPerson* from the Prices table to the fourth *Field* text box.
2. Insert the following calculated field entry in the fifth *Field* text box: *Amount: [NumberOfPeople]\*[PricePerPerson]*.
3. Run the query.
4. Save the query and name it *EventAmounts*.
5. Print and then close the query.

## Assessment 6 Design a Query with Aggregate Functions

1. With the **Cornerstone.accdb** database open, create a query in Design view using the EventAmounts query with the following specifications:
   a. At the Cornerstone : Database window, click the Create tab and then click the Query Design button.
   b. At the Show Tables dialog box, click the Queries tab.
   c. Double-click *EventAmounts* in the list box and then click the Close button.
   d. Insert the *Amount* field to the first, second, third, and fourth *Field* text boxes.
   e. Click the Totals button in the Show/Hide group.
   f. Insert *Sum* in the first *Group By* list box in the *Total* row.
   g. Insert *Avg* in the second *Group By* list box in the *Total* row.
   h. Insert *Min* in the third *Group By* list box in the *Total* row.
   i. Insert *Max* in the fourth *Group By* list box in the *Total* row.
2. Run the query.
3. Automatically adjust the column widths.
4. Save the query and name it *AmountTotals*.
5. Print and then close the query.

## Assessment 7 Design a Query Using Fields from Tables and a Query

1. With the **Cornerstone.accdb** database open, create a query in Design view using the Employees table, the Clients table, the Events table, and the EventAmounts query with the following specifications:
   a. At the Cornerstone : Database window, click the Create tab and then click the Query Design tab.
   b. At the Show Tables dialog box, double-click *Employees*.
   c. Double-click *Clients*.
   d. Double-click *Events*.
   e. Click the Queries tab, double-click *EventAmounts* in the list box, and then click the Close button.
   f. Insert the *LastName* field from the Employees table to the first *Field* text box.
   g. Insert the *ClientName* field from the Clients table to the second *Field* text box.
   h. Insert the *Amount* field from the EventAmounts query to the third *Field* text box.

i. Insert the *DateOfEvent* field from the Events table to the fourth *Field* text box.
2. Run the query.
3. Save the query and name it *EmployeeEvents*.
4. Close the query.
5. Using the Crosstab Query Wizard, create a query that summarizes the total amount of events by employee by client using the following specifications:
   a. At the first Crosstab Query Wizard dialog box, click the *Queries* option in the *View* section, and then click *Query: EmployeeEvents* in the list box.
   b. At the second Crosstab Query Wizard dialog box, click *Last Name* in the *Available Fields* list box and then click the button containing the greater than (>) symbol.
   c. At the third Crosstab Query Wizard dialog box, make sure *ClientName* is selected in the list box.
   d. At the fourth Crosstab Query Wizard dialog box, make sure *Amount* is selected in the *Fields* list box, and then click *Sum* in the *Functions* list box.
   e. At the fifth Crosstab Query Wizard dialog box, type **AmountsByEmployeeByClient** in the *What do you want to name your query?* text box.
6. Automatically adjust the column widths and change the orientation to landscape.
7. Print and then close the AmountsByEmployeeByClient query.

### Assessment 8 Use the Find Duplicates Query Wizard

1. With the **Cornerstone.accdb** database open, use the Find Duplicates Query Wizard to find employees who are responsible for at least two events with the following specifications:
   a. At the first wizard dialog box, double-click *Table: Events* in the list box.
   b. At the second wizard dialog box, click *Employee#* in the *Available fields* list box and then click the button containing the greater than (>) symbol.
   c. At the third wizard dialog box, move the *DateOfEvent* field and the *NumberOfPeople* field from the *Available fields* list box to the *Additional query fields* list box.
   d. At the fourth wizard dialog box, name the query *DuplicateEvents*.
2. Print and then close the DuplicateEvents query.

### Assessment 9 Use the Find Unmatched Query Wizard

1. With the **Cornerstone.accdb** database open, use the Find Unmatched Query Wizard to find any employees who do not have an upcoming event scheduled with the following specifications:
   a. At the first wizard dialog box, click *Table: Employees* in the list box.
   b. At the second wizard dialog box, click *Table: Events* in the list box.
   c. At the third wizard dialog box, make sure *Employee#* is selected in the *Fields in 'Employees'* list box and in the *Fields in 'Events'* list box.
   d. At the fourth wizard dialog box, click the button containing the two greater than symbols (>>) to move all fields from the *Available fields* list box to the *Selected fields* list box.
   e. At the fifth wizard dialog box, click the Finish button. (Let the wizard determine the query name: *Employees Without Matching Events*.)
2. Print and then close the *Employees Without Matching Events* query.

# WRITING activities

The following activity gives you the opportunity to practice your writing skills along with demonstrating an understanding of some of the important Access features you have mastered in this unit. Use correct grammar, appropriate word choices, and clear sentence constructions.

## Create a Payroll Table and Word Report

The manager of Cornerstone Catering has asked you to add information to the **Cornerstone.accdb** database on employee payroll. You need to create another table that will contain information on payroll. The manager wants the table to include the following (you determine the appropriate field name, data type, field size, and description):

Employee Number: 10
Status: Full-time
Monthly Salary: $2,850

Employee Number: 14
Status: Part-time
Monthly Salary: $1,500

Employee Number: 19
Status: Part-time
Monthly Salary: $1,400

Employee Number: 21
Status: Full-time
Monthly Salary: $2,500

Employee Number: 24
Status: Part-time
Monthly Salary: $1,250

Employee Number: 26
Status: Part-time
Monthly Salary: $1,000

Print and then close the payroll table. Open Word and then write a report to the manager detailing how you created the table. Include a title for the report, steps on how the table was created, and any other pertinent information. Save the completed report and name it **Access_U01_Act01**. Print and then close **Access_U01_Act01.docx**.

# INTERNET research

## Vehicle Search

In this activity you will search the Internet for information on different vehicles before doing actual test drives. Learning about a major product, such as a vehicle, can increase your chances of finding a good buy, can potentially guide you away from a poor purchase, and can help speed up the process of narrowing the search to the type of vehicle that will meet your needs. Before you begin, list the top five criteria you would look for in a vehicle. For example, it must be a four-door vehicle, needs to be four-wheel drive, etc.

Using key search words, find at least two Web sites that list vehicle reviews. Use the search engines provided within the different review sites to find vehicles that fulfill the criteria you listed to meet your particular needs. Create a database in Access and create a table in that database that will contain the results from your vehicle search. Design the table keeping in mind what type of data you need to record for each vehicle that meets your requirements. Include at least the make, model, year, price, description, and special problems in the table. Also, include the ability to rate the vehicle as poor, fair, good, or excellent. You will decide on the rating of each vehicle depending on your findings.

## Level 1

# Microsoft® access

## Unit 2:    Creating Forms and Reports

➤ Creating Forms

➤ Creating Reports and Mailing Labels

➤ Modifying, Filtering, and Viewing Data

➤ Importing and Exporting Data

Access

# Benchmark Microsoft® Access 2007 Level 1

## Microsoft Certified Application Specialist Skills—Unit 2

| Reference No. | Skill | Pages |
|---|---|---|
| **2** | **Creating and Formatting Database Elements** | |
| 2.5 | Create forms | |
| 2.5.3 | Create multiple item forms | 168-169 |
| 2.5.4 | Create split forms | 166-167 |
| 2.5.6 | Create PivotTable forms | 229-231 |
| 2.5.7 | Create forms using Layout view | 154-166 |
| 2.5.8 | Create simple forms | 147-152 |
| 2.6 | Create reports | |
| 2.6.1 | Create reports as a simple report | 183-185 |
| 2.6.2 | Create reports using the Report Wizard | 198-203 |
| 2.6.6 | Set the print layout | 185-186 |
| 2.6.7 | Create labels using the Label Wizard | 203-206 |
| 2.7 | Modify the design of reports and forms | |
| 2.7.7 | Apply AutoFormats to forms and reports | 164-166, 194, 196-198 |
| **3** | **Entering and Modifying Data** | |
| 3.2 | Navigate among records | 149-150 |
| 3.5 | Import data | |
| 3.5.1 | Import data from a specific source | 260-261 |
| 3.5.2 | Link to external data sources | 262-263 |

*Note:* The Level 1 and Level 2 texts each address approximately half of the Microsoft Certified Application Specialist skills. Complete coverage of the skills is offered in the combined Level 1 and Level 2 text titled *Benchmark Series Microsoft® Access 2007: Levels 1 and 2,* which has been approved as certified courseware and which displays the Microsoft Certified Application Specialist logo on the cover.

# Creating Forms

**CHAPTER**
**5**

## PERFORMANCE OBJECTIVES

**Upon successful completion of Chapter 5, you will be able to:**

- Create a form using the Form button
- Change views in a form
- Print and navigate in a form
- Add records to and delete records from a form
- Customize a form with options at the Form Layout Tools Format tab
- Create a form using the Simple Form button
- Create a form using the Multiple Items button
- Create a form using the Form Wizard

**Tutorial 5.1**
Creating Forms
**Tutorial 5.2**
Customizing Forms and Using
the Form Wizard

In this chapter, you will learn to create forms from database tables, improving the data display and making data entry easier. Access offers several methods for presenting data on the screen for easier data entry. You will create a form using the Form, Split Form, and Multiple Items buttons as well as the Form Wizard. You will also learn how to customize control objects in a form.

*Note: Before beginning computer projects, copy to your storage medium the Access2007L1C5 subfolder from the Access2007L1 folder on the CD that accompanies this textbook and make Access2007L1C5 the active folder.*

## Project 1 Create Forms with the Form Button

You will use the Form button to create forms with fields in the Clients, Representatives, and Sales tables. You will also add, delete, and print records and use buttons in the Form Layout Tools Format tab to apply formatting to control objects in the forms.

**QUICK STEPS**

**Create a Form with Form Button**
1. Click desired table.
2. Click Create tab.
3. Click Form button.

# Creating a Form

Access offers a variety of options for presenting data in a more easily read and attractive format. When entering data in a table in Datasheet view, multiple records display at the same time. If a record contains several fields, you may not be able to view all fields within a record at the same time. If you create a form, generally all fields for a record are visible on the screen. Several methods are available for creating a form. In this section, you will learn how to create a form using the Form, Split Form, and Multiple Items buttons as well as the Form Wizard.

**HINT**

A form allows you to focus on a single record at a time.

**HINT**

Save a form before making changes or applying formatting to the form.

Form

## Creating a Form with the Form Button

You can view, add, or edit data in a table in Datasheet view. You can also perform these functions on data inserted in a form. A form is an object you can use to enter and edit data in a table or query and is a user-friendly interface for viewing, adding, editing, and deleting records. A form is also useful in helping prevent incorrect data from being entered and it can be used to control access to specific data.

You can use a variety of methods to create a form. The simplest method to create a form is to click the Create tab and then click the Form button in the Forms groups. Figure 5.1 displays the form you will create in Project 1a with the Clients table in the Deering.accdb database. Access creates the form using all fields in the table in a vertical layout and displays the form in Layout view with the Form Layout Tools Format tab active.

**Figure 5.1** Form Created from Data in the Clients Table

Form Layout Tools Format tab

Clients form created with the Clients table

Record navigation bar

## Changing Views

When you click the Form button to create a form, the form displays in Layout view. This is one of three views you can use when working with forms. Use the Form view to enter and manage records. Use the Layout view to view the data as well as modify the appearance and contents of the form and use the Design view to view the structure of the form and modify the form. Change views with the View button in the Views group in the Form Layout Tools Format tab or with buttons in the view area located at the right side of the Status bar.

## Printing a Form

Print all records in the form by clicking the Quick Print button on the Quick Access toolbar or by displaying the Print dialog box with *All* selected in the *Print Range* section and then clicking OK. If you want to print a specific record, display the desired record and then display the Print dialog box. At the Print dialog box, click the *Selected Record(s)* option and then click OK. You can also print a range of records by clicking the *Pages* option in the *Print Range* section of the Print dialog box and then entering the beginning record number in the *From* text box and the ending record number in the *To* text box.

**Print Specific Record**
1. Display form.
2. Click Office button, Print.
3. Click *Selected Record(s)*.
4. Click OK.

## Navigating in a Form

When a form displays in either Form view or Layout view, navigation buttons display along the bottom of the form in the Record navigation bar as identified in Figure 5.1. Using these navigation buttons, you can display the first record in the form, the previous record, the next record, the last record, and a new record.

Along with the Record navigation bar, you can display records in a form using the keyboard. Press the Page Down key to move forward a single record or press the Page Up key to move back a single record. Press Ctrl + Home to display the first record or Press Ctrl + End to display the last record.

First record    Previous record

Next record    Last record

---

## Project 1a   Creating a Form with the Clients Table

1. Display the Open dialog box with Access2007L1C5 on your storage medium the active folder.
2. Open the **Deering.accdb** database.
3. Create a form with the Clients table by completing the following steps:
   a. Click the Clients table in the Navigation pane.
   b. Click the Create tab.
   c. Click the Form button in the Forms group.

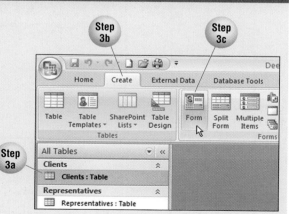

4. Switch to the Form view by clicking the View button in the Views group in the Form Layout Tools Format tab.

Step 4

5. Navigate in the form by completing the following steps:
   a. Click the Next record button in the Record navigation bar to display the next record.
   b. Click the Last record button in the Record navigation bar to display the last record.
   c. Click the First record button in the Record navigation bar to display the first record.

Step 5a

6. Save the form by completing the following steps:
   a. Click the Save button on the Quick Access toolbar.
   b. At the Save As dialog box, with *Clients* inserted in the *Form Name* text box, click OK.

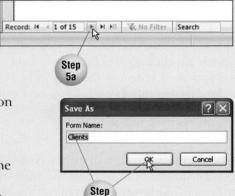

Step 6b

7. Change orientation and print the current record in the form by completing the following steps:
   a. Display Print Preview, change the orientation to landscape, and then close Print Preview.
   b. Click the Office button and then click *Print* at the drop-down menu.
   c. At the Print dialog box, click the *Select Record(s)* option in the *Print Range* section and then click OK.

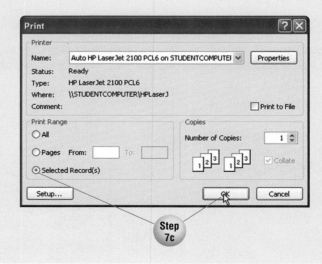

Step 7c

## Adding and Deleting Records

Add a new record to the form by clicking the New (blank) record button (contains a right arrow followed by a yellow asterisk) that displays in the Record navigation bar along the bottom of the form. You can also add a new record to a form by clicking the Home tab and then clicking the New button in the Records group. To delete a record, display the record, click the Home tab, click the Delete button arrow in the Records group, and then click *Delete Record* at the drop-down list. At the message telling you that the record will be deleted permanently, click Yes.

## Sorting Records

You can sort data in a form by clicking in the field containing data on which you want to sort and then clicking the Ascending button or Descending button in the Sort & Filter group in the Home tab. Click the Ascending button to sort text in alphabetic order from A to Z or numbers from lowest to highest or click the Descending button to sort text in alphabetic order from Z to A or numbers from highest to lowest.

## Project 1b    Adding and Deleting Records in a Form

1. With the Clients form open and the first record displayed, add a new record by completing the following steps:
   a. Click the New (blank) record button located in the Record navigation bar.
   b. At the new blank record, type the following information in the specified fields (move to the next field by pressing Tab or Enter; move to the previous field by pressing Shift + Tab):

   | | | |
   |---|---|---|
   | *ClientID* | = | 116 |
   | *RepID* | = | 14 |
   | *Client* | = | Gen-Erin Productions |
   | *StreetAddress* | = | 1099 15th Street |
   | *City* | = | Muncie |
   | *State* | = | IN |
   | *ZipCode* | = | 473067963 |
   | *Telephone* | = | 7655553120 |
   | *Email* | = | gep@emcp.net |

2. Print the current record in the form by completing the following steps:
   a. Click the Office button and then click *Print* at the drop-down menu.
   b. At the Print dialog box, click the *Select Record(s)* option in the *Print Range* section and then click OK.

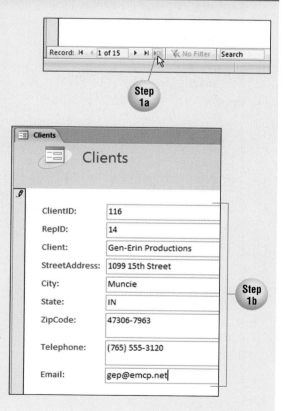

3. Delete the second record (ClientID 102) by completing the following steps:
   a. Click the First record button in the Record navigation bar.
   b. Click the Next record button in the Record navigation bar.
   c. With Record 2 active, click the Home tab.
   d. Click the Delete button arrow and then click *Delete Record* at the drop-down list.

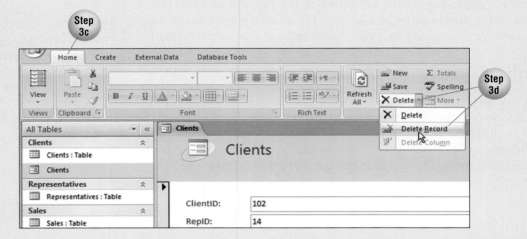

   e. At the message telling you that you will not be able to undo the delete operation, click Yes.
4. Click the New (blank) record button in the Record navigation bar and then type the following information in the specified fields.

   | | | |
   |---|---|---|
   | *ClientID* | = | 102 |
   | *RepID* | = | 11 |
   | *Client* | = | Sunrise Corporation |
   | *StreetAddress* | = | 14432 Center Avenue |
   | *City* | = | Indianapolis |
   | *State* | = | IN |
   | *ZipCode* | = | 462381744 |
   | *Telephone* | = | 3175555640 |
   | *Email* | = | sc@emcp.net |

5. Sort the records in the form by completing the following steps:
   a. Click in the field containing the data *Sunrise Corporation* and then click the Ascending button in the Sort & Filter group in the Home tab.
   b. Click in the field containing the data *Indianapolis* and then click the Descending button in the Sort & Filter group.
   c. Click in the field containing the data *47306-4839* and then click the Ascending button in the Sort & Filter group.
   d. Click in the field containing the data *114* and then click the Ascending button in the Sort & Filter group.
6. Click the Save button on the Quick Access toolbar.
7. Close the Clients form by clicking the Close button located in the upper right corner of the forms window.

# Creating a Form with a Related Table

When you created the form with the Clients table, only the Clients table fields displayed in the form. If you create a form with a table that has a one-to-many relationship established, Access adds a datasheet to the form that is based on the related table. For example, in Project 1c, you will create a one-to-many relationship between the Clients table and the Representatives table and then create a form with the Representatives table. Since it is related to the Clients table by a one-to-many relationship, Access inserts a datasheet at the bottom of the form containing all of the records in the Clients table. Figure 5.2 displays the form you will create in Project 1c. Notice the datasheet that displays at the bottom of the form.

If you have created only a single one-to-many relationship, the datasheet for the related table displays in the form. If you have created more than one relationship in a table, Access will not display any datasheets when you create a form with the table.

**Figure 5.2** Representatives Form with Clients Datasheet

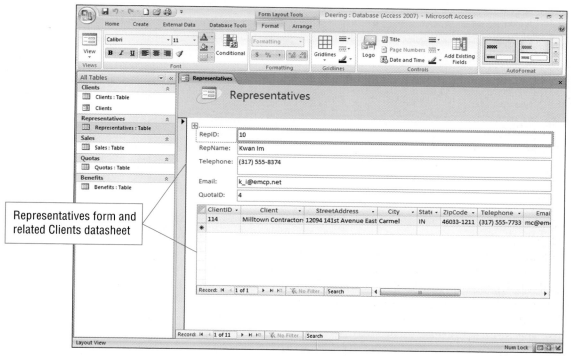

Representatives form and related Clients datasheet

## Project 1c  Creating a Form with a Related Table

1. With the **Deering.accdb** database open, create a one-to-many relationship where the *RepID* field in the Representatives table is the "one" and the *RepID* field in the Clients table is the "many." Save and then close the relationships window.
2. Create a form with the Representatives table by completing the following steps:
   a. Click the Representatives table in the Navigation pane.
   b. Click the Create tab.
   c. Click the Form button in the Forms group.

3. Insert a new record in the Clients table for representative 12 (Catherine Singleton) by completing the following steps:
   a. Click twice on the Next record button in the Record navigation bar at the bottom of the form window (not the Record navigation bar in the Clients datasheet) to display the record for Catherine Singleton.
   b. Click in the cell immediately below *113* in the *ClientID* field in the Clients datasheet.
   c. Type the following information in the specified fields:

   | | | |
   |---|---|---|
   | *ClientID* | = | 117 |
   | *Client* | = | Dan-Built Construction |
   | *StreetAddress* | = | 903 James Street |
   | *City* | = | Carmel |
   | *State* | = | IN |
   | *ZipCode* | = | 46033-9050 |
   | *Telephone* | = | (317) 555-1122 |
   | *Email* | = | dc@emcp.net |

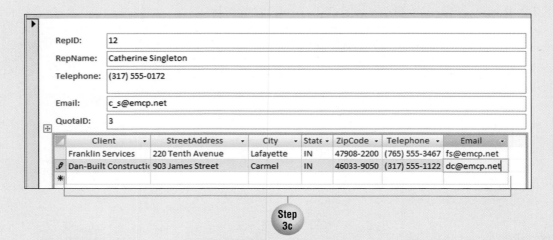

Step
3c

4. Click the Save button on the Quick Access toolbar and at the Save As dialog box with *Representatives* in the *Form Name* text box, click OK.
5. Print the current record in the form by completing the following steps:
   a. Click the Office button and then click *Print* at the drop-down menu.
   b. At the Print dialog box, click the *Select Record(s)* option in the *Print Range* section and then click OK.
6. Close the Representatives form.

# Customizing a Form

A form is comprised of a series of control objects, which are objects that display titles or descriptions, accept data, or perform actions. You can customize control objects with buttons in the Form Layout Tools Format tab. This tab is active when you display a form in Layout view and contains buttons for changing the font, alignment, and formatting of text; applying gridlines; and inserting controls such as a logo, title, and the date and time.

To customize an individual control object, click the object to select it. A selected control object displays with an orange border. To apply formatting to multiple objects, hold down the Shift key while clicking each object. To select all objects in a column, click the first object, position the mouse pointer at the top of the selected object until the pointer turns into a black, down-pointing arrow, and then click the left mouse button.

## Changing the Font

With buttons in the Font group, you can change the font, font style, font size, and font color. You can also change the alignment of text in a field and apply fill to fields. The Font group also contains a Format Painter button to copy formatting and apply it to other data.

### Project 1d  Applying Font Formatting to a Form

1. With the **Deering.accdb** database open, open the Clients form by completing the following steps:
   a. Click the Navigation pane Menu bar.
   b. Click *Object Type* at the drop-down list. (This option displays the objects grouped by type—Tables, Queries, Forms, and Reports. The **Deering.accdb** database only contains tables and forms, so you will see only those two types in the Navigation pane.)
   c. Double-click *Clients* in the *Forms* section of the Navigation pane.
2. Click the Layout View button located at the right side of the Status bar. (The form must display in Layout view to display the Form Layout Tools Format tab.)
3. Change the font and alignment formatting of form elements by completing the following steps:
   a. Click the *ClientID* control object.
   b. Hold down the Shift key.
   c. Click each of the field names through *Email*.
   d. With the nine control objects selected, click the Font button arrow in the Font group and then click *Candara* at the drop-down list.
   e. Click the Bold button and then click the Italic button in the Font group.
   f. Click the Align Text Right button in the Font group.
   g. Click the Font Color button arrow and then click *Maroon 5* at the drop-down color palette. (See image at the right.)
4. Change the font and width of control objects by completing the following steps:
   a. Click the control object containing the text *101*.
   b. Position the mouse pointer at the top of the selected object until the mouse pointer displays as a black, down-pointing arrow and then click the left mouse button.

c. With the nine control objects selected, position the mouse pointer on the right edge of any of the selected control objects until the pointer changes to a left- and right-pointing arrow, drag the right border left to the approximate width shown in the image below, and then release the mouse button.

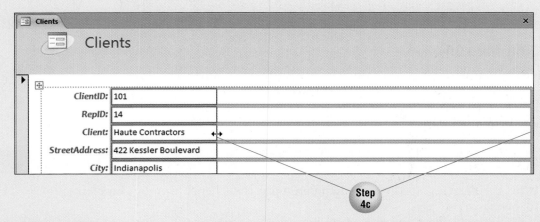

Step 4c

d. Click the Font Color button arrow and then click *Dark Blue* at the drop-down color palette (second color from the *right* in the bottom row of the *Standard Colors* section).

e. Click the Fill/Back Color button arrow and then click *Maroon 1* at the drop-down color palette.

f. Click outside the selected control objects to deselect them.

5. Click the Save button on the Quick Access toolbar.

6. Click the Next record button in the Record navigation bar to display the next record. Continue navigating through the records to view the records with the font formatting applied.

7. Click the First record button in the Record navigation bar.

## Applying Conditional Formatting

Conditional

Click the Conditional button in the Font group in the Form Layout Tools Format tab and the Conditional Formatting dialog box displays as shown in Figure 5.3. In the *Default Formatting* section, specify the type of formatting you want applied to the control object if the condition (or conditions) is not met. A preview box displays in the *Default Formatting* section showing you how the control object will display if the condition is not met. Use options in the *Condition 1* section of the dialog box to specify a criterion and choose the formatting you want applied to data in a control object that meet the criterion. For example, in Project 1e you will specify that you want any *Indianapolis* entries in the *City* field to display in red.

Click the down-pointing arrow at the right side of the second option box in a condition section and a drop-down list displays with the options *between*, *not between*, *equal to*, *not equal to*, *greater than*, *less than*, *greater than or equal to*, and *less than or equal to*. Use these options when creating conditional formatting.

**Figure 5.3** Conditional Formatting Dialog Box

Use options in this dialog box to apply conditions to text in a form.

**Conditional Formatting** ? ✕

Default Formatting
This format will be used if no conditions are met:    AaBbCcYyZz    **B** *I* <u>U</u> | ◇ ▾ | **A** ▾ | ▣

Condition 1
Field Value Is ▾    between    ▾    [            ] and [            ]
Preview of format to use when condition is true:    No Format Set    **B** *I* <u>U</u> | ◇ ▾ | **A** ▾ | ▣

Add >>    Delete...    OK    Cancel

Click the Add button to insert up to two additional conditions.

## Project 1e  Applying Conditional Formatting

1. With the **Deering.accdb** database open, the Clients form open, and the first record displayed, click the control object containing the word *Indianapolis*.
2. Click the Conditional button in the Font group in the Form Layout Tools Format tab.
3. At the Conditional Formatting dialog box, click the down-pointing arrow in the second list box in the *Condition 1* section (the list box containing the word *between*) and then click *equal to* at the drop-down list.
4. Click in the text box immediately right of the option box containing *equal to* and then type Indianapolis.
5. Click the Fill/Back Color button in the *Condition 1* section (this inserts light maroon fill in the preview cell).
6. Click the Font/Fore Color button arrow in the *Condition 1* section and then click the red color at the drop-down color palette (second color from the left in the bottom row).
7. Click OK to close the dialog box.
8. Navigate through the records and notice that *Indianapolis* in the *City* field displays in red while the other cities display in the dark blue color your chose in the previous project.
9. Save the Clients form.
10. Click the First record button in the Record navigation bar and then print the record.
11. Close the Clients form.

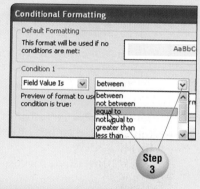

Step 3

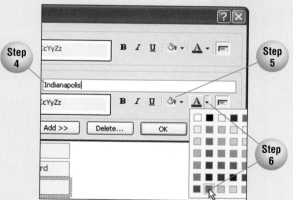

Step 4

Step 5

Step 6

## Adding Additional Conditions

In Project 1e you created one condition for the *City* field—if the field is equal to *Indianapolis* then the font color changes to red. At the Conditional Formatting dialog box, you can create up to three conditions. Click the Add button in the dialog box to insert additional conditions. For example, in Project 1f you will create two conditions specifying that if an amount is greater than $99,999 then the font color changes to green and if an amount is less than $100,000 then the font color changes to red.

## Formatting Numbers and Applying Gridlines

Use options in the Formatting group of the Form Layout Tools Format tab to apply Currency, Percentage, or Comma formatting to numbers and choose a number style from the Format option drop-down list. With options in the Gridlines group, you can apply gridlines to control objects and then change the width, style, and color of the lines. To apply gridlines, you must select at least one control object to make active the buttons in the Gridline group. By default, Access applies formatting to all control objects in the form.

## Project 1f  Formatting Numbers and Applying Gridlines and Conditional Formatting

1. With the **Deering.accdb** database open, create a form with the Sales table by completing the following steps:
   a. Click the Sales table in the Navigation pane.
   b. Click the Create tab.
   c. Click the Form button in the Forms group.
2. Decrease the number of decimals in the *Sales2008* and *Sales2009* fields by completing the following steps:
   a. Make sure the form displays in Layout view.
   b. Click in the control object containing the number $289,563.00.
   c. Click twice on the Decrease Decimals button in the Formatting group in the Form Layout Tools Format tab.
   d. Click in the control object containing the number $327,541.00.
   e. Click twice on the Decrease Decimals button in the Formatting group in the Form Layout Tools Form tab.
3. Change the width of form control objects by completing the following steps:
   a. Click the control object containing the text *101*.
   b. Hold down the Shift key and then click each of the two remaining control objects containing money amounts.

c. With the three control objects selected, position the mouse pointer on the right edge of any of the selected control objects until the pointer changes to a left- and right-pointing arrow, drag the right border left to the approximate width shown in the image below, and then release the mouse button.

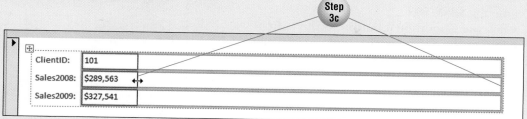

d. Click the Font Color button arrow and then click *Dark Blue* at the drop-down color palette (second color from the *right* in the bottom row of the *Standard Colors* section).

e. Click the Fill/Back Color button arrow and then click *Maroon 1* at the drop-down color palette.

f. Click outside the selected control objects to deselect them.

4. Format the three field name control objects by completing the following steps:

a. Select the *ClientID*, *Sales2008*, and *Sales2009* control objects.

b. Click the Font Color button arrow and then click *Maroon 5* at the drop-down color palette.

c. Click the Bold button and the Italic button in the Font group.

d. Click the Align Text Right button in the Font group.

e. Click outside the selected control objects to deselect them.

5. Apply and format gridlines by completing the following steps:

a. Click the *ClientID* control object.

b. Click the Gridlines button in the Gridlines group and then click *Horizontal* at the drop-down list.

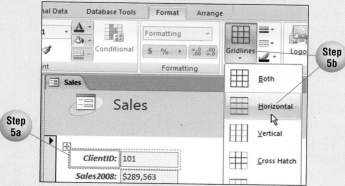

c. Click the Width button in the Gridlines group and then click the *Hairline* option (top option in the drop-down list).

d. Click the Style button in the Gridlines group and then click the *Dashes* option (third option from the top of the drop-down list).

e. Click the Color button arrow in the Gridlines group and then click *Dark Blue* at the drop-down color gallery.

f. After looking at the gridlines, you decide to change them by clicking the Gridlines button and then clicking *Cross Hatch* at the drop-down list.

6. Scroll through the records and notice the formatting you applied to the control objects.

7. Click the Save button on the Quick Access toolbar and at the Save As dialog box with *Sales* in the *Form Name* text box, click OK.

8. Apply conditional formatting by completing the following steps:
   a. Click the First record button in the Record navigation bar.
   b. Click the control object containing the amount *$289,563*.
   c. Click the Conditional button in the Font group in the Form Layout Tools Format tab.
   d. At the Conditional Formatting dialog box, click the down-pointing arrow in the second list box in the *Condition 1* section (the list box containing the word *between*) and then click *greater than* at the drop-down list.
   e. Click in the text box immediately right of the option box containing *greater than* and then type 99999.
   f. Click the Bold button
   g. Click the Fill/Back Color button in the *Condition 1* section (this inserts light maroon fill in the preview cell).
   h. Click the Font/Fore Color button arrow in the *Condition 1* section and then click the green color at the drop-down color palette (sixth color from the left in the bottom row).
   i. Click the Add button. (This inserts a *Condition 2* section toward the bottom of the dialog box.)
   j. Click the down-pointing arrow in the second list box in the *Condition 2* section and then click *less than* at the drop-down list.
   k. Click in the text box immediately right of the option box containing *less than* and then type 100000.
   l. Click the Bold button.
   m. Click the Fill/Back Color button in the *Condition 2* section (this inserts light maroon fill in the preview cell).
   n. Click the Font/Fore Color button arrow in the *Condition 2* section and then click the red color at the drop-down color palette (second color from the left in the bottom row).
   o. Click OK to close the dialog box.
9. Complete steps similar to those in Step 8 to apply the same conditional formatting to the field containing the *Sales2009* amount *$327,541*.
10. Scroll through the records and notice the conditional formatting applied to amounts in the *Sales2008* and *Sales2009* fields.
11. Click the First record button and then print the current record.
12. Save and then close the *Sales* form.

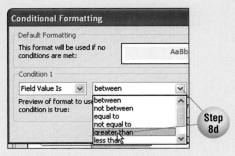

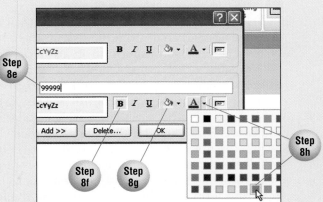

## Formatting Controls

With options in the Controls group in the Form Layout Tools Format tab, you can insert a logo, form title, page numbers, and date and time. You can also apply lines to control objects and then change the line thickness, type, and color.

Click the Add Existing Fields button in the Controls group and the Field List window opens and displays at the right side of the screen. This window displays the fields available in the current view, fields available in related tables, and fields available in other tables. Figure 5.4 presents the Field List window you display in Project 1g. You can add fields to the form by double-clicking a field or by dragging the field from the Field List window into the form.

**Figure 5.4** Field List Window

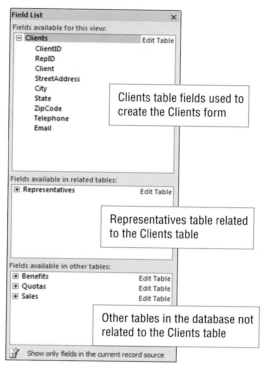

In the *Fields available for this view* section, Access displays all fields in any tables used to create the form. So far, you have been creating a form with all fields in one table. In the *Fields available in related tables*, Access displays tables that are related to the table(s) used to create the form. To display the fields in the related table, click the plus symbol that displays before the table name in the Field List window and the list expands to display all field names. To add a field to the form, double-click the desired field in the Field List window. This inserts the field below the existing fields in the form.

You can also drag a field from the Field List window into the form. To do this, position the mouse pointer on the desired field in the Field List window, hold down the left mouse button, drag into the form window, and then release the mouse button. A horizontal gold bar displays as you drag the field in the existing fields in the form. When the gold bar is positioned in the desired location, release the mouse button. You can insert multiple fields in a form from the Field List window. To do this, hold down the Ctrl key while clicking the desired fields and then drag the fields into the form.

If you try to drag a field from a table in the *Fields available in other tables* section, the Specify Relationship dialog box will display. To move a field from the Field List window to the form, the field must be located in a table that is related to the table(s) used to create the form.

## Changing Field Order

When you drag a field from the Field List window into the form window, a horizontal gold bar displays as you drag in the existing fields in the form. Position the gold bar at the location where you want the field inserted and then release the mouse button. You can also change the order of existing fields by clicking the field control object and then dragging the field to the desired position.

## Sizing a Control Object

You can change the size of a selected control object. To do this, select the object and then position the mouse pointer on the object border until the mouse pointer displays as a double-headed arrow pointing in the desired direction. Drag in or out to decrease or increase the size of the object.

## Moving a Control Object in the Form Header

A form contains a form header that is the top portion of the form containing the logo container control object and the form title. You can move control objects in a form header to different locations within the header. To move a control object in a header, click the object to select it and then drag it with the mouse to the desired position.

## Project 1g    Formatting Controls in a Form

1. With the **Deering.accdb** database open, right-click the Clients form in the Navigation pane and then click *Layout View* at the shortcut menu. (Make sure you right-click the Clients form and not the Clients table.)
2. Insert a logo image by completing the following steps:
   a. Click the logo container control object that displays in the upper left corner of the form (in the form header).
   b. Click the Logo button in the Controls group in the Form Layout Tools Format tab.

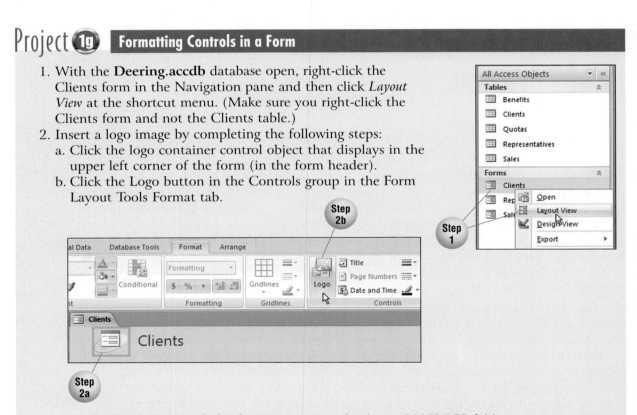

c. At the Insert Picture dialog box, navigate to the Access2007L1C5 folder on your storage medium and then double-click *Mountain.jpg*.

3. Increase the size of the logo control object by completing the following steps:
   a. With the logo control object selected, position the mouse pointer on the bottom right corner of the object until the mouse pointer displays as a diagonally-pointing two-headed arrow.
   b. Drag down and to the right until the logo control object is approximately the size shown at the right and then release the mouse button.

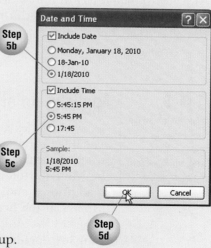

Step
3b

4. Change the form title and format the title by completing the following steps:
   a. Click the Title button in the Controls group.
   b. With *Clients* selected, type **Deering Industries Clients**.

Step
4a

   c. Click the Font Color button arrow in the Font group and then click the *Maroon 5* color at the drop-down color palette.

Step
4b

   d. Click the Bold button in the Font group.
   e. Click the Line Thickness button in the Controls group and then click the *2 pt* option (third option from the top).
   f. Click the Line Type button in the Controls group and then click the *Dashes* option (third option from the top).

Step
4h

   g. Click the Line Color button arrow and then click *Dark Blue* at the color palette.
   h. Drag the title control object so it is centered vertically in the form header.

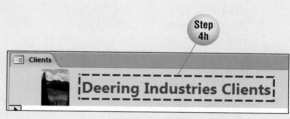

5. Insert and format the date and time by completing the following steps:
   a. Click the Date and Time button in the Controls group.
   b. At the Date and Time dialog box, click the bottom option in the *Include Date* section.
   c. Click the middle option in the *Include Time* section.
   d. Click OK to close the dialog box.
   e. Click the date control object, hold down the Shift key, and then click the time control object.
   f. Click the Font color button in the Font group. (This applies the *Maroon 5* color you choose in Step 4c.)
   g. Click the Bold button in the Font group.
   h. Click outside the control objects to deselect them.

Step
5b

Step
5c

Step
5d

6. Insert an additional field into the Clients form from the Representatives table by completing the following steps:
   a. Click the Add Existing Fields button in the Controls group.

b. Click the plus symbol that displays immediately left of the Representatives table name located in the *Fields available in related tables* section of the Field List window. (If this section does not display, click the <u>Show all tables</u> hyperlink that displays at the bottom of the Field List window.)

c. Position the mouse pointer on the *RepName* field, hold down the left mouse button, drag into the form until the gold horizontal bar displays immediately below the *RepID* field in the form, and then release the mouse button. (This inserts the field with a down-pointing arrow at the right side. Access inserts the field as a Lookup field.)

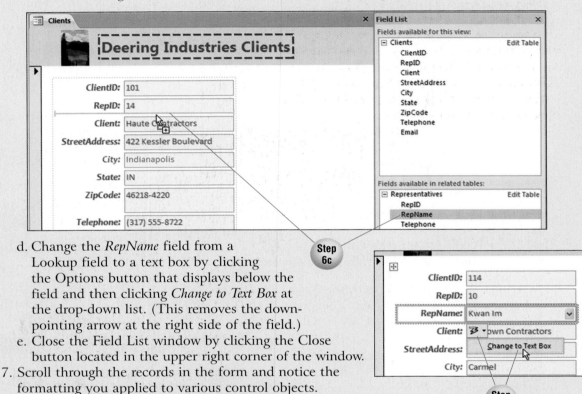

d. Change the *RepName* field from a Lookup field to a text box by clicking the Options button that displays below the field and then clicking *Change to Text Box* at the drop-down list. (This removes the down-pointing arrow at the right side of the field.)

e. Close the Field List window by clicking the Close button located in the upper right corner of the window.

7. Scroll through the records in the form and notice the formatting you applied to various control objects.

8. Click the First record button in the Record navigation bar.

9. Save the form and then print the current record.

10. Close the Clients form.

## Applying AutoFormats

**HINT**

Autoformats have the same names as themes in Word, Excel, and PowerPoint and apply similar formatting.

Access includes autoformats you can apply to a form. These autoformats are available in the AutoFormat group of the Form Layout Tools Format tab. Generally, two autoformats display—the Access 2003 and the Access 2007 autoformats. Click the More button at the right side of the autoformats to display a drop-down list of additional choices. Hover the mouse pointer over an autoformat and the name displays in the ScreenTip. The names of the autoformats align with the theme names in Word, Excel, and PowerPoint. To maintain a consistent appearance in company documents, you can apply the same autoformat to a form that matches the theme you apply to a Word document, Excel spreadsheet, or PowerPoint presentation.

1. With the **Deering.accdb** database open, *right-click* the Representatives form and then click *Layout View* at the shortcut menu. (Make sure you right-click the Representatives form and not the Representatives table.)
2. Apply an autoformat by clicking the More button located at the right side of the AutoFormat group and then clicking the *Urban* autoformat at the drop-down list.
3. After looking at the formatting, you decide that you want to change the autoformat. To do this, click the More button at the right side of the AutoFormat group and then click *Equity* at the drop-down list.

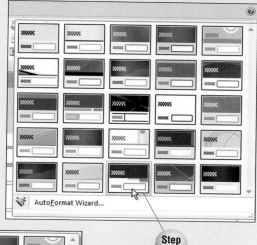

Step 2

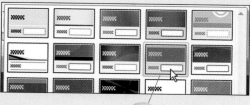

Step 3

4. Apply conditional formatting to the numbers in the *QuotaID* field by completing the following steps:
   a. Click the First record button in the Record navigation bar.
   b. Click the *QuotaID* control object containing the number *4*.
   c. Click the Conditional button in the Font group in the Form Layout Tools Format tab.
   d. At the Conditional Formatting dialog box, click the down-pointing arrow in the second list box in the *Condition 1* section (the list box containing the word *between*) and then click *equal to* at the drop-down list.
   e. Click in the text box immediately right of the option box containing *equal to* and then type *2*.
   f. Click the Font/Fore Color button arrow in the *Condition 1* section and then click the purple color at the drop-down color palette (last color in the bottom row).

Step 4d

Step 4e

Step 4f

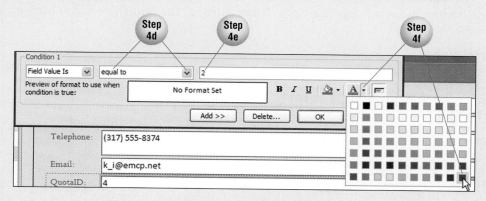

   g. Click the Add button. (This inserts a *Condition 2* section toward the bottom of the dialog box.)

h. Click the down-pointing arrow in the second list box in the *Condition 2* section and then click *equal to* at the drop-down list.

i. Click in the text box immediately right of the option box containing *equal to* and then type 3.

j. Click the Font/Fore Color button arrow in the *Condition 2* section and then click the green color at the drop-down color palette (sixth color from the left in the bottom row).

k. Click the Add button. (This inserts a *Condition 3* section toward the bottom of the dialog box.)

l. Click the down-pointing arrow in the second list box in the *Condition 3* section and then click *equal to* at the drop-down list.

m. Click in the text box immediately right of the option box containing *equal to* and then type 4.

n. Click the Font/Fore Color button arrow in the *Condition 3* section and then click the red color at the drop-down color palette (second color from the left in the bottom row).

o. Click OK to close the dialog box.

5. Scroll through the records and notice the coloring of the quote ID number.

6. Save the Representatives form.

7. Click the First record button in the Record navigation bar and then print the record.

8. Close the Representatives form.

9. Open the Clients form by right-clicking the Clients form name in the Navigation pane and then clicking *Layout View* at the shortcut menu.

10. Apply the Equity format by clicking the More button located at the right side of the AutoFormat group and then clicking *Equity* option at the drop-down list. (Position the date and time on the orange background.)

11. Make the first record active and then print the current record.

12. Save and then close the Clients form.

13. Open the Sales form in Layout view, apply the Equity autoformat, and then save the form.

14. Print the first record in the form and then close the form.

15. Close the **Deering.accdb** database.

## Project 2 Create Forms with the Split Form and Multiple Items Buttons and the Form Wizard

You will create a form with the Split Form button, the Multiple Form button, and the Form Wizard.

**QUICK STEPS**

**Create a Split Form**
1. Click desired table.
2. Click Create tab.
3. Click Split Form button.

Split Form

## Creating a Split Form

You can create a form with the Split Form button in the Forms group in the Create tab. When you use this button to create a form, Access splits the screen in the work area and provides two views for the form. The top half of the work area displays the form in Layout view and the bottom half of the work area displays the form in Datasheet view. The two views are connected and are synchronous, which means that displaying or modifying a specific field in the Form view portion will cause the same action to occur in the field in the Datasheet view portion. Figure 5.5 displays the split form you will create for Project 2a.

**Figure 5.5** Split Form

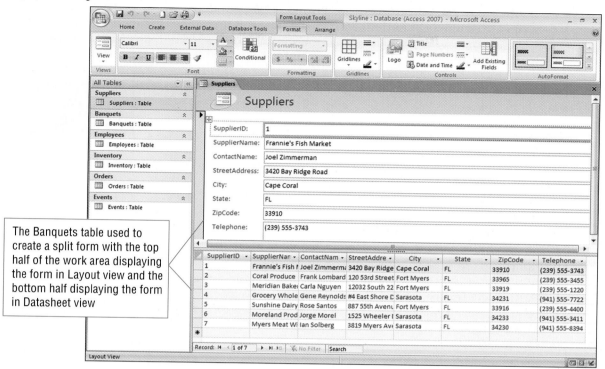

The Banquets table used to create a split form with the top half of the work area displaying the form in Layout view and the bottom half displaying the form in Datasheet view

## Project 2a   Creating a Split Form

1. Display the Open dialog box with Access2007L1C5 on your storage medium the active folder.
2. Open the **Skyline.accdb** database.
3. Create a split form with the Suppliers table by completing the following steps:
   a. Click the Suppliers table in the Navigation pane.
   b. Click the Create tab.
   c. Click the Split Form button in the Forms group.
   d. Click several times on the Next record button in the Record navigation bar. (Notice that as you scroll through records, the current record in Form view in the top portion of the window is the same record selected in Datasheet view in the lower portion of the window.)
4. Apply an autoformat by completing the following steps:
   a. Make sure the form displays in Layout view.
   b. Click the More button located at the right side of the AutoFormat group.
   c. Click the *Flow* autoformat at the drop-down list.

Step 3b

Step 3c

Step 3a

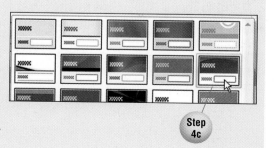

Step 4c

5. Insert a logo image by completing the following steps:
   a. Click the logo container control object that displays in the upper left corner of the form.
   b. Click the Logo button in the Controls group in the Form Layout Tools Format tab.
   c. At the Insert Picture dialog box, navigate to the Access2007L1C5 folder on your storage medium and then double-click *Cityscape.jpg*.
6. Increase the size of the logo so it displays as shown in the image at the right.
7. Change the form title and format the title by completing the following steps:
   a. Click the Title button in the Controls group.
   b. With *Suppliers* selected, type **Skyline Suppliers**.
   c. Click the Font Color button arrow in the Font group and then click the *White* color at the drop-down color palette (first color from the left in the first row of the *Standard Colors* section).
   d. Click the Bold button in the Font group.
   e. Click the Font Size button arrow and then click *24* at the drop-down list.
8. Insert a new record in the Suppliers form by completing the following steps:
   a. Click the Form View button located in the lower right corner of the Status bar.
   b. Click the New (blank) record button in the Record navigation bar.
   c. Click in the *SupplierID* field in the Form view portion of the window and then type the following information in the specified fields:

   | | | |
   |---|---|---|
   | *Supplier10* | = | 8 |
   | *SupplierName* | = | Jackson Produce |
   | *ContactName* | = | Marshall Jackson |
   | *StreetAddress* | = | 5790 Cypress Avenue |
   | *City* | = | Fort Myers |
   | *State* | = | FL |
   | *ZipCode* | = | 33917 |
   | *Telephone* | = | 2395555002 |

9. Click the Save button on the Quick Access toolbar and save the form with the name *Suppliers*.
10. Print the current form by completing the following steps:
    a. Display the Print dialog box.
    b. At the Print dialog box, click the Setup button.
    c. At the Page Setup dialog box, click Print Form Only and then click OK.
    d. At the Print dialog box, click the Selected Record(s) option and then click OK.
11. Close the *Suppliers* form.

**QUICK STEPS**

**Create a Multiple Item Form**
1. Click desired table.
2. Click Create tab.
3. Click Multiple Items button.

## Creating a Multiple Item Form

When you create a form with the Form button, a single record displays. You can use the Multiple Items button in the Forms group in the Create tab to create a form that displays multiple records. The advantage to creating a multiple item form over displaying the table in Datasheet view is that you can customize the form using options in the Form Layout Tools Format tab.

1. With the **Skyline.accdb** database open, create a multiple item form by completing the following steps:
   a. Click the Orders table in the Navigation pane.
   b. Click the Create tab.
   c. Click the Multiple Items button in the Forms group.
2. Apply the Flow autoformat to the form.
3. Insert the **Cityscape.jpg** image as the logo.
4. Insert the title *Skyline Orders* and turn on bold.
5. Insert the date and time in the form header. Change the font color of the date and time to white, turn on bold, and then drag the date and time so they are right-aligned with the SupplierID heading.
6. Save the form with the name *Orders*.
7. Print the first record in the form by completing the following steps:
   a. Display the Print dialog box.
   b. Click the *Pages* option in the *Print Range* section.
   c. Type 1 in the *From* text box, press the Tab key, and then type 1 in the *To* text box.
   d. Click OK.
   e. At the message that displays, click OK.
8. Close the Orders form.

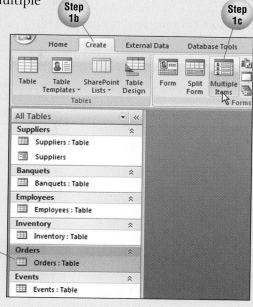

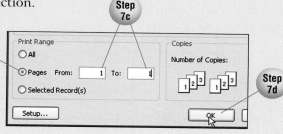

# Creating a Form Using the Form Wizard

Access offers a Form Wizard that will guide you through the creation of a form. To create a form using the Form Wizard, click the Create tab, click the More Forms button in the Forms group, and then click *Form Wizard* at the drop-down list. At the first Form Wizard dialog box, shown in Figure 5.6, specify the table and then the fields you want included in the form. To select the table, click the down-pointing arrow at the right side of the *Tables/Queries* option box and then click the desired table. Select the desired field in the *Available Fields* list box and then click the button containing the greater than symbol (>). This inserts the field in the *Selected Fields* list box. Continue in this manner until you have inserted all desired fields in the *Selected Fields* list box. If you want to insert all fields into the *Selected Fields* list box at one time, click the button containing the two greater than symbols (>>). After specifying fields, click the Next button.

**QUICK STEPS**

**Create a Form Using Form Wizard**
1. Click Create tab.
2. Click More Forms button.
3. Click *Form Wizard* at drop-down list.
4. Choose desired options at each of the Form Wizard dialog boxes.

**HINT**
Using the Form Wizard, you can be more selective about what fields you insert in a form.

**Figure 5.6** First Form Wizard Dialog Box

Click this down-pointing arrow and then click the desired table at the drop-down list.

Add a field to the *Selected Fields* list box by clicking the desired field in the *Available Fields* list box and then clicking the button with the > symbol.

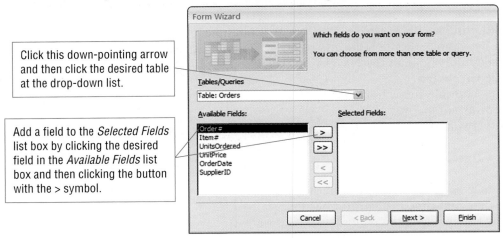

At the second Form Wizard dialog box, shown in Figure 5.7, specify the layout for the records. You can choose from *Columnar, Tabular, Datasheet,* and *Justified* (with *Columnar* the default). After choosing the layout, click the Next button.

**Figure 5.7** Second Form Wizard Dialog Box

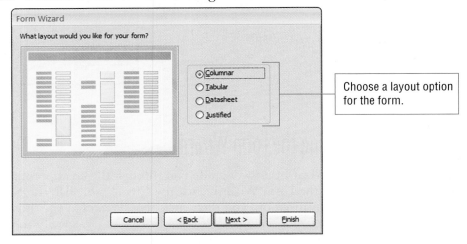

Choose a layout option for the form.

At the third Form Wizard dialog box, shown in Figure 5.8, choose an autoformat style. These are the same autoformats that are available in the AutoFormat group in the Form Layout Tools Format tab. Click a format style and the results of the style display in the preview box. After selecting the desired format style, click the Next button.

**Figure 5.8** Third Form Wizard Dialog Box

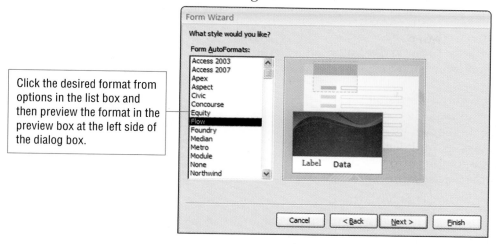

Click the desired format from options in the list box and then preview the format in the preview box at the left side of the dialog box.

At the final Form Wizard dialog box, shown in Figure 5.9, the Form Wizard offers a title for the form and also provides the option *Open the form to view or enter information*. Make any necessary changes in this dialog box and then click the Finish button.

**Figure 5.9** Fourth Form Wizard Dialog Box

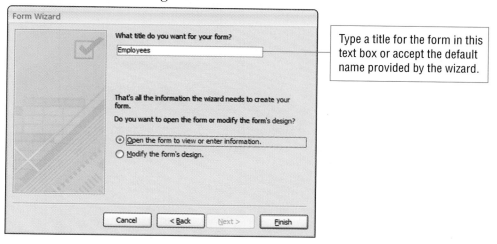

Type a title for the form in this text box or accept the default name provided by the wizard.

# Project 2c  Creating a Form Using the Form Wizard

1. With the **Skyline.accdb** database open, create a form with the Form Wizard by completing the following steps:

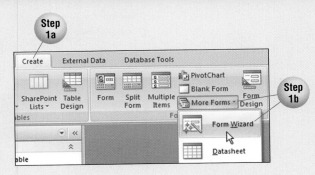

Step 1a

Step 1b

a. Click the Create tab.

b. Click the More Forms button in the Forms group and then click *Form Wizard* at the drop-down list.

c. At the first Form Wizard dialog box, click the down-pointing arrow at the right side of the *Tables/Queries* option box and then click *Table: Employees* at the drop-down list.

d. Specify that you want all fields included in the form by clicking the button containing the two greater than symbols (>>).

e. Click the Next button.

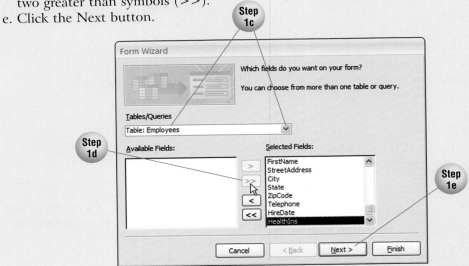

Step 1c

Step 1d

Step 1e

f. At the second Form Wizard dialog box, click the Next button. (This leaves the layout at the default of *Columnar*.)

g. At the third Form Wizard dialog box, make sure the Flow autoformat is selected in the list box and then click the Next button.

h. At the fourth Form Wizard dialog box, leave the options at the default, and then click the Finish button.

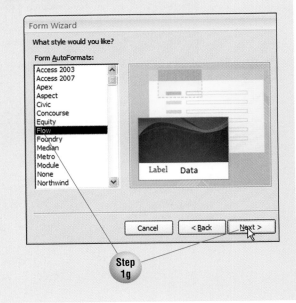

Step 1g

2. When the first record displays, click the New (blank) record button and then add the following records:

| | | |
|---|---|---|
| EmployeeID | = | 11 |
| LastName | = | Thompson |
| FirstName | = | Carol |
| StreetAddress | = | 6554 Willow Drive, Apt. B |
| City | = | Fort Myers |
| State | = | FL |
| ZipCode | = | 33915 |
| Telephone | = | 2395553719 |
| HireDate | = | 12/1/2007 |
| HealthIns | = | *(Click in the check box to insert a check mark.)* |

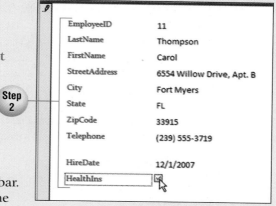

| | | |
|---|---|---|
| EmployeeID | = | 12 |
| LastName | = | Hahn |
| FirstName | = | Eric |
| StreetAddress | = | 331 South 152nd Street |
| City | = | Cape Coral |
| State | = | FL |
| ZipCode | = | 33906 |
| Telephone | = | 2395558107 |
| HireDate | = | 12/1/2007 |
| HealthIns | = | *(Leave blank.)* |

3. Click the Save button on the Quick Access toolbar.
4. Print the record for Eric Hahn and then print the record for Carol Thompson.
5. Close the Employees form.

# Creating a Form with Fields from Related Tables

In Project 2c you used the Form Wizard to create a form with all of the fields in one table. If tables are related, you can create a form using fields from related tables. At the first Form Wizard dialog box (see Figure 5.6), choose fields from the selected table and then choose fields from a related table. To change to the related table, click the down-pointing arrow at the right of the *Tables/Queries* option box and then click the name of the desired table.

## Project 2d — Creating a Form with Related Tables

1. With the **Skyline.accdb** database open, create the following relationships:

| Field Name | "One" Table | "Many" Table |
|---|---|---|
| EmployeeID | Employees | Banquets |
| EventID | Events | Banquets |

2. Create a form with fields from related tables by completing the following steps:
   a. Click the Create tab.
   b. Click the More Forms button in the Forms group and then click *Form Wizard* at the drop-down list.
   c. At the first Form Wizard dialog box, click the down-pointing arrow at the right of the *Tables/Queries* option box and then click *Table: Banquets*.
   d. Click *ResDate* in the *Available Fields* list box and then click the button containing the greater than symbol (>). (This inserts *ResDate* in the *Selected Fields* list box.)
   e. Click *AmountTotal* in the *Available Fields* list box and then click the button containing the greater than symbol.
   f. Click *AmountPaid* in the *Available Fields* list box and then click the button containing the greater than symbol.
   g. Click the down-pointing arrow at the right side of the *Tables/Queries* option box and then click *Table: Events* at the drop-down list.
   h. Click *Event* in the *Available Fields* list box and then click the button containing the greater than symbol.
   i. Click the down-pointing arrow at the right side of the *Tables/Queries* option box and then click *Table: Employees* at the drop-down list.
   j. Click *LastName* in the *Available Fields* list box and then click the button containing the greater than symbol.
   k. Click the Next button.
   l. At the second Form Wizard dialog box, click the Next button.
   m. At the third Form Wizard dialog box, click the Next button.
   n. At the fourth Form Wizard dialog box, make sure *Flow* is selected in the list box and then click the Next button.
   o. At the fifth Form Wizard dialog box, select the text in the *What title do you want for your form?* text box, type **Upcoming Banquets**, and then click the Finish button.

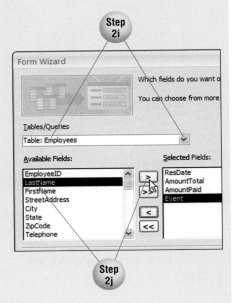

Step 2i

Step 2j

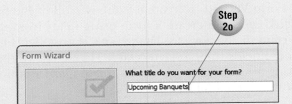

Step 2o

3. When the first record displays, print the record.
4. Save and then close the form.
5. Close the **Skyline.accdb** database.

# CHAPTER summary

- A form generally improves the ease with which data is entered into a table. Some methods for creating a form include using the Form, Split Form, or Multiple Items buttons or the Form Wizard.

- A form is an object you can use to enter and edit data in a table or query and to help prevent incorrect data from being entered in a database.

- The simplest method for creating a form is to click a table in the Navigation pane, click the Create button, and then click the Form button in the Forms group.

- When you create a form, it displays in Layout view. Use this view to display data as well as modify the appearance and contents of the form. Other form views include Form view and Design view. Use Form view to enter and manage records and use Design view to view the structure of the form and modify the form.

- Print a form with options at the Print dialog box or by clicking the Quick Print button. To print an individual record, display the Print dialog box, click the *Select Record(s)* option, and then click OK.

- Navigate in a form with buttons in the Record navigation bar.

- Add a new record to a form by clicking the New Record button in the Record navigation bar or by clicking the Home tab and then clicking the New button in the Records group.

- Delete a record from a form by displaying the record, clicking the Home tab, clicking the Delete button arrow, and then clicking *Delete Record* at the drop-down list.

- If you create a form with a table that has a one-to-many relationship established, Access adds a datasheet at the bottom of the form.

- A form is comprised of a series of control objects and you can customize these control objects with buttons in the Form Layout Tools Format tab, which is active when you display a form in Layout view.

- Use options in the Font group in the Form Layout Tools Format tab to change the font, font style, font size, and font color. Use the Conditional button to apply specific formatting to data that matches a specific criterion.

- Format numbers and apply and customize gridlines with buttons in the Formatting group in the Form Layout Tools Format tab.

- With options in the Controls group in the Form Layout Tools Format tab, you can insert a logo, form title, page numbers, and date and time; apply lines to control objects; and customize the lines.

- Click the Add Existing Fields button in the Controls group to display the Field List window. Add fields to the form by double-clicking on or dragging the field from the window.

- Change the order of fields in a form by dragging the field to the desired position.

- Change the size of a selected control object by dragging a border of the object with the mouse.

- Move a selected control object by dragging the object with the mouse.

- Apply an autoformat to a form by clicking one of the two autoformats that display in the Form Layout Tools Form tab or by clicking the More button at the right side of the autoformats and then clicking the desired autoformat at the drop-down list.
- Create a split form by clicking the Split Form button in the Forms group in the Create tab. Access displays the form in Form view in the top portion of the work area and the form in Datasheet view in the bottom of the work area. The two views are connected and are synchronous.
- Create a form with the Multiple Items button and the form displays multiple records.
- The Form Wizard walks you through the steps for creating a form and lets you specify the fields you want included in the form, a layout for the records, the desired formatting, and a name for the form.
- You can create a form with the Form Wizard that contains fields from tables connected by a one-to-many relationship.

# COMMANDS review

| FEATURE | RIBBON TAB, GROUP | BUTTON, OPTION |
|---|---|---|
| Form | Create, Forms | |
| Conditional Formatting dialog box | Form Layout Tools Format, Font | |
| Field List window | Form Layout Tools Format, Controls | |
| Split Form | Create, Forms | |
| Multiple Items form | Create, Forms | |
| Form Wizard | Create, Forms | More Forms ▾ , Form Wizard |

# CONCEPTS check

## Test Your Knowledge

**Completion:** In the space provided at the right, indicate the correct term, symbol, or command.

1. The simplest method to create a form is to click this tab and then click the Form button.

_____

2. When you click the Form button to create a form, the form displays in this view.

_____

3. To print the current record in a form, click this option at the Print dialog box and then click OK.

_____

4. Navigate in a form using buttons in this bar.

_____

5. Click this button to add a new record to a form.

_____

6. The Form Layout Tools Format tab is active when a form displays in this view.

_____

7. The Conditional button is located in this group in the Form Layout Tools Format tab.

_____

8. Click the Add Existing Fields button in the Controls group in the Form Layout Tools Format tab and this window displays.

_____

9. The top portion of the form containing the logo container control object and the form title is referred to as this.

_____

10. When you create a form with the Split Form button, the form displays in this view in the top half of the work area.

_____

11. Click this button in the Forms group in the Create tab to create a form that displays multiple records.

_____

12. Click this button in the Forms group in the Create tab to display a drop-down list containing the option *Form Wizard*.

_____

# SKILLS check
## *Demonstrate Your Proficiency*

## 1 CREATE AND CUSTOMIZE A SALES FORM

1. Display the Open dialog box with Access2007L1C5 on your storage medium the active folder.
2. Open the **OutdoorOptions.accdb** database.
3. Use the Form button in the Forms group in the Create tab to create a form with the Suppliers table.
4. Switch to Form view and then add the following records to the Suppliers form:

   | | | |
   |---|---|---|
   | *Supplier#* | = | 12 |
   | *SupplierName* | = | Seaside Suppliers |
   | *StreetAddress* | = | 4120 Shoreline Drive |
   | *City* | = | Vancouver |
   | *Province* | = | BC |
   | *PostalCode* | = | V2V 8K4 |
   | *Email* | = | ss@emcp.net |

   | | | |
   |---|---|---|
   | *Supplier#* | = | 34 |
   | *SupplierName* | = | Carson Company |
   | *StreetAddress* | = | 120 Plaza Center |
   | *City* | = | Vancouver |
   | *Province* | = | BC |
   | *PostalCode* | = | V2V 1K6 |
   | *Email* | = | cc@emcp.net |

5. Delete the record containing information on Manning, Inc.
6. Switch to Layout view and then apply the Civic autoformat to the form.
7. Select the seven field names (from *Supplier#* through *Email*) and then change the font color to Aqua Blue 5, alignment to Align Text Right, and turn on bold.
8. Click in the *City* field entry and then apply conditional formatting that changes the font color to red and turns on bold for any *City* field that contains the name *Calgary*.
9. Insert the image named **River.jpg** in the logo container control object.
10. Change the name of the form title to *Company Suppliers*. Change the font color of the title to Aqua Blue 5 and turn on bold.
11. Insert the date and time in the form header. Change the font color of the date and time to Aqua Blue 5 and turn on bold.
12. Save the form with the name *Suppliers*.
13. Print the first record in the form in landscape orientation and then close the Suppliers form.

## 2 CREATE AND CUSTOMIZE AN ORDERS FORM AND A PRODUCTS FORM

1. With the **OutdoorOptions.accdb** database open, create a form with the Orders table using the Form button in the Create tab.
2. Make the following changes to the form:
   a. Display the Field List window and then, if necessary, click the <u>Show all tables</u> hyperlink (located toward the bottom of the window). Expand the Suppliers table in the *Fields available in related tables* section and then drag the field named *SupplierName* into the form and position it between *Supplier#* and *Product#*.
   b. Apply the Civic autoformat to the form.
   c. Apply horizontal gridlines to the form.
   d. Select the seven field names (from *Order#* through *OrderDate*) and then change the font color to Aqua Blue 5, the alignment to Align Text Right, and turn on bold.
   e. Apply conditional formatting that changes the font color to green for any *Amount* field entry that contains an amount greater than $999 and changes the font color to blue for any amount less than $1000. (Do not use the dollar sign when specifying the conditions.)
   f. Insert the image named **River.jpg** in the logo container control object.
3. Save the form with the name *Orders*.
4. Print the first record in the form and then close the Orders form.
5. Create a form with the Products table using the Split Form button in the Create tab with the following specifications:
   a. Apply the Civic autoformat to the form.
   b. Apply horizontal gridlines to the form.
   c. Select the six field names (from *Product#* through *ReorderLevel*) and then change the font color to Aqua Blue 5, the alignment to Align Text Right, and turn on bold.
   d. Change to Form view, create a new record, and then enter the following information in the specified fields:

   | | | |
   |---|---|---|
   | *Product#* | = | 303 |
   | *Product* | = | Ski helmet |
   | *Supplier#* | = | 68 |
   | *UnitsInStock* | = | 12 |
   | *UnitsOnOrder* | = | 0 |
   | *ReorderLevel* | = | 10 |

6. Save the form with the name *Products*.
7. Print the current record (the record you just typed). (Hint: Display the Print dialog box, click the Setup button, and then click the *Print Form Only* option. Click *Selected Record(s)* at the Print dialog box.)
8. Close the Products form.

## Assessment

### 3 CREATE A FORM USING THE FORM WIZARD

1. With the **OutdoorOptions.accdb** database open, create a form from two related database tables using the Form Wizard with the following specifications:
   a. At the first Form Wizard dialog box, insert the following fields in the *Selected Fields* list box:
      From the Products table:
         *Product#*
         *Product*
         *UnitsOnOrder*
      From the Suppliers table:
         *Supplier#*
         *SupplierName*
         *StreetAddress*
         *City*
         *Province*
         *PostalCode*
   b. Do not make any changes at the second Form Wizard dialog box.
   c. Do not make any changes at the third Form Wizard dialog box.
   d. Do not make any changes at the fourth Form Wizard dialog box.
   e. At the fifth Form Wizard dialog box, select the text in the *What title do you want for your form?* text box, type the name Units On Order, and then click the Finish button.
   f. Switch to the Layout view and then apply the Civic autoformat.
2. Print only the first record.
3. Close the Units On Order form.
4. Create a form with the Suppliers table using the Form Wizard with the following specifications:
   a. At the first Form Wizard dialog box, insert all of the Suppliers table fields in the *Selected fields* list box.
   b. At the second Form Wizard dialog box, specify that you want the layout of the form to be *Tabular*.
   c. At the third Form Wizard dialog box, make sure *Civic* is selected.
   d. At the fourth Form Wizard dialog box, select the text in the *What title do you want for your form?* text box, type the name Company Suppliers, and then click the Finish button.
5. Print the form.
6. Close the Company Suppliers form and then close the **OutdoorOptions.accdb** database.

# CASE study

## Apply Your Skills

You are the office manager at the Lewis Vision Care Center and your center is switching over to Access to manage files. You have already created four basic tables and now need to create relationships and enter data. Open the **LewisCenter.accdb** database and then create the following relationships between tables:

| Field Name | "One" Table | "Many" Table |
|---|---|---|
| *Patient#* | Patients | Billing |
| *ServiceID* | Services | Billing |
| *Doctor#* | Doctors | Billing |

Save and then print the relationships.

Before entering data in the tables, create a form for each table and apply the same autoformat to each form. Apply any additional formatting to enhance the visual appeal of each form. Using the forms, insert the information on the next page in the correct fields in the specified forms. After entering the information in the forms, print the first record of each form.

## Part 3

Apply the following conditions to fields in forms:

- In the Patients form, apply the condition that the city *Tulsa* displays in red and the city *Broken Arrow* displays in blue in the *City* field.
- In the Billing form, apply the condition that amounts in the *Fee* field over $99 display in green.

Print the first record of the form. Close the Patients form and then close the **LewisCenter.accdb** database.

Your center has a procedures manual that describes processes and procedures in the center. Open Word and then create a document for the procedures manual that describes the formatting and conditions you applied to the forms in the **LewisCenter.accdb** database. Save the completed document and name it **Access_C5_CS_P4**. Print and then close **Access_C5_CS_P4.docx**.

## Patients form

Patient number 030
Rhonda J. Mahler
130 East 41st Street
Tulsa, OK 74155
(918) 555-3107

Patient number 076
Patrick S. Robbins
3281 Aspen Avenue
Tulsa, OK 74108
(918) 555-9672

Patient number 092
Oren L. Vargas
21320 Tenth Street
Broken Arrow, OK 74012
(918) 555-1188

Patient number 085
Michael A. Dempsey
506 Houston Street
Tulsa, OK 74142
(918) 555-5541

Patient number 074
Wendy L. Holloway
23849 22nd Street
Broken Arrow, OK 74009
(918) 555-8842

Patient number 023
Maggie M. Winters
4422 South 121st
Tulsa, OK 74142
(918) 555-8833

## Doctors form

Doctor number 1
Carolyn Joswick
(918) 555-4772

Doctor number 2
Gerald Ingram
(918) 555-9890

Doctor  number 3
Kay Feather
(918) 555-7762

Doctor number 4
Sean Granger
(918) 555-1039

Doctor number 5
Jerome Deltoro
(918) 555-8021

## Services form

Co = Consultation

V = Vision Screening

G = Glaucoma Testing

C = Cataract Testing

S = Surgery

E = Emergency

## Billing form

Patient number 076
Doctor number 2
Date of visit = 04/01/2010
Service ID = C
Fee = $85

Patient number 076
Doctor number 3
Date of visit = 04/01/2010
Service ID = V
Fee = $150

Patient number 085
Doctor number 1
Date of visit = 04/01/2010
Service ID = Co
Fee = $0

Patient number 074
Doctor number 3
Date of visit = 4/1/2010
Service ID = V
Fee = $150

Patient number 023
Doctor number 5
Date of visit = 04/01/2010
Service ID = S
Fee = $750

Patient number 092
Doctor number 1
Date of visit = 04/01/2010
Service ID = G
Fee = $85

# Creating Reports and Mailing Labels

## PERFORMANCE OBJECTIVES

**Upon successful completion of Chapter 6, you will be able to:**

- Create a report using the Report button
- Display a report in Print Preview
- Create a report with a query
- Format and customize a report
- Group and sort records in a report
- Create a report using the Report Wizard
- Create mailing labels using the Label Wizard

**Tutorial 6.1**
Working with Reports and
Creating Mailing Labels

In this chapter, you will learn how to prepare reports from data in a table using the Report button in the Reports group in the Create tab and with the Report Wizard. You will also learn how to format and customize a report with options in the Report Layout Tools Format tab and create mailing labels using the Label Wizard.

*Note: Before beginning computer projects, copy to your storage medium the Access2007L1C6 subfolder from the Access2007L1 folder on the CD that accompanies this textbook and make Access2007L1C6 the active folder.*

## Project 1 Create and Customize Reports Using Tables and Queries

You will create reports with the Report button using tables and queries. You will change the report views; select, move, and resize control objects; sort records; customize reports; apply conditional formatting; and group and sort fields in a report.

## Creating a Report

The primary purpose for inserting data in a form is to improve the display of the data and to make data entry easier. You can also insert data in a report. The purpose for this is to control what data appears on the page when printed. Reports generally answer specific questions (queries). For example, a report could answer the question

**QUICK STEPS**

**Create a Report**
1. Click Create tab.
2. Click desired table or query in Navigation pane.
3. Click Report button.

**HINT**

Create a report to control what data appears on the page when printed.

*What customers have submitted claims?* or *What products do we currently have on order?* You can use the Report button in the Reports group in the Create tab to create a report based on a table or query. You can also use the Report Wizard that walks you through the process of creating a report.

## Creating a Report with the Report Button

To create a report with the Report button, click the desired table or query in the Navigation pane, click the Create tab, and then click the Report button in the Reports group. This displays the report in columnar style in Layout view with the Report Layout Tools Format tab active as shown in Figure 6.1. Access creates the report using all of the fields in the table.

**Figure 6.1** Report Created with Sales Table

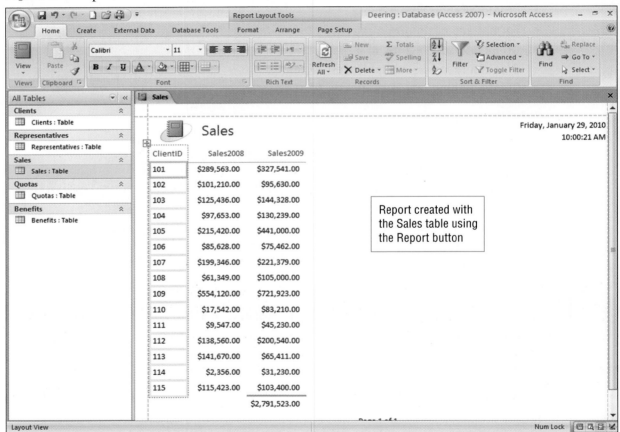

1. Display the Open dialog box with Access2007L1C6 on your storage medium the active folder.
2. Open the **Deering.accdb** database.
3. Create a report by completing the following steps:
   a. Click the Sales table in the Navigation pane.
   b. Click the Create tab.
   c. Click the Report button in the Reports group.

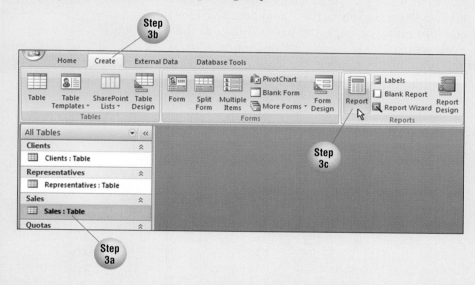

Step 3b

Step 3c

Step 3a

4. Print the report by clicking the Quick Print button on the Quick Access toolbar.
5. Save the report by clicking the Save button on the Quick Access toolbar, making sure *Sales* displays in the *Report Name* text box in the Save As dialog box, and then clicking OK.

## Displaying a Report in Print Preview

When you create a report, the report displays in the work area in Layout view. This is one of four views available including Report view, Print Preview, and Design view. Use Print Preview to display the report as it will appear when printed. To change to Print Preview, click the Print Preview button in the view area located at the right side of the Status bar. You can also click the View button arrow in the Views group in either the Home tab or the Report Layout Tools Format tab and then click *Print Preview* at the drop-down list.

At the Print Preview tab, send the report to the printer by clicking the Print button. Use options in the Page Layout group to specify the size, orientation, and margins of the printed report. Click the Size button and a drop-down list of size choices displays. By default, a report prints in portrait orientation. Click the Landscape button if you want the report printed in landscape orientation. Change margins with the Margins button in the Page Layout group and click the Page Setup button to display a dialog box with page layout options. If you want to print only the report data and not the column headings or report title, click the *Print Data Only* check box to insert a check mark. Use options in the Zoom group to display specific

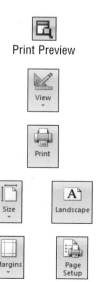

Print Preview

View

Print

Size

Landscape

Margins

Page Setup

locations in the report. The Print Preview tab also contains options for exporting a report to Word or to a text format. You will learn more about exporting data in Chapter 8.

## Project 1b    Displaying a Report in Print Preview

1. With the Sales report open, click the Print Preview button in the view area at the right side of the Status bar.
2. Click the Two Pages button in the Zoom group. (Since this report contains only one page, the page displays at the left side of the work area.)
3. Click the Zoom button arrow in the Zoom group and then click *50%* at the drop-down list.

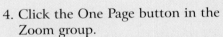

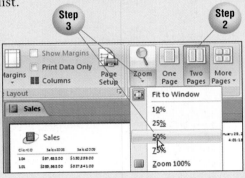

4. Click the One Page button in the Zoom group.
5. Click the Landscape button in the Page Layout group.
6. Click the Margins button in the Page Layout group and then click the *Wide* option at the drop-down list.
7. Print the report by clicking the Print button in the Print Preview tab and then clicking OK at the Print dialog box.
8. Close Print Preview by clicking the Close Print Preview button located at the right side of the Print Preview tab.

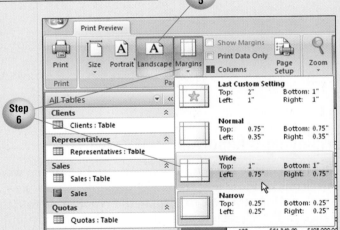

9. Close the Sales report.
10. Create a report with the Clients table by completing the following steps:
    a. Click the Clients table in the Navigation pane.
    b. Click the Create tab.
    c. Click the Report button in the Reports group.
11. Click the Print Preview button in the view area at the right side of the Status bar.
12. Click the Two Pages button in the Zoom group.
13. Change the setup of the report by completing the following steps:
    a. Click the Page Setup button in the Page Layout group.

b. At the Page Setup dialog box with the Print Options tab selected, change the *Top*, *Bottom*, *Left*, and *Right* measurements to 1.

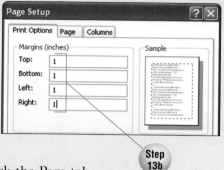

Step 13c

Step 13d

Page Setup

Print Options | Page | Columns

Margins (inches)
Top: 1
Bottom: 1
Left: 1
Right: 1

Sample

Step 13b

Page Setup

Print Options | Page | Columns

Orientation
○ Portrait    ⊙ Landscape

Paper
Size: Letter
Source: Automatically Select

Printer for Clients
⊙ Default Printer
○ Use Specific Printer    Printer...

OK    Cancel

Step 13e

c. Click the Page tab.
d. At the Page Setup dialog box with the Page tab selected, click the *Landscape* option.
e. Click OK to close the dialog box.
14. After looking at the report, you decide to return to portrait orientation by clicking the Portrait button in the Page Layout group.
15. Print the report by clicking the Print button in the Print Preview tab and then clicking OK at the Print dialog box.
16. Close Print Preview by clicking the Close Print Preview button.
17. Save the report with the name *Clients*.
18. Close the Clients report.

# Creating a Report with a Query

Since one of the purposes of a report is to answer specific questions, design and run a query and then create a report based on that query. Create a report from a query in the same manner as creating a report from a table.

## Project 1c    Creating a Report with a Query

1. With the **Deering.accdb** database open, create the following one-to-many relationships:

| Field Name | "One" Table | "Many" Table |
|---|---|---|
| *RepID* | Representatives | Clients |
| *RepID* | Benefits | Clients |
| *QuotaID* | Quotas | Representatives |

2. Create a one-to-one relationship between the *ClientID* field in the Clients table and the Sales table.
3. Save and then close the relationships window.
4. Design a query that extracts records from two tables with the following specifications:
   a. Add the Clients and Sales tables to the query window.
   b. Insert the *Client* field from the Clients table to the first *Field* text box.
   c. Insert the *StreetAddress* field from the Clients table to the second *Field* text box.

d. Insert the *City* field from the Clients table to the third *Field* text box.

e. Insert the *State* field from the Clients table to the fourth *Field* text box.

f. Insert the *ZipCode* field from the Clients table to the fifth *Field* text box.

g. Insert the *Sales2008* field from the Sales table to the sixth *Field* text box.

h. Insert the criterion *Indianapolis Or Muncie* in the *Criteria* text box in the *City* column.

i. Insert the criterion *>75000* in the *Criteria* text box in the *Sales2008* column.

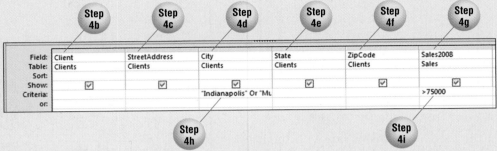

j. Run the query.

k. Save the query and name it *IndianapolisMuncieSalesOver$75000*.

l. Close the query.

5. Create a report with the query by completing the following steps:

a. Click the IndianapolisMuncieSalesOver$75000 query in the Navigation pane.

b. Click the Create tab.

c. Click the Report button in the Reports group.

d. Click the View button arrow in the Views group at the left side of the Report Layout Tools Format tab and then click *Print Preview* at the drop-down list.

e. Click the Landscape button in the Page Layout group.

f. Click the Margins button in the Page Layout group and then click the *Wide* option at the drop-down list.

g. Close Print Preview by clicking the Close Print Preview button.

6. Save the report and name it *IndianapolisMuncieSales*.

7. Print and then close the report.

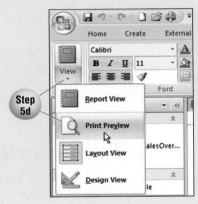

# Selecting Control Objects

To apply formatting to specific control objects in a report, click the object to select it. If you click a data field in the report, Access selects all data in the column except the column heading. To select all control objects in a report, press Ctrl + A. You can also select multiple objects in a report by holding down the Shift key as you click each object.

## Sizing and Moving a Control Object

Change the size of a selected control object by positioning the mouse pointer on the object border until the mouse pointer displays as a double-headed arrow and then drag in or out to decrease or increase the size of the object. A report, like a form, contains a report header that is the top portion of the report containing the logo container control object, the report title, and the current date and time. You can move a control object in a report header by clicking the object to select it and then dragging with the mouse to the desired location.

## Changing the Width and Order of a Column

You can change the width of columns in a report. To do this, click in any data field in the column, position the mouse pointer on the right border of the column until the mouse pointer displays as a two-headed arrow pointing left and right, hold down the left mouse button, drag in or out to decrease or increase the width of the column, and then release the mouse button.

You can change the order of columns in a report. To do this, click the desired column heading, position the mouse pointer in the column heading until the pointer displays with a four-headed arrow attached, and then drag the column left or right to the desired position. As you drag the column, a vertical orange bar displays indicating the location at which the column will be placed when you release the mouse button.

## Sorting Records

You can sort data in a report by clicking in the field containing data on which you want to sort and then clicking the Ascending button or Descending button in the Sort & Filter group in the Home tab. Click the Ascending button to sort text in alphabetic order from A to Z or numbers from lowest to highest, or click the Descending button to sort text in alphabetic order from Z to A or numbers from highest to lowest.

**Sort Records**
1. Click in field containing data.
2. Click Ascending or click Descending button.

Ascending

Descending

Project **1d**  Sizing, Moving, and Sorting Control Objects

1. With the **Deering.accdb** database open, open the Sales report by right-clicking the Sales report in the Navigation pane and then clicking *Layout View* at the shortcut menu.
2. Close the Navigation pane by clicking the Shutter Bar Open/Close Button located in the upper right corner of the pane.

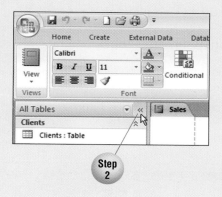

Step 2

3. Move the date control object by completing the following steps:
   a. Click the current date that displays in the upper right corner of the report.
   b. Position the mouse pointer inside the selected object (mouse displays with a four-headed arrow attached), drag to the left to the approximate location shown in the image below, and then release the mouse button.
4. Complete steps similar to those in Step 3 to move the time control object so it is right-aligned with the date (see image below).

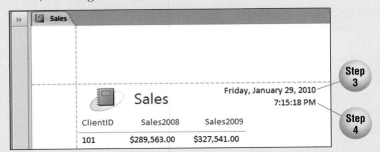

5. Change the width of the *ClientID* column by completing the following steps:
   a. Click the *ClientID* column heading.
   b. Position the mouse pointer on the right border of the *ClientID* column until the mouse pointer displays as a double-headed arrow pointing left and right.
   c. Hold down the left mouse button, drag to the right the approximate distance shown in the image at the right, and then release the mouse button.
6. Reverse the order of the *Sales2008* and *Sales2009* columns by completing the following steps:
   a. Click the *Sales2009* column heading.
   b. Position the mouse pointer inside the *Sales2009* column heading until the pointer displays with a four-headed arrow attached.
   c. Hold down the left mouse button, drag to the left until the vertical orange bar displays between *ClientID* and *Sales2008*, and then release the mouse button.

7. Sort the records in the report by completing the following steps:
   a. Click in the field containing the amount *$289,563.00* (located below the *Sales2008* column heading).
   b. Click the Home tab.
   c. Click the Ascending button in the Sort & Filter group.

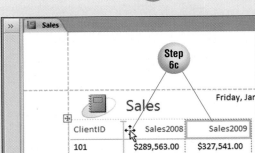

# Customizing a Report

A report, like a form, is comprised of a series of control objects, which are objects that display titles or descriptions, accept data, or perform actions. You can customize control objects with buttons in the Report Layout Tools Format tab.

## Changing the Font

Use options in the Font group to change the font, font style, font size, and font color of the selected control object in the report. You can also change the alignment of text and apply fill to fields in the report.

## Applying Conditional Formatting

Click the Conditional button in the Font group in the Report Layout Tools Format tab and the Conditional Formatting dialog box displays. This is the same dialog box that displays when you click the Conditional button in the Font group in the Form Layout Tools Format tab. With the options at this dialog box, specify the formatting you want applied to control objects that meet a specific criterion (condition).

## Totaling Numbers

You can use the Totals button in the Grouping & Totals group in the Report Layout Tools Format tab to perform functions such as finding the sum, average, maximum, or minimum of the numbers in a column. To use the Totals button, click the column heading of the column containing data you want to total, click the Totals button in the Grouping & Totals group, and then click the desired function at the drop-down list.

## Formatting Numbers and Applying Gridlines

The Report Layout Tools Format tab contains numbering and gridline options similar to those in the Form Layout Tools Format tab. Use options in the Formatting group to apply Currency, Percent, or Comma Number formatting to numbers and choose a number style from the Format option drop-down list. Use options in the Gridlines group to apply and customize gridlines to control objects.

## Formatting Controls

Use options in the Controls group in the Report Layout Tools Format tab to insert a logo, title, or date and time. The group also contains buttons for applying lines to control objects and then changing the line thickness, type, and color. Click the

Add Existing Fields button in the Controls group and the Field List window displays. This window displays the fields available in the current view, fields available in related tables, and fields available in other tables.

## Project 1e  Applying Fonts and Conditional Formatting to a Report

1. With the Sales report open, change the font for all control objects in the report by completing the following steps:
   a. Press Ctrl + A to select all control objects in the report (an orange border displays around objects).
   b. Click the Font button arrow in the Font group in the Report Layout Tools Format tab and then click *Cambria* at the drop-down list. (You will need to scroll down the list to display *Cambria*.)
2. Change the font style and alignment of the column headings by completing the following steps:
   a. Click *ClientID* to select the control object (orange border surrounds the object).
   b. Hold down the Shift key, click *Sales2009*, and then click *Sales2008*.
   c. Click the Center button in the Font group.
   d. Click the Bold button in the Font group.

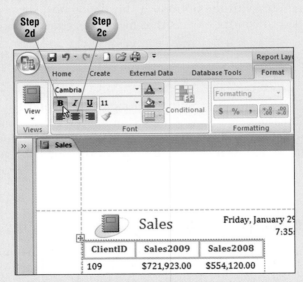

3. Change the alignment of data in the *ClientID* column by clicking *109* (below the *ClientID* column heading) and then clicking the Center button in the Font group.
4. Format amounts and apply conditional formatting to the amounts in the report by completing the following steps:
   a. Click the control object containing the amount *$721,923.00*. (This selects all of the amounts in the column.)
   b. Hold down the Shift key and then click the control object containing the amount *$554,120.00*.

c. Click twice on the Decrease Decimals button in the Formatting group in the Report Layout Tools Format tab.

d. Click the Conditional button in the Font group.

e. At the Conditional Formatting dialog box, click the down-pointing arrow in the second list box in the *Condition 1* section and then click *greater than* at the drop-down list.

f. Click in the text box immediately right of the option box containing *greater than* and then type 199999.

g. Click the Fill/Back Color button arrow and then click the seventh color option from the left in the third row (light green).

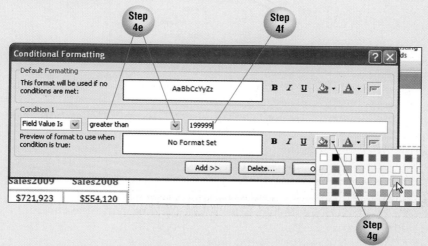

h. Click the Add button. (This inserts a *Condition 2* section toward the bottom of the dialog box.)

i. Click the down-pointing arrow in the second list box in the *Condition 2* section and then click *less than* at the drop-down list.

j. Click in the text box immediately right of the option containing *less than* and then type 200000.

k. Click the Fill/Back Color button arrow and then click the sixth color from the left in the second row (light red).

l. Click OK to close the dialog box.

5. Apply and format gridlines by completing the following steps:

a. Click the *ClientID* column heading, hold down the Shift key, click *Sales2009*, and then click *Sales2008*.

b. Click the Gridlines button in the Gridlines group in the Report Layout Tools Format tab and then click *Cross Hatch* at the drop-down list.

c. Click the Color button arrow in the Gridlines group and then click the purple color at the drop-down list (last color in the bottom row in the *Standard Colors* section).

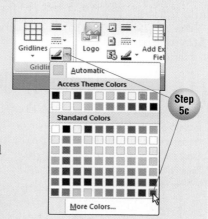

d. Click in the control object containing the number *109*, hold down the Shift key, click the amount *$721,923*, and then click the amount *$554,120*.

e. Click the Gridlines button in the Gridlines group and then click *Cross Hatch* at the drop-down list.

f. Click the Color button. (This applies the purple color to the line.)

6. Sum the totals in the *Sales2008* column by completing the following steps:
   a. Click in the *Sales2008* column heading.
   b. Click the Totals button and then click *Sum* at the drop-down list.

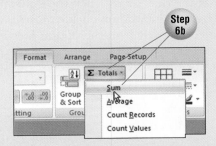

7. Insert a logo image by completing the following steps:
   a. Click the logo container content control object.
   b. Click the Logo button in the Controls group.
   c. At the Insert Picture dialog box, navigate to the Access2007L1C6 folder on your storage medium and then double-click **Mountain.jpg**.
8. Insert a title by completing the following steps:
   a. Click the Title button in the Controls group.
   b. Type 2008-2009 Sales.
   c. Click the Bold button in the Font group.
   d. If the title overlaps the date and time, select the date and time control objects and then move them to the right.
9. Save, print, and then close the Sales report.
10. Display the Navigation pane by clicking the Shutter Bar Open/Close Button.

**Apply AutoFormat**
1. Click Report Layout Tools Format tab.
2. Click AutoFormat button.
3. Click desired autoformat at drop-down list.

## Applying AutoFormats

Click the AutoFormat button in the Report Layout Tools Format tab to display a list of autoformats. These are the same autoformats available in the Form Layout Tools Format tab. The names of the autoformats align with the theme names in Word, Excel, and PowerPoint. Apply an autoformat by clicking the AutoFormat button and then clicking the desired autoformat at the drop-down list.

## Changing Page Setup

**HINT**
Autoformats apply formatting similar to themes in Word, Excel, and PowerPoint.

The Print Preview tab contains options for changing page setup options such as margins, orientation, and size. Many of these options are also available in the Report Layout Tools Page Setup tab. Display this tab by opening a report in Layout view and then clicking the Page Setup tab in the Report Layout Tools tab.

AutoFormat

# Grouping and Sorting Records

A report presents database information in a printed form and generally displays data that answers a specific question. To make the data in a report easy to understand you can divide the data into groups. For example, you can divide data in a report by region, sales, dates, or any other division that helps identify the data to the reader. Access contains a powerful group and sort feature you can use in a report. In this section you will complete basic group and sort functions. For more detailed information on grouping and sorting, please refer to the Access help files.

Click the Group & Sort button in the Grouping & Totals group in the Report Layout Tools Format tab and the Group, Sort, and Total pane displays at the bottom of the work area as shown in Figure 6.2. Click the Add a group button in the Group, Sort, and Total pane and Access adds a new grouping level row to the pane along with a list of available fields. Click the field on which you want to group data in the report and Access adds the grouping level in the report. With options in the grouping level row, you can change the group, specify the sort order, and expand the row to display additional options.

## QUICK STEPS

**Group and Sort Records**
1. Open desired report in Layout view.
2. Click Report Layout Tools Format tab.
3. Click Group & Sort button.
4. Click Add a group button.
5. Click desired group field.

**HINT**
Grouping allows you to separate groups of records visually.

**Figure 6.2** Group, Sort, and Total Pane

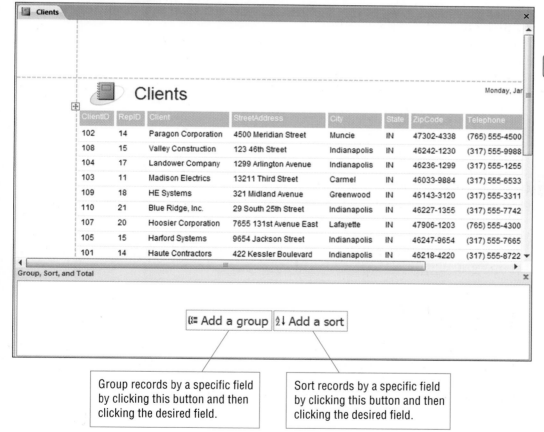

Group records by a specific field by clicking this button and then clicking the desired field.

Sort records by a specific field by clicking this button and then clicking the desired field.

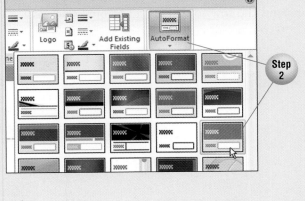

When you specify a grouping level, Access automatically sorts that level in ascending order (from A to Z or from lowest to highest). You can then sort additional data within the report by clicking the Add a sort button in the Group, Sort, and Total pane. This inserts a sorting row in the pane below the grouping level row along with a list of available fields. At this list, click the field on which you want to sort. For example, in Project 1f you will specify that a report is grouped by city (which will display in ascending order) and then specify that the client names display in alphabetical order within the city.

To delete a grouping or sorting level in the Group, Sort, and Total pane, click the Delete button that displays at the right side of the level row. After specifying the grouping and sorting levels, close the Group, Sort, and Total pane by clicking the close button located in the upper right corner of the pane.

## Project 1f    Applying an AutoFormat and Grouping and Sorting Data

1. With the **Deering.accdb** database open, open the Clients report in Layout view.
2. Click the AutoFormat button in the AutoFormat group in the Report Layout Tools Format tab and then click *Northwind* at the drop-down list.
3. Click each of the column headings individually and then decrease the size of each column so the right border of the column is just right of the longest entry in each column.
4. Change the orientation to landscape by completing the following steps:
   a. Click the Report Layout Tools Page Setup tab.
   b. Click the Landscape button in the Page Setup group.
5. Group the report by RepID and then sort by clients by completing the following steps:
   a. Click the Report Layout Tools Format tab.
   b. Click the Group & Sort button in the Grouping & Tools group.
   c. Click the Add a group button in the Group, Sort, and Total pane.
   d. Click the *RepID* field in the list box.
   e. Scroll through the report and notice that the records are grouped by the *RepID* field. Also, notice that the client names within each RepID group are not in alphabetic order.
   f. Click the Add a sort button in the Group, Sort, and Total pane.
   g. Click the *Client* field in the list box.
   h. Scroll through the report and notice that client names are now alphabetized within RepID groups.

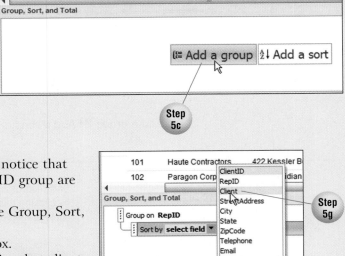

i. Close the Group, Sort, and Total pane by clicking the Close button located in the upper right corner of the pane.

6. Save, print, and then close the Clients report.

7. Open the IndianapolisMuncieSales report in Layout view.

8. Click the AutoFormat button in the AutoFormat group in the Report Layout Tools Format tab and then click *Northwind* at the drop-down list.

9. Click each of the column headings individually and then decrease the size of each column so the right border of the column is near the longest entry in each column.

10. Group the report by city and then sort by clients by completing the following steps:
   a. Click the Group & Sort button in the Grouping & Tools group in the Report Layout Tools Format tab.
   b. Click the Add a group button in the Group, Sort, and Total pane.
   c. Click the *City* field in the list box.
   d. Click the Add a sort button in the Group, Sort, and Total pane and then click the *Client* field in the list box.
   e. Close the Group, Sort, and Total pane by clicking the Close button located in the upper right corner of the pane.

11. Save, print, and then close the IndianapolisMuncieSales report.

12. Close the **Deering.accdb** database.

13. Display the Open dialog box with Access2007L1C6 on your storage medium the active folder.

14. Open the **LegalServices.accdb** database.

15. Design a query that extracts records from three tables with the following specifications:
   a. Add the Billing, Clients, and Rates tables to the query window.
   b. Insert the *LastName* field from the Clients table to the first *Field* text box.
   c. Insert the *Date* field from the Billings table to the second *Field* text box.
   d. Insert the *Hours* field from the Billings table to the third *Field* text box.
   e. Insert the *Rate* field from the Rates table to the fourth *Field* text box.
   f. Click in the fifth *Field* text box, type Total: [Hours]*[Rate], and then press Enter.

Step 15b    Step 15c    Step 15d    Step 15e    Step 15f

| Field: | LastName | Date | Hours | Rate | Total: [Hours]*[Rate] |
|---|---|---|---|---|---|
| Table: | Clients | Billing | Billing | Rates | |
| Sort: | | | | | |
| Show: | ☑ | ☑ | ☑ | ☑ | ☑ |
| Criteria: | | | | | |

g. Run the query.

h. Save the query and name it *ClientBilling*.

i. Close the query.

16. Create a report with the query by completing the following steps:
   a. Click the ClientBilling query in the Navigation pane.
   b. Click the Create tab.
   c. Click the Report button in the Reports group.

17. Click the AutoFormat button in the Report Layout Tools Format tab and then click *Median* at the drop-down list.

Step 17

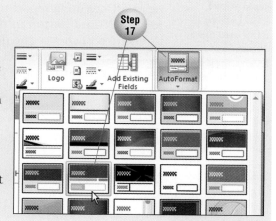

18. Click each of the column headings individually and then decrease the size of each column so the right border of the column is near the longest entry.
19. Click in the first field below the *Total* column (the field containing the data *262.5*) and then click the Apply Currency Format button in the Formatting group. If necessary, increase the column width to display all amounts.
20. Group the report by last name by completing the following steps:
    a. Click the Group & Sort button in the Grouping & Tools group.
    b. Click the Add a group button in the Group, Sort, and Total pane.
    c. Click the *LastName* field in the list box.
    d. Click the Add a sort button in the Group, Sort, and Total pane.
    e. Click the *Date* field in the list box.
    f. Close the Group, Sort, and Total pane by clicking the Close button located in the upper right corner of the pane.
21. Save the report and name it *ClientBillingReport*.
22. Print and then close the report.
23. Close the **LegalServices.accdb** database.

Step 19

---

# Project ❷ Use Wizards to Create Reports and Labels

**You will create reports using the Report Wizard and prepare mailing labels using the Label Wizard.**

---

QUICK STEPS

## Creating a Report Using the Report Wizard

**Create a Report Using Report Wizard**
1. Click Create tab.
2. Click Report Wizard button.
3. Choose desired options at each of the Report Wizard dialog boxes.

Access offers a Report Wizard that will guide you through the steps for creating a report. To create a report using the wizard, click the Create tab and then click the Report Wizard button in the Reports group. At the first wizard dialog box, shown in Figure 6.3, choose the desired table with options from the *Tables/Queries* option box. Specify the fields you want included in the report by inserting them in the *Selected Fields* list box and then clicking the Next button.

**HINT**
Use the Report Wizard to select specific fields and specify how data is grouped and sorted.

**Figure 6.3** First Report Wizard Dialog Box

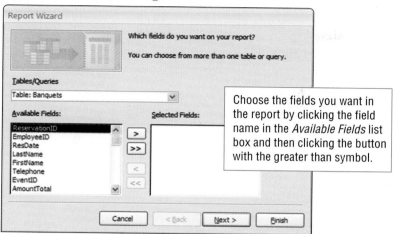

Choose the fields you want in the report by clicking the field name in the *Available Fields* list box and then clicking the button with the greater than symbol.

At the second Report Wizard dialog box, shown in Figure 6.4, you can specify the grouping level of data in the report. To group data by a specific field, click the field in the list box at the left side of the dialog box and then click the button containing the greater than symbol. Use the button containing the left-pointing arrow to remove an option as a grouping level. Use the up-pointing and down-pointing arrows to change the priority of the field.

**Figure 6.4** Second Report Wizard Dialog Box

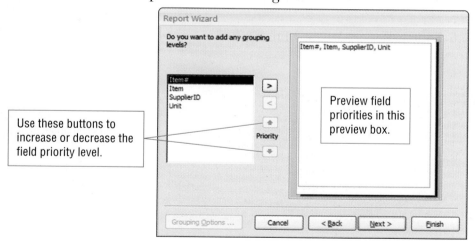

Use these buttons to increase or decrease the field priority level.

Preview field priorities in this preview box.

Specify a sort order with options at the third Report Wizard dialog box shown in Figure 6.5. To specify a sort order, click the down-pointing arrow at the right of the option box preceded by a number 1 and then click the field name. The default sort is done in ascending order. You can change this to descending by clicking the button that displays at the right side of the text box. After identifying the sort order, click the Next button.

**Figure 6.5** Third Report Wizard Dialog Box

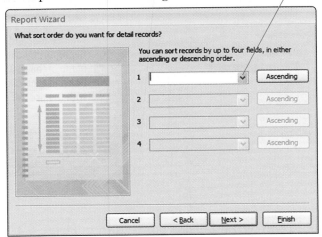

Specify a sort order by clicking this down-pointing arrow and then clicking the desired field name.

Use options at the fourth Report Wizard dialog box as shown in Figure 6.6 to specify the layout and orientation of the report. The *Layout* option has a default setting of *Stepped*. You can change this to *Block* or *Outline*. By default the report will print in *Portrait* orientation. You can change this to *Landscape* in the *Orientation* section of the dialog box. Access will adjust field widths in the report so all fields fit on one page. If you do not want Access to make the adjustment, remove the check mark from the *Adjust the field width so all fields fit on a page* option.

**Figure 6.6** Fourth Report Wizard Dialog Box

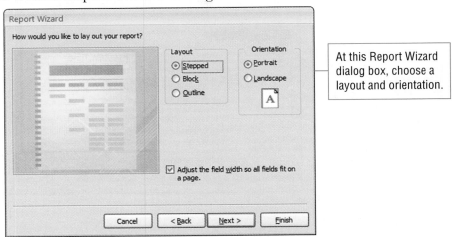

At this Report Wizard dialog box, choose a layout and orientation.

Choose an autoformat for the report at the fifth Report Wizard dialog box. By default, Access selects the autoformat that was previously applied to a report. Click the desired autoformat and then click the Next button. At the final Report Wizard dialog box, type a name for the report and then click the Finish button.

1. Display the Open dialog box with Access2007L1C6 on your storage medium the active folder.
2. Open the **Skyline.accdb** database.
3. Create a report using the Report Wizard by completing the following steps:
   a. Click the Create tab.
   b. Click the Report Wizard button in the Reports group.
   c. At the first Report Wizard dialog box, click the down-pointing arrow at the right side of the *Tables/Queries* option box and then click *Table: Inventory* at the drop-down list.
   d. Click the button containing the two greater than symbols to insert all Inventory fields in the *Selected Fields* list box.
   e. Click the Next button.

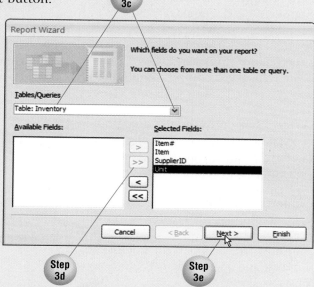

Step 3c

Step 3d

Step 3e

f. At the second Report Wizard dialog box, click the *SupplierID* field in the list box at the left side of the dialog box and then click the button containing the greater than symbol. (This tells Access that you want data in the report grouped by the supplier identification number.)

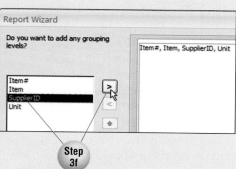

Step 3f

g. Click the Next button.
h. At the third Report Wizard dialog box, click the Next button. (You want to use the sorting defaults.)
i. At the fourth Report Wizard dialog box, click the *Block* option in the *Layout* section and then click the Next button.
j. At the fifth Report Wizard dialog box, click *Concourse* in the style list box and then click the Next button.
k. At the sixth Report Wizard dialog box, make sure *Inventory* displays in the *What title do you want for your report?* text box and then click the Finish button.
4. Change to Layout view. (If the *Field List* option box displays, close it.)
5. Decrease the column width for the *Item* and *Unit* columns so the right border of the column is just right of the longest entry.
6. Save, print, and then close the Inventory report.

If you create a report with fields from only one table, you will choose options from six Report Wizard dialog boxes. If you create a report with fields from more than one table, you will choose options from seven Report Wizard dialog boxes. After choosing the tables and fields at the first dialog box, the second dialog box that displays asks how you want to view the data. For example, if you specify fields from a Suppliers table and fields from an Orders table, the second Report Wizard dialog box will ask you if you want to view data "by Suppliers" or "by Orders."

## Project 2b  Creating a Report with Fields from Multiple Tables

1. With the **Skyline.accdb** database open, create the following one-to-many relationships:

   | Field Name | "One" Table | "Many" Table |
   | --- | --- | --- |
   | *SupplierID* | Suppliers | Orders |
   | *EmployeeID* | Employees | Banquets |
   | *EventID* | Events | Banquets |

2. Save and then close the relationships window.
3. Create a report with the Report Wizard by completing the following steps:
   a. Click the Create tab.
   b. Click the Report Wizard button in the Reports group.
   c. At the first Report Wizard dialog box, click the down-pointing arrow at the right side of the *Tables/Queries* option box and then click *Table: Events* at the drop-down list.
   d. Click the *Event* field in the *Available Fields* list box and then click the button containing the greater than (>) symbol.
   e. Click the down-pointing arrow at the right side of the *Tables/Queries* option box and then click *Table: Banquets* at the drop-down list.
   f. Insert the following fields in the *Selected Fields* list box:
      *ResDate*
      *LastName*
      *FirstName*
      *Telephone*
      *AmountTotal*
      *AmountPaid*
   g. After inserting the fields, click the Next button.
   h. At the second Report Wizard dialog box, make sure *by Events* is selected and then click the Next button.
   i. At the third Report Wizard dialog box, click the Next button. (The report preview shows that the report will be grouped by event.)

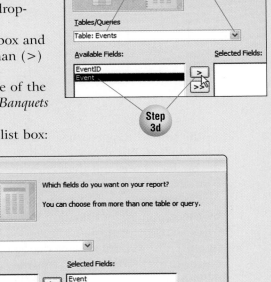

j. At the fourth Report Wizard dialog box, click the Next button. (You want to use the sorting defaults.)

k. At the fifth Report Wizard dialog box, click the *Block* option in the *Layout* section, click *Landscape* in the *Orientation* section, and then click the Next button.

l. At the sixth Report Wizard dialog box, make sure *Concourse* is selected in the style list box and then click the Next button.

m. At the seventh Report Wizard dialog box, select the current name in the *What title do you want for your report?* text box, type BanquetEvents, and then click the Finish button.

4. Change to Layout view.

5. Increase and/or decrease the size of each column to display the longest entry in each column.

6. Save, print, and then close the BanquetEvents report.

7. Close the **Skyline.accdb** database.

# Preparing Mailing Labels

**QUICK STEPS**

**Create Mailing Labels Using Label Wizard**
1. Click Create tab.
2. Click Labels button.
3. Choose desired options at each of the Label Wizard dialog boxes.

Access includes a mailing label wizard that walks you through the steps for creating mailing labels with fields in a table. To create mailing labels, click the Create tab and then click the Labels button in the Reports group. At the first Label Wizard dialog box shown in Figure 6.7, specify the label size, units of measure, and the label type, and then click the Next button.

**Figure 6.7** First Label Wizard Dialog Box

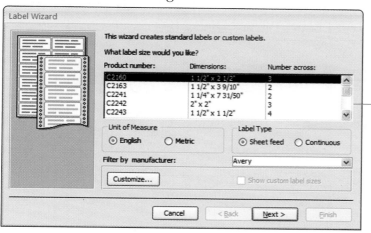

At the second Label Wizard dialog box shown in Figure 6.8, specify the font name, size, weight, and color, and then click the Next button.

**Figure 6.8** Second Label Wizard Dialog Box

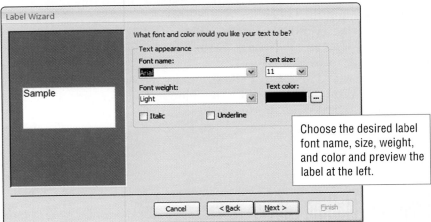

Choose the desired label font name, size, weight, and color and preview the label at the left.

Specify the fields you want included in the mailing labels at the third Label Wizard dialog box shown in Figure 6.9. To do this, click the field in the *Available fields* list box, and then click the button containing the greater than symbol (>). This moves the field to the *Prototype label* box. Insert the fields in the *Prototype label* box as you want the text to display on the label. After inserting the fields in the *Prototype label* box, click the Next button.

**Figure 6.9** Third Label Wizard Dialog Box

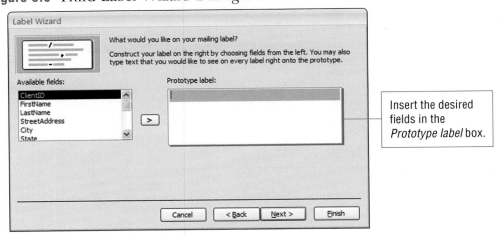

Insert the desired fields in the *Prototype label* box.

At the fourth Label Wizard dialog box, shown in Figure 6.10, you can specify a field from the database by which the labels are sorted. If you want the labels sorted (for example, by last name, postal code, etc.), insert the field by which you want the fields sorted in the *Sort by* list box and then click the Next button.

**Figure 6.10** Fourth Label Wizard Dialog Box

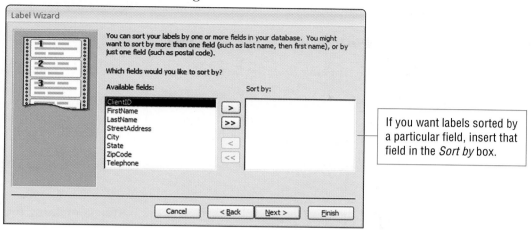

If you want labels sorted by a particular field, insert that field in the *Sort by* box.

At the last Label Wizard dialog box, type a name for the label file, and then click the Finish button. After a few moments, the labels display on the screen in Print Preview. Print the labels and/or close Print Preview.

## Project 2c  Preparing Mailing Labels

1. Open the **LegalServices.accdb** database.
2. Click the Clients table in the Navigation pane.
3. Click the Create tab and then click the Labels button in the Reports group.
4. At the first Label Wizard dialog box, make sure *English* is selected in the *Unit of Measure* section, *Avery* is selected in the *Filter by manufacturer* list box, *Sheet feed* is selected in the *Label Type* section, *C2160* is selected in the *Product number* list box, and then click the Next button.

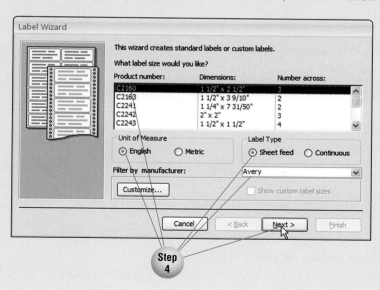

Step 4

5. At the second Label Wizard dialog box, if necessary, change the font size to 11, and then click the Next button.
6. At the third Label Wizard dialog box, complete the following steps to insert the fields in the *Prototype label* box:
   a. Click *FirstName* in the *Available fields* list box and then click the button containing the greater than symbol (>).
   b. Press the spacebar, make sure *LastName* is selected in the *Available fields* list box, and then click the button containing the greater than symbol (>).
   c. Press the Enter key (this moves the insertion point down to the next line in the *Prototype label* box).
   d. With *StreetAddress* selected in the *Available fields* list box, click the button containing the greater than symbol (>).
   e. Press the Enter key.
   f. With *City* selected in the *Available fields* list box, click the button containing the greater than symbol (>).
   g. Type a comma (,) and then press the spacebar.
   h. With *State* selected in the *Available fields* list box, click the button containing the greater than symbol (>).
   i. Press the spacebar.
   j. With *ZipCode* selected in the *Available fields* list box, click the button containing the greater than symbol (>).

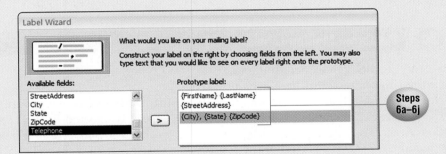

Steps
6a–6j

   k. Click the Next button.
7. At the fourth Label Wizard dialog box, sort by ZIP code. To do this, click *ZipCode* in the *Available fields* list box and then click the button containing the greater than symbol (>).
8. Click the Next button.
9. At the last Label Wizard dialog box, click the Finish button. (The Label Wizard automatically names the label report *Labels Clients*.)
10. Print the labels by clicking the Quick Print button on the Quick Access toolbar.
11. Close the labels report and then close the **LegalServices.accdb** database.

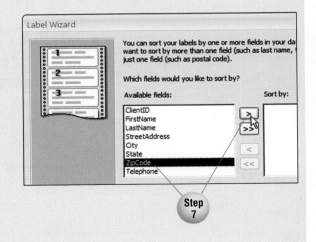

Step
7

# CHAPTER summary

- You can create a report with data in a table or query to control how data appears on the page when printed.
- Create a report with the Report button in the Reports group in the Create tab.
- Four views are available for viewing a report—Report view, Print Preview, Layout view, and Design view.
- Use options in the Print Preview tab to specify how a report prints.
- In Layout view, you can select a report control object and then size or move the object. You can also change column width by clicking a column heading and then dragging the border to the desired width.
- Sort data in a record using the Ascending or Descending buttons in the Sort & Filter group in the Home tab.
- Customize a report with options in the Report Layout Tools Format tab.
- Apply font formatting to a report with options in the Font group in the Report Layout Tools Format tab.
- Apply conditional formatting to a report with options at the Conditional Formatting dialog box. Display this dialog box by clicking the Conditional button in the Font group in the Report Layout Tools Format tab.
- Use the Totals button in the Grouping & Totals group in the Report Layout Tools Format tab to perform functions such as finding the sum, average, maximum, or minimum of the numbers in a column.
- Apply formatting to numbers with options in the Formatting group in the Report Layout Tools Format tab and apply gridline formatting with options in the Gridlines group.
- Use options in the Controls group in the Report Layout Tools Format tab to insert a logo, title, or the date and time. Click the Add Existing Fields button in the Controls group to display the Field List window.
- Click the AutoFormat button in the Report Layout Tools Format tab to display a list of autoformats.
- Use options in the Report Layout Tools Page Setup tab to change the page setup for a report.
- To make data in a report easier to understand, divide the data into groups using the Group, Sort, and Total pane. Display this pane by clicking the Group & Sort button in the Grouping & Totals group in the Report Layout Tools Format tab.
- Use the Report Wizard to guide you through the steps for creating a report. Begin the wizard by clicking the Create tab and then clicking the Report Wizard button in the Reports group.
- Create mailing labels with data in a table using the Label Wizard. Begin the wizard by clicking the Create tab and then clicking the Labels button in the Reports group.

# COMMANDS review

| FEATURE | RIBBON TAB, GROUP | BUTTON, OPTION |
|---|---|---|
| Report | Create, Reports | |
| Conditional Formatting dialog box | Report Layout Tools Format, Font | |
| Field List window | Report Layout Tools Format, Controls | |
| Group, Sort, and Total pane | Report Layout Tools Format, Grouping & Totals | |
| Report Wizard | Create, Reports | Report Wizard |
| Labels Wizard | Create, Reports | Labels |

# CONCEPTS check

## Test Your Knowledge

**Completion:** In the space provided at the right, indicate the correct term, symbol, or command.

1. Create a report with the Report button in the Create tab and the report displays in the work area in this view. _____

2. Layout view is one of four views available in a report including Report view, Design view, and this. _____

3. Press these keys to select all control objects in a report in Layout view. _____

4. The Ascending button is located in this group in the Home tab. _____

5. Click the Conditional button in the Font group in the Report Layout Tools Format tab and this dialog box displays. _____

6. Click this button in the Grouping & Totals group in the Report Layout Tools Format tab to perform functions such as finding the sum, average, maximum, or minimum of the numbers in a column. _____

7. Click the Add Existing Fields button in the Controls group in the Report Layout Tools Format tab and this displays. _____

8. The Group & Sort button is located in this group in the Report Layout Tools Format tab.

   _____

9. Click the Group & Sort button and this pane displays.

   _____

10. Use this to guide you through the steps for creating a report.

   _____

# SKILLS check
## Demonstrate Your Proficiency

### Assessment

## 1 CREATE AND FORMAT REPORTS IN THE HILLTOP DATABASE

1. Open the **Hilltop.accdb** database.
2. Create a report with the Inventory table.
3. With the report in Layout view, apply the following formatting:
   a. Center the data below each of the following column headings: *Equipment#*, *AvailableHours*, *ServiceHours*, and *RepairHours*.
   b. Select all of the control objects and then change the font to Constantia.
   c. Select the date control object and then move the object so the right side aligns with the right side of the *RepairHours* column.
   d. Select the time control object and then move the object so the right side aligns with the right side of the date.
   e. Select the money amounts below the *PurchasePrice* column heading and then decrease the decimal so the money amounts display without a decimal point.
   f. Click in the $473,260.00 amount and then decrease the decimal so the amount displays without a decimal.
   g. Apply horizontal gridlines to the column headings and the data below each column heading (except the amount *$473,260*).
   h. Change the title of the report to *Inventory Report*.
4. Save the report and name it *Inventory Report*.
5. Print and then close Inventory Report.
6. Create a query in Design view with the following specifications:
   a. Add the Customers, Equipment, Invoices, and Rates tables to the query window.
   b. Insert the *Customer* field from the Customers table in the first *Field* text box.
   c. Insert the *Equipment* field from the Equipment table in the second *Field* text box.
   d. Insert the *Hours* field from the Invoices table in the third *Field* text box.
   e. Insert the *Rate* field from the Rates table in the fourth *Field* text box.
   f. Click in the fifth *Field* text box, type Total: [Hours]*[Rate], and then press Enter.
   g. Run the query.
   h. Save the query and name it *CustomerRentals* and then close the query.
7. Create a report with the CustomerRentals query using the Report button.

8. With the report in Layout view, apply the following formatting:
   a. Decrease the width of columns so the right border of each column displays near the right side of the longest entry.
   b. Select the money amounts and then decrease the decimal so the amounts display with no decimal point.
   c. Click in the 8305 amount (located at the bottom of the Total column), click the Apply Currency Format button, and then decrease the decimal so the amount displays without a decimal point.
   d. Display the Group, Sort, and Total pane, group the records by *Customer*, sort by *Equipment*, and then close the pane.
   e. Apply the Apex autoformat.
   f. Select the date control object and the time control object, change the font color to black, and then drag the objects to the left so the right border of the objects aligns with the right side of the *Total* column.
   g. Select the five column headings and then change the font color to white and turn on bold.
   h. Change the title to *Rentals*.
   i. Make sure the margins are set to *Narrow*.
   j. Display the report in Print Preview and make sure the data will print on one page, and then change to Layout view.
9. Save the report and name it *Rental Report*.
10. Print and then close Rental Report.

## Assessment

## 2 CREATE REPORTS USING THE REPORT WIZARD

1. With the **Hilltop.accdb** database open, create a report using the Report Wizard with the following specifications:
   a. At the first Report Wizard dialog box, insert the following fields in the *Selected Fields* list box:

      From the Equipment table:
         *Equipment*
      From the Inventory table:
         *Purchase Date*
         *Purchase Price*
         *Available Hours*

   b. Do not make any changes at the second Report Wizard dialog box.
   c. Do not make any changes at the third Report Wizard dialog box.
   d. At the fourth Report Wizard dialog box, choose the *Columnar* option.
   e. At the fifth Report Wizard dialog box, make sure the Apex autoformat is selected.
   f. At the last Report Wizard dialog box, click the Finish button. (This accepts the default report name of *Equipment*.)
2. Print and then close the report.
3. Create a report using the Report Wizard with the following specifications:
   a. At the first Report Wizard dialog box, insert the following fields in the *Selected Fields* list box:

      From the Customers table:
         *Customer*

From the Invoices table:
> *BillingDate*
> *Hours*

From the Equipment table:
> *Equipment*

From the Rates table:
> *Rate*

   b. Do not make any changes at the second Report Wizard dialog box.
   c. Do not make any changes at the third Report Wizard dialog box.
   d. Do not make any changes at the fourth Report Wizard dialog box.
   e. At the fifth Report Wizard dialog box, choose the *Block* option.
   f. At the sixth Report Wizard dialog box, make sure the Apex autoformat is selected.
   g. At the last Report Wizard dialog box, name the report *Rentals*.

4. Increase or decrease column widths to display column data.
5. Print and then close the report.

## Assessment

## 3   CREATE MAILING LABELS

1. With the **Hilltop.accdb** database open, click the Customers table in the Navigation pane.
2. Use the Label Wizard to create mailing labels (you determine the label type) with the customer names and addresses and sorted by customer names. Name the mailing label report *Customer Mailing Labels*.
3. Print the mailing labels.
4. Close the mailing labels.

## Assessment

## 4   ADD A FIELD TO A REPORT

1. In Chapter 5, you added a field list to an existing form using the Field List window. Experiment with adding a field to an existing report and then complete the following:
   a. Open the report named Rental Report (created in Assessment 1) in Layout view.
   b. Display the Field List window and display all tables.
   c. Drag the *BillingDate* field from the Invoices table so the field is positioned between the *Equipment* column and the *Hours* column.
   d. At the message indicating that Access will modify the RecordSource property and asking if you want to continue, click Yes.
2. Decrease the widths of the columns to ensure that all columns will fit on one page.
3. Save, print, and then close the report.
4. Close the **Hilltop.accdb** database.

# CASE study

## Apply Your Skills

**Part 1**

As the office manager at Millstone Legal Services, you need to enter records for three new clients in the **MillstoneLegal.accdb** database. Using the following information, enter the data in the appropriate tables:

Client number 42
Martin Costanzo
1002 Thomas Drive
Casper, WY 82602
(307) 555-5001
Mr. Costanzo saw Douglas Sheehan regarding divorce proceedings on 3/14/2010 with a fee of $150.

Client number 43
Susan Nordyke
23193 Ridge Circle East
Mills, WY 82644
(307) 555-2719
Ms. Nordyke saw Loretta Ryder regarding support enforcement on 3/14/2010 with a fee of $75.

Client number 44
Monica Sommers
1105 Riddell Avenue
Casper, WY 82609
(307) 555-1188
Ms. Sommers saw Anita Leland regarding a guardianship on 3/15/2010 for a fee of $150.

**Part 2**

Create the following queries, reports, and labels:

- Create a report with the Clients table. Apply formatting to enhance the visual appeal of the report.
- Create a query that displays the client ID, first name, and last name; attorney last name; date of visit; and fee. Name the query *ClientBilling*.
- Create a report with the ClientBilling query. Group the records in the report by attorney last name (the second *LastName* field in the drop-down list) and sort alphabetically in ascending order by client last name (the first *LastName* field in the drop-down list). Apply formatting to enhance the visual appeal of the report.
- Create a telephone directory by creating a report that includes client last names, first names, and telephone numbers. Sort the records in the report alphabetically by last name and in ascending order.
- Edit the ClientBilling query so it includes a criterion that displays only visits between 3/01/2010 and 3/05/2010. Save the query with Save As and name it *ClientBilling01-05*.
- Create a report with the ClientBilling01-05 query. Apply formatting to enhance the visual appeal of the report.
- Create mailing labels for the clients.

**Part 3**

Apply the following conditions to fields in reports:

- In the Clients report, apply the condition that the city *Casper* displays in red and the city *Mills* displays in blue in the *City* field.
- In the ClientBilling report, apply the condition that amounts over $99 display in green and amounts less than $100 display in blue.

**Part 4**

Your center has a procedures manual that describes processes and procedures in the center. Open Word and then create a document for the procedures manual that describes the process for creating a report using the Report button, the Report Wizard, and the process for preparing mailing labels using the Label Wizard. Save the completed document and name it **Access_C6_CS_P4**. Print and then close **Access_C6_CS_P4.docx**.

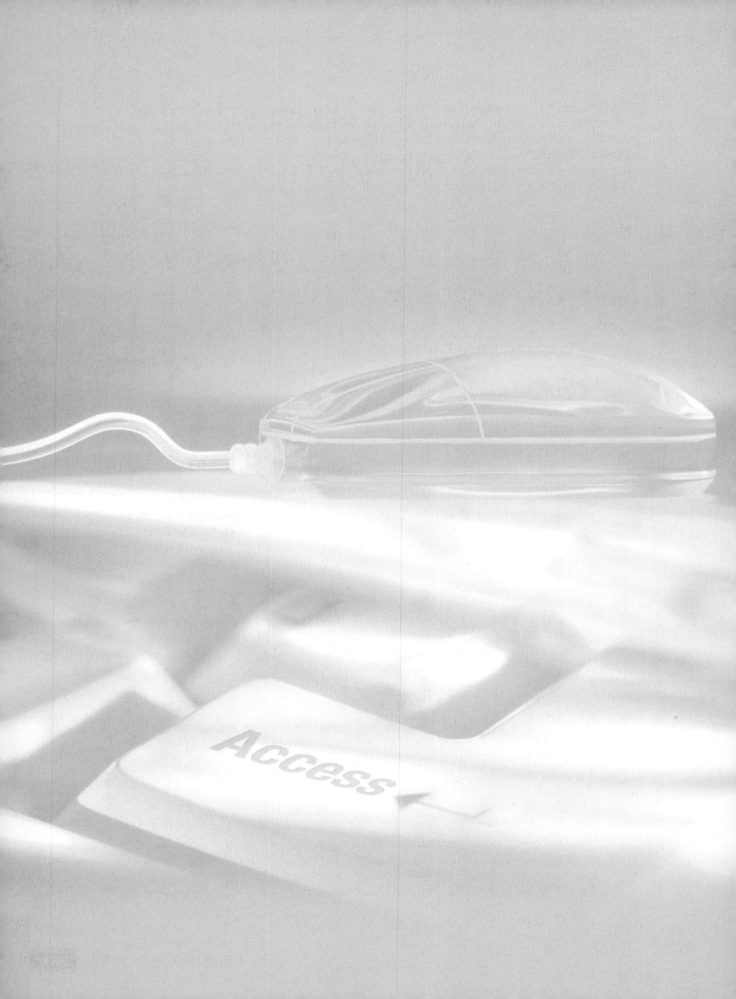

# Modifying, Filtering, and Viewing Data

## PERFORMANCE OBJECTIVES

**Upon successful completion of Chapter 7, you will be able to:**

- **Filter data by selection and by form**
- **Remove a filter**
- **Summarize and analyze data in PivotTable view**
- **Summarize and analyze data in a PivotTable form**
- **Summarize and analyze data in PivotChart view**
- **View and customize document properties**
- **View object dependencies**

access Chapter 7

SNAP

**Tutorial 7.1**
Modifying and Viewing Data

You can filter data in a database object to view specific records without having to change the design of the object. In this chapter, you will learn how to filter data, filter by selection, and filter by form. You will also learn how to summarize and analyze data in an object in PivotTable and PivotChart view and view document properties and object dependencies.

*Note: Before beginning computer projects, copy to your storage medium the Access2007L1C7 subfolder from the Access2007L1 folder on the CD that accompanies this textbook and make Access2007L1C7 the active folder.*

## Project 1 Filter Records

You will filter records in a table, query, and report in the Skyline database using the Filter button, Selection button, Toggle Filter button, and shortcut menu. You will also remove filters and filter by form.

## Filtering Data

You can place a set of restrictions, called a *filter*, on records in a table, query, form, or report to isolate temporarily specific records. A filter, like a query, lets you view specific records without having to change the design of the table, query, form, or report. Access provides a number of buttons and options for filtering data. You can filter data using the Filter button in the Sort & Filter group in the Home tab, right-click specific data in a record and then specify a filter, and use the Selection and Advanced buttons in the Sort & Filter group.

**Filter Records**
1. Open desired object.
2. Click in entry of desired field column to filter.
3. Click Filter button.
4. Select desired sorting option at drop-down list.

## Filtering Using the Filter Button

You can use the Filter button in the Sort & Filter group in the Home tab to filter records in an object (table, query, form or report). To use this button, open the desired object, click in any entry in the field column on which you want to filter and then click the Filter button. This displays a drop-down list with sorting options and a listing of all of the field entries. Figure 7.1 displays the drop-down list that displays when you click in the *City* field and then click the Filter button. To sort on a specific criterion, click the *(Select All)* check box to move all check marks from the list of field entries. Click the item in the list box on which you want to sort and then click OK.

**Figure 7.1** City Field Drop-down List

To filter on the *City* field, click in any entry in the field column and then click the Filter button. This displays a drop-down list with sorting options and a listing of all field entries.

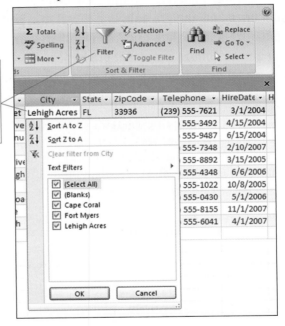

**HINT**

Filters available depend on the type of data selected in a column.

When you open a table, query, or form, the Record navigation bar contains the dimmed words *No Filter* preceded by a filter icon with a delete symbol (an X). If you filter records in one of these objects, *Filtered* displays in place of *No Filter*, the delete symbol is removed, and the text and filter icon display with an orange background. In a report, the word *Filtered* displays at the right side of the Status bar if you apply a filter to records.

# Removing a Filter

When you filter data, the underlying data in the object is not deleted. You can switch back and forth between the data and the filtered data by clicking the Toggle Filter button in the Sort & Filter group in the Home tab. If you click the Toggle Filter button and turn off the filter, all of the data in a table, query, or form displays and the message *Filtered* in the Record navigation bar changes to *Unfiltered*.

Clicking the Toggle Filter button may redisplay all data in an object but it does not remove the filter. To remove the filter, click in the field column containing the filter and then click the Filter button in the Sort & Filter group in the Home tab. At the drop-down list that displays, click the *Clear filter from xxx* (where *xxx* is the name of the field). You can remove all filters from an object by clicking the Advanced button in the Sort & Filter group and then clicking the *Clear All Filters* option.

**QUICK STEPS**

**Remove a Filter**
1. Click in field column containing filter.
2. Click Filter button.
3. Click *Clear filter from xxx*.
OR
1. Click Advanced button.
2. Click *Clear All Filters* at drop-down list.

Toggle Filter

Advanced ▾

## Project 1a   Filtering Records in a Table, Form, and Report

1. Display the Open dialog box with Access2007L1C7 on your storage medium the active folder.
2. Open the **Skyline.accdb** database.
3. Filter records in the Employees table by completing the following steps:
   a. Open the Employees table.
   b. Click in any entry in the *City* field.
   c. Click the Filter button in the Sort & Filter group in the Home tab. (This displays a drop-down list in the *City* field.)
   d. Click the *(Select All)* check box in the filter drop-down list box. (This removes all check marks from the list options.)
   e. Click the *Fort Myers* check box in the list box. (This inserts a check mark in the check box.)

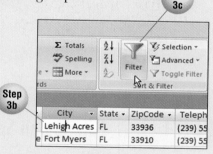

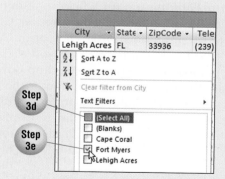

   f. Click OK. (Access displays only those records with a city field of *Fort Myers* and also displays *Filtered* and the filter icon with an orange background in the Record navigation bar.)
   g. Click the Quick Print button on the Quick Access toolbar.
4. Toggle the display of filtered data by clicking the Toggle Filter button in the Sort & Filter group in the Home tab. (This redisplays all data in the table.)

5. Remove the filter by completing the following steps:
   a. Click in any entry in the *City* field.
   b. Click the Filter button in the Sort & Filter group.
   c. Click the *Clear filter from City* option at the drop-down list. (Notice that the message on the Record navigation bar changes to *No Filter* and dims the words.)
6. Save and then close the Employees table.
7. Create a form by completing the following steps:
   a. Click the Orders table in the Navigation pane.
   b. Click the Create tab and then click the Form button in the Forms group.
   c. Click the Form View button in the view area at the right side of the Status bar.
   d. Save the form and name it Orders.
8. Filter the records and display only those records with a supplier identification number of 2 by completing the following steps:
   a. Click in the *SupplierID* field containing the text *2*.
   b. Click the Filter button in the Sort & Filter group.
   c. At the filter drop-down list, click *(Select All)* to remove all of the check marks from the list options.
   d. Click the *2* option to insert a check mark.
   e. Click OK.
   f. Navigate through the records and notice that only the records with a supplier identification number of 2 display.
   g. Close the Orders form.

Step 5b

Step 5c

**HINT**

Hover the mouse over a column heading to display a tip showing the filter criterion.

## Filtering on Specific Values

When you filter on a specific field, you can display a list of unique values for that field. If you click the Filter button for a field containing text, the drop-down list for the specific field will contain a *Text Filters* option. Click this option and a values list displays next to the drop-down list. The options in the values list will vary depending on the type of data in the field. If you click the Filter button for a field containing number values, the option in the drop-down list displays as *Number Filters* and if you are filtering dates, the option at the drop-down list displays as *Date Filters*. Use options in the values list to refine further a filter for a specific field. For example, you can use the values list to display money amounts within a specific range or order dates between certain dates. You can use the values list to find fields that are "equal to" or "not equal to" text in the current field.

1. With the **Skyline.accdb** database open, create the following one-to-many relationships:

   | Field Name | "One" Table | "Many" Table |
   |---|---|---|
   | *EmployeeID* | Employees | Banquets |
   | *Item#* | Inventory | Orders |
   | *SupplierID* | Suppliers | Orders |
   | *EventID* | Events | Banquets |

2. Create a query in Design view with the following specifications:
   a. Add the Banquets and Events tables to the query window.
   b. Insert the *ResDate* field from the Banquets table to the first *Field* text box.
   c. Insert the *LastName* field from the Banquets table to the second *Field* text box.
   d. Insert the *FirstName* field from the Banquets table to the third *Field* text box.
   e. Insert the *Telephone* field from the Banquets table to the fourth *Field* text box.
   f. Insert the *Event* field from the Events table to the fifth *Field* text box.
   g. Insert the *EmployeeID* field from the Banquets table to the sixth *Field* text box.
   h. Run the query.
   i. Save the query and name it *BanquetReservations*.

3. Filter records of reservations before July 15, 2010, in the query by completing the following steps:
   a. With the BanquetReservations query open, make sure the first entry is selected in the *ResDate* field.
   b. Click the Filter button in the Sort & Filter group in the Home tab.
   c. Point to the *Date Filters* option in the drop-down list box.
   d. Click *Before* in the values list.

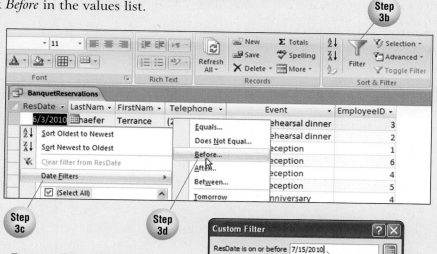

   e. At the Custom Filter dialog box, type 7/15/2010 and then click OK.
   f. Print the filtered query by clicking the Quick Print button on the Quick Access toolbar.

4. Remove the filter by clicking the filter icon that displays at the right side of the *ResDate* column heading and then clicking *Clear filter from ResDate* at the drop-down list.

5. Save and then close the BanquetReservations query.

6. Create a report by completing the following steps:
   a. Click the BanquetReservations query in the Navigation pane.
   b. Click the Create tab and then click the Report button in the Reports group.
   c. With the report in Layout view, decrease the column widths so the right column border displays near the longest entry in each column.
   d. Click the Report View button in the view area at the right side of the Status bar.
   e. Save the report and name it *BanquetReport*.
7. Filter the records and display all records of events except *Other* events by completing the following steps:
   a. Click in the first entry in the *Event* field.
   b. Click the Filter button in the Sort & Filter group.
   c. Point to the *Text Filters* option in the drop-down list box and then click *Does Not Equal* at the values list.

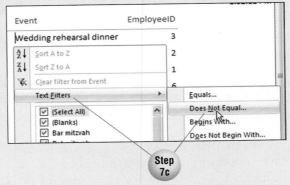

**Step 7c**

   d. At the Custom Filter dialog box, type **Other** and then click OK.
8. Further refine the filter by completing the following steps:
   a. Click in the first entry in the *EmployeeID* field.
   b. Click the Filter button.
   c. At the filter drop-down list, click the *(Select All)* check box to remove all of the check marks from the list options.
   d. Click the *3* check box to insert a check mark.
   e. Click OK.
9. Click the Quick Print button on the Quick Access toolbar.
10. Save and then close the BanquetReport report.

# Filtering by Selection

If you click in a field in an object and then click the Selection button in the Sort & Filter group in the Home tab, a drop-down list displays below the button with options for filtering on the data in the field. For example, if you click in a field containing the city name *Fort Myers*, clicking the Selection button will cause a drop-down list to display as shown in Figure 7.2. Click one of the options at the drop-down list to filter records. You can select specific text in a field entry and then filter based on the specific text. For example, in Project 1c you will select the word *peppers* in the entry *Green peppers* and then filter records containing the word *peppers*.

**Figure 7.2** Selection Button Drop-down List

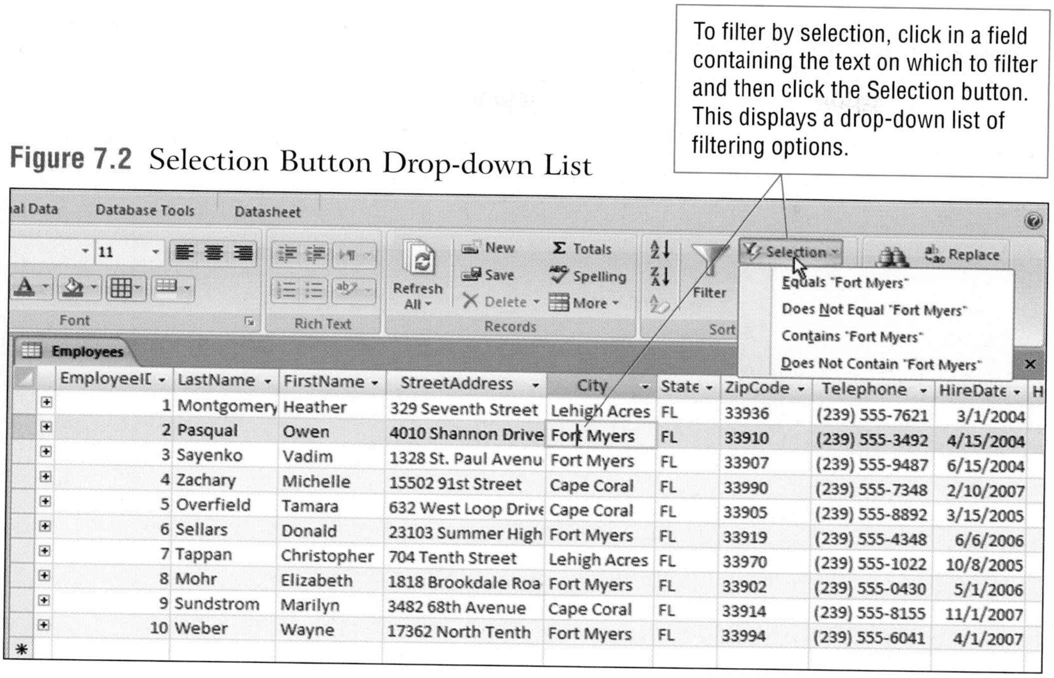

> To filter by selection, click in a field containing the text on which to filter and then click the Selection button. This displays a drop-down list of filtering options.

## Filtering by Shortcut Menu

If you right-click on a field entry, a shortcut menu displays with options to sort the text, display a values list, or filter on a specific value. For example, if you right-click the field entry *Schaefer* in the *LastName* field, a shortcut menu displays as shown in Figure 7.3. Click a sort option to sort text in the field in ascending or descending order, point to the *Text Filters* option to display a values list, or click one of the values filters located toward the bottom of the menu. You can also select specific text within a field entry and then right-click the selection to display the shortcut menu.

**Figure 7.3** Filtering Shortcut Menu

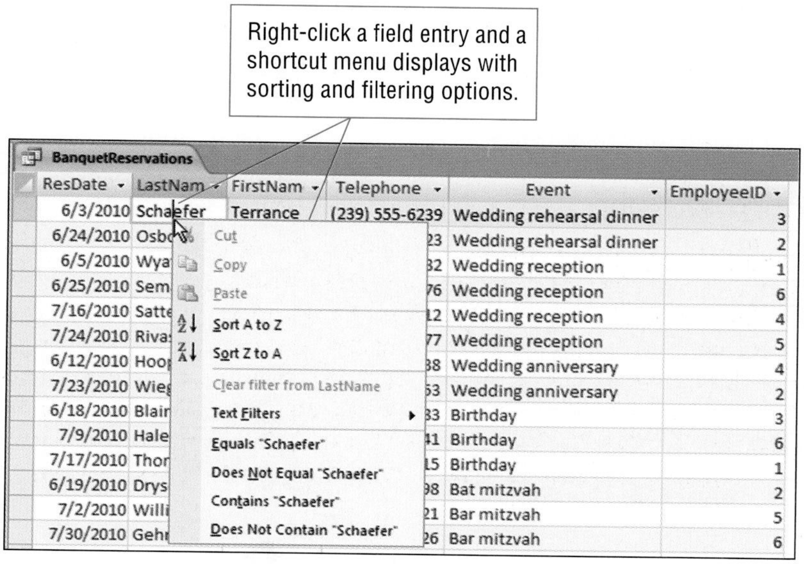

> Right-click a field entry and a shortcut menu displays with sorting and filtering options.

1. Open the Inventory table.
2. Filter only those records with a supplier number of 6 by completing the following steps:
   a. Click in the first entry containing *6* in the *SupplierID* field.
   b. Click the Selection button and then click *Equals "6"* at the drop-down list.
   c. Click the Quick Print button on the Quick Access toolbar.
   d. Click the Toggle Filter button in the Sort & Filter group.

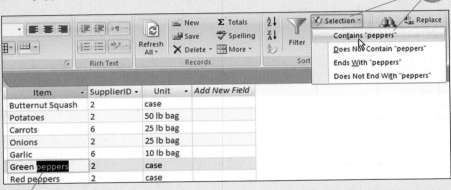

3. Filter any records in the *Item* field containing the word "pepper" by completing the following steps:
   a. Click in the entry in the *Item* field containing the entry *Green peppers*.
   b. Using the mouse, select the word *peppers*.
   c. Click the Selection button and then click *Contains "peppers"* at the drop-down list.

   d. Click the Quick Print button on the Quick Access toolbar.
4. Close the Inventory table without saving the changes.
5. Open the BanquetReservations query.
6. Filter records in the *Event* field except *Wedding reception* by completing the following steps:
   a. Right-click in the first *Wedding reception* entry in the *Event* field.
   b. Click *Does Not Equal "Wedding reception"* at the shortcut menu.
   c. Click the Quick Print button on the Quick Access toolbar.
   d. Click the Toggle Filter button in the Sort & Filter group.

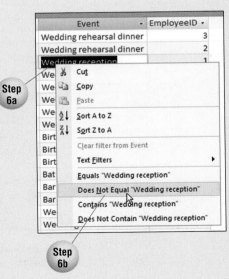

7. Filter any records in the *Event* field containing the word *mitzvah* by completing the following steps:
   a. Click in the entry in the *Event* field containing the entry *Bar mitzvah*.
   b. Using the mouse, select the word *mitzvah*.
   c. Right-click on the selected word and then click *Contains "mitzvah"* at the shortcut menu.
   d. Click the Quick Print button on the Quick Access toolbar.
8. Close the BanquetReservations query without saving the changes.

# Using Filter By Form

QUICK STEPS

**Use Filter By Form**
1. Click Advanced button.
2. Click *Filter By Form* at drop-down list.
3. Click in empty field below desired column to filter.
4. Click down-pointing arrow.
5. Click on item to filter.

One of the options from the Advanced button drop-down list is *Filter By Form*. Click this option and a blank record displays in a Filter by Form window in the work area. In the Filter by Form window, the *Look for* and *Or* tabs display toward the bottom of the form. The *Look for* tab is active by default and tells Access to look for whatever data you insert in a field. Click in the empty field below the desired column and a down-pointing arrow displays at the right side of the field. Click the down-pointing arrow and then click the item on which you want to filter. Click the Toggle Filter button to display the desired records. Add an additional value to a filter by clicking the *Or* tab at the bottom of the form.

## Project 1d Using Filter By Form to Display Specific Records

1. With the **Skyline.accdb** database open, open the Banquets table.
2. Filter records for a specific employee identification number by completing the following steps:
   a. Click the Advanced button in the Sort & Filter group in the Home tab and then click *Filter By Form* at the drop-down list.
   b. At the Filter by Form window, click in the blank record below the *EmployeeID* field.
   c. Click the down-pointing arrow at the right side of the field and then click *3* at the drop-down list.
   d. Click the Toggle Filter button in the Sort & Filter group.
3. Print the filtered table by completing the following steps:
   a. Click the Office button, point to *Print*, and then click *Print Preview* at the side menu.
   b. Click the Landscape button in the Page Layout group.
   c. Click the Print button and then click OK at the Print dialog box.
   d. Click the Close Print Preview button.
4. Close the Banquets table without saving the changes.
5. Open the Inventory table.
6. Filter records for supplier numbers 2 or 7 by completing the following steps:
   a. Click the Advanced button in the Sort & Filter group in the Home tab and then click *Filter By Form* at the drop-down list.

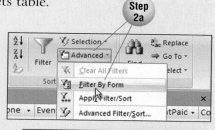

Step 2a

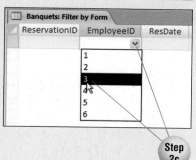

Step 2c

    b. At the Filter by Form window, click in the blank record below the *SupplierID* field.

    c. Click the down-pointing arrow at the right side of the field and then click *2* at the drop-down list.

    d. Click the *Or* tab located toward the bottom of the form.

    e. If necessary, click in the blank record below the *SupplierID* field.

    f. Click the down-pointing arrow at the right side of the field and then click *7* at the drop-down list.

    g. Click the Toggle Filter button in the Sort & Filter group.

    h. Click the Quick Print button on the Quick Print toolbar.

    i. Click the Toggle Filter button to redisplay all records in the table.

    j. Click the Advanced button and then click *Clear All Filters* from the drop-down list.

7. Close the Inventory table without saving the changes.
8. Close the **Skyline.accdb** database.

# Project 2  Summarize and Analyze Data in PivotTable and PivotChart Views

You will view and analyze data in the OutdoorOptions database in PivotTable view and create a PivotTable form. You will also save an object as a different object and with a new name and view and analyze data in PivotChart view.

**Display PivotTable View**
1. Open table or query.
2. Click PivotTable View button in view area at right side of Status bar.
OR
1. Open table or query.
2. Click View button arrow.
3. Click PivotTable View at drop-down list.

PivotTable View

# Summarizing Data by Changing Views

Access provides additional views in a table and query that you can use to summarize data. Change to the PivotTable view to create a PivotTable, which is an interactive table that organizes and summarizes data. Use the PivotChart view to create a PivotChart that summarizes data in a graph.

## Summarizing Data Using PivotTable View

A PivotTable is an interactive table that organizes and summarizes data based on the fields you designate for row headings, column headings, and source record filtering. In PivotTable view, you can easily add aggregate functions to the table such as sum, avg, and count. A PivotTable provides more options for viewing data than a Crosstab query because you can easily change the results by filtering data by an item in a row, a column, or for all source records. This interactivity allows you to analyze the data for numerous scenarios.

    To create a PivotTable, open a table or query in Datasheet view and then click the PivotTable View button in the view area at the right side of the Status bar. You can also display a table or query in PivotTable view by clicking the View button arrow in the Views group in the Home tab and then clicking *PivotTable View* at the drop-down list. This displays the datasheet in PivotTable layout with four sections along with a *PivotTable Field List* box as shown in Figure 7.4. Dimmed text in each section describes the types of fields you should drag and drop.

**Figure 7.4** PivotTable Layout

Drag the desired item from this list box and drop it in the appropriate location.

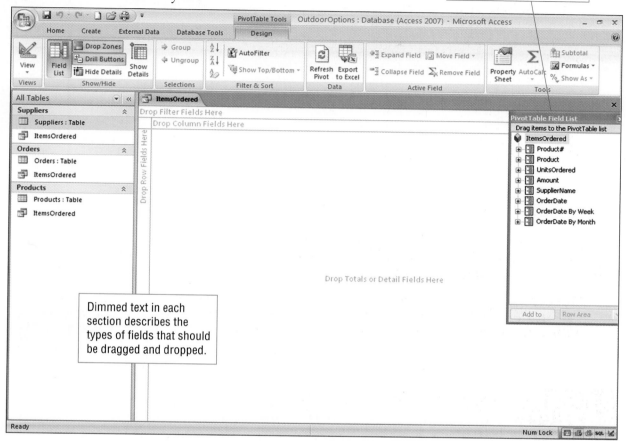

Dimmed text in each section describes the types of fields that should be dragged and dropped.

Drag the fields from the *PivotTable Field List* box to the desired locations in the PivotTable layout. The dimmed text in the PivotTable layout identifies the field you should drop in the location. In Project 2a, you will drag the *SupplierName* field to the Row field section, the *Product* field to the Column field section, the *Amount* field to the Totals or Details field section, and the *OrderDate* to the Filter section. The PivotTable will then display as shown in Figure 7.5.

**Figure 7.5** PivotTable for Project 2a

| ItemsOrdered | | | | | | | ✕ |
|---|---|---|---|---|---|---|---|
| OrderDate ▼ | | | | | | | |
| All | | | | | | | |
| | **Product ▼** | | | | | | |
| | Backpack | Ski goggles | Snowboard | Two-person tent | Wool ski hats | Grand Total | |
| | + − | + − | + − | + − | + − | + − | |
| SupplierName ▼ | Amount ▼ | Amount ▼ | Amount ▼ | Amount ▼ | Amount ▼ | No Totals | |
| Freedom Corporation | | $1,100.00 | | | $687.50 | | |
| KL Distributions | $1,906.25 | | | ▶ $1,137.50 | | | |
| Rosewood, Inc. | | | $2,800.00 | | | | |
| Grand Total | | | | | | | |

1. Display the Open dialog box with Access2007L1C7 on your storage medium the active folder.
2. Open the **OutdoorOptions.accdb** database.
3. Create a new query in Design view with the following specifications:
   a. Add the Orders, Products, and Suppliers tables to the design grid.
   b. Add the following fields from the specified tables:

   | | | |
   |---|---|---|
   | *Product#* | = | Orders table |
   | *Product* | = | Products table |
   | *UnitsOrdered* | = | Orders table |
   | *Amount* | = | Orders table |
   | *SupplierName* | = | Suppliers table |
   | *OrderDate* | = | Orders table |

   Step 3b

   | Field: | Product# | Product | UnitsOrdered | Amount | SupplierName | OrderDate | ☑ |
   |---|---|---|---|---|---|---|---|
   | Table: | Orders | Products | Orders | Orders | Suppliers | Orders | |
   | Sort: | | | | | | | |
   | Show: | ☑ | ☑ | ☑ | ☑ | ☑ | ☑ | |
   | Criteria: | | | | | | | |
   | or: | | | | | | | |

   c. Run the query.
   d. Save the query and name it *ItemsOrdered*.
4. Click the PivotTable View button in the view area at the right side of the Status bar.

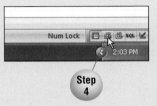

Step 4

5. At the PivotTable layout, drag and drop the *SupplierName* field to the Row field section by completing the following steps:
   a. Position the mouse pointer on the *SupplierName* field in the *PivotTable Field List* box.
   b. Hold down the left mouse button, drag to the dimmed text *Drop Row Fields Here* located at the left side of the query window, and then release the mouse button.

Step 5b

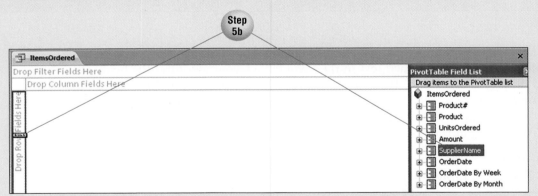

6. Complete steps similar to those in Step 5 to drag and drop the following fields:
   a. Drag the *Product* field from the *PivotTable Field List* box and drop it on the dimmed text *Drop Column Fields Here*.
   b. Drag the *Amount* field from the *PivotTable Field List* box and drop it on the dimmed text *Drop Totals or Detail Fields Here*.
   c. Drag the *OrderDate* field from the *PivotTable Field List* box and drop it on the dimmed text *Drop Filter Fields Here*.

7. Remove the *PivotTable Field List* box from the screen by clicking the Field List button in the Show/Hide group in the PivotTable Tools Design tab. (Your PivotTable should look like the one shown in Figure 7.5.)
8. Click the Quick Print button on the Quick Access toolbar to print the query in PivotTable view.
9. Click the View button arrow in the Views group in the Home tab and then click *Datasheet View* at the drop-down list.
10. Save and then close the query.

When you create a PivotTable in a query or table, it becomes a part of and is saved with the table or query. The next time you open the table or query, display the PivotTable by clicking the PivotTable View button in the view area on the Status bar or by clicking the View button arrow in the Views group in the Home tab and then clicking *PivotTable View* at the drop-down list. If you make changes to data in fields that are part of the table or query (and PivotTable), the data is automatically updated in the table or query.

The power of a PivotTable is the ability to analyze data for numerous scenarios. For example, in the PivotTable you created in Project 2a, you can display orders for a specific date or isolate a specific supplier. Use the plus and minus symbols that display in a row or column heading to show (plus symbol) or hide (minus symbol) data. Use the down-pointing arrow (called the **filter arrow**) that displays in a field to display specific data in the field. You can also use buttons in the PivotTable Tools Design tab to perform actions such as filtering data and performing calculations on data.

## Project 2b  Analyzing Data in PivotTable View

1. With the **OutdoorOptions.accdb** database open, open the Orders table.
2. Add the following records to the table:

| | | |
|---|---|---|
| Order# | = | (AutoNumber) |
| Supplier# | = | 68 |
| Product# | = | 558 |
| UnitsOrdered | = | 25 |
| Amount | = | $550 |
| OrderDate | = | 2/26/2010 |

| | | |
|---|---|---|
| Order# | = | (AutoNumber) |
| Supplier# | = | 70 |
| Product# | = | 897 |
| UnitsOrdered | = | 10 |
| Amount | = | $1,120 |
| OrderDate | = | 2/26/2010 |

3. Close the Orders table.
4. Double-click the ItemsOrdered query in the *Orders* list box.

5. With the query open, click the View button arrow in the Views group in the Home tab and then click *PivotTable View* at the drop-down list. (Notice the PivotTable reflects the two new order records you inserted in the Orders table.)
6. Display only items ordered on February 26 by completing the following steps:
    a. Click the filter arrow (down-pointing arrow) at the right of the *OrderDate* field (located in the upper left corner of the query window).
    b. At the drop-down list that displays, click the *(All)* check box to remove the check mark before each date.
    c. Click the check box to the left of *2/26/2010*.
    d. Click the OK button.
    e. Click the Quick Print button on the Quick Access toolbar.
    f. Redisplay all items by clicking the filter arrow at the right of the *OrderDate* field, clicking the check box to the left of *(All)*, and then clicking OK.
7. Display only those order amounts for Freedom Corporation by completing the following steps:
    a. Click the filter arrow at the right of the *SupplierName* field.
    b. At the drop-down list, click the *(All)* check box to remove the check mark before each supplier name.
    c. Click the check box to the left of *Freedom Corporation*.
    d. Click the OK button.
    e. Click the Quick Print button on the Quick Access toolbar.
    f. Redisplay all supplier names by clicking the filter arrow at the right of the *SupplierName* field, clicking the check box to the left of *(All)*, and then clicking OK.
8. Display subtotals and totals of order amounts by completing the following steps:
    a. Position the mouse pointer on any *Amount* column heading until the pointer displays with a four-headed arrow attached and then click the left mouse button. (This displays all the *Amount* column headings and amounts with a light blue background.)
    b. Click the AutoCalc button in the Tools group in the PivotTable Tools Design tab and then click *Sum* at the drop-down list. (This inserts subtotals and totals in the PivotTable.)
9. Save, print, and then close the PivotTable.

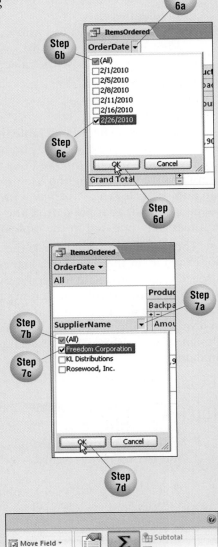

# Summarizing and Analyzing Data in a PivotTable Form

When you create a PivotTable in a query or table, the PivotTable settings are saved and become part of the table or query. When you open a table or query in which you have created a PivotTable and then switch to PivotTable view, the table or query displays with the PivotTable settings you created. If you want to view different fields or perform other functions in PivotTable view, you have to edit the last settings. For example, if you created a PivotTable in an Employees query that summed the salary field by department by year of hire, and then wanted to sum by month, you would have to edit the previous PivotTable. If you want to view data by year and month or other date, consider creating a PivotTable form. A PivotTable form is a separate object from the query or table, so you could create one showing the sum by year and another showing the sum by month.

To create a PivotTable form, click the desired object in the Navigation pane and then click the Create tab. Click the More Forms button in the Forms group and then click *PivotTable* at the drop-down list. This displays the object in PivotTable layout. Click the Field List button in the Show/Hide group to display the *PivotTable Field List* box. (You may need to click the button twice to display the list box.)

Field List

## *Saving Objects*

If you want to create an object that is similar to another object in the database, use the *Save As* option from the Office button drop-down list. For example, if you want to save a query as a form, open the query, click the Office button, and then click *Save As*. At the Save As dialog box, type a name for the new object, click the down-pointing arrow at the right side of the *As* list box, click the desired object type, and then click OK. If you want to save an open object with a new name, click the Office button, and then click *Save As*. At the Save As dialog box, type a new name for the object, leave the *As* list box as the default, and then click OK.

---

## Project 2c    Creating a PivotTable Form

1. With the **OutdoorOptions.accdb** database open, save the ItemsOrdered query as a form by completing the following steps:
   a. Click the ItemsOrdered query in the Navigation pane.
   b. Click the Office button and then click *Save As* at the drop-down list.
   c. At the Save As dialog box, type ItemsOrdered in the *Save 'ItemsOrdered' to* text box.
   d. Click the down-pointing arrow at the right side of the *As* list box and then click *Form* at the drop-down list.
   e. Click OK.
   f. Close the ItemsOrdered form.

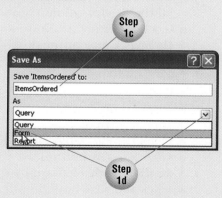

Step 1c

Step 1d

2. Create a PivotTable form by completing the following steps:
    a. Click the ItemsOrdered form in the Navigation pane.
    b. Click the Create tab.
    c. Click the More Forms button in the Forms group and then click *PivotTable* at the drop-down list.

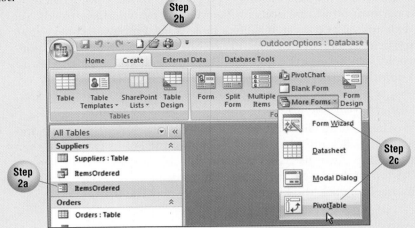

    d. At the PivotTable form, click twice on the Field List button in the Show/Hide group in the PivotTable Tools Design tab.
    e. Drag the *SupplierName* field in the *PivotTable Field List* box and drop it on the dimmed text *Drop Row Fields Here*.
    f. Drag the *Product* field from the *PivotTable Field List* box and drop it on the dimmed text *Drop Column Fields Here*.
    g. Drag the *Amount* field from the *PivotTable Field List* box and drop it on the dimmed text *Drop Totals or Detail Fields Here*.
    h. Drag the *OrderDate* field from the *PivotTable Field List* box and drop it on the dimmed text *Drop Filter Fields Here*.
    i. Close the PivotTable Field List box.
3. Display subtotals and totals of order amounts by completing the following steps:
    a. Position the mouse pointer on any *Amount* column heading until the pointer displays with a four-headed arrow attached and then click the left mouse button. (This displays all the *Amount* column headings and amounts with a light blue background.)
    b. Click the AutoCalc button in the Tools group in the PivotTable Tools Design tab and then click *Sum* at the drop-down list. (This inserts subtotals and totals in the PivotTable.)
4. Display only the order amounts for Freedom Corporation by completing the following steps:
    a. Click the filter arrow at the right of the *SupplierName* field.
    b. At the drop-down list, click the *(All)* check box to remove the check mark before each supplier name.
    c. Click the check box to the left of *Freedom Corporation*.
    d. Click the OK button.
5. Save the PivotTable form by completing the following steps:
    a. Click the Save button on the Quick Access toolbar.
    b. At the Save As dialog box, type FreedomOrders and then click OK.

6. Display only the order amounts for KL Distributions by completing the following steps:
   a. Click the filter arrow at the right of the *SupplierName* field.
   b. At the drop-down list, click the *Freedom Corporation* check box to remove the check mark.
   c. Click the check box to the left of *KL Distributions*.
   d. Click the OK button.

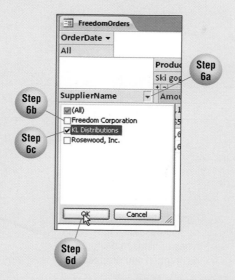

7. Save and print the PivotTable form by completing the following steps:
   a. Click the Office button and then click *Save As* at the drop-down list.
   b. At the Save As dialog box, type **KLOrders** and then click OK.
   c. Click the Quick Print button on the Quick Access toolbar.
8. Complete steps similar to those in Steps 6 and 7 to save and print a PivotTable form that displays order amounts for Rosewood, Inc. and name the form *RosewoodOrders*.
9. Close the RosewoodOrders PivotTable form.

## Summarizing Data Using PivotChart View

A PivotChart performs the same function as a PivotTable with the exception that Access displays the source data in a graph instead of a table or query. You create a chart by dragging fields from the *Chart Field List* box to the Filter, Data, Category, and Series sections of the chart. As with a PivotTable, you can easily alter the PivotChart using the filter arrows.

   To create a PivotChart, open a table or query in Datasheet view, click the PivotChart View button in the view area at the right side of the Status bar or click the View button arrow in the Views group in the Home tab, and then click PivotChart View at the drop-down list. This changes the datasheet to PivotChart layout, which contains four sections, and displays the *Chart Field List* box. Dimmed text in each section describes the types of fields that you should drag and drop. Figure 7.6 displays the PivotChart layout you will be using in Project 2d.

**Display PivotChart View**
1. Open table or query.
2. Click PivotChart View button in view area at right side of Status bar.
OR
1. Open table or query.
2. Click View button arrow.
3. Click PivotChart View at drop-down list.

PivotChart View

**Figure 7.6** PivotChart Layout

Drag the desired item from this list box and drop it in the appropriate location.

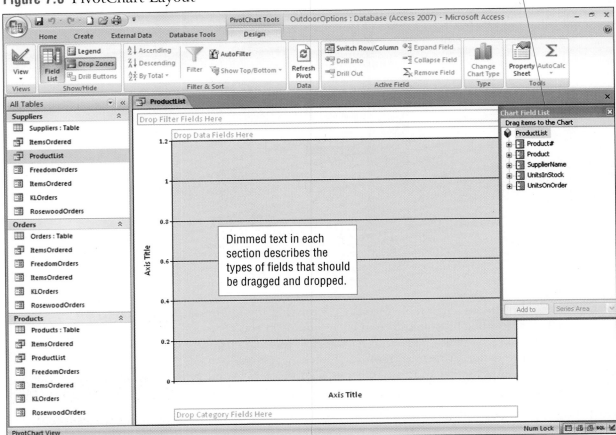

Dimmed text in each section describes the types of fields that should be dragged and dropped.

# HINT

A PivotTable is linked dynamically to a PivotChart. Changes made to the filter settings in PivotChart view are also updated in PivotTable view.

Drag the fields from the *Chart Field List* box to the desired locations in the PivotChart layout. The dimmed text in the PivotChart layout identifies the field you should drop in the location. In Project 2d, you will drag the *SupplierName* field to the Row field section, the *Product* field to the Column field section, the *Amount* field to the Totals or Details field section, and the *OrderDate* to the Filter section. The PivotChart will then display as shown in Figure 7.7. When you create a PivotChart, Access automatically creates a PivotTable. View a PivotTable based on a PivotChart by changing to PivotTable view.

**Figure 7.7** PivotChart for Project 2d

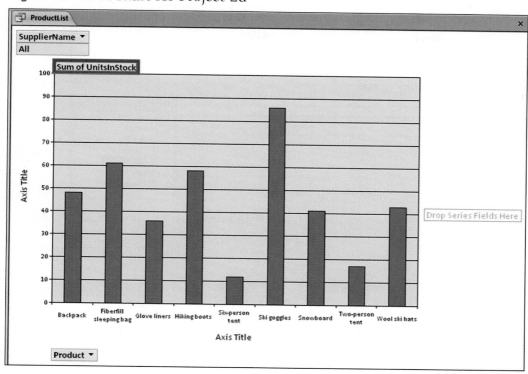

## Project ② Summarizing Data Using PivotChart View

1. With the **OutdoorOptions.accdb** database open, create a new query in Design view with the following specifications:
   a. Add the Products and Suppliers tables to the design grid.
   b. Add the following fields from the specified tables:

   | | | |
   |---|---|---|
   | *Product#* | = | Products table |
   | *Product* | = | Products table |
   | *SupplierName* | = | Suppliers table |
   | *UnitsInStock* | = | Products table |
   | *UnitsOnOrder* | = | Products table |

   c. Run the query.
   d. Save the query and name it *ProductList*.
2. Click the View button arrow in the Views group in the Home tab and then click *PivotChart View* at the drop-down list.

3. At the PivotChart layout, drag and drop the following fields:
   a. Drag the *SupplierName* field from the *Chart Field List* box and drop it on the dimmed text *Drop Filter Fields Here*.

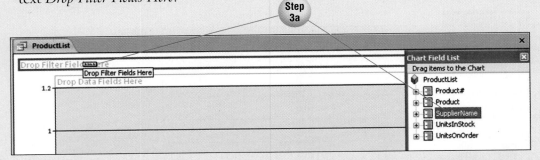

   b. Drag the *Product* field from the *Chart Field List* box and drop it on the dimmed text *Drop Category Fields Here*.
   c. Drag the *UnitsInStock* field from the *Chart Field List* box and drop it on the dimmed text *Drop Data Fields Here*.
4. Remove the *Chart Field List* box from the screen by clicking the Field List button in the Show/Hide group. (Your PivotChart should look like the PivotChart shown in Figure 7.7.)
5. Click the Quick Print button on the Quick Access toolbar to print the query in PivotChart view.
6. Display specific items on order by completing the following steps:
   a. Click the filter arrow at the right of the *Product* field (located in the lower left corner of the query window).
   b. At the pop-up list that displays, click the *(All)* check box to remove the check mark before each date.
   c. Click the check box to the left of *Ski goggles*.
   d. Click the check box to the left of *Snowboard*.
   e. Click the check box to the left of *Wool ski hats*.
   f. Click the OK button.

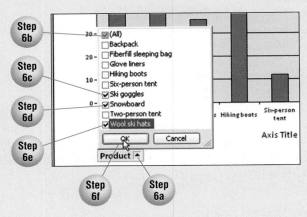

   g. Click the Quick Print button on the Quick Access toolbar.
   h. Redisplay all items by clicking the filter arrow at the right of the *Product* field, clicking the check box to the left of *(All)*, and then clicking OK.

7. Display only those products ordered from KL Distributions by completing the following steps:
   a. Click the filter arrow at the right of the *SupplierName* field.
   b. At the drop-down list, click the *(All)* check box to remove the check mark before each supplier name.
   c. Click the check box to the left of *KL Distributions*.
   d. Click the OK button.
   e. Click the Quick Print button in the Quick Access toolbar.
   f. Redisplay all supplier names by clicking the filter arrow at the right of the *SupplierName* field, clicking the check box to the left of *(All)*, and then clicking OK.
8. Click the View button arrow in the Views group and then click *PivotTable View* at the drop-down list. (This displays the chart in PivotTable view.)
9. Click the Quick Print button in the Quick Access toolbar.
10. Click the View button arrow in the Views group and then click *Datasheet View* at the drop-down list. (This returns the query to the Datasheet view.)
11. Save and then close the query.
12. Close the **OutdoorOptions.accdb** database.

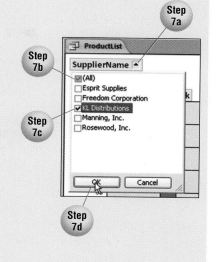

# Project ❸ View Document Properties and Object Dependencies

You will view and customize document properties for the OutdoorOptions database and view object dependencies in the Hilltop database.

# Viewing and Customizing Document Properties

The Properties dialog box contains **metadata**, which is data that describes other data. Data in the Properties dialog box describes details about the database such as title, author name, and subject, and contains options you can use to further describe or identify the database. You can display properties for the current database or display properties for a database at the Open dialog box.

## Viewing Properties at the Open Dialog Box

View properties for a database at the Open dialog box by clicking the Tools button located in the lower left corner of the Open dialog box and then clicking *Properties* at the drop-down list. This displays the Properties dialog box similar to what you see in Figure 7.8. The Properties dialog box with the General tab selected displays information about the document type, size, and location.

**View Properties at Open Dialog Box**
1. Display Open dialog box.
2. Click desired database.
3. Click Tools button.
4. Click *Properties* at drop-down list.

**Figure 7.8** OutdoorOptions.accdb Properties Dialog Box

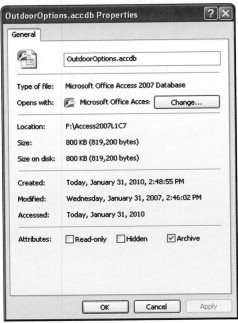

Click the ***OutdoorOptions.accdb*** database in the Open dialog box list box, click the Tools button, and then click *Properties*, and this dialog box displays.

If you display the properties for a database saved on the hard drive, the Properties dialog box will display the Summary tab along with the General tab. The Summary tab contains fields where you can enter the title, subject, category, keywords, and comments about the database. Move the insertion point to a field by clicking in the field or by pressing the Tab key until the insertion point is positioned in the desired field.

## Project ③ᵃ    Viewing Database Properties

1. At the *Getting Started with Microsoft Office Access* window, click the Open button on the Quick Access toolbar.
2. At the Open dialog box, make sure the Access2007L1C7 folder on your storage medium is active and then click ***OutdoorOptions.accdb*** in the list box.
3. Click the Tools button located in the lower left corner of the dialog box and then click *Properties* at the drop-down list.
4. At the Properties dialog box, read the information that displays in the dialog box with the General tab selected and then click the Cancel button.
5. Click ***Skyline.accdb*** in the list box, click the Tools button, and then click *Properties*.
6. Read the information that displays and then click the Cancel button.
7. Close the Open dialog box.

# Viewing and Customizing Properties for the Current Database

**View Properties of Current Database**
1. Open desired database.
2. Click Office button, point to *Manage*, click *Database Properties*.

To view properties for the currently open database, click the Office button, point to *Manage*, and then click *Database Properties*. This displays the Properties dialog box similar to what you see in Figure 7.9. The Properties dialog box for an open database contains additional tabs with information on the database. The General tab contains the same options as the Properties dialog box that displays when you click the Tools button in the Open dialog box and then click *Properties*. Click the Summary tab and fields display such as title, subject, author, category, keywords, and comments. Some fields may contain data and others may be blank. You can insert, edit, or delete text in the fields. Move the insertion point to a field by clicking in the field or by pressing the Tab key until the insertion point is positioned in the desired field.

Click the Statistics tab and information displays such as dates for when the database was created, modified, accessed, and printed. You can view the objects in the database by clicking the Contents tab. The *Document contents* section displays the objects in the database including tables, queries, form, reports, macros, and modules.

**Figure 7.9** Current Database Properties Dialog Box

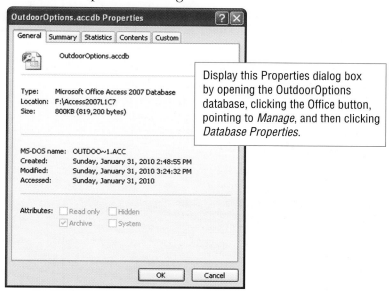

Use options at the Properties dialog box with the Custom tab selected to add custom properties to the database. For example, you can add a property that displays the date the database was completed, information on the department in which the database was created, and much more. The list box below the *Name* option box displays the predesigned properties provided by Access. You can choose a predesigned property or create your own.

To choose a predesigned property, select the desired property in the list box, specify what type of property it is (value, date, number, yes/no), and then type a value. For example, to specify the department in which the database was created, you would click *Department* in the list box, make sure the *Type* displays as *Text*, click in the *Value* text box, and then type the name of the department.

1. Open the **OutdoorOptions.accdb** database.
2. Display database properties by clicking the Office button, pointing to *Manage*, and then clicking *Database Properties*.

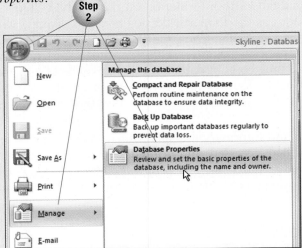

3. At the Properties dialog box, make sure the General tab is selected and then read the information that displays in the dialog box.
4. Click the Summary tab and then type the following text in the specified text boxes:

   *Title* = OutdoorOptions database
   *Subject* = Outdoor equipment and supplies
   *Author* = (type your first and last names)
   *Category* = Retail store
   *Keywords* = retail, equipment, products, suppliers
   *Comments* = This database contains information on Outdoor Options suppliers, products, and orders.

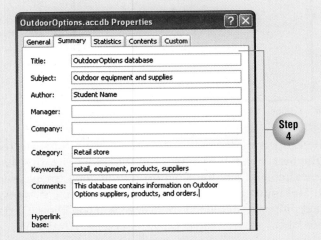

5. Click the Statistics tab and read the information that displays in the dialog box.
6. Click the Contents tab and notice that the *Document contents* section of the dialog box displays the objects in the database.

7. Click the Custom tab and then create custom properties by completing the following steps:
   a. Click the *Date completed* option in the *Name* list box.
   b. Click the down-pointing arrow at the right of the *Type* option box and then click *Date* at the drop-down list.
   c. Click in the *Value* text box and then type the current date in this format: *##/##/####*.
   d. Click the Add button.

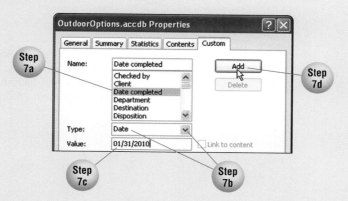

   e. With the insertion point positioned in the *Name* text box, type **Course**.
   f. Click the down-pointing arrow at the right of the *Type* option box and then click *Text* at the drop-down list.
   g. Click in the *Value* text box, type your current course number, and then press Enter.
   h. Click OK to close the dialog box.

# Viewing Object Dependencies

The structure of a database is comprised of table, query, form, and report objects. Tables are related to other tables by creating relationships. Queries, forms, and reports draw the source data from records in the tables to which they have been associated and forms and reports can include subforms and subreports which further expand the associations between objects. A database with a large number of interdependent objects is more complex to work with. Viewing a list of the objects within a database and viewing the dependencies between objects can be beneficial to ensure an object is not deleted or otherwise modified causing an unforeseen effect on another object.

Display the structure of a database, including tables, queries, forms, and reports as well as relationships, at the Object Dependencies task pane. Display this task pane by opening the database, clicking the Database Tools tab, and then clicking the Object Dependencies button in the Show/Hide group. The Object Dependencies task pane in Figure 7.10 displays the objects for the Hilltop database.

**QUICK STEPS**

**View Object Dependencies**
1. Open desired database.
2. Click Database Tools tab.
3. Click Object Dependencies button.

**Figure 7.10** Object Dependencies Task Pane

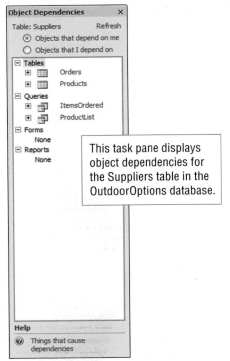

This task pane displays object dependencies for the Suppliers table in the OutdoorOptions database.

By default, *Objects that depend on me* is selected in the Object Dependencies task pane and the list box displays the names of objects for which the Employee Dates and Salaries table is the source. Next to each object in the task pane list is an expand button (plus symbol). Clicking the expand button will show objects dependent at the next level. For example, if a query is based upon the Employee Dates and Salaries table and the query is used to generate a report, clicking the expand button next to the query name would show the report name.

Clicking an object name in the Object Dependencies task pane opens the object in Design view so that you can remove the dependency by deleting bound fields, controls, or otherwise changing the source from which the data is obtained. Relationships between tables are deleted by opening the Relationships window (as you learned in Chapter 2).

1. With the **OutdoorOptions.accdb** database open, display the structure of the database by completing the following steps:

   a. Click the Suppliers table in the Navigation pane.

   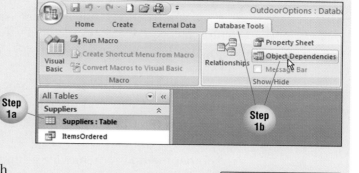

   b. Click the Database Tools tab and then click Object Dependencies in the Show/Hide group. (This displays the Object Dependencies task pane. By default, *Objects that depend on me* is selected and the task pane lists the names of objects for which the Suppliers table is the source.)

   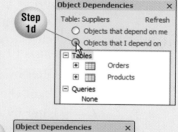

   c. Click the expand button (plus symbol) to the left of *Orders* in the Tables section. (This displays all objects that are dependent on the Orders table.)

   d. Click the *Objects that I depend on* option located toward the top of the Object Dependencies task pane.

   e. Click the Products table in the Navigation pane.

   f. Click the Refresh hyperlink located in the upper right corner of the Object Dependencies task pane.

   g. Click the *Objects that depend on me* option located toward the top of the Object Dependencies task pane. Notice the objects that are dependent on the Products table.

   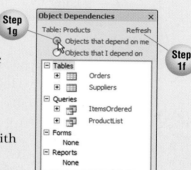

   h. Close the Object Dependencies task pane.

2. Delete the relationship between the Orders table and the Products table by completing the following steps:

   a. Click the Relationships button in the Show/Hide group with the Database Tools tab selected.

   b. Right-click the black join line between the Orders and Products tables.

   c. At the shortcut menu that displays, click *Delete*.

   d. At the message asking if you are sure you want to permanently delete the relationship, click Yes.

   e. Close the Relationships window.

   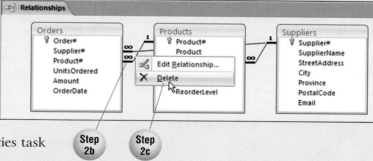

3. Display the Object Dependencies task pane for the Invoices table by completing the following steps:

   a. Click the Orders table in the Navigation pane.

   b. Click the Database Tools tab and then click Object Dependencies in the Show/Hide group. (Notice that the Products table is not listed in the Tables section of the Object Dependencies task pane.)

4. Close the Object Dependencies task pane.

5. Close the **OutdoorOptions.accdb** database.

# CHAPTER summary

- A set of restrictions, called a filter, can be set on records in a table or form. A filter lets you select specific field values.
- You can filter records with the Filter button in the Sort & Filter group in the Home tab.
- Click the Toggle Filter button in the Sort & Filter group to switch back and forth between data and filtered data.
- Remove a filter by clicking the Filter button in the Sort & Filter group and then clicking the *Clear filter from xxx* (where *xxx* is the name of the field).
- Another method for removing a filter is to click the Advanced button in the Sort & Filter group and then click *Clear All Filters*.
- Display a list of filter values by clicking the Filter button and then pointing to *Text Filters* (if the data is text), *Number Filters* (if the data is numbers), or *Date Filters* (if the data is a date).
- Filter by selection by clicking the Selection button in the Sort & Filter group.
- Right-click a field entry to display a shortcut menu with filtering options.
- Filter by form by clicking the Advanced button in the Sort & Filter group and then clicking *Filter By Form* at the drop-down list. This displays a blank record with the two tabs *Look for* and *Or*.
- A PivotTable is an interactive table that organizes and summarizes data. Create a PivotTable for an object to analyze data for numerous scenarios. Change to the PivotTable view to create a PivotTable.
- A PivotTable you create in a query or table is saved with the object. You can also create a PivotTable form that is saved as a separate object from the table or query.
- You can save an open object as a different object with the *As* option at the Save As dialog box. Display this dialog box by clicking the Office button and then clicking *Save As* at the drop-down list.
- Create a PivotTable form by clicking the More Forms button in the Forms group in the Create tab and then clicking *PivotTable* at the drop-down list.
- Create a PivotChart to analyze data in a chart rather than a table or query. Change to the PivotChart view to create a PivotChart.
- View database properties by displaying the Open dialog box, clicking the desired database, clicking the Tools button, and then clicking *Properties* at the drop-down list.
- To view properties for the currently open database, click the Office button, point to *Manage*, and then click *Database Properties*.
- Customize database properties with options at the Properties dialog box with the Custom tab selected.
- Display the structure of a database and the relationship between objects at the Object Dependencies task pane. Display this task pane by clicking the Database Tools tab and then clicking the Object Dependencies button in the Show/Hide group.

# COMMANDS review

| FEATURE | RIBBON TAB, GROUP | BUTTON, OPTION |
|---|---|---|
| Filter | Home, Sort & Filter | |
| Toggle filter | Home, Sort & Filter | Toggle Filter |
| Remove filter | Home, Sort & Filter | , Clear filter from *xxx*, OR  Advanced , Clear All Filters |
| Filter by selection | Home, Sort & Filter | Selection |
| Filter by form | Home, Sort & Filter | Advanced , Filter By Form |
| PivotTable view | Home, Views | , PivotTable View |
| PivotTable form | Create, Forms | More Forms , PivotTable |
| PivotChart | Home, Views | , PivotChart View |
| Object Dependencies task pane | Database Tools, Show/Hide | Object Dependencies |

# CONCEPTS check

## Test Your Knowledge

**Completion:** In the space provided at the right, indicate the correct term, symbol, or command.

1. The Filter button is located in this group in the Home tab.                                                        _____

2. If you filter data, you can switch between the data and the filtered data by clicking this button.                 _____

3. Remove filtering from an object with the Filter button or by clicking this button and then clicking *Clear All Filters*.   _____

4. In the Filter By Form window, these two tabs display toward the bottom of the form.                                _____

5. Display a table or query in this view to summarize data based on the fields you designate for row headings, column headings, and source record filtering.   _____

6. To create a PivotTable form, click this button in the Forms group and then click *PivotTable* at the drop-down list.   _____

7. Click this button in the Show/Hide group in the PivotTable Tools Design tab to display the *PivotTable Field List* box.   _____

8. Use this view to display data in a graph.                                                                          _____

9. View properties for a database at the Open dialog box by clicking this button located in the lower left corner of the dialog box and then clicking *Properties*.   _____

10. Display the structure of a database at this task pane.                                                            _____

# SKILLS check
## Demonstrate Your Proficiency

## Assessment

### 1 FILTER RECORDS IN TABLES

1. Display the Open dialog box with Access2007L1C7 on your storage medium the active folder.
2. Open the **LegalServices.accdb** database.
3. Open the Clients table and then filter the records to display the following records:
    a. Display only those records of clients who live in Renton. When the records of clients in Renton display, print the results and then remove the filter.
    b. Display only those records of clients with the Postal Code of 98033. When the records of clients with the ZIP code 98033 display, print the results in landscape orientation and then remove the filter. (Hint: Change to landscape orientation in Print Preview.)
4. Close the Clients table without saving the changes.
5. Open the Billing table and then filter records by selection to display the following records:
    a. Display only those records with a Category of CC. Print the CC records and then remove the filter.
    b. Display only those records with an Attorney ID of 12. Print the records and then remove the filter.
    c. Display only those records between the dates 6/1/2010 and 6/10/2010. Print the records and then remove the filter.
6. Close the Billing table without saving the changes.
7. Open the Clients table and then use Filter By Form to display clients in Auburn or Renton. (Be sure to use the Or tab at the very bottom of the table.) Print the table in landscape orientation and then remove the filter.
8. Close the Clients table without saving the changes.
9. Open the Billing table and then use Filter By Form to display categories G or P. Print the table and then remove the filter.
10. Close the Billing table without saving the changes.
11. Close the **LegalServices.accdb** database.

## Assessment

### 2 VIEW AND ANALYZE DATA IN PIVOTTABLE AND PIVOTCHART VIEW

1. Open the **Hilltop.accdb** database.
2. Create a query in Design view with the following specifications:
    a. Add the Invoices, Customers, Equipment, and Rates tables to the design grid.
    b. Add the following fields from the specified tables:

    | | | |
    |---|---|---|
    | *BillingDate* | = | Invoices table |
    | *Customer* | = | Customers table |
    | *Equipment* | = | Equipment table |
    | *Hours* | = | Invoices table |
    | *Rate* | = | Rates table |

c. Click in the sixth *Field* text and then insert a calculation to total the rental hour amounts by typing **Total: [Hours]\*[Rate]**. (Press the Tab key to move to the next field.)

d. Run the query.

e. Save the query and name it *RentalTotals*.

3. Display the query in PivotTable view.

4. At the PivotTable layout, drag and drop the fields as follows:

   a. Drag the *Equipment* field to the *Drop Row Fields Here* section.

   b. Drag the *Customer* field to the *Drop Column Fields Here* section.

   c. Drag the *Total* field to the *Drop Totals or Detail Fields Here* section.

   d. Drag the *BillingDate* field to the *Drop Filter Fields Here* section.

5. Remove the *PivotTable Field List* box from the screen.

6. Click the Quick Print button on the Quick Access toolbar to print the query in PivotTable view. (If the total amounts in the Cascade Enterprises and Country Electrical columns print as number symbols instead of amounts, increase the size of the Total column by dragging to the right the border at the right side of the Total heading below Cascade Enterprises.)

7. In the *BillingDate* field, display only equipment rentals for May 1, 2010.

8. Print the PivotTable and then redisplay all rental dates.

9. In the *Equipment* field, display records only for the Hydraulic Pump and Pressure Sprayer.

10. Print the PivotTable and then redisplay all equipment.

11. Switch to Datasheet view, save the query, and then close the query.

12. Create a query in Design view with the following specifications:

    a. Add the Equipment, Customers, and Invoices tables to the design grid.

    b. Add the following fields from the specified tables:

    | | | |
    |---|---|---|
    | *Equipment* | = | Equipment table |
    | *Customer* | = | Customers table |
    | *Hours* | = | Invoices table |

    c. Run the query.

    d. Save the query and name it *CustomerHours*.

13. Click the View button arrow in the Views group in the Home tab and then click *PivotChart View* at the drop-down list.

14. At the PivotChart layout, drag and drop the following fields:

    a. Drag the *Equipment* field to the *Drop Filter Fields Here* section.

    b. Drag the *Customer* field to the *Drop Category Fields Here* section.

    c. Drag the *Hours* field to the *Drop Data Fields Here* section.

15. Remove the *Chart Field List* box from the screen.

16. Click the Quick Print button on the Quick Access toolbar to print the query in PivotChart view.

17. In the *Equipment* field, display only records for Backhoe, print the PivotChart, and then redisplay all equipment.

18. In the *Customer* field, display only the customers Allied Builders and Cascade Enterprises, print the PivotChart, and then redisplay all customers.

19. Save the PivotChart, switch to Datasheet view, and then close the query.

20. Create a PivotTable form with the RentalTotals query and drag and drop the following fields in the PivotTable layout:

    a. Drag the *Equipment* field to the *Drop Row Fields Here* section.

    b. Drag the *Customer* field to the *Drop Column Fields Here* section.

    c. Drag the *Total* field to the *Drop Totals or Detail Fields Here* section.

    d. Drag the *BillingDate* field to the *Drop Filter Fields Here* section.

21. Save the PivotTable form and name it *CustomerRentals*.
22. Display only those records for Able Construction. Save the PivotTable form with Save As and name it *AbleConstruction*. Print the form.
23. Display only those records for Cascade Enterprises. Save the PivotTable form with Save As and name it *CascadeEnterprises*. Print and then close the form.

## Assessment

### 3 DELETE AND RENAME OBJECTS

1. With the **Hilltop.accdb** database open, experiment with the options in the shortcut menu that displays when you right-click an object and then complete the following:
   a. Delete the AbleConstruction form.
   b. Rename the CascadeEnterprises form to *CascadeHours*.
   c. Rename the RentalTotals query to *RentalHoursTotals*.
2. Close the **Hilltop.accdb** database.

# CASE study
## *Apply Your Skills*

### Part 1

As the office manager at the Summit View Medical Services, you are responsible for maintaining clinic records. Open the **SummitView.accdb** database and then insert the following additional services into the appropriate table:

- Edit the *Doctor visit* entry in the Services table so it displays as *Clinic visit*.
- Add the entry *X-ray* with a service identification of *X*.
- Add the entry *Cholesterol screening* with a service identification of *CS*.

Add the following new patient information in the database in the appropriate tables or forms:

Patient number 118
Brian M. Gould
2887 Nelson Street
Helena, MT 59604
(406) 555-3121
Mr. Gould saw Dr. Wallace for a clinic visit on 4/5/2010, which has a fee of $75.

Patient number 119
Ellen L. Augustine
12990 148th Street
East Helena, MT 59635
(406) 555-0722
Ms. Augustine saw Dr. Kennedy for cholesterol screening on 4/5/2010, which has a fee of $90.

Patient number 120
Jeff J. Masura
3218 Eldridge Avenue
Helena, MT 59624
(406) 555-6212
Mr. Masura saw Dr. Rowe for an x-ray on 4/5/2010, which has a fee of $75.

Add the following information to the Billing form:

- Patient 109 came for cholesterol screening with Dr. Kennedy on 4/5/2010 with a $90 fee.
- Patient 106 came for immunizations with Dr. Pena on 4/5/2010 with a $100 fee.
- Patient 114 came for an x-ray with Dr. Kennedy on 4/5/2010 with a $75 fee.

## Part 2

Create the following filters, queries, PivotTable, and PivotChart:

- Open the Billing table and then filter and print the records for the date 04/01/2010. Clear the filter and then filter and then print the records with a doctor number of 18. Save and then close the table.
- Create a report that displays the patient's first name, last name, street address, city, state, and ZIP code. Apply formatting to enhance the visual appeal of the report. Filter and print the records of those patients living in Helena and then filter and print the records of those patients living in East Helena. Close the report.
- Design a query that includes the doctor number, doctor last name, patient number, date of visit, and fee. Save the query with the name *DoctorBillingFees* and then print the query.
- Create a PivotTable with the DoctorBillingFees query with the following specifications: Drop the *DateOfVisit* field in the Filter Fields section, the *Patient#* field in the Column Fields section, the *LastName* field in the Row Fields, and the *Fee* field in the Totals or Detail Fields. Save and then print the PivotTable.
- Filter records in the PivotTable for Dr. Kennedy and Dr. Pena. Print the filtered PivotTable.
- Remove the filter and then filter records for the dates 4/1/2010 and 4/2/2010. Print the filtered table. Save and then close the query.

## Part 3

Using the PivotTable layout you designed in the DoctorBillingFees query in Part 2, create a PivotTable form in the same layout. Save the PivotTable form and name it *BillingFees* and then print the PivotTable form. Decide on two different filters you can apply to the data in the PivotTable form. Complete each filter and save the filtered PivotTable form with a new name and print the form.

## Part 4

Your clinic has a procedures manual that describes processes and procedures in the center. Open Word and then create a document for the procedures manual that describes the process for creating the PivotTable form you created in Part 3. Save the completed document and name it **Access_C7_CS_P4**. Print and then close **Access_C7_CS_P4.docx**.

# Importing and Exporting Data

## PERFORMANCE OBJECTIVES

**Upon successful completion of Chapter 8, you will be able to:**

- Export Access data to Excel
- Export Access data to Word
- Merge Access data with a Word document
- Import data to a new table
- Link data to a new table
- Use the Office Clipboard
- Save a database in an earlier version of Access

**Tutorial 8.1**
Exporting Data
**Tutorial 8.2**
Importing Data and Viewing
    Object Dependencies

Microsoft Office 2007 is a suite of programs that allows easy data exchange between programs. In this chapter you will learn how to export data from Access to Excel and Word, merge Access data with a Word document, import and link data to a new table, and copy and paste data between programs. You will also learn how to copy and paste data between applications and save a database in an earlier version of Access.

*Note: Before beginning computer projects, copy to your storage medium the Access2007L1C8 subfolder from the Access2007L1 folder on the CD that accompanies this textbook and make Access2007L1C8 the active folder.*

## Project ① Export Data to Excel and Export and Merge Data to Word

You will export a table and query to Excel and export a table and report to Word. You will also merge data in an Access table and query with a Word document.

## Exporting Data

One of the advantages of a suite like Microsoft Office is the ability to exchange data between one program and another. Access, like other programs in the suite, offers a feature to export data from Access into Excel and/or Word. The Export group in the External Data tab contains buttons for exporting a table, query, form, or report to other programs such as Excel and Word.

# Exporting Data to Excel

**Export Data to Excel**
1. Click the desired table, query, or form.
2. Click the External Data tab.
3. Click Excel button in Export group.
4. Make desired changes at Export - Excel Spreadsheet dialog box.
5. Click OK.

Use the Excel button in the Export group in the External Data tab to export data in a table, query, or form to an Excel worksheet. Click the object containing data you want to export to Excel, click the External Data tab, click the Excel button in the Export group and the first Export - Excel Spreadsheet wizard dialog box displays as shown in Figure 8.1.

Click the Browse button and then navigate to the desired folder and file.

**Figure 8.1** Export - Excel Spreadsheet Dialog Box

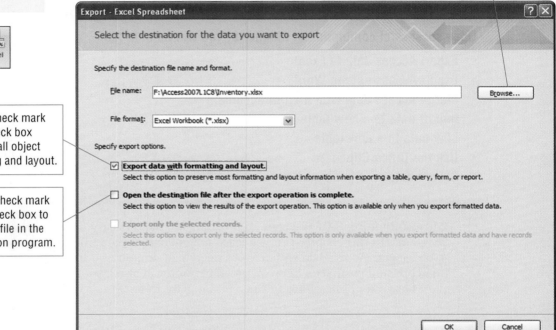

Insert a check mark in this check box to export all object formatting and layout.

Insert a check mark in this check box to open the file in the destination program.

**HINT**
Data exported from Access to Excel is saved as an Excel workbook with the .xlsx extension.

**HINT**
You can export only one database object at a time, and you cannot export reports to Excel.

At the first wizard dialog box, Access uses the name of the object as the Excel workbook name. You can change this by selecting the current name and then typing a new name and you can specify the file format with the *File format* option. Click the *Export data with formatting and layout* check box to insert a check mark. This exports all data formatting to the Excel workbook. If you want Excel to open with the exported data, click the *Open the destination file after the export operation is complete* option to insert a check mark. When you have made all desired changes, click the OK button. This opens Excel with the data in a workbook. Make any desired changes to the workbook and then save, print, and close the workbook. Exit Excel and Access displays with a second wizard dialog box asking if you want to save the export steps. At this dialog box, insert a check mark in the *Save export steps* if you want to save the export steps, or leave the option blank and then click the Close button.

1. Display the Open dialog box with Access2007L1C8 on your storage medium the active folder.
2. Open the **Hilltop.accdb** database.
3. Save the Inventory table as an Excel worksheet by completing the following steps:
   a. Click the Inventory table in the Navigation pane.
   b. Click the External Data tab and then click the Excel button in the Export group.

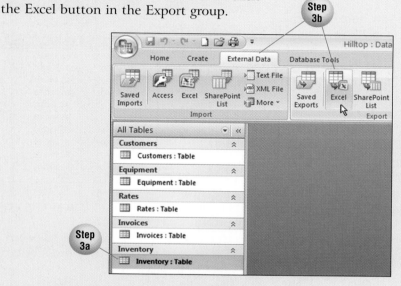

   c. At the Export - Excel Spreadsheet dialog box, click the Browse button.
   d. At the File Save dialog box, navigate to the Access2007L1C8 folder on your storage medium and then click the Save button.
   e. Click the *Export data with formatting and layout* option to insert a check mark in the check box.
   f. Click the *Open the destination file after the export operation is complete* option to insert a check mark in the check box.

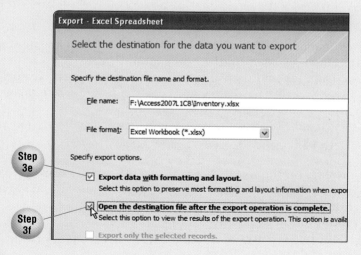

   g. Click OK.

h. When the data displays on the screen in Excel as a worksheet, select cells A2 through A11 and then click the Center button in the Alignment group in the Home tab.

i. Select cells D2 through F11 and then click the Center button.

j. Click the Save button on the Quick Access toolbar.

k. Click the Quick Print button on the Quick Access toolbar.

l. Close the worksheet and then exit Excel.

4. In Access, click the Close button to close the second wizard dialog box.

5. Design a query that extracts records from three tables with the following specifications:

a. Add the Invoices, Customers, and Rates tables to the query window.

b. Insert the *BillingDate* field from the Invoices table to the first *Field* text box.

c. Insert the *Customer* field from the Customers table to the second *Field* text box.

d. Insert the *Hours* field from the Invoices table to the third *Field* text box.

e. Insert the *Rate* field from the Rates table to the fourth *Field* text box.

f. Click in the fifth *Field* text box, type **Total: [Hours]*[Rate]** and then press Enter.

| | A | B | C | D | |
|---|---|---|---|---|---|
| 1 | Equipment# | PurchaseDate | PurchasePrice | AvailableHours | Se |
| 2 | 10 | 05-Feb-06 | $65,540.00 | 120 | |
| 3 | 11 | 01-Sep-07 | $105,500.00 | 125 | |
| 4 | 12 | 01-Jun-05 | $55,345.00 | 140 | |
| 5 | 13 | 05-May-08 | $86,750.00 | 120 | |
| 6 | 14 | 15-Jul-07 | $4,500.00 | 160 | |
| 7 | 15 | 01-Oct-05 | $95,900.00 | 125 | |
| 8 | 16 | 01-Dec-08 | $3,450.00 | 150 | |
| 9 | 17 | 10-Apr-07 | $5,600.00 | 160 | |
| 10 | 18 | 15-Jun-08 | $8,000.00 | 150 | |
| 11 | 19 | 30-Sep-06 | $42,675.00 | 120 | |
| 12 | | | | | |

| Field: | BillingDate | Customer | Hours | Rate | Total: [Hours]*[Rate] |
|---|---|---|---|---|---|
| Table: | Invoices | Customers | Invoices | Rates | |
| Sort: | | | | | |
| Show: | ✓ | ✓ | ✓ | ✓ | ✓ |
| Criteria: | | | | | |
| or: | | | | | |

g. Run the query.

h. Save the query and name it *CustomerInvoices*.

i. Close the query.

6. Export the CustomerInvoices query to Excel by completing the following steps:

a. Click the CustomerInvoices query in the Navigation pane.

b. Click the External Data tab and then click the Excel button in the Export group.

c. At the Export - Excel Spreadsheet dialog box, click the *Export data with formatting and layout* option to insert a check mark in the check box.

d. Click the *Open the destination file after the export operation is complete* option to insert a check mark in the check box.

e. Click OK.

f. When the data displays on the screen in Excel as a worksheet, select cells A2 through A20 and then click the Center button in the Alignment group in the Home tab.

g. Select cells C2 through C20 and then click the Center button.

h. Click the Save button on the Quick Access toolbar.

i. Click the Quick Print button on the Quick Access toolbar.

j. Close the worksheet and then exit Excel.

7. In Access, click the Close button to close the second wizard dialog box.

# Exporting Data to Word

Export data from Access to Word in the same manner as exporting to Excel. To export data to Word, select the desired object in the Navigation pane, click the External Data tab, and then click the Word button in the Export group. At the Export - RTF File dialog box, make desired changes and then click OK. Word automatically opens and the data displays in a Word document that is saved automatically with the same name as the database object. The difference is that the file extension .rtf is added to the name. An RTF file is saved in "rich-text format," which preserves formatting such as fonts and styles. You can export a document saved with the .rtf extension in Word and other Windows word processing or desktop publishing programs.

**QUICK STEPS**

**Export Data to Word**
1. Click the desired table, query, form, or report.
2. Click External Data tab.
3. Click Word button in Export group.
4. Make desired changes at Export - RTF File dialog box.
5. Click OK.

**HINT**
Data exported from Access to Word is saved with the .rtf file extension.

## Project 1b   Exporting a Table and Report to Word

1. Click the Invoices table in the Navigation pane.
2. Click the External Data tab and then click the Word button in the Export group.

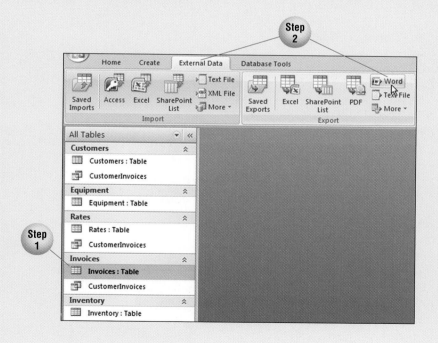

3. At the Export - RTF File wizard dialog box, click the Browse button.
4. At the File Save dialog box, navigate to the Access2007L1C8 folder on your storage medium and then click the Save button.
5. At the Export - RTF File wizard dialog box, click the *Open the destination file after the export operation is complete* check box.

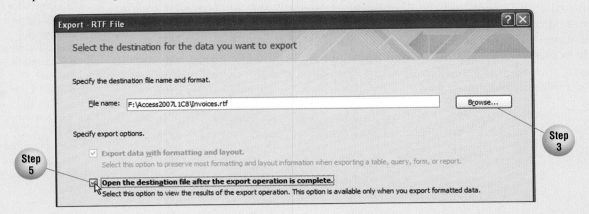

6. Click OK.
7. With the **Invoices.rtf** file open in Word, click the Quick Print button on the Quick Access toolbar.
8. Close the **Invoices.rtf** file and then exit Word.
9. Click the Close button to close the wizard dialog box.
10. Create a report with the Report Wizard by completing the following steps:
    a. Click the Create tab and then click the Report Wizard button in the Reports group.
    b. At the first Report Wizard dialog box, insert the following fields in the *Selected Fields* list box:

    From the Customers table:
      *Customer*
    From the Equipment table:
      *Equipment*
    From the Invoices table:
      *BillingDate*
      *Hours*

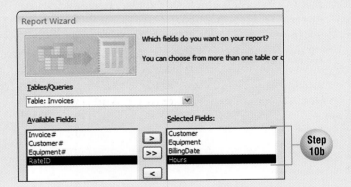

c. After inserting the fields, click the Next button.

d. At the second Report Wizard dialog box, make sure *by Customers* is selected in the list box in the upper left corner and then click the Next button.

e. At the third Report Wizard dialog box, click the Next button.

f. At the fourth Report Wizard dialog box, click the Next button.

g. At the fifth Report Wizard dialog box, click *Block* in the *Layout* section and then click the Next button.

h. At the sixth Report Wizard dialog box, click *Solstice* in the list box and then click the Next button.

i. At the seventh Report Wizard dialog box, select the current name in the *File name* text box, type **CustomerReport**, and then click the Finish button.

j. When the report displays in Print Preview, click the Layout View button located in the view area at the right side of the Status bar.

k. Click the *Customer* column heading and then increase the width of the column so all of the customer names display in the fields.

l. Click the Quick Print button on the Quick Access toolbar.

m. Save and then close the CustomerReport report.

11. Export the CustomerReport report to Word by completing the following steps:

a. Click the CustomerReport report in the Navigation pane.

b. Click the External Data tab and then click the Word button in the Export group.

c. At the Export - RTF File wizard dialog box, click the *Open the destination file after export operation is complete* option to insert a check mark in the check box and then click OK.

d. When the data displays on the screen in Word, click the Quick Print button on the Quick Access toolbar.

e. Save and then close the CustomerReport document.

f. Exit Word.

12. In Access, click the Close button to close the second wizard dialog box.

# Merging Access Data with a Word Document

You can merge data from an Access table with a Word document. When merging data, the data in the Access table is considered the data source and the Word document is considered the main document. When the merge is completed, the merged documents display in Word. To merge data, click the desired table in the Navigation pane and then click the External Data tab. Click the More button in the Export group and then click the *Merge it with Microsoft Office Word* option at the drop-down list. When merging Access data, you can either type the text in the main document or merge Access data with an existing Word document.

**Merge Data with Word**

1. Click the desired table or query.
2. Click External Data tab.
3. Click More button, *Merge it with Microsoft Office Word*.
4. Make desired choices at each wizard dialog box.

1. Click the Customers table in the Navigation pane.
2. Click the External Data tab.
3. Click the More button in the Export group and then click the *Merge it with Microsoft Office Word* option at the drop-down list.

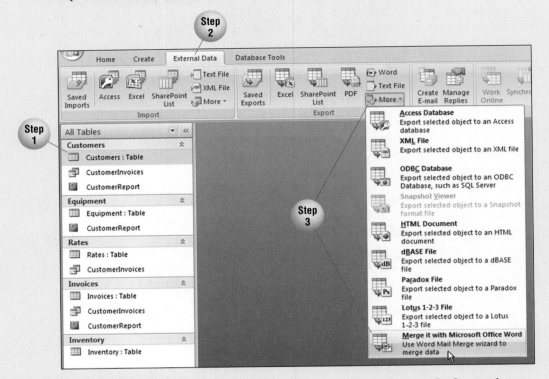

4. At the Microsoft Word Mail Merge Wizard dialog box, make sure *Link your data to an existing Microsoft Word document* is selected and then click OK.
5. At the Select Microsoft Word Document dialog box, make the Access2007L1C8 folder on your storage medium the active folder and then double-click the document named **HilltopLetter.docx**.
6. Click the Maximize button located at the right side of the HilltopLetter.docx title bar and then close the Mail Merge task pane.
7. Press the down arrow key six times (not the Enter key) and then type the current date.
8. Press the down arrow key five times and then insert fields for merging from the Customers table by completing the following steps:

   a. Click the Insert Merge Field button arrow located in the Write & Insert Fields group and then click *Customer1* in the drop-down list. (This inserts the «*Customer1*» field in the document. The drop-down list contains a *Customer* and a *Customer1* option. The first *Customer* option is actually the *Customer#* field. Word dropped the # symbol from the field name and added the *1* to the second *Customer* field to differentiate the two fields.)

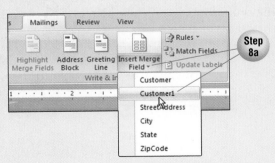

b. Press Enter, click the Insert Merge Field button arrow, and then click *StreetAddress* in the drop-down list.

c. Press Enter, click the Insert Merge Field button arrow, and then click *City* in the drop-down list.

d. Type a comma (,) and then press the spacebar.

e. Click the Insert Merge Field button arrow and then click *State* in the drop-down list.

f. Press the spacebar, click the Insert Merge Field button arrow, and then click *ZipCode* in the drop-down list.

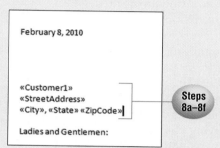

g. Replace the letters *XX* that display toward the bottom of the letter with your initials.

h. Click the Finish & Merge button in the Finish group and then click *Edit Individual Documents* in the drop-down list.

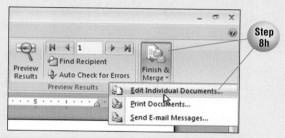

i. At the Merge to New Document dialog box, make sure *All* is selected and then click OK.

j. When the merge is completed, save the new document and name it **AccessL1_C8_P1a** in the Access2007L1C8 folder on your storage medium.

9. Print just the first two pages (two letters) of **AccessL1_C8_P1a.docx**.

10. Close **AccessL1_C8_P1a.docx** and then close **HilltopLetter.docx** without saving the changes.

11. Exit Word.

## Merging Query Data with a Word Document

You can perform a query in a database and then use the query to merge with a Word document. In Project 1d you merged a table with an existing Word document. You can also merge a table or query and then type the Word document. You will create a query in Project 1e and then merge data in the query with a new document in Word.

1. Perform a query with the Query Wizard and modify the query by completing the following steps:
   a. Click the Create tab and then click the Query Wizard button in the Other group.
   b. At the New Query dialog box, make sure Simple Query Wizard is selected and then click OK.
   c. At the first Simple Query Wizard dialog box, click the down-pointing arrow at the right of the *Tables/Queries* option box and then click *Table: Customers*.
   d. Click the button containing the two greater than symbols (>>) to insert all of the fields in the *Selected Fields* list box.
   e. Click the Next button.
   f. At the second Simple Query Wizard dialog box, make the following changes:
      1) Select the current name in the *What title do you want for your query?* text box and then type **DenverCustomersQuery**.
      2) Click the *Modify the query design* option.
      3) Click the Finish button.
   g. At the query window, click in the *Criteria* text box in the *City* column, type **Denver**, and then press Enter.

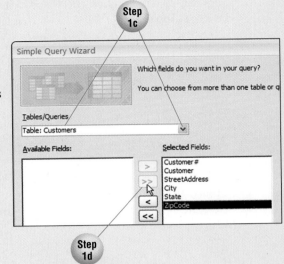

Step 1c

Simple Query Wizard

Which fields do you want in your query?

You can choose from more than one table or q

Tables/Queries

Table: Customers

Available Fields:

Selected Fields:

Customer #
Customer
StreetAddress
City
State
ZipCode

Step 1d

| Field: | [Customer#] | [Customer] | [StreetAddress] | [City] | [State] | [ZipCode] |
|---|---|---|---|---|---|---|
| Table: | Customers | Customers | Customers | Customers | Customers | Customers |
| Sort: | | | | | | |
| Show: | ☑ | ☑ | ☑ | ☑ | ☑ | ☑ |
| Criteria: | | | | "Denver" | | |
| or: | | | | | | |

   h. Click the Run button in the Results group. (Those customers located in Denver will display.)

Step 1g

   i. Save and then close the DenverCustomersQuery query.
2. Click the DenverCustomersQuery query in the Navigation pane.
3. Click the External Data tab, click the More button in the Export group, and then click the *Merge it with Microsoft Office Word* option at the drop-down list.
4. At the Microsoft Word Mail Merge Wizard dialog box, click the *Create a new document and then link the data to it.* option and then click OK.
5. Click the Maximize button located at the right side of the Document1 title bar and then close the Mail Merge task pane.

Step 4

Microsoft Word Mail Merge Wizard

This wizard links your data to a Microsoft Word document, so that you can print form letters or address envelopes.

OK

Cancel

What do you want the wizard to do?

○ Link your data to an existing Microsoft Word document.

◉ Create a new document and then link the data to it.

6. Complete the following steps to type text and insert fields in the blank Word document:
   a. Click the Home tab and then click the No Spacing style in the Styles group.
   b. Press Enter six times.

c. Type the current date.

d. Press Enter five times.

e. Click the Mailings tab.

f. Insert the following fields at the left margin in the order shown below (start by clicking the Insert Merge Field button arrow in the Write & Insert Fields group):

    *«Customer1»*
    *«StreetAddress»*
    *«City», «State» «ZipCode»*

g. Press Enter twice and then type the salutation Ladies and Gentlemen:.

h. Press Enter twice and then type the following paragraphs of text:

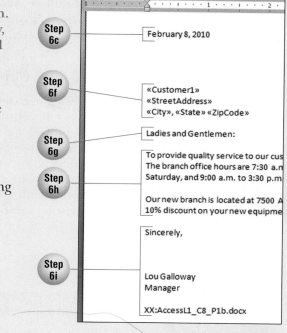

To provide quality service to our customers, we have opened a new branch office in downtown Denver. The branch office hours are 7:30 a.m. to 7:00 p.m. Monday through Friday, 8:00 a.m. to 5:00 p.m. Saturday, and 9:00 a.m. to 3:30 p.m. Sunday.

Our new branch is located at 7500 Alameda Avenue. Stop by during the next two weeks and receive a 10% discount on your next equipment rental.

i. Press Enter twice and then type the following complimentary close (at the left margin):

Sincerely,

Lou Galloway
Manager

XX:AccessL1_C8_P1b.docx

j. Click the Finish & Merge button in the Finish group and then click *Edit Individual Documents* in the drop-down menu.

k. At the Merge to New Document dialog box, make sure *All* is selected, and then click OK.

l. When the merge is complete, save the new document as **AccessL1_C8_P1b** in the Access2007L1C8 folder on your storage medium.

7. Print the first two pages (two letters) of **AccessL1_C8_P1b.docx**.

8. Close **AccessL1_C8_P1b.docx**.

9. Save the main document as **AccessHilltopLetter** in the Access2007L1C8 folder on your storage medium and then close the document.

10. Exit Word.

11. Close the **Hilltop.accdb** database.

# Project ② Import and Link Excel Worksheets with an Access Table

You will import an Excel worksheet into an Access table. You will also link an Excel worksheet into an Access table and then add a new record to the Access table.

## Importing and Linking Data to a New Table

In this chapter, you learned how to export Access data to Excel and Word. You can also import data from other programs into an Access table. For example, you can import data from an Excel worksheet and create a new table in a database using data from the worksheet. Data in the original program is not connected to the data imported into an Access table. If you make changes to the data in the original program, those changes are not reflected in the Access table. If you want the imported data connected to the original program, link the data.

## Importing Data to a New Table

To import data, click the External Data tab and then determine where you would like to retrieve data with options in the Import group. At the Import dialog box that displays, click Browse and then double-click the desired file name. This activates the Import Wizard and displays the first wizard dialog box. The appearance of the dialog box varies depending on the file selected. Complete the steps of the Import Wizard specifying information such as the range of data, whether or not the first row contains column headings, whether you want to store the data in a new table or store it in an existing table, the primary key, and the name of the table.

## Project ②a  Importing an Excel Worksheet into an Access Table

1. Display the Open dialog box with Access2007L1C8 on your storage medium the active folder.
2. Open the **SouthwestInsurance.accdb** database.
3. Import an Excel worksheet into a new table in the **SouthwestInsurance.accdb** database by completing the following steps:
   a. Click the External Data tab and then click the Excel button in the Import group.
   b. At the Get External Data - Excel Spreadsheet dialog box, click Browse and then make the Access2007L1C8 folder on your storage medium the active folder.
   c. Double-click *ExcelC08_01.xlsx* in the list box.
   d. Click OK at the Get External Data - Excel Spreadsheet dialog box.

Step 3a

e. At the first Import Spreadsheet Wizard dialog box, click the Next button.
f. At the second Import Spreadsheet Wizard dialog box, make sure the *First Row Contains Column Headings* option contains a check mark and then click the Next button.
g. At the third Import Spreadsheet Wizard dialog box, click the Next button.
h. At the fourth Import Spreadsheet Wizard dialog box, click the *Choose my own primary key* option (this inserts *Policy#* in the text box located to the right of the option) and then click the Next button.

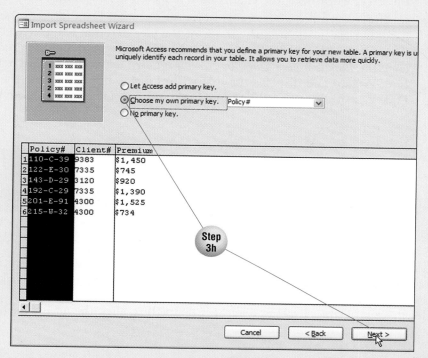

i. At the fifth Import Spreadsheet Wizard dialog box, type **Policies** in the *Import to Table* text box and then click the Finish button.

j. At the Get External Data - Excel Spreadsheet dialog box, click the Close button.
4. Open the new Policies table in Datasheet view.
5. Print and then close the Policies table.

## QUICK STEPS

**Link Data to Excel Worksheet**
1. Click External Data tab.
2. Click Excel button in Import group.
3. Click Browse button.
4. Double-click desired file name.
5. Click *Link to a data source by creating a linked table.*
6. Make desired choices at each wizard dialog box.

# Linking Data to an Excel Worksheet

Imported data is not connected to the source program. If you know that you will use your data only in Access, import it. However, if you want to update data in a program other than Access, link the data. Changes made to linked data in the source program file are reflected in the destination program file. For example, you can link an Excel worksheet with an Access table and when you make changes in the Excel worksheet, the changes are reflected in the Access table.

To link data to a new table, click the External Data tab and then click the Excel button in the Import group. At the Get External Data - Excel Spreadsheet dialog box, click the Browse button, double-click the desired file name, and then click the *Link to a data source by creating a linked table* option. This activates the Link Wizard and displays the first wizard dialog box. Complete the steps of the Link Wizard, specifying the same basic information as the Import Wizard.

Excel

# Project 2b    Linking an Excel Worksheet with an Access Table

1. With the **SouthwestInsurance.accdb** database open, click the External Data tab and then click the Excel button in the Import group.
2. At the Get External Data - Excel Spreadsheet dialog box, click the Browse button, navigate to the Access2007L1C8 folder on your storage medium, and then double-click **ExcelC08_01.xlsx**.
3. At the Get External Data - Excel Spreadsheet dialog box, click the *Link to the data source by creating a linked table* option and then click OK.

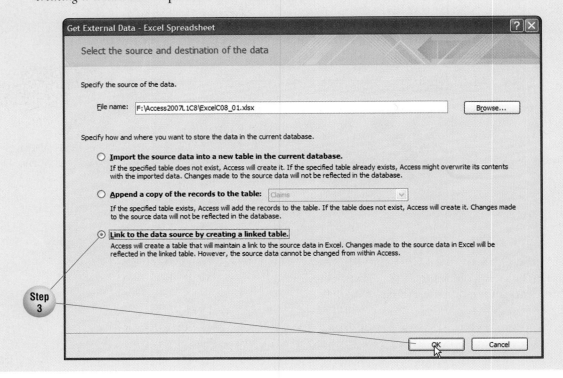

4. At the first Link Spreadsheet Wizard dialog box, make sure *Show Worksheets* and *Sheet 1* are selected in the list box and then click the Next button.
5. At the second Link Spreadsheet Wizard dialog box, make sure the *First Row Contains Column Headings* option contains a check mark and then click the Next button.
6. At the third Link Spreadsheet Wizard dialog box, type LinkedPolicies in the *Linked Table Name* text box and then click the Finish button.
7. At the message stating the linking is finished, click OK.
8. Open the new LinkedPolicies table in Datasheet view.
9. Close the LinkedPolicies table.
10. Open Excel, open the **ExcelC08_01.xlsx** workbook and then make the following changes:
    a. Change the amount *$745* in cell C3 to *$850*.
    b. Add the following information in the specified cells:
       A8 = 227-C-28
       B8 = 3120
       C8 = $685

| | A | B | C | D |
|---|---|---|---|---|
| 1 | Policy# | Client# | Premium | |
| 2 | 110-C-39 | 9383 | $1,450 | |
| 3 | 122-E-30 | 7335 | $850 | |
| 4 | 143-D-29 | 3120 | $920 | |
| 5 | 192-C-29 | 7335 | $1,390 | |
| 6 | 201-E-91 | 4300 | $1,525 | |
| 7 | 215-W-32 | 4300 | $734 | |
| 8 | 227-C-28 | 3120 | $685 | |
| 9 | | | | |

Step 10a
Step 10b

11. Save, print, and then close **ExcelC08_01.xlsx**.
12. Exit Excel.
13. With Access the active program and the **SouthwestInsurance.accdb** database open, open the LinkedPolicies table. Notice the changes you made in Excel are reflected in the table.
14. Close the LinkedPolicies table and then close the **SouthwestInsurance.accdb** database.

## Project 3 Collect Data in Word and Paste in an Access Table

You will open a Word document containing Hilltop customer names and addresses and then copy the data and paste it into an Access table.

# Using the Office Clipboard

Use the Office Clipboard to collect and paste multiple items. You can collect up to 24 different items in Access or other programs in the Office suite and then paste the items in various locations. To copy and paste multiple items, display the Clipboard task pane shown in Figure 8.2 by clicking the Clipboard group dialog box launcher.

Select data or an object you want to copy and then click the Copy button in the Clipboard group in the Home tab. Continue selecting text or items and clicking the Copy button. To insert an item from the Clipboard task pane to a field in an Access table, make the desired field active and then click the button in the task pane representing the item. If the copied item is text, the first 50 characters display. When all desired items are inserted, click the Clear All button to remove any remaining items from the Clipboard task pane.

You can copy data from one object to another in an Access database or from a file in another program to an Access database. In Project 3a, you will copy data from a Word document and paste it into a table. You can also collect data from other programs such as PowerPoint and Excel.

QUICK STEPS

**Display Clipboard Task Pane**
Click Clipboard group dialog box launcher.

**Figure 8.2** Office Clipboard Task Pane

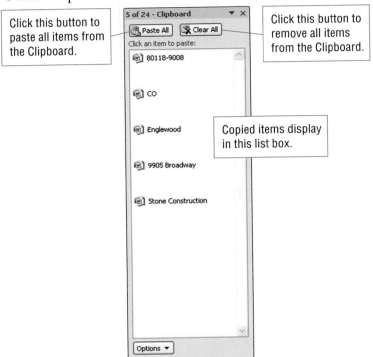

Click this button to paste all items from the Clipboard.

Click this button to remove all items from the Clipboard.

Copied items display in this list box.

Project **3a** **Collecting Data in Word and Pasting it in an Access Table**

1. Open the **Hilltop.accdb** database.
2. Open the Customers table.
3. Copy data from Word and paste it into the Customers table by completing the following steps:
   a. Open Word, make the Access2007L1C8 folder active, and then open **HilltopCustomers.docx**.
   b. Make sure the Home tab is active.
   c. Click the Clipboard group dialog box launcher to display the Clipboard task pane.
   d. Select the first company name, *Stone Construction*, and then click the Copy button in the Clipboard group.
   e. Select the street address, *9905 Broadway*, and then click the Copy button.

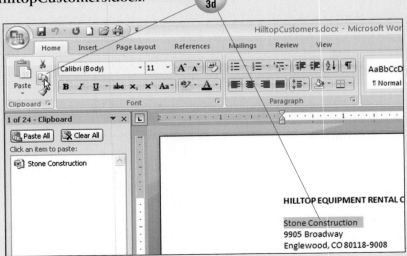

Step 3d

f. Select the city, *Englewood*, and then click the Copy button.

g. Select the state, *CO* (select only the two letters and not the space after the letters), and then click the Copy button.

h. Select the ZIP code, *80118-9008*, and then click the Copy button.

i. Click the button on the Taskbar representing Access. (Make sure the Customer table is open and displays in Datasheet view.)

j. Click in the first empty cell in the *Customer#* field and then type 178.

k. Display the Clipboard task pane by clicking the Clipboard group dialog box launcher.

l. Close the Navigation pane by clicking the Shutter Bar Open/Close Button.

m. Click in the first empty cell in the *Customer* field and then click *Stone Construction* in the Clipboard task pane.

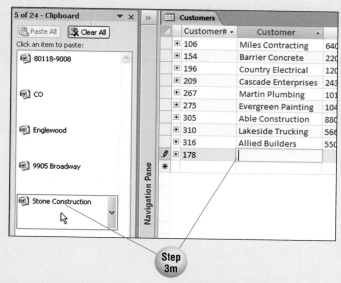

Step 3m

n. Click in the *StreetAddress* field and then click *9905 Broadway* in the Clipboard task pane.

o. Click in the *City* field and then click *Englewood* in the Clipboard task pane.

p. Click in the *State* field and then click *CO* in the Clipboard task pane.

q. Click in the *ZipCode* field, make sure the insertion point is positioned at the left side of the field, and then click *80118-9008* in the Clipboard task pane.

Step 3r

r. Click the Clear All button in the Clipboard task pane. (This removes all entries from the Clipboard.)

4. Complete steps similar to those in 3c through 3q to copy the information for Laughlin Products and paste it into the Customers table. (The Customer# is 225.)

5. Click the Clear All button in the Clipboard task pane.

6. Close the Clipboard task pane by clicking the Close button (contains an *X*) located in the upper right corner of the task pane.

7. Save, print, and then close the Customers table.

8. Open the Navigation pane by clicking the Shutter Bar Open/Close Button.

9. Make Word the active program, close **HilltopCustomers.docx** without saving changes, and then exit Word.

**Save a Database in a Previous Version Format**
1. Click Office button.
2. Point to *Save As*.
3. Click desired version.

# Saving a Database in a Previous Version Format

If you need to share an Access 2007 database with someone who is using an earlier version of Access, you will need to save the database in a different format. An Access 2007 database is saved with the .accdb file extension. Earlier versions of Access such as versions 2003, 2002, or 2000 save a database with the .mdb file extension. To save an Access 2007 database in an earlier version, open the database, click the Office button, point to *Save As*, and then click the desired version at the side menu shown in Figure 8.3.

**Figure 8.3** Save As Side Menu

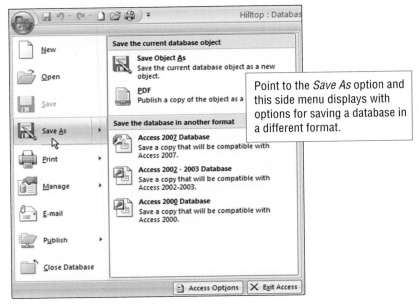

Point to the *Save As* option and this side menu displays with options for saving a database in a different format.

If you want to create a database in an earlier version, change the *Default file format* at the Access Options dialog box with the *Popular* option selected. To display this dialog box, click the Office button and then click the Access Options button located toward the bottom right side of the drop-down list. At the Access Options dialog box with *Popular* selected, click the down-pointing arrow at the right side of the *Default file format* option and then click *Access 2000* or *Access 2002 - 2003* at the drop-down list. This default format change remains in effect even if you exit and then open Access.

# Project 3b  Saving a Database in a Previous Version

1. With the **Hilltop.accdb** database open, save the database in a previous version of Access by completing the following steps:

   a. Click the Office button, point to *Save As*, and then click *Access 2002 - 2003 Database* at the side menu.

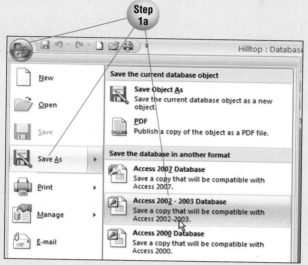

Step 1a

   b. At the Save As dialog box, type Hilltop2003Format.

   c. Notice that the *Save as type* option displays as *Microsoft Access Database (2002-2003) (*.mdb)*.

   d. Click the Save button.

2. Notice the Title bar displays the database file name *Hilltop2003Format : Database (Access 2002 - 2003 file format)*.

3. Close **Hilltop2003Format.mdb**.

# CHAPTER summary

- Use the Excel button in the Export group in the External Data tab to export data in a table, query, or form to an Excel worksheet.
- Use the Word button in the Export group in the External Data tab to export data in a table, query, form, or report to a Word document. Access exports the data to an RTF (rich-text format) file.
- You can merge Access data with a Word document. The Access data is the data source and the Word document is the main document. To merge data, click the desired table or query and then click the External Data tab. Click the More button in the Export group and then click *Merge it with Microsoft Office Word* at the drop-down list.
- Use the Excel button in the Import group in the External Data tab to import Excel data to an Access table.
- You can link imported data. Changes made to the data in the source program file are reflected in the destination source file.
- If you want to link imported data, click the *Link to the data source by creating a linked table* option at the Get External Data dialog box.
- Use the Clipboard task pane to collect up to 24 different items in Access or other programs and paste them in various locations.
- Display the Clipboard task pane by clicking the Clipboard group dialog box launcher.
- Save an Access database in an earlier version of Access by clicking the Office button, pointing to *Save As,* and then clicking *Access 2002 - 2003 Database* or *Access 2000 Database* at the side menu.

# COMMANDS review

| FEATURE | RIBBON TAB, GROUP | BUTTON, OPTION |
|---|---|---|
| Export object to Excel | External Data, Export | |
| Export object to Word | External Data, Export | Word |
| Merge Access data with Word | External Data, Export | More , Merge it with Microsoft Office Word |
| Import Excel data | External Data, Import | |
| Clipboard task pane | Home, Clipboard | |
| Save as 2002 - 2003 database | | , Save As, Access 2002 - 2003 Database |
| Save as 2000 Database | | , Save As, Access 2000 Database |

# CONCEPTS check

## Test Your Knowledge

**Completion:** In the space provided at the right, indicate the correct term, symbol, or command.

1. Click this tab to display the Export group.

    _____

2. Click this button in the Export group to display the Export - Excel Spreadsheet wizard dialog box.

    _____

3. At the first Export - Excel Spreadsheet wizard dialog box, click this option if you want Excel to open with the exported data.

    _____

4. When you export Access data to Word, the document is saved with this file format.

    _____

5. When merging data, the data in the Access table is considered this.

    _____

6. To merge data, click the More button in the Export group and then click this option.

    _____

7. If you want imported data connected to the original program, do this to the data.

    _____

8. Use this task pane to collect and paste multiple items.

    _____

9. To save a database in the 2003 format, click the Office button, point to *Save As*, and then click this option at the side menu.

    _____

10. To create a database in an earlier version, change the *Default file format* option at this dialog box with the *Popular* option selected.

    _____

# SKILLS check

*Demonstrate Your Proficiency*

## Assessment

## 1 EXPORT A FORM TO EXCEL AND A REPORT TO WORD

1. Display the Open dialog box with Access2007L1C8 on your storage medium the active folder.
2. Open the **LegalServices.accdb** database.
3. Create a form named *Billing* using the Form Wizard with the following fields:
   From the Billing table:
   > *Billing#*
   > *ClientID*
   > *Date*
   > *Hours*
   From the Rates table:
   > *Rate*
4. When the form displays, close it.
5. Create an Excel worksheet with the Billing form.
6. Make the following changes to the Excel Billing worksheet:
   a. Select columns A through E and then autofit the column widths.
   b. Select cells A2 through B28 and then click the Center button in the Alignment group in the Home tab.
   c. Save the Billing worksheet.
   d. Print and then close the Billing worksheet.
   e. Exit Excel.
7. In Access, close the Export Wizard.
8. Create a report named *ClientBilling* using the Report Wizard with the following fields:
   From the Clients table:
   > *FirstName*
   > *LastName*
   From the Billing table:
   > *Date*
   > *Hours*
   From the Rates table:
   > *Rate*
9. Apply the Foundry autoformat to the report.
10. When the report displays, change to Layout view and then decrease the size of the columns so the right border of the column displays just right of the longest entry in the column.
11. Save and then close the report.
12. Create a Word document with the ClientBilling report and save it to the Access2007L1C8 folder on your storage medium with the default name. In the Word document, make the following changes:
    a. Press Ctrl + A to select the entire document, change the font color to black, and then deselect the text.
    b. Insert a space between *Client* and *Billing* in the title.
    c. Position the insertion point immediately right of the word *Billing*, press the spacebar, and then type of Legal Services.

13. Save and then print **ClientBilling.rtf**.
14. Close the document and then exit Word.
15. In Access, close the wizard dialog box.

## Assessment

# 2   MERGE TABLE AND QUERY DATA WITH A WORD DOCUMENT

1. With the **LegalServices.accdb** database open, merge data in the Clients table to a new Word document using the *Merge it with Microsoft Office Word* option.
2. Maximize the Word document, close the Mail Merge task pane, and then compose a letter with the following elements:
   a. Click the Home tab and then click the No Spacing style in the Styles group.
   b. Press Enter six times, type the current date, and then press Enter five times.
   c. Click the Mailings tab and then insert the proper field names for the recipient's name and address. *Hint: Use the Insert Merge Field button in the Write & Insert Fields group.*
   d. Insert a proper salutation.
   e. Compose a letter to clients that includes the following information:

   The last time you visited our offices, you may have noticed how crowded we were. To alleviate the overcrowding, we are leasing new offices in the Meridian Building and will be moving in at the beginning of next month.

   Stop by and see our new offices at our open house planned for the second Friday of next month. Drop by any time between 2:00 and 5:30 p.m. We look forward to seeing you.

   f. Include an appropriate complimentary close for the letter. Use the name and title *Marjorie Shaw, Senior Partner* for the signature and add your reference initials and the document name (**AccessL1_C8_A2a.docx**).
3. Merge to a new document and then save the document with the name **AccessL1_C8_A2a**.
4. Print only the first two letters in the document and then close **AccessL1_C8_A2a.docx**.
5. Save the main document and name it **AccessL1_C8_A2_MD1**, close the document, and then exit Word.
6. At the LegalServices database, extract the records from the Clients table of those clients located in Kent and then name the query *KentQuery*.
7. Merge the KentQuery to a new Word document using the *Merge it with Microsoft Office Word* option.
8. Maximize the Word document, close the Mail Merge task pane, and then compose a letter with the following elements:
   a. Click the Home tab and then click the No Spacing style in the Styles group.
   b. Press Enter six times, type the current date, and then press Enter five times.
   c. Click the Mailings tab and then insert the proper field names for the inside address.
   d. Insert a proper salutation.

e. Compose a letter to clients that includes the following information:
   The City of Kent Municipal Court has moved from 1024 Meeker Street to a new building located at 3201 James Avenue. All court hearings after the end of this month will be held at the new address. If you need directions to the new building, please call our office.

f. Include an appropriate complimentary close for the letter. Use the name *Thomas Zeiger* and the title *Attorney* in the complimentary close and add your reference initials and the document name (**AccessL1_C8_A2b.docx**).

9. Merge the letter to a new document and then save the document with the name **AccessL1_C8_A2b**.

10. Print only the first two letters in the document and then close **AccessL1_C8_A2b.docx**.

11. Save the main document and name it **AccessL1_C8_A2_MD2**, close the document, and then exit Word.

## Assessment

### 3   IMPORT AND LINK AN EXCEL WORKBOOK

1. At the **LegalServices.accdb** database, import and link **ExcelC8_02.xlsx** into a new table named *Cases*.
2. Open the Cases table in Datasheet view.
3. Print and then close the Cases table.
4. Open Excel, open the **ExcelC08_02.xlsx** workbook and then add the following data in the specified cell:

| | | |
|---|---|---|
| A8 | = | 57-D |
| B8 | = | 130 |
| C8 | = | $1,100 |
| | | |
| A9 | = | 42-A |
| B9 | = | 144 |
| C9 | = | $3,250 |
| | | |
| A10 | = | 29-C |
| B10 | = | 125 |
| C10 | = | $900 |

5. Save, print, and then close **ExcelC08_02.xlsx**.
6. Exit Excel.
7. In Access, open the Cases table in Datasheet view. (Notice the changes you made in Excel are reflected in the table.)
8. Print and then close the Cases table.

# CASE study

## Apply Your Skills

**Part 1**

As the office manager at Woodland Dermatology Center, you are responsible for managing the center database. In preparation for an upcoming meeting, open the **Woodland.accdb** database and prepare the following with data in the database:

- Create a query that displays the patient number, first name, and last name; doctor last name; date of visit; and fee. Name the query *PatientBilling*.
- Export the PatientBilling query to an Excel worksheet. Apply formatting to enhance the appearance of the worksheet and then print the worksheet.
- Create mailing labels for the patients.
- Export the patient labels to a Word (.rtf) document and then print the document.
- Import and link the **WoodlandPayroll.xlsx** Excel worksheet to a new table named *WeeklyPayroll*. Print the WeeklyPayroll table.

You have been given some updated information about the weekly payroll and need to make the following changes to the **WoodlandPayroll.xlsx** worksheet: Change the hours for Irene Vaughn to *30*, change the wage for Monica Saunders to *$10.50*, and change the hours for Dale Jorgensen to *20*. After making the changes, open, print, and then close the WeeklyPayroll table.

**Part 2**

The center is expanding and will be offering cosmetic dermatology services at the beginning of next month to residents in the Altoona area. Design a query that extracts records of patients living in the city of Altoona and then merge the query with Word. At the Word document, write a letter describing the new services which include microdermabrasion, chemical peels, laser resurfacing, sclerotherapy, and photorejuvenation as well as an offer for a free facial and consultation. Insert the appropriate fields in the document and then complete the merge. Save the merged document and name it **Access_C8_CS_P2**. Print the first two letters of the document and then close the document. Close the main document without saving it and then exit Word.

**Part 3**

You need to save objects in the Woodland database in a format that can be read by employees that do not have Access available. You have researched the various file formats available and have determined that the PDF format is the most universal. Use the Access Help feature to learn how to save a database object in PDF format. (You may need to download an add-in to save an object in PDF format.) Save the Patients table in PDF format and then print the PDF file. Save the Doctors table in PDF format and then print the PDF file.

**Part 4**

Since you are responsible for updating the clinic procedures manual, you decide to create a Word document that describes the steps for saving an object in PDF format. Save the completed document and name it **Access_C8_CS_P4**. Print and then close **Access_C8_CS_P4.docx**.

# Creating Forms and Reports

## ASSESSING proficiency

In this unit, you have learned to create forms, reports, and mailing labels; filter data; and summarize and analyze data in PivotTable and PivotChart view as well as create a PivotTable form. You also learned how to modify document properties; view object dependencies; and export, import, and link data between programs.

*Note: Before beginning unit assessments, copy to your storage medium the Access2007L1U2 subfolder from the Access2007L1 folder on the CD that accompanies this textbook and then make Access2007L1U2 the active folder.*

### Assessment 1 Create Tables in a Clinic Database

1. Use Access to create a database for clients of a mental health clinic. Name the database **LancasterClinic**. Create a table named *Clients* that includes the following fields (you determine the field name, data type, field size, and description):

   *ClientNumber* (primary key)
   *ClientName*
   *StreetAddress*
   *City*
   *State*
   *ZipCode*
   *Telephone*
   *DateOfBirth*
   *DiagnosisID*

2. After creating the table, switch to Datasheet view and then enter the following data in the appropriate fields:

   | | |
   |---|---|
   | *ClientNumber:* 1831 | *ClientNumber:* 3219 |
   | George Charoni | Marian Wilke |
   | 3980 Broad Street | 12032 South 39th |
   | Philadelphia, PA 19149 | Jenkintown, PA 19209 |
   | (215) 555-3482 | (215) 555-9083 |
   | *DateOfBirth:* 4/12/1958 | *DateOfBirth:* 10/23/1981 |
   | *DiagnosisID:* SC | *DiagnosisID:* OCD |
   | | |
   | *ClientNumber:* 2874 | *ClientNumber:* 5831 |
   | Arthur Shroeder | Roshawn Collins |
   | 3618 Fourth Avenue | 12110 52nd Court East |

Philadelphia, PA 19176    Cheltenham, PA 19210
(215) 555-8311            (215) 555-4779
*DateOfBirth:* 3/23/1958    *DateOfBirth:* 11/3/1965
*DiagnosisID:* OCD        *DiagnosisID:* SC

*ClientNumber:* 4419      *ClientNumber:* 1103
Lorena Hearron         Raymond Mandato
3112 96th Street East     631 Garden Boulevard
Philadelphia, PA 19132   Jenkintown, PA 19209
(215) 555-3281           (215) 555-0957
*DateOfBirth:* 7/2/1984     *DateOfBirth:* 9/20/1979
*DiagnosisID:* AD         *DiagnosisID:* MDD

3. Save, print, and then close the Clients table.
4. Create a table named *Diagnoses* that includes the following fields:
   *DiagnosisID* (primary key)
   *Diagnosis*
5. After creating the table, switch to Datasheet view and then enter the following data in the appropriate fields:

   | | | |
   |---|---|---|
   | *DiagnosisID* | = | AD |
   | *Diagnosis* | = | Adjustment Disorder |
   | | | |
   | *DiagnosisID* | = | MDD |
   | *Diagnosis* | = | Manic-Depressive Disorder |
   | | | |
   | *DiagnosisID* | = | OCD |
   | *Diagnosis* | = | Obsessive-Compulsive Disorder |
   | | | |
   | *DiagnosisID* | = | SC |
   | *Diagnosis* | = | Schizophrenia |

6. Save, print, and then close the Diagnoses table.
7. Create a table named *Fees* that includes the following fields (you determine the field name, data type, field size, and description):
   *FeeCode* (primary key)
   *HourlyFee*
8. After creating the table, switch to Datasheet view and then enter the following data in the appropriate fields:

   | | | |
   |---|---|---|
   | *FeeCode* | = | A |
   | *HourlyFee* | = | $75.00 |
   | | | |
   | *FeeCode* | = | B |
   | *HourlyFee* | = | $80.00 |
   | | | |
   | *FeeCode* | = | C |
   | *HourlyFee* | = | $85.00 |
   | | | |
   | *FeeCode* | = | D |
   | *HourlyFee* | = | $90.00 |

$$FeeCode = E$$
$$HourlyFee = \$95.00$$

$$FeeCode = F$$
$$HourlyFee = \$100.00$$

$$FeeCode = G$$
$$HourlyFee = \$105.00$$

$$FeeCode = H$$
$$HourlyFee = \$110.00$$

9. Save, print, and then close the Fees table.
10. Create a table named *Employees* that includes the following fields (you determine the field name, data type, field size, and description):
      *ProviderNumber* (primary key)
      *ProviderName*
      *Title*
      *Extension*
11. After creating the table, switch to Datasheet view and then enter the following data in the appropriate fields:

   *ProviderNumber:* 29                  *ProviderNumber:* 15
   *ProviderName:* James Schouten        *ProviderName:* Lynn Yee
   *Title:* Psychologist                 *Title:* Child Psychologist
   *Extension:* 399                      *Extension:* 102

   *ProviderNumber:* **33**              *ProviderNumber:* 18
   *ProviderName:* Janice Grisham        *ProviderName:* Craig Chilton
   *Title:* Psychiatrist                 *Title:* Psychologist
   *Extension:* 11                       *Extension:* 20

12. Save, print, and then close the Employees table.
13. Create a table named *Billing* that includes the following fields (you determine the field name, data type, field size, and description):
      *BillingNumber* (primary key; identify the data type as *AutoNumber*)
      *ClientNumber*
      *DateOfService* (apply the Date/Time data type)
      *Insurer*
      *ProviderNumber*
      *Hours*
      *FeeCode*
14. After creating the table, switch to Datasheet view and then enter the following data in the appropriate fields:

   *ClientNumber:* 4419                  *ClientNumber:* 1831
   *DateOfService:* 3/1/2010             *DateOfService:* 3/1/2010
   *Insurer:* Health Plus                *Insurer:* Self
   *ProviderNumber:* 15                  *ProviderNumber:* 33
   *Hours:* 2                            *Hours:* 1
   *FeeCode:* B                          *FeeCode:* H

ClientNumber: 3219  
DateOfService: 3/2/2010  
Insurer: Health Plus  
ProviderNumber: 15  
Hours: 1  
FeeCode: D  

ClientNumber: 5831  
DateOfService: 3/2/2010  
Insurer: Penn-State Health  
ProviderNumber: 18  
Hours: 2  
FeeCode: C  

ClientNumber: 4419  
DateOfService: 3/3/2010  
Insurer: Health Plus  
ProviderNumber: 15  
Hours: 1  
FeeCode: A  

ClientNumber: 1103  
DateOfService: 3/3/2010  
Insurer: Penn-State Health  
ProviderNumber: 18  
Hours: 0.5  
FeeCode: A  

ClientNumber: 1831  
DateOfService: 3/4/2010  
Insurer: Self  
ProviderNumber: 33  
Hours: 1  
FeeCode: H  

ClientNumber: 5831  
DateOfService: 3/4/2010  
Insurer: Penn-State Health  
ProviderNumber: 18  
Hours: 0.5  
FeeCode: C  

15. Save, print, and then close the Billing table.

## Assessment 2 Relate Tables and Create Forms in a Clinic Database

1. With the **LancasterClinic.accdb** database open, create the following one-to-many relationships:
   a. *ClientNumber* in the Clients table is the "one" and *ClientNumber* in the Billing table is the "many."
   b. *DiagnosisID* in the Diagnoses table is the "one" and *DiagnosisID* in the Clients table is the "many."
   c. *ProviderNumber* in the Employees table is the "one" and *ProviderNumber* in the Billing table is the "many."
   d. *FeeCode* in the Fees table is the "one" and *FeeCode* in the Billing table is the "many."
2. Create a form with the data in the Clients table.
3. After creating the form, add the following record to the Clients form:
   ClientNumber: 1179  
   Timothy Fierro  
   1133 Tenth Southwest  
   Philadelphia, PA 19178  
   (215) 555-5594  
   DateOfBirth: 12/7/1987  
   DiagnosisID: AD
4. Save the form as Clients, print the form, and then close the form.
5. Add the following records to the Billing table:
   ClientNumber: 1179  
   DateOfService: 3/8/2010  
   Insurer: Health Plus  
   ProviderNumber: 15  
   Hours: 0.5  
   FeeCode: C  

   ClientNumber: 1831  
   DateOfService: 3/8/2010  
   Insurer: Self  
   ProviderNumber: 33  
   Hours: 1  
   FeeCode: H  
6. Save and then print the Billing table.
7. Close the Billing table.

## Assessment 3 Create Forms Using the Form Wizard

1. With the **LancasterClinic.accdb** database open, create a form with fields from related tables using the Form Wizard with the following specifications:
   a. At the first Form Wizard dialog box, insert the following fields in the Selected Fields list box:
      From the Clients table:
         *ClientNumber*
         *DateOfBirth*
         *DiagnosisID*
      From the Billing table:
         *Insurer*
         *ProviderNumber*
   b. Do not make any changes at the second Form Wizard dialog box.
   c. Do not make any changes at the third Form Wizard dialog box.
   d. You determine the format style at the fourth Form Wizard dialog box.
   e. At the fifth Form Wizard dialog box, type the name ProviderInformation in the *Form* text box.
2. When the first record displays, print the first record.
3. Close the form.

## Assessment 4 Create Labels with the Label Wizard

1. With the **LancasterClinic.accdb** database open, use the Label Wizard to create mailing labels with the client names and addresses and sorted by ZIP code. Name the mailing label file **ClientMailingLabels**.
2. Print the mailing labels.
3. Close the mailing labels file.

## Assessment 5 Filter Records in Tables

1. With the **LancasterClinic.accdb** database open, open the Billing table and then filter the records to display the following records:
   a. Display only those records with the Health Plus insurer. Print the results and then remove the filter.
   b. Display only those records with the 4419 client number. Print the results and then remove the filter.
2. Filter records by selection to display the following records:
   a. Display only those records with a C fee code. Print the results and then remove the filter.
   b. Display only those records between the dates of 3/1/2010 and 3/3/2010. Print the results and then remove the filter.
3. Close the Billing table without saving the changes.
4. Open the Clients table and then use Filter By Form to display clients in Jenkintown or Cheltenham. Print the results and then remove the filter.
5. Close the Clients table without saving the changes.

## Assessment 6 View and Analyze Data in PivotTable View

1. With the **LancasterClinic.accdb** database open, create a query in Design view with the following specifications:
   a. Add the Billing, Employees, and Clients tables to the design grid.
   b. Add the following fields from the specified tables:

| | | | |
|---|---|---|---|
| *DateOfService* | = | Billing table | |
| *ProviderNumber* | = | Employees table | |
| *ClientNumber* | = | Clients table | |
| *Hours* | = | Billing table | |

    c. Run the query.

    d. Save the query and name it *ProviderHours*.

2. Display the query in PivotTable view.
3. At the PivotTable layout, drag and drop the fields as follows:

    a. Drag the *ProviderNumber* field to the *Drop Row Fields Here* section.

    b. Drag the *ClientNumber* field to the *Drop Column Fields Here* section.

    c. Drag the *Hours* field to the *Drop Totals or Detail Fields Here* section.

    d. Drag the *DateOfService* field to the *Drop Filter Fields Here* section.

4. Remove the *PivotTable Field List* box from the screen.
5. Click the Quick Print button to print the query in PivotTable view.
6. In the *ProviderNumber* field, display only the hours for provider number 15.
7. Print the PivotTable and then redisplay all providers.
8. In the *DateOfService* field, display only hours for March 2, 2010.
9. Print the PivotTable and then redisplay all rental dates.
10. Switch to Datasheet view, save the query, and then close the query.

## Assessment 7 Export a Table to Excel

1. With the **LancasterClinic.accdb** database open, export the Billing table to an Excel workbook.
2. Apply formatting to the cells in the Excel workbook to enhance the appearance of the data.
3. Change the page orientation to landscape.
4. Save, print, and then close the workbook.
5. Exit Excel.

## Assessment 8 Merge Records to Create Letters in Word

1. With the **LancasterClinic.accdb** database open, merge data in the Clients table to a blank Word document. ***Hint: Use the* Merge it with Microsoft Office Word *option from the More button in the Export group in the External Data tab.*** You determine the fields to use in the inside address and an appropriate salutation. Type March 10, 2010 as the date of the letter and type the following text in the body of the document:

> The building of a new wing for the Lancaster Clinic will begin April 1, 2010. We are excited about this new addition to our clinic. With the new facilities, we will be able to offer additional community and group services along with enhanced child-play therapy treatment.
>
> During the construction, the main entrance will be moved to the north end of the building. Please use this entrance until the construction of the wing is completed. We apologize in advance for any inconvenience this causes you.

Include an appropriate complimentary close for the letter. Use the name and title *Marianne Lambert, Clinic Director* for the signature and add your reference initials and the document name (**AccessL1_U2_A8.docx**).

2. Merge to a new document and then save the document with the name **AccessL1_U2_A8**.
3. Print the first two letters of the document and then close **AccessL1_U2_A8.docx**.
4. Save the main document as **ConstructionLetter** and then close **ConstructionLetter.docx**.
5. Exit Word.

## Assessment 9 Import and Link Excel Data to an Access Table

1. With the **LancasterClinic.accdb** database open, import and link **ExcelU02_01.xlsx** into a new table named *StaffHours*.
2. Open the StaffHours table in Datasheet view.
3. Print and then close the StaffHours table.
4. Open **ExcelU02_01.xlsx** in Excel.
5. Insert a formula in cell D2 that multiplies B2 with C2 and then copy the formula down to cells D3 through D7.
6. Save and then close **ExcelU02_01.xlsx**.
7. Exit Excel.
8. In Access with the **LancasterClinic.accdb** database open, open the StaffHours table.
9. Print and then close the StaffHours table.

# WRITING activities

The following activities give you the opportunity to practice your writing skills along with demonstrating an understanding of some of the important Access features you have mastered in this unit. Use correct grammar, appropriate word choices, and clear sentence constructions.

## Activity 1 Add a Table to the Clinic Database

The director at Lancaster Clinic has asked you to add information to the **LancasterClinic.accdb** database on insurance companies contracted by the clinic. You need to create a table that will contain information on insurance companies. The director wants the table to include the insurance company name, address, city, state, and ZIP code along with a telephone number and the name of a representative. You determine the field names, data types, field sizes, and description for the table and then include the following information (in the appropriate fields):

Health Plus
4102 22nd Street
Philadelphia, PA 19166
(212) 555-0990
Representative: Byron Tolleson

Penn-State Health
5933 Lehigh Avenue
Philadelphia, PA 19148
(212) 555-3477
Representative: Tracey Pavone

Quality Medical
51 Cecil B. Moore Avenue
Philadelphia, PA 19168
(212) 555-4600
Representative: Lee Stafford

Delaware Health
4418 Front Street
Philadelphia, PA 19132
(212) 555-6770
Representative: Melanie Chon

Save, print, and then close the insurance company table. Open Word and then write a report to the clinic director detailing how you created the table. Include a title for the report, steps on how you created the table, and any other pertinent information. Save the completed report and name it **AccessL1_U2_Act1**. Print and then close **AccessL1_U2_Act1.docx**.

## Activity 2 Merge Records to Create Letters to Insurance Companies

Merge data in the insurance company database to a blank Word document. You determine the fields to use in the inside address and an appropriate salutation. Compose a letter to the insurance companies informing them that Lancaster Clinic is providing mental health counseling services to people with health insurance through their company. You are sending an informational brochure about Lancaster Clinic and are requesting information from the insurance companies on services and service limitations. Include an appropriate complimentary close for the letter. Use the name and title *Marianne Lambert, Clinic Director* for the signature and add your reference initials. When the merge is completed, name the document containing the merged letters **AccessL1_U2_Act2**. Print the first two letters in the merged document and then close **AccessL1_U2_Act2.docx**. Close the main document without saving it and then exit Word. Close the **LancasterClinic.accdb** database.

## Health Information Search

In this activity, you will search the Internet for information on a health concern or disease that interests you. You will be looking for specific organizations, interest groups, or individuals who are somehow connected to the topic you have chosen. Your topic may be an organization that raises money to support research, it may be a support group that posts information or answers questions, or you may find information about clinics or doctors who specialize in your topic. Try to find at least ten different groups that support the health concern you are researching.

Create a database in Access and create a table that includes information from your search. Design the table so that you can store the name, address, phone number, and Web address of the organizations you find. You will also want to identify the connection the group has to your topic (supports research, interest group, treats patients, etc.). Create a report to summarize your findings. In Microsoft Word, create a letter that you can use to write for further information about the organization. Use the names and addresses in your database to merge with the letter. Select and then print the first two letters that result from the merge. Finally, write a paragraph describing information you learned about the health concern that you previously did not know.

## City Improvement Projects

In this activity, you are working with the city council in your area to keep the public informed of the progress being made on improvement projects throughout the city. These projects are paid for through tax dollars voted on by the public, and the city council feels that an informed public leads to a good voter turnout when it is time to make more improvements.

Your job is to create a database and a table in the database that will store the following information for each project: a project ID number, a description of the project, the budgeted dollar amount to be spent, the amount spent so far, the amount of time allocated to the project, and the amount of time spent so far. Enter five city improvement projects into the table (sample data created by you). Create a query based on the table that calculates the percent of budgeted dollars spent so far and the percent of budgeted time spent so far. Print the table and the query.

# A

Access
  closing, 18
  data management with, 7
  security features in, 10
Access data: merging with Word
    document, 255–257, 268
Access database
  copying data from one object
    to another in, 263
  saving in earlier version of
    Access, 268
Access Help window, 90
Access Options button, 87, 266
Access Options dialog box, 266
Access screen: elements within,
    9, 10
Access table
  collecting data in Word and
    pasting it in, 264–265
  importing Excel data to, 268
  importing Excel worksheet
    into, 260–261
  inserting item from Clipboard
    task pane to field in, 263
  linking Excel worksheet with,
    262–263
Access 2003 autoformats, 164
Access 2007 autoformats, 164
Add a group button, 195
Add a sort button, 196
Add button, 160
Add Existing Field button, 161,
    163, 175, 192
Advanced button, 217, 242
Aggregate function list:
    displaying, 118, 129
Aggregate functions, 129
  adding to tables, in
    PivotTable view, 224
  designing queries with, 118
  using and grouping records,
    120–121
  using in queries, 119–120
Alignment
  changing, in form fields, 155
  changing, in reports, 191
Align Text Right button, 155,
    159
And criteria: designing queries
    with, 111–112, 129
Ascending button, 92, 151,
    189, 190, 207
Attachment data type, 67
AutoCalc button, 228
AutoCorrect feature, 82
AutoFormat button, 194, 196,
    197, 207
AutoFormat group, 164
AutoFormats
  applying to forms, 164–166,
    176
  applying to reports, 194,
    196–198
  selection of, for reports, 200
Autoformat styles: choosing in
    Form Wizard dialog box,
    170, 172
AutoNumber data type, 67

Avg aggregate function, 121, 129
  including in queries, 118

# B

Backing up databases, 86,
    88–89, 92, 93
Blank Database button, 8
Bold button, 155, 159, 160,
    163, 168, 192
Browse button, 262
Build button, 73

# C

Calculated fields
  creating, 116
  creating, in a query, 116–118
  inserting in Field text boxes,
    129
Capitalizations: irregular, 82
Cascade Delete Related Records
    option, 42, 43, 48
Cascade Update Related Fields
    option, 42, 43, 48
Center button, 192
City field drop-down list, 216
Clear All button, 263
Clients datasheet:
    Representatives form with,
    153
Clients table: creating a form
    with, 149–150
Clipboard group dialog box
    launcher, 263, 268
Clipboard task pane, 268
Close button, 18
Closing
  Access, 18
  databases, 8, 11–12, 30
  objects, 11–12
Collapse indicator, 54, 58
Color
  applying in forms, 159, 160
  font, in reports, 191
  line, in reports, 193
Color button, 193
Color button arrow, 159
Columnar layout: specifying in
    Form Wizard dialog box,
    170, 172
Columns: changing width and
    order of, in reports, 189
Column widths: changing in
    reports, 207
Comma (,): exclusion of, from
    field names, 13
Comma Number formatting:
    applying to numbers in
    reports, 191
Compacting and repairing
    databases, 87–89, 92, 93
Complex query wizards, 100
Conditional button, 156, 160,
    175, 191
Conditional formatting:
    applying in forms,
    156–157, 158–160
Conditional formatting:
    applying to reports, 191,
    192–194, 207

Conditional Formatting dialog
    box, 156, 157, 176, 191,
    193, 207, 208
Conditions, additional, adding,
    158
Control objects
  customizing, in forms,
    154–155, 175
  moving, 175
  moving, in form header, 162
  selecting, 188
  sizing and moving in reports,
    188–191
  sizing in forms, 162, 175
Controls
  formatting, in forms,
    160–161, 162–164
  formatting, in reports,
    191–192
Controls group, 160, 175
Copy button, 263
Count aggregate function, 129
  including in queries, 118
Create button, 17, 42, 175
Criterion
  establishing, 101
  examples of, 102
Crosstab queries: creating,
    121–123, 129
Crosstab Query Wizard, 130
Crosstab Query Wizard dialog
    box, 123
Crosstab Wizards, 100
Currency data type, 67
Currency formatting: applying
    to numbers in reports, 191
Current Database Properties
    dialog box, 237
Custom Filter dialog box, 219,
    220
Customize Quick Access
    Toolbar button, 22
Customizing
  control objects in forms, 147
  database properties, 242
  database properties for
    current database, 238–239
  document properties,
    235–239
  forms, 154–155
  properties for the current
    database, 237
  reports, 191–192, 207

# D

Data
  analyzing in PivotTable view,
    227–228
  entering in a table, 19–21
  exporting, 249
  exporting, to Excel, 249, 250
  exporting, to Word, 249,
    253–255
  filtering, 215–216
  finding and replacing, 83
  grouping and sorting in
    reports, 196–198
  importing to a new table, 260
  inserting in reports, 183

linking to Excel worksheet, 262
organizing in Access, 29
organizing in tables, 13–19
specific, finding, 85–86
summarizing, in PivotChart
    view, 231–235
summarizing, in PivotTable
    view, 224–227
summarizing and analyzing,
    in PivotTable form, 229
Database management system
    software, 7, 13, 29
Database objects, 10
Database properties: viewing,
    236, 242
Databases
  backing up, 86, 88–89, 92, 9?
  closing, 30
  compacting and repairing,
    87–89, 92, 93
  components of, 8
  creating in an earlier version,
    266
  flat file, 36
  opening and closing, 8,
    11–12, 29
  planning, 36
  previously created, opening,
  saving, 18, 29, 30
  saving, in a previous version
    format, 266–267, 268
Database tables
  checking spelling in, 83
  creating, 7–30
  planning, 58
Datasheet layout: specifying in
    Form Wizard dialog box,
    170
Datasheets: total rows inserted
    into, 70, 71–72
Datasheet view, 15, 19, 29, 30?
    148
  adding fields in, 92
  deleting fields in, 67
Data Type column, 16
Data types
  assigning, 67
  assigning, to fields, 14–15
Date and time: inserting in
    reports, 207
Date and Time button, 163
Date and Time dialog box, 16?
Date/Time data type, 67
  assignment of, to fields, 14
Decrease Decimals button, 15?
    193
Default margins: changing, 23?
Default value: assigning, 70,
    71–72
Default Value property, 92
Delete button, 151
Delete button arrow, 26
Delete Rows button, 67, 92, 9?
Delete symbol: filtering and, 2?
Deleting
  fields, 67, 93
  forms in records, 151–152
  grouping or sorting levels, 1?
  records, 29, 30
  records, from forms, 175

fonts changed in, 191
formatting numbers and
  applying gridlines in, 191
naming, 200
printing, 207
record sorting in, 189
specifying grouping level of
  data in, 199
totaling numbers in, 191
Reports group, 183, 184, 198, 207
Report view, 185, 207
Report Wizard, 183, 184, 208
  reports created with,
    198–201, 207
Report Wizard button, 198, 201
Report Wizard dialog boxes,
  201, 202
Restrictions: filters as, 215, 242
Results group, 109, 110, 116
Returning queries, 102
Ribbon, 9, 10
Rich-text format, 253, 268
Rows
  adding for new fields in
    Design view, 66–67
  selecting, 92
RTF files: saving in rich-text
  format, 253
Run button, 101, 109, 110, 116
Run query, 130

## S

Save As dialog box, 15, 17, 86,
  109, 242
Save As side menu, 266
Save button, 16, 109
Saved queries: modifying, 109
Saving databases, 18, 29, 30
Security features: in Access
  2007, 10
Selection button, 220, 242
Selection button drop-down list,
  221
Shortcut menu: filtering by, 221
Show/Hide group, 41, 46, 51,
  118
Show Table button, 46
Show Table dialog box, 41, 45,
  46, 120
  query window with, 100
Show Table list box, 100
Shutter Bar Open/Close button,
  189, 194
Simple Query Wizard, 100,
  112, 115, 129, 130
  performing and modifying a
    query with, 115–116
  performing a query with,
    112–115
Simple Query Wizard dialog
  boxes, 112, 113, 114
Simple query wizards, 100
Size: changing in reports, 194
Size button, 185
Size option: at Page Setup
  dialog box, 29

Sizing
  control objects, 188–191
  control objects in forms, 162
Social Security numbers: Text
  data types and, 14
Sort Ascending button, 80
Sort Descending button, 80
Sort & Filter group, 80, 92,
  151, 189, 190, 207, 216,
  217, 220, 242
Sorting
  mailing labels, 204
  records, 80
  records in forms, 151
Sort order: specifying for
  reports, 199, 200
SouthwestInsurance.accdb
  database, 36, 38, 44
SouthwestInsurance database:
  relating tables in, 44
Spaces, in field names, 13
Specify Relationship dialog box,
  161
Spelling button, 82, 92
Spelling checker, 92, 93
Spelling checks
  completing, 82
  in database tables, 83
Spelling dialog box, 82
Split Form button, 166, 176
  forms created with, 147, 148,
    175
Split forms, creating, 166–168,
  176
Square brackets ([]): exclusion
  of, from field names, 13
Standard page size, 23
Start button, 8
Start pop-up menu, 7
Status bar, 9, 10
Style button, 159
Subdatasheets, 58
  related records displayed in,
    54–55
  turning off display of, 56, 58
  viewing and editing, 56–57
Sum aggregate function, 121,
  129
  including in queries, 118
Summary tab: in Properties
  dialog box, 236
Suppliers table, open, 12
Symbols
  in Criteria text box, 102
  delete, 216
  in field names, 13
  infinity, 42, 43
  plus and minus, 227
Synchronous viewing: with split
  forms, 166, 176

## T

Table orientation: changing, 24
Tables, 8, 10
  creating, 15–18, 38–40
  creating, and defining one-to-
    one relationship, 51–54
  creating PivotTable in, 227

data entered in, 19–21
data organized in, 13–19
deleting records in, 26–28
in Design view, 15
determining fields for, 13–14,
  29
displaying in Design view, 66
editing or deleting
  relationships between, 58
establishing relationships
  between, 40–41
exporting data in, to Excel
  worksheet, 268
exporting to Excel, 251–252
exporting to other programs,
  249
exporting to Word, 253–255
filtering records in, 217–218
importing data to, 260
maintaining, 26, 29
modifying, 66–70, 68–70, 92
moving fields in, 79–80
multiple, creating reports
  with fields from, 202–203
page layout changed in,
  23–24
performing queries on,
  103–105
previewing, 22
primary, 41
printing, 22, 29, 30
records added to, 26–28
related, 41
relating, in
  SouthwestInsurance
  database, 44
sorting records in, 92
with subdatasheet displayed,
  55
viewing object dependencies
  and, 239
Table Tools Datasheet tab, 15,
  66
Table Tools Design tab, 16, 66
Tabs, 9, 10
Tabular layout: specifying in
  Form Wizard dialog box,
  170
Taskbar, Start button on, 8
Telephone numbers: Text data
  types and, 14
Template Categories section: of
  Getting Started with
  Microsoft Office Access
  screen, 8, 9
Text data type, 67
  assignment of, to fields, 14
Themes: autoformats matched
  to, 164
Title bar, 9, 10
Titles
  inserting in forms, 175
  inserting in reports, 207
Titles for forms: choosing in
  Form Wizard dialog box,
  171
Toggle filter, 243
Toggle Filter button, 217, 223,
  242

Tools button, 235, 236, 242
Tools group, 37, 92
Totaling numbers: in reports,
  191
Total rows
  adding to query design, 130
  inserting, 70, 71–72
Totals button, 70, 92, 118, 121,
  191, 194, 207
Trust Center dialog box, 10
Trusted locations, 10
Two Pages button, 186

## U

Undo button, 67
Unmatched queries, 129
  creating, 127–128
Unmatched Query Wizards,
  100

## V

Validation rule, 92
Validation Rule property, 70, 92
Validation Text property, 92
View button, 15, 16, 17, 39,
  66, 109, 129, 149
View button arrow, 66, 227
Viewing: subdatasheets, 56–57
Views: changing in forms, 149
Views group, 66

## W

Width button, 159
Wildcard character: query
  criteria and, 103, 129
Word
  Access data merged with, 268
  collecting data in, and
    pasting it in Access table,
    264–265
  exporting a table and report
    to, 253–255
  exporting data to, 253
  exporting objects to, 268
Word button, 268
Word document
  Access data merged with,
    255–257, 268
  performing a query and then
    merging with, 258–259
  query data merged with, 257
Work area
  in Access screen, 9, 10
  opening more than one
    document in, 11

## Y

Yes/No data type, 67

## Z

ZipCode field, 73
ZIP codes: Text data types and,
  14
Zoom button arrow, 186
Zoom group, 185, 186

# Microsoft® PowerPoint®

## Making PowerPoint Work for You!

Being an effective communicator is one of the most marketable job skills you can possess. Whether your audience is a few colleagues in a small meeting room or a larger gathering in a conference center, you can enhance your message through the use of visual aids created with presentation software. Microsoft PowerPoint 2007 is the presentation graphics program included in the Microsoft Office 2007 suite. Content created in PowerPoint can be projected through a computer to a large screen or output in various formats, including slides, transparencies, or hard copy.

## Organizing Information

PowerPoint 2007 offers several views in which you can organize the content of your topic. Each view is suited for specific tasks, but you can choose to work in the view in which you are most comfortable. For example, if you have a lot of typing to do, use Normal view with the Outline tab selected in the Slides/Outline pane. Switch to Slide Sorter view to rearrange several slides by dragging slide miniatures to new positions in the presentation. Use Notes Page view to add speaker notes to your slides. Insert and position graphics in Normal view with the Slides tab selected in the Slides/Outline pane. Preview the presentation in Slide Show view.

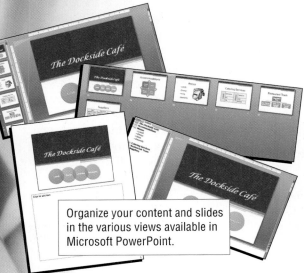

Organize your content and slides in the various views available in Microsoft PowerPoint.

Changing slide formatting such as the font, font size, and color is made easier with the use of *slide masters*. Open a presentation in Slide Master view to make global changes—changes you want applied to all slides. Changes can be made before or after content has been added. A slide master can also be used to add a graphic object, such as a company logo, to the same position in each slide. Use slide masters whenever possible to reduce the number of steps needed to make changes to all slides in a presentation.

# Analyzing Information

In today's global workplace, two or more people commonly collaborate on a presentation. Send a PowerPoint file to others in a workgroup for review by placing the presentation on a network share folder and use options in the Review tab to insert, edit, and delete comments. With other options in the Review tab you can research information, use the thesaurus, and translate text into other languages.

Editing slides by rearranging the progression of content is easily accomplished using a drag and drop technique in either Slide Sorter view or Outline view. Use the Spelling feature to help find common misspellings. Everyone remembers the speaker with the slides that had typos. Make sure your audience remembers you for the brilliant insight you gave about your topic and not for the typing errors!

Rearrange the order of slides using a drag and drop technique.

Use the Rehearse Timings feature to set up a self-running presentation that has to synchronize times in which to advance slides. Display the Rehearsal toolbar and use buttons on the toolbar to set the appropriate amount of time each slide should display on the screen.

# Presenting Information

Creating an eye-catching, thought-provoking presentation has never been easier. Microsoft PowerPoint 2007 includes several professionally created design theme templates that you can easily apply to your content. You don't have to be knowledgeable about choosing complementary colors or scaling font sizes for readability to create a background or interesting bullet style—design theme templates have all of these features incorporated for you. Click the Design tab, click the More button at the right side of the themes styles, and then browse through the themes until you find one that intrigues you. Click the theme and it is instantly applied to your presentation. Want to preview more design themes? Click the option *More Themes on Microsoft Office Online* to browse the Web site where you can download additional design theme templates. This site is constantly updated, so check back often for creative new offerings.

No one wants to sit and watch a presentation that is text, text, and more text! Add interest to your presentation by inserting objects such as clip art, pictures, SmartArt diagrams, charts, photographs, movies, sounds, and more. Display the Clip Art task pane and search both your computer's media Gallery and the Microsoft Office Online Gallery for the right media clip to spruce up that text-only slide.

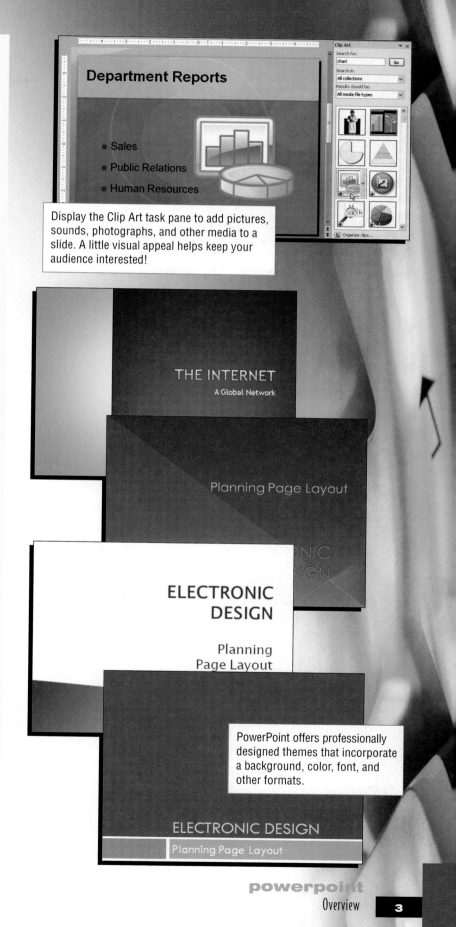

Display the Clip Art task pane to add pictures, sounds, photographs, and other media to a slide. A little visual appeal helps keep your audience interested!

PowerPoint offers professionally designed themes that incorporate a background, color, font, and other formats.

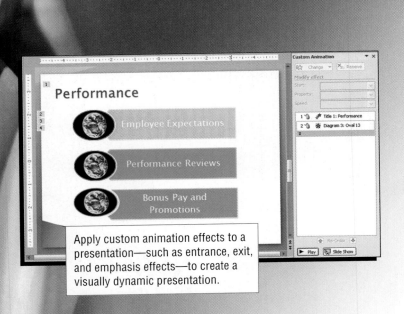

Apply custom animation effects to a presentation—such as entrance, exit, and emphasis effects—to create a visually dynamic presentation.

After adding objects such as clip art, charts, or photographs to your slides, consider adding animation effects to maintain audience interest, create focus, or signal changes in content. Microsoft PowerPoint includes built-in animation effects you can apply to a presentation. Want more control over animation? Use options in the Custom Animation task pane to further animate objects in your presentation. Apply entrance, exit, and emphasis effects; display objects one at a time or all at once; display individual elements within an object such as a SmartArt diagram or chart; and apply a "build" to text in a slide to keep your audience focused on the current topic.

Set up your slide show presentation by creating a custom show. Add or modify action buttons to control slide progression or hide slides that you do not want the audience to view. On the day you are to deliver your presentation, use the slide show features to advance slides and use the pointer options to focus attention on a slide element by drawing with a ballpoint pen, felt tip pen, or highlighter.

Get started and have fun learning to use Microsoft PowerPoint. You will soon be amazing audiences with your ability to produce effective and visually appealing presentations that help make your point!

# Microsoft® PowerPoint®

## Unit 1: Creating and Formatting PowerPoint Presentations

- ➤ Preparing a PowerPoint Presentation
- ➤ Modifying a Presentation and Using Help
- ➤ Formatting Slides
- ➤ Inserting Elements in Slides

# Benchmark Microsoft® PowerPoint 2007

## Microsoft Certified Application Specialist Skills—Unit 1

| Reference No. | Skill | Pages |
|---|---|---|
| **1** | **Creating and Formatting Presentations** | |
| 1.1 | Create new presentations | |
| 1.1.1 | Create presentations from blank presentations | 27-29 |
| 1.1.2 | Create presentations from templates | 10-11, 14-16 |
| 1.1.3 | Create presentations from existing presentations | 22-24 |
| 1.4 | Create and change presentation elements | |
| 1.4.1 | Change presentation orientation | 54-56 |
| 1.4.2 | Add, change, and remove transitions between slides at the presentation level | 29-32 |
| 1.4.3 | Set slide size | 95-97 |
| 1.5 | Arrange slides | 48-50 |
| **2** | **Creating and Formatting Slide Content** | |
| 2.1 | Insert and format text boxes | |
| 2.1.1 | Insert and remove text boxes | 120-124 |
| 2.1.2 | Size text boxes | 120, 122-123 |
| 2.1.3 | Format text boxes | 120-126 |
| 2.1.4 | Select text orientation and alignment | 122, 124, 128 |
| 2.1.5 | Set margins | 123 |
| 2.1.6 | Create columns in text boxes | 123-126 |
| 2.2 | Manipulate text | |
| 2.2.1 | Cut, copy, and paste text | 41-45 |
| 2.2.2 | Apply Quick Styles from the Style Gallery | 88-92 |
| 2.2.3 | Format font attributes | 70-74 |
| 2.2.4 | Use the Format Painter to format text | 74-75 |
| 2.2.5 | Create and format bulleted and numbered lists | 76-79, 84-88 |
| 2.2.6 | Format paragraphs | 76-88 |
| 2.2.7 | Insert and modify WordArt | 145-148 |
| 2.3 | Add and link existing content to presentations | |
| 2.3.1 | Reuse slides from an existing presentation | 52-53 |
| 2.3.2 | Copy elements from one slide to another | 41-44, 50, 129-133 |
| **3** | **Working With Visual Content** | |
| 3.3 | Insert illustrations and shapes | |
| 3.3.1 | Insert pictures from file | 137 |
| 3.3.2 | Insert shapes | 126-135 |
| 3.3.3 | Insert clip art | 140-144 |
| 3.3.4 | Add text to shapes | 127, 132 |
| 3.4 | Modify illustrations | |
| 3.4.1 | Apply Quick Styles to shapes and pictures | 127, 131, 135, 138 |
| 3.4.2 | Add change and remove illustration effects | 138, 139 |
| 3.5 | Arrange illustrations and other content | |
| 3.5.1 | Size, scale, and rotate illustrations and other content | 136-138, 142-144 |
| 3.5.2 | Order illustrations and other content | 136-138 |
| 3.5.3 | Group and align illustrations and other content | 134-135 |
| 3.5.4 | Use gridlines and guides to arrange illustrations and other content | 129-135 |
| **4** | **Collaborating on and Delivering Presentations** | |
| 4.3 | Secure and share presentations | |
| 4.3.5 | Compress images | 135-138 |
| 4.4 | Prepare printed materials | |
| 4.4.2 | Print a presentation in various formats | 19-20, 32 |
| 4.5 | Prepare for and rehearse presentation delivery | |
| 4.5.3 | Use presentation tools | 17-18, 21-24 |

# Preparing a PowerPoint Presentation

## PERFORMANCE OBJECTIVES

**Upon successful completion of Chapter 1, you will be able to:**

- Create a PowerPoint presentation with an installed template
- Open, save, run, print, close, and delete a presentation
- Plan a presentation
- Create a presentation using a theme template
- Insert slides, insert text in slides, and choose slide layouts
- Change presentation views
- Navigate and edit slides
- Create a presentation from an existing presentation
- Apply a design theme to slides in a presentation
- Prepare a presentation from a blank presentation
- Prepare a presentation in Slides/Outline pane
- Add transitions and sounds to a presentation

**Tutorial 1.1**
Creating, Saving, and Printing a
    Presentation
**Tutorial 1.2**
Organizing and Enhancing
    Presentations

During a presentation, the person doing the presenting may use visual aids to strengthen the impact of the message as well as help organize the presentation. Visual aids may include transparencies, slides, photographs, or an on-screen presentation. With Microsoft's PowerPoint program, you can easily create visual aids for a presentation and then print copies of the aids as well as run the presentation. PowerPoint is a presentation graphics program that you can use to organize and present information.

*Note: Before beginning computer projects, copy to your storage medium the PowerPoint2007C1 subfolder from the PowerPoint2007 folder on the CD that accompanies this textbook. Steps on how to copy a folder are presented on the inside of the back cover of this textbook. Do this every time you start a chapter's projects.*

## roject  Open and Run a Template Presentation

You will open an installed template presentation, run the presentation, and then close the presentation.

# Creating a PowerPoint Presentation

PowerPoint provides several methods for creating a presentation. You can create a presentation using an installed template or using a theme template and prepare a presentation from a blank presentation or from an existing presentation. The steps you follow to create a presentation will vary depending on the method you choose, but will probably follow these basic steps:

1. Open PowerPoint.
2. Choose the desired installed template or theme or open an existing presentation or start with a blank presentation.
3. Type the text for each slide, adding additional elements as needed such as graphic images.
4. If necessary, apply a design theme.
5. Save the presentation.
6. Print the presentation as slides, handouts, notes pages, or an outline.
7. Run the presentation.
8. Close the presentation.
9. Exit PowerPoint.

## Understanding the PowerPoint Window

When you choose the specific type of presentation you want to create, you are presented with the PowerPoint window in the Normal view. What displays in the window will vary depending on the type of presentation you are creating. However, the PowerPoint window contains some consistent elements as shown in Figure 1.1.

**Figure 1.1** PowerPoint Window

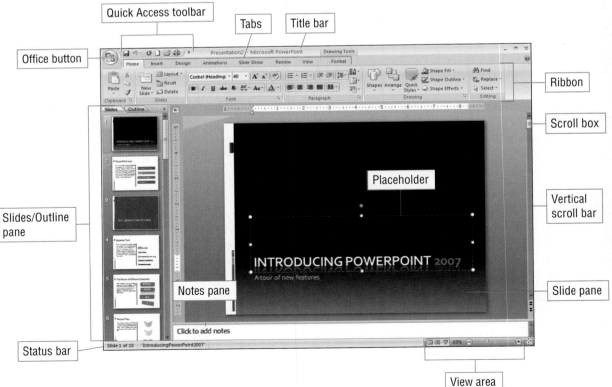

The PowerPoint window contains many elements that are similar to other Microsoft Office programs such as Word and Excel. For example, the PowerPoint window, like the Word window, contains an Office button, Quick Access toolbar, tabs, ribbon, vertical and horizontal scroll bars, and a Status bar. The PowerPoint window elements are described in Table 1.1.

**Table 1.1** PowerPoint Window Elements

| Feature | Description |
|---|---|
| Office button | Displays as a Microsoft Office logo and, when clicked, displays a list of options along with the most recently opened presentations. |
| Quick Access toolbar | Contains buttons for commonly used commands. |
| Title bar | Displays presentation name followed by the program name. |
| Tabs | Contains commands and features organized into groups. |
| Ribbon | Area containing the tabs and commands divided into groups. |
| Slides/Outline pane | Displays at the left side of the window with two tabs—Slides and Outline. With the Slides tab selected, slide miniatures (thumbnails) display in the pane; with the Outline tab selected, presentation contents display in the pane. |
| Slide pane | Displays the slide and slide contents. |
| Notes pane | Add notes to a presentation in this pane. |
| Vertical scroll bar | Display specific slides using this scroll bar. |
| I-beam pointer | Used to move the insertion point or to select text. |
| Insertion point | Indicates the location of the next character entered at the keyboard. |
| View area | Located toward the right side of the Status bar and contains buttons for changing the presentation view. |
| Status bar | Displays the slide number and number of slides, name of the applied design theme, view buttons, and the Zoom slider bar. |

PowerPoint, like other Microsoft Office programs, provides enhanced ScreenTips for buttons and options. Hover the mouse pointer on a button or option and, after approximately one second, an enhanced ScreenTip displays near the button or option. The enhanced ScreenTip displays the name of the button or option, any shortcut command if one is available, and a description of the button or option.

# Opening a Presentation

**Open a Presentation**
1. Click Open button.
2. Navigate to desired folder or drive.
3. Double-click presentation.

**Open an Installed Template**
1. Click Office button, *New.*
2. Click *Installed Templates* option.
3. Double-click desired presentation.

When you create and then save a presentation, you can open the presentation at the Open dialog box. Display this dialog box by clicking the Open button on the Quick Access toolbar or click the Office button and then click *Open* at the drop-down list. (If the Open button does not display on the Quick Access toolbar, click the Customize Quick Access Toolbar button located at the right side of the toolbar and then click *Open* at the drop-down list.) At the Open dialog box, navigate to the desired folder and then double-click the desired presentation in the list box. By default, PowerPoint displays the nine most recently opened presentations in the Office button drop-down list. To open one of these presentations, click the Office button and then click the desired presentation in the *Recent Documents* section. If you want a presentation to remain in the drop-down list, "pin" the presentation to the drop-down list by clicking the pin button that displays at the right side of the presentation name. This changes the dimmed gray stick pin to a green stick pin. To "unpin" the presentation, click the pin button to change it from a green pin to a gray pin.

## Opening an Installed Template

Office button

Open

Microsoft provides a number of predesigned presentation templates you can view and also use as a basis for preparing your own presentation. To display the installed templates, click the Office button and then click *New* at the drop-down list. At the New Presentation dialog box, click the *Installed Templates* option in the *Templates* section. To open a template presentation, double-click the desired presentation in the *Installed Templates* list box.

# Starting a Presentation

QUICK STEPS

**Run a Presentation**
1. Click Slide Show button in view area on Status bar.
2. Click left mouse button to advance slides.

**Close a Presentation**
1. Click Office button.
2. Click *Close.*
OR
Press Ctrl + F4.

When you open a presentation, the presentation displays in Normal view. In this view, you can edit and customize the presentation. To run the presentation, click the Slide Show button in the view area on the Status bar or click the Slide Show tab and then click the From Beginning button in the Start Slide Show group. Navigate through slides in the presentation by clicking the left mouse button.

# Closing a Presentation

To remove a presentation from the screen, close the presentation. You can close a presentation by clicking the Office button and then clicking *Close* at the drop-down list. You can also close a presentation with the keyboard shortcut Ctrl + F4. To use this shortcut, hold down the Ctrl key on the keyboard, press the F4 function key located toward the top of the keyboard, and then release the Ctrl key. If you made any changes to the presentation, you will be asked if you want to save the presentation.

1. Open PowerPoint.
2. Click the Office button and then click *New* at the drop-down list.
3. At the New Presentation dialog box, click the *Installed Templates* option in the *Templates* section.
4. Double-click *Introducing PowerPoint 2007* in the *Installed Templates* list box.
5. Run the presentation by completing the following steps:
   a. Click the Slide Show button in the view area on the Status bar.
   b. Read the information in the first slide in the presentation and then click the left mouse button.
   c. Continue reading information in slides and clicking the left mouse button to advance slides.
   d. At the black screen with the message "End of slide show, click to exit." click the left mouse button. (This returns the presentation to Normal view.)
6. Close the presentation by clicking the Office button and then clicking *Close* at the drop-down list.

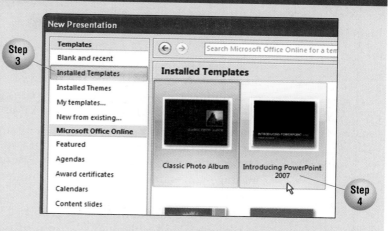

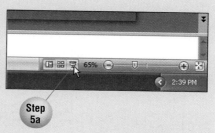

Project **2** | **Create an Internet Presentation Using a Theme Template**

**You will use a theme template to create a presentation, insert text in slides in the presentation, choose a slide layout, insert new slides, change views, navigate through the presentation, edit text in slides, and then print the presentation.**

# Planning a Presentation

With PowerPoint, you can create slides for an on-screen presentation and you can print handouts of the presentation, print an outline, or print the entire presentation. When planning a presentation, first define the purpose of the presentation. Is the intent to inform? educate? sell? motivate? and/or entertain? Additionally, consider the audience who will be listening to and watching the presentation. Determine the content of the presentation and also the medium that will be used to convey the message. Will a computer be used to display the slides of a presentation or will overhead transparencies be created from the slides? Some basic guidelines to consider when preparing the content of the presentation include:

- **Determine the main purpose of the presentation.** Do not try to cover too many topics—this may strain the audience's attention or cause confusion. Identifying the main point of the presentation will help you stay focused and convey a clear message to the audience.

- **Determine the output.** Is the presentation going to be presented in PowerPoint? Will slides be used? Or will black and white or color transparencies be made for an overhead? To help decide the type of output needed, consider the availability of equipment, the size of the room where the presentation will be made, and the number of people who will be attending the presentation.

- **Show one idea per slide.** Each slide in a presentation should convey only one main idea. Too many thoughts or ideas on a slide may confuse the audience and cause you to stray from the purpose of the slide. Determine the specific message you want to convey to the audience and then outline the message to organize ideas.

- **Maintain a consistent layout.** A consistent layout and color scheme for slides in a presentation will create continuity and cohesiveness. Do not get carried away by using too many colors and too many pictures or other graphic elements.

- **Keep slides easy to read and uncluttered.** Keep slides simple and easy for the audience to read. Keep words and other items such as bullets to a minimum.

- **Determine the output needed.** Will you be providing audience members with handouts? If so, will these handouts consist of a printing of each slide? an outline of the presentation? a printing of each slide with space for taking notes?

# Creating a Presentation Using a Theme Template

PowerPoint provides a variety of predesigned theme templates you can use when creating slides for a presentation. These theme templates include formatting such as color, background, fonts, and so on. You can choose a theme template at the New Presentation dialog box. To do this, click the Office button and then click *New* at the drop-down list. At the New Presentation dialog box, click *Installed Themes* in the *Templates* section and then double-click the desired theme template in the list box.

# Inserting Text in Slides

When you choose a theme template at the New Presentation dialog box or start with a blank presentation, click the Design tab and then click the desired theme in the Themes group, a slide displays in the Slide pane in Normal view. The slide displays with a Title default slide layout. This layout contains placeholders for entering the slide title and the slide subtitle. To insert text in a placeholder, click the placeholder text. This moves the insertion point inside the placeholder, removes the default placeholder text, and selects the placeholder. A selected placeholder displays surrounded by a dashed border with sizing handles and a green rotation handle. Figure 1.2 displays a selected placeholder.

**Figure 1.2** Selected Placeholder

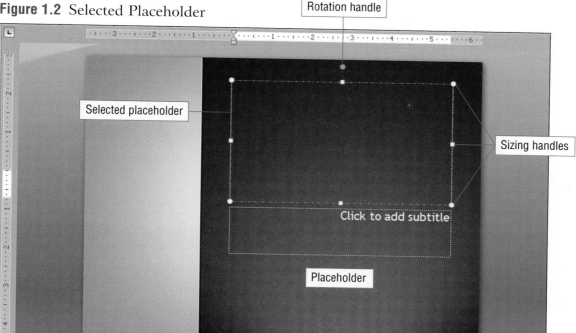

With the insertion point positioned in a placeholder, type the desired text. Edit text in a placeholder in the same manner as editing text in a Word document. Press the Backspace key to delete the character immediately left of the insertion point and press the Delete key to delete the character immediately right of the insertion point. Use the arrow keys on the keyboard to move the insertion point in the desired direction.

# Choosing a Slide Layout

When you choose a theme template or a theme in a blank presentation, the slide displays in the Title Slide layout. This layout provides two placeholders for text — title text and subtitle text. You can change the slide layout with the Layout button in the Slides group in the Home tab. Click the Layout button and a drop-down list of layouts displays. Click the desired layout at the drop-down list and the layout is applied to the current slide.

# Inserting a New Slide

Create a new slide in a presentation by clicking the New Slide button in the Slides group in the Home tab. By default, PowerPoint inserts a new slide with the Title and Content layout. You can choose a different slide layout for a new slide by clicking the New Slide button arrow and then clicking the desired layout at the drop-down list. You can also change the slide layout by clicking the Layout button in the Slides group in the Home tab and then clicking the desired layout at the drop-down list.

**QUICK STEPS**

**Choose a Slide Layout**
1. Click Layout button.
2. Click desired layout option in drop-down list.

**Insert a New Slide**
Click New Slide button.

**HINT**
PowerPoint includes nine built-in standard layouts.

**Save a Presentation**
1. Click Save button.
2. Navigate to desired folder.
3. Type presentation name in *File name* text box.
4. Click Save button.

# Saving a Presentation

After creating a presentation, save it by clicking the Save button on the Quick Access toolbar or by clicking the Office button and then *Save As*. This displays the Save As dialog box. At the Save As dialog box, type a name for the presentation in the *File name* text box. Click the down-pointing arrow at the right side of the *Save in* option, click the drive containing your storage medium, and then click the Save button.

Save

## Project 2a  Creating a Presentation Using a Theme Template

1. With PowerPoint open, click the Office button and then click *New* at the drop-down list.
2. At the New Presentation dialog box, click *Installed Themes* in the *Templates* section of the dialog box.
3. Scroll down the *Installed Themes* list box and then double-click *Opulent*.

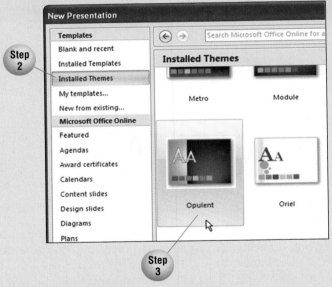

Step 2

Step 3

Step 6

4. Click in the placeholder text *CLICK TO ADD TITLE* and then type the internet (the design theme changes the text to uppercase letters).
5. Click in the placeholder text *Click to add subtitle* and then type A Global Network.
6. Click the New Slide button in the Slides group in the Home tab (this inserts a slide with the Title and Contents layout).

7. Click the placeholder text *CLICK TO ADD TITLE* and then type communications (the design theme changes the text to uppercase letters).
8. Click the placeholder text *Click to add text* and then type E-mail.
9. Press the Enter key (this moves the insertion point to the next line and inserts a bullet) and then type Chat Rooms.
10. Press the Enter key and then type Instant Messaging.
11. Press the Enter key and then type Blogs.
12. Press the Enter key and then type Electronic Bulletin Boards.

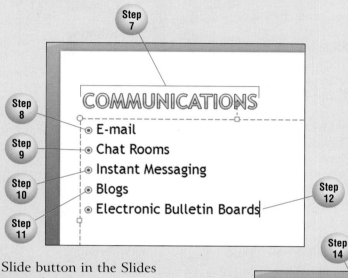

13. Click the New Slide button in the Slides group in the Home tab.
14. Click the placeholder text *CLICK TO ADD TITLE* and then type entertainment.
15. Click the placeholder text *Click to add text* and then type Online Games.
16. Press the Enter key and then type Online Gambling.
17. Press the Enter key and then type Music.
18. Press the Enter key and then type Video.
19. Click the New Slide button arrow and then click the Title Slide layout.

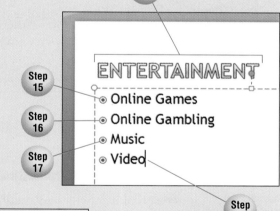

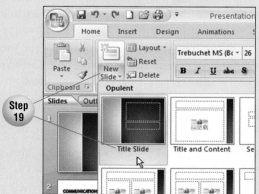

20. Click the placeholder text *CLICK TO ADD TITLE* and then type internet issues.
21. Click the placeholder text *Click to add subtitle* and then type Community and Policy Issues.
22. Click the New Slide button.
23. Click the placeholder text *CLICK TO ADD TITLE* and then type community issues.
24. Click the placeholder text *Click to add text* and then type Flaming.
25. Press the Enter key and then type Netiquette.
26. Press the Enter key and then type Moderated Environments.
27. Click the New Slide button in the Slides group in the Home tab.
28. Click the placeholder text *CLICK TO ADD TITLE* and then type policy issues.

29. Click the placeholder text *Click to add text* and then type Privacy Issues.
30. Press the Enter key and then type Security Protection.
31. Press the Enter key and then type Viruses.
32. Press the Enter key and then type Copyright Infringement.
33. Click in the Slide pane but outside the slide. (This deselects the placeholder.)
34. Save the presentation by completing the following steps:
    a. Click the Save button on the Quick Access toolbar.
    b. At the Save As dialog box type PP_C1_P2 (for PowerPoint, Chapter 1, Project 2).
    c. Click the down-pointing arrow at the right side of the *Save in* option and then click the drive containing your storage medium.
    d. Click the Save button.

**HINT**

In Normal view, you can increase or decrease the size of the Slides/Outline pane and the Notes pane.

## Changing Views

PowerPoint provides a variety of viewing options for a presentation. You can change the view with buttons in the view area on the Status bar or with options in the Presentation Views group in the View tab. The viewing choices include:

- **Normal view:** This is the default view and displays three panes—Slides/Outline, Slide, and Notes. With these three panes, you can work with all features in one place. This view is also referred to as tri-pane view.
- **Slide Sorter view:** Choosing the Slide Sorter view displays all slides in the presentation in slide miniatures. In this view, you can easily add, move, rearrange, and delete slides.
- **Notes Page view:** Change to the Notes Page view and an individual slide displays on a page with any added notes displayed below the slide.
- **Slide Show view:** Use the Slide Show view to run a presentation. When you choose this view, the slide fills the entire screen.

The view area on the Status bar contains three buttons for changing the view—Normal, Slide Sorter, and Slide Show with the active button displaying with a light orange background. You can also change views with buttons in the View tab. The Presentation Views group in the View tab contains a number of buttons for changing views. Four buttons in the group include the Normal, Slide Sorter, Notes Page, and Slide Show button. Click the Notes Page button and the active slide displays along with a space below the slide for inserting text. Click the text *Click to add text* that displays in the box below the slide and then type the desired note. When running the presentation, you can display any note attached to the slide.

Normal

Normal

## Navigating in a Presentation

Slide Sorter

In the Normal view, change slides by clicking the Previous Slide or Next Slide buttons located at the bottom of the vertical scroll bar. You can also change to a different slide using the mouse pointer on the vertical scroll bar. To do this, position the mouse pointer on the scroll box on the vertical scroll bar, hold down the left mouse button, drag up or down until a box displays with the desired slide number, and then release the button.

Slide Show

Notes Page

Previous Slide    Next Slide

You can also use the keyboard to display slides in a presentation. In Normal view, press the Down Arrow or Page Down key to display the next slide or press the Up Arrow or Page Up key to display the previous slide in the presentation. Press the Home key to display the first slide in the presentation and press End to display the last slide in the presentation. Navigate in the Slides/Outline pane by clicking the desired slide thumbnail. Navigate in the Slide Sorter view by clicking the desired slide or using the arrow keys on the keyboard.

Project **2b**    **Navigating and Editing Slides in a Presentation**

1. With **PP_C1_P2.pptx** open, navigate in the presentation by completing the following steps:
   a. Make sure that a placeholder in the slide is not selected.
   b. Press the Home key to display Slide 1 in the Slide pane.
   c. Click the Next Slide button located toward the bottom of the vertical scroll bar.
   d. Press the End key to display the last slide in the Slide pane.
   e. Click the Slide Sorter button in the view area on the Status bar.

Step 1c

Step 1e

   f. Click Slide 1. (Notice that the active slide displays with a dark orange border.)
   g. Double-click Slide 5. (This closes Slide Sorter view and displays the presentation in Normal view with Slide 5 active.)
2. Insert text in slides by completing the following steps:
   a. Click on any character in the bulleted text. (This selects the placeholder.)
   b. Move the insertion point so it is positioned immediately right of *Flaming*.

c. Press the Enter key and then type E-mail Pointers.

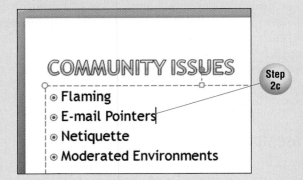

d. Click Slide 3 in the Slides/Outline pane. (This displays Slide 3 in the Slide pane.)
e. Click on any character in the bulleted text.
f. Move the insertion point so it is positioned immediately right of *Video*.
g. Press the Enter key and then type Travel.
3. Type a note in the Notes pane by completing the following steps:
a. Click Slide 6 in the Slides/Outline pane.
b. Click the text *Click to add notes* that displays in the Notes pane.
c. Type Discuss the Digital Millennium Copyright Act of 1998.

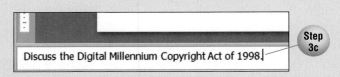

d. Display the slide in Notes Page view by clicking the View tab and then clicking the Notes Page button in the Presentation Views group. (Notice the note you typed displays below the slide in this view.)

e. Return to Normal view by clicking the Normal button in the view area on the Status bar.
f. Press the Home key to make Slide 1 the active slide.
4. Save the presentation by clicking the Save button on the Quick Access toolbar.

# Printing a Presentation

You can print a PowerPoint presentation in a variety of formats. You can print each slide on a separate piece of paper; print each slide at the top of the page, leaving the bottom of the page for notes; print up to nine slides or a specific number of slides on a single piece of paper; or print the slide titles and topics in outline form. Use the *Print what* option at the Print dialog box, shown in Figure 1.3, to specify what you want printed. To display the Print dialog box, click the Office button and then click *Print* at the drop-down list. At the Print dialog box, click the down-pointing arrow at the right side of the *Print what* option box and then click the desired printing format.

To print specific slides in a presentation, click the *Slides* option in the *Print range* section and then type the slide number in the *Slides* text box. Print a range of slides using the hyphen and print specific slides using a comma. For example, to print Slides 2 through 6, you would type *2-6* in the *Slides* text box. To print Slides 1, 3 and 7, you would type *1,3,7*. You can combine a hyphen and comma. For example, to print Slides 1 through 4 and Slide 8, you would type *1-4,8*.

If you want to send the presentation directly to the printer, click the Quick Print button on the Quick Access toolbar. (If this button does not display on the toolbar, click the Customize Quick Access Toolbar button located at the right side of the toolbar and then click *Quick Print* at the drop-down list.)

**HINT**
Printing a hard copy of your presentation and distributing it to your audience helps reinforce your message.

Quick Print

**Figure 1.3** Print Dialog Box

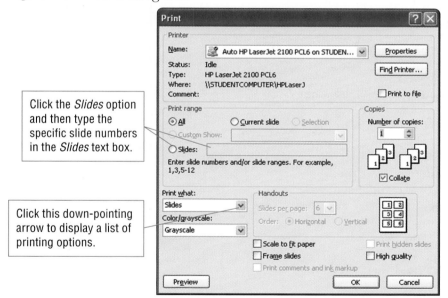

Click the *Slides* option and then type the specific slide numbers in the *Slides* text box.

Click this down-pointing arrow to display a list of printing options.

# Project 2c — Printing a Presentation

1. With **PP_C1_P2.pptx** open, print the presentation as a handout with six slides per page by completing the following steps:
   a. Click the Office button and then click *Print* at the drop-down list.
   b. At the Print dialog box, click the down-pointing arrow at the right side of the *Print what* option and then click *Handouts* at the drop-down list.
   c. Make sure the number *6* displays in the *Slides per page* text box in the *Handouts* section of the dialog box.
   d. Click OK.

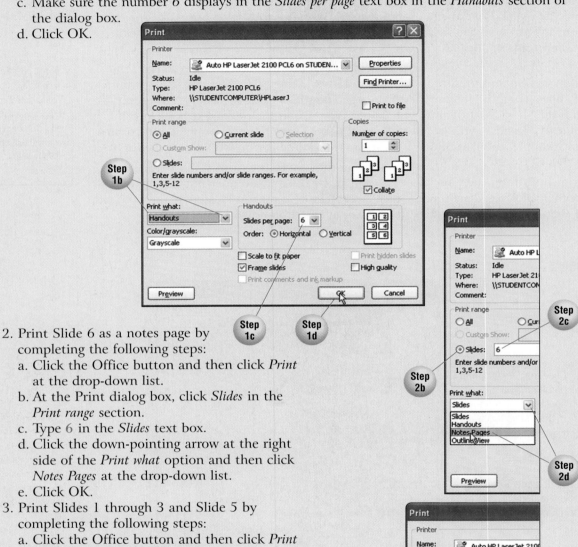

2. Print Slide 6 as a notes page by completing the following steps:
   a. Click the Office button and then click *Print* at the drop-down list.
   b. At the Print dialog box, click *Slides* in the *Print range* section.
   c. Type *6* in the *Slides* text box.
   d. Click the down-pointing arrow at the right side of the *Print what* option and then click *Notes Pages* at the drop-down list.
   e. Click OK.

3. Print Slides 1 through 3 and Slide 5 by completing the following steps:
   a. Click the Office button and then click *Print* at the drop-down list.
   b. At the Print dialog box, click *Slides* in the *Print range* section.
   c. Type *1-3,5* in the *Slides* text box.
   d. Change the *Print what* option to *Slides*.
   e. Click OK.

4. Close the presentation by clicking the Office button and then clicking *Close* at the drop-down list.

roject **3** **Create a Planning Presentation from an Existing Presentation**
You will create a presentation from an existing presentation, apply a design theme
to the presentation, run the presentation, and then delete the presentation.

# Running a Slide Show

As you learned earlier in this chapter, run a presentation by clicking the Slide Show button in the view area on the Status bar or by clicking the Slide Show tab and then clicking the From Beginning button in the Start Slide Show group. This group also contains a From Current Slide button. Use this button to begin running the slide show with the currently active slide rather than the first slide in the presentation.

From Beginning

From Current Slide

PowerPoint offers a wide variety of options for navigating through slides in a presentation. Figure 1.4 displays the Slide Show Help window that contains keyboard commands for running a presentation.

**Figure 1.4** Slide Show Help Menu

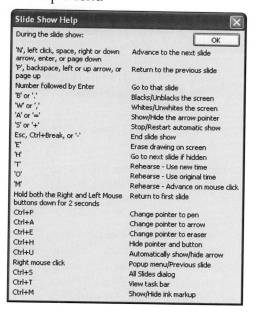

**Slide Show Help**

During the slide show:

[OK]

| | |
|---|---|
| 'N', left click, space, right or down arrow, enter, or page down | Advance to the next slide |
| 'P', backspace, left or up arrow, or page up | Return to the previous slide |
| Number followed by Enter | Go to that slide |
| 'B' or '.' | Blacks/Unblacks the screen |
| 'W' or ',' | Whites/Unwhites the screen |
| 'A' or '=' | Show/Hide the arrow pointer |
| 'S' or '+' | Stop/Restart automatic show |
| Esc, Ctrl+Break, or '-' | End slide show |
| 'E' | Erase drawing on screen |
| 'H' | Go to next slide if hidden |
| 'T' | Rehearse - Use new time |
| 'O' | Rehearse - Use original time |
| 'M' | Rehearse - Advance on mouse click |
| Hold both the Right and Left Mouse buttons down for 2 seconds | Return to first slide |
| Ctrl+P | Change pointer to pen |
| Ctrl+A | Change pointer to arrow |
| Ctrl+E | Change pointer to eraser |
| Ctrl+H | Hide pointer and button |
| Ctrl+U | Automatically show/hide arrow |
| Right mouse click | Popup menu/Previous slide |
| Ctrl+S | All Slides dialog |
| Ctrl+T | View task bar |
| Ctrl+M | Show/Hide ink markup |

In addition to the methods described in the Slide Show Help window, you can also navigate in a presentation using buttons on the Slide Show toolbar shown in Figure 1.5. To display this toolbar, run the presentation, and then move the mouse pointer. Click the right arrow button on the toolbar to display the next slide and click the left arrow button to display the previous slide. Click the slide icon button and a pop-up list displays with the following options: *Next, Previous, Last Viewed, Go to Slide, Custom Show, Screen, Help, Pause,* and *End Show.* Use these options to navigate to a particular slide in the presentation, display the Slide Show Help window, and pause or end the show. Click the pen button and a pop-up list displays with the following options: *Arrow, Ballpoint Pen, Felt Tip Pen, Highlighter, Ink Color, Eraser, Erase All Ink on Slide,* and *Arrow Options.*

**QUICK STEPS**

**Use Pen/Highlighter during Presentation**
1. Run presentation.
2. Display desired slide.
3. Click pen button on Slide Show toolbar.
4. Click pen or highlighter option.
5. Drag to draw line or highlight text.

**HINT**

If you use the pen or highlighter on a slide when running a presentation, choose an ink color that the audience can see easily.

**Figure 1.5**  Slide Show Toolbar

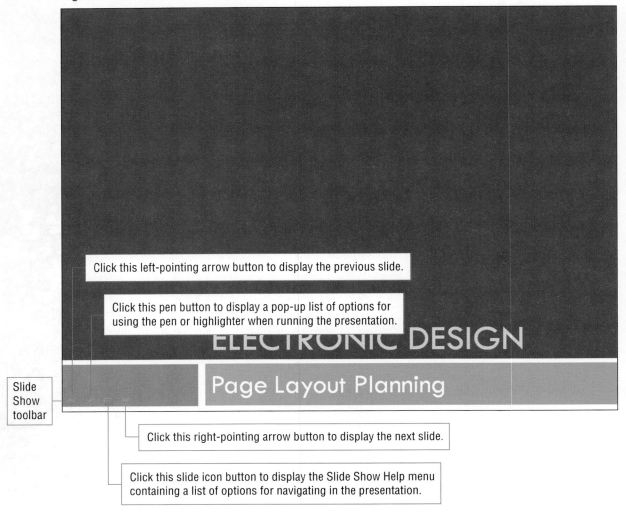

Click this left-pointing arrow button to display the previous slide.

Click this pen button to display a pop-up list of options for using the pen or highlighter when running the presentation.

Slide Show toolbar

ELECTRONIC DESIGN

Page Layout Planning

Click this right-pointing arrow button to display the next slide.

Click this slide icon button to display the Slide Show Help menu containing a list of options for navigating in the presentation.

When running a presentation, the mouse pointer is set, by default, to be hidden automatically after three seconds of inactivity. The mouse pointer will appear again when you move the mouse. You can change this default setting by clicking the pen button on the Slide Show toolbar, pointing to *Arrow Options*, and then clicking *Visible* if you want the mouse pointer always visible or *Hidden* if you do not want the mouse to display at all as you run the presentation. The *Automatic* option is the default setting.

**Create a Presentation from an Existing Presentation**
1. Click Office button, *New*.
2. Click *New from existing* option.
3. Double-click desired presentation.
4. Edit presentation.
5. Save presentation with new name.

## Creating a Presentation from an Existing Presentation

You can create a presentation from an installed template, an installed theme, a blank presentation, or from an existing presentation. To create a presentation from an existing presentation, click the Office button and then click *New* at the drop-down list. At the New Presentation dialog box, click the *New from existing* option in the *Templates* section. This displays the New from Existing Presentation dialog box with options similar to the Open dialog box. Double-click the desired presentation in the dialog box list box. This opens a new presentation based on the existing presentation and the Title bar displays *Presentation* followed by a number. Edit the presentation and then save the presentation with a new name.

## Project ③ⓐ  Creating and Running a Presentation from an Existing Presentation

1. Click the Office button and then click *New* at the drop-down list.
2. At the New Presentation dialog box, click the *New from existing* option in the *Templates* section.
3. At the New from Existing Presentation dialog box, navigate to the PowerPoint2007C1 folder on your storage medium and then double-click *PlanningPresentation.pptx*.
4. Save the presentation by completing the following steps:
   a. Click the Save button on the Quick Access toolbar.
   b. At the Save As dialog box, make sure the PowerPoint2007C1 folder on your storage medium is active and then type **PP_C1_P3** in the *File name* text box.
   c. Press Enter or click the Save button.
5. Run the presentation by completing the following steps:
   a. Click the Slide Show button in the view area on the Status bar.
   b. When Slide 1 fills the screen, move the mouse to display the Slide Show toolbar. (This toolbar displays in a dimmed manner in the lower left corner of the slide.)
   c. Click the button containing the right arrow. (This displays the next slide.)
   d. Continue clicking the button containing the right arrow until a black screen displays.
   e. Click the left mouse button. (This displays the presentation in Normal view.)

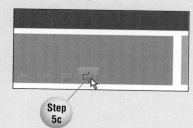

Step 5c

6. Run the presentation from the current slide and use the pen and highlighter to emphasize specific words by completing the following steps:
   a. Click Slide 2 in the Slides/Outline pane. (This makes Slide 2 active.)
   b. Click the Slide Show tab.
   c. Click the From Current Slide button in the Start Slide Show group.

Step 6b

Step 6c

   d. With Slide 2 active, use the felt tip pen to underline a word by completing the following steps:
      1) Move the mouse to display the Slide Show toolbar.
      2) Click the pen button on the Slide Show toolbar and then click *Felt Tip Pen* at the pop-up list. (This changes the mouse pointer to a small circle.)

Step 6d2

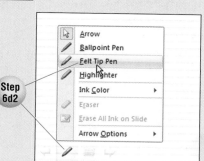

3) Using the mouse, draw a circle around the text *STEP 1*.

4) Draw a line below the word *identify*.

5) Click the pen button on the Slide Show toolbar and then click *Arrow* at the pop-up list. (This returns the mouse pointer to an arrow.)

e. Erase the pen markings by clicking the pen button on the Slide Show toolbar and then clicking *Erase All Ink on Slide* at the pop-up list.

f. Click the pen button on the Slide Show toolbar and then click *Ballpoint Pen* at the pop-up list.

g. Change the color of the ink by clicking the pen button, pointing to *Ink Color*, and then clicking the purple color (first option from the right in the bottom row).

h. Draw a circle around *STEP 1*.

i. Click the pen button on the Slide Show toolbar and then click *Arrow* at the pop-up list.

j. Click the left mouse button to display the next slide (Slide 3).

k. Click the pen button in the Slide Show toolbar and then click *Highlighter* at the pop-up list.

l. Drag through the word *target* to highlight it.

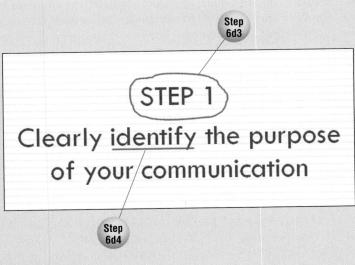

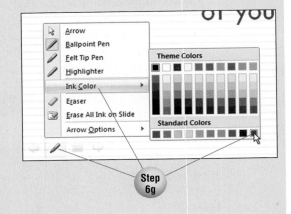

m. Click the button in the Slide Show toolbar containing the right arrow. (This displays Slide 4.)

n. Drag through the words *best format* to highlight them.

o. Click the pen button on the Slide Show toolbar and then click *Arrow* at the pop-up list.

7. Continue clicking the left mouse button to run the presentation.

8. At the black screen, click the left mouse button.

9. At the message asking if you want to keep your ink annotations, click the Discard button.

10. Save **PP_C1_P3.pptx**.

# Applying a Design Theme

**Apply a Design Theme**
1. Click Design tab.
2. Click desired theme in Themes group.

As you learned, PowerPoint provides a variety of predesigned theme templates you can use when creating slides for a presentation. You can choose a theme template at the New Presentation dialog box or with options in the Themes group in the Design tab. Click the Design tab and theme thumbnails display in the Themes group. Click one of these themes to apply it to the current presentation. To display additional themes, click the More button that displays at the right side of the visible themes. You can also click the up-pointing or down-pointing arrow at the right side of the visible themes to scroll through the list. Hover your mouse pointer over a theme and the active slide in the presentation displays with the theme formatting applied. This is an example of the *live preview* feature, which allows you to see how theme formatting affects your presentation.

Themes similar to the ones available in PowerPoint are also available in Word, Excel, and Outlook. When you hover the mouse pointer over a theme thumbnail, a ScreenTip displays (after approximately a second) containing the theme name. Theme names in PowerPoint are similar in Word, Excel, and Outlook and apply similar formatting. With the availability of the themes across these applications, you can "brand" your business files such as documents, workbooks, and presentations with a consistent and uniform appearance.

**HINT**

Design themes were designed by professional graphic artists who understand the use of color, space, and design.

## Project 3b  Applying Design Themes

1. With **PP_C1_P3.pptx** open, make Slide 1 active, and make sure the presentation displays in Normal view.
2. Apply a different design theme to the presentation by completing the following steps:
   a. Click the Design tab.
   b. Hover the mouse pointer over the third theme thumbnail in the Themes group and notice the theme formatting applied to the slide in the Slide pane.
   c. Hover the mouse pointer over the remaining visible theme thumbnails and notice the formatting applied to the active slide.
   d. Click the *Civic* theme.

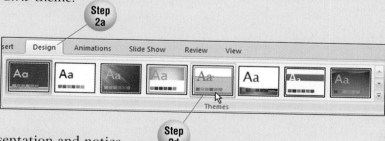

Step 2a

Step 2d

3. Run the presentation and notice the formatting applied by the theme.
4. After running the presentation, you decide you do not like the formatting applied by the theme. Click the *Flow* theme in the Themes group.
5. Run the presentation and notice the formatting applied by the theme.

6. With the presentation in Normal view, apply a different design theme by completing the following steps:
   a. Click the More button that displays at the right side of the theme thumbnails.
   b. Click *Verve* at the drop-down gallery.

Step 6a

7. Run the presentation.
8. Print the presentation as a handout by completing the following steps:
   a. Click the Office button and then click *Print* at the drop-down list.
   b. At the Print dialog box, click the down-pointing arrow at the right side of the *Print what* option and then click *Handouts* at the drop-down list.
   c. Make sure the number *6* displays in the *Slides per page* text box in the *Handouts* section of the dialog box.
   d. Click OK.
9. Save and then close **PP_C1_P3.pptx**.

## Deleting a Presentation

**Delete a Presentation**
1. Click Office button, *Open*.
2. Navigate to desired folder or drive.
3. Click the presentation.
4. Click Delete button.
5. Click Yes.

File management tasks in PowerPoint can be performed at the Open or Save As dialog box. To delete a PowerPoint presentation (presentation must be closed), display the Open dialog box, click the presentation you want deleted, and then click the Delete button on the dialog box toolbar. At the message asking if you are sure you want to delete the presentation, click the Yes button.

## Project 3c    Deleting PowerPoint Presentation

1. Click the Open button on the Quick Access toolbar to display the Open dialog box. (If the Open button does not display on the Quick Access toolbar, click the Customize Quick Access Toolbar button located at the right side of the toolbar and then click *Open* at the drop-down list.)
2. At the Open dialog box, make sure the PowerPoint2007C1 folder on your storage medium is the active folder, and then click **PlanningPresentation.pptx** in the list box.
3. Click the Delete button on the dialog box toolbar.

Step 2          Step 3

| Open | |
|---|---|
| Look in: | PowerPoint2007C1 |
| My Recent Documents | PlanningPresentation.pptx |
| | PP_C1_P2.pptx |
| Desktop | PP_C1_P3.pptx |

4. At the message asking if you are sure you want to delete the presentation, click Yes.
5. Click the Cancel button to close the Open dialog box.

# Project 4 Create a Technology Presentation in the Slides/Outline Pane

You will create a computer technology presentation in the Slides/Outline pane with the Outline tab selected, add and remove transitions and sounds to the presentation, and set up the presentation to advance slides automatically after a specified amount of time.

## Preparing a Presentation from a Blank Presentation

When you first open PowerPoint, a blank presentation displays in which you can enter text in slides. You can also display a blank presentation by clicking the Office button and pointing to *New*. At the New Presentation dialog box, click the *Blank Presentation* option in the *Blank and recent* section and then click the Create button that displays in the lower right corner of the dialog box. You can also double-click *Blank Presentation*.

**QUICK STEPS**

**Prepare a Presentation from a Blank Presentation**
1. Click Office button, *New*.
2. Click *Blank Presentation* option.
3. Click Create button.

## Preparing a Presentation in the Slides/Outline Pane

In Normal view, you can enter text in a slide in the Slide pane and you can also enter text in a presentation in the Slides/Outline pane with the Outline tab selected. To create a slide in the Outline/Slides pane, click the Outline tab, click in the pane, and then type the text. Press the Tab key to move the insertion point to the next tab stop. This moves the insertion point and also changes the formatting. The formatting will vary depending on the theme you chose. Press Shift + Tab to move the insertion point to the previous tab stop and change the formatting. Moving the insertion point back to the left margin will begin another slide. Slides are numbered at the left side of the screen and are followed by a slide icon.

## Project 4a  Preparing a Presentation in the Slides/Outline Pane

1. At a blank screen, click the Office button and then click *New* at the drop-down list.
2. At the New Presentation dialog box, double-click the *Blank Presentation* option in the *Blank and recent* section.
3. At the blank presentation, click the Outline tab in the Slides/Outline pane.

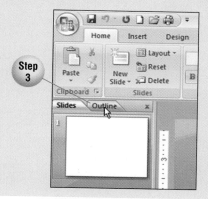

4. Click immediately right of the Slide 1 icon in the Slides/Outline pane, type the first slide title shown in Figure 1.6 *(Computer Technology)*, and then press Enter.
5. Type the second slide title shown in Figure 1.6 *(The Motherboard)* and then press Enter.
6. Press the Tab key, type the text after the first bullet in Figure 1.6 *(Buses)*, and then press Enter.
7. Continue typing the text as it displays in Figure 1.6. Press the Tab key to move the insertion point to the next tab stop or press Shift + Tab to move the insertion point back to a previous tab stop.

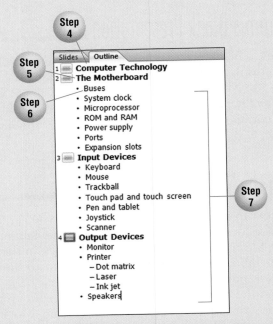

8. After typing all of the information as shown in Figure 1.6, click the Slides tab in the Slides/Outline tab.
9. Click Slide 1 in the Slides/Outline pane. (This displays Slide 1 in the Slide pane.)
10. Apply a design theme by completing the following steps:
   a. Click the Design tab.
   b. Click the More button that displays at the right side of the design theme thumbnails.
   c. Click *Module* at the drop-down gallery.
11. Save the presentation with Save As and name it **PP_C1_P4**.
12. Run the presentation.

**Figure 1.6  Project 4a**

1  Computer Technology
2  The Motherboard
   - Buses
   - System clock
   - Microprocessor
   - ROM and RAM
   - Power supply
   - Ports
   - Expansion slots
3  Input Devices
   - Keyboard
   - Mouse
   - Trackball
   - Touch pad and touch screen
   - Pen and tablet
   - Joystick
   - Scanner
4  Output Devices
   - Monitor
   - Printer
     - Dot matrix
     - Laser
     - Ink jet
   - Speakers

# Adding Transition and Sound Effects

You can apply interesting transitions and sounds to a presentation. A transition is how one slide is removed from the screen during a presentation and the next slide is displayed. You can apply transitions such as fades, wipes, push, cover, stripes, and bar. To add transitions and sounds, open a presentation, and then click the Animations tab. This displays transition buttons and options as shown in Figure 1.7.

**Figure 1.7** Animations Tab

Transitions and sounds apply by default to the active slide. If you want transitions and sound to affect all slides, click the Apply To All button in the Transition to This Slide group. In Slide Sorter view, you can select all slides by pressing Ctrl + A (or by clicking the Home tab, clicking the Select button, and then clicking *Select All* at the drop-down list) and then applying the desired transition and/or sound.

## Adding Transitions

**QUICK STEPS**

**Apply Transition to Slides**
1. Click Animations tab.
2. Click desired transition in Transition to This Slide group.
3. Click Apply To All button.

**Apply Sound to Slides**
1. Click Animations tab.
2. Click down-pointing arrow at right of *Transition Sound* option.
3. Click desired sound.
4. Click Apply To All button.

To add a transition, click a transition thumbnail in the Transition to This Slide group in the Animations tab. Hover the mouse pointer over a transition thumbnail and the transition displays in the slide in the Slide pane. Use the down-pointing and up-pointing arrows at the right side of the transition thumbnails to display additional transitions. Click the More button that displays at the right side of the visible transitions and a drop-down gallery displays with additional transition options. Use the Transition Speed option to specify the speed slides transition when running the presentation. Click the down-pointing arrow at the right side of the Transition Speed option box and you can choose *Slow*, *Medium*, or *Fast*.

When you apply a transition to slides in a presentation, animation icons display below the slides in the Slides/Outline pane and in Slide Sorter view. Click an animation icon for a particular slide and the slide will display the transition effect.

## Adding Sounds

**HINT**

Make a presentation more appealing by adding effects such as transitions and sounds.

As a slide is removed from the screen and another slide is displayed, you can add a sound. To add a sound, click the down-pointing arrow at the right side of the *Transition Sound* option box and then click the desired sound at the drop-down gallery. Hover your mouse pointer over a sound in the list box and you can hear the sound.

## Removing Transitions and Sounds

You can remove a transition and sound from specific slides or from all slides in a presentation. To remove a transition, click the More button that displays at the right side of the transition thumbnails and then click the *No Transition* option at the drop-down gallery. To remove transitions from all slides, click the Apply To All button in the Apply to This Slide group. To remove sound from a slide, click the down-pointing arrow at the right side of the *Transition Sound* option and then click *[No Sound]* at the drop-down gallery. To remove sound from all slides, click the Apply To All button.

1. With **PP_C1_P4.pptx** open, click the Animations tab.
2. Hover the mouse pointer over each of the transition thumbnails (except the first one) and notice how the transition displays in the slide in the Slide pane.
3. Apply transitions and sound to all slides in the presentation by completing the following steps:

   a. Click the More button at the right side of the transition thumbnails and then click the second option from the left in the fourth row in the *Wipes* section *(Wheel Clockwise, 8 Spokes)*.

   b. Click the down-pointing arrow at the right side of the *Transition Speed* option box and then click *Slow* at the drop-down list.

   c. Click the down-pointing arrow at the right side of the *Transition Sound* option box in the Transition to This Slide group and then click *Chime* at the drop-down gallery.

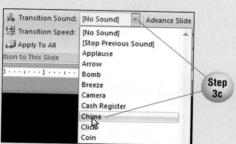

   d. Click the Apply To All button in the Transition to This Slide group.
4. Run the presentation. (Notice the transitions and sounds as you move from slide to slide.)
5. With the presentation in Normal view and the Animations tab active, remove the transitions and sound by completing the following steps:

   a. Click the More button at the right side of the transition thumbnails and then click *No Transition* at the drop-down gallery.

   b. Click the down-pointing arrow at the right side of the *Transition Sound* option box and then click *[No Sound]* at the drop-down gallery.

   c. Click the Apply To All button.
6. Apply transitions and sounds to specific slides by completing the following steps:

   a. Make sure the presentation displays in Normal view.

   b. Click Slide 1 in the Slides/Outline pane.

   c. Hold down the Shift key and then click Slide 2. (Slides 1 and 2 will display with orange backgrounds).

d. Click the More button at the right side of the transition thumbnails and then click a transition of your choosing.

e. Click the down-pointing arrow at the right side of the *Transition Sound* option box and then click a sound of your choosing.

f. Click Slide 3 in the Slides/Outline pane.

g. Hold down the Shift key and then click Slide 4.

h. Click the More button at the right side of the transition thumbnails and then click a transition of your choosing.

i. Click the down-pointing arrow at the right side of the *Transition Sound* option box and then click a sound of your choosing.

7. Run the presentation from the beginning.

8. Remove the transitions and sounds from all slides. (Refer to Step 5.)

9. Save **PP_C1_P4.pptx**.

**Advance Slides Automatically**

1. Click Animations tab.
2. Click *Automatically after* check box.
3. Insert desired number of seconds in text box.
4. Click Apply To All button.

## Advancing Slides Automatically

You can advance slides in a slide show after a specific number of seconds with options in the Transition to This Slide group in the Animations tab. To advance slides automatically, click in the *Automatically after* check box and then insert the desired number of seconds in the text box. You can select the current time in the text box and then type the desired time or click the up- or down-pointing arrow to increase or decrease the time. If you want the transition time to affect all slides in the presentation, click the Apply To All button. In Slide Sorter view, the transition time displays below each affected slide.

## Project 4c  Advancing Slides Automatically

1. With **PP_C1_P4.pptx** open, make sure the Animations tab is active.
2. Click in the *Automatically After* check box in the Apply to This Slide group to insert a check mark.
3. Click in the *On Mouse Click* check box to remove the check mark.
4. Click the up-pointing arrow at the right side of the *Automatically After* option box until *00:04* displays in the box.
5. Click the Apply To All button.
6. Run the presentation. (Each slide will advance automatically after four seconds.)
7. At the black screen, click the left mouse button.
8. Print the presentation as an outline by completing the following steps:
   a. Click the Office button and then click *Print* at the drop-down list.
   b. At the Print dialog box, click the down-pointing arrow at the right side of the *Print what* option and then click *Outline View* at the drop-down list.
   c. Click OK.
9. Print the presentation as a handout with six slides per page.
10. Save and then close **PP_C1_P4.pptx**.

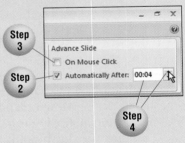

# CHAPTER summary

- PowerPoint is a software program you can use to create slides for an on-screen presentation.

- Open a presentation at the Open dialog box. Display this dialog box by clicking the Open button on the Quick Access toolbar or by clicking the Office button and then clicking *Open*. The Office button drop-down list displays the nine recently opened presentations.

- Predesigned presentation templates are available at the New Presentation dialog box. Display this dialog box by clicking the Office button and then clicking *New*.

- Start running a presentation by clicking the Slide Show button in the view area on the Status bar or by clicking the View tab and then clicking the From Beginning button.

- Close a presentation by clicking the Office button and then clicking *Close* or with the keyboard shortcut, Ctrl + F4.

- Before creating a presentation in PowerPoint, plan the presentation by defining the purpose and determining the content and medium.

- You can use a predesigned theme template to create a presentation. A theme template provides slides with formatting such as color, background elements, and fonts.

- To insert text in a slide, click the desired placeholder and then type text.

- A slide layout provides placeholders for specific data in a slide. Choose a slide layout by clicking the Layout button in the Slides group in the Home tab.

- Insert a new slide in a presentation with the Title and Content layout by clicking the New Slide button in the Slides group in the Home tab. Insert a new slide with a specific layout by clicking the New Slide button arrow and then clicking the desired layout at the drop-down list.

- Save a presentation by clicking the Save button on the Quick Access toolbar or clicking the Office button and then clicking *Save As*. At the Save As dialog box, type a name for the presentation.

- View a presentation in one of the following four views: Normal view, which is the default and displays three panes — Slides/Outline, Slide, and Notes; Slide Sorter view, which displays all slides in the presentation in slide miniatures; Notes Page view, which displays an individual slide with any added notes displayed below the slide; and Slide Show view, which runs the presentation.

- Navigate to various slides in a presentation using the mouse and/or keyboard. You can use the Previous Slide and Next Slide buttons located at the bottom of the vertical scroll bar, the scroll box on the vertical scroll bar, arrow keys on the keyboard, and the Page Up and Page Down buttons on the keyboard.

- With options at the Print dialog box, you can print presentations with each slide on a separate piece of paper; each slide at the top of the page, leaving room for notes; all or a specific number of slides on a single piece of paper; or slide titles and topics in outline form.

- The Slide Show toolbar contains buttons and options for running a presentation. You can navigate to slides, make ink notations on slides, and display a Help menu. Click the slide show icon on the toolbar and then click *Help* and the Slide Show Help menu displays with options for using the keyboard to navigate in a presentation.
- Apply a design theme to a presentation by clicking the Design tab and then clicking the desired theme in the Themes group. Click the More button to display additional themes.
- Delete a presentation at the Open dialog box by clicking the presentation file name and then clicking the Delete button on the dialog box toolbar.
- At the New Presentation dialog box you can choose to prepare a presentation from an existing presentation or a blank presentation.
- You can type text in a slide in the Slide pane or in the Slides/Outline pane with the Outline tab selected.
- Enhance a presentation by adding transitions (how one slide is removed from the screen and replaced with the next slide) and sound. Add transitions and sound to a presentation with options in the Transition to This Slide group in the Animations tab.
- Advance slides automatically in a slide show by removing the check mark from the *On Mouse Click* check box in the Animations tab, inserting a check mark in the *Automatically After* check box, and then specifying the desired time in the time option box.
- Click the Apply To All button to apply transitions, sounds, and/or time settings to all slides in a presentation.

# COMMANDS review

| FEATURE | RIBBON TAB, GROUP | BUTTON | QUICK ACCESS TOOLBAR | OFFICE BUTTON DROP-DOWN LIST | KEYBOARD SHORTCUT |
|---|---|---|---|---|---|
| Open dialog box | | | 📂 | Open | Ctrl + O |
| New Presentation dialog box | | | | New | |
| Run presentation | Slide Show, Start Slide Show | ▶ | | | F5 |
| Close presentation | | | | Close | Ctrl + F4 |
| Slide layout | Home, Slides | Layout ▾ | | | |
| New slide | Home, Slides | | | | Ctrl + M |
| Save As dialog box | | | 💾 | Save As | Ctrl + S |
| Normal view | View, Presentation Views | | | | |
| Slide Sorter view | View, Presentation Views | | | | |
| Notes page | View, Presentation Views | | | | |
| Print dialog box | | | 🖨 | Print | Ctrl + P |
| Design theme | Design, Themes | | | | |
| Transition | Animation, Transition to This Slide | | | | |
| Sound | Animation, Transition to This Slide | Transition Sound: [No Sound] ▾ | | | |
| Transition speed | Animation, Transition to this Slide | Transition Speed: Fast ▾ | | | |

# CONCEPTS check

## Test Your Knowledge

**Completion:** In the space provided at the right, indicate the correct term, command, or number.

1. Click this button to display a list of options along with the most recently opened presentations. _____

2. This toolbar contains buttons for commonly used commands. _____

3. This area contains the tabs and commands divided into groups. _____

4. Display installed templates in this dialog box. _____

5. This is the keyboard shortcut to close a presentation. _____

6. Apply a theme to a presentation by clicking this tab and then clicking the desired theme in the Themes group. _____

7. Insert a new slide by clicking the New Slide button in this group in the Home tab. _____

8. Change to this view to view displays of all slides in the presentation in slide miniatures. _____

9. This is the default view and displays three panes. _____

10. The Previous Slide or Next Slide buttons display in this location. _____

11. To print six slides on a page, change the *Print what* option to this. _____

12. To run a presentation beginning with Slide 1, click this button in the Slide Show tab. _____

13. In Normal view, you can enter text in a slide in this pane or in the Slides/Outline pane with the Outline tab selected. _____

14. To add a transition, click a transition in the Transition to This Slide group in this tab. _____

15. When you apply a transition to slides in a presentation, these display below the slides in the Slides/Outline pane. _____

16. To advance slides automatically, insert a check mark in this option and then insert the desired number of seconds. _____

# SKILLS check
## Demonstrate Your Proficiency

## Assessment

### 1 CREATE A DEDUCTIBLE INCOME EXCEPTIONS PRESENTATION

1. Create a presentation with the text shown in Figure 1.8 by completing the following steps:
   a. With PowerPoint open, click the Office button and then click *New*.
   b. At the New Presentation dialog box, click the *Installed Themes* option, and then double-click *Paper* in the list box. (You may need to scroll down the list to display this theme.)
   c. Create slides with the text shown in Figure 1.8. Choose the *Title Slide* layout when inserting new slides.
2. Save the completed presentation in the PowerPoint2007C1 folder on your storage medium and name the presentation **PP_C1_A1**.
3. Apply the *Blinds Vertical* transition (second option from left in the *Stripes and Bars* row) to all slides in the presentation.
4. Change the transition speed to *Medium*.
5. Apply the *Laser* sound to all slides in the presentation.
6. Run the presentation.
7. Print the presentation as a handout with six slides per page.
8. Save and then close **PP_C1_A1.pptx**.

**Figure 1.8  Assessment 1**

| Slide 1 | Title | = | DEDUCTIBLE INCOME |
| | Subtitle | = | Exceptions to Deductible Income |
| | | | |
| Slide 2 | Title | = | EXCEPTION 1 |
| | Subtitle | = | Any cost of living increase if increase becomes effective while disabled |
| | | | |
| Slide 3 | Title | = | EXCEPTION 2 |
| | Subtitle | = | Reimbursement for hospital, medical, or surgical expense |
| | | | |
| Slide 4 | Title | = | EXCEPTION 3 |
| | Subtitle | = | Reasonable attorney's fees incurred in connection with a claim for deductible income |
| | | | |
| Slide 5 | Title | = | EXCEPTION 4 |
| | Subtitle | = | Benefits from any individual disability insurance policy |
| | | | |
| Slide 6 | Title | = | EXCEPTION 5 |
| | Subtitle | = | Group credit or mortgage disability insurance benefits |

## Assessment

### 2 CREATE A PRESENTATION ON PREPARING A COMPANY NEWSLETTER PRESENTATION

1. At the blank screen, click the Office button and then click *New*.
2. At the New Presentation dialog box, double-click the *Blank Presentation* option in the *Blank and recent* section.
3. Create slides with the text shown in Figure 1.9.
4. Apply a design theme of your choosing.
5. Run the presentation.
6. Print the presentation as a handout with six slides per page.
7. Make the following changes to the presentation:
   a. Apply a different design theme.
   b. Add a transition of your choosing to all slides.
   c. Add a sound of your choosing to all slides.
   d. Specify that all slides advance automatically after five seconds.
8. Run the presentation.
9. Save the presentation and name it **PP_C1_A2**.
10. Close **PP_C1_A2.pptx**.

**Figure 1.9 Assessment 2**

Slide 1　　Title　　=　　PREPARING A COMPANY NEWSLETTER
　　　　　　Subtitle　=　　Planning and Designing the Layout

Slide 2　　Title　　=　　Planning a Newsletter
　　　　　　Bullets　=　　◆ If a scanner is available, use pictures of different people from your organization in each issue.
　　　　　　　　　　　　◆ Distribute contributor sheets soliciting information from employees.
　　　　　　　　　　　　◆ Keep the focus of the newsletter on issues of interest to employees.

Slide 3　　Title　　=　　Planning a Newsletter
　　　　　　Bullets　=　　◆ Make sure the focus is on various levels of employment; do not focus on top management only.
　　　　　　　　　　　　◆ Conduct regular surveys to see if your newsletter provides a needed source of information.

Slide 4　　Title　　=　　Designing a Newsletter
　　　　　　Bullets　=　　◆ Maintain consistent elements from issue to issue such as:
　　　　　　　　　　　　　　- Column layout
　　　　　　　　　　　　　　- Nameplate formatting and location
　　　　　　　　　　　　　　- Formatting of headlines
　　　　　　　　　　　　　　- Use of color

Slide 5　　Title　　=　　Designing a Newsletter
　　　　　　Bullets　=　　◆ Consider the following elements when designing a newsletter:
　　　　　　　　　　　　　　- Focus
　　　　　　　　　　　　　　- Balance
　　　　　　　　　　　　　　- White space
　　　　　　　　　　　　　　- Directional flow

Slide 6　　Title　　=　　Creating a Newsletter Layout
　　　　　　Bullets　=　　◆ Choose paper size
　　　　　　　　　　　　◆ Choose paper weight
　　　　　　　　　　　　◆ Determine margins
　　　　　　　　　　　　◆ Specify column layout

# CASE study

## *Apply Your Skills*

**Part 1**

You work for Citizens for Consumer Safety, a non-profit organization providing information on household safety. Your supervisor, Melinda Johansson, will be presenting information on smoke detectors at a community meeting and has asked you to prepare a PowerPoint presentation. Open the Word document named **PPSmokeDetectors.docx**. Read over the information and then use the information to prepare a presentation. Consider the information in the *Planning a Presentation* section of this chapter and then prepare at least five slides. Apply an appropriate design theme and add a transition and sound to all slides. Save the presentation and name it **PP_C1_CS_P1**. Run the presentation and then print the presentation as a handout with all slides on one page.

**Part 2**

Ms. Johansson has looked at the printout of the presentation and has asked you to print the presentation with two slides per page and a frame around each slide. Display the Print dialog box, click the Help button that displays in the upper right corner of the dialog box (white question mark on a blue background), and then navigate through hyperlinks to read information about printing in Microsoft Office PowerPoint. After reading the information, print the presentation with two slides per page and the slides framed.

**Part 3**

Ms. Johansson would like to provide information to participants at the presentation on online companies that sell smoke detectors. Using the Internet, locate at least three online stores that sell smoke detectors. Insert a new slide in the presentation that includes the names of the stores, Web addresses, and any additional information you feel is important. Save the presentation and then print the presentation in Outline view. Close the presentation.

# CHAPTER 2

# Modifying a Presentation and Using Help

## PERFORMANCE OBJECTIVES

**Upon successful completion of Chapter 2, you will be able to:**

- Check spelling
- Insert and delete text in slides
- Find and replace text in slides
- Cut, copy, and paste text in slides
- Rearrange text in the Slides/Outline pane
- Size and rearrange placeholders
- Insert, delete, move, and copy slides
- Copy slides between presentations
- Duplicate slides
- Reuse slides
- Preview a presentation
- Use the Help feature

**Tutorial 2.1**
Working with Text
**Tutorial 2.2**
Organizing Slides and Using Help

When preparing a presentation, you may need to modify a presentation by inserting and deleting text in slides or finding and replacing specific text. Improve the quality of your presentation by completing a spelling check to ensure that the words in your presentation are spelled correctly. Additional modifications you may need to make to a presentation include sizing and rearranging placeholders and rearranging, inserting, deleting, or copying slides. In this chapter, you will learn how to make these modifications to a presentation as well as how to preview a presentation and use the Help feature.

*Note: Before beginning computer projects, copy to your storage medium the PowerPoint2007C2 subfolder from the PowerPoint2007 folder on the CD that accompanies this textbook and then make PowerPoint2007C2 the active folder.*

# Project 1 Check Spelling and Manage Text in a Design Presentation

You will open a presentation on steps for planning a design publication, complete a spelling check on the text in the presentation, and find and replace specific text in slides.

## QUICK STEPS

**Complete a Spell Check**
1. Click Review tab.
2. Click Spelling button.
3. Change or ignore errors.
4. Click OK.

ABC
Spelling

# Checking Spelling

When preparing a presentation, perform a spelling check on text in slides using PowerPoint's spelling feature. The spelling feature compares words in slides in a presentation with words in its dictionary. If a match is found, the word is passed over. If a match is not found, the spelling checker selects the word and offers replacement suggestions. To perform a spelling check on a PowerPoint presentation, click the Review tab and then click the Spelling button in the Proofing group. You can also start the spelling checker by pressing the F7 function key on the keyboard.

When you begin spell checking text in a presentation in Project 1a, the spelling checker will stop at the misspelled word *Layuot* and display the Spelling dialog box as shown in Figure 2.1. The options available in the Spelling dialog box are described in Table 2.1.

**Figure 2.1** Spelling Dialog Box

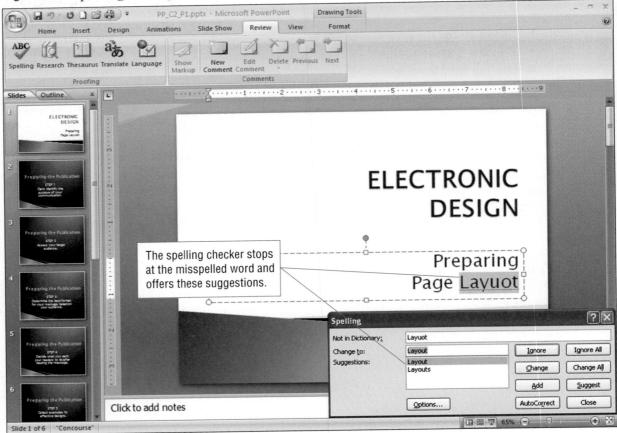

**Table 2.1** Spelling Dialog Box Options

| Button | Function |
| --- | --- |
| Ignore | Skips that occurrence of the word. |
| Ignore All | Skips that occurrence of the word and all other occurrences of the word in slides. |
| Change | Replaces selected word in slide with selected word in *Suggestions* list box. |
| Change All | Replaces selected word in slide with selected word in *Suggestions* list box and all other occurrences of the word. |
| Add | Adds selected word to the main spelling check dictionary. |
| Suggest | Makes active the first suggestion in the *Suggestions* list box. |
| AutoCorrect | Inserts selected word and correct spelling of word in AutoCorrect dialog box. |
| Close | Closes the Spelling dialog box. |
| Options | Displays PowerPoint Options dialog box with *Proofing* selected that contains options for customizing a spelling check. |

## Project 1a  Checking the Spelling in a Presentation

1. Open **ElectronicDesign.pptx** (located in the PowerPoint2007C2 folder on your storage medium) and then save the presentation and name it **PP_C2_P1**.
2. With the presentation in Normal view, complete a spelling check by completing the following steps:
   a. Click the Review tab.
   b. Click the Spelling button in the Proofing group.
   c. When the spelling checker selects the misspelled word *Layuot* and displays the correct spelling (*Layout*) in the *Change to* text box, click the Change button (or Change All button).
   d. When the spelling checker selects the misspelled word *Clerly* and displays the correct spelling (*Clearly*) in the *Change to* text box, click the Change button (or Change All button).

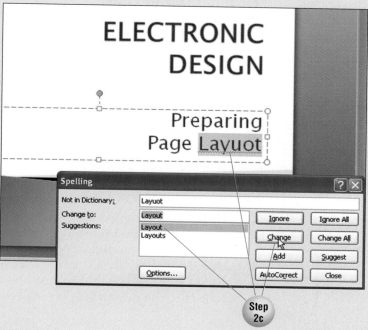

e. When the spelling checker selects the misspelled word *massege*, click *message* in the *Suggestions* list box and then click the Change button (or Change All button).

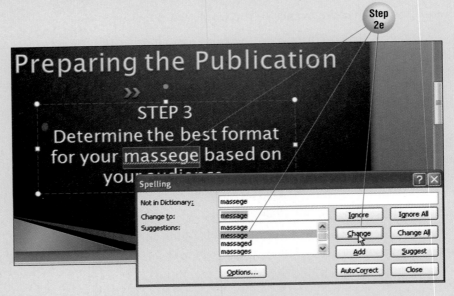

f. When the spelling checker selects the misspelled word *fo* and displays the correct spelling (*of*) in the *Change to* text box, click the Change button.

g. At the message telling you that the spelling check is complete, click the OK button.

3. Save **PP_C2_P1.pptx**.

## Managing Text in Slides

As you enter text in slides or as you manage existing slides, you may need to edit, move, copy, or delete text from slides. You may also want to find specific text in slides and replace with other text. Text is generally inserted in a slide placeholder and this placeholder can be moved, sized, and/or deleted.

### Inserting and Deleting Text in Slides

To insert or delete text in an individual slide, open the presentation, edit the text as needed, and then save the presentation again. If you want to delete more than an individual character, consider selecting the text first. Several methods can be used for selecting text as shown in Table 2.2.

Text in a slide is positioned inside of a placeholder. Slide layouts provide placeholders for text and generally display with a message suggesting the type of text to be entered in the slide. For example, the Title and Content slide layout contains a placeholder with the text *Click to add title* and another with the text *Click to add text*. Click placeholder text and the insertion point is positioned inside the placeholder, the default text is removed, and the placeholder is selected.

**Table 2.2** Selecting Text

| To do this | Perform this action |
|---|---|
| Select text mouse pointer passes through | Click and drag mouse |
| Select entire word | Double-click word |
| Select entire paragraph | Triple-click anywhere in paragraph |
| Select entire sentence | Ctrl + click anywhere in sentence |
| Select all text in selected placeholder | Click Select, Select All or press Ctrl + A |

## Project 1b  Inserting and Deleting Text in Slides

1. With **PP_C2_P1.pptx** open and the presentation in Normal view, click the Previous Slide button (or Next Slide button) located at the bottom of the vertical scroll bar until Slide 5 displays.
2. Edit Slide 5 by completing the following steps:
   a. Position the I-beam pointer on the sentence below *STEP 4* and then click the left mouse button. (This selects the placeholder.)
   b. Edit the sentence so it reads *Decide what steps you want readers to take after reading the message.* (Use deleting and inserting commands to edit this sentence.)

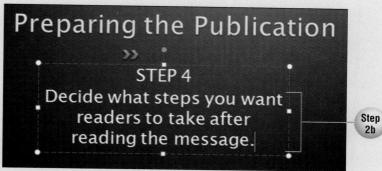

3. Click the Next Slide button to display Slide 6 and then edit Slide 6 in the Outline/Slides pane by completing the following steps:
   a. Click the Outline tab in the Slides/Outline pane.
   b. Click in the sentence below *STEP 5* and then edit the sentence so it reads *Collect and assess examples of effective designs.*
   c. Click the Slides tab.
4. Save **PP_C2_P1.pptx**.

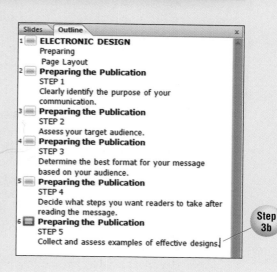

# Finding and Replacing Text in Slides

Use the find feature to look for specific text in slides in a presentation and use the find and replace feature to look for specific text in slides in a presentation and replace with other text. Begin a find by clicking the Find button in the Editing group in the Home tab. This displays the Find dialog box shown in Figure 2.2. In the *Find what* text box, type the text you want to find and then click the Find Next button. Continue clicking this button until a message displays telling you that the search is complete. At this message, click OK.

**Figure 2.2** Find Dialog Box

In this text box, type the text for which you are searching.

Use options at the Replace dialog box shown in Figure 2.3 to search for text and replace it with other text. Display this dialog box by clicking the Replace button in the Home tab. Type the text you want to find in the *Find what* text box, press the Tab key, and then type the replacement text in the *Replace with* text box. Click the Find Next button to find the next occurrence of the text or click the Replace All button to replace all occurrences in the presentation.

**Figure 2.3** Replace Dialog Box

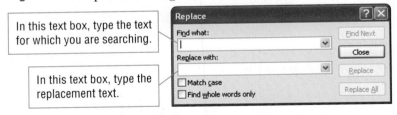

In this text box, type the text for which you are searching.

In this text box, type the replacement text.

Both the Find and Replace dialog boxes contain two additional options for conducting a find and a find and replace. Insert a check mark in the *Match case* check box to specify that the text should exactly match the case of the text entered in the *Find what* text box. For example, if you search for *Planning*, PowerPoint will stop at *Planning* but not *planning* or *PLANNING*. Insert a check mark in the *Find whole words only* check box to specify that the text is a whole word and not part of a word. For example, if you search for *plan*, and did not check the *Find whole words only* option, PowerPoint would stop at ex*plan*ation, *planned*, *plan*et, and so on.

1. With **PP_C2_P1.pptx** open, make Slide 1 active.
2. Find all occurrences of *Preparing* in the presentation and replace with *Planning* by completing the following steps:
   a. With Slide 1 active, click the Replace button in the Home tab.
   b. At the Replace dialog box, type Preparing in the *Find what* text box.
   c. Press the Tab key.
   d. Type Planning in the *Replace with* text box.
   e. Click the Replace All button.
   f. At the message telling you that six replacements were made, click OK.
   g. Click the Close button to close the Replace dialog box.
3. Find all occurrences of *Publication* and replace with *Newsletter* by completing steps similar to those in Step 2.
4. Save the presentation.
5. Apply a transition and sound of your choosing to all slides in the presentation.
6. Run the presentation.
7. Print Slide 1 by completing the following steps:
   a. Click the Office button and then click *Print* at the drop-down list.
   b. At the Print dialog box, click the *Slides* option in the *Print range* section and then type 1 in the text box.
   c. Click OK.
8. Print the presentation as a handout with six slides per page. (Change the *Print what* option at the Print dialog box to *Handouts*.)
9. Save and then close **PP_C2_P1.pptx**.

Step 2b

Step 2d

Step 2e

---

**P**roject **2**  **Cut, Copy, Paste, Rearrange, and Manage Slides in a Network Presentation**

**You will open a network evaluation presentation and then cut, copy, and paste text in slides; rearrange text in the Slides/Outline pane; size and rearrange placeholders in slides; and manage slides by inserting, deleting, moving, and copying slides. You will also copy slides between presentations.**

---

## Cutting, Copying, and Pasting Text in Slides

With buttons in the Clipboard group in the Home tab and also with shortcut menu options, you can cut, copy, and/or paste text in slides. For example, to move text in a slide, click once in the placeholder containing the text to be moved, select the text, and then click the Cut button in the Clipboard group. Position the insertion point where you want the text inserted and then click the Paste button in the Clipboard group. To cut and paste with the shortcut menu, select the text you want to move, right-click the text, and then click *Cut* at the shortcut menu.

**HINT**
Ctrl + X is the keyboard shortcut to cut selected text, Ctrl + C is the keyboard shortcut to copy selected text, and Ctrl + V is the keyboard shortcut to paste cut or copied text.

Cut   Copy

Position the insertion point where you want the text inserted, right-click the location, and then click *Paste* at the shortcut menu. Complete similar steps to copy and paste text except click the Copy button instead of the Cut button or click the *Copy* option at the shortcut menu instead of the *Cut* option.

Paste

## Project 2a   Cutting, Copying, and Pasting Text in Slides

1. Open **NetworkSystem.pptx** located in the PowerPoint2007C2 folder on your storage medium and then save the presentation and name it **PP_C2_P2**.
2. Insert a new slide by completing the following steps:
   a. Make Slide 4 active.
   b. Click the New Slide button in the Slides group in the Home tab.
   c. Click the *Click to add title* placeholder and then type TIME.
3. Cut text from Slide 3 and paste it into Slide 5 by completing the following steps:
   a. Make Slide 3 active.
   b. Click on any character in the bulleted text (in the Slide pane).
   c. Using the mouse, select the text following the bottom three bullets. (The bullets will not be selected.)
   d. With the text selected, click the Cut button in the Clipboard group in the Home tab.

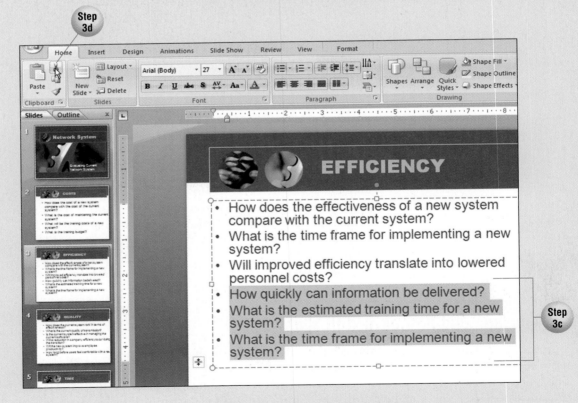

   e. Make Slide 5 the active slide (contains the title *TIME*).
   f. Click the *Click to add text* placeholder.

g. Click the Paste button in the Clipboard group.

h. If the insertion point is positioned below the third bulleted item following a bullet, press the Backspace key twice. (This removes the bullet and deletes the blank line below the bullet.)

4. Insert a new slide by completing the following steps:

a. With Slide 5 the active slide, click the New Slide button in the Slides group in the Home tab.

b. Click the *Click to add title* placeholder and then type EASE OF USE.

5. Cut text from Slide 4 and paste it into Slide 6 by completing the following steps:

a. Make Slide 4 active.

b. Click on any character in the bulleted text.

c. Select the text following the bottom three bullets.

d. Click the Cut button in the Clipboard group.

e. Make Slide 6 active (contains the title *EASE OF USE*).

f. Click the *Click to add text* placeholder.

g. Click the Paste button in the Clipboard group.

h. If the insertion point is positioned below the third bulleted item following a bullet, press the Backspace key twice.

6. Copy text from Slide 3 to Slide 5 by completing the following steps:

a. Make Slide 3 active.

b. Click on any character in the bulleted text.

c. Position the mouse pointer on the last bullet until the pointer turns into a four-headed arrow and then click the left mouse button. (This selects the text following the bullet.)

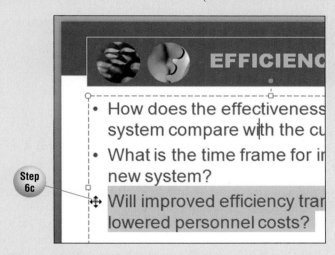

Step
6c

d. Click the Copy button in the Clipboard group.

e. Make Slide 5 active.

f. Click in the bulleted text and then move the insertion point so it is positioned immediately right of the question mark in the second bulleted item.

g. Press the Enter key. (This moves the insertion point down to the next line and inserts another bullet.)

h. Click the Paste button in the Clipboard group.

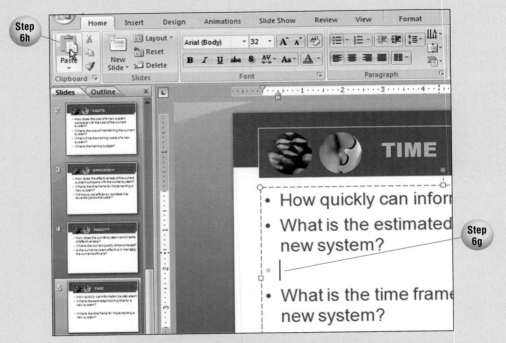

i. If a blank line is inserted between the third and fourth bullets, press the Backspace key twice.

7. Save **PP_C2_P2.pptx**.

## Rearranging Text in the Slides/Outline Pane

**HINT**
Press Ctrl + Shift + Tab to switch between the Slides and Outline tabs in the Slides/Outline pane.

You can use the mouse to move text in the Slides/Outline pane with the Outline tab selected. To do this, position the mouse pointer on the slide icon or bullet at the left side of the text until the arrow pointer turns into a four-headed arrow. Hold down the left mouse button, drag the arrow pointer (a thin horizontal line displays) to the desired location, and then release the mouse button.

If you position the arrow pointer on the slide icon and then hold down the left mouse button, all of the text in the slide is selected. If you position the arrow pointer on the bullet and then hold down the left mouse button, all text following that bullet is selected.

Dragging selected text with the mouse moves the selected text to a new location in the presentation. You can also copy selected text. To do this, click the slide icon or click the bullet to select the desired text. Position the arrow pointer in the selected text, hold down the Ctrl key, and then the left mouse button. Drag the arrow pointer (displays with a light gray box and a plus sign attached) to the desired location, release the mouse button, and then release the Ctrl key.

1. With **PP_C2_P2.pptx** open, make Slide 1 active.
2. Click the Outline tab in the Slides/Outline pane.
3. Move the first bulleted item in Slide 4 to the end of the list by completing the following steps:
   a. Position the mouse pointer on the first bullet below *QUALITY* until it turns into a four-headed arrow.
   b. Hold down the left mouse button, drag the arrow pointer down until a thin horizontal line displays below the last bulleted item, and then release the mouse button.

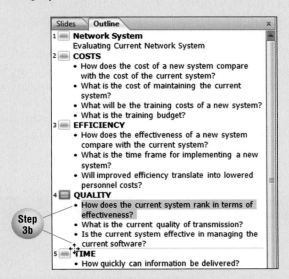

Step 3b

4. Copy and paste text by completing the following steps:
   a. In the Slides/Outline pane, move the insertion point to the end of the text in Slide 6 and then press the Enter key. (This inserts a new bullet in the slide.)
   b. Scroll up the Slides/Outline pane until the last bulleted item in Slide 2 is visible in the Slides/Outline pane as well as the last bullet in Slide 6.
   c. Position the mouse pointer on the fourth bullet below *COSTS* until it turns into a four-headed arrow and then click the left mouse button. (This selects the text.)
   d. Position the mouse pointer in the selected text, hold down the left mouse button, hold down the Ctrl key, and then drag down until the arrow pointer and light blue vertical line display on the blank line below the text in Slide 6.
   e. Release the mouse button and then release the Ctrl key.
5. Click the Slides tab in the Slides/Outline pane.
6. Save **PP_C2_P2.pptx**.

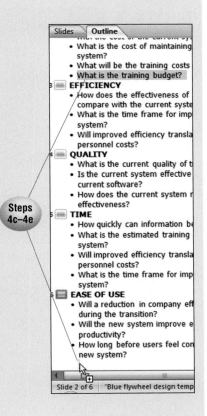

Steps 4c–4e

# Sizing and Rearranging Placeholders in a Slide

Click inside a placeholder to select it and white sizing handles and a green rotation handle display around the placeholder border. With the sizing handles, you can increase or decrease the size of the placeholder. You can also move a placeholder by dragging it with the mouse. Increase or decrease the size of a placeholder by positioning the arrow pointer on a sizing handle until the pointer turns into a double-headed arrow and then dragging the placeholder border to the desired size. To move a placeholder, position the arrow pointer on the placeholder border until the arrow pointer displays with a four-headed arrow attached. Hold down the left mouse button, drag the outline of the placeholder to the desired position, and then release the mouse button.

Dragging a selected placeholder with the mouse moves the placeholder. If you want to copy a placeholder, hold down the Ctrl key while dragging the placeholder. When the outline of the placeholder is in the desired position, release the mouse button, and then release the Ctrl key. If you make a change to the size and/or location of a placeholder, click the Reset button in the Slides group in the Home tab to return the formatting of the placeholder back to the default.

## Project 2c    Sizing and Rearranging Placeholders

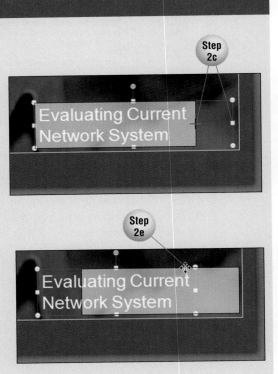

**Step 2c**

**Step 2e**

1. With **PP_C2_P2.pptx** open, make Slide 1 active.
2. Size and move a placeholder by completing the following steps:
   a. Click on any character in the subtitle *Evaluating Current Network System*.
   b. Position the arrow pointer on the sizing handle that displays in the middle of the right border until the pointer turns into a left- and right-pointing arrow.
   c. Hold down the left mouse button, drag to the left until the right border displays just to the right of the text in the placeholder, and then release the mouse button (see image at right).
   d. Position the arrow pointer on the border of the placeholder until the pointer turns into a four-headed arrow.
   e. Hold down the left mouse button, drag the placeholder to the right so the placeholder is positioned as shown at the right, and then release the mouse button.
3. Make Slide 4 active.
4. Size and move a placeholder by completing the following steps:
   a. Click on any character in the bulleted text.
   b. Position the arrow pointer on the sizing handle that displays in the middle of the right border until the pointer turns into a left- and right-pointing arrow.

c. Hold down the left mouse button and then drag to the left until the right border displays just to the right of the word *in* in the third bulleted text (see image below).

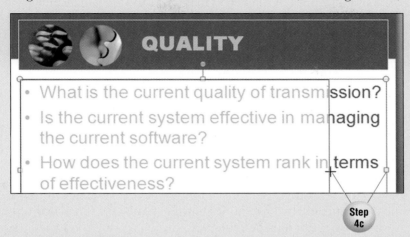

Step
4c

d. Drag the middle sizing handle on the bottom border up until the bottom border of the placeholder displays just below the last bulleted text.
e. Position the arrow pointer on the border of the placeholder until the pointer turns into a four-headed arrow.
f. Hold down the left mouse button and then drag the placeholder to the right so the placeholder is positioned approximately in the middle of the white portion of the slide.

Step
4f

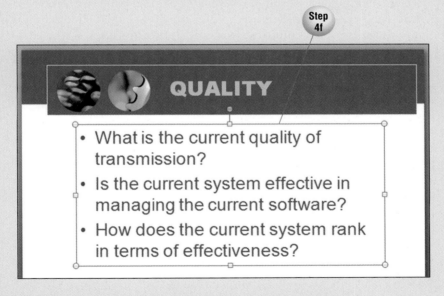

5. Print the presentation as a handout with six slides per page.
6. Save **PP_C2_P2.pptx**.

# Managing Slides

As you edit a presentation, you may need to reorganize slides and insert a new slide or delete an existing slide. You can manage slides in the Slides/Outline pane or in Slide Sorter view. Switch to Slide Sorter view by clicking the Slide Sorter button in the view area on the Status bar or by clicking the View tab and then clicking Slide Sorter in the Presentation Views group.

## Inserting and Deleting Slides

As you learned in Chapter 1, click the New Slide button in the Slides group in the Home tab to insert a new slide in the presentation immediately following the currently active slide. You can also insert a new slide in Slide Sorter view. To do this, click the slide that will immediately precede the new slide and then click the New Slide button in the Slides group. Delete a slide in Normal view by clicking the slide miniature in the Slides/Outline pane and then clicking the Delete button in the Slides group in the Home tab or by pressing the Delete key. You can also delete a slide by switching to Slide Sorter view, clicking the slide miniature, and then clicking the Delete button or pressing the Delete key.

## Moving Slides

Move slides in a presentation in Normal view or Slide Sorter view. In Normal view, click the desired slide in the Slides/Outline pane (with the Slides tab selected) and then position the mouse pointer on the selected slide. Hold down the left mouse button, drag up or down until a thin horizontal line displays in the desired location, and then release the mouse button. In Slide Sorter view, click the desired slide and then position the mouse pointer on the selected slide. Hold down the left mouse button, drag with the mouse until a thin vertical line displays in the desired location, and then release the mouse button.

## Copying a Slide

Slides in some presentations may contain similar text, objects, and formatting. Rather than create a new slide, consider copying a slide. To do this, display the presentation in either Slide Sorter view or in Normal view with the Slides tab selected in the Slides/Outline pane. Position the arrow pointer in the slide, hold down the Ctrl key and then the left mouse button. Drag to the location where you want the slide copied, then release the mouse button and then the Ctrl key.

1. With **PP_C2_P2.pptx** open in Normal view, move slides by completing the following steps:
   a. Make sure the Slides tab is selected in the Slides/Outline pane.
   b. Click Slide 3 (*EFFICIENCY*) in the Slides/Outline pane.
   c. Position the mouse pointer on Slide 3, hold down the left mouse button, drag up until a thin horizontal line displays between Slides 1 and 2, and then release the mouse button.
   d. Click Slide 4 (*QUALITY*) in the Slides/Outline pane.
   e. Position the mouse pointer on Slide 4, hold down the left mouse button, drag down until a thin horizontal line displays below Slide 6, and then release the mouse button.
2. Move and copy slides in Slide Sorter view by completing the following steps:
   a. Click the Slide Sorter button in the view area on the Status bar.
   b. Click Slide 4 to make it the active slide (slide displays with orange border).
   c. Position the mouse pointer on Slide 4, hold down the left mouse button, drag to the left until the thin vertical line displays between Slides 1 and 2, and then release the mouse button.

Step 1c

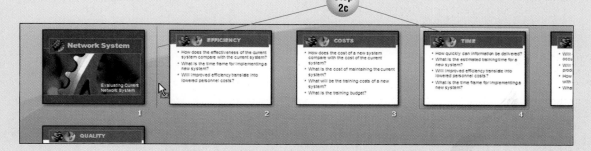

Step 2c

   d. Click Slide 1 to make it the active slide.
   e. Position the mouse pointer on Slide 1, hold down the left mouse button, and then hold down the Ctrl key.
   f. Drag down and to the right until the thin vertical line displays immediately right of Slide 6.
   g. Release the mouse button and then the Ctrl key.
3. Click the Normal button in the view area on the Status bar.
4. Save **PP_C2_P2.pptx**.

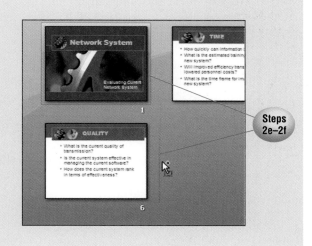

Steps 2e–2f

## Copying a Slide between Presentations

You can copy slides within a presentation as well as between presentations. To copy a slide, click the slide you want to copy (either in Slide Sorter view or in Normal view with the Slides tab selected in the Slides/Outline pane) and then click the Copy button in the Clipboard group in the Home tab. Open the presentation into which the slide is to be copied (in either Slide Sorter view or Normal view with the Slides tab selected in the Slides/Outline pane). Click in the location where you want the slide positioned and then click the Paste button. The copied slide will take on the design theme of the presentation into which it is copied.

---

### Project 2e   Copying Slides between Presentations

1. With **PP_C2_P2.pptx** open, open the presentation named **EvaluatingNetwork.pptx** located in the PowerPoint2007C2 folder on your storage medium.
2. Copy Slide 2 to the **PP_C2_P2.pptx** presentation by completing the following steps:
   a. Click Slide 2 in the Slides/Outline pane to make it the active slide.
   b. Click the Copy button in the Clipboard group in the Home tab.
   c. Click the button on the Taskbar representing the **PP_C2_P2.pptx** presentation.
   d. Click Slide 4 (*COSTS*) in the Slides/Outline pane.
   e. Click the Paste button in the Clipboard group.
   f. Click the button on the Taskbar representing the **EvaluatingNetwork.pptx** presentation.
3. Copy Slide 3 to the **PP_C2_P2.pptx** by completing the following steps:
   a. Click Slide 3 in the Slides/Outline pane.
   b. Position the mouse pointer on Slide 3 and then click the right mouse button. (This displays a shortcut menu.)
   c. Click *Copy* at the shortcut menu.
   d. Click the button on the Taskbar representing the **PP_C2_P2.pptx** presentation.
   e. Right-click Slide 3 in the Slides/Outline pane.
   f. Click *Paste* at the shortcut menu.

Step
3c

4. Click the button on the Taskbar representing the **EvaluatingNetwork.pptx** presentation.
5. Close the presentation.
6. With **PP_C2_P2.pptx** open, delete Slide 9 by completing the following steps:
   a. If necessary, scroll down the Slides/Outline pane until Slide 9 is visible.
   b. Click Slide 9 to select it.
   c. Press the Delete key.
7. Save the presentation.
8. Print the presentation as a handout with nine slides per page.
9. Close **PP_C2_P2.pptx**.

# Project ③ Insert and Manage Slides in an Adventure Tours Presentation

You will open a presentation on Adventure Tours and then insert additional slides in the presentation by duplicating existing slides in the presentation and reusing slides from another presentation. You will also preview the presentation, make changes to the presentation in Print Preview, and then print the presentation.

## Duplicating Slides

In Project 2, you used the Copy and Paste buttons in the Clipboard group and also options from a shortcut menu to copy slides in a presentation. You can also copy slides in a presentation using the *Duplicate Selected Slides* option from the New Slide button drop-down list. This option is useful if you are copying more than one slide. To use the option, select the desired slides in the Slides/Outline pane with the Slides tab selected, click the New Slide button arrow, and then click *Duplicate Selected Slides* at the drop-down list.

To select adjacent (sequential) slides, click the first slide in the Slides/Outline pane, hold down the Shift key, and then click the last in the sequence. For example, if you want to duplicate Slides 3 through 6, you would click Slide 3, hold down the Shift key, and then click Slide 6. To select nonadjacent (nonsequential) slides, hold down the Ctrl key while clicking each desired slide.

**QUICK STEPS**

**Duplicate Slides**
1. Select desired slides in Slides/Outline pane.
2. Click New Slide button arrow.
3. Click *Duplicate Selected Slides* at drop-down list.

## Project ③a  Duplicating Selected Slides

1. Open **AdventureTours.pptx** and then save the presentation and name it **PP_C2_P3**.
2. Make sure the presentation displays in Normal view and that the Slides tab is active in the Slides/Outline pane.
3. Select and then duplicate slides by completing the following steps:
   a. Click Slide 1 in the Slides/Outline pane.
   b. Hold down the Ctrl key.
   c. Click Slide 3, Slide 4, and Slide 5.
   d. Release the Ctrl key.
   e. Click the New Slide button arrow and then click *Duplicate Selected Slides* at the drop-down list.
4. With Slide 6 active in the Slide pane, change *Fiji Tour* to *Costa Rica Tour*.
5. Make Slide 7 active, select and delete the bulleted text, and then type the following bulleted text:
   - Round-trip airfare from Los Angeles to San Jose, Costa Rica
   - 8 days and 7 nights in Costa Rica
   - Monthly tours
   - Prices from $1099 to $1599

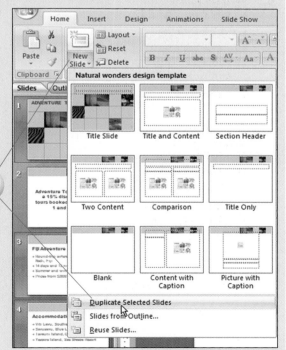

Step 3e

6. Make Slide 8 active, select and delete the bulleted text, and then type the following bulleted text:
   - San Jose, Emerald Suites
   - Tortuguero, Plantation Spa and Resort
   - Fortuna, Pacific Resort
   - Jaco, Monteverde Cabanas
7. Make Slide 9 active, select and delete the bulleted text, and then type the following bulleted text:
   - San Jose city tour
   - Rainforest tram
   - Canal cruise
   - Forest hike
8. Save **PP_C2_P3.pptx**.

**Reuse Slides**
1. Click New Slide button arrow.
2. Click *Reuse Slides.*
3. Click Browse button, *Browse File.*
4. Navigate to desired folder.
5. Double-click desired presentation.
6. Click desired slide in Reuse Slides task pane.

# Reusing Slides

PowerPoint provides another method for copying slides from one presentation to another. Click the New Slide button arrow and then click the *Reuse Slides* option at the drop-down list and the Reuse Slides task pane displays at the right side of the screen as shown in Figure 2.4. At this task pane, click the Browse button, click *Browse File* at the drop-down list, and the Browse dialog box displays. At this dialog box, navigate to the desired folder and then double-click the desired presentation. This inserts the presentation slides in the Reuse Slides task pane. Click a slide in the Reuse Slides task pane to insert it in the currently open presentation.

**Figure 2.4** Reuse Slides Task Pane

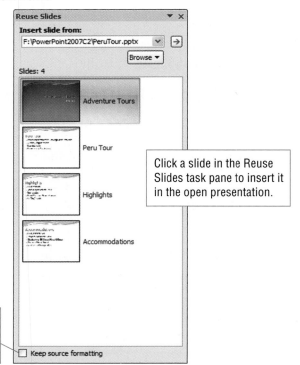

Click a slide in the Reuse Slides task pane to insert it in the open presentation.

Insert a check mark in this check box if you want the inserted slide to maintain source formatting.

By default, the slides you insert from the Reuse Slides task pane into the currently open presentation take on the formatting of the current presentation. If you want the slides to retain their original formatting when inserted in the presentation, insert a check mark in the *Keep source formatting* check box located toward the bottom of the Reuse Slides task pane.

## Project 3b   Reusing Slides

1. With **PP_C2_P3.pptx** open, click the New Slide button arrow and then click *Reuse Slides* at the drop-down list. (This displays the Reuse Slides task pane at the right side of the screen.)
2. Click the Browse button in the Reuse Slides task pane and then click *Browse File* at the drop-down list.
3. At the Browse dialog box, navigate to the PowerPoint2007C2 folder on your storage medium and then double-click *PeruTour.pptx*.
4. In the Slides/Outline pane, scroll down the slide thumbnails until Slide 9 displays and then click below Slide 9. (This inserts a thin, horizontal line below the Slide 9 thumbnail in the Slides/Outline pane.)
5. Click the first slide thumbnail (*Adventure Tours*) in the Reuse Slides task pane. (This inserts the slide in the open presentation immediately below Slide 9.)
6. Click the second slide thumbnail (*Peru Tour*) in the Reuse Slides task pane.
7. Click the fourth slide thumbnail (*Accommodations*) in the Reuse Slides task pane.
8. Click the third slide thumbnail (*Highlights*) in the Reuse Slides task pane.
9. Close the Reuse Slides task pane by clicking the Close button (contains an X) located in the upper right corner of the task pane.
10. Save **PP_C2_P3.pptx**.

Step 2

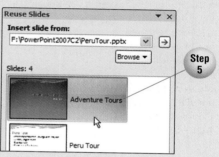

Step 5

## Previewing a Presentation

Before printing a presentation, consider previewing the presentation. In Print Preview you can specify printing options, change the zoom display, and display specific slides. To display a presentation in Print Preview, click the Office button, point to *Print*, and then click *Print Preview*. The Print Preview tab, shown in Figure 2.5, displays toward the top of the screen. Click the Print button to send the presentation to the printer. Click the Options button and a drop-down list displays with options for inserting a header or footer, changing from color to grayscale, scaling the presentation to fit on a page, framing the slides, and specifying a print order. Use the Print What button to specify whether you want to print slides, handouts, notes pages, or an outline.

**QUICK STEPS**

**Print Preview**
1. Click Office button.
2. Point to *Print*.
3. Click *Print Preview*.

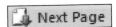

With the Orientation button you can choose to print the presentation on paper in portrait or landscape orientation. At the portrait orientation, data is printed on a page that is 11 inches tall and 8.5 inches wide. At the landscape orientation, the page is 8.5 inches tall and 11 inches wide. Click the Zoom button and the Zoom dialog box displays with options for changing the zoom by percentage. Click the Fit to Window button to return the display to the default. Use the Next Page or Previous Page buttons to navigate through the presentation and click the Close Print Preview button to close the preview window.

**Figure 2.5** Print Preview Window

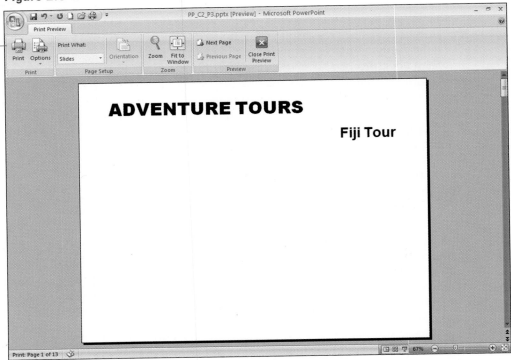

## Inserting Headers and Footers

You can choose to print a presentation as individual slides, handouts, notes pages, or an outline. If you print a presentation as handouts or an outline, PowerPoint will automatically print the current date in the upper right corner of the page and the page number in the lower right corner. If you print the presentation as notes pages, PowerPoint will automatically print the page number in the lower right corner. PowerPoint does not insert the date or page number when you print individual slides.

You can modify existing header and footer elements or insert additional elements with options in the Header and Footer dialog box. If *Slides* is selected in the *Print What* option box, the Header and Footer dialog box displays with the Slide tab selected. If *Handouts*, *Notes Pages*, or *Outline* is selected in the *Print What* option, the Header and Footer dialog box displays with the Notes and Handouts tab selected as shown in Figure 2.6. The options in the dialog box are similar with either tab selected.

With options at the Header and Footer dialog box, you can insert the date and time, a header, a footer, and page numbers. If you insert the date and time in a presentation, you can choose the *Update automatically* option if you want the date and time updated each time the presentation is opened. Choose the date and

**QUICK STEPS**

**Insert Header/Footer**
1. Display presentation in Print Preview.
2. Click Options button, *Header and Footer.*
3. Make desired changes at dialog box.
4. Click Apply to All button.

time formatting by clicking the down-pointing arrow at the right side of the *Update automatically* option box and then choose the desired formatting at the drop-down list. If you choose the *Fixed* option, type the desired date and/or time in the *Fixed* text box. Type header text in the *Header* text box and type footer text in the *Footer* text box. If you want to print the slide number on slides, insert a check mark in the *Slide number* check box in the Header and Footer dialog box with the Slide tab selected. If you want to include page numbers on handouts, notes pages, or outline pages, insert a check mark in the *Page number* check box in the Header and Footer dialog box with the Notes and Handouts tab selected. If you want all changes you make to the Header and Footer dialog box to apply to all slides or all handouts, notes pages, and outline pages, click the Apply to All button located in the upper right corner of the dialog box.

**Figure 2.6** Header and Footer Dialog Box with the Notes and Handouts Tab Selected

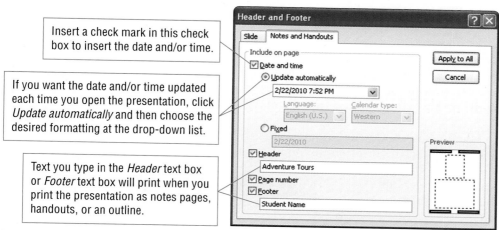

Insert a check mark in this check box to insert the date and/or time.

If you want the date and/or time updated each time you open the presentation, click *Update automatically* and then choose the desired formatting at the drop-down list.

Text you type in the *Header* text box or *Footer* text box will print when you print the presentation as notes pages, handouts, or an outline.

## Project 3c  Previewing a Presentation

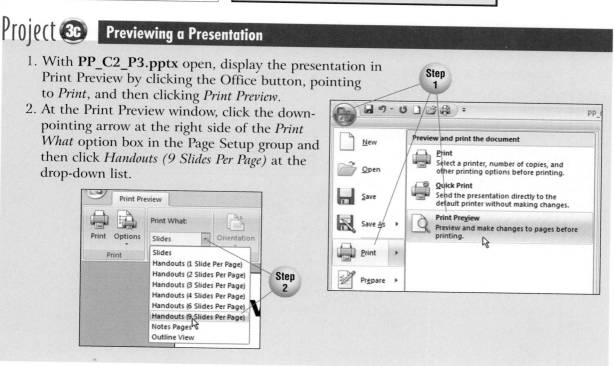

1. With **PP_C2_P3.pptx** open, display the presentation in Print Preview by clicking the Office button, pointing to *Print*, and then clicking *Print Preview*.
2. At the Print Preview window, click the down-pointing arrow at the right side of the *Print What* option box in the Page Setup group and then click *Handouts (9 Slides Per Page)* at the drop-down list.

3. Click the Options button in the Print group, point to *Color/Grayscale*, and then click *Color (On Black and White Printer)*.
4. Click the Options button in the Print group, point to *Printing Order*, and then click *Vertical*.
5. Click the Orientation button in the Page Setup group and then click *Landscape* at the drop-down list.

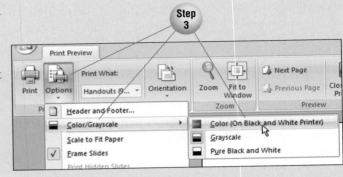

6. Change the Zoom by completing the following steps:
   a. Click the Zoom button in the Zoom group.
   b. At the Zoom dialog box, click *100%* in the *Zoom to* group.
   c. Click OK.
7. Click the Fit to Window button in the Zoom group.
8. Click the Options button in the Print group, point to *Color/Grayscale*, and then click *Grayscale*.
9. Make changes at the Header and Footer dialog box by completing the following steps:

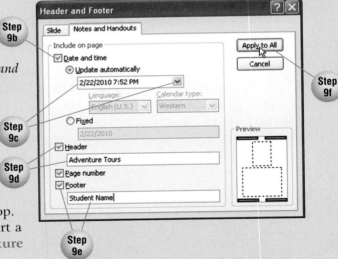

   a. Click the Options button in the Print group and then click *Header and Footer* at the drop-down list.
   b. At the Header and Footer dialog box with the Notes and Handouts tab selected, click the *Date and time* option.
   c. Click the down-pointing arrow at the right side of the *Update automatically* option box and then click the eighth option from the top.
   d. Click the *Header* check box to insert a check mark and then type Adventure Tours in the *Header* text box.
   e. Click the *Footer* check box to insert a check mark and then type your first and last names in the *Footer* text box.
   f. Click the Apply to All button located in the upper right corner of the dialog box.
10. Click the Print button in the Print group and then click OK at the Print dialog box.
11. Click the down-pointing arrow at the right side of the *Print What* option box in the Page Setup group and then click *Slides* at the drop-down list.

12. Make changes at the Header and Footer dialog box by completing the following steps:
   a. Click the Options button in the Print group and then click *Header and Footer* at the drop-down list.
   b. At the Header and Footer dialog box with the Slide tab selected, click the *Date and time* check box to insert a check mark.
   c. Click the *Update automatically* option.
   d. Click the *Slide number* check box to insert a check mark.
   e. Click the *Footer* check box to insert a check mark and then type your first and last names in the *Footer* text box.
   f. Click the *Don't show on title slide* check box to insert a check mark.
   g. Click the Apply to All button located in the upper right corner of the dialog box.
   h. Click the Next Page button in the Preview group to display the next slide. (Notice the date, your name, and the slide number that displays along the bottom of the slide.)
   i. Click the Next Page button a couple of more times to view other slides.
13. Click the Print button in the Print group and then click OK at the Print dialog box.
14. Click the Close Print Preview button.
15. Add a transition and sound of your choosing to all slides in the presentation.
16. Run the presentation.
17. Save and then close **PP_C2_P3.pptx**.

**Header and Footer**

Slide | Notes and Handouts

Include on slide

☑ Date and time — **Step 12b**
　　◉ Update automatically — **Step 12c**
　　　2/22/2010 ▾
　　　Language: | Calendar type:
　　　English (U.S.) ▾ | Western ▾
　　○ Fixed

☑ Slide number — **Step 12d**
☑ Footer — **Step 12e**
　　Student Name
☑ Don't show on title slide — **Step 12f**

Apply to All — **Step 12g**
Apply
Cancel

Preview

# Project 4  Use the PowerPoint Help Feature and Create a Presentation

You will use the Help feature to learn more about the options in the Save As dialog box. You will also use the PowerPoint Help window to find information on keyboard shortcuts and then use the information to create a presentation.

# Using Help

PowerPoint provides a Help feature you can use to find information on specific options in a dialog box or on PowerPoint features and commands. You can use the Help button to find information about specific features in a dialog box and you can use the Microsoft Office PowerPoint Help button to find information on PowerPoint features.

**HINT**
Press F1 to display the PowerPoint Help window.

## Getting Help in a Dialog Box

**Dialog Box Help**

Some dialog boxes contain a Help button you can click to display information in the PowerPoint Help window that is specific to the dialog box. This button is located in the upper right corner of the dialog box and displays as a question mark inside a square. Click this button and the PowerPoint Help window displays with topics related to the dialog box.

## Project 4a    Using a ScreenTip to Access Help

1. At a blank presentation, click the Office button and then click *Save As* at the drop-down list.
2. At the Save As dialog box, click the Help button located in the upper right corner of the dialog box.
3. At the PowerPoint Help window, click the *Save As* hyperlink.

Step 2

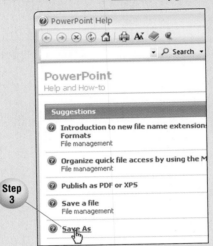

Step 3

4. In the Save As list box, click *Microsoft Office PowerPoint*.
5. Read the information that displays about saving in PowerPoint and then click the Close button to close the PowerPoint Help window.
6. Close the Save As dialog box.

## Using the Microsoft Office PowerPoint Help Button

PowerPoint's Help feature is an on-screen reference manual containing information about all PowerPoint features and commands. PowerPoint's Help feature is similar to the Windows Help and the Help features in Word, Excel, and Access. Get help by clicking the Microsoft Office PowerPoint Help button located in the upper right corner of the screen (a question mark in a circle) or by pressing the keyboard shortcut, F1. This displays the PowerPoint Help window. In this window, type a topic, feature, or question in the *Search* text box and then press Enter. Topics related to the search text display in the Help window. Click a topic that interests you. If the topic window contains a Show All hyperlink in the upper right corner, click this hyperlink and the information expands to show all help information related to the topic. When you click the Show All hyperlink, it becomes the Hide All hyperlink.

1. At a blank presentation screen, click the Microsoft Office PowerPoint Help button located in the upper right corner of the screen.

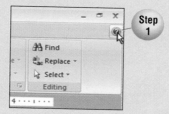

2. At the PowerPoint Help window, type keyboard shortcuts in the *Search* text box.
3. Press the Enter key.
4. When the list of topics displays, click the *Keyboard shortcuts for PowerPoint 2007* hyperlink. (The location of this hyperlink may vary.)

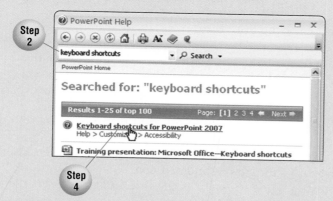

5. Click the Show All hyperlink that displays in the upper right corner of the window.

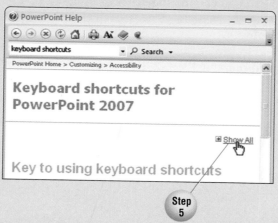

6. Scroll through the PowerPoint Help window and notice the information that displays about keyboard shortcuts.
7. Scroll back to the beginning of the Help text and then click the Hide All hyperlink.

8. Scroll down toward the bottom of the list and then click the <u>Delete and copy text and objects</u> hyperlink. (This option is located in the *Common tasks in Microsoft Office PowerPoint* section.)
9. Click the Print button that displays on the PowerPoint Help window toolbar.

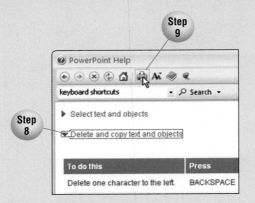

10. At the Print dialog box, click the Print button.
11. Click the Close button to close the PowerPoint Help window.
12. At the blank presentation, create a presentation with the information you printed that contains the following information:
    a. Slide 1: Insert the text PowerPoint Help as the title and Keyboard Shortcuts as the subtitle.
    b. Slide 2: Insert the text Delete Text as the title and then insert the four delete keyboard shortcuts as bulleted text.
    c. Slide 3: Insert the text Cut, Copy, Paste Text as the title and then insert the three cut, copy, and paste keyboard shortcuts as bulleted text.
    d. Slide 4: Insert the text Undo and Redo as the title and then insert the two undo and redo keyboard shortcuts as bulleted text.
    e. Slide 5: Insert the text Copy and Paste Formatting as the title and then insert the three copy and paste formatting keyboard shortcuts as bulleted text.
13. Apply a design theme of your choosing. Check each slide to make sure the text displays appropriately on each slide.
14. Apply a transition and sound to all slides in the presentation.
15. Save the presentation and name it **PP_C2_P4**.
16. Run the presentation.
17. Print the presentation as a handout with six slides per page.
18. Close **PP_C2_P4.pptx**.

# CHAPTER summary

- Use the spelling feature to check spelling of slides in a presentation. Begin the spelling checker by clicking the Review tab and then clicking the Spelling button in the Proofing group.

- Refer to Table 2.1 for methods for selecting text in slides.

- Text in a placeholder is positioned inside of a placeholder. Click in a placeholder to select the placeholder and position the insertion point inside.

- Display the Find dialog box by clicking the Find button in the Editing group in the Home tab.

- Display the Replace dialog box by clicking the Replace button in the Editing group in the Home tab.

- With buttons in the Clipboard group or with options from a shortcut menu, you can cut and paste or copy and paste text in slides.

- You can use the mouse to move text in the Slides/Outline pane. You can select and then drag it to a new location or hold down the Ctrl key while dragging to copy text to a new location.

- Use the sizing handles that display around a selected placeholder to increase or decrease the size of the placeholder. You can use the mouse to drag a selected placeholder to a new location in the slide.

- Use the New Slide button in the Home tab to insert a slide in a presentation.

- Delete a selected slide by clicking the Delete button in the Slides group in the Home tab or by pressing the Delete button.

- You can move or delete a selected slide in Normal view in the Slides/Outline pane or in Slide Sorter view.

- Copy a selected slide by holding down the Ctrl key while dragging the slide to the desired location.

- Use the Copy and Paste buttons in the Clipboard group in the Home tab to copy a slide between presentations.

- Select adjacent slides in the Slides/Outline pane or in Slide Sorter view by clicking the first slide, holding down the Shift key, and then clicking the last slide. Select nonadjacent slides by holding down the Ctrl key while clicking each desired slide.

- Duplicate slides in a presentation by selecting the desired slides in the Slides/Outline pane, clicking the New Slide button arrow, and then clicking the *Duplicate Selected Slides* option.

- You can copy slides from a presentation into the open presentation with options at the Reuse Slides task pane. Display this task pane by clicking the New Slide button arrow and then clicking *Reuse Slides* at the drop-down list.

- Display a presentation in Print Preview by clicking the Office button, pointing to *Print*, and then clicking *Print Preview*.

- In Print Preview, display the Header and Footer dialog box by clicking the Options button and then clicking *Header and Footer* at the drop-down list. Use options in the dialog box to insert the date and time, a header, a footer, slide numbers, or page numbers. The options will vary depending on which tab is selected—*Slide* or *Notes and Handouts*.
- Click the Help button in a dialog box and the PowerPoint Help window displays with information specific to the dialog box.
- Click the Microsoft Office Word Help button or press F1 to display the PowerPoint Help window.

# COMMANDS review

| FEATURE | TAB, GROUP | BUTTON, OPTION | OFFICE BUTTON DROP-DOWN LIST | KEYBOARD SHORTCUT |
|---------|-----------|----------------|------------------------------|-------------------|
| Spelling check | Review, Proofing | ABC | | F7 |
| Find dialog box | Home, Editing | Find | | Ctrl + F |
| Replace dialog box | Home, Editing | Replace | | Ctrl + H |
| Cut text or slide | Home, Clipboard | | | Ctrl + X |
| Copy text or slide | Home, Clipboard | | | Ctrl + C |
| Paste text or slide | Home, Clipboard | | | Ctrl + V |
| Duplicate slide | Home, Slides | , Duplicate Selected Slides | | |
| Reuse Slides task pane | Home, Slides | , Reuse Slides | | |
| Print Preview | | | Print, Print Preview | |
| PowerPoint Help window | | | | F1 |

# CONCEPTS check

## Test Your Knowledge

**Completion:** In the space provided at the right, indicate the correct term, symbol, or command.

1. The Spelling button is located in the Proofing group in this tab.  _____

2. This is the keyboard shortcut to select all text in a placeholder.  _____

3. The Find button is located in this group in the Home tab.  _____

4. In the Slides/Outline pane with the Outline tab selected, hold down the left mouse button on this to select all text in the slide.  _____

5. To copy text to a new location in the Slides/Outline pane with the Outline tab selected, hold down this key while dragging text.  _____

6. The border of a selected placeholder displays these handles as well as a green rotation handle.  _____

7. You can reorganize slides in a presentation in the Slides/Outline pane or in this view.  _____

8. You can copy selected slides in a presentation using this option from the New Slide button drop-down list.  _____

9. To select adjacent slides, click the first slide, hold down this key, and then click the last slide.  _____

10. Click the New Slide button arrow and then click the *Reuse Slides* option at the drop-down list and this displays.  _____

11. Display the presentation in Print Preview by clicking the Office button, pointing to this option, and then clicking *Print Preview*.  _____

12. In Print Preview, display the Header and Footer dialog box by clicking this button in the Print Preview tab and then clicking *Header and Footer* at the drop-down list.  _____

13. This is the keyboard shortcut to display the PowerPoint Help window.  _____

# SKILLS check

*Demonstrate Your Proficiency*

## Assessment

## 1 CREATE AN ELECTRONIC DESIGN PRESENTATION

1. Create the presentation shown in Figure 2.7 using a design theme of your choosing. (When typing bulleted text, press the Tab key to move the insertion point to the desired tab level.)
2. After creating the slides, complete a spelling check on the text in the slides.
3. Save the presentation into the PowerPoint2007C2 folder on your storage medium and name the presentation **PP_C2_A1**.
4. Run the presentation.
5. Preview the presentation, change the *Print What* option to *Handouts (4 Slides Per Page)*, change the orientation to landscape, and then print the presentation.
6. Make the following changes to the presentation:
   a. Change to Slide Sorter view and then move Slide 3 between Slides 1 and 2.
   b. Move Slide 4 between Slides 2 and 3.
   c. Search for the word *document* and replace it with the word *brochure*. (Make Slide 1 active and then capitalize the "b" in "brochure.")
   d. Add a transition and sound of your choosing to each slide.
7. Save the presentation.
8. Display the Reuse Slides task pane, browse to the PowerPoint2007C2 folder on your storage medium, and then double-click **LayoutTips.pptx**.
9. Insert the *Layout Punctuation Tips* slide below Slide 4.
10. Insert the *Layout Tips* slide below Slide 5.
11. Close the Reuse Slides task pane.
12. Find all occurrences of *Layout* and replace with *Design*. (Insert a check mark in the *Match case* check box.)
13. Move Slide 5 between Slides 1 and 2.
14. Move Slide 6 between Slides 2 and 3.
15. Save the presentation.
16. Print the presentation as a handout with six slides per page.
17. Close **PP_C2_A1.pptx**.

**Figure 2.7  Assessment 1**

Slide 1  Title    =  Electronic Design and Production
         Subtitle =  Designing a Document

Slide 2  Title    =  Creating Balance
         Bullets  =  
- Symmetrical balance: Balancing similar elements equally on a page (centered alignment) of the document
- Asymmetrical balance: Balancing contrasting elements on a page of the document

Slide 3  Title    =  Creating Focus
         Bullets  =  
- Creating focus with titles, headings, and subheads in a document
- Creating focus with graphic elements in a document
  - Clip art
  - Watermarks
  - Illustrations
  - Photographs
  - Charts
  - Graphs

Slide 4  Title    =  Providing Proportion
         Bullets  =  
- Evaluating proportions in a document
- Sizing graphic elements in a document
- Using white space in a document

## Assessment

## 2  CREATE A NETIQUETTE PRESENTATION

1. Create a presentation with the text shown in Figure 2.8. You determine the design template and the slide layout.
2. If necessary, size and move placeholders so the text is positioned attractively on the slide.
3. Select Slides 4 through 6 and then duplicate the slides.
4. Type the following text in place of the existing text in the identified slides:
   a. Slide 7: Select the placeholder netiquette rule text and then type Do not plagiarize.
   b. Slide 8: Select the netiquette rule text in the placeholder and then type Respect and accept people's differences.
   c. Slide 9: Select the netiquette rule text in the placeholder and then type Share expert knowledge.
5. Complete a spelling check on text in the presentation.
6. Save the presentation and name it **PP_C2_A2**.
7. Print the presentation as a handout with nine slides per page.

8. Make the following edits to the presentation:
   a. Display the presentation in Slide Sorter view.
   b. Move Slide 3 between Slide 5 and Slide 6.
   c. Move Slide 7 between Slide 3 and Slide 4.
9. Add a transition and sound of your choosing to all slides in the presentation.
10. Save the presentation.
11. Run the presentation.
12. Print the presentation as a handout with nine slides per page.
13. Close **PP_C2_A2.pptx**.

**Figure 2.8  Assessment 2**

| Slide 1 | Title | = | INTERNET APPLICATIONS |
| | Subtitle | = | Internet Community |

| Slide 2 | Title | = | Community Issues |
| | Bullets | = | • Flaming |
| | | | • E-mail |
| | | | • Moderated environments |
| | | | • Netiquette |

| Slide 3 | Title | = | Netiquette Rule |
| | Subtitle | = | Remember you are dealing with people. |

| Slide 4 | Title | = | Netiquette Rule |
| | Subtitle | = | Adhere to the same standards of behavior online that you follow in real life. |

| Slide 5 | Title | = | Netiquette Rule |
| | Subtitle | = | Know where you are in cyberspace. |

| Slide 6 | Title | = | Netiquette Rule |
| | Subtitle | = | Respect others' time and bandwidth. |

## Assessment

### 3  DOWNLOAD A DESIGN THEME

1. If your computer is connected to the Internet, Microsoft Office Online provides a number of design themes you can download to your computer.
2. Display the New Presentation dialog box and then click *Design slides* in the *Microsoft Office Online* section. Browse through the design themes and then download a design theme that interests you.
3. Open **PP_C2_A2.pptx** and then save the presentation and name it **PP_C2_A3**.
4. Apply the design theme you downloaded to the presentation.
5. Check each slide to make sure the text displays in an attractive manner on the slide.
6. Run the presentation.
7. Print Slide 1 and Slide 5 of the presentation.
8. Save and then close **PP_C2_A3.pptx**.

# CASE study

## *Apply Your Skills*

You are the office manager at the Company Connections agency. One of your responsibilities is to conduct workshops for preparing individuals for the job search process. A coworker has given you a presentation for the workshop but the presentation needs some editing and modifying. Open **JobAnalysis.pptx** and then save the presentation and name it **PP_C2_CS_P1**. Check each slide in the presentation and then make modifications to maintain consistency in the size and location of placeholders (consider using the Reset button to reset the formatting and size of the placeholders), maintain consistency in heading text, move text from an overcrowded slide to a new slide, complete a spelling check, apply a design theme, and make any other modifications to improve the presentation. Save **PP_C2_CS_P1.pptx**.

After reviewing the presentation, you realize that you need to include slides on resumes. Open the **ResumePresentation.pptx** presentation and then copy Slides 2 and 3 into the **PP_C2_CS_P1.pptx** presentation. You want to add additional information on resume writing tips and decide to use the Internet to find information. Locate information on the Internet with tips on writing a resume and then create a slide (or two) with the information you find. Add a transition and sound to all slides in the presentation. Save the **PP_C2_CS_P1.pptx** presentation.

You know that Microsoft Word offers a number of resume templates you can download from the Microsoft Office Online site. You decide to include information in the presentation on how to download resumes. Open Microsoft Word, click the Office button, and then click *New* at the drop-down list. At the New Document dialog box, click the Help button that displays in the upper right corner of the dialog box. Read the information on downloading templates and then experiment with downloading a template. With the **PP_C2_CS_P1.pptx** presentation open, add an additional slide to the end of the presentation that provides steps on how to download a resume in Microsoft Word. Print the presentation as a handout with six slides per page. Save, run, and then close the **PP_C2_CS_P1.pptx** presentation.

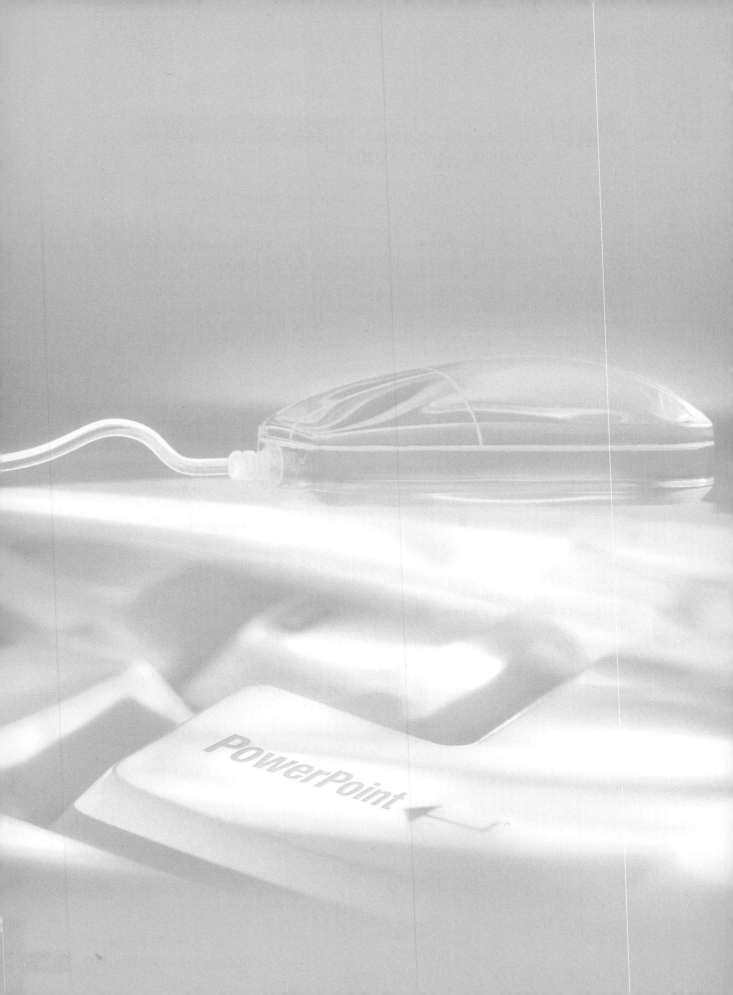

# Formatting Slides

## PERFORMANCE OBJECTIVES

Upon successful completion of Chapter 3, you will be able to:

- Apply font and paragraph formatting to text in slides
- Apply formatting with the Mini toolbar and Format Painter
- Customize bullets and numbers
- Modify theme colors and fonts
- Change slide background
- Change page setup
- Create custom themes including custom theme colors and theme fonts
- Delete custom themes

**Tutorial 3.1**
Formatting Slide Content
**Tutorial 3.2**
Formatting Slide Appearance

The Font and Paragraph groups in the Home tab contain a number of buttons and options you can use to format text in slides. PowerPoint also provides a Mini toolbar and the Format Painter feature to help you format text. You can modify the design theme colors and fonts provided by PowerPoint and you can create your own custom themes. You will learn to use these features in this chapter along with how to change page setup options.

*Note: Before beginning computer projects, copy to your storage medium the PowerPoint2007C3 subfolder from the PowerPoint2007 folder on the CD that accompanies this textbook and then make PowerPoint2007C3 the active folder.*

## Project 1 Format an E-commerce Presentation

You will open an e-commerce presentation, apply font and paragraph formatting, apply formatting with Format Painter, apply column formatting to text in placeholders, and rotate and vertically align text in placeholders.

# Formatting a Presentation

PowerPoint provides a variety of design themes you can apply to a presentation. These themes contain formatting such as font, color, and graphics. In some situations, the formatting provided by the theme is appropriate; in other situations, you may want to change or enhance the formatting of a slide.

## Applying Font Formatting

The Font group in the Home tab contains a number of buttons for applying font formatting to text in a slide such as changing the font, font size, color, and applying font effects. Table 3.1 describes the buttons in the Font group along with any keyboard shortcuts to apply font formatting.

### *Changing Fonts*

Design themes apply a font to text in slides. You may want to change this default to some other font for such reasons as changing the mood of a presentation, enhancing the visual appeal of slides, and increasing the readability of the text in slides. Change the font with the Font and Font Size buttons in the Font group in the Home tab.

When you select text and then click the Font button arrow, a drop-down gallery displays with font options. Hover your mouse pointer over a font option and the selected text in the slide displays with the font applied. You can continue hovering your mouse pointer over different font options to see how the selected text displays in the specified font. The Font button drop-down gallery is an example of the *live preview* feature, which allows you to see how the font formatting affects your text without having to return to the presentation. The live preview feature is also available when you click the Font Size button arrow.

Fonts may be decorative or plain and generally fall into one of two categories: *serif* or *sans serif*. A serif is a small line at the end of a character stroke. A serif font is easier to read and is generally used for large amounts of text. A sans serif font does not have serifs (*sans* is French for *without*) and is generally used for titles and headings.

In addition to buttons in the Font group in the Home tab, you can use options at the Font dialog box shown in Figure 3.1 to apply character formatting to text. Display the Font dialog box by clicking the Font group dialog box launcher or with the keyboard shortcut Ctrl + Shift + F. (The dialog box launcher is the small button containing a diagonal arrow that displays in the lower right corner of the group.) Use options at the Font dialog box to choose a font, font style, font size, and to apply special effects to text in slides such as Superscript, Subscript, and Double Strikethrough.

**HINT**
Consider using a sans serif typeface for titles and headings and a serif typeface for body text.

**HINT**
Use options at the Font dialog box with the Character Spacing tab selected to increase or decrease spacing between characters and to apply kerning to text.

**Table 3.1** PowerPoint Home Tab Font Group Buttons

| Button | Name | Function | Keyboard Shortcut |
|---|---|---|---|
| Calibri (Body) ▾ | Font | Changes selected text to a different font | |
| 32 ▾ | Font Size | Changes selected text to a different font size | |
| A▴ | Increase Font Size | Increases font size of selected text to next available larger size | Ctrl + Shift + > |
| A▾ | Decrease Font Size | Decreases font size of selected text to next available smaller size | Ctrl + Shift + < |
| ✐▾ | Clear All Formatting | Clears all character formatting from selected text | Ctrl + Spacebar |
| **B** | Bold | Adds or removes bold formatting to or from selected text | Ctrl + B |
| *I* | Italic | Adds or removes italic formatting to or from selected text | Ctrl + I |
| U ▾ | Underline | Adds or removes underline formatting to or from selected text | Ctrl + U |
| abc | Strikethrough | Inserts or removes a line through the middle of selected text | |
| S | Text Shadow | Adds or removes shadow formatting to or from selected text | |
| AV↔ ▾ | Character Spacing | Adjusts spacing between characters | |
| Aa ▾ | Change Case | Changes the case of selected text | Shift + F3 |
| A ▾ | Font Color | Changes the font color for selected text | |

**Figure 3.1** Font Dialog Box

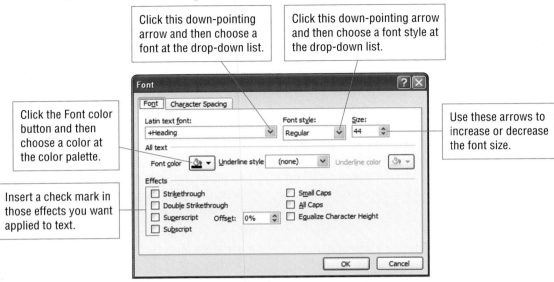

Click this down-pointing arrow and then choose a font at the drop-down list.

Click this down-pointing arrow and then choose a font style at the drop-down list.

Click the Font color button and then choose a color at the color palette.

Use these arrows to increase or decrease the font size.

Insert a check mark in those effects you want applied to text.

## *Formatting with the Mini Toolbar*

When you select text, the Mini toolbar displays in a dimmed fashion above the selected text. Hover the mouse pointer over the Mini toolbar and it becomes active. Click a button on the Mini toolbar to apply formatting to selected text. If you do not want the Mini toolbar to display when you select text, you can turn it off. To do this, click the Office button and then click the PowerPoint Options button that displays in the lower right corner of the drop-down list. At the PowerPoint Options dialog box with the *Popular* option selected in the left panel, click the *Show Mini Toolbar on selection* check box to remove the check mark.

## Project 1a  Applying Font Formatting to Text

1. Open **E-Commerce.pptx** and then save the presentation and name it **PP_C3_P1**.
2. Apply the Urban design theme to the presentation.
3. Change the font formatting of the Slide 1 subtitle by completing the following steps:
    a. With Slide 1 active, click any character in the subtitle *Online Services*.
    b. Select *Online Services*.
    c. Click the Home tab.
    d. Click the Font button arrow, scroll down the drop-down gallery, and then click *Trebuchet MS*.

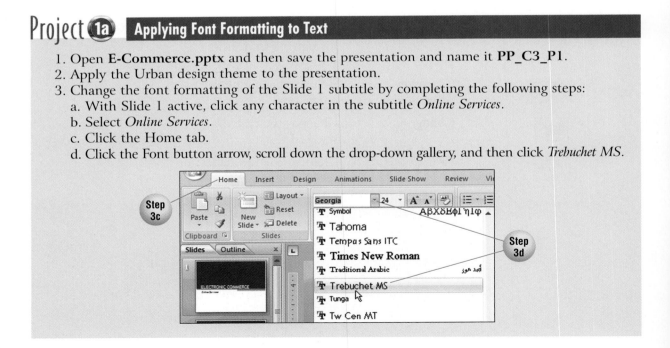

Step 3c

Step 3d

e. Click the Font Size button arrow and then click *40* at the drop-down gallery.
f. Click the Bold button.
g. Click the Text Shadow button in the Font group.
h. Click the Font Color button arrow and then click the *Blue-Gray, Accent 6, Darker 25%* option as shown below.

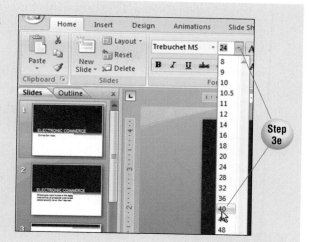

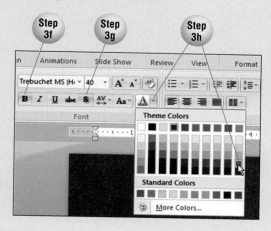

4. Change the size of the title text by completing the following steps:
   a. Click any character in the title *ELECTRONIC COMMERCE* and then select the title.
   b. Click the Increase Font Size button in the Font group.
5. Change the case of text by completing the following steps:
   a. Make Slide 2 active.
   b. Click in the title *ELECTRONIC COMMERCE* and then select the title.
   c. Click the Change Case button in the Font group and then click *Capitalize Each Word* at the drop-down list.

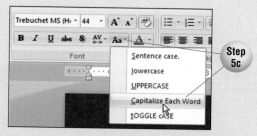

6. Apply and clear formatting to text by completing the following steps:
   a. Make Slide 3 active.
   b. Click in the bulleted text placeholder.
   c. Select *m-commerce* located in the parentheses.
   d. Click the Underline button in the Font group in the Home tab.
   e. Click the Bold button in the Font group.
   f. After looking at the text set with underlining and bold formatting, you decide to remove the formatting by clicking the Clear All Formatting button in the Font group.
   g. With the text still selected, click the Italic button in the Font group in the Home tab.

7. Apply italic formatting with the Mini toolbar by completing the following steps:
   a. Select *B2C*, hover the mouse pointer over the Mini toolbar to make it active, and then click the Italic button.
   b. Select *B2B*, hover the mouse pointer over the Mini toolbar to make it active, and then click the Italic button.
8. Save **PP_C3_P1.pptx**.

# Electronic Commerce Terminology

- Mobile commerce (*m-comm*
- Business-to-consumer (B2C) electronic commerce

Step 7a

## Formatting with Format Painter

If you apply character and/or paragraph formatting to text in a slide and want to apply the same formatting to text in the slide or other slides, use the Format Painter. With Format Painter, you can apply the same formatting in more than one location in a slide or slides. To use the Format Painter, apply the desired formatting to text, position the insertion point anywhere in the formatted text, and then double-click the Format Painter button in the Clipboard group in the Home tab. Using the mouse, select the additional text to which you want the formatting applied. After applying the formatting in the desired locations, click the Format Painter button to deactivate it. If you need to apply formatting in only one other location, click the Format Painter button once. The first time you select text, the formatting is applied and the Format Painter is deactivated.

**Project 1b**   **Applying Formatting with Format Painter**

1. With **PP_C3_P1.pptx** open, make sure Slide 3 is active.
2. Apply formatting to the title by completing the following steps:
   a. Click in the title text and then select the title *Electronic Commerce Technology*.
   b. Click the Font group dialog box launcher.

Step 2b

c. At the Font dialog box, click the down-pointing arrow at the right side of the *Font style* option box and then click *Bold Italic* at the drop-down list.

d. Select the current number in the *Size* text box and then type 36.

e. Click the Font color button and then click the *Blue-Gray, Accent 6, Darker 25%* option.

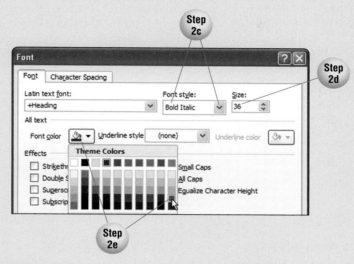

f. Click OK to close the dialog box.

3. Click on any character in the title.

4. Double-click the Format Painter button in the Clipboard group.

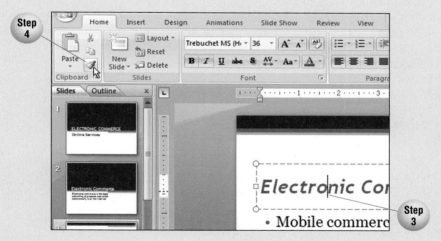

5. Make Slide 8 active.

6. Using the mouse, select the title *Advantages of Online Shopping*. (The mouse pointer displays as an I-beam with a paintbrush attached. You can also click each word in the title to apply the formatting.)

7. Make Slide 9 active and then select the title (or click each word in the title).

8. Make Slide 10 active and then select the title (or click each word in the title).

9. Click the Format Painter button to deactivate it.

10. If necessary, deselect the text.

# Formatting Paragraphs

The Paragraph group in the Home tab contains a number of buttons for applying paragraph formatting to text in a slide such as applying bullets and numbers, increasing and decreasing list levels, changing the horizontal and vertical alignment of text, changing line spacing, and rotating text in a placeholder. Table 3.2 describes the buttons in the Paragraph group along with any keyboard shortcuts.

**Table 3.2** PowerPoint Home Tab Paragraph Group Buttons

| Button | Name | Function | Keyboard Shortcut |
|---|---|---|---|
| | Bullets | Adds or removes bullets to or from selected text | |
| | Numbering | Adds or removes numbers to or from selected text | |
| | Decrease List Level | Moves text to the previous tab stop (level) | Shift + Tab |
| | Increase List Level | Moves text to the next tab stop (level) | Tab |
| | Line Spacing | | |
| | Align Text Left | Left-aligns text | Ctrl + L |
| | Center | Center-aligns text | Ctrl + E |
| | Align Text Right | Right-aligns text | Ctrl + R |
| | Justify | Justifies text | |
| | Columns | Splits text into two or more columns | |
| | Text Direction | Rotates or stacks text | |
| | Align Text | Changes the alignment of text within a text box | |
| | Convert to SmartArt Graphic | Converts selected text to a SmartArt graphic | |

1. With **PP_C3_P1.pptx** open, change bullets by completing the following steps:
   a. Make Slide 3 active.
   b. Click on any character in the bulleted text.
   c. Select the bulleted text.
   d. Click the Bullets button arrow and then click the *Filled Square Bullets* option at the drop-down gallery.

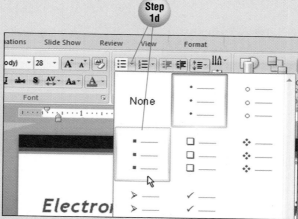

Step 1d

2. Change bullets to numbers by completing the following steps:
   a. Make Slide 8 active.
   b. Click on any character in the bulleted text.
   c. Select the bulleted text.
   d. Click the Numbering button arrow in the Paragraph group in the Home tab and then click the *A. B. C.* option at the drop-down gallery.

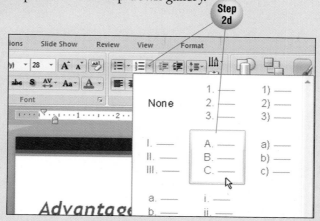

Step 2d

   e. After looking at the numbering, you decide to change to numbers by clicking the Numbering button arrow and then clicking the *1. 2. 3.* option at the drop-down gallery.
3. Decrease and increase list levels by completing the following steps:
   a. With Slide 8 active and the numbered text selected, click the Increase List Level button in the Paragraph group in the Home tab.
   b. With the text still selected, click the Font Color button arrow and then click the Dark Blue color (second color from the right in the bottom row).

c. Make Slide 10 active.

d. Click on any character in the bulleted text.

e. Move the insertion point so it is positioned immediately left of the *J.* in *J.C. Penney*.

f. Click the Decrease List Level button in the Paragraph group in the Home tab.

g. Move the insertion point so it is positioned immediately left of the *M* in *Macy's*.

h. Press Shift + Tab.

i. Move the insertion point so it is positioned immediately left of the first *L.* in *L.L. Bean*.

j. Click the Increase List Level button in the Paragraph group.

k. Move the insertion point so it is positioned immediately left of the *T* in *The Gap*.

l. Press the Tab key.

m. Complete similar steps to those in 3h or 3i to indent the following text to the next level: *Bloomingdale's, Expedia, Travelocity,* and *Orbitz.*

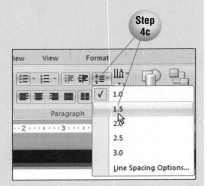

4. Change text line spacing by completing the following steps:

a. Make Slide 3 active.

b. Click in the bulleted text and then select the bulleted text.

c. Click the Line Spacing button in the Paragraph group in the Home tab and then click *1.5* at the drop-down list.

d. Make Slide 8 active.

e. Click in the bulleted text and then select the bulleted text.

f. Click the Line Spacing button and then click *2.0* at the drop-down list.

5. Change paragraph alignment by completing the following steps:

a. Make Slide 3 active, click on any character in the title, and then click the Center button in the Paragraph group.

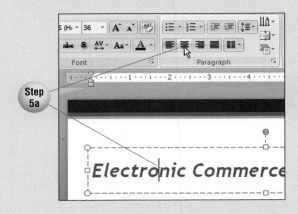

b. Make Slide 8 active, click on any character in the title, and then click the Center button.

c. Make Slide 9 active, click on any character in the title, and then click the Center button.

d. Make Slide 10 active, click on any character in the title, and then click the Center button.

6. Split text into two columns by completing the following steps:
   a. Make Slide 9 active.
   b. Click in the bulleted text and then select the bulleted text.
   c. Click the Columns button in the Paragraph group and then click *Two Columns* at the drop-down list.

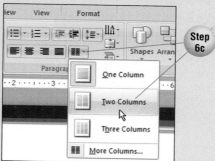

   d. Select the first sentence in the first bulleted paragraph (the sentence *Clear selling terms.*) and then click the Bold button.
   e. Select and then bold the first sentence in the remaining bulleted paragraphs of text in Slide 9.
7. Save **PP_C3_P1.pptx**.

## Customizing Paragraphs

If you want more control over paragraph alignment, indenting, and spacing, click the Paragraph group dialog box launcher. This displays the Paragraph dialog box with the Indents and Spacing tab selected as shown in Figure 3.2. You can also display this dialog box by clicking the Line Spacing button in the Paragraph group and then clicking *Line Spacing Options* at the drop-down list. Use options at this dialog box to specify text alignment, paragraph indention, spacing before and after paragraphs, and line spacing.

Line Spacing

**Figure 3.2** Paragraph Dialog Box with Indents and Spacing Tab Selected

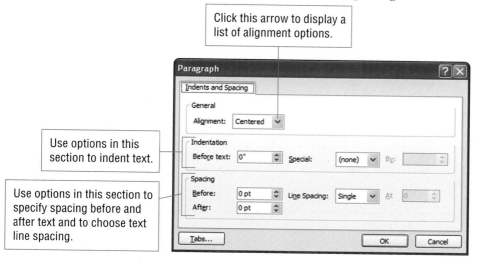

Columns

## Customizing Columns

Click the Columns button in the Paragraph group and you can choose one, two, or three columns. If you want to choose a number for columns other than the three choices or if you want to control spacing between columns, click the *More Columns* option at the drop-down list. This displays the Columns dialog box shown in Figure 3.3. With options in this dialog box, you can specify the number of columns and the spacing measurement between columns.

**Figure 3.3** Columns Dialog Box

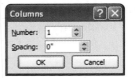

Specify the number of columns and spacing between columns in this dialog box.

## Project 1d   Customizing Paragraph and Column Formatting

1. With **PP_C3_P1.pptx** open, change line and paragraph spacing by completing the following steps:
   a. Make Slide 3 active.
   b. Click in the bulleted text and then select the bulleted text.
   c. Click the Paragraph group dialog box launcher.
   d. At the Paragraph dialog box, click twice on the up-pointing arrow at the right side of the *Before text* measurement box. (This inserts *0.6"* in the measurement box.)
   e. Click twice on the up-pointing arrow at the right side of the *After* measurement box in the *Spacing* section. (This inserts *12 pt* in the box.)
   f. Click the down-pointing arrow at the right side of the *Line Spacing* option box and then click *Multiple* at the drop-down list.
   g. Select the current measurement in the *At* text box and then type 1.8.
   h. Click OK.

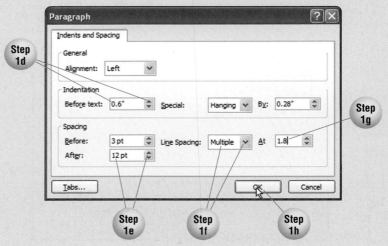

2. Format text in columns by completing the following steps:
   a. Make Slide 10 active.
   b. Click in the bulleted text and then select the text.
   c. Click the Columns button in the Paragraph group and then click *More Columns*.
   d. At the Columns dialog box, click once on the up-pointing arrow at the right side of the *Number* option. (This inserts a *2* in the text box.)
   e. Click the up-pointing arrow at the right side of the *Spacing* measurement box until *0.5″* displays in the box.
   f. Click OK.
   g. With the text still selected, click the Paragraph group dialog box launcher.
   h. At the Paragraph dialog box, click once on the up-pointing arrow at the right side of the *After* measurement box in the *Spacing* section. (This inserts *6 pt* in the box.)
   i. Click OK.
3. Save **PP_C3_P1.pptx**.

Step 2d

Step 2f

Step 2e

## *Rotating and Vertically Aligning Text*

If you click the Text Direction button in the Paragraph group, a drop-down list displays with options for rotating and stacking text. Click *More Options* at the drop-down list and the Format Text Effects dialog box with *Text Box* selected in the left panel displays as shown in Figure 3.4. Use options in this dialog box to specify vertical alignment and text direction, autofit contents, and change internal margins. Click the Align Text button in the Paragraph group and a drop-down list displays with options for changing the alignment to top, middle, or bottom of the placeholder. Click *More Options* that displays at the bottom of the drop-down list and the Format Text Effects dialog box shown in Figure 3.4 displays.

Text Direction

Align Text

**Figure 3.4** Format Text Effects Dialog Box with Text Box Selected

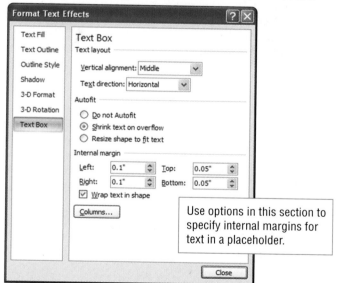

Use options in this section to specify internal margins for text in a placeholder.

1. With **PP_C3_P1.pptx** open, change vertical alignment by completing the following steps:
   a. Make Slide 9 active.
   b. Click on any character in the bulleted text.
   c. Click the Align Text button in the Paragraph group and then click *Middle* at the drop-down list.

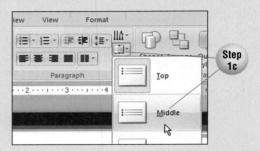

2. Modify Slide 8 so it displays as shown in Figure 3.5 by completing the following steps:
   a. Click in the numbered text and then select the numbered text.
   b. Click the Bullets button arrow and then click the *Filled Square Bullets* option.
   c. Decrease the size of the bulleted text placeholder so the placeholder borders display just outside the text.
   d. Drag the placeholder so the bulleted text is positioned as shown in Figure 3.5.
   e. Click on any character in the title *Advantages of Online Shopping*.
   f. Delete *of Online Shopping*.
   g. Select *Advantages* and then change the font size to 60.
   h. Drag in the right border of the placeholder to the left so it is positioned just outside the text.
   i. Click the Text Direction button in the Paragraph group and then click *Rotate all text 270°*.

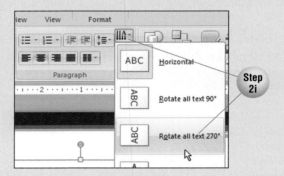

   j. Using the sizing handles that display around the title placeholder, increase the height and decrease the width of the placeholder and then drag the placeholder so the title displays as shown in Figure 3.5.
3. Apply a transition and sound to all slides in the presentation.
4. Display the presentation in Print Preview and insert the date, header, and footer in handouts pages by completing the following steps:
   a. Click the Office button, point to *Print*, and then click *Print Preview*.
   b. At the Print Preview window, click the down-pointing arrow at the right of the *Print What* option box in the Page Setup group and then click *Handouts (6 Slides Per Page)* at the drop-down list.

c. Click the Options button in the Print group in the Print Preview tab and then click *Header and Footer* at the drop-down list.

d. At the Header and Footer dialog box with the Notes and Handouts tab selected, click the *Date and time* check box to insert a check mark.

e. Click the *Header* check box to insert a check mark and then type Electronic Commerce in the *Header* text box.

f. Click the *Footer* check box to insert a check mark and then type your first and last names in the *Footer* text box.

g. Click the Apply to All button located in the upper right corner of the dialog box.

h. Click the Print button in the Print group and then click OK at the Print dialog box.

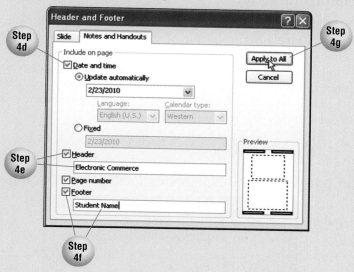

5. Save and then close **PP_C3_P1.pptx**.

**Figure 3.5  Project 1e, Slide 8**

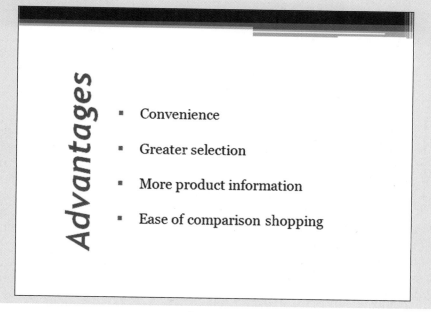

# Project ② Customize Bullets and Numbers in a Color Presentation

You will open a presentation on using colors in publications and then create and apply custom bullets and numbering.

## QUICK STEPS

**Customize Bullets**
1. Click in bulleted text.
2. Click Bullets button arrow.
3. Click *Bullets and Numbering* at drop-down gallery.
4. Make desired changes.
5. Click OK.

## Customizing Bullets

Each design theme contains a Title and Content slide layout containing bullets. The appearance and formatting of the bullets varies with each design theme. You can choose to use the bullet provided by the design theme or create custom bullets. Customize bullets with options at the Bullets and Numbering dialog box with the Bulleted tab selected as shown in Figure 3.6. Display this dialog box by clicking in a bulleted list placeholder, clicking the Bullets button arrow and then clicking *Bullets and Numbering* at the drop-down gallery.

Bullets

**Figure 3.6** Bullets and Numbering Dialog Box with Bulleted Tab Selected

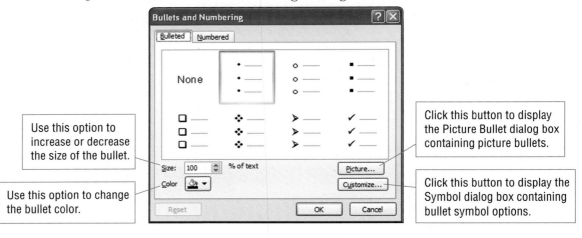

Use this option to increase or decrease the size of the bullet.

Use this option to change the bullet color.

Click this button to display the Picture Bullet dialog box containing picture bullets.

Click this button to display the Symbol dialog box containing bullet symbol options.

**HINT**
Choose a custom bullet that matches the theme or mood of the presentation.

At the Bullets and Numbering dialog box, choose one of the predesigned bullets from the list box, change the size of the bullets by percentage in relation to the text size, change the bullet color, and display bullet pictures and characters. Click the Picture button located toward the bottom of the dialog box and the Picture Bullet dialog box displays. Click the desired bullet in the list box and then click OK. Click the Customize button located toward the bottom of the Bullets and Numbering dialog box and the Symbol dialog box displays. Choose a symbol bullet option at the Symbol dialog box and then click OK. Picture or symbol bullets are particularly effective in adding visual interest.

If you want to move the insertion point down to the next line without inserting a bullet, press Shift + Enter. This inserts a line break without inserting a bullet. If you press the Enter key, bulleting is turned back on.

# Project 2a   Customizing Bullets and Numbers

1. Open **ColorPresentation.pptx** and then save the presentation and name it **PP_C3_P2**.
2. Increase list level and create custom bullets by completing the following steps:
   a. Make Slide 2 active.
   b. Select the second, third, and fourth bulleted paragraphs.
   c. Click the Increase List Level button in the Paragraph group.
   d. With the three bulleted paragraphs still selected, click the Bullets button arrow and then click *Bullets and Numbering* at the drop-down list.
   e. At the Bullets and Numbering dialog box with the Bulleted tab selected, click the up-pointing arrow at the right side of the *Size* option until *75* displays in the text box.
   f. Click the Picture button located toward the bottom right corner of the dialog box.
   g. At the Picture Bullet dialog box, click the first bullet option from the left in the third row (gold, square bullet).
   h. Click OK to close the Picture Bullet dialog box and the Bullets and Numbering dialog box.

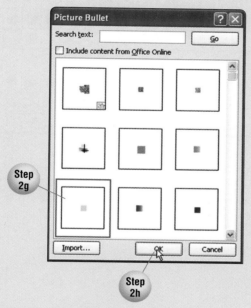

Step 2g

Step 2h

3. Insert symbol bullets by completing the following steps:
   a. Make Slide 3 active.
   b. Select all of the bulleted text.
   c. Click the Bullets button arrow and then click *Bullets and Numbering* at the drop-down list.
   d. At the Bullets and Numbering dialog box with the Bulleted tab selected, click the up-pointing arrow at the right side of the *Size* option until *80* displays in the text box.
   e. Click the Customize button located toward the bottom right corner of the dialog box.

f. At the Symbol dialog box, click the down-pointing arrow at the right side of the *Font* option box, scroll down the drop-down list, and then click *Wingdings*. (This option is located toward the bottom of the list.)

g. Scroll to the bottom of the Symbol dialog box list box until the last row of symbols displays and then click the second symbol from the right in the bottom row (check mark inside of a square).

h. Click OK.

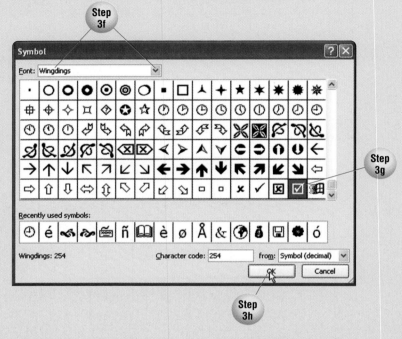

i. At the Bullets and Numbering dialog box, click the Font Color button and then click the Red color (second color from the left in the *Standard Colors* section).

j. Click OK to close the Bullets and Numbering dialog box. (This applies the red check mark symbol bullets to the selected text.)

4. Save **PP_C3_P2.pptx**.

**QUICK STEPS**

**Customize Numbering**
1. Click in numbered text.
2. Click Numbering button arrow.
3. Click *Bullets and Numbering* at drop-down gallery.
4. Make desired changes.
5. Click OK.

## Customizing Numbering

Click the Numbering button arrow in the Paragraph group and several numbering options display in a drop-down gallery. You can customize numbering with options at the Bullets and Numbering dialog box with the Numbered tab selected as shown in Figure 3.7. Display this dialog box by clicking the Numbering button arrow and then clicking *Bullets and Numbering* at the drop-down gallery. Use options at this dialog box to change the size and color of numbers as well as the starting number.

If you want to move the insertion point down to the next line without inserting a number, press Shift + Enter. If you press Enter, numbering is turned back on.

Numbering

**Figure 3.7** Bullets and Numbering Dialog Box with Numbered Tab Selected

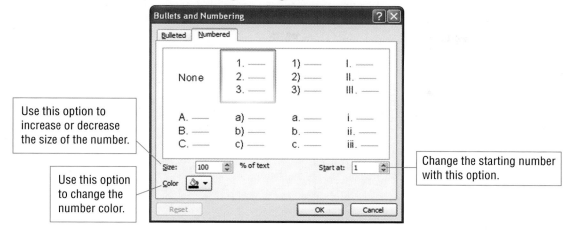

Use this option to increase or decrease the size of the number.

Use this option to change the number color.

Change the starting number with this option.

## Project 2b  Customizing Numbers

1. With **PP_C3_P2.pptx** open, make sure the presentation displays in Normal view.
2. Customize and insert numbers by completing the following steps:
   a. Make Slide 4 active.
   b. Select the bulleted text in the slide.
   c. Click the Numbering button arrow in the Home tab and then click the *Bullets and Numbering* option at the drop-down list.
   d. At the Bullets and Numbering dialog box with the Numbered tab selected, click the *1. 2. 3.* option (second option from the left in the top row).
   e. Click the up-pointing arrow at the right side of the *Size* option until *80* displays in the text box.
   f. Click the Font Color button and then the Dark Red color (first color option from the left in the *Standard Colors* row).
   g. Click OK.

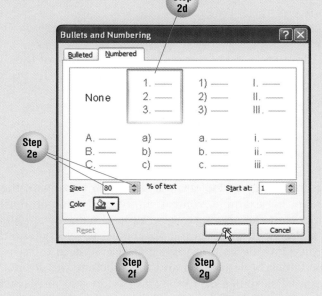

Step 2d

Step 2e

Step 2f

Step 2g

h. Make Slide 5 active.

i. Select the bulleted text in the slide.

j. Click the Numbering button arrow and then click the *Bullets and Numbering* option at the drop-down list.

k. At the Bullets and Numbering dialog box with the Numbered tab selected, click the *1. 2. 3.* option (second option from the left in the top row).

l. Click the up-pointing arrow at the right side of the *Size* option until *80* displays in the text box.

m. Click the Font Color button and then click the Dark Red color (first color option from the left in the *Standard Colors* row).

n. Click the up-pointing arrow at the right of the *Start at* option until *6* displays in the text box.

o. Click OK.

3. Add a transition and sound of your choosing to all slides in the presentation.

4. Run the presentation.

5. Display the presentation in Print Preview and insert the date, header, and footer in handouts pages by completing the following steps:

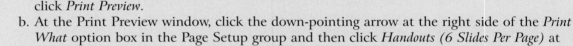

a. Click the Office button, point to *Print*, and then click *Print Preview*.

b. At the Print Preview window, click the down-pointing arrow at the right side of the *Print What* option box in the Page Setup group and then click *Handouts (6 Slides Per Page)* at the drop-down list.

c. Click the Options button in the Print group in the Print Preview tab and then click *Header and Footer* at the drop-down list.

d. At the Header and Footer dialog box with the Notes and Handouts tab selected, click the *Date and time* check box to insert a check mark.

e. Click the *Header* check box to insert a check mark and then type Company Publications in the *Header* text box.

f. Click the *Footer* check box to insert a check mark and then type your first and last names in the *Footer* text box.

g. Click the Apply to All button located in the upper right corner of the dialog box.

h. Click the Print button in the Print group and then click OK at the Print dialog box.

6. Save **PP_C3_P2.pptx**.

**HINT**
You can also use options in the Drawing Tools Format tab to customize a placeholder.

## Customizing Placeholders

You can customize a placeholder in a slide with buttons in the Drawing group in the Home tab. For example, you can apply a fill color, an outline, and an effect to a placeholder. You can also customize a placeholder by applying a Quick Style. To customize a placeholder, click in the placeholder to select it and then click the desired button in the Drawing group. Apply a Quick Style to the selected placeholder by clicking the Quick Styles button and then clicking the desired style at the drop-down gallery. Click the *Other Theme Fills* option that displays at the bottom of the drop-down gallery and a side menu displays with additional fills.

In addition to the Quick Styles button, you can use the Shape Fill, Shape Outline, and Shape Effects buttons in the Drawing group in the Home tab to customize a placeholder. Click the Shape Fill button arrow and a drop-down gallery displays with options for applying a color, picture, gradient, or texture to the placeholder. Use the Shape Outline button to apply an outline to a placeholder and specify the outline color, weight, and style. With the Shape Effects button, you can choose from a variety of effects such as shadow, reflection, glow, and soft edges.

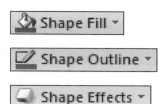

## Changing Internal Margins

When you apply formatting to a placeholder, you may need to move text within the placeholder. You can do this with the internal margins measurements in the Format Text Effects dialog box with the *Text Box* option selected in the left panel (shown in Figure 3.4). Use the *Left*, *Right*, *Top*, and *Bottom* measurements boxes to specify internal margins for text inside the placeholder.

Project 2c   **Customizing Placeholders**

1. With **PP_C3_P2.pptx** open, customize the title placeholder in Slide 1 by completing the following steps:
   a. If necessary, make Slide 1 active.
   b. Click in the title to select the placeholder.
   c. If necessary, click the Home tab.
   d. Click the Quick Styles button in the Drawing group.
   e. Click the *Moderate Effect - Accent 1* option at the drop-down gallery (second option from the left in the fifth row).

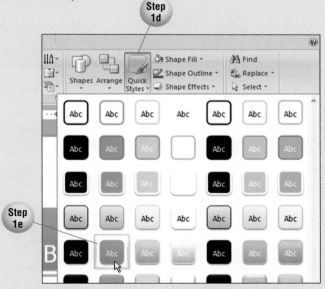

   f. Click the Shape Outline button arrow in the Drawing group and then click *Blue* in the *Standard Colors* section.

g. Click the Shape Outline button arrow, point to *Weight*, and then click *3 pt* at the side menu.

h. Click the Shape Effects button, point to *Bevel*, and then click *Cool Slant* at the side menu (last option in the top row in the *Bevel* section).

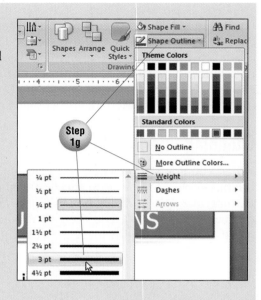

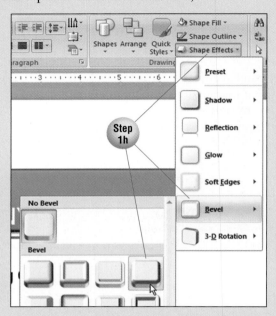

i. After looking at the fill color, you decide to change it by clicking the Quick Styles button in the Drawing group, pointing to *Other Theme Fills* that displays at the bottom of the drop-down gallery, and then clicking *Style 11* at the side menu (third option from the left in the bottom row).

2. Change the internal margins for the text in the title placeholder by completing the following steps:

a. With the title placeholder selected, click the Text Direction button in the Paragraph group in the Home tab and then click *More Options* at the drop-down list.

b. At the Format Text Effects dialog box with *Text Box* selected in the left panel, click the up-pointing arrow at the right side of the *Left* measurement box until *0.3"* displays in the measurement box.

c. Click the up-pointing arrow at the right side of the *Right* measurement box until *0.3"* displays in the measurement box.

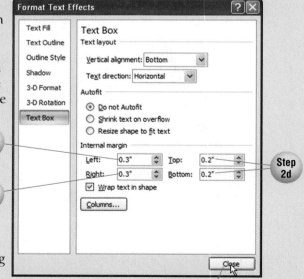

d. Complete similar steps to change the measurement in the *Top* box and the *Bottom* box to *0.2"*.

e. Click the Close button to close the dialog box.

f. Decrease the size of the placeholder border so the border displays an equal distance from text along the top, bottom, left, and right sides.

3. Customize the subtitle placeholder by completing the following steps:
   a. Click in the subtitle text to select the placeholder.
   b. Click the Shape Fill button arrow in the Drawing group, point to *Texture*, and then click *Water droplets* at the drop-down gallery (first option from the left in the second row).
   c. Click the Shape Effects button, point to *Bevel*, and then click *Cool Slant* at the side menu (last option in the top row in the *Bevel* section).

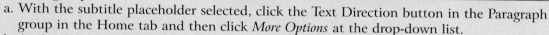

4. Change the internal margins for the text in the subtitle placeholder by completing the following steps:
   a. With the subtitle placeholder selected, click the Text Direction button in the Paragraph group in the Home tab and then click *More Options* at the drop-down list.
   b. At the Format Text Effects dialog box with *Text Box* selected in the left panel, click the up-pointing arrow at the right side of the *Left* measurement box until *0.5″* displays in the measurement box.
   c. Click the up-pointing arrow at the right side of the *Right* measurement box until *0.5″* displays in the measurement box.
   d. Complete similar steps to change the measurement in the *Top* box and the *Bottom* box to *0.2″*.
   e. Click the Close button to close the dialog box.
   f. Decrease the size of the placeholder border so the border displays an equal distance from text along the top, bottom, left, and right sides.
   g. Position the placeholders attractively in the slide.

5. Make Slide 3 active and then change the spacing after paragraphs by completing the following steps:
   a. Select the bulleted text.
   b. Click the Paragraph group dialog box launcher.
   c. At the Paragraph dialog box, click the up-pointing arrow at the right side of the *After* option in the *Spacing* section to display *6 pt* in the option box.
   d. Click OK to close the dialog box.

6. Customize the placeholder by completing the following steps:
   a. With the bulleted text placeholder selected, click the Quick Styles button in the Drawing group and then click *Subtle Effect - Accent 6* at the drop-down gallery (last option in the fourth row).
   b. Click the Shape Effects button, point to *Soft Edges*, and then click *2.5 Point* at the side menu.

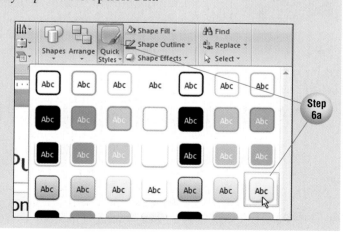

   c. Click the Text Direction button and then click *More Options* at the drop-down list.

   d. At the Format Text Effects dialog box, change the left, right, top, and bottom measurements to *0.4".*

   e. Click the Close button to close the dialog box.

   f. Move the placeholder so it is positioned attractively in the slide.

7. Run the presentation.

8. Print the presentation as a handout with six slides per page.

9. You decide that you do not like the appearance of the formatting of the subtitle placeholder in Slide 1 so you decide to remove the formatting by completing the following steps:

   a. Make Slide 1 active.

   b. Click on any character in the subtitle placeholder text.

   c. Make sure the Home tab is selected.

   d. Click the Quick Styles button in the Drawing group and then click the *Colored Outline - Accent 3* option (fourth option from the left in the top row).

10. Print Slide 1.

11. Save and then close **PP_C3_P2.pptx**.

---

# Project 3 Modify the Theme and Slide Background of a Job Search Presentation

You will open a job search presentation, apply a design theme, and then change the theme colors and fonts. You will also apply and customize a background style.

---

## Modifying Theme Colors and Fonts

A design theme is a set of formatting choices that includes a color theme (a set of colors), a font theme (heading and text fonts), and an effects theme (a set of lines and fill effects). Use buttons at the right side of the Themes group to change design theme colors, fonts, and effects.

A theme contains specific color formatting, which you can change with options from the Colors button in the Themes group. Click this button and a drop-down gallery displays with named color schemes. The names of the color schemes correspond to the names of the themes. Each theme applies specific fonts, which you can change with options from the Fonts button in the Themes group. Click this button and a drop-down gallery displays with font choices. Each font group in the drop-down gallery contains two choices. The first choice in the group is the font that is applied to slide titles and the second choice is the font that is applied to slide subtitles and text. If you are formatting a presentation that contains graphic elements such as illustrations, pictures, clip art, or text boxes, you can specify theme effects with options at the Effects drop-down gallery.

# Changing Slide Background

The Background group in the Design tab contains a button and an option for customizing the background of slides in a presentation. Click the Background Styles button and a drop-down gallery of background styles displays. Click the desired style at this drop-down gallery or click the *Format Background* option to display the Format Background dialog box shown in Figure 3.8. You can also display the dialog box by clicking the Background group dialog box launcher. Use options in this dialog box to customize background fill, gradient, direction, and color. If you make changes to the slide background, you can reset the background to the default by clicking the Reset Background button in the Format Background dialog box. You can also reset the background to the default by clicking the Background Styles button and then clicking *Reset Slide Background* at the drop-down gallery.

**Change Slide Background**
1. Click Design tab.
2. Click Background Styles button.
3. Click desired style at drop-down gallery.

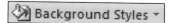

**Figure 3.8** Format Background Dialog Box

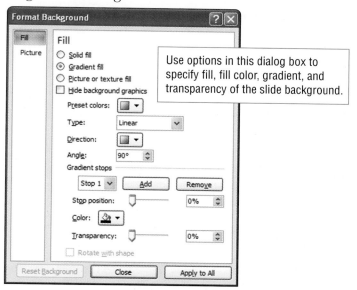

> Use options in this dialog box to specify fill, fill color, gradient, and transparency of the slide background.

Some of the design themes provided by PowerPoint contain a background graphic. You can remove this graphic from a slide by clicking the *Hide Background Graphics* check box in the Background group. This removes the background from the currently active slide. If you want to remove the background from more than one slide, select the slides. You can also remove background graphics from all slides by inserting a check mark in the Hide background graphics check box in the Format Background dialog box and then clicking the Apply to All button.

## Project 3a    Customizing Theme Colors and Fonts

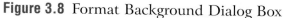

1. Open **JobSearch.pptx** and then save the presentation and name it **PP_C3_P3**.
2. Apply a design theme by completing the following steps:
   a. Click the Design tab.
   b. Click the More button at the right side of the design themes and then click *Metro* at the drop-down gallery.

3. Change the theme colors by clicking the Colors button in the Themes group and then clicking *Paper* at the drop-down gallery.

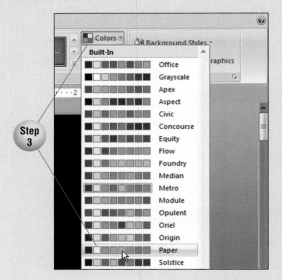

4. Change the theme fonts by clicking the Fonts button in the Themes group, scrolling down the drop-down gallery, and then clicking *Solstice*.

5. Change the background style by clicking the Background Styles button in the Background group and then clicking *Style 10* at the drop-down gallery.
6. With Slide 1 active, run the presentation and notice the formatting applied by the theme, theme colors, theme fonts, and background style.
7. With the presentation in Normal view, change the background style by clicking the Background Styles button in the Background group in the Design tab and then clicking *Style 7* at the drop-down gallery.

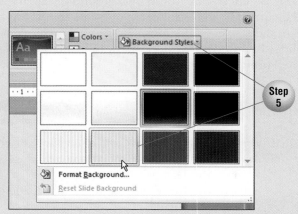

8. Apply and customize a background style by completing the following steps:
   a. Click the Background group dialog box launcher.
   b. At the Format Background dialog box, click the *Hide background graphics* check box to insert a check mark.
   c. Click the down-pointing arrow to the right of the *Type* option box and then click *Path* at the drop-down list.
   d. Drag the button on the *Stop position* slider bar until *85%* displays in the percentage box at the right.
   e. Click the Color button and then click *Black, Background 1, Lighter 35%* at the drop-down list (first color option from the left in the third row).
   f. Drag the button on the *Transparency* slider bar until *15%* displays in the percentage box at the right. (You can also click the up-pointing arrow at the right side of the percentage box until *15%* displays.)
   g. Click the Apply to All button.
   h. Click the Close button.
9. Run the presentation and notice the background formatting.
10. Save **PP_C3_P3.pptx**.

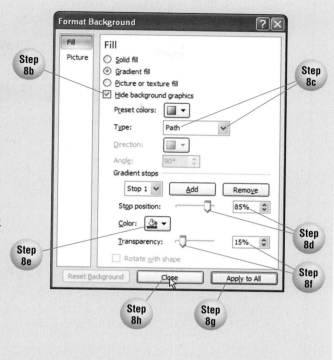

# Changing Page Setup

As you learned in Chapter 2, the Print Preview tab contains buttons for changing orientation and page setup options. You can also control page setup and the orientation of slides with buttons in the Page Setup group in the Design tab. The default slide orientation is *Landscape*. You can change this to *Portrait* with the Slide Orientation button. Click the Page Setup button and the Page Setup dialog box displays as shown in Figure 3.9. With options at this dialog box, you can specify how you want the slides sized. By default, slides are sized for an on-screen show with a 4:3 ratio. Click the down-pointing arrow at the right side of the *Slides sized for* option and a drop-down list displays with options for changing the slide size ratio and choosing other paper sizes. With other options in the dialog box, you can specify slide width and height and change the starting slide number. You can also change the orientation of slides and the orientation of notes, handouts, and outline pages.

Slide Orientation

Page Setup

**Figure 3.9** Page Setup Dialog Box

Click this down-pointing arrow and choose a slide size at the drop-down list.

Use these options to specify the slide width and height measurements.

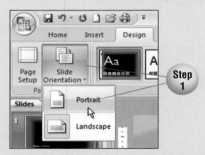

## Project 3b    Changing Orientation and Page Setup

1. With **PP_C3_P3.pptx** open, change slide orientation by clicking the Design tab, clicking the Slide Orientation button, and then clicking *Portrait* at the drop-down list.

Step 1

2. Run the presentation and notice how the slides appear in portrait orientation.
3. After running the presentation, click the Slide Orientation button and then click *Landscape* at the drop-down list.
4. Suppose you are going to run the presentation on a wide screen monitor. To do this, you decide to change the slide size ratio by completing the following steps:
   a. Click the Page Setup button in the Page Setup group in the Design tab.
   b. At the Page Setup dialog box, click the down-pointing arrow at the right side of the *Slides sized for* option and then click *On-screen Show (16:10)*. (Notice that the slide height changed from *7.5* to *6.25*.)
   c. Click OK.

Step 4b    Step 4c

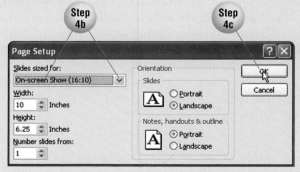

5. Run the presentation.
6. Specify slide width and height by completing the following steps:
   a. Click the Page Setup button.
   b. At the Page Setup dialog box, click the down-pointing arrow at the right side of the *Width* measurement box until *9* displays in the box.
   c. Click the down-pointing arrow at the right side of the *Height* measurement box until *6* displays in the box.
   d. Click OK.
7. Run the presentation.
8. Return the slide size to the default by completing the following steps:
   a. Click the Page Setup button.
   b. At the Page Setup dialog box, click the down-pointing arrow at the right side of the *Slides sized for* option and then click *On-screen Show (4:3)*.
   c. Click OK.
9. Save and then close **PP_C3_P3.pptx**.

 **roject** **4** **Create and Apply Custom Themes to Presentations**

You will create custom theme colors and custom theme fonts and then save the changes as a custom theme. You will then apply the custom theme to a job search presentation and a resume writing presentation.

# Creating Custom Themes

If the default themes, theme colors, and theme fonts do not provide the formatting you desire for your presentation, you can create your own custom theme colors, custom theme fonts, and a custom theme. A theme you create will display in the Themes drop-down gallery under the *Custom* section. To create a custom theme, change the theme colors, theme fonts, and/or theme effects.

The buttons at the right side of the Themes group in the Design tab display a visual representation of the current theme. If you change the theme colors, the colors are reflected in the small color squares on the Colors button. If you change the theme fonts, the A on the Fonts button reflects the change.

## Creating Custom Theme Colors

To create custom theme colors, click the Design tab, click the Colors button in the Themes group, and then click *Create New Theme Colors* at the drop-down gallery. This displays the Create New Theme Colors dialog box similar to the one shown in Figure 3.10. Theme colors contain four text and background colors, six accent colors, and two hyperlink colors as shown in the *Themes color* section of the dialog box. Change a color in the list box by clicking the color button at the right side of the color option and then clicking the desired color at the color palette.

QUICK STEPS

**Create Custom Theme Colors**
1. Click Design tab.
2. Click Theme Colors button.
3. Click *Create New Theme Colors*.
4. Change to desired background, accent, and hyperlink colors.
5. Type name for custom theme colors.
6. Click Save button.

**Figure 3.10** Create New Theme Colors Dialog Box

Click the Reset button to reset color back to the default.

Change a theme color by clicking the color button and then clicking the desired color at the drop-down palette.

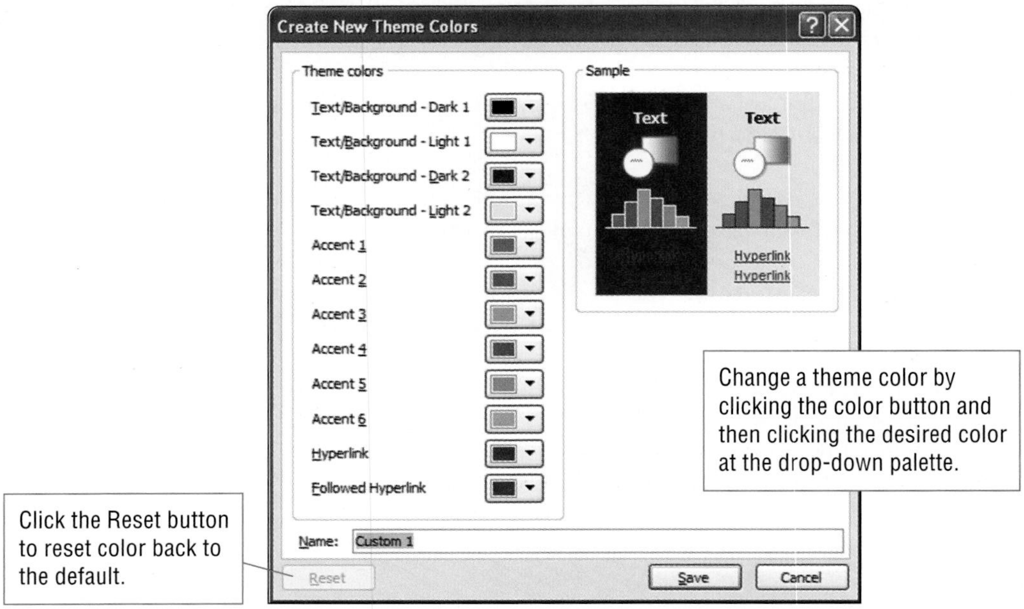

After you have made all desired changes to colors, click in the *Name* text box, type a name for the custom theme colors, and then click the Save button. This saves the custom theme colors and applies the color changes to the currently open presentation. Display the custom theme colors by clicking the Colors button in the Themes group in the Design tab. Your custom theme colors will display toward the top of the drop-down gallery in the *Custom* section. If you make changes to colors at the Create New Theme Colors dialog box and then decide you do not like the color changes, click the Reset button located in the lower left corner of the dialog box.

When you create custom theme colors, you can apply the theme to your presentation by clicking the Colors button in the Themes group in the Design tab and then clicking the custom theme colors that display toward the top of the drop-down gallery in the *Custom* section.

*Note: If you are running PowerPoint 2007 on a computer connected to a network in a public environment such as a school, you may need to complete all of Project 4 during the same session. Network system software may delete your custom themes when you exit PowerPoint. Check with your instructor.*

## Project 4a  Creating Custom Theme Colors

1. At a blank presentation, click the Design tab, click the More button at the right side of the Themes group, and then click *Technic* at the drop-down gallery.
2. Create custom theme colors by completing the following steps:
   a. Click the Colors button in the Themes group and then click the *Create New Theme Colors* option at the drop-down gallery.

b. At the Create New Theme Colors dialog box, click the color button that displays at the right side of the *Text/Background - Dark 1* option and then click the *Olive Green, Accent 4, Lighter 60%* option.

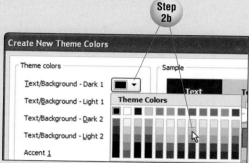

c. Click the color button that displays at the right side of the *Text/Background - Light 1* option and then click the *Gold, Accent 2, Lighter 80%* option.
d. Click the color button that displays at the right side of the *Text/Background - Dark 2* option and then click the *Lavender, Accent 3, Darker 25%* option.

3. Save the custom colors by completing the following steps:
   a. Select the current text in the *Name* text box.
   b. Type your first and last names.
   c. Click the Save button.

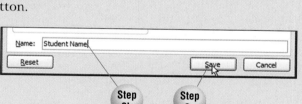

4. Save the presentation and name it **CustomTheme**.

## Creating Custom Theme Fonts

To create custom theme fonts, click the Design tab, click the Fonts button, and then click *Create New Theme Fonts* at the drop-down gallery. This displays the Create New Theme Fonts dialog box similar to the one shown in Figure 3.11. At this dialog box, choose a heading font and a font for body text. Type a name for the custom theme fonts in the *Name* box and then click the Save button.

**QUICK STEPS**

**Create Custom Fonts**
1. Click Design tab.
2. Click Theme Fonts button.
3. Click *Create New Theme Fonts*.
4. Choose desired fonts.
5. Type name for custom theme fonts.
6. Click Save button.

**Figure 3.11** Create New Theme Fonts Dialog Box

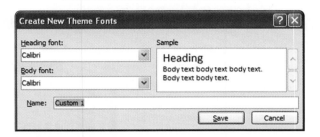

Choose a heading font and body font, type a new name for the theme in the *Name* text box, and then click Save.

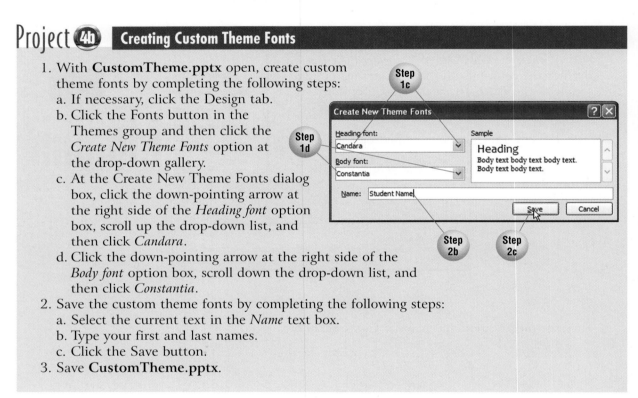

## Project 4b  Creating Custom Theme Fonts

1. With **CustomTheme.pptx** open, create custom theme fonts by completing the following steps:
   a. If necessary, click the Design tab.
   b. Click the Fonts button in the Themes group and then click the *Create New Theme Fonts* option at the drop-down gallery.
   c. At the Create New Theme Fonts dialog box, click the down-pointing arrow at the right side of the *Heading font* option box, scroll up the drop-down list, and then click *Candara*.
   d. Click the down-pointing arrow at the right side of the *Body font* option box, scroll down the drop-down list, and then click *Constantia*.
2. Save the custom theme fonts by completing the following steps:
   a. Select the current text in the *Name* text box.
   b. Type your first and last names.
   c. Click the Save button.
3. Save **CustomTheme.pptx**.

---

**QUICK STEPS**

**Saving a Custom Theme**

**Save a Custom Theme**
1. Click Design tab.
2. Click More button in Themes group.
3. Click *Save Current Theme*.
4. Type name for custom theme.
5. Click Save button.

When you have customized theme colors and fonts, you can save these as a custom theme. To do this, click the More button at the right side of the Themes group in the Design tab and then click *Save Current Theme*. This displays the Save Current Theme dialog box with many of the same options as the Save As dialog box. Type a name for your custom theme in the *File name* text box and then click the Save button. To apply a custom theme, click the More button and then click the desired theme in the *Custom* section of the drop-down gallery.

1. With **CustomTheme.pptx** open, save the custom theme colors and fonts as a custom theme by completing the following steps:
   a. If necessary, click the Design tab.
   b. Click the More button at the right side of the themes thumbnails in the Themes group.
   c. Click the *Save Current Theme* option that displays at the bottom of the drop-down gallery.
   d. At the Save Current Theme dialog box, type **C3** and then type your last name in the *File name* text box.
   e. Click the Save button.

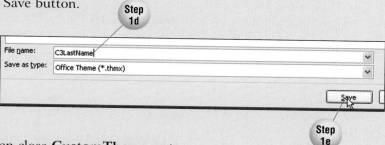

2. Save and then close **CustomTheme.pptx**.
3. Open **JobSearch.pptx** and then save the presentation and name it **PP_C3_P4a**.
4. Apply your custom theme by completing the following steps:
   a. Click the Design tab.
   b. Click the More button that displays at the right side of the themes thumbnails.
   c. Click the custom theme that begins with *C3* followed by your last name. (The theme will display in the *Custom* section of the drop-down gallery.)

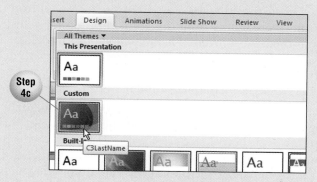

5. Run the presentation and notice how the slides display with the custom theme applied.
6. Print Slide 1 of the presentation.
7. Save and then close **PP_C3_P4a.pptx**.
8. Open **ResumePresentation.pptx** and then save the presentation and name it **PP_C3_P4b**.
9. Apply your custom theme (the theme that displays beginning with *C3* followed by your last name).
10. Make Slide 2 active and then adjust the placeholder containing the bulleted text so it is positioned attractively on the slide.
11. Make Slide 1 active and then run the presentation.
12. Print Slide 1 of the presentation.
13. Save and then close **PP_C3_P4b.pptx**.

# Editing Custom Themes

**Edit Custom Theme Colors**
1. Click Design tab.
2. Click Theme Colors button.
3. Right-click desired custom theme.
4. Click *Edit*.
5. Make desired changes.
6. Click Save button.

**Edit Custom Theme Fonts**
1. Click Page Layout tab.
2. Click Theme Fonts button.
3. Right-click desired custom theme.
4. Click *Edit*.
5. Make desired changes.
6. Click Save button.

You can edit the custom theme colors and custom theme fonts. To edit the custom theme colors, click the Colors button in the Themes group in the Design tab. At the drop-down gallery of custom and built-in themes, right-click your custom theme and then click *Edit* at the shortcut menu. This displays the Edit Theme Colors dialog box that contains the same options as the Create New Theme Colors dialog box shown in Figure 3.10. Make the desired changes to theme colors and then click the Save button.

To edit custom theme fonts, click the Fonts button in the Themes group in the Design tab, right-click your custom theme fonts, and then click *Edit* at the shortcut menu. This displays the Edit Theme Fonts dialog box that contains the same options as the Create New Theme Fonts dialog box shown in Figure 3.11. Make the desired changes and then click the Save button.

# Deleting Custom Themes

QUICK STEPS

**Delete Custom Theme Colors**
1. Click Design tab.
2. Click Theme Colors button.
3. Right-click desired custom theme.
4. Click *Delete*.
5. Click Yes.

**Delete Custom Theme Fonts**
1. Click Design tab.
2. Click Theme Fonts button.
3. Right-click desired custom theme.
4. Click *Delete*.
5. Click Yes.

**Delete Custom Theme**
1. Click Design tab.
2. Click More button in Themes group.
3. Click *Save Current Theme*.
4. Click custom theme.
5. Click Delete button.
6. Click Yes.

You can delete custom theme colors from the Colors button drop-down gallery, delete custom theme fonts from the Fonts drop-down gallery, and delete custom themes from the Save Current Theme dialog box. To delete custom theme colors, click the Colors button, right-click the theme you want to delete, and then click *Delete* at the shortcut menu. At the message asking if you want to delete the theme colors, click Yes. Complete similar steps to delete custom theme fonts.

Delete a custom theme at the Save Current Theme dialog box. To display this dialog box, click the More button at the right side of the Themes group in the Design tab and then click *Save Current Theme* at the drop-down gallery. At the dialog box, click the custom theme file name and then click the Delete button on the dialog box toolbar. At the message asking if you are sure you want to send the theme to the Recycle Bin, click Yes.

# Project 4d  Deleting Custom Themes

1. At a blank presentation, delete the custom theme colors by completing the following steps:
   a. Click the Design tab.
   b. Click the Colors button in the Themes group.
   c. Right-click the custom theme colors named with your first and last names.
   d. Click *Delete* at the shortcut menu.

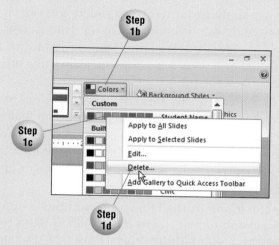

Step 1b

Step 1c

Step 1d

   e. At the question asking if you want to delete the theme colors, click Yes.
2. Complete steps similar to those in Step 1 to delete the custom theme fonts you created named with your first and last names.
3. Delete the custom theme by completing the following steps:
   a. Click the More button that displays at the right side of the themes thumbnails.
   b. Click *Save Current Theme* located toward the bottom of the drop-down gallery.
   c. At the Save Current Theme dialog box, click the custom theme that begins with *C3* followed by your last name.
   d. Click the Delete button on the dialog box toolbar.

Step 3d

Step 3c

   e. At the message asking if you are sure you want to send the theme to the Recycle Bin, click Yes.
   f. Click the Cancel button to close the dialog box.
4. Close the presentation without saving it.

# CHAPTER summary

- The Font group in the Home tab contains buttons for applying character formatting to text in slides. Refer to Table 3.1 for a listing of the Font group buttons, a description of the button function, and keyboard shortcuts.

- Design themes apply a font to text in slides. You can change this default font with the Font and Font Size buttons in the Font group.

- Some buttons, such as the Font and Font Size buttons, contain the *live preview* feature, which allows you to see how the formatting affects your text without having to return to the presentation.

- You can also apply character formatting with options at the Font dialog box. Display this dialog box by clicking the Font group dialog box launcher.

- Select text in a slide and the Mini toolbar displays above the selected text in dimmed fashion. Move the mouse pointer to the toolbar and it becomes active.

- Use the Format Painter feature to apply formatting to more than one location in a slide or slides.

- The Paragraph group in the Home tab contains a number of buttons for applying paragraph formatting to text in slides. Refer to Table 3.2 for a listing of the Paragraph group buttons, a description of the button function, and keyboard shortcuts.

- Customize paragraph formatting with options at the Paragraph dialog box with the Indents and Spacing tab selected. Display this dialog box by clicking the Paragraph group dialog box launcher or by clicking the Line Spacing button in the Paragraph group and then clicking *Line Spacing Options* at the drop-down list.

- Use the Columns button in the Paragraph group or options at the Columns dialog box to format selected text into columns. Display the Columns dialog box by clicking the Columns button and then clicking *More Columns* at the drop-down list.

- Use the Text Direction button or options at the Format Text Effects dialog box to rotate or stack text in a slide. Display the Format Text Effects dialog box by clicking the Text Direction button and then clicking *More Options* at the drop-down list.

- Use the Align Text button or options at the Format Text Effects dialog box to vertically align text in a slide.

- Customize bullets with options at the Bullets and Numbering dialog box with the Bulleted tab selected. Display this dialog box by clicking the Bullets button arrow and then clicking *Bullets and Numbering* at the drop-down list.

- Customize numbering with options at the Bullets and Numbering dialog box with the Numbered tab selected. Display this dialog box by clicking the Numbering button arrow and then clicking *Bullets and Numbering* at the drop-down list.

- Click the Quick Styles button in the Drawing group in the Home tab to apply formatting to a placeholder. The Drawing group also contains the Shape Fill, Shape Outline, and Shape Effects buttons you can use to customize a placeholder.

- Use the Colors button in the Themes group in the Design tab to change the theme colors and use the Fonts button to change the theme fonts.

- Use the Background Styles button in the Background group in the Design tab to customize the background of slides and insert a check mark in the *Hide Background Graphics* check box to remove the slide background graphic.

- Click the Page Setup button in the Design tab and the Page Setup dialog box displays containing options for changing the slide size and ratio, starting slide number, and the orientation of slides and notes, handouts, and outline pages.

- Create custom theme colors with options at the Create New Theme Colors dialog box. Display this dialog box by clicking the Colors button in the Themes group in the Design tab and then clicking *Create New Theme Colors* at the drop-down gallery.

- Create custom theme fonts with options at the Create New Theme Fonts dialog box. Display this dialog box by clicking the Fonts button in the Themes group in the Design tab and then clicking *Create New Theme Fonts* at the drop-down gallery.

- Save a custom theme at the Save Current Theme dialog box. Display this dialog box by clicking the Themes button in the Themes group in the Design tab and then clicking *Save Current Theme* at the drop-down gallery.

- Edit custom theme colors with options at the Edit Theme Colors dialog box and edit custom theme fonts with options at the Edit Theme Fonts dialog box.

- Delete custom theme colors by clicking the Theme Colors button, right-clicking the custom theme, and then clicking the *Delete* option.

- Delete custom theme fonts by clicking the Theme Fonts button, right-clicking the custom theme, and then clicking the *Delete* option.

- Delete a custom theme at the Save Current Theme dialog box. Display this dialog box by clicking the Themes button and then clicking *Save Current Theme* at the drop-down gallery.

# COMMANDS review

| FEATURE | RIBBON TAB, GROUP | BUTTON, OPTION | KEYBOARD SHORTCUT |
|---|---|---|---|
| Font dialog box | Home, Font | | Ctrl + Shift + F |
| Format Painter | Home, Clipboard | | |
| Paragraph dialog box | Home, Paragraph | | |
| Columns dialog box | Home, Paragraph | , More Columns | |
| Format Text Effects dialog box | Home, Paragraph | , More Options | |
| Bullets and Numbering dialog box with Bulleted tab selected | Home, Paragraph | , Bullets and Numbering | |
| Bullets and Numbering dialog box with Numbered tab selected | Home, Paragraph | , Bullets and Numbering | |
| Format Background dialog box | Design, Background | | |
| Page Setup dialog box | Design, Page Setup | | |
| Create New Theme Colors dialog box | Design, Themes | Colors, Create New Theme Colors | |
| Create New Theme Fonts dialog box | Design, Themes | A Fonts, Create New Theme Fonts | |
| Save Current Theme dialog box | Design, Themes | , Save Current Theme | |

# CONCEPTS check

## Test Your Knowledge

**Completion:** In the space provided at the right, indicate the correct term, symbol, or command.

1. The Font button drop-down gallery is an example of this feature, which allows you to see how the font formatting affects your text without having to return to the presentation. _____

2. Click this button to clear character formatting from selected text. _____

3. Click this to display the Font dialog box. _____

4. Select text in a slide and this displays in a dimmed fashion above the selected text. _____

5. The Format Painter button is located in this group in the Home tab. _____

6. Press this key to move text to the next tab stop (level). _____

7. Use options at this dialog box to change text alignment, indention, and spacing. _____

8. Click this button in the Paragraph group and a drop-down list displays with options for rotating and stacking text. _____

9. Customize numbering with options at the Bullets and Numbering dialog box with this tab selected. _____

10. Use the Align Text button or options at this dialog box to vertically align text in a slide. _____

11. The Quick Styles button is located in this group in the Home tab. _____

12. Click this button to apply fill to a placeholder. _____

13. Create custom theme colors with options at this dialog box. _____

14. Save a custom theme at this dialog box. _____

# SKILLS check
## *Demonstrate Your Proficiency*

## Assessment

### 1   CREATE, FORMAT, AND MODIFY A BENEFITS PRESENTATION

1. At a blank presentation, create the slides shown in Figure 3.12.
2. Apply the Oriel design theme.
3. Make Slide 1 active and then make the following changes:
   a. Select the title *BENEFITS PROGRAM*, change the font to Candara, the font size to 48, the font color to Ice Blue, Accent 5, Darker 50%, and apply italic formatting.
   b. Select the subtitle *Change to Plans*, change the font to Candara, the font size to 32, the font color to Orange, Accent 1, Darker 50%, and apply shadow formatting.
   c. Click the title placeholder and then drag the placeholder up until the title is vertically centered on the slide.
   d. Click the subtitle placeholder and then drag the placeholder up so the subtitle is positioned just below the title.
4. Make Slide 2 active and then make the following changes:
   a. Select the title *INTRODUCTION*, change the font to Candara, the font size to 48 points, and apply shadow formatting.
   b. Using Format Painter, apply the title formatting to the titles in the remaining slides.
5. Center-align the titles in Slides 2 through 5.
6. Make Slide 2 active, select the bulleted text, and then change the line spacing to *2.0*.
7. Make Slide 3 active, select the bulleted text, and then change the line spacing to *2.0*.
8. Make Slide 4 active, select the bulleted text, and then change the line spacing to *1.5*.
9. Make Slide 5 active, select the bulleted text, and then change the spacing after paragraphs to *18 pt*. **Hint: Do this at the Paragraph dialog box.**
10. Make Slide 2 active and then select the bulleted text. Display the Bullets and Numbering dialog box with the Numbered tab selected, choose the *1. 2. 3.* option, change the size to *85%*, and then close the dialog box.
11. Make Slide 3 active and then select the bulleted text. Display the Bullets and Numbering dialog box with the Numbered tab selected, choose the *1. 2. 3.* option, change the size to *85%*, change the starting number to *5*, and then close the dialog box.
12. Make Slide 4 active, select the bulleted text, and then change the bullets to *Hollow Square Bullets*.
13. Make Slide 5 active, select the bulleted text, and then change the bullets to *Hollow Square Bullets*.
14. Apply the *Style 5* background style to slides.
15. Save the presentation and name it **PP_C3_A1**.
16. Run the presentation.
17. Print the presentation as a handout with six slides per page.
18. Change the theme colors to *Solstice*.

19. Apply the *Style 2* background style to slides.
20. Apply a transition and sound of your choosing to each slide.
21. Run the presentation.
22. Print the presentation as a handout with six slides per page.
23. Save and then close **PP_C3_A1.pptx**.

**Figure 3.12  Assessment 1**

Slide 1     Title       =     BENEFITS PROGRAM
            Subtitle    =     Changes to Plans

Slide 2     Title       =     INTRODUCTION
            Bullets     =     • Changes made for 2010
                              • Description of eligibility
                              • Instructions for enrolling new members
                              • Overview of medical and dental coverage

Slide 3     Title       =     INTRODUCTION
            Bullets     =     • Expanded enrollment forms
                              • Glossary defining terms
                              • Telephone directory
                              • Pamphlet with commonly asked questions

Slide 4     Title       =     WHAT'S NEW
            Bullets     =     • New medical plans
                                 - Plan 2010
                                 - Premiere Plan
                              • Changes in monthly contributions
                              • Paying with pretax dollars
                              • Contributions toward spouse's coverage

Slide 5     Title       =     COST SHARING
            Bullets     =     • Increased deductible
                              • New coinsurance amount
                              • Higher coinsurance amount for retail prescription drugs
                              • Co-payment for mail-order medicines
                              • New stop loss limit

## Assessment

# 2  FORMAT AND MODIFY A PERENNIALS PRESENTATION

1. Open **PerennialsPresentation.pptx** and then save the presentation and name it **PP_C3_A2**.
2. Change the theme fonts to *Opulent*.
3. Make Slide 3 active, select the bulleted text, and then create and apply a custom bullet using a flower symbol in a complementary color. (You can find a flower symbol in the *Wingdings* font in the Symbol dialog box.)

4. With Slide 3 active, format the bulleted text into two columns and change the line spacing to *2*. Make sure each column contains four bulleted items. If not, make any spacing or other corrections to make the columns even.

5. Make Slide 4 active and then arrange the bulleted text more attractively on the slide. (You determine the formatting and position.)

6. Make Slide 5 active and then format the bulleted text into two columns with three bulleted items in each column. Make any spacing or formatting changes to improve the visual appeal of the slide.

7. Make Slide 6 active and then format the bulleted text into two columns with three bulleted items in each column. Make any spacing or formatting change to improve the visual appeal of the slide.

8. Make any other changes to slides to improve the visual appeal of each slide.

9. Display the presentation in Print Preview, change the *Print What* option to *Handouts (4 Slides Per Page)*, add a header that prints *Perennial Presentation* on all pages and a footer that prints your first and last names on all pages.

10. Print the presentation.

11. Add a transition and sound of your choosing to all slides in the presentation.

12. Run the presentation.

13. Save and then close **PP_C3_A2.pptx**.

## Assessment

## 3 CREATE AND APPLY A CUSTOM THEME TO A TRAVEL PRESENTATION

1. At a blank presentation, apply the *Opulent* design.

2. Create custom theme colors named with your first and last names that changes the following colors:
   a. At the Create New Theme Colors dialog box, change the *Text/Background - Light 1* option to *Gold, Accent 4, Lighter 80%*.
   b. Change the *Text/Background - Dark 2* option to *Green* (sixth color from the left in the *Standard Colors* row).

3. Create custom theme fonts named with your first and last names that applies the following fonts:
   a. At the Create New Theme Fonts dialog box, change the *Heading font* to *Copperplate Gothic Bold*.
   b. Change the *Body font* to *Rockwell*.

4. Save the current theme as a custom theme named with your first and last names. **Hint: Do this at the Save Current Theme dialog box.**

5. Close the presentation without saving it.

6. Open **TravelEngland.pptx** and then save the presentation and name it **PP_C3_A3**.

7. Apply the custom theme named with your first and last names.

8. Improve the visual display of the bulleted text in Slides 2 and 3 by increasing the spacing between items and positioning the bulleted item placeholders attractively in the slides.

9. Make Slide 4 active, increase the spacing between bulleted items and then format the text into two columns. Make sure that each column contains three bulleted items. Consider decreasing the size of the placeholder.

10. Format the bulleted text in Slides 5 and 6 into two columns with four bulleted items in each column. Consider decreasing the size of the placeholder.

11. Display the presentation in Print Preview, change the *Print What* option to *Handouts (3 Slides Per Page)*, add a header that prints *Traveling in England* on all pages and a footer that prints your first and last names on all pages.
12. Print the presentation.
13. Add a transition and sound of your choosing to all slides in the presentation.
14. Run the presentation.
15. Save and then close **PP_C3_A3.pptx**.
16. Display a blank presentation and then delete the custom theme colors, custom theme fonts, and custom theme you created for this assessment.
17. Close the presentation without saving it.

## Assessment

## 4 PREPARE AND FORMAT A PRESENTATION AT THE FONT DIALOG BOX

1. At a blank presentation, click in a placeholder in the blank slide and then click the Font group dialog box launcher.
2. At the Font dialog box, click the Help button that displays in the upper right corner of the dialog box.
3. Click the Microsoft Office PowerPoint hyperlink, click the Font tab hyperlink, click the Character Spacing tab hyperlink, and then print the Help information.
4. Using the information you printed, create a PowerPoint presentation with the following specifications:
   a. Create a slide with the title of your presentation. Type your name as the subtitle of the presentation.
   b. Create slides (you determine the number of slides) that summarize the information you printed. (Make sure that the slides are not crowded with too much information.) Include a definition for *kerning* on one of the slides.
   c. Apply a design theme of your choosing.
   d. Change the design theme colors.
   e. Change the design theme fonts.
   f. Apply a transition and sound of your choosing to all slides.
5. Save the presentation and name it **PP_C3_A4**.
6. Run the presentation.
7. Print the presentation as an outline.
8. Close **PP_C3_A4.pptx**.

# CASE study
## Apply Your Skills

**Part 1**

You are the assistant to Gina Coletti, manager of La Dolce Vita, an Italian restaurant. She has been working on a new lunch menu and wants to present the new menu at the upcoming staff meeting. She has asked you to prepare a presentation she can use at the meeting. Open the Word document named **LunchMenu.docx** and then print the document. Close the document and then exit Word. Using the information you printed, create a presentation and apply the Civic design theme to the presentation. Make any formatting changes to improve the visual appeal of the presentation. Save the presentation and name it **PP_C3_CS_P1**.

**Part 2**

Ms. Coletti has looked over the presentation and has asked you to apply color and font formatting consistent with other restaurant publications. With **PP_C3_CS_P1.pptx** open, create custom theme colors that change the *Text/Background - Light 2* color to a light yellow and the *Accent 3* color to a green of your choosing. Make sure the colors are complementary. Create custom theme fonts that apply Monotype Corsiva as the heading font and Garamond as the body font. Save the custom theme and name it *LaDolceVita* followed by your initials. Add a transition and sound to all slides in the presentation. Display the presentation in Print Preview, specify that you want the presentation printed as a handout (you determine the number of slides) insert a header and footer of your choosing, and then print the presentation. Save and then close **PP_C3_CS_P1.pptx**.

**Part 3**

Ms. Coletti needs further information for the meeting. She wants you to use the Internet and search for two companies that print restaurant menus, two companies that design restaurant menus, and the names of two restaurant menu design software programs. Prepare a presentation with the information you find on the Internet and then apply your custom theme to the presentation. Make any formatting changes to improve the visual appeal of each slide. Add a transition and sound to each slide in the presentation. Save the information and name it **PP_C3_CS_P3.pptx**. Print the presentation in the same manner as you printed **PP_C3_CS_P1.pptx**. Close **PP_C3_CS_P3.pptx**.

**Part 4**

When running **PP_C3_CS_P3.pptx**, Ms. Coletti would like to link to a couple of the sites you list in the presentation. Use PowerPoint's Help feature to learn how to insert a hyperlink in a slide to a Web page or Web site. Create at least two hyperlinks between sites you list in the presentation and the Web page or Web site. Print the slide(s) containing the hyperlinks. Save and then close **PP_C3_CS_P3.pptx**.

# Inserting Elements in Slides

## PERFORMANCE OBJECTIVES

Upon successful completion of Chapter 4, you will be able to:

- Insert, format, select, and align a text box
- Set tabs in a text box
- Insert, format, and copy shapes
- Display rulers, gridlines, and guides
- Group and ungroup objects
- Insert, crop, size, move, and format a picture
- Insert a picture as a slide background
- Insert, size, scale, rotate, and position a clip art image
- Create and format WordArt text
- Insert objects such as a header, footer, date, slide number, and symbol

**Tutorial 4.1**
Working with Shapes
**Tutorial 4.2**
Working with Images and with
Headers and Footers

A presentation consisting only of text slides may have important information in it that will be overlooked by the audience because a slide contains too much text. Adding visual elements, where appropriate, can help deliver the message to your audience by adding interest and impact to the information. In this chapter, you will learn how to create visual elements on slides such as text boxes, shapes, pictures, clip art images, and WordArt text. These elements will make the delivery of your presentation a dynamic experience for your audience.

*Note: Before beginning computer projects, copy to your storage medium the PowerPoint2007C4 subfolder from the PowerPoint2007 folder on the CD that accompanies this textbook and then make PowerPoint2007C4 the active folder.*

# Project 1 — Create a Company Presentation Containing Text Boxes, Shapes, and Images

You will create a company presentation that includes slides with text boxes, a slide with tabbed text in a text box, slides with shapes and text, slides with pictures, and slides with clip art images. You will also insert elements in slides such as slide numbers, headers, footers, date, and symbols.

**QUICK STEPS**

**Draw a Text Box**
1. Click Insert tab.
2. Click Text Box button.
3. Drag in slide to create box.
OR
1. Click Insert tab.
2. Click Text Box button.
3. Click in slide.

## Inserting and Formatting Text Boxes

Many of the slide layouts contain placeholders for entering text and other elements in a document. Along with placeholders, you can insert and format a text box. To insert a text box in a slide, click the Insert tab, click the Text Box button in the Text group, and the mouse pointer displays as a thin, down-pointing arrow. Using the mouse, drag in the slide to create the text box. You can also click in the desired location and a small text box is inserted in the slide.

## Formatting a Text Box

**HINT**

Use a text box to place text anywhere in a slide.

When you insert a text box in the document, the Home tab displays. Use options in the Drawing group to format the text box by applying a Quick Style or adding a shape fill, outline, or effect. Format a text box in a manner similar to formatting a placeholder. In addition to the options in the Drawing group, you can also apply formatting to a text box with options in the Drawing Tools Format tab. Click this tab and the ribbon displays as shown in Figure 4.1. The Shape Styles group contains the same options as the Drawing group in the Home tab. With other options in the tab, you can apply WordArt formatting to text and arrange and size the text box.

**Figure 4.1** Drawing Tools Format Tab

Move a text box in the same manner as you move a placeholder. Click the text box to select it, position the mouse pointer on the text box border until the pointer displays with a four-headed arrow attached, and then drag the text box to the desired position. Change the size of a selected text box using the sizing handles that display around the box. You can also use the *Shape Height* and *Shape Width* measurement boxes in the Size group in the Drawing Tools Format tab to specify the text box height and width.

You can apply the same formatting to text in a text box that you apply to text in a placeholder. For example, you can use the buttons in the Paragraph group in the Home tab to align text horizontally and vertically in a text box, change text direction, set text in columns, and set internal margins for the text in the text box.

## Selecting Multiple Objects

You can select multiple text boxes and other objects in a slide and then apply formatting or align and arrange the objects in the slide. To select all objects in a slide, click the Select button in the Editing group in the Home tab and then click *Select All* at the drop-down list. You can also select all objects in a slide with the keyboard shortcut, Ctrl + A. To select specific text boxes or objects in a slide, click the first object, hold down the Shift key, and then click each of the other desired objects.

## Aligning Text Boxes

With the Align button in the Arrange group in the Drawing Tools Format tab, you can align the edge of multiple objects in a slide. Click the Align button and a drop-down list of alignment options displays including options for aligning objects vertically and horizontally and distributing objects.

## Project 1a — Inserting and Formatting Text Boxes

1. At a blank presentation, apply a design and change colors by completing the following steps:
   a. Click the Design tab.
   b. Click the More button that displays at the right side of the themes thumbnails and then click *Technic* at the drop-down gallery.
   c. Click the Colors button in the Themes group and then click *Trek* at the drop-down gallery.
2. Click in the title placeholder, type Addison, press the Enter key, and then type Industries.
3. Click in the subtitle placeholder and then type Annual Report.
4. Insert a text box in the slide by completing the following steps:
   a. Click the Insert tab.
   b. Click the Text Box button in the Text group.
   c. Click in the lower right corner of the slide. (This inserts a small, selected text box in the slide.)
   d. Type January, 2010.
   e. Click outside the text box to deselect it.
5. After looking at the slide, you decide to delete the text box by completing the following steps:
   a. Click in the text box to select it.
   b. Position the mouse pointer on the text box border until the mouse pointer displays with a four-headed arrow attached and then click the left mouse button (this changes the text box border from a dashed border line to a solid border line).
   c. Press the Delete key.

Step 4c

6. Insert a new slide with the *Blank* layout by completing the following steps:
   a. Click the Home tab.
   b. Click the New Slide button arrow.
   c. Click the *Blank* layout at the drop-down list.
7. Insert and format the *Safety* text box shown in Figure 4.2 by completing the following steps:
   a. Click the Insert tab.
   b. Click the Text Box button in the Text group.
   c. Click in the slide. (This inserts a small, selected text box in the slide.)
   d. Type **Safety**.
   e. Select the text and then change the font to Copperplate Gothic Bold, the font size to 36, and the font color to Orange (third color option from the left in the *Standard Colors* row).
   f. Click the Text Direction button in the Paragraph group in the Home tab and then click *Stacked* at the drop-down list.

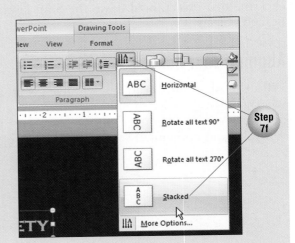

Step 7f

   g. Click the Drawing Tools Format tab.
   h. Click the down-pointing arrow at the right side of the *Shape Height* measurement box in the Size group until *4"* displays in the box. (Make sure the measurement in the *Shape Width* box is *0.86".*)
   i. Click the More button that displays at the right side of the styles thumbnails in the Shape Styles group and then click the *Moderate Effect - Accent 6* option (last option in the fifth row).
   j. Drag the text box so it is positioned as shown in Figure 4.2.

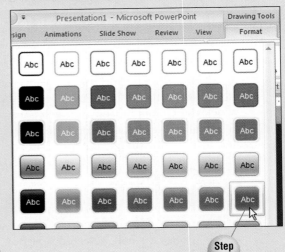

Step 7i

8. Insert and format the other text box shown in Figure 4.2 by completing the following steps:
   a. Click the Insert tab.
   b. Click the Text Box button in the Text group.
   c. Drag in the slide to create a text box. (Drag to the approximate width of the text box in Figure 4.2.)
   d. Type the text shown in the text box as shown in Figure 4.2 in a single column. Type the text in the first column and then type the text in the second column. (Your text will display as shown at the right in one column, in a smaller font, and in a different line spacing than you see in the figure.)
   e. Select the text and then change the font size to 32.

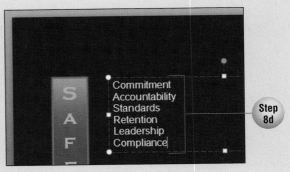

Step 8d

f. Click the Line Spacing button in the Paragraph group and then click *2.0* at the drop-down list. (The text may flow off the slide.)

g. Click the Columns button in the Paragraph group and then click *Two Columns* at the drop-down list.

h. Click the Drawing Tools Format tab.

i. Click the down-pointing arrow at the right side of the *Shape Height* measurement box until *4″* displays in the box.

j. Click the up- or down-pointing arrow at the right side of the *Shape Width* measurement box until *7″* displays in the box.

k. Click the Shape Fill button arrow in the Shape Styles group and then click *Orange, Accent 6, Lighter 40%* at the drop-down gallery.

l. Click the Shape Fill button arrow, point to *Gradient*, and then click *Linear Up* in the *Dark Variations* section at the side menu.

m. Click the Shape Outline button arrow in the Shape Styles group and then click *Dark Red* at the drop-down gallery (first color from the left in the *Standard Colors* row).

n. Click the Shape Effects button in the Shape Styles group, point to *Shadow*, and then click *Inside Diagonal Top Right* at the side menu (last option in the top row of the *Inner* section).

o. Change the internal margins by completing the following steps:
   1) Click the Home tab.
   2) Click the Text Direction button and then click *More Options* at the drop-down list.
   3) In the *Internal margin* section of the Format Text Effects dialog box, change the *Left* measurement to *0.6″* and the *Top* and *Bottom* measurements to *0.4″*.
   4) Click the Close button to close the dialog box.
   5) Click in the slide outside the text boxes.

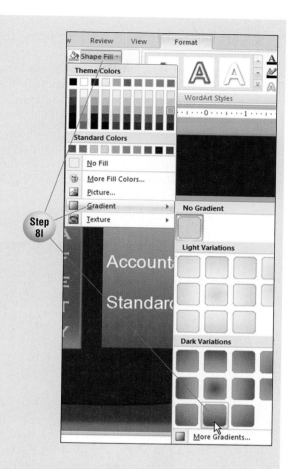

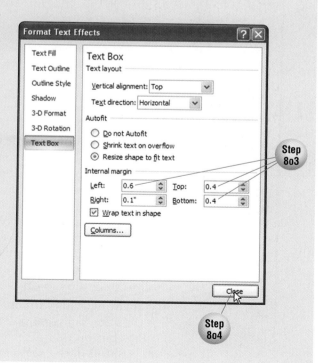

9. Arrange the text boxes by completing the following steps:
   a. Press Ctrl + A to select both text boxes.
   b. Click the Drawing Tools Format tab.
   c. Click the Align button in the Arrange group and then click *Align Middle* at the drop-down list.
   d. Drag both boxes to the approximate location in the slide as shown in Figure 4.2.
10. Save the presentation and name it **PP_C4_P1**.

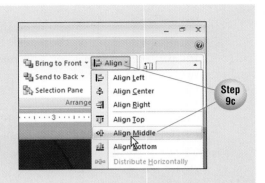

**Figure 4.2  Project 1a, Slide 2**

## Setting Tabs in a Text Box

**HINT**
Tab stops help you align your text in a slide.

Left Tab

Center Tab

Right Tab

Inside a text box, you may want to align text in columns using tabs. A text box, by default, contains left alignment tabs that display as light gray marks along the bottom of the horizontal ruler. You can change these default left alignment tabs to center, right, or decimal. To change to a different tab alignment, click the Alignment button located at the left side of the horizontal ruler. Display the desired tab alignment symbol and then click at the desired position on the horizontal ruler. When you set a tab on the horizontal ruler, any default tabs to the left of the new tab are deleted. You can move tabs on the horizontal ruler by using the mouse to drag the tab to the desired position. To delete a tab, use the mouse to drag the tab off of the ruler.

You can also set tabs with options at the Tabs dialog box. To display this dialog box, click the Paragraph group dialog box launcher. At the Paragraph dialog box, click the Tabs button that displays in the lower left corner. At the Tabs dialog box, type a tab position in the *Tab stop position* text box, choose a tab alignment with options in the *Alignment* section, and then click the Set button. Clear a specific tab by typing the tab stop position in the *Tab stop position* text box and then clicking the Clear button. Clear all tabs from the horizontal ruler by clicking the Clear All button. When all desired changes are made, click OK to close the Tabs dialog box and then click OK to close the Paragraph dialog box.

## Project 1b  Creating a Text Box and Setting Tabs

1. With **PP_C4_P1.pptx** open, make Slide 1 active and then click the Home tab.
2. Click the New Slide button arrow and then click the *Title Only* layout.
3. Click in the placeholder text *Click to add title* and then type Executive Officers.
4. Draw a text box by completing the following steps:
   a. Click the Insert tab.
   b. Click the Text Box button in the Text group.
   c. Draw a text box in the slide that is approximately 8 inches wide and 0.5 inch tall.
5. Change tabs in the text box by completing the following steps:
   a. With the insertion point inside the text box, make sure the horizontal ruler displays. (If not, click the View tab and then click the *Ruler* check box in the Show/Hide group.)
   b. Check the alignment button at the left side of the horizontal ruler and make sure the left tab symbol displays.
   c. Position the tip of the mouse pointer on the horizontal ruler below the 0.5-inch mark and then click the left mouse button.
   d. Click once on the Alignment button to display the Center alignment symbol.
   e. Click on the horizontal ruler immediately below the 4-inch mark on the horizontal ruler.
   f. Click once on the Alignment button to display the Right alignment symbol.
   g. Click on the horizontal ruler immediately below the 7.5-inch mark. (You may need to expand the size of the text box to set the tab at the 7.5-inch mark.)

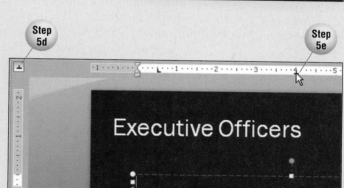

6. Type the text in the text box as shown in the slide in Figure 4.3. Make sure you press the Tab key before typing text in the first column (this moves the insertion point to the first tab, which is a left alignment tab). Bold the three column headings—*Name, Title,* and *Number.*
7. When you are finished typing the text in the text box, press Ctrl + A to select all of the text in the text box and then change the line spacing to 1.5.
8. With the text still selected, drag the left alignment marker on the horizontal ruler from the 0.5-inch mark to the 0.25-inch mark and then drag the right alignment marker on the horizontal ruler from the 7.5-inch mark on the ruler to the 7-inch mark.
9. Save **PP_C4_P1.pptx**.

**Figure 4.3 Project 1b, Slide 2**

## Executive Officers

| Name | Title | Number |
|------|-------|--------|
| Taylor Hallowell | Chief Executive Officer | 555-4321 |
| Gina Rodgers | Chief Financial Officer | 555-4203 |
| Samuel Weinberg | President | 555-4421 |
| Leslie Pena | Vice President | 555-3122 |
| Leticia Reynolds | Vice President | 555-3004 |
| Gerald Yuan | Vice President | 555-2310 |
| Michael Anderson | Vice President | 555-3877 |

**QUICK STEPS**

**Insert a Shape**
1. Click Shapes button.
2. Click desired shape at drop-down list.
3. Drag in slide to create shape.

**HINT**

Many shapes have an adjustment handle you can use to change the most prominent feature of the shape.

Shapes

# Inserting and Formatting Shapes

You can draw shapes in a slide using the Shapes button in the Drawing group or with the Shapes button in the Illustrations group in the Insert tab. With the Shapes button drop-down list, you can choose to draw shapes including lines, basic shapes, block arrows, flow chart symbols, callouts, stars, and banners. Click a shape and the mouse pointer displays as crosshairs (plus sign). Click in the slide to insert the shape or position the crosshairs in the slide and then drag to create the shape. Apply formatting to a shape in a manner similar to formatting a text box. Use buttons in the Drawing group in the Home tab and/or buttons in the Drawing Tools Format tab (shown in Figure 4.1).

If you choose a shape in the *Lines* section of the drop-down list, the shape you draw is considered a ***line drawing***. If you choose an option in the other sections of the drop-down list, the shape you draw is considered an ***enclosed object***. When drawing an enclosed object, you can maintain the proportions of the shape by holding down the Shift key while dragging with the mouse to create the shape.

## Project 1c  Drawing and Formatting Lines and Shapes

1. With **PP_C4_P1.pptx** open, make Slide 3 active.
2. Click the New Slide button arrow and then click the *Blank* layout at the drop-down list.
3. Insert and format the square shown in the lower left corner of the slide in Figure 4.4 by completing the following steps:
   a. Make sure the Home tab is selected.

b. Click the Shapes button in the Drawing group.

c. Click the Rectangle shape in the *Rectangles* section of the drop-down list.

d. Hold down the Shift key and then draw a square the approximate size of the square shown in Figure 4.4.

e. With the square selected, click the Quick Styles button in the Drawing group and then click *Moderate Effect - Accent 1* (second option from the left in the fifth row).

f. Click the Drawing Tools Format tab.

g. Change the *Shape Height* and *Shape Width* to *1.6"*.

h. If necessary, drag the square so it is positioned as shown in Figure 4.4.

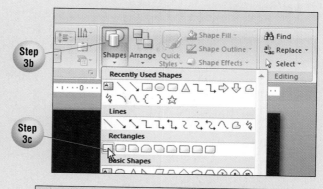

4. Insert the word *Safety* in the square by completing the following steps:

a. With the Drawing Tools Format tab selected, click the Text Box button in the Insert Shapes group.

b. Click inside the square.

c. Click the Home tab.

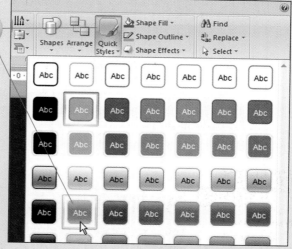

d. Change the font to Copperplate Gothic Bold, change the font size to 24, and change the font color to Brown, Accent 2, Darker 50%.

e. Type Safety.

5. Draw and format the line shown in Figure 4.4 by completing the following steps:

a. Click the Insert tab.

b. Click the Shapes button in the Illustrations group and then click *Arrow* in the *Lines* section.

c. Position the mouse pointer (cross hairs) in the upper right corner of the square and then drag up to the approximate location shown in Figure 4.4.

d. With the arrow line selected, click the Drawing Tools Format tab.

e. Click the Shape Outline button arrow in the Shape Styles group, point to *Weight*, and then click *4½ pt* at the side menu.

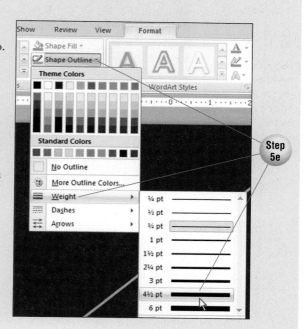

f. Click the Shape Effects button in the Shape Styles group, point to *Bevel*, and then click *Circle* at the side menu (first option from the left in the top row in the *Bevel* section).
6. Draw a text box and type the text shown in the upper left corner of the slide by completing the following steps:
   a. Click the Text Box button in the Insert Shapes group in the Drawing Tools Format tab.
   b. Click in the upper left side of the slide.
   c. Click the Home tab, change the font size to 28, and then click the Bold button.
   d. Click the Align Text Right button in the Paragraph group.
   e. Type 2009, press the Enter key, and then type Safety Training.
   f. If necessary, drag the text box so it is positioned as shown in Figure 4.4.
7. Draw and format the text box shown near the arrow line by completing the following steps:
   a. Click the Insert tab.
   b. Click the Text Box button in the Text group.
   c. Click in the slide (you determine the position).
   d. Change the font size to 24, click the Bold button, and then change the font color to Orange.
   e. Type 1,000 ASA-trained employees.
   f. Position the mouse pointer on the green rotation handle, hold down the left mouse button, and then rotate the text box so it is angled as shown in Figure 4.4.
   g. Drag the text box so it is positioned next to the arrow line.
8. Save **PP_C4_P1.pptx**.

**Figure 4.4  Project 1c, Slide 4**

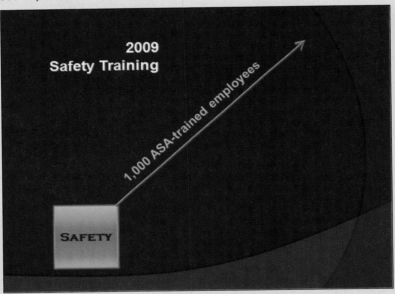

## Copying Shapes

To copy a shape, select the shape and then click the Copy button in the Clipboard group in the Home tab. Position the insertion point at the location where you want the copied image and then click the Paste button. You can also copy a selected shape by holding down the Ctrl key while dragging the shape to the desired location.

## Displaying Rulers, Gridlines, and Guides

To help position objects such as placeholders, text boxes, and shapes, consider displaying horizontal and vertical rulers, gridlines, and/or drawing guides as shown in Figure 4.5. You can turn the horizontal and vertical ruler on and off with the Ruler check box in the Show/Hide group in the View tab. The Show/Hide group also contains a Gridlines check box. Insert a check mark in this check box and gridlines display in the active slide. Gridlines are intersecting lines that create a grid on the slide and are useful for aligning objects. You can also turn the display of gridlines on and off with the keyboard shortcut, Shift + F9.

### QUICK STEPS

**Copy a Shape**
1. Select desired shape.
2. Click Copy button.
3. Position insertion point at desired location.
4. Click Paste button.
OR
1. Select desired shape.
2. Hold down Ctrl key.
3. Drag shape to desired location.

**Figure 4.5** Rulers, Gridlines, and Drawing Guides

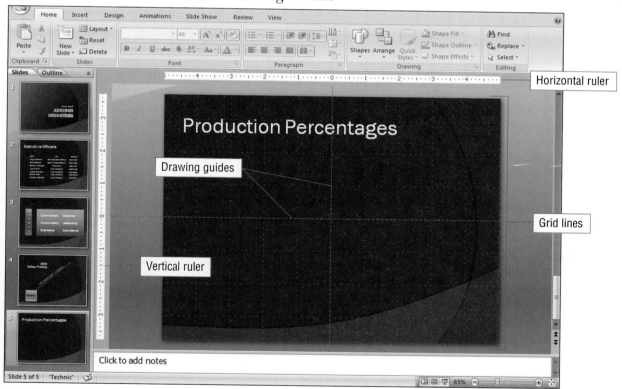

Turn on drawing guides to help position objects on a slide. Drawing guides are horizontal and vertical dashed lines that display on the slide in the Slide pane as shown in Figure 4.5. To turn on the drawing guides, display the Grid and Guides dialog box shown in Figure 4.6. Display this dialog box by selecting an object in the slide, clicking the Drawing Tools Format tab, clicking the Align button in the Arrange group, and then clicking *Grid Settings* at the drop-down list. At the dialog box, insert a check mark in the *Display drawing guides on screen* check box. By default, the horizontal and vertical drawing guides intersect in the middle of the slide. You can move these guides by dragging the guide with the mouse. As you drag the guide, a measurement displays next to the mouse pointer. Drawing guides and gridlines display on the slide but do not print.

You can turn on gridlines with the Gridlines check box in the View tab and you can also turn them on by inserting a check mark in the *Display grid on screen* check box. The horizontal and vertical spacing between the gridlines is 0.083 inch by default. You can change this measurement with the *Spacing* option at the Grid and Guides dialog box.

**Figure 4.6** Grid and Guides Dialog Box

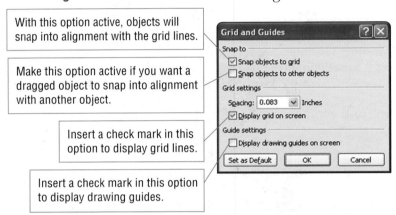

With this option active, objects will snap into alignment with the grid lines.

Make this option active if you want a dragged object to snap into alignment with another object.

Insert a check mark in this option to display grid lines.

Insert a check mark in this option to display drawing guides.

As you drag or draw an object on the slide, it is pulled into alignment with the nearest intersection of gridlines. This is because the *Snap objects to grid* option at the Grid and Guides dialog box is active by default. If you want to position an object precisely, you can remove the check mark from the *Snap objects to grid* to turn the feature off or you can hold down the Alt key while dragging an object. If you want an object to be pulled into alignment with another object, insert a check mark in the *Snap objects to other objects* check box.

## Project 1d  Drawing and Formatting Shapes and Text Boxes

1. With **PP_C4_P1.pptx** open, make sure Slide 4 is active and then insert a new slide by clicking the New Slide button arrow and then clicking *Title Only* at the drop-down list.
2. Turn on the display of gridlines by clicking the View tab and then clicking *Gridlines* to insert a check mark in the check box.

Step 2

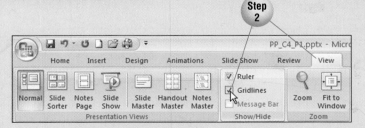

3. Click in the title placeholder and then type Production Percentages.

4. With the placeholder selected, turn on drawing guides and turn off the snap-to-grid feature by completing the following steps:

a. Click the Drawing Tools Format tab.

b. Click the Align button in the Arrange group.

c. Click the *Grid Settings* option at the drop-down list.

d. At the Grid and Guides dialog box, click the *Snap objects to grid* check box to remove the check mark.

e. Click the *Display drawing guides on screen* to insert a check mark in the check box.

f. Click OK.

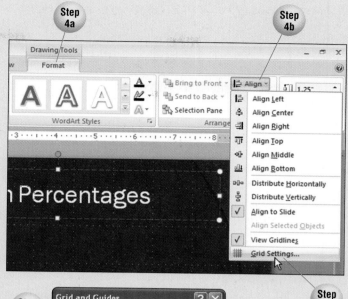

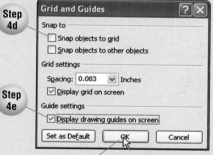

5. Draw the arrow at the left in the slide in Figure 4.7 by completing the following steps:

a. Click outside the title placeholder to deselect it.

b. Click the Insert tab.

c. Click the Shapes button and then click the *Up Arrow* shape (third shape from the left in the top row of the *Block Arrows* section).

d. Position the crosshairs on the intersection of the horizontal drawing guide and the first vertical gridline from the left.

e. Hold down the left mouse button, drag down and to the right until the crosshairs are positioned on the intersection of the third vertical line from the left and the first horizontal line from the bottom, and then release the mouse button. (Your arrow should be the approximate size shown in Figure 4.7.)

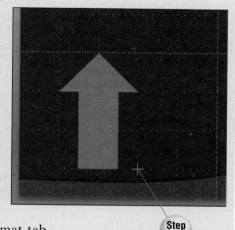

f. With the arrow selected, click the Drawing Tools Format tab.

g. Click the Shape Fill button arrow and then click *Light Blue* at the drop-down gallery (seventh color option from the left in the *Standard Colors* section).

h. Click the Shape Fill button arrow, point to *Gradient*, and then click the *Linear Up* option in the *Dark Variations* section (second option from the left in the bottom row of the *Dark Variations* section).

i. Click the Shape Effects button, point to *Bevel*, and then click the *Soft round* option (second option from the left in the second row in the *Bevel* section).

6. Insert a text box in the arrow by completing the following steps:
   a. Click the Insert tab.
   b. Click the Text Box button in the Text group.
   c. Drag to create a text box toward the top of the arrow the approximate size shown at the right.
   d. With the Home tab selected, change the font size to 20, turn on Bold, and then change the font color to Dark Blue.
   e. Click the Center button in the Paragraph group.
   f. Type Plant 3, press the Enter key, and then type 48%.
   g. Move and/or size the text box so the text is positioned in the arrow as shown in Figure 4.7.
7. Copy the arrow and text box by completing the following steps:
   a. With the text box selected, hold down the Shift key and then click the arrow. (This selects the arrow and the text box.)
   b. Position the mouse pointer on the border of the selected arrow or text box until the mouse pointer displays with a four-headed arrow attached.
   c. Hold down the Ctrl key, drag the arrow and text box to the right so the tip of the arrow is positioned at the intersection of the horizontal and vertical drawing guides.

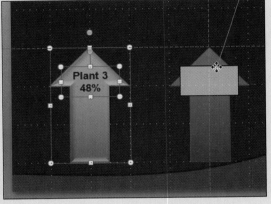

8. Move the vertical drawing guide and then copy the arrow and text box by completing the following steps:
   a. Click outside the arrow to deselect the arrow and the text box.
   b. Position the mouse pointer on the vertical drawing guide, hold down the left mouse button, drag right until the mouse pointer displays with 3.00 and a right-pointing arrow in a box, and then release the mouse button.

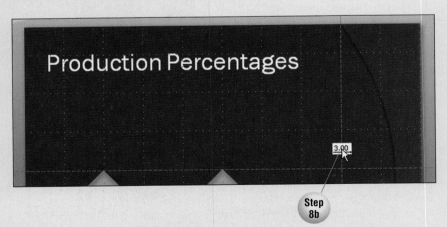

   c. Click the arrow at the right, hold down the Shift key, and then click the text box inside the arrow.
   d. Hold down the Ctrl, drag the arrow and text box to the right so the tip of the arrow is positioned at the intersection of the horizontal and vertical drawing guides.

9. Increase the height of the middle arrow by completing the following steps:
   a. Click the middle arrow to select it.
   b. Using the mouse, drag the top middle sizing handle up to the next horizontal gridline.
   c. Click the text box in the middle arrow and then drag the text box up to the position shown in Figure 4.7.
   d. Complete similar steps to increase the height of the arrow at the right to the second horizontal gridline. Drag the text box to the position shown in Figure 4.7.
   e. Change the text in the text box in the middle arrow to *Plant 1 72%* and change the text in the text box in the arrow at the right to *Plant 2 91%* (see Figure 4.7).
10. Turn off gridlines, drawing guides, and turn on the snap-to-grid feature by completing the following steps:
   a. Click the text in the title placeholder.
   b. Click the Drawing Tools Format tab.
   c. Click the Align button in the Arrange group.
   d. Click the *Grid Settings* option at the drop-down list.
   e. At the Grid and Guides dialog box, click the *Snap objects to grid* check box to insert a check mark.
   f. Click the *Display grid on screen* option to remove the check mark.
   g. Click the *Display drawing guides on screen* to remove the mark in the check box.
   h. Click OK.
11. Save **PP_C4_P1.pptx**.

**Figure 4.7  Project 1d, Slide 5**

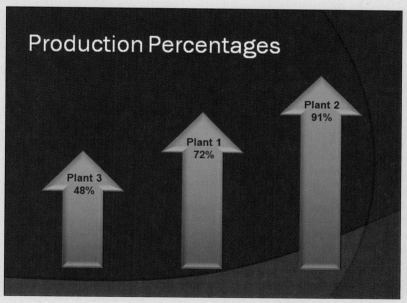

**Group Objects**
1. Select desired objects.
2. Click Drawing Tools Format tab.
3. Click Group button.
4. Click *Group* at drop-down list.

HINT

Group objects so you can move, size, flip, or rotate objects at one time.

# Grouping/Ungrouping Objects

If you want to apply the same formatting or make the same adjustments to the size or rotation of objects, group the objects. If you group objects and then apply a formatting such as a shape fill, effect, or shape style, the formatting is applied to each object within the group. With objects grouped, you can apply formatting more quickly to objects in the slide. To group objects, select the objects you want included in the group. You can do this by clicking each object while holding down the Shift key or you can draw a border around the objects you want included. With the objects selected, click the Drawing Tools Format tab, click the Group button in the Arrange group, and then click *Group* at the drop-down list.

You can format an individual object within a group. To do this, click any object in the group and the group border displays around the objects. Click the individual object and then apply the desired formatting. If you no longer want objects grouped, click the group to select it, click the Drawing Tools Format tab, click the Group button in the Arrange group, and then click *Ungroup* at the drop-down list.

## Project 1e — Grouping and Formatting Objects

1. With **PP_C4_P1.pptx** open, make Slide 3 active.
2. Group the objects and apply formatting by completing the following steps:
   a. Using the mouse, draw a border around the two text boxes in the slide.
   b. Click the Drawing Tools Format tab.
   c. Click the Group button in the Arrange group and then click *Group* at the drop-down list.

**Step 2c**

   d. Click the More button at the right side of the shape style thumbnails and then click *Intense Effect - Accent 2* at the drop-down gallery (third option from the left in the bottom row).
   e. Click the Shape Outline button arrow and then click *Brown, Accent 3, Darker 50%*.
   f. Click the Shape Outline button arrow, point to *Weight*, and then click *4½ pt*.
3. Make Slide 4 active and then group and format objects by completing the following steps:
   a. Using the mouse, draw a border around all objects in the slide.
   b. Click the Drawing Tools Format tab.
   c. Click the Group button in the Arrange group and then click *Group* at the drop-down list.
   d. Click the Home tab.
   e. Click the Font Color button arrow and then click the *Orange, Accent 1, Lighter 60%* option.
4. Make Slide 1 active and then run the presentation.
5. After running the presentation you decide that you want to change the color of the square shape and the arrow in Slide 4. Do this by completing the following steps:
   a. Make Slide 4 active.
   b. Click any object in the slide. (This selects the border around all of the objects.)
   c. Click the gold square located in the lower left corner of the slide.
   d. Click the Drawing Tools Format tab.

e. Click the More button at the right side of the shape style thumbnails and then click *Intense Effect - Accent 2* at the drop-down gallery (third option from the left in the bottom row).

6. Ungroup the objects by completing the following steps:

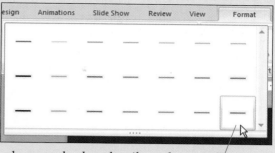

a. With the group and square selected, click the Group button in the Arrange group and then click *Ungroup* at the drop-down list.

b. Click outside any object to deselect the objects.

c. Click the arrow line.

d. Click the More button at the right side of the shape style thumbnails and then click the *Intense Line - Accent 6* option (last option in the bottom row).

Step 6d

7. You also decide that you do not like the light yellow border (outline) around the three arrows in Slide 5. Remove the outlines by completing the following steps:

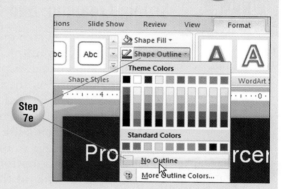

a. Make Slide 5 active.

b. Using the mouse, draw a border around the three arrows in the slide.

c. Click the Drawing Tools Format tab.

d. Click the Group button in the Arrange group and then click *Group* at the drop-down list.

e. Click the Shape Outline button in the Shape Styles group and then click *No Outline* at the drop-down gallery.

Step 7e

8. Save **PP_C4_P1.pptx**.

# Inserting an Image

You can insert an image such as a picture or clip art in a slide with buttons in the Illustrations group in the Insert tab. Click the Picture button to display the Insert Picture dialog box where you can specify the desired picture file or click the Clip Art button and then choose from a variety of images available at the Clip Art task pane.

## Customizing and Formatting an Image

When you insert an image in a slide, the image is selected and the Picture Tools Format tab is active as shown in Figure 4.8. Use buttons in this tab to apply formatting to the image. With options in the Adjust group in the Picture Tools Format tab you can recolor the picture or clip art image and change the brightness and contrast of the image. You can also reset the picture or clip art back to its original color or change to a different image. Use the Compress Pictures button to compress the size of the image file. Compressing a picture makes the color take up fewer bits per pixel without any loss of quality.

PowerPoint provides predesigned styles you can apply to your image. These styles are available in the Picture Styles group along with buttons for changing the image border and applying effects to the image. Use options in the Arrange group to position the image on the page, specify text wrapping in relation to the image, align the image with other objects in the document, and rotate the image. Use the Crop button in the Size group to remove any unnecessary parts of the image and specify the image size with the *Shape Height* and *Shape Width* measurement boxes.

**Figure 4.8** Picture Tools Format Tab

## QUICK STEPS

**Insert Picture**
1. Click Insert tab.
2. Click Picture button.
3. Navigate to desired folder.
4. Double-click desired picture.

## HINT

Insert a picture from your camera by downloading the picture to your computer and then copying the picture into PowerPoint.

# Sizing, Cropping, and Moving an Image

You can change the size of an image with the *Shape Height* and *Shape Width* measurement boxes in the Size group in the Picture Tools Format tab or with the sizing handles that display around the selected image. To change size with a sizing handle, position the mouse pointer on a sizing handle until the pointer turns into a double-headed arrow and then hold down the left mouse button. Drag the sizing handle in or out to decrease or increase the size of the image and then release the mouse button. Use the middle sizing handles at the left or right side of the image to make the image wider or thinner. Use the middle sizing handles at the top or bottom of the image to make the image taller or shorter. Use the sizing handles at the corners of the image to change both the width and height at the same time.

The Size group in the Picture Tools Format tab contains a Crop button. Use this button to remove portions of an image. Click the Crop button and the mouse pointer displays with the crop tool attached, which is a black square with overlapping lines, and the image displays with cropping handles around the border. Drag a cropping handle to remove a portion of the image.

Move a selected image by dragging it to the desired location. Move the image by positioning the mouse pointer on the image border until the arrow pointer turns into a four-headed arrow. Hold down the left mouse button, drag the image to the desired position, and then release the mouse button. You can use the arrow keys on the keyboard to move the image in the desired direction. If you want to move the image in small increments (called ***nudging***), hold down the Ctrl key while pressing an arrow key.

Use the rotation handle to rotate an image by positioning the mouse pointer on the green, round rotation handle until the pointer displays as a circular arrow. Hold down the left mouse button, drag in the desired direction, and then release the mouse button.

# Arranging Objects

If you want to layer one object on top of another, use the Bring to Front or Send to Back buttons in the Arrange group in the Drawing Tools Format tab or Picture Tools Format tab. For example, if you want an image to display behind a text box, select the image and then click the Send to Back button. If you want a selected object to display on top of other objects in the slide, click the Bring to Front button.

# Inserting a Picture

To insert a picture in a document, click the Insert tab and then click the Picture button in the Illustrations group. At the Insert Picture dialog box, navigate to the folder containing the desired picture and then double-click the picture. Use buttons in the Picture Tools Format tab to format and customize the picture.

Picture

## Project 11 · Inserting and Formatting a Picture

1. With **PP_C4_P1.pptx** open, make Slide 5 active and then click the Home tab.
2. Insert a new slide by clicking the New Slide button arrow and then clicking *Blank* at the drop-down list.
3. Insert a text box by completing the following steps:
   a. Click the Insert tab.
   b. Click the Text Box button in the Text group.
   c. Click in the middle of the slide.
   d. Change the font to Arial Black and the font size to 36.
   e. Click the Center button in the Paragraph group.
   f. Type Alternative, press the Enter key, and then type Energy Resources.
   g. With the text box selected, click the Drawing Tools Format tab.
   h. Click the Align button and then click *Distribute Horizontally* at the drop-down list.
   i. Click the Align button and then click *Distribute Vertically* at the drop-down list.

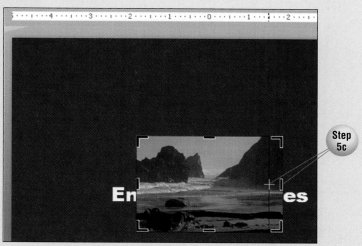

Step 3h

4. Insert a picture by completing the following steps:
   a. Click the Insert tab.
   b. Click the Picture button in the Illustrations group.
   c. At the Insert Picture dialog box, navigate to the PowerPoint2007C4 folder on your storage medium and then double-click *Ocean.jpg*.
5. Crop the picture by completing the following steps:
   a. With the picture selected, click the Crop button in the Size group in the Picture Tools Format tab.
   b. Position the mouse pointer (displays with the crop tool attached) on the cropping handle in the middle of the right side of the picture.
   c. Hold down the left mouse button and then drag to the left approximately 0.25 inch. (Use the guideline that displays on the horizontal ruler to crop the picture 0.25 inch.)

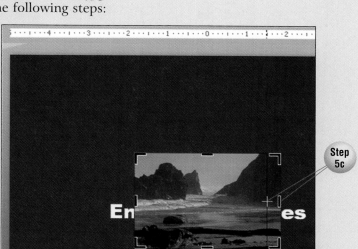

Step 5c

d. Complete steps similar to those in Steps 5b and 5c to crop approximately 0.25 inch from the top of the picture. (Use the guideline that displays on the vertical ruler to crop the picture 0.25 inch.)

e. Click the Crop button to turn off cropping.

6. Click in the *Shape Height* measurement box in the Size group, type 5, and then press Enter.

7. Click the Send to Back button in the Arrange group. (This moves the picture behind the text in the text box.)

8. Align the picture by completing the following steps:

a. With the picture selected, click the Home tab.

b. Click the Arrange button in the Drawing group, point to *Align* at the drop-down list, and then click *Distribute Horizontally*.

c. Click the Arrange button, point to *Align*, and then click *Distribute Vertically*.

9. Format the picture by completing the following steps:

a. With the picture selected, click the Picture Tools Format tab, click the Recolor button in the Adjust group, and then click the *Accent color 6 Dark* option (last option in the *Dark Variations* row).

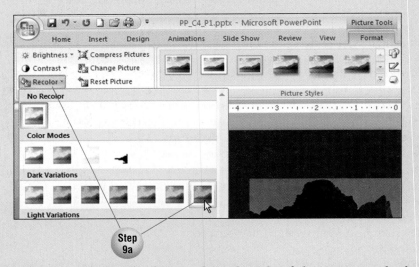

b. Click the More button that displays at the right side of the picture style thumbnails and then click *Soft Edge Oval* at the drop-down gallery (second option from the left in the fourth row).

c. Click the Brightness button in the Adjust group and then click *+10%* at the drop-down list.

d. Click the Contrast button in the Adjust group and then click *+20%* at the drop-down list.

e. Click the Compress Pictures button in the Adjust group. At the Compress Pictures dialog box, click OK.

10. Save **PP_C4_P1.pptx**.

# Inserting a Picture as a Slide Background

You can insert a picture as the background in an entire slide. To do this, click the Design tab, click the Background Styles button in the Background group, and then click *Format Background* at the drop-down list. At the Format Background dialog box, click the *Picture or texture fill* option in the *Fill* section and then click the File button. At the Insert Picture dialog box, navigate to the desired folder, and then double-click the picture. Click the Close button to close the Format Background dialog box. If you want the picture background to display on all slides, click the Apply to All button at the Format Background dialog box.

**Insert Picture as Slide Background**
1. Click Design tab.
2. Click Background Styles button, *Format Background*.
3. Click *Picture or texture fill* option.
4. Click File button.
5. Navigate to desired folder.
6. Double-click desired picture.
7. Click Close button.

## Project 1g  Inserting a Picture as a Slide Background

1. With **PP_C4_P1.pptx** open, make sure Slide 6 is active, and then click the Home tab.
2. Click the New Slide button arrow and then click the *Blank* layout at the drop-down list.
3. Insert a picture background on Slide 7 by completing the following steps:
   a. Click the Design tab.
   b. Click the Background Styles button in the Background group and then click *Format Background* at the drop-down gallery.
   c. At the Format Background dialog box, click the *Picture or texture fill* option in the *Fill* section.
   d. Click the File button that displays near the middle of the dialog box.
   e. At the Insert Picture dialog box, navigate to the PowerPoint2007C4 folder on your storage medium and then double-click *EiffelTower.jpg*.
   f. Click the Close button to close the Format Background dialog box.
   g. Remove the background graphic by clicking the *Hide Background Graphics* check box in the Background group in the Design tab to insert a check mark.
4. Insert a text box by completing the following steps:
   a. Click the Insert tab.
   b. Click the Text Box button in the Text group.
   c. Click in the upper left corner of the slide.
   d. Change the font size to 40.
   e. Type European and then press Enter.
   f. Type Division 2010.
   g. Drag the text box so it is positioned attractively on the slide in the upper left corner.
5. Change the formatting of slides and slide objects by completing the following steps:
   a. Make Slide 3 active.
   b. Click the Design tab.
   c. Click the Colors button in the Themes group and then click *Office* at the drop-down gallery.
   d. Click in the lower right corner of the text box containing the text in columns (this selects the group).

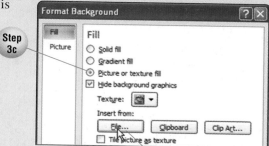

Step 3c

Step 3d

e. Click the Drawing Tools Format tab.

f. Click the More button at the right side of the shape style thumbnails and then click the *Moderate Effect - Accent 1* option (second option from the left in the fifth row).

g. Make Slide 4 active, select the square and the line arrow, click the Drawing Tools Format tab, and then apply the *Moderate Effect - Accent 1* option (second option from the left in the fifth row).

h. Using the mouse, draw a border around all of the objects in the slide, click the Home tab, and then change the font color to Orange.

i. Make Slide 6 active and then click the picture to select it.

j. Click the Picture Tools Format tab.

k. Click the Recolor button in the Adjust group and then click the *No Recolor* option.

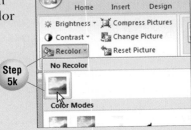

Step 5k

6. Save **PP_C4_P1.pptx**.

## Inserting a Clip Art Image

**Insert Clip Art Image**
1. Click Insert tab.
2. Click Clip Art button.
3. Type search word or topic.
4. Press Enter.
5. Click desired image.

Microsoft Office includes a gallery of media images you can insert in a slide such as clip art, photographs, and movie images, as well as sound clips. To insert a clip art image in a slide, click the Insert tab and then click the Clip Art button in the Illustrations group. This displays the Clip Art task pane at the right side of the screen as shown in Figure 4.9. You can also choose a slide layout that contains a content placeholder with a Clip Art button.

**Figure 4.9** Clip Art Task Pane

Search for specific images by typing the desired category in this text box and then clicking the Go button.

To view all picture, sound, and motion files, make sure the *Search for* text box in the Clip Art task pane does not contain any text and then click the Go button. When the desired image is visible, click the image to insert it in the document. Use buttons in the Picture Tools Format tab shown in Figure 4.8 to format and customize the clip art image.

If you are searching for specific images, click in the *Search for* text box, type the desired topic, and then click the Go button. For example, if you want to find images related to business, click in the *Search for* text box, type **business**, and then click the Go button. Clip art images related to *business* display in the viewing area of the task pane. If you are connected to the Internet, Word will search for images at the Office Online Web site matching the topic.

By default (unless it has been customized), the Clip Art task pane displays all media images and sound clips found in all locations. You can narrow the search to specific locations and to specific images. The *Search in* option at the Clip Art task pane has a default setting of *All collections*. This can be changed to *My Collections*, *Office Collections*, and *Web Collections*. The *Results should be* option has a default setting of *Selected media file types*. Click the down-pointing arrow at the right side of this option to display media types. To search for a specific media type, remove the check mark before all options at the drop-down list except the desired type. For example, if you are searching only for photograph images, remove the check mark before Clip Art, Movies, and Sound.

## Project 1h  Inserting and Formatting a Clip Art Image

1. With **PP_C4_P1.pptx** open, make Slide 1 active.
2. Insert a clip art image by completing the following steps:
   a. Click the Insert tab.
   b. Click the Clip Art button in the Illustrations group.
   c. At the Clip Art task pane, click the down-pointing arrow at the right side of the *Results should be* option box and then click in the *Photographs*, *Movies*, and *Sounds* check boxes to remove the check marks. (The *Clip Art* check box should be the only one with a check mark.)
   d. Select any text that displays in the *Search for* text box, type **industry**, and then press Enter.
   e. Click the clip art image in the list box as shown at the right.
   f. Click the down-pointing arrow at the right side of the *Results should be* option box and then click in the *All media types* check box to insert a check mark.
   g. Close the Clip Art task pane by clicking the Close button (contains an X) located in the upper right corner of the task pane.
3. Arrange, size, and position the clip art image by completing the following steps:
   a. With the clip art image selected, click the Rotate button in the Arrange group and then click *Flip Horizontal*.

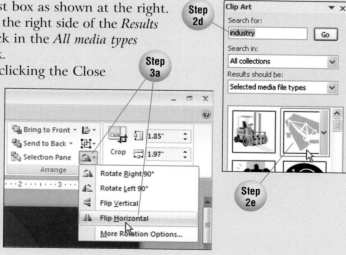

b. Click in the *Shape Height* measurement box, type 4.5, and then press Enter.

c. Click the Recolor button in the Adjust group and then click the *Accent color 5 Light* option at the drop-down gallery (second option from the right in the *Light Variations* section).

d. Click the Contrast button in the Adjust group and then click *+30%* at the drop-down gallery.

e. Click the Send to Back button in the Arrange group.

f. Drag the clip art image so it is positioned as shown in Figure 4.10.

4. Save **PP_C4_P1.pptx**.

**Figure 4.10  Project 1h, Slide 1**

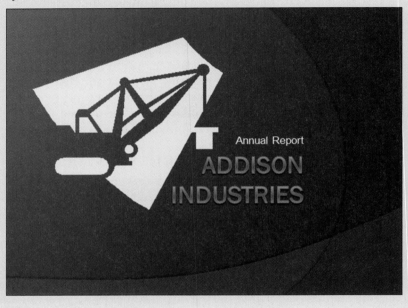

## Sizing, Rotating, and Positioning Objects

As you have learned in this chapter, you can use the sizing handles that display around an object to increase and decrease the size, and use the *Shape Height* and *Shape Width* measurement boxes. You also learned to position objects by dragging the object with the mouse. You can also size and position objects with options at the Size and Position dialog box shown in Figure 4.11. Display this dialog box by clicking the Size group dialog box launcher in the Picture Tools Format tab or the Drawing Tools Format tab.

**Figure 4.11** Size and Position Dialog Box

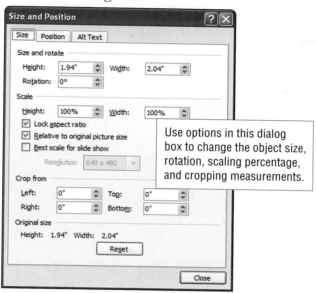

Use options in this dialog box to change the object size, rotation, scaling percentage, and cropping measurements.

Use options at the Size and Position dialog box with the Size tab selected to specify the object size, rotation degree, scaling percentage, and cropping measurements. The Size and Position dialog box with the Position tab selected contains options for specifying the horizontal and vertical position of the object in the slide.

## Project 1i  Inserting and Formatting a Clip Art Image

1. With **PP_C4_P1.pptx** open, make Slide 7 active.
2. Click the New Slide button arrow and then click the *Two Content* layout at the drop-down list.
3. Click the placeholder text *Click to add title* and then type Technology.
4. Click the placeholder text *Click to add text* located in the right side of the slide.
5. Click the Bullets button in the Paragraph group to turn off bullets.
6. Change the font size to 36, turn on bold, and change the font color to Orange.
7. Press the Enter key.
8. Type Equipment and then press the Enter key twice.
9. Type Software and then press the Enter key twice.
10. Type Personnel.
11. Insert a clip art image by completing the following steps:
    a. Click the Clip Art button that displays in the middle of the placeholder at the left side of the slide.

Step 11a

b. At the Clip Art task pane, select any text that displays in the *Search for* text box, type technology, and then press Enter.

c. Click the clip art image in the list box as shown at the right.

d. Close the Clip Art task pane by clicking the Close button (contains an X) located in the upper right corner of the task pane.

12. Scale, rotate, and position the clip art image by completing the following steps:

a. With the clip art image selected, click the Size group dialog box launcher.

b. Click the down-pointing arrow at the right of the *Rotation* option until *–20%* displays in the option box.

c. Select the current percentage in the *Height* option box in the *Scale* section and then type 225.

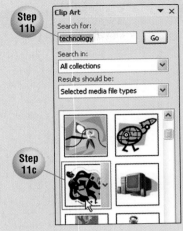

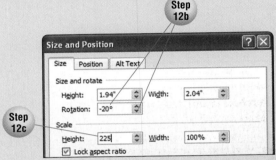

d. Click the Position tab.

e. Click the down-pointing arrow at the right side of the *Horizontal* option until *0.7″* displays in the option box.

f. Click the down-pointing arrow at the right side of the *Vertical* option until *1.9″* displays in the option box.

g. Click the Close button to close the dialog box.

13. Bring the text in front of the clip art image by completing the following steps:

a. Click in the text to select the text placeholder.

b. Click the Drawing Tools Format tab.

c. Click the Bring to Front button in the Arrange group.

14. Save **PP_C4_P1.pptx**.

## Copying Objects within and between Presentations

Earlier in this chapter you learned how to copy shapes within a slide. You can also copy shapes as well as other objects to other slides within the same presentation or to slides in another presentation. To copy an object, select the object and then click the Copy button in the Clipboard group in the Home tab. Make the desired slide active or open another presentation and display the desired slide and then click the Paste button in the Clipboard group. You can also copy an object by right-clicking the object and then clicking *Copy* at the shortcut menu. To paste the object, make the desired slide active, click the right mouse button, and then click *Paste* at the shortcut menu.

## Project 1j  Copying an Object within and between Presentations

1. With **PP_C4_P1.pptx** open, make Slide 1 active.
2. Click the clip art image to select it and then press the Delete key.
3. Open **Addison.pptx**.
4. Click the clip art image located in Slide 1 and then click the Copy button in the Clipboard group.
5. Click the button on the Taskbar representing the **PP_C4_P1.pptx** and then click the Paste button. (This inserts the clip art image in Slide 1.)
6. Make the **Addison.pptx** presentation active and then close the presentation.
7. With the **PP_C4_P1.pptx** open and the clip art image selected, make Slide 2 active and then click the Paste button.
8. Decrease the size and position the clip art by completing the following steps:
   a. Click the Picture Tools Format tab.
   b. Click in the *Shape Height* measurement text box, type 0.8, and then press Enter.
   c. Drag the clip art image so it is positioned in the upper right corner of the slide.

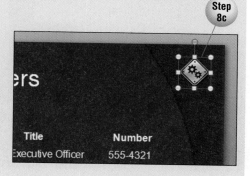

Step 8c

9. Copy the clip art image to other slides by completing the following steps:
   a. With the clip art image selected in Slide 2, click the Copy button in the Clipboard group in the Home tab.
   b. Make Slide 3 active and then click the Paste button in the Clipboard group.
   c. Make each of the following slides active and then paste the clip art image: Slide 4, 5, 6, and 8.
10. Save **PP_C4_P1.pptx**.

# Creating WordArt Text

Use the WordArt feature to insert preformatted, decorative text in a slide. You can also use WordArt to modify text to conform to a variety of shapes. Consider using WordArt to create a company logo, letterhead, flier title, or heading. Insert WordArt in a slide by clicking the Insert tab and then clicking the WordArt button in the Text group. This displays the WordArt drop-down list as shown in Figure 4.12. Click the desired WordArt style at this drop-down list and a text box is inserted in the slide containing the text *Your Text Here*. Type the desired WordArt text and then use the options in the Drawing Tools Format tab to customize the WordArt.

**Create WordArt Text**
1. Click Insert tab.
2. Click WordArt button.
3. Click desired WordArt style.
4. Type WordArt text.

**HINT**
Use WordArt to create interesting text effects in slides.

WordArt

**Figure 4.12** WordArt Drop-down List

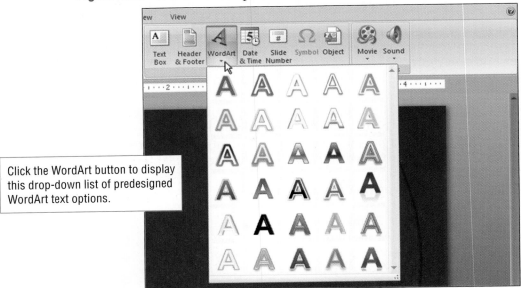

Click the WordArt button to display this drop-down list of predesigned WordArt text options.

## HINT

Edit WordArt by double-clicking the WordArt text.

Text Fill

Text Outline

Text Effect

## Formatting WordArt Text

When you insert WordArt text in a document, the Drawing Tools Format tab is active. Use options and buttons in this tab to format the WordArt text. Use the WordArt styles to apply predesigned formatting to the WordArt text. Customize the text with the Text Fill, Text Outline, and Text Effects buttons in the WordArt Styles group. Use the Text Fill button to change the fill color, the Text Outline button to change the text outline color, and use the Text Effects button to apply a variety of text effects and shapes.

Click the Text Effects button and then point to *Transform* and a side menu displays with shaping and warping options as shown in Figure 4.13. Use these options to conform the WordArt text to a specific shape.

**Figure 4.13** Text Effects Transform Side Menu

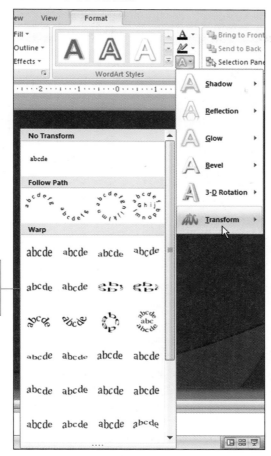

Click an option at this side menu to conform the WordArt text to a specific shape.

## Project 1k  Inserting and Formatting WordArt

1. With **PP_C4_P1.pptx** open, make sure Slide 8 is active and then click the Home tab.
2. Click the New Slide button arrow and then click the *Blank* layout.
3. Click the Insert tab.
4. Click the WordArt button in the Text group and then click the *Gradient Fill - Accent 6, Inner Shadow* option (second option from the left in the fourth row).
5. Type Addison Industries, press the Enter key, and then type 2010.
6. Click the WordArt text border to change the border from a dashed line to a solid line. (This selects the text box.)

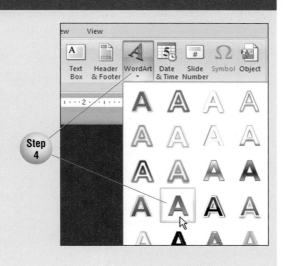

Step 4

7. Click the Text Outline button arrow in the WordArt Styles group and then click the *Dark Blue* color in the *Standard Colors* section.

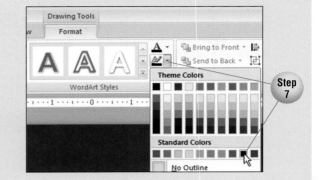

8. Click the Text Effects button, point to *Glow*, and then click *Accent color 1, 11 pt glow* at the side menu (first option from the left in the third row in the *Glow Variations* section).

9. Click the Text Effects button, point to *Transform*, and then click the *Triangle Up* option (third option from the left in the top row of the *Warp* section).

10. Click in the *Shape Height* measurement box, type 3, and then press Enter.

11. Click in the *Shape Width* measurement box, type 8, and then press Enter.

12. Click the Align button and then click *Distribute Horizontally*.

13. Click the Align button and then click *Distribute Vertically*.

14. Make Slide 6 active.

15. Apply WordArt formatting to the text in the text box by completing the following steps:
    a. Click in the text to select the text box.
    b. Click the text box border to change the border line from a dashed line to a solid line.
    c. With the Drawing Tools Format tab selected, click the More button at the right side of the WordArt style thumbnails, and then click *Fill - Accent 6, Warm Matte Bevel* option (second option from the left in the bottom row).

16. Save **PP_C4_P1.pptx**.

# Inserting Text Objects

In Chapter 2 you learned how to insert headers, footers, the date and time, and slide numbers using the Options button in Print Preview. You can also insert these objects in a presentation with buttons in the Text group in the Insert table. Click the Header & Footer button and the Header and Footer dialog box displays with the Slide tab selected. Click the Date & Time or Slide Number button and the same dialog box displays. Use options at this dialog box to insert a header, footer, date, time, and slide number in the active slide or all slides in the presentation. Click the Notes and Handouts tab if you want the objects inserted in handouts, notes pages, and outline pages.

The Text group in the Insert tab also includes a Symbol button. Click this button and the Symbol dialog box displays. Choose a symbol font with the *Font* option in the dialog box, click the desired symbol in the list box, click the Insert button, and then click the Close button. This closes the dialog box and inserts the symbol in the slide at the location of the insertion point.

1. With **PP_C4_P1.pptx** open, make Slide 1 active.
2. Insert slide numbers on each slide by completing the following steps:
   a. Click the Insert tab.
   b. Click the Slide Number button in the Text group.
   c. At the Header and Footer dialog box with the Slide tab selected, click the *Slide Number* check box to insert a check mark.
   d. Click the Apply to All button.
3. Insert your name as a footer that prints on handout pages by completing the following steps:
   a. Click the Header & Footer button in the Text group.
   b. At the Header and Footer dialog box, click the Notes and Handouts tab.
   c. Click the *Footer* check box to insert a check mark and then type your first and last names.
   d. Click the Apply to All button.
4. Insert the current date as a header that prints on handout pages by completing the following steps:
   a. Click the Date & Time button in the Text group.
   b. At the Header and Footer dialog box, click the Notes and Handouts tab.
   c. Click the *Date and Time* check box to insert a check mark.
   d. Click the Apply to All button.
5. Insert a symbol by completing the following steps:
   a. Make Slide 2 active.
   b. Click in the text containing the names, titles, and telephone numbers. (This selects the text box.)
   c. Delete the *n* in *Pena* (the fourth last name).
   d. Click the Insert tab and then click the Symbol button.
   e. At the Symbol dialog box, click the down-pointing arrow at the right side of the *Font* option box and then click *(normal text)* at the drop-down list (first option in the list).
   f. Scroll down the symbol list box and then click the ñ symbol (first symbol from the left in the twelfth row).
   g. Click the Insert button and then click the Close button.

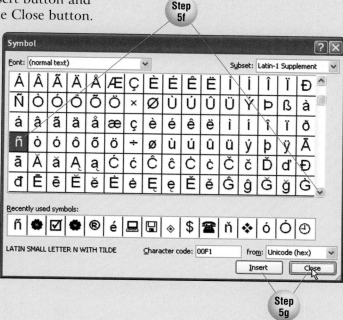

Step 5f

Step 5g

6. Insert a text box and a symbol by completing the following steps:
   a. With Slide 2 active, click the Text Box button in the Text group in the Insert tab.
   b. Click in the lower right corner of the slide below the telephone number column.
   c. Change the font size to 24 and the font color to black.
   d. Click the Insert tab.
   e. Click Symbol button.
   f. At the Symbol dialog box, click the down-pointing arrow at the right side of the *Font* option, scroll to the end of the list box, and then click *Wingdings*.
   g. Click the telephone symbol ☏ located in the top row.
   h. Click the Insert button and then click the Close button.
7. Apply a transition and sound of your choosing to all slides.
8. Run the presentation.
9. Print Slide 2.
10. Print the presentation as handouts with six slides per page.
11. Save and then close **PP_C4_P1.pptx**.

# CHAPTER summary

- Insert a text box in a slide using the Text Box button in the Text group in the Insert tab.

- Format a text box with options in the Drawing group in the Home tab or with options in the Drawing Tools Format tab.

- Select all objects in a slide by clicking the Select button in the Editing group in the Home tab and then clicking *Select All* or with the keyboard shortcut, Ctrl + A.

- Align selected objects with options from the Align button in the Arrange group in the Drawing Tools Format tab.

- Set tabs in a text box by clicking the Alignment button at the left side of the horizontal ruler until the desired symbol displays and then clicking on a specific location on the ruler. You can set a left, center, right, or decimal tab.

- Insert a shape in a slide with options at the Shapes button in the Drawing group in the Home tab or the Shapes button in the Illustrations group in the Insert tab.

- With options in the Shapes button drop-down list, you can draw a line, basic shapes, block arrows, flow chart symbols, callouts, stars, and banners.

- Copy a shape by selecting the shape, clicking the Copy button in the Clipboard group, positioning the insertion point in the desired position, and then clicking the Paste button in the Clipboard group. You can also copy a shape by holding down the Ctrl key and then dragging the shape to the desired location.

- Turn the horizontal and vertical rulers on and off with the *Ruler* check box in the Show/Hide group in the View tab and turn gridlines on and off with the *Gridlines* check box. You can also turn gridlines as well as drawing guides and the snap-to-grid feature on and off with options at the Grid and Guides dialog box. Display this dialog box by clicking the Align button in the Drawing Tools Format tab and then clicking *Grid Settings* at the drop-down list.

- You can group objects and then apply the same formatting to objects in the group. To group objects, select the objects, click the Group button in the Arrange group in the Drawing Tools Format tab, and then click *Group* at the drop-down list.

- Size images with the *Shape Height* and *Shape Width* measurement boxes in the Picture Tools Format tab or with the sizing handles that display around a selected image.

- Use the Crop button in the Size group in the Picture Tools Format tab to remove portions of an image.

- Move an image by dragging it to the new location. Move an imagine in small increments, called nudging, by holding down the Ctrl key while pressing an arrow key.

- Click the Bring to Front button in the Arrange group in the Drawing Tools Format tab or Picture Tools Format tab to move the selected object on top of other objects in the slide. Click the Send to Back button to move the selected image behind other objects in the slide.

- Insert a picture in a slide with the Picture button in the Illustrations group in the Insert tab.

- Insert a picture as a slide background with options at the Format Background dialog box. Display this dialog box by clicking the Background Styles button in the Background group in the Design tab and then clicking *Format Background*.
- Insert a clip art image with options in the Clip Art task pane. Display this task pane by clicking the Clip Art button in the Illustrations group in the Insert tab or clicking the Clip Art button in a layout content placeholder.
- Size, scale, rotate, and position an object with options in the Size and Position dialog box. Display this dialog box by clicking the Size group dialog box launcher in the Picture Tools Format tab or Drawing Tools Format tab.
- Use the WordArt feature to distort or modify text to conform to a variety of shapes. Insert WordArt by clicking the WordArt button in the Illustrations group in the Insert tab and then clicking the desired option at the drop-down list. Format WordArt text with options in the Drawing Tools Format tab.
- Click the Header & Footer button, Date & Time button, or Slide Number button in the Text group in the Insert tab to display the Header and Footer dialog box with the Slide tab selected.
- Insert a symbol in a slide with options at the Symbol dialog box. Display this dialog box by clicking the Symbol button in the Text group in the Insert tab.

# COMMANDS review

| FEATURE | TAB, GROUP | BUTTON, OPTION | KEYBOARD SHORTCUT |
|---|---|---|---|
| Text box | Insert, Text | A | |
| Shape | Insert, Illustrations or Home, Drawing | | |
| Gridlines | View, Show/Hide | ☑ Gridlines | Shift + F9 |
| Rulers | View, Show/Hide | ☑ Ruler | |
| Grid and Guides dialog box | Drawing Tools Format, Arrange | Align ▾ , Grid Settings | |
| Picture | Insert, Illustrations | | |
| Format Background dialog box | Design, Background | Background Styles ▾ , Format Background | |
| Clip Art task pane | Insert, Illustrations | | |
| Size and Position dialog box | Drawing Tools Format, Size or Picture Tools Format, Size | | |
| WordArt | Insert, Text | A | |
| Header and Footer | Insert, Text | | |
| Date and Time | Insert, Text | | |
| Slide number | Insert, Text | # | |
| Symbol dialog box | Insert, Text | Ω | |

# CONCEPTS check

## Test Your Knowledge

**Completion:** In the space provided at the right, indicate the correct term, symbol, or command.

1. The Text Box button is located in the Text group in this tab.                    _____

2. Use the sizing handles or these measurement boxes to change the size of a text box.                    _____

3. This is the keyboard shortcut to select all objects in a slide.                    _____

4. A text box, by default, contains tabs with this alignment.                    _____

5. The Drawing group in the Home tab and the Illustrations group in this tab each contain a Shapes button.                    _____

6. When dragging a shape to change the size, hold down this key to maintain the proportions of the shape.                    _____

7. Copy a shape by holding down this key while dragging the shape to the desired location.                    _____

8. Turn drawing guides on and off with options in this dialog box.                    _____

9. The Group button is located in this group in the Drawing Tools Format tab.                    _____

10. Click the Clip Art button and this displays at the right side of the screen.                    _____

11. Use this button in the Size group in the Picture Tools Format tab to remove any unnecessary parts of an image.                    _____

12. Use this feature to distort or modify text to conform to a variety of shapes.                    _____

# SKILLS check
## Demonstrate Your Proficiency

## 1 FORMAT AND ADD ENHANCEMENTS TO A TRAVEL PRESENTATION

1. Open **TravelEngland.pptx** and then save the presentation and name it **PP_C4_A1**.
2. Apply the Solstice design theme.
3. Insert the slide shown in Figure 4.14 with the following specifications:
   a. Make Slide 6 active and then insert a new slide with the *Title Only* layout.
   b. Type the title *Travel England* as shown in the slide.
   c. Draw a text box in the slide and then type the text shown in Figure 4.14. Select and then change the text font size to 40 and change the font color to Brown, Accent 5, Darker 50%.
   d. Apply *Gold, Accent 2, Lighter 80%* shape fill to the text box.
   e. Apply the *Accent color 1, 18 pt glow* shape effect (from the *Glow* side menu).
   f. Size and position the text box so it displays as shown in Figure 4.14.
4. Insert the slide shown in Figure 4.15 with the following specifications:
   a. Make Slide 1 active and then insert a new slide with the *Title Only* layout.
   b. Type the title *Upcoming Tours* as shown in the slide.
   c. Draw a text box in the slide and then set a left tab at the *0.5"* mark on the horizontal ruler, a center tab at the *4.0"* mark, and a right tab at the *7"* mark.
   d. Type the text in columns as shown in Figure 4.15. Bold the heading text *Dates*, *Duration*, and *Price*.
   e. After typing the text, select the text, change the font size to 20, the font color to Brown, Accent 5, Darker 50%, and change the line spacing to 1.5.
   f. Size and position the text box so it displays as shown in Figure 4.15.
5. Insert a picture in Slide 6 as shown in Figure 4.16 with the following specifications:
   a. Insert the picture named **WhiteHorse.jpg**.
   b. Size and move the picture so it displays as shown in Figure 4.16.
6. Insert a picture in Slide 4 as shown in Figure 4.17 with the following specifications:
   a. Insert the picture named **Stonehenge.jpg**.
   b. Crop the picture so it displays as shown in Figure 4.17.
   c. Send the picture behind the text.
   d. Size and move the bulleted text placeholder so it displays as shown in Figure 4.17.
   e. Size and move the picture so it displays as shown in Figure 4.17.
7. Insert a clip art image in Slide 7 as shown in Figure 4.18 with the following specification:
   a. In the Clip Art task pane, search only for clip art images that match the topic *Spring*.
   b. Click the image shown in the Clip Art task pane as shown in Figure 4.18 to insert it in the slide. (The original image contains pink blossoms in the tree instead of green.) If this image is not available, choose another clip art image related to "spring."
   c. Recolor the picture to Accent color 4 Light in the *Light Variations* section.
   d. Size and move the clip art image so it displays as shown in Figure 4.18.

8. Insert a picture as background in Slide 1 as shown in Figure 4.19 with the following specifications:
    a. Click the Design tab, click the Background Styles button, and then click *Format Background* at the drop-down list.
    b. At the Format Background dialog box, insert a check mark in the *Hide background graphics*.
    c. Click the File button, navigate to the PowerPoint2007L1C4 folder on your storage medium and then double-click **BigBen.jpg**.
    d. At the Format Background dialog box, click the down-pointing arrow at the right side of the *Bottom* option box in the *Stretch Options* section until -*100%* displays in the box.
    e. Close the dialog box.
    f. Size and move the title placeholder so the title displays as shown in Figure 4.19.
    g. Size and move the subtitle placeholder so the subtitle displays as shown in Figure 4.19.
9. Insert the slide shown in Figure 4.20 with the following specifications:
    a. Make Slide 8 active and then insert a new slide with the *Title Only* layout.
    b. Type the title *Travel Discounts!* as shown in Figure 4.20.
    c. Draw the shape shown in the slide in Figure 4.20 using the *Up Ribbon* shape.
    d. Apply the *Subtle Effect - Accent 1* shape style to the shape.
    e. Apply the *Accent color 2, 8 pt glow* shape effect (from the *Glow* side menu).
    f. Create a text box in the shape and then type the text shown in Figure 4.20. Change the font size for the text to 28 and change the font color to Brown, Accent 5, Darker 50%.
    g. Size and position the shape and text box so they display as shown in Figure 4.20.
10. Insert a new slide at the beginning of the presentation with the *Blank* layout. **Hint: Click above the Slide 1 miniature in the Slides/Outline pane and then click the New Slide button arrow.** Insert a logo from another presentation by completing the following steps:
    a. Open **FCTCruise.pptx** and then copy the First Choice Travel logo from Slide 1 to Slide 1 in the **PP_C4_A1.pptx** presentation.
    b. Close **FCTCruise.pptx**.
    c. With Slide 1 of **PP_C4_A1.pptx** active and the logo selected, recolor the logo (picture) to Accent color 1 Light.
    d. Position the logo attractively on the slide.
11. Apply a transition and sound of your choosing to each slide.
12. Insert slide numbers on each slide.
13. Insert a footer for notes and handouts pages that prints your first and last names.
14. Run the presentation.
15. Print the presentation as a handout with six slides per page.
16. Save and then close **PP_C4_A1.pptx**.

**Figure 4.14  Assessment 1 Step 3**

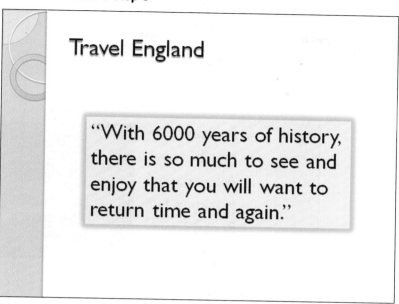

## Travel England

"With 6000 years of history, there is so much to see and enjoy that you will want to return time and again."

**Figure 4.15  Assessment 1 Step 4**

## Upcoming Tours

| Dates | Duration | Price |
|---|---|---|
| April 17 – 24 | 8 days, 7 nights | $2499 pp |
| May 15 – 22 | 8 days, 7 nights | $2499 pp |
| June 12 – 19 | 8 days, 7 nights | $2999 pp |
| July 8 – 18 | 11 days, 10 nights | $3599 pp |
| July 24 – 31 | 8 days, 7 nights | $3099 pp |

**Figure 4.16  Assessment 1 Step 5**

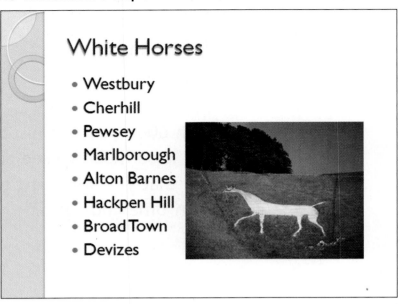

**Figure 4.17  Assessment 1 Step 6**

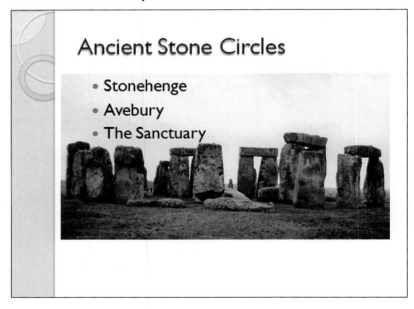

**Figure 4.18  Assessment 1 Step 7**

**Figure 4.19  Assessment 1 Step 8**

**Figure 4.20 Assessment 1 Step 9**

## Assessment

### 2 FORMAT AND ADD ENHANCEMENTS TO A GARDENING PRESENTATION

1. Open **PerennialsPresentation.pptx** and then save the presentation and name it **PP_C4_A2**.
2. Insert the slide shown in Figure 4.21 with the following specifications:
   a. Make Slide 2 active and then insert a new slide with the *Blank* layout.
   b. Hide the background graphics.
   c. Insert the WordArt text using *Gradient Fill - Accent 6, Inner Shadow* (second option from the left in the fourth row).
   d. Change the shape of the WordArt to *Wave 1*.
   e. Change the height of the WordArt to *3″* and the width to *9″*.
   f. Display the Format Background dialog box (for help, see Assessment 1, Step 8), click the *Gradient fill* option in the *Fill* section, change the *Preset colors* option to *Daybreak*, and then close the dialog box.
   g. Position the WordArt text as shown in Figure 4.21.
3. Insert the slide shown in Figure 4.22 with the following specifications:
   a. Make Slide 8 active and then insert a new slide with the *Title Only* layout.
   b. Insert the title *English/French Translations* as shown.
   c. Insert a text box, change the font size to 28, change the font color to Light Blue, Accent 5, Darker 25%, set left tabs at the 0.5″ and the 4″ mark on the horizontal ruler, and then type the text in columns. Bold the headings *English Name* and *French Name* and use the Symbol dialog box to insert the special symbols in the French names.
   d. If necessary, move the text box so it is positioned as shown in Figure 4.22.

4. Make Slide 4 active and then make the following changes:
   a. Select the bulleted text and then change the line spacing to 2.0.
   b. With the bulleted text selected, set the bulleted text in two columns. ***Hint: Refer to Project 1c in Chapter 3.***
   c. Make sure four bulleted items display in each column.
5. Make Slide 5 active and then insert a clip art image related to *garden* or *gardening*. Size and position the clip art attractively in the slide.
6. Select and then delete Slide 10.
7. Insert the slide shown in Figure 4.23 with the following specifications:
   a. Make Slide 9 active and then insert a new slide with the *Title Only* layout.
   b. Insert the title *Gardening Magazines*.
   c. Create the top shape using the *Bevel* shape.
   d. Draw a text box inside the shape, change the font size to 32, turn on bold, turn on italic, change the alignment to Center, and then type the text in the top shape.
   e. Select the shape and the text box and then copy them two times.
   f. Change the text in the second and third shapes to match what you see in Figure 4.23.
   g. Size and position the shapes and text boxes as shown in Figure 4.23
8. Make Slide 7 active and then insert a clip art image of your choosing.
9. Run the presentation.
10. Print the presentation as a handout with six slides per page.
11. Save **PP_C4_A2.pptx**.

**Figure 4.21  Assessment 2 Step 2**

**Figure 4.22  Assessment 2 Step 3**

**Figure 4.23  Assessment 2 Step 7**

# 3 COPY A PICTURE FROM A WEB SITE TO A PRESENTATION

1. With **PP_C4_A2.pptx** open, make Slide 6 active.
2. Use the Help feature to find information on copying a picture from a Web page. (Begin by entering "insert a picture or clip art" in the PowerPoint Help window and then press Enter. Click the <u>Insert a picture or clip art</u> hyperlink and then click the "<u>Copy a picture from a Web page</u>" hyperlink.)
3. Using the information you learned about copying a Web page, open your Web browser and then use a search engine of your choosing to search for a picture of at least one flower mentioned in the slide.
4. Copy the picture to the slide and then size and move the picture so it is positioned attractively in the slide. (Consider inserting at least one more picture of one of the flowers mentioned.)
5. Print only Slide 6.
6. Run the presentation.
7. Save and then close **PP_C4_A2.pptx**.

# CASE study
## *Apply Your Skills*

## Part 1

You work for Honoré Financial Services and the Office Manager, Jason Monroe, has asked you to prepare a presentation for a community workshop he will be conducting next week. Open the Word document named **HonoreFinancialServices.docx** and then use the information in the document to create a presentation with the following specifications:

- Slide 1: Include the company name Honoré Financial Services (use the Symbol feature to create the é in Honoré) and the subtitle *Managing Your Money*.
- Slide 2: Insert the word *Budgeting* as WordArt.
- Slides 3, 4, and 5: Use the bulleted and numbered information to create these slides.
- Slide 6: Create a text box, set tabs, and then type the information in the *Managing Records* section that is set in columns.
- Slide 7: Create a shape and then insert a text box inside the shape with the following slogan "*Retirement Planning Made Easy*".
- Include at least one picture and one clip art in the presentation.

Apply a design theme of your choosing and add any additional features to improve the visual appeal of the presentation. Insert a transition and sound to each slide and then run the presentation. Save the presentation and name it **PP_C4_CS_P1.pptx**. Print the presentation as a handout with four slides per page.

**Part 2**

Mr. Monroe will be conducting a free workshop titled *Financial Planning for the College Student*. Create a slide in the **PP_C4_CS_P1.pptx** presentation (make it the last slide in the presentation) that includes a shape with a text box inside and include information about the workshop inside the text box. You determine the day, the time, and the location for the workshop. Print the slide.

**Part 3**

Mr. Monroe would like to post the information about the workshop in various locations in the community and wants to print a number of copies. You decide to copy the shape and the text box and then insert them in a blank Word document. In Word, change the orientation of the page to landscape, increase the size of the shape and text box, and then drag the shape and text box to the middle of the page. Save the Word document and name it **PP_C4_CS_P3**. Print and then close **PP_C4_CS_P3.docx**.

**Part 4**

Mr. Monroe has asked you to locate online finance and/or budgeting resources such as newsletters and magazines. He would like you to locate resources and then create a slide with hyperlinks to the resources. Locate at least two online resources and then insert this information with the hyperlinks in a new slide at the end of the **PP_C4_CS_P1.pptx** presentation. Print the slide and then save and close the presentation.

# Creating and Formatting PowerPoint Presentations

## ASSESSING proficiency

In this unit, you have learned to create, print, save, close, open, view, run, edit, and format a PowerPoint presentation. You also learned how to add transitions and sound to presentations; rearrange slides; customize presentations by changing the design theme; and add visual appeal to slides by inserting text boxes, shapes, pictures, clip art, and symbols.

*powerpoint Unit 1*

*Note: Before beginning computer assessments, copy to your storage medium the PowerPoint2007U1 folder from the PowerPoint2007 folder on the CD that accompanies this textbook and then make PowerPoint2007U1 the active folder.*

### Assessment 1 Prepare, Format, and Enhance a Conference Presentation

1. Create a presentation with the text shown in Figure U1.1 using a design theme of your choosing. Use the appropriate slide layout for each slide. After creating the slides, complete a spelling check on the text in slides.
2. Add a transition and sound of your choosing to all slides.
3. Save the presentation and name it **PP_U1_A1**.
4. Run the presentation.
5. Make Slide 1 active and then find all occurrences of *Area* and replace it with *Market*.
6. Make the following changes to Slide 2:
   a. Type Net Income per Common Share over *Net Income*.
   b. Delete *Return on Average Equity*.
7. Make the following changes to Slide 4:
   a. Delete *Shopping*.
   b. Type Business Finance between *Personal Finance* and *E-mail*.
8. Rearrange the slides in the presentation so they are in the following order (only the slide titles are shown below):
   Slide 1  =  CORNERSTONE SYSTEMS
   Slide 2  =  Corporate Vision
   Slide 3  =  Future Goals
   Slide 4  =  Industrial Market
   Slide 5  =  Consumer Market
   Slide 6  =  Financial Review
9. Increase spacing to 1.5 for the bulleted text in Slides 2, 3, 5, and 6.
10. Make Slide 4 active, increase the spacing to 2.0 for the bulleted text, and then format the bulleted text into two columns with three entries in each column.

11. Apply a different theme color to the presentation.
12. Save and then run the presentation.
13. Print the presentation as a handout with six slides per page.
14. Display the Reuse Slides task pane, browse to the PowerPoint2007U1 folder on your storage medium, and then double-click *MarketingPresentation.pptx*.
15. Insert the *Department Reports* slide below Slide 4.
16. Insert the *Services* slide below Slide 2.
17. Close the Reuse Slides task pane.
18. Make Slide 8 active, select the bulleted text, and then create and apply a custom bullet using a money symbol in a complementary color. (You can find a money symbol in the normal font in the Symbol dialog box.)
19. With Slide 8 active, insert a clip art image related to *money* or *finances*. Size and position the clip art attractively in the slide.
20. Move Slide 4 (*Future Goals*) to the end of the presentation.
21. Insert a new slide with the *Title and Content* layout at the end of the presentation with the following specifications:
    a. Insert *Future Goals* as the title.
    b. Type International Market as the first bulleted item and then press Enter.
    c. Copy *Acquisitions*, *Production*, *Technology*, and *Marketing* from Slide 8 and paste them in the content area of the new slide below the first bulleted text. (When copied, the items should be preceded by a bullet. If a bullet displays on a blank line below the last text item, press the Backspace key twice.)
    d. Select the bulleted text and then change the line spacing to 1.5.
22. Make Slide 8 active, select the bulleted items, and then apply numbering.
23. Make Slide 9 active, select the bulleted items, and then apply numbering and change the beginning number to 6.
24. With Slide 9 active, create a new slide with the *Blank* layout with the following specifications:
    a. Insert the picture named *Nightscape.jpg* as a background picture and hide the background graphics. *Hint: Do this with the Background Styles button in the Design tab.*
    b. Create a text box toward the top of the slide, change the font color to white, increase the font size to 36, and then change the alignment to center.
    c. Type National Sales Meeting, press Enter, type New York City, press Enter, and then type March 3 - 6, 2010.
    d. Move and/or size the text box so the text is positioned centered above the buildings in the picture.
25. Insert slide numbers on each slide.
26. Insert a footer for notes and handouts pages that prints your first and last names.
27. Save and then run the presentation.
28. Print the presentation as a handout with six slides per page.
29. Close **PP_U1_A1.pptx**.

**Figure U1.1  Assessment 1**

Slide 1    Title    =    CORNERSTONE SYSTEMS
          Subtitle =    Executive Conference

Slide 2    Title    =    Financial Review
          Bullets  =
- Net Revenues
- Operating Income
- Net Income
- Return on Average Equity
- Return on Average Asset

Slide 3    Title    =    Corporate Vision
          Bullets  =
- Expansion
- Increased Productivity
- Consumer Satisfaction
- Employee Satisfaction
- Area Visibility

Slide 4    Title    =    Consumer Area
          Bullets  =
- Travel
- Shopping
- Entertainment
- Personal Finance
- E-mail

Slide 5    Title    =    Industrial Area
          Bullets  =
- Finance
- Education
- Government
- Production
- Manufacturing
- Utilities

Slide 6    Title    =    Future Goals
          Bullets  =
- Domestic Area
- Acquisitions
- Production
- Technology
- Marketing

## Assessment 2 Format and Enhance a Kraft Artworks Presentation

1. Open **ArtworksPresentation.pptx** and then save the presentation and name it **PP_U1_A2**.
2. With Slide 1 active, insert the text *Kraft Artworks* as WordArt and apply at least the following formatting:
   a. Change the shape of the WordArt.
   b. Change the size so the WordArt better fills the slide.
   c. Change the fill to a purple color.
   d. Apply any other formatting to improve the visual appeal of the WordArt.
3. Duplicate Slides 2 and 3.
4. Change the goal number in Slide 4 from *1* to *3* and change the goal text to *Conduct six art workshops at the Community Center.*
5. Change the goal number in Slide 5 from *2* to *4* and change the goal text to *Provide recycled material to public schools for art classes.*
6. With Slide 5 active, insert a new slide with the *Title Only* layout with the following specifications:
   a. Insert the title *Clients* and then format, size, and position the title in the same manner as the title in Slide 5.
   b. Insert a text box, change the font to Comic Sans MS, the font size to 20, the font color to purple, and then type the following text in columns (you determine the tab settings):

   | School | Contact | Number |
   |---|---|---|
   | Logan Elementary School | Maya Jones | 555-0882 |
   | Cedar Elementary School | George Ferraro | 555-3211 |
   | Sunrise Elementary School | Avery Burns | 555-3444 |
   | Hillside Middle School | Joanna Myers | 555-2211 |
   | Douglas Middle School | Ray Murphy | 555-8100 |

   c. Select all of the text in the text box and then change the line spacing to 1.5.
7. With Slide 6 active, insert a new slide with the *Blank* layout, hide the background graphic, and then create the slide shown in Figure U1.2 with the following specifications:
   a. Use the *Explosion 1* shape to create the first shape.
   b. Change the fill color of the shape to Gold, Accent 2, Lighter 40% and apply the *Accent color 3, 18 pt glow* effect.
   c. Insert a text box inside the shape, change the font to 40-point Comic Sans MS bold in purple color, change the alignment to center, and then type the text shown in Figure U1.2.
   d. Copy the shape and the text box twice.
   e. Type the appropriate text in each text box as shown in Figure U1.2.
8. With Slide 7 active, insert a new slide with the *Blank* layout, hide the background graphic, and then create the slide shown in Figure U1.3 with the following specifications:
   a. Set the text in the two text boxes at the left and right side of the slide in 54-point Comic Sans MS bold and in purple color. Rotate, size, and position the two text boxes as shown in Figure U1.3.
   b. Use the *Explosion 1* shape to create the shape in the middle of the slide.
   c. Change the fill color of the shape to Gold, Accent 2, Lighter 40%, apply the *Perspective Diagonal Upper Left* shadow effect, and change the shape outline color to purple and the weight to 2¼ pt.

d. Insert a text box in the middle of the shape, change the font to 28-point Comic Sans MS bold in purple color, change the alignment to center, and then type the text inside the shape as shown in Figure U1.3.

9. Create a footer that prints your first and last names and the current date on handout pages.

10. Print the presentation as a handout with four slides per page.

11. Save and then close **PP_U1_A2.pptx**

**Figure U1.2 Assessment 2, Slide 7**

**Figure U1.3 Assessment 2, Slide 8**

## Assessment 3 Create and Apply a Custom Theme to a Job Search Presentation

1. At a blank presentation, apply the *Civic* design.
2. Create custom theme colors named with your first and last names that change the following colors:
   a. Change the Text/Background - Dark 1 color to Dark Yellow, Followed Hyperlink, Lighter 80%.
   b. Change the Text/Background - Dark 2 color to White, Text 1.
   c. Change the Text/Background - Light 2 color to Turquoise, Hyperlink, Darker 25%.
   d. Change the Accent 1 color to Dark Red.
   e. Change the Accent 2 and the Accent 3 color to Red, Accent 1, Darker 50%.
3. Create custom theme fonts named with your first and last names that changes the *Heading font* to Constantia and the *Body font* to Cambria.
4. Save the current theme as a custom theme named with your first and last names. **Hint: Do this at the Save Current Theme dialog box.**
5. Close the presentation without saving it.
6. Open **JobSearch.pptx** and then save the presentation and name it **PP_U1_A3**.
7. Apply the custom theme named with your first and last names.
8. Insert a clip art image in Slide 5 related to *telephone*, *people*, or *Internet*. You determine the size and position of the image.
9. Insert a clip art image in Slide 6 related to *clock* or *time*. You determine the size and position of the image.
10. Improve the visual display of text in Slides 2, 3, 7, 8, and 9 by increasing the spacing between items and positioning the text placeholders attractively in the slides.
11. Insert the current date and slide number on all slides in the presentation. (The slide numbers will appear in the round circle that is part of the design theme.)
12. Create the header *Job Search Seminar*, the footer *Employment Strategies*, and insert the date and page number for notes and handouts.
13. Add the speaker note *Hand out list of Internet employment sites.* to Slide 5.
14. Apply a transition and sound of your choosing to all slides in the presentation.
15. Save and then run the presentation.
16. Print the presentation as a handout with six slides per page.
17. Print Slide 5 as notes pages.
18. Save and then close **PP_U1_A3.pptx**.
19. Display a blank presentation and then delete the custom theme colors, custom theme fonts, and custom theme you created for this assessment.
20. Close the presentation without saving it.

## Assessment 4 Format and Enhance a Medical Plans Presentation

1. Open **MedicalPlans.pptx** and then save the presentation and name it **PP_U1_A4**.
2. Apply a design theme of your choosing.
3. Create a new Slide between Slides 1 and 2 that contains a shape with the text *Medical Plans 2009 - 2010* in a text box inside the shape. You determine the format, position, and size of the shape and text box.

4. Change the bullets to custom bullets (you determine the picture or symbol) for the bullets in Slides 3, 4, and 5.

5. Insert a clip art image related to *medicine* in Slide 4. You determine the color, size, and position of the image.

6. Make Slide 5 active, and then apply the following formatting:

    a. Move the insertion point to the beginning of *Eugene* and then press the Enter key.

    b. Select all of the bulleted text and then change the line spacing to 2.0.

    c. With the bulleted text selected, format the text into two columns. (Make sure each column contains four entries.)

    d. Size and/or move the placeholder so the bulleted text displays attractively in the slide.

7. Apply any additional formatting or elements to improve the visual appeal of the slides.

8. Add a transition and sound of your choosing to the presentation.

9. Run the presentation.

10. Print the presentation as a handout with three slides per page.

11. Save and then close **PP_U1_A4.pptx**.

# WRITING activities

The following activities provide you with the opportunity to practice your writing skills along with demonstrating an understanding of some of the important PowerPoint features you have mastered in this unit. Use correct spelling, grammar, and appropriate word choices.

## Activity 1 Prepare and Format a Health Plan Presentation

Open Word and then open, print, and close **KeyLifeHealthPlan.docx**. Looking at the printing of this document, create a presentation in PowerPoint that presents the main points of the plan. (Use bullets in the presentation.) Add a transition and sound to the slides. Apply formatting and/or insert images to enhance the visual appeal of the presentation. Save the presentation and name it **PP_U1_Act01**. Run the presentation. Print the presentation as a handout with six slides per page. Save and then close **PP_U1_Act01.pptx**.

## Activity 2 Prepare and Format a Clip Art Presentation

At a blank presentation, use the Help feature to find information on inserting a picture or clip art image. *Hint: Display the PowerPoint Help window, type* insert picture or clip art*, press Enter, and then click the* Insert a picture or clip art *hyperlink that displays in the window.* Print and then read the information and then use the information to create a presentation that includes at least four slides. Format and add visual appeal to the presentation. With the presentation still open, display the Clip Art task pane and then click the Clip art on Office Online hyperlink that displays at the bottom of the task pane. (Your computer needs to be connected to the Internet to complete this activity.) Look over the information that displays at the Microsoft Office Online Clip Art Web site and then create at least three additional slides that contain information on the site. For example, you might create a slide that summarizes the options at the left side of the page, create a slide that includes a clip art from the featured collection, and a slide that lists some interesting clip art categories. Save the completed presentation and name it **PP_U1_Act02**. Add a transition and sound of your choosing to each slide and then run the presentation. Print the presentation as a handout with four slides per page. Close the **PP_U1_Act02.pptx** presentation.

### Analyze a Magazine Web Site

Make sure you are connected to the Internet and then explore the Time® magazine Web site at www.time.com. Discover the following information for the site:

- Magazine sections
- The type of information presented in each section
- Services available
- Information on how to subscribe

Use the information you discovered about the Time magazine Web site and create a PowerPoint presentation that presents the information in a clear, concise, and logical manner. Add formatting and enhancements to the presentation to make it more interesting. When the presentation is completed, save it and name it **PP_U1_TimeMag**. Run, print, and then close the presentation.

Microsoft®

# PowerPoint®

## Unit 2: Customizing and Enhancing PowerPoint Presentations

➤ Creating Tables, Charts, and SmartArt Graphics

➤ Using Slide Masters and Action Buttons

➤ Applying Custom Animation and Setting Up Shows

➤ Integrating, Reviewing, Protecting, and Saving Presentations

PowerPoint

# Benchmark Microsoft® PowerPoint 2007

## Microsoft Certified Application Specialist Skills—Unit 2

| Reference No. | Skill | Pages |
|---|---|---|
| **1** | **Creating and Formatting Presentations** | |
| 1.1 | Create new presentations | |
| 1.1.2 | Create presentations from templates | 235-237 |
| 1.1.4 | Create presentations from Microsoft Office Word outlines | 298-299 |
| 1.2 | Customize slide masters | |
| 1.2.1 | Apply themes to slide masters | 222-224 |
| 1.2.2 | Format slide master backgrounds | 223-226 |
| 1.3 | Add elements to slide masters | 221-235 |
| **2** | **Creating and Formatting Slide Content** | |
| 2.2 | Manipulate text | |
| 2.2.1 | Cut, copy, and paste text (paste special) | 305-307 |
| 2.3 | Add and link existing content to presentations | |
| 2.3.1 | Reuse slides from an existing presentation (apply slide masters) | 226-227 |
| 2.3.3 | Insert hyperlinks | 247-249 |
| 2.3.4 | Insert media clips | 285-288 |
| 2.4 | Apply, customize, modify, and remove animations | |
| 2.4.1 | Apply built-in animations | 260-261 |
| 2.4.2 | Modify animations | 261, 265-268 |
| 2.4.3 | Create custom animations | 262-272 |
| **3** | **Working with Visual Content** | |
| 3.1 | Create SmartArt diagrams | |
| 3.1.1 | Create a SmartArt diagram | 184-187, 189-192 |
| 3.1.2 | Create SmartArt diagrams from bullet points | 189-191 |
| 3.2 | Modify SmartArt diagrams | |
| 3.2.1 | Add text to SmartArt diagrams | 185, 187, 191-192 |
| 3.2.2 | Change theme colors | 187-188, 190, 192 |
| 3.2.3 | Add effects using SmartArt Styles | 187-188, 192 |
| 3.2.4 | Change the layout of diagrams | 186 |
| 3.2.5 | Change the orientation of charts | 188, 190 |
| 3.2.6 | Add or remove shapes within SmartArt | 185, 190 |
| 3.2.7 | Change diagram types | 186 |
| 3.6 | Insert and modify charts | |
| 3.6.1 | Insert charts | 192-202 |
| 3.6.2 | Change chart types | 196-197 |
| 3.6.3 | Format fill and other effects | 199-201 |
| 3.6.4 | Add chart elements | 197-199 |
| 3.7 | Insert and modify tables | |
| 3.7.1 | Insert tables in a slide | 176-178 |
| 3.7.2 | Apply Table Styles to tables | 178-180 |
| 3.7.3 | Change alignment and orientation of table text | 180-183 |
| 3.7.4 | Add images to tables | 182 |
| **4** | **Collaborating on and Delivering Presentations** | |
| 4.1 | Review presentations | |
| 4.1.1 | Insert, delete, and modify comments | 309-312 |
| 4.1.2 | Show and hide markup | 310-312 |
| 4.2 | Protect presentations | |
| 4.2.1 | Add digital signatures to presentations | 316-319 |
| 4.3 | Secure and share presentations | |
| 4.3.1 | Identify presentation features not supported by previous versions | 319-321 |
| 4.3.2 | Remove inappropriate information using Document Inspector | 314-316 |
| 4.3.3 | Restrict permissions to a document using Information Rights Management (IRM) | 320-321 |
| 4.3.4 | Mark presentations as final | 319, 321 |
| 4.3.6 | Save presentations as appropriate file types | 322-323, 325-330 |
| 4.4 | Prepare printed materials | |
| 4.4.1 | Customize handout masters | 237-239 |
| 4.5 | Prepare for and rehearse presentation delivery | |
| 4.5.1 | Show only specific slides in presentations | 280-284 |
| 4.5.2 | Rehearse and time the delivery of a presentation | 277-278 |
| 4.5.4 | Package presentations for a CD | 331-332 |
| 4.5.5 | Set slide show options | 276-282 |

# CHAPTER 5

# Creating Tables, Charts, and SmartArt Graphics

## PERFORMANCE OBJECTIVES

**Upon successful completion of Chapter 5, you will be able to:**

- Create and format a table
- Modify the design and layout of a table
- Insert an image in a table
- Create SmartArt diagrams
- Modify the design and layout of SmartArt
- Create a SmartArt graphic with bulleted text
- Create and format charts
- Modify the design and layout of charts
- Select and format chart elements
- Create, edit, and format a photo album

powerpoint Chapter 5

**Tutorial 5.1**
Graphically Representing and
Arranging Data

If you want to present numbers and lists in a slide, consider inserting the information in a table. Use the Tables feature to create data in columns and rows in a manner similar to a spreadsheet. Display data in a slide in a more visual way by creating a SmartArt diagram. The SmartArt feature provides a number of predesigned diagrams and organizational charts. You can create a SmartArt diagram and then modify the design and layout of the diagram.

While a table does an adequate job of representing data, you can create a chart from data to provide a more visual representation of the data. A chart is sometimes referred to as a *graph* and is a picture of numeric data. If you have Microsoft Excel installed on your computer, you can create a chart in a PowerPoint slide. If you do not have Excel installed on your computer, PowerPoint uses the Microsoft Graph feature to create your chart. Projects and assessments in this chapter assume that you have Excel installed on your computer.

You can create a photo album presentation to attractively display personal or business photographs. With the Photo Album feature you can insert pictures and then format the appearance of the pictures in the presentation.

*Note: Before beginning computer projects, copy to your storage medium the PowerPoint2007C5 folder from the PowerPoint2007 folder on the CD that accompanies this textbook and then make PowerPoint2007C5 the active folder.*

# roject ❶ Create a Company Sales Conference Presentation

You will create a sales conference presentation for Nature's Way that includes a table, a column chart, a pie chart, and four SmartArt graphics.

## QUICK STEPS

**Insert a Table**
1. Click Insert Table button in content placeholder.
2. Type number of columns.
3. Press Tab.
4. Type number of rows.
5. Click OK.
OR
1. Click Insert tab.
2. Click Table button.
3. Drag in grid to desired number of columns and rows.

**HINT**

Add a row to the bottom of a table by positioning the insertion point in the last cell and then pressing the Tab key.

Table

**HINT**

You can move text to a different cell by selecting the text and then dragging the selected text to a different cell.

# Creating a Table

Use the Tables feature to create boxes of information called *cells*. A cell is the intersection between a row and a column. A cell can contain text, characters, numbers, data, graphics, or formulas. If you want to arrange the content of a slide in columns and rows, insert a new slide with the slide layout that includes a content placeholder. Click the Insert Table button in the content placeholder and the Insert Table dialog box displays. At the Insert Table dialog box, type the number of columns, press the Tab key, type the number of rows, and then press Enter. You can also insert a table using the Table button in the Tables group in the Insert tab. Click the Table button, drag the mouse down and to the right to select the desired number of columns and rows, and then click the left mouse button.

When you create a table, the insertion point is located in the cell in the upper left corner of the table. Cells in a table contain a cell designation. Columns in a table are lettered from left to right, beginning with *A*. Rows in a table are numbered from top to bottom beginning with *1*. The cell in the upper left corner of the table is cell A1. The cell to the right of A1 is B1, the cell to the right of B1 is C1, and so on.

## Entering Text in Cells

With the insertion point positioned in a cell, type or edit text. Move the insertion point to other cells with the mouse by clicking in the desired cell. If you are using the keyboard, press the Tab key to move the insertion point to the next cell or press Shift + Tab to move the insertion point to the previous cell.

If the text you type does not fit on one line, it wraps to the next line within the same cell. Or, if you press Enter within a cell, the insertion point is moved to the next line within the same cell. The cell vertically lengthens to accommodate the text, and all cells in that row also lengthen. Pressing the Tab key in a table causes the insertion point to move to the next cell in the table. If you want to move the insertion point to a tab stop within a cell, press Ctrl + Tab. If the insertion point is located in the last cell of the table and you press the Tab key, PowerPoint adds another row to the table.

# Selecting Cells

You can apply formatting to an entire table or to specific cells, rows, or columns in a table. To identify cells for formatting, select the specific cells using the mouse or the keyboard. Press the Tab key to select the next cell or press Shift + Tab to select the previous cell. Refer to Table 5.1 for additional methods for selecting in a table.

**Table 5.1** Selecting in a Table

| To select this | Do this |
|---|---|
| A cell | Position the mouse pointer at left side of cell until pointer turns into a small, black arrow, and then click the left mouse button. |
| A row | Position the mouse pointer outside the table at the left edge of the row until the pointer turns into a small, black arrow pointing right, and then click the left mouse button. Drag to select multiple rows. |
| A column | Position the mouse pointer outside the table at the top of the column until the pointer turns into a small, black arrow pointing down, and then click the left mouse button. Drag to select multiple columns. |
| All cells in a table | Drag to select all cells or press Ctrl + A. |
| Text within a cell | Position the mouse pointer at the beginning of the text and then hold down the left mouse button as you drag the mouse across the text. (When a cell is selected, the cell background color changes to blue. When text within cells is selected, only those lines containing text are selected.) |

## Project 1a  Creating a Table

1. Open **Conference.pptx** and then save the presentation and name it **PP_C5_P1**.
2. Make Slide 4 active.
3. Insert a table in the slide and enter text into the cells by completing the following steps:
   a. Click the Insert Table button located in the middle of the slide in the content placeholder.
   b. At the Insert Table dialog box, type 2 in the *Number of columns* text box.
   c. Press the Tab key.
   d. Type 5 in the *Number of rows* text box.
   e. Click OK or press Enter.

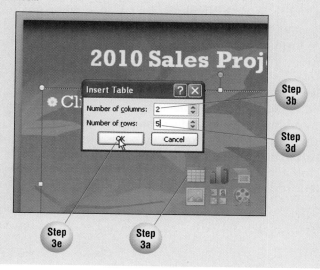

Step 3b
Step 3d
Step 3e
Step 3a

f. Type the text as displayed in the table below. Press the Tab key to move the insertion point to the next cell or press Shift + Tab to move the insertion point to the previous cell. Do not press Tab after typing the last cell entry.

**2010 Sales Projections**

**Step 3f** →

| Region | Sales |
|--------|-------|
| North | $1,683,000 |
| South | $1,552,000 |
| East | $1,778,000 |
| West | $1,299,000 |

4. Apply formatting to text in specific cells by completing the following steps:
   a. With the insertion point positioned in the table, press Ctrl + A to select all of the text in the table.
   b. Click the Home tab and then change the font size to 32.
   c. Looking at the text set in 32 point size, you decide that you want the text below the headings set in a smaller point size. To do this, position the mouse pointer at the left edge of the second row (to the left of the cell containing *North*) until the pointer turns into a small, black, right-pointing arrow. Hold down the left mouse button, drag down so the remaining rows are selected, and then change the font size to 28.
   d. Click outside the table to deselect it.
5. Save **PP_C5_P1.pptx**.

**HINT**
Draw a freeform table by clicking the Insert tab, clicking the Table button, and then clicking the *Draw Table* option. Drag in the document to create the table.

Draw Table

Eraser

Shading

Borders

Effects

# Changing Table Design

When you create a table, the Table Tools Design tab is selected that contains a number of options for enhancing the appearance of the table as shown in Figure 5.1. With options in the Table Styles group, apply a predesigned style that applies color and border lines to a table. Maintain further control over the predesigned style formatting applied to columns and rows with options in the Table Style Options group. For example, if you want your first column to be formatted differently than the other columns in the table, insert a check mark in the *First Column* check box. Apply additional design formatting to cells in a table with the Shading, Borders, and Effects buttons in the Table Styles group. Draw a table or draw additional rows and/or columns in a table by clicking the Draw Table button in the Draw Borders group. Click this button and the mouse pointer turns into a pencil. Drag in the table to create the desired columns and rows. Click the Eraser button and the mouse pointer turns into an eraser. Drag through the column and/or row lines you want to erase in the table.

**Figure 5.1** Table Tools Design Tab

## Project 1b  Modifying the Table Design

1. With **PP_C5_P1.pptx** open, make sure Slide 4 is active, the table is selected, and the Table Tools Design tab is selected.
2. Click the *First Column* check box in the Table Style Options group to insert a check mark. (This applies bold formatting to the text in the first column.)
3. Click the More button that displays at the right side of the Table Styles thumbnails and then click the *Themed Style 1 - Accent 6* option (last option in the top row).

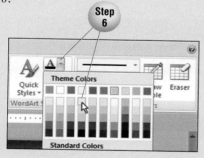

4. Select the first row of the table.
5. Click the Quick Styles button in the WordArt Styles group and then click *Fill - Accent 3, Outline - Text 2* option (last option in the top row).
6. Click the Text Fill button arrow in the WordArt Styles group and then click *Light Yellow, Text 2, Darker 10%*.

7. Click the Text Outline button arrow in the WordArt Styles group and then click *Green, Accent 6, Lighter 40%*.
8. Click the Pen Weight button arrow in the Draw Borders group and then click *2¼ pt*. (This activates the Draw Table button.)
9. Click the Pen Color button in the Draw Borders group and then click *Green, Accent 6, Darker 25%*.

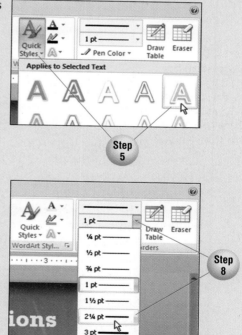

10. Draw along the border that separates the two columns from the top of the first row to the bottom of the last row.
11. Draw along the border that separates the first row from the second row.
12. Click the Draw Table button to deactivate it.
13. Save **PP_C5_P1.pptx**.

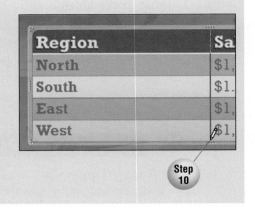

Step 10

**HINT**

If you make a mistake while formatting a table, immediately click the Undo button on the Quick Access toolbar.

# Changing Table Layout

To further customize a table consider changing the table layout by inserting or deleting columns and rows and specifying cell alignments. Change table layout with options at the Table Tools Layout tab shown in Figure 5.2. Use options and buttons in the tab to select specific cells, delete and insert rows and columns, merge and split cells, specify cell and table height and width and text alignment in cells, and arrange elements in a slide.

**Figure 5.2** Table Tools Layout Tab

## Project 1c  Modifying Table Layout

1. With **PP_C5_P1.pptx** open, make sure Slide 4 is active.
2. Click in any cell in the table and then click the Table Tools Layout tab.
3. Click in the cell containing the word *East*.
4. Click the Insert Above button in the Rows & Columns group.
5. Type Central in the new cell at the left, press the Tab key, and then type $1,024,000 in the new cell at the right.
6. Click in the cell containing the word *Region*.
7. Click the Insert Left button in the Rows & Columns group.
8. Click the Merge Cells button in the Merge group.
9. Type Sales Projections in the new cell.

Step 4

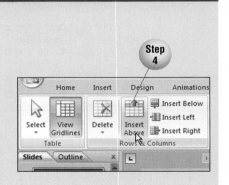

10. Click the Text Direction button in the Alignment group and then click *Rotate all text 270°* at the drop-down list.

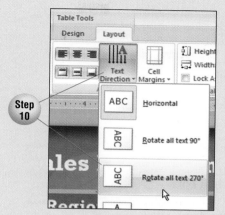

Step 10

11. Click the Center button in the Alignment group and then click the Center Vertically button in the Alignment group.
12. Click in the *Table Column Width* measurement box in the Cell Size group, type 1.2, and then press Enter.
13. Click the Table Tools Design tab.
14. Click the Borders button arrow in the Table Styles group (the name of the button changes depending on the last action performed) and then click *Bottom Border* at the drop-down list.

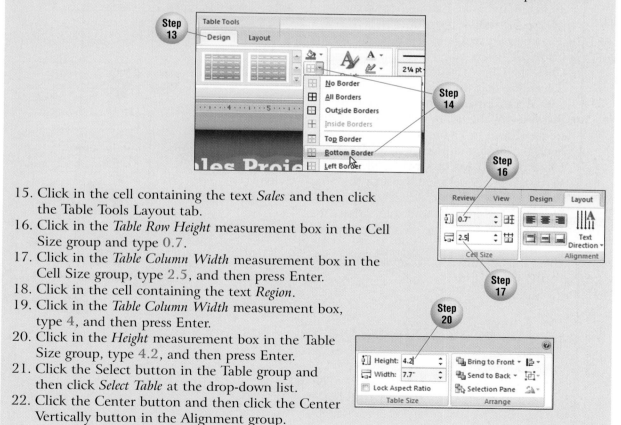

Step 13

Step 14

Step 16

Step 17

Step 20

15. Click in the cell containing the text *Sales* and then click the Table Tools Layout tab.
16. Click in the *Table Row Height* measurement box in the Cell Size group and type 0.7.
17. Click in the *Table Column Width* measurement box in the Cell Size group, type 2.5, and then press Enter.
18. Click in the cell containing the text *Region*.
19. Click in the *Table Column Width* measurement box, type 4, and then press Enter.
20. Click in the *Height* measurement box in the Table Size group, type 4.2, and then press Enter.
21. Click the Select button in the Table group and then click *Select Table* at the drop-down list.
22. Click the Center button and then click the Center Vertically button in the Alignment group.

23. After looking at the text in cells, you decide that you want the text in the second column left-aligned. To do this, complete the following steps:
   a. Click in the cell containing the text *Region*.
   b. Click the Select button in the Table group and then click *Select Column* at the drop-down list.
   c. Click the Align Text Left button in the Alignment group.
   d. Click in any cell in the table.

24. Align the table by completing the following steps:
   a. Click the Home tab.
   b. Click the Arrange button in the Drawing group, point to *Align*, and then click *Distribute Horizontally*.
   c. Click the Arrange button, point to *Align*, and then click *Distribute Vertically*.
   d. Looking at the table, you decide that it should be moved down in the slide. To do this, position the mouse pointer on the table border until the pointer displays with a four-headed arrow attached. Hold down the left mouse button, drag down approximately one-half inch, and then release the mouse button.

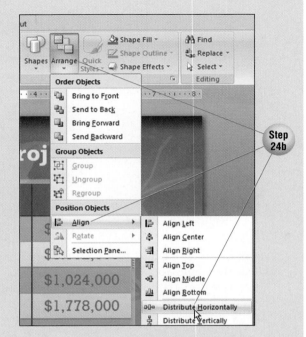

Step 24b

25. Insert a clip art image in the table by completing the following steps:
   a. Click the Insert tab.
   b. Click the Clip Art button in the Illustrations group.
   c. Select any text that displays in the *Search for* text box in the Clip Art task pane, type **sales**, and then press Enter.
   d. Scroll down the list of clip art images and then click the image shown in Figure 5.3. (If this image is not available, choose a similar clip art image related to sales.)
   e. Close the Clip Art task pane.
   f. With the image selected, click in the Shape Height measurement box in the Size group in the Picture Tools Format tab, type 2.8, and then press Enter.
   g. Drag the clip art image so it is positioned in the table as shown in Figure 5.3.
   h. Click outside the clip art image to deselect it.

26. Save **PP_C5_P1.pptx**.
27. Print Slide 4.

Step 25c

Step 25d

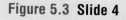

**Figure 5.3  Slide 4**

## Creating SmartArt

With the SmartArt feature you can insert diagrams and organizational charts in a slide. SmartArt offers a variety of predesigned diagrams and organizational charts that are available at the Choose a SmartArt Graphic dialog box shown in Figure 5.4. Display the Choose a SmartArt Graphic dialog box by clicking the Insert SmartArt Graphic button that displays in a content placeholder or by clicking the Insert tab and then clicking the SmartArt button in the Illustrations group. At the dialog box, *All* is selected in the left panel and all available predesigned diagrams display in the middle panel.

### Modifying SmartArt Design

Predesigned diagrams display in the middle panel of the Choose a SmartArt Graphic dialog box. Use the scroll bar at the right side of the middle panel to scroll down the list of diagram choices. Click a diagram in the middle panel and the name of the diagram displays in the right panel along with a description of the diagram type. SmartArt includes diagrams for presenting a list of data; showing data processes, cycles, and relationships; and presenting data in a matrix or pyramid. Double-click a diagram in the middle panel of the dialog box and the diagram is inserted in the slide.

**QUICK STEPS**

**Insert a SmartArt Diagram**
1. Click Insert SmartArt Graphic button in content placeholder.
2. Double-click desired diagram.
OR
1. Click Insert tab.
2. Click SmartArt button.
3. Double-click desired diagram.

**HINT**
Use SmartArt to communicate your message and ideas in a visual manner.

**Figure 5.4** Choose a SmartArt Graphic Dialog Box

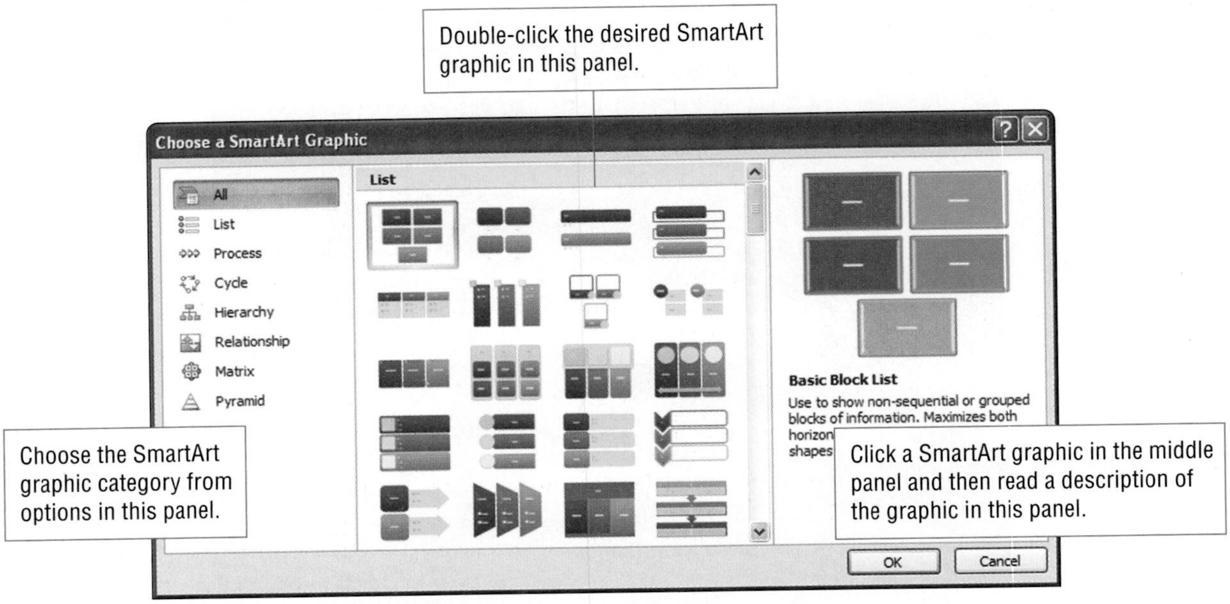

Double-click the desired SmartArt graphic in this panel.

Choose the SmartArt graphic category from options in this panel.

Click a SmartArt graphic in the middle panel and then read a description of the graphic in this panel.

**HINT**

Limit the number of shapes and the amount of text to key points.

When you double-click a diagram at the dialog box, the diagram is inserted in the slide and a text pane may display at the left side of the diagram. You can type text in the text pane or directly in the diagram. Apply design formatting to a diagram with options at the SmartArt Tools Design tab shown in Figure 5.5. This tab is active when the diagram is inserted in the slide. With options and buttons in this tab you add objects, change the diagram layout, apply a style to the diagram, and reset the diagram back to the original formatting.

**Figure 5.5** SmartArt Tools Design Tab

**Project 1d** **Inserting and Modifying a SmartArt Diagram**

1. With **PP_C5_P1.pptx** open, make sure Slide 4 is active and then insert a new slide with the *Title and Content* layout.
2. Click in the title placeholder and then type Division Reorganization.
3. Click the Insert SmartArt Graphic button located in the middle of the slide in the content placeholder.

4. At the Choose a SmartArt Graphic dialog box, click *Hierarchy* in the left panel of the dialog box.

5. Double-click the *Horizontal Hierarchy* option (first option from the left in the second row).

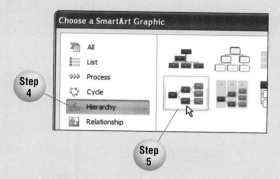

6. If a *Type your text here* window displays at the left side of the organizational chart, close the pane by clicking the Text Pane button in the Create Graphic group.

7. Delete one of the boxes in the organizational chart by clicking the border of the top box at the right side of the slide (the top box of the three stacked boxes) and then pressing the Delete key. (Make sure that the selection border that surrounds the box is a solid line and not a dashed line. If a dashed line displays, click the box border again. This should change it to a solid line.)

8. Click *[Text]* in the first box at the left, type Andrew Singh, press the Enter key, and then type Director. Click in each of the remaining boxes and type the text as shown below.

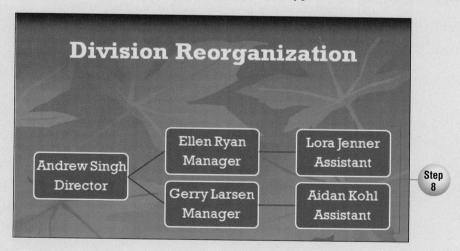

9. Click the More button located at the right side of the styles in the SmartArt Styles group and then click the *Polished* style in the *3-D* section (first option from the left in the top row of the *3-D* section).

10. Click the Change Colors button in the SmartArt Styles group and then click *Gradient Range - Accent 2* (third option from the left in the *Accent 2* section).
11. Change the layout of the organizational chart by clicking the *Table Hierarchy* layout in the Layouts group. Your slide should now look like the slide shown in Figure 5.6.

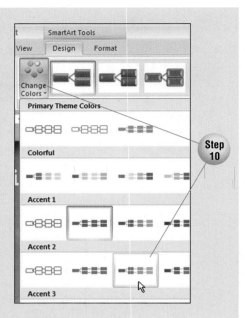

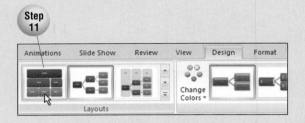

12. Save **PP_C5_P1.pptx**
13. Print Slide 5.

**Figure 5.6  Slide 5**

# Formatting SmartArt

Apply formatting to a SmartArt diagram with options at the SmartArt Tools Format tab shown in Figure 5.7. With options and buttons in this tab you can change the size and shape of objects in the diagram; apply shapes styles and WordArt styles; change the shape fill, outline, and effects; and arrange and size the diagram. Move the diagram by positioning the arrow pointer on the diagram border until the pointer turns into a four-headed arrow, holding down the left mouse button, and then dragging the diagram to the desired location.

HINT
Nudge selected shape(s) with the up, down, left, or right arrow keys on the keyboard.

**Figure 5.7** SmartArt Tools Format Tab

## Project 1e   Inserting and Formatting a Diagram

1. With **PP_C5_P1.pptx** open, make Slide 1 active.
2. Click the Insert tab and then click the SmartArt button in the Illustrations group.
3. At the Choose a SmartArt Graphic dialog box, click *Relationship* in the left panel of the dialog box.
4. Double-click the *Basic Venn* option shown below.

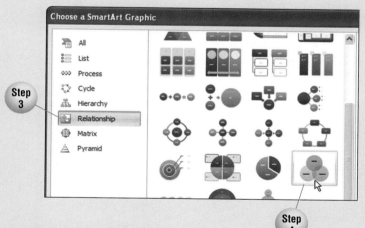

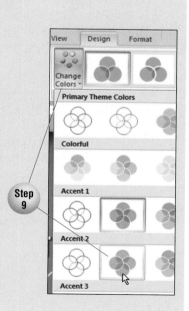

5. Click in the top shape and type Health.
6. Click in the shape at the left and type Happiness.
7. Click in the shape at the right and type Harmony.
8. Click inside the SmartArt border but outside of any shape.
9. Click the Change Colors button and then click *Colored Fill - Accent 2* (second option from the left in the *Accent 2* section).

10. Click the More button at the right side of the SmartArt Styles group and then click *Polished* at the drop-down gallery (first option from the left in the top row of the *3-D* section).
11. Click the SmartArt Tools Format tab.
12. Click the More button at the right side of the WordArt Styles thumbnails and then click *Fill - Accent 3, Powder Bevel* at the drop-down gallery (fourth option from the left in the *Applies to All Text in the Shape* section).
13. Click the Text Outline button arrow and then click *Light Yellow, Text 2, Darker 25%*.
14. Click the Size button, click in the *Height* measurement box, and then type 3.6.
15. Click in the *Width* measurement box, type 5.5, and then press Enter.
16. Click the Arrange button and then click the Send to Back button that displays in the drop-down list.
17. Drag the SmartArt so it is positioned as shown in Figure 5.8.
18. Drag the title and subtitle placeholders so they are positioned as shown in Figure 5.8.
19. You decide to experiment with rotating and changing the orientation of text in a shape. To do this, complete the following steps:
    a. Click the shape containing the word *Happiness*.
    b. Click the Arrange button in the SmartArt Tools Format tab, click *Rotate* at the drop-down list, and then click *Rotate Left 90°*.
    c. Click the shape containing the word *Harmony*.
    d. Click the Arrange button, click *Rotate* at the drop-down list, and then click *Rotate Left 90°*.
    e. You decide you do not like the text rotated. Return the text to normal orientation by clicking twice on the Undo button on the Quick Access toolbar.
20. Save **PP_C5_P1.pptx**.
21. Print Slide 1.

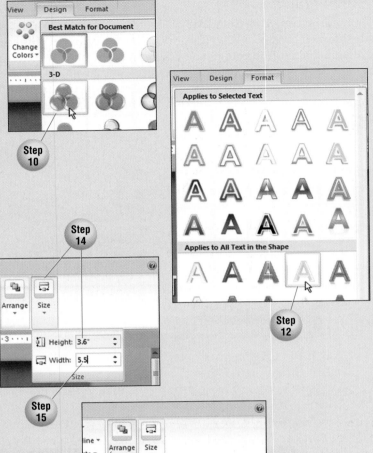

**Figure 5.8 Slide 1**

## Creating a SmartArt Graphic with Bulleted Text

To improve the visual display of text and to create a professionally-designed image, consider converting bulleted text to a SmartArt graphic. To do this, select the placeholder containing the text you want to convert and then click the Convert to SmartArt Graphic button that displays in the Paragraph group in the Home tab. Click the desired SmartArt graphic at the drop-down gallery or click the *More SmartArt Graphics* option that displays at the bottom of the drop-down gallery. This displays the Choose a SmartArt Graphic dialog box where you can choose a SmartArt graphic.

Project **1f**   **Creating a SmartArt Graphic with Bulleted Text**

1. With **PP_C5_P1.pptx** open, make Slide 6 active.
2. Click on any character in the bulleted text.
3. If necessary, click the Home tab.

4. Click the Convert to SmartArt Graphic button that displays in the Paragraph group.
5. At the drop-down gallery that displays, click the *More SmartArt Graphics* option that displays at the bottom of the gallery.

Step
4

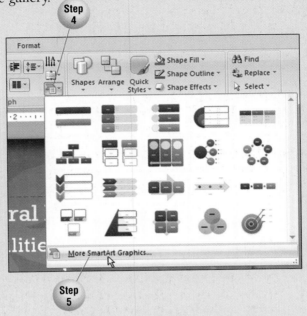

Step
5

6. At the Choose a SmartArt Graphic dialog box, click *Cycle* in the left panel, and then double-click *Diverging Radial* in the middle panel.

Step
6

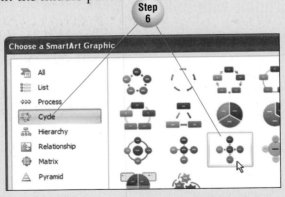

7. Click the Add Shape button in the Create Graphic group in the SmartArt Tools Design tab and then type **Supplies** in the new shape.
8. Change the order of the text in the shapes at the left and right sides of the graphic by clicking the Right to Left button in the Create Graphic group.
9. Click the Change Colors button in the SmartArt Styles group and then click *Colorful Range - Accent Colors 2 to 3* (second option from the left in the *Colorful* section).
10. Click the More button at the right of the SmartArt Styles thumbnails and then click *Inset* (second option from the left in the *3-D* section).

Step
9

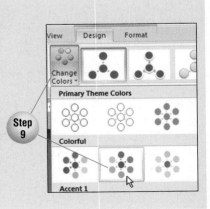

11. Click the SmartArt Tools Format tab.
12. Click the middle circle (contains the text *Central Division*).
13. Click three times on the Larger button in the Shapes group.
14. Click inside the SmartArt border but outside of any shape.
15. Click the Size button, click in the *Height* measurement box, and then type 6.6.
16. Click in the *Width* measurement box, type 8.2, and then press Enter.
17. Click the Home tab.
18. With the SmartArt graphic selected, click the Arrange button in the Drawing group, point to *Align*, and then click *Distribute Horizontally*.
19. Click the Arrange button in the Drawing group, point to *Align*, and then click *Distribute Vertically*.
20. Click the Bold button in the Font group.
21. Save **PP_C5_P1.pptx**.
22. Print Slide 6.

Step 13

## Inserting Text in the Text Pane

You can enter text in a SmartArt shape by clicking in the shape and then typing the text. You can also insert text in a SmartArt shape by typing text in the Text pane. Display the Text pane by clicking the Text Pane button in the Create Graphic group in the SmartArt Tools Design tab.

## Project 1g   Creating a SmartArt Graphic and Inserting Text in the Text Pane

1. With **PP_C5_P1.pptx** open, make sure Slide 6 is active and then insert a new slide with the *Title and Content* layout.
2. Click the title placeholder and type Division Planning.
3. Click the Insert SmartArt Graphic button in the content placeholder.
4. At the Choose a SmartArt Graphic dialog box, click *Process* in the left panel, and then double-click *Alternating Flow* (last option in the top row).
5. If necessary, click the Text Pane button in the Create Graphic group in the SmartArt Tools Design tab to display the *Type your text here* text pane.
6. With the insertion point positioned after the top bullet in the *Type your text here* text pane, type Facility.
7. Click *[Text]* that displays below *Facility* and then type Research market.
8. Continue clicking occurrences of *[Text]* and typing text so the text pane displays as shown at the right.
9. Close the text pane by clicking the Close button (contains an X) that displays up in the upper right corner of the pane. (You can also click the Text Pane button in the Create Graphic group.)

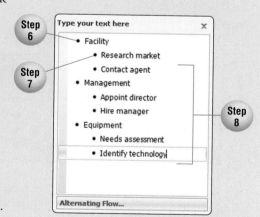

Step 6
Step 7
Step 8

10. Click inside the diagram border but outside any shape. (This deselects any shapes but keeps the diagram selected.)
11. If necessary, click the SmartArt Tools Design tab.
12. Click the Change Colors button in the SmartArt Styles group and then click *Dark 2 Fill*, the last option in the *Primary Theme Colors* section.
13. Click the *Intense Effect* thumbnail that displays in the SmartArt Styles group (if this style is not visible, click the More button at the right side of the SmartArt Styles group and then click the last option in the *Best Match for Document* section).

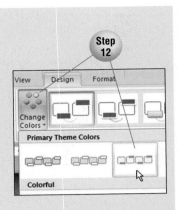

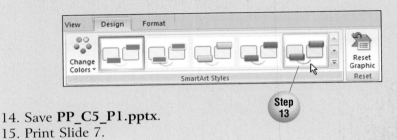

14. Save **PP_C5_P1.pptx**.
15. Print Slide 7.

# Creating a Chart

You can create a variety of charts including bar and column charts, pie charts, area charts, and much more. Table 5.2 describes the eleven basic chart types you can create in PowerPoint. To create a chart, click the Insert Chart button in a content placeholder or click the Insert tab and then click the Chart button in the Illustrations group. This displays the Insert Chart dialog box shown in Figure 5.9. At this dialog box, choose the desired chart type in the list at the left side, click the chart style, and then click OK.

**Figure 5.9** Insert Chart Dialog Box

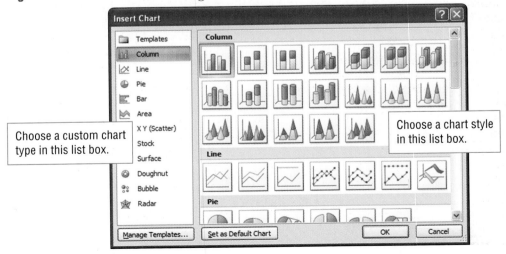

**Table 5.2** Types of Charts

| | |
|---|---|
| **Area** | An area chart emphasizes the magnitude of change, rather than time and the rate of change. It also shows the relationship of parts to a whole by displaying the sum of the plotted values. |
| **Bar** | A bar chart shows individual figures at a specific time, or shows variations between components but not in relationship to the whole. |
| **Bubble** | A bubble chart compares sets of three values in a manner similar to a scatter chart, with the third value displayed as the size of the bubble marker. |
| **Column** | A column chart compares separate (noncontinuous) items as they vary over time. |
| **Doughnut** | A doughnut chart shows the relationship of parts of the whole. |
| **Line** | A line chart shows trends and change over time at even intervals. It emphasizes the rate of change over time rather than the magnitude of change. |
| **Pie** | A pie chart shows proportions and relationships of parts to the whole. |
| **Radar** | A radar chart emphasizes differences and amounts of change over time and variations and trends. Each category has its own value axis radiating from the center point. Lines connect all values in the same series. |
| **Stock** | A stock chart shows four values for a stock—open, high, low, and close. |
| **Surface** | A surface chart shows trends in values across two dimensions in a continuous curve. |
| **XY (Scatter)** | A scatter chart either shows the relationships among numeric values in several data series or plots the interception points between $x$ and $y$ values. It shows uneven intervals of data and is commonly used in scientific data. |

When you click OK at the Insert Chart dialog box, a sample chart is inserted in your slide and Excel opens with sample data as shown in Figure 5.10. Type the desired data in the Excel worksheet cells over the existing data. As you type data, the chart in the slide reflects the typed data. To type data in the Excel worksheet, click in the desired cell, type the data, and then press the Tab key to make the next cell active, press Shift + Tab to make the previous cell active, or press Enter to make the cell below active.

Cells used by Excel to create the chart are surrounded by a blue border and the message "To resize chart data range, drag lower right corner of range." displays below the border. If you need to change the data range, position the mouse pointer on the bottom right corner of the border until the mouse pointer displays as a double-headed arrow pointing diagonally. Hold down the left mouse button and then drag up, down, left, and/or right until the border is in the desired location. You can also click in a cell immediately outside the border and, when you insert data, the border will expand. When all data is entered in the worksheet, click the Close button that displays in the upper right corner of the screen. This closes the Excel window and displays the chart in the slide.

**QUICK STEPS**

**Insert a Chart**
1. Click Insert Chart button in content placeholder.
2. Click desired chart style and type.
3. Enter data in Excel spreadsheet.
4. Close Excel.
OR
1. Click Insert tab.
2. Click Chart button.
3. Click desired chart style and type.
4. Enter data in Excel spreadsheet.
5. Close Excel.

**Figure 5.10** Sample Chart

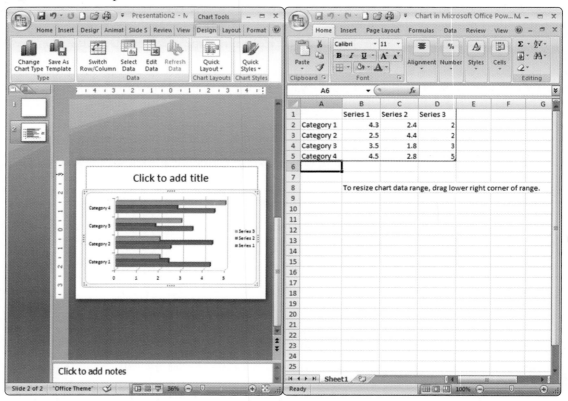

Enter data in cells in the Excel worksheet. The data entered is reflected in the PowerPoint presentation chart.

## Project ① Creating a Chart

1. With **PP_C5_P1.pptx** open, make Slide 3 active.
2. Click the Insert Chart button in the content placeholder.
3. At the Insert Chart dialog box, click *Bar* in the left panel.
4. Click the *Clustered Bar in 3-D* option that displays in the *Bar* section (fourth option from the left) in the middle panel and then click OK.

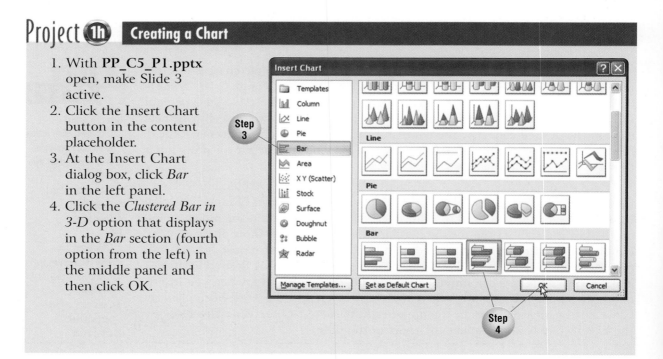

5. In the Excel worksheet, position the mouse pointer on the bottom right corner of the blue border until the mouse pointer displays as a double-headed arrow pointing diagonally. Hold down the left mouse button, drag to the left until the border displays at the right side of column C, and then release the mouse button.

6. Position the mouse pointer on the bottom right corner of the blue border until the pointer displays as a double-headed arrow and then drag down until the border displays at the bottom of row 6.

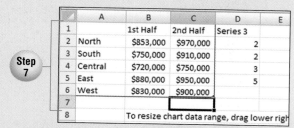

Step 6

7. Type the text in cells as shown at the right by completing the following steps:
   a. Click in cell B1 in the Excel worksheet, type 1st Half, and then press the Tab key.
   b. With cell C1 active, type 2nd Half and then press the Tab key.
   c. In cell A2, type North and then press the Tab key.
   d. Type $853,000 and then press the Tab key.
   e. Type $970,000 and then press the Tab key.
   f. Continue typing the remaining data in cells as indicated above.

8. Click the Close button that displays in the upper right corner of the Excel window.

9. Save PP_C5_P1.pptx.

Step 7

Step 8

## Changing Chart Design

When the chart is inserted in the slide, the Chart Tools Design tab is active as shown in Figure 5.11. Use options in this tab to change the chart type, edit chart data, change the chart layout, and apply a chart style.

**Figure 5.11** Chart Tools Design Tab

**Change Chart Type and Style**
1. Make the chart active.
2. Click Chart Tools Design tab.
3. Click Change Chart Type button.
4. Click desired chart type.
5. Click desired chart style.
6. Click OK.

**HINT**

Click the Save As Template button in the Chart group in the Chart Tools Design tab to save the current chart as a template.

Change Chart Type

Edit Data

After you create a chart, you can change the chart type by clicking the Change Chart Type button in the Type group in the Chart Tools Design tab. This displays the Change Chart Type dialog box. This dialog box contains the same options as the Insert Chart dialog box shown in Figure 5.9. At the Change Chart Type dialog box, click the desired chart type in the left panel and click the desired chart style at the right.

Use options in the Data group in the Chart Tools Design tab to change the order of the data in the chart, select specific data, edit data, and refresh the data. When you create a chart, the cells in the Excel worksheet are linked to the chart in the slide. If you need to edit data in the chart, click the Edit Data button and the Excel worksheet opens. Make the desired changes to cells in the Excel worksheet and then click the Close button.

The chart feature provides a number of predesigned chart layouts and styles you can apply to a chart. Click one of the chart layouts that displays in the Chart Layouts group or click the More button and then click the desired layout at the drop-down list. Apply a chart style to a chart by clicking one of these styles in the Chart Styles group or by clicking the More button and then clicking the desired style at the drop-down list.

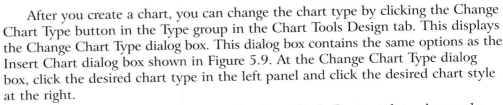

Project **1i** **Changing the Chart Type and Editing Data**

1. With **PP_C5_P1.pptx** open, make sure Slide 3 is active.
2. Delete the title placeholder by completing the following steps:
   a. Click on any character in the title *2009 Sales by Region*.
   b. Position the mouse pointer on the placeholder border until the pointer displays with a four-headed arrow attached and then click the left mouse button. (This changes the placeholder border from a dashed line to a solid line.)
   c. Press the Delete key. (This removes the title *2009 Sales by Region* and displays the placeholder text *Click to add title*.)
   d. Position the mouse pointer on the placeholder border until the pointer displays with a four-headed arrow attached and then click the left mouse button. (This changes the placeholder border from a dashed line to a solid line.)
   e. Press the Delete key.
3. Click near the chart (but outside any chart elements) to select the chart. (A light turquoise border displays around the chart.)
4. Click the Chart Tools Design tab.
5. Looking at the chart, you decide that the bar chart was not the best choice for the data and decide to change to a column chart. To do this, click the Change Chart Type button in the Type group.

6. At the Change Chart Type dialog box, click the *Column* option in the left panel.
7. Click the *3-D Clustered Column* option (fourth option from the left in the top row in the *Column* section of the dialog box).

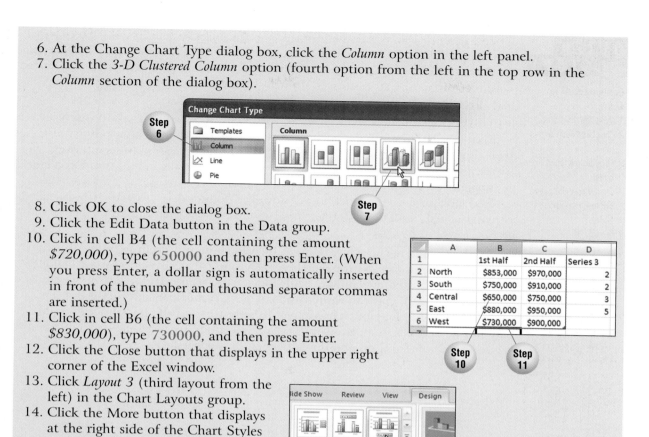

8. Click OK to close the dialog box.
9. Click the Edit Data button in the Data group.
10. Click in cell B4 (the cell containing the amount *$720,000*), type 650000 and then press Enter. (When you press Enter, a dollar sign is automatically inserted in front of the number and thousand separator commas are inserted.)
11. Click in cell B6 (the cell containing the amount *$830,000*), type 730000, and then press Enter.
12. Click the Close button that displays in the upper right corner of the Excel window.
13. Click *Layout 3* (third layout from the left) in the Chart Layouts group.
14. Click the More button that displays at the right side of the Chart Styles group and then click the *Style 18* option (second option from the left in the third row).
15. Save **PP_C5_P1.pptx**.

## Formatting Chart Layout

Click the Chart Tools Layout tab and options display for changing and customizing chart elements as shown in Figure 5.12. With options in this tab you can specify chart elements, insert objects, add labels to the chart, customize the chart background, and add analysis items to the chart.

To format or modify a specific element in a chart, select the element. Do this by clicking the element or by clicking the Chart Elements button in the Current Selection group in the Chart Tools Layout tab. With the element selected, apply the desired formatting. Click the Format Selection button in the Current Selection group and a dialog box displays with options for formatting the selected element.

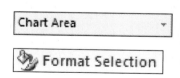

**Figure 5.12** Chart Tools Layout Tab

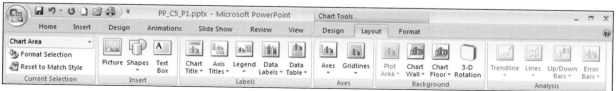

Insert objects in a chart with buttons in the Insert group in the Chart Tools Layout tab. Click the Picture button and the Insert Picture dialog box displays. At this dialog box, navigate to the desired folder and then double-click the desired picture. Use the Shapes button to draw a shape in the chart and use the Draw Text Box button to insert a text box in the chart.

Use options in the Labels group in the Chart Tools Layout tab to insert and position labels. For example, click the Chart Title button and a drop-down list displays with options for removing the chart title, centering the title and overlaying on the chart, and displaying the title above the chart. You can also position a label by dragging it. To do this, select the label, position the mouse pointer over the selected label or over the label border until the pointer displays with a four-headed arrow attached, hold down the left mouse button, and then drag the label to the desired location.

With buttons in the Axes, Background, and Analysis groups, you can further customize a chart. Use buttons in the Axes group to specify if you want major and/or minor horizontal and vertical lines in the chart. With buttons in the Background group, you can format the chart wall and floor and rotate the chart. Depending on the type of chart, some of the buttons in the Background group may not be active. Use buttons in the Analysis group to add analysis elements such as trendlines and up and down bars and error bars.

## Project 1i    Modifying Chart Layout

1. With **PP_C5_P1.pptx** open, make sure Slide 3 is active and the chart is selected.
2. Click the Chart Tools Layout tab.
3. Click the Text Box button in the Insert group.
4. Click in the lower left corner of the chart (outside any chart elements).
5. Change the font size to 16, turn on bold, change the font color to Green, Accent 6, Darker 50%, and then type Nature's Way.
6. Click the Drawing Tools Format tab.
7. Click in the *Shape Height* measurement box and then type 0.4.
8. Click in the *Shape Width* measurement box, type 1.7, and then press Enter.
9. Drag the text box down to the lower left corner of the chart.
10. Click inside the chart border but outside any chart elements and then click the Chart Tools Layout tab.
11. Click the Chart Elements button arrow and then click *Chart Title* at the drop-down list.
12. Type 2009 Regional Sales.

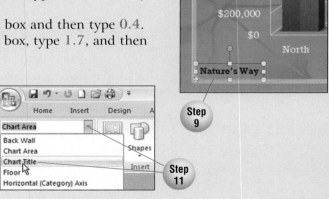

13. Click the Data Table button in the Labels group and then click the *Show Data Table with Legend Keys* option at the drop-down list.
14. After looking at the data table, you decide to remove it by clicking the Data Table button in the Labels group and then clicking *None* at the drop-down list.
15. Click the Gridlines button in the Axes group, point to *Primary Vertical Gridlines*, and then click *Major & Minor Gridlines* at the side menu.

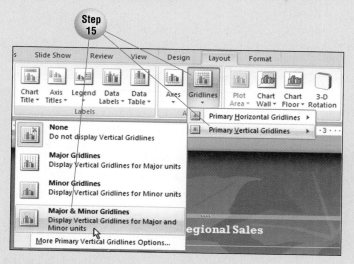

16. Increase the height of the chart by positioning the mouse pointer on the four dots that display in the middle of the top border until the pointer displays as a two-headed arrow pointing up and down. Hold down the left mouse button, drag up approximately one inch, and then release the mouse button.
17. Click on any character in the chart title *2009 Regional Sales*.
18. Click the Home tab, change the font size to 32, and change the font color to Light Yellow, Text 2, Darker 10%.
19. Save **PP_C5_P1.pptx**.

## Changing Chart Formatting

Customize the format of the chart and chart elements with options in the Chart Tools Format tab as shown in Figure 5.13. The tab contains the same Current Selection group as the Chart Tools Layout tab. With the other options in the tab you can apply a predesigned style to a shape, a predesigned WordArt style to text, and arrange and size the chart.

**Figure 5.13** Chart Tools Format Tab

The Shape Styles group in the Chart Tools Format tab contains predesigned styles you can apply to shapes in the chart. Click the More button at the right side of the style in the group and a drop-down gallery displays of shape styles. Use the buttons that display at the right side of the Shape Styles group to apply fill, an outline, and an effect to a selected shape. The WordArt Styles group contains predesigned styles you can apply to text in a chart. Use the buttons that display at the right side of the WordArt Styles group to apply fill, an outline, or an effect to text in a chart.

## Project 1k  Changing Chart Formatting

1. With **PP_C5_P1.pptx** open, make sure Slide 3 is the active slide and the chart is selected.
2. Click the Chart Tools Format tab.
3. Click the Chart Elements button arrow in the Current Selection group and then click *Series "2nd Half"* at the drop-down list. (This selects the green bars in the chart representing second half sales.)
4. Click the More button at the right side of the Shapes Style thumbnails and then click the *Colored Fill - Dark 1* option (first option from the left in the second row).

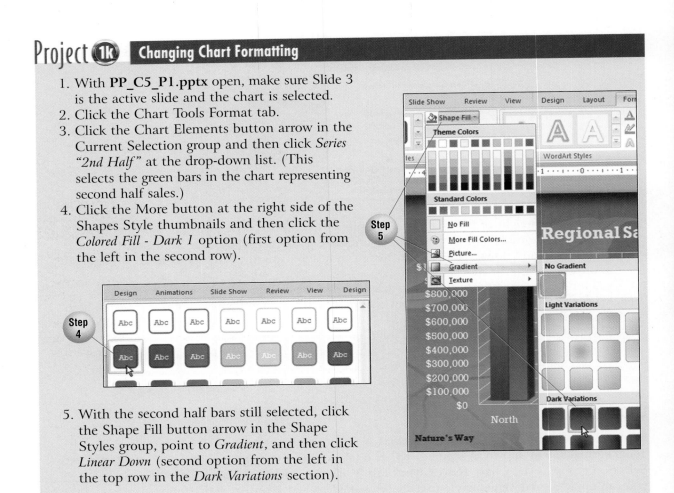

5. With the second half bars still selected, click the Shape Fill button arrow in the Shape Styles group, point to *Gradient*, and then click *Linear Down* (second option from the left in the top row in the *Dark Variations* section).

6. With the second half bars still selected, click the Shape Effects button in the Shape Styles group, point to *Bevel*, and then click the *Circle* option (first option from the left in the *Bevel* section of the side menu).
7. Click one of the teal bars that represent the first half sales amounts. (This selects all teal bars in the chart.)
8. Click the Shape Fill button arrow in the Shape Styles group and then click *Light Yellow, Text 2, Darker 10%*.
9. With the first half bars still selected, click the Shape Effects button in the Shape Styles group, point to *Bevel*, and then click the *Circle* option at the side menu.
10. Save **PP_C5_P1.pptx**.
11. Print Slide 3.

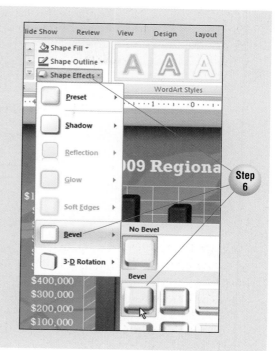

Step 6

Use buttons in the Arrange group to send the chart behind other objects, move it to the front of other objects, specify the alignment, and rotate the chart. You can size a chart by selecting the chart and then dragging a border. You can also size a chart to specific measurements with the Shape Height and Shape Width measurement boxes in the Size group in the Chart Tools Format tab. Change the height or width by clicking the up- or down-pointing arrows that display at the right side of the measurement box or click the current measurement in the measurement box and then type a specific measurement.

**QUICK STEPS**

**Change Chart Height and/or Width**
1. Make the chart active.
2. Click Chart Tools Format tab.
3. Insert desired height and/or width in *Shape Height* and/or *Shape Width* measurement boxes.

Shape Height

Shape Width

## Project 11  Creating and Formatting a Pie Chart

1. With **PP_C5_P1.pptx** open, make Slide 6 active and then insert a new slide with the *Title and Content* layout.
2. Click the title placeholder text and then type Division Budget.
3. Click the Insert tab and then click the Chart button in the Illustrations group.
4. At the Insert Chart dialog box, click *Pie* in the left panel.
5. Click the *Pie in 3-D* option (second option from the left in the *Pie* section) and then click OK.

6. In the Excel worksheet, position the mouse pointer on the bottom right corner of the border until the mouse pointer displays as a double-headed arrow pointing diagonally. Hold down the left mouse button and then drag down until the border displays at the bottom of row 7.

| | A | B | C |
|---|---|---|---|
| 1 | | Sales | |
| 2 | 1st Qtr | 8.2 | |
| 3 | 2nd Qtr | 3.2 | |
| 4 | 3rd Qtr | 1.4 | |
| 5 | 4th Qtr | 1.2 | |
| 6 | | | |
| 7 | | | |
| 8 | | To resize chart data ra | |

Step 6

7. Type the text in cells as shown at the right.
8. When all data is entered, click the Close button that displays in the upper right corner of the Excel window.
9. With the Chart Tools Design tab selected, click the More button at the right side of the Chart Styles group and then click the *Style 26* option (second option from the left in the fourth row).

Step 7

| | A | B | C |
|---|---|---|---|
| 1 | | Percentage | |
| 2 | Salaries | 41% | |
| 3 | Benefits | 10% | |
| 4 | Facilities | 23% | |
| 5 | Equipment | 12% | |
| 6 | Supplies | 9% | |
| 7 | Miscellaneous | 5% | |
| 8 | | To resize chart data ra | |
| 9 | | | |

10. Click the Chart Tools Layout tab.
11. Click the Chart Title button in the Labels group and then click *None* at the drop-down list.
12. Click the Data Labels button in the Labels group and then click *Inside End* at the drop-down list.

Step 12

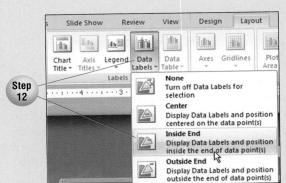

13. Click the Chart Tools Format tab.
14. Click the piece of pie containing *10%*. (Make sure only the one piece of pie is selected.)
15. Click the Shape Fill button arrow in the Shape Styles group and then click *Light Yellow, Text 2, Darker 75%*.
16. Click the piece of pie containing *9%*. (Make sure only the one piece of pie is selected.)
17. Click the Shape Fill button arrow in the Shape Styles group and then click *Light Green, Accent 5, Darker 50%*.
18. Click the piece of pie containing *12%*. (Make sure only the one piece of pie is selected.)
19. Click the Shape Fill button arrow in the Shape Styles group and then click *Dark Teal, Accent 1, Lighter 40%*.
20. Click the Chart Elements button in the Current Selection group and then click *Chart Area* at the drop-down list.
21. Click in the *Shape Height* measurement box in the Size group, type 6, and then press Enter.
22. Click the Align button in the Arrange group and then click *Distribute Vertically*.
23. Drag the chart down approximately one-half inch.
24. Apply a transition and sound of your choosing to all slides in the presentation.
25. Save **PP_C5_P1.pptx**.
26. Run the presentation.
27. Print Slide 7 and then close **PP_C5_P1.pptx**.

# Project ② Create and Format a Travel Photo Album

You will use the photo album feature to create a presentation containing travel photographs. You will also apply formatting and insert elements in the presentation.

## Creating a Photo Album

With PowerPoint's photo album feature, you can create a presentation containing personal or business pictures. You can customize and format the appearance of pictures by applying interesting layouts, frame shapes, and themes and you can also insert elements such as captions and text boxes. To create a photo album, click the Insert tab, click the Photo Album button arrow, and then click *New Photo Album* at the drop-down list. This displays the Photo Album dialog box as shown in Figure 5.14.

To insert pictures in the photo album, click the File/Disk button and the Insert New Pictures dialog box displays. At this dialog box, navigate to the desired folder and then double-click the picture you want inserted in the album. This inserts the picture name in the *Pictures in album* list box in the dialog box and also previews the picture in the *Preview* section. As you insert pictures in the photo album, the picture names display in the *Pictures in album* list box in the order in which they will appear in the presentation. When you have inserted the desired pictures in the photo album, click the Create button. This creates the photo album as a presentation and displays the first slide. The photo album feature creates the first slide with the title *Photo Album* and inserts the user's name.

### QUICK STEPS

**Create Photo Album**
1. Click Insert tab.
2. Click Photo Album button arrow.
3. Click *New Photo Album*.
4. Click File/Disk button.
5. Double-click desired pictures.
6. Make desired changes at Photo Album dialog box.
7. Click Create button.

Photo Album ▾

**Figure 5.14** Photo Album Dialog Box

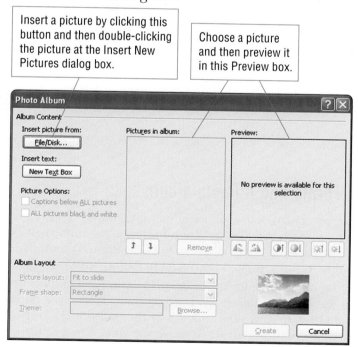

Insert a picture by clicking this button and then double-clicking the picture at the Insert New Pictures dialog box.

Choose a picture and then preview it in this Preview box.

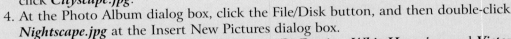

1. At a blank screen, click the Insert tab, click the Photo Album button arrow, and then click *New Photo Album* at the drop-down list.
2. At the Photo Album dialog box, click the File/Disk button.
3. At the Insert New Pictures dialog box, navigate to the PowerPoint2007C5 folder on your storage medium and then double-click ***Cityscape.jpg***.
4. At the Photo Album dialog box, click the File/Disk button, and then double-click ***Nightscape.jpg*** at the Insert New Pictures dialog box.
5. Insert the following images: ***Stonehenge.jpg***, ***BigBen.jpg***, ***WhiteHorse.jpg***, and ***VictoriaBC.jpg***.
6. Click the Create button. (This opens a presentation with each image in a slide and the first slide containing the default text *Photo Album* followed by your name (or the user name for the computer).

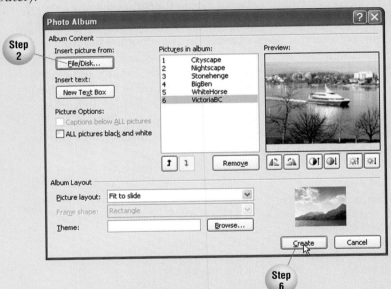

7. Save the presentation and name it **PP_C5_P2.pptx**.
8. Run the presentation.

---

**QUICK STEPS**

### Editing and Formatting a Photo Album

**Edit Photo Album**
1. Click Insert tab.
2. Click Photo Album button arrow.
3. Click *Edit Photo Album*.
4. Make desired changes at Edit Photo Album dialog box.
5. Click Update button.

If you want to make changes to a photo album presentation, open the presentation, click the Insert tab, click the Photo Album button arrow, and then click *Edit Photo Album* at the drop-down list. This displays the Edit Photo Album dialog box, which contains the same options as the Photo Album dialog box.

Rearrange the order of slides in the photo album presentation by clicking the desired slide in the *Pictures in album* list box and then clicking the button containing the up-pointing arrow to move the slide up in the order or clicking the button containing the down-pointing arrow to move the slide down in the order. Remove a slide by clicking the desired slide in the list box and then clicking the Remove button. With the buttons below the *Preview* box in the Edit Photo Album dialog box, you can rotate the picture in the slide, increase or decrease the contrast, and increase or decrease the brightness of the picture.

The *Picture layout* option in the *Album Layout* group has a default setting of *Fit to slide*. At this setting the picture in each slide will fill most of the slide. You can change this setting by clicking the down-pointing arrow at the right side of the option. With options at the drop-down list, you can specify that you want one picture inserted in the slide, two pictures, or four pictures. You can also specify that you want the one, two, or four pictures inserted in slides with titles.

If you change the *Picture layout* option to something other than the default of *Fit to slide*, the *Frame shape* option becomes available. Click the down-pointing arrow at the right side of the option and a drop-down list displays with framing options. You can choose a rounded frame, single frame, double frame, or a soft or shadow effect frame.

You can apply a theme to the photo album presentation by clicking the Browse button located at the right side of the *Theme* option box and then double-clicking the desired theme in the Choose Theme dialog box. This dialog box contains the predesigned themes provided by PowerPoint.

If you want to include a caption with the pictures, change the *Picture layout* to one, two, or four slides, and then click the *Captions below ALL pictures* check box located in the *Picture Options* section of the dialog box. PowerPoint will insert a caption below each picture that contains the name of the picture. You can edit the caption in the slide in the presentation. If you want to display all of the pictures in your photo album in black and white, click the *ALL pictures black and white* check box in the *Picture Options* section.

Click the New Text Box button in the Edit Photo Album dialog box and a new slide containing a text box is inserted in the presentation. In the presentation, you can edit the information in the text box. When all changes are made to the photo album, click the Update button located toward the bottom right side of the dialog box.

## Project 2b    Editing and Formatting a Photo Album

1. With **PP_C5_P2.pptx** open, click the Insert tab, click the Photo Album button arrow, and then click *Edit Photo Album* at the drop-down list.
2. At the Edit Photo Album dialog box, make the following changes:
   a. Click *VictoriaBC* in the *Pictures in album* list box and then click three times on the up-pointing arrow that displays below the list box. (This moves *VictoriaBC* so it is positioned between *Nightscape* and *Stonehenge*).

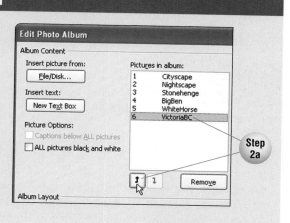

b. Click the down-pointing arrow at the right side of the *Picture layout* option and then click *1 picture* at the drop-down list.

c. Click the down-pointing arrow at the right side of the *Frame shape* option and then click *Center Shadow Rectangle* at the drop-down list.

d. Click the Browse button located at the right side of the *Theme* option box. At the Choose Theme dialog box, scroll down the list box and then double-click *Trek.thmx*.

e. Click the *Captions below ALL pictures* check box to insert a check mark.

f. Click *WhiteHorse* in the *Pictures in album* list box and then click the New Text Box button that displays at the left side of the list box. (This inserts a new slide containing a text box at the end of the presentation.)

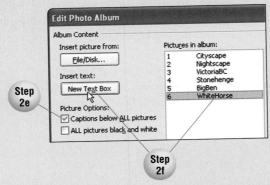

g. Click the Update button located in the lower right corner of the dialog box.

3. At the presentation, make the following formatting changes:
   a. Click the Design tab.
   b. Click the Colors button in the Themes group and then click *Metro* at the drop-down gallery.
   c. Click the Background Styles button in the Background group and then click *Style 2* at the drop-down list.

4. Make Slide 1 active and then make the following changes:
   a. Select the text *PHOTO ALBUM* and then type travel album. (The text will display in all caps.)
   b. Select any text that displays after the word *by* and then type your first and last names.
   c. Click the Insert tab and then click the Picture button.
   d. At the Insert Picture dialog box, navigate to the PowerPoint2007C5 folder on your storage medium and then double-click *FCTLogo.jpg*.
   e. Click the Recolor button in the Adjust group in the Picture Tools Format tab and then click *Set Transparent Color* at the drop-down list.

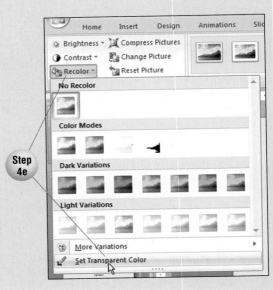

f. Move the mouse pointer (pointer displays with a tool attached) to any white portion of the logo and then click the left mouse button. (This changes the white fill to transparent fill and allows the blue background to show through.)

g. Change the height of the logo to *3.5"* and then position the logo attractively in the slide.

5. Make Slide 2 active and then edit the caption by completing the following steps:
   a. Click on any character in the caption *Cityscape*.
   b. Select *Cityscape* and then type New York City Skyline.

6. Complete steps similar to those in Step 5 to change the following captions:
   a. Slide 3: Change *Nightscape* to *New York City at Night*.
   b. Slide 4: Change *VictoriaBC* to *Victoria, British Columbia*.
   c. Slide 5: Change *Stonehenge* to *Stonehenge, Wiltshire County*.
   d. Slide 6: Change *BigBen* to *Big Ben, London*.
   e. Slide 7: Change *WhiteHorse* to *White Horse, Wiltshire County*.

7. Make Slide 8 active and then make the following changes:
   a. Select the text *Text Box* and then type Call First Choice Travel at 555-4500 to book your next travel tour.
   b. Select the text, change the font size to 48, change the font color to Blue, and change the alignment to Center.

8. Apply a transition and sound of your choosing to each slide.
9. Run the presentation.
10. Save **PP_C5_P2.pptx**.

# Formatting Pictures

If you format slides in the presentation instead of the Edit Photo Album dialog box, you may lose some of those changes if you subsequently display the Edit Photo Album dialog box, make changes, and then click the Update button. Consider making your initial editing and formatting changes at the Edit Photo Album dialog box and then make final editing and formatting changes in the presentation.

Since a picture in a slide in a photo album is an object, you can format it with options at the Drawing Tools Format tab and the Picture Tools Format tab. With options at the Drawing Tools Format tab, you can insert shapes, apply a shape style to the picture and caption (if one is displayed), apply a WordArt style to caption text, and arrange and size the picture. Use options in the Picture Tools Format tab to adjust the color of the picture, apply a picture style, and arrange and size the picture.

## Project 2c  Formatting Pictures in a Presentation

1. With **PP_C5_P2.pptx** open, make Slide 2 active.
2. Format the picture in Slide 2 by completing the following steps:
   a. Click the picture to select it.
   b. Click the Drawing Tools Format tab.

c. Click the More button at the right side of the shape styles and then click *Subtle Effect - Accent 1* (second option from the left in the fourth row).

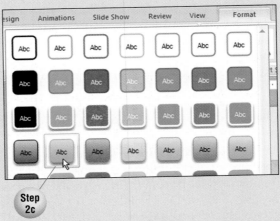

Step
2c

3. Apply the same style to the pictures in Slides 3 through 7 by making each slide active, clicking the picture, and then pressing F4. (Pressing F4 repeats the style formatting.)
4. Make Slide 2 active and then apply a WordArt style to the caption text by completing the following steps:
   a. With Slide 2 active, click the picture to select it.
   b. Click the Drawing Tools Format tab.
   c. Click the More button at the right side of the WordArt styles and then click *Gradient Fill - Accent 4, Reflection* (last option in the fourth row).
5. Apply the same WordStyle style to caption text in Slides 3 through 7 by making each slide active, clicking the picture, and then pressing F4.
6. Run the presentation
7. Print the presentation as a handout with four slides per page.
8. Save and then close **PP_C5_P2.pptx**.

# CHAPTER summary

- Use the Tables feature to create columns and rows of information. Create a table with the Insert Table button in a content placeholder or with the Table button in the Tables group in the Insert tab.

- A cell is the intersection between a row and a column. Columns in a table are lettered from left to right beginning with *A*. Rows are numbered from top to bottom beginning with *1*.

- Change the table design with options and buttons in the Table Tools Design tab.

- Change the table layout with options and buttons in the Table Tools Layout tab.

- Use the SmartArt feature to insert predesigned diagrams and organizational charts in a slide. Click the Insert SmartArt Graphic button in a content placeholder or click the SmartArt button in the Illustrations group in the Insert tab to display the Choose a SmartArt Graphic dialog box.

- When you insert a SmartArt diagram in a slide, the SmartArt Tools Design tab is active. Use options and buttons in this tab to change the diagram layout, apply a style to the diagram, and reset the diagram back to the original formatting.

- Use buttons in the SmartArt Tools Format tab to change the size and shapes of objects in the diagram; apply shape styles; change the shape fill, outline, and effects; and arrange and size the diagram.

- Create a SmartArt graphic with bulleted text by clicking in the bulleted text placeholder, clicking the Convert to SmartArt Graphic button in the Paragraph group in the Home tab, and then clicking the desired SmartArt diagram at the drop-down gallery.

- You can insert text directly into a SmartArt diagram shape or at the Text pane. Display this pane by clicking the Text Pane button in the Create Graphic group in the SmartArt Tools Design tab.

- A chart is a visual presentation of data and you can create a variety of charts as described in Table 5.2.

- To create a chart, display the Insert Chart dialog box by clicking the Insert Chart button in a content placeholder or clicking the Chart button in the Illustrations group in the Home tab.

- Enter chart data in an Excel worksheet. When entering data, press Tab to make the next cell active, press Shift + Tab to make the previous cell active, and press Enter to make the cell below active.

- Modify a chart design with options and buttons in the Chart Tools Design tab. Change the chart type with the Change Chart Type button, change the order of data in a chart with options in the Data group, apply a chart layout with options in the Chart Layouts group, and apply styles to a chart with options in the Chart Styles group.

- Cells in the Excel worksheet used to create a chart are linked to the chart in the slide. To edit chart data, click the Edit Data button in the Chart Tools Design tab and then make changes to text in the Excel worksheet.

- The Chart Tools Layout tab contains options and buttons for inserting objects in a chart such as a picture, shape, or text box and inserting and removing labels, axes, gridlines, and backgrounds.
- Customize the format of a chart and chart elements with options and buttons in the Chart Tools Format tab. You can select the chart or a specific element, apply a style to a shape, apply a WordArt style to text, and arrange and size the chart.
- Use the Photo Album feature to create a presentation containing pictures and then edit and format the pictures. Create a Photo Album by clicking the Insert tab, clicking the Photo Album button arrow, and then clicking *New Photo Album* at the drop-down list.
- At the Photo Album dialog box (or the Edit Photo Album dialog box), insert pictures and then use options to customize the photo album.
- Edit a photo album presentation by opening the presentation, clicking the Insert tab, clicking the Photo Album button arrow, and then clicking *Edit Photo Album* at the drop-down list.
- Use options in the Drawing Tools Format tab and the Picture Tools Format tab to format pictures in a photo album presentation.

# COMMANDS review

| FEATURE | RIBBON TAB, GROUP | BUTTON, OPTION | PLACEHOLDER BUTTON |
|---|---|---|---|
| Insert Table dialog box | Insert, Tables | , Insert Table | |
| Choose a SmartArt Graphic dialog box | Insert, Illustrations | | |
| Convert bulleted text to SmartArt | Home, Paragraph | | |
| Text pane | SmartArt Tools Design, Create Graphic | Text Pane | |
| Insert Chart dialog box | Insert, Illustrations | | |
| Create photo album | Insert, Illustrations | , New Photo Album | |
| Edit photo album | Insert, Illustrations | , Edit Photo Album | |

# CONCEPTS check

## Test Your Knowledge

**Completion:** In the space provided at the right, indicate the correct term, symbol, or command.

1. Display the Insert Table dialog box by clicking this button in a content placeholder.

   _____

2. This term refers to the intersection between a row and a column.

   _____

3. Use this keyboard shortcut to move the insertion point to the next cell.

   _____

4. This is the keyboard shortcut to select all cells in a table.

   _____

5. The Table Styles group is located in this tab.

   _____

6. Use options and buttons in this tab to delete and insert rows and columns and merge and split cells.

   _____

7. Click this button in a content placeholder to display the Choose a SmartArt Graphic dialog box.

   _____

8. When you insert a SmartArt diagram in a slide, this tab is active.

   _____

9. Create a SmartArt diagram with bulleted text by clicking in the text placeholder, clicking this button, and then clicking the desired SmartArt graphic at the drop-down list.

   _____

10. Click the Chart button in this group in the Insert tab to display the Insert Chart dialog box.

    _____

11. Insert a chart in a slide and this tab is active.

    _____

12. To edit data in a chart, click the Edit Data button in this group in the Chart Tools Design tab.

    _____

13. This group in the Chart Tools Format tab contains predesigned styles you can apply to shapes in a chart.

    _____

14. This group in the Chart Tools Format tab contains predesigned styles you can apply to chart text.

    _____

15. To create a photo album, click the Insert tab, click the Photo Album button arrow, and then click this at the drop-down list.

_____

16. To insert captions below pictures in a photo album, insert a check mark in this check box in the Edit Photo Album dialog box.

_____

17. Click the down-pointing arrow at the right of this option in the Edit Photo Album dialog box to display a list of framing choices.

_____

# SKILLS check
## *Demonstrate Your Proficiency*

## Assessment

### 1  CREATE AND FORMAT TABLES AND SMARTART IN A RESTAURANT PRESENTATION

1. Open **Dockside.pptx** and save the presentation and name it **PP_C5_A1**.
2. Make Slide 6 active and then create the table shown in the slide in Figure 5.15 with the following specifications:
   a. Create a table with three columns and six rows.
   b. Type the text in cells as shown in Figure 5.15.
   c. Apply the *Medium Style 4 - Accent 3* style to the table.
   d. Select all of the text in the table, center the text vertically, change the font size to 20 points, and change the font color to Turquoise, Accent 2, Darker 50%.
   e. Change the height of the table to 3.7 inches. (The width should be set at 9 inches.)
   f. Center the text in the first row.
   g. Center the text in the third column.
   h. Position the table as shown in Figure 5.15.
3. Make Slide 4 active and then create the table shown in the slide in Figure 5.16 with the following specifications:
   a. Create a table with four columns and three rows.
   b. Select the entire table, change the vertical alignment to center, and then change the font size to 28.
   c. Merge the cells in the first column, change the text direction to *Rotate all text 270°*, change the alignment to center, change the font size to 40, and then type **Lunch**.
   d. Merge the cells in the third column, change the text direction to *Rotate all text 270°*, change the alignment to center, change the font size to 40, and then type **Dinner**.
   e. Type the remaining text in cells as shown in Figure 5.16.
   f. Change the height of the table to 3 inches.
   g. Change the width of the first and third columns to 1.2 inches.
   h. Change the width of the second and fourth columns to 2.5 inches.

   i. Insert a check mark in the *Banded Columns* check box in the Table Style Options group in the Table Tools Design tab and remove the check marks from the other check boxes in the group.

   j. Apply the *Medium Style 4 - Accent 3* style to the table.

   k. Select all of the text in the table and then change the font color to Turquoise, Accent 2, Darker 50%.

   l. Position the table on the slide as shown in Figure 5.16.

4. Make Slide 5 active and then create the SmartArt organizational chart shown in the slide in Figure 5.17 with the following specifications:

   a. Choose the *Organization Chart* diagram at the Choose a SmartArt Graphic dialog box.

   b. Delete the second box so your chart appears with the same number of boxes and in the same order as the organizational chart in Figure 5.17.

   c. Type the text in the boxes as shown in Figure 5.17.

   d. Change the color to Colorful Range – Accent Colors 3 to 4.

   e. Apply the *Cartoon* SmartArt style.

   f. Apply the *Fill - White, Drop Shadow* WordArt style to text.

   g. Change the height of the organizational chart to 5 inches and change the width to 8.5 inches.

   h. Position the organizational chart in the slide as shown in Figure 5.17.

5. Make Slide 1 active and then format the title and create the SmartArt diagram shown in the slide in Figure 5.18 with the following specifications:

   a. Select the title *The Dockside Café* and then change the font to Lucida Calligraphy.

   b. Create the SmartArt diagram with the *Linear Venn* option located in the *Relationship* group. Type the text in the shapes as shown in Figure 5.18.

   c. Change the colors to *Colorful - Accent Colors*.

   d. Apply the *Intense Effect* SmartArt style.

   e. Apply the *Fill - White, Drop Shadow* WordArt style to text.

   f. Change the height of the diagram to 4.2 inches and the width to 6.8 inches.

   g. Position the SmartArt diagram on the slide as shown in Figure 5.18.

6. Make Slide 2 active, select the bulleted text placeholder, and then convert the bulleted text to a *Basic Matrix* diagram as shown in the slide in Figure 5.19 with the following specifications:

   a. Change the colors to *Colorful - Accent Colors*.

   b. Apply the *Cartoon* SmartArt style.

   c. Apply the *Fill - White, Drop Shadow* WordArt style to text.

   d. Change the height of the diagram to 4.8 inches and the width to 5.5 inches.

   e. Position the SmartArt diagram on the slide as shown in Figure 5.19.

7. Make Slide 3 active and then insert a clip art image related to "menu." Size and position the image attractively on the slide.

8. Apply a transition and sound of your choosing to all slides in the presentation.

9. Run the presentation.

10. Print the presentation as a handout with six slides per page.

11. Save and then close **PP_C5_A1.pptx**.

**Figure 5.15  Assessment 1, Slide 6**

## Suppliers

| Supplier | Contact Person | Telephone |
|---|---|---|
| Seaside Fish Market | Iliana Kovich | 253-555-4331 |
| MacDougal's Bakery | Joseph Loeberg | 253-555-0099 |
| Oakridge Winery | Michelle Woodring | 206-555-3156 |
| Tanner Supplies | Rose Patterson | 425-555-1165 |
| Pier 90 Company | Miguel Trujillo | 206-555-7761 |

**Figure 5.16  Assessment 1, Slide 4**

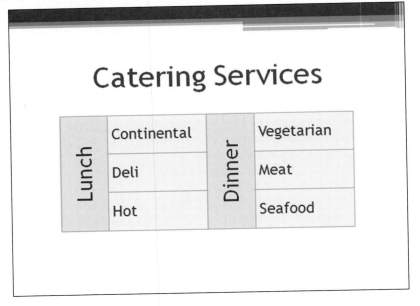

## Catering Services

| Lunch | Continental | Dinner | Vegetarian |
|---|---|---|---|
| | Deli | | Meat |
| | Hot | | Seafood |

**Figure 5.17** Assessment 1, Slide 5

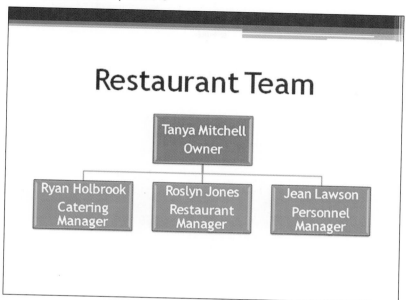

**Figure 5.18** Assessment 1, Slide 1

**Figure 5.19 Assessment 1, Slide 2**

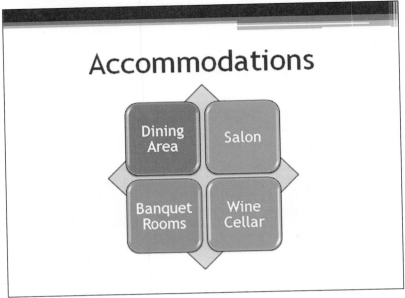

## Assessment

## 2 CREATE AND FORMAT CHARTS IN A MARKETING PRESENTATION

1. Open **MarketingPresentation.pptx** and save the presentation and name it **PP_C5_A2**.
2. Make Slide 2 active, insert a new slide with the *Title and Content* layout, and then create the chart shown in the slide in Figure 5.20 with the following specifications:
   a. Type the slide title as shown in Figure 5.20.
   b. Use the pie chart option *Pie in 3-D* to create the chart.
   c. Type the following information in the Excel worksheet:

   |              | Amount |
   |--------------|--------|
   | Salaries     | 47%    |
   | Equipment    | 18%    |
   | Supplies     | 4%     |
   | Production    | 21%    |
   | Distribution | 10%    |

   d. Change the chart layout to *Layout 3*.
   e. Insert data labels on the outside end.
   f. Change the shape fill of the piece of pie containing *10%* to *White, Accent 3, Darker 35%*.
3. Print Slide 3.
4. After looking at the slide, you realize that two of the percentages are incorrect. Edit the Excel data and change *47%* to *42%* and change *10%* to *15%*.
5. With Slide 3 active, insert a new slide with the *Title and Content* layout and then create the chart shown in the slide in Figure 5.21 with the following specifications:
   a. Type the slide title as shown in Figure 5.21.
   b. Use the line chart option *Line with Markers* to create the chart.

c. Type the following information in the Excel worksheet:

|        | Revenues  | Expenses  |
|--------|-----------|-----------|
| 1st Qtr | $789,560 | $670,500 |
| 2nd Qtr | $990,450 | $765,000 |
| 3rd Qtr | $750,340 | $780,000 |
| 4th Qtr | $980,400 | $875,200 |

d. Apply the *Style 42* chart style.

e. Click the Data Table button in the Chart Tools Layout tab and then click the *Show Data Table with Legend Keys* option.

f. Select and then delete the legend.

g. Insert major and minor vertical gridlines.

h. Select the plot area and then change the shape fill color to Light Green, Accent 1, Lighter 80%. (The Shape Fill button is located in the Chart Tools Format tab.)

i. Select the chart area and then change the shape fill color to Green, Accent 2, Darker 50%.

j. Select the expenses line (*Series "Expenses"*) and then change the shape fill to Red and the shape outline to Red.

k. Select the revenues line (*Series "Revenues"*) and then change the shape fill and the shape outline to Light Green, Accent 1, Darker 50%.

6. Apply a transition and sound of your choosing to each slide in the presentation.

7. Run the presentation.

8. Print the presentation as a handout with three slides per page.

9. Save and then close **PP_C5_A2.pptx**.

**Figure 5.20  Assessment 2, Slide 3**

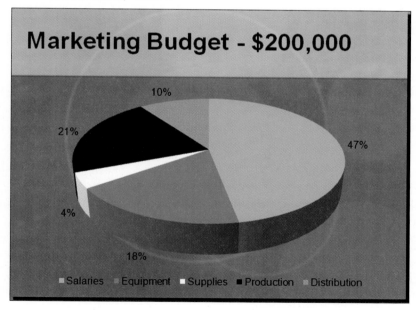

**Figure 5.21  Assessment 2, Slide 4**

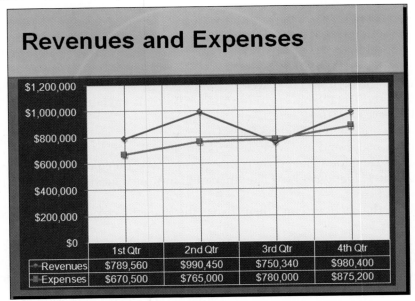

## Assessment

### 3 CREATE A SCENERY PHOTO ALBUM

1. At a blank screen, create a new photo album.
2. At the Photo Album dialog box, insert the following images:
   **AlderSprings.jpg**
   **CrookedRiver.jpg**
   **Mountain.jpg**
   **Ocean.jpg**
   **Olympics.jpg**
   **River.jpg**
3. Change the *Picture layout* option to *1 picture with title*.
4. Change the *Frame shape* option to *Simple Frame, White*.
5. Apply the *Paper* theme.
6. Click the Create button.
7. At the presentation, change the theme colors to *Solstice* and the background style to *Style 8*. **Hint: Do this with buttons in the Design tab.**
8. Insert the following titles in the specified slides:
   Slide 2 = Alder Springs, Oregon
   Slide 3 = Crooked River, Oregon
   Slide 4 = Mt. Rainier, Washington
   Slide 5 = Pacific Ocean, Washington
   Slide 6 = Olympic Mountains, Washington
   Slide 7 = Salmon River, Idaho
9. Make Slide 1 active, select any name that follows *by*, and then type your first and last names.
10. Save the presentation and name it **PP_C5_A3**.
11. Print the presentation as a handout with four slides per page.
12. Close **PP_C5_A3.pptx**.

## 4  CREATE A SALES AREA CHART

1. Open **PP_C5_A2.pptx** and then save the presentation and name it **PP_C5_A4**.
2. Make Slide 4 active and then insert a new slide with the *Title and Content* layout.
3. Use Excel's Help feature to learn more about chart types and then create an area chart (use the *Area* chart type) with the data shown below. Apply design, layout, and/or formatting to improve the visual appeal of the chart. Type **Sales by Region** as the slide title.

|            | Region 1  | Region 2  | Region 3  |
|------------|-----------|-----------|-----------|
| Sales 2007 | $650,300  | $478,100  | $225,500  |
| Sales 2008 | $623,100  | $533,600  | $210,000  |
| Sales 2009 | $725,600  | $478,400  | $296,500  |

4. Print Slide 5.
5. Save and then close **PP_C5_A4.pptx**.

# CASE study

## *Apply Your Skills*

**Part 1**

You are an administrator for Terra Energy Corporation and you are responsible for preparing a presentation for a quarterly meeting. Open the Word document named **TerraEnergy.docx** and then use the information to prepare a presentation with the following specifications:

- Create the first slide with the company name and the subtitle of *Quarterly Meeting*.
- Create a slide that presents the Executive Team information in a table.
- Create a slide that presents the phases information in a table (the three columns of text in the *Research and Development* section). Insert a column at the left side of the table that includes the text *New Product* rotated.
- Create a slide that presents the development team information in a SmartArt organizational chart.
- Create a slide that presents the revenues information in a chart (you determine the type of chart).
- Create a slide that presents the United States sales information in a chart (you determine the type of chart).

Apply a design theme of your choosing and add any additional features to improve the visual appeal of the presentation. Insert a transition and sound to each slide and then run the presentation. Save the presentation and name it **PP_C5_CS_P1.pptx**. Print the presentation as a handout with four slides per page.

**Part 2**

Last year, a production project was completed and you want to display a graphic that illustrates the primary focus of the project. Create a slide and insert a *Funnel* SmartArt graphic (in the *Relationship* group) with the following information in the shapes inside the funnel (turn on the Text pane to type the information in the shapes):

Updated Systems
Safety Programs
Market Expansion

Insert the information *Higher Profits* below the funnel. Apply formatting to the SmartArt graphic to improve the visual appeal. Print the slide and then save **PP_C5_CS_P1.pptx**.

**Part 3**

The presentation should include information on the corporation's stock. Use the Help feature to learn about stock charts and then create a high-low-close stock chart with the following information:

| Date | High | Low | Close |
|------|------|-----|-------|
| 01/01/2010 | 23 | 20.25 | 21.875 |
| 02/01/2010 | 28.625 | 25.25 | 26.375 |
| 03/01/2010 | 32.375 | 28 | 30.125 |
| 04/01/2010 | 27.125 | 24.5 | 26.375 |
| 05/01/2010 | 25.125 | 22.875 | 24.25 |

Apply formatting to the chart to improve the readability and appeal of the chart. Print the slide and then save **PP_C5_CS_P1.pptx**.

**Part 4**

You have created an Excel chart containing information on department costs. You decide to improve the visual appeal of the chart and then create a link from the presentation to the chart. Open Excel and then open **DepartmentCosts.xlsx**. Apply additional formatting to the pie chart to make it easy to read and understand the data. Save and then close the workbook and exit Excel. Create a new slide in the **PP_C5_CS_P1.pptx** presentation that includes a hyperlink to the **DepartmentCosts.xlsx** workbook. Run the presentation and when the slide displays containing the hyperlinked text, click the hyperlink, view the chart in Excel, and then exit Excel. Print the presentation as a handout with four slides per page. Save and then close **PP_C5_CS_P1.pptx**.

# Using Slide Masters and Action Buttons

## PERFORMANCE OBJECTIVES

**Upon successful completion of Chapter 6, you will be able to:**

- Format slides in Slide Master view
- Apply themes and backgrounds in Slide Master view
- Delete placeholders and slide master layouts
- Insert elements in Slide Master view
- Create and rename a custom slide layout
- Insert a new slide master
- Save a presentation as a template
- Customize a handout in Handout Master view
- Customize notes pages in Notes Master view
- Insert action buttons
- Create hyperlinks

powerpoint Chapter 6

**Tutorial 6.1**
Working with Masters
**Tutorial 6.2**
Creating and Customizing a
Presentation

If you make design or formatting changes and you want the changes to affect all slides in the presentation, consider making the changes in a slide master in the Slide Master view. Along with the Slide Master view, you can make changes to all pages in a handout with options in the Handout Master view and all notes pages in the Notes Master view. You can insert action buttons in a presentation to connect to slides within the same presentation, connect to another presentation, connect to a Web site, or connect to another program. You can also connect to a Web site by inserting a hyperlink to the site.

*Note: Before beginning computer projects, copy to your storage medium the PowerPoint2007C6 folder from the PowerPoint2007 folder on the CD that accompanies this textbook and then make PowerPoint2007C6 the active folder.*

You will apply formatting to a blank presentation in Slide Master view, insert slides in the presentation, insert elements in Slide Master view, insert a custom slide layout, and insert a new slide master.

**QUICK STEPS**

**Display Slide Master View**
1. Click View tab.
2. Click Slide Master button.

**HINT**

Create a consistent look to your slides by customizing slides in Slide Master view.

## Customizing Slide Masters

When creating a presentation, you can apply a design theme to the presentation to provide colors and formatting. If you make changes to a slide and want the changes to affect all slides in the presentation, make the change in a slide master. You can customize a slide master by changing the theme, theme colors, and/or theme fonts; changing the location of and inserting placeholders; applying a background style; and changing the page setup and slide orientation. If you know you want to customize slides, consider making the changes in Slide Master view before you create each slide. If you apply a slide master to an existing presentation, some items on slides may not conform to the new formatting.

To display the Slide Master view, click the View tab and then click the Slide Master button in the Presentation Views group. This displays the Slide Master tab, a blank slide master in the Slide pane, and inserts slide master thumbnails in the slide thumbnail pane. The largest thumbnail in the pane is the slide master and the other thumbnails represent associated layouts. Position the mouse pointer on a slide thumbnail and the name of the thumbnail displays in a box by the thumbnail. Figure 6.1 displays a blank presentation in Slide Master view. To specify the slide master or layout you want to customize, click the desired thumbnail in the slide thumbnail pane. With the slide master layout displayed in the Slide pane, make the desired changes and then click the Close Master View button.

### Applying Themes to Slide Masters

You can apply themes, theme colors, theme fonts, and theme effects with buttons in the Edit Theme group in the Slide Master tab. Click the Themes button and a drop-down list displays with available predesigned themes and also any custom themes you have created. Click the desired theme and the theme formatting is applied to the slide master. Complete similar steps to apply theme colors, theme fonts, and theme effects.

**Figure 6.1** Slide Master View

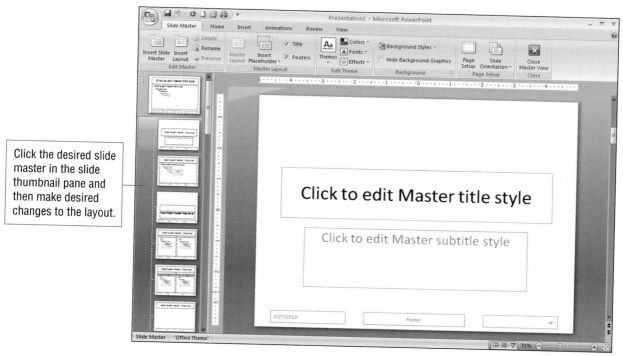

Click the desired slide master in the slide thumbnail pane and then make desired changes to the layout.

## Project 1a  Formatting a Slide Master

1. Display a blank presentation.
2. Click the View tab and then click the Slide Master button in the Presentation Views group.

**Step 2**

**Step 4**

3. Click the top (and largest) slide master thumbnail in the slide thumbnail pane (*Office Theme Slide Master*). (This displays the slide master layout in the Slide pane.)
4. Click the Themes button in the Edit Theme group in the Slide Master tab.
5. Click *Solstice* at the drop-down gallery.
6. Click the Colors button in the Edit Theme group and then click *Metro* at the drop-down gallery.
7. Click the Fonts button in the Edit Theme group and then click the *Foundry* option at the drop-down gallery.
8. Change the font color and alignment for the title style by completing the following steps:
   a. Select the text *Click to edit Master title style* that displays in the slide master in the Slide pane.

**Step 5**

b. Click the Home tab.

c. Click the Font Color button arrow and then click the *Turquoise, Accent 4, Darker 25%* option.

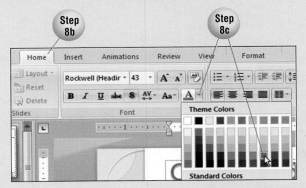

Step
8b

Step
8c

d. Click the Center button in the Paragraph group.

9. Change the font color by completing the following steps:

   a. Select all of the bulleted text in the slide master.

   b. Make sure the Home tab is selected.

   c. Click the Font Color button arrow and then click the *Periwinkle, Accent 5, Darker 50%* option.

10. Change the color of the first two bullets by completing the following steps:

   a. Select the text following the first two bullets.

   b. Click the Bullets button arrow in the Paragraph group in the Home tab and then click *Bullets and Numbering* at the drop-down gallery.

   c. At the Bullets and Numbering dialog box with the Bulleted tab selected, click the Color button and then click the *Turquoise, Accent 4, Darker 25%* color option.

   d. Click OK to close the dialog box.

11. Click the Slide Master tab.

12. Click the Close Master View button.

13. Save the presentation and name it **TravelMaster.pptx**.

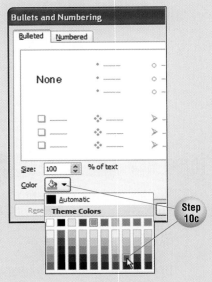

Step
10c

# HINT

# Applying and Formatting Backgrounds

Like the Background group in the Design tab, the Background group in the Slide Master tab contains the Background Styles button and the *Hide Background Graphics* check box. If you want to change the background graphic for all slides, make the change at the slide master. To do this, display the presentation in Slide Master view and then click the desired slide master layout in the slide thumbnail pane. Click the Background Styles button and then click a background at the drop-down gallery. Or, click the *Format Background* option and choose the desired options at the Format Background dialog box. If you want to remove the background graphic for slides, click the *Hide Background Graphics* check box to insert a check mark.

## Deleting Placeholders

If you want to remove a placeholder for all slides in a presentation, consider deleting the placeholder in the Slide Master view. To do this, display the presentation in Slide Master view, click the desired slide master layout in the slide thumbnail pane, click the placeholder border (make sure the border displays as a solid line), and then press the Delete key. You can also remove a title placeholder from a slide master by clicking the *Title* check box in the Master Layout group to remove the check mark. Remove footer placeholders by clicking the *Footer* check box to remove the check mark.

**QUICK STEPS**

**Delete Slide Master Layouts**
1. Display presentation in Slide Master view.
2. Click desired slide layout thumbnail.
3. Click Delete button.

## Deleting Slide Master Layouts

In Slide Master view, a slide master displays for each available layout. If you know that you will not be using a particular layout in the presentation, you can delete the layout slide master. To do this, display the presentation in Slide Master view, click the desired slide layout thumbnail in the slide thumbnail pane, and then click the Delete button in the Edit Master group.

**HINT**

You can also delete a slide layout by right-clicking the layout in the slide thumbnail pane and then clicking *Delete Layout* at the shortcut menu.

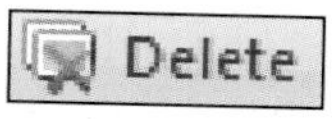


## Project 1b Applying and Formatting Background Graphics

1. With **TravelMaster.pptx** open, click the View tab and then click the Slide Master button in the Presentation Views group.
2. Click the top slide layout thumbnail (*Solstice Slide Master*) in the slide thumbnail pane.
3. Format the background by completing the following steps:
   a. Click the Background Styles button in the Background group and then click *Format Background* at the drop-down gallery.
   b. At the Format Background dialog box, click the *Gradient fill* option.
   c. Click the *Preset colors* button and then click the *Fog* option at the drop-down list (last option in the second row).
   d. Click the down-pointing arrow at the right side of the *Type* option and then click *Path* at the drop-down list.
   e. Click the Close button.

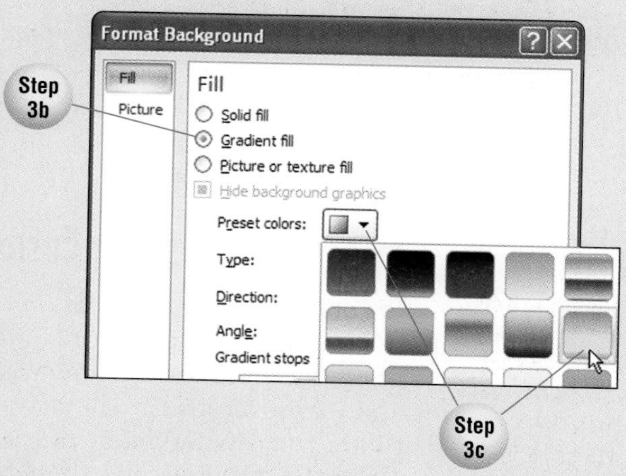


4. Apply a picture to the background of the title slide layout (the picture will appear only on this layout) by completing the following steps:
   a. Click the second slide layout thumbnail (*Title Slide Layout*) in the slide thumbnail pane.
   b. Click the *Hide Background Graphics* check box to insert a check mark.
   c. Click the Background Styles button in the Background group and then click *Format Background* at the drop-down list.
   d. At the Format Background dialog box, click the *Picture or texture fill* option.

e. Click the File button (located below the *Insert from* option).

f. At the Insert Picture dialog box, navigate to the PowerPoint2007C6 folder on your storage medium and then double-click **Stonehenge.jpg**.

g. Click the Close button to close the Format Background dialog box.

h. Remove the two small green circles that appear in the slide master in the Slide pane by clicking each circle and then pressing the Delete key.

i. Click on any character in the text *Click to edit Master title style* and then press Ctrl + E. (This is the keyboard shortcut for centering.)

j. Drag the placeholder so it is positioned above the stones and centered horizontally. (Make sure the bottom border of the placeholder is positioned above the stones.)

5. Delete the Master subtitle style placeholder by clicking the placeholder border (make sure the border displays as a solid line) and then pressing the Delete key.

6. Remove the footer placeholders from the layout by clicking the *Footers* check box in the Master Layout group to remove the check mark.

Step
6

Step
7d

7. Delete slide layouts that you will not be using in the presentation by completing the following steps:

a. Click the fourth slide layout thumbnail in the slide thumbnail pane.

b. Scroll down the pane until the last slide layout thumbnail is visible.

c. Hold down the Shift key and then click the last slide layout thumbnail.

d. Click the Delete button in the Edit Master group. (The slide thumbnail pane should contain the slide master and two associated layouts.)

8. Click the Close Master View button.

9. Delete the slide that currently displays in the Slide pane. (This displays a blue background with the text *Click to add first slide*. The presentation does not contain any slides, just formatting.)

10. Save **TravelMaster.pptx**.

## Inserting Slides in a Customized Presentation

If you customize slides in a presentation in Slide Master view, you can use the presentation formatting in other presentations. You can save the formatted presentation as a template or you can save the presentation in the normal manner and then open the presentation, save it with a new name, and then type text in slides. You can also insert slides into the current presentation using the Reuse Slides task pane. (You learned about this task pane in Chapter 2.) To use this task pane, click the Home tab, click the New Slide button arrow, and then click *Reuse Slides* at the drop-down list. This displays the Reuse Slides task pane at the right side of the screen. Click the Browse button and then click the *Browse File* option at the drop-down list. At the Browse dialog box, navigate to the desired folder and then double-click the desired presentation. Insert slides into the current presentation by clicking the desired slide in the task pane.

1. With **TravelMaster.pptx** open, save the presentation with Save As and name it **PP_C6_P1**.
2. Make sure the Home tab is active, click the New Slide button arrow, and then click *Title Slide* at the drop-down list.
3. Click the *Click to add title* text in the current slide and then type Wiltshire, England.
4. Insert slides into the current presentation from an existing presentation by completing the following steps:

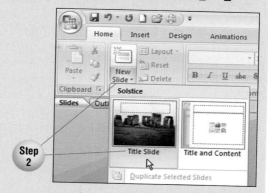

Step 2

   a. Click the New Slide button arrow and then click *Reuse Slides* at the drop-down list.
   b. Click the Browse button in the Reuse Slides task pane and then click *Browse File* at the drop-down list.
   c. At the Browse dialog box, navigate to the PowerPoint2007C6 folder on your storage medium and then double-click **TravelEngland.pptx**.

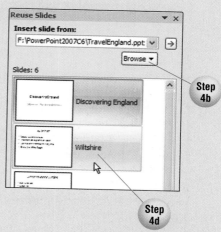

Step 4b

Step 4d

   d. Click the *Wiltshire* slide in the Reuse Slides task pane. (This inserts the slide in the presentation and applies the custom formatting to the slide.)
   e. Click the *Ancient Stone Circles* slide in the Reuse Slides task pane.
   f. Click the *Ancient Wiltshire* slide in the Reuse Slides task pane.
   g. Click the *White Horses* slide in the Reuse Slides task pane.
   h. Click the Close button located in the upper right corner of the Reuse Slides task pane to close the task pane.
5. With Slide 5 active, format the bulleted text into two columns by completing the following steps:
   a. Click in any character in the bulleted text.
   b. Move the insertion point so it is positioned immediately following *Marlborough*.
   c. Press the Enter key (to insert a blank line) and then click the Bullets button in the Paragraph group in the Home tab to remove the bullet.
   d. Press Ctrl + A to select all of the bulleted text.
   e. Click the Line Spacing button in the Paragraph group and then click *2.0* at the drop-down list.
   f. Click the Columns button in the Paragraph group and then click *Two Columns* at the drop-down list.
6. With Slide 5 active, insert a new slide by completing the following steps:
   a. Click the New Slide button arrow and then click the *Title Slide* layout at the drop-down list.
   b. Click in the text *Click to add title* and then type Call Lucy at 555-4500.
7. Save **PP_C6_P1.pptx**.
8. Print the presentation as a handout with six slides per page. (The picture backgrounds will not print.)

## Inserting Elements in a Slide Master

As you learned in Chapter 2, you can display a presentation in Print Preview and then insert a header, footer, or the date and time that print on every slide in the presentation. You can also insert these elements in a slide master. For example, to insert a header or footer in slides, display the presentation in Slide Master view, click the Insert tab, and then click the Header & Footer button in the Text group. At the Header and Footer dialog box with the Slide tab selected, make the desired changes, click the Notes and Handouts tab, make the desired changes, and then click the Apply to All button. You can also insert additional elements in the Slide Master view such as a picture, clip art image, shape, SmartArt graphic, or chart. Insert any of these elements in the normal manner in a slide in Slide Master view.

### Project 1d  Inserting Elements in Slide Master View

1. With **PP_C6_P1.pptx** open, insert a header, a footer, and the date and time by completing the following steps:
   a. Click the View tab.
   b. Click the Slide Master button in the Presentation Views group.
   c. Click the slide master thumbnail (the top slide thumbnail in the slide thumbnail pane).
   d. Click the Insert tab.
   e. Click the Header & Footer button in the Text group.
   f. At the Header and Footer dialog box with the Slide tab selected, click the *Date and time* check box to insert a check mark.
   g. Make sure the *Update automatically* option is selected. (With this option selected, the date and/or time will automatically update each time you open the presentation.)
   h. Click the *Slide number* check box to insert a check mark.
   i. Click the *Footer* check box to insert a check mark and then type your first and last names in the *Footer* text box.

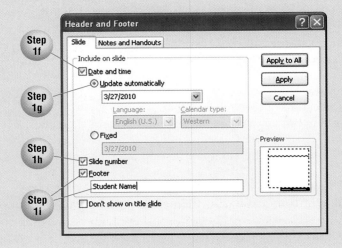

j. Click the Notes and Handouts tab.

k. Click the *Date and time* check box to insert a check mark.

l. Make sure the *Update automatically* option is selected.

m. Click the *Header* check box and then type the name of your school.

n. Click the *Footer* check box and then type your first and last names.

o. Click the Apply to All button.

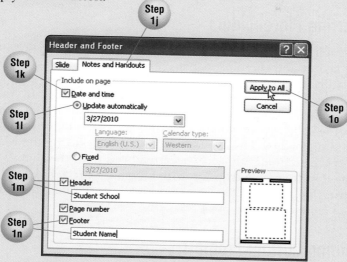

2. Insert the First Choice Travel logo in the lower left corner of the slide master by completing the following steps:

a. Click the Picture button in the Illustrations group.

b. At the Insert Picture dialog box, navigate to the PowerPoint2007C6 folder on your storage medium and then double-click **FCTLogo.jpg**.

c. Click in the *Shape Height* measurement box in the Size group in the Picture Tools Format tab, type **0.55**, and then press Enter.

d. Drag the logo so it is positioned in the lower left corner of the slide as shown at the right.

e. Click the Send to Back button in the Arrange group.

f. Click outside the logo to deselect it.

3. With the Slide Master tab selected, click the Close Master View button.

4. Run the presentation and notice the logo and other elements in the slides.

5. Print the presentation as a handout with six slides per page.

6. Save **PP_C6_P1.pptx**.

# Creating and Renaming a Custom Slide Layout

You can create your own custom slide layout in Slide Master view and then customize the layout by inserting or deleting elements and applying formatting to placeholders and text. To create a new slide layout, click the Insert Layout button in the Edit Master group in the Slide Master tab. This inserts in the Slide pane a new slide containing a Master title style placeholder and footer placeholders. Customize the layout by inserting or deleting placeholders and applying formatting to placeholders.

Insert Layout

PowerPoint will automatically assign the name *Custom Layout* to a slide layout you create. If you create another slide layout, PowerPoint will name it *1_Custom Layout*, and so on. Consider renaming your custom layout to a name that describes the layout. To rename a layout, make sure the desired slide layout is active, and then click the Rename button in the Edit Master group. At the Rename Layout dialog box, type the desired name, and then click the Rename button.

## Inserting Placeholders

You can insert placeholders in a predesigned slide layout or you can insert a custom slide layout and then insert placeholders. Insert a placeholder by clicking the Insert Placeholder button arrow in the Master Layout group and then clicking the desired placeholder option at the drop-down list. If you click the slide master, the Insert Placeholder button is dimmed. If you delete a placeholder from the slide master, you can reinsert the placeholder with options at the Master Layout dialog box. Display this dialog box by clicking the Master Layout button and any placeholder that has been removed from the slide master displays in the dialog box as an active option with an empty check box. Reinsert the placeholder by inserting a check mark in the desired placeholder check box and then clicking OK to close the dialog box.

## Creating Custom Prompts

Some placeholders in a custom layout may contain generic text such as *Click to add Master title style* or *Click to edit Master text styles*. In Slide Master view, you can select this generic text and replace it with custom text. You might want to insert text that describes what you want entered into the placeholder.

## Project 1e   Inserting a Layout and Placeholder

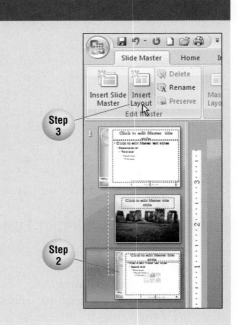

1. With **PP_C6_P1.pptx** open, click the View tab and then click the Slide Master button in the Presentation Views group.
2. Click the bottom slide layout thumbnail in the slide thumbnail pane.
3. Click the Insert Layout button in the Edit Master group. (This inserts in the Slide pane a new slide with a Master title style placeholder, the logo, and the footer information.)
4. Format and move the placeholder by completing the following steps:
   a. Select the text *Click to edit Master title style*.
   b. Click the Home tab, click the Text Shadow button (to turn off shadowing), turn on bold, change the font to Tahoma, change the font size to 28 points, and change the font color to Light Blue.

Step 3

Step 2

c. Move the placeholder so it is positioned along the bottom of the slide just above the footer placeholder.

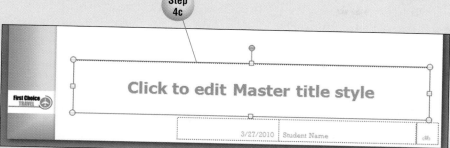

Step 4c

5. Click the Slide Master tab.
6. Insert a Picture placeholder by completing the following steps:
   a. Click the Insert Placeholder button arrow.
   b. Click *Picture* at the drop-down list.
   c. Drag in the slide in the Slide pane to create a placeholder that is approximately 7.5 inches wide and 3.5 inches high.
   d. Click the Drawing Tools Format tab.
   e. Click in the *Shape Height* measurement box and then type 3.5.
   f. Click in the *Shape Width* measurement box, type 7.5, and then press Enter.
   g. Drag the placeholder so it is balanced in the slide.
   h. Click outside the placeholder to deselect it.
   i. Position the mouse pointer immediately left of the word *Picture* in the placeholder until the pointer turns into an I-beam and then click the left mouse button. (This removes the word *Picture* and inserts the insertion point in the placeholder.)
   j. Type Insert company logo.
7. Remove the footer and slide number placeholders by completing the following steps:
   a. Click the footer placeholder (located along the bottom of the slide in the Slide pane).
   b. Click the border of the placeholder to select it (the border turns into a solid line) and then press the Delete key.
   c. Click the slide number placeholder, click the placeholder border, and then press the Delete key.
   d. Drag the date placeholder so it is positioned at the right side of the slide.
8. If necessary, click the Slide Master tab.
9. Rename the custom slide layout by completing the following steps:
   a. Click the Rename button in the Edit Master group.
   b. At the Custom Layout dialog box, type Logo Layout.
   c. Click the Rename button.
10. Click the Close Master View button.
11. Insert a slide using the new slide layout by completing the following steps:
    a. Make Slide 6 active.

Step 6a

Step 6b

Step 6e

Step 6f

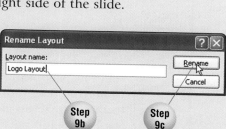

Step 9b

Step 9c

b. Click the New Slide button arrow.
c. Click the *Logo Layout* option at the drop-down list.
d. Click the Insert Picture from File button in the slide.
e. At the Insert Picture dialog box, navigate to the PowerPoint2007C6 folder on your storage medium and then double-click ***FCTLogo.jpg***.
f. Click in the text *Click to add title* and then type Monthly special – 20% discount on Wiltshire tour.

12. Save **PP_C6_P1.pptx**.

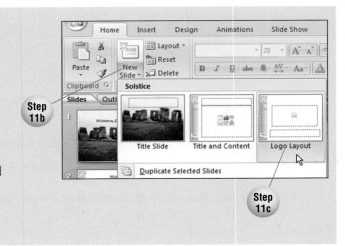

## Inserting a New Slide Master

A PowerPoint presentation can contain more than one slide master (and associated layouts). To insert a new slide master, display the presentation in Slide Master view and then click the Insert Slide Master button in the Edit Master group. This inserts the slide master and all associated layouts below the existing slide master and layouts in the slide thumbnail pane. You can also insert a slide master and all associated layouts with a design theme applied. To do this, click below the existing slide master and associated layouts, click the Themes button in the Edit Theme group, and then click the desired theme at the drop-down gallery. A slide master containing the chosen design theme is inserted below the existing thumbnails.

## Preserving Slide Masters

**Preserve Slide Master**
1. Display presentation in Slide Master view.
2. Click desired slide master thumbnail.
3. Click Preserve button.

If you delete all slide layouts that follow a slide master, PowerPoint will automatically delete the slide master. You can protect a slide master from being deleted by "preserving" the master. To do this, click the desired slide master thumbnail and then click the Preserve button in the Edit Master group. If you insert a slide master using the Insert Slide Master button, the Preserve button is automatically active. When a slide master is preserved, a preservation icon displays below the slide number in the slide thumbnail pane.

## Changing Page Setup

The Page Setup group in the Slide Master tab contains two buttons. By default, slides display in the landscape orientation (wider than tall). You can change this to portrait orientation (taller than wide) by clicking the Slide Orientation button in the Page Setup group and then clicking *Portrait* at the drop-down list. Click the Page Setup button and the Page Setup dialog box displays with options for changing slide width and height; slide numbering; and applying slide orientation to slides or notes, handouts, and outline pages.

# Project 1f  Applying a Second Slide Master and Changing Slide Numbering

Step 1b

1. With **PP_C6_P1.pptx** open, insert a second slide master by completing the following steps:
   a. Click the View tab and then click the Slide Master button in the Presentation Views group.
   b. Click below the bottom slide layout in the slide thumbnail pane. (You want the slide master and associated layouts to display below the original slide master and not take the place of the original.)
   c. Click the Themes button in the Edit Theme group and then click *Flow* at the drop-down gallery. (Notice the slide master and associated layouts that display in the slide thumbnail pane below the original slide master and associated layouts and notice the preservation icon that displays below the slide master number 2.)
   d. Click the Colors button in the Edit Theme group and then click *Apex* at the drop-down gallery.
   e. Click the Fonts button and then click *Foundry* at the drop-down gallery.
2. Insert a footer, the date and time, and slide numbers in the slide master by completing the following steps:
   a. Click the Insert tab.
   b. Click the Header & Footer button in the Text group.
   c. At the Header and Footer dialog box with the Slide tab selected, click the *Date and time* check box to insert a check mark.
   d. Make sure the *Update automatically* option is selected. (With this option selected, the date and/or time will automatically update each time you open the presentation.)
   e. Click the *Slide number* check box to insert a check mark.
   f. Click the *Footer* check box to insert a check mark and then type your first and last names in the *Footer* text box.
   g. Click the Apply to All button.
3. Click the Slide Master tab.
4. Click the third layout below the new slide master (*Section Header Layout*), scroll down to the bottom of the slide thumbnail pane, hold down the Shift key, click the bottom thumbnail, and then click the Delete button in the Edit Master group. (This deletes all but two of the associated layouts with the new slide master.)
5. Format the slide layout below the new slide master by completing the following steps:
   a. Click the layout (Title Slide Layout) below the new slide master.
   b. Click the Background Styles button in the Background group and then click *Format Background*.
   c. At the Format Background dialog box, click the *Picture or texture fill* option.
   d. Click the File button (located below the *Insert from* option).
   e. At the Insert Picture dialog box, navigate to the PowerPoint2007C6 folder on your storage medium and then double-click **Nightscape.jpg**.
   f. Click the *Hide background graphics* check box to insert a check mark.
   g. Click the Close button.
   h. Click in the text *Click to edit Master title style* and then press Ctrl + E. (This centers the text.)
   i. Drag the placeholder up so the text displays above the buildings.
   j. Select and then delete the subtitle placeholder.
   k. Click the *Footers* check box in the Master Layout group to remove footer placeholders.
6. Click the Close Master View button.

7. Insert a new slide by completing the following steps:
   a. Make Slide 7 active.
   b. Click the New Slide button arrow and then click the Flow Title Slide (the slide with the image of the New York City night skyline).
   c. Click in the text *Click to add title* and then type New York City Tour.
8. Insert a new slide by completing the following steps:
   a. With Slide 8 active, click the New Slide button. (This inserts the Flow Title and Content layout.)
   b. Click the text *Click to add title* and then type Manhattan Tour.
   c. Click the text *Click to add text* and then type the following bulleted text:
      - Times Square
      - Madison Square Garden
      - Greenwich Village
      - Soho
      - Little Italy
      - Battery Park
9. Insert the following text in slides using the Flow Title and Content layout:
   Slide 10    Dinner Cruise
      - Three-hour cruise
      - Manhattan skyline
      - Five-course gourmet dinner
      - Entertainment
      - Dancing
   Slide 11    City Pass
      - Empire State Building
      - Statue of Liberty
      - Ellis Island
      - Rockefeller Center
      - United Nations Building
      - Bronx Zoo
   Slide 12    Museum Passes
      - Museum of Modern Art
      - Guggenheim Museum
      - American Museum of Natural History
      - Metropolitan Museum of Art
      - Ellis Island Museum
      - Brooklyn Museum of Art
10. Insert a new slide by completing the following steps:
    a. With Slide 12 active, click the New Slide button arrow and then click the Flow Title Slide (the slide with the image of the New York City night skyline).
    b. Click in the text *Click to add text* and then type Call Beth at 555-4500.

11. Insert a new slide with the Logo Layout by completing the following steps:
   a. With Slide 13 active, click the New Slide button arrow and then click the Solstice Logo Layout.
   b. Click the Insert Picture from File button in the slide.
   c. At the Insert Picture dialog box, navigate to the PowerPoint2007C6 folder on your storage medium and then double-click *FCTLogo.jpg*.
   d. Click in the text *Click to add title* and then type Complimentary airport shuttle when you book your New York tour.

12. Assume that the presentation is going to be inserted into a larger presentation and that the starting slide number will be 12 (instead of 1). Change the beginning slide number by completing the following steps:
   a. Click the View tab and then click the Slide Master button.
   b. Click the top slide master in the slide thumbnail pane.
   c. Click the Page Setup button in the Page Setup group.
   d. At the Page Setup dialog box, select the current number in the *Number slides from* text box and then type 12.
   e. Click OK to close the dialog box.
   f. Click the Close Master View button.

13. Print the presentation as a handout with six slides per page.

14. Save and then close **PP_C6_P1.pptx**.

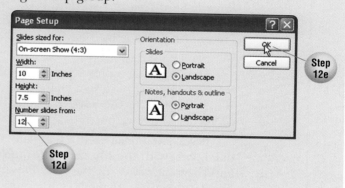

Step 12e

Step 12d

---

P roject ❷ **Save a Template and Create a Travel Presentation with the Template**

You will save a travel presentation as a template and then use the template to create and format a travel presentation. You will insert elements in the presentation in Handout Master view and Notes Master view, change the presentation zoom, and view the presentation in grayscale and black and white.

## Saving a Presentation as a Template

If you create custom formatting that you will use for future presentations, consider saving the presentation as a template. The advantage to saving your presentation as a template is that you cannot accidentally overwrite the presentation. When you open a template and then click the Save button on the Quick Access toolbar, the Save As dialog box automatically displays.

To save a presentation as a template, click the Office button and then click *Save As*. At the Save As dialog box, click the down-pointing arrow at the right side of the *Save as type* option and then click *PowerPoint Template (*.potx)* at the drop-down list. Type a name for the template in the *File name* text box and then click

**QUICK STEPS**

**Save Presentation as a Template**
1. Click Office button, *Save As*.
2. Click *Save as type* option.
3. Click *PowerPoint Template (*.potx)*.
4. Type presentation name.
5. Click Save button.

the Save button. The template is automatically saved in the C:\Program Files\Microsoft Office\Templates\ folder. If you want to save the template to another location, navigate to the desired folder in the Save As dialog box and then save the template.

To create a presentation based on a template, click the Office button and then click *New*. Recently used templates display in the *Recently Used Templates* section of the dialog box. If the desired template displays in this section, double-click the template (or click the template and then click the Create button). If the desired template does not display in the *Recently Used Templates* section, click the *My Templates* option in the *Templates* section. At the New Presentation dialog box with the My Templates tab selected, double-click the desired template.

If you created a template in a location other than the default, open a presentation based on the template by clicking the Office button and then clicking *New*. At the New Presentation dialog box, double-click the desired template in the *Recently Used Templates* section. If the template does not display in the section, click the *New from existing* option in the *Templates* section. At the New from Existing Presentation dialog box, navigate to the desired folder and then double-click the desired template.

After opening a presentation template, insert the desired slides and make any other formatting or design changes and then click the Save button on the Quick Access toolbar. At the Save As dialog box, type a name for the presentation and then click the Save button.

If you no longer need a template, delete the template at the New Presentation dialog box with the My Templates tab selected. To do this, click the Office button and then click *New*. At the New Presentation dialog box, click *My Templates* in the *Templates* section. At the New Presentation dialog box with the My Templates tab selected, right-click the template you want to delete and then click *Delete* at the shortcut menu. At the message asking if you want to delete the template, click the Yes button. If you saved a template to a location other than the default, delete the template in the same manner as you delete a presentation. To do this, display the Open dialog box, navigate to the desired folder, click the template you want to delete, click the Delete button on the dialog box toolbar, and then click Yes at the message that displays.

## Project 2a   Saving a Presentation as a Template

1. Open **TravelMaster.pptx**.
2. Click the Office button and then click *Save As* at the drop-down list.
3. At the Save As dialog box, click the down-pointing arrow at the right side of the *Save as type* option and then click *PowerPoint Template (*.potx)* at the drop-down list.

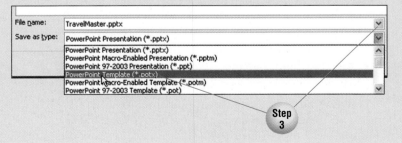

4. Navigate to the PowerPoint2007C6 folder on your storage medium.
5. Select the name that currently displays in the *File name* text box and then type **XXXTravelTemplate** (type your initials rather than the *XXX*).
6. Click the Save button.

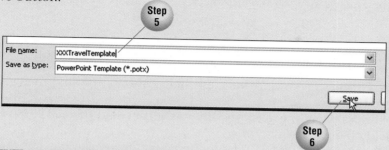

**Step 5**

File name: XXXTravelTemplate

Save as type: PowerPoint Template (*.potx)

Save

**Step 6**

7. Close the **XXXTravelTemplate.potx** template.
8. Open the template and save it as a presentation by completing the following steps:
   a. Click the Office button and then click *New* at the drop-down list.
   b. At the New Presentation dialog box, click the *New from existing* option in the *Templates* section.
   c. At the New from Existing Presentation dialog box, navigate to the PowerPoint2007C6 folder on your storage medium and then double-click *XXXTravelTemplate.potx*.
9. Save the presentation and name it **PP_C6_P2**.

# Customizing the Handout Master

As you learned in Chapter 2, you can choose to print a presentation as individual slides, handouts, notes pages, or an outline. If you print a presentation as handouts or an outline, PowerPoint will automatically print the current date in the upper right corner of the page and the page number in the lower right corner. You can customize the handout with options in the Print Preview tab and you can also customize a handout in the Handout Master view. Display a presentation in Handout Master view by clicking the View tab and then clicking the Handout Master button in the Presentation Views group. With options in the Handout Master tab, you can move, resize, and format header and footer placeholders, change page orientation, and specify the number of slides you want printed on each page.

Handout Master

With buttons in the Page Setup group, you can display the Page Setup dialog box with options for changing the size and orientation of the handout page, changing the handout and/or slide orientation, and specifying the number of slides you want printed on the handout page. By default, a handout will contain a header, footer, date, and page number placeholder. You can remove any of these placeholders by removing the check mark before the placeholder option in the Placeholders group. For example, to remove the page number placeholder, click the *Page Number* check box in the Placeholders group to remove the check mark.

The Edit Theme group contains buttons for changing the theme color, font, and effects. Click the Themes button and the options in the drop-down gallery are dimmed, indicating that the themes are not available for the handout. If you apply a background style to the handout master, you can change theme colors by clicking the Colors button and then clicking the desired color theme at the drop-down gallery. Apply theme fonts by clicking the Fonts button and then clicking the desired fonts theme at the drop-down gallery.

Apply a background style to the handout page by clicking the Background Styles button in the Background group and then clicking one of the predesigned styles. You can also click the *Format Background* option and then make changes at the Format Background dialog box. Remove any background graphics by clicking the *Hide background graphics* check box to insert a check mark.

## Project 2b   Customizing the Handout Master

1. With **PP_C6_P2.pptx** open, click the New Slide button arrow and then click *Reuse Slides* at the drop-down list.
2. In the Reuse Slides task pane, click the Browse button, and then click the *Browse File* option at the drop-down list.
3. Navigate to the PowerPoint2007C6 folder on your storage medium and then double-click ***ParisTour.pptx***.
4. Insert the second, third, fourth, and fifth slides from the Reuse Slides task pane into the current presentation.
5. Close the Reuse Slides task pane.
6. Edit the Title Slide Layout in Slide Master view by completing the following steps:
   a. Click the View tab and then click the Slide Master button.
   b. Click the second thumbnail in the slide thumbnail pane (*Title Slide Layout*).
   c. Click the Background Styles button in the Background group and then click *Format Background* at the drop-down list.
   d. At the Format Background dialog box, click the File button (displays below the *Insert from* text).
   e. At the Insert Picture dialog box, navigate to the PowerPoint2007C6 folder on your storage medium and then double-click ***EiffelTower.jpg***.
   f. Click the Close button to close the Format Background dialog box.
   g. Select the text *Click to edit Master title style*, click the Home tab, click the Font Color button arrow, and then click *Turquoise, Accent 4, Lighter 60%* at the drop-down gallery.
   h. Click the Slide Master tab.
   i. Click the Close Master View button.
7. Make Slide 1 active, click in the text *Click to add title*, and then type Paris Tour.
8. Size and move the text placeholder so *Paris Tour* displays in a blue area on the slide (not over the tower).
9. Display each slide and then make adjustments to the position of clip art images and/or placeholders.
10. Make Slide 5 active and then create a new slide with the *Title Slide* layout. Type Call Greg at 555-4500.
11. Save **PP_C6_P2.pptx**.
12. Click the View tab and then click the Handout Master button in the Presentation Views group.

13. Click the Handout Orientation button in the Page Setup group and then click *Landscape* at the drop-down list.
14. Click in the Header placeholder on the page and then type your first and last names.
15. Click in the Footer placeholder and then type *Paris Tour*.
16. Click the Background Styles button and then click *Style 10* at the drop-down list (second option from the left in the third row).
17. Click the Colors button in the Edit Theme group and then click *Metro* at the drop-down list.
18. Click the Fonts button in the Edit Theme group and then click *Foundry* at the drop-down list.
19. Edit the header text by completing the following steps:
    a. Click in the header placeholder and then click on any character in your name.
    b. Move the insertion point so it is positioned immediately right of the last character in your last name.
    c. Type a comma, press the spacebar, and then type your course number and title.
    d. Click in the handout page outside of any placeholder.
20. Click the Close Master View button.
21. Print the presentation as a handout with four slides per page. (The handout background style and the pictures will not print.)
22. Save **PP_C6_P2.pptx**

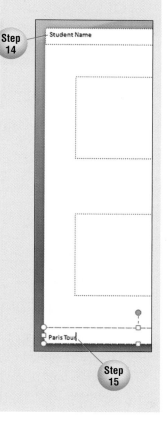

Step 14

Student Name

Paris Tour

Step 15

## Customizing the Notes Master

You can insert notes in a presentation and then print the presentation as notes pages and the notes will print below the slide. If you want to insert or format text or other elements as notes on all slides in a presentation, consider making the changes in the Notes Master view. Display this view by clicking the View tab and then clicking the Notes Master button in the Presentation Views group. This displays a notes page along with the Notes Master tab. Many of the buttons and options in this tab are the same as the ones in the Handout Master tab.

Notes Master

## Project 2c    Customizing the Notes Master

1. With **PP_C6_P2.pptx** open, click the View tab and then click the Notes Master button in the Presentation Views group.
2. Click the *Body* check box in the Placeholders group to remove the check mark.
3. Click the Fonts button in the Edit Theme group and then click *Foundry* at the drop-down list.
4. Click the Insert tab.

| Notes Master | Home | Insert | Review | View |

Page Setup    Notes Page Orientation    Slide Orientation

☑ Header    ☑ Date
☑ Slide Image    ☐ Body
☑ Footer    ☑ Page Number

Page Setup    Placeholders

Step 2

5. Click the Text Box button in the Text group.
6. Click in the notes page below the slide.
7. Type Visit www.first-choice.emcp.net for a listing of all upcoming tours.
8. Size and position the text box below the slide.

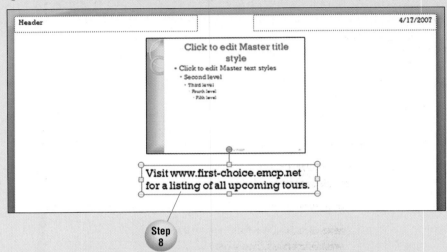

Step
8

9. Click the Insert tab and then click the Picture button in the Illustrations group.
10. At the Insert Picture dialog box, navigate to the PowerPoint2007C6 folder on your storage medium and then double-click *FCTLogo.jpg*.
11. Change the height of the logo to *0.5"*. (This changes the width to *1"*.)
12. Drag the logo so it is positioned below the text.

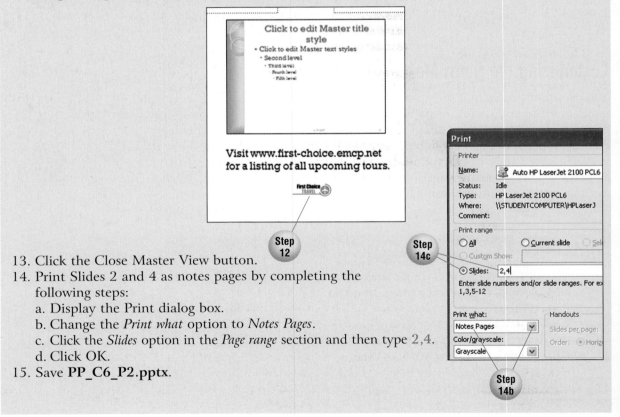

Step
12

Step
14c

Step
14b

13. Click the Close Master View button.
14. Print Slides 2 and 4 as notes pages by completing the following steps:
   a. Display the Print dialog box.
   b. Change the *Print what* option to *Notes Pages*.
   c. Click the *Slides* option in the *Page range* section and then type *2,4*.
   d. Click OK.
15. Save **PP_C6_P2.pptx**.

# Using View Tab Options

You have used buttons in the Presentation Views group in the View tab to display your presentation in various views such as Normal, Slide Sorter, Slide Master, Handout Master, and Notes Master. In addition to viewing buttons, the View tab includes options for showing or hiding the ruler and gridlines; zooming in or out in the slide; viewing the slide in color, grayscale, or black and white; and working with windows including arranging, splitting, and switching windows.

## Changing the Zoom

You can change the display size of the slide in the Slide pane or slides in the Slides/Outline pane with the Zoom button in the View tab and also with the Zoom slider bar located at the right side of the Status bar. Click the Zoom button in the View tab and the Zoom dialog box displays. Use options in this dialog box to increase or decrease the display size of slides in the Slides/Outline pane or the slide in the Slide pane. To change the zoom with the Zoom slider bar, use the mouse to drag the slider bar button to the left to decrease the display size or to the right to increase the display size. Click the button with the minus symbol that displays at the left side of the Zoom slider bar to decrease the display percentage or click the button with the plus symbol that displays at the right side of the Zoom slider bar to increase the display percentage. Click the percentage number that displays at the left side of the slider bar and the Zoom dialog box displays.

Zoom

## Project 2d — Viewing a Presentation

1. With **PP_C6_P2.pptx** open, make Slide 1 active and then click the slide in the Slide pane.
2. Click the View tab.
3. Increase and decrease the zoom by completing the following steps:
   a. Click the Zoom button. (This displays the Zoom dialog box.)
   b. At the Zoom dialog box, click the *33%* option and then click OK.
   c. Click the Zoom button, click the *66%* option in the Zoom dialog box, and then click OK.
   d. Click the Slide 2 thumbnail in the Slides/Outline pane.
   e. Click the Zoom button, click the *66%* option in the Zoom dialog box, and then click OK. (Because the slide in the Slides/Outline pane was active, the percentage display changed for the thumbnails in the pane.)
   f. Position the mouse pointer on the Zoom slider bar button (located at the right side of the Status bar), drag the button to the right to increase the size of the slide in the Slide pane, and then drag the slider bar to the left to decrease the size of the slide.
   g. Click the percentage number that displays at the left side of the Zoom slider bar (this displays the Zoom dialog box).
   h. Click the *66%* option in the Zoom dialog box and then click OK.
   i. Click the Slide 3 thumbnail in the Slide/Outline pane.
   j. Click the Zoom button in the View tab.
   k. Type *45* in the *Percentage* text box and then click OK.

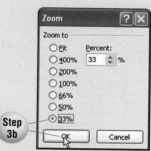

Step 3b

4. View the slides in grayscale by completing the following steps:
   a. Click the slide in the Slides pane to make it active and then click the Grayscale button in the Color/Grayscale group in the View tab.

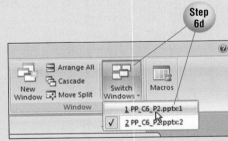

Step 4a

   b. Click some of the buttons in the Grayscale tab to display the slides in varying grayscale options.
   c. Click the Back To Color View button.
5. View the slides in black and white by completing the following steps:
   a. Click the View tab and then click the Pure Black and White button in the Color/Grayscale group in the View tab.
   b. Click some of the buttons in the Black And White tab to display the slides in varying black and white options.
   c. Click the Back To Color View button.
6. Open a new window and arrange the windows by completing the following steps:
   a. Click the View tab and then click the New Window button in the Window group in the View tab. (This opens the same presentation in another window. Notice that the name on the title bar displays followed by a colon and the number 2.)

Step 6a

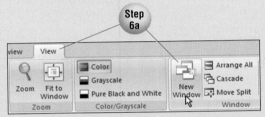

   b. Click the Arrange All button to arrange the two presentation windows. (This arranges the presentations as tiles with the title bar of each presentation visible as well as a portion of each presentation.)
   c. Click the Cascade button. (This arranges the two presentations with the presentations overlapping with the title bar for each presentation visible as well as a portion of the top presentation.)

Step 6d

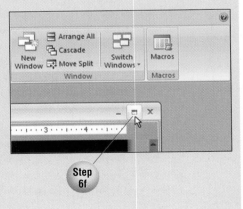

   d. Click the Switch Windows button and then click the *PP_C6_P2.pptx:1* option at the drop-down list. (Notice the presentation name in the title bar now displays followed by a colon and the number 1.)
   e. Click the Close button that displays in the upper right corner of the currently active presentation. (The Close button contains an X.)
   f. Click the Maximize button that displays in the upper right corner of the presentation window. (The Maximize button displays immediately left of the Close button.)
7. With the View tab active, click the Grayscale button in the Color/Grayscale group and then click the Inverse Grayscale button in the Change Selected Object group.
8. Print the presentation as a handout with six slides per page.
9. Click the Back To Color View button.

Step 6f

10. Save and then close **PP_C6_P2.pptx**.

# Project ③ Insert Action Buttons and Hyperlinks in a Job Search Presentation

You will open a job search presentation and then insert action buttons that display the next slide, the first slide, and another presentation. You will also create a hyperlink from text in a slide to a site on the Internet.

## Inserting Action Buttons

Action buttons are drawn objects on a slide that have a routine attached to them which is activated when the viewer or the speaker clicks the button. For example, you could include an action button that displays the next slide in the presentation, a file in another program, or a specific Web page. Creating an action button is a two-step process. You draw the button using an Action Button shape in the Shapes button drop-down list and then you define the action that will take place with options in the Action Settings dialog box. You can customize an action button in the same manner as customizing a drawn object. When the viewer or speaker moves the mouse over an action button during a presentation, the pointer changes to a hand with a finger pointing upward to indicate clicking will result in an action.

To display the available action buttons, click the Insert tab and then click the Shapes button in the Illustrations group. Action buttons display at the bottom of the drop-down list. Hover the mouse pointer over a button and the name as well as the action it performs displays in a box above the button. The action attached to an action button occurs when you run the presentation and then click the button.

**QUICK STEPS**

**Create Action Button**
1. Make desired slide active.
2. Click Insert tab.
3. Click Shapes button.
4. Click desired action button.
5. Drag in slide to create button.
6. Make desired changes at Action Settings dialog box.

**HINT**
Apply formatting to an action button with options in the Drawing Tools Format tab.

## Project ③a  Inserting Action Buttons

1. Open **JobSearch.pptx** and then save the presentation with the name **PP_C6_P3**.
2. Make the following changes to the presentation:
   a. Display the presentation in Slide Master view.
   b. Click the top slide master in the slide thumbnail pane.
   c. Change the theme to *Verve*.
   d. Change the theme colors to *Metro*.
   e. Change the theme fonts to *Concourse*.
   f. Click the Insert tab and then click the Header & Footer button.
   g. At the Header and Footer dialog box with the Slide tab selected, click the *Date and time* check box and make sure *Update automatically* is selected.
   h. Click the *Slide number* check box to insert a check mark.
   i. Click the Notes and Handouts tab.
   j. Click the *Date and time* check box.
   k. Click the *Header* check box and then type the name of your school.
   l. Click the *Footer* check box and then type your first and last names.
   m. Click the Apply to All button.
   n. Click the Slide Master tab and then close Slide Master view.

3. Insert an action button in Slide 1 that will display the next slide by completing the following steps:
   a. Make Slide 1 active.
   b. Click the Insert tab and then click the Shapes button.
   c. At the drop-down list, click *Action Button: Forward or Next* (second option from the left) that displays at the bottom of the drop-down list.
   d. Move the crosshair pointer to the lower right corner of the slide and then drag to create a button as shown below.

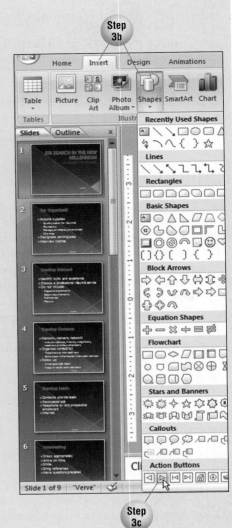

Step
3b

Step
3c

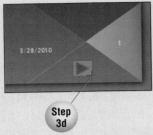

Step
3d

   e. At the Action Settings dialog box, click OK. (The default setting is *Hyperlink to Next Slide*.)
   f. With the button selected, click the Home tab.
   g. Click the Quick Styles button in the Drawing group in the Drawing Tools Format tab and then click the *Colored Outline - Accent 1* option (second option from the left in the top row).

Step
3g

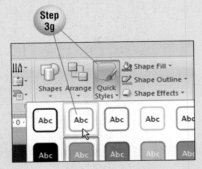

4. Insert an action button in Slide Master view that will display the next slide by completing the following steps:
   a. Display the presentation in Slide Master view.
   b. Click the top slide master thumbnail.

c. Click the Insert tab and then click the Shapes button.

d. At the drop-down list, click *Action Button: Forward or Next* (second option from the left).

e. Move the crosshair pointer to the lower right corner of the slide master and then drag to create a button as shown at the right.

Step 4e

f. At the Action Settings dialog box, click OK. (The default setting is *Hyperlink to Next Slide*.)

g. Click the Slide Master tab and then click the Close Master View button.

5. Make Slide 1 active and then run the presentation, clicking the action button to advance slides. When you click the action button on the last slide (Slide 9) nothing happens because it is the last slide. Press the Esc key to end the presentation.

6. Change the action button on Slide 9 by completing the following steps:

a. Make Slide 9 active.

b. Click the Insert tab and then click the Shapes button.

c. At the drop-down list, click *Action Button: Home* (fifth button from the left).

d. Drag to create a button on top of the previous action button.

e. At the Action Settings dialog box with the *Hyperlink to: First Slide* option selected, click OK.

f. Deselect the button.

7. Display Slide 1 in the Slide pane and then run the presentation. Navigate through the slide show by clicking the action button. When you click the action button on the last slide, the first slide displays. End the slide show by pressing the Esc key.

8. Print the presentation as a handout with six slides per page.

9. Save **PP_C6_P3.pptx**.

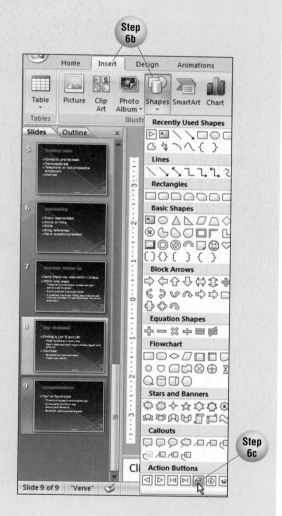

Step 6b

Step 6c

## Linking to a Web Site

You can specify that an action button links to a Web site during a presentation. To do this, draw an Action button. At the Action Settings dialog box, click the *Hyperlink to* option, click the down-pointing arrow at the right side of the *Hyperlink to* option box, and then click *URL* at the drop-down list. At the Hyperlink To URL dialog box, type the Web address in the URL text box, and then click OK. Click OK to close the Action Settings dialog box. Other actions you can link to using the *Hyperlink to* drop-down list include: Next Slide, Previous Slide, First Slide, Last Slide, Last Slide Viewed, End Show, Custom Show, Slide, Other PowerPoint Presentation, and Other File.

---

## Project 3b — Linking to a Web Site and Another Presentation

1. With **PP_C6_P3.pptx** open, add an action button that will link to another presentation by completing the following steps:
   a. Make Slide 4 active.
   b. Click the Insert tab and then click the Shapes button.
   c. At the drop-down list, click *Action Button: Help* (second button from the right).
   d. Draw the action button to the left of the existing button located in the lower right corner of the slide.
   e. At the Action Settings dialog box, click the *Hyperlink to* option.
   f. Click the down-pointing arrow at the right side of the *Hyperlink to* option box and then click *Other PowerPoint Presentation* at the drop-down list. (You will need to scroll down the list to display this option.)

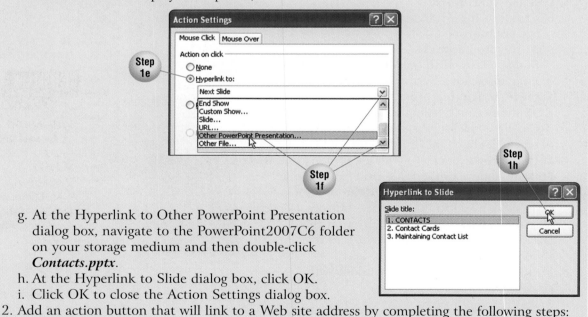

   g. At the Hyperlink to Other PowerPoint Presentation dialog box, navigate to the PowerPoint2007C6 folder on your storage medium and then double-click **Contacts.pptx**.
   h. At the Hyperlink to Slide dialog box, click OK.
   i. Click OK to close the Action Settings dialog box.
2. Add an action button that will link to a Web site address by completing the following steps:
   a. Make Slide 5 active.
   b. Click the Insert tab and then click the Shapes button.
   c. At the drop-down list, click *Action Button: Information* (sixth from the left).

d. Draw the action button to the left of the existing button located in the lower right corner of the slide.

e. At the Action Settings dialog box, click the *Hyperlink to* option.

f. Click the down-pointing arrow at the right of the *Hyperlink to* option box, and then click *URL* at the drop-down list.

g. At the Hyperlink To URL dialog box, type **www.usajobs.gov** and then click OK.

h. Click OK to close the Action Settings dialog box.

i. Click outside the button to deselect it.

3. Run the presentation by completing the following steps:

a. Make sure you are connected to the Internet.

b. Make Slide 1 active.

c. Click the Slide Show button in the view area on the Status bar.

d. Navigate through the slide show to Slide 4.

e. Click the action button in Slide 4 containing the question mark. (This displays Slide 1 of **Contacts.pptx**.)

f. Navigate through the three slides in **Contacts.pptx**. Continue clicking the mouse button until you return to Slide 4 of **PP_C6_P3.pptx**.

g. Display Slide 5 and then click the action button containing the lowercase *i*. (If you are connected to the Internet, the job site of the United States Federal Government displays.)

h. Click a few links at the Web site.

i. When you are finished viewing the Web site, close your Web browser.

j. Continue viewing the remainder of the presentation.

k. When Slide 1 displays, press the Esc key to end the presentation.

4. Print the presentation as a handout with nine slides per page.

5. Save **PP_C6_P3.pptx**.

# Creating Hyperlinks

In Project 3b, you created hyperlinks using action buttons. You can also create hyperlinks with options at the Insert Hyperlink dialog box shown in Figure 6.2. To display this dialog box, select a key word or phrase in a slide, click the Insert tab, and then click the Hyperlink button in the Links group. You can also display the Insert Hyperlink dialog box with the keyboard shortcut Ctrl + K. At the Insert Hyperlink dialog box, type the Web address in the *Address* text box and then click OK.

**QUICK STEPS**

**Create Hyperlink**
1. Make desired slide active.
2. Select text.
3. Click Insert tab.
4. Click Hyperlink button.
5. Type Web address or file name in *Address* text box.

**HINT**
Hyperlinks are active when running the presentation, not when creating it.

Hyperlink

**Figure 6.2** Insert Hyperlink Dialog Box

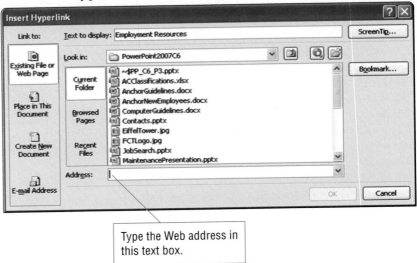

Type the Web address in this text box.

Project **3c** | **Inserting Hyperlinks**

1. With **PP_C6_P3.pptx** open, insert a new slide by completing the following steps:
   a. Make Slide 5 active.
   b. Click the Home tab.
   c. Click the New Slide button arrow and then click the *Title Slide* layout.
   d. Click the text *Click to add title* and then type Internet Job Resources.
   e. Click the text *Click to add subtitle* and then type Employment Resources, press Enter, and then type America's Job Bank.
2. Add a hyperlink to the Employment Resources site by completing the following steps:
   a. Select *Employment Resources* in Slide 6.
   b. Click the Insert tab and then click the Hyperlink button in the Links group.
   c. At the Insert Hyperlink dialog box, type www.employment-resources.com in the *Address* text box. (PowerPoint automatically inserts *http://* at the beginning of the address.)

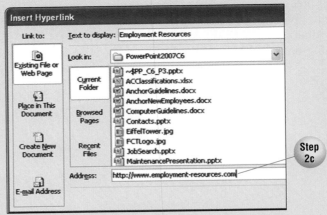

Step 2c

   d. Click OK to close the Insert Hyperlink dialog box.

3. Add a hyperlink to the America's Job Bank site by completing the following steps:
   a. Select *America's Job Bank* in Slide 6.
   b. Click the Hyperlink button in the Links group in the Insert tab.
   c. At the Insert Hyperlink dialog box, type www.ajb.dni.us in the *Address* text box.
   d. Click OK to close the Insert Hyperlink dialog box.
4. Copy the action button in Slide 1 to Slide 6 by completing the following steps:
   a. Make Slide 1 active.
   b. Click the action button to select it.
   c. Press Ctrl + C to copy the button.
   d. Make Slide 6 active.
   e. Press Ctrl + V to paste the button.
5. Run the presentation by completing the following steps:
   a. Make sure you are connected to the Internet.
   b. Make Slide 1 active.
   c. Click the Slide Show button in the view area on the Status bar.
   d. Navigate through the slides. When you reach Slide 6, click the <u>Employment Resources</u> hyperlink.
   e. Scroll through the employment site and then close the Web browser.
   f. Click the <u>America's Job Bank</u> hyperlink.
   g. Scroll through the America's Job Bank site and then close the Web browser.
   h. Continue viewing the remainder of the presentation. (When Slide 1 displays, press the Esc key to end the presentation.)
6. Print only Slide 6 of the presentation.
7. Save and then close **PP_C6_P3.pptx**.

# CHAPTER summary

- Display a presentation in Slide Master view by clicking the View tab and then clicking the Slide Master button in the Presentation Views group.
- Close Slide Master view by clicking the Close Master View button.
- In Slide Master view, slide master thumbnails display in the slide thumbnail pane.
- Use buttons in the Edit Theme group in the Slide Master tab to apply a design theme, theme colors, and theme fonts.
- Use buttons in the Background group in the Slide Master tab to apply a predesigned background style, display the Format Background dialog box with options for applying background styles, and hide background graphics.
- Delete a placeholder by clicking in the placeholder, clicking the placeholder border, and then pressing the Delete key.
- Delete a slide master in Slide Master view by clicking the desired slide master thumbnail in the slide thumbnail pane and then clicking the Delete button in the Edit Master group.
- In Slide Master view, you can display the Header and Footer dialog box with the Slide tab selected and then insert the date and time, slide number, and/or a footer. At the Header and Footer dialog box with the Notes and Handouts tab selected, you can insert the date and time, a header, page numbers, and/or a footer.
- Create a custom slide layout by clicking the Insert Layout button in the Edit Master group in the Slide Master tab. Rename the custom slide layout by clicking the Rename button in the Edit Master group, typing the desired name at the Rename Layout dialog box, and then clicking the Rename button.
- Insert placeholders in a slide layout or custom slide layout by clicking the Insert Placeholder button arrow in the Master Layout group and then clicking the desired placeholder at the drop-down list. To reinsert a deleted placeholder, click the Master Layout button, click the check box of the desired placeholder in the drop-down list, and then click OK to close the dialog box.
- In Slide Master view, create custom prompts by selecting generic text in a placeholder and then typing the desired text.
- Click the Insert Slide Master button in Slide Master view to insert a new slide master and associated slide layouts. You can also insert a new slide master by applying a design theme in Slide Master view.
- Save a presentation as a template by changing the *Save as type* option at the Save As dialog box to *PowerPoint Template (*.potx)*.
- To open a presentation based on a template, click the Office button and then click *New*. At the New Presentation dialog box, double-click the desired template in the *Recently Used Templates* section. If the desired template is not visible, click the *My Templates* option and, at the New Presentation dialog box with the My Templates tab selected, double-click the desired template.

- To open a presentation based on a template saved in a location other than the default location, double-click the desired template in the *Recently Used Templates* section of the New Presentation dialog box or click the *New from existing* option. At the New from Existing Presentation dialog box, navigate to the desired folder and then double-click the desired template.

- Delete a template by displaying the New Presentation dialog box with the My Templates tab selected, right-clicking the theme, and then clicking *Delete* at the shortcut menu. Delete a template saved in a location other than the default in the same manner as deleting a presentation.

- You can customize a handout with options in the Handout Master view. Display this view by clicking the View tab and then clicking the Handout Master button in the Presentation Views group.

- You can customize notes pages with options in the Notes Master view. Display this view by clicking the View tab and then clicking the Notes Master button in the Presentation Views group.

- In addition to changing the view, you can use buttons in the View tab to show/hide the ruler and/or gridlines; change the zoom display; view slides in color, grayscale, or black and white; and arrange, split, and switch windows.

- Action buttons are drawn objects in a slide that have a routine attached, such as displaying the next slide, the first slide, a Web site, or another PowerPoint presentation.

- Create an action button by clicking the Insert tab, clicking the Shapes button, clicking the desired button at the drop-down list, and then dragging in the slide to create the button.

- Create a hyperlink in a slide by selecting text in the slide, clicking the Insert tab, and then clicking the Hyperlink button in the Links group. At the Insert Hyperlink dialog box, type the Web site address or file location and then click OK.

# COMMANDS review

| FEATURE | RIBBON TAB, GROUP | BUTTON, OPTION | KEYBOARD SHORTCUT |
|---|---|---|---|
| Slide Master view | View, Presentation Views | | |
| New Presentation dialog box | | , New | |
| New Presentation dialog box with My Templates tab selected | | , New, My Templates | |
| Handout Master view | View, Presentation Views | | |
| Notes Master view | View, Presentation Views | | |
| Action buttons | Insert, Illustrations | | |
| Insert Hyperlink dialog box | Insert, Links | | Ctrl + K |

# CONCEPTS check

## Test Your Knowledge

**Completion:** In the space provided at the right, indicate the correct term, symbol, or command.

1. To display a presentation in Slide Master view, click this tab and then click the Slide Master button.

   _____

2. Click this button to close Slide Master view.

   _____

3. This group in the Slide Master tab contains buttons for applying a theme, theme colors, and theme fonts.

   _____

4. This dialog box with the Slide tab selected contains options for inserting the date and time, a slide number, and a footer.

   _____

5. To create a new slide layout in Slide Master view, click this button in the Edit Master group.

   _____

6. To save a presentation as a template, choose this option at the *Save as type* drop-down list at the Save As dialog box.

   _____

7. Delete a template at the New Presentation dialog box with this tab selected.

   _____

8. Change to this view to customize handouts.

   _____

9. Change to this view to customize notes pages.

   _____

10. The Zoom slider bar is located at the right side of this bar.

    _____

11. Click this button to display a drop-down list that includes action buttons.

    _____

12. Insert this action button in a slide to display the next slide in the presentation.

    _____

13. Insert this action button in a slide to display the first slide in the presentation.

    _____

14. This is the keyboard shortcut to display the Insert Hyperlink dialog box.

    _____

# SKILLS check

## Demonstrate Your Proficiency

### 1 FORMAT A PRESENTATION IN SLIDE MASTER VIEW AND THEN SAVE THE PRESENTATION AS A TEMPLATE

1. Display a blank presentation, click the View tab, and then click the Slide Master button.
2. Click the top slide master thumbnail in the slide thumbnail pane.
3. Apply the *Urban* theme, change the theme colors to *Paper*, and change the theme fonts to *Flow*.
4. Apply the *Style 2* background style.
5. Select the text *Click to edit Master title style*, click the Home tab, change the font color to Olive Green, Accent 1, Darker 50%, and then turn on bold.
6. Select the text *Second level* in the slide master, click the Home tab, and then change the font color to Orange, Accent 2, Darker 50%.
7. Insert the **WELogo.jpg** in the master slide, change the height of the logo to 0.5″, and drag the logo to the lower left corner of the slide master. (With the logo selected, change the background of the logo to transparent by clicking the Recolor button in the Picture Tools Format tab, clicking the *Set Transparent Color* option, and then clicking on a white portion of the logo. This removes the white background so the yellow slide background displays.)
8. Select the date placeholder and then move the placeholder to the lower right corner of the slide.
9. Select the footer placeholder and then drag it down to the lower right corner of the slide immediately left of the date placeholder.
10. Click the Slide Master tab.
11. Click the first slide layout below the slide master.
12. Click the *Footers* check box in the Master Layout group to remove the footer and date placeholders.
13. Select and then delete the slide layouts from the third layout below the slide master (the *Section Header Layout*) to the last layout.
14. Preserve the slide masters by clicking the top slide master in the slide thumbnail pane, clicking the Slide Master tab, and then clicking the Preserve button in the Edit Master group.
15. Click the Close Master View button.
16. Save the presentation as a template to the PowerPoint2007C6 folder on your storage medium and name the template **XXXPublicationTemplate** (use your initials in place of the *XXX*).
17. Close **XXXPublicationTemplate.potx**.

# Assessment

## 2 USE A TEMPLATE TO CREATE A PUBLICATIONS PRESENTATION

1. Open **XXXPublicationTemplate.potx**. (To do this, display the New Presentation dialog box and then click *New from existing*. At the New from Existing Presentation dialog box, navigate to the PowerPoint2007C6 folder on your storage medium, and then double-click ***XXXPublicationTemplate.potx***.)
2. Save the presentation and name it **PP_C6_A2**.
3. Click the *Click to add title* text in the current slide and then type Worldwide Enterprises.
4. Click the *Click to add subtitle* text and then type Company Publications.
5. Display the Reuse Slides task pane, browse to PowerPoint2007C6 folder on your storage medium, and then double-click **Publications.pptx**.
6. Insert the second, third, fourth, and fifth slides from the Reuse Slides task pane into the current presentation and then close the task pane.
7. Insert a second slide master with the following specifications:
   a. Display the presentation in Slide Master view.
   b. Click in the slide thumbnail pane below the bottom slide layout.
   c. Change the theme to *Foundry*, the colors to *Paper*, and the fonts to *Flow*.
   d. Apply the *Style 2* background style.
   e. Select the *Click to edit Master title style* text, click the Home tab, turn off text shadow, turn on bold, and change to left alignment.
   f. Select the text *Second level* and then change the font color to Orange, Accent 2, Darker 50%.
   g. Click the Slide Master tab.
8. Select and then delete slide layouts from the third layout (*Section Header Layout*) below the new slide master to the last layout.
9. Insert headers, footers, slide numbers, and dates with the following specifications:
   a. Click the Insert tab, display the Header and Footer dialog box with the Slide tab selected, insert the date and time to update automatically (choose a format that inserts the date and time in figures), and insert slide numbers.
   b. Click the Notes and Handouts tab, insert the date and time to update automatically (choose a format that inserts the date and time in figures), insert a header that prints your first and last names, insert a footer that prints *Worldwide Enterprises*, and then click the Apply to All button.
   c. Click the top slide master in the slide thumbnail pane and then increase the width of the date and time placeholder so the date and time display on one line.
10. Close Slide Master view.
11. Make Slide 5 active and then insert a new slide using the new Foundry Title Slide layout and then type *Worldwide Enterprises* as the title and *Preparing the Company Newsletter* as the subtitle.
12. Insert the following text in slides using the Foundry Title and Content layout:
    Slide 7        Preparing the Newsletter
    - Maintain consistent elements from issue to issue
    - Consider the following when designing the newsletter
      - Focus
      - Balance
      - White space
      - Directional flow

Slide 8          Preparing the Newsletter
- Choose paper size and weight
- Determine margins
- Specify column layout
- Choose nameplate layout and format
- Specify heading format
- Determine newsletter colors

13. Select the bulleted text in Slide 8 and then change the line spacing to *1.5*.
14. Make Slide 7 active and then insert a clip art image related to newsletters.
15. Insert a transition and sound of your choosing to the presentation.
16. Run the presentation.
17. Print the presentation as a handout with four slides per page.
18. Save and then close **PP_C6_A2.pptx**.


## Assessment

# 3 INSERT ACTION BUTTONS IN A GARDENING PRESENTATION

1. Open **PerennialsPresentation.pptx** and then save the presentation with the name **PP_C6_A3**.
2. Make Slide 1 active and then insert an action button in the lower right corner of the slide that displays the next slide.
3. Display the presentation in Slide Master view, click the top slide master in the slide thumbnail pane, create an action button in the lower right corner of the slide that displays the next slide, and then close Slide Master view.
4. Make Slide 8 active and then create an action button that displays the first slide in the presentation.
5. Make Slide 2 active and then insert a second action button in the lower right corner that will link to the presentation **MaintenancePresentation.pptx** (located in the PowerPoint2007C6 folder on your storage medium).
6. Display Slide 8 and then make the following changes:
   a. Delete text *Better Homes and Gardens*® and then type Organic Gardening®.
   b. Select *Organic Gardening*® and then create a hyperlink with the text to the Web site www.organicgardening.com.
7. Make sure you are connected to the Internet and then run the presentation beginning with Slide 1. Navigate through the slide show by clicking the next action button and display the connected presentation by clicking the information action button. At Slide 8, click the *Organic Gardening*® hyperlink (if you are connected to the Internet). Scroll through the site and click a couple different hyperlinks that interest you. After viewing a few Web pages in the magazine, close your Web browser. When you click the action button on the last slide, the first slide displays. End the slide show by pressing the Esc key.
8. Print the presentation as a handout with four slides per page.
9. Save and then close **PP_C6_A3.pptx**.

## 4 CREATE AN ACTION BUTTONS PRESENTATION

1. In this chapter, you learned to insert a number of action buttons in a slide. Experiment with the other action buttons (click the Insert tab, click the Shapes button, and then point to Action Buttons) and then prepare a PowerPoint presentation with the following specifications:
   a. The first slide should contain the title of your presentation.
   b. Include one slide for each of the eleven action buttons that includes the specific name as well as an explanation of the button.
   c. Apply a design theme of your choosing to the presentation.
2. Save the presentation and name it **PP_C6_A4**.
3. Print the presentation as a handout with six slides per page.
4. Close **PP_C6_A4.pptx**.

# CASE study
## *Apply Your Skills*

**Part 1**

You are the training manager for Anchor Corporation and one of your job responsibilities is conducting new employee orientations. You decide that a PowerPoint presentation will help you deliver information to new employees during the orientation. You know that you will be creating other PowerPoint presentations so you decide to create a template. Create a presentation template with attractive formatting that includes a design theme, theme colors, theme fonts, and include an anchor clip art image in the lower left corner of most of the slides. Apply any other formatting or design elements to increase the appeal of the presentation. Save the presentation as a template on your storage medium with the name **AnchorTemplate** and make sure it contains the file extensions *.potx*. Close the template.

**Part 2**

You have a document with notes about information on types of employment appointments, employee performance, and compensation. Open the Word document named **AnchorNewEmployees.docx** and then use the information to prepare a presentation using the **AnchorTemplate.potx** template. Save the completed presentation with the name **PP_C6_CS_P2** and make sure it has the file extension *.pptx*. Apply a transition and sound to each slide in the presentation, print the presentation as a handout, and then close the presentation.

**Part 3**

Open the Word document named **AnchorGuidelines.docx** and then use the information in the document to prepare a presentation using the **AnchorTemplate.potx** template. Save the completed presentation with the name **PP_C6_CS_P3** and make sure it contains the file extension *.pptx*. Apply a transition and sound to each slide in the presentation, print the presentation as a handout, and then close the presentation.

**Part 4**

During the new employee presentation you want to refer to a chart of employee classifications, so you decide to create a link to an Excel spreadsheet. Open the **PP_C6_CS_P2.pptx** presentation and then create a new slide that contains a hyperlink to the Excel workbook named **ACClassifications.xlsx**. Run the presentation, link to the Excel chart, and then continue running the remaining slides in the presentation. Print only the new slide and then save and close **PP_C6_CS_P2.pptx**.

**Part 5**

The information you used to create the **PP_C6_CS_P3.pptx** presentation was taken from a document that is part of a new employee handbook. You decide that you want to create a link in your presentation to the Word document to show employees the additional information in the document. Create a new slide in the **PP_C6_CS_P3.pptx** presentation that includes an action button that links to the Word document named **ComputerGuidelines.docx**. Include other action buttons for navigating in the presentation. Run the presentation, link to the Word document, and then continue running the remaining slides in the presentation. Print only the new slide and then save and close **PP_C6_CS_P3.pptx**.

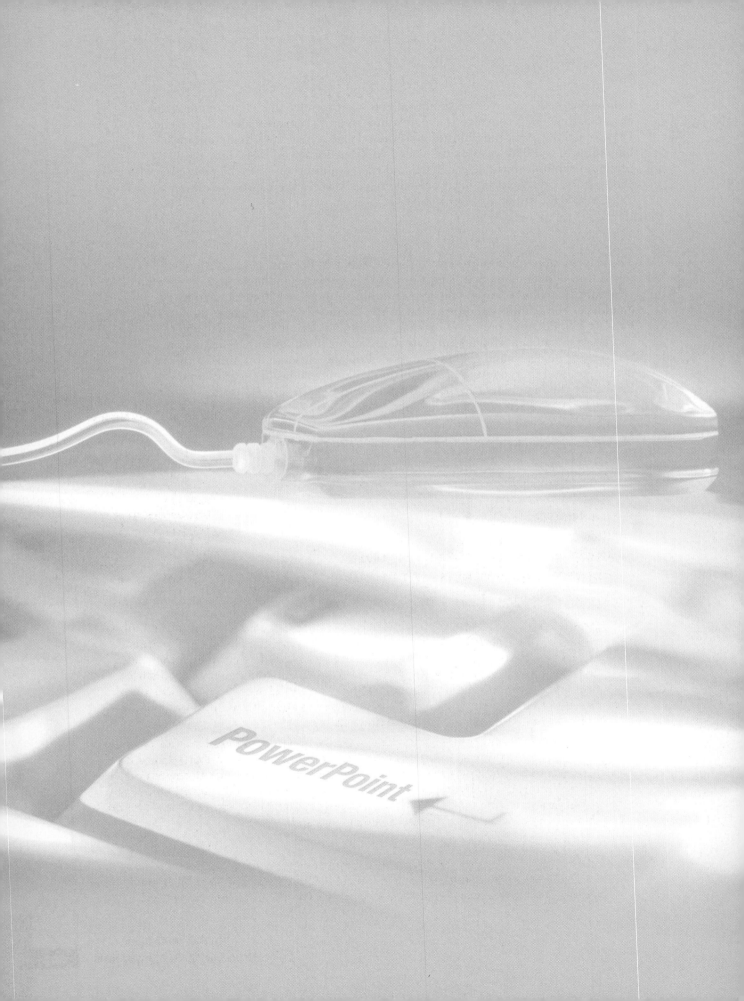

# Applying Custom Animation and Setting Up Shows

## PERFORMANCE OBJECTIVES

**Upon successful completion of Chapter 7, you will be able to:**

- Apply built-in animations
- Modify and remove animations
- Create custom animations
- Apply custom animation effects
- Modify and remove animation effects
- Animate shapes, images, SmartArt, and chart elements
- Apply a build
- Draw motion paths
- Set up a slide show
- Set rehearse timings for slides
- Hide slides
- Create, run, edit, and print a custom show
- Insert and customize sounds and movie clips

**Tutorial 7.1**
Enhancing Presentations
**Tutorial 7.2**
Using Special Features
**Tutorial 7.3**
Maintaining Presentations and
Creating Custom Shows

Animation or movement will add visual appeal and interest to your presentation when used appropriately. PowerPoint provides a number of built-in animation effects as well as custom animation effects you can apply to elements in a slide. You can apply animation effects with options in the Animations tab and with options in the Custom Animation task pane. In this chapter, you will learn how to apply built-in and custom animation effects as well as how to insert sound and media clips to create dynamic presentations.

In some situations, you may want to prepare a self-running presentation where the presentation runs on a continuous loop. You can customize a presentation to run continuously and also rehearse the time you want each slide to remain on the screen. You can also create a custom slide show to present only specific slides in a presentation. In this chapter, you will learn how to prepare self-running presentations and how to create and edit custom slide shows.

*Note: Before beginning computer projects, copy to your storage medium the PowerPoint2007C7 folder from the PowerPoint2007 folder on the CD that accompanies this textbook and then make PowerPoint2007C7 the active folder.*

# Project 1  Apply Animation Effects to Elements in Marketing Presentation

You will open a marketing presentation and then apply built-in animation effects to the title slide and apply animation effects in Slide Master view to the remaining slides. You will remove some of the animation effects and then apply custom animation effects to elements in slides such as entrance and emphasis effects.

**Apply Built-in Animation**
1. Click desired item.
2. Click Animations tab.
3. Click *Animate* option.
4. Click desired animation at drop-down list.

**HINT**
You can animate text, objects, graphics, SmartArt diagrams, charts, hyperlinks, and sound.

**HINT**
When you apply an animation effect to an object in a slide, an animation icon displays below the slide number in the Slides/Outline pane.

Preview

## Applying Built-in Animation Effects

You can animate items such as text or objects in a slide to add visual interest to your presentation. Displaying items one at a time helps your audience focus on a single topic or point as you present it. PowerPoint includes a number of built-in animations you can apply to items in a slide. These built-in animations can be modified to fit your specific needs. You may want items to appear one right after the other or in groups. You can control the direction that the item comes from and the rate of speed. Try not to overwhelm your audience with too much animation. In general, you want them to remember the content of your presentation and not the visual effects.

To animate an item, click the desired item, click the Animations tab, and then click the *Animate* option in the Animations group. At the drop-down list that displays, click the desired animation. Built-in animations are grouped into three categories—*Fade*, *Wipe*, and *Fly In*. Depending on the item selected, each group may contain a list of specific items. For example, if you select a placeholder containing bulleted text, each group contains the choices *All At Once* and *By 1st Level Paragraphs*. If you select an object such as a chart, each group contains choices for animating specific chart items. If you want to apply animation effects to slides created with the same layout, apply the effect in Slide Master view.

If you want to see the animation effects in your slide without running the presentation, click the Preview button in the Animations tab. Click this button and the animation effect you applied to the active slide displays on the slide in the Slide pane. When you apply animation effects to items in a slide, an animation icon displays below the slide number in the Slides/Outline pane.

1. Open **MarketingPresentation.pptx** and save the presentation with the name **PP_C7_P1**.
2. Make sure Slide 1 is active and then apply built-in animations to the title and subtitle by completing the following steps:
   a. Click in the title *CORNERSTONE SYSTEMS*.
   b. Click the Animations tab.
   c. Click the down-pointing arrow at the right of the *Animate* option in the Animations group and then click *Fade* at the drop-down list. (If you hover the mouse pointer over the option, the slide in the Slide pane will preview the animation.)

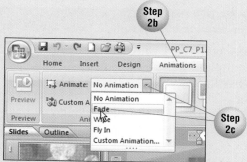

Step 2b

Step 2c

   d. Click in the subtitle *Marketing Report*.
   e. Click the down-pointing arrow at the right side of the *Animate* option and then click *All At Once* in the *Fade* group at the drop-down list.
   f. Click the Preview button in the Animations tab to see the animation effect in the slide in the Slide pane.

Step 2e

3. Apply animations to Slides 2 through 4 in Slide Master view by completing the following steps:
   a. Click the View tab and then click the Slide Master button in the Presentation Views group.
   b. Click the third slide master layout in the slide thumbnail pane (*Title and Content Layout*).
   c. Click in the text *Click to edit Master title style*.
   d. Click the Animations tab, click the down-pointing arrow at the right side of the *Animate* option, and then click *Fly In* at the drop-down list.
   e. Click in the bulleted text.
   f. Click the down-pointing arrow at the right side of the *Animate* option and then click *By 1st Level Paragraphs* in the *Fly In* group in the drop-down list.
   g. Click the Slide Master tab and then click the Close Master View button.

Step 3f

4. Make Slide 1 active and then run the presentation. Click the mouse button to advance items in slides and to advance slides. Notice how the bulleted text in Slides 2 through 4 displays one item at a time.
5. Save **PP_C7_P1.pptx**.

## Removing Built-in Animations

Remove the built-in animation effect from an item by clicking the item, clicking the down-pointing arrow at the right side of the *Animate* option, and then clicking *No animation* at the drop-down list. If you applied animation in Slide Master view, display the presentation in Slide Master view, click the slide master layout containing the animation, click the desired item, and then remove the animation.

Project **1b**   **Removing Animations**

1. With **PP_C7_P1.pptx** open, make Slide 1 active and then remove the animation from the title and subtitle by completing the following steps:
   a. Click the title *CORNERSTONE SYSTEMS*.
   b. Click the Animations tab.
   c. Click the down-pointing arrow at the right of the *Animate* option in the Animations group and then click *No Animation*.
   d. Click the subtitle *Marketing Report*, click the down-pointing arrow at the right side of the *Animate* option, and then click *No Animation*.
2. Remove the animation effect for Slides 2 through 4 by completing the following steps:
   a. Click the View tab and then click the Slide Master button.
   b. Click the third slide master layout in the slide thumbnail pane (*Title and Content Layout*).
   c. Click in the text *Click to edit Master title style*.
   d. Click the Animations tab, click the down-pointing arrow at the right side of the *Animate* option drop-down list, and then click *No Animation* at the drop-down list.
   e. Click the Slide Master tab and then click the Close Master View button.
3. Make Slide 1 active and then run the presentation.
4. Save **PP_C7_P1.pptx**.

## Applying Custom Animations

If you want to customize animation effects and have more control over the order of animations in a slide, use options at the Custom Animation task pane shown in Figure 7.1. Display this task pane by clicking the Custom Animation button in the Animations group in the Animations tab. You can also display the Custom Animation task pane by clicking the down-pointing arrow at the right side of the Animate option in the Animations tab and then clicking *Custom Animation*.

**Figure 7.1** Custom Animation Task Pane

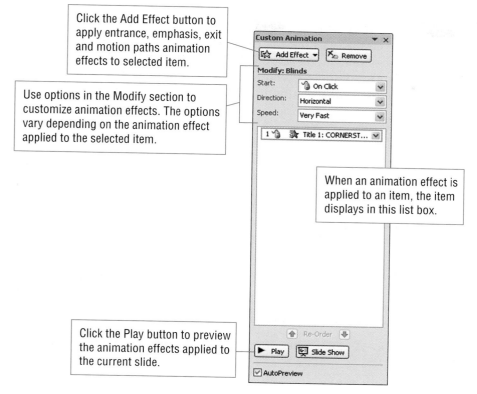

Click the Add Effect button to apply entrance, emphasis, exit and motion paths animation effects to selected item.

Use options in the Modify section to customize animation effects. The options vary depending on the animation effect applied to the selected item.

When an animation effect is applied to an item, the item displays in this list box.

Click the Play button to preview the animation effects applied to the current slide.

## Applying Effects

The Add Effect button in the Custom Animation task pane provides four types of effects you can apply to custom animation settings for items. You can apply an effect as an item *enters* the slide and also as an item *exits* the slide. You can apply *emphasis* to an item that is already visible, and you can also apply a *motion path* to an item that will cause it to move in a specific pattern or even off the slide.

To apply an entrance effect to an item, click the Add Effect button in the Custom Animation task pane, point to *Entrance*, and then click one of the options that displays in the side menu. The list of options in the side menu varies and displays the most recently used options. An animation icon displays at the left side of the option in the side menu and provides a visual representation of the animation effect. Click the *More Effects* option at the bottom of the side menu and the Add Entrance Effect dialog box displays containing additional entrance effects.

Click the Add Effect button, point to *Exit*, and a side menu displays with the same options as the side menu for *Entrance* effects. Click the *More Effects* option at the bottom of the side menu and the Add Exit Effect dialog box displays containing additional exit effects.

Click the Add Effect button, point to *Emphasis* and a side menu displays with options to emphasize the text or item. The options in the side menu vary depending on the most recently used options. If a text item is selected, options display for changing the font, font style, or font size and growing, shrinking, or spinning the text. If an object item is selected, options such as grow, shrink, or spin display.

**QUICK STEPS**

**Apply Entrance Effect**
1. Click desired item.
2. Click Add Effect button in Custom Animation task pane.
3. Point to *Entrance*.
4. Click desired option at side menu.

**Apply Exit Effect**
1. Click desired item.
2. Click Add Effect button in Custom Animation task pane.
3. Point to *Exit*.
4. Click desired option at side menu.

**Apply Emphasis Effect**
1. Click desired item.
2. Click Add Effect button in Custom Animation task pane.
3. Point to *Emphasis*.
4. Click desired option at side menu.

**HINT**
You can apply both an entrance and an exit animation effect to an object in a slide.

**Apply Motion Path**
1. Click desired item.
2. Click Add Effect button in Custom Animation task pane.
3. Point to *Motion Paths.*
4. Click desired option at side menu.

Click the *More Effects* option at the bottom of the side menu and the Add Emphasis Effect dialog box displays containing additional emphasis effects.

With options from the *Motion Paths* side menu, you can specify a path you want an item to follow as it is appearing on the slide. Click the Add Effect button, point to *Motion Paths,* and a side menu displays with options for drawing a motion path in a specific direction. For example, if you want an item to move left when running the presentation, click the Add Effect button, point to *Motion Paths,* and then click *Left* at the side menu. Choose the *Freeform* option if you want to draw your own path in the slide. Click the *More Motion Paths* option at the bottom of the side menu and the Add Motion Path dialog box displays with additional motion options.

When you apply an animation effect or effects to a slide, you can play the animations by clicking the Play button located toward the bottom of the task pane. The animation effect displays in the slide in the Slide pane and a time indicator displays along the bottom of the task pane with a vertical line indicating the progression of time (in seconds). You can begin a presentation from the task pane by clicking the Slide Show button located toward the bottom of the task pane.

## Project 1c  Applying Animation Effects

1. With **PP_C7_P1.pptx** open, apply an animation effect to the title and subtitle in Slide 1 by completing the following steps:
   a. Make Slide 1 active.
   b. Click the Animations tab and then click the Custom Animation button in the Animations group. (This displays the Custom Animation task pane at the right side of the screen. The task pane list box should be empty.)
   c. Click the title *CORNERSTONE SYSTEMS.*
   d. Click the Add Effect button, point to *Entrance,* and then click an option in the side menu (you choose the option). (The list of options varies and displays the most recently used options.)
   e. Click the subtitle *Marketing Report.*
   f. Click the Add Effect button, point to *Exit,* and then click an option in the side menu.
2. Apply an animation effect to the title of Slides 2 through 4 by completing the following steps:
   a. Click the View tab and then click the Slide Master button.
   b. Click the third slide master layout in the slide thumbnail pane (*Title and Content Layout*).
   c. Click in the bulleted text.
   d. Click the Animations tab, click the down-pointing arrow at the right side of the *Animate* option, and then click *No Animation* at the drop-down list.
   e. Click in the text *Click to edit Master title style.*
   f. Click the Add Effect button in the Custom Animation task pane, point to *Emphasis,* and then click *Spin.* (The location of the *Spin* option may vary.)

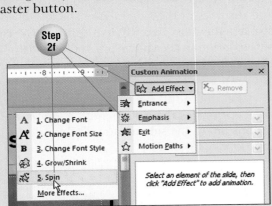

g. Click in the bulleted text, click the Add Effect button, point to *Entrance*, and then click an option in the side menu.

h. Click the Slide Master tab and then click the Close Master View button.

3. Click the Play button located toward the bottom of the Custom Animation task pane to view the animation effects. (Notice the time indicator along the bottom of the task pane and the vertical line indicating the progression of time.)

Step 3

4. Make Slide 1 active and then run the presentation by clicking the Slide Show button located toward the bottom of the task pane. Click the mouse button to begin animation effects and to advance slides.

5. Close the Custom Animation task pane.

6. Save **PP_C7_P1.pptx**.

## Modifying Animation Effects

When you apply an effect to an item, modification options display in the task pane below the Add Effect button. The options that display vary depending on the effect applied. For example, if you apply an entrance effect, the Modify section of the task pane displays with options for customizing when the item starts animating, the direction of the animation, and the speed of the animation. Change a modification option by clicking the down-pointing arrow at the right side of the option and then clicking the desired option at the drop-down list.

When you apply an animation effect to an item, the item name or description displays in the task pane list box. Hover the mouse pointer over an item and a description of the animation effect applied to the item displays in a box above the item. If you click the down-pointing arrow at the right side of an item in the list box, a drop-down list displays with options for modifying or customizing the animation effect. For example, you can use options at the drop-down list to specify when you want the item inserted in the slide. Generally, items display in a slide when you click the mouse button. You can change this to *With Previous* or *With Next* and the item will appear on the slide with the previous item or the next item.

## Changing Animation Effects

When you apply an effect to an item using the Add Effect button in the Custom Animation task pane, the item name or description displays in the task pane list box. If you want to change the animation effect applied to an item, click the item in the list box, click the Change button (previously the Add Effect button), and then apply the desired entrance, emphasis, exit, or motion path effect.

## Removing an Animation Effect

If you want to remove an animation effect from an item, click the item in the task pane list box and then click the Remove button that displays toward the top of the task pane. You can also remove animation from an item by clicking the down-pointing arrow at the right side of the item in the list box and then clicking *Remove* at the drop-down list.

**Change Animation Effect**
1. Click item in Custom Animation task pane list box.
2. Click Change button.
3. Apply animation.

**Remove Animation Effect**
1. Click item in Custom Animation task pane list box.
2. Click Remove button.

QUICK
STEPS

**Reorder Animation Items**

1. Click item in Custom Animation task pane list box.
2. Click Up Re-Order arrow or Down Re-Order arrow.

# Reordering Items

When you apply an effect to an item using the Add Effect button in the Custom Animation task pane, the item name or description displays in the task pane list box preceded by a number. This number indicates the order in which items will appear in the slide. When more than one item displays in the list box, you can change the order of an item by clicking the item in the list box and then clicking the Up Re-Order arrow or the Down Re-Order arrow located below the task pane list box.

## Project 1d    Removing, Modifying, and Reordering Animation Effects

1. With **PP_C7_P1.pptx** open, make Slide 1 active.
2. Modify the start setting for the slide title animation effect by completing the following steps:
   a. Display the Custom Animation task pane by clicking the Animations tab and then clicking the Custom Animation button.
   b. Click the Title 1 item that displays in the task pane list box.
   c. Click the down-pointing arrow at the right side of the *Start* option in the *Modify* section of the task pane and then click *With Previous*. (At this setting the title animation effect will begin as soon as the slide displays without you having to click the mouse button. Notice that the number 1 preceding the item in the list box changed to a zero.)

3. Change the animation effect to the subtitle and modify the animation effect by completing the following steps:
   a. Click the Marketing Report item in the task pane list box.
   b. Click the Change button in the task pane, point to *Emphasis*, and then click *Grow/Shrink* at the side menu. (The location of the *Grow/Shrink* may vary.)
   c. Click the down-pointing arrow at the right side of the *Start* option in the *Modify* section of the task pane and then click *With Previous*.
   d. Click the down-pointing arrow at the right side of the *Speed* option and then click *Fast*.

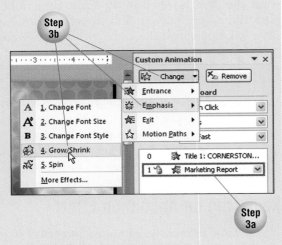

4. Remove animations from slides in Slide Master view by completing the following steps:
   a. Click the View tab and then click the Slide Master button.
   b. Click the third slide master layout in the slide thumbnail pane (*Title and Content Layout*).

c. Click the Title 1 item in the task pane list box and then click the Remove button.

d. Click the content placeholder item in the task pane list box and then click the Remove button.

e. Click the Slide Master tab and then click the Close Master View button.

5. Make Slide 2 active and then apply and customize animation effects by completing the following steps:

a. Click the title *Department Reports*.

b. Click the Add Effect button in the Custom Animation task pane, point to *Entrance* and then click *More Effects*.

c. At the Add Entrance Effect dialog box, scroll down the list box and then click *Spiral In* in the *Exciting* section.

d. Click OK to close the dialog box.

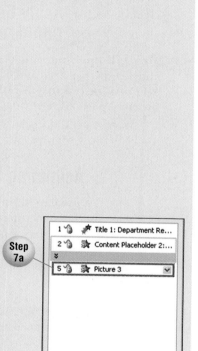

e. Click in the bulleted text.

f. Click the Add Effect button, point to *Entrance*, and then click an option in the side menu.

g. Click the clip art image.

h. Click the Add Effect button, point to *Entrance*, and then click an option in the side menu.

6. Click the Play button to view the animation effects.

7. After viewing the animation effects, you decide that you want the clip art to animate before the bulleted text and you want the animation effects to begin with the previous animation (instead of a mouse click). With Slide 2 active, complete the following steps:

a. Click the Picture 3 item in the task pane list box.

b. Click the Up Re-Order button located toward the bottom of the task pane. (This moves the *Picture 3* item between the Title 1 and the content placeholder items.)

c. Click the down-pointing arrow at the right side of the *Start* option in the *Modify* section of the task pane and then click *With Previous*.

d. Click the Title 1 item in the task pane list box, click the down-pointing arrow at the right side of the item, and then click *Start With Previous* at the drop-down list.

8. Apply to Slides 3 and 4 animation effects similar to those you applied to Slide 2.

9. Make Slide 1 active and then run the presentation. After running the presentation, make any changes or modifications to animation effects.

10. Close the Custom Animation task pane.

11. Save and then close **PP_C7_P1.pptx**.

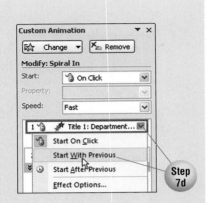

# Project ② Apply Custom Animation Effects to Elements in Slides in an Online Learning Presentation

**You will open an online learning presentation and then apply animation effects to shapes, a clip art image, elements in SmartArt graphics, and elements in a chart. You will also apply a build to bulleted text that dims a previous point and draw a motion path in a slide.**

## Animating Shapes and Images

You can animate individual shapes or images such as clip art images in a slide in the same manner as animating a title or text content placeholder. You can select more than one shape and then apply the same animation effect to the shapes. To select more than one shape, click the first shape, hold down the Shift key, and then click any additional shapes.

## Project 2a  Animating Shapes and a Clip Art Image

1. Open **OnlineLearning.pptx** and then save the presentation and name it **PP_C7_P2**.

2. Make Slide 8 active (this slide contains one large object with three smaller objects hidden behind it) and then animate objects and apply exit effects by completing the following steps:

a. Display the Custom Animation task pane by clicking the Animations tab and then clicking the Custom Animation button.

b. Click the large object in the slide.

c. Click the Add Effect button, point to *Exit*, and then click the *More Effects* option.

d. At the Add Exit Effect dialog box, click the *Spiral Out* option in the *Exciting* section, watch the animation effect in the slide, and then click OK.

e. With the large object selected, drag it down the slide to display a portion of the three objects behind.

f. Click the small object at the left, click the Add Effect button, point to *Entrance*, and then click *More Effects*.

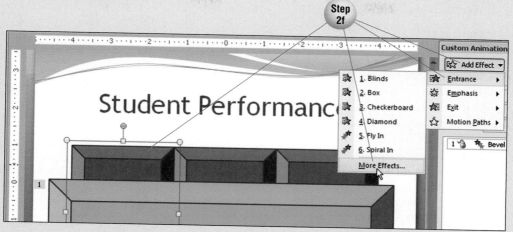

g. At the Add Entrance Effect dialog box, click *Spinner* in the *Moderate* section, and then click OK.

h. Select the middle object, hold down the Shift key, and then click the object at the right. (This selects both objects.)

i. Click the Add Effect button, point to *Entrance*, and then click *Spinner* at the side menu. (Notice that the two objects are numbered 3 in the task pane list box and are set to enter the slide at the same time. You will change this in the next step.)

j. Click the bottom item in the task pane list box, click the down-pointing arrow at the right side of the item, and then click *Start On Click* at the drop-down list.

k. Apply emphasis to the middle object by clicking the middle object, clicking the Add Effect button, pointing to *Emphasis*, and then clicking *Grow/Shrink* at the side menu. (The bottom two items in the task pane list box are the two effects applied to the middle object. Notice that the animation icons are different, indicating different effects. Hover the mouse pointer over an item to view a description of the animation effect.)

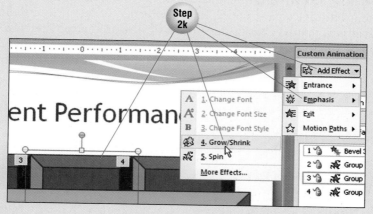

l. Reposition the large object over the three smaller objects.
m. Click the Play button to play the animation effects in the slide.

3. Make Slide 9 active and apply and modify animation effects and change animation order by completing the following steps:

a. Apply an entrance animation effect of your choosing to the text box containing the text *Online learning continues to evolve!*

b. Apply an entrance animation effect of your choosing to the text box containing the text *Stay tuned!*

c. Click the clip art image to select it.

d. Apply the *Spin* emphasis animation effect.

e. Click the down-pointing arrow at the right side of the *Amount* option in the *Modify* section of the task pane and then click *Two Spins* at the drop-down list.

f. Click the down-pointing arrow at the right side of the *Speed* option and then click *Fast*.

g. Click once on the Up Re-Order Arrow (located toward the bottom of the task pane). This moves the clip art image item in the list box above the *Stay tuned!* text box item.

h. Click the Play button to play the animation effects in the slide.

4. Save **PP_C7_P2.pptx**.

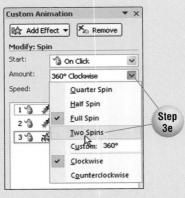

## Animating a SmartArt Graphic

**QUICK STEPS**

**Animate SmartArt Graphic**
1. Click SmartArt graphic.
2. Apply desired animation effect.
3. Click SmartArt graphic item in Custom Animation task pane list box.
4. Click down-pointing arrow at right of item.
5. Click *Effect Options*.
6. Click down-pointing arrow at right of *Group graphic*.
7. Click desired grouping option.

You can apply animation effects to a SmartArt graphic and animate the graphic or individual elements in the graphic. To animate a specific element in a graphic, select the element and then apply an animation effect. Click the item in the task pane list box, click the down-pointing arrow at the right side of the item, and then click *Effect Options* at the drop-down list. This displays the effect options dialog box with a SmartArt Animation tab. Click this tab and then use the *Group graphic* option to specify whether you want the elements grouped as one object, all at once, one by one, from the center at once, or from the center one by one. The name of the effect options dialog box varies depending on the animation effect applied. For example, when you apply the *Ease In* entrance animation effect to the SmartArt graphic in Project 2b, the Effect Options dialog box displays with the name Ease In.

## Project 2b  Animating SmartArt

1. With **PP_C7_P2.pptx** open, make Slide 4 active and then animate objects in the SmartArt graphic by completing the following steps:

a. Click the shape in the SmartArt graphic containing the word *Convenient*. (Make sure the white sizing handles display only around the shape.)

b. Click the Add Effect button in the task pane, point to *Entrance*, and then click the *More Effects* option.

c. At the Add Entrance Effect dialog box, click *Ease In* in the *Moderate* section of the dialog box.

d. Click OK to close the dialog box.

e. Click the down-pointing arrow at the right side of the content placeholder item in the task pane list box and then click *Effect Options*.

f. At the Ease In effect options dialog box, click the SmartArt Animation tab.

g. Click the down-pointing arrow at the right side of the *Group graphic* option and then click *One by one* at the drop-down list. (This will allow you to apply different effects to the four objects in the SmartArt graphic.)

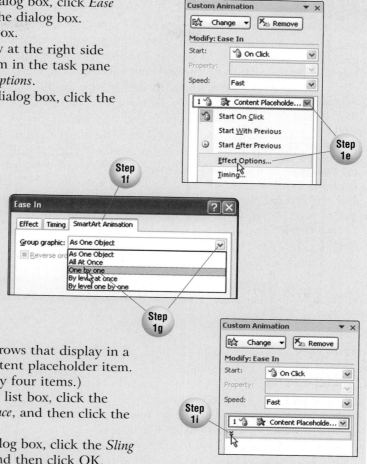

h. Click OK to close the dialog box. (Watch the animation effect play in the slide in the Slide pane.)

i. Expand the list of SmartArt graphic objects in the list box by clicking the small double arrows that display in a blue shaded box below the content placeholder item. (This expands the list to display four items.)

j. Click in the second item in the list box, click the Change button, point to *Entrance*, and then click the *More Effects* option.

k. At the Add Entrance Effect dialog box, click the *Sling* option in the *Exciting* section and then click OK.

l. Click the third item in the list box, click the Change button, point to *Entrance*, and then click *Sling* at the side menu. (The *Sling* option was added to the side menu.)

m. Click the fourth item in the list box, click the Change button, point to *Entrance*, and then click *Sling* at the side menu.

2. Make Slide 6 active and then apply and modify animation effects by completing the following steps:

a. Click the shape containing the text *Multi-Media*.

b. Apply the *Circle* entrance animation effect to the shape. (This effect is located in the *Basic* section of the Add Entrance Effect dialog box.)

c. Click the content placeholder item in the list box, click the down-pointing arrow at the right side of the option, and then click *Effect Options* at the drop-down list.

d. At the Circle dialog box, click the SmartArt Animation tab.

e. Click the down-pointing arrow at the right side of the *Group graphic* option and then click *One by one* at the drop-down list.

f. Click OK to close the dialog box.

g. Click the down-pointing arrow at the right side of the *Speed* option in the *Modify* section of the task pane and then click *Fast* at the drop-down list.

3. Save **PP_C7_P2.pptx**.

# Animating a Chart

**Animate Chart**
1. Click chart.
2. Apply desired animation effect.
3. Click chart item in Custom Animation task pane list box.
4. Click down-pointing arrow at right of item.
5. Click *Effect Options*.
6. Click down-pointing arrow at right of *Group graphic*.
7. Click desired grouping option.

Like a SmartArt graphic, you can animate a chart or elements in a chart. Displaying data in a chart may have a more dramatic effect if the chart is animated. Bringing in one element at a time also allows you to discuss each piece of the data as it displays. Specify how you want the chart animated in the slide with options in the effect options dialog box. Apply an animation effect to a chart, click the down-pointing arrow at the right of the chart item in the Custom Animation task pane list box, and then click *Effect Options*. At the effect options dialog box (the name varies depending on the animation effect applied to the chart), click the Chart Animation tab and then specify how you want chart elements grouped. For example, you can group chart elements on one object or by series or category. Click the Effect tab and the dialog box displays with options for applying enhancements to the animation such as sound. Click the Timing tab to display options for controlling the timing of the animation effects such as the start time, amount of delay, and speed.

## Project 2c   Animating Elements in a Chart

1. With **PP_C7_P2.pptx** open, make Slide 3 active and then animate chart elements by completing the following steps:
   a. Click in the chart placeholder to select the chart. (Make sure you do not have a chart element selected.)
   b. Add the *Dissolve In* entrance animation effect (located in the *Basic* section of the Add Entrance Effect dialog box).
   c. Click the down-pointing arrow at the right side of the content placeholder item in the list box and then click *Effect Options*.
   d. At the Dissolve In dialog box with the Effect tab selected, click the down-pointing arrow at the right side of the *Sound* option, scroll down the drop-down list, and then click the *Click* option.

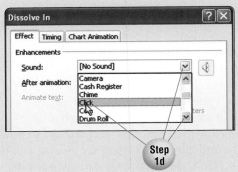

Step 1d

   e. Click the Timing tab.
   f. Click the down-pointing arrow at the right side of the *Speed* option and then click *1 seconds (Fast)* at the drop-down list.
   g. Click the Chart Animation tab.
   h. Click the down-pointing arrow at the right side of the *Group chart* option and then click *By Category* at the drop-down list.
   i. Click OK to close the dialog box.
2. Save **PP_C7_P2.pptx**.

## Applying a Build

In Project 1a, you applied a ***build*** to bulleted text in a slide. A build displays important points on a slide one point at a time keeping the audience's attention focused on the current point. You can further customize a build by causing a previous point to dim when the next point displays. To customize a build, choose a color option with the *After animation* option in the effect options dialog box with the Effect tab selected.

**HINT**

You can group text (in a bulleted text placeholder) at the effect options dialog box by first, second, third, fourth, or fifth levels.

## Project 2d  Applying a Build Animation

1. With **PP_C7_P2.pptx** open, make Slide 7 active and then apply an animation effect and modify the effect by completing the following steps:
   a. Click in the bulleted text.
   b. Apply the *Fly In* entrance animation effect.
   c. Click the down-pointing arrow at the right side of the *Direction* option in the *Modify* section of the task pane and then click *From Left* at the drop-down menu.
   d. Click the down-pointing arrow at the right side of the content placeholder item in the task pane list box and then click *Effect Options* at the drop-down list.
   e. At the Fly In dialog box, make sure the Effect tab is selected, click the down-pointing arrow at the right side of the *After animation* option and then click the yellow color (second color from the right).
   f. Click OK to close the dialog box.
2. Make Slide 2 active and then complete steps similar to those in Step 1 to apply a build animations effects to the bulleted text in the slide.
3. Save **PP_C7_P2.pptx**.

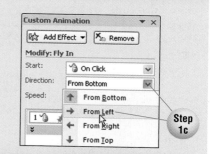

Step 1c

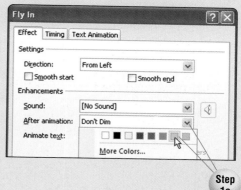

Step 1e

## Drawing Motion Paths

One of the options at the Add Effect button drop-down list is *Motion Paths*. Point to this option and a side menu displays with an option for specifying an animation motion for an object in the slide. You can choose one of the predesigned motion paths or you can choose to draw your own path. To draw your own motion path, point to *Draw Custom Path* and then click *Freeform*. Using the mouse, drag in the slide to create the path. When the path is completed, double-click the mouse button.

**QUICK STEPS**

**Draw Motion Path**
1. Click Add Effect button in Custom Animation task pane.
2. Point to *Motion Paths*.
3. Point to *Draw Custom Path*.
4. Click *Freeform*.
5. Drag in slide to create path.
6. Double-click mouse.

1. With **PP_C7_P2.pptx** open, make Slide 5 active and then animate the star on the map by completing the following steps:
   a. Click the star object in the slide (located below the heading *North America*).
   b. Click the Add Effect button, point to *Motion Paths*, point to *Draw Custom Path*, and then click *Freeform*.

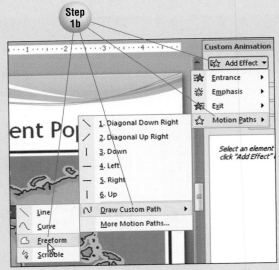

   c. Position the mouse pointer (displays as crosshairs) on the star, hold down the left mouse button, draw a path through each of the five locations on the map ending back in the original location, and then double-click the left mouse button. (If a Custom Path dialog box displays, click the Cancel button.)
   d. Click the Play button to play the animation effect in the slide.
2. Save **PP_C7_P2.pptx**.
3. Run the presentation and click the mouse button to advance slides and elements on slides as needed.
4. Print the presentation as a handout with six slides per page.
5. Close the Custom Animation task pane.

# Setting Up a Slide Show

Control how the presentation displays with options at the Set Up Show dialog box shown in Figure 7.2. With options at this dialog box, you can set slide presentation options, specify how you want slides to advance, and set screen resolution.

**Figure 7.2** Set Up Show Dialog Box

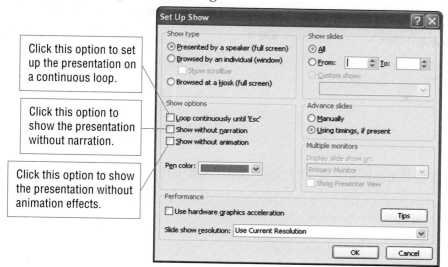

Click this option to set up the presentation on a continuous loop.

Click this option to show the presentation without narration.

Click this option to show the presentation without animation effects.

**Run Presentation without Animation**
1. Click Slide Show tab.
2. Click Set Up Slide Show button.
3. Click *Show without animation*.
4. Click OK.

Set Up Slide Show

# Running a Presentation without Animation

If a presentation contains numerous animation effects, you can choose to run the presentation without the animations. To do this, click the Slide Show tab and then click the Set Up Slide Show button in the Set Up group. At the Set Up Show dialog box, click the *Show without animation* check box to insert a check mark, and then click OK. Changes you make to the Set Up Show dialog box are saved with the presentation.

## Project ② Running a Presentation without Animation

1. With **PP_C7_P2.pptx** open, specify that you want to run the presentation without animation by completing the following steps:
   a. Click the Slide Show tab.
   b. Click the Set Up Slide Show button in the Set Up group.
   c. At the Set Up Show dialog box, click the *Show without animation* check box to insert a check mark.
   d. Click OK to close the dialog box.
2. Run the presentation and notice that the animation effects do not play.
3. Specify that you want the presentation to run with animations by completing the following steps:
   a. Click the Slide Show tab and then click the Set Up Slide Show button.
   b. At the Set Up Show dialog box, click the *Show without animation* check box to remove the check mark and then click OK.
4. Save and then close **PP_C7_P2.pptx**.

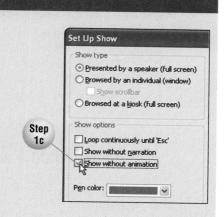

Step 1c

# Project 3 — Prepare a Self-Running Adventure Presentation and Create Custom Shows

You will open a travel tour presentation and then customize it to be a self-running presentation set on a continuous loop. You will also hide slides and create and edit custom shows.

## QUICK STEPS

**Loop Presentation Continuously**
1. Click Slide Show tab.
2. Click Set Up Slide Show button.
3. Click *Loop continuously until 'Esc'*.
4. Click OK.

**HINT**
Use a self-running presentation to communicate information without a presenter.

## Setting Up a Presentation to Loop Continuously

In Chapter 1, you learned how to set automatic times for advancing slides. Insert a check mark in the *Automatically After* check box in the Advance Slide section in the Animations tab and then insert the desired number of seconds in the time box. If you want to have the ability to advance a slide more quickly than the time applied, leave the check mark in the *On Mouse Click* option. With this option active, you can let the slide advance the specified number of seconds or you can click the left mouse button to advance the slide sooner. Remove the check mark from the *On Mouse Click* button if you do not want to advance slides with the mouse.

In some situations, such as at a trade show or convention, you may want to prepare a self-running presentation. A self-running presentation is set up on a continuous loop and does not require someone to run the presentation. To design a self-running presentation, display the Set Up Show dialog box and then insert a check mark in the *Loop continuously until 'Esc'* option. With this option active, the presentation will continue running until you press the Esc key.

## Project 3a — Preparing a Self-Running Presentation

1. Open **AdventureTours.pptx** and then save the presentation with the name **PP_C7_P3**.
2. Insert slides by completing the following steps:
   a. Click below the last slide miniature in the Slides/Outline pane.
   b. Make sure the Home tab is selected, click the New Slide button arrow, and then click *Reuse Slides* at the drop-down list.
   c. At the Reuse Slides task pane, click the Browse button and then click *Browse File*.
   d. At the Browse dialog box, navigate to the PowerPoint2007C7 folder on your storage medium and then double-click *PeruTour.pptx*.
   e. Click each slide in the Reuse Slides task pane in the order in which they display beginning with the top slide.
   f. Close the Reuse Slides task pane.
3. Add transition and sound effects and specify a time for automatically advancing slides by completing the following steps:
   a. Click the Animations tab.
   b. Click in the *Automatically After* check box to insert a check mark.
   c. Click the up-pointing arrow at the right side of the time box until *00:05* displays.

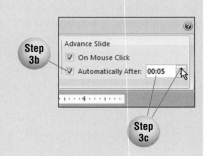

Step 3b

Step 3c

d. Click the *On Mouse Click* check box to remove the check mark.

e. Click the *Fade Smoothly* slide transition (second slide transition option from the left) in the Transition to This Slide group.

f. Click the down-pointing arrow at the right side of the *Transition Sound* option and then click *Breeze* at the drop-down list.

g. Click the Apply To All button in the Transition to This Slide group.

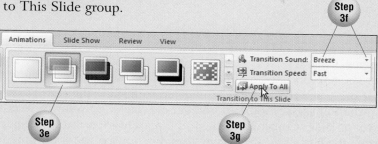

4. Set up the presentation to run continuously by completing the following steps:

a. Click the Slide Show tab.

b. Click the Set Up Slide Show button in the Set Up group.

c. At the Set Up Show dialog box, click in the *Loop continuously until 'Esc'* check box to insert a check mark. (Make sure *All* is selected in the *Show slides* section and *Using timings, if present* is selected in the *Advance slides* section.)

d. Click OK to close the dialog box.

5. Click Slide 1 to select it and then run the presentation. (The slides will advance automatically after five seconds.)

6. After viewing the presentation at least twice, press the Esc key on the keyboard.

7. Save **PP_C7_P3.pptx**.

# Setting Automatic Times for Slides

Applying the same time to all slides is not very practical unless the same amount of text occurs on every slide. In most cases, some slides should be left on the screen longer than others. Apply specific times to a slide with buttons on the Rehearsal toolbar. Display this toolbar by clicking the Slide Show tab and then clicking the Rehearse Timings button in the Set Up group. This displays the first slide in the presentation in Slide Show view with the Rehearsal toolbar located in the upper left corner of the slide. The buttons on the Rehearsal toolbar are identified in Figure 7.3.

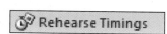

**Figure 7.3** Rehearsal Toolbar

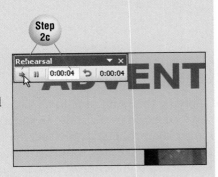

Slide Time

Next

Pause    Repeat

**Set Automatic Times for Slides**
1. Click Slide Show tab.
2. Click Rehearse Timings button.
3. Using Rehearsal toolbar, specify time for each slide.
4. Click Yes.

Next    Pause

Repeat

When the slide displays on the screen, the timer on the Rehearsal toolbar begins. Click the Next button on the Rehearsal toolbar when the slide has displayed for the appropriate amount of time. If you want to stop the timer, click the Pause button. Click the Pause button again to resume the timer. Use the Repeat button on the Rehearsal toolbar if you get off track and want to reset the time for the current slide. Continue through the presentation until the slide show is complete. After the last slide, a message displays showing the total time for the presentation and asks if you want to record the new slide timings. At this message, click Yes to set the times for each slide recorded during the rehearsal. If you do not want to use the rehearsed timings when running a presentation, click the Slide Show tab and then click in the Use Rehearsed Timings check box to remove the check mark.

Project **3b**   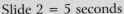  **Setting Rehearse Timings for Slides**

1. With **PP_C7_P3.pptx** open, remove the automatic times for slides by completing the following steps:
   a. Click the Slide Show tab.
   b. Click the Set Up Slide Show button.
   c. At the Set Up Show dialog box, click the *Loop continuously until 'Esc'* check box to remove the check mark.
   d. Click OK to close the dialog box.
2. Set times for the slides to display during a slide show by completing the following steps:
   a. Make Slide 1 active.
   b. With the Slide Show tab active, click the Rehearse Timings button in the Set Up group.
   c. The first slide displays in Slide Show view and the Rehearsal toolbar displays. Wait until the time displayed for the current slide reaches four seconds and then click Next. (If you miss the time, click the Repeat button to reset the clock back to zero for the current slide.)
   d. Set the times for remaining slides as follows:
      Slide 2 = 5 seconds
      Slide 3 = 6 seconds
      Slide 4 = 5 seconds
      Slide 5 = 6 seconds
      Slide 6 = 3 seconds
      Slide 7 = 6 seconds
      Slide 8 = 7 seconds
      Slide 9 = 7 seconds

Step 2c

Rehearsal    0:00:04    0:00:04
ADVENT

e. After the last slide displays, click Yes at the message asking if you want to record the new slide timings.

f. Click the Normal button in the view area on the Status bar.

3. Click the Set Up Slide Show button to display the Set Up Show dialog box, click the *Loop continuously until 'Esc'* check box to insert a check mark, and then click OK to close the dialog box.

4. Run the presentation. (The slide show will start and run continuously.) Watch the presentation until it has started for the second time and then end the show by pressing the Esc key.

5. Save **PP_C7_P3.pptx**.

## Recording Narration

QUICK STEPS

**Record Narration**
1. Click Slide Show tab.
2. Click Record Narration button.
3. Click OK.
4. Narrate slides.
5. Click Save.

You can record narration with your presentation that will play when the presentation is running. To record narration you must have a microphone connected to your computer. To begin the narration, click the Record Narration button in the Set Up group in the Slide Show tab. At the Record Narration dialog box, click the Set Microphone Level button. At the Microphone Check dialog box, dictate the text in quotes so the microphone setup wizard can make sure your microphone is working properly and to adjust the volume levels. Click OK to close the Microphone Check dialog box and then click OK to close the Record Narration dialog box. Your presentation begins and the first slide fills the screen. Begin your narration, clicking the mouse button to advance to each slide. When you have narrated all of the slides in the presentation, a message displays telling you that the narrations have been saved with each slide and asking if you want to save the slide timings. At this message, click the Save button.

The narration in a presentation plays by default when you run the presentation. You can run the presentation without the narration by displaying the Set Up Show dialog box and then inserting a check mark in the *Show without narration* check box in the *Show options* section.

## Project 3c   Recording Narration

**This is an optional project. Before beginning the project, check with your instructor to determine if you have a microphone available for recording.**

1. With **PP_C7_P3.pptx** open, save the presentation and name it **PP_C7_C3Narration**.

2. Remove the continuous loop option and remove timings by completing the following:

a. Click the Slide Show tab.

b. Click the Set Up Slide Show button.

c. At the Set Up Show dialog box, click the *Loop continuously until 'Esc'* check box to remove the check mark.

d. Click OK to close the dialog box.

e. Click the Animations tab.

f. Click the down-pointing arrow at the right side of the time box until *00:00* displays.

g. Click the *Automatically After* check box to remove the check mark.

h. Click the *On Mouse Click* option to insert a check mark.

i. Click the Apply To All button.

3. Make Slide 1 active and then record narration by completing the following steps:

a. Click the Slide Show tab and then click the Record Narration button in the Set Up group.

b. At the Record Narration dialog box, click the Set Microphone Level button.

c. At the Microphone Check dialog box, dictate the text in quotes, and then click the OK button.

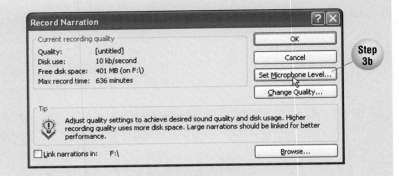

Step 3b

d. At the Record Narration dialog box, click OK.

e. When the first slide displays, either read the information or provide your own narrative of the slide and then click the left mouse button.

f. At the next slide, continue your narration and then click the left mouse button when completed.

g. Continue narrating each slide (either using some of the information in the slides or creating your own narration).

h. After narrating the last slide (the slide about accommodations for the Peru tour), press the Esc key.

i. At the message telling you that the narrations have been saved with each slide and asking if you want to save the slide timings, click the Save button.

4. With Slide 1 active, run the presentation. If your computer has speakers, you will hear your narration as the presentation runs.

5. Run the presentation without narration by completing the following steps:

a. Click the Set Up Slide Show button in the Slide Show tab.

b. At the Set Up Show dialog box, click in the *Show without narration* check box to insert a check mark.

c. Click OK.

d. Run the presentation beginning with Slide 1. (The presentation will run automatically with the timing established when you were recording your narration but without the narration.)

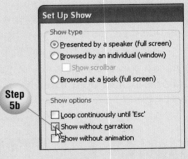

Step 5b

6. Save and then close **PP_C7_P3Narration.pptx**.

## Hiding Slides

**Hide Slide**
1. Make slide active.
2. Click Slide Show tab.
3. Click Hide Slide button.

Hide Slide

A presentation you create may be presented to a number of different groups or departments. In some situations, you may want to hide specific slides in a presentation depending on the audience. To hide a slide in a presentation, make the desired slide active, click the Slide Show tab, and then click the Hide Slide button in the Set Up group. When a slide is hidden, a square with a slash through it displays behind the slide number in the Slides/Outline pane. The slide is visible in the Slides/Outline pane in Normal view and also in the Slide Sorter view. To remove the hidden icon and redisplay the slide when running a presentation, click the slide miniature in the Slides/Outline pane, click the Slide Show tab, and then click the Hide Slide button.

# Setting Up Monitors

With options in the Monitors group in the Slide Show tab, you can specify screen resolution and show the presentation on two different monitors. The Resolution option in the Slide Show tab displays the current resolution for your monitor. If you hover your mouse over the option, an expanded ScreenTip displays with information telling you that you can choose a screen resolution and that a smaller resolution generally displays faster while a larger resolution generally displays the presentation slower but with more visual detail.

If you have two monitors connected to your computer or are running PowerPoint on a laptop with dual-display capabilities, you can choose the *Presenter View* option in the Monitors group. With this option active, you display your presentation in full-screen view on one monitor and display your presentation in a special speaker view on the other.

## Project 3d — Changing Monitor Resolution

**Check with your instructor before completing this project to determine if you can change monitor resolution.**

1. Open **PP_C7_P3.pptx**.
2. Remove the continuous loop option and remove timings by completing the following:
   a. Click the Slide Show tab.
   b. Click the Set Up Slide Show button.
   c. At the Set Up Show dialog box, click the *Loop continuously until 'Esc'* check box to remove the check mark.
   d. Click OK to close the dialog box.
   e. Click the Animations tab.
   f. Click the down-pointing arrow at the right side of the time box until *00:00* displays.
   g. Click the *Automatically After* check box to remove the check mark.
   h. Click the *On Mouse Click* option to insert a check mark.
   i. Click the Apply To All button.
3. Hide Slide 2 by completing the following steps:
   a. Click the Slide 2 miniature in the Slides/Outline pane.
   b. Click the Slide Show tab and then click the Hide Slide button in the Set Up group.
4. Change the monitor resolution by completing the following steps:
   a. Note the current monitor resolution that displays in the *Resolution* option box in the Monitors group.
   b. Click the down-pointing arrow at the right side of the *Resolution* option and then click *800 × 600* at the drop-down list.

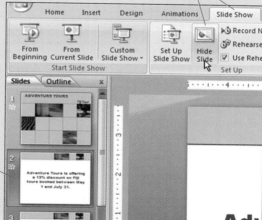

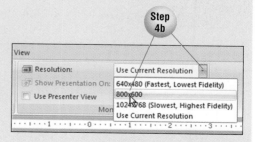

5. Run the presentation and notice the resolution and that Slide 2 does not display (since it is hidden).
6. Unhide Slide 2 by clicking the Slide 2 miniature in the Slides/Outline pane and then clicking the Hide Slide button in the Set Up group in the Slide Show tab.
7. Return the monitor resolution to the original setting by clicking the down-pointing arrow at the right side of the *Resolution* option in the Monitors group in the Slide Show tab and then clicking the original resolution at the drop-down list.
8. Save **PP_C7_P3.pptx**.

**HINT**

Create custom shows to customize a presentation for a variety of audiences.

## Creating a Custom Show

You can select specific slides within a presentation to create a presentation within a presentation. This might be useful in situations where you want to show only a select number of slides to a particular audience. To create a custom show, click the Slide Show tab, click the Custom Slide Show button in the Start Slide Show group, and then click *Custom Shows* at the drop-down list. At the Custom Shows dialog box, click the New button and the Define Custom Show dialog box displays similar to what you see in Figure 7.4.

**Figure 7.4** Define Custom Show Dialog Box

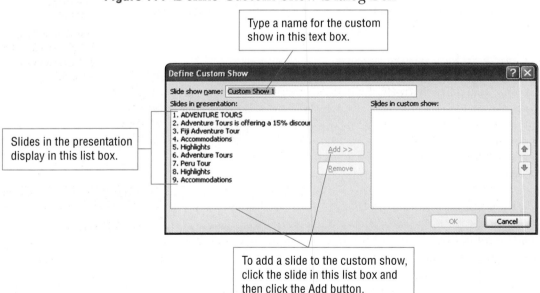

Type a name for the custom show in this text box.

Slides in the presentation display in this list box.

To add a slide to the custom show, click the slide in this list box and then click the Add button.

At the Define Custom Show dialog box, type a name for the custom presentation in the *Slide show name* text box. To insert a slide in the custom show, click the slide in the *Slides in presentation* list box and then click the Add button. This inserts the slide in the *Slides in custom show* list box. Continue in this manner until all desired slides are added to the custom show. If you want to change the order of the slides in the *Slides in custom show* list box, click one of the arrow keys to move the selected slide up or down in the list box. When the desired slides are inserted in the *Slides in custom show* list box and in the desired order, click OK. You can create more than one custom show in a presentation.

## Running a Custom Show

To run a custom show within a presentation, click the Custom Slide Show button in the Slide Show tab and then click the desired custom show at the drop-down list. You can also choose a custom show by displaying the Set Up Show dialog box and then clicking the *Custom show* option. If the presentation contains more than one custom show, click the down-pointing arrow at the right of the *Custom show* option and then click the show name at the drop-down list.

## Editing a Custom Show

A custom show is saved with the presentation and can be edited. To edit a custom show, open the presentation, click the Custom Slide Show button in the Slide Show tab, and then click *Custom Shows* at the drop-down list. At the Custom Shows dialog box, click the custom show name you want to edit and then click the Edit button. At the Define Custom Show dialog box, make the desired changes to the custom show such as adding or removing slides or changing the order of slides. When all changes have been made, click the OK button.

## Printing a Custom Show

You can print a custom show with the *Custom Show* option in the Print dialog box. To do this, display the Print dialog box, click the *Custom Show* option in the *Print range* section, and then click OK. If the presentation includes more than one show, click the down-pointing arrow at the right side of the *Custom Show* option at the Print dialog box, click the desired show, and then click OK.

**QUICK STEPS**

**Create Custom Show**
1. Click Slide Show tab.
2. Click Custom Slide Show button.
3. Click *Custom Shows*.
4. Click New button.
5. Make desired changes at Define Custom Show dialog box.
6. Click OK.

**Run Custom Show**
1. Click Slide Show tab.
2. Click Custom Slide Show button.
3. Click desired custom show.

**Edit Custom Show**
1. Click Slide Show tab.
2. Click Custom Slide Show button.
3. Click desired custom show.
4. Click Edit button.
5. Make desired changes at Define Custom Show dialog box.
6. Click OK.

**Print Custom Show**
1. Display Print dialog box.
2. Click *Custom Show*.
3. Click OK.

Project **3e**   **Creating, Editing, and Running Custom Shows**

1. With **PP_C7_P3.pptx** open, save the presentation and name it **PP_C7_P3Custom**.
2. Create two custom shows by completing the following steps:
   a. Click the Slide Show tab, click the Custom Slide Show button, and then click *Custom Shows* at the drop-down list.
   b. At the Custom Shows dialog box, click the New button.

Step 2b

c. At the Define Custom Show dialog box, type **PeruTourCustom** in the *Slide show name* text box.

d. Click Slide 6 in the *Slides in presentation* list box and then click the Add button. (This adds the slide to the *Slides in custom show* list box.)

e. Click each of the remaining slides in the list box (Slides 7, 8, and 9) and click the Add button.

f. Click OK to close the Define Custom Show dialog box.

g. At the Custom Shows dialog box, click the New button.

h. At the Define Custom Show dialog box, type **FijiTourCustom** in the *Slide show name* text box.

i. Add Slides 1 through 5 to the *Slides in custom show* list box.

j. Click OK to close the dialog box.

k. Click the Close button to close the Custom Shows dialog box.

3. Run the *PeruTourCustom* custom show by completing the following steps:

a. Click the Custom Slide Show button in the Slide Show tab and then click *PeruTourCustom* at the drop-down list.

b. Click the left mouse button to advance slides.

c. Click the Custom Slide Show button, click *FijiTourCustom* at the drop-down list, and then view the presentation. (Click the left mouse button to advance slides.)

4. Edit the FijiTourCustom custom slide show by completing the following steps:

a. Click the Custom Slide Show button in the Slide Show tab and then click *Custom Shows* at the drop-down list.

b. At the Custom Shows dialog box, click *FijiTourCustom* in the *Custom shows* list box and then click the Edit button.

c. At the Define Custom Show dialog box, click Slide 2 in the *Slides in custom show* list box and then click three times on the down-pointing arrow at the right side of the list box. (This moves the slide to the bottom of the list.)

d. Click OK to close the dialog box.

e. Click the Close button to close the Custom Shows dialog box.

5. Run the FijiTourCustom custom show.

6. Save and then close **PP_C7_P3Custom.pptx**.

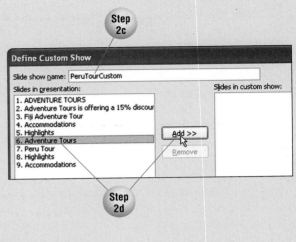

Step 2c

Step 2d

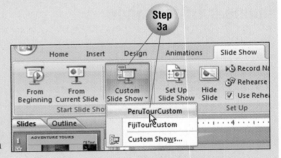

Step 3a

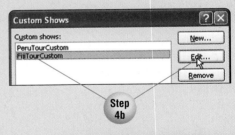

Step 4b

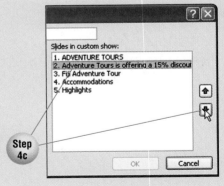

Step 4c

 roject **4** **Insert a Sound and a Movie Clip in a Presentation**

You will open a presentation and then insert a sound clip, movie clip, and clip art image with motion. You will also customize the sound and movie clips to play automatically when running the presentation.

# Inserting Sounds and Movie Clips

Adding sound and/or movie clips to a presentation will turn a slide show into a true multimedia experience for your audience. Including a variety of elements in a presentation will stimulate interest in your presentation and keep the audience motivated.

To add a sound to your presentation, click the Insert tab and then click the Sound button in the Media Clips group. At the Insert Sound dialog box, navigate to the desired folder and then double-click the sound file. You can also insert a sound by clicking the Sound button arrow and then clicking an option at the drop-down list. With the list options you can choose to insert a sound from a file or clipboard, play an audio track, or record a sound.

When you insert a sound from the Insert Sound dialog box, a message displays asking how you want the sound to start when the slide displays in the slide show. Click the Automatically button if you want the sound to begin when the slide displays or click the When Clicked button if you want the sound to begin when you click the sound icon.

A sound file in a slide can be embedded or linked. PowerPoint will embed only sound files with the file extension *.wav* (waveform audio data) and all other sound file types are linked to the slide. If you move a linked sound file, PowerPoint may not be able to locate the file. If possible, save the sound file in the same folder as the presentation so PowerPoint can find the sound file when you run the presentation.

Adding a movie clip is a similar process to adding sound. Click the Movie button in the Media Clips group in the Insert tab to display the Insert Movie dialog box. At this dialog box, navigate to the folder containing the movie clip file and then double-click the file. You can also click the Movie button arrow and then click *Movie from File* to display the Insert Movie dialog box or click the *Movie from Clip Organizer* to display the Clip Art task pane with images containing motion.

**Insert Sound Clip**
1. Click Insert tab.
2. Click Sound button.
3. Double-click desired sound file.

Sound

**Insert Movie Clip**
1. Click Insert tab.
2. Click Movie button.
3. Double-click desired movie file.

Movie

1. Open **PotentialPresentation.pptx** and then save the presentation with the name **PP_C7_P4**.
2. Insert a movie clip and sound in a new slide by completing the following steps:
   a. Make Slide 6 active.
   b. Click the New Slide button arrow and then click the *Blank* layout.
   c. Click the Insert tab.
   d. Click the Movie button in the Media Clips group.
   e. At the Insert Movie dialog box, navigate to the SoundandVideo folder on the CD that accompanies this textbook, and then double-click the file named *TakeOff.mpeg*.
   f. At the message asking how you want the movie to start, click the Automatically button.
   g. Resize the image so it fills the entire slide.
3. Add a sound clip to the new slide (Slide 7) that will automatically play by completing the following steps:
   a. Click the Sound button in the Media Clips group.
   b. At the Insert Sound dialog box, navigate to the SoundandVideo folder on the CD that accompanies this textbook, and then double-click the file named *Greatfire.mid*.
   c. At the message asking how you want the sound to start, click the Automatically button.
4. Insert a clip art image with motion (the motion will display when you run the presentation) by completing the following steps:
   a. Make Slide 2 active.
   b. Click the Movie button arrow and then click *Movie from Clip Organizer* at the drop-down list.
   c. Click the clip art image shown at the right. (If this image is not available, choose another.)
   d. Close the Clip Art task pane.
   e. With the image selected in the slide, click the Recolor button and then click *Accent color 2 Dark* (third from the left in the *Dark Variations* section).
   f. Click in the *Shape Height* measurement box in the Size group, type 1.8, and then press Enter.
   g. Move the image so it is positioned below and to the right of the bulleted text.
5. Display Slide 1 in the Slide pane and then run the presentation. When the last slide (Slide 7) displays, watch the movie clip, listen to the sound (the sound plays after the movie clip plays), and then press the Esc key to end the slide show.
6. Save **PP_C7_P4.pptx**.

Step 4b

Step 4c

## Customizing Sounds and Movie Clips

When you insert a sound clip in a slide, you can customize the sound with options in the Sound Tools Options tab. With options in this tab, you can change the sound volume, specify sound options, and arrange and size the sound icon. When you insert a movie clip, the Movie Tools Options tab is available. This tab contains many of the same options as the Sound Tools Options tab.

## Project 4h  Customizing a Sound and Movie Clip

1. With **PP_C7_P4.pptx** open, assume that you want the sound and movie clips to play continuously. To do this, complete the following steps:
   a. Make Slide 7 active.
   b. Click the movie clip in the slide.
   c. Click the Movie Tools Options tab.
   d. Click the *Loop Until Stopped* check box in the Movie Options group.

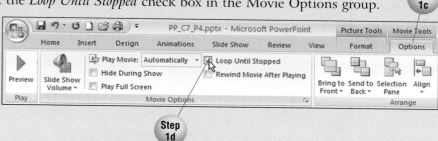

   e. Click the sound icon and then click the Sound Tools Options tab.
   f. Click the *Loop Until Stopped* check box in the Sound Options group.
   g. Click the *Hide During Show* check box in the Sound Options group.
2. You want the sound and movie clip to play when Slide 7 displays during the presentation. To do this, you will need to customize the start options in the Custom Animation task pane by completing the following steps:
   a. Click the Animations tab.
   b. Click the Custom Animation button.
   c. Click the Greatfire.mid item in the task pane list box.
   d. Click the down-pointing arrow at the right side of the Greatfire.mid item and then click the *Start With Previous* option.
   e. Close the Custom Animation tab.

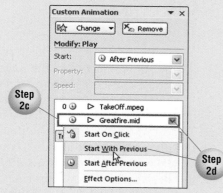

3. Make Slide 1 active and then run the presentation. When you reach Slide 7, watch the movie clip and listen to the sound and then end the slide show.
4. Print the slides as handouts with four slides per page.
5. Save and then close the presentation.

## Project 5  Play a Sound throughout a Presentation

You will open a job search presentation, set it up as a self-running presentation, and then insert a sound that plays throughout the presentation.

## Playing a Sound throughout a Presentation

In Project 4a, you inserted a sound object that played when a specific slide displayed. You can also insert a sound file in a presentation and have the sound continue through all slides in a presentation. Generally, you would add a sound for the entire presentation when setting up a self-running presentation. To include a sound clip in a self-running presentation, insert the sound, click the down-pointing arrow at the right side of the *Play Sound* option in the Sound Tools Options tab, and then click *Play across slides* at the drop-down list.

## Project 5 — Inserting Sound and Playing throughout Presentation

1. Open **JobSearch.pptx** and then save the presentation with the name **PP_C7_P5**.
2. Apply the *Module* design theme.
3. Suppose you are going to display this presentation at a trade show and you want to set it up as a self-running presentation. To do this, complete the following steps:
   a. Click the Animations tab.
   b. Click in the *On Mouse Click* check box to remove the check mark.
   c. Click in the *Automatically After* check box to insert a check mark.
   d. Click the up-pointing arrow at the right side of the time box until *00:05* displays.
   e. Click the *Fade Through Black* transition (third from left) in the Transition to This Slide group.
   f. Click the Apply To All button in the Transition to This Slide group.
   g. Click the Slide Show tab and then click the Set Up Slide Show button in the Set Up group.
   h. At the Set Up Show dialog box, click in the *Loop continuously until 'Esc'* option check box to insert a check mark. (Make sure *All* is selected in the *Show slides* section and *Using timings, if present* is selected in the *Advance slides* section.)
   i. Click OK to close the dialog box.

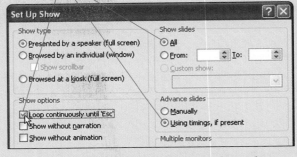

4. To add more interest to the presentation, you decide to add a sound that plays throughout the presentation. To do this, complete the following steps:
   a. Make Slide 1 the active slide.
   b. Click the Insert tab and then click the Sound button in the Media Clips group.
   c. At the Insert Sound dialog box, navigate to the SoundandVideo folder on the CD that accompanies this textbook, and then double-click the file named **Greenspace.mid**.
   d. At the message asking how you want the sound to start, click the Automatically button.
   e. Click the down-pointing arrow at the right side of the *Play Sound* option in the Sound Tools Option tab and then click *Play across slides* at the drop-down list.

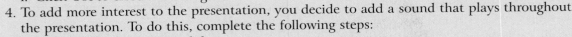

   f. Move the sound icon down to the bottom right corner of the slide.
5. With Slide 1 the active slide, run the presentation.
6. After viewing the presentation at least twice, press the Esc key on the keyboard.
7. Print the presentation as a handout with nine slides per page.
8. Save and then close **PP_C7_P5.pptx**.

# CHAPTER summary

- Apply a built-in animation to an item in a slide by clicking the Animations tab, clicking the down-pointing arrow at the right side of the *Animate* option in the Animations group, and then clicking the desired animation at the drop-down list.

- Click the Preview button in the Animations tab to view animation effects in a slide without running the presentation.

- Remove a built-in animation effect from an item by clicking the item, clicking the down-pointing arrow at the right side of the *Animate* option in the Animations tab, and then clicking *No animation*.

- Apply custom animation effects with options at the Custom Animation task pane. Display this task pane by clicking the Animations tab and then clicking the Custom Animation button.

- With the Add Effect button in the Custom Animation task pane you can apply entrance, emphasis, exit, and motion path effects to an item in a slide.

- Click the Play button located toward the bottom of the Custom Animation task pane to play any animation effects in the current slide.

- Modify animation effects with options in the *Modify* section in the Custom Animation task pane. The options in the *Modify* section vary depending on the effect applied.

- Change animation effects by clicking the item in the Custom Animation task pane and then clicking the Change button, remove an animation effect by clicking the Remove button, and reorder items by clicking the Up Re-Order arrow or Down Re-Order arrow.

- Animate a shape or image by clicking the object and then applying the desired animation effects.

- Animate specific elements in a SmartArt graphic with options in the effect options dialog box with the SmartArt tab selected. To display this dialog box, apply an animation effect to the SmartArt element, click the item in the task pane representing the element, click the down-pointing arrow at the right side of the item, and then click *Effect Options*.

- Animate specific elements in a chart with options in the effect options dialog box with the Chart Animation tab selected.

- Apply a build that dims the previous item in a slide with the *After animation* option at the effect options dialog box with the Effect tab selected.

- Draw a custom motion path in a slide by clicking the Add Effect button in the Custom Animation task pane, pointing to *Motion Paths*, pointing to *Draw Custom Path*, and then clicking *Freeform*. Using the mouse, drag in the slide to create the path.

- Customize a slide show with options in the Set Up Show dialog box. Display this dialog box by clicking the Set Up Slide Show button in the Set Up group in the Slide Show tab.

- To prepare a self-running presentation, display the Set Up Show dialog box and insert a check mark in the *Loop continuously until 'Esc'* option.

- To apply specific times to slides, click the Rehearse Timings button in the Set Up group in the Slide Show. This displays the first slide in the presentation with a rehearsal toolbar in the upper left corner. Use buttons on this toolbar to set, pause, or repeat timings.

- To record a narration for a presentation, click the Slide Show tab, click the Record Narration button, make any desired changes at the Record Narration dialog box, and then click OK.

- Hide or unhide a slide in a presentation by clicking the Hide Slide button in the Set Up group in the Slide Show tab.

- Specify screen resolutions with the *Resolution* option in the Monitors group in the Slide Show tab.

- Create a custom slide show, which is a presentation within a presentation, with options in the Define Custom Shows dialog box. Display this dialog box by clicking the Slide Show tab, clicking the Custom Slide Show button, and then clicking *Custom Shows*. At the Custom Shows dialog box, click the New button.

- To run a custom slide show, click the Custom Slide Show button in the Slide Show tab and then click the desired custom show at the drop-down list. You can also run a custom slide show by choosing the desired show with the *Custom show* option in the Set Up Show dialog box.

- Edit a custom show by clicking the custom show name in the Custom Shows dialog box, clicking the Edit button, and then making desired changes at the Define Custom Show dialog box.

- Print a custom show with the *Custom Show* option in the Print dialog box.

- To insert a sound file in a slide, click the Insert tab, click the Sound button, and then double-click the desired sound file at the Insert Sound dialog box.

- To insert a movie clip in a slide, click the Insert tab, click the Movie button, and then double-click the desired movie clip file at the Insert Movie dialog box.

- Customize sound with options in the Sound Tools Options tab and customize a movie clip with options in the Movie Tools Options tab.

- To play a sound throughout a self-running presentation, insert the sound, click the down-pointing arrow at the right side of the *Play Sound* option in the Sound Tools Options tab, and then click *Play across slides* at the drop-down list.

# COMMANDS review

| FEATURE | RIBBON TAB, GROUP | BUTTON, OPTION |
|---------|-------------------|----------------|
| Built-in animations | Animations, Animations | Animate: No Animation |
| Custom Animation task pane | Animations, Animations | Custom Animation |
| Set Up Show dialog box | Slide Show, Set Up | |
| Rehearsal toolbar | Slide Show, Set Up | Rehearse Timings |
| Record Narration dialog box | Slide Show, Set Up | Record Narration |
| Hide/unhide slide | Slide Show, Set Up | |
| Define Custom Show dialog box | Slide Show, Start Slide Show | , Custom Shows |
| Insert Sound dialog box | Insert, Media Clips | |
| Insert Movie dialog box | Insert, Media Clips | |

# CONCEPTS check

## Test Your Knowledge

**Completion:** In the space provided at the right, indicate the correct term, symbol, or command.

1. To display built-in animations, click the down-pointing arrow at the right side of this option in the Animations tab.

   _____

2. Click this button in the Animations tab to view the animation effects applied to elements in the current slide.

   _____

3. Click the Add Effect button in the Custom Animation task pane and four options display—*Entrance, Exit, Motion Paths,* and this.

   _____

4. Use this option in the Effect Options dialog box with the SmartArt Animation tab selected to specify a grouping.

   _____

5. When animating chart elements, click this tab at the Effect Options dialog box to apply enhancements to the animation such as sound.

   _____

6. This term refers to displaying important points one at a time in a slide when running a presentation.

   _____

7. To display a presentation without animation effects, insert a check mark in the *Show without animation* check box in this dialog box.

   _____

8. Click this button in the Slide Show tab to display the first slide in the presentation in Slide Show view with the Rehearsal toolbar visible.

   _____

9. The Hide Slide button is located in this tab.

   _____

10. Specify the slides you want included in a custom show with options at this dialog box.

    _____

11. Print a custom slide show by clicking the *Custom Show* option in this section of the Print dialog box.

    _____

12. The Sound button and Movie button are located in this group in the Insert tab.

    _____

13. Customize a sound file with options in this tab.

    _____

14. To play a sound throughout a presentation, insert the sound, click the down-pointing arrow at the right side of the *Play Sound* option in the Sound Tools Options tab, and then click this option.

    _____

# SKILLS check
## Demonstrate Your Proficiency

## Assessment

### 1  APPLY BUILT-IN ANIMATION EFFECTS TO A TRAVEL PRESENTATION

1. Open **FCTCruise.pptx** and then save the presentation with the name **PP_C7_A1**.
2. Make Slide 1 active, click the company logo, and then apply the *Fade* built-in animation.
3. Display the presentation in Slide Master view, click the top slide master layout in the slide thumbnail pane, and then apply the following animations:
   a. Apply the *Fade* built-in animation to the title style.
   b. Apply the *By 1st Level Paragraphs* in the *Wipe* section to the bulleted text.
   c. Close the Slide Master view.
4. Run the presentation.
5. Save and then close **PP_C7_A1.pptx**.

## Assessment

### 2  APPLY CUSTOM ANIMATION EFFECTS TO AN EMPLOYEE ORIENTATION PRESENTATION

1. Open **GlobalEmployeeOrientation.pptx** and then save the presentation with the name **PP_C7_A2**.
2. Make Slide 2 active and then apply the following custom animations to the SmartArt graphic:
   a. Apply the *Blinds* entrance animation effect.
   b. Change the SmartArt animation so the graphic is grouped *One by one*. **Hint: Do this at the Blinds dialog box. Display this dialog box by clicking the content placeholder item in the Custom Animation task pane list box, clicking the down-pointing arrow at the right side of the item, and then clicking Effect Options at the drop-down list.**
   c. Change the direction to *Vertical* and the speed to *Fast*.
3. Make Slide 3 active and then apply the following custom animations to the organizational chart:
   a. Apply the *Blinds* entrance animation effect.
   b. Change the SmartArt animation so the graphic is grouped *By branch one by one*.
   c. Change the speed to *Fast*.
4. Make Slide 4 active and then apply the following custom animations to the bulleted text (click on any character in the bulleted text):
   a. Apply the *Color Typewriter* entrance animation effect.
   b. Set the text to dim after animation to a light blue color.
5. Apply the following custom animations to the clip art image in Slide 4:
   a. Apply the *Spin* emphasis animation effect.
   b. Set the amount of spin for the clip art image to *Two Spins* and the speed to *Very Fast*.
   c. Change the *Start* option to *With Previous*.
   d. Reorder the items in the task pane list box so the clip art displays first when running the presentation.

6. Make Slide 5 active, select the SmartArt graphic, and apply a custom animation effect so the elements in the SmartArt graphic fade in one by one.

7. Make Slide 6 active and then apply the following custom animation effects to the images with the following specifications:

    a. Apply the *Fly Out* exit animation effect to the *Free Education* gift package, change the direction to *To Right*, and change the speed to *Fast*.

    b. Apply the *Box* entrance animation effect to the diploma/books clip art image.

    c. Move the *Free Education* gift package so the bulleted text underneath displays, apply the *Descend* entrance animation effect to the bulleted text, and then move the gift package back to the original location.

    d. Apply the *Fly Out* exit animation effect to the *Free Toys and Fitness* gift package, change the direction to *To Left*, and change the speed to *Fast*.

    e. Apply the *Box* entrance animation effect to the notebook computer clip art image.

    f. Move the *Free Toys and Fitness* gift package so the bulleted text underneath displays, apply the *Descend* entrance animation effect to the bulleted text, and then move the gift package back to the original location.

8. Make Slide 1 active and then run the presentation.

9. Save **PP_C7_A2.pptx**.

10. Display the presentation in Slide Master view, click the top slide master layout in the slide thumbnail pane, apply an entrance animation effect of your choosing to the title, and then close Slide Master view.

11. Make Slide 1 active and then apply the following custom animation effects:

    a. Click the globe clip art image and then draw a freeform motion path so the image will circle around the slide and return back to the original location.

    b. Apply the *Spiral In* entrance animation effect to the *New Employee Orientation* placeholder.

12. Run the presentation.

13. Print the presentation as a handout with all slides on one page.

14. Save and then close **PP_C7_A2.pptx**.


## Assessment

### 3   APPLY ANIMATION EFFECTS AND SOUND TO A JOB SEARCH PRESENTATION

1. Open **JobSearch.pptx** and then save the presentation with the name **PP_C7_A3**.

2. Apply a design theme of your choosing to the presentation.

3. Add appropriate clip art to one or two slides.

4. Apply animation effects to slides in the presentation.

5. Insert the **Greenspace.mid** sound clip (located in the SoundandVideo folder on the CD that accompanies this textbook) in Slide 9 so it plays when you click the sound icon.

6. Create a custom show named *Interview* that contains Slides 1, 3, 6, 7, and 9.

7. Run the Interview custom show. (After you have displayed all elements on Slide 9, click the sound icon to play the music. After listening to the music for a period of time, end the presentation.)

8. Print the Interview custom show as a handout with all slides on one page.

9. Edit the Interview custom show by removing Slide 2.

10. Print the Interview custom show again as a handout with all slides on one page.

11. Save and then close **PP_C7_A3.pptx**.

# 4 INSERT A SOUND FROM THE CLIP ORGANIZER INTO A TRAVEL PRESENTATION

1. Experiment with inserting sounds from the clip organizer and then open **HawaiiTour.pptx** and save the presentation with the name **PP_C7_A4**.
2. Insert a song from the sound clip organizer (such as *Hawaii Farewell*, *Hawaii Song*, *Light Piano*, or any other song of your choosing) into the first slide in the presentation.
3. Set up the presentation to run on an endless loop and the sound to play across all slides and continuously as long as the presentation is running. (Display the Custom Animation task pane and make sure the song item displays at the beginning of the list and is set to *Start With Previous*.)
4. Run the presentation.
5. Print the presentation as a handout with all slides on one page.
6. Save and then close **PP_C7_A4**.

# CASE study
## *Apply Your Skills*

**Part 1**

You are a trainer in the Training Department at Riverside Services. You are responsible for coordinating and conducting software training in the company. Your company hires contract employees and some of those employees work at home and need to have a computer available. You will be conducting a short training for contract employees on how to purchase a personal computer. Open the Word document named **PCBuyingGuidelines.docx** and then use the information in the document to prepare your presentation. Make sure you keep the slides uncluttered and easy to read. Consider inserting clip art or other images in some of the slides. Insert custom animation effects to each slide in the presentation. Run the presentation and then make any necessary changes to the animation effects. Save the presentation and name it **PP_C7_CS_P1**. Print the presentation as a handout.

**Part 2**

Some training sessions on purchasing a personal computer are only scheduled for twenty minutes. For these training sessions, you want to cover only the information about selecting computer hardware components. With the **PP_C7_CS_P1.pptx** presentation open, create a custom show (you determine the name) that contains only the slides pertaining to selecting hardware components. Run the custom show and then print the custom show. Save **PP_C7_CS_P1.pptx**.

**Part 3**

You would like to insert a sound file that plays at the end of the presentation and decide to find free sound files on the Internet. Log on to the Internet and then use a search engine to search for "free sound clips" or "free audio clips." When you find a site, make sure that you can download and use the sound clip without violating copyright laws. Download a sound clip and then insert it in the last slide in your presentation. Set up the sound clip to play after all of the elements display on the slide. Save and then close **PP_C7_CS_P1.pptx**.

**Part 4**

The training manager has asked you to view the Microsoft training tutorial on adding sound effects to a presentation. She wants you to complete the tutorial and also complete the practice session on inserting sound files into a presentation. (The training will take approximately 45 minutes to an hour.) Display the PowerPoint Help window, type Add sound effects to a presentation, and then press Enter. Click the Add sound effects to a presentation hyperlink in the PowerPoint Help window. Complete the tutorial and then complete the practice on inserting sound files. When you have completed the practice steps, save the presentation to the PowerPoint2007C7 folder on your storage medium and name it **PC_C7_CS_P4**. Run the presentation and then print the presentation as a handout with six slides per page. Save and then close the presentation.

# Integrating, Reviewing, Protecting, and Saving Presentations

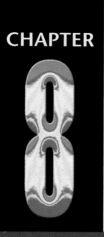

## PERFORMANCE OBJECTIVES

**Upon successful completion of Chapter 8, you will be able to:**

- Import a Word outline into a presentation
- Export a presentation to Word
- Copy and paste data
- Copy and paste data using the Clipboard task pane
- Link and embed objects
- Download design templates
- Insert, edit, and delete comments
- Modify presentation properties
- Inspect, encrypt, mark as final, and add a digital signature to a presentation
- Run the compatibility checker
- Save presentations in different formats
- Save slides as images
- Save a presentation as a Web page
- Package a presentation for a CD

powerpoint Chapter 8

**Tutorial 8.1**
Embedding and Linking Objects
**Tutorial 8.2**
Sharing Data and Comments
**Tutorial 8.3**
Preparing Presentations for
Remote Delivery

Share objects between programs in the Microsoft Office suite by importing and exporting data, copying and pasting objects, copying and embedding objects, or copying and linking objects. The method you choose depends on how you use the information and whether the data is static or dynamic. If you use PowerPoint in a workgroup environment, you may want to insert comments in a presentation and then share the presentation with others in your group. In a workgroup environment, you might also want to protect presentations and prepare presentations for distribution. In this chapter, you will learn how to complete these tasks as well as how to download design templates from Microsoft Office Online, save a presentation in various formats, and package a presentation for a CD.

*Note: Before beginning computer projects, copy to your storage medium the PowerPoint2007C8 folder from the PowerPoint2007 folder on the CD that accompanies this textbook and then make PowerPoint2007C8 the active folder.*

# $P$roject ①  Import a Word Outline and Copy and Paste Items between Programs

You will create a PowerPoint presentation using a Word document and then copy and paste an Excel chart and a Word table into slides in the presentation.

**QUICK STEPS**

**Import a Word Outline**
1. Open blank presentation.
2. Click New Slide button arrow.
3. Click *Slide from Outline.*
4. Double-click desired document.

## Importing a Word Outline

You can import a Word document containing text formatted with heading styles into a PowerPoint presentation. Text formatted with a Heading 1 style becomes the title of a new slide. Text formatted with a Heading 2 style becomes first level text, paragraphs formatted with a Heading 3 style become second level text, and so on. To import a Word outline, open a blank presentation, click the New Slide button arrow in the Slides group in the Home tab, and then click *Slides from Outline* at the drop-down list. At the Insert Outline dialog box, navigate to the folder containing the Word document and then double-click the document. If text in the Word document does not have heading styles applied, PowerPoint creates an outline based on each paragraph of text in the document.

You can import an outline document from a Word 97-2003 document (.doc), a Word 2007 document (.docx), or a rich text format document (.rtf) into a PowerPoint presentation.

## $P$roject ①a    Importing a Word Outline

1. At a blank presentation, click the New Slide button arrow and then click *Slides from Outline* at the drop-down list.
2. At the Insert Outline dialog box, navigate to the PowerPoint2007C8 folder on your storage medium and then double-click *WordOutline01.docx*.
3. Apply the *Solstice* design theme, apply the *Metro* colors theme, and apply the *Foundry* fonts theme.
4. Delete Slide 1.
5. Format the current Slide 1 by completing the following steps:
   a. Change the slide layout by clicking the Layout button in the Slides group in the Home tab and then clicking the *Title Only* layout at the drop-down list.
   b. Click the text *Adventure Tours* to select the placeholder and then drag the placeholder down toward the bottom of the slide and center the text horizontally (click the Center button in the Paragraph group in the Home tab).

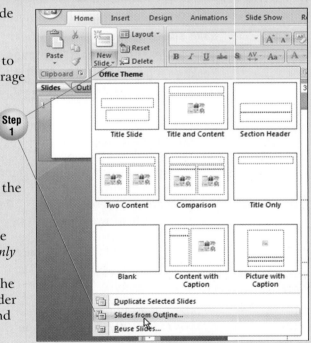

c. Insert the **FCTLogo.jpg** (do this with the Picture button in the Insert tab) and then increase the size of the logo so it fills a good portion of the upper part of the slide.

d. Recolor the logo (picture) to Accent color 4 Light. ***Hint: Do this with the Recolor button in the Adjust group in the Picture Tools Format tab.***

6. Make Slide 2 active and then change the layout to *Title Only*.

7. Make Slide 3 active, change the line spacing to 2.0 for the bulleted text, and then insert a clip art image of your choosing related to *travel* or *spring*.

8. Make Slide 4 active and then change the line spacing to 1.5 for the bulleted text.

9. Save the presentation and name it **PP_C8_P1**.

# Exporting a Presentation to Word

You can export a PowerPoint presentation to a Word document and you can edit and format the presentation in Word. You can print slides as handouts in PowerPoint; however, you may prefer to export the presentation to Word to have greater control over the formatting of the handouts. To export the presentation that is currently open, click the Office button, point to *Publish*, and then click *Create Handouts in Microsoft Office Word*. At the Send To Microsoft Office Word dialog box shown in Figure 8.1, select the page layout you want to use in Word and then click OK.

The first four page layout options will export slides as they appear in PowerPoint with lines to the right or below the slides. The last option will export the text only as an outline. If you select the *Paste link* option, the Word document will be automatically updated whenever changes are made to the PowerPoint presentation.

**Export a Presentation to Word**
1. Click Office button.
2. Point to *Publish*.
3. Click *Create Handouts in Microsoft Office Word*.
4. Select page layout.
5. Click OK.

**Figure 8.1** Send To Microsoft Office Word Dialog Box

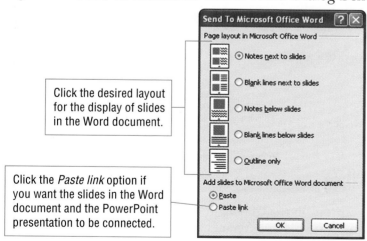

Click the desired layout for the display of slides in the Word document.

Click the *Paste link* option if you want the slides in the Word document and the PowerPoint presentation to be connected.

1. With **PP_C8_P1.pptx** open, click the Office button, point to *Publish*, and then click *Create Handouts in Microsoft Office Word*.

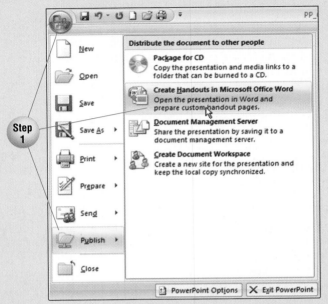

2. At the Send To Microsoft Office Word dialog box, click the *Blank lines next to slides* option and then click OK.
3. When all of the slides are inserted in the Word document, select the first column (the presentation was inserted in a table in Word) and then turn on bold.
4. Select the third column (contains the lines) and then change the font color to Red.
5. Save the document and name it **PP_C8_P1_Word**.
6. Print and then close **PP_C8_P1_Word.docx**.
7. Exit Word.

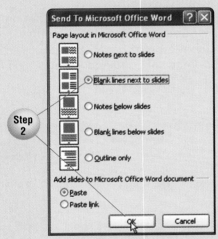

# Copying and Pasting Data

Use the Copy and Paste buttons in the Clipboard group in the Home tab to copy data such as text or an object from one program and then paste it into another program. For example, in Project 1c, you will copy an Excel chart and then paste it into a PowerPoint slide. You can move and size a copied object, such as a chart, like any other object.

# Project 1C  Copying an Excel Chart to a Slide

1. With **PP_C8_P1.pptx** open, make Slide 2 active.
2. Open Excel and then open the workbook named **Top5Tours.xlsx** located in the PowerPoint2007C8 folder on your storage medium.
3. Click the chart to select it. (Make sure you select the chart and not an element in the chart.)
4. Click the Copy button in the Clipboard group in the Home tab.

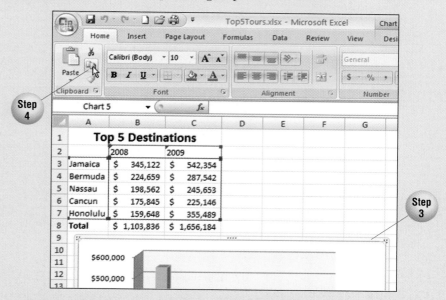

5. Close the **Top5Tours.xlsx** workbook and exit Excel.
6. In PowerPoint, with Slide 2 active, click the Paste button in the Clipboard group in the Home tab.
7. Resize and move the chart so it fills a good portion of the slide below the title and to the right of the slide design background.
8. Modify the chart by completing the following steps:
   a. Make sure the chart is selected and then click the Chart Tools Design tab.
   b. Click the More button at the right side of the chart styles thumbnails and then click *Style 38* at the drop-down gallery (sixth option from the left in the fifth row).
   c. Click the Chart Tools Format tab.
   d. Click the Shape Outline button arrow in the Shape Styles group and then click *No Outline* at the drop-down gallery.

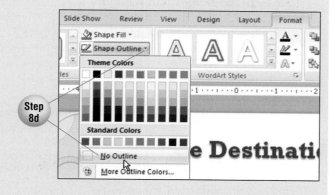

9. Display Slide 1 in the Slide pane and then run the presentation.
10. Print only Slide 2.
11. Save **PP_C8_P1.pptx**.

# Using the Clipboard Task Pane

Use the Clipboard task pane to collect and paste multiple items. You can collect up to 24 different items and then paste them in various locations. Turn on the display of the Clipboard task pane by clicking the Clipboard group dialog box launcher. The Clipboard task pane displays at the left side of the screen as shown in Figure 8.2.

**Figure 8.2** Clipboard Task Pane

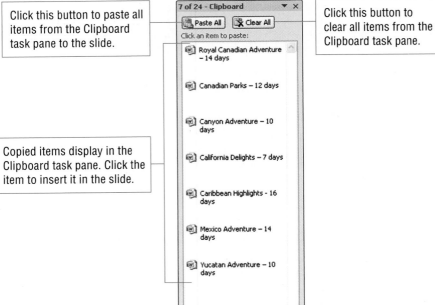

Click this button to paste all items from the Clipboard task pane to the slide.

Click this button to clear all items from the Clipboard task pane.

Copied items display in the Clipboard task pane. Click the item to insert it in the slide.

Select data or an object you want to copy and then click the Copy button in the Clipboard group. Continue selecting text or items and clicking the Copy button. To insert an item, position the insertion point in the desired location and then click the button in the Clipboard task pane representing the item. If the copied item is text, the first 50 characters display. When all desired items are inserted, click the Clear All button to remove any remaining items from the Clipboard task pane. If you want to paste all items from the Clipboard task pane at once, click the Paste All button.

**Project** **1d** **Collecting and Pasting Text between a Document and a Presentation**

1. With **PP_C8_P1.pptx** open, make Slide 4 active and then insert a new slide with the *Title and Content* layout.
2. Click the text *Click to add title* and then type Spring Treks. Select *Spring Treks* and then turn on bold.
3. Copy text from Word by completing the following steps:
   a. Open Word and then open **AdventureTreks.docx**.
   b. Click the Clipboard group dialog box launcher to display the Clipboard task pane.
   c. If any data displays in the Clipboard task pane, click the Clear All button located toward the top of the task pane.
   d. Select the text *Yucatan Adventure – 10 days* (including the paragraph mark following the text—consider turning on the display of nonprinting characters) and then click the Copy button in the Clipboard group.

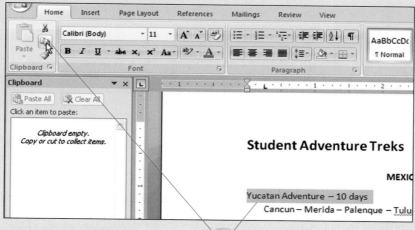

Step 3d

   e. Select the text *Mexico Adventure – 14 days* and then click the Copy button.
   f. Select the text *Caribbean Highlights – 16 days* and then click the Copy button.
   g. Select the text *California Delights – 7 days* and then click the Copy button.
   h. Select the text *Canyon Adventure – 10 days* and then click the Copy button.
   i. Select the text *Canadian Parks – 12 days* and then click the Copy button.
   j. Select the text *Royal Canadian Adventure – 14 days* and then click the Copy button.
4. Click the button on the Taskbar representing **PP_C8_P1.pptx** and then paste items from the Clipboard task pane by completing the following steps:
   a. With Slide 5 active, click the text *Click to add text*.
   b. Click the Clipboard group dialog box launcher to display the Clipboard task pane.
   c. Click the *California Delights* item in the Clipboard task pane.
   d. Click the *Canadian Parks* item in the Clipboard task pane.
   e. Click the *Caribbean Highlights* item in the Clipboard task pane.
   f. Click the *Mexico Adventure* item in the Clipboard task pane.

Step 4c

g. Click the *Yucatan Adventure* item in the Clipboard task pane. (Press the Backspace key twice to remove the bullet below *Yucatan Adventure* and the blank line.)

5. Select the bulleted text, change the line spacing to 1.5, change the font color to Periwinkle, Accent 5, Darker 25%, and turn on bold.

6. Clear the Clipboard task pane by clicking the Clear All button located in the upper right corner of the task pane.

Step 6

7. Close the Clipboard task pane by clicking the Close button (contains an *X*) located in the upper right corner of the task pane.

8. Make Slide 1 the active slide and then run the presentation.

9. Print the presentation as a handout with all slides on one page.

10. Save and then close **PP_C8_P1.pptx**.

11. Make Word the active program, close **AdventureTreks.docx**, and then exit Word.

---

# Project 2 — Embed and Link Excel Charts to a Presentation

You will open a company funds presentation and then copy an Excel pie chart and embed it in a PowerPoint slide. You will also copy and link an Excel column chart to a slide and then update the chart in Excel.

## Linking and Embedding Objects

One of the reasons the Microsoft Office suite is used extensively in business is because it allows data from an individual program to seamlessly integrate into another program. For example, a chart depicting the sales projections created in Excel can easily be added to a slide in a presentation to the company board of directors on the new budget forecast.

Integration is the process of completing a file by adding parts to it from other sources. Duplicating data that already exist in another program should be a rare instance. Copy and paste objects from one application to another when the content is not likely to change. If the content is dynamic, the copy and paste method becomes problematic and prone to error. To illustrate this point, assume one of the outcomes from the presentation to the board of directors is a revision to the sales projections. The chart that was originally created in Excel has to be updated to reflect the new projections. The existing chart in PowerPoint needs to be deleted and then the revised chart in Excel copied and pasted to the slide. Both Excel and PowerPoint need to be opened and edited to reflect this change in projection. In this case, copying and pasting the chart was not efficient.

To eliminate the inefficiency of the copy and paste method, you can integrate data between programs using **object linking and embedding**. Object linking and embedding (OLE) is the sharing of data from one program to another. An object can be text in a presentation, data in a table, a chart, a picture, a slide, or any combination of data that you would like to share between programs. The program that was used to create the object is called the **source** and the program the object is linked or embedded to is called the **destination**.

Embedding and linking are two methods you can use to integrate data in addition to the copy and paste method. When an object is embedded, the content in the object is stored in both the source and the destination programs. When you edit an embedded object in the destination program, the source program in which the program was created opens. If the content in the object is changed in the source program, the change is not reflected in the destination program and vice versa. Linking inserts a code into the destination file connecting the destination to the name and location of the source object. The object itself is not stored within the destination file. If a change is made to the content in the source program, the destination program reflects the change automatically.

Your decision to integrate data by embedding or linking will depend on whether the data is dynamic or static. If the data is dynamic, then linking the object is the most efficient method of integration. You can embed or copy and paste static data from the source to the destination program.

## Embedding Objects

An object that is embedded will be stored in both the source *and* the destination programs. The content of the object can be edited in *either* the source or the destination; however, a change made in one will not be reflected in the other. The difference between copying and pasting and embedding is that embedded objects can be edited with the source program's editing tabs and options.

Since embedded objects are edited within the source program, the source program must reside on the computer when the presentation is opened for editing. If you are preparing a presentation that will be edited on another computer, you may want to check before embedding any objects to verify that the other computer has the same programs.

To embed an object, open both programs and both files. In the source program, click the desired object and then click the Copy button in the Clipboard group in the Home tab. Click the button on the Taskbar representing the destination program file and then position the insertion point at the location where you want the object embedded. Click the Paste button arrow in the Clipboard group and then click *Paste Special* at the drop-down list. At the Paste Special dialog box, click the source of the object in the *As* list box and then click OK.

You can edit an embedded object by double-clicking the object. This displays the object with the source program tabs and options. Make any desired changes and then click outside the object to exit the source program tabs and options. You can apply animation effects to an embedded object with the same techniques you learned in Chapter 7.

### QUICK STEPS

**Embed an Object**
1. Open source program.
2. Select desired object.
3. Click Copy button.
4. Open destination program.
5. Click Paste button arrow.
6. Click *Paste Special*.
7. Click source of object.
8. Click OK.

## Project 2a | Embedding an Excel Chart in a Presentation

1. Open **FundsPresentation.pptx** and then save the presentation with the name **PP_C8_P2**.
2. Open Excel and then open the workbook named **Funds01.xlsx** located in the PowerPoint2007C8 folder on your storage medium.
3. Click the chart to select it. (Make sure the chart is selected and not an element in the chart.)
4. Click the Copy button in the Clipboard group in the Home tab.
5. Click the button on the Taskbar representing **PP_C8_P2.pptx**.

6. Make Slide 4 active.
7. Click the Paste button arrow and then click *Paste Special* at the drop-down list.
8. At the Paste Special dialog box, make sure *Microsoft Office Graphic Object* is selected in the *As* list box and then click OK.

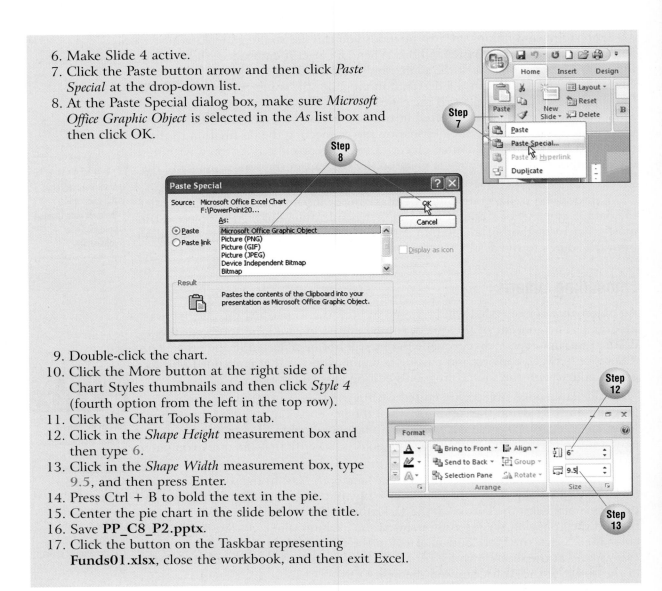

9. Double-click the chart.
10. Click the More button at the right side of the Chart Styles thumbnails and then click *Style 4* (fourth option from the left in the top row).
11. Click the Chart Tools Format tab.
12. Click in the *Shape Height* measurement box and then type 6.
13. Click in the *Shape Width* measurement box, type 9.5, and then press Enter.
14. Press Ctrl + B to bold the text in the pie.
15. Center the pie chart in the slide below the title.
16. Save **PP_C8_P2.pptx**.
17. Click the button on the Taskbar representing **Funds01.xlsx**, close the workbook, and then exit Excel.

## Linking Objects

**QUICK STEPS**

**Link an Object**
1. Open source program.
2. Select desired object.
3. Click Copy button.
4. Open destination program.
5. Click Paste button arrow.
6. Click *Paste Special*.
7. Click *Paste link* option.
8. Click OK.

If the content of the object that you will integrate between programs is likely to change, then link the object from the source program to the destination program. Linking the object establishes a direct connection between the source and destination program. The object is stored in the source program only. The destination program will have a code inserted into it that indicates the name and location of the source of the object. Whenever the presentation containing the link is opened, a message displays saying that the presentation contains links and the user is prompted to update the links. This process of updating links is referred to as *Dynamic Data Exchange* (DDE).

To link an object, open both programs and open both program files. In the source program file, click the desired object and then click the Copy button in the Clipboard group in the Home tab. Click the button on the Taskbar representing the destination program file and then position the insertion point in the desired location. Click the Paste button arrow in the Clipboard group in the Home tab and then click *Paste Special* at the drop-down list. At the Paste Special dialog box, click the source program for the object in the *As* list box, click the *Paste link* option located at the left side of the *As* list box, and then click OK.

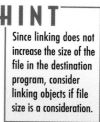

**HINT**

Since linking does not increase the size of the file in the destination program, consider linking objects if file size is a consideration.

## Project 2b  Linking an Excel Chart to a Presentation

1. With **PP_C8_P2.pptx** open, open Excel and then open **Funds02.xlsx** located in the PowerPoint2007C8 folder on your storage medium.
2. Save the workbook with Save As and name it **MoneyMarketFunds**.
3. Copy and link the chart to a slide in the presentation by completing the following steps:
   a. Click the chart to select it.
   b. Click the Copy button in the Clipboard group in the Home tab.
   c. Click the button on the Taskbar representing **PP_C8_P2.pptx**.
   d. Make Slide 5 active.
   e. Click the Paste button arrow and then click *Paste Special* at the drop-down list.
   f. At the Paste Special dialog box, click the *Paste link* option.
   g. Make sure *Microsoft Office Excel Chart Object* is selected in the *As* list box.
   h. Click OK.

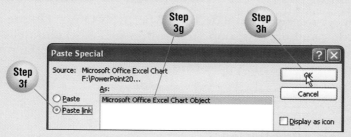

   i. Increase the size of the chart in the slide so it fills a good portion of the slide below the title. Move the chart so it appears balanced below the title.
4. Click the button on the Taskbar representing **MoneyMarketFunds.xlsx**.
5. Close **MoneyMarketFunds.xlsx** and exit Excel.
6. Make Slide 1 active and then run the presentation.
7. Print Slide 5.
8. Save and then close **PP_C8_P2.pptx**.

## Editing Linked Objects

Edit linked objects in the source program in which they were created. Open the document, workbook, or presentation containing the object, make the changes as required, and then save and close the file. If both the source and destination programs are open at the same time, the changed content is reflected immediately in both programs.

## Project 2c  Editing Linked Data

1. Open Excel and then open **MoneyMarketFunds.xlsx**.
2. Make the following changes to data in the following cells:
   a. Change B2 from *13%* to *17%*.
   b. Change B3 from *9%* to *12%*.
   c. Change B6 from *10%* to *14%*.
3. Click the Save button on the Quick Access toolbar to save the edited workbook.
4. Close **MoneyMarketFunds.xlsx** and then exit Excel.
5. In PowerPoint, open **PP_C8_P2.pptx**.
6. At the message telling you that the presentation contains links, click the Update Links button.
7. Print the presentation as a handout with all of the slides on one page.
8. Save and then close **PP_C8_P2.pptx**.

|   | A | B | C |
|---|---|---|---|
| 1 |   | Percentage |   |
| 2 | 2005 | 17% |   |
| 3 | 2006 | 12% |   |
| 4 | 2007 | 18% |   |
| 5 | 2008 | 4% |   |
| 6 | 2009 | 14% |   |

Step 2a
Step 2b
Step 2c

## Project 3  Download and Apply a Design Template to a Presentation and Prepare the Presentation for Distribution

You will download a design template from Microsoft Office Online and apply the template to a company presentation. You will insert, edit, and delete comments in the presentation; modify the presentation properties; inspect the presentation; and encrypt the presentation with a password.

**QUICK STEPS**

**Download a Design**
1. Click Office button.
2. Click *New*.
3. Click *Design slides* option.
4. Click desired category.
5. Click desired design.
6. Click Download button.

**HINT**
Microsoft checks the validity of your Microsoft Office software each time you download a template.

## Downloading Designs

PowerPoint 2007 provides a number of design templates you can apply to a presentation. The Microsoft Office Online site contains additional design templates you can download and apply to a presentation. To view the available design templates for downloading, click the Office button and then click *New* at the drop-down list. At the New Presentation dialog box, click the *Design slides* option in the *Microsoft Office Online* section in the left panel. This displays categories of design templates in the middle panel. Click a category and design templates in the category display in the middle panel with information about the design in the right panel.

Some design thumbnails in the middle panel may contain a small logo of shoulders and a head indicating that the design template was created by a member of the Microsoft Office Online Community and Microsoft cannot guarantee that the design will work or that the design template is free from viruses or defects.

To download a design template, click the desired template in the middle panel and then click the Download button located in the lower right corner of the dialog box. At the message that displays telling you that templates are only available to customers running genuine Microsoft Office, click the Continue button. When the download is complete, the design template is applied to the open presentation and is also available in the Themes group in the Design tab.

*Note: Check with your instructor before downloading a design template. To download a template you must have access to the Internet and access to the hard drive. If the* Target the market design template *is already downloaded, skip steps 1 through 10 below. If you do not have access to the design template or cannot download, open ISPresentation.pptx, save it with the name PP_C8_P3, apply a design theme of your choosing, and then continue with step 11.*

1. At a blank presentation, click the Office button and then click *New* at the drop-down list.
2. At the New Presentation dialog box, click the *Design slides* option in the *Microsoft Office Online* section in the left panel.
3. Click the *Business* option in the *Design slides* section in the middle panel.
4. Scroll down the list of design templates and then click the *Target the market design template* (shown at the right).
5. Click the Download button that displays in the lower right corner of the dialog box.
6. At the message telling you that the templates are only available to customers running genuine Microsoft Office, click the Continue button. (This applies the design template to the current presentation.)
7. Close the presentation without saving it.
8. Open **ISPresentation.pptx** and then save the presentation with the name **PP_C8_P3**.

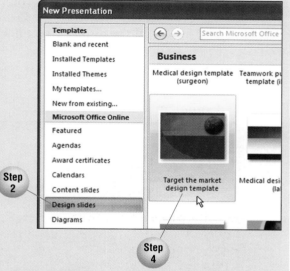

Step 2

Step 4

9. Apply the new design template by clicking the Design tab, clicking the More button at the right side of the theme thumbnails, and then clicking the *Target the market design template* theme that displays in the *Custom* section of the drop-down gallery.
10. Click the Colors button in the Themes group and then click *Office Theme 5* at the drop-down gallery.
11. Make each slide active and then make any formatting changes to elements so they appear attractively in the slide.
12. Save **PP_C8_P3.pptx**.

# Inserting Comments

If you are sending out a presentation for review and want to ask reviewers specific questions or provide information about slides in a presentation, insert a comment. To insert a comment, display the desired slide and then position the insertion point where you want the comment to appear. Click the Review tab and then click the New Comment button in the Comments group. At the comment box that displays, similar to the one shown in Figure 8.3, type the desired comment. After typing the desired comment, click outside the comment box and a small yellow box displays with the user's initials and a comment number. Comments by individual users are numbered sequentially beginning with 1.

**Insert a Comment**
1. Click Review tab.
2. Click New Comment button.
3. Type comment text.

New Comment

**HINT**

Move a comment by selecting the comment box and then dragging it to the desired location.

Show Markup

Next     Previous

To print comments, display the Print dialog box, choose how you want slides printed with the *Print what* option, and then make sure the *Print comments and ink markup* check box contains a check mark. Comments print on a separate page after the presentation is printed.

By default, the Show Markup button is active (displays with an orange background) in the Comments group in the Review tab. With this button active, comment boxes display in slides. If you want to hide comment boxes, click the Show Markup button to deactivate it. You can use the Next button and the Previous button in the Comments group in the Review tab to display comments in a presentation. Click the Next button to display the next comment in the presentation or click the Previous button to display the previous comment. If you turn off the display of comment boxes, you can use the Next and Previous buttons to display comments.

**Figure 8.3** Comment Box

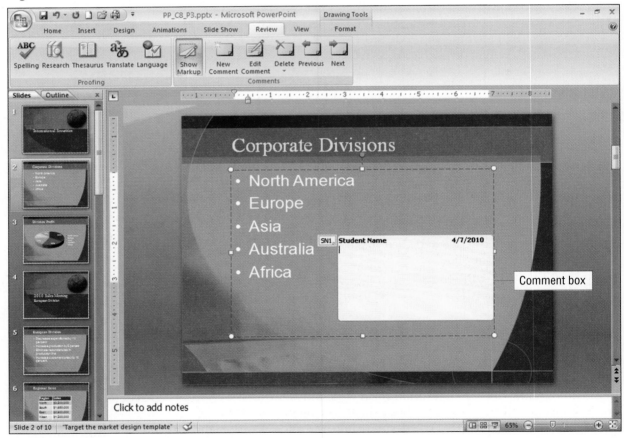

# Project 3b  Inserting Comments

1. With **PP_C8_P3.pptx** open, make Slide 2 active and then insert a comment by completing the following steps:
   a. Position the insertion point immediately right of the word *Australia*.
   b. Click the Review tab.
   c. Click the New Comment button in the Comments group.
   d. Type the following in the comment box: Include information on New Zealand branch.

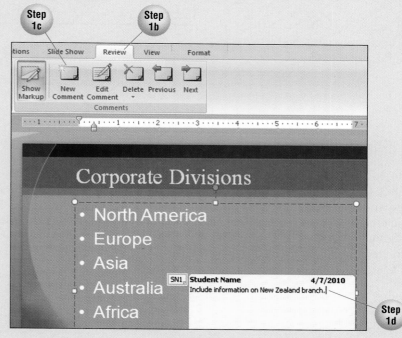

2. Make Slide 3 active and then insert a comment by completing the following steps:
   a. Click in the chart to select it. (Make sure you select the chart and not a chart element.)
   b. Click the New Comment button in the Comments group.
   c. Type the following in the comment box: Include a chart showing profit amounts.
3. Make Slide 5 active, position the insertion point immediately right of the word *line* at the end of the third bulleted item, and then insert the comment Provide detailed information on how this goal will be accomplished.
4. Make Slide 8 active, position the insertion point immediately right of the word *Singapore* in the second bulleted item, and then insert the comment Who will be managing the Singapore office?
5. Click the Previous button in the Comments group to display the comment box in Slide 5.
6. Click the Previous button to display the comment box in Slide 3.
7. Click the Show Markup button in the Comments group in the Review tab to turn off the display of comment boxes.

8. Click Slide 5 and notice that the comment box is not visible.
9. Click the Next button to display the comment box in Slide 2.
10. Click the Show Markup button to turn on the display of comment boxes.

11. Print the presentation and the comments by completing the following steps:
    a. Click the Office button and then click *Print*.
    b. At the Print dialog box, change the *Print what* to *Handouts* with six slides per page.
    c. Make sure the *Print comments and ink markup* check box contains a check mark.
    d. Click OK.
12. Make Slide 1 active and then run the presentation beginning with Slide 1.
13. Save **PP_C8_P3.pptx**.

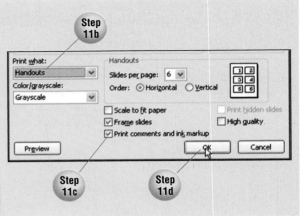

Step 11b

Step 11c

Step 11d

## Editing and Deleting Comments

Edit Comment

Delete

To edit text in a comment box, click the comment box you want to edit and then click the Edit Comment button in the Comments group in the Review tab. This expands the comment box and positions the insertion point inside the box. To delete a comment from a slide, click the small box containing the user's initials and comment number and then click the Delete button in the Comments group in the Review tab. You can also right-click the box containing the initials and then click Delete at the shortcut menu.

## Project 3c   Editing and Deleting Comments

1. With **PP_C8_P3.pptx** open, make Slide 8 active and then edit the comment by completing the following steps:
   a. Click the comment box containing the user's initials and comment number.
   b. Make sure the Review tab is active and then click the Edit Comment button in the Comments group.
   c. Select and delete the text in the comment box and then type Check with Sandy Cates to determine who will be appointed branch manager.
2. Delete the comment in Slide 3 by completing the following steps:
   a. Click twice on the Previous button to display Slide 3 and the comment in the slide.
   b. Click the Delete button in the Comments group in the Review tab.
3. Print the presentation as a handout with six slides per page and make sure the comments print.
4. Save **PP_C8_P3.pptx**.

Step 2b

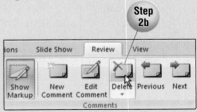

# Preparing a Presentation for Distribution

If you work with other employees or colleagues, you may want to share and distribute your presentations. You can prepare your presentation for distribution with options at the Office button Prepare side menu, which you can display by clicking the Office button and then pointing to *Prepare*.

## Modifying Presentation Properties

Each presentation you create has properties information attached to the presentation such as the type and location of the presentation and when the presentation was created, modified, and accessed. Along with this information, you can add additional properties information such as a presentation title, subject, category, and keywords. Add additional properties information at the document information panel similar to the one shown in Figure 8.4. Display this panel by clicking the Office button, pointing to *Prepare*, and then clicking the *Properties* option at the side menu. You can type specific information in each of the text boxes in the properties panel to describe the presentation and to help you search for the presentation at a later date. To move the insertion point to the next text box, press the Tab key. To move the insertion point to the previous text box, press Shift + Tab.

**Figure 8.4** Document Information Panel

Type information about the presentation in the text boxes in the document information panel.

| Document Properties ▼ | | | Location: F:\PowerPoint2007C8\PP_C8_P3.pptx | | | * Required field ✕ |
|---|---|---|---|---|---|---|
| Author: | Title: | Subject: | Keywords: | Category: | Status: | |
| Comments: | | | | | | |

Along with the document information panel, you can also insert specific information about the presentation with options at the Properties dialog box. To display this dialog box, click the Document Properties button that displays in the upper left corner of the document information panel and then click *Advanced Properties*. At the Properties dialog box, click a specific tab and then insert the desired information or read the information that displays.

# Project 3d  Inserting Document Properties

1. With **PP_C8_P3.pptx** open, display the document information panel by clicking the Office button, pointing to *Prepare*, and then clicking *Properties* at the side menu.
2. Select the name that appears in the *Author* text box (unless it is your name) and then type your first and last names.
3. Press the Tab key twice (this makes the *Subject* text box active) and then type International Securities Corporate Meeting.
4. Press the Tab key and then type the following words in the *Keywords* text box: International Securities, sales, divisions.
5. Press the Tab key and then type sales meeting in the *Category* text box.
6. Press the Tab key twice and then type the following in the *Comments* text box: This is a presentation prepared for the corporate meeting.

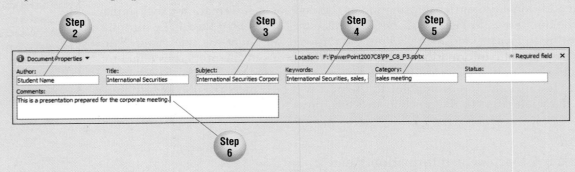

7. Close the document information panel by clicking the Close button located in the upper right corner of the panel.
8. Save **PP_C8_P3.docx**.

## Inspecting a Presentation

**HINT**

Inspect your document for personal and hidden data before distributing it to others.

PowerPoint includes a document inspection feature you can use to inspect your presentation for personal data, hidden data, and metadata. Metadata is data that describes other data such as presentation properties information. You may want to remove some personal or hidden data before you share your presentation with other people. Check your presentation for personal or hidden data by clicking the Office button, pointing to *Prepare*, and then clicking *Inspect Document* at the side menu. This displays the Document Inspector dialog box shown in Figure 8.5.

**Figure 8.5** Document Inspector Dialog Box

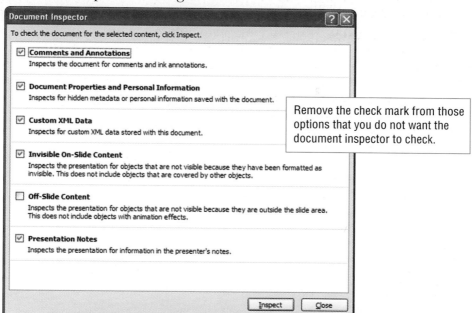

Remove the check mark from those options that you do not want the document inspector to check.

By default, the document inspector will check all of the items listed in the dialog box. If you do not want the inspector to check a specific item in your presentation, remove the check mark. For example, if you know your presentation contains comments and/or annotations, click the *Comments and Annotations* check box to remove the check mark. Click the Inspect button located toward the bottom of the dialog box and the document inspector scans the presentation identifying information.

When the inspection is complete, the results display in the dialog box. A check mark before an option indicates that the inspector did not find the specific items. If an exclamation point is inserted before an option, the inspector found items and displays a list of the items. If you want to remove the found items, click the Remove All button that displays at the right side of the desired option. Click the Close button to close the Document Inspector dialog box.

**Inspect a Presentation**
1. Click Office button, *Prepare, Inspect Document.*
2. Remove check marks from items you do not want checked.
3. Click Inspect button.

# Project 3e Inspecting a Presentation

1. With **PP_C8_P3.pptx** open, click the Office button, point to *Prepare*, and then click *Inspect Document*.
2. At the Document Inspector dialog box, you decide you do not want to check the presentation for XML data, so click the *Custom XML Data* check box to remove the check mark.

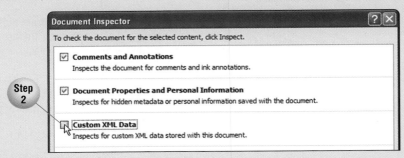

3. Click the Inspect button.
4. Read through the inspection results and then remove all comments by clicking the Remove All button that displays at the right side of the *Comments and Annotations* section.

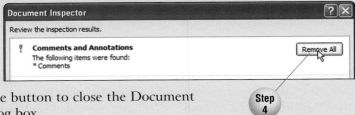

5. Click the Close button to close the Document Inspector dialog box.
6. Save **PP_C8_P3.pptx**.

**QUICK STEPS**

**Encrypt a Presentation**
1. Click Office button, *Prepare, Encrypt Document.*
2. Type a password.
3. Press Enter.
4. Type same password again.
5. Click OK.

## Encrypting a Presentation

You can insert a password in a presentation to ensure that the presentation is opened only by someone who knows the password. You can protect a presentation with a password with the *Encrypt Document* option at the Office button Prepare side menu. Click the *Encrypt Document* option at the Prepare side menu and the Encrypt Document dialog box displays as shown in Figure 8.6. In the dialog box, type a password and then press the Enter key. At the Confirm Password dialog box, type the password again and then click OK.

You can also insert a password in a presentation by displaying the Save As dialog box, clicking the Tools button located in the lower left corner of the dialog box, and then clicking *General Options*. At the General Options dialog box, type a password in the *Password to open* text box, press the Tab key, type the same password in the *Password to modify* text box, and then click OK.

**HINT**

A strong password contains a mix of uppercase and lowercase letters as well as numbers and symbols.

**Figure 8.6** Encrypt Document Dialog Box

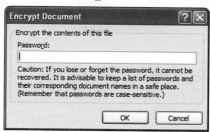

## Project ③ Encrypting a Presentation with a Password

1. With **PP_C8_P3.pptx** open, click the Office button, point to *Prepare*, and then click *Encrypt Document*.
2. At the Encrypt Document dialog box, type your initials in all uppercase letters.
3. Press the Enter key.
4. At the Confirm Password dialog box, type your initials again in uppercase letters and then click OK.
5. Save and then close **PP_C8_P3.pptx**.
6. Open **PP_C8_P3.pptx**. At the Password dialog box, type your initials in uppercase letters and then press Enter.
7. Close **PP_C8_P3.pptx**.

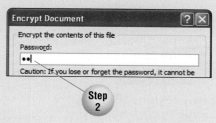

Step 2

## Project ④ Protect and Check Compatibility of an Online Learning Presentation

You will open an online learning presentation, add a digital signature to the presentation, mark it as final, and run a compatibility check on the presentation.

## Adding a Digital Signature to a Presentation

You can apply a digital signature to a presentation to authenticate the presentation and ensure that the content of the presentation has not been changed or tampered with after it was digitally signed. When you apply a digital signature to a presentation, the presentation is locked so that it cannot be edited or changed unless you remove the digital signature. Before applying a digital signature, you must obtain a signature. You can obtain a digital signature from a commercial certification authority or you can create your own digital signature. When you create your digital signature, it is saved on the hard drive or the network. Depending on how your system is set up, you might be prevented from using a certificate.

To add a digital signature, click the Office button, point to *Prepare*, and then click *Add a Digital Signature* at the side menu. At the message displaying information about the digital signature, click OK. At the Signs dialog box, shown in Figure 8.7,

**QUICK STEPS**

**Insert a Digital Signature**
1. Click Office button, Prepare, Add a Digital Signature.
2. Type purpose for signing document.
3. Click Sign.
4. Click OK.

Signatures

type text in the *Purpose for signing this document* text box that identifies the reason for the signature and then click the Sign button. At the message telling you that the signature was successfully saved with the presentation, click OK. This opens the Signatures task pane at the right side of the screen and also inserts a Signatures button toward the left side of the Status bar. Turn on or off the Signatures task pane by clicking the Signatures button on the Status bar.

**Figure 8.7** Sign Dialog Box

Type in this text box the explanation of why a digital signature is attached to the presentation.

**QUICK STEPS**

**Remove a Digital Signature**
1. Click Signatures button at left side of Status bar.
2. Hover mouse pointer over signature in Signatures task pane.
3. Click down-pointing arrow at right of signature.
4. Click *Remove Signature* at drop-down list.

To remove a digital signature from a presentation, click the Signatures button on the Status bar to turn on the display of the Signatures task pane. Move the mouse pointer over the signature in the Signatures task pane list box, click the down-pointing arrow at the right side of the signature, and then click *Remove Signature* at the drop-down list. At the message asking if you are sure you want to remove permanently the digital signature, click Yes. At the message telling you that the signature has been removed, click OK and then close the Signatures task pane.

## Project 4a  Adding and Removing a Digital Signature

*Check with your instructor before completing this project.*

1. Open the presentation named **OnlineLearning.pptx** and then save the presentation and name it **PP_C8_P4**.
2. Click the Office button, point to *Prepare*, and then click *Add a Digital Signature*.
3. At the message displaying information about the digital signature, click OK.
4. At the Sign dialog box, type **Presentation prepared for training seminar by Student Name.** (Type your first and last names in place of *Student Name*.)
5. Click the Sign button.

Step 4

Step 5

6. At the message telling you that the signature was successfully saved, click OK.
7. Close the Signatures task pane by clicking the Close button located in the upper right corner of the task pane.
8. Click each of the tabs in the ribbon and notice that most buttons and options are not active since the digital signature prevents the presentation from being altered.

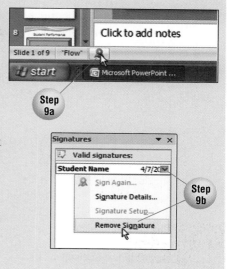

9. Remove the digital signature by completing the following steps:
   a. Click the Signatures button located toward the left side of the Status bar. (This displays the Signatures task pane.)
   b. Hover the mouse pointer over the signature in the Signatures task pane, click the down-pointing arrow at the right side of the signature, and then click *Remove Signature* at the drop-down list.
   c. At the message asking if you are sure you want to remove permanently the digital signature, click Yes.
   d. At the message telling you that the signature has been removed, click OK.
   e. Close the Signatures task pane.
10. Save **PP_C8_P4.pptx**.

## Marking a Presentation as Final

You can save your presentation as a read-only presentation and mark it as final with the *Mark as Final* option at the Office button Prepare side menu. To use this feature, click the Office button, point to *Prepare*, and then click *Mark as Final*. At the message telling you that the presentation will be marked as final and then saved, click the OK button. A message box displays with information telling you that the presentation is marked as final to indicate that editing is complete and that it is the final version of the presentation. The message further indicates that when a presentation is marked as final, the status property is set to "Final" and typing, editing, commands, and proofing marks are turned off. It also tells you that you can identify a presentation marked as final when the *Mark As Final* icon displays toward the left side of the Status bar. At this message, click OK.

**QUICK STEPS**

**Mark a Presentation as Final**
1. Click Office button, Prepare, Mark as Final.
2. Click OK.
3. Click OK.

## Running the Compatibility Checker

PowerPoint includes a compatibility checker that will check your presentation and identify elements that are not supported or will act differently in previous versions of PowerPoint. Some features not supported by previous versions of PowerPoint include custom slide layouts; heading and body fonts; and some shapes, pictures, objects, and SmartArt. For example, if you save a presentation containing heading and body fonts and a SmartArt graphic as a PowerPoint 2003 presentation, the heading and body are converted to static formatting and the SmartArt graphic is converted to an uneditable picture.

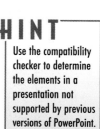

**HINT**
Use the compatibility checker to determine the elements in a presentation not supported by previous versions of PowerPoint.

To determine the compatibility of the features in your presentation, click the Office button, point to *Prepare*, and then click *Run Compatibility Checker*. This displays the Microsoft Office PowerPoint Compatibility Checker dialog box similar to the one shown in Figure 8.8. This dialog box displays a summary of the elements in the presentation that are not compatible with previous versions of PowerPoint and indicates what will occur with the elements when the presentation is saved and then opened in a previous version. By default, PowerPoint will run the compatibility checker when you save a presentation in an earlier version of PowerPoint. If you do not want the compatibility checker to check your presentations, remove the check mark from the *Check compatibility when saving in PowerPoint 97-2003 formats* option at the Microsoft Office PowerPoint Compatibility Checker dialog box.

**Figure 8.8** Microsoft Office PowerPoint Compatibility Checker Dialog Box

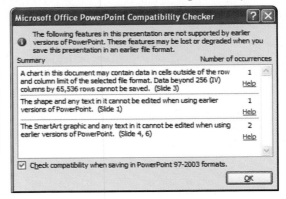

This dialog box displays information on what will happen to text or elements if the presentation is saved in a previous version of PowerPoint.

## Restricting Permissions to a Presentation

In Microsoft Office 2007, Information Rights Management (IRM) is used to restrict permissions to a presentation. Permissions is the term given to the viewing and editing rights that you assign to an individual. You can grant one person the ability to read but not change the presentation and another person the ability to read and edit but not print the presentation. By restricting the presentation you can prevent confidential data from being changed, printed, or copied. You can also add an expiration date on a presentation so that after the specified date, the presentation is no longer available.

To be able to use the Restrict Permission feature, you must have previously installed the Windows Rights Management Software (RMS). The computer that you are using requires the RMS client. You also need the ability to connect to a Windows 2003 or later server running RMS. The server is used to distribute licenses to individuals who want to access a restricted presentation. For example, if you grant permission to a person to edit a presentation, the first time the individual opens the restricted presentation, he or she connects to the server for authentication and downloads a license.

If you have the RMS client software and access to a licensing server, you can restrict permissions to the active presentation by clicking the Office button, pointing to *Prepare*, pointing to *Restrict Permission*, and then clicking *Do Not Distribute*. This opens the Permission dialog box. Click the *Restrict permission to this document* check box and then assign the access rights you want to grant to individual users. Users are identified by e-mail address. The following permission levels are available:

- *Read.* Individual can read the presentation but cannot edit, print, or copy.
- *Change.* Individual can read, edit, and save changes but cannot print.
- *Full Control.* Individual can read, edit, save changes, and print; essentially any task that the author can do is also available to a person granted full control permission.

If you receive a presentation that is restricted, a *Do Not Distribute* message appears in the message bar when the presentation is opened.

## Project 4b — Checking the Compatibility of Elements and Marking a Presentation as Final

1. With **PP_C8_P4.pptx** open, you need to send the presentation to a colleague who is using Microsoft PowerPoint 2003 and decide to check the compatibility of the presentation to determine what will happen to elements not supported by the 2003 version. Run the compatibility checker by completing the following steps:
   a. Click the Office button, point to *Prepare*, and then click *Run Compatibility Checker* at the side menu.
   b. At the Microsoft Office PowerPoint Compatibility Checker dialog box, read the information about the elements not supported by 2003 and what will happen to the elements.
   c. Click OK to close the dialog box.
2. Mark the presentation as final by completing the following steps:
   a. Click the Office button, point to *Prepare*, and then click *Mark as Final*.
   b. At the message telling you that the presentation will be marked as final and then saved, click OK.
   c. At the message that displays, click OK.
   d. Click each of the tabs in the ribbon and notice that most of the buttons and options are dimmed and unavailable.
3. Close **PP_C8_P4.pptx**

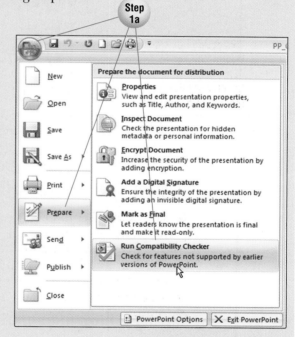

Step 1a

## Project 5 — Save Presentations in Different Formats and Package a Presentation for CD

You will save presentations in a number of formats including PowerPoint Show, a previous version of PowerPoint, PDF format, and save slides as graphic images. You will also save a presentation as a Web page and then package the presentation for a CD.

# Saving Presentations in Different Formats

**HINT**

PowerPoint 2007 does not support saving to PowerPoint 95 or earlier versions.

With the *Save as type* option at the Save As dialog box, you can choose to save a presentation in a variety of formats such as an earlier version of PowerPoint, as a PowerPoint show, as a PDF file, or as a Web page. You can also save a presentation in other formats using the Office button Save As side menu. Click the Office button, point to *Save As*, and a side menu displays as shown in Figure 8.9. The first option in the side menu, *PowerPoint Presentation*, will save a presentation in the default format (*.pptx).

**Figure 8.9** Save As Side Menu

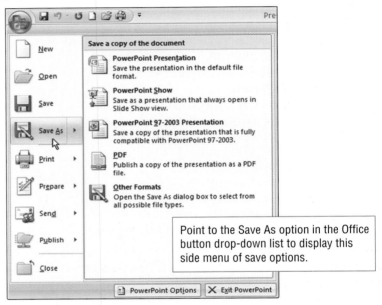

Point to the Save As option in the Office button drop-down list to display this side menu of save options.

## Saving a Presentation as a PowerPoint Show

Choose the *PowerPoint Show* option to save a presentation in the *.ppsx* format, which will open a presentation in Slide Show view without opening PowerPoint. For example, you can save a presentation in PowerPoint Show format, display My Computer in Windows, double-click the presentation, and it automatically opens on the screen in Slide Show view.

## Project 5a — Saving a Presentation as a PowerPoint Show

1. Open **OnlineLearning.pptx** and then save the presentation with the name **PP_C8_P5**.
2. Click the Office button, point to *Save As*, and then click *PowerPoint Show*.
3. At the Save As dialog box, type PP_C8_P5_Show and then press Enter.
4. Close **PP_C8_P5_Show.ppsx**.
5. Display the My Computer window by clicking the Start button and then clicking *My Computer*.
6. In the My Computer window, double-click the drive representing your storage medium.
7. Navigate to the PowerPoint2007C8 folder on your storage medium and then double-click *PP_C8_P5_Show.ppsx*. (This starts the presentation in Slide Show view.)
8. Run the presentation.
9. Close the My Computer window.

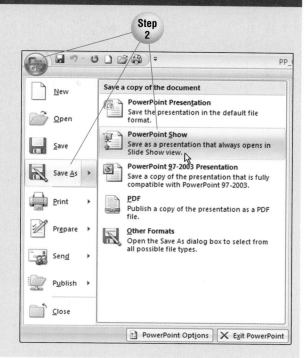

## Saving a Presentation in a Previous Version

If you create presentations that others will open in a previous version of PowerPoint, consider saving the presentation in the PowerPoint 97-2003 format. If you save a presentation in a previous version, the presentation name displays in the title bar followed by the words *[Compatibility Mode]*. In this mode, some PowerPoint 2007 features may not be available.

## Project 5b — Saving a Presentation in a Previous Version

1. Open **PP_C8_P5.pptx**.
2. Click the Office button, point to *Save As*, and then click *PowerPoint 97-2003 Presentation* at the side menu.
3. At the Save As dialog box, type PP_C8_P5_2003format and then press Enter.
4. At the Microsoft Office PowerPoint Compatibility Checker dialog box, click the Continue button.
5. Close **PP_C8_P5_2003format.ppt**.

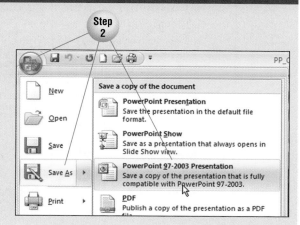

## Saving in PDF Format

The portable document format (PDF) was developed by Adobe Systems® and is a format that captures all of the elements of a file as an electronic image. You can view a PDF file on any application on any computer, making this format the most widely used for transferring files to other users. A presentation saved in PDF format is printer-friendly and most, if not all, of the presentation's original appearance is maintained.

Before saving a PowerPoint presentation in PDF format, you must install an add-in download from the Microsoft Web site. To determine whether or not the download is installed, click the Office button and then point to the *Save As* option. If the add-in is installed, you will see the option *PDF or XPS* in the side menu. If the add-in is not downloaded, you will see the option *Find add-ins for other file formats* in the side menu. To download the add-in, click the *Find add-ins for other file formats* option at the side menu. This displays the PowerPoint Help window with information on how to download the add-in.

When you save a presentation in PDF format, the presentation opens in Adobe Reader, which is an application designed to view your presentation. You will be able to navigate in the presentation but you will not be able to make any changes to it.

## Project 5c    Saving a Presentation in PDF Format

1. Open **PP_C8_P5.pptx**.
2. Click the Office button, point to *Save As*, and then click *PDF or XPS* in the side menu. (If this option does not display, the PDF add-in download has not been installed.)

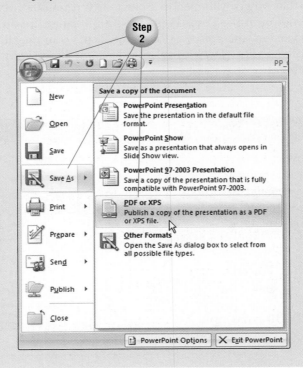

3. At the Save As dialog box with the *Save as type* option set at *PDF (\*.pdf)*, click the Publish button.

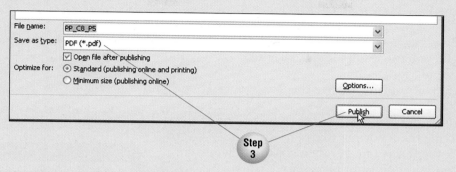

4. Scroll through the presentation in Adobe Reader.
5. Click the Close button located in the upper right corner of the window to close Adobe Reader.

## Saving Slides as Images

You can save a PowerPoint presentation in a variety of formats including saving slides within a presentation as graphic images. Some graphic image formats you can use to save a presentation include GIF (Graphics Interchange Format), JPEG (Joint Photographic Experts Group), and TIF (Tag Image File).

The GIF format is limited to 256 colors and is more effective for scanned images, line drawings, and black and white images rather than color photographs. The JPEG file format supports 16 million colors and is effective for photographs and complex graphics. The TIF file format is best for storing bit-mapped images on personal computers and can be any resolution, black and white, grayscale, and color.

To save a slide or all slides in a presentation in a graphic format, open the presentation, display the Save As dialog box, and then change the *Save as type* option to the desired format. Type a name for the slide or presentation and then press Enter or click Save. At the message that displays, click the Every Slide button if you want every slide in the presentation saved as a graphic image or click the Current Slide Only button if you want only the current slide saved as a graphic image.

If you click the Every Slide button, a message displays telling you that all slides in the presentation were saved as separate files in a folder. The name of the folder is the name that you type in the *File name* text box in the Save As dialog box.

## Project 5d   Saving Slides as Graphic Images

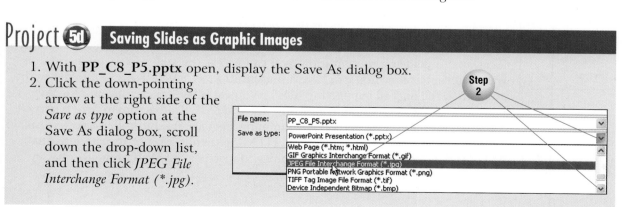

1. With **PP_C8_P5.pptx** open, display the Save As dialog box.
2. Click the down-pointing arrow at the right side of the *Save as type* option at the Save As dialog box, scroll down the drop-down list, and then click *JPEG File Interchange Format (\*.jpg)*.

3. Select the current name in the *File name* text box and then type OnlinePresentationSlides.
4. Click the Save button.
5. At the message that displays, click the Every Slide button.
6. At the message telling you that each slide has been saved as a separate file in the OnlinePresentationSlides folder, click OK.
7. Open Word.
8. At a blank document, change the font size to 18, turn on bold, change the alignment to center, and then type Online Learning – It just makes sense!
9. Press the Enter key twice and then insert one of the slides saved in JPEG format by completing the following steps:
   a. Click the Insert tab and then click the Picture button in the Illustrations group.
   b. At the Insert Picture dialog box, navigate to the OnlinePresentationSlides folder in the PowerPoint2007C8 folder on your storage medium and then double-click *Slide3.JPG*.

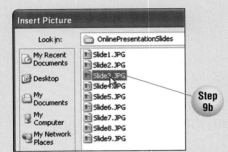

Step 9b

10. Format the image in the document by completing the following steps:
   a. Click in the *Shape Height* measurement box in the Size group in the Picture Tools Format tab, type 2.8, and then press Enter.
   b. Click the *Drop Shadow Rectangle* option in the Picture Styles group.
11. Press Ctrl + End to move the insertion point to the end of the document, press the Enter key, and then complete steps similar to those in Steps 9 and 10 to insert the image *Slide4.JPG* in the document.

Step 10b

12. Save the document and name it **PP_C8_P5_Word**.
13. Print and then close **PP_C8_P5_Word.docx**.
14. Exit Word.

**HINT**

Publish your presentation to the Web to make it available to colleagues for viewing.

## Saving a Presentation as a Web Page

The Internet is fast becoming a preferred choice as a presentation medium. Once a presentation has been published to the Internet, anyone around the world with Internet access can view your presentation. If you are traveling to several remote locations to deliver a presentation, you can access the slides from any computer with Internet access. You can save a presentation as a Web page as a folder with an HTML file and all supporting files or you can save a presentation as a Web page as a single file with all supporting files. *HTML* is an acronym for Hypertext Markup Language, which is the programming language used to code pages to display graphically on the World Wide Web. HTML is a collection of instructions that includes *tags* applied to text and graphics to instruct the Web browser software how to properly display the page.

Fortunately, PowerPoint will translate the slides into Web pages for you so you can publish presentations to the Internet without having to learn HTML programming. To do this, open the presentation you want to save as a Web page, display the Save As dialog box, change the *Save as type* option to *Single File Web Page (\*.mht; \*.mhtml)*, and the Save As dialog box displays as shown in Figure 8.10.

**Figure 8.10** Save As Dialog Box

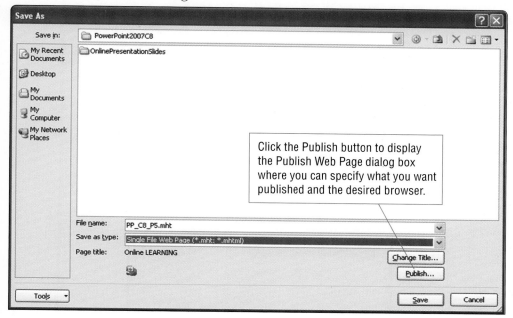

Click the Publish button to display the Publish Web Page dialog box where you can specify what you want published and the desired browser.

At the Save As dialog box, click the Publish button and the Publish as Web Page dialog box displays as shown in Figure 8.11. If you do not want to convert all of the slides in the presentation, specify the starting slide number in the *Slide number* text box and the ending slide number in the *through* text box in the *Publish what?* section. You can convert to specific versions of Web browser software with the options in the *Browser support* section. Click the Web Options button to display the Web Options dialog box displayed in Figure 8.12.

**Figure 8.11** Publish as Web Page Dialog Box

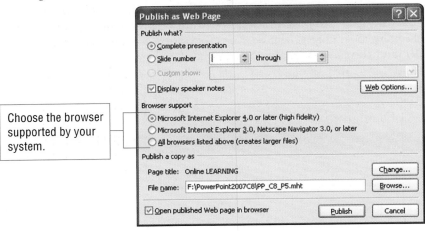

Choose the browser supported by your system.

**Figure 8.12** Web Options Dialog Box

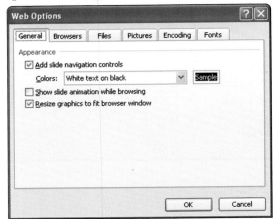

When PowerPoint converts the presentation to HTML format, navigation buttons are created for users to navigate through the slides in the Web browser. The default colors for the navigation buttons are *White text on black*. You can select different color schemes with the *Colors* option at the Web Options dialog box with the General tab selected. If the target browser is Microsoft Internet Explorer version 4.0 or later, you can select *Show slide animation while browsing*.

Click the Files tab at the Web Options dialog box and options display for determining how the Web page files will be organized. By default, PowerPoint creates a folder in the conversion process and stores all of the files in the folder. The screen size can be set at the dialog box with the Pictures tab selected. Click the down-pointing arrow to the right of the *Screen size* text box and then click a screen resolution from the drop-down list. Use options at the Web Options dialog box with the Encoding tab selected to specify a different language code for saving the Web page.

When a presentation is converted to HTML with *All browsers listed above* as the Browser support option at the Publish as Web Page dialog box, additional files are created from the original presentation as follows: separate graphic files are created for each slide; separate graphic files are created for the navigation buttons and other navigation assistance tools; separate HTML files are created for each slide; a text-only version is created for each page for browser software that does not support graphics; and finally, an outline page is created that becomes the index frame where the user can select the page titles for each slide. The outline page is the opening page in the left frame that is displayed in the Web browser. A single presentation file can result in several files being created after conversion to Web pages.

If you are directly connected to a company intranet or Web server, contact the system administrator to find out the destination folder you need to specify in the *Publish a copy as File name* text box. Use the Browse button next to the *File name* option box to navigate to the correct folder. If you are not directly connected to an intranet or Web server, specify a folder on your system to copy the files so that you can later send to a Web server by modem or disk.

Click the Publish button in the Publish as Web Page dialog box to begin the conversion once all of the options have been set. If you would like to view the completed Web pages in your Web browser software when the conversion is complete, click the *Open published Web page in browser* check box before clicking the Publish button. Navigate through the presentation using the slide titles in the left frame of the browser window or the navigation buttons located along the bottom of the window.

## Project 5e  Saving a Presentation as a Web Page

1. With **PP_C8_P5.pptx** open, display the Save As dialog box and then change the *Save as type* option to *Single File Web Page (*.mht; *.mhtml)*.
2. Click the Publish button.

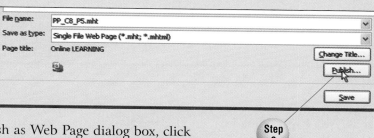

3. At the Publish as Web Page dialog box, click the Web Options button in the *Publish what?* section.

Step 2

4. At the Web Options dialog box with the General tab selected, click the down-pointing arrow at the right of the *Colors* text box and then click *Black text on white* at the drop-down list.
5. Click OK to close the Web Options dialog box.
6. At the Publish as Web Page dialog box, choose the target browser in the *Browser support* section that applies to your school. Check with your instructor if you are not sure which target browser you should be using. The default selection is *Microsoft Internet Explorer 4.0 or later*.

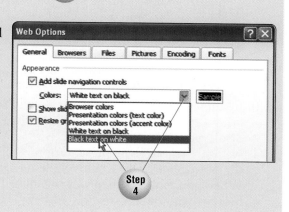

Step 4

7. Click the Browse button next to the *File name* option box, make sure the correct folder is displayed for storing the presentation, and then click OK.

8. If necessary, click the *Open published Web page in browser* check box to insert a check mark.

9. Click the Publish button.

10. In a few moments, the conversion will be complete and the Microsoft Internet Explorer or other default browser window will open with the opening page of the presentation displayed.

11. Navigate through the presentation by clicking the slide titles along the left frame, or using the Next Slide and Previous Slide navigation buttons along the bottom of the window. When you have finished viewing all of the slides, close the Internet Explorer or other browser window.

12. Close **PP_C8_P5.pptx** without saving the changes.

13. Open **GlobalEmployeeOrientation.pptx**.

14. Display the Save As dialog box and then change the *Save as type* option to *Web Page (*.htm; *.html)*.

15. Click the Publish button.

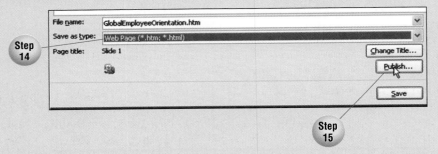

16. At the Publish as Web Page dialog box, choose the target browser in the *Browser support* section that applies to your school. Check with your instructor if you are not sure which target browser you should be using. The default selection is *Microsoft Internet Explorer 4.0 or later*.

17. Click the Browse button next to the *File name* option box, make sure the correct folder is displayed for storing the presentation, and then click OK.

18. Make sure the *Open published Web page in browser* check box contains a check mark.

19. Click the Publish button.

20. In a few moments, the conversion will be complete and the Microsoft Internet Explorer or other default browser window will open with the opening page of the presentation displayed.

21. Navigate through the presentation by clicking the slide titles along the left frame, or using the Next Slide and Previous Slide navigation buttons along the bottom of the window. When you have finished viewing all of the slides, close the Internet Explorer or other browser window.

22. Close **GlobalEmployeeOrientation.pptx** without saving the changes.

# Packaging a Presentation for a CD

The safest way to transport a PowerPoint presentation to another computer is to use the Package for CD feature. With this feature, you can copy a presentation including all of the linked files, fonts used, and PowerPoint Viewer program in case the destination computer does not have PowerPoint installed on it onto a CD or to a folder or network location. To use the Package for CD feature, click the Office button, point to *Publish*, and then click the *Package for CD* option at the side menu. This displays the Package for CD dialog box shown in Figure 8.13.

**Figure 8.13** Package for CD Dialog Box

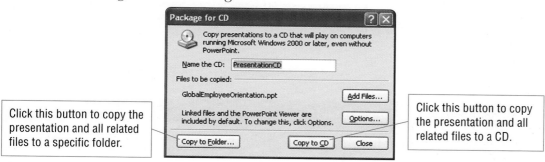

Click this button to copy the presentation and all related files to a specific folder.

Click this button to copy the presentation and all related files to a CD.

At the Package for CD dialog box, type a name in the *Name the CD* text box and then click the Copy to CD button. If you want to copy the presentation to a specific folder (instead of a CD), click the Copy to Folder button.

Click the Options button at the Package for CD dialog box and the Options dialog box displays as shown in Figure 8.14. Insert a check mark in the check box for those features you want to be included on the CD or in the folder or remove the check mark from those you do not want to include. If the computer you will be using does not contain the PowerPoint program, make sure the *Viewer Package* option is selected. The PowerPoint Viewer allows you to run a presentation on a computer that does not contain PowerPoint. (By default, the PowerPoint Viewer is installed when you install PowerPoint.) If charts or other files are linked to the presentation, insert a check mark in the *Linked files* check box and, if the destination computer does not have the same fonts installed, insert a check mark in the *Embedded TrueType fonts* check box.

**HINT**

PowerPoint Viewer does not support files that are formatted for Microsoft PowerPoint 97 or earlier versions.

**Figure 8.14** Options Dialog Box

Make sure this option is selected if you want the PowerPoint Viewer saved with the presentation.

Insert a check mark in this option to ensure that any linked files are saved with the presentation.

Insert a check mark in this option if the presentation contains TrueType fonts.

**Options**

Package type
- ⊙ Viewer Package (update file formats to run in PowerPoint Viewer)
  - Select how presentations will play in the viewer:
  - [Play all presentations automatically in the specified order ▾]
- ○ Archive Package (do not update file formats)

Include these files
(These files will not display in the Files to be copied list)
- ☑ Linked files
- ☐ Embedded TrueType fonts

Enhance security and privacy
- Password to open each presentation: [          ]
- Password to modify each presentation: [          ]
- ☐ Inspect presentations for inappropriate or private information

[ OK ]  [ Cancel ]

---

## Project 5f  Using the Package for CD Feature

1. Open **GlobalEmployeeOrientation.pptx**.
2. Click the Office button, point to *Publish*, and then click *Package for CD*. (If a dialog box displays with information about the PowerPoint Viewer, click OK.)
3. At the Package for CD dialog box, type **PP_C8_P5_CD** in the *Name the CD* text box.
4. Click the Options button.
5. At the Options dialog box, make sure the *Linked files* option contains a check mark.
6. Insert a check mark in the *Embedded TrueType fonts* check box.
7. Click OK to close the Options dialog box.
8. At the Package for CD dialog box, click the Copy to Folder button.
9. At the Copy to Folder dialog box, click the Browse button.
10. Navigate to your storage medium.
11. Click the Select button.
12. At the Copy to Folder dialog box, click OK.
13. At the message asking if you want to include linked files in the presentation, click the Yes button.
14. After the presentation is saved, close the Package for CD dialog box by clicking the Close button.
15. Close **GlobalEmployeeOrientation.pptx**.

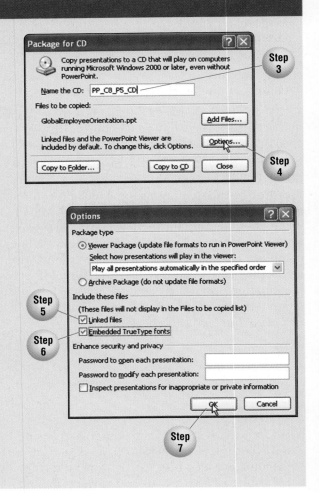

**Package for CD**

Copy presentations to a CD that will play on computers running Microsoft Windows 2000 or later, even without PowerPoint.

Name the CD: [PP_C8_P5_CD]  — Step 3

Files to be copied:

GlobalEmployeeOrientation.ppt   [ Add Files... ]

Linked files and the PowerPoint Viewer are included by default. To change this, click Options.   [ Options... ]  — Step 4

[ Copy to Folder... ]   [ Copy to CD ]   [ Close ]

**Options**

Package type
- ⊙ Viewer Package (update file formats to run in PowerPoint Viewer)
  - Select how presentations will play in the viewer:
  - [Play all presentations automatically in the specified order ▾]
- ○ Archive Package (do not update file formats)

Include these files  — Step 5
(These files will not display in the Files to be copied list)
- ☑ Linked files
- ☑ Embedded TrueType fonts  — Step 6

Enhance security and privacy
- Password to open each presentation: [          ]
- Password to modify each presentation: [          ]
- ☐ Inspect presentations for inappropriate or private information

[ OK ]  [ Cancel ]  — Step 7

# CHAPTER summary

- Import a Word outline document into a presentation by clicking the New Slide button arrow and then clicking *Slides from Outline*. At the Insert Outline dialog box, double-click the desired Word document.

- Export a PowerPoint presentation to a Word document by clicking the Office button, pointing to *Publish*, and then clicking *Create Handouts in Microsoft Office Word*. At the Send To Microsoft Office Word dialog box, select the desired page layout, and then click OK.

- Use the Copy and Paste buttons in the Clipboard group to copy data from one program to another.

- Use the Clipboard task pane to collect and paste up to 24 items. Click the Clipboard group dialog box launcher to turn on the display of the task pane.

- Integration is the process of completing a file by adding parts to it from other sources.

- An object created in one program of the Microsoft Office suite can be copied, linked, or embedded to another program in the suite. The program containing the original object is called the source and the program the object is pasted to is called the destination.

- An embedded object is stored in both the source and the destination programs.

- Link an object if the content is subject to change. Linking will ensure that the content in the destination always reflects the current content in the source. A linked object is stored in the source program only. The destination program contains a code indicating the name and location of the source.

- The content in a link is edited by opening the presentation containing the linked object in the source program, making the required changes, and then saving and closing the file.

- Download design templates at the New Presentation dialog box. To download, click the *Design slides* option in the dialog box, click a category, click the desired template, and then click the Download button.

- Insert, edit, and delete comments with buttons in the Comments group in the Review tab.

- Click the Show Markup button in the Comments group in the Review tab to turn on/off the display of comments.

- Modify document properties at the document information panel. Display this panel by clicking the Office button, pointing to *Prepare*, and then clicking *Properties*.

- Inspect a presentation for personal data, hidden data, and metadata with options at the Document Inspector dialog box. Display this dialog box by clicking the Office button, pointing to *Prepare*, and then clicking *Inspect Document* at the side menu.

- Insert a password in a presentation to ensure that the presentation is opened only by someone who knows the password. Insert a password in the Encrypt Document dialog box, which you can display by clicking the Office button, pointing to *Prepare*, and then clicking *Encrypt Document*.

- Apply a digital signature to a presentation to vouch for the authenticity of the presentation. Once a digital signature is applied to a presentation, the presentation is locked and cannot be edited or changed without first removing the digital signature.

- Run the compatibility checker to check your presentation and identify elements that are not supported or will act differently in previous versions of PowerPoint. Run the checker by clicking the Office button, pointing to *Prepare*, and then clicking *Run Compatibility Checker*.

- Save presentations in different formats with options at the Office button Save As side menu. You can also save presentations in different formats with the *Save as type* option at the Save As dialog box.

- Save a presentation as graphic images by saving the presentation in a format such as GIF, JPEG, or TIF. Use the *Save as type* option at the Save As dialog box to specify the file format. You can choose to save an individual slide within a presentation or all slides in the presentation.

- You can save a presentation as a Web page using either the *Single File Web Page (*.mht; *mhtml)* or *Web Page (*htm; *.html)* file format available from the *Save as type* option in the Save As dialog box.

- Use the Package for CD feature to copy a presentation including all of the linked files, fonts used, and PowerPoint Viewer onto a CD or to a folder or network location. To use the feature, click the Office button, point to *Publish*, and then click *Package for CD*.

# COMMANDS review

| FEATURE | RIBBON TAB, GROUP | BUTTON, OPTION |
|---------|-------------------|----------------|
| Insert Outline dialog box | Home, Slides | [icon], Slides from Outline |
| Send To Microsoft Office Word dialog box | | [icon], Publish, Create Handouts in Microsoft Office Word |
| Clipboard task pane | Home, Clipboard | [icon] |
| Paste Special dialog box | Home, Clipboard | [icon], Paste Special |
| New Presentation dialog box | | [icon], New |
| Insert comment | Review, Comments | [icon] |
| Edit comment | Review, Comments | [icon] |
| Delete comment | Review, Comments | [icon] |
| Previous comment | Review, Comments | [icon] |
| Next comment | Review, Comments | [icon] |
| Document information panel | | [icon], Prepare, Properties |
| Document Inspector dialog box | | [icon], Prepare, Inspect Document |
| Encrypt Document dialog box | | [icon], Prepare, Encrypt Document |
| Digital signature | | [icon], Prepare, Add a Digital Signature |
| Microsoft Office PowerPoint Compatibility Checker dialog box | | [icon], Prepare, Run Compatibility Checker |
| Package for CD | | [icon], Publish, Package for CD |

# CONCEPTS check

## Test Your Knowledge

**Completion:** In the space provided at the right, indicate the correct term, symbol, or command.

1. Display the Insert Outline dialog box by clicking the New Slide button arrow and then clicking this option. _____

2. Display the Send To Microsoft Office Word dialog box by clicking the Office button, pointing to this option, and then clicking Create Handouts in Microsoft Office Word. _____

3. To link or embed an object, open this dialog box in the destination program after copying the source object. _____

4. Display this dialog box to display and download design templates from Microsoft Office Online. _____

5. The New Comment button is located in the Comments group in this tab. _____

6. Click the Office button, point to *Prepare*, and then click *Properties* and this displays. _____

7. Display the Document Inspector dialog box by clicking the Office button, pointing to *Prepare*, and then clicking this option. _____

8. Apply this to a presentation to vouch for the authenticity of the presentation. _____

9. Choose this option at the Office button Save As side menu to save a presentation with the *.ppsx* file extension. _____

10. The letters PDF are an acronym for this. _____

11. Three graphic image formats include GIF, TIF, and this. _____

12. HTML is an acronym for this, which is a programming language used to code pages to display graphically on the World Wide Web. _____

13. Use this feature to copy a presentation onto a CD or to a folder or network location. _____

# SKILLS check
## Demonstrate Your Proficiency

## Assessment

### 1 COPY WORD AND EXCEL DATA INTO A SALES CONFERENCE PRESENTATION

1. Open **HerbalPresentation.pptx** and then save the presentation and name it **PP_C8_A1**.
2. Make Slide 2 active and then complete the following steps:
   a. Open Excel and then open the workbook named **SalesProjections.xlsx** (located in your PowerPoint2007C8 folder on your storage medium).
   b. Copy the chart and paste it into Slide 2.
   c. Resize the chart so it fills most of the slide below the title.
   d. Close the workbook and exit Excel.
3. Make Slide 4 active and then complete the following steps:
   a. Draw a text box in the slide.
   b. Open Word and then open the document named **HerbalRemedies.docx**.
   c. Copy the first three terms and the paragraph below each term in the document to the text box in Slide 4.
   d. Select the text in the placeholder, change the font to Rockwell, and then change the font size to 24. (If necessary, size and move the text box so the text is positioned attractively on the slide.)
   e. Move and/or resize the placeholder so it fills most of the slide below the title.
4. Make Slide 5 active and then complete the following steps:
   a. Draw a text box in the slide.
   b. Make active the **HerbalRemedies.docx** Word document.
   c. Copy the last two terms and the paragraph below each term in the document and paste them into Slide 5.
   d. Select the text in the placeholder, change the font to Rockwell, and then change the font size to 24.
   e. Move and/or resize the placeholder so it fills most of the slide below the title.
5. Make Word active, close **HerbalRemedies.docx,** and then exit Word.
6. Make PowerPoint active and then apply custom animation effects to each slide.
7. Run the presentation.
8. Save **PP_C8_A1.pptx**.
9. Export the presentation to a Word document that prints blank lines next to slides.
10. Save the Word document and name it **PP_C8_A1_Word**.
11. Print and then close **PP_C8_A1_Word.docx**.
12. Save and then close **PP_C8_A1.pptx**.

## Assessment

## 2 COPY AND LINK WORD AND EXCEL DATA INTO A COMMUNICATIONS PRESENTATION

1. Open **CommunicationPresentation.pptx** and then save the presentation with the name **PP_C8_A2**.
2. Open Word and then open the document named **VerbalSkills.docx** (located in the PowerPoint2007C8 folder on your storage medium).
3. Copy the table and embed it (use the Paste Special dialog box) into Slide 5.
4. Resize the table so it better fills the slide.
5. Make Word active, close the **VerbalSkills.docx** document, and then exit Word.
6. Open Excel and then open the workbook named **NonverbalCues.xlsx** (located in the PowerPoint2007C8 folder on your storage medium).
7. Copy the chart and link it to Slide 6. Resize the chart so it fills a majority of the slide below the title.
8. Save and then close **PP_C8_A2.pptx**.
9. Make the following change to the chart in **NonverbalCues.xlsx**:
   a. Select the chart and then apply the *Style 18* chart style. **Hint: Do this in the Chart Tools Design tab.**
   b. Apply the *Gradient Fill-Accent 4, Reflection* WordArt style. **Hint: Do this in the Chart Tools Format tab.**
   c. Change the shape outline to *No Outline*.
   d. Change the amount in B2 from *35%* to *38%*.
   e. Change the amount in B3 from *25%* to *22%*.
10. Save and then close **NonverbalClue.xlsx** and then exit Excel.
11. In PowerPoint, open **PP_C8_A2.pptx**. (At the message that displays when you open the presentation, click the Update Links button.)
12. Make Slide 2 active and then insert the following comment after the second bulleted item: Ask Lauren to provide a specific communication example.
13. Make Slide 4 active and then insert the following comment after the third bulleted item: Insert a link here to the writing presentation prepared by Sylvia.
14. Make Slide 8 active and then insert the following comment after the third bulleted item: Distribute evaluation forms to audience.
15. Run the presentation.
16. Save the presentation and then print the presentation as a handout with all slides on one page and make sure the comments print.
17. Delete the comments.
18. Run the compatibility checker.
19. Save the presentation in *PowerPoint 2003-2007 Presentation* format and name it **PP_C8_A2_2003format**.
20. Close **PP_C8_A2_2003format.ppt**.

# Assessment

## 3 SAVE SLIDES IN JPEG FORMAT AND INSERT SLIDES IN A TRAVEL PRESENTATION

1. Open **FCTTours.pptx**, save all slides in the presentation in the JPEG graphic format, and then close **FCTTours.pptx**.
2. Open **FCTQtrMeeting.pptx** and then save the presentation with the name **PP_C8_A3**.
3. Make Slide 4 active and then insert each of the four slides you saved in JPEG format in Step 1 with the following specifications:
   a. Use the Picture button in the Insert tab to insert each JPEG graphic slide.
   b. Change the height of each JPEG slide image to *2.4"*.
   c. Position all four JPEG graphic slides in Slide 4 so they are balanced in the slide and do not overlap the slide background graphic or title.
4. Make Slide 1 active and then run the presentation.
5. Save **PP_C8_A3.pptx**.
6. Save **PP_C8_A3.pptx** with Save As and name it **PP_C8_A3_Animation**.
7. Apply an animation effect of your choosing to the logo and the subtitle in Slide 1.
8. Apply an animation effect of your choosing to the titles in Slides 2, 3, 5, and 6.
9. Apply a custom build animation to the bulleted text in Slides 2, 3, 5, and 6 that causes the previous point to dim when the next point displays.
10. Make Slide 1 active and then run the presentation.
11. Save and then close **PP_C8_A3_Animation.pptx**.
12. Open **PP_C8_A3.pptx** and then save the presentation as a single file Web page.
13. In your browser, navigate through the presentation.
14. After viewing all of the slides, close your browser window and then close **PP_C8_A3.pptx** without saving the changes.

# Assessment

## 4 DOWNLOAD AND FILL IN A COURSE COMPLETION CERTIFICATE

1. Display the New Presentation dialog box and look for award certificates you can download from the Microsoft Office Online site.
2. Download the award certificate named *Certificate of completion for course*. (If this certificate is not available, download one of your choosing.)
3. Fill in the certificate with the appropriate information. (Use your school's name for the company name.)
4. Save the completed certificate and name it **PP_C8_A4**.
5. Print and then close **PP_C8_A4.pptx**.

# CASE study
## Apply Your Skills

**Part 1**

You work for Rocky Mountain Family Medicine and are responsible for preparing education and training materials and publications for the center. You want to be able to insert the center logo in publications so you decide to save the logo as a graphic image. To do this, open the presentation (one slide) named **RMFMLogo.pptx** and then save the slide as a JPEG graphic image.

**Part 2**

You are responsible for presenting information on childhood diseases at an education class at a local community center. Open the Word document named **ChildhoodDiseases.docx** and then use the information to create a presentation with the following specifications:

- Apply the *Flow* design theme.
- Change the layout for the first slide to *Title Only*, type an appropriate title for the presentation, and then move the title to the bottom of the slide. Insert the **RMFMLogo.jpg** graphic image in the first slide and then size and position the logo attractively on the slide. (Consider setting transparent color to the background of the logo graphic image. Do this with the *Set Transparent Color* option in the Recolor button drop-down list in the Picture Tools Format tab.)
- Create additional slides with the information in the **ChildhoodDiseases.docx** Word document.
- Apply any additional enhancements to improve the presentation.

Run the presentation and then save the presentation with the name **PP_C8_CS_P2**. Print the presentation as a handout with six slides per page and then close the presentation.

**Part 3**

You need to prepare a presentation for an upcoming education and training meeting. Import the Word outline document named **RMFMOutline.docx** into a PowerPoint presentation and then make the following changes:

- Apply the *Flow* design theme.
- Create the first slide with the *Title Only* layout, insert the **RMFMLogo.jpg** graphic image, and then size and position the logo in the same manner as the first slide in **PP_C8_CS_P2.pptx**. Insert the title *Education and Training* in the title placeholder.
- Change the layout to *Title Only* for the Community Contacts slide and then copy the table from the Word document **RMFMContacts.docx** and paste it into the Community Contacts slide. Increase the size of the table so it better fills the slide.
- Change the layout to *Title Only* for the Current Enrollment slide and then copy the chart from the Excel workbook **RMFMEnrollment.xlsx** and link it to the Current Enrollment slide.
- Apply any additional enhancements to improve the presentation.

Run the presentation and then save the presentation with the name **PP_C8_CS_P3**. Print the presentation as a handout with six slides per page and then close the presentation. You check the enrollments for classes and realize that more people have enrolled so you need to update the numbers in the Excel workbook. Open the **RMFMEnrollment.xlsx** Excel workbook and then change *46* to *52*, *38* to *40*, and *24* to *27*. Save and then close the workbook. Open the **PP_C8_CS_P3.pptx** presentation and then update the links. Print only the Current Enrollment slide and then close the presentation.

**Part 4**

You decide that you want to include information in the **PP_C8_CS_P2.pptx** presentation on measles. Using the Internet, search for information on measles such as symptoms, complications, transmission, and prevention. Include this information in new slides in the **PP_C8_CS_P2.pptx** presentation. Run the presentation and then print only the new slides. Save and then close the presentation.

**Part 5**

Rocky Mountain Family Medicine has a Web site that contains information about the center as well as educational information. You decide to save the childhood diseases presentation as a Web page that visitors to the Web site can view. Open **PP_C8_CS_P2.pptx** and then save the presentation as a single file Web page. View the presentation in your default browser and then close the presentation.

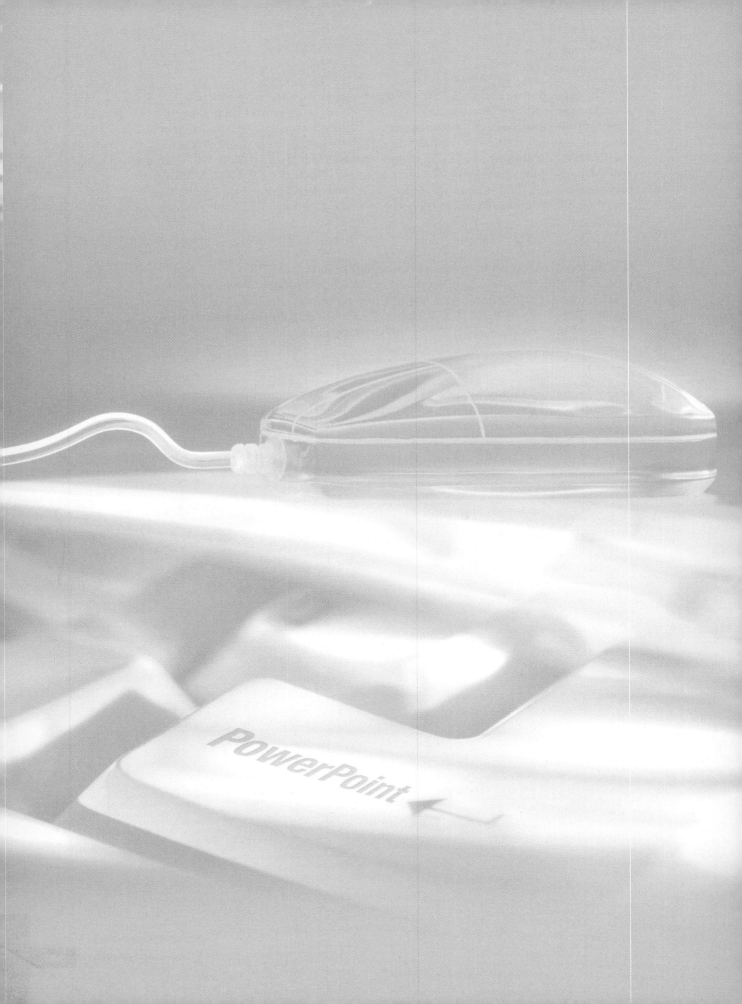

# Customizing and Enhancing PowerPoint Presentations

# ASSESSING proficiency

In this unit, you have learned to add visual elements to presentations such as tables, charts, and SmartArt graphics; create a photo album; apply formatting in Slide Master view; insert action buttons; apply custom animation effects; and set up slide shows. You also learned how to copy, embed, and link data between programs; how to insert comments; and how to protect and prepare a presentation.

powerpoint Unit 2

*Note: Before beginning computer assessments, copy to your storage medium the PowerPoint2007U2 folder from the PowerPoint2007 folder on the CD that accompanies this textbook and then make PowerPoint2007U2 the active folder.*

## Assessment 1 Save a Slide in JPEG Format and Copy and Link Objects in a Presentation

1. Open **GreenSpaceLogo.pptx**, save the only slide in the presentation as a JPEG graphic image, and then close **GreenSpaceLogo.pptx**.
2. Open **GreenSpacePresentation.pptx** and then save the presentation with the name **PP_U2_A1**.
3. Display the presentation in Slide Master view and then make the following changes:
   a. Click the top slide master thumbnail.
   b. Select the text *CLICK TO EDIT MASTER TITLE STYLE* and then change the font color to *Green*.
   c. Select the text *Click to edit Master text styles*, change the font color to Gold, Accent 3, Darker 50%, and then change the bullet color to Green.
   d. Close Slide Master view.
4. Make Slide 1 active and then make the following changes:
   a. Insert the **GreenSpaceLogo.jpg** graphic image.
   b. Set transparent color for the logo background. (Do this with the *Set Transparent Color* option at the Recolor button drop-down list in the Picture Tools Format tab.)
   c. Size and position the logo so it is positioned attractively on the slide. (Consider offsetting the image slightly to the right to balance it with the slide title.)
5. Make Slide 6 active and then insert the following data in a table. You determine the formatting of the table and the formatting of the data in the table:

| Project | Contact | Completion Date |
|---|---|---|
| Moyer-Sylvan Complex | Barry MacDonald | 07/31/2010 |
| Waterfront Headquarters | Jasmine Jefferson | 02/15/2011 |
| Linden Square | Marion Van Horn | 09/30/2011 |
| Village Green | Parker Alderton | 12/31/2011 |
| Cedar Place Market | Gerry Halderman | 03/31/2012 |

6. Make Slide 7 active and then insert the following data in a SmartArt organizational chart. You determine the organization and formatting of the chart:

**Avery Trinidad**
**Lead Designer**

| Mary Pirone | Craig Stafford | Kenneth Chan |
|---|---|---|
| Structural Engineer | Ergonomic Designer | Urban Designer |

Diana Warren
Research Assistant

Justin Charone
Draftsperson

7. Make Slide 5 active and then create a column chart with the following data. Delete the chart title and chart legend. You determine the formatting and layout of the chart.

| | Revenues |
|---|---|
| 1st Qtr. | $25,250,000 |
| 2nd Qtr. | $34,000,000 |
| 3rd Qtr. | $22,750,000 |
| 4th Qtr. | $20,500,000 |

8. Make Slide 8 active and then insert a SmartArt diagram with the *Repeating Bending Process* diagram (found in the *Process* group) with the following information. You determine the design and formatting of the SmartArt diagram.
   - Mission Analysis
   - Requirements Analysis
   - Function Allocation
   - Design
   - Verification

9. Check each slide and make any changes that improve the visual appeal of the slide.

10. Make Slide 1 active and then run the presentation.

11. Make Slide 3 active, click immediately right of the slide title, and then insert the comment Check with Marilyn about adding River View Mall to this list.

12. Make Slide 4 active, click immediately right of the word *Australia* in the bulleted text, and then insert the comment What happened to the plans to open an office in Sydney?

13. Print the presentation as a handout with four slides per page and make sure the comments print.

14. Save and then close **PP_U2_A1.pptx**.

## Assessment 2 Copy and Paste Data between Programs and Insert Action Buttons in a Telecommunications Presentation

1. Open **TelecomPresentation.pptx** and then save the presentation with the name **PP_U2_A2**.
2. Make Slide 6 active and then create a new Slide 7 (with the Title and Content layout) with the following specifications:
   a. Insert the title *APPLICATION* in the slide.
   b. Open Word and then open **WordConcepts.docx**.
   c. Display the Clipboard task pane. (Make sure the task pane is empty. If not, click the Clear All button.)
   d. Select and then copy *RECEIVING* and the paragraph below it.
   e. Select and then copy *STORING* and the paragraph below it.
   f. Select and then copy *TRANSMITTING* and the paragraph below it.
   g. Display the **PP_U2_A2.pptx** presentation.
   h. Click in the bulleted text *Click to add text*.
   i. Turn on the display of the Clipboard task pane.
   j. Paste the *TRANSMITTING* item in the slide.
   k. Paste the *RECEIVING* item in the slide.
   l. Clear and then close the Clipboard.
   m. Select all of the bulleted text and then change the font size to 28. Delete the bullet below the last paragraph.
   n. Make the **WordConcepts.docx** document active, close the Clipboard task pane, close the document, and then exit Word.
3. Make Slide 1 active and then insert an action button with the following specifications:
   a. Use the *Action Button: Forward or Next* option to draw the button.
   b. Draw the button in the lower right corner of the slide and make it approximately one-half inch in size.
   c. Change the shape fill of the button to Blue, Accent 2, Lighter 40%.
4. Display the presentation in Slide Master view and then make the following changes:
   a. Click the top slide master thumbnail.
   b. Insert an action button in the lower right corner of the slide with the same specifications as those in Step 3.
   c. Close Slide Master view.
5. Run the presentation. (Use the action buttons to advance slides. At the last slide, press the Esc key.)
6. Create a footer that prints your first and last names and include the date in the upper right corner on handout pages.
7. Print the presentation as a handout with four slides per page.
8. Save and then close **PP_U2_A2.pptx**

## Assessment 3 Save a Template Presentation and Copy, Embed, and Link Objects between Programs

1. Display a blank presentation, click the View tab, and then click the Slide Master button.
2. Click the top slide master thumbnail in the slides thumbnail pane.
3. Apply the *Technic* theme and change the theme colors to *Median*.
4. Apply the *Style 8* background style.
5. Insert **ISLogo.jpg** in the master slide (use the Picture button in the Insert tab), change the height of the logo to one inch, and drag the logo to the

lower left corner of the slide master. Set transparent color for the logo background. (Do this with the *Set Transparent Color* option at the Recolor button drop-down list in the Picture Tools Format tab.)

6. Close Slide Master view.

7. Save the presentation as a template to the PowerPoint2007U2 folder on your storage medium and name the template **XXXISTemplate** (use your initials in place of the *XXX*).

8. Close **XXXISTemplate.potx**.

9. Open **XXXISTemplate.potx**. (To do this, display the New Presentation dialog box and then click *New from existing*. At the New from Existing Presentation dialog box, navigate to the PowerPoint2007U2 folder on your storage medium and then double-click ***XXXISTemplate.potx***.)

10. Save the presentation and name it **PP_U2_A3**.

11. Create the first slide with the following specifications:
    a. Choose the *Blank* layout.
    b. Use WordArt to create the text *International Securities*. (You determine the shape and formatting of the WordArt text.)

12. Create the second slide with the following specifications:
    a. Choose the *Title Slide* layout.
    b. Type European Division as the subtitle.
    c. Type 2010 SALES MEETING as the title.

13. Create the third slide with the following specifications:
    a. Choose the *Title Only* layout.
    b. Type REGIONAL SALES as the title.
    c. Open Excel and then open **ISWorkbook01.xlsx**.
    d. Save the workbook with Save As and name it **ISSalesWorkbook**.
    e. Select cells A1 through D5 (the cells containing data) and then copy and embed the cells in Slide 3.
    f. Increase the size of the cells so they better fill the slide.

14. Create the fourth slide with the following specifications:
    a. Choose the *Title and Content* layout.
    b. Type 2011 GOALS as the title.
    c. Type the following as the bulleted items:
       ♦ Increase product sales by 15 percent
       ♦ Open a branch office in Spain
       ♦ Hire one manager and two additional account managers
       ♦ Decrease production costs by 6 percent

15. Create the fifth slide with the following specifications:
    a. Choose the *Title and Content* layout.
    b. Type HIRING TIMELINE as the title.
    c. Create a table with two columns and five rows and then type the following text in the cells in the table. (You determine the formatting of the cells.)

| Task | Date |
| --- | --- |
| Advertise positions | 03/01/2010 to 04/30/2010 |
| Review resumes | 05/15/2010 to 06/01/2010 |
| Conduct interviews | 06/15/2010 to 07/15/2010 |
| Hire personnel | 08/01/2010 |

16. Create the sixth slide with the following specifications:
    a. Choose the *Title Only* layout.
    b. Type PRODUCTION EXPENSES as the title.
    c. Make Excel the active program and then close **ISSalesWorkbook.xlsx**.
    d. Open **ISWorkbook02.xlsx**.

e. Save the workbook with Save As and name it **ISExpensesWorkbook**.

f. Copy and then link the pie chart in **ISExpensesWorkbook.xlsx** to Slide 6.

g. Increase the size of the pie chart so it better fills the slide.

h. Make Excel active, close **ISExpensesWorkbook.xlsx**, and then exit Excel.

17. Run the presentation.

18. Create a footer that prints your first and last names in the lower left corner and include the current date in the upper right corner on handout pages.

19. Print the presentation as a handout with four slides per page.

20. Save and then close **PP_U2_A3.pptx**.

21. Open Excel and then open **ISExpensesWorkbook.xlsx**.

22. Make the following changes:

a. B2: Change *38% to 41%*

b. B3: Change *35% to 32%*

c. B4: Change *18% to 21%*

d. B5: Change *9% to 6%*

23. Save, print, and close **ISExpensesWorkbook.xlsx** and then exit Excel.

24. With PowerPoint the active program, open **PP_U2_A3.pptx**. (At the message that displays, click the Update Links button.)

25. Display Slide 3, double-click the cells, and then make the following changes to the data in the embedded cells:

a. C2: Change *2,678,450 to 2,857,300*

b. C3: Change *1,753,405 to 1,598,970*

c. C4: Change *1,452,540 to 1,635,400*

26. Run the presentation.

27. Print the slides as a handout with four slides per page.

28. Save **PP_U2_A3.pptx**.

29. Apply a transition and sound of your choosing to all slides in the presentation.

30. Use the Rehearse Timings feature to set the following times for the slides to display during a slide show:

      Slide 1 = 3 seconds

      Slide 2 = 3 seconds

      Slide 3 = 6 seconds

      Slide 4 = 5 seconds

      Slide 5 = 6 seconds

      Slide 6 = 5 seconds

31. Set up the slide show to run continuously.

32. Run the presentation beginning with Slide 1. Watch the slide show until the presentation has started for the second time and then end the show.

33. Save and then close the presentation.

## Assessment 4 Apply Custom Animation Effects to a Travel Presentation

1. Open **AustraliaTour.pptx** and then save the presentation with the name **PP_U2_A4**.

2. With Slide 1 active, apply a *Fly In* entrance animation effect to the title *Australia Tour* that has the title fly in from the bottom.

3. Display the presentation in Slide Master view and then make the following changes:

a. Click the third slide master thumbnail.

b. Apply a *Fly In* entrance animation effect to the title that has the title fly in from the top.

c. Apply a *Fly In* entrance animation effect to the bulleted text that has the text fly in from the left and then dim when the next bullet displays.

d. Close Slide Master view.

4. Make Slide 5 active, select the sun shape that displays above *Sydney*, and then draw a freeform motion path from Sydney to Melbourne, Tasmania, Adelaide, Perth, Derby, Darwin, Cairns, and then back to Sydney. Change the speed to *Very Slow*.

5. Make Slide 6 active and then make the following changes:

a. Click the bottom shape to select it. (You may want to move the top two shapes out of the way.)

b. Apply a *Fly In* entrance animation effect that has the shape fly in from the left. Apply a *Fly Out* exit animation effect that has the shape fly out to the right.

c. Click the middle shape to select it and then apply a *Fly In* entrance animation effect that has the shape fly in from the left. Apply a *Fly Out* exit animation effect that has the shape fly out to the right.

d. Click the top shape to select it and then apply a *Fly In* entrance animation effect that has the shape fly in from the left.

e. Position the shapes so they are stacked on top of each other so you do not see a portion of the shapes behind.

6. Save **PP_U2_A4.pptx**.

7. Make Slide 1 active, run the presentation, and make sure the custom animation effects play correctly.

8. Print the presentation as a handout with all slides on one page.

9. Close **PP_U2_A4.pptx**.

### Assessment 5 Inspect a Presentation and Save a Presentation in Different Formats

1. Open **PP_U2_A1.pptx** and then save the presentation with the name **PP_U2_A5**.

2. Inspect the presentation using the Document Inspector dialog box and remove comments from the presentation.

3. Run the compatibility checker.

4. Save the presentation in *PowerPoint 97-2003* format and name it **PP_U2_A5_2003format**. (Click the Continue button at the compatibility checker message.)

5. Close **PP_U2_A5_2003format.ppt**.

6. Open **PP_U2_A5.pptx** and then save the presentation as a single file Web page.

7. Run the presentation in your Web browser.

8. After viewing all of the slides, close your browser window.

9. Close **PP_U2_A5.pptx** without saving the changes.

# WRITING activities

The following activities give you the opportunity to practice your writing skills along with demonstrating an understanding of some of the important PowerPoint features you have mastered in this unit. Use correct grammar, appropriate word choices, and clear sentence structure.

## Activity 1 Prepare and Format a Travel Presentation

You work for First Choice Travel and you are responsible for preparing a presentation on travel vacations. Open the Word document named **TravelVacations.docx** and then print the document. Close the document and then exit Word. Using the information in the document, prepare a PowerPoint presentation with the following specifications:

1. Create a presentation that presents the main points of the document.
2. Rehearse and set times for the slides to display during a slide show. You determine the number of seconds for each slide.
3. Insert a song into the first slide from the sound clip organizer (or from any resource available to you).
4. Set up the presentation to run on an endless loop and the sound to play across all slides and continuously as long as the presentation is running.
5. Run the presentation. (The slide show will start and run continuously.) Watch the presentation until it has started for the second time and then end the show by pressing the Esc key.
6. Save the presentation and name it **PP_U2_Act01**.
7. Print the presentation as a handout with six slides per page.
8. Close **PP_U2_Act01.pptx**.

## Activity 2 Prepare and Format a Presentation on Media Files

Using PowerPoint's Help feature, learn more about types of media files you can add to a PowerPoint presentation and compatible multimedia file formats. (Search specifically for *types of media files you can add* and *compatible multimedia file formats*.) Using the information you find in the Help files, create a presentation with *at least* the following specifications:

- Slide containing the title of the presentation and your name
- Create at least two slides that contain file types you can add to the Microsoft Clip Organizer. (Search for additional information on file types, search for *file formats that are supported in PowerPoint 2007*. Use this additional information to further describe file types.)
- Create at least three slides each containing information on a compatible audio file format including the file format, extension, and a brief description of the format.
- Create at least three slides each containing information on a compatible video file format including the file format, extension, and a brief description of the format.
- If you are connected to the Internet, search for Web sites where you can download free audio clips and then include this information in a slide as well as a hyperlink to the site.

Save the completed presentation and name it **PP_U2_Act02**. Run the presentation and then print the presentation as a handout with six slides per page. Close **PP_U2_Act02.pptx**.

## Presenting Office 2007

Make sure you are connected to the Internet and then explore the Microsoft Web site at www.microsoft.com. Browse the various categories and links on the Web site to familiarize yourself with how information is organized.

Create a PowerPoint presentation that could be delivered to someone who has just purchased Office 2007 and wants to know how to find more information about the software from the Microsoft Web site. Include points or tips on where to find product release information and technical support. Include hyperlinks to important pages at the Microsoft Web site. Add formatting and enhancements to make the presentation as dynamic as possible. Save the presentation and name it **PP_U2_Office2007**. Run the presentation and then print the presentation as a handout with six slides per page. Close **PP_U2_Office2007.pptx**.

## Creating a Skills Presentation

You are preparing a presentation that you will use when presenting information on jobs at your local job fair. Open the Word document named **JobDescriptions.docx**, print the document, and then close the document and exit Word. Use the information in the document to prepare slides that describe each job (do not include the starting salary). Using the Internet, locate information on two other jobs that interest you and then create a slide for each job that provides information on job responsibilities. Determine the starting salary for the two jobs and then use that information along with the starting salary information for the jobs in the Word document to create a chart that displays the salary amounts. Locate at least two online job search Web sites and then include them in your presentation along with hyperlinks to the sites. Insert action buttons to move to the next page for the first slide through the second from the end. On your final slide, create an action button to return to the first slide.

Save the presentation and name it **PP_U2_JobStudy**. Run the presentation and then print the presentation as a handout with six slides per page. Close **PP_U2_JobStudy.pptx**.

# Office 2007 –
# Integrated Project

Now that you have completed the chapters in this textbook, you have learned to create documents in Word, build worksheets in Excel, organize data in Access, and design presentations in PowerPoint. To learn the various programs in the Microsoft Office 2007 suite, you have completed a variety of projects, assessments, and activities. This integrated project is a final assignment that allows you to apply the knowledge you have gained about the programs in the Office suite to produce a variety of documents and files.

## Situation

You are the vice president of Classique Coffees, a gourmet coffee company. Your company operates two retail stores that sell gourmet coffee and related products to the public. One retail store is located in Seattle, Washington, the other in Tacoma. The company is three years old and has seen approximately a 10- to 20-percent growth in profit each year. Your duties as the vice president of the company include researching the coffee market; studying coffee buying trends; designing and implementing new projects; and supervising the marketing, sales, and personnel managers.

### Activity 1  Write Persuasively

Using Word, compose a memo to the president of Classique Coffees, Leslie Steiner, detailing your research and recommendations:

- Research has shown a 20-percent growth in the iced coffee market.
- The target population for iced coffees is people from ages 18 to 35.
- Market analysis indicates that only three local retail companies sell iced coffees in the greater Seattle-Tacoma area.
- The recommendation is that Classique Coffees develops a suite of iced coffees for market consumption by early next year. (Be as persuasive as possible.)

Save the completed memo and name it **ProjectAct01**. Print and then close **ProjectAct01.docx**.

### Activity 2  Design a Letterhead

You are not satisfied with the current letterhead used by your company. Design a new letterhead for Classique Coffees using Word and include the following information:

- Use a clip art image in the letterhead. (Consider downloading a clip art image from Microsoft Office Online.)
- Include the company name—Classique Coffees.
- Include the company address—355 Pioneer Square, Seattle, WA 98211.
- Include the company telephone number—(206) 555-6690.
- Include the company e-mail address—ccoffees@emcp.net.
- Create a slogan that will help your business contacts remember your company.
- Add any other information or elements that you feel are appropriate.

When the letterhead is completed, save it and name it **ProjectAct02**. Print and then close **ProjectAct02.docx**.

## Activity 3 **Prepare a Notice**

Using Word, prepare a notice about an upcoming marketing seminar. Include the following information in the notice:

- Name of the seminar—Marketing to the Coffee Gourmet
- Location of the seminar—Conference room at the corporate office, 355 Pioneer Square, Seattle, WA 98211
- Date and time of seminar—Friday, October 19, 2010, 9:00 a.m. to 2:30 p.m.
- Topics that will be covered at the seminar:
    > identifying coffee-drinking trends
    > assessing the current gourmet coffee market
    > developing new products
    > analyzing the typical Classique Coffees customer
    > marketing a new product line
- Consider including a clip art image in the notice. (You determine an appropriate clip art image.)

When the notice is completed, save it and name it **ProjectAct03**. Print and then close **ProjectAct03.docx**.

## Activity 4 **Create an Organizational Chart**

In preparation for an upcoming meeting, you need to prepare an organizational chart for the organization of the leadership team at Classique Coffees. Create an organizational chart using a SmartArt graphic that includes the following:

President

Vice President

| Marketing Manager | Sales Manager | Personnel Manager |
| --- | --- | --- |
| Marketing Assistants | Sales Associates | Assistant Manager |

Apply formatting to improve the visual appeal of the chart. Save the chart and name it **ProjectAct04**. Print and then close **ProjectAct04.docx**.

## Activity 5  Create a SmartArt Graphic

In addition to the organizational chart, you also want to create a SmartArt graphic that illustrates the steps in a marketing plan. Those steps are:

- Planning
- Development
- Marketing
- Distribution

Apply formatting to improve the visual appeal of the graphic. Save the SmartArt graphic and name it **ProjectAct05**. Print and then close **ProjectAct05.docx**.

## Activity 6  Build a Budget Worksheet

Using Excel, prepare a worksheet with the following information:

**Annual Budget:** $1,450,000

| Department | Percent of Budget | Total |
|---|---|---|
| Administration | 10% | |
| Purchasing | 24% | |
| Sales | 21% | |
| Marketing | 23% | |
| Personnel | 12% | |
| Training | 10% | |

Insert formulas that will calculate the total amount for each department based on the specified percentage of the annual budget. When the worksheet is completed, save it and name it **ProjectAct06** and then print **ProjectAct06.xlsx**.

Determine the impact of a 10-percent increase in the annual budget on the total amount for each department. With the amounts displayed for a 10-percent increase, save, print, and then close **ProjectAct06.xlsx**.

## Activity 7  Determine Sales Quota Increases

The Marketing Department for Classique Coffees employs seven employees who market the company products to customers. These employees are given a quota for yearly sales that they are to meet. You have determined that the quota needs to be raised for the upcoming year. You are not sure whether the quotas should be increased 5 percent or 10 percent. Using Excel, prepare a worksheet with the following information:

### CLASSIQUE COFFEES
#### Sales Quotas

| Employee | Current Quota | Projected Quota |
|---|---|---|
| Berenstein | $125,000 | |
| Evans | $100,000 | |
| Grayson | $110,000 | |

| | |
|---|---|
| Lueke | $135,000 |
| Nasson | $125,000 |
| Phillips | $150,000 |
| Samuels | $175,000 |

Insert a formula to determine the projected quotas at 5 percent more than the current quota. Save the worksheet and name it **ProjectAct07A** and then print **ProjectAct07A.xlsx**. Determine the projected quotas at 10 percent more than the current quota. Save the worksheet and name it **ProjectAct07B**. Print and then close **ProjectAct07B.xlsx**.

## Activity 8  Build a Sales Worksheet and Create a Chart

Using Excel, prepare a worksheet with the following information:

| Type of Coffee | Percent of Sales |
|---|---|
| Regular blend | 22% |
| Espresso blend | 12% |
| Regular blend decaf | 17% |
| Espresso blend decaf | 10% |
| Flavored blend | 25% |
| Flavored blend decaf | 14% |

Save the completed worksheet and name it **ProjectAct08** and then print **ProjectAct08.docx**. With the worksheet still displayed, create a pie chart as a new sheet with the data in the worksheet. Title the pie chart *Year 2010 Percentage of Sales*. When the chart is completed, save the worksheet (now two sheets) with the same name (**ProjectAct08.docx**). Print only the sheet containing the pie chart and then close **ProjectAct08.docx**.

## Activity 9  Build a Projected Sales Worksheet and Create a Chart

Using Excel, prepare a worksheet with the following information:

| Type of Coffee | Percent of Sales |
|---|---|
| Regular blend | 21% |
| Espresso blend | 10% |
| Regular blend decaf | 16% |
| Espresso blend decaf | 8% |
| Flavored blend | 24% |
| Flavored blend decaf | 13% |
| Iced | 5% |
| Iced decaf | 3% |

Create a pie chart as a new sheet with the data in the worksheet. Title the pie chart *Year 2011 Projected Percentage of Sales*. When the chart is completed, save the worksheet (two sheets) and name it **ProjectAct09**. Print and then close **ProjectAct09.xlsx**.

Analyze the sales data by comparing and contrasting the pie charts created in **ProjectAct08.xlsx** and **ProjectAct09.xlsx**. What areas in the projected sales percentages have changed? What do these changes indicate? Assume that the projected 2011 annual income for Classique Coffees is $2,200,000. What amount of that income will come from iced coffees (including decaf iced coffees)? Does this amount warrant marketing this new product? Prepare a memo in Word to Leslie Steiner that includes your analysis. Add any other interpretations you can make from analyzing the pie charts. Save the memo and name it **WordProject09**. Print and then close **WordProject09.docx**.

## Activity 10  Design and Create a Presentation

Using PowerPoint, prepare a marketing slide presentation. Include the following information in the presentation:

- Classique Coffees 2011 Marketing Plan (title)
- Company reorganization (insert the organizational chart you created in Activity 4)
- 2010 sales percentages (insert into the slide the pie chart that is part of the **ProjectAct08.xlsx** worksheet)
- 2011 projected sales percentages (insert into the slide the pie chart that is part of the **ProjectAct09.xlsx** worksheet)
- Iced coffee marketing strategy
  > target customer
  > analysis of competition
  > wholesale resources
  > pricing
  > volume
- Product placement
  > stocking strategies
  > shelf allocation
  > stock rotation schedule
  > seasonal display

When preparing the slide presentation, you determine the presentation design theme and the layouts. Include any clip art images that might be appropriate and apply an animation scheme to all slides. When the presentation is completed, save it and name it **ProjectAct10**. Run the presentation and then print the presentation with six slides on a page.

## Activity 11  Create a Database File and Organize Data

Use Access to create a database for Classique Coffees that contains information on suppliers and products. Include the following fields in the Suppliers table and the Products table (you determine the specific field names):

**Suppliers table:**
> *Supplier#*
> *SupplierName*
> *Address*
> *City*

*State*
*ZipCode*
*Email*

**Products table:**
*Product#*
*Product*
*Supplier#*

Type the following data in the Suppliers table:

| | | | | | | |
|---|---|---|---|---|---|---|
| *Supplier#* | = | 24 | | *Supplier#* | = | 62 |
| *SupplierName* | = | Gourmet Blends | | *SupplierName* | = | Sure Shot Supplies |
| *Address* | = | 109 South Madison | | *Address* | = | 291 Pacific Avenue |
| *City* | = | Seattle | | *City* | = | Tacoma |
| *State* | = | WA | | *State* | = | WA |
| *ZipCode* | = | 98032 | | *ZipCode* | = | 98418 |
| *Email* | = | gblends@emcp.net | | *Email* | = | sssupplies@emcp.net |
| | | | | | | |
| *Supplier#* | = | 36 | | *Supplier#* | = | 41 |
| *SupplierName* | = | Jannsen Company | | *SupplierName* | = | Bertolinos |
| *Address* | = | 4122 South Sprague | | *Address* | = | 11711 Meridian East |
| *City* | = | Tacoma | | *City* | = | Seattle |
| *State* | = | WA | | *State* | = | WA |
| *ZipCode* | = | 98402 | | *ZipCode* | = | 98109 |
| *Email* | = | jannsen@emcp.net | | *Email* | = | bertolino@emcp.net |

Type the following data in the Products table:

| | | | | | | |
|---|---|---|---|---|---|---|
| *Product#* | = | 12A-0 | | *Product#* | = | 59R-1 |
| *Product* | = | Premium blend | | *Product* | = | Vanilla syrup |
| *Supplier#* | = | 24 | | *Supplier#* | = | 62 |
| | | | | | | |
| *Product#* | = | 12A-1 | | *Product#* | = | 59R-2 |
| *Product* | = | Cappuccino blend | | *Product* | = | Raspberry syrup |
| *Supplier#* | = | 24 | | *Supplier#* | = | 62 |
| | | | | | | |
| *Product#* | = | 12A-2 | | *Product#* | = | 59R-3 |
| *Product* | = | Hazelnut blend | | *Product* | = | Chocolate syrup |
| *Supplier#* | = | 24 | | *Supplier#* | = | 62 |
| | | | | | | |
| *Product#* | = | 21B-2 | | *Product#* | = | 89T-3 |
| *Product* | = | 12-oz cup | | *Product* | = | Napkins, 500 ct |
| *Supplier#* | = | 36 | | *Supplier#* | = | 41 |

| | | | | | | |
|---|---|---|---|---|---|---|
| *Product#* | = | 21B-3 | | *Product#* | = | 89T-4 |
| *Product* | = | 16-oz cup | | *Product* | = | 6-inch stir stick |
| *Supplier#* | = | 36 | | *Supplier#* | = | 41 |

Print both the Suppliers table and the Products table in landscape orientation. Prepare a report with the following information: supplier name, supplier #, supplier e-mail, and product.

Merge the records of those suppliers that are located in Tacoma to a blank Word document. You determine the fields to use in the inside address and an appropriate salutation. Compose a business letter that you will send to the contacts in Tacoma that includes the following information:

- Explain that Classique Coffees is interested in selling iced coffees in the greater Seattle/Tacoma area.
- Ask if the company offers any iced coffee products.
- If the company does not currently offer any iced coffee products, will these products be available in the future?
- Ask the company to send any materials on current products and specifically on iced coffees.
- Ask someone at the company to contact you at the Classique Coffees address, by telephone at (206) 555-6690, or by e-mail at ccoffees@emcp.net.
- Include any other information you think appropriate to the topic.

Merge to a new document and then save the document with the name **ProjectAct11**. Print and then close **ProjectAct11.docx**. Save the main document as **IcedCoffeeLtrMD** and then close **IcedCoffeeLtrMD.docx**.

## Activity 12  Assess Your Work

Review the documents you developed and assess your own work in writing. In order to develop an objective perspective of your work, openly solicit constructive criticism from your teacher, peers, and contacts outside of school. Your self-assessment document should specify the weaknesses and strengths of each piece and your specific recommendations for revision and improvement.